THE OXFORD HANDBOOK OF

JORGE LUIS BORGES

THE OXFORD HANDBOOK OF

JORGE LUIS BORGES

Edited by
DANIEL BALDERSTON
and
NORA BENEDICT

OXFORD
UNIVERSITY PRESS

Oxford University Press is a department of the University of Oxford. It furthers
the University's objective of excellence in research, scholarship, and education
by publishing worldwide. Oxford is a registered trade mark of Oxford University
Press in the UK and certain other countries.

Published in the United States of America by Oxford University Press
198 Madison Avenue, New York, NY 10016, United States of America.

© Oxford University Press 2024

All rights reserved. No part of this publication may be reproduced, stored in
a retrieval system, or transmitted, in any form or by any means, without the
prior permission in writing of Oxford University Press, or as expressly permitted
by law, by license, or under terms agreed with the appropriate reproduction
rights organization. Inquiries concerning reproduction outside the scope of the
above should be sent to the Rights Department, Oxford University Press, at the
address above.

You must not circulate this work in any other form
and you must impose this same condition on any acquirer.

Library of Congress Cataloging-in-Publication Data
Names: Balderston, Daniel, 1952– editor. | Benedict, Nora, editor.
Title: The Oxford handbook of Jorge Luis Borges / edited by Daniel
Balderston and Nora Benedict.
Other titles: Handbook of Jorge Luis Borges
Description: New York : Oxford University Press, 2024. |
Series: Oxford handbooks series | Includes bibliographical references and index. |
Identifiers: LCCN 2024023067 (print) | LCCN 2024023068 (ebook) |
ISBN 9780197535271 (hardback) | ISBN 9780197535301 |
ISBN 9780197535295 (epub)
Subjects: LCSH: Borges, Jorge Luis, 1899–1986—Criticism and interpretation.
Classification: LCC PQ7797.B635 Z79674 2024 (print) |
LCC PQ7797.B635 (ebook) | DDC 863/.62—dc23/eng/20240604
LC record available at https://lccn.loc.gov/2024023067
LC ebook record available at https://lccn.loc.gov/2024023068

DOI: 10.1093/oxfordhb/9780197535271.001.0001

The manufacturer's authorized representative in the EU for product safety is
Oxford University Press España S.A., Parque Empresarial San Fernando de Henares,
Avenida de Castilla, 2 – 28830 Madrid (www.oup.es/en or product.safety@oup.com).
OUP España S.A. also acts as importer into Spain of products made by the manufacturer.

CONTENTS

About the Volume Editors	ix
List of Contributors	xi
Introduction	xiii
DANIEL BALDERSTON AND NORA BENEDICT	
Chronology	xxi

PART I. BORGES: FAMILY, WORKING LIFE

1. Borges: Biography and Its Discontents   3
DANIEL BALDERSTON

2. The Secret Sharer: Borges as Reader   13
MAGDALENA CÁMPORA AND MARIANA DI CIÓ

3. From the Other Side of the Library: Borges in Newspapers and
Magazines   33
SYLVIA SAÍTTA

4. Developing an Argentine Style in Form and Content:
Jorge Luis Borges and Editorial Proa   52
NORA BENEDICT

5. Borges: Three Times a Translator   73
PATRICIA WILLSON

6. Borges's Lectures: Literature, Travels, and Orality   95
MARIELA BLANCO

7. Works and Days: Jorge Luis Borges and the Library as a Scene
for Literary Production   114
LAURA ROSATO AND GERMÁN ÁLVAREZ

PART II. REPRESENTATIVE WORKS

8. Orality and Literacy in Borges: Two Manuscripts of "Del culto de los libros" [On the Cult of Books] 135
DANIEL BALDERSTON

9. The 1920s Poetry of Jorge Luis Borges: Remapping, Nostalgia, and Mythification 153
SEBASTIÁN HERNAIZ

10. The Art of Recapitulation: The Early Essays (1920–1936) 177
NICOLÁS LUCERO

11. Inventing Authors, Imagining Books: An Invisible Literary History 197
JULIO PREMAT

12. Knives, Vendettas, Bifurcations: Detective Fiction in Borges 217
JÚLIO PIMENTEL PINTO

13. Borges, Anthologizer of the Fantastic 236
EMRON ESPLIN

14. Anthologies of the Self: Borges's Self-Figuration Process between 1935 and 1960 254
SEBASTIÁN URLI

15. The Middle Essays and Reviews 269
DARDO SCAVINO

16. Virgil's Keepsakes: Memory and Oblivion in Poetic Form 287
SILVIO MATTONI

17. Borges's Self-Figuration Process in the Late Fiction (1970–1983) 301
EVELYN FISHBURN

PART III. COLLABORATION

18. The Bustos Domecq Cycle: Going With and Against the Flow 319
MARIANO GARCÍA

19. Jorge Luis Borges and the Interview as Theater 333
CODY C. HANSON

CONTENTS vii

20. Borges and the Creative Economy of the Apocryphal 351
ALFREDO ALONSO ESTENOZ

PART IV. RECEPTION

IN LITERATURE

21. A History of Borges's Reception in Argentina 373
SERGIO PASTORMERLO

22. Borges and the Crucible of Aesthetic Autonomy in Latin America 388
HÉCTOR HOYOS

23. Borges's Reception in Europe and the USA 405
EDWIN WILLIAMSON

24. Borges in the Eastern Bloc 423
LÁSZLÓ SCHOLZ

25. Borges and the Formation of the Literary Global South 441
JAY CORWIN

IN OTHER FIELDS

26. "Nueva refutación del tiempo" [A New Refutation of Time] and the
Portrayal of an Ironic Fate 457
MARINA MARTÍN

27. Borges and Postcolonial Studies: Toward the Universal and Back 471
GUIDO HERZOVICH

28. Borges in French Theory 483
BRUNO BOSTEELS

29. Borges, Gender, and Sexuality 503
AMY KAMINSKY

30. Xul Solar and Jorge Luis Borges in the *Revista Multicolor
de los Sábados* [*Multicolor Saturday Magazine*] 519
PATRICIA M. ARTUNDO

31. Borges, Bewitched by Film   538
GONZALO AGUILAR

32. Political Theory and Borges's Work   552
ALEJANDRA M. SALINAS

33. Bird, Schedule, Name: On Some Media in Borges   567
JOHN DURHAM PETERS

34. Mirror. Lens. Puzzlebox. Metaphor.   582
WILLIAM GOLDBLOOM BLOCH

35. Faithfulness and Betrayal: Community, Legitimacy, and
Identity in Stories by Jorge Luis Borges   596
LEONARDO PITLEVNIK

Index   615

ABOUT THE VOLUME EDITORS

Daniel Balderston is Andrew W. Mellon Professor of Modern Languages at the University of Pittsburgh, where he directs the Borges Center and its journal *Variaciones Borges*. He earned his BA in English from the University of California-Berkeley and his MA and PhD in Comparative Literature from Princeton. He has published or edited fifteen books on Borges and has published widely on other writers including José Bianco, Silvina Ocampo, Augusto Roa Bastos, Ricardo Piglia, Juan José Saer, and Juan Carlos Onetti, as well as on translation studies and sexuality studies. Much of his recent work focuses on Borges's manuscripts. The book *Cuadernos*, a selection of Borges's notebooks, co-edited by Balderston, Blanco, Alonso Estenoz, Esplin, and María Celeste Martín, is in press with the Borges Center.

Nora Benedict is Assistant Professor of Spanish and Digital Humanities at the University of Georgia. She received her MA in Spanish from the University of Wisconsin-Madison and her PhD in Spanish from the University of Virginia. Her research centers on Latin American literature, book history, and digital and print cultures. Her first monograph, *Borges and the Literary Marketplace* (Yale University Press, 2021), explains how the Argentine author Jorge Luis Borges's general involvement in the publishing industry influenced his formation as a writer and global book markets. Beyond her research on Borges, her second monograph in progress, *Taking a Page from Their Books*, examines how international publishing firms in the Global North capitalized on the economic, political, and cultural opportunities available to them in the book industry in Latin America.

Contributors

Gonzalo Aguilar, Universidad de Buenos Aires

Alfredo Alonso Estenoz, Luther College

Germán Álvarez, Biblioteca Nacional Mariano Moreno

Patricia M. Artundo, Universidad de Buenos Aires

Daniel Balderston, University of Pittsburgh

Nora Benedict, University of Georgia

Mariela Blanco, Universidad Nacional de Mar del Plata/CONICET

William Goldbloom Bloch, Wheaton College

Bruno Bosteels, Columbia University

Magdalena Cámpora, Universidad Católica Argentina/CONICET

Jay Corwin, University of Cape Town

Mariana Di Ció, Université Sorbonne Nouvelle

John Durham Peters, Yale University

Emron Esplin, Brigham Young University

Evelyn Fishburn, University College London

Mariano García, Universidad Católica Argentina/CONICET

Cody C. Hanson, Indiana State University

Sebastián Hernaiz, Universidad de Buenos Aires

Guido Herzovich, Universidad de Buenos Aires/CONICET

Héctor Hoyos, Stanford University

Amy Kaminsky, University of Minnesota

Nicolás Lucero, University of Georgia

Marina Martín, College of Saint Benedict and Saint John's University

Silvio Mattoni, Universidad Nacional de Córdoba/CONICET

Sergio Pastormerlo, Universidad Nacional de La Plata

Júlio Pimentel Pinto, Universidade de São Paulo

Leonardo Pitlevnik, Universidad de Buenos Aires

Julio Premat, Université Paris 8/Institut Universitaire de France/CONICET

Laura Rosato, Biblioteca Nacional Mariano Moreno

Sylvia Saítta, Universidad de Buenos Aires

Alejandra M. Salinas, Universidad Nacional de Tres de Febrero/
Facultad de Ciencias Sociales, UCA

Dardo Scavino, Université de Pau et des Pays de l'Adour

László Scholz, Eötvös Loránd University/Oberlin College

Sebastián Urli, Bowdoin College

Edwin Williamson, University of Oxford

Patricia Willson, Université de Liège

INTRODUCTION

DANIEL BALDERSTON AND NORA BENEDICT

JORGE Luis Borges (Buenos Aires 1899–Geneva 1986) stands out as one of the most widely regarded and inventive authors in world literature. His short stories and philosophical essays, most notably *El jardín de senderos que se bifurcan* [*The Garden of Forking Paths*] (1941), *Ficciones* [*Fictions*] (1944), *El Aleph* [*The Aleph*] (1949), and *Otras inquisiciones* [*Other Inquisitions*] (1952), have influenced numerous writers, including Michel Foucault, Jacques Derrida, George Steiner, Susan Sontag, and Umberto Eco. This volume shifts the emphasis to the ways in which his thousands of short texts were produced in relation to his working life, particularly his jobs with magazines, newspapers, and publishers. For instance, while many studies mention his contributions to periodicals or edited volumes, they exclusively center on the articles, essays, or literary works that he published in these outlets, not the roles that he played in selecting or editing texts for their final publication. In addition, our commitment to assessing Borges's impact outside of Latin American and world literature results in a more well-rounded account of Borges, both as writer and as public intellectual. What makes our volume ambitious and impactful is our consideration of Borges's less-visible labor in shaping and crafting not only his own works and words, but also those of other writers both within and outside of Argentina.

In this volume, we approach Borges's work through new critical and theoretical lenses, including those of material, textual, and editorial studies that have yet to be applied systematically to his writings. In addition to discussing the textual variations in his written works, the essays in this volume examine certain polemical facets of his life, such as his ever-changing public personae and his varied political activities. Finally, this *Handbook* carves out space in which to evaluate Borges's impact on not only Latin American and world literature, but also on a wide variety of other fields ranging from political science and philosophy to media studies and mathematics. This volume, similar to all other *Oxford Handbooks*, offers fresh perspectives on the state of the field through a series of innovative, original studies that advance new lines of scholarly inquiry. The essays in this volume carefully situate Borges's work in particular moments and locales while simultaneously providing a diachronic look at the themes and mediums of his literary production. They also explore how slight shifts and changes in his craft attracted new types of readers from around the globe and across disciplinary lines.

xiv   INTRODUCTION

WHY BORGES? WHY NOW?

Since a number of Borges's extant manuscripts have come to light recently, thanks in great part to Daniel Balderston's research for *How Borges Wrote* (2018) and *Lo marginal es lo bello* (2022), there is the need for a more nuanced consideration of his processes of production. Several new lines of research include the careful analysis of his drafts and notes, the reconstruction of a hypothetical Borges library, the mapping of his talks from 1949 onward, and the relations between oral and periodical versions of his texts and subsequent book publications. In particular, Balderston and a team of scholars—many of whom are collaborators here—are editing a large volume of selections from Borges's notebooks from 1949 to 1955, which show in detail his research for his oral presentations during this period. Because of Borges's prodigious memory, he called upon this research in hundreds of talks and interviews—not to mention published materials—in the period after he became blind, for the purposes of reading and writing, in 1955. Complementing the notebooks project, the work of Mariela Blanco and others has established a much more complete chronology of Borges's career as an itinerant public speaker, as seen in the growing database of these talks on the Borges Center website (https://www.borges.pitt.edu/talks-borges) and the website of the National Library of Argentina (http://centroborges.bn.gob.ar). Borges's compositional practices have also been the subject of important new work that shows that he was indeed convinced that literary texts are always already unfinished and provisional, or "open" to use Umberto Eco's term. Essays in this volume highlight Borges's improvisational approach to writing, quite a different idea than previously thought, by continuing these lines of inquiry concerning his manuscripts, talks, interviews, and public performances.

Attention to Borges's working life has brought into sharp focus his activities in the publishing industry and for various periodicals. Borges was not a man of means and depended on his editorial positions, his work as a translator, and his activities as a public speaker to earn a living. His professional life became somewhat more stable after 1955, with his appointment to director of the National Library and later as a professor of English literature at the University of Buenos Aires; as he notes in "Poema de los dones" [Poem of the Gifts] this less precarious status came after he had lost his sight. His world fame, which naturally came with countless invitations to speak around the world and to teach as a visiting professor, refashioned him as a blind seer, the dominant image of him in world culture. Ironically, the work of this period has been somewhat less influential than his works from the 1940s and early 1950s.

The reader of this volume will note that our contributors have commented frequently on some of the same texts, not only those that are most canonical ("Pierre Menard, autor del Quijote" [Pierre Menard, Author of the *Quixote*], "Tlön, Uqbar, Orbis Tertius," "La biblioteca de Babel" [The Library of Babel], "El escritor argentino y la tradición" [The Argentine Writer and Tradition]), but also on such other texts as "Historia de la

Table I.1 Most frequently cited volumes and individual texts across chapters in the Handbook

Most cited volumes	Most cited individual texts
1. *El jardín de senderos que se bifurcan*	1. "Pierre Menard, autor del Quijote"
2. *Ficciones*	2. "Tlön, Uqbar, Orbis Tertius"
3. *El Aleph*	3. "El milagro secreto"
4. *Otras inquisiciones*	4. "El escritor argentino y la tradición"
5. *Historia universal de la infamia*	5. "La muerte y la brújula"
6. *Discusión*	6. "El Aleph"
7. *Historia de la eternidad*	7. "Emma Zunz"
8. *El informe de Brodie*	8. "El idioma analítico de John Wilkins"
9. *El hacedor*	9. "El Zahir"
10. *El libro de arena*	10. "Nota sobre Walt Whitman"

eternidad" [A History of Eternity], "Nueva refutación del tiempo" [A New Refutation of Time], and "Del culto de los libros" [On the Cult of Books] (see Table I.1 for the most cited works across the volume).

Moreover, when the canonical works appear, sometimes more than once in the course of the handbook, they look quite different in the discussion of the various topics covered. For example, "Tlön, Uqbar, Orbis Tertius" is discussed in both Julio Premat's chapter on imaginary books and Emron Esplin's chapter on the fantastic, yet these authors approach this short story from distinct angles: the creation of literary history versus the creation of actual books. By organizing each chapter around concepts and ideas, rather than around Borges's published books, our volume provides a more thoroughgoing and accurate representation of Borges's literary production. The volume as a whole benefits from our collaborators' examinations of clusters of texts that allow new thinking about famous issues in Borges studies.

Broadly conceived, this volume highlights current debates among Borges scholars as a way to reevaluate how the physical forms and sociopolitical contexts of Borges's writings both shaped and determined specific readerships around the world. Alongside these novel approaches to Borges's fictions and nonfictions, this volume is the first of its kind to dedicate space to the reception of Borges's works in the fields of philosophy, the visual arts, film, political science, media theory, mathematics, and law. Our collection also goes further to trace Borges's activity in the public sphere, including local and national politics and the functioning of cultural institutions. To date, no other collection devoted to his writings or life addresses these issues in depth, nor do they consider how his affiliations and interests change over the course of his long life. Incorporating these broader perspectives into this *Handbook* serves to bring out tensions, continuities, and discontinuities in Borges's work, allowing for a much more nuanced understanding of it.

xvi INTRODUCTION

This *Handbook* includes thirty-five chapters (some translated from Spanish and Portuguese by Leah Leone Anderson), organized into four main categories: Borges's life (his family, education, working life, late fame, and iconic status); his representative works traced across the many decades of his writing, grouped around such categories as fake reviews and obituaries, crime fiction, and the fantastic; his work in collaboration, including anthologies and manuals; and his reception in literature (Argentina, Latin America, the Global North, the Socialist Bloc, the Global South) and in other disciplines (philosophy, the sciences, and the social sciences).

The first section of this book considers Borges's life and working career (Balderston), with attention to his activities as editor and publisher (Saítta; Benedict), translator (Willson), librarian (Rosato and Álvarez), reader (Cámpora and Di Ció), and public speaker (Blanco). The next section surveys his representative works in the genres of poetry (Hernaiz; Urli; Mattoni), essays (Lucero; Scavino), and short fiction (Premat; Pimentel Pinto; Esplin; Fishburn), while also problematizing the boundaries of these genres in Borges (Balderston). The third section underlines the importance of Borges's work in collaboration (García); his performances in interviews, particularly those from the 1960s onward (Hanson); and the mischievous presence of apocryphal texts and authors in his writings and in subsequent continuations of it by other writers (Alonso Estenoz). The fourth is twofold: Borges's reception in literature around the world (Pastermerlo on Argentina; Hoyos on Latin America; Williamson on the Global North; Scholz on the Socialist Bloc; Corwin on the Global South) and his reception in other fields (Martín and Bosteels on philosophy and critical theory; Herzovich on postcolonial studies; Kaminsky on gender and sexuality; Artundo on the visual arts; Aguilar on cinema; Salinas on political theory; Peters on media studies; Goldbloom Bloch on mathematics and the hard sciences; and Pitlevnik on the law).

A volume like this necessarily leaves some things out, though glimmers of work on those omissions do pop up in footnotes (e.g., references to Lou Yu's work on Borges in China in Scholz's and Corwin's chapters or references to Quian Quiroga's work on cognitive science and Alberto Rojo's reflections on Borges and quantum physics in Goldbloom Bloch's chapter). Other lines of inquiry include Borges's impact on painting (Jorge J. E. Gracia), digital studies (Sassón-Henry; Basile; Sosa Escudero), and music (Turci-Escobar; Favali; Schvartzman). The "specter" of Borges haunts many fields, from Aníbal Jarkowski's novel on the relationship between Borges and Estela Canto to Christopher Nolan's uses of Borges in his cinema to Foucault's invocation of him at the beginning of *Les mots et les choses*, to his cameos in many works of popular culture (the McLuhan cameo on Borges in Woody Allen's *Annie Hall*, Lucas Nine's graphic novel on Borges as inspector of poultry and rabbits, Sol LeWitt's and Mirta Kupfermic's illustrated editions of Borges works, the image of Borges in Google Doodles, and the presence of many businesses in Buenos Aires whose names invoke his works).

INTRODUCTION   xvii

THE FUTURE OF BORGES STUDIES

Borges himself states emphatically that literature exists as rough drafts and that final versions are an illusion. As such, a major problem in approaching Borges's work is establishing the texts that are pertinent for a given study. For many Borges poems, essays, and stories, his writing process includes very rough drafts with multiple false starts and alternatives (see Balderston [Chapter 8]), then fair copies, handwritten by Borges for submission to newspapers and magazines. Then those first published versions were revised and collected into books. Sometimes the manuscripts reveal precise readings that Borges had in mind but that are not mentioned explicitly in the published versions. A different kind of textual problem are those texts that Borges changed in tone and content (see Hernaiz [Chapter 9]). By the 1950s, various friends and editors (José Bianco and José Edmundo Clemente first, and later Carlos Frías) assisted in the process of selecting the versions that then were collected into the so-called *Obras completas*. A major decision that seems to have been made at that point was the omission of the first three books of essays (*Inquisiciones* [*Inquisitions*], *El tamaño de mi esperanza* [*The Extent of My Hope*], *El idioma de los argentinos* [*The Language of Argentines*]) and the inclusion of the 1940s revised version of *Fervor de Buenos Aires*. The first three books of essays would only be reprinted more than a decade after Borges's death, but they are pivotal for an understanding of his early work and evolving prose style. Other posthumous collections of hundreds of other works, particularly book reviews and cultural journalism, have rounded out the published materials; a crucial example has been the recovery of Borges's writings in the magazine *El Hogar* from 1936 to 1939, which provide a rich and nuanced perspective on his reading and thinking in the period immediately before his most famous writing.

Almost all of Borges's works were published first in periodicals (magazines and newspapers); for many of them, there are surviving manuscripts of first drafts (usually with many variants) and subsequent versions and sometimes also fair copies in Borges's hand with a note "Para *Sur*" [For *Sur*] or "Para *La Nación*" [For *La Nación*]. He rewrote a fair amount from periodical to book publication and sometimes used copies of the published works to rewrite, although in the cases of "La lotería en Babilonia" [The Lottery in Babylon]and *Inquisiciones* the hundreds of changes were never incorporated into subsequent published versions. As Balderston showed in *How Borges Wrote* and *Lo marginal es lo más bello*, the working drafts included numerous possibilities, sometimes as many as fifteen for a word and twenty-six for a line of poetry; taking stock of this textual proliferation could, as Dirk van Hulle and Hans Walter Gabler have discussed in recent books, be taxing to the eye and difficult for the brain to process. It would be helpful to have a web version with the full genetic dossiers of each text, with a judicious approach to how to present the variants in the print version.

First compiled by Emecé Editores in the 1950s as a series of single volumes, the *Obras completas* were collected into a 1,161-page single-volume edition in 1974. All the subsequent editions, some in three and then four volumes, even the sloppy "edición crítica" [critical edition] of 2015, derive from this single-volume edition, sometimes adding new typographical errors to the ones that were already there, sometimes adding posthumous materials (though it is impossible to know what criteria were employed). All of these editions also follow the chaotic way in which the single volumes for Emecé were collected: after publishing *El Aleph* in 1949, and adding more stories in 1951, Borges wrote three more stories that were added to the second edition of *Ficciones* (originally from 1944) in 1956. Similarly, essays that were published after *Otras inquisiciones* in 1952 were added to the second edition of *Discusión* [*Discussion*] (originally from 1932) in 1957. The important proto-fiction "El acercamiento a Almotásim" [The Approach to Al-Mu'tasim] had been mischievously published in the 1936 book of essays *Historia de la eternidad* [*A History of Eternity*], but was then included in *El jardín de senderos que se bifurcan* in 1941 and *Ficciones* in 1944; in the later Emecé edition, it disappears from *Ficciones*, where it really belongs, and returns to *Historia de la eternidad*. To say nothing of what happened to the poetry: the early books were rewritten, with many poems suppressed and a few added, but (except for in the footnotes to the "edición crítica") the earlier versions disappeared from the complete works. (A bit as if we only had access to Whitman's "deathbed edition" of *Leaves of Grass*.) And no attempt has ever been made to correct errors that have been signaled over and over in the enormous body of criticism of the Argentine author, like the misprint of "julio" [July] for "junio" [June] at the beginning of "El jardín de senderos que se bifurcan" or the bowdlerization of the "necesidades fecales" [fecal necessities] as "necesidades finales" [final necessities] in "La biblioteca de Babel" (examples of this kind abound).

Iván Almeida and Cristina Parodi proposed, in a brief article in *Variaciones Borges*, that a way of supplying a critical apparatus would be to publish a 1,161-page book with a big hole in it, in which the 1974 edition could be inserted; Balderston made an analogous proposal in *Innumerables relaciones: cómo leer con Borges* in 2010, though in that piece the *Obras completas* structure would be abandoned in favor of a rigorous chronological ordering of the texts, from the first published poem in 1919 to the last works published before Borges's death. The latter proposal would have the virtue of incorporating the three volumes of suppressed essays and the many texts that have been collected in the three volumes of *Textos recobrados* and the like, thereby providing a better guide to the evolution of Borges's writing. In the case of the first book of poems, *Fervor de Buenos Aires*, Balderston proposed that the 1923 edition be published early in the new edition, with the 1943 and 1969 revisions appearing later (as is the case with the Whitman example mentioned earlier).

Because of this fractious and cloudy picture, it behooves us to think about what a future edition of Borges would look like. In particular, how it would treat the manuscript materials; how the notebooks that are housed in various libraries and private collections might be incorporated; and what kinds of annotations and introductions should be included. As we have noted, this is a purely intellectual exercise for the moment. A modest proposal, then: a rigorously chronological presentation of all of Borges's work, with variants, explanatory notes, and critical introductions on the provenance of each piece and its textual history. The introductions would discuss the relations between the published pieces and the surviving manuscripts and notebooks. The notes would clarify the source for each quotation and reference (which in the case of Borges run to the hundreds of thousands).

An issue for the next decades in Borges studies, then, is the preparation of a better standard reading text in Spanish (which could then be the basis for new translations of the work into the many languages where there are readers of Borges). Since we now know a lot more about his reading notes and manuscripts, this information needs to be made more widely available. A deeper look needs to be taken into the books that he read, with a complete survey of his reading notes (as has happened with the personal library of the Portuguese poet Fernando Pessoa). Other lines of inquiry, some of them sketched out here, are the relation between Borges's writing and his oral performances (public speaking and interviews), a deeper look at his professional activities, a fuller list of the books in his various libraries (and the friends' libraries he consulted), a clearer account of how his writing (and his family's trips) were financed, and new biographies (in various languages) that take into account what we know now that was not known when the existing biographies were written. No one has attempted a biography since the publication of the Bioy diary (1,663 pages in 2006, with a shortened version in 2016, English version forthcoming), or the Rosato and Álvarez book of some of his reading notes, or the extensive work on his manuscripts and research notes. Borges's status as a key figure in modern letters is beyond doubt. The large, varied, and international readership, and the abundant scholarly work, guarantee that Borges studies will continue to be a lively area for intellectual debate.

Chronology

1899
Born on August 24 in Buenos Aires. His name appears in the Civil Registry as Jorge Francisco Isidoro Borges.

1900
Baptized on June 20 as Jorge Francisco Luis Isidoro Borges.

1901
Borges's sister, Leonor Fanny Borges Haslam ("Norah"), is born on March 4.

1905
Death of Isidoro Acevedo Laprida, maternal grandfather. First writings, in English and Spanish.

1910
Borges publishes his translation of Oscar Wilde's "The Happy Prince" in the Buenos Aires newspaper *El País* on June 25.

1911
School records show Borges enrolled on March 2 at a primary school in the Palermo neighborhood of Buenos Aires. He withdraws the following year after being bullied.

1913
Passes the entrance exams for the Colegio Nacional de Buenos Aires. Publishes his first story, "El rey de la selva" [King of the Jungle] in the magazine of the Colegio under the pseudonym "Nemo."

1914
Borges family travels to Europe in February. Borges studies at the Collège Calvin in Geneva from 1914 to 1918.

1918
Death in Geneva of Leonor Suárez Haedo de Acevedo, maternal grandmother. End of studies at Collège Calvin without taking final exams or getting a high school diploma. Travels in Switzerland and France.

1919
Travels in Italy and Spain. Periodical publications in Geneva and Seville.

1920
Borges family leaves Mallorca for Seville and Madrid, where Borges joins up with the *ultraísta* groups, a Spanish avant-garde movement.

1921
Borges family returns to Buenos Aires in March.

1922
The end of Borges's *ultraísta* period. Many periodical publications, including *Prisma* and the first *Proa*.

1923
Borges family embarks on their second trip to Europe in July. Publication of *Fervor de Buenos Aires* [*Fervor of Buenos Aires*] shortly before departure.

xxii   CHRONOLOGY

1924

Borges family returns to Buenos Aires in July. Founding of the journal *Martín Fierro* by Evar
Méndez and others.

1925

Meets Victoria Ocampo. Publication of *Inquisiciones* and *Luna de enfrente* [*Moon Across
the Way*].

1926

Proa ceases publication. Publication of *El tamaño de mi esperanza* [*The Extent of My Hope*] and
(edited with Alberto Hidalgo and Vicente Huidobro) *Índice de la nueva poesía americana*
[*Index of New American Poetry*].

1927

End of *Martín Fierro*. Periodical publications and postscript for the *Antología de la moderna
poesía uruguaya, 1900–1927* [*Anthology of Modern Uruguayan Poetry, 1900–1927*] (edited by
Ildefonso Pereda Valdés). Political activity in favor of Hipólito Yrigoyen.

1928

Borges's sister, Norah, marries Guillermo de Torre. Publication of *El idioma de los argentinos*
[*The Language of Argentines*].

1929

Wins the Segundo Premio Municipal de Literatura for *El idioma de los argentinos*. Publication
of *Cuaderno San Martín* [*San Martín Notebook*].

1930

Meets Adolfo Bioy Casares (at Ocampo's home). Publication of *Evaristo Carriego*.

1931

Borges starts writing reviews for Ocampo's literary journal *Sur*, which launched in 1931.

1932

Publication of *Discusión* [*Discussion*].

1933

Becomes co-director, with Ulises Petit de Murat, of the *Revista Multicolor de los Sábados*
[*Multicolor Saturday Magazine*] (1933–1934). Publication of *Las Kenningar* [*The Kenning*]
(later republished as *Los Kenningar*).

1934

Final months of the *Revista Multicolor*; travels in Uruguay with Enrique Amorim.

1935

Death of Fanny Haslam, paternal grandmother, on June 20; deterioration of father's health.
Publication of *Historia universal de la infamia* [*A Universal History of Infamy*].

1936

Borges starts his regular work for *El Hogar* [*The Home*] (1936–1939); edits and contributes to
Destiempo with Bioy Casares. Publication of *Historia de la eternidad* [*A History of Eternity*].

1937

Publication of *Antología clásica de la literatura argentina* [*Classic Anthology of Argentine
Literature*] (with Pedro Henríquez Ureña).

1938

Death of Borges's father, Jorge Guillermo Borges Haslam, on February 24. Borges starts
working at the Miguel Cané Municipal Library; suffers from septicemia after an accident in
December.

1939

End of collaboration with *El Hogar*; continues working at Miguel Cané until 1946.

CHRONOLOGY xxiii

1940

Edits the *Antología de la literatura fantástica* [*Anthology of Fantastic Literature*] with Silvina Ocampo and Bioy Casares.

1941

Publication of *El jardín de senderos que se bifurcan* [*The Garden of Forking Paths*] and, with Silvina Ocampo and Adolfo Bioy Casares, the *Antología poética argentina* [*Anthology of Argentine Poetry*].

1942

Presents *El jardín de senderos que bifurcan* for the Premio Nacional de Literatura (does not win the prize because the collection was considered insufficiently Argentine). *Sur* publishes a special issue on Borges. Publication of *Seis problemas para don Isidro Parodi* [*Six Problems for Mr. Isidro Parodi*] (with Bioy Casares) under the pseudonym H. Bustos Domecq.

1943

Publication of *Poemas, 1922–1943* [*Poems, 1922–1943*] and *Los mejores cuentos policiales* [*The Best Detective Stories*] (edited with Bioy Casares).

1944

Publication of *Ficciones* [*Fictions*], which wins the Gran Premio de Honor from the Sociedad Argentina de Escritores (SADE).

1945

Complex involvement with Estela Canto. Publication of *El compadrito* [*The Thug*] (edited with Silvina Bullrich). First public talk, on gauchesque poetry, in Montevideo; read by José Pedro Díaz.

1946

Resigns from his position at the Miguel Cané; begins directing *Los Anales de Buenos Aires* [*The Annals of Buenos Aires*]. Publication of *Dos fantasías memorables* [*Two Memorable Fantasies*] (H. Bustos Domecq) and *Un modelo para la muerte* [*A Model for Death*] (B. Suárez Lynch) in collaboration with Bioy Casares. Psychoanalysis with Dr. Miguel Kohan-Miller (for two years).

1947

Publication of *Nueva refutación del tiempo* [*A New Refutation of Time*].

1948

End of *Los Anales de Buenos Aires*. Borges's mother and sister are arrested for participating in an unauthorized demonstration against the new Peronist constitution.

1949

Elected member of the Goethe Academy of São Paulo, Brazil. Publication of *El Aleph* [*The Aleph*]. In March, gives the first of more than a hundred public talks (beginning of career as public speaker).

1950

Elected president of the SADE (1950–1953). Teaches English literature at the Asociación Argentina de Cultura Inglesa and various courses at the Colegio Libre de Estudios Superiores. Publication of *Aspectos de la literatura gauchesca* [*Aspects of Gaucho Literature*].

1951

Paul Verdevoye translates *Ficciones* into French. Publication of *Los mejores cuentos policiales. Segunda serie* (edited with Bioy Casares), *Antiguas literaturas germánicas* [*Ancient Germanic Literatures*] (written in collaboration with Delia Ingenieros), and *La muerte y la brújula* [*Death and the Compass*].

xxiv   CHRONOLOGY

1952
Publication of *Otras inquisiciones* [*Other Inquisitions*].

1953
Beginning of publication of *Obras completas* as a set of individual volumes, under the direction of José Edmundo Clemente. Publication of *El "Martín Fierro"* [*The "Martín Fierro"*].

1954
Adolfo Prieto publishes the first critical monograph on Borges; Leopoldo Torre Nilsson films *Días de odio* [*Days of Hate*], an adaptation of "Emma Zunz."

1955
Fall of Perón. Borges is named director of the National Library (a post he will hold until 1973) and becomes a member of the Academia Argentina de Letras. Publication of *Cuentos breves y extraordinarios* [*Extraordinary Tales*] (edited with Bioy Casares), *Los orilleros* [*The Hoodlums*], *El paraíso de los creyentes* [*The Paradise of Believers*] (film scripts with Bioy Casares), and *Nueve poemas* [*Nine Poems*]. Blindness prevents him from reading and writing.

1956
Named professor of English literature at the Universidad de Buenos Aires. Receives a doctorate *honoris causa* from the Universidad del Cuyo in Mendoza and the Premio Nacional de Literatura.

1957
Restarts the magazine *La Biblioteca*, founded by Paul Groussac. French translation of *Otras inquisiciones*. Publication of *Manual de zoología fantástica* [*The Book of Imaginary Beings*] (with Margarita Guerrero; later expanded as *El libro de los seres imaginarios*).

1958
Publication of *Límites* [*Limits*].

1959
Publication of *Poemas* [*Poems*].

1960
Publication of *El hacedor* [*Dreamtigers*] and *Libro del cielo y del infierno* [*Book of Heaven and Hell*] (with Bioy Casares).

1961
Wins the Formentor Prize, in conjunction with Samuel Beckett. Italian government recognizes Borges with title of Commendatore. First trip to the United States, where he teaches at the University of Texas and lectures at other universities. Publication of *Antología personal* [*A Personal Anthology*].

1962
Recognition by the French government. René Mugica makes a film version of "Hombre de la esquina rosada" [Man on Pink Corner]. Publication of *Labyrinths* (edited by Donald Yates and James Irby).

1963
Trip to Europe with his mother. Receives doctorate *honoris causa* from the Universidad Nacional de Colombia in Bogotá and speaks in Medellín. Publication of *El lenguaje de Buenos Aires* [*The Language of Buenos Aires*] (with José Edmundo Clemente).

1964
Travels to West Germany, France, England, and Spain. *L'Herne* publishes a massive special issue on Borges. Publication of *El otro, el mismo* [*The Other, the Same*].

CHRONOLOGY   XXV

1965
First trip to Peru. Various international prizes. Trip to Colombia and Chile, accompanied by Esther Zemborain de Torres. Gives four lectures on the tango in Buenos Aires. Publication of *Para las seis cuerdas* [*For the Six Strings*], *Literaturas germánicas medievales* [*Medieval Germanic Literatures*] (with María Esther Vázquez), and *Introducción a la literatura inglesa* [*Introduction to English Literature*] (also with Vázquez).

1966
Prizes in Milan and New York. Publication of *Seis poemas escandinavos* [*Six Scandinavian Poems*] and *Obra poética, 1923–1966* [*Poetic Works, 1923–1966*].

1967
Marriage on September 21 to Elsa Astete Millán. Norton Lectures at Harvard University. Publication of *Crónicas de Bustos Domecq* [*Chronicles of Bustos Domecq*] (with Bioy Casares), *Introducción a la literatura norteamericana* [*Introduction to North American Literature*] (with Esther Zemborain de Torres), *El libro de los seres imaginarios* [*The Book of Imaginary Beings*] (with Margarita Guerrero), and *Siete poemas* [*Seven Poems*].

1968
Continuation of Norton Lectures at Harvard. Travels in the United States, Chile, Europe, and Israel. Publication of *Nueva antología personal* [*A New Personal Anthology*].

1969
Travels to Israel and the United States. Publication of *Elogio de la sombra* [*In Praise of Darkness*]. *Invasión* by Hugo Santiago (film script by Borges and Bioy Casares).

1970
Receives the Premio Literario Iberoamericano in São Paulo. Separation from Elsa Astete Millán (but not divorce since divorce was not legal in Argentina). Named member of the Hispanic Society of America. Publication *El informe de Brodie* [*Doctor Brodie's Report*] and the "Autobiographical Notes."

1971
Fourth trip to the United States. Columbia University bestows a doctorate *honoris causa* and Yale hosts an "Encuentro con Jorge Luis Borges." Trip to Iceland, Scotland, and England with María Kodama. Oxford gives him a doctorate *honoris causa*. Named "Ciudadano Ilustre" by the city of Buenos Aires. Wins the Jerusalem Prize.

1972
Return to the United States to receive a doctorate *honoris causa* from the University of Michigan. Visits to Texas and New York. Publication of *El oro de los tigres* [*The Gold of the Tigers*].

1973
Resigns as the director of the National Library and donates part of his library to this institution. Travels to Madrid and Mexico City; receives the Premio Alfonso Reyes. *La Nación* dedicates a supplement to the fiftieth anniversary of *Fervor de Buenos Aires*.

1974
Les autres (film script written with Bioy Casares, for Hugo Santiago). Publication of the one-volume *Obras completas*.

1975
Death of mother, Leonor Acevedo Suárez de Borges, on July 8. Travels to Michigan State University where he teaches for the fall semester, giving numerous talks at other US universities. Publication of *El libro de arena* [*The Book of Sand*], *La rosa profunda* [*The Deep Rose*], and *Prólogos con un prólogo de prólogos* [*Prologue with a prologue of prologues*].

xxvi   CHRONOLOGY

1976

Travels to Spain, the United States, Mexico, and Chile. Receives doctorates *honoris causa* from the University of Cincinnati and the Universidad de Santiago in Chile. Receives the Orden de Mérito de Bernardo O'Higgins from the Pinochet government in Chile. Publication of *Qué es el budismo* [*What is Buddhism*] (with Alicia Jurado) and *La moneda de hierro* [*The Iron Coin*].

1977

Travels to Italy, France, and Switzerland. Awarded doctorate *honoris causa* from the Universidad Nacional de Tucumán. Publication of *Historia de la noche* [*History of the Night*] and *Nuevos cuentos de Bustos Domecq* [*New Tales of Bustos Domecq*] (with Bioy Casares).

1978

The Sorbonne awards him a doctorate *honoris causa*. Travels to Mexico, Colombia, Egypt, and Ecuador. Publication of *Breve antología anglosajona* [*Brief Anglosaxon Anthology*].

1979

Awards in Germany, France, and Iceland. Trip to Japan with María Kodama, and to New York, invited by the PEN Club. Publication of *Obras completas en colaboración* and *Borges, oral*.

1980

Cervantes Prize (with Gerardo Diego) awarded in Spain. Other literary prizes in Buenos Aires and Paris. Travels in the United States. Publication of *Siete noches* [*Seven Nights*].

1981

Travels to Rome, New Orleans, Mexico City. Doctorate *honoris causa* from the University of Puerto Rico. Publication of *La cifra* [*The Limit*].

1982

Receives an award in Portugal. Publication of *Nueve ensayos dantescos* [*Nine Dantesque Essays*] and *La memoria de Shakespeare* [*Shakespeare's Memory*].

1983

Awards in France, Spain, and the United States. Publication of "*Veinticinco Agosto 1983*" *y otros cuentos* [*"August 25, 1983" and Other Stories*].

1984

Prizes in Italy. Speaks at the opening of an exhibit on Kafka at the Pompidou Center. Travels to Morocco to an international conference of poets. Publication of *Atlas*.

1985

Travels to Madrid and Barcelona to present *Los conjurados* [*The Conspirators*]. In November, departs for Geneva, accompanied by María Kodama. Publication of *Los conjurados*.

1986

Borges marries María Kodama (by proxy, through the Paraguayan consulate in Geneva) on April 26. Death in Geneva on June 14. Publication of *Textos cautivos*.

PART I

BORGES
Family, Working Life

CHAPTER 1

....

BORGES

Biography and Its Discontents

....

DANIEL BALDERSTON

BORGES eloquently discusses the difficulties of writing a biography twice. First, in his 1930 book *Evaristo Carriego* (which is a sort of biography of the poet, though it focuses more on the poetry than on the life), he writes,

> Que un individuo quiera despertar en otro individuo recuerdos que no pertenecieron más que a un tercero, es una paradoja evidente. Ejecutar con despreocupación esa paradoja, es la inocente voluntad de toda biografía. Creo también que el haberlo conocido a Carriego no rectifica en este particular la dificultad del propósito. Poseo recuerdos de Carriego: recuerdos de recuerdos de otros recuerdos, cuyas mínimas desviaciones originales habrán oscuramente crecido en cada nuevo ensayo. (*OC* I: 113)

> [That one person should want to inspire in another person memories relating only to a third person is an obvious paradox. To pursue this paradox freely is the harmless intention of all biography. The fact that my having known Carriego does not, I contend—not in this particular case—modify the difficulty of this undertaking. I have in my possession memories of Carriego: memories of memories of other memories, whose slightest distortions, at the very outset, may have increased imperceptibly at each retelling.] (*Evaristo Carriego* 51)

And, second, in "Sobre el 'Vathek' de William Beckford" [On William Beckford's "Vathek"], he writes,

> Wilde atribuye la siguiente broma a Carlyle: una biografía de Miguel Ángel que omitiera toda mención de las obras de Miguel Ángel. Tan compleja de la realidad, tan fragmentaria y tan simplificada la historia, que un observador omnisciente podría redactar un número indefinido, y casi infinito, de biografías de un hombre, que destacan hechos independientes y de las que tendríamos que leer muchas antes de comprender que el protagonista es el mismo. (*OC* II: 107)

[Wilde attributes this joke to Carlyle: a biography of Michelangelo that would make no mention of the works of Michelangelo. So complex is reality, and so fragmentary and simplified is history, that an omniscient observer could write an indefinite, almost infinite, number of biographies of a man, each emphasizing different facts; we would have to read many of them before we realized that the protagonist was the same.] (*SNF* 236)

He goes on to posit biographies that focus on different aspects of a life: "Nadie se resigna a escribir la biografía literaria de un escritor, la biografía militar de un soldado, todos prefieren la biografía genealógica, la biografía económica, la biografía psiquiátrica, la biografía quirúrgica, la biografía tipográfica" [No one today resigns himself to writing a literary biography of an author or the military biography of a soldier; everyone prefers the genealogical biography, the economic biography, the psychiatric biography, the surgical biography, the typographical biography] (*OC* II: 107; *SNF* 236). He himself would, nevertheless, write dozens of the "biografías infames" [infamous biographies] of *Historia universal de la infamia* [*A University History of Infamy*] (1935) as well as the short "biografías sintéticas" [concise biographies] in his columns in *El Hogar* [*The Home*] from 1936 to 1939, and he often includes biographical information, however brief, in his writings.[1] His healthy skepticism about the highly selective nature of biography will inform what follows: despite the various biographies of Borges, their accounts of his life (and its relation to his work) vary widely—as we will see, a position that resonates with his general skepticism about the unity of the writing subject.[2]

Nevertheless, Norman Thomas di Giovanni prevailed upon Borges to dictate what was first titled "Autobiographical Notes," then renamed an "Autobiographical Essay" when it was included at the end of the English translation of *The Aleph and Other Stories*.[3] It is a very problematic text, full of mistakes that can be attributed to di Giovanni, the amanuensis, but also with a number of embellishments or fabrications that Borges was fond of in his many interviews in this period: the notion that he learned German by reading Heinrich Heine poems with a dictionary (when he had studied that language for four years at the Collège Calvin), the demonstrably false statement that he read *Don Quixote* first in English (the edition mentioned is by Garnier Hermanos in Paris, and it is in Spanish), the dubious assertion that he intended to write a book of "red psalms" in honor of the Bolshevik Revolution (when there are only four extant poems that could have made up that book), and the unsubstantiated notion that Borges was "promoted" from his post at the Biblioteca Municipal Miguel Cané to a job as inspector of poultry and rabbits at the municipal market (when he was offered a job that no doubt appealed to him more in the year 1946, that of editing the magazine *Los Anales de Buenos Aires* [*The Annals of Buenos Aires*]). Many of these issues will be taken up in subsequent chapters in this volume (Williamson, Hanson, Rosato, and Álvarez); what is worth arguing is that this so-called autobiography, dictated fairly late in life by a blind man and presumably never corrected by him, has proven a notoriously unreliable source for information on his life.

Despite his skepticism about biography, Borges has been the subject of numerous biographies, which range as widely as the hypothetical biographies in the essay on Beckford. No one has attempted a biography since the publication, in 2006, of Adolfo Bioy Casares's massive *Borges* and Rosato and Álvarez's first systematic look at his reading notes (2010). Now, with the publication of a significant number of Borges's manuscripts and notes for talks and courses, with the publication of several writings by family members,[4] and with significant research into Borges's work as editor and publisher, the existing biographies all come up quite short. And none grapples with their subject's diffident attitude about the possibility of writing a biography. In what follows, I will try to say what we know for sure.[5]

Borges's father, Jorge Guillermo Borges (1874–1938), was the son of a military officer, Francisco Isidoro Borges (1834–1874) who was killed in a civil war when Borges's father was a baby, so he was brought up (in English) by his mother Frances Haslam de Borges (1842–1935), known as Fanny Haslam. She survived as a widow with two sons by keeping a boarding house for English-speaking teachers who came to Argentina, mostly from the United States, as part of the afterlife of Domingo Faustino Sarmiento's admiration for the educational innovations of Horace Mann (Sarmiento was friends with Mann's widow, Mary Peabody Mann, who translated a version of the *Facundo*). Jorge Guillermo and his brother Francisco or "Frank" (later a naval officer) grew up, then, in a pocket of Anglophone Argentina (and Francisco would marry a woman of Scandinavian descent, Estela Erfjord[6]). Borges's mother, Leonor Acevedo de Borges (1876–1975), was descended from an Argentine and Uruguayan family that included a few minor luminaries in the independence war (her grandfather, Colonel Isidoro Suárez) and later civil wars in the region (her father, Isidoro Acevedo), both subjects of later poems by Borges. Jorge Guillermo was a freethinker and a Spencerian anarchist, Leonor a devout Catholic. The father would publish a translation of Omar Khayyam (not from the Arabic but from Edward FitzGerald's translation of the *Rubaiyat*) and several poems, but the main literary work published in his lifetime was a novel of rural Argentina, *El caudillo* [*The Leader*], which, when it was published in 1921, was already somewhat anachronistic, in the vein of the nineteenth-century fiction of Eugenio Cambaceres and others. He also left behind an unpublished philosophical work, *La senda* [*The Path*], which was written in 1917, in Geneva, and sheds new light on his thinking about the individual and the state, but also on such topics as the education of one's children.[7] Leonor wrote a series of letters to Esther Haedo in Uruguay recounting her early life, and she also was interviewed at length by Alicia Jurado late in her (very long) life; these sources have recently been assembled by Martín Hadis as her "memoirs," though the book does not inform its readers which parts come from the letters to Haedo, which come from the Jurado interviews, and what has been put together by Hadis.

Ricardo Piglia famously wrote about Borges's "two lineages," the intellectual and the military, and Borges himself wove elements of the family history into the first paragraph of the 1953 story "El Sur" [The South], but obviously that is something of a simplification, since the military ancestors (Francisco Borges and Isidoro Suárez) were long dead when

6   DANIEL BALDERSTON

Borges was born, and Isidoro Acevedo was at best a minor figure in the civil wars of the end of the nineteenth century. Similarly, Hadis's book on Borges's English ancestors, *Literatos y excéntricos: los ancestros ingleses de Jorge Luis Borges* (2006), finds a number of minor intellectuals from the area of the Midlands known as "the Potteries," but it is a stretch to think that Borges inherited his vocation as a writer from any of them. The fact that Jorge Guillermo Borges was an aspiring writer who never quite made it is significant, though, since early in his career young Borges made it his business to appropriate the memory of his parents' friend Evaristo Carriego (who had died in 1912, when Borges was twelve) and to cultivate the friendship of his father's law school classmate (and fellow anarchist) Macedonio Fernández (1874–1952), Borges's mentor of sorts for metaphysical speculation and literary experimentation, particularly in the 1920s and 1930s.

It is also worth noting that in the Borges family, as it was constituted by the time of the first trip to Europe in 1914, Leonor and Borges's sister, Norah, were predominantly Spanish speakers and both very Catholic, while Borges and his father were atheists and spoke with grandmother Fanny (who was Methodist) in English. The rich texture of these cultural differences within the family come into Borges's work obliquely on numerous occasions, with atheists who are deeply interested in theology, bilingual people who serve as translators and mediators (sometimes to their detriment, as is the case of Baltasar Espinosa in "El Evangelio según Marcos" [The Gospel According to Mark]), people caught between polar opposites (the English grandmother conversing with the English "captive" in "Historia del guerrero y de la cautiva" [Story of the Warrior and the Captive]), and the librarian who accepts a challenge to a knife fight (in "El Sur").

Borges went to public school in Buenos Aires for only one year, to a school on Calle Thames in Palermo (where he met Roberto Godel, to whom he would write enthusiastically a few years later about the Bolshevik and the ultimately unsuccessful German revolutions; he would write a preface for a volume of Godel's poetry in 1932). He was accepted to the Colegio Nacional Buenos Aires (the most prestigious public secondary school in the Argentine capital), but their parents decided to go to Europe in 1914, an inauspicious moment to do so; they would end up in neutral Switzerland. Borges studied for four years at the Collège de Genève,[8] though he never graduated because some sort of nervous breakdown in late 1918 and early 1919 prevented him from presenting himself for the final exams.[9] At the school in Geneva, instruction was in French (which young Borges learned as quickly as he could), with courses in Latin and German; his close friends there were both Jewish, Maurice Abramowicz (1901–1981, later a socialist politician in Switzerland) and Simon Jichlinski (1902–1994, later a physician in Geneva). While Borges was studying there, his sister, Norah, began studying art; both siblings were talented writers and artists, but there seems to have been an implicit decision between them that Jorge Luis's career was to be in letters and Norah's in the visual arts. Norah would meet the young Spanish intellectual Guillermo de Torre (1900–1971) during both siblings' involvement with the avant garde movement Ultraísmo (Norah would design many book and magazine covers for the publications of the *ultraístas*); they married in 1928 and lived in Spain until the Spanish Civil War (1936–1939). De Torre would work for many years as an editor, first with José Ortega y Gasset at the *Revista de*

Occidente and then with Gonzalo Losada at Editorial Losada in Buenos Aires.[10] The relations between Borges and de Torre were marked by conflict (an early poem is dedicated "a Guillermo de Torre, por contraste"), and Borges would later joke that they got along fine once de Torre was deaf and Borges was blind: "Él no me puede oír y yo no lo puedo ver" [He can't hear me and I can't see him], which has the sly second meaning of "I can't stand him."

After a period in northern Italy, presumably for Borges to recover from his nervous breakdown (but also coinciding with the death of his maternal grandmother, Leonor Suárez de Acevedo, who may have helped finance the years in Europe), the Borges family went to Spain, ending up for some months in Mallorca (where the siblings became friends with Jacobo and Elvira Sureda, the children of an artsy family in Valldemossa), and then mostly in Madrid. In this period, from late 1919 to 1921, both siblings were intensely involved with Ultraísmo, the brother as a poet and writer of manifestoes (and translator of German expressionist poetry) and the sister as the creator of woodcuts that graced the covers and the interior of various magazines, most prominently *VLTRA* (1921–1922). When the family returned to Buenos Aires in March 1921, both were centrally involved in the founding of an Argentine *ultraísta* group, which published the first *Proa* in 1922–1923, the two editions of the "revista mural" *Prisma* in 1921–1922, and later the second series of *Proa* (no longer really an organ of Ultraísmo) between 1924 and 1927. Borges's fervor for the rather formulaic avant garde poetry of Ultraísmo had largely cooled by the time he (self-) published his first book, *Fervor de Buenos Aires* [*Fervor of Buenos Aires*], in 1923, shortly before the family went to Europe for a second, briefer, trip from June 1923 to July 1924, this time accompanied by Fanny Haslam (who would see her native country for the first time since her immigration to Argentina in 1870).

One of the enigmas of the family history I have just narrated is how all of this was financed. Leonor Suárez de Acevedo had inherited land (and perhaps a modest fortune), and she and her husband Isidoro Acevedo (a municipal official in Buenos Aires) bought the lot in Palermo where the Borges family built a house and lived for a decade until their departure for Europe in 1914; it was then rented out until they sold it sometime in the 1920s. They lived in rented apartments between 1921 and 1923 and in the period from 1924 until Borges's mother bought the small apartment at Calle Maipú 994 in central Buenos Aires where she would live with her son from 1947 until her death in 1975 (Williamson 263). He would live there (except for a brief hiatus from 1967 to 1970, when he lived in an apartment at Avenida Belgrano 1377 with his wife Elsa Astete Millán)[11] until his departure for Geneva in 1985, already sick with the liver cancer that would kill him there.[12] Jorge Guillermo studied law but did not practice; he got a job teaching at the Instituto de Lenguas Vivas (where his aunt Carolina Haslam also worked), but eventually would have to give that up in the late 1920s, when he went blind. Borges himself would have some rather precarious jobs, first as co-editor (with Ulises Petit de Murat) at the *Revista Multicolor de los Sábados* [*Saturday Multicolor Magazine*] of the evening mass-circulation newspaper *Crítica* (1933–1934),[13] then at the Biblioteca Municipal Miguel Cané from 1938 to 1946.[14] Even though the Argentine peso was a strong currency in the early part of the twentieth century, the family's finances must have always been rather precarious; Leonor

8   DANIEL BALDERSTON

Acevedo would buy a modest summer house in Adrogué in 1944, but then have to sell it in 1952 (it is now the Casa Museo Borges, owned by the municipality of Almirante Brown).

A life in letters, certainly, but also a rather agitated one in its public dimensions, as will be explored in some of the following chapters. Abrupt changes in his esthetics, in his politics, in his work life, all precede blindness and world fame; any sort of financial stability or steady work would come to Borges late in life. His writings were published almost all first in magazines and newspapers, then collected in a rather haphazard way in the long series of his books; there were enough published but uncollected works to fill several posthumous volumes (the three volumes of *Textos recobrados*; the reviews and short essays in *Textos cautivos* and *Borges en El Hogar*; and the many other uncollected essays, translations, and reviews in *Borges en Sur*). He was never a rich man and depended on the generosity of friends who bought books or lent them to him from their libraries (early on Xul Solar, later Adolfo Bioy Casares, among others); summer vacations were at friends' properties (the Bioy Casares/Silvina Ocampo house in Mar del Plata and their ranch Rincón Viejo in Pardo, Las Nubes in Salto, Uruguay, the summer home of his cousin Esther Haedo and her writer husband Enrique Amorim; and briefer stays elsewhere). Between 1924, when the family returned from the second sojourn in Europe, and 1961, when Borges was invited to the University of Texas at Austin for a semester as a visiting professor, he would not leave the River Plate region, though he traveled extensively within Argentina to give talks in the period from 1949 to 1955,[15] and also went to Uruguay for the same purpose in 1945 and again late in the Peronist decade (see "Talks by Borges" on the Borges Center website). A polemicist (and polemical figure) as early as the Ultraísta period, Borges was deeply involved in cultural work that had a political dimension, as becomes very clear during the Peronist decade (1946–1955).[16]

Borges says in a famous preface that his childhood was spent in the rather inauspicious neighborhood of Palermo.

> Yo creí, durante años, haberme criado en un suburbio de Buenos Aires, un suburbio de calles aventuradas y de ocasos visibles. Lo cierto es que me crié en un jardín, detrás de una verja con lanzas, y en una biblioteca de ilimitados libros ingleses. Palermo del cuchillo y de la guitarra andaba (me aseguran) por las esquinas, pero quienes poblaron mis mañanas y dieron agradable horror a mis noches fueron el bucanero ciego de Stevenson, agonizando bajo las patas de los caballos, y el traidor que abandonó a su amigo en la luna, y el viajero del tiempo, que trajo del porvenir una rosa marchita, y el genio encarcelado durante siglos en el cántaro salomónico, y el profeta velado del Jorasán, que detrás de las piedras y de la seda ocultaba la lepra.
>
> ¿Qué había, mientras tanto, del otro lado de la verja con lanzas? ¿Qué destinos vernáculos y violentos fueron cumpliéndose a unos pasos de mí, en el turbio almacén o en el azaroso baldío? ¿Cómo fue aquel Palermo o cómo hubiera sido hermoso que fuera? (*OC* I: 101)

> [For years I believe I had grown up in a suburb of Buenos Aires, a suburb of dangerous streets and showy sunsets. The truth is that I grew up in a garden, behind a fence of iron palings, and in a library of endless English books. The Palermo of the knife and guitar throve (I am told) just around the corner, but those who populated

BIOGRAPHY AND ITS DISCONTENTS   9

my days and gave a pleasant shiver to my nights were Stevenson's blind buccaneer, dying under the horses' hooves, and the traitor who left his friend behind on the moon, and the time traveler who brought back from the future a withered flower, and the genie imprisoned for centuries in a Solomonic jar, and the Veiled Prophet of Khurasan, who hid his leprosy behind silk and precious stones.

What was going on, meanwhile, on the other side of the iron palings? What everyday lives were fulfilling their violent destinies only a few steps away from me in some unsavory saloon or ominous vacant lot? What was Palermo like then, and how beautiful would it really have been?] (*Evaristo Carriego* 33)

This preface, added to *Evaristo Carriego* when it was republished in the series of small volumes from Emecé in the 1950s that were later collected in the 1974 so-called *Obras completas*, is a retrospective look at a life, only a few years of which were actually lived in that house in Palermo. The bookish child looking out was certainly not the only Borges that the writer could have conjured up in the 1950s, nor is it an adequate account of the person he was by then. But the assertion of looking at life, as Emily Dickinson said, "slant" does perhaps describe an important facet of the life he lived, at the threshold of experience, looking up from his reading.[17]

In the chapters that follow, many aspects of Borges's working and writing life will be taken up, showing that he strayed far from the boy in that garden. But perhaps his evocation of that self, and of the world outside that he perhaps barely knew in the years in that house and garden (from age four to fourteen), is a good way to start this handbook. The reader looking up from the book: an evocative self-portrait of a boy from a complicated family and in a rapidly changing city (and nation). Borges would return several times late in his life to evocations of his early selves, most famously in the 1974 story "El otro" [The Other], in which an older Borges sits on a bench by the Charles River in Cambridge next to a boy who turns out to be his own younger self, but who is sitting on a bench by the Rhône River in Geneva. He would write numerous evocations of his ancestors, of which perhaps the most eloquent is "Poema conjetural" [Conjectural Poem], about Francisco Narciso de Laprida (he was descended from Laprida's sister), but there were also texts about his parents and grandparents and delicate and rather diffident references to his sister. There are also numerous ironic self-portraits, or cameo appearances, in his fiction. The man Jorge Luis Borges (or, as his birth records show, Jorge Francisco Isidoro, the Luis being added a year later in his baptismal record) would be conjured up as a double or a specter. "Borges y yo" [Borges and I], one of the brief prose texts that are included in the 1960 book *El hacedor* [*Dreamtigers*], would define the relationship between the self and the man Borges, perhaps the public figure, as antagonistic, but also as the opportunity for flight ("fuga").[18] Is Borges evoking the art of the fugue here, the quintessence of baroque music? In 1950, he would give a talk on "La literatura alemana en la época de Bach" [German Literature in the Age of Bach] (published in 1953), and his writings are full of references to the baroque. He presents emphatic images of himself throughout his career, though they differ and contradict each other. "No hay tal yo de conjunto" [there is no such self as a whole], he writes in the early essay "La nadería de la personalidad" [The Nothingness of Personality] in 1922, and, in the epigraph to *Evaristo Carriego*, he quotes De Quincey's "mode of truth, not of truth coherent and central, but angular and splintered." Late in his life he performed the role of the blind seer but also wrote (in several of the texts in *El hacedor*) that such a performance could be a simulacrum, with nothing inside. There is still no adequate biography of Borges, but I guess there's no reason why there should be: the subject resists closure, is elusive, hides many enigmas.

NOTES

1. There are also numerous brief biographies in his prefaces to Arturo Jauretche, Gloria Alcorta, Franz Kafka, Domingo Faustino Sarmiento, and Henry James, to mention just a few.
2. An early biography is Alicia Jurado's *Genio y figura de Jorge Luis Borges* (1964). Emir Rodríguez Monegal's *Jorge Luis Borges: A Literary Biography* (1978) was well-regarded at the time of its publication but has not fared well since then. Estela Canto's *Borges a contraluz* (1987) provided important first-hand information about Borges's life from a close friend, a woman he wanted to marry in the 1940s; another close friend who wrote about Borges's life was María Esther Vázquez. *Los dos Borges: Vida, sueños, enigmas* (1996) is an interesting biography by the Chilean communist Volodia Teitelboim. James Woodall (*Borges: A Life*, 1996) and Jason Wilson (*Borges*, 2006) are useful, though the most detailed account of Borges's life is Edwin Williamson's *Borges: A Life* (2004). Alejandro Vaccaro has written several volumes about Borges, of which the most complete is *Borges: Vida y literatura* (2006).
3. Di Giovanni gives his account of the writing of the text in *The Lesson of the Master* (141–57).
4. See, e.g., Miguel de Torre Borges's *Borges, manuscritos y fotografías* (1987, then 2004 under a slightly different title), *Un día de Jorge Luis Borges* (1995), and *Apuntes de familia* (2004, expanded edition 2019); and Martín Hadis's *Memorias de Leonor Acevedo de Borges: Los recuerdos de la madre del más grande escritor argentino* (2021).
5. For a detailed chronology of Borges's life and work set in the context of Argentine and wider history, see the timeline on the homepage of the Borges Center website: www.borges.pitt.edu.
6. Her surname appears in several texts including "Tres versiones de Judas" [Three Versions of Judas], "Los teólogos" [The Theologians], and "El Congreso" [The Congress]. See Williamson for an account of the Lange and Erfjord connections (98–99, 126).
7. The Borges Center published this work in 2015.
8. Founded by Jean Calvin in 1559, it is often referred to as the Collège Calvin.
9. On this, see Yates and Williamson, among others.
10. Their son Miguel, who died in 2022, would work at Losada himself after his father's death; he edited books of his uncle's manuscripts and the family photo album, as well as the two small books of family memories already mentioned.
11. See the rather catty account of the marriage by Norman Thomas di Giovanni, *Georgie & Elsa: Jorge Luis Borges and His Wife: The Untold Story* (2014).
12. He is buried in the municipal Cimetière Plainpalais (or Cimetière des Rois), reserved for illustrious figures connected one way or another to Geneva. His tomb there is near that of the reformer Jean Calvin; a new neighbor is the "Écrivain Peintre Prostituée" Grisélidis

Réal (1929–2005). See Martín Hadis's *Siete guerreros nortumbrios* (2011) for information on Borges's tombstone.
13. See work on this by Sylvia Saítta here and elsewhere.
14. See the Rosato and Álvarez chapter in this volume.
15. See Mariela Blanco in her chapter in this volume and elsewhere.
16. See my later chapter in this volume.
17. On this, see the chapter by Magdalena Cámpora and Mariana Di Ció in this volume.
18. On this famous text, see the article by Donald Yates.

WORKS CITED

Bioy Casares, Adolfo. *Borges*, edited by Daniel Martino. Destino, 2006.

Borges, Jorge Luis. "Autobiographical Essay." *The Aleph and Other Stories, 1933–1969, Together with Commentaries and an Autobiographical Essay*. E. P. Dutton, 1970, pp. 203–62.

Borges, Jorge Luis. "Autobiographical Notes," with Norman Thomas di Giovanni. *The New Yorker*, September 19, 1970, pp. 40–99.

Borges, Jorge Luis. *Evaristo Carriego*, translated by Norman Thomas di Giiovanni. E. P. Dutton, 1984.

Borges, Jorge Luis. "La nadería de la personalidad." *Proa* (first series), 1922. Later included in *Inquisiciones*. Editorial Proa, 1925.

Borges, Jorge Luis. *Obras completas*. 4 vols. Emecé, 1996.

Borges, Jorge Luis. *Selected Non-Fictions*, edited by Eliot Weinberger. Viking, 1999.

Canto, Estela. *Borges a contraluz*. Espasa-Calpe, 1989.

de Torre Borges, Miguel. *Apuntes de familia: Mis padres, mi tío, mi abuela, mi madrina*. Losada, 2019.

de Torre Borges, Miguel. *Borges, fotos y manuscritos*. Alloni/Proa, 2006.

de Torre Borges, Miguel. *Un día de Borges*. Buenos Aires, 1995.

Di Giovanni, Norman Thomas. *Georgie & Elsa: Jorge Luis Borges and His Wife: The Untold Story*. The Friday Project, 2014.

Di Giovanni, Norman Thomas. *The Lesson of the Master: On Borges and his Work*. Continuum Books, 2003.

Hadis, Martín. *Literatos y excéntricos: Los ancestros ingleses de Jorge Luis Borges*. Editorial Sudamericana, 2006.

Hadis, Martín. *Memorias de Leonor Acevedo de Borges: Los recuerdos de la madre del más grande escritor argentino*. Claridad, 2021.

Hadis, Martín. *Siete guerreros nortumbrios*. Emecé, 2011.

Jurado, Alicia. *Genio y figura de Jorge Luis Borges*. Eudeba, 1964.

Piglia, Ricardo. "Ideología y ficción en Borges." *Punto de Vista*, vol. 2, no. 5, 1979, pp. 3–6.

Rodríguez Monegal, Emir. *Jorge Luis Borges: A Literary Biography*. E. P. Dutton, 1978.

Rosato, Laura and Germán Álvarez. *Borges, libros y lecturas*. Biblioteca Nacional, 2010.

Teitelboim, Volodia. *Los dos Borges: Vida, sueños, enigmas*. Editorial Hermes/Editorial Sudamericana Chilena, 1996.

Vaccaro, Alejandro. *Borges: Vida y literatura*. Edhasa, 2006.

Vázquez, María Esther. *Borges: Esplendor y derrota*. Tusquets, 1996.

Williamson, Edwin. *Borges: A Life*. Viking, 2004.

Wilson, Jason. *Jorge Luis Borges*. Reaktion Books, 2006.

Woodall, James. *Borges: A Life*. Basic Books, 1996. [Original British title: *Man in the Mirror of the Book*. Hodden and Stoughton, 1996.]

Yates, Donald A. "Behind 'Borges and I.'" *Modern Fiction Studies*, vol. 19, no. 3, 1973, pp. 317–24.

Yates, Donald A. "Jorge Guillermo Borges (1874–1938): Two Notes." *Variaciones Borges*, vol. 32, 2011, pp. 215–20.

Yates, Donald A. *Jorge Luis Borges: Life, Work and Criticism*. York Press, 1985.

CHAPTER 2

THE SECRET SHARER
Borges as Reader

MAGDALENA CÁMPORA AND MARIANA DI CIÓ

BEFORE THE PUBLIC

THE constant reader, the child in the library, the most bountiful reader (be it for pleasure, for work, or in quantity), the reader who went blind: reading is perhaps the most dramatic and transformative event in the life of Jorge Luis Borges. Yet drama—or pathos, as he would have called it—was not the tone with which he described events, and acceptance and humility can be sensed in the verses of his 1969 poem, "Un lector" [A Reader]: "Que otros se jacten de las páginas que han escrito; / a mí me enorgullecen las que he leído" [Let others boast of pages they have written / I take pride in those I've read] (*OC* II: 394; *In Praise* 121). Within this poem appear two constants in Borges's reflections on reading: memory and the physical book. Memory works with the material he has read and inserts it in new contexts, allowing his readings to nourish his writing. And the book (its "gravitación amistosa" [friendly gravitation] [*OC* IV: 170]) refers to readings situated in specific editions, singularized by affection.[1] A place (*that* book), any place (reading): Michel de Certeau, quoting Borges, described the reader as a traveler and reading as a space outside the text, where imagination and thought move away from the page to create one's own enjoyment. For Borges that magic, which begins when readers lift their eyes from the page, gives them primacy over everything else: the author, the interpretative community, the institution.

His ideas in this regard are well known. The book is an "eje de innumerables relaciones" [an axis of innumerable relationships] (*OC* II: 152; *Labyrinths* 214), and it is the reader who weaves these networks. Reading modifies texts; to read *Don Quixote* as does Pierre Menard in Nîmes in 1934 (or in Buenos Aires in 1939) is to turn the novel Cervantes wrote somewhere in Castile, three centuries earlier, into another book. Hence, "una literatura difiere de otra, ulterior o anterior, menos por el texto que por la manera de ser leída: si me fuera otorgado leer cualquier página actual—ésta, por ejemplo—como la leerán el año 2000 yo sabría cómo será la literatura del año 2000" [one literature differs from another, prior or posterior, less because of the text than because of the way in which it is read: if I were granted the possibility of reading any present-day page—this one, for example—as it will be read in the year two thousand, I would know what the literature of the year two thousand will be like] (*OC* II: 152; *Labyrinths* 214). Elsewise, reading occupies a central place in Borges's poetics, and the very experience of reading is a primary motif. "Tema del traidor y del héroe" [Theme of the Traitor and the Hero], "El evangelio según Marcos" [The Gospel According to Mark], "Tlön, Uqbar, Orbis Tertius": in these stories, Borges writes about people who read and, by reading, intervene in the world. In his essays and reviews, analyzing ways of reading allows for the discussion of literary superstitions, which are attempts to stabilize meaning. In poetry, the evocation of reading allows for an indirect and modest way of conveying one's affections: such a passage from the Gospel, from the *Comedy*, from *Don Quixote*.

That Borges flaunts his readings when he writes is something that the most candid reader perceives almost sensorially due to his habit of quotation, the presence of titles and authors' names, the bibliographical references in the body of the text or in footnotes. Strictly speaking, it is difficult to think of Borges at all without thinking of "Borges the Reader": his readings cover the work, just like the map of the empire covers the territory in "Del rigor en la ciencia" [On Exactitude in Science]. This bewildering abundance of references created a sense of alienation in his first readers and distrust in those who followed. Suspicions regarding apocryphal quotation and mystification were part of the creation of Borges's singular public figure, which was both accessible and enigmatic. As his appearances in the mass media began to multiply from the 1960s onward,[2] there also arose the commonplace understanding of Borges as a "difficult" author who had devoted his personal life to literature and whose references were complicated—when not made up.

In parallel, within literary criticism, analyzing the ways reading was integrated into Borges's creative process generated analytical categories that are still relevant to both literary studies and in Borges scholarship: the semantic productivity of the text, which projects the utopia of anonymous creation and nourishes concepts that are central to Structuralism, such as intertextuality and hypertext (Genette); the art of "allusion" (Christ); "the pleasure of interpolation" and of "jumbled up erudition" (Molloy); quotation as rewriting (Lafon); a possible typology of his reading erudition (Louis 2016, *Borges*); and the networking, in encyclopedias and dictionaries, of the partial and fragmented elements that constitute a fictional reality composed of other texts (Balderston, *The Literary Universe*; Fishburn and Hughes).

After his death in 1986, and the subsequent publication of those writings (mostly his early work) that Borges had discarded during his lifetime—including his first three books of essays, his "recovered texts," most of the work published in newspapers and journals—, the author's personal encyclopedia was expanded. The new records, which no longer depended on his personal editing and curating, allowed for the analysis of unknown connections that fostered his writing. Familiarity with his readings also served to historicize those cultural contributions Borges made locally, which he contributed through his editorial work (print media, directorship of publishers' themed collections, prefaces, anthologies), critical work (reviews and essays not published in book form), and translations. Between the 1930s and the 1950s, these mediations, which were generally linked to his remunerated labor, allowed him to propose bold reorganizations of literary historiography, both national and foreign. Thus, critics' interest turned to the affinities and strategic uses (in aesthetic and political terms) of texts and authors who were appearing in Borges's work, whose frontiers were increasingly expanding (Louis, *Borges face au fascisme*; Balderston, *Innumerables relaciones*; and Schwartz).

A third perspective for the study of Borges as a reader was unveiled in 2010, from the Biblioteca Nacional Mariano Moreno (Argentina), with the publication of the *catalogue raisonné* entitled *Borges, libros y lecturas* by Laura Rosato and Germán Álvarez. This archive contains the personal library that Borges donated to the National Library during his time as Director (1955–1973) and consists of some three hundred entries of books annotated by Borges. They are, for the most part, instrumental records (generally on the flyleaves) where what was read served as a basis for writing. Markers or signposts of future ideas or images, the annotations in these books acquire meaning for those who specialize in Borges, allowing them to map that territory based on the published work. While this library of writing material (in a process that is still in progress) was reemerging from the now distant time when Borges was still an autonomous and solitary reader, his manuscripts also returned from the past. Since the 2000s, Daniel Balderston has undertaken the collection and systematic study of the existing manuscripts,[3] scattered around the world in libraries and private collections. Their margins covered with references to other texts, the manuscripts also allow for an intimate study of Borges as a reader—the evanescent scene that is the dialogue between texts he read and his own writing. However, it is not so much a matter of recuperating the fetish of the "infinitesimal" moment of "la invención" [the invention] (*TR* 2: 122), but rather of accessing new registers that illuminate the elaboration of his writing and allow for the critical evaluation of the formal markers of his readings' aesthetic impact. These records are complemented by access to notebooks with notes, drafts, and reading citations preserved in places including university libraries in the United States; with the publication of the courses he gave at the Colegio Libre de Estudios Superiores (CLES); and with the identification of the lectures and courses he gave between 1946 and 1955, partly consigned by Borges himself on the title page of a *Life of Schopenhauer*, in the National Library of Argentina's collection.[4]

The annotated library, notebooks, lectures, courses, manuscripts—in the light of these other scenes of reading and creation, Borges's published work becomes the outer peel of a series of layers or stages in the elaboration of ideas and forms, for which we now have material records. We knew what Borges read: the new archives allow us to think about *how* he read. The possibility of using these materials to analyze the dynamics of writing and reading feeding one another before publication—Borges reads, jots down, reformulates, invents, prepares notes for a lecture—opens new critical spaces that were unthinkable until a few years ago. This is largely because, beyond the intertextual relationship or co-presence in the final published text, these new materials prove that reading in Borges is a submerged continent, a cognitive process that continues to work even from absence, such as in that text of *El hacedor* [*Dreamtigers*] where the captive remained "trabajado por el desierto" [chiseled by the desert] (*OC* II: 177).

READING ON THE STREETCAR (READING AND WORKING)

Making Borges uniquely singular as a reader is the fact that, owing to his work, there is a near weekly record of what he was reading. The thirty years prior to achieving international fame in the 1960s and prior to the blindness which, after 1955, prevented him from reading directly, were in fact marked by a clear-cut task: reading in order to write. He wrote to Estela Canto at the end of 1944, "Me abruman las tareas. . . un prólogo para las *Novelas ejemplares*, otro para el *Paradise Lost*, otro para un libro de Emerson, . . . la lectura (nominal) de cuatro volúmenes para el Premio Nacional de Filosofía, la de otras tantas piezas de teatro para un certamen, la innumerable redacción de solapas, noticias y contratapas" [I am overwhelmed by tasks. . . a prologue for the *Novelas ejemplares*, another for *Paradise Lost*, another for a book by Emerson, . . . the (nominal) reading of four books for the National Prize in Philosophy, and a bunch of plays for a contest, the countless number of book flaps, notes and back covers] (123). Additionally, the essays, reviews, capsule biographies in *El Hogar* [The Home], *Sur*, and other publications give an account of his readings; Bioy Casares's diary detailing his relationship with Borges often recorded what they were reading; his notebooks valuably preserve his notes: for the historian of reading, Borges is a wish fulfilled, a dream come true.

There is a whole area of his production where reading is linked to paid work. Unlike other writers of his close circle (Bioy Casares, Silvina and Victoria Ocampo, María Rosa Oliver) Borges was not independently wealthy and had to work in exchange for money; as we know, in 1938, he became first assistant at the Miguel Cané Library. This situation was complicated for him, less because of the effort involved in reading and working with books and more because of potentially feeling humiliated by needing to receive a salary. The social burden of the poor gentleman "hidalgo," descended from warriors for Argentina's Independence, who now lived frugally with his mother amid ancient criollo furniture, was undoubtedly intensified by having his salary paid by the State, particularly when it came from a Peronist government. In the story he tells Norman Thomas Di Giovanni in 1970, in his "Autobiographical Notes," the issue comes up time and again: how little money he earned at the municipal library, the money that his society friends told him he could earn at another job, the large sum of money that "an old English lady" who read his tea leaves predicted he would earn by lecturing, how funny this prophecy seemed to him and his mother. The discourse surrounding Borges's inability to earn money is also a discourse about class, but the truth is that the remuneration he obtained from the exercise of letters and the oratorical arts (arduously achieved, according to his automythography) was the result of an immensely pragmatic approach to availing himself of resources. Michel Lafon (1990), referring to the author's poetics, has mentioned Borges's gifts as a rewriter; the same could be said of his gifts as a re-reader when considering the ways that he managed and organized his texts and readings. Borges recovered, reassembled, economized texts according to each instance's need. Lectures, courses, newspaper and journal articles—every space served for the argumentative and rhetorical development of whatever concepts or thoughts had been revealed in his reading: the textual economy supplied the domestic economy. A clear example can be found in what he logged in his notebooks. As several of the *Variaciones Borges* studies devoted to notebooks have shown (2021, number 52), the Borges of the *late style* would frequently rely upon the notes he had taken earlier, when he was still able to see. Daniel Balderston notes, "Borges's compositional notebooks were in a locked cabinet in Leonor Acevedo de Borges's bedroom at Maipú 994 for many years" (*How Borges Wrote* 50). Those notes were re-read for him when he could no longer do so, and they served to structure courses and conferences in Argentina and eventually around the world when he became an international figure. Thus, reading and study patterned by the demands of oral presentations or publications between the 1930s and 1950s became a reservoir for later lectures and writings. "Un libro se lee para la memoria" [A book is read to be remembered] (*OC* IV: 183), he would say in his 1978 lecture on the book.

Before his blindness, Borges read while working and jotted his notes down everywhere: back and front covers, notebooks, book covers—all of which served to organize lists of books, to translate by condensing, to accumulate references in several languages. What also emerges from these bountiful papers is the *libido scribendi* that possessed him, the urge that led him to take notes on any sheet of paper he had at hand after reading: it was the impulse of writing as it happened, with penmanship that today reveals signs of adrenaline when Borges was encountering a discovery, his handwriting in such moments moving beyond his famous, insect-like script. We now have an archive of, as Balderston calls it, Borges's "chaotic and irregular" calligraphy (*How Borges Wrote* 17). There is something stirring in this dialogue with paper and book, in this solitary and autonomous life of writing with its private jokes. For example, Borges transcribed and recorded the texts sold to magazines or newspapers in the "credit" column of an accounting notebook; he recorded the lectures he had given throughout Argentina on the title page of a *Life of Schopenhauer*: the philosopher who turns boredom and pain into parts of the world reflects the hard-working life of the scholar, who regards his task with jocular irony.

None of it was ever expressed as a burden or a thankless task, but as an area of joy in a time—the 1940s—when he still exercised sovereignty over his own body and lived in full, harmonious solitude with books, ink, and paper: Borges as a stationery man, figuratively and literally. A consumer of notebooks, spiral-bound or buckled, of various brands (Avon, Lanceros Argentinos de 1910, Carabela, 33 Orientales); a connoisseur of paper, graph or plain; a reader and annotator of books whose inside covers bear the blue, black, or burgundy marbling of the bookbinders. And while his maternal great-grandfather Colonel Suarez led a regiment of lancers at the siege of Colonia in 1827, in the nationalist and Catholic Argentina of the 1940s, Borges's reading notes on Leibniz's and Fritz Mauthner's perspectives on the gratuitousness of evil are taken in a school notebook branded "Lanceros Argentinos" [Argentine Lancers]. In the active stillness of the intellectual task, the materials signify and suggest a joyful, almost sensory relationship with the paper, in rare harmony with life itself: the "casi intolerables memorias de un ángulo de tu sonrisa . . ., de tus dedos rasgando el papel" [almost intolerable memories of an angle of your smile . . . of your fingers tearing the paper] he then wrote to Estela Canto (125). Borges stated countless times that reading was happiness: in the notebooks, where he appropriates greatly malleable images taken from works of philosophy or theology, where the speed of the connections he forms is enhanced by his network of quotations and other memories of reading—such enjoyment is tangible. They were books and notebooks never intended to be seen by anyone; today, they are the material traces of moments of plenitude in the process of reading.

Borges's relationship with books between the 1930s and the 1950s is not removed from the cultural events of his time, particularly from the processes of democratization of reading and the new forms of book consumption. He read *La Divina Comedia* on Line 76 of Buenos Aires's streetcar system, on which he traveled to and from work on a route that took "a couple of hours each day" ("Autobiographical Essay" 170) between Almagro and downtown. The "natural" scene for reading within his social class of origin was, however, something quite different. It is a scene that he sets in his father's library and in his childhood, a setting that also appears in the memoirs of his contemporaries María Rosa Oliver[5] and Victoria Ocampo: Jorge Guillermo Borges's library "was in a room of its own, with glass-fronted shelves, and must have contained several thousand volumes" ("Autobiographical Notes" 42). But the adult worker Borges now must read in the midst of others who do not know who he is, or during the hours he would "steal away" at work, when he would read Gibbon or Vicente Fidel López in the basement or on the roof (depending on the weather) ("Autobiographical Notes" 42). A certain contingency marks his readings of the contemporary books given to him to review or his fortuitous encounter with the books he wanted to read: "leía todas las traducciones que encontraba" [I read all the translations I could find], he says of *The Divine Comedy* (*Seven Nights* 209). In reality, his access to books was no different from that of any educated, low-income reader from the middle classes in modernizing Argentina. Books by Garnier Hermanos published in Spanish in Europe (such as his children's edition of *Don Quixote*), libraries of classics (for example, Clásicos Jackson, where he collaborated), the *Encyclopaedia Britannica*, the twenty-five volumes of the Spanish-American dictionary by Montaner y Simón, the English pocket editions of Everyman's Library, handbooks, manuals or introductions to various disciplines and authors[6]: these were the books Borges had access to as well, and he read them sitting on the floor of the English bookstores, at Mitchell's on calle Cangallo (today Perón), at Mackern on calle Reconquista, "donde era conocido y se le permitía revolver todo lo que quisiera" [where he was known and allowed to rummage through anything he wanted] (Canto 30), or at the German bookstore in Buenos Aires. He also read at the public library in the Almagro neighborhood and in the private libraries of rich friends like Bioy and Silvina Ocampo, who had the books he wanted brought to them.

This breadth in reading experiences, this mixing among social classes and scenarios, sharpened Borges's perception of readers with different degrees of literacy and access to books, which will later appear in among the Gutres ("El evangelio según Marcos"), Emma Zunz ("Emma Zunz"), Alejandro Villari ("La espera" [The Wait]), Red Scharlach ("La muerte y la brújula" [Death and the Compass]), Julius Rothe ("El milagro secreto" [The Secret Miracle]), Yu Tsun ("El jardín de senderos que se bifurcan" [The Garden of Forking Paths]), the illiterate possessor of the book of sand ("El libro de arena" [The Book of Sand]), and so many more. What is remarkable is that the lower the literacy level of the character, the greater is their fictional activity and the better they handle the world and its violence. The Gutres, who cannot read, sacrifice Espinosa, who translates and declaims with rhetorical dexterity (two literati skills that cause his end); Julius Rothe, the Nazi censor who misreads symbolic capital, condemns Jaromir Hladík to death because he mistakenly considers him an important translator (in "El evangelio según Marcos" and "El milagro secreto," translation is a practice for which one can die). Yu Tsun reads a name in a phone book and that reading implies the bombing of a city and the death of a man who has spent his life reading (in "El jardín de senderos que se bifurcan," reading is a practice that can kill). The worker Emma Zunz, like her namesake Emma Bovary, knows how to "plot" and "imagine" a perfect plot to kill Aaron Loewenthal.[7] Alejandro Villari, who reads *The Divine Comedy* naively (as Borges advised readers do in his lectures), manages to escape pre-death anguish because he does not distinguish between fiction and reality. But perhaps Red Scharlach is the most complete example of this dynamic between access to texts, new readers, and action: he conceives the trap against Lönnrot because he reads in "los diarios de la tarde . . . las explicaciones rabínicas" [in the evening papers about the rabbinical explanations] of the murders and because "uno de esos tenderos que han descubierto que cualquier hombre se resigna a comprar cualquier libro, publicó una edición popular de la *Historia de la secta de los Hasidim*" [one of those shopkeepers who have found that any given man may be persuaded to buy any given book published a popular edition of the *A History of the Hasidim*] (*OC* I: 537; *CF* 149). The Argentine publishing and media landscape is drawn in filigree—the popular publishers that supply autodidacts. There also is the allegory of access to knowledge by a criminal who uses reading to inform his crime.

Who reads better: The reader of taste, or the efficient reader who reads and perceives according to interest?[8] All the ambivalence of the anti-modern Borges, who collaborates in the newspaper *Crítica* and publishes with TOR, appears in this twist where the sophisticated reading is not of the high culture—like that of Lönnrot, the reasoning son of Auguste Dupin—but of the "más ilustre de los pistoleros del Sur" [the most famous gunman of the Southside] (*OC* I: 606; *CF* 152) a self-taught reader, a child of local literacy campaigns, who gets a popular edition of the *History of the Sect of the Hasidim*, reads it shrewdly and puts it at the service of his revenge. Just as Baudelaire slights photography (that mass-producing technique) in "The Modern Public and Photography" (1862) and then poses for Felix Nadar's camera on more than twenty occasions, Borges distrusts the masses as a political actor—that "Gran Perro Bonzo" [Big Dog Bonzo] as he calls the public in "La fiesta del monstruo" [The Monster's Party] in 1947—but makes one of its members the most brilliant and effective of readers (*Nuevos Cuentos* 91). "Leí la *Historia de la secta de los Hasidim*" [I read the *A History of the Hasidim*] (*OC* I: 543; *CF* 155) says Red Scharlach. Within that illegitimate reading by the plebian is condensed the entire process of the democratization of books in Argentina in the first half of the twentieth century: the formation of new readers; Law 1420 requiring compulsory and free education; the professionalization of publishing, bookstores, and kiosks; popular publishing; the resistance and fascination of the literati in the face of that process. Where must Red Scharlach have purchased the book? Did he read the afternoon papers standing next to a kiosk, as depicted in so many photos of the time? On that background, which he keeps in twilight between Rue de Toulon and Triste-le-Roy, Borges embeds the perfect miniature of his fictions (Cámpora 2024).

The Secret Reader

If Borges's tendency to quote is already legendary, the appearance of the new materials discussed above allows for more accurate and less conjectural study—at least somewhat more preserved from the traps of authorial meta-discourse—of Borges's way of thinking about reading not only as a practice, but also as an essential aspect of the task of writing. The annotations and underlining in the books included in *Borges, libros y lecturas* (Rosato and Álvarez), as well as the three volumes of manuscripts published by the Borges Center (Balderston and Martín), corroborate references generally already known to Borges's readers, but, above all, they allow us to nuance the erudition he deploys as well as to glimpse certain writing techniques in which readings and previous documentation interact with or even generate his texts.

It is not about rebuilding a catalog with the multiple sources that appear in his texts, but rather about studying certain methods of projection, reappropriation, or diversion with the aim of illustrating, from a microanalysis of specific texts, some of the ways in which Borges filters and even hides references while using those same readings as a discrete underlying layer for the writing of his fictions. A particularly interesting field of study is a corpus that Borges always kept at a distance: French literature, which is cited ironically throughout all his work, written and oral, making it highly illustrative of Borges as a secret reader. The sixteen-page manuscript of handwritten notes for the course "La obra de Flaubert" [The Work of Flaubert], recently edited by Daniel Balderston and Mariana Di Ció (*Ensayos* 60–143), is particularly revelatory because it is a lecture series on a single author, thus comparable to other of the author's great lectures that were published as essays (Dante, Evaristo Carriego, *Martín Fierro*), but which, in this particular case, Borges nevertheless chose to leave largely unpublished. In addition to demonstrating his familiarity with the French language and the enormous bibliographic material he consults for this occasion, the interest of these pages lies in the fact that this material was never originally intended for publication, therefore making it extremely useful in laying bare Borges's compositional procedures. According to Carlo Ginzburg's indicative paradigm (1978), as these were moments in which less control was exercised over what was written, the annotations, the symbols, and the nimble, often unintentional marks that we find in these working notes are useful for studying the covert use Borges made of his readings and, in particular, his readings of French literature—not least because this was a subject with which Borges always maintained an ambiguous relationship.[9]

Critics have already profusely analyzed the way in which Borges makes an "exhibición desaforada de la literatura como procedimiento" [unbridled exhibition of literature as a process] (Pezzoni 37), as directed by a modus operandi that displays the documentation he consulted as a matter of course. By systematically incorporating bibliographical references, be they parceled, recycled, or sifted through narratives that in one way or another thematize the act of reading, Borges constructs in his texts a sort of ideal library that would seem to embody or coincide with "el horizonte—o la ambición o el ideal—del conjunto de la cultura letrada" [the horizon—or ambition or ideal—of the whole of lettered culture] (Premat 225). A "dimensión hiperbólica" [hyperbolic dimension] (Premat 225) of what is read emerges from his texts, which constructs and reinforces an erudite image in which there seems to be no room for other types of readings.

Fueled then by the meta-poetic discourse itself and by the often theatrical exhibition of certain sources that the author himself makes rather than by a true analysis of the texts, the horizon of expectations of Borges's readers is usually based on subjective impressions and reading effects that take his erudition for granted or on implicit representations that reproduce values commonly associated with erudition: culture, elitism, hermeticism, and academicism (Pauls and Helft 141). Ricardo Piglia's stance in this regard is visionary: a few pages of *Respiración artificial* dedicated to fictionalizing and discussing the topic of Borgesian erudition argue, by means of his alter ego, Renzi, that the story "El indigno" [The Unworthy] is, in reality, an unintended, if not unimaginable, homage to Arlt, whom he even takes the luxury of (almost) quoting by naming his fictional detective Alt: "una transposición típicamente borgeana, esto es, una miniatura del tema de *El juguete rabioso*. . . . El núcleo temático es el mismo en los dos textos . . . y la delación es la clave en los dos textos" [a typically Borgesian transposition, that is, a miniature of the plot of *The Furious Toy*. . . . The thematic core is the same in both texts . . . and betrayal is the key for both texts] (Piglia 135–36).

Conversely, another operation employed by Borges to hide his references is disqualification. The case of the French critic Albert Thibaudet, author of *Histoire de la littérature française de 1789 à nos jours*, a work Borges would refer to on several occasions throughout the years, merits discussion. In March 1937, that is, just a few months after this handbook's posthumous publication, Borges notes its appearance in *El Hogar* (*Borges en El Hogar* 39); he refers to it again to contrast the text with Benjamin Ifor Evans's handbook of English literature to illustrate the way French literature tends to be produced as a function of literary history (*BS* 238).[10] In the prologue to the *Antología poética argentina*, which he published with Bioy Casares and Silvina Ocampo in 1941, he

22   MAGDALENA CÁMPORA AND MARIANA DI CIÓ

sharpens his criticism of this type of codification with the same kind of scathing irony found in his essay, "El arte de injuriar" [The Art of Insult], in terms that were nearly the verbatim of what he had written in his Ifor Evans review the previous year.

> Los franceses han contaminado de realismo (en el sentido escolástico de la palabra) la crítica literaria de nuestro tiempo. La exornan con metáforas militares (brigadas, retaguardia, vanguardia) y con metáforas políticas (centro, izquierdas, derechas). Niegan los individuos; sólo ven generaciones, escuelas. La *reductio ad absurdum* de ese "método" es cierto venerado manual de Albert Thibaudet, que tolera subtítulos como éste: *El proceso Dreyfus,* y hasta como éste: *Reservistas. Paul Valéry.*[11] (*Textos recobrados* 192)

> [The French have contaminated the literary criticism of our time with realism (in the scholastic sense of the word). They embellish it with military metaphors (brigades, rearguard, vanguard) and with political metaphors (center, left, right). They deny individuals; they only see generations, schools. The *reductio ad absurdum* of this "method" is a certain venerated manual by Albert Thibaudet, which tolerates subtitles such as this: *The Dreyfus Process,* and even this: *Reservists. Paul Valéry.*]

Despite his criticism, the notes Borges prepared for the lectures he gave in 1952 on Flaubert at the Colegio Libre de Estudios Superiores confirm that he read Thibaudet abundantly: he respects his chronologies and occasionally mentions him, although most of the time he translates and even glosses what the French critic says about Flaubert, most of the time without ever specifying his source (see *Ensayos* 94–143). And yet Borges always seemed very critical of Thibaudet's opinions, and many years later would maliciously quote him in the prologue to *The Temptations of Saint Anthony* included in his Personal Library in 1985: "Albert Thibaudet ha escrito que las *Tentaciones* es una colosal 'flor del mal'. ¿Qué no hubiera dicho Flaubert sobre esta temeraria y torpe metáfora?" [Albert Thibaudet has written that the *Temptations* is a colossal 'flower of evil.' What wouldn't Flaubert have said about this reckless and clumsy metaphor?] (*OC* IV: 517). Borges writes this carefully failing to note that Thibaudet was referring only to the first version of the text, nor that the author justified the comparison between the two writers not in aesthetic terms but according to the ways in which, when faced with nature's abyss, both are subjected to temptation and must confront their inner evil while being deprived of grace—a stance that the French critic qualifies as "catolicismo estético" [aesthetic Catholicism] (Thibaudet 182).

Regardless of the objections that Borges formulates toward Thibaudet, the truth is that, on many other occasions, he seems not only to adhere to the French critic's positions, but even to take him as a guide. Moreover, a meticulous analysis of the overwhelming documentation that Borges relied upon when preparing the lectures on Flaubert (*Ensayos*) suggests that his frequent dismissal of Thibaudet actually served to obscure—through the meticulous orchestration of his notes—those references that were most important or useful for him in developing his own poetics.

Let us look at an example. In the third lecture of this series, dedicated to *L'Éducation sentimentale,* Borges simply notes "Thibaudet 295" (*Essays* 74), although the page number does not seem to refer to the French critic's manual, which was used abundantly as a source for these classes, but to the study on Flaubert from which Borges extracted the quotation about *Les Fleurs du mal*, which, thirty years later, he would use to deride Thibaudet. What interests Borges in this text is the end of the essay. After transcribing a letter to Louise Colet in which Flaubert reflects on prose as a new genre and particularly on the future of the novel, Thibaudet adds, incorporating the examples to which Flaubert alluded in his letter, the following comment: "¿Acaso no diríamos que prevé a Marcel Proust? La prosa de Proust no se encaminó hacia esos rumbos. Pero en el límite de Flaubert había lugar, en efecto, para potencias más libres que las suyas y para una prosa más espesa. Podemos imaginar un *Satiricón* y un *Asno de oro* saliendo de *La educación* y de *La tentación*" [Might we not say that he predicts Marcel Proust? Proust's prose did not go in that direction. But within Flaubert's borders there was indeed room for powers freer than his own and for denser prose. We can imagine a *Satyricon* and a *Golden Ass* emerging out of *Education* and *Temptation*] (*Ensayos* 98).[12]

While it is true that this way of thinking about the interaction of literary works is already present in T. S. Eliot's famous essay ("Tradition and the Individual Talent"), which Borges reviews and comments upon in 1933 (*TR* 78–84), it is also undeniable that Thibaudet's formulation comes unmistakably close to the central idea of "Kafka y sus precursores" [Kafka and his Precursors], a text he worked on exactly when he was researching for the Flaubert lectures.[13] "El hecho es que cada escritor *crea* a sus precursores. Su labor modifica nuestra concepción del pasado, como ha de modificar el futuro" [The fact is that each writer *creates* his precursors. His work modifies our conception of the past, as it will modify the future] (*OC* II: 95; *SNF* 365) writes Borges in this essay, before adding, in a footnote, the explicit reference to Eliot from an anthology of essays. However, he says nothing of Thibaudet's formulation—which, by including concrete examples, is perhaps even more eloquent than Eliot's—for presenting Flaubert's successors. Borges seems to insist on Eliot as a source but conveniently hides Thibaudet, who is not only overlooked, but even reviled. And while it may seem paradoxical, it is perhaps no accident that one of the primary and most frequently recurring points of derision that Borges had for Thibaudet, whom he uses almost metonymically to represent all French criticism, is precisely the way in which he approaches literature in terms of literary historiography. In this way, he conveniently eclipses or hides Thibaudet's primary and quite prescient concept: that literature—Flaubert's in this case—is capable not only of engendering descendants but even of "generating" works of the past such as *The Golden Ass* or the *Satyricon*. Or, to put it in Borgesian terms, of generating "precursors."

BORGES AS RE-READER

A text like the 1927 essay "La fruición literaria" [Literary Joy] allows us to see that, from very early on, Borges associates reading with the passage of time. The starting point is a heterogeneous list of formative texts he had read, presented in a fairly chronological progression and accompanied by some autobiographical comments. But the text quickly moves into praise for re-reading and the "recordativo placer" [reminiscent pleasure] ("Fruición" 186) it generates until reaching what seems to be the essay's true axis: a reflection on time and literature as an art that aspires to eternity. If reading is, as defined in "Pierre Menard," an "arte detenido y rudimentario" [a slow and rudimentary art] (*OC* I: 482; *CF* 95), Borges undeniably practices the art of re-reading as well, and does so abundantly. In both his fiction and his essays, the explicit reference to re-reading sometimes functions as part of the writing process itself, considering other possibilities as a means of nuancing what has been said ("Releo lo anterior y temo no haber destacado bastante las virtudes del libro" [I re-read what I have just written and I fear I have not been sufficiently explicit in the virtues of the book] [*OC* I: 499; *CF* 86]); as a way to introduce documentation he consulted ("Releo, para mejor investigación de lo clásico, el párrafo de Gibbon" [I re-read, in my investigation of the classic, the above paragraph by Gibbon] [*OC* I: 255; *SNF* 61]); or as a rhetorical device to move toward a conclusion ("Releo estas negaciones y pienso" [I re-read these negative remarks and I realize] [*OC* I: 239; *SNF* 55]).

The 1946 postscript that accompanies *Artificios* [*Artifices*] also ends with a list of authors to whom Borges confesses he returns again and again: "Schopenhauer, De Quincey, Stevenson, Mauthner, Shaw, Chesterton, Léon Bloy, forman el censo heterogéneo de los autores que continuamente releo. En la fantasía cristológica titulada 'Tres versiones de Judas' creo percibir el remoto influjo de este último" [Schopenhauer, De Quincey, Stevenson, Mauthner, Shaw, Chesterton, Léon Bloy—this is the heterogeneous list of writers that I am continually re-reading. In the Christological fantasy titled 'Three Versions of Judas,' I think I can perceive the remote influence of the last of these] (*OC* I: 517; *CF* 130). Despite not appearing in any of the many lists of preferred authors that he cites over the years, Borges quotes Flaubert regularly from *Luna de enfrente* [*Moon Across the Way*] (1925) onward. Thus, his sixteen handwritten pages on this author constitute invaluable material not only for studying the way in which Borges carries out a monumental research project (more than seventy authors and critics consulted) that allows him to dialogue with those authors he considers his "amistades escritas" [written friends] ("Fruición" 186) but also to reflect on the way he strategically uses his readings and re-readings to develop his own "problemático ejercicio de la literatura" [problematic pursuit of literature] (*OC* I: 546; *CF* 158) and insert himself among world literature's most prominent figures.

Aligning with the dynamics of textual recovery and reuse, and with the readings that we have already mentioned, Borges's first and last lectures on Flaubert serve as the basis for two articles ("Vindicación de *Bouvard et Pécuchet*" [Vindication of *Bouvard et Pécuchet*][14] and "Flaubert y su destino ejemplar" [Flaubert and His Exemplary Destiny]) that would be published in the newspaper *La Nación* (the last lecture given appearing in print first) and then in the reprint of *Discusión* [*Discussion*] (1957). In its own way, the order of publication of the two articles on Flaubert encourages readers not only to re-read the French author starting with his last novel, but also to consider all his work in light of his "precursors"—an idea that closes Borges's notes for the first lecture: "Ascendencia escandinava de Flaubert – Las sagas/ El autorretrato" [Flaubert's Scandinavian ancestry – The Sagas/The Self-Portrait] (*Ensayos* 109). Relatively frequent in Borges, this strategy of displacing and chronologically reorganizing texts obliges one to re-read the essays in *Discusión* in light of these additions to the reprint. Such a reading thus favors dialogue with "El escritor argentino y la tradición" [The Argentine Writer and Tradition], which comes just after these two essays, but also with a text such as "Las versiones homéricas" [The Homeric Versions], where he analyzes the effect that the passage of time has on certain images or metaphors, and particularly on the Homeric adjectives that reappear "conmovedoramente a destiempo" [inopportunely moving] (*OC I* 253; *SNF* 70). They likewise cause us to reconsider "Nota sobre Walt Whitman" [Note on Walt Whitman] where, as in the first lecture on Flaubert, he discusses the existence of two Whitmans (the man of flesh and blood; the immortal poet) and the possibility of an "libro absoluto" [absolute book] that includes all (*OC I*: 262).

Significantly, he leaves unpublished, and therefore in the shadows, the core of this course, which nevertheless enters into perfect dialogue with other past and future texts by Borges, as we will see below. More than on the individual analysis of the texts, Borges's focus seems to be on Flaubert's handling of temporality and, in particular, on the attempt to "rebasar la sucesión histórica" [surpass historical succession], as Enrique Pezzoni has likewise identified in *Evaristo Carriego* (36). Following the critic Dumesnil, Borges again demonstrates this desire in the *Tres cuentos* by pointing out that Flaubert "parte del presente y va alejándose y retrocediendo en el tiempo" [starts from the present and moves away and backwards in time] (*Ensayos* 122). But, in addition to these considerations of the internal temporality of the French writer's work, Borges is interested above all in Flaubert's interaction with his predecessors and with his successors: "Flaubert, en la historia de la literatura de Francia y de la literatura del mundo, es más que un episodio espléndido; prepara y admite el porvenir y recibe y justifica el pasado" [Flaubert, in the history of the literature of France and of the literature of the world, is more than a splendid episode; he prepares and admits the future and receives and justifies the past] (*Ensayos* 107–08). He then notes, in the upper margin of one of the manuscripts: "Mira, como Jano bifronte, el pasado y el porvenir" [He looks, like Janus bifrons, at the past and the future] (*Ensayos* 105) along with the pagination corresponding to the *Classical Dictionary of Proper Names Mentioned in Ancient Authors* by John Lemprière (1788), from which the reference was taken.

From this perspective, *Bouvard et Pécuchet*, Flaubert's last and unfinished work, seems to be of particular interest to Borges. In summarizing the plot of this novel in which not much "happens," Borges writes: "Flaubert les hace leer una biblioteca, <u>para que no la entiendan</u>" [Flaubert makes them read a library, <u>so they are unable to understand it</u>] (*Ensayos* 139, emphasis in the original). Flaubert's characters are two "imbéciles" [stupid] copyists who not only copy, but read. Their stupidity is not based, then, on a lack of reading but rather on a profound lack of understanding ("superstición") of what they have read. But what is a motive for mockery will eventually become a paradoxical and unexpected sharpness of spirit, until arriving at the crucial moment when Flaubert "se reconcilia con Bouvard y Pécuchet, Dios con sus criaturas" [is reconciled with Bouvard and Pécuchet, God with his creatures] (*OC* I: 275). While Borges states that this is, perhaps, typical of all works of art, he insists on Flaubert's specificity: "aquí sorprendemos el instante en que el soñador, por decirlo con una metáfora afín, nota que está soñándose y que las formas de su sueño son él" [here we are surprised by the instant in which the dreamer, to use a related metaphor, notices that he is dreaming himself and that the forms of his dream are him] (*OC* I: 275). And though he never establishes direct comparisons to his own work, we can note that Borges makes use of oneiric metaphors similar to those often employed in his own texts: "Flaubert, según Faguet, soñó una epopeya de la idiotez humana" [Flaubert, according to Faguet, dreamed an epic of human idiocy]; "renuncian a su enciclopédico sueño" [they abandon their encyclopedic dream] (*OC* I: 274; *Ensayos* 140), a procedure that we also notice when he presents Flaubert as a writer "consagrado" [consecrated] to literature (*Ensayos* 140) or in his commentary on *Salammbô*. The way in which Borges refers to the historical reconstruction of Carthage, which ends up imposing itself upon and replacing reality, seems almost a confirmation of what, in Tlön, was only a prediction: "Cartago es, ahora, la Cartago del sueño de Flaubert" [Carthage is now the Carthage of Flaubert's dream] (*Ensayos* 116).[15]

If the plot of *Bouvard et Pécuchet* is, in Borges's words, "engañosamente simple" [deceptively simple] (*OC* I: 274), the ending is no less so: "desencantados (ya veremos que la 'acción' no ocurre en el tiempo sino en la eternidad), encargan al carpintero un doble pupitre, y se ponen a copiar, como antes" [disenchanted (we will see that the 'action' does not occur in time but in eternity), they order the carpenter to make a double desk, and they start copying, as before] (*OC* I: 274). At this point, he fails to state what it is the two copyists are working on, but, later in the text, Borges will clarify that it is the famous *Sottisier*, a compilation that includes the notes of previously read authors, old papers (newspapers, lost letters, posters) purchased per kilo from a neighboring paper mill, and specimens of texts of every style. Among the things copied by the two "imbéciles" is a confidential letter that, in a way, summarizes all the actions and thoughts of these two "irresponsables fantoches" [irresponsible puppets] (*Ensayos* 142), whom he will categorize in the same vein as Don Quixote and Sancho or Candide and Pangloss, among other references. In short, it is a *mise en abyme* in which, based on what Flaubert projected in his manuscript, the reader is offered both the synthesis and the critique of the whole work, an approach analogous to the ambition of the "absolute book" that Borges envisions in his "Nota sobre Walt Whitman" ("un libro de los libros que incluya a todos como un arquetipo platónico, un objeto cuya virtud no aminoren los años" [a book of books that includes all books as a Platonic archetype, an object whose virtue is not diminished by the years] [*OC* I: 262]). To some extent, a parallel can also be drawn to the utopia of a "total library," to the totalizing zeal of the encyclopedia, of Pascal's sphere or even of the Aleph,[16] as each represents the impossible quest to concentrate the entire universe in a single point.

At the beginning of the lecture notes on *Bouvard et Pécuchet*, we read in the upper margin, although without any indication of where this comment should be inserted: "La historia de Francia y la historia universal se detienen para que P y B ejecuten sus vagos experimentos" [The history of France and universal history stop to allow P and B to carry out their vague experiments] (*Ensayos* 141). Although, strictly speaking, this idea does not appear as such in Flaubert,[17] the reflection is reminiscent of "El milagro secreto," when time stops so that Jaromir Hladík can finish the play he is writing, which, not by chance, takes place in a library. In addition to a certain carelessness in the writing of this note—in contrast with the careful handwriting most commonly found in this manuscript—the fact that no other such mention or allusion appears in the development of this lecture suggests that this is an idea that probably arose later.[18] In another sense, we see that, during the course, Borges's attempts to link Flaubert's last work with the present time, an aspect that he will later discard from the published version: "el lector de mil novecientos cincuenta y tantos tiene un poco la sensación de Laurel y Hardy ensayando con entusiasmo idiota la jardinería, la química, la gimnasia, la hidroterapia, el magnetismo animal, el espiritismo y la mnemotecnia, y previsiblemente fracasando en cada episodio" [the reader of nineteen fifty-something gets a bit of a sense of Laurel and Hardy attempting, with idiotic enthusiasm, gardening, chemistry, gymnastics, hydrotherapy, animal magnetism, spiritualism and mnemonics, and predictably failing in each episode] (*Ensayos* 140).

Rather than referring to a time that has stopped, Borges's reading attempts to extract the novel from temporality[19]: "ya veremos que la 'acción' no 'ocurre' en el tiempo sino en la eternidad" [we will see that the 'action' does not 'occur' in time but in eternity] (*OC* I: 274); "el tiempo de Bouvard y Pécuchet se inclina a la eternidad" [the time of Bouvard and Pécuchet inclines to eternity] (*OC* I: 277). And if he regards this work with those "tan resucitadores ojos de la historia" [so resuscitating eyes of history] of which he spoke in "La fruición literaria" (189) it is not so much (or not only) because this novel constitutes a masterful example of that *late style* about which Edward Said would theorize several decades later, but fundamentally because Borges sees in *Bouvard et Pécuchet* a book that is capable of anticipating not only its own end, but also the crisis and the end of the novel as a genre, that he includes in the novel itself:

> Las negligencias o desórdenes o libertades del último Flaubert han desconcertado a los críticos; yo creo ver en ellas un símbolo. El hombre que con *Madame Bovary* forjó la novela realista fue también el primero en romperla. Chesterton, apenas ayer, escribía: "La novela bien puede morir con nosotros". El instinto de Flaubert presintió esa muerte, que ya está aconteciendo. . . . Por eso, el tiempo en *Bouvard y Pécuchet* se inclina a la eternidad; por eso, los protagonistas no mueren y seguirán copiando, cerca de Caen, su anacrónico *Sottisier*, tan ignorantes de 1914 como de 1870; por eso la obra mira, hacia atrás, a las parábolas de Voltaire y de Swift y de los orientales y, hacia delante, a las de Kafka. (*OC* I: 277)

> [The negligence or disorder or liberties of the late Flaubert have puzzled critics; I think I see in them a symbol. The man who forged the realistic novel with *Madame Bovary* was also the first to break it. Chesterton, only yesterday, wrote: "The novel may well die with us." Flaubert's instinct foresaw that death, which is already happening. . . . That is why time in *Bouvard and Pécuchet* is inclined toward eternity; that

is why the protagonists do not die and will continue to copy, near Caen, their anachronistic *Sottisier*, as ignorant of 1914 as of 1870; that is why the work looks backward to the parables of Voltaire and Swift and the Orientals and forward to those of Kafka.]

The ending foreseen by Flaubert, "*Copier comme autrefois—Ils s'y mettent*," which Borges quoted in French in the previous lecture on *The Temptations of Saint Anthony*, suggests that the characters renew the copying they had been doing at the beginning of the novel, but now do so for pleasure or necessity rather than employment. Thus is suggested the project of a unique and circular book, of a book in which all temporalities coexist and which, for this very reason, inclines toward the infinite, even though—just as the text copied by Pierre Menard is not the same text as *Don Quixote* despite coinciding word for word—the copyists are no longer what they were at the beginning because they have been modified by the passage of time and by their readings.

"Emerson dijo que una biblioteca es un gabinete mágico en el que hay muchos espíritus hechizados" [Emerson said that a library is a magic cabinet in which there are many bewitched spirits] (*OC* III: 301) Borges wrote some twenty-five years after the lecture series in which he invites us to read, sifted through his own work, the oeuvre of Flaubert. Out of time, those books that "despiertan cuando los llamamos" [awaken when we call them] (*OC* III: 301) are like the timeless Bouvard and Pécuchet that Flaubert "dreams" and like this or that "visitado escritor" [visited writer] that Borges, the "lector hedónico" [hedonic reader] (*OC* I: 246), reads or re-reads or asks to have read to him throughout his life. And if today we can access the material traces of a good part (though certainly not all) of the sources with which he has nourished his "vista de lector y de escritor" [reader's and writer's view] (*OC* III: 331), his published texts also contain the memory, visible and invisible, of these readings where all temporalities coexist, in anachronistic or, rather, in timeless dialogue with him. To read Borges is not, therefore, only to go through the lines of each of the pages that Borges wrote, but also, even if we do not always realize it, to read and re-read with him each of the pages that Borges read.

Notes

1. "No sé si hay otra vida; si hay otra, deseo que me esperen en su recinto los libros que he leído bajo la luna con las mismas cubiertas y las mismas ilustraciones, quizá con las mismas erratas, y los que me depara aún el futuro" [I don't know if there is another life. If there is another, I hope there waits for me in their corner the books I have read in the moonlight with the covers and the same illustrations, perhaps even with the same errors, and those the future still has in store for me] (Borges, "Prólogo" 33). In her study on Borges and the publishing market, Nora Benedict rightly defines Borges as a bibliographer, not a bibliophile (14–15). Indeed, his interest in the materiality of the book seems to be linked to the processes of constructing meaning in the text, rather than the historical value of various editions.
2. See the works of Annick Louis (2020) and Sylvia Saítta (2018), as well as Lucas Adur's current research on "pop" Borges.

THE SECRET SHARER 29

3. Michel Lafon edited the manuscripts of "Tlön, Uqbar, Orbis Tertius" and "El sur" [The South], which are at the Fondation Bodmer in a facsimile edition, in 2010.

4. Some results of these new perspectives of study can be seen in the team work presented in issue 52 (2021), dedicated to the notebooks, and in issue 54 (2022), dedicated to the conferences, of the journal *Variaciones Borges*; in the facsimiles *Poesías, Cuentos, Ensayos* published by Daniel Balderston with the Borges Center; and in the website dedicated to the conferences put together by Mariela Blanco and her team at the Centro Borges de la Biblioteca Nacional Mariano Moreno (Argentina).

5. "Casi la mitad de las horas de mi infancia transcurrieron entre paredes cubiertas de libros . . . tras los cristales biselados se alineaban las bien encuadernadas colecciones de los clásicos griegos, latinos, castellanos y franceses" [Almost half the hours of my childhood were spent within walls covered with books . . . behind beveled glass panes were lined the well-bound collections of Greek, Latin, Castilian and French classics] (125) writes María Rosa Oliver, who was a child around 1910, in *Mundo, mi casa*.

6. A microcosm of that library in Flores Maio's 2018 book.

7. In addition to their own names, the link between the two goes through what Peter Brooks (1976) called "melodramatic imagination": sentimental novels for Bovary, Hollywood movies for Zunz.

8. Borges takes from his readings of Fritz Mauthner the idea that interest conditions knowledge. See the work of Silvia Dapía (197).

9. On this ambiguity, see the works collected in the book *Borges-Francia* (2011).

10. See also "La paradoja de Apollinaire," in *Los Anales de Buenos Aires*, Buenos Aires, vol. 1, no. 8, August 1946, p. 31; and in J. L. Borges, *Ficcionario*, Mexico, Fondo de Cultura Económica, 1985 (*Textos recobrados* 247–50).

11. In the entry for July 13, 1963, Bioy noted in his diary: "Habla de los errores a que llegan los profesores e historiadores de la literatura con su afán de clasificaciones—de las clasificaciones por generaciones, por zonas geográficas, etcétera—: 'Thibaudet fue el campeón, pero astutamente dijo que él no creía en las clasificaciones. Yo escribí en *Sur* sobre su *Historia de la literatura francesa* y señalé absurdos subtítulos de ese libro: 'Los reservistas: Paul Valéry', 'Los politécnicos'. Pero nadie notó nada'" [He speaks of the mistakes made by professors and historians of literature in their eagerness to classify— classifications by generations, by geographical zones, etc.—: 'Thibaudet was the champion, but he wisely said that he didn't believe in classifications. I wrote in *Sur* about his *History of French Literature*, pointing out the absurd subtitles of that book: 'The Reservists: Paul Valéry', 'The Polytechnicians'. But nobody noticed anything'] (921).

12. "Ne dirait-on pas qu'il prévoit Marcel Proust? Sa prose à lui ne s'est pas tournée de ce côté. Mais à la limite de Flaubert, il y avait place en effet pour des puissances plus libres que les siennes et pour une prose plus étoffée. On peut imaginer un *Satyricon* et un *Âne d'or* sortant de l'*Éducation* et de la *Tentation*" (Thibaudet 295).

13. See *Ensayos* 97–98.

14. The version published in *Discusión* includes a change of conjunction in the title, a subtle indication that Borges wishes to quote the work in its original French.

15. Although we could say that he always uses his readings as an argument of authority, sometimes he is forced to justify them explicitly: "recuerdo esas combustiones y resurrecciones de la leyenda porque no es menos maravilloso lo que Flaubert quiso hacer con Cartago" [I remember those combustions and resurrections of the legend because it is no less wonderful what Flaubert wanted to do with Carthage] (*Ensayos* 110).

16. For further development of this approach, see Di Ció (2011).

17. The published version attempts to deepen this idea on the basis of critical documentation: "René Descharmes ha examinado, y reprobado, la cronología de *Bouvard y Pécuchet*. La acción requiere unos cuarenta años; los protagonistas tienen sesenta y ocho cuando se entregan a la gimnasia, el mismo año en que Pécuchet descubre el amor. En un libro tan poblado de circunstancias, el tiempo, sin embargo, está inmóvil . . . faltan las vicisitudes comunes y la fatalidad y el azar. 'Las comparsas del desenlace son las del preámbulo; nadie viaja, nadie se muere,' observa Claude Digeon" [René Descharmes has examined, and rejected, the chronology of *Bouvard and Pécuchet*. The action requires about forty years; the protagonists are sixty-eight years old when they dedicate themselves to gymnastics, the same year in which Pécuchet discovers love. In a book so populated by circumstances, time, however, is immobile . . . common vicissitudes and fatality and chance are missing. 'The characters in the denouement are those found in the preamble; no one travels, no one dies,' observes Claude Digeon] (*OC* I: 277).

18. It is not impossible that, as Bouvard and Pécuchet were copyists, the formulation in these terms may have arisen by association with "Pierre Menard," where, as we have already pointed out, he defines reading precisely as an "arte detenido" [slow/detained art].

19. In the lecture on *Sentimental Education*, Borges rightly emphasizes the fact that Frédéric remains oblivious to the historical events of 1848, which he perceives as "a spectacle" (*Ensayos* 118).

WORKS CITED

AA.VV. *Variaciones Borges*, vol. 52, "Cuadernos," 2021.

AA.VV. *Variaciones Borges*, vol. 54, "Conferencias," 2022.

Balderston, Daniel. *How Borges Wrote*. University of Virginia Press, 2018.

Balderston, Daniel. *Innumerables relaciones: Cómo leer con Borges*. Universidad Nacional del Litoral, 2010.

Balderston, Daniel. *The Literary Universe of Jorge Luis Borges: An Index to References and Allusions to Persons, Titles, and Places in His Writings*. Greenwood, 1986.

Benedict, Nora C. *Borges and the Literary Marketplace: How Editorial Practices Shaped Cosmopolitan Reading*. Yale University Press, 2021.

Bioy Casares, Adolfo. *Borges*, edited by Daniel Martino. Destino, 2006.

Borges, Jorge Luis. "Autobiographical Notes." *The New Yorker*, September 19, 1970, pp. 40–99.

Borges, Jorge Luis. *Collected Fictions*, translated by Andrew Hurley. Penguin, 1999.

Borges, Jorge Luis. *Deux Fictions: Tlön, Uqbar, Orbis Tertius et El Sur*. Edición facsimilar de los manuscritos, edited by Michel Lafon. PUF/Fondation Bodmer, 2010.

Borges, Jorge Luis. *In Praise of Darkness*, translated by Norman Thomas di Giovanni. E. P. Dutton, 1974.

Borges, Jorge Luis. *Borges en* El Hogar *(1935-1958)*. Emecé, 2000.

Borges, Jorge Luis. *Labyrinths*, translated by James Irby. New Directions, 1964.

Borges, Jorge Luis. "La fruición literaria". *El idioma de los argentinos* (1928). Edited by Debolsillo, 2012, pp. 185–90.

Borges, Jorge Luis. "La génesis de "El Cuervo" de Poe" (1935). *Textos recobrados (1931–1955)*. Emecé, 2001, pp. 120–123.

Borges, Jorge Luis. *Obras completas*. 4 vols. Emecé, 1996.

Borges, Jorge Luis. *Poemas & Prosas breves*, transcription, editing, and notes by Daniel Balderston and María Celeste Martín. Borges Center, 2018.

Borges, Jorge Luis. *Ensayos*, transcription, editing, and notes by Daniel Balderston and María Celeste Martín. Borges Center, 2019.

Borges, Jorge Luis. *Cuentos*, transcription, editing, and notes by Daniel Balderston and María Celeste Martín. Borges Center, 2020.

Borges, Jorge Luis. "Prólogo." *Tesoros de España* (1985), *Ten Centuries of Spanish Books. The New York Public Library* (Oct. 12–Dec. 30, 1985), Madrid, Ministerio de Cultura, Dirección General del Libro y Bibliotecas, p. 33.

Borges, Jorge Luis. *Selected Non-Fictions*, edited by Eliot Weinberger, translated by Esther Allen, Suzanne Jill Levine, and Eliot Weinberger. Penguin, 1999.

Borges, Jorge Luis. *Textos recobrados (1931–1955)*. Emecé, 2001.

Brooks, Peter. *The Melodramatic Imagination. Balzac, Henry James, Melodrama and the Mode of Excess*. Yale University Press, 1976.

Cámpora, Magdalena. *El intérprete imprevisto: Clásicos franceses en ediciones populares argentinas (1901–1955)*. Ampersand, Colección "Scripta Manent," 2024.

Cámpora, Magdalena, and Javier Roberto González, eds. *Borges-Francia*. Publicaciones de la Facultad de Filosofía y Letras, Universidad Católica Argentina/Selectus, 2011.

Canto, Estela. *Borges a contraluz*. Espasa-Calpe, 1989.

Certeau, Michel de. "Lire: un braconnage." *L'invention du quotidien. I. Arts de faire*. 10/18, pp. 279–96.

Christ, Ronald. *The Narrow Act: Borges' Art of Allusion*. New York University Press, 1969.

Dapía, Silvia. "La presencia de Fritz Mauthner en el ensayismo de Borges." *Revista de Crítica Literaria Latinoamericana*, vol. 21, no. 42, 1995, pp. 189–206.

Di Ció, Mariana. "Carlos Argentino Daneri y su destino ejemplar." *Borges-Francia*. Edited by Magdalena Cámpora and J. R. González, Universidad Católica Argentina/Selectus, 2011, pp. 487–96.

Fishburn, Evelyn, and Psiche Hughes. *A Dictionary of Borges*. Duckworth, 1990.

Flores Maio, Fernando. *La biblioteca de Borges*. Paripé Books/Fundación Jorge Luis Borges, 2018.

Genette, Gérard. "L'utopie littéraire." *Figures*. Edited by Seuil, 1966, pp. 123–32.

Ginzburg, Carlo. "Indicios. Raíces de un paradigma de inferencias indiciales." *Mitos, emblemas, indicios. Morfología e historia*. Edited by Gedisa, [1978], 2008, pp. 185–239.

Lafon, Michel. *Borges ou la réécriture*. Seuil, 1990.

Lafon, Michel, ed. *Jorge Luis Borges. Tlön, Uqbar, Orbis Tertius. El Sur*. Presses Universitaires de France / Fondation Martin Bodmer, 2010.

Louis, Annick. *Borges face au fascisme*. 2 vols: *1. Les causes du présent. 2. Les fictions du contemporain*. Aux lieux d'être, 2006.

Louis, Annick. "De l'érudition borgésienne dans la fiction." *Lire Borges aujourd'hui. Autour de* Ficciones *et* El hacedor. Edited by Roland Béhar and Annick Louis, Rue d'Ulm, 2016, pp. 69–86.

Louis, Annick. "A momentary lapse of history. Borges y la crítica moderna argentina bajo la última dictadura y en la postdictadura (1976–1986)." *Letras, Dossier "Borges, sus ensayos: lógicas textuales y archivos de época,"* Facultad de Filosofía y Letras, Universidad Católica Argentina, vol. 81, 2020, pp. 270–338.

Molloy, Sylvia. *Las letras de Borges*. Sudamericana, 1979.

Oliver, María Rosa. *Mundo, mi casa (Recuerdos de infancia)*. Falco Librero Editor, 1965.

Pauls, Alan, and Nicolas Helft. *El factor Borges: Nueve ensayos ilustrados*. FCE, 2000.

Pezzoni, Enrique. *Enrique Pezzoni, lector de Borges. Lecciones de literatura 1984–1988*, compiled and prologue by Annick Louis. Sudamericana, 1999.

Piglia, Ricardo. *Respiración artificial*. Pomaire, 1980.

Premat, Julio. *Borges: La reinvención de la literatura*. Paidós, 2022.

Rosato, Laura, and Germán Álvarez. *Borges, libros y lecturas: catálogo de la colección Jorge Luis Borges en la Biblioteca Nacional Buenos Aires*. Ediciones Biblioteca Nacional, 2010.

Saítta, Sylvia. "Borges mediático." *Variaciones Borges*, University of Pittsburgh, vol. 46, 2018, pp. 3–21.

Schwartz, Jorge, ed. *Borges babilônico: Uma Enciclopedia*. Companhia das Letras, 2017.

Thibaudet, Albert. *Gustave Flaubert*, collection "Leurs Figures." Gallimard, 1935.

CHAPTER 3

FROM THE OTHER SIDE OF THE LIBRARY

Borges in Newspapers and Magazines

SYLVIA SAÍTTA

FROM his literary beginnings until the end of his life, Jorge Luis Borges's essays, poems, and short stories appeared in literary magazines, newspapers, and periodicals before they were published in book form. The hypothesis of this chapter is that Borges circulated his literature through cultural journalism and mass media and, in doing so, not only created his image as a writer and reader through his contributions to aesthetic polemics and ideological debates but also found a means of *earning a living*. Outside the library, as of the early 1920s, Borges's essays, poems, and stories circulated in newspapers and magazines, which constituted, as Annick Louis states, the first contexts for his publications: each poem, each story, each essay "is not presented in isolation, but surrounded by other writings, sometimes accompanied by illustrations, in a medium with an aesthetic and political orientation, aimed at a particular audience, with a specific circulation" (*Obras y maniobras* 24). Outside the library as well, during the times when working in libraries was another way of *earning a living*, Borges was interviewed by the press and on radio and television programs; he directed magazines and cultural supplements; he participated as a juror in literary contests held by newspapers, publishing houses, and weeklies; he wrote film scripts, posed for photographers, signed autographs and participated in book fairs and public events. Juan José Saer, referring to the reviews and capsule biographies that Borges published in *El Hogar* between 1936 and 1940, states that it was "gracias a las obligaciones didácticas de esos artículos periodísticos que el barroquismo un poco decorativo de su prosa juvenil adquiere la sencillez y la precisión incomparable de los grandes textos de las dos décadas venideras" [thanks to the educational requirements of those periodical articles that his somewhat decoratively baroque early prose acquired the simplicity and incomparable precision found in his great texts of the following two decades] (23).

Simply citing a few references from Borges's biography is enough to confirm that, from a very young age, he wished to publish in newspapers and magazines—and not always successfully. In 1918, from Switzerland, Borges sent the parables "El Profeta" [The Prophet] and "El Héroe" [The Hero] to *Caras y Caretas* [*Faces and Masks*] in Buenos Aires, and the following year, a story about a werewolf to *La Esfera* in Madrid (*Georgie* 134). His search finally paid off in Spain: in Seville, Borges published his first poem "Himno del Mar" [Hymn of the Sea] in the journal *Grecia* (1919), thus initiating what Vaccaro considers a crucial stage "ya que comenzó a ver su producción reflejada en las páginas de las revistas más representativas de entonces" [as he began to see his work reflected in the pages of the era's most representative magazines] (*Georgie* 192). Both in Seville and, months later, in Madrid, Borges published relentlessly in Spain's leading ultraist journals—*Grecia*, *Última Hora*, *VLTRA*—and participated in the literary gatherings led by Isaac del Vando-Villar in Seville and Rafael Cansinos Assens in Madrid. Consequently, the Borges who returned to his country in March 1921, after seven years' absence, in addition to suitcases and books brought an aesthetic agenda for Argentine literature: "La llegada del joven poeta de 22 años al puerto de Buenos Aires" writes Martín Prieto, "fue, para la evolución de la literatura argentina, tan importante como lo fueron los desembarcos de Echeverría en los años treinta, y de Rubén Darío en 1893" [The arrival of the young 22-year-old poet to the port of Buenos Aires was, for the evolution of Argentine literature, as important as the arrival of Echeverría in the 1830s, and of Rubén Darío in 1893] (213).

Though his manifesto entitled "Ultraísmo" [Ultraism], which Borges published in the celebrated journal *Nosotros* in December 1921, would provoke strongest impact, just weeks before, he had helped found *Prisma* with Norah Borges, Guillermo Juan, Eduardo González Lanuza, and Guillermo de Torre. Argentina's first ultraist magazine debuted in November 1921, pasted on Buenos Aire's street walls. In his *Autobiografía*, Borges recalls,

> Nuestro pequeño grupo ultraísta estaba ansioso de poseer una revista propia, pero una verdadera revista era algo que estaba más allá de nuestros medios. Noté cómo se colocaban anuncios en las paredes de la calle, y se me ocurrió la idea de que podríamos imprimir también una revista mural, que nosotros mismos pegaríamos sobre las paredes de los edificios, en diferentes partes de la ciudad. Cada edición era una sola hoja grande y contenía un manifiesto y unos seis u ocho poemas breves y lacónicos, impresos con mucho blanco en derredor y con un grabado hecho por mi hermana. Salíamos de noche—González Lanuza, Piñero, mi primo y yo—armados de tarros de goma y de brochas que aportaba mi madre y caminando a lo largo de millas, los pegábamos en las calles Santa Fe, Callao, Entre Ríos y México. (62)

> [Our small ultraist group was eager to have a magazine of its own, but a real magazine was beyond our means. I had noticed billboard ads, and the thought came to me that we might similarly print a "mural magazine" and paste it up ourselves on the walls of buildings in different parts of town. Each issue was a large single sheet and contained a manifesto and some six or eight short, laconic poems, printed with plenty of white space around them, and a woodcut by my sister. We sallied forth at night—Gonzalez Lanuza, Piñero, my cousin, and I—armed with pastepots and brushes provided by my mother, and, walking miles on end, slapped them up along Santa Fe, Callao, Entre Rios, and Mexico Streets.] ("Autobiographical Essay" 163)

BORGES IN NEWSPAPERS AND MAGAZINES 35

Prisma was the first avant-garde magazine in Argentina to anticipate, as early as 1921, two trends: the incorporation of advertising techniques in the world of literature and the uses of urban public space as both a theme and as a mode of aesthetic circulation by the young writers and poets of the 1920s. Its first issue is preceded by a "Proclamation" written by Borges in numerous and disparate typefaces, but signed by Guillermo de Torre, Eduardo González Lanuza, Guillermo Juan, and Jorge Luis Borges; the formal structure of the text follows the model of Guillermo de Torre's "Manifiesto Vertical Ultraísta" [Ultraist Vertical Manifesto]:

> En su forma más evidente i automática, el juego de entrelazar palabras campea en esa entablillada nadería que es la literatura actual. Los poetas sólo se ocupan de cambiar de sitio los cachivaches ornamentales que los rubenianos heredaron de Góngora—las rosas, los cisnes, los faunos, los dioses griegos, los paisajes ecuánimes i enjardinados—i engarzar millonariamente los flojos adjetivos inefable, divino, azul, misterioso. Cuánta socarronería i cuánta mentira en ese manosear de ineficaces i desdibujadas palabras, cuánto miedo altanero de adentrarse verdaderamente en las cosas, cuánta impotencia en esa vanagloria de símbolos ajenos. Mientras tanto los demás líricos, aquellos que no ostentan el tatuaje azul rubeniano, ejercen un anecdotismo gárrulo, i fomentan penas rimables que barnizadas de visualidades oportunas venderán después con un gesto de amaestrada sencillez i de espontaneidad prevista.[1] ("Proclama")

> [In its most evident and automatic form, the game of interweaving words is played in that constricted nothingness that is today's literature. The poets merely concern themselves with exchanging the places of the ornamental odds and ends that the Ruben Dario's disciples inherited from Góngora—roses, swans, fawns, Greek gods, and serene and well-groomed landscapes—and millioniarily stringing together the weak adjectives "ineffable," "divine," "blue," "mysterious." What cynicism, and what mendacity in that manhandling of inefficacious and indistinct words, what haughty fear of truly delving into things, what impotence in that vainglory of other people's symbols. In the meantime, the other poems, those that don't boast the Rubenian blue tattoo, perform a garrulous anecdotism, and foment rhyming embarrassments that, once varnished with opportune visualities, will then be sold with gesture of demure simplicity and foreseen spontaneity.]

In addition to the unorthodox spellings and the use of neologisms so characteristic of the early Borges, one can already note, apart from his disdain for *rubenismo* and *modernismo*, several features that, through their negation, define Borges's future literature: he is against the psychological novel, against rhyme, against the excessive length of the story, against the first person, against exoticism, against sentimental literature:

> Escriben dramas i novelas abarrotadas de encrucijadas espirituales, de gestos culminantes i de apoteosis donde se remansa definitivamente el vivir. Han inventado ese andamiaje literario—la estética—según la cual hay que preparar las situaciones i empalmar las imágenes. . . . Idiotez que les hace urdir un soneto para colocar una línea, i decir en doscientas páginas lo cabedero en dos renglones. ("Proclama")

[They write plays and novels crammed with spiritual crossroads, culminating gestures and apotheosis where life is definitively made stagnant. They have invented this literary framework—the aesthetic—according to which you have to prepare the situations and connect the images. . . . Nonsense which makes them concoct a sonnet to house a single line, and say in two-hundred pages what could fit in two sentences.]

In December, as mentioned above, Borges again takes up the arguments made in "Proclama" in the *Nosotros* essay, in which he synthesizes the principles of the movement (though this time using *correct* Spanish): reducing poetry to its core element: metaphor; eliminating connecting phrases, nexuses, and useless adjectives; the abolition of ornamental devices, proselytization, and overwrought opaqueness; and the synthesis of two or more images in one, broadening their suggestive capacity.

The second and final issue of *Prisma* came out in April 1922; no third issue followed, but a new ultraist journal, *Proa*, appeared in August 1922. Three issues were published (the second, in December 1922 and the third, in July 1923, when the Borges siblings traveled to Spain), consisting of three pages "desplegables como ese espejo triple que hace movediza y variada la gracia inmóvil de la mujer que refleja" [that unfold like a three-way mirror that shifts and varies the immovable grace of the woman it reflects] (Borges, "Acotaciones" 3). The first issue was subtitled *Revista de Literatura* [Journal of Literature]; the other two, *Revista de Renovación Literaria* [Journal of Literary Renewal]. Directed by Borges, Guillermo Juan, Norah Lange, and Eduardo González Lanuza, *Proa* was described by the newspaper *Crítica* as follows: "Figúrese el lector tres hojas puestas en fila, o una hoja muy ancha doblada en tres pedacitos que, multiplicados por dos— pues ya es sabido que toda hoja tiene dos páginas—, hacen seis planos de sabrosa lectura animada por la rareza de unos grabados en boje" [Let the reader imagine three pages in a row, or a very wide sheet of paper folded in three pieces that, multiplied by two—as of course every sheet has two pages—make six planes of delectable reading, animated by the exquisiteness of several woodcut engravings] (7). *Proa*'s agenda, as Borges outlines it in his review of a Norah Lange book, which he published in *Martín Fierro*, reasserts *Prisma*'s major points: "Hartos estábamos de la insolencia de palabras y de la musical indecisión que los poetas del novecientos amaron y solicitamos un arte impar y eficaz en que la hermosura fuese innegable como la alacridad que el mes de octubre insta en la carne juvenil y en la tierra. Ejercimos la imagen, la sentencia, el epíteto, rápidamente compendiosos" [We were fed up with the insolence of words and with musical indecision that the poets of the 1890s adored and we asked for a matchless, efficient art in which beauty was as undeniable as the alacrity with which the month of October urges springtime in youthful flesh and across the land. We perform the image, the sentence, the epithet—rapidly condensed] (3).

The second run of *Proa* was published the following year, between August 1924 and January 1926. Headed by Borges, Ricardo Güiraldes, Alfredo Brandán Caraffa, and Pablo Rojas Paz, its fifteen issues differed notably from the first *Proa* because they had a different aim: it was no longer an ultraist journal but rather sought to become a "tribuna serena y sin prejuicios" [a tribune serene, and without prejudices], "amplia y sin barreras" [ample and without barriers], that would include all voices and opinions, to set itself above the polemics that were already beginning to fracture the incipient literary scene with the well-known dispute between Florida and Boedo. Consequently, in its first issue in August 1924, *Proa* asserts that "quiere ser el primer exponente de la unión de los jóvenes" [it seeks to be the leading model of unity of young people], as demonstrated by its having been founded by "cuatro jóvenes formados en distintos ambientes" [four young people raised in different environments] who seek to realize a work of synthesis (4). *Proa* then defined its stance by differentiating itself as much from *Prisma* as from its own first iteration, distancing itself primarily from ultraism. Borges, who had already published *Fervor de Buenos Aires* [*Fervor of Buenos Aires*] in 1923 and had begun his search into the voices, ghosts, and characters populating the city limits, reviewed González Lanuza's book *Prismas* in the first issue of the new *Proa* to explain and separate his distance and that of the journal's second incarnation from ultraism:

> He leído sus versos admirables, he paladeado la dulce mansedumbre de su música, he sentido cumplidamente la grandeza de algunas traslaciones, pero también he comprobado que, sin quererlo, hemos incurrido en otra retórica, tan vinculada como las antiguas al prestigio verbal. . . . González Lanuza ha hecho el libro ejemplar del ultraísmo y ha diseñado un meandro de nuestro unánime sentir. Su libro, pobre de intento personal, es arquetípico de una generación. . . . González ha logrado el libro nuestro, el de nuestra hazaña en el tiempo y el de nuestra derrota en lo absoluto. (32)

> [I have read his admirable verses, I have savored the sweet docility of his music, I have fully felt the grandness of some passages, but I have also confirmed that, without meaning to, we have fallen into another rhetoric, as tied to verbal prestige as those that came before. . . . González Lanuza has produced Ultraism's emblematic book and he has designed a meander of our unanimous feeling. His book, lacking in personal intent, is archetypical of a generation. . . . González has achieved our book, that of our victory in time and that of our defeat in the absolute.]

Cunning in the "art of injury," with a flourish of his pen, Borges destroyed the aesthetic movement he himself had proposed as Argentina's national literature. He instead became involved in co-directing a journal that advanced dialogue with contemporary European writers (primarily between Valery Larbaud and Güiraldes, or between Ramón Gómez de la Serna and Borges); platforming Latin American writers and poets such as Alfonso Reyes, Fernán Silva Valdés, Pedro Leandro Ipuche, Ildefonso Pereda Valdés, Pablo Neruda, and Xavier Villaurrutia; and including writers from different aesthetic schools, as demonstrated by the journal's advanced publication of sections from Roberto Arlt's *El juguete rabioso* [*The Furious Toy*], "El rengo" and "El poeta parroquial," Luis Emilio Soto's review of Álvaro Yunque's *Versos de la calle*, or socially committed stories, like Edgardo Casella's "El estudiante que murió de rabia." Among the various schools and distinctive voices stands out a young Borges attempting a *criollismo* that, he writes, is conversador del mundo y del yo, de Dios y de la muerte" [conversant with the world and the self, with God and with death] and uses an oral orthography to recreate the sounds of *arrabalero* [Buenos Aires inhabitant of a poor neighborhood] speech: "ciudá" for *ciudad* [city], "cotidianidá" for *cotidianidad* [everyday life]. Owing to the journal's international reach and its desire to combine the best of Argentine literature with the newest literature coming out of Latin America and Europe, *Proa* is the best, though not always recognized, antecedent for the journal *Sur*. It is also the first scene upon which two of Argentina's great writers, Borges and Arlt, would meet and from whom, according to Ricardo Piglia, "se arman todas las genealogías, los parentescos y las intrigas de la literatura argentina contemporánea" [are derived all of the genealogies, the relationships and the intrigues of contemporary Argentine literature] (Costa 40). It is because of this encounter that Borges mentions Arlt's first novel in two essays published before *El juguete rabioso* [*The Furious Toy*] was even released—"La pampa y el suburbio son dioses" [The Pampa and the Suburbs are Gods] (*Proa*, no. 15, January 1926), and "Invectiva contra el arrabalero" [Invective Against the Slang of the Suburbs] (*La Prensa*, June 6, 1926)—which can be read as a kind of separate prologue to Arlt's beginnings as a writer. Because of this encounter, Borges would rewrite "El rengo" [The Lame] decades later when he publishes "El indigno" [The Unworthy] in *El informe de Brodie* [*Doctor Brodie's Report*], provocatively citing Arlt in the book's prologue (dated April 19, 1970), after countless pages of literary criticism had turned Borges and Arlt into a cipher for one of the many antinomies with which Argentine literary critics would quite comfortably cast one or the other, on the side of civilization or that of barbarism. Among his final stories, Borges would do something with Arlt's work that was reminiscent of the former's October 1953 story "El fin" [The End], in which he displaced José Hernández's gaucho Martín Fierro from the pampa to the urban outskirts. With "El indigno," Borges displaced Arlt's traitor from the working-class Flores neighborhood to the city's outer limits, past the Maldonado stream, and turns Arlt's lumpen character—a parking attendant at the Flores market—into a *compadrito* [thug]. According to Emilio Renzi, the protagonist of Piglia's *Respiración artificial*, Borges "escribe en términos de ficción sus homenajes y sus lecturas de la literatura argentina" [writes his homages and his readings of Argentine literature in fictional terms] and, at the same time, confirms the extraordinary consistency of his literary choices (140).

In addition to being one of the directors of *Proa*, Borges participated in the periodical *Martín Fierro*, headed by Evar Méndez, between February 1924 and November 1927. Borges's presence at the periodical was important but, despite what critics have tended to purport, far from central. While Borges published twenty-three items—poems, essays, prologues, and reviews, as well as "Leyenda policial," the predecessor for his first fictional story "Hombre de la esquina rosada" (Walker 33, 34)—it was Oliverio Girondo who published *Martín Fierro*'s most important contributions which, as Martín Greco argues, "revolucionaron el programa originario, hasta convertirlo en la condición de posibilidad y el dispositivo para la producción, distribución y difusión de las teorías del arte y la literatura de vanguardia" [revolutionized the creative movement to the point of making it the condition of possibility and the mechanism for the production, distribution and dissemination of theories of avant-garde art and literature] (12).

As is well known, *Martín Fierro* operated as the central point in organizing and reorganizing the lines of force traversing the literary field of the 1920s. Because there was *Martín Fierro*, there was Florida, which went from being the name of an elegant street in the city of Buenos Aires to designating a cultural group and a program of renewal and avant-garde aesthetics that, at the same time, maintained nostalgia for a *criollo* world that selfsame modernity was leaving behind. In *Martín Fierro, martinfierrismo* was born, which backed various manifestations of avant-garde art, European cinema, experimental theater, and new architectural forms and insinuated the decline of the *modernista* movement despite the journal's director, Evar Méndez, being a product of Latin American *modernismo*.

At the same time, *Martín Fierro* was the site of confluence of at least three great movements: that of Oliverio Girondo, which was established in the periodical's fourth issue (May 15, 1924) in its program-defining "Manifiesto de *Martín Fierro*"; that of the Ultraists, led by González Lanuza y Norah Lange; and that of Borges and his urban avant-garde *criollismo*. The disagreements among the different sectors came to a head at the end of 1927, after *Proa* had shut down, when *Crítica* published a commentary about the "new generation's" adherence to *yrigoyenismo* and the creation of the "Comité Irigoyenista (sic) de Intelectuales Jóvenes" [*Irigoyenista* (sic) Committee of Young Intellectuals], whose president was none other than Jorge Luis Borges. *Crítica* notes that the committee's first meeting was held at the "provisional headquarters" located at Avenida Quintana 222, none other than the house with barred windows and garden where the Borges family had been living since 1924 ("La 'nueva generación'" 3). The note, as García and Greco understand it, provoked a response from Evar Méndez in the pages of *Martín Fierro* in what would prove to be—though no one yet realized— the periodical's final issue: the journal was "absolutely non-political." The dissident leaders—Borges, Leopoldo Marechal, and Francisco Luis Bernárdez—responded in turn with their "desmemoria" [anti-memoir] of *Martín Fierro* published in *Crítica*, where they also announce the revival of *Proa* that coming March (80). Borges made clear, in a personal letter to Vicente Rossi dated June 1928, that the group hadn't "deseo ni el derecho de usurpar el nombre o la jefatura" [the desire nor the right to usurp the name or the leadership] of *Martín Fierro* (García and Greco 82). This was also reiterated in an article that Guillermo de Torre published contemporaneously in *La Gaceta Literaria de Madrid*, where he claimed that

> tres de sus miembros más conspicuos—Borges, Bernárdez y Marechal— separáronse radicalmente. Los tres escritores, confederados, proyectan ahora, como inminente, la reaparición de la revista *Proa*, tercera época de aquella juvenil publicación.... *Proa* vendrá muy a su hora para congregar una falange de jóvenes escritores con filiación homogénea, que representan un nuevo estado de espíritu más firme y maduro, con relación a los extremismos de sus orígenes. (García and Greco 86)

> [three of its most conspicuous members—Borges, Bernárdez and Marechal— radically separated themselves. The three newly confederated writers, now projected the imminent reappearance of the journal *Proa*, the third run of that youthful publication.... *Proa* will prove just the thing to bring together a throng of young, similarly aligned writers who represent a new spiritual state that is stronger and more mature when compared to the extremisms of its origins.]

Yet *Proa* did not reappear and the fraternity of the three confederates did not last long: owing to ideological and religious issues, only Marechal and Bernárdez would go on to edit the only issue of *Libra*, and not *Proa*, in August 1929.

Over the decades, Borges only grew further from *Martín Fierro*, both through omission and through open confrontation. In his *Autobiografía*, for example, Borges describes first his discomfort with everything the periodical represented:

> En 1924 me vinculé con dos grupos literarios diferentes. Uno, del que conservo un buen recuerdo, era el de Ricardo Güiraldes, quien todavía no había escrito *Don Segundo Sombra*.... El otro grupo, del que más bien me arrepiento, fue el de la revista *Martín Fierro*. No me gustaba lo que representaba *Martín Fierro*: la idea francesa de que la literatura se renueva continuamente, que Adán renace todas las mañanas, y de que si en París había cenáculos que promovían la publicidad y las disputas, nosotros teníamos que actualizarnos y hacer lo mismo. (89–90)

> [In 1924, I found my way into two different literary sets. One, whose memory I still enjoy, was that of Ricardo Güiraldes, who was yet to write *Don Segundo Sombra*.... The other set, which I rather regret, was that of the magazine *Martin Fierro*. I disliked what *Martin Fierro* stood for, which was the French idea that literature is being continually renewed—that Adam is reborn every morning, and also for the idea that, since Paris had literary cliques that wallowed in publicity and bickering, we should be up to date and do the same.] ("Autobiographical Essay" 164–65)

Second, he chooses not to mention it when he discusses his work during the 1920s:

> Ese período de 1921 a 1930 fue de gran actividad, aunque buena parte de esa actividad fue quizá imprudente y hasta inútil. Escribí y publiqué nada menos que siete libros: cuatro de ensayos y tres de poemas. También fundé tres revistas y escribí con regularidad para una docena de publicaciones periódicas, entre ellas *La Prensa*, *Nosotros*, *Inicial*, *Criterio* y *Síntesis*. Esta productividad hoy me asombra tanto como el hecho de que sólo siento una remota afinidad con la obra de aquellos años. (79)

> [This period, from 1921 to 1930, was one of great activity, but much of it was perhaps reckless and even pointless. I wrote and published no less than seven books—four of them essays and three of them verse. I also founded three magazines and contributed with fair frequency to nearly a dozen other periodicals, among them *La Prensa*, *Nosostros*, *Initial*, *Criteria*, and *Sintesis*. This productivity now amazes me as much as the fact that I feel only the remotest kinship with the work of these years.] ("Autobiographical Essay" 159)

In 1931, Borges joined the editorial board of *Sur*, a journal to which he would contribute over the course of forty-nine years (1931–1980), with a total of 175 texts including essays and commentaries, stories and book reviews, poems and translations, film reviews, and articles about crime fiction (*Borges en Sur* 7). As Beatriz Sarlo notes, Borges's collaborations "muestran que *Sur* fue un verdadero laboratorio donde a la vez que construía su poética del relato ensayaba el pasaje a la ficción narrativa que finalmente resultó decisivo para su consagración internacional" [show that *Sur* was a true laboratory where at the same time he was constructing his poetics of storytelling he was endeavoring a move to narrative fiction that would ultimately be a decisive factor in his international canonization] ("Una poética de la ficción" 20). Even while writing for *Sur* and other publications, Borges did not hold a stable, paid job until 1937, when he began working at the Biblioteca Municipal Miguel Cané. Perhaps owing to this freedom, in 1933, he accepted the offer to co-direct with Ulises Petit de Murat, la *Revista Multicolor de los Sábados* [*Multicolor Saturday Magazine*], the cultural supplement to *Crítica*, the newspaper in which Borges had published his first autobiography in 1926: "Natalio Botana me pagó generosamente: trescientos pesos al mes. Yo le pregunté qué horario había y él me dijo que ninguno. Que lo importante era que yo entregara la revista con una semana de anticipación" [Natalio Botana paid me generously: three hundred pesos a month. I asked him what the schedule was and he said there was none. That what mattered was that I submit the magazine a week ahead of time] (*Borges el memorioso* 217). Soon thereafter, Borges agreed to head up the "Libros y autores extranjeros" [Foreign Books and Authors] page of *El Hogar* [*The Home*] magazine between 1936 and 1939, where he wrote 326 reviews (Borges 1986).

At both venues, Borges undertook the tasks of a cultural journalist: writing reviews of recently published books, translating foreign stories, selecting material to be published. Yet it was the *Revista Multicolor de los Sábados* where the radically new would break into Borges's life and work. He became the director of the cultural supplement of the most popular and the most scandalous evening newspaper in Argentina (Saítta 1998), placing himself—not only in aesthetic and literary terms—at the polar opposite of Eduardo Mallea, who directed the formal and distinguished cultural supplement of *La Nación* between 1931 and 1956 and was an author of the long, psychological novels that Borges so abhorred. It might now be difficult to imagine that insertion of the avant-garde poet into the plebian universe of the "voice of the people" that *Crítica* represented in its motley pages, overflowing with huge headlines, scabrous illustrations, galleries of fear-inspiring murderers, social campaigns in tenements and poor neighborhoods, and shrill announcements of sporting event results. It is undeniable, however, that it was in the offices of *Crítica*, and through directing *Revista Multicolor de los Sábados*, that Borges learned the new trade of being an editor and a proofreader: "aprendí a leer los linotipos, como un espejo. Y aprendí a armar una página, también. Yo podía armar una página entonces.... Armar páginas, corregir pruebas: todo eso lo hacía yo" [I learned to read linotypes, like a mirror. And I learned to put a page together too. I could set a page then.... Setting pages, correcting proofs: I did it all] (*Borges el memorioso* 218).

The first issue of *Revista Multicolor de los Sábados* came out on August 12, 1933, and it is an essential chapter in the history of Argentine literature and journalism for its ability to combine highly sophisticated avant-garde literature, translations, and book reviews with the newspaper's mass appeal. Like a "*mezcla rara de Museta y de Mimí*," as Carlos Gardel sings in his tango song "Griseta" [a strange mix of Museta and Mimí], referencing two characters from Puccini's "La Bohème," *Revista Multicolor de los Sábados* published Argentine short stories and translations of foreign writers in which the fantastic genre, detective stories, Asian legends, and fictional essays shared pages with articles on popular science, notes on cinema and popular music, and miscellaneous sections, all held together with a profusion of illustrations. Striking images in bright colors were contributed by the great illustrators of the age such as Arístides Rechain, Juan Sorazábal, Premiani, Parpagnoli, Pascual Güida, Lorenzo Molas, Pedro Rojas, and Andrés Guevara. The supplement also included three comic strips: "Peloponeso y Jazmín," by Vincent T. Hamlin; "El nuevo rico," by Héctor Rodríguez; and "Nuevas aventuras del capitán y sus dos sobrinos," by Rudolph Dirks, which, even if they were translations of US comics, as Louis has noted, referenced points close to the Argentine reader through the process of modifying the original text (*Louis, oeuvre et manoeuvres* 293). Borges's imprint on the magazine was decisive, especially when compared to its first iteration, which had been published under the title *Revista Multicolor de los Sábados* between March 1931 and February 1932, very likely under Enrique González Tuñón. In that era of the supplement, social literature prevailed, and the bulk of the texts and poems were signed by writers close to the Boedo group: Álvaro Yunque, César Tiempo, Lorenzo Stanchina, Roberto Mariani, Alberto Gerchunoff, Cayetano Córdova Iturburu, Enrique, and Raúl González Tuñón. In contrast, under new leadership, most of the stories issued from among Borges's favorite authors—Rudyard Kipling, G. K. Chesterton, H. G. Wells, Marcel Schwob, Oscar Wilde, Jonathan Swift, Bernard Shaw, Heinrich Mann, Gustav Meyrink, Novalis, and Carl Sandburg—including translations of fantastic tales and stories of the Orient that soon thereafter would be included in the *Antología de la literatura fantástica* [*Anthology of Fantastic Literature*] and the *Cuentos breves y extraordinarios* [*Extraordinary Tales*].[2]

With respect to his own work, the *Revista Multicolor de los Sábados* implies a before and an after; it is in this communicative context that Borges published his first fictional stories, the very texts that would be published, with corrections, in 1935 under the title *Historia universal de la infamia* [*A Universal History of Infamy*] with the likewise mass-oriented press Tor (Balderston 274). These first fictions, these "ejercicios de prosa narrativa," which Borges deemed the "irresponsable juego de un tímido que no se animó a escribir cuentos y que se distrajo en falsear y tergiversar (sin justificación estética alguna vez) ajenas historias" [irresponsible game of a shy man who dared not write stories and so amused himself by falsifying and distorting (without any aesthetic justification whatever) the tales of others] (*Historia universal* 10; *A Universal History* 11–12), appeared at the time in the supplement of a newspaper read by three-hundred thousand readers, defining a poetics and mode of narration that would be reaffirmed in his future books. In these stories, says Sylvia Molloy, Borges works with texts that are apart from, on the margins of "great literature"—encyclopedia entries, tales of outlaws, myths of the Orient—which underlie his fiction not only as prior pretexts but as functional pre-texts (32). These are, to Sarlo's mind, Borges's most avant-garde stories: he selected second-hand materials from the margins of great literary traditions, casting doubt on the idea of originality by working with others' texts, versions, and repetitions of stories that did not belong to him (*Borges* 115). It was, in Borges's words, the true beginning of his career as a storyteller because those exercises "asumían la forma de falsificaciones y seudo-ensayos" [were in the nature of hoaxes and pseudo-essays] which led him "poco a poco a la escritura de cuentos legítimos" [very slowly . . . to legitimate stories] (*Autobiografía* 101). Thus, these stories that were destined not for publication in a book but for mass consumption in *Crítica* have "el valor secreto—además del placer que me dio escribirlas—[que] consiste en el hecho de que son ejercicios narrativos. Ya que los argumentos o las circunstancias generales me habían sido dados, sólo tenía que tramar vívidas variaciones" [the secret value of those sketches—apart from the sheer pleasure the writing gave me—lay in the fact that they were narrative exercises. Since the general plots or circumstances were all given me, I had only to embroider sets of vivid variations] (*Autobiografía* 101–2). In these very pages, Borges published his first story, "Hombre de la esquina rosada" [Man on Pink Corner], which he titles "Hombres de las orillas" [Men of the Neighborhoods] and signs—out of timidity, because he thought it was beneath him, because he knew his mother "desaprobaría el tema de manera terminante" [would heartily disapprove of the subject matter]—using the pseudonym Francisco Bustos, the name of one of this great-grandfathers (*Autobiografía* 101).

After his time with *Crítica*, Borges co-edited, along with Adolfo Bioy Casares, the journal *Destiempo*, whose three issues were published in 1936 and 1937. While Borges and Bioy Casares continued publishing in *Sur*, it is quite possible—though difficult to prove—that they thought of *Destiempo* as an alternative space, one more in line with their own literary interests. John King was the first scholar to point out the somewhat peripheral nature of the group Borges led at Sur before May 1938, when José Bianco replaced Guillermo de Torre as chief editor. Bianco recalls, "cuando yo entré en *Sur* me propuse de común acuerdo con Victoria Ocampo que la revista publicaría más literatura de imaginación, que aparecieran cuentos que trataran de evocar la realidad y no se contentaran con describirla, que fueran, en suma, más allá de la mera verosimilitud sin invención. Se publicaron más cuentos que hasta entonces" [when I began at *Sur* I was determined—in agreement with Victoria Ocampo—that the journal publish more literature of the imagination, that it have stories that attempted to evoke reality rather than settle for describing it, that went, in other words, beyond mere verisimilitude without invention. We published more stories than there had been previously] (369).

Destiempo is Borges's and Bioy Casares's first attempt at co-directing a journal. It was a nearly secret undertaking because the two were not named as its directors. Rather, Ernesto Pissavini, a complete unknown, was listed as editor-in-chief. This individual, who was in fact the superintendent of the building where Bioy Casares lived, also financed the journal, as indicated by its advertisements for "La Martona." The first two issues were published in October and November 1936; the third and final issue in December of the following year. Bioy Casares writes,

> En 1936 fundamos la revista *Destiempo*. El título indicaba nuestro anhelo de sustraernos a supersticiones de la época. Objetábamos particularmente la tendencia de algunos críticos a pasar por alto el valor intrínseco de las obras y a demorarse en aspectos folklóricos, telúricos o vinculados a la Historia literaria o a las disciplinas y estadísticas sociológicas. Creíamos que los preciosos antecedentes de una escuela eran a veces tan dignos de olvido como las probables, o inevitables, trilogías sobre el gaucho, la modista de clase media, etcétera. La mañana de septiembre en que salimos

de la imprenta de Colombo, en la calle Hortiguera, con el primer número de la revista, Borges propuso, un poco en broma, un poco en serio, que nos fotografiáramos para la Historia. Así lo hicimos en una modesta galería de barrio. Tan rápidamente se extravió esa fotografía, que ni siquiera la recuerdo. *Destiempo* reunió en sus páginas a escritores ilustres y llegó al número 3. (29)

[In 1936 we founded *Destiempo* magazine. The title indicated our desire to distance ourselves from the superstitions of the time. We particularly objected to the tendency of some critics to overlook the intrinsic value of the works and to dwell on folkloric, telluric aspects or those linked to literary history or sociological disciplines and statistics. We believed that the rarified antecedents of a literary movement were sometimes as worthy of forgetting as the likely, or inevitable, trilogies about the gaucho, the middle-class seamstress, and so on. The September morning when we left the Colombo printing house, on Calle Hortiguera, with the first issue of the magazine, Borges suggested, half joking, half serious, that we have a picture taken of ourselves for History. That's what we did, in a modest neighborhood gallery. That photograph was lost so fast that I don't even remember it. *Destiempo* brought together illustrious writers in its pages and made it to three issues.]

Those "illustrious" writers were the intellectuals closest to Borges's and Bioy Casares's most intimate circle: Silvina Ocampo, Macedonio Fernández, Alfonso Reyes, Manuel Peyrou. In addition to translations and film and literary criticism, the journal included an unsigned miscellaneous section entitled "Museo," which years later would reappear in *Los Anales de Buenos Aires* [*The Annals of Buenos Aires*], signed by B. Lynch Davis. This journal, belonging to Sara de Ortiz Basualdo, came under Borges's leadership in March 1946, after he left the Biblioteca Municipal Miguel Cané. Fabiana Sabsay-Herrera argues that the name B. Lynch Davis is reminiscent of B. Suárez Lynch, a pseudonym created by Borges and Bioy Casares, whose first and only appearance was made that same year as the author of *Un modelo para la muerte* [*A Model for Death*]. Evidently, Borges would have said that the B. represented the first letter of both his and Bioy Casares's last names; Suárez was one of his ancestors and Lynch was one of Bioy Casares's. Davis happened to be a distant relative on the English side of Borges's family (113).

The twenty-three issues of *Los Anales de Buenos Aires* were published between January 1946 and the beginning of 1948 by the cultural organization of the same name, which sought to promote connections with French culture by taking Paris's *Journal de L'Université des Annales* as its model. Its content reveals an intentional balance among stories, essays, and poetry, as well as between national and international contributors. Borges's preferences dominated its translations: stories or autobiographical excerpts from G. K. Chesterton, O. Henry, D. H. Lawrence, Jack London, and Thomas de Quincey; prose writings by Kafka; and an essay by Schopenhauer (Rasi 136–37). As with *Destiempo*, the majority of the texts published issued from the circle of the directors' friends: Silvina Ocampo, Xul Solar, Ulises Petit de Murat, Manuel Peyrou (in charge of the film section), Enrique Amorim, Ramón Gómez de la Serna, Ezequiel Martínez Estrada. The differences, Mariela Blanco finds, reside in *Los Anales de Buenos Aires* publishing new texts written specifically for the journal and in its listing Borges as editor-in-chief in its third to eleventh issues, published at the end of 1946, and in its last issue, published in 1948. In this venue, Borges published some of this most important stories and essays: "Los inmortales" [The Immortals], "Los teólogos" [The Theologians], "La casa de Asterión" [The House of Asterion], "El Zahir," "Nota sobre el Ulises en español" [A Note about Ulysses in Spanish], "La paradoja de Apollinaire" [The Paradox of Apollinaire], "El primer Wells" [The First Wells], "Sobre Oscar Wilde" [On Oscar Wilde], "Nota sobre Walt Whitman" [Note on Walt Whitman], and "Nota sobre Chesterton" [Note on Chesterton].

After the 1955 coup d'état, Borges's life, work, and public presence took a major turn with his appointment as Director of the National Library, a position he held until October 1973, and his being hired at the College of Philosophy and Letters at the University of Buenos Aires, where he taught English Literature courses until 1967. While Adolfo Prieto's 1956 book *Sociología del público argentino* [Sociology of the Argentine Public] may have demonstrated the non-specialized public's lack of familiarity with Borges's work when pointing out that, like other Argentine writers, he had failed to break down "la prevención con que el público mira la literatura argentina contemporánea, prevención que pareciera considerar la producción literaria como quehacer de enigmáticas élites" [the reticence with which the public views contemporary Argentine literature, reticence that seems to consider literary creation to be an enigmatically elite task] (77)—it is around this same time that Borges burst onto the scene as one of Argentina's great public figures.

Borges took over as Director of the National Library, with José Edmundo Clemente as Deputy Director, on October 25, 1955. Laura Rosato and Germán Álvarez hold that Borges's leadership brought the Library unprecedented cultural capital and international fame: the Mariano Moreno reading room became the setting for symposia and cultural events, and, in his Director's office, Borges dictated poems, essays, and prologues; revised his texts for the completion of his *Obras completas* [*Complete Works*]; worked on translations; prepared anthologies; received the national and international press; and even celebrated his birthday every August 24 (19). As of October 1955, as Borges himself told a journalist from *Siete Días*, the National Library became his place in the world:

> Toda mi producción literaria del 55 en adelante la preparé aquí, ayudado por mis secretarias y el dictáfono. Mi último libro, *El oro de los tigres* (del cual no puedo anticipar nada porque así lo convine con la empresa editora), aparecerá en un par de meses. Creo que quienes lean atentamente su nota (y recuerden que sólo veo los amarillos) pueden colegir de qué se trata. Pero no vaya a creer que vine a esta casa a escribir solamente. Siempre me preocuparon sus problemas, en especial el magro sueldo que ganan los empleados. . . . Recuerdo que en una oportunidad visité al ex presidente Roberto Levingston para exponerle esa carencia. Entonces le conté la historia de un ordenanza que había muerto, en una villa de emergencia de Boulogne, en la provincia de Buenos Aires, roído por la enfermedad y la miseria. Yo siempre voy a pedir que a mi sueldo (y le confieso que no sé cuánto gano) lo repartan por ley entre los operarios de la sección Maestranza. (26)

> [All of my literary output from '55 on I produced here, with the help of my secretaries and a Dictaphone. My latest book, *El oro de los tigres* (which I can't say anything about because that's what I agreed with the publisher) will be out in a few months. I think that those who read its author's note carefully (and remember, I can only see shades of

yellow) will figure out what it is about. But don't think that I came here just to write. I have always been concerned about its problems, especially the meager salaries of the library's employees. . . . I remember one time I visited the former president Roberto Levingston to point out how low these wages were. Then I told him the story of an assistant who had died, in the Boulogne slum in Buenos Aires province, wracked by illness and poverty. I am always going to ask that my salary (and I confess I don't know how much I make) be legally distributed among the maintenance workers.]

In addition to his tasks as Director and working on his writing, Borges decided to launch the second run of the journal *La Biblioteca*, which, despite the great enthusiasm he showed for it in many of the interviews he gave during this time, had only a brief life. He told Rafael R. de Stéfano, a reporter for *Propósitos*, that, unlike the journal's first iteration, whose only function was to "reimprimir documentos del archivo" [reprint documents from the archive] its second incarnation would have "un carácter más amplio" [a more ample nature] and that its pages would have "cabida toda expresión intelectual que se halle representada en la Biblioteca" [room for all of the intellectual expression that is represented in the National Library] (3). Indeed, in the five issues published between the first quarter of 1957 and June 1961, the journal published literary, historical, and philosophical essays, stories, and poems by Manuel Peyrou, Marcos Victoria, Bonifacio del Carril, Adolfo Bioy Casares, Guillermo de Torre, César Dabove, Arturo Capdevila, Felix Della Paolera, Jaime Rest, Julio César Caillet-Bois, Alicia Jurado, Adolfo Bioy Casares, César Fernández Moreno, Juan Carlos Ghiano, Luisa Mercedes Levinson, Raúl Castagnino, León Dujovne, and Ángel Battistessa, among others. Borges published his own texts in four of the five issues: "El simulacro" [The Simulacrum], "Borges y yo" [Borges and I], and "Delia Elena San Marco" (no. 1, spring 1957); "Diálogo de muertos" [Dead Men's Dialogue], "La trama" [The Plot], and "Un problema" [A Problem] (no. 2, fall 1957); "El hacedor" [The Maker] (no. 3, 1958); "Composición escrita en un ejemplar de la Gesta de Beowulf" [Written in a Copy of the Geste of Beowulf]; and the translation and notes for "Un diálogo anglosajón del siglo XI" [A Ninth-Century Anglo-Saxon Dialogue] (no. 5, 1961).

The political use of an institutional journal such as the National Library's is evident, because Borges does not publish *just any* story, but chooses—for the first issue no less— to include "El simulacro" (later included in his 1960 book *El hacedor*). One of his most explicitly political stories, this text in turn unleashed a series of literary representations of Eva Perón—one of Peronism's most powerful sources of symbolic production— whose signifying potential still shapes ideological positions today both within and outside the Peronist movement. Eva Perón's image has long formed the basis for interpretive historical-political and cultural essays and has fueled controversies at the level of literary, film, television, and visual criticism surrounding her figure. "El simulacro" is a short story that narrates, through the form its title suggests, the funeral of Eva Perón. In a ranch in a small town in the Argentine province of Chaco, Eva Perón's wake is staged in a reproduction in which everything is simulated: Evita's coffin is "una caja de cartón con una muñeca de pelo rubio" [a cardboard box with a doll with blonde hair] and a tall, lean man in mourning with "Indian" features represents Perón, who receives the condolences of desperate old women, boys, and field laborers. It is a "fúnebre farsa" [funereal farce] that, when reiterated in various parts of the country, deems all Argentine politics during Peronism to have been a simulation and a farce. From that first story published by Borges, and for decades after, the literary representation of Eva Perón became central to Argentine literature because stories, poems, novels, and plays were both referring to and configuring areas of the political and social imaginary, either in line with the Peronist versions of history or in frank dissent with them.

In addition to his tasks as director of the National Library and as a professor of English literature, Borges continued publishing poems, short stories, and essays in the mass media, as Jorge Emilio Gallardo well recalls, in a 1986 tribute in *La Nación*:

> Borges llegaba cualquier tarde a *La Nación*, imprevistamente . . . se sentaba en un sillón bajo en el despacho del Suplemento Literario, en el viejo edificio de la calle San Martín, con las manos fijas sobre el bastón alto, y apuntaba vagamente su humor y su mentón hacia el interlocutor invisible. Entregaba casi con humildad un borrador ya pasado a máquina, que le era leído en voz alta y al cual sobre la marcha añadía correcciones. Leída una vez más, daba a la versión por definitiva o modificaba todavía una palabra, un mínimo detalle. . . . Durante más de sesenta años este diario anticipó buena parte de lo que sería su obra total. . . . En una época en la cual ya muy pocos colaboradores de este Suplemento Literario revisaban las pruebas de galera de sus colaboraciones (o las pruebas de página, cuando nuevas técnicas de impresión liquidaron las galeras), el viejo poeta ciego no dudaba en renovar su visita artesanal al diario de siempre para corregir las pruebas del texto entregado pocos días antes por su misma mano. (4)

> [Borges would arrive at *La Nación* any afternoon, unexpectedly . . . he would sit in a low chair in the office of the Literary Supplement, in the old building on San Martín Street, with his hands fixed on his tall cane, and vaguely point his humor and his chin at the invisible interlocutor. He would almost humbly hand over a typewritten draft, which would be read aloud to him and to which he would add corrections as he went along. Read once again, the version would be declared definitive or require a modification to one word, a minute detail. . . . For more than sixty years this newspaper had the first look at a good part of what would be his total work. . . . At a time when very few collaborators of this Literary Supplement still reviewed the galley proofs of their contributions (or the page proofs, when new printing techniques eliminated the galleys), the old blind poet never thought twice about continuing his customary author's visits the newspaper to correct the proofs of the handwritten texts he had dropped off a few days before.]

From the 1960s until his death, Borges's presence in the media multiplied and diversified in other ways: not only was he a prize jury member in detective story contests in the popular magazine *Vea y Lea* in 1961, and for *La Nación*'s prizes for short stories, essays, plays, and novels between 1960 and 1974, he also became a public figure who was photographed, interviewed, and honored for an extraordinarily diverse array of topics and in the most varied sorts of media, from large national newspapers and

48   SYLVIA SAÍTTA

cultural magazines to illustrated weeklies, neighborhood newspapers, and the sensationalist press. Only an extreme closeness to the media—which in those years also included television programs—explains Borges's presence even in the outer limits of print journalism, as evidenced by an article published in *Así*, one of Argentina's most sensationalist magazines, created by Héctor Ricardo García, owner of the extremely popular *Crónica* newspaper. For the first time since its release on the street in October 1955, on September 1, 1970, the cover of *Así* did not display photos of murderers, accidents, crime scenes, or corpses, but rather, under the crass title "Borges's divorce: Argentine candidate for the Nobel Prize couldn't stand his wife" along with two photographs, it announced the recent separation of Jorge Luis Borges and Elsa Astete Millán. Four photograph-filled pages included two interviews with the ex-spouses: "Borges's Failure. Famous elite writer couldn't bear married life" the title of the interview with Borges; and "'Two opposite poles' Mrs. Borges, in an exclusive interview, reveals what led her to divorce the writer" for the one with Astete Millán. For a number of reasons, the feature in itself was a scandalous event: it was about Borges, an established writer who was also Director of the National Library; around 1970, writers' intimate lives were still considered private; the two interviews pruriently reveal the details of the couple's private life, showing in turn the violence done to the tabloid's interviewees. The feature reads,

> Borges estaba muy lejos de suponer que su divorcio pudiera prevalecer como tema en una entrevista. ¿Por qué no dialogar sobre su último libro *El informe de Brodie* o sobre los 25 mil cruceros del premio interamericano de literatura Matarazzo-Sobrinho que acaba de recibir en Río de Janeiro? ¿O en alguna medida sobre política, o sus estudios de inglés antiguo y escandinavo? Hablar sobre su divorcio le parece trivial, ahondar en sus causas carece de sentido, porque no remedia nada. . . . Como es lógico, el abrupto tema del divorcio no fue tratado a quemarropa. . . . Antes Borges, como recreándose, habló de *El informe de Brodie*.

> [Borges couldn't have imagined his divorce would be a major topic for an interview. Why not talk about his latest book, *El informe de Brodie*, or about the 25,000 Brazilian *cruzeiros* he just won in Rio de Janeiro for the Matarazzo-Sobrinho Inter-American Literature Prize? Or a bit about politics, or his studies of Old English and Old Norse? Talking about his divorce seemed trivial to him, delving into the causes for it was meaningless, that wouldn't help anything. . . . Of course, the subject of divorce wasn't brought up point blank. . . . Before that, Borges, seemingly amusing himself, spoke on *El informe de Brodie*.]

The journalist listened to Borges talk about books and literature while silently preparing to shoot, this time, at point blank: "¿Por qué no nos habla de su divorcio?" [Why don't you tell us about your divorce?]. Borges, giving up, responded: "Nos separamos como amigos. Entre mi esposa y yo no hay una situación hostil. Somos dos mundos distintos, que no tenemos punto de contacto" [We parted ways as friends. There is no hostility between my wife and me. We are two different worlds, with no points of contact]. A more improbable, sentimental, and mawkish Borges, committing to the media rhetoric of scandal and verging on impudence, added: "Es cierto que soy sensible. Muy romántico, pero es un defecto ser así, porque uno no llega a nada. La sensibilidad es un camino que no conduce a nada positivo. . . . ¿Va a publicar todo esto? . . . No quisiera hablar más de esto, por favor" [It is true that I am sensitive. Very romantic, but it's a defect to be this way, because it comes to nothing. Sensitivity isn't a path that leads to anything positive. . . . Are you going to publish all this? . . . I don't want to talk about this anymore, please]. This feature, like many that preceded and came after it, constructed the other side of Borges's public figure. It is far—due to its tone, its themes, the emphasis of his voice—from his first autobiography published in *Crítica*—but not in its extreme proximity to mass, popular media.

In this heterogeneous network of texts and photographs, critical readings of his literary work coexist in happy harmony with the media's updates on his private life; the reviews of his newest books alongside the minute details of his marriage and subsequent separation; and coverage of his national and international conferences, with photos of him receiving awards, traveling the world, attending a public event, signing books, or simply walking down *calle* Florida or perhaps Maipú. Books, libraries, and the streets of Buenos Aires, as they were in the twenties; mass media, film studios, and television sets, beginning in the sixties: a Borges for all, a high-profile and popular Borges.

Notes

1. TN: As part of Borges's avant-garde aesthetics of the early 1920s, the word "y" [and] has been spelled phonetically as [i].
2. See Emron Esplin's chapter in this volume for more on the fantastic and these collections.

Works Cited

Balderston, Daniel. "Puntos suspensivos: sobre el manuscrito de 'Hombre de la esquina rosada." *Cuarenta Naipes*, no. 1, 2019, pp. 260–74.
Bianco, José. *Ficción y reflexión*. Fondo de Cultura Económica, 1988.
Bioy Casares, Adolfo. *Borges*. Edición al cuidado de Daniel Martino. Destino, 2006.
Blanco, Mariela. "Borges crítico en *Los Anales de Buenos Aires*." *Letras*, no. 81, January–June 2020, pp. 204–23.
Borges, Jorge Luis. "Acotaciones." *Proa*, no. 1, August 1924, pp. 30–32.
Borges, Jorge Luis. *A Universal History of Infamy*, translated by Norman Thomas di Giovanni, Dutton, 1979.
Borges, Jorge Luis. *Autobiografía (1899–1970)*, translated by Marcial Souto and Norman Thomas di Giovanni. El Ateneo, 1999.
Borges, Jorge Luis. *Historia universal de la infamia* [1935]. Alianza, 1979.
Borges, Jorge Luis. "Leyenda policial." *Martín Fierro*, no. 38, February 26, 1927, p. 4.
Borges, Jorge Luis. "Nora Lange." *Martín Fierro*, no. 10–11, October 9, 1924, p. 3.
Borges, Jorge Luis. "Proclama." *Prisma*, no. 1, December 11, 1921.

Borges, Jorge Luis. *Textos cautivos: Ensayos y reseñas en El Hogar (1936–1939)*, edited by Enrique Sacerio-Garí and Emir Rodríguez Monegal. Tusquets, 1986.

Borges, Jorge Luis. *The Aleph and Other Stories, 1933–1969: Together with Commentaries and an Autobiographical Essay*. Trans. Norman Thomas di Giovanni, Bantam Books, 1971.

Borges, Jorge Luis. "Ultraísmo." *Nosotros*, no. 151, December 1921, pp. 466–71.

Borges el memorioso. Conversaciones de Jorge Luis Borges con Antonio Carrizo. Fondo de Cultura Económica, 1983.

Borges en Sur, 1931–1980, edited by Sara Luisa del Carril and Mercedes Rubio de Socchi. Emecé, 1999.

Costa, Marithelma. "Entrevista a Ricardo Piglia." *Hispamerica*, no. 44, August 1986, pp. 39–54.

De Stéfano, Rafael R. "Flamante director de la Biblioteca" (entrevista a Jorge Luis Borges). *Propósitos*, November 3, 1955, p. 3.

"El divorcio de Borges: Candidato argentino al premio Nobel no fue capaz de soportar a su esposa." *Así*, no. 743, September 1, 1970.

Gallardo, Jorge Emilio. "El creador en *La Nación*." *La Nación*, June 22, 1986, section 4, Homenaje a Jorge Luis Borges, p. 4.

García, Carlos, and Martín Greco. *La ardiente Aventura: Cartas y documentos inéditos de Evar Méndez, director del periódico Martín Fierro*. Albert editor, 2017.

Greco, Martín, "Prólogo." *El periódico Martín Fierro*. Edited by Oliverio Girondo, EUDEBA, 2018, pp. 11–28.

King, John. *Sur. A Study of the Argentine Literary Journal and Its Role in the Development of a Culture, 1931–1970*. Cambridge University Press, 1986.

"La Biblioteca Nacional y su futuro edificio. Historia en 1.600.000 tomos." *Siete Días Ilustrados*, no. 364, July 10, 1972, pp. 25–6.

"La glosa del día. Al margen de *Proa*." *Crítica*, December 12, 1922, p. 7.

"La 'nueva generación' se ha adherido al irigoyenismo. Constituyó una entidad con el nombre de Comité Irigoyenista de Intelectuales Jóvenes." *Crítica*, December 20, 1927, p. 3.

Louis, Annick. *Jorge Luis Borges: Obras y maniobras*. UNL, 2013.

Louis, Annick. *Jorge Luis Borges: oeuvre et manoeuvres*. L'Harmattan, 1997.

Molloy, Sylvia. *Las letras de Borges y otros ensayos*. Beatriz Viterbo, 1999.

Piglia, Ricardo. *Respiración artificial*. Sudamericana, 1980.

Piglia, Ricardo. "Sobre Borges." *Crítica y ficción*. Siglo veinte, 1990.

Prieto, Adolfo. *Sociología del público literario*. Leviatán, 1956.

Prieto, Martín. *Breve historia de la literatura argentina*. Taurus, 2006.

"Proa." *Proa*, no. 1, August 1924.

Rasi, Humberto M. "Jorge Luis Borges y la Revista *Los Anales de Buenos Aires*." *Revista Interamericana de Bibliografía*, no. 2, April–June 1977, pp. 135–41.

Rosato, Laura, and Germán Álvarez, eds. *Borges, libros y lecturas: catálogo de la colección Jorge Luis Borges en la Biblioteca Nacional*. Biblioteca Nacional, 2010, pp. 19–40.

Sabsay-Herrera, Fabiana. "Para la prehistoria de H. Bustos Domecq. *Destiempo*, una colaboración olvidada de Jorge Luis Borges y Adolfo Bioy Casares." *Variaciones Borges*, no. 5, 1998, pp. 106–22.

Saer, Juan José. "Borges francófobo." *Punto de Vista*, no. 36, December 1989, pp. 22–4.

Saítta, Sylvia. *Regueros de tinta. El diario Crítica en la década de 1920*. Sudamericana, 1998.

Sarlo, Beatriz. *Borges, un escritor en las orillas*. Ariel, 1995.

Sarlo, Beatriz. *Una modernidad periférica. Buenos Aires, 1920 y 1930*. Nueva Visión, 1988.

Sarlo, Beatriz. "Una poética de la ficción." *El oficio se afirma. Historia crítica de la literatura argentina*, vol. 9. Edited by Sylvia Saítta. Emecé, 2004, pp. 19–38.

Sarlo, Beatriz. "Vanguardia y criollismo: la aventura de *Martín Fierro*." Edited by Carlos Altamirano and Beatriz Sarlo, *Ensayos argentinos. De Sarmiento a la vanguardia*, CEAL, 1983, pp. 127–81.

Vaccaro, Alejandro. *Georgie 1890–1930: Una vida de Jorge Luis Borges*. Editorial Proa-Alberto Casares, 1996.

Vaccaro, Alejandro. "Georgie: Sevilla." *Variaciones Borges*, no. 2, 1996, pp. 192–6.

Walker, Carlos. "Jorge Luis Borges: de *Martín Fierro* a *Sur* (1924–1935)." *Iberoamericana*, no. 41, 2011, pp. 25–42.

CHAPTER 4

DEVELOPING AN ARGENTINE STYLE IN FORM AND CONTENT

Jorge Luis Borges and Editorial Proa

NORA BENEDICT

> "Ya se sabe que el mayor énfasis de una palabra, su más reverente pronunciación, es destacarla para nombre de un libro"
>
> [It is already known that the best emphasis of a word, its most reverent pronunciation, is to assign it as the name of a book.]
>
> —Jorge Luis Borges, *Cuaderno San Martín* [*San Martín Notebook*] (1929)

JORGE Luis Borges is known for his frequent use of complex themes, yet he returns time and time again to two ideas more than others: books and his native Buenos Aires. In this chapter I link his fascination with these two concepts to his earliest participation in the world of publishing. In particular, works such as *Inquisiciones* [*Inquisitions*] (1925), *El tamaño de mi esperanza* [*The Size of My Hope*] (1926), and *Cuaderno San Martín* (1929) all demonstrate Borges's unique Argentine style, which emerges from his involvement with Editorial Proa. While critics have written on his Argentine voice in these early works, there is a dearth of scholarship pertaining to the physical presentation of these books, Borges's crucial role in their production, and the central link between these concepts. As such, I detail here how Borges's marked Argentine style, which incorporates themes, language, and physical presentation, emerges from his exposure to the burgeoning publishing industry in Argentina. More specifically, both the form and content of Editorial Proa's works serve to highlight Borges's early engagement with the book as a cultural object and vehicle for Argentine expression.

A Brief History of Editorial Proa

Evar Méndez, along with Oliverio Girondo and Ricardo Güiraldes, founded Editorial Proa in 1924 as an offshoot of the periodical *Martín Fierro* (1924–1927).[1] Although these two cultural endeavors shared a desire to highlight up-and-coming young Argentine writers and renovate the artistic environment of Buenos Aires, the creation of Editorial Proa is, from the start, described as an "organismo totalmente autónomo, independiente del periódico [*Martín Fierro*]" [totally autonomous organism, independent from the journal] ("Editoriales Proa y Martín Fierro" 5). We see Méndez's knowledge of the publishing industry in the same print announcement for Editorial Proa that appears in *Martín Fierro*:

> A esto se agregó el designio de abaratar el libro nacional, revolucionando el mercado al lanzar a la plaza ediciones, al menor precio posible, de un tipo de libro especialmente estudiado, con carácter propio, de primera calidad como papeles, tipografía, impresión, estilo, y en las mejores condiciones de presentación por medio de prospectos críticos, fajas anunciadoras, carteles de propaganda, organización de exposiciones en vitrinas de librerías, garantizando de tal modo una excelente difusión, beneficiosa para autor, librero y editor. La práctica demostró el pleno éxito del sistema. ("Editoriales Proa y Martín Fierro" 5)

> [To this is added the plan to reduce the price of the Argentine book, revolutionizing the market by launching editions, at the cheapest price possible, of primarily studied books, with their own character and of the highest quality with regard to their paper, typography, style, and presented in the best conditions through critical reviews, promotional sashes, advertising posters, organized displays in bookstore windows, all of which will guarantee an excellent dissemination that will be beneficial to the author, the bookseller, and the editor. These customs demonstrated the full success of the system.]

Not only did Méndez go to great lengths to outline the benefits for authors, but he also explained how works produced by Editorial Proa would benefit booksellers with a very detailed breakdown of their potential commissions. Along with Méndez's emphasis on the publishing industry as a type of system that requires a detailed plan of action, we also see his interest in producing books of the highest quality in terms of their physical composition. Premium quality paper, elegant typography, and a clean style became synonymous with Editorial Proa. There was also a strong emphasis placed on not only this high quality but also accessibility. In other words, Méndez hoped to produce beautiful books at the lowest price possible, so that many people could have access to them. In addition to the attention to cost, Méndez also stressed the importance of establishing fair and consistent copyright laws to protect authors, which, up to that point, were very rarely followed. Instead, the norm for many editors would be to register works in their own names and, thus, rob authors of not only the rights to reproduce and copy their own works but also the ability to receive adequate royalties and payment. Even though Méndez's intentions for elevating national literature and book culture were noble, the fact that he was not interested in monetary gain, which meant that he did not go to great lengths to develop a sustainable and organized operations plan for Editorial Proa, ultimately led to its demise.

During its eight years of existence, Editorial Proa published a total of twenty-one works. The sixteen works in table 4.1 formed part of what might be deemed their general collection. In a letter to Victoria Ocampo dated January 9, 1927, we learn that Méndez had approached this prominent Argentine about publishing with Editorial Proa as well (García and Greco 224). We also discover in this same letter than Méndez had several other works in mind for his firm that never came to fruition, including a translation of *The Young Visitors* by Daisy Ashford (with illustrations by Norah Borges), a work by Xul Solar entitled *64 signos [64 Signs]*, and a second edition of Güiraldes's *Cencerro de cristal [Crystal Bell]* (García and Greco 224).[2] Moreover, in the January 24, 1925, issue of *Martín Fierro* we find an announcement of books that would be published throughout the year, many of which were slated to appear with Editorial Proa, yet the majority of them never materialized. A similar announcement appeared in the May 5, 1925, issue of *Martín Fierro* with a few newly added works such as Norah Borges's *Su obra plástica [Her Plastic Work]* and the promise of editions by foreign authors including Rubén Darío, Ramón del Valle Inclán, Ramón Gómez de la Serna, Rafael Cansinos Assens, Remy de Gourmont, Rudyard Kipling, Valery Larbaud, Aldo Polazzeschi, and Luigi Pirandello. None of these works ended up forming part of Editorial Proa's literary output.

In terms of their physical features, the majority of Editorial Proa's published books share similar design elements, which highlights Méndez's stylistic preferences for his publishing house. While the covers might differ in color (blue, yellow, red, orange, etc.), the typographical layout and presentation of these volumes is virtually uniform from one work to the next. Thus, we find the name of the author along the top edge of the cover, and the title of the work—in a slightly larger typeface—about an inch below this name. Printed in the bottom third of the cover are two horizontal black lines, with the top line being nearly twice as thick as the lower one, directly above the name of the publisher along with the location and the date of publication (see Figures 4.1).

The clean lines and simplicity of each of these books distinguish Editorial Proa from all other Argentine firms at the time and signal a crucial moment in the development of Buenos Aires book culture. While some covers show a slight variation from these stylistic elements, with additional details such as a black dot below the title or a second thinner horizontal line below the publication information, the overall presence of shared and unifying design features provides Editorial Proa with an aesthetic trademark.[3]

There are no cover illustrations and the typefaces used are modern with almost hairline serifs and an extreme level of vertical stress and contrast, which has the effect of drawing the eye up and down rather than side to side. Furthermore, the amount of balance between the units of typography and the overall use of space on the cover give these

Table 4.1 Editorial Proa titles, 1925–1932

Author	Work	Printer	Date	Copies
Jorge Luis Borges	*Inquisiciones*	El Inca	1925	505
Francisco Luis Bernárdez	*Alcándara* [*The Falcon's Perch*]	El Inca	1925	505
Jorge Luis Borges	*Luna de enfrente* [*Moon across the Way*]	G. Ricordi E. C.	1925	300
Sergio Piñero, hijo	*El puñal de Orión* [*Orion's Dagger*]	G. Ricordi E. C.	1925	
Ricardo Güiraldes	*Don Segundo Sombra*	Francisco A. Colombo	1926	7,090
Jorge Luis Borges	*El tamaño de mi esperanza*	Ernesto A. Petenello	1926	500
Leopoldo Hurtado	*Sketches*	Porter Hermanos	1927	1,020
Norah Lange	*Voz de la vida* [*The Voice of Life*]	Porter Hermanos	1927	520
Ricardo E. Molinari	*El imaginero* [*The Religious Painter*]	Porter Hermanos	1927	520
Nydia Lamarque	*La elegía del gran amor* [*Elegy of Great Love*]	Porter Hermanos	1927	510
Andrés L. Caro	*Mapa Mundi*	Porter Hermanos	1928	254
Guillaume Apollinaire	*32 poemas*[a] [*32 Poems*]	Porter Hermanos	1929	252
María de Villarino	*Calle apartada*[b] [*Remote Street*]	Francisco A. Colombo	1929	302
Norah Lange	*El rumbo de la rosa* [*The Direction of the Rose*]	Francisco A. Colombo	1930	450
Ricardo E. Molinari	*Panegírico* [*Panegyric*]	Francisco A. Colombo	1930	200
Oliverio Girondo	*Espantapájaros* [*Scarecrow*]	Francisco A. Colombo	1932	5,065

[a] Translated by Lisandro Z. D. Galtier.

[b] The differing design features of María de Villarino's work, whose only reference to Editorial Proa is in the printed colophon, can easily be explained by Méndez himself in a letter he writes to Alfonso Reyes on May 15, 1929 (García and Greco 269).

works a level of elegance. The pronounced type stands out even more against the subtle colors of the covers. The interior pages also exhibit a level of elegance in both the typographical diagramming of the text and the selection of paper for printing. More specifically, the text blocks are justified and aligned on the page to allow for a maximum amount of margin space, which is a traditional sign of luxury since paper is, historically speaking, an expensive commodity. Along with the central text block placement,

FIGURE 4.1 Two books produced by Editorial Proa (1925–1927).

Source: Photo courtesy of Nora Benedict.

each of Editorial Proa's books introduces continuous typographical ornaments at the head of each page, in the form of two horizontal black lines, which echo the horizontal lines above the publication information on the covers and title pages. Most of the earlier editions do not contain running titles in addition to these typographical ornaments, but a few later works, including Nydia Lamarque's *La elegía del gran amor*, introduce these textual elements above the two horizontal lines.

Although these common features might suggest the handiwork of one printer or typesetter, that is not the case. Rather, the colophons of each of these works demonstrate that Méndez used the following five printers for his Editorial Proa books: "El Inca," "G. Ricordi E. C.," "Ernesto A. Petenello," "Francisco A. Colombo," and "Porter Hermanos." This sense of variety curiously contradicts the original plan of Editorial Proa, as outlined in *Martín Fierro*, to rely on Casa Ricordi to print their books ("Editoriales Proa y Martín Fierro" 5). As opposed to becoming a sort of house printer for Editorial Proa, we find that Casa Ricordi only printed two of Editorial Proa's twenty-one books: *Luna de enfrente* (1925) and *El puñal de Orión* (1925). This is the same number of titles printed by El Inca (two) and only one more than Ernesto A. Petenello (one). In contrast, Porter Hermanos prints nearly one third of all of Editorial Proa's titles (six of the twenty-one) and Francisco A. Colombo prints nearly half of the titles (ten of the twenty-one). Even though the use of various printers goes against the initial scripted publishing plan for Editorial Proa, this diversity reveals that the signature design elements of these works were not just the product of one printer or typographer but, rather, can be traced directly to the house style that Méndez created for his firm.

When viewed together, all these aspects demonstrate Méndez's success in defining "una nueva escuela gráfica" [a new graphic school] and works that were *productos de* "un nuevo arte" [products of a new art] (Buonocore 109). What is more, the decision to include detailed information about the number of copies produced, the types of papers used, and how many books in each print run were "fuera de comercio" [not for sale] distinguishes the book production of Editorial Proa from virtually all other Argentine firms in operation during the first part of the twentieth century. More specifically, we find that the majority of Editorial Proa's books, including both the regular works and those that formed part of the "Cuadernos del Plata" series, contain a printed reference to between two and thirty copies produced that were not for sale. These noncirculating copies were printed on various types of paper including Japanese paper, Vergé laid paper, Fabriano paper, Wathman paper, and Hammermill paper.[4] This level of detail and transparency with regard to the physical production process, which is uncommon in early 1920s Argentine book production, highlights the value of Editorial Proa's books not only for their content but also for their artistic forms. The only three distinct exceptions to what I would call this house style are the following works: Jorge Luis Borges's *Luna de enfrente* (1925), Nydia Lamarque's *La elegía del gran amor* (1928), and Oliverio Girondo's *Espantapájaros* (1932). Although Borges's work is the only one of the three that is officially designated as a luxury edition, the inclusion of illustrations and multiple ink colors throughout the other two titles set them apart from the rest of Editorial Proa's books. Moreover, Lamarque's work was published as a private edition, which may account for its unique design features. As for Girondo's work, it was tied to a unique marketing plan, which included the creation of a three-foot-tall papier mâché replica of the figure adorning the book's cover that Girondo marched through the streets of Buenos Aires to help boost sales.[5] This novel sales tactic worked well and Girondo sold more than 5,000 copies within the first month of the book's initial release.

Alongside these elegantly produced titles, Méndez also enlisted his friend Alfonso Reyes to direct a special series for Editorial Proa, "Cuadernos del Plata," which appears to amplify Méndez's already known interest in up-and-coming Argentine writers. That said, the extant correspondence between Reyes and Méndez reveals that Reyes never truly felt like the real director of this collection due to Méndez's almost militant control over all aspects of publication (García and Greco 272). Even though Reyes reviewed all of the galley proofs and weighed in on certain design features, such as the initial capitals used throughout Güiraldes's *Seis relatos*, Méndez was the one who spoke directly with Francisco A. Colombo, the official printer for the collection (García and Greco 217). Méndez also was the one who arranged orders with various booksellers including Viau y Zona, Palacio del Libro, and the Amigos del Arte (García and Greco 270). Moreover, their correspondence also shows that Méndez took the lead on deciding how to market and sell these new books, which consisted of making the luxury editions available first and then releasing the common copies a few weeks later.

The first known announcement of this collection appeared in the "Notas y Notabilidades" section of the Argentine periodical *La Vida Literaria*. Here we discover that Francisco A. Colombo was to print all the works, which immediately links these forthcoming books with the immense success of *Don Segundo Sombra*.[6] The short note lists *Siete cuentos* [*Seven Stories*][7] de Ricardo Güiraldes as the first publication in the "Cuadernos del Plata" collection, along with several books that never actually appear in print with this series for Editorial Proa including a work by Victoria Ocampo entitled *Epistolario* [*Epistolary*], a work by Xul Solar entitled *San Signos* [*Holy Signs*], an anthology of North American poets, and a work by Alfonso Reyes himself entitled *Culto a Mallarmé* [*Cult of Mallarmé*].[8] The five works in table 4.2 were the only ones published as a part of this separate series. Looking to the covers of these works, we find that they are all virtually identical in terms of their design features, which seems to be a characteristic trait for Méndez's publishing house (see Figures 4.2).

Although their use of a sans-serif typeface is distinct from the rest of Editorial Proa publications, the typographical layout is reminiscent of the earlier books produced by this firm. In contrast to the austere and modern covers, the interior pages of each book use a softer, serif typeface, continuous page numbers, and double-barred type ornaments for the headers, all of which recall the style of the rest of Editorial Proa's works. What is more, each of these works includes a visual rendering of its author in the form of either a drawing or a photograph on glossy paper, facing the title page.

Table 4.2 Works published in the "Cuadernos del Plata" series, 1929–1939

Author	Work	Date	Copies
Ricardo Güiraldes	*Seis relatos* [*Six Stories*]	1929	550
Jorge Luis Borges	*Cuaderno San Martín*	1929	250
Macedonio Fernández	*Papeles de Recienvenido* [*Newcomer Papers*]	1929	465
Ricardo E. Molinari	*El pez y la manzana* [*The Fish and the Apple*]	1930	155
Gilberto Owen	*Línea* [*Line*]	1930	320

BORGES AND EDITORIAL PROA

Editorial Proa is the first publisher that Borges worked with throughout his long career, and as a result, his first experiences with the ins and outs of the Argentine publishing industry can be traced to this firm.[9] In a sense, by publishing with Editorial Proa, Borges gained not only first-hand experience with the entire book industry but also the opportunity to work alongside someone who was very much concerned with the highest quality in all aspects of the book. Even though Méndez and Borges did not see eye to eye on many issues, and eventually had a severe falling out, their initial interactions served as a foundation for the young Argentine writer's understanding of the book as a physical object and his marked interested in a simple style for book design.[10]

Borges published four works with Editorial Proa during the 1920s: *Inquisiciones* (1925), *Luna de enfrente* (1925), *El tamaño de mi esperanza* (1926), and *Cuaderno San Martín* (1929). Although each of these works possesses its own unique traits and varies in form from prose to poetry, they can be linked by their shared Argentine style, which shines through in both their linguistic texts and their physical features. Moving chronologically, *Inquisiciones* is not only Borges's first published collection of prose but also Editorial Proa's first published work. Borges called the work an "ejecutoria parcial de mis veinticinco años" [partial final judgement of my twenty-five years] in the prologue and cited his first collection of poetry, *Fervor de Buenos Aires*, as its poetic counterpart. Throughout the essays, or "borradores" [drafts] as Borges calls them in this same prologue, we see three central thematic groupings: European literary traditions, the Ultraist movement, and *criollismo*. His interest in European writers such as Francisco de Quevedo ("Menoscabo y Grandeza de Quevedo" [Quevedo's Diminution and Greatness]), James Joyce ("El 'Ulises' de Joyce" [Joyce's 'Ulysses']), and even Sir Thomas Browne ("Sir Thomas Browne") is a natural extension of his schooling and travels throughout Europe and, in a sense, speaks to the fact that such authors might have been fresh in his mind as his family had just returned to Buenos Aires in 1924 after a second trip to the Continent. In a similar vein, his writings on "Norah Lange" and "E. González Lanuza," among others, along with several pieces on the value of the form of the metaphor ("Después de las imágenes" [After Images]), all

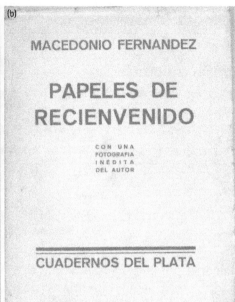

FIGURE 4.2 Books in the "Cuadernos del Plata" series (1929).

Source: Photo courtesy of Nora Benedict.

highlight his interest in the Ultraist movement, as well as the efforts he expended to bring its literary tenets from Spain to his native Argentina.[11] The final thematic thread that runs throughout *Inquisiciones* is Borges's *criollismo*, which emerges most clearly in essays such as "Queja de todo criollo" [Every *Criollo*'s Complaint], "Buenos Aires," "Interpretación de Silva Valdés" [Interpretation of Silva Valdés], "La criolledad en Ipuche" [The *criollo*ness in Ipuche], and "Ascasubi." Although many of his contemporaries praise this early collection of essays for its universal themes and philosophical metaphysics, they also note their dislike of his strong use of such local color (Piñero 4). Borges himself later rejected virtually all these earlier collections for these same reasons.[12]

As the first published work for Editorial Proa, many of the physical features found throughout Borges's *Inqusiciones* establish the firm's house style, yet, as we shall see, certain elements that appear in this volume become more refined, or are eliminated entirely, in their later books. Aside from the tripartite typographical cover design (author name—title—publisher's information), the interior pages of this work print the title of each essay in a sans-serif typeface, along with the first letter of the essay, while the remainder of the text is a bolded serif. Each text block is justified with a large amount of marginal space, and the page numbers are continuous throughout. Double-bar types of ornaments are used in the headers of each page, which ties the interior design features of the work to the exterior ones, namely, the typographical elements on the cover. There are no blank pages between each of the essays, and there is a fair amount of poor title spacing throughout the book, which renders certain words illegible.[13] In addition, there are several typographical errors, such as "*Defininición* de Cansinos Asséns" [*Defininition* of Cansinos Assens] and the variant spelling of "Norah Lange" as "Nora." Although there is a *fe de erratas* [errata sheet] at the close of the work, there is no mention of either of these errors.

The second work that Borges published with Editorial Proa, *Luna de enfrente*, is also the firm's first and only officially deemed luxury edition. From the opening prologue we discover that Borges homes in on the *criollo* of his native Buenos Aires in this collection: "Muchas composiciones de este libro hay habladas en criollo; no en gauchesco ni arrabalero, sino en la heterogénea lengua vernácula de la charla porteña" [Many of the compositions in this book are spoken in *criollo*, the local vernacular; not in gaucho or in the slang of the outskirts, but in the heterogeneous vernacular language of *porteño* speech] (7). In contrast with the essays in *Inquisiciones*, which tend to focus on themes, histories, and persons who call to mind a *criollo* spirit or way of being, Borges's poems in this collection center on linguistic features that evoke certain aspects of Buenos Aires life. As Rafael Olea Franco noted, "the use of self-consciously *criollo* words illustrates Borges's innovative and experimental kind of writing, which was integral to his project to establish a new *criollo* aesthetic" (177). From the very first poem, "Calle con almacén rosao" [Street with a Pink Corner Store], we thus see an emphasis on capturing the Argentine manner of speaking (*rosao*), which is one of the defining features of *Luna de enfrente*. Coupled with the use of unique Argentine phrases throughout the work, many of which are almost untranslatable, are marked orthographic choices such as a "j" instead of a "g" in Borges's first name ("Jorje") and the constant substitution of "y" for "i," both of which call to mind Andrés Bello's desired orthographic reform that would more accurately align written language with spoken language. This phenomenon can also be seen in the shortening of words such as "dualidá" [duality] and "oscuridá" [oscurity] to reflect their regional pronunciation. Curiously, the most frequently occurring word in the entire work is "mi(s)" [my], which appears forty-two times. In a sense, this "I"-focused frequency can be mapped onto Borges's personal desire to poetically embody the *criollo* of his native Buenos Aires.[14]

Whereas the physical features of *Luna de enfrente* are unique and do not resemble Editorial Proa's house style, it is important to note the presence of four original illustrations by Borges's sister, Norah, which call to mind her cover art for his first book of poems, *Fervor de Buenos Aires*. On the cover we find a rendering of the pampa, complete with a figure on horseback and two typical one-story homes. The use of a clay-like red color for this illustration also ties it to the land and the earth. Turning to the colophon, another one of Norah's illustrations depicts the city streets of Buenos Aires with a park bench and a one-story home with a signature black-and-white tiled floor. There is a prominent moon in each image that serves to link the visual elements to the thematic and textual elements that make up the work. In a letter to Evar Méndez, Borges describes his vacillation between two similar titles for the work, *Lunario* [*Moon Calendar*] and *Luna de enfrente*, both of which point to the central role of the moon.[15] He also writes about the rediscovery of his native Buenos Aires upon returning from Europe in 1924: "redescubro la ciudad, en dulces calles de arrabal enternecida [sic] de árboles y ocasos. Yo he estado siempre en Buenos Aires" [I rediscovered the city, in the sweet streets of the tender suburbs filled with trees and sunsets. I have always been in Buenos Aires] (cited in García and Greco 163). His words are tinged with not only a sense of déjà vu but also a longing for how the city was when he was a young boy. Although there are certain thematic echoes between his earlier *Fervor de Buenos Aires* and *Luna de enfrente*, the latter carries more nostalgic rumination and pain for what has been lost.

The third work that Borges published with Editorial Proa, *El tamaño de mi esperanza* (1926), is the most explicit collection of *criollo* prose that he produced. This message is clear from the very first lines of his opening prologue: "A los criollos les quiero hablar: a los hombres que en esta tierra se sienten vivir y morir, no a los que el sol y la luna están en Europa" [I want to speak to the *criollos*: to the men that feel life and death in this land, not to those for whom the sun and the moon are in Europe] (5). He describes his aim in compiling this collection of essays as working to "encontrarle [a Buenos Aires] la poesía y la música y la pintura y la religión y la metafísica que con su grandeza se avienen" [find poetry, music, painting, religion, and metaphysics that evoke the grandeur of Buenos Aires] (9). In essence, he wants to home in on the cultural roots of Buenos Aires, of the *criollo*, which tend to emerge as feelings of nostalgia for the pampa and the land. The collection opens with an essay on Estanislao del Campo's *Fausto* [*Faust*], which Borges praises as the best American rendering of the famous German legend and, as a result, marks it as a type of bedrock for the Argentine literature that will follow and build upon its themes and ideas. From here we find a variety of essays detailing everything from central Argentine archetypes ("La pampa y el suburbio son dioses" [The Pampa and the Suburbs are Gods]) and writers ("Carriego y el sentido del arrabal" [Carriego and the Sense of the Suburb]) to *rioplatense* poetics ("Las coplas acriolladas" [Nativized Poems]) and *criollo* linguistics ("Invectiva contra el arrabalero" [Invective Against the

Slang of the Suburbs]). While the majority of the essays that comprise *El tamaño de mi esperanza* focus on the essence of the *criollo*, there are a few outliers, such as "Milton y su condenación de la rima" [Milton and his Condemnation of Rhyme], "Ejercicio de ánalisis" [Analytical Exercise], "Balada de la cárcel de Reading" [The Ballad of Reading Gaol], and "Examen de un soneto de Góngora" [An Examination of a Sonnet of Góngora], whose philosophical musings and universal themes appear better suited for Borges's earlier *Inquisiciones*.[16] That said, these few pieces do not take away from the overall emphasis placed on the local color and culture of Buenos Aires.

The design features of *El tamaño de mi esperanza* echo what we saw in *Inquisiciones* and reflect what I call Editorial Proa's house style. In other words, there are double-bar types of ornaments in the headers of each page, bolded serif typefaces for the main text blocks, and continuous page numbers throughout. The main stylistic difference between this work and the earlier collection of essays is the use of the same serif typeface not only for the text blocks but also for the titles of the essays. What is more, there are five original illustrations by Xul Solar throughout the collection.[17] The recurring motifs of flags, banners, and human figures are reminiscent of some sort of carnivalesque ritual and are also a signature Xul Solar creation, which makes their inclusion even more Argentine in style.[18]

The final work that Borges published with Editorial Proa, *Cuaderno San Martín*, formed part of their separate "Cuadernos del Plata" series. Once again, we find a distinct *criollo* narrative throughout each of the twelve poems that make up the volume. In contrast with the more linguistic (and orthographical) idiosyncrasies of *Luna de enfrente*, Borges's works in *Cuaderno San Martín* focus on historical events, places, and, as the opening poem ("Fundación mitológica . . .") indicates, mythologies of his native city. In addition, the collection takes on a more somber tone, which is most evident through the inclusion of various compositions about death. There are also several mournful elegies concerning the changing landscape of modernity and memories of a former splendor.

In terms of its physical features, this collection of poetry resembles the other four works in the "Cuadernos del Plata" series, which, to a certain extent, also echoes much of the general production of Editorial Proa. In other works, these works all showcase an aesthetic preference for clean lines and simplicity. Many of these features also align with Borges's later preferences for the design features of his own works, and, perhaps, much of the technical experience he received from working with Evar Méndez (and Alfonso Reyes). Although the galley proofs and other printing ephemera from Editorial Proa are no longer extant, the correspondence between Méndez and Reyes points to a high level of editorial involvement on the part of Borges.[19]

Ekphrastic Texts and Bibliographical Evidence

A notable difference between *Cuaderno San Martín* and the other three books that Borges published with Editorial Proa[20] is the presence of five annotations that explain certain historical or literary references that appear throughout the work.[21] Four of these notes contextualize historical figures, places, or literary works that are mentioned in the poems: translations of the FitzGerald quote that serves as an epigraph to the book; information about Borges's maternal grandfather, Isidoro Acevedo, who is the subject of a poem; a personal anecdote about an encounter in a club where a guitar player sings about death; an explanation of Richard Rothe's speculation about the existence of supernatural realms; and a conceptual outline of a poem, "El Ángel de la Guarda en Avellaneda" [The Guardian Angel in Avellaneda] which does not make it into the collection. The remaining note, which happens to be the first in the section, stands apart from the rest for its detailed description of the common Argentine schoolbook for which Borges names his collection, a "Cuaderno San Martín." He wrote:

> Hay objetos que parecen vivirnos vicariamente; el cuaderno San Martín es uno. Es cariño tan entreverado en mí que no puedo reducirlo a otros elementos, facilitarlo. El museíto de la tapa—el medallón del prócer, la guarda griega transversal, el pajarito sobre la rama caligráfica sin sostén, la casi imperceptible resolución escolar Labor omnia vincit, los bien sombreados arrequives, el jarrón con la palma—es, antepuesto a las desabridas páginas rayadas o cuadriculadas, un símbolo de lo travieso en lo pobre. Algo como la balaustrada o la copa en la edificación popular. Tal vez, pero básteme nombrar, no inquirir. Ya se sabe que el mayor énfasis de una palabra, su más reverente pronunciación, es destacarla para nombre de un libro. (55)

> [There are some objects that seem to live through us religiously; San Martín's notebook is one of them. It is an affection so much a part of me that I cannot reduce it to other elements, cannot obtain it. The little museum on the cover—the forefather's medallion, the diagonal Greek adornment, the small bird perched on an unsupported calligraphic branch, the almost imperceptible scholarly resolve of *Labor omnia vincit*, the well-shaded trimmings, the vase with the palm—is, preceding the bland lined or graph paper, a symbol of the lively in the scanty. Something like the balustrade or the crown in popular buildings. Perhaps, but it's enough to name, not inquire. It is already known that the best emphasis of a word, its most reverent pronunciation, is to assign it as the name of a book.]

Instead of simply pointing out that the title of his work is drawn from a popular Argentine notebook, he presents his readers with what can only be called an ekphrastic description of the object itself. It seems odd that Borges would go to such pains to describe such a commonplace item that most local readers would recognize from their own schooling, especially since *Cuaderno San Martín* most likely had little circulation outside Argentina when it was first published. When we compare Borges's description with an actual example of a "Cuaderno San Martín" schoolbook, the similarities are astonishing.

The level of detail that Borges captures in his text points to the fact that he had one of these notebooks on hand at the time he composed the poems within his collection.[22] This ekphrastic text, coupled with a manuscript in the Borges Collection at the University of Virginia, support the latter claim, and confirm the fact that this Argentine writer was very much involved in the physical presentation of his works (see Figure 4.3).

DEVELOPING AN ARGENTINE STYLE   65

Unlike other surviving Borges manuscripts that the author composed on varying types of notebook paper, this document consists of fragments of phrases and notes written on the covers of a "Cuaderno Chacabuco," which was a typical schoolbook in Argentina much like the "Cuaderno San Martín" (see Figure 4.4).[23]

In general terms, each of the four pages of this manuscript contains unique handwritten material. The first, second, and fourth pages contain fragments of phrases or numerical equations while the third page contains two drawn figures. Each of the pages of this manuscript deserves a more detailed description, yet I devote my attention here to the second page (or back side of the front cover), which, given its contents, is crucial to the present study.

On the page in question, we find two basic types of information: a preliminary list of contents for Borges's 1929 book of poetry, *Cuaderno San Martin*, and a series of numerical calculations related to the physical layout of this volume (Figure 4.5). It might be commonplace for an author to decide on the individual works to be included in a collection of poetry, but unless an author was also an editor, it seems somewhat rarer for an author to decide on the number of lines per page and, as a result, how many pages will be necessary for the entire book.

This is exactly the type of computation, clearly written in Borges's distinctive hand, that we find in the above manuscript: "26 reglones por página y 50 renglones por composición, preciso para 48 páginas (3 plieges [sic])" [26 lines per page and 50 lines per poem, makes for 48 pages (3 gatherings)]. Besides the already mentioned peculiarity of an author designating a specific number of lines per page, the fact that Borges has already converted his total number of pages into "3 gatherings" is undoubtedly a significant bibliographical detail. In an effort to compare his initial calculations for the layout of his *Cuaderno San Martín* with the first printed edition of the work, I returned to Special Collections at the University of Virginia. Even though the Borges collection holds not just one but two copies of this first printed edition, each of them has been rebound, which makes it quite difficult to determine their format. That said, the fact that they each has sixty-four pages, plus an additional insert of a drawing of Borges by Silvina Ocampo, indicates that a fourth "pliegue" [gathering] was added to Borges's initial calculations. Even more puzzling is the fact that of the list of possible poems in this manuscript, only ten appear in the printed first edition of *Cuaderno San Martín*, which points to a reduction in the necessary number of pages, as opposed to an increase.

Another interesting aspect of this hard-to-read manuscript is the following parenthetical note that appears alongside "Viñetas cardinales de Buenos Aires" [Cardinal Vignettes of Buenos Aires], one of the possible titles to be included in the collection: "(con anotaciones marginales como *The ancient mariner*)" [(with marginal notes like *The Ancient Mariner*)]. Since "Viñetas cardinales de Buenos Aires" was cut from the contents of the printed versions of *Cuaderno San Martín*, it is challenging to narrow down the edition of *The Rime of the Ancient Mariner* that Borges was referencing from a design standpoint. That said, when we consider the publication history of Coleridge's poem, it is most likely that Borges was alluding to the revised second edition, first published in 1817 as part of *Sibylline Leaves*, that incorporated a gloss that was not present in the first edition. Borges's desire to have his poem annotated *in the style of* this well-known work highlights his strong preferences toward the physical presentation of the words on the page.

FIGURE 4.3 Example of a "Cuaderno San Martín" schoolbook.
Source: Reprinted with permission from Albert and Shirley Small Special Collections Library, University of Virginia.

The elegance and simplicity of Editorial Proa's house style marks not only a clear turning point in the history of the book in Argentina but also an essential formative period in Borges's early career. This newfound material evidence highlights the need to describe and analyze the physical features of Borges's various publications in

FIGURE 4.4 Cover of Borges's "Cuaderno Chacabuco."
Source: Reprinted with permission from the Albert and Shirley Small Special Collections Library, University of Virginia.

more detail, especially since he might have had a greater role in their production than was initially thought. In a televised interview in 1976, Borges commented on how his early works, especially *Fervor de Buenos Aires*, and by extension all of those in which he crafts his *criollo* voice, would simultaneously define and contain everything that

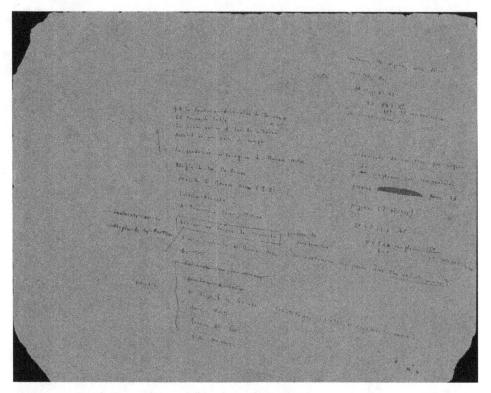

FIGURE 4.5 Inside Cover of Borges's "Cuaderno Chacabuco."
Source: Reprinted with permission from the Albert and Shirley Small Special Collections Library, University of Virginia.

Table 4.3 A selection of works by Borges, 1930–1960

Work	Publisher	Printer	Date
Evaristo Carriego	Manuel Gleizer	Francisco A. Colombo	1930
Historia universal de la infamia [A Universal History of Infamy]	Editorial TOR	Editorial TOR	1935
Seis problemas para don Isidro Parodi [Six Problems for Mr. Isidro Parodi]	Editorial SUR	Imprenta Iglesias y Matera	1942
El Hacedor [Dreamtigers]	Emecé Editores	Imprenta López	1960

he would later produce.[24] In a sense, through a careful reading between these early (poetic) lines, Borges suggests that his readers will discover all the themes and ideas that he would return to again and again throughout his impressive literary career. By looking to Editorial Proa's literary production from the early part of the twentieth century, I would argue that this close, careful reading between the lines must also consider the physical media themselves and their characteristic design features. In fact, similar to the recurring themes that we find throughout Borges's writings that emerge from this early part of his career, many of the design features of his books parallel those established by Editorial Proa. Consider, for instance, the works in table 4.3, which were all published by different firms and produced by unique printers (see Figures 4.6).

FIGURE 4.6 Selection of covers of Borges's works (1930–1960).

Source: Photo Courtesy of Nora Benedict.

Even though there are slight aesthetic variations between these works, they all capture the simple, elegant design features that define Borges's early publications with Editorial Proa. Moreover, when we look to the general catalogues of these later publishers and printers, we find a large amount of variety in their design features, which suggests, at the very least, Borges's active influence on his printers and publishers.[25] Sara del Carril, who worked closely with Borges at Emecé Editores, noted that virtually all his books that this firm published in the 1950s and 1960s "salieron con tapa gris tipográfica (a Borges no le gustaban las tapas ilustradas)" [appeared with a gray typographical cover (Borges did not like illustrated covers)] (125). In a sense, Borges's initial exposure to the world of publishing through his interactions with Evar Méndez and Editorial Proa establishes him as a writer concerned with not only the content of his works but also their physical form and overall presentation.

NOTES

1. Méndez created two distinct publishing houses as offshoots of his periodical *Martín Fierro*: Editorial Proa and Editorial Martín Fierro. The latter firm, which existed for only two years (1925–1926), published a total of three works and had less of a focus on an exacting physical presentation. The former, in contrast, produced a much larger number of works, stressed the physical features and overall crafting of the book, and had a longer run (1924–1932).
2. Méndez also proposes what appears to be the same work by Xul Solar for Editorial Proa's "Cuadernos del Plata" series, but with the slightly revised title of *San Signos*.
3. The following four works produced by Editorial Proa include both a small black dot below the title as well as an additional horizontal line below the publication information: Norah Lange's *Voz de la vida*, Leopoldo Hurtado's *Sketches*, Ricardo E. Molinari's *El imaginero*, and Guillaume Apollinaire's *32 poemas*.
4. No information about print runs or papers used is found for *El puñal de Orión* (1925). The fact that this printer produced another work for Editorial Proa, *Luna de enfrente*, which does include the number of copies printed, suggests that it was not the decision of the printer to exclude this information. In addition to the lack of detail in this work, Ricardo E. Molinari's *Panegírico* (1930) does not mention any special copies printed that were not for commercial circulation since the entire work was produced as a private edition according to the page opposite the title page.
5. Girondo's papier mâché figure is housed at the National Library in Buenos Aires: https://www.cultura.gob.ar/el-espantapajaros-de-girondo-y-una-historia-curiosa_3400/.
6. Within months of its initial release, *Don Segundo Sombra* (1926) had sold two entire print runs (totaling well over 5,000 copies) and was slated for a third before the end of 1926.
7. The final published version of this book is *Seis relatos*, which suggests that an initial composition was cut from the work.
8. It is unclear whether Ocampo's projected work was ever published. Xul Solar's visions, which must have been a large part of his slated *San Signos*, were not published until the posthumous edition (*Los San Signos: Xul Solar y el I Ching*, 2012). Alfonso Reyes's book on Mallarmé never appeared with Editorial Proa, but what appears to have been the same work appeared a few years later with Editorial Destiempo (1938). That said, in a letter to

Reyes, dated July 12, 1929, Méndez mentions a ream of Auvergne paper he acquired for his work on Mallarmé, which seems rather curious since this specific book never materialized as part of the "Cuadernos del Plata" series (García and Greco 271).

9. Borges self-published his first work, *Fervor de Buenos Aires* [*Fervor of Buenos Aires*] (1923), simply by sending it to a printer. The edition was rather sloppy in presentation and lacked pagination.

10. García and Greco suggest that we even see the strained relationship between Borges and Méndez with regard to galley proofs and corrections (87).

11. See Hernaiz (ch. 9) for more on Borges and *criollismo*.

12. He referenced this earlier *criollo* voice as something he had tried to forget in his 1951 talk, "El escritor argentino y la tradición" [The Argentine Writer and Tradition].

13. See, for instance, "Menoscabo y grandeza de Quevedo" (39).

14. A similar distant reading of *Fervor de Buenos Aires*, which is commonly read as the more *intimate* of these two early poetry collections, reveals that "calle(s)" [street(s)] is the most recurring word, appearing twenty-eight times in the work, while "mi(s)" is only the third most common word (19), right behind *tarde* [afternoon] (22).

15. Despite Borges's antipathy toward Lugones's poetics in the 1920s, he considers the title *Lunario*, which would have been an explicit allusion to *Lunario sentimental* [*Sentimental Moon Calendar*] (1909).

16. Borges goes so far as to refer directly to this early collection of essays in the pages of "Ejercicio de análsis" [Analytical exercise]: "En mis Inquisiciones (página 157-9) he señalado la diferencia entre el concepto clásico de la noche y el que hoy nos rige" [In my book *Inquisiciones* I have noted the difference between the classic concept of night and our present one] (112).

17. These are found at the end of each of the following essays: "La pampa y el suburbio son dioses" (25), "Carriego y el sentido del arrabal" (25), "La adjetivación" [Adjectivization] (50), "Milton y su condenación de la rima" (115), and "La balada de la cárcel de Reading" (131).

18. The facsimile edition of Xul Solar's personal copy of Borges's later work, *El idioma de los argentinos* (1928), is adorned with similar shapes, figures, and patterns: https://www.bell asartes.gob.ar/museo/novedades/17/04/26/edicion-facsimilar-de-el-idioma-de-los-arg entinos.

19. García and Greco also noted Reyes's frequent mentions of Borges's help in correcting proofs with him for Editorial Proa.

20. Parts of this section draw and expand on arguments made in Benedict, *Borges and the Literary Marketplace*.

21. These additional notes only appear in the first edition of the work, the 1943 Losada edition of *Poemas, 1923–1943* and the 1953 Emecé edition, and then are not reproduced again until 1995.

22. In fact, we know that he had two on hand given the extant notebooks at Michigan State and the University of Virginia.

23. The Cuaderno Chacabuco notebook at Michigan State also contains part of the *Cuaderno San Martín* manuscript, including the notes. For more on Borges's compositional practices and the types of papers that he used most frequently, see Balderston.

24. "Encuentro con las artes y las letras," *RTVE*, 1976.

25. Editorial Sur maintains this distinctive style for most of their works produced in the 1930s and early 1940s, which is precisely when Borges was most actively involved with the firm as a member of their editorial committee.

Works Cited

Balderston, Daniel. *How Borges Wrote*. University of Virginia Press, 2018.

Benedict, Nora C. *Borges and the Literary Marketplace: How Editorial Practices Shaped Cosmopolitan Reading*. Yale University Press, 2021.

Borges, Jorge Luis. *Cuaderno San Martín*. Editorial Proa, 1929.

Borges, Jorge Luis. *Inquisiciones*. Editorial Proa, 1925.

Borges, Jorge Luis. *Luna de enfrente*. Editorial Proa, 1925.

Borges, Jorge Luis. "Al tal vez lector." *Martín Fierro* (segunda época) 2, no. 25, November 14, 1925, p. 4.

Borges, Jorge Luis. *El tamaño de mi esperanza*. Editorial Proa, 1926.

Borges, Jorge Luis. "Two Covers of a Cuaderno Chacabuco with Manuscript Notes and Original Drawings by the Author." n.d. Manuscript in the Borges Collection of the Albert and Shirley Small Special Collections Library, University of Virginia.

Buonocore, Domingo. *Libreros, editores e impresores de Buenos Aires*. Librería el Ateneo, 1944.

"Cuadernos del Plata." *La Vida Literaria*, May 10, 1929, p. 8.

del Carril, Sara Luisa. "Borges en Emecé." *Proa* 42, 1999, pp. 125–27.

"Editoriales Proa y Martín Fierro." *Martín Fierro* (segunda época) 3, no. 34, October 5, 1926, p. 5.

García, Carlos, and Martín Greco. *La ardiente aventura: Cartas y documentos inéditos de Evar Méndez, director del periódico Martín Fierro*. Alberto Editor, 2017.

Marechal, Leopoldo. "'Luna de enfrente', por Jorge Luis Borges." *Martín Fierro* (segunda época) 2, no. 26, December 29, 1925, p. 4.

Olea Franco, Rafael. "The early poetry (1923–1929)." *The Cambridge Companion to Jorge Luis Borges*. Edited by Edwin Williamson, Cambridge University Press, 2013, pp. 172–85.

Piñero, Sergio (hijo). "'Inquisiciones', por Jorge Luis Borges." *Martín Fierro* (segunda época) 2, no. 18, June 26, 1925, p. 4.

CHAPTER 5

....

BORGES

Three Times a Translator

....

PATRICIA WILLSON

How to picture the figure of Borges as translator? The subject of abundant discussion, this image is usually held as the decisive proof of a recurring critical hypothesis: Borges translated in a certain way because he wrote certain texts about translation, and vice versa. This ubiquitous and recursive focus on the relationships between Borges's translations and his "direct writings" is based on a handful of foundational texts read in some specific ways: as an illustration of the paradoxes posed by the classic dichotomy of literal versus free translation, as metaphors for translation, and as allegories for untranslatability. In "Las dos maneras de traducir" [The Two Ways of Translating] (1926), Borges discusses the conceptions of literature and of the writer that underpin free or literal translation methods; in "Las versiones homéricas" [The Homeric Versions] (1932) and "Los traductores de las 1001 Noches" [The Translators of the 1001 Nights] (1936), he reflects on the text's status of "originality," on the fact that each text is inscribed in a determined historical context, as are the ways of evaluating them. "Pierre Menard, autor del Quijote" [Pierre Menard, Author of the Quixote] (1939) is one of criticism's most frequently deployed metaphors for translation: Menard "writes" Don Quixote, but one could argue that he translates it since his copy will be read in new space-time coordinates, as happens with all translations with respect to their source texts. "La busca de Averroes" [Averroes's Search] (1947) is an allegorical fiction of the problem of *realia* when translating: a cultural object exists in the source culture but does not exist—or at least lacks a name—in the receiving culture. In this story, the "things" that do not exist in the culture of the translating language are tragedy and comedy. The story also stages an indirect translation since Averroes does not know Aristotle's Greek and comments on it from translations into other languages.[1]

The monographic works on Borges as translator differ in their approaches, but they are based on this same conceptual matrix. Frances Aparicio, in her book on four Latin American translator writers (Valencia, Borges, Cortázar, Paz), proposes reading Borges's translations from the standpoint of literary pantheism. As will be seen later, this same hypothesis predominates in Aparicio's reading of the Borgesian version of Whitman. Efraín Kristal explores Borges's translations of the German Expressionists and outlines a Borgesian theory of translation. Sergio Waisman hypothesizes the influence of the periphery on Borges's freedom in receiving (and translating) foreign literature. Borges's translation work in *Sur* has also been thought of as yet another instance of his literary avant-gardes (Willson). Among the more indirect references to translation, which may be less subject to a "theory," criticism still tends to favor those that revolve around topics mentioned above, leaving aside the more normative, less "Borgesian" comments.[2]

Translation also tinges the "biographical myth of Borges." According to Beatriz Sarlo, this myth is based on the appropriation of literature: "Don Quixote, read for the first time in English translation when he was a child; his version, at age nine, of an Oscar Wilde story; his fascination with Chesterton, Kipling and Stevenson; his translations of Kafka, Faulkner, and Virginia Woolf . . . " (my translation, 10–11).[3] Of all the possible forms of appropriation of literature, however, translation is one of the most radical, if not *the* most radical.

Analysis of the Borgesian versions, comparing source texts to the translations and reexamining the discursive and material contexts in which they appeared, reveals other aspects that merit interrogation. To do so, some analytical tools will be necessary: first, the *scene of translation*, both aesthetic and ideological, in which the translations occur. The notion of "scene of translation" was used in 1998 by Nora Catelli and Marietta Gargatagli in *El tabaco que fumaba Plinio*. In this pioneering book, the authors define the scene of translation as the simulacrum of a happy or, at the least, peaceable cultural encounter which, in fact, serves to hide a conflict. Among the scenes studied is Borges's 1925 translation of James Joyce, which labored not under the weight of an immediate, all-encompassing Anglo-Saxon tradition, as did Joyce, but rather Latin America's "heavy nineteenth-century stories, rustic and conventional prose, bombastic and empty versification" (Catelli and Gargatagli 425). The reconstruction of a scene of translation thus consists of "detecting and analyzing that conflict around which the conceptions and functions of translation, the actors at stake and their particular interests will be defined" (my translation, Falcón 12).

Second, we must consider the *publishing discourse (énonciation éditoriale)*,[4] understood as the set of actions surrounding text publication that establish, transform, and transmit a work with the intent of influencing the conditions and modalities of its reception. This notion refers to the concept of "plural construction" or "polyphonic collaboration," capable of intervening in the conception and production of a book or of any paratext or device that associates either text and image or text, image, and sound (Souchier 141). Publishing discourse, in its materiality, affects the understanding of the translator's work, sometimes masking its agents, other times foregrounding them. A translator's name on a book cover or its absence from the copyright page are examples of this discourse's location within time or space, differentially revealing the authorial status of the translation. Often escaping readers' notice, the "transubstantiation of the text into a book"—as termed by Pascal Durand and Anthony Glinoer (Ouvry-Vial 70)—has been addressed both by book and publishing historians and by media and communications scholars.[5]

Finally, there are *translation strategies*, conceived as the effect of a persona—in the sense of a mask or a character (Toury 215)—which enables critics to overcome an important analytical hurdle: distinguishing what belongs to the editor and what to the translator. The persona Borges translates Jack London, Henri Michaux, and Walt Whitman deploying procedures related to realia, onomastics, titles, lexical choices, breaks with the narrator—in other words, the textual places in which that persona can effectuate analyzable and systematizable changes. Translation strategies reveal, when comparing a text and its translation, the relevance given to culturally specific items when interpreting the original; they also reveal conceptions of literature and of the reader, of the power relations between the translated and the receiving literatures, and among the geographical varieties of the language of translation. In short, they are the source of a surplus of meaning that can only be revealed by an approach that seeks, without prescriptive intent, to compare translations with the texts from which they originate. These three groups of features—those pertaining to the scene of translation, the publishing discourse surrounding a translation, and a given version's strategies—afford the *figure of the translator* a depth that is overlooked when Borges's translations are approached through the closed system mentioned above, where relationships are assumed a priori.

A few preliminary words to define what is meant here by "translation" and thus differentiate this practice from rewriting and other textual maneuvers, but without resorting to essentialist terms based on a postulated relationship between a source or original text. The most contingent definition would be to affirm that a translation is what, at a given moment in a cultural space, is believed to be a translation, including pseudo-translations.[6] But it is possible to opt for a more normative definition: translation is the practice by which a text is obtained in language B that is equivalent, both semantically and pragmatically, to one written in language A. The first definition highlights—and, at the same time, neutralizes—the problem of false attributions; the second raises the problem of equivalence or, at minimum, the commensurability of the translation with the text from which it departs. Both definitions will come into play in this analysis.

In the pages that follow, Borges the Translator will be removed from the unifying and retrospectively established matrix of a literary life, which neatly integrates and gives coherence to his translation work in a single persona. As a result, my analysis will not automatically aspire to "exhaustion," nor will Borges's very first translations necessarily bear traces of the universal writer he would eventually become. Rather, seeking to move Borges's translation work out from under the long shadow cast by his classic essays about translation and translating, this chapter will propose three representative figures of the translator. To illustrate each of these figures, a translation by or attributed to Borges will be discussed, focusing on his translation strategies, reconstructing the context in which each translation occurred, and examining the publishing discourse framing the publication of each.

FIGURE ONE: THE MAGAZINE TRANSLATOR

Critics have widely pointed out the interest and complexity of the *Revista Multicolor de los Sábados* [*Multicolor Saturday Magazine*] as a cultural object. As a cross between "high" and popular cultures, of fiction and information (Saítta, "Estudio preliminar"); as a place where genres, themes, motifs, and modes of writing partial to this diverse space for book dissemination are configured and renewed; as a "Peninsular" continuation of the main section of the newspaper *Crítica* (though also sometimes considered an "islet"; Mascioto, *Nuevos modos* 43); as a testing ground for the young Borges and his infamous fictions; and as a place of interaction between two semiotic systems, the verbal and the visual (Louis, *Obras y maniobras*). However, the subject of this section is not "Borges in the *Revista Multicolor de los Sábados* (*RMS*)," but rather the figure of the translator who emerges from his contributions within the framework of this magazine.[7]

The literary and cultural landscape of Buenos Aires in the 1930s, as the scene in which these versions of Borges were produced, has also been the subject of a vast reconstruction. A "peripheral and uneven modernity," where innovative and traditional elements coexist, according to Beatriz Sarlo (*modernidad*); a "dynamic decade," but at the same time, one distanced from the optimistic tone of the preceding decade, according to María Teresa Gramuglio; the 1930s bear witness to Borges's debut into narrative fiction with the stories of *Historia universal de la infamia* [*A Universal History of Infamy*], first published in the *RMS* and collected by Editorial Tor in 1935. Gramuglio discusses the images of the Thirties that have become cemented in criticism; among them, a Borges who takes refuge in the "literature of evasion" (212). In fact, Borges sought to contend for space among the realistic and psychological trends then dominant in Argentine narrative, represented by Manuel Gálvez and Eduardo Mallea, through a campaign to promote popular genres: the adventure story, crime fiction, and fantastic narrative (Gramuglio 214). According to Ricardo Piglia, Borges's perpetual reading of Stevenson, of Conrad, of crime fiction, was a method of creating a space where his texts could be read in the context in which they operated (19).

Published between August 1933 and October 1934, the *RMS* functioned as a laboratory for producing the "availability" of certain foreign authors and texts. In this scene of translation, the availability afforded by translation did not entail publishing foreign authors' texts in book form, but rather in a much more effective medium: the cultural supplement of a popular newspaper. In the *RMS*, the translator figure comprised by co-directors Borges and Ulises Petit de Murat is versatile: they select, translate, correct (Saítta, "Estudio preliminar"). Borges's impetus to anthologize would find its continuation in book form with the *Antología de la literatura fantástica* [*Anthology of Fantastic Literature*] (1940) and *Los mejores cuentos policiales* [*The Best Detective Stories*] (1943), also compiled in collaboration. However, there are differences in the material and, consequently, in what is significant about the fantastic literature published in the *RMS* and that published in book form in the *Antología de la literatura fantástica* by Borges, Adolfo Bioy Casares, and Silvina Ocampo (Mascioto, "Literatura fantástica"). There are also differences in the successive publication variations of Jack London's "The Minions of Midas" ([1901] 1906), translated as "Las muertes eslabonadas" in the 38th issue of *RMS*, published April 28, 1934. This translation will serve as a representative example of the literary importation that characterizes the figure of Borges the Translator of Magazines.

In a progression of versions that could be called "las *traducciones* eslabonadas" [the linked translations], this first ever Spanish translation of London's story underwent several changes in Borges's and Bioy's subsequent editions of *Los mejores cuentos policiales*, starting with the story's title: as of 1943, becoming "Las muertes concéntricas" [A Thousand Deaths].[8] When comparing versions, one can observe that these changes, including the free translation of the title, only serve to corroborate their common origin, perhaps in an attempt to hide it. Without a doubt, comparative analysis reveals a system of appropriation that culminates in the collaboration with Bioy. With this first figure of the translator, and according to the first definition of translation given in the introductory section to this chapter, considerations of actual authorship of the translation are not relevant nor is the prescriptivist search for semantic or pragmatic equivalences with the source text.

Once past those limitations, what are the translation strategies deployed by this figure? Some examples reveal the dual impacts of the scene of translation and of the discourse surrounding it. In the 1930s, the translation of onomastics (i.e., of proper names) is a mark of the era: only in the 1940s does some fluctuation begin to occur—sometimes within the same translated text—between character names being translated or left in the original form. Hence the "John" in later versions had been "Juan" in the *RMS*, and likewise, "Pete" had been "Pedro." Notably, the criticism inherent in the title "The Minions of Midas" is obscured when transformed to "Las muertes eslabonadas." Likewise, the capitalist Eben Hale, the *money baron,* receives the epithet "plutócrata" [plutocrat] in the translation. Both choices point to the figure of Borges the Translator of Magazines, having privileged the crime fiction aspects of the story, more in keeping with the section of the *RMS* in which the version was published: "Un cuento policial" [A detective story]. In other words, the publishing discourse manifest in the story's layout in the *RMS* aligns with the translation strategy employed for its title and its description of Eben Hale, both reinforcing a specific type of reading: that of the murder mystery.

Indeed, Borges is not satisfied with privileging or imposing certain authors: he also seeks to guide how those works are read, as happened with Wells, whose science fiction he preferred to his social criticism (Willson 73). Readings are thus guided by specific literary interests and by the very novelty offered by the *RMS*: its emphasis on stories about crime and murder (Saítta, "Estudio preliminar"). Yet it might also be a reading apt for that era: that same year, Madrid's *Revista Literaria. Novelas y cuentos* published their own translation of London's "The Minions of Midas" as "Los hijos de Midas," calling it a "detective novel" (Issue 309, December 1934).

We know for certain that, in its successive installments, the *RMS* published numerous foreign authors in translation, some of whom are still well-known literary names (Robert Blake, Marcel Schwob, O. Henry, Jean Rostand, Anton Chekov, Euclides da Cunha, Henry de Montherlant, for example). However, there is also a large group of authors whose names must be spelled any number of ways to track them down in library catalogs or in the indexes of magazines such as *The American Mercury* or the *Revue générale internationale, scientifique, littéraire et artistique*: Erik Wickenburg, (Henry) Cuyler Bunner, Arlington B. Conway, Luis (Louis) Gastin, Jim Tully, Xavier de Hautecloque, Alejandra (Alexandra) Roubé-Janski, Claude Farrère, Walter White, Ernest (Ernst) Sorge, Rémy Saint-Maurice, James Greenwood, Raimundo Moraes, Luis (Louis) W. Larsen, among others. Of this list of foreign authors, the scholarship and criticism has primarily focused on the most outstanding names, but even those who have fallen into obscurity today still created part of a literary context, just like national authors.

The two full-color illustrations by Juan Sorazábal that accompany "Las muertes eslabonadas" are a key element of the publishing discourse created by the *RMS*, which privileged the crime fiction aspects of London's story. In the first image, a man is outstretched, dying in a nocturnal urban setting; in the second, we see the back of another man walking down a deserted street at night, wielding a knife. The story—the name of the *RMS* section, the title of the story, mention of the author and illustrator, as well as the illustrations—all fit on one page of the magazine. The names of the author and of the illustrator are given equal prominence at the bottom of the page, mirroring one another in font, size, and color. The translator's name is conspicuous for its absence (Figure 5.1).

In this version of London's story in the *RMS*, rather than seek out equivalences or lack thereof with the source text, let us instead highlight a series of syntactic, lexical, and ortho-typographic features that reveal transformations in the register and even in the observance of grammatical rules, as can be seen in the examples below.

> *Nevertheless, we have entered the arena.*
> Sin embargo, entramos a la cancha.
> [Back translation: Nevertheless, we enter/entered the playing field.]
> *We leave the eventuality to time and law.*
> Dejamos la eventualidad al tiempo y a Dios.
> [Back translation: We leave the eventuality to time and God.]
> *Had there been any scandal in the dead man's family, or had his sons been wild or undutiful, then there might have been a glimmering of reasons in this most unusual action.*
> Si hubieran habido escándalos en la familia Hale, o sus hijos fueran unos díscolos e irrespetuosos, habría habido alguna excusa para esta inusitada acción póstuma.
> [Back translation: If there had been scandals in Hale's family, or his children been a bunch of scoundrels and disrespectful, there might have been some excuse for this unheard-of posthumous action.]

With the translation "*hubieran habido,*" the incorrectness in the impersonal verb *haber* (when used existentially to signify "there is," Spanish grammar dictates that the verb always be conjugated in the singular) is another of the marks that the publishing discourse imprints on the translation as a text. The translation's division into paragraphs also fails to follow that of the source text, except for those that separate the new messages from the Minions of

THREE TIMES A TRANSLATOR   79

FIGURE 5.1   Image of the page of *RMS* 38 (1934) with London's story.
Source: Archivo Histórico de Revistas Argentinas (https://ahira.com.ar/).

Midas, the formatting appears to show more concern with fitting the entire story on a single page. To the procedures found in the direct writings of the magazine, characterized by the practices of cutting, fragmentation, and summarizing (Mascioto, "Borges editor" 209), the translation adds another dimension: interlinguistic paraphrasing and adaptation.

With "Las muertes eslabonadas," the figure of Borges as translator in the *RMS* most closely aligns with the translation theory proposed in his most famous essays on the subject: that the source text is but a pretext for literary creation. In the following sections, however, other features will appear that require us to employ, once again, the analytical tools used in the examination of this first figure.

Figure Two: The Translator on Commission

Just after his versions in *RMS* come Borges's translations for the publishers Sur and Sudamericana (although these three figures of Borges the translator are presented chronologically, it is not time but rather each figure's function that organizes their presentation). *Un cuarto propio* (Virignia Woolf's *A Room of One's Own* [1929]) was published in installments in the cultural journal *Sur*, beginning in December 1935— the same year as the book-form publication of Borges's *Historia universal de la infamia*. With this second figure of the translator, a new form appears—the book—as do two new genres—the novel and the volume of essays.[9] *Un cuarto propio* [*A Room of One's Own*] and *Orlando* (1928/1936), by Virginia Woolf; *Las palmeras salvajes* (1940) [*The Wild Palms* (1939)], by William Faulkner; *Un bárbaro en Asia* (1941) [*Un barbare en Asie* (1933)], by Henri Michaux, some of them previously published in installments in the journal *Sur*, make up the corpus of translations belonging to this second figure. In this discussion, we are not focusing on "Borges in *Sur*," a complex topic that has already been extensively addressed by other scholars[10]; rather, we seek to uncover the specificities of this translator figure.

The list of texts translated by Borges for the publishing houses Sur and Sudamericana has led Sylvia Saítta to a hypothesis, which she herself describes as unprovable: *Destiempo*—a literary journal published with Bioy that released just three issues between 1936 and 1937—is actually where Borges found material more in tune with his literary interests at the time (Saítta, "Borges mediático" 12).[11] Conjectures about aesthetic distance with translated material are frequent in studies of commissioned translations and the publishing sector, calling into question the principle of empathy between the translated author and the translator. The reference to literary interests is important because, as Saítta points out, Borges only found his first permanent job in 1937. Several of the translations for Sur were produced during this "professional" period for Borges, in the sense that he translated texts that others had selected. The notion of "commissioned translation" brings with it another agent: the "commissioner" or "initiator." In this case, the "initiator" is most likely Victoria Ocampo. As critics have shown from various perspectives, Ocampo's cultural and publishing project involved literary importation, although its subjects did not necessarily correspond to Borges's interests. In 1941, in addition to *Un barbare en Asie* by Henri Michaux, Sur published a biography of Federico García Lorca by Alfredo de la Guardia; the second series of *Testimonios* (1935–1941) and *San Isidro* by Victoria Ocampo; *Changer la vie ou changer l'homme?* by Denis de Rougemont; H. G. Wells's *The Fate of Homo Sapiens*; and *Three Guineas* by Virginia Woolf. The Michaux translation occurred between the publications of Borges's two anthologies, fantastic literature in 1940 and crime fiction in 1943, both created in collaboration. At the same time, with his critique of Américo Castro's *La peculiaridad lingüística rioplatense y su sentido histórico* (*Sur* 86 [1941]: 66–70), Borges had also just begun an ongoing debate about "proper" Spanish with the famous Spanish philologist.

Of the translations produced by this second figure of Borges in translation, the text least analyzed by critics is, without a doubt, *Un bárbaro en Asia*. Henri Michaux published the text with Gallimard in 1933, after his trip to India, China, and Japan. In 1936, he visited Uruguay and Argentina; in September of that year, as guest of honor for Belgium, he attended the Buenos Aires PEN Club conference, where he met Victoria Ocampo.[12] As an object, the book published by Sur in 1941 resembles the one published by Gallimard in 1933, with the exception of their colors: a uniform cream color in Gallimard, a uniform green in Sur—with the author's name first, followed by the title in larger letters and the publisher's name at the bottom. The publishing discourse thus provides similar models for the French text and its version in Spanish (Figures 5.2 and 5.3).

Un Barbare en Asie, an idiosyncratic travel book, is divided into nine sections, with titles that seem to overlap: "Un barbare aux Indes" (which, in later editions, became "Un barbare en Inde"), "Himalayan Railway," "L'Inde méridionale," "Un Barbare à Ceylan," "Histoire naturelle," "Un Barbare en Chine," "Un Barbare au Japon," "Un Barbare chez les Malais," and "Post-face," per Gallimard's first edition, before the author's revision in the 1960s. In Borges's translation, these sections are reordered—in their layout, if not in their content—into four long chapters: "A Barbarian in India," "A Barbarian in China," "A Barbarian in Ceylon," "A Barbarian in Japan."

Years later, Borges mentions Michaux in prologues and even in a 1983 conference in Paris (attended by Michaux himself—one of the French writer's last public appearances). However, in the first run, the translation is published without any translator's paratext. According to Daniel Balderston, Michaux's translation should be understood as one more episode in Borges's relationship with the world (56). This hypothesis does not force a stylistic approximation between Borges and Michaux, who, according to Eberhard Geisler, could be Borges's other—or vice versa. If both writers represent the vertigo of the infinite in some of their works (Geisler 103), Borges's representation always returns to the rational. Paradox, unlike what happens in Michaux, does not need the pragmatics of exclamation to reveal its ability to draw readers in. In his style of short sentences, without phrasal subordination, sometimes even without an inflected verb, Michaux often makes use of emphatic astonishment. However, in the midst of this writing, which

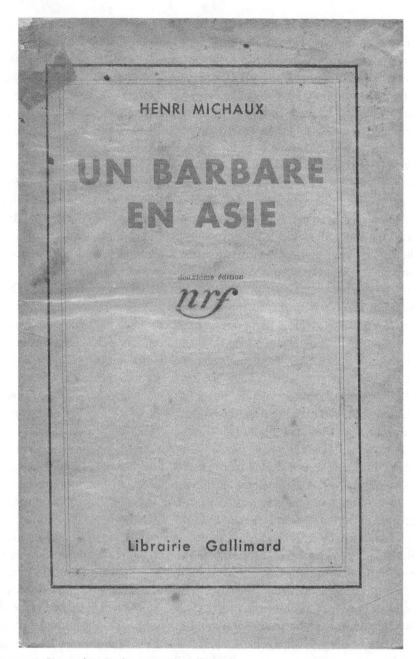

FIGURE 5.2 Cover of *Un Barbare en Asie*, Gallimard.

Source: Photo Courtesy of Patricia Willson.

FIGURE 5.3 Cover of *Un bárbaro en Asia*, Sur.

Source: Photo Courtesy of Nora Benedict.

does not have strong ties with that of Borges, this antecedent of the Argentine's anomalous enumerations appears:

Un Barbare en Asie (45)	Un bárbaro en Asia (39), Borges's Version	An English Translation of Borges's Version
« Vénérable Nagarena, quelles qualités doit posséder un disciple? » (Question du roi Milinda.) Réponse:	Venerable Nagarena, ¿qué cualidades debe poseer un discípulo? (Pregunta del rey Milindo). Respuesta:	Venerable Nagarena, what qualities should a diciple possess? (Question by King Milindo). Answer:
1) une qualité de l'âne	1) Una cualidad del asno.	1) One quality of the ass.
2) deux du coq	2) dos del gallo.	2) two of the rooster.
3) une de l'écureuil	3) una de la ardilla.	3) one of the squirrel.
4) une de la panthère femelle	4) una de la pantera hembra.	4) one of the female panther.
5) deux de la panthère mâle	5) dos de la pantera macho.	5) two of the male panther.
6) cinq de la tortue	6) cinco de la tortuga.	6) five of the tortoise.
7) une du bambou	7) una del bambú.	7) one of the bamboo.
8) une de l'oie	8) una del ganso.	8) one of the goose.
9) deux du corbeau	9) dos del cuervo.	9) two of the crow.
10) deux d'un singe, etc., etc.	10) dos del mono, etc., etc.	10) two of the monkey, etc., etc.
34) deux de l'ancre, etc., etc.	34) dos del ancla, etc., etc.	34) two of the anchor, etc., etc.
36) trois du pilote	36) tres del piloto.	36) three of the pilot.
37) une du mât, etc., etc., etc.	37) una del mástil, etc., etc.	37) one of the mast, etc., etc. etc.
61) deux de la sémence, etc., etc., etc.	61) dos de la simiente, etc., etc., etc.	61) two of the seed, etc., etc.
Il y a soixante-sept divisions, plus de cent qualités.	Hay 67 divisiones y más de cien cualidades.	There are 67 divisions and more than one hundred qualities.

Given the relative proximity between French and Spanish, Michaux's writing, with few exceptions, admits literal translation throughout. The translator's intervention is more crucial at the lexical level since it often refers to exotic referents captured by a surprised traveler. The coherence or accuracy in the name of the referent reveals a certain negligence: for example, not following exactly Michaux's alternations among *indien/hindou/hindi* when deploying his translations "indio" and "hindú"; preferring hypernyms (words denoting broader categories) to the more precise names of animal species; and not maintaining consistency in the spellings of demonyms (adjectives of geographic place). As in other of his prose translations, Borges, the commissioned translator, intervenes in the length of the paragraphs, sometimes splitting them, other times merging them. In the description of *the other* from India, Ceylon, China, and Japan, the translation at times anticipates that of Brodie, the improvised ethnologist of the Yahoos.[13] Comparisons between Asians and Westerners reveal, in Michaux and Borges, the conventional nature of religion, the unintentional nature of customs.

Figure Three: The Retranslator of Whitman

In 1969, Juárez Editor published Borges's version of *Leaves of Grass* in Buenos Aires. This partial version of Whitman's book was preceded by, most notably, Francisco Alexander's complete text (1953) and León Felipe's version of "Song of Myself" (1941). Unlike the first and second figures, this Borges does not translate: he retranslates.

His retranslation of Whitman occurs between his publications of *Elogio de la sombra* [*In Praise of Darkness*] (1969) and *El oro de los tigres* [*The Gold of the Tigers*] (1972). If his works in collaboration are taken into account, the texts published closest in time to the retranslation are *Literaturas germánicas medievales* [*Medieval Germanic Literatures*] (1966, with María Ester Vázquez) and *El libro de los seres imaginarios* [*The Book of Imaginary Beings*] (1967, with Margarita Guerrero). Blindness and Borges's subsequent preference for brief literary forms, especially poetry, occurred contemporaneously with his rise to international celebrity, which was definitively consolidated throughout the 1960s. Borges had already won in 1961—*ex aequo* with Samuel Beckett—the Formentor Literary Prize. In 1964, *Cahiers de L'Herne* dedicated a volume to him. His fictions had found readers all over the world and had already been translated into several languages. The three prologues that he wrote for the reeditions of his first poetry collections— also released in 1969, in August—evoke, through their rejection of his past work, the practice of rewriting. The prologue to *Fervor de Buenos Aires* [*Fervor of Buenos Aires*] begins with the statement: "No he reescrito el libro. He mitigado sus excesos barrocos, he limado asperezas, he tachado sensiblerías y vaguedades" [I have not rewritten the book. I have mitigated its baroque excesses, I have filed down rough bits; I have omitted sentimentalisms and vaguenesses] (*OC* I: 13). In the prologue for *Luna de enfrente* [*Moon Across the Way*] there arises the purported need for a dictionary, specifically of Argentinisms: "que me suministraron palabras que hoy puedo apenas descifrar: *madrejón, espadaña, estaca pampa* . . . " [that provided me words that today I can barely decipher: *madrejón* (dry river bed), *espadaña* (bell gable), *estaca pampa* (horizontally buried stake for tying up horses on the pampa) . . .] (*OC* I: 55). As will soon be seen, the theme of the dictionary and its illusory contribution to lexical equivalence reappears in the prologue that Borges writes for his translation of Whitman.

However, the scene of translation in which Borges the Retranslator appears is defined not only by the discourses of universal consecration and the Olympic distance that Borges sought to put between himself and his early writing, but favored instead a vision of literature less anchored in the local. For, at the same time, books in the national language were on the rise, and publishing projects, such as the Centro Editor de América Latina and Jorge Álvarez, made such collections available to a wide readership. The rebelliousness motivating writers of the time—full of strikes, syndicalism, and journalism—has been analyzed by historians of Latin American thought and literature (Terán; Gilman). From the perspective of the history of editorial translation, Alejandrina Falcón, in her work specifically on 1969, focuses on Argentine translations of that year and reveals the tendency to acclimatize and, more specifically, to "Argentinize" those works.

Faulkner received the Nobel Prize ten years after Borges's translation of *The Wild Palms*; he was writing some of his best novels at the time Borges was translating it (though, ironically, in English, *The Wild Palms* is by no means considered one of them); Michaux was an active writer until the 1980s. To the contrary, Whitman, a poet of the nineteenth century, had a complete and unanimously celebrated oeuvre. In Borges's version of *Leaves of Grass*, does the consecrated poet translate the consecrated poet? Some criticism seems to answer this question in the affirmative, postulating an empathy that went far beyond the manifest differences. Fernando Alegría, in his commentary on Borges's version of "Song of Myself," states: "Of all the Whitman followers in Latin America, I think Borges was the one who understood him the best" (209). In the name of that empathy, Alegría would argue, literalness, liberty, slips of meaning, and even omissions, must necessarily be the best possible solution. Precisely because Borges understands Whitman better than anyone, Alegría would have any manipulation of the source text be due to a meeting of essences. This type of criticism, with its attendant implications about who can translate the great authors and who cannot, has also been applied to Borges's translation of Faulkner (Willson 170–71; Rodríguez Monegal 373). Some criticism also presupposes that, in contrast to previous Spanish versions, Borges transposes Whitman's pantheism more fully, the later Borges of 1969 himself being a literary pantheist (Aparicio 134–41). It has also been proposed that the translation of *Leaves of Grass* offered Borges the opportunity to "be" Whitman and to express feelings that do not appear in his own work (Miller 144–45; Tcherepashenets 189).

The copyright page of the book published by Juárez Editor lists the source text: it is from Modern Library, making it the 1891–1892 edition of *Leaves of Grass*. In the colophon, it is noted that Borges "selected and translated," but, which sections and poems did he select? From the *Inscriptions* section he translates the first part of "Starting from Paumanok" and, in full, the long poem *Song of Myself*. While the *Children of Adam* section is also fully translated, from the others, Borges relentlessly discards poems. From *Calamus*, he only translates "Recorders Ages Hence," "When I Heard at the Close of the Day," "Behold this Swarthy Face," "I Saw in Louisiana a Live-Oak Growing," "No Labor Saving Machine," and "Full of Life Now." He then moves on to *Autumn Rivulets*, from which he translates "To a Common Prostitute." From *Songs of Parting* he translates "So Long!," which closes the volume. The choice of *Song of Myself* seems motivated by the relative autonomy of this long poem from the rest of *Leaves of Grass*. Regarding the selection of the other poems, it was likely motivated by Borges's own preferences for those poems he returned to time and again. Three features of the publishing discourse complete the materiality of the translation itself. The book has a 24 x 32 cm format, the edition is illustrated with engravings by Antonio Berni and the foreword—extensive, erudite, and at bit pedantic—was written by Guillermo Nolasco Juárez, quite possibly the owner of the publishing house.

Leaves of Grass as a book was an anomaly for the publishing house Juárez Editor. According to the records from the Biblioteca Nacional Mariano Moreno, the publisher had only one collection, "Literature," directed by Borges, Ernesto Sábato, and Lysandro Galtier. The same catalog includes eight entries related to Guillermo Nolasco Juárez; as the author of two monographs (*La ciudad de Buenos Aires comparada con Madrid y París. Apremios y otros ensañamientos contra los contribuyentes porteños* [1996] and *Confrontaciones: el desarrollo económico y las inversiones sociales: El Área de Libre Comercio* [1997]); and as author of the foreword to *Hojas de hierba* (1969 and successive editions). Records from the Biblioteca Nacional Mariano Moreno also reveal that Juárez Editor's most prolific year was, no less, 1969, with titles including the Whitman translation, a volume of *Cuentos chinos con fantasmas, Dinastías Tan a Tsing,* and the reedition of *Filo, contrafilo y punta,* by Arturo Jauretche.

At the thresholds that turn a text into a book, in addition to the foreword by Nolasco Juárez, there is also a prologue by Borges, in which he reviews his own readings of Whitman. Toward the end, he writes,

> En cuanto a mi traducción . . . Paul Valéry ha dejado escrito que nadie como el ejecutor de una obra conoce a fondo sus deficiencias. Pese a la superstición comercial de que el traductor más reciente siempre ha dejado atrás a sus ineptos predecesores, no me atreveré a declarar que mi traducción aventaje a las otras. No las he descuidado, por lo demás; he consultado con provecho la de Francisco Alexander (Whitman, 1953) que sigue pareciéndome la mejor, aunque suele incurrir en excesos de literalidad, que podemos atribuir a la reverencia o tal vez a un abuso del diccionario inglés-español. (1969, 31)

> [As for my translation . . . Paul Valéry has written that no one is as fully aware of the deficiencies of a work as the person who carried it out; despite the commercial superstition that the most recent translator has always left his inept predecessors far behind, I shall not have the temerity to declare that my translation surpasses the others. Nor have I neglected them; I have consulted and profited from the version by Francisco Alexander (Whitman, 1953), which still strikes me as the best, though it often falls into an excess of literalness which we may attribute to reverence or perhaps to an overreliance on the Spanish-English Dictionary.] (*SNF* 448–49)

The "commercial superstition" is a formulation that anticipates—by refuting it—what years later would become the *retranslation hypothesis,* which argues: with translations subject to expiration or at least to aging, successive versions or retranslations of a work are often presented to readers as surpassing previous translations (Berman 1). In any case, it is not only the prologue that evokes the presence of Alexander's version; the choice of "Canto de mí mismo" and not the reiteration of León Felipe's[14] option, "Canto a mí mismo," also constitutes the first sign of that presence. Another reference point provided by the book as

FIGURE 5.4 Cover of *Hojas de hierba*, translation by Alexander.

Source: Photo Courtesy of Patricia Willson.

an object is that both Borges and Alexander translated from the same edition of the source text, which enables comparisons of their versions (Figures 5.4 and 5.5).

With respect to syntax, both versions are conspicuously alike, except for Alexander's use of enclitics ("velozmente eleváronse"), a technique never used by Borges in this translation, and for the simplification of hypothetical clauses, as in the following example:

> *It may be if I had known them I would have loved them* (Whitman 28)[15]
>
> Acaso, si yo los hubiere conocido, los habría amado (Alexander 37)
>
> Acaso, si estuvieran aquí, yo los amaría (Borges, *Hojas de hierba* 45)

FIGURE 5.5 Cover of *Hojas de hierba*, translation by Borges.

Source: Photo Courtesy of Patricia Willson.

The more substantial difference appears, rather, in their lexical choices. Borges's choice of words in comparison to Alexander's is always less erudite, more "plain," as can be seen in the following examples taken from "Started from Paumanok," which opens the collection, and *Song of Myself*:

Starting from fish-shape Paumanok where I was born (Whitman 12)

Al partir de la Paumanok pisciforme donde yo nací (Alexander 15)

Saliendo de Paumanok, la isla en forma de pez donde yo nací (Borges 35)

The atmosphere is not a perfume, it has no taste of the distillation, it is odourless (Whitman 24)

La atmósfera no es un perfume, no tiene el gusto de la esencia, es inodora (Alexander 32)

El aire no es un aroma, no huele a nada (Borges 40)

The sound of the belch'd words of my voice loos'd to the eddies of the wind (Whitman 25)

El sonido de las palabras, emitidas con regüeldos, de mi voz, que se pierden en los remolinos del viento (Alexander 32)

El áspero sonido de las palabras en mi boca que se pierden en los remolinos del viento (Borges 40)

Have you felt so proud to get at the meaning of poems? (Whitman 25)

¿Te has vanagloriado de penetrar el significado de los poemas? (Alexander 32)

¿Te enorgullece comprender el sentido de los poemas? (Borges 40)

I have no mockings or arguments, I witness and wait (Whitman 27)

No empleo pullas ni sofismas: observo y espero (Alexander 35)

En mí no hay burlas ni razones, miro y espero (Borges 43)

These examples and others like them highlight Borges's interpretation of *Leaves of Grass*. If, despite the ambitious poetic project animating them, Whitman's poems manage to circumvent "el mero fárrago de la acumulación y del caos" [the mere barrage of accumulation and of chaos] as Borges asserts in his prologue to the retranslation (29), this was also the result of the translation strategies that led him to, in places he judged it necessary, "mitigar excesos barrocos" [mitigate baroque excesses] to "limar asperezas" [file down rough bits], and, above all, avoid the "abuso del diccionario inglés-español" [abuse of the English-Spanish dictionary], in contrast to Alexander's translation. This is a translation strategy that seems to contradict Nolasco Juárez's foreword, the first threshold to Borges's translation.

CONCLUSION

In his extensive relationship with the concrete practice of translation, Borges embodies at minimum three dissimilar figures. Such is the hypothesis articulated in this chapter. These three figures, with their varying outlines formed by the translation strategies of each, the aesthetic-ideological scenes in which they unfolded, and the publishing discourses that gave them materiality, could not be summed up in just one persona. The versions analyzed here have been republished and consequently bear changes, both in the translation scenes and in the publishing discourses.

In the light of these new contexts, the translation strategies—which affect the textual level—were redefined. Although a text is always read from the present, in this chapter, we have sought to return to the moment of production of Borges's versions and reconstruct the original contexts. Translating for the *RMS* in the 1930s brought about the erasure of the agents except for the author and the illustrator. Borges's theories of translation, to which we alluded in the first paragraphs of this chapter, are more in line with the first of the three figures—Borges the Translator of Magazines. In other words, it is within the framework of *Crítica*'s literary supplement where the agenda implied in Borges's famous essays on translation is most fully deployed. There is, to be sure, a reckoning with the prose of psychological and realistic causality. In the second figure, Borges the Translator on Commission, only a few subversive gestures reveal the transposition of the aesthetic conflict that separated Borges from the famous authors that the Sur and Sudamericana publishing houses commissioned him to translate: Woolf, Faulkner, and Michaux, whose textualities were so foreign to Borges's own literary project in the 1930s and 1940s. With the third figure, Borges the Retranslator, another point of comparison appears: in addition to the original text, we cannot avoid consideration of the previous translation by Francisco Alexander, which Borges confesses in his prologue to *Hojas de hierba* have "consultado con provecho" (31) [consulted and profited from (*SNF* 449)]. The "triangulation" of the analysis affords us access to the new approaches to reading Whitman proposed by this persona. These plural methods of approaching "Borges the Translator" as a subject in no way exhaust the possible interpretations of this matter. They but seek to facilitate new interpretations of Borges's practices of literary appropriation.

NOTES

1. Regarding the relationships among these Borges texts and translation, see, among others Pastormerlo; Pauls y Helft; Arrojo; Leone; Climer. Regarding Borges's actual translation practices, see in particular Aparicio, Kristal, Willson; Waisman, whose main hypotheses will be discussed later in this chapter.
2. Herein lies the value of Claudia Fernández Speier's research into the relationships between Borges and translation that can be found in other sources—interviews, for example—that lie outside the traditional canon of texts referenced on this topic.

3. Sarlo goes on to list a series of appropriations that go beyond translation, as it is understood in this chapter: "his youthful friendship, in Spain, with ultraism; his familiarity with gauchesque poetry and his aversion for tango lyrics; his capricious and productive relationship with Evaristo Carriego, a modest poet his father often read; his devotion to Macedonio Fernández and his enjoyment of 'strange,' marginal and minor writers; the anthologies he prepared with his friends Adolfo Bioy Casares and Silvina Ocampo; the *criollismo* of *Don Segundo Sombra* sounding false to his ear; his fascination with Scandinavian literatures; the Thousand and One Nights and the Odissey [*sic*]; his Buenos Aires infused translation of the last pages of Ulysses; his veneration for the Kabbalah and for the Divine Comedy" (Sarlo, "Introducción" 11). As commented on elsewhere in this volume, the idea that Borges first read the *Qujote* in English is a frequent misconception.

4. In the source text for this chapter, the author uses "enunciation" in Émile Benveniste's terms, understood as the set of conditions in which a message is produced, which is notoriously difficult to translate into English (Joseph). We have decided to use "discourse" as a term that refers not only to culturally and contextually determined patterns of linguistic production but also to the material consequences created by the rhetorical approaches motivating and resulting from language use.

5. See, for example, Brigitte Ouvry-Vial and de Diego, and of course, work by Roger Chartier, which will not be cited here, but is the predecessor for this field of analysis.

6. This is one of polysystem theory's main contributions to translation studies (Toury 45). By focusing on the target culture and the function of translations within that culture, polysystems theorists are freed from the problem of equivalence and hence from judgments about a translation's success in rendering its source.

7. Key to this research is material collected in the online portal *AHiRA* (Historical Archive of Argentine Journals), which provides visual access to magazines published in Argentina over more than a century: https://ahira.com.ar/. On this digital platform, in addition to viewing every issue of the *RMS*, one can also find studies by Louis and Gargatagli.

8. See Camps, whose analysis of the version published in the anthology with Bioy focuses on the ideological context of the source text, including London's conversion to socialism.

9. We do not include here Borges's translations of poetry that appeared in *Sur* that did not go on to be collected in book form.

10. See, for example, King, Willson, Sarlo (*Escritos*) and Gramuglio.

11. On Borges as editor of *Destiempo*, see Mascioto ("Borges Editor") and Benedict.

12. This and all other information about Michaux are taken from Carion and Outers. Regarding his conference at the PEN Club, see Weibel Richard (Fédération international des P.E.N.). This involvement is significant as it situates Michaux within the category of "bendian" intellectuals—in reference to Julien Benda and his essay *La Trahison des clercs* (1927), a debate discussed in several issues of *Sur* over the 1930s.

13. In Borges's 1970 story, "El informe de Brodie" [Doctor Brodie's Report], Scottish missionary David Brodie encounters the tribe of the Yahoos whose apparently brutal customs highlight the relativity of cultural constructions of propriety.

14. The 1941 "La pajarita de papel" published by Losada with a poetic prologue by León Felipe, an epilogue by Guillermo de Torre, and illustrations by Attilio Rossi.

15. All citations are taken from the 1921 edition of *Leaves of Grass*, used by both translators. From this point on, citation will only be of page numbers.

Works Cited

Primary Works Cited

Borges, Jorge Luis. "Walt Whitman, *Leaves of Grass.*" *Selected Non-Fictions.* Edited by Eliot Weinberger, translated by Esther Allen, Penguin, 1999, pp. 445–49.

London, Jack. "Las muertes concéntricas." *Los mejores cuentos policiales.* Edited by Emecé Editores, 1943, pp. 71–85.

London, Jack. "Las muertes eslabonadas." *Revista Multicolor de los Sábados,* vol. 1, no. 38, 1934, p. x. http://ahira.com.ar.

London, Jack. "Los hijos de Midas." *Revista Literaria de Novelas y Cuentos,* vol. 39, 1934, p. x.

London, Jack. "The Minions of Midas." In *Moon Face and Other Stories.* Sonoma University Press, [1901] 1906.

Michaux, Henri. *Un Barbare en Asie.* Gallimard, 1933.

Michaux, Henri. Un bárbaro en Asia, translated by Jorge Luis Borges. Editorial Sur, 1941.

Whitman, Walt. *Canto a mí mismo,* translated by León Felipe. Editorial Losada, 1941.

Whitman, Walt. *Hojas de hierba,* translated by Francisco Alexander. Casa de la Cultura Ecuatoriana, 1953.

Whitman, Walt. Hojas de hierba, translated by Jorge Luis Borges. Juárez Editor, 1969.

Whitman, Walt. *Leaves of Grass.* [1892] Modern Library, 1921.https://archive.org/details/leav esofgrass00whit/page/n3/mode/2up?ref=ol&view=theater.

Secondary Works Cited

Alegría, Fernando. "Borges's 'Song of Myself.'" *Cambridge Companion to Walt Whitman.* Edited by Ezra Greenspan. Cambridge University Press, 2006, pp. 208–20.

Aparicio, Francis. "Versiones, interpretaciones y creaciones." *Instancias de la traducción literaria en Hispanoamérica en el siglo veinte.* Hispamérica, 1991.

Arrojo, Rosmary. "Translation, Transference, and the Attraction to Otherness. Borges, Menard, Whitman." *Diacritics,* vol. 34, no. 3/4, Fall-Winter 2004, pp. 31–53.

Benedict, Nora. "(In)visible Collaborations between *los hermanos* Borges and *los* Bioy." *Variaciones Borges,* vol. 49, 2020, pp. 89–116.

Camps, Valentina. "'The Minions of Midas' and 'Las muertes concéntricas.'" *Variaciones Borges,* vol. 25, 2008, pp. 187–204.

Carion, Jacques, and Jean-Luc Outers. *Henri Michaux. Face à face.* La Lettre volée, 2016.

Catelli, Nora, and Ana Gargatagli. *El tabaco que fumaba Plinio.* Ediciones del Serbal, 1998.

Climer, Claire. "'Un fuego sin luz': La paradoja y el error en 'La busca de Averroes.'" *Latin American Literary Review,* vol. 44, no. 88, 2017, pp. 59–70.

De Diego, José Luis. *Los autores no escriben libros: Nuevos aportes a la historia de la edición.* Ampersand, 2019.

Falcón, Alejandrina. *Traductores del exilio: Argentinos en editoriales españolas: Traducciones, escrituras por encargo y conflicto lingüístico* (1974–1983). Iberoamericana Vervuert, 2018.

Fédération internationale des P.E.N. "Clubs." 14th Congrès international des P.E.N. clubs, 5–15 septembre 1936, discours et débats. Translated by R. Weibel-Richard. 1937. https://gallica. bnf.fr/ark:/12148/bpt6k373794w/f1.image (accessed October 5, 2022).

Fernández Speier, Claudia. *Las traducciones argentinas de la Divina Comedia.* Eudeba, 2019.

Gargatagli, Ana. "Borges en Crítica. Invención y escritura de Las mil y una noches." *Letras*, vol. 81, enero-junio 2020, pp. 155–70.

Geisler, Eberhard. "El otro de Borges, Michaux." *Jorge Luis Borges: variaciones interpretativas sobre sus procedimientos literarios y bases epistemológicas*. Edited by Karl Alfred Blüher, Alfonso de Toro, Degruyter, 1995, pp. 95–118.

Gramuglio, María Teresa. *Nacionalismo y cosmopolitismo en la literatura argentina*. Editorial Municipal de Rosario, 2013.

King, John. *Sur. Estudio de la revista argentina y de su papel en el desarrollo de una cultura, 1931–1970*. Fondo de Cultura Económica, 1989.

Kristal, Efraín. *Invisible Work: Borges and Translation*. Vanderbilt University Press, 2002.

Leone Anderson, Leah. *Borges's Creative Infidelities: Translating Joyce, Woolf and Faulkner*. Bloomsbury, 2024.

Louis, Annick. "Instrucciones para buscar a Borges en la *Revista Multicolor de los Sábados*." *Variaciones Borges*, vol. 5, 1998, pp. 246–64.

Louis, Annick. *Jorge Luis Borges: Œuvre et manœuvres*. L'Harmattan, 1997.

Mascioto, María de los Ángeles. "Borges Editor." *Anclajes*, vol. 22, no. 2, 2018, pp. 57–68.

Mascioto, María de los Ángeles. "Literatura fantástica entre el diario Crítica y la Editorial Sudamericana: Políticas editoriales, materialidad de los textos y modos de escritura." *Revista chilena de literatura*, vol. 93, 2016, pp. 127–53.

Mascioto, María de los Ángeles. *Nuevos modos de escritura en la Revista Multicolor de los Sábados (1933–1934)*. Universidad Nacional de La Plata, PhD dissertation, 2019.

Miller, Andrea. "Borges canta a Whitman." *Variaciones Borges*, vol. 30, 2010, pp. 145–59.

Ouvry-Vial, Brigitte. "L'acte éditorial: Vers une théorie du geste." *Communication and Languages*, vol. 154, 2007, pp. 67–82.

Pastormerlo, Sergio. "Borges y la traducción." 1999. *Borges Studies Online*. http://www.borges.pitt.edu/bsol/pastorm1.php.

Pauls, Alan y Nicolás Helft. *El factor Borges*. Fondo de Cultura Económica, 1999.

Rodríguez Monegal, Emir. *Jorge Luis Borges: A Literary Biography*. Dutton, 1978.

Saítta, Sylvia. "Borges mediático." *Variaciones Borges*, vol. 46, 2018, pp. 3–21.

Saítta, Sylvia. "Estudio preliminar." *Crítica, Revista Multicolor de los Sábados*. Edición complete en CD-Rom. Fondo Nacional de las Artes, 1999, pp. 10–38.

Sarlo, Beatriz. *Borges, un escritor en las orillas*. Ariel, 1995.

Sarlo, Beatriz. *Escritos sobre literatura argentina*. Siglo XXI, 2007.

Sarlo, Beatriz. *"Introducción a El informe de Brodie."* Borges Studies Online. Borges Center for Studies & Documentation, April 14, 2001. http://www.borges.pitt.edu/bsol/bsbrodie.php.

Sarlo, Beatriz. *Una modernidad periférica: Buenos Aires 1920–1930*. Nueva Visión, 1988.

Souchier, Emmanuel. "L'image du texte. Pour une théorie de l'énonciation éditoriale." *Les Cahiers de Médiologie*, vol. 6, no. 2, 1998, pp. 137–145.

Tcherepashenets, Nataly. "Borges on Poetry and Translation in Theory and Practice." *Variaciones Borges*, vol. 19, 2005, pp. 183–94, http://www.jstor.org/stable/24880559.

Toury, Gideon. *Descriptive Translation Studies and Beyond*. John Benjamins. 1995.

Waisman, Sergio. *Borges y la traducción: La irreverencia de la periferia*. Adriana Hidalgo, 2005.

Willson, Patricia. *La Constelación del Sur: Traductores y traducciones en la literatura argentina del siglo veinte*. Siglo XXI, 2004/2017.

CHAPTER 6

BORGES'S LECTURES

Literature, Travels, and Orality

MARIELA BLANCO

TRAUMA, MODESTY, AND ORALITY

THE history of Borges's work as a lecturer began in 1945, with his celebrated inaugural conference on gauchesque literature, which would both mark a new stage in his career and shed new light on his obstacles.[1] It is an absurd paradox: the first lecture Borges gave could not be read by Borges himself. Borges would step into this new role, which had so many surprises in store, by skirting its key duty. Emir Rodríguez Monegal, one of the main cultural forces in strengthening ties between Borges and Uruguay from this time on, explains how this experience would begin a new stage in Borges's academic life.

> Había sido invitado por el servicio cultural del Ministerio de Instrucción Pública para dar en la universidad una charla sobre literatura gauchesca. Tímido e introvertido, Borges nunca se había confiado a su propia voz en público. Se negaba a dar conferencias, y en las raras ocasiones en que se vio obligado a hacerlo, escribió un texto cuidadosamente ensayado, y luego pidió a un amigo que lo leyera en su lugar. (347)[2]

> [He had been invited through the Ministry of Public Instruction's cultural service to give a talk at the university about gauchesque literature. Timid and introverted, Borges never trusted his own voice in public. He refused to give conferences, and on the rare occasions he found himself obligated to do so, he would write a carefully crafted text and then ask a friend to read it in his place.]

Through the correspondence between Borges and this first event's organizer, Marta Muller, director of *Arte y Cultura Popular de Montevideo*, which has been studied by Pablo Rocca, the background for this very first of Borges's lectures can be reconstructed (211). The first invitation dates back to 1937, and only after Muller's persistent attempts did Borges, after much delay, accept the invitation in 1945. There would be nothing particularly strange about the excuses he gave were it not for what followed: the outlandish request that the reading of his lecture be delegated to someone else. The first choice would have been Borges's old friend Pedro Leandro Ipuche, who declined the request saying it would be too monotonous to hear just his voice because he also was introducing the speaker. Ultimately it would be the young scholar José Pedro Díaz who read the lecture:

> En carta fechada el 24 de octubre de 1945, María V. de Muller, directora de "Arte y Cultura Popular" (Ministerio de Instrucción Pública) le escribe a Díaz informándole que Gervasio Guillot Muñoz ha propuesto su nombre para leer el texto de Borges, quien recientemente había sido operado de la vista. En la misma se aclara que "Ipuche no quiere leer ese trabajo, pues cree indispensable otro timbre de voz, para evitar la monotonía para el público y la radio." "Precisamos un buen lector," añade, "que destaque las ideas y los conceptos de Borges, y le dé a la lectura todo el relieve y claroscuro necesario para que llegue el pensamiento de Borges en toda su plenitud." Y aún en la posdata agrega: "será todo un acontecimiento literario, ya que Borges nunca ha dado una conferencia en Montevideo." (Alzugarat 92)

> [In a letter dated 24 October 1945, María V. de Muller, director of "Arte y Cultura Popular" (Ministry of Public Instruction) wrote to Díaz informing him that Gervasio Guillot Muñoz had suggested his name as the person to read the text on behalf of Borges, who had recently had eye surgery. In the same letter she clarifies that "Ipuche doesn't want to read this lecture, because he thinks an additional tone of voice indispensable for avoiding monotony for the audience and the radio." "We need a good reader," she adds, "who can highlight Borges's ideas and concepts and give the reading all of the relief and chiaroscuro needed for Borges's thought to evoked in full." And in the postscript she adds, "this is going to be a major literary event because Borges has never given a lecture in Montevideo."]

Rodríguez Monegal uses a marvelous image to condense the situation into a single scene: "Mientras José Pedro Díaz, un joven profesor de literatura, leía el largo discurso con dicción impecable y una voz bella y sonora, Borges permanecía sentado al fondo, apuntándole el texto invisible e inaudiblemente. Fue una curiosa función, como la de un ventrílocuo que controlara a su muñeco desde cierta distancia" [While José Pedro Díaz, a young literature professor, read the long speech with impeccable diction and beautiful, sonorous voice, Borges sat in the back, invisibly and inaudibly prompting him the text. It was a curious function, like that of a ventriloquist controlling his doll from afar] (347). I find two concepts particularly interesting—the theatricality and the sense of ventriloquism—in the way they synthesize two fundamental aspects of orality that are crucial for analyzing the phenomenon of Borges as lecturer.[3] In that vein, Mladen Dólar's reflections eloquently apply when considering that close connection between orality and subjectivity that so impacted Borges's elaboration of this practice:

> Uno debería renunciar a la noción trivial de una realidad primordial, plenamente constituida, donde la vista y el oído se complementaran armoniosamente entre sí: en

cuanto ingresamos al orden simbólico, una hiancia insalvable separa para siempre a cuerpo humano de "su" voz. La voz adquiere una autonomía espectral, nunca termina de pertenecer del todo al cuerpo que vemos, de modo que incluso cuando vemos hablar a una persona en vivo, siempre hay un mínimo de ventrilocuismo en juego: es como si la propia voz del hablante lo vaciara y de algún modo hablara "por sí misma," a través de él. En otras palabras, su relación es mediada por una imposibilidad: en última instancia, oímos cosas porque no podemos ver todo. (11–12)

[One must renounce the trivial notion of a primordial, fully constituted reality, where sight and hearing harmoniously complement each other: as soon as we enter the symbolic order, an insurmountable gap forever separates the human body from "its" voice. The voice acquires a spectral autonomy, it never fully belongs to the body we see, so that even when we see a live person speak, there is always a modicum of ventriloquism at play: it is as if the speaker's own voice left the body and, in a way, speaks "for itself," through it. In other words, the relationship is mediated by an impossibility: ultimately, we hear things because we cannot see everything.]

To better manage this relationship with his own voice, Borges began therapy with psychoanalyst Miguel Kohan Miller in 1946, as Estela Canto attests in *Borges a contraluz*. According to Julio Woscoboinik, "el tratamiento fue de dos sesiones por semana y duró 2 o 3 años" [the treatment was two sessions per week and lasted 2 or 3 years] (260). In line with this time frame, and despite the fact that Borges cited vision problems in Montevideo as a hindrance to reading his own lecture, it is evident that his reluctance to own the gap and the emotions his own voice caused him were the trigger for him to start treatment with Kohan Miller, who had previously been his old friend's, the writer Manuel Peyrou, therapist as well.

What, in 1945, had been attempted as a novelty, as of 1946, would become a necessity. The new political context, marked by the inauguration of Juan Domingo Perón, forced Borges to stop working at the Biblioteca Miguel Cané, a small neighborhood library in Buenos Aires. Rather than go into detail about the political situation, suffice it now to highlight that this had been Borges's only stable job, apart from itinerant, related tasks such as consulting for the Emecé publishing house and, eventually, translating and contributing pieces for graphic media. In this new political context, some friends suggested that he start giving lectures, particularly at an institution with which Borges would maintain a strong and lasting link, the Argentine Association of English Culture (AACI).

Added to Borges's political and material conditions is, unquestionably, his emotional state. Such can be gleaned from Estela Canto's aforementioned book, a personal biography that consistently ties the biographical details she notes to Borges's sexuality. However, even if there is plenty of evidence for the hypothesis that Borges's issues with shyness were sexual in nature and particularly linked to a traumatic experience in his youth—as the psychoanalyst himself suggests in the conversations that Canto reproduces—there appears to be little need to delve into them. Far more than such details, what is interesting is that Borges seems to find, if not a way to end his shyness, a way to cope with it when speaking in public—so much so that he manages to transform his initial stuttering into a very unique personal style that many witnesses describe with admiration. Take, for example, the description given by Benigno Herrera Almada, assistant to the course "English Authors" (July 4 to September 26, 1949):

> Mientras [Borges] habla, con el busto un poco inclinado hacia adelante, coloca las manos en posición ojival. O desliza una sobre otra, como si se calzara un guante. Rara vez recurre al libro, abandonado sobre el pupitre, y cuando lo hace es para citar un texto, siempre brevísimo. Sólo al comienzo de algunos períodos vacila contados segundos en la dicción. Tiene una voz cálida, de entonación uniforme: una voz vigilada, para impedir que cualquiera de sus juicios adquiera preponderancia sobre los demás. (*Borges en El Hogar* 169)

> [While he speaks, with his torso leaning forward a bit, he arranges his hands in a pointed arch. Or he places one on top of the other, as if trying on a glove. Very rarely does he refer to the book, abandoned on the desk, and when he does so, it is to read a quote from text, always extremely brief. He has a warm voice, with uniform intonation: a voice he closely monitors, to prevent any of his judgments from taking preponderance over any other.]

Much had happened between that first conference in Uruguay and this first course he gave at the educational institution Colegio Libre de Estudios Superiores (CLES), where he would go on to establish a stable position. At this point, there is no doubt that therapy had been successful with respect to his development as an orator. This much is made clear by anecdotes from his conference's attendees, such as those collected by Borges's friend Carlos Mastronardi:

> El vivo interés que su palabra, oral y escrita, despierta en quienes lo siguen, acaso tenga fiel reflejo en la suelta confesión del muchacho que, luego de oírlo, al trasponer la puerta de la sala de conferencias, le dice a un amigo, también joven: "Esto me ayuda mucho. Con una frase de Borges puedo vivir una semana." (35)

> [The lively interest that his word, both spoken and written, awakens in those who follow him, might best be reflected in the unguarded confession of a young man who, after hearing him, said to a friend, also young, after exiting through the conference room's door: "That helps me a lot. I can live for a week on a line of Borges's."]

From this point forward, Borges would go on to develop a method that would make the lecture circuit his main occupation for the following years, especially between 1949 and 1955, at which point he was named director of the National Library subsequent to Perón's government being overthrown by a civil-military coup. This method would continue to be defined by personal circumstances, such as blindness. To begin to describe his approach, even briefly, Canto's observations serve as a starting point:

> Una institución privada, el Colegio Libre de Estudios Superiores, le propuso una serie de conferencias. Acicateado por el doctor Cohen Miller [sic], Borges preparó cinco o seis conferencias y aprendió de memoria los textos. Solía recitarlos con sus

BORGES'S LECTURES   99

amigas, mientras daba vueltas a la manzana donde estaba el edificio del lugar en que iba a hablar, generalmente la Sociedad Científica Argentina, en la calle Santa Fe.

La primera conferencia le costó un tremendo esfuerzo, pero acatando las órdenes de su médico y ayudado por una copita de caña de durazno oriental —que le fue dada por la poetisa uruguaya Ema Risso Platero—, muy efectiva en el organismo de un abstemio total, logró hablar y siguió hablando por el resto de los cuarenta años de vida que aún le quedaban. (118)

[A private institution, the Free College of Higher Education, offered him a series of lectures. Encouraged by Doctor Cohen Miller [sic], Borges prepared five or six lectures and memorized them all. He used to practice them with his female friends, reciting them while circling the block where the building in which he was going to speak was located, generally the Argentine Scientific Society on Santa Fe Street.

The first lecture took him tremendous effort, but following his doctor's orders and with the help of a little shot of local peach cane spirits—given him by the Uruguayan poet Ema Risso Platero, which was very effective in the body of a person who was a complete teetotaler—he managed to speak and to keep speaking for the remaining forty years still ahead of him.]

The help of the alcohol would become a colorful detail incessantly repeated by attendees of Borges's courses and lectures, perhaps because they witnessed it first-hand or perhaps because they were seduced by the story itself. What is striking is the reliance on writing as a primary scaffold and then on memorization as a form of mediating and conquering his fears and shyness. Whether this preparation was on Kohan Miller's recommendation or not, owing to the progress of the research group that I direct at the National University of Mar del Plata, which focuses exclusively on Borges's lectures, we are able to corroborate that Borges conducted very thorough research for each of the topics on which he would lecture and would record his notes in his very idiosyncratic notebooks, as I detail at the end of this chapter. This practice would become essential both for the period I am focusing on here and after 1955, when he would lose his sight for reading and writing purposes. From that point on, we can conjecture—and also on the basis of many firsthand accounts—that these notes would become even more crucial and would transcend the mere function of memory and recitation aid to become a kind of symphonic score that would allow him to return to the themes and sources he consulted repeatedly and accurately. Borges's mother would become the other foundational pillar supporting this work because she was charged with both taking notes on new topics and reading her son's old notes in order to update their content and offer new applications to new audiences (Jurado, "Borges and I" 327).

Thanks to this new career in lecturing, between 1949 and 1955, Borges undertook numerous trips to the interior of Argentina and to Montevideo on a regular basis. He was thus able to visit many cities, some central, such as Córdoba and Rosario, and others less populous, such as Nogoyá, Gualeguay, Olavarría, or Azul, among others, several of which he likely had not visited prior to giving these talks. It is worth asking how all these travels might have influenced his subjectivity. Beyond the happiness that he expressed in some statements, they undoubtedly helped to increase Borges's sociability, which would have also helped improve his self-esteem and, in turn, his confidence when facing the public. Indeed, numerous journalistic notes refer to the intense applause he received upon finishing his talks.

Little by little, Borges would go on to become a performer, a traveler taking his word from town to town with a few books under his arm, as shown in research by Rosato and Álvarez (171), to preach to an audience that was much larger and much closer than any he was used to prior to this experience. Borges sometimes traveled alone and sometimes accompanied by his mother or a female friend, but he was always feted by the locals, who painstakingly prepared for this writer who was becoming a central figure in Argentine literature. When he did not travel with his mother, he would write her postcards recounting details of everyday life, such as this:

> Dearest Mother: De Resistencia, que no es una gran ciudad (y quizás, agregaría Paul Groussac, el epíteto huelga), te dará una idea suficientemente monótona y desarreglada la imagen del reverso. El hotel es una versión territorial del hotel provinciano de Santiago. La gente es muy simpática: anoche comí con una hija de Gerchunoff y con su marido. Ayer hablé (entiendo que bien) sobre los poetas gauchescos. "Vaya un cielito rabioso," etc.; hoy sobre Almafuerte, mañana sobre Banchs y Lugones. Afectos y un abrazo,
> ¿Qué tal *Folio on Mary White*, o lo que sea? Georgie
> Los días son calurosos, las noches (a juzgar por la única que he pasado) son más bien frías. (Helft 127)[4]

> [Dearest Mother: From Resistencia which is not a large city (and perhaps, Paul Groussac might add, its name is fitting), you will get a sufficiently monotonous and messy idea from the image on the other side. The hotel is a small-town version of the provincial hotel in Santiago. The people are very agreeable: last night I had dinner with a daughter of Gerchunoff's and her husband. Yesterday I spoke (apparently well) about the gauchesque poets. "*Vaya un cielito rabioso,*"[5] etc.; today on Almafuerte, tomorrow on Banchs and Lugones. Fondly and a hug,
> How about *Folio on Mary White* or something? Georgie
> The days are hot, and the nights (judging by the only one I have had here so far) are rather cold.]

In these kinds of recollections, details about his activities abound: themes, company, landscape, venues, and, not least, observations about his performance. Without question, lecturing was an endeavor tightly bound up with his emotions and feelings, as can be noted in the postcards sent to his closest friends and family, for example, this one, to Wally Zinner:

> Señora Wally Leonor de Aparicio/ Chacabuco 3337/ Mar del Plata/ E.C.S.
> Querida y admirada Wally: Perdone el horror del anverso.[6] Esta noche, Madre y yo nos vamos a Montevideo; el dieciséis diré o balbucearé o acaso emitiré una conferencia sobre literatura americana, en el Colegio Libre. Luis Reissig me ha

invitado a esa empresa, que encaro con temor y curiosidad. Saludos a los suyos. La ciudad la extraña infinitamente. Borges. (Helft 128)

[Señora Wally Leonor de Aparicio/ Chacabuco 3337/ Mar del Plata/ E.C.S.

Dearest and admired Wally: Pardon the horror on the other side. Tonight, Mother and I are going to Montevideo; on the sixteenth I will give or blubber or possibly broadcast a lecture on American literature at the Colegio Libre. Luis Reissig invited me to undertake this venture, which I face with fear and curiosity. Greetings to your loved ones. The city misses you infinitely. Borges]

As can be noted, in the years between 1949 and 1955, lecturing became a central activity, one that became an increasingly deeper part of Borges's subjectivity, such that the "fear" continually moves closer to "curiosity."

The Anti-Peronist Platform

Borges's relationship with politics proved decisive in his new role as a lecturer. Indeed, both he and his biographers have taken it upon themselves to spread the story that he was forced to undertake his career as a lecturer after learning he was about to be appointed to the position of poultry inspector, as he recounts in his famous speech published in *Sur*.[7] On the basis of a conversation with a municipal employee, Borges mythologizes the origin of what would be his long and contentious relationship with Peronism from the moment its leader, Juan Domingo Perón, came to power in 1946.

En algún resquicio de esa tarde única, yo temerariamente firmé alguna declaración democrática; hace un día o un mes o un año platónico, me ordenaron que prestara servicios en la policía municipal. Maravillado por ese brusco avatar administrativo, fui a la Intendencia. Me confiaron, ahí, que esa metamorfosis era un castigo por haber firmado aquellas declaraciones. (*Borges en Sur* 303)

[At some breaking point that unique afternoon, I recklessly signed some democratic declaration; a day or a month or a Platonic year later, I was ordered to serve in the municipal police. Amazed by that abrupt administrative change, I went to Headquarters. They confided to me, there, that this metamorphosis was a punishment for having signed those declarations.]

His account is marked not only by the temporal indeterminacy, a feature so typical of his fictions, that gives this scene a mythical nature, but particularly by its parallelism with one of his favorite stories, Kafka's "The Trial," an emblematic statement of the kind of future the state had in store for him. In all likelihood, Borges had signed a petition in favor of the Democratic Union, a political party fronted by the Tamborini-Mosca ticket, which opposed the de facto government under Edelmiro Farrell at that time as well as Perón's ticket for the presidency in 1946. Borges would have been sanctioned for this act, but the consequences of this significant intervention into the political field ended up being far greater than mere administrative action. Thus, once again, beyond the veracity of the facts, what matters here is the way in which Borges makes public this turning point in his career and, consequently, in his daily life. Borges would abandon office work and its obligatory routine to begin his work as a professor and lecturer—a place from which he would construct a platform characterized throughout this period by shots against Peronism.

His relationship with Peronism started off on the wrong foot and, over time, would only get worse. Borges would throw himself into other activities once definitively separated from the Boedo library, until, in 1948, an extraordinary event would make this relationship irreversibly one of pure scorn. I am referring here to Borges's sister and mother being arrested on Florida Street for having sung verses of Argentina's national anthem, signaling their support of the 1853 constitution at a time when the reigning party was looking to introduce reforms that would allow Perón a second term. Upon refusing to stop singing, the police accused them of disorderly conduct, punishable by thirty days' imprisonment. Norah Borges was confined to Buen Pastor jail, and Borges's mother was placed under house arrest owing to her advanced age (she was seventy-two) (Vaccaro 467).[8]

Consequently, even if—as Borges has taken pains to point out many times—he refused to include himself among the committed writers of the time given his fear of being subjected to an ideology that would impose themes or leanings he had to follow, his performances as a lecturer did place him squarely in the political arena. And, it would seem, we can confidently argue that his speaking engagements and conferences should be considered performances; they were ephemeral, public, and diverged significantly from what he himself thought should be included in written works, as made clear by how few oral texts he would publish during his lifetime. It is clear that, in orality, in contrast with his writings, Borges found a more comfortable, more suitable venue for offering his political opinions.

One of the clearest examples of how politics seeps into this work is the use of Borges's "Poema conjetural" [Conjectural Poem] as the finishing touch on the published version from his talks on a gauchesque literature in Montevideo. The poem had been published in the newspaper *La Nación* in 1943, but it was repurposed here as an epilogue for the talk, whose individual talks Borges would publish in three issues of the Uruguayan journal *Marcha* (numbers 306, 307, and 308, in 1945) as well as in booklet form through Ediciones Número press in 1950.[9] The words preceding the work eloquently resignify this powerful narrative poem, making it a weapon loaded with ink and aimed at a specific reading that Borges sought to reinforce, one assigning Peronism the same negative association with barbarity that the liberal independence movement had been promoting since the nineteenth century:

> Muchas noches giraron sobre nosotros y aconteció lo que no ignoramos ahora. Entonces comprendí que no le había sido negada a mi patria la copa de amargura y de hiel. Comprendí que otra vez nos encarábamos con la sombra y con la aventura.

Pensé que el trágico año 20 volvía, pensé que los varones que se midieron con su barbarie, también sintieron estupor ante el rostro de un inesperado destino que sin embargo no rehuyeron. En esos días escribí este poema. Lo diré, como quien pone una viñeta al pie de una página. (*Aspectos* 34)

[Many nights turned their wheel above us and the thing we now know happened. I then understood my country had not been denied its cup of bitterness and bile. I understood we were once again facing off against darkness and danger. I thought the tragic year 1820 was back, I thought that the men who measured themselves by their barbarity were also stupefied when facing an unexpected destiny, and yet they did not shrink from it. I wrote this poem in those days. I will speak it, like a person who stamps a vignette at the bottom of a page.]

In this way, the imaginary recreation of Laprida's death at the hands of Aldao's guerilla forces served to metaphorize the barbarity that had returned to the present with ghostly hues to assail the forces of civilization, now defended by anti-Peronist intellectuals. Many writers joined these ranks, taking refuge in institutions that sought to remain outside the auspices of Peronism and within linked networks of solidarity, as will be made evident in the next section.

The special homage paid to Esteban Echeverría on January 19, 1951, is especially interesting for its political symbolism. According to Tulio Halperín Dongui, this event was the liberal intellectuals' response against Peronism's homages to San Martín celebrated throughout 1950 (233). Effectively, ample coverage by the anti-Peronist newspaper *La Prensa* described in detail how the event, organized by the Comisión Central de Homenaje en el Monumento del Parque Tres de Febrero (Central Tribute Commission for the February Third Park Monument), was affected by its scheduled speakers being forbidden to give their talks. Numerous institutions stood up against this censorship. Among them was the Sociedad Argentina de Escritores (SADE), led by its president, Jorge Luis Borges, and accompanied by other intellectuals like José Luis Lanuza and Carlos Erro who had been most involved in the organization. The writers flocked to Echeverría's monument to "dejar, en silencio, el testimonio de su homenaje" [offer, in silence, the witness of their homage] ("En el centenario" 6). The newspaper published the words of Borges and the other participants who, despite the prohibition, gave at the park the talks they were supposed to have given at La Casa del Escritor. Borges's words are clearly oriented toward the same goal of drawing a parallel between the two "dictatorships": Rosas's, against which Echeverría fought, and Peron's, against which, in this case, Borges would be a leading voice of the opposition: "Echeverría, al escribir su obra, no cantaba pintorescos temas exóticos; historiaba la dolorosa realidad de su tiempo. Su retórica no era, naturalmente, la que hoy emplearíamos; su convicción de estar en un mundo terrible, en un mundo sin esperanza, puede coincidir con la nuestra" [Echeverría, upon writing his work, did not intone picturesque exotic themes; he told the story of the painful reality of his time. His rhetoric was not, naturally, what we would use today; his conviction of being in a terrible world, a world without hope, can coincide with our own] ("La conmemoración" 5).

With respect to Borges's public persona, which was becoming increasingly visible—not to mention audible—especially after becoming president of SADE in 1950, María Esther Vázquez recalls,

> A Borges lo seguía un policía, siempre dos pasos atrás. Un día, el escritor le pidió permiso para tomarse de su brazo a fin de cruzar una avenida; desde esa tarde caminaron juntos, charlando como dos amigos. A sus conferencias asistían siempre dos agentes, que tomaban notas. Muchas veces me he preguntado qué entenderían cuando Borges hablaba de los místicos orientales. (199)

> [A police officer used to follow Borges, always two steps behind. One day, the writer asked him if he might take his arm to cross the avenue; from that point on, the two walked together, chatting like two friends. Two officers always attended his lectures, taking notes. I have often wondered what they might have understood when Borges spoke on the Eastern mystics.]

Those who attended his classes at CLES, such as Marcelo Abadi, whom I was able to interview, confirm Vázquez's story, emphasizing how strange the agents' presence was to other attendees. The audience, in turn, never doubted who the agents were, even though the undercover officers circulated with everyone else in the auditorium. In the same sense, a succession of Peronist rulings in 1952 only confirmed Borges's hypothesis that he was being persecuted. In July 1952, by Federal Police order—reportedly in response to disorderly noise—the CLES locale was closed. That same year, an administrative decision was made to require passports to travel to Uruguay, which curtailed the job market for many intellectuals who crossed the Río de la Plata regularly to give talks. In Borges's case, this resulted in a decrease in the number of talks given during this time, especially in the city of Buenos Aires.

It seems likely that the lectures' virulent tone did not go unnoticed by some government sectors. Indeed, it can be noted that, after the final conference at CLES in 1951, which closed with the diatribe that eventually became one of his hallmark texts, "El escritor argentino y la tradición" [The Argentine Writer and Tradition], his lectures began to revolve more frequently around the role of writers in relation to their individual context.

In his book, *Oratoria y evocación*, Ansolabehere focuses on the intense oratory activity that marked the consolidation of the Argentine national state as well as on how the genre lost importance throughout the twentieth century to such a degree that it disappeared from literary histories. For Ansolabehere, Ricardo Rojas is the only outstanding Argentine orator. Among his correct characterizations, Rojas does correspond to the archetypical orator and poet. Ansolabehere attributes this development to the professionalization of the writer, which would go hand in hand with literary autonomy (78). Borges's lecturing activity, which he was only able to pursue after abandoning a state-funded position, is a tremendous example of autonomy. Nevertheless, his interventions owe much to the platform these talks permitted him, especially because he transformed the spaces of the assembly halls and auditoriums into places for exercising political proselytization (Ansolabehere 40). Beyond the fact that his figure is very close to that of the "orator-poet," the limited interest in publishing his lectures (very few of them are published, and many of them reach the press in the form of shorthand versions that someone salvages, as CLES did on some occasions) seems to show that Borges was more interested in separating his public interventions from his writing.

All these considerations allow us to begin outlining a profile of these talks. To do so, Fernando Degiovanni's hypothesis is suggestive when analyzing talks given by Latin American intellectuals, as in the case of Ugarte. Degiovanni refers to "activism" as a method of creating and consolidating a community with shared interests: "Giving speeches and lectures became a way of transforming the writer into an activist who abandoned a contemplative position in favor of a political activity whose public platform was the balcony, the auditorium, and the private hall" (23).

In a similar way, Borges traveled throughout Argentina and assiduously visited Montevideo to consolidate a community of ideas, but also of feelings, among those for whom rallying around the rejection of Peronism required little inducement. In this light, the debate against nationalism that Borges promoted with "El escritor argentino y la tradición," which ended activities at CLES and constituted a direct attack on the dominant discourses during the Peronist government, should not surprise us.[10] It is even less surprising that this virulence would only intensify in the following years as the party responded to perceived criticisms with ever more closures that came very close to outright censorship. In this regard, I want to highlight one of Borges's last lectures at CLES as part of his "El escritor y nuestro tiempo" [The Writer and Our Times] course, in which he openly upholds the need for writers to militate:

> Creo que queda algo más, mucho más, queda el artista. Creo que el artista tiene el deber de militar, pero creo que puede hacerlo de un modo más eficaz, diremos. Por lo pronto creo que el artista no debe hacer nada que se parezca a una complicidad con aquellos de que abomina. Creo que estamos empeñados en una guerra, una guerra de lo que es un episodio—ojalá efímero—lo que está ocurriendo ahora en este país, creo que la guerra en que está empeñada la humanidad es la que profetizó hace más de medio siglo Herbert Spencer en su obra *El individuo contra el estado*. Creo que si el artista se siente como me siento yo, un individuo, no debe hacer nada que pueda apoyar o ayudar a la fuerza del estado. ("El escritor" inédito)

> [I believe there remains something more, much more for the artist. I believe the artist has the duty to be an activist, but I think they can do so in a, let's say, more effective way. For the time being, I believe the artist should do nothing that appears complicit with those whom they abhor. I believe we are engaged in a war, an episode—hopefully brief—of which is what is happening in this country now; I believe the war in which humanity is engaged is what Herbert Spencer prophesized more than a half century ago with his work *The Man Versus the State*. I believe that if the artist feels as I—an individual man—do, they should do nothing that can uphold or help the power of the state.]

It is this "war" that compels Borges to abandon the slightest hint of nationalism. And the direct allusions in his oratory that openly identify the enemy make evident how the

Argentine experienced lecturing as a civic practice and the degree to which he used it as a platform for undertaking a pedagogical effort. In this sense, his work fits into the vast tradition Tom Wright calls "lecture culture" (26), and it is characterized by, among other aspects, its impact within the consolidation of democratic practice when taken as a mode of intervention into public life by disseminating power among the common people. It is not my goal here to enter into the discussion surrounding the conceptualization of the intellectual in a framework as vast as World War II, but I do want to acknowledge that figure's relationship to oratory in its being a genre associated with the public. Borges would feel comfortable enough to deploy his style—monotonous and monotone, according to the descriptions of those who attended (which also harkens back to the style of Protestant sermons that felt familiar to Borges, owing to his blood ties)—not in any political arena but at art associations, educational institutions such as CLES and its branches in the interior, and other cultural institutions. Organizations such as these would come to constitute a network united by their anti-Peronism, and it was within this network that Borges chose to build up his public figure—which began to grow disproportionately at both national and regional levels, anticipating what will be his launch to international fame in the 1960s.

Exponential Gains: Travels, Friends, and Money

In January 1938, Borges began as a temporary employee at the Biblioteca Miguel Cané. He was recommended for the job by Adolfo Bioy, father of the writer Adolfo Bioy Casares. His first tasks were to catalog and classify its bibliographical holdings until August of that same year, when he was made assistant librarian of periodicals. Another important job he would hold during these years would be as editor of *Los Anales de Buenos Aires* [*The Annals of Buenos Aires*].[11] This journal, launched by Sara de Ortiz Basualdo, arose as a source of dissemination for an artistic society that sought to promote ties to French culture, taking as its model the *Journal de l'Université des Annales de París*. Nineteen issues were published between January 1946 and the beginnings of 1948, numbering from 1 to 23. Borges is listed as the director of issues 3 to 11, printed toward the end of 1946. As of issue number 12, Borges becomes a "consultant," but, curiously, for the last issue published, the only one to come out in 1948, he is once again listed as "Director." His work with *Los Anales de Buenos Aires* was interrupted in 1948. To this is added the situation María Esther Vázquez describes: "las notas en *Sur* y *La Nación* económicamente significaban poco" [his reviews in *Sur* and *La Nación* mean little economically] (194).[12]

With this period coming to an end, a stage of major transformations began in Borges's life given the significant shift in his means of making a living. After quitting his post at the Biblioteca Miguel Cané in 1946, which had guaranteed him a set monthly income, Borges was forced to look beyond whatever he might charge for his newspaper and journal articles to secure an income stream that could maintain the home he shared with his mother, Leonor Acevedo. His high-society friends, the most notable including Victoria Ocampo and Esther Zamborain de Torres Duggan, began recommending him to various cultural institutions to give courses and lectures, as famous foreign intellectuals had done a decade before when visiting Argentina.[13] We have since found that these lectures not only became the writer's main source of income, but they also allowed him to live a little more comfortably (though not abounding in luxury, as this would have gone against his own class consciousness). The oft-referenced *pudor* (or modesty) which Borges claimed as a feature distinctive to Argentine people in "El escritor argentino y la tradición" (269)[14] also translated into terms of economic austerity.

A relevant piece of information that reveals the impact the conferences had on Borges's lifestyle: while his pre-tax monthly salary at the library was 210 pesos (199 net), we have been able to confirm that at CLES he received 200 pesos for each class. And he was giving at least one a week, in addition to all the lectures he was giving at other institutions, making it clear that his income had multiplied exponentially.

Given the intimacy of her relationship with Borges, Estela Canto was the witness who most closely noted the impact of finances on his personal life—indeed she describes how monetary factors bore upon Borges's sadness during the years he worked as a librarian, as well the contrast that arose once he began to have success as a lecturer. The figures he made at one job versus the other shed much light on this change of spirits, not least because they offered him, it would seem, the possibility of considering independence. From his mother? Possibly. From the Argentine state? Unquestionably.

Another record of the amount that Borges collected per lecture is found in the correspondence of Canal Feijóo, an old comrade from the journal *Martín Fierro*, who became a cultural organizer and promoted Borges's work because of his ties to Canal Feijóo's native province, Santiago del Estero. Once again, from within his most intimate circle of friends came the efforts to organize a lecturing circuit—in this case, a tour through the north of Argentina. In his exchange with those charged with receiving Borges at the Sarmiento Library in 1949, Canal Feijóo writes,

> Los temas serán los que se indican en la hojita adjunta, que Uds. repartirán entre las entidades patrocinantes. "La Cábala" podría ser para esa sociedad Israelita en la que puede determinar las cosas el Dr. Rosestein. Les ruego hablar enseguida con el Dr. Rosestein y el Dr. Rava y arreglar las cosas en firme; se tratará de pagarle a Borges por esa conferencia unos 250 o 300 pesos. Les ruego hablar también enseguida con el Dr. Nano Paz para que arregle lo del Jockey, estando convenido en principio con él que también allí se abonarán 300 pesos. (Carta de B. Canal Feijóo, 22 de septiembre de 1949)[15]

> [The topics will be those indicated on the insert I have included, which you will hand out among sponsoring organizations. "The Kabbalah" could be for that Israelite organization where Dr. Rosestein can decide how things should go. I would ask you to please speak with Dr. Rosestein and Dr. Rava right away to settle things; for this talk it will be some 250 or 300 pesos. I would also ask you to contact Dr. Nano Paz right

away so he can arrange things with the Jockey Club, as it has been agreed with him in principle that there too they will pay him 300 pesos.]

In addition to the financial yield, which becomes more evident when considering that, on the northern mini-tour, Borges would give eight lectures in twelve days, there are other aspects that stand out about the organization of these events. I am referring to the publicity and the strategies deployed by friends and organizers to "sell" these talks. While at institutions such as CLES the teaching staff itself already constituted an assurance of quality among its members and friends, when Borges traveled to Argentina's interior—given that he was not yet enjoying the fame he would attain in a few years—his image had to be sold. Canal Feijóo, for example, described Borges as "el conferenciante más original y más interesante de Bs. As.; todas sus conferencias se convierten en verdaderas puebladas, y terminan en aclamaciones" [the most original and most interesting speaker in Buenos Aires; all of his talks become total mobs and they all end in cheers]. In addition to this, Borges was able to manage everything from the tickets to the license through the British Embassy (for which he was teaching) and thus obtain the permission to take off work that would allow him to make this trip to the north of Argentina.

Generally, Borges's lectures were open and free of charge, with the exception of the courses he taught at CLES and the Asociación de Cultura Inglesa. In its function as a marketing strategy, the choice of topics that would be of interest to the potential audience becomes relevant here. In fact, archival research allows us to affirm that the topics chosen depended both on the knowledge of the lecturer and the interests of the institutions that invited him, as well as the audience. This can be seen in the case of the Jewish cultural institutions, in which Borges referred to topics related to the Kabbalah, or with the lectures he gave on various writers' birthdays when he was director of the SADE. The CLES, one of the main institutions promoting his courses, provides particularly interesting data with its 1950 member survey selecting course topics for the following year. It is worth noting that Borges had an average of some eighty students enrolled in these courses.

The institutions at which Borges spoke on subjects as diverse as English literature, French literature, the Kabbalah, the mystics, detective novels, Buddhism, and Germanic literatures, among others, were varied, but it is clear that they formed a network linked through social actors and, largely, through their positions in opposition to Peronism. The intellectual field of the time is undoubtedly marked by the dispute over the definition of culture that would divide the waters at a social level and, in the more concrete framework we are describing, among writers. This confrontation can be seen in the division within the SADE that took place around 1948, when several writers spoke out about being expelled for their Peronist sympathies and eventually joined the Argentine Writers Association (ADEA). The federal distribution of Borges's lectures is also of relevance: while most of the talks took place at organizations in Buenos Aires, Borges visited more than eighteen Argentine cities in addition to his frequent trips to Montevideo.

The Lecturing Writer: Toward the Total Work

I think it is important to point out that, beyond the already attention-getting debate with Peronism that Borges developed during this period, we can define this stage as a kind of prehistory to the international era of his lecturing career. After being made Director of the National Library in 1955, and after his texts were translated into various foreign languages abroad, he would be flooded with invitations to teach classes and give lectures in other parts of the world. Borges would not cease lecturing—a practice which both helped him conquer his fear of public speaking and led him to travel constantly—until his death.

Then again, this is the era during which Borges would write his conferences, as stated by the majority of his biographers and proved by existing manuscripts.[16] Given the magnitude and complexity of this material, an international team led by Daniel Balderston has recently begun to draw partial conclusions, from which we can affirm that Borges developed a method for preparing lectures in the following way: (1) taking detailed notes including references to quotations that he planned to use; (2) reviewing the notes to be able to improve orally; and (3) the performance stage, which is marked by the instance of pure orality, during which he did not read, according to witness testimony, with the exception of a random passage from a book which he always had on hand as a kind of guide. The importance of this period thus takes on new dimensions for being the one in which Borges sketched the maps, the itinerary of what would be future repetitions with variations based on the research conducted during these early years in his speaking career.

This statement is supported by the marginalia in these texts, where Borges carefully noted the sources from which he extracted nearly every detail of what he would share with his audience. His famed trait of being a great reader would make his method one that honored a precept held by Quintilian, a master orator:

> El oficio de orador es arduo y requiere una preparación muy estricta: de hecho *Institución oratoria* es un texto pedagógico que dedica muchas de sus páginas a la enseñanza de los niños y a puntuales recomendaciones para los maestros. Por eso el buen orador, antes que nada, como lo dice Cicerón, debe ser un gran lector, alguien preparado en disciplinas muy diversas, no sólo la de su especialidad, sobre todo la filosofía: "sin filosofía, nadie puede ser elocuente," sentencia en *Diálogos de orador*. (Ansolabehere 22)

> [The role of orator is arduous and requires strict preparation: indeed *Institutio Oratoria* is a pedagogical text that dedicates many of its pages to teaching young people and to timely recommendations for teachers. This is why a good orator, must, as Cicero says, before anything else, be a great reader, someone well-read in very diverse disciplines, not just that of one's own area of specialization, and especially in

philosophy: "without philosophy, no one can be eloquent," he says in his *Dialogus de oratoribus.*]

Borges's notes allow us to understand his lectures as a montage in which his voice intertwines with that of others' voices and those of his readings.

At this point, it is interesting to reconsider Ansolabehere's observations when analyzing the speeches given by public figures in the nineteenth century. They highlight how, with the increasing overdetermination of writing over oral genres, oratory ceased to be a referent for the figure of the twentieth century intellectual. Borges himself plays with this dialectic between orality and writing in many of his talks, as he notes in a life of Schopenhauer, where he focuses on the close tie that exists between discourse and life.[17]

As more talks and their paratexts continue to appear, it is clear that we need to attend to them to truly consider Borges's "complete" works. On the one hand, we can point to the vast number of texts that were born as talks and that, after some modifications, became articles in newspapers or journals and eventually came to be published as books (*Otras inquisiciones* [*Other Inquisitions*] is perhaps the most emblematic of these); there are also those lectures that directly became books such as *Borges, oral* (1979) or *Siete noches* [*Seven Nights*] (1980); or the lectures given at universities in the United States.[18] Likewise, texts such, *Antiguas literaturas germánicas* [*Ancient Germanic Literatures*] or *Qué es budismo* [*What is Buddhism*] had their origin in courses offered at the CLES. On the other hand, we now must add to this list the countless talks that have been uploaded to YouTube that exceed the scope of the period we have studied (1949–1955), during which audiovisual recording technology was not available for these kinds of events. Finally, in addition to the lectures that keep appearing, we have already uncovered more than four hundred talks that must be included when considering Borges's "total work" if we truly wish to have a complete panorama of the themes and tasks that mattered to him.

NOTES

1. This chapter presents the results of the project I directed at the National University of Mar del Plata, in collaboration with researchers from the National Library of Argentina and with the support of CONICET. The aim of the research was to trace the itinerary of the lectures Borges gave in Argentina and one of its neighboring countries, Uruguay, between 1945 and 1955.
2. Some antecedents for this modus operandi are described by Alicia Jurado (*Genio* 24, 50). Another famous example is the "Palabras pronunciadas por Jorge Luis Borges en la comida que le ofrecieron los escritores" [Words given by Jorge Luis Borges at the meal given in his honor by writers] (*Borges en Sur* 303–04). The way in which Borges reconstructs this particular event in his "Autobiographical Notes" is interesting in that, when confessing that shyness had prevented him from giving the talk himself, he claims to have asked Pedro Henríquez Ureña to do so (85). As Daniel Fitzgerald makes clear, it is impossible for this information to be accurate, given the date of Henríquez Ureña's death (78).

3. See Hanson's chapter in this volume for the theatrical element in Borges's interviews.

4. Although Helft does not date the postcards, thanks to our research, these lines can be dated August 8, 1950, since the lecture on gauchesque literature was given on August 7.

5. This is a line from the epic poem *Paulino Lucero o Los gauchos del Río de la Plata cantando y combatiendo contra los tiranos de la República Argentina y oriental del Uruguay (1839 a 1851)* by leading gauchesque poet Hilario Ascasubi.

6. Photo of the Kavanagh building in Buenos Aires.

7. María Esther Vázquez summarizes the various discontinuous versions of this story: on the one hand, Borges himself and his biographers, Alicia Jurado and Emir Rodríguez Monegal, maintain that he had been transferred to the Abasto market as a poultry inspector; on the other hand, the then Secretary of Culture of the Municipality, Raúl Salinas, maintains that he does not remember very well, but that in order not to fire him—given that Miguel Ángel Echeverrigaray and Francisco Luis Bernárdez had intervened on Borges's behalf—he had been transferred to the Municipality's Beekeeping School (Jurado, *Genio* 191). What is certain is that the magazines of the time broadcast the incident (Vaccaro 449–51).

8. *El grito sagrado* by Adela Grondona, one of the women who shared a cell with Norah, offers details about life during those days they were in jail. What is funny about the "advanced age" of Leonor is that she would live until 1975.

9. Perón assumed his first presidency on June 4, 1946.

10. Cfr. Balderston "Detalles circunstanciales" and Blanco.

11. See https://ahira.com.ar/revistas/los-anales-de-buenos-aires/.

12. To see the activities and publications that Borges carried out at the same time, see the Borges Center's *Timeline* (https://www.borges.pitt.edu/timeline/13) and Benedict.

13. Aguilar and Siskind.

14. For a thorough exploration of *pudor* (modesty) as national trait of Argentine people, see Helft and Pauls (47–56).

15. This material comes to us thanks to the generosity of Daniel Guzmán, Director of the Sarmiento Library of Santiago del Estero.

16. The notebooks that form part of the Donald Yates collection at Michigan State University are essential for this work (MSS 678). See issue 52 of *Variaciones Borges* for the initial results of a projected headed by Daniel Balderston which considers Borges's notes as they relate to his lectures.

17. In this regard, two features are significant: Schopenhauer's phrase underlined by Borges the reader, "Das Leben ist eine Sprache" (Life is a speech) and the fact that he chose that space to record the list of lectures that served as a starting point for this research (Rosato and Álvarez 380).

18. Other books that collect Borges's lectures include: *Borges: el misterio esencial* (1981), *Conferencias de Jorge Luis Borges en el I.I.C.C.A.I.* (1988), *Recuerdos de mi amigo Xul Solar* (1990), *Borges en la Escuela Freudiana de Buenos Aires* (1993), *This Craft of Verse* (2000), *Borges profesor* (2000), *El aprendizaje del escritor* (2014), and *El tango* (2016).

WORKS CITED

Aguilar, Gonzalo, and Mariano Siskind. "Viajeros culturales en la Argentina (1928–1942)." *Historia crítica de la literatura argentina*, vol. 6. Edited by María Teresa Gramuglio, Emecé, 2002, pp. 367–89.

Alzugarat, Alfredo, ed. *Diario de José Pedro Díaz (1942–1956; 1971; 1998)*. Biblioteca Nacional-Ediciones de la Banda Oriental, 2011.

Ansolabehere, Pablo. *Oratoria y evocación*. Santiago Arcos, 2012.

Balderston, Daniel. "Detalles circunstanciales: Sobre dos borradores de 'El escritor argentino y la tradición.'" *Cuadernos Lírico*, vol. 9, 2013, http://lirico.revues.org/1111.

Balderston, Daniel. *How Borges Wrote*. University of Virginia Press, 2018.

Balderston, Daniel. *Lo marginal es lo más bello*. EUDEBA, 2022.

Balderston, Daniel. "Revelando las falacias del nacionalismo: de 'Viejo hábito argentino' a 'Nuestro pobre individualismo.'" *Variaciones Borges*, no. 46, 2018, pp. 135–55.

Balderston, Daniel. *Timeline y Finder's Guide*. http://www.borges.pitt.edu.

Benedict, Nora C. *Borges and the Literary Marketplace: How Editorial Practices Shaped Cosmopolitan Reading*. Yale University Press, 2021.

Blanco, Mariela. *Invención de la nación en Borges y Marechal. Nacionalismo, liberalismo y populismo*. Eduvim, 2020.

Borges, Jorge Luis. *Aspectos de la literatura gauchesca*. Número, 1950.

Borges, Jorge Luis. "Autobiographical Notes." *The New Yorker*, no. 3, September 1970, pp. 40–99.

Borges, Jorge Luis. *Borges en El Hogar*. Emecé, 2000.

Borges, Jorge Luis. *Borges en Sur*. Emecé, 1999.

Borges, Jorge Luis. "El escritor y nuestro tiempo." Curso inédito, 1952.

Canal Feijóo, Bernardo. "Carta." September 22, 1949. Biblioteca Sarmiento de Santiago del Estero.

Canto, Estela. *Borges a contraluz*. Espasa Calpe, 1989.

Degiovanni, Fernando. *Vernacular Latin Americanisms: War, the Market, and the Making of a Discipline*. University of Pittsburgh Press, 2018.

Dolar, Mladen. *Una voz y nada más*. Manantial, 2006.

"En el centenario de su muerte hónrase a Esteban Echeverría." *La Prensa*, January 1, 1951, p. 6.

Fitzgerald, Daniel. "El 'escritor y nuestro tiempo': la conferencia, Entre Ríos 1952". *Variaciones Borges*, no. 42, 2016, pp. 59–85.

Gargatagli, Marietta. "Borges oral." *Cuadernos Hispanoamericanos*, no. 505, March 1999, pp. 51–58.

Grondona, Adela. *El grito sagrado (30 días en la cárcel)*. Francisco A. Colombo, 1957.

Halperín Dogui, Tulio. *Son memorias*. Siglo XXI, 2008.

Helft, Nicolás. *Borges. Postales de una biografía*. Emecé, 2013.

Helft, Nicolás, and Alan Pauls. *El factor Borges*. FCE, 2000.

Jurado, Alicia. *Genio y figura de Jorge Luis Borges*. EUDEBA, 1996.

Jurado, Alicia. "Borges and I" (Donald Yates, ed.). *Variaciones Borges*, no. 35, 2013, pp. 315–32.

"La conmemoración de Echeverría en el centenario de su muerte," *La Prensa*, January 19, 1951, p. 5.

Mastronardi, Carlos. *Borges*. Academia Argentina de Letras, 2007.

Rodríguez Monegal, Emir. *Borges: Una biografía literaria*. FCE, 1987.

Rocca, Pablo, ed. *El Uruguay de Borges: Borges y los uruguayos (1925–1974)*. Universidad de la República, 2002.

Rocca, Pablo. *El Uruguay de Borges: Borges y los uruguayos 1925–1974*. Instituto de Humanidades y Ciencias de la Educación, Universidad de la República, 2011.

Rocca, Pablo. "*Sur* y las revistas uruguayas (la conexión Borges, 1945–1965)." *Revista Iberoamericana*, vol. 70, no. 208–209, July–December 2004, pp. 811–24.

Rosato, Laura, and Germán Álvarez, eds. *Borges, libros y lecturas*. Biblioteca Nacional, 2010.

Vaccaro, Alejandro. *Borges. Vida y literatura*. Edhasa, 2006.

Vázquez, María Esther. *Borges. Esplendor y derrota*. Tusquets, 1996.

Woscoboinik, Julio. *El secreto de Borges. Indagación psicoanalítica de su obra*. Grupo Editor Latinoamericano, 1989.

Wright, Tom, ed. *The Cosmopolitan Lyceum: Lecture, Culture and the Globe in Nineteenth-Century America*. University of Massachusetts Press, 2013.

CHAPTER 7

WORKS AND DAYS

Jorge Luis Borges and the Library as a Scene for Literary Production

LAURA ROSATO AND GERMÁN ÁLVAREZ

LIBRARIES abound in Borges's writing. Limitless, atrocious, total, paradisiacal; they are the subject matter of his work, but they are also the place where the author chose to situate himself. If the series of personal libraries he described throughout his life constitute an aesthetic manifesto, libraries as institutions constitute a political one. Hence, the Miguel Cané Municipal Library and the Mariano Moreno National Library (BNMM) are identified with distinct stages in Borges's writing production, but also with the creation of his public image as writer—one who did not avoid the events occurring in his social and political context but manipulated them to assimilate it to his fictional imaginary. Borges has so labored over the story of his time in those archives that, on more than one occasion, he has conflated the modest job in the Miguel Cané Municipal Library and the position of high-ranking state official at the BNMM. A disambiguation of the positions and institutions will allow a more accurate reconstruction of the context and processes of production of his work.

Borges was almost forty years old when, out of necessity, to help support his family, he entered the world of paid work. He previously had paid collaborations in magazines and literary supplements, but this was more a strategy to participate in the intellectual marketplace than a formal job (Saítta 77). Borges belonged to a traditionally lettered family and enjoyed a certain economic comfort, but he was not part of the ruling class, as were many of his colleagues and friends in the *Sur* group. He had to work for a living, but he could do so—due to his social ties and particular skills—in the comfort of public employment, far from the rigors of factories or newspaper offices. Thus, Borges took advantage of the environment of a job not associated with the demands of productivity to make a shift in his own work—to transform his style and enhance his literary career such that, by the time he left the Miguel Cané Library, he had already written and published many of his most important short stories. He would likewise, as we shall see, take advantage of the position to tie his departure from municipal employment to high politics.

In 1955, Borges joined the BNMM, no longer as a public employee but as a state official, assuming the position of Director. His time at these institutions, then, occurred in different political and social contexts and led to two distinct moments in his literary production, both united by his desire to create a writerly public image that was consistent with his work. This chapter aims to give an account of his time at these libraries, first as a simple employee of a municipal library in a neighborhood far from downtown, and later his arrival as a government official to direct the main bibliographic repository of Argentina. Both periods, although very different, can be understood as time Borges used to read, write, and engage in politics, all intertwined in a single motion. Consequently, what he did and wrote while at the Miguel Cané Municipal Library was used to construct his public figure as a writer, which would ultimately be raised up as mythology at the BNMM. To understand how this came to be, we must first interrogate certain issues regarding how and in what political and social contexts Borges attained these positions while balancing the facts with the elements of his personal story. Then, we must identify the traces he left of his time at these institutions, how those places effectuated an intrinsic dynamic in his writing methods, and, finally, how they made their way into his work.

THE MIGUEL CANÉ MUNICIPAL LIBRARY

The Miguel Cané Municipal Public library is located on a block of low buildings on Carlos Calvo street, just meters away from La Plata Avenue, in the neighborhood of Boedo. Inaugurated in 1927, it was the first public library in what is now called the Red de Bibliotecas de la Ciudad de Buenos Aires [Library Network of the City of Buenos Aires]. Its primary mission was to promote culture through reading; entrance and home lending was free of charge, and there were reference services on site. On January 8, 1938, Jorge Luis Borges joined the staff of this library. His confirmation as first assistant was signed on August 18 of the same year. Borges's entry into his first paid job coincides with what we can consider the foundational stage of his work and his name as a writer. Prior to his employment at Miguel Cané, Borges had solely undertaken small publishing tasks, his only paid work up to that moment. Among these were his co-direction of the *Revista Multicolor de los Sábados* [*Multicolor Saturday Magazine*] (1933–1934) with Ulises Petit de Murat, his book review section in *El Hogar* [*The Home*] (1936–1939), and some other minor publications.

At the time he started this first full-time job, Borges was thirty-nine years old. It clearly weighed on him that he was not able to contribute to his household; moreover, his latest book had been a failure in terms of sales.[1] Like many Argentine writers and intellectuals of the time who did not come from well-to-do families, work on behalf of the State was the only avenue for his late entry into the labor market; public employment seemed an opportunity to enter the world of work without giving up his artistic aspirations. The nature of the work did not demand too much time, and, in some cases, the time commitment was minimal.[2] Regardless, the year he started at the library was a singular one in the life of Jorge Luis Borges. A few days after his appointment, he was devastated by his father's death.[3] Additionally, the death of Jorge Guillermo Borges occurred almost simultaneously with the suicide of writer Leopoldo Lugones, leaving Borges doubly orphaned, literally and symbolically.[4]

The work environment was also bleak. In his memory, his colleagues "no se interesaban en otra cosa que en las carreras de caballos, en el fútbol, en los chistes verdes" [were interested in nothing but horse racing, soccer matches, and smutty stories] (*Autobiografía* 106; "Autobiographical" 169). He even recounts how, on one occasion, a woman was raped in the restroom and that the other employees justified it, arguing that the ladies' and men's restrooms were adjoined, making it inevitable that this kind of thing would happen. The library staff resembled the characters in his tales of knifemen and *compadritos* [thugs] but lacked any kind of epic or heroic nature. Contrary to his stories, the more real and sordid, the less interesting he found them. Later in his life, during an interview, Borges reflected about this period only to conclude: "Toda esa atmósfera me deprimió" [The entire atmosphere depressed me] (Irby 8). Consequently, much of the aesthetic of the urban outskirts, with the marginality, violence, and brutality that had characterized Borges's literature between the 1920s and 1930s was, paradoxically, diluted the moment he was actually confronted with those realities. Although some critics note that this distancing involved a rejection of the mass culture that led up to the political movement known as Peronism, we believe that we cannot ignore the impact of this mediocre work environment, from which he distanced himself by going off alone to write in the library basement or, when the weather permitted, on the sunny rooftop.

Literary Production

It appears quite likely that the combination of disappointments at work and the deep sadness he felt at the death of his father compelled Borges to move away from his old *Ars poetica* of the *arrabal*, or slum, to instead deepen his push toward new types of writing, represented in a series of stories that land somewhere between fiction and philosophical essay. At that time, the Miguel Cané Library was also the *locus* of some of the stories that appeared in *Sur*.

Text	Date
"Pierre Menard, autor del Quijote" [Pierre Menard, author of the *Quixote*]	May 1939
"La biblioteca total" [The Total Library]	August 1939
"Tlön, Uqbar, Orbis Tertius"	May 1940
"Las ruinas circulares" [The Circular Ruins]	December 1940
"La lotería en Babilonia" [The Lottery in Babylon]	January 1941
"Examen de la obra de Herbert Quain" [An Examination of the Work of Herbert Quain]	April 1941
"La muerte y la brújula" [Death and the Compass]	May 1942
"El milagro secreto" [The Secret Miracle]	February 1943
"Tema del traidor y del héroe" [Theme of the Traitor and the Hero]	February 1944
"Tres versiones de Judas" [Three Versions of Judas]	August 1944
"Biografía de Tadeo Isidoro Cruz" [Biography of Tadeo Isidoro Cruz]	December 1944
"El Aleph" [The Aleph]	September 1945
"Deutsches Requiem"	February 1946

If we consider this list, it undeniably contains the hard, central core of stories (and an essay that is a kind of preliminary version of a later story) that constitute the backbone of Borges's work: *El jardín de senderos que se bifurcan* [*The Garden of Forking Paths*] (1941), later integrated into *Ficciones* [*Fictions*] (1944), and three of the main stories in *El Aleph* (1949). We now focus on two stories from *El jardín de senderos que se bifurcan* (1941), "La lotería en Babilonia" [The Lottery in Babylon] and "La biblioteca de Babel" [The Library of Babel], as well as on the dedicated writing that physically took place in the Boedo library and which, faithful to Borges's *pathos*, permeated, in a sublimated form, the composition and background of the fiction.

"La biblioteca de Babel" is iconic; to a great extent, the concept of a library-universe is associated with Borges because of this story. The theme of the story had been dealt with shortly before in "La biblioteca total" (1939). There, Borges gave an account of the different iterations of an invention (an innumerable quantity of texts resulting from the multiple combinations of all typographic characters) and, particularly, its latest variant, which he deemed to be Kurd Lasswitz's book of fantastic stories *Traumkristalle*.[5] The sensation underlying the possibility that this infinite set, and a library containing it, might be real—the resulting "subaltern horror" and its emotional consequences (*Borges en Sur* 27) are all that "La biblioteca total" and "La biblioteca de Babel" have in common.

"La biblioteca de Babel" is indebted to Franz Kafka's claustrophobic and biblically reminiscent parables, but even more so to the "realidad atroz o banal" [horrifying or banal truth] (*OC* I: 431; *CF* 68) that Borges experienced every day at the Miguel Cané Library. The story offers clues regarding his employment at the library that no one may have perceived at the time, details such as the arrangement of the shelves in this infinite library or the location in space of the toilets and their uses, or the customs of the employees (*OC* I: 465). The monstrous architecture of the story replicates the form and distribution of the Buenos Aires library. The librarian's habits mimic Borges's own habit of writing during work hours, stolen away to isolate and protect himself from his colleagues' incomprehension (*OC* I: 470). In the text we also find references to the classification of books, a task he performed regularly: "También hay letras en el dorso de cada libro; esas letras no indican o prefiguran lo que dirán las páginas. Sé que esa inconexión, alguna vez, pareció misteriosa" [There are also letters on the front cover of each book; those letters neither indicate nor prefigure what the pages inside will say. I am aware that that lack of correspondence once struck men as mysterious] (*OC* I: 466; *CF* 113). However, beyond these relevant examples, what prevails is the "sensación general de desesperanza, de monotonía y de horror, que el cuento transmite con tanta eficacia" [general sense of hopelessness, of monotony and horror, which the story conveys so effectively] (Rodríguez Monegal 283).

The other story associated with "La biblioteca de Babel," due to the point in time at which it was composed and its narrative continuity, is "La lotería en Babilonia." Both stories' titles include locations in the ancient Middle East that can be related to Biblical tradition. We sense this as a dogmatic way of creating distance, both historically and geographically, allowing him to approach issues in his own life by obscuring them in allegory. As Ricardo Piglia states, "Los grandes relatos de Borges giran sobre la incertidumbre del recuerdo personal y la experiencia artificial. La clave de este universo paranoico es la manipulación de la memoria y de la identidad. Tenemos la sensación de habernos extraviado en una red que remite a un centro cuya sola arquitectura es malvada" [Borges's great stories revolve around the uncertainty of personal memory and artificial experience. The key to this paranoid universe is the manipulation of memory and identity. We get the sensation of having lost our way in a network that leads to a center whose only architecture is evil] (*Formas breves* 51). For Beatriz Sarlo, Borges's literature performs a sort of "ordenamiento fantástico al desvío irracional de Occidente" [fantastic ordering of the West's skew toward the irrational] (*Borges, un escritor* 47), related to the rise of totalitarian movements and democracy of the masses, embodied in a populist state. A state that manifested itself in its most domestic form in the Miguel Cané Library's banal bureaucracy, with its phantasmagorical pyramid of hierarchical positions; its nebulous, meaningless tasks designed to give the "apariencia de trabajo" [semblance of work] (*Autobiografía* 106; "Autobiographical" 169); and its rewards in the vile form of "pequeños regalos de arriba" [small gifts from above] (*Autobiografía* 107; "Autobiographical" 170).

In "La lotería en Babilonia," Borges refers to these events as an invisible conspiracy, a plot of the Company, which ruled and surveilled by means of lottery tickets. The logical and rhetorical figures—paradox and oxymoron—prevalent in the narrative suggest the semantic contradiction implied in Babylon's dystopian society being governed by chance. As Daniel Balderston points out, "Borges estaba profundamente interesado en la interacción entre la lógica y el azar en el mundo social. Era quizás una manera de refugiarse del mundo infernal de 1941" [Borges was deeply interested in the interplay between logic and chance in the social world. It was perhaps a way of taking refuge from the hellish world of 1941] (148). We have mentioned Kafka's work as an inspiration for these stories, the atmosphere and the use of the parable—which emanates from Kafka's sphere but belongs to Judaism. Borges even explicitly inserts his name by means of a latrine called "Qaphqa," where the Company investigates the desires and denunciations of the people. As a final argument for this influence, on the backflap of a book by Max Brod on Kafka,[6] we find his peculiar *marginalia*, which, as Beatriz Sarlo says, "marca citas que hoy llamaríamos 'borgeanas,' frases que podrían ser suyas" [marks quotes that today we would call 'Borgesian' phrases that could be his] ("Lector esquivo" 10), which perfectly describes the mood that gave rise to the idea of the story: "Schreiben als Form des Gebetes" [Writing as a form of prey]. With "The Lottery in Babylon," which functions as the narrative counterpart of "The Library of Babel," Borges solidifies his political-aesthetic stance of rejection of populism and definitively distances himself from the so-called literature of the *suburbio* [urban outskirts].

THE JOB AND THE WORKS

The collections of the Miguel Cané retain few if any material traces of Borges's activity at work, much less any books with his annotations in them. It could be conjectured that, even for one who had long been introducing marginalia into his reading materials—belonging, as he was, to that singular species of extractive reader—the need to keep his first formal job outside of literature implied he must abide rules forbidding writing in books that were public property. Moreover, as this is a lending library whose holdings have been systematically renewed and purged over time, the chances that it retains a copy with Borges's handwritten notes are slim compared to other archives in which he worked. Borges's indexing notations have been identified in just a few philosophy texts and some others in which the call numbers have been proofed and replaced, a crease in the paper being the only trace that has survived to testify to the classification tasks he performed at that library and which he chronicled in his work.[7] Despite not being enriched by his marginalia, the composition of the municipal library's holdings was, in part, determined by Borges's reading aesthetics. Part of his work was to assemble the desiderata requesting purchase of the complete collection—during those years—of the *Everyman's Library*, which is still preserved today in a small shelf to one side of the reading room.[8] Beyond these artifacts, little remains of his time at this institution. Borges's professional performance at Miguel Cané can unambiguously be defined as mediocre, to the degree that his ambition was focused exclusively on elaborating his own works of writing.[9]

In another order of things, the Miguel Cané as a *locus* for his writing is also revealed in the materiality of the supplies used for drafting some of his manuscripts. We know that Borges used flyleaves, the insides of front and back covers, and even the backs of books

120   LAURA ROSATO AND GERMÁN ÁLVAREZ

and notebooks for his marginalia, pre-texts, and pre-writing compositions. He generally used different types of school notebooks, such as the Avon or Lanceros Argentinos
brand of 1910. We also know from the discovery of the manuscript of "La muerte y la
brújula" (1942) on a letterhead titled "Comisión Honoraria de Bibliotecas Públicas
Municipales" [Honorary Commission of Municipal Public Libraries] (Helft 115) that he
used the official stationery he had on hand in the library for his writing. Additionally,
the manuscript of "La lotería en Babilonia," preserved in Buenos Aires, is written on
letterhead from "Impuestos Argentinos de la Nación" [Argentine National Tax Office]
(Balderston 149). Borges also included the use of official stationery in his fiction. In "El
Aleph," Carlos Argentino Daneri, epitome of the mediocre litterateur, writes his would-
be poetic masterpiece on letterhead from the fictitious "Biblioteca Juan Crisóstomo
Lafinur."

In Borges's case, creative processes are represented as interchangeable links in a living
chain connecting reading and writing. During his time at the Miguel Cané Library, the
work environment was also a place for creation and reading:

> Hacía todo el trabajo de la biblioteca en una hora y después me escapaba al sótano,
> donde pasaba las otras cinco horas leyendo o escribiendo. Así leí los seis volúmenes
> de la *Historia de la decadencia y caída del Imperio Romano* de Gibbon y la *Historia de
> la República Argentina* de Vicente Fidel López. Leí a Léon Bloy, a Claudel, a Groussac
> y a Bernard Shaw. (*Autobiografía* 108)

> [I would do all my library work in the first hour and then steal away to the basement
> and pass the other five hours in reading or writing. I remember in this way rereading
> the six volumes of Gibbon's *Decline and Fall* and the many volumes of Vicente Fidel
> Lopez's *History of the Argentine Republic*. I read Léon Bloy, Claudel, Groussac, and
> Bernard Shaw.] ("Autobiographical" 170)

The lack of annotation in the volumes of the Miguel Cané collection leads us to believe
that, as he would during his time at the BNMM, Borges used books he had at home
during this period.[10] A large part of these volumes in his personal library undoubtedly
belong to the period of his greatest literary production, which coincides exactly with the
years of work in the Miguel Cané library.

If we follow the marks that are unequivocally those that Borges's used to date when he
read a given copy from his library, we can reconstruct a map of the authors and themes
that interested him during those years of work and literary production. For the year 1938,
which coincides with his start at the library, the readings of eclectic subjects stand out,
ranging from an analysis of the dream world, to popular nonfiction books by the famous
philosopher of science Hermann von Helmholtz, a classic study on metrics in English poetry, and several books by H. G. Wells, which he later reviewed for *La Nación* (Rosato and
Álvarez, *Borges, libros y lecturas* 354). In 1939, what stands out are *Conversations of Goethe
with Eckermann* (128), which he discussed at length with Bioy Casares; a book of essays on
James Joyce's last work, *Our Exagmination Round his Factification for Incamination of Work
in Progress* (257), whose notes he will use to write "El último libro de Joyce" [Joyce's Latest

Book] (*El Hogar*, June 16, 1939) and "Joyce y los neologismos" [Joyce and Neologisms] (*Sur*, November 1939); and Bertrand Russell's *The Principles of Mathematics* (301), used in the argument for his essay "Los avatares de la tortuga" [Avatars of the Tortoise] (*Sur*, December 1939).

In 1940, he noted a book by Ernst Cassirer (Rosato and Álvarez, *Borges, libros y lecturas* 85) from which he took the argument of Pietro Damiani, attributed to San Anselmo, which he would use in the short story "La otra muerte" [The Other Death] (*El Aleph* [1949]). Of more immediate use was the reading of *Pain, Sex and Time* by Gerald Heard (184), a book whose review will appear in *Sur* (May 1941), or Edmund Gosse's book *Father and Son* (166), whose notes form the essay "La creación y P. H. Gosse" [Creation and P. H. Gosse] (*Sur*, June 1941). The following year is prodigious and miscellaneous in titles and authors: Samuel Butler (82), Cicero's *De Natura Deorum* (87), Rabelais' *Gargantua et Pantagruel* (272), Paul Deussen's edition of Schopenhauer's magnum opus *Die Welt als Wille und Vorstellung* (304); as well, he read and annotated a critical work on Edgar Allan Poe and the essays of Oscar Wilde. Between 1942 and 1945, the number of readings found decreases markedly and then increases sharply in 1946, which coincides with his last period at the post and his departure in June of that year.

THE FALL

Borges's departure from the Miguel Cané library had nothing to do with his work performance, and, while the historical account insists on representing the episode as a duel between Borges and Perón, the incident was just another pawn in the conflict between the enlightened elites and, in this case, nationalist groups aligned with Peronism. To understand the true story of Borges's estrangement from the Miguel Cané Library, we must refer to the National Literature Awards of the 1939–1941 triennium, where *El jardín de senderos que se bifurcan* [*The Garden of Forking Paths*] did not even receive a mention. In an article explaining this exclusion, Roberto Giusti, a member of the Advisory Commission of the awards, cited the jury's conclusions that Borges's book was a "juego cerebral" [cerebral game], "literatura deshumanizada" [dehumanized literature] and an "obra exótica y de decadencia" [exotic and decadent work] ("Los premios" 116). A month before, when reviewing his friend's book, Adolfo Bioy Casares had conjectured the possibility of an unfavorable reading. The article so presciently anticipated the jury's objections that it is not unreasonable to imagine he had prior information about the discussions surrounding the prize (Bioy Casares, "Jorge Luis Borges" 62–63). What is certain is that, in 1942, Sur publishing house's big bet was on *El jardín de senderos que se bifurcan*, and this relegation sat very poorly with the intellectuals gathered there. In July 1942, the journal *Sur* published a special issue known as "Desagravio a Borges" [Reparation to Borges]. An atmosphere of incomprehension and dismissal began to surround Borges, which would permeate the closed-mindedness of the officials in office.[11]

In August 1946, Borges was subjected to a new affront. This time, according to some sources (not entirely reliable, as we will discuss below), he was removed from his modest position and transferred to the poultry and rabbit inspection office "en el mercado público de la calle Córdoba" [at the public market on Calle Córdoba] (Rodríguez Monegal 352).[12] Strictly speaking, this was a promotion from second assistant to inspector. However, accounts by friends such as Alicia Jurado and Victoria Ocampo do not coincide with the formal aspect of the *affaire*, nor with the dates (Jurado 55; Ocampo 22–23). If we read Jurado carefully, we are inclined to date the episode to the days prior to June 4, 1946, the days of General Farrell's provisional presidency, before Perón took office. However, none of this can be proved because "por lo menos bajo la forma de registraciones o datos administrativos fehacientes, como la publicación del acto desencadenante en el *Boletín Oficial*, al uso de la época" [at least in the form of records or reliable administrative data, such as the publication of the promotion in the *Official Gazette*, in use at the time], there is no trace of the transfer from library assistant to "Inspector de aves y huevos" [Inspector of Poultry and Rabbits] (Rivera 36). This is rather curious, because other transfers to the Civil Registry between June and December 1941 are mentioned (Rivera 36). Although there is no record that this actually took place (Vaccaro 354), given this lack of documentary evidence, we suspect that the real background for Borges's removal from office was his signature— as an active member of the Unión Democrática political party—on several petitions calling for the prevention of the rise to power of what he considered to be populist totalitarianism.[13]

On January 8, 1946, while there was a decree in force that prohibited public employees from participating in political parties, Borges signed an adherence to the Unión Democrática in the newspaper *La Prensa* (Rivera 35). That same month, the Dirección de Sumarios [Directorate of Disciplinary Action] requested a copy of his work record and initiated disciplinary action for his being an "infringer" of the rules. Shortly thereafter, by means of a decree dated April 15, 1946, under file number 669/46, Borges was sanctioned with the minimum penalty, "atenuada por su condición de empleado que goza de un concepto inmejorable y por su competencia, dedicación y condiciones personales" [mitigated by his condition as an employee who enjoys an incomparable reputation and by his competence, dedication and personal conditions] (Rivera 35–6). Thus, being disciplined for exercising a civic right, rather than being transferred under the Peronist government, was the real reason for Borges's resignation between June 4 and 28, 1946 (Rivera 36).

At the beginning of August, at a banquet offered by the Sociedad Argentina de Escritores [Argentine Society of Writers] (SADE), Borges gave a talk that marked the beginning of his official account of the events leading to his removal from office. The text was reproduced by the magazine *Argentina Libre*[14] under the title "Dele, dele":

> Nueve años concurrí a esa biblioteca, nueve años que serán en el recuerdo una sola tarde, una tarde monstruosa en cuyo decurso clasifiqué un número infinito de libros

y el Reich devoró a Francia y el Reich no devoró las islas Británicas, y el nazismo, arrojado de Berlín, buscó nuevas regiones. En algún resquicio de esa tarde única, yo temerariamente firmé alguna declaración democrática; hace un día o un mes o un año platónico, me ordenaron que prestara servicios en la policía municipal. Maravillado por ese brusco avatar administrativo, fui a la Intendencia. Me confiaron, ahí, que esa metamorfosis era un castigo por haber firmado aquellas declaraciones. Mientras yo recibía la noticia con debido interés, me distrajo un cartel que decoraba la solemne oficina. Era rectangular y lacónico, de formato considerable, y registraba el interesante epigrama *Dele-Dele*. No recuerdo la cara de mi interlocutor, no recuerdo su nombre, pero hasta el día de mi muerte recordaré esa estrafalaria inscripción. *Tendré que renunciar*, repetí, al bajar las escaleras de la Intendencia, pero mi destino personal me importaba menos que ese cartel simbólico. (5)

[Nine years I went to that library, nine years that will remain in my memory a single afternoon, a monstrous afternoon in the course of which I catalogued an infinite number of books and the Reich devoured France, and the Reich did not devour the British Isles, and Nazism, thrown out of Berlin, sought new regions. At some breaking point that single afternoon, I recklessly signed some democratic declaration; a day or a month or a platonic year later, I was ordered to serve in the municipal police. Amazed by that abrupt administrative change, I went to the city hall. They confided to me, there, that this metamorphosis was a punishment for having signed those declarations. While I received the news with due interest, I was distracted by a poster decorating the solemn office. It was rectangular and laconic, of considerable format, and it stated the interesting epigram *Dele-Dele*. I don't remember the face of my interlocutor, I don't remember his name, but until the day I die I will remember that bizarre inscription. *I will have to resign*, I repeated, as I descended the stairs from the city hall, but my personal fate mattered less to me than that symbolic sign.]

That "laconic" poster, and the "bizarre" inscription that serves as the title of the text, contain a key symbol that would determine the version of what happened from here on. It refers to a slogan that manifested itself in graffiti and cheers of "Dele, dele, general," which, in the government of the 1943 revolution, celebrated the appointment of the then Colonel Juan Domingo Perón as Secretary of Labor and Welfare. But, in time, in a single move, Borges would change the sequence of events: the warning for supporting the Unión Democrática, which was in favor of the Allies, and the alleged transfer to market inspector.

With his departure from the Miguel Cané Municipal Library, Borges shored up his image as an intellectual opponent of General Perón's "regime" and began a new period of resistance through his work, especially through the lectures and courses he gave in Buenos Aires and the interior of Argentina.[15] In these lectures and from the SADE, over which he presided between 1950 and 1953, Borges put his aesthetic-political position into play against the Peronist "dictatorship" and in favor of liberties and civil rights. Perhaps, unconsciously, he was preparing the ground for his future as a government official in charge of the most important public library in the country.

The National Library

With the so-called Revolución Libertadora of 1955 and the fall of the Peronist government, Borges became Director of the BNMM. In 1957, Arturo Jauretche, always attentive to the uncertain twists and turns in Argentine history, reasoned—not without some sarcasm,

> Yo no digo que Borges no tenga motivos para estar enojado; lo echaron de un empleíto que tenía en la Municipalidad, con una revolución. Con otra lo hicieron director de la Biblioteca Nacional. Algo hemos ganado, porque lo veo más para director de biblioteca que para andar mirando balanzas y almacenes rosados. (80)

> [I am not saying that Borges has no reason to be angry; he was fired from a little job he had with the Municipality with one revolution. With the other, they made him director of the National Library. We've gained something, because I see him more suited to be a library director than to go around looking at scales and pink stores.]

In the polemic style he was known for, Jauretche is referring to the 1943 revolution that saw Borges removed from his post at the Miguel Cané. Borges, for his part, gave his version of events in his "An Autobiographical Essay," where he had the opportunity to present his memories, tailored to the measure of his myth: "Dos amigas muy queridas, Esther Zemborain de Torres y Victoria Ocampo, concibieron la posibilidad de que se me nombrara director de la Biblioteca Nacional. Pensé que era un disparate: esperaba como mucho que me dieran la dirección de una pequeña biblioteca de barrio, preferentemente por el sur de la ciudad" [Two very dear friends of mine, Esther Zemborain de Torres and Victoria Ocampo, dreamed up the possibility of my being appointed Director of the National Library. I thought the scheme a wild one, and hoped at most to be given the directorship of some small-town library, preferably to the south of the city] (*Autobiografía* 124; "Autobiographical Essay" 176). Indeed, Borges suggested the possibility of an appointment in the municipal library of Adrogué or Lomas de Zamora, towns far to the south in the province of Buenos Aires.[16] "No sea estúpido Borges; pediremos la Biblioteca Nacional" [Don't be stupid Borges; we will ask for the National Library] was Victoria Ocampo's categorical response to this surprising lack of ambition.

Thus, although Borges, for ethical reasons or for modesty, had not personally applied for a position in the government for which he had militated, he did not object when an intermediary with strong political connections, such as Victoria Ocampo, demanded what she considered appropriate for him. Bioy Casares, in his diary, sums up his friend's mood: "la alegría de Borges era sin matices; no podía uno hablar de otra cosa, porque parecía inoportuno" [Borges's joy was without nuance; you couldn't speak of anything else, because it seemed rude] (Bioy Casares 143). His inauguration took place on October 26, 1955, in the building at 564 Mexico Street. In spite of the government's reticence due to his blindness and his lack of academic credentials, the appointment was more than correct; Jorge Luis Borges's management, which lasted eighteen years despite the country's transition through several governments, created a position for the library in the world that was commensurate with the author's rise to international fame (Vaccaro 528).[17] From his office, Borges would dedicate himself to writing under the influence and inspiration of the new government, which only deepened the stylistic turn he had already made, highlighting his opposition to the previous government's slogan: "Alpargatas sí; libros no" [Espadrilles yes; books no]. He expressed as much, when he was interviewed by *Propósitos* immediately after assuming leadership of the library in November 1955.

> La revolución tiene que traer un renacimiento en nuestra cultura. No es un hecho exclusivamente político-militar. Es un proceso que se ha realizado en cada uno de nosotros; un proceso emocional. Los escritores tienen una magnífica oportunidad para dejar de retrotraerse a la figura del gaucho que no han tenido ocasión de analizar, o al ambiente del arrabal que no han vivido. Ahora viven instantes que cobrarán con el tiempo carácter de mito. . . . Laten en mí poemas de la Revolución que pronto saldrán a la luz. (*Textos recobrados* 377)

> [The revolution has to bring about a renaissance in our culture. It is not an exclusively political-military event. It is a process that has taken place in each one of us; an emotional process. Writers have a magnificent opportunity to stop returning to the figure of the gaucho who they've never had the opportunity to analyze, or to the atmosphere of the urban outskirts they've never lived in. Now they are living moments that will eventually take on a mythological character. . . . There beat in my heart poems of the Revolution that will soon come to light.]

WRITING IN THE LIBRARY

Borges indeed felt compelled to "Apoyar la obra de la Revolución" [Support the work of the Revolution] as he stated in a survey included in the November 2, 1956, issue of *El Hogar*. To this end, he embarked on the publication of a series of texts, some new and others already published, in what was unquestionably a gesture of political commitment. He reissued "Poema conjetural" [Conjectural Poem] (*La Nación*, July 4, 1943), a powerfully symbolic text with respect to nationalism and, especially, to Peronism. This poem had already been included as an epilogue in *Aspectos de la literatura gauchesca* [*Aspects of Gauchesque Literature*] (1950), then in *Nueve poemas* [*Nine Poems*] (1955), in *Antología personal* [*Personal Anthology*] (1961), and in the fourth edition of *El otro, el mismo* [*The Other, The Same*] (1964). The same happened with "El escritor argentino y la tradición" [The Argentine Writer and Tradition], which had appeared in the January-February-March 1953 issue of the journal *Cursos y Conferencias* and was included again in *Sur*'s January-February 1955 issue. Borges applied Pierre Menard's concept, proposing to re-read these texts in a new context in order to disrupt—or point out—their multiple interpretations. In other words, the context changed the meaning, intensified it, or turned the same into different.

More direct is the text he published in the second period of *La Biblioteca*, the BNMM's magazine, entitled "El simulacro" [The Simulacrum] (1957).[18] There, he describes Peronism as "una crasa mitología" [a crass and ignoble mythology] (*OC* II: 167; *CF* 302) that defined "la cifra de una época irreal" [the symbol of an unreal time] (*OC* II: 167; *CF* 301). The story evokes the national funeral rites for the death of Eva Perón as a farce "para el crédulo amor de los arrabales" [for the credulous love of the working class] (*OC* II: 167; *CF* 302). It is written in a violently crude style impregnated with an atmosphere of unreality comparable to that of "La fiesta del monstruo" [The Monster's Party], which Bioy Casares and Borges wrote toward the end of the 1940s, although it was not published until 1955.

By that time, as a palpable consequence of his blindness, he had also returned to classical metrical verse, which he considered portable (*Autobiografía* 128). His second in charge, José Edmundo Clemente,[19] left a valuable testimony of Borges's method of literary production at the Library:

> Borges se acostumbró, por la imposición física, al trabajo corto, pequeño, que podía ser memorizado. Entonces él solía dar vueltas por la sala de lectura de la Biblioteca Nacional, la sala grande, paseándose hablando solo. Estaba recitándose a sí mismo y corrigiendo su memoria. Y cuando tenía el texto bien armado llamaba a su secretaria y se lo dictaba. Después, la secretaria lo tenía que recitar y él hacía las correcciones que correspondía. (25)

> [Borges became accustomed, because of physical need, to works that were short, small, that could be memorized. So he would circle the reading room of the National Library, the big room, walking around talking to himself. He was reciting to himself and correcting his memory. And when he had the text really well assembled, he would call his secretary and dictate it to her. Afterwards, the secretary had to recite it and he would make the corrections needed.]

Among all he produced during this period, the "Poema de los dones" [Poem of the Gifts] of 1959, which summarizes the essence of the moment and, at the same time, unites his name with that of his predecessor, Paul Groussac, is remarkable (*OC* II: 188).

This procedure was part of what we might define as the "inclusion of his name," that is, his inserting himself into a legacy to thus form part of that tradition. Such is particularly the case when he writes the "Intenciones" [Intentions] for the revival of the National Library's magazine *La Biblioteca*. Yet the most intimate book from that period is *El hacedor* (1960), a text miscellaneous in nature, composed of poems and short pieces of limpid prose that still "abunda en reflejos e interpolaciones" [abounds in reflections and interpolations] (*OC* II: 232; *CF* 327). From the volume's very first text, which gives *El hacedor* its name, Borges seeks to identify himself with Homer, the blind bard of classical culture. This piece functions as *El hacedor*'s opening and its poetic manifesto. The book has a dedication to Leopoldo Lugones, which describes a dream that, transcending space and time, conjures an "escena imposible" [scene that is impossible]: a meeting between Borges and Lugones that blurs the boundaries between them and entangles their official offices while at the same time serving as a tribute (*OC* II: 157; *CF* 291). Borges feels that he is closing the circle he began to forge many years before, and that, finally, he might begin to inscribe his name next to that of the man often described as Argentina's greatest writer.

As Ricardo Piglia points out, the years of work at the Miguel Cané municipal library coincide with the period of Borges's best work. The time he spent directing the BNMM was the period of his international consolidation, during which he was transformed from a moderately recognized local writer to an author whose international fame exceeded literary representations. This process was closely aligned with the organization and translation of Borges's work, which occurred simultaneously with his management of the National Library. Borges felt secure and happy in his position at the BNMM and was invited by foreign institutions to give lectures and teach classes.[20] Additionally, he alternated these activities with his teaching duties as a professor of English Literature at the Faculty of Philosophy and Letters of the University of Buenos Aires, a position he had held since 1957.

Around this same time, he began writing short stories again. Borges had not published any new material in this genre since 1953, though "no dejaba de elaborar mentalmente" [he never stopped working on it mentally] (di Giovanni 28). He spent his days directing the BNMM between the translation of his work into English and the edition of his *Obras completas* for Emecé. International recognition was arriving simultaneously with the consolidation of his work and his image at the national level.

THE LIBRARY OF DREAMS

The southern neighborhoods of Buenos Aires embodied, for Borges, the true and secret center of the city—the outskirts he describes in his early poetry books. His relationship to the Library as building was so dear that, at some point at the beginning of his administration, he contemplated moving—as previous directors had done—to live on the second floor of that house of books. In his 1984 book *Atlas*, Borges states that the building remained in his dreams: "Nunca sueño con el presente sino con un Buenos Aires pretérito y con las galerías y claraboyas de la Biblioteca Nacional en la calle México" [I never dream of the present but of a Buenos Aires of the past and of the galleries and skylights of the National Library on Calle Mexico] (63). Parodically, like the play within a play immortalized by Shakespeare, those rooms also function as a stage set for some of the dreams and nightmares found in Borges's fiction of that time. In this regard, we analyze a few stories from the book Borges used to bid farewell to his directorship of the BNMM, *El libro de arena* [*The Book of Sand*] (1975), "El Congreso" [The Congress], "Utopía de un hombre que está cansado" [A Weary Man's Utopia], and the eponymous "El libro de arena."

"El Congreso" is "quizás la más ambiciosa de las fábulas de este libro" [perhaps the most ambitious of the fables in this book] (*OC* III: 72; *CF* 484). For biographer James Woodall, the tale "da la impresión de una nueva versión urbana de 'La biblioteca de Babel'" [gives the impression of an updated, urban version of 'La biblioteca de Babel'] (313). In fact, if we extrapolate, "El Congreso" and "El libro de arena" function—in Borges's work and in their respective periods—similarly to "La biblioteca de Babel" and "La lotería en Babilonia." He points out the Kafkaesque atmosphere that, beginning with their titles, associates them with "The Castle" or "The Trial." He also includes himself in the plot by placing a version of himself in his post: "El nuevo director de la Biblioteca, me dicen, es un literato que se ha consagrado al estudio de las lenguas antiguas, como si las actuales no fueran suficientemente rudimentarias, y a la exaltación demagógica de un imaginario Buenos Aires de cuchilleros. Nunca he querido conocerlo" [The new director of the library, I am told, is a literary gentleman who has devoted himself to the study of antique languages, as though the languages of today were not sufficiently primitive, and to the demagogical glorification of an imaginary Buenos Aires of knife fighters. I have never wished to meet him] (*OC* III: 20; *CF* 422–23). Details such as the Kafkaesque atmosphere or "la crisis de misticismo" [the crisis of mysticism] that Borges sees in himself are revealed again; the author-character is reliving the experience of being estranged from Miguel Cané and its pathos associated with state bureaucracy, this time pertaining to his directorship of the National Library and his being forced to leave the position in the wake of Peronism's return to power.

In "Utopía de un hombre que está cansado," Borges creates a future where books, languages, the humanities, cities, museums, libraries, history itself, are abolished. In other words, memory. Borges once said that libraries represented the world's memory; with this story, he reveals his position on Peronism's return to power—and his subsequent sorrow at being removed from his position at the Library.[21] As in the previous story, Borges provides some autobiographical details. In closing, he ends up in one of the rooms in the Library: "En mi escritorio de la calle México guardo la tela que alguien pintará, dentro de miles de años, con materiales hoy dispersos en el planeta" [In my study on Calle Mexico still hangs the canvas that someone will paint, thousands of years from now, with substances that now are scattered around the planet] (*OC* III: 56; *CF* 465). Moreover, with the final lines of "La biblioteca de Babel," Borges anticipates the theme of the closing story in the 1975 volume, making "El libro de arena" function as an interchangeable or equivalent variation of the 1941 story (*OC* I: 471; *CF* 118). So the character Borges, who has already retired from the National Library, decides to rid himself of the object that "infamaba y corrompía la realidad" [defiled and corrupted reality] taking direction from a quote from Chesterton's "The Sign of the Broken Sword": "que el mejor lugar para ocultar una hoja es un bosque" [that the best place to hide a leaf is in the forest] (*OC* III: 71; *CF* 483). He loses the volume among the basement shelves of the building on Mexico Street, a practice that was not, in fact, foreign to him.[22]

Origin of the Collection

In March 1973, Peronism, with its party leader in Spain, ran for and won national elections in Argentina. Héctor Cámpora assumed the presidency while preparing for the return of the exiled Juan Domingo Perón, who was ultimately elected president in September of the same year. Borges, from his office, inferred that his time at the head of the National Library was coming to an end but speculated about the right time and the right way to leave office. Repeating the exit strategy he used when leaving the Miguel Cané Library, Borges stayed in his post, hoping the new government, from its position of power, would make the first move: "No voy a renunciar. Dejaré que me echen y que carguen con la impopularidad de la opinión mundial que el hecho pueda traerles" [I won't resign. I'll let them throw me out and they can live with the unpopularity that brings them in world opinion] (Bioy Casares 1402). On October 8 of that year, and in the absence of any reaction on the part of the government, he requested his retirement, which was granted in the record time of seventy-two hours. In a last act of generosity toward the Library, Borges left the set of books from his personal library that had informed his literary production during his tenure at the BNMM. In keeping with his personal ethics, he bequeathed these books as a "secret donation," leaving no administrative record. These volumes had accumulated in Paul Groussac's former office, which Borges had implemented as an extension of his home. The set included readings from his childhood, books inherited from his father's mythical library, and a few works he requested for consultation and reference from the Library's general stacks. He had brought them over from his home to assist in the editing process of his *Obras completas* and in the English translations of his work, both of which required cross-checking the sources he used to compose his early texts and the readings he had relied on that inspired the main corpus of his work, as well as new publications, such as the first version of *El libro de los seres imaginarios* [*The Book of Imaginary Beings*] (1967), called *Manual de zoología fantástica* (1957). Anthologies such as *El libro del cielo y el infierno* [*The Book of Heaven and Hell*] (1960), a volume on the theme of the double (which never materialized) and the late *El libro de sueños* [*The Book of Dreams*] (1976) also required having the readings cataloguing these types of texts on hand.

Consequently, the Jorge Luis Borges Collection of the BNMM is the documentary legacy of the writer's literary work during the years he was director of the National Library. It includes books from Borges's youth in Europe until the 1970s, when he left the BNMM. As a manner of structuring the work, most of the volumes' dates coincide with the most prolific stage of Borges's literary production, spanning the 1930s and 1940s. These books represent the link between the campaign of reading and writing that Borges undertook while working at the Miguel Cané—which we define as the creation of the foundational corpus of his work—and his second campaign, once at the BNMM, of revising, consolidating, and organizing the texts to be included in his *Obras completas*. This collection is one of the most important documentary testimonies of Borges's *modus legendi*, and it holds the keys to the internal scaffolding upon which he built his work.

We indicated at the beginning of this chapter the need to disambiguate the Miguel Cané Library from the BNMM and to distinguish the two workplaces in terms of Borges's stages of literary production and the social and political context in which they took place. However, despite the differences, we can perceive a movement that traverses both periods, the rigorous construction of an oeuvre and a public image. Thus, the aesthetic and political decisions made during his time at the Miguel Cané determined both the subsequent reception of Borges's work and the consolidation of his position as a diehard opponent of the most relevant political movement in Argentina since the mid-twentieth century and up to the present. The distance from the aesthetics of the *arrabal* [outskirt slums], the systematic expurgation of "local color," and the identification, if not always explicit, with Kafka, the author who best represents the *zeitgeist*, are some of the keys to the universal character of Borges's work. At the same time, the choice of the library as the locus of his fictions, the double value—nightmare/paradise—attributed to this space in "La biblioteca de Babel" and the "Poema de los dones" directly relates to his life and is less the product of a "cerebral game" than a fictionalized version of his work experiences. Given this choice, the image of the blind librarian, locked up in his high house of books and willfully ignorant of the vicissitudes of daily life, gives way to that of the intellectual committed to his political ideals.

Notes

1. *Historia de la eternidad* [*A History of Eternity*] (1936) had sold only thirty-seven copies a year later.
2. Public employment was not only exercised by intellectuals related to the Argentine elite, as was the case of Paul Groussac. This practice was extended over time and thus, those young literary figures coming from the middle class or petty bourgeoisie could access their first job thanks to a low-ranking public position, which they complemented with paid literary collaborations. Some other examples are Leopoldo Lugones, Ezequiel Martinez Estrada, and, closer to Borges, Francisco Luis Bernárdez and Horacio Schiavo, both colleagues at the Miguel Cané.
3. On February 24, 1938, Jorge Guillermo Borges died. A few days after his death Borges wrote the poem "A mi padre" [To my father]. See Balderston and Martín 87–90.
4. On February 18, the writer Leopoldo Lugones committed suicide. See Borges's obituary in *Sur* (no. 41, feb. 1938, pp. 57–58).
5. *Traumkristalle: Neue Märchen* (Rie und Immer, 2), Leipzig, B. Clischer Nachfolger, n.d. The story referred to is "Die Universalbibliothek." A copy of this work that belonged to Borges and is dated 1937 can be found in the National Library.
6. *Franz Kafkas Glauben und Lehre: (Kafka und Tolstoi).* Winterthur, Mondial Verlag, 1948 (*Borges, libros y lecturas* 70).
7. In the 1952 postscript to the "Epilogue" of *The Aleph*, Borges recalls how the plot of "La espera" [The Wait] came about, "una crónica policial que Alfredo Doblas me leyó, hará diez años, mientras clasificábamos libros según el manual del Instituto Bibliográfico de Bruselas, código del que todo he olvidado, salvo que a Dios le corresponde la cifra 231" [a true police story that Alfredo Doblas read me, some ten years ago, while we were

WORKS AND DAYS   131

classifying books—following the manual of the Bibliographic Institute of Brussels, I might add, a code I have entirely forgotten save for the detail that God can be found under the number 231] (*OC* I: 630; *CF* 288).

8. In this case, at the time of ordering the purchase, Borges criteria for the selection was considerably more humanistic than corresponded to a library of Miguel Cané's nature.

9. A copy of his service record found in the library's records cites multiple warnings for his repeated, often unexcused absences.

10. José Edmundo Clemente, deputy director of the National Library, testifies that Borges, in his day-to-day work, "used his personal library," the one he had had since his youth (Clemente 43).

11. For more on this issue of *Sur*, see Podlubne.

12. In fact, it was called Mercado de Concentración Municipal de Aves, Huevos y Afines (Rivera 31).

13. Formed by a broad coalition between the Radical Civic Union and sectors of conservative parties.

14. The magazine was a liberal anti-fascist publication. The text is also reproduced in *Sur*, August 1946, with the title "Palabras pronunciadas por Jorge Luis Borges en la comida que le ofrecieron los escritores" [Words pronounced by Jorge Luis Borges at the dinner given to writers].

15. See Blanco's chapter in this volume for more on Borges's talks.

16. He was offered the directorship of the Cultural Commission of the Province of Buenos Aires, which he declined.

17. Shortly thereafter, in April 1956, he was awarded his first honorary doctorate by the University of Cuyo.

18. Later included in *El hacedor* [*Dreamtigers*] (1960).

19. Writer and professional librarian who had worked with Borges at Emecé between 1948 and 1955. He was responsible for having convinced Bonifacio del Carril, in 1953, to start editing Borges's *Complete Works* at the same publishing house. He was appointed deputy director of the BNMM, in charge of operational management tasks.

20. In 1961, Borges was invited to teach a semester at the University of Texas, and he returned to the United States again in 1967 and 1969. In 1963, he traveled to England and Scotland. This decade thus saw the start of a long international tour that would not cease until the end of his days.

21. The story first appeared in *La Nación*, Buenos Aires, May 5, 1974.

22. In 2013, six unbound copies of the journal *Sur* with corrections in Borges's handwriting were located at the BNMM.

Works Cited

Balderston, Daniel. *El método Borges*. Ampersand, 2021.

Balderston, Daniel, and María Celeste Martín. *Poemas & prosas breves. Jorge Luis Borges*. Borges Center, 2018.

Bioy Casares, Adolfo. *Borges*. Destino, 2006.

Bioy Casares, Adolfo. "Jorge Luis Borges. *El jardín de senderos que se bifurcan*." *Sur*, no. 92, May 1942, pp. 60–65.

Borges, Jorge Luis. *Autobiografía*. El Ateneo, 1999.

Borges, Jorge Luis. "An Autobiographical Essay." *The Aleph and Other Stories, 1933–1969: Together with Commentaries and an Autobiographical Essay*. Edited by di Giovanni, Thomas, Bantam, 1971, pp. 135–88.

Borges, Jorge Luis. *Borges en Sur (1931–1980)*. Emecé, 1999.

Borges, Jorge Luis. *Collected Fictions*, translated by Andrew Hurley. Penguin, 1998.

Borges, Jorge Luis. *Obras completas*. 4 vols. Emecé, 1996.

Borges, Jorge Luis. *Textos recobrados (1931–1955)*. Emecé, 2001.

Borges, Jorge Luis, and María Kodama. *Atlas*. Editorial Sudamericana, 1984.

Clemente, José Edmundo, and Oscar Sbarra Mitre. *Borges: Director de la Biblioteca Nacional*. Ediciones Biblioteca Nacional, 1998.

Di Giovanni, Norman Thomas. *La lección del maestro*. Editorial Sudamericana, 2002.

Giusti, Roberto. "Los premios nacionales de literatura." *Nosotros*, vol. 2, no. 76, July 1942, pp. 114–16.

Helft, Nicolás. *Borges: Postales de una biografía*. Emecé, 2013.

Irby, James E. "Entrevista con Borges." *Revista de la Universidad de México*, 16.10 1962, pp. 4–10.

Jauretche, Arturo. *Los profetas del odio*. Ediciones Trafac, 1957.

Jurado, Alicia. *Genio y figura de Jorge Luis Borges*. EUDEBA, 1997.

Ocampo, Victoria. "Visión de Jorge Luis Borges." *Cahiers de L'Herne*, no. 4, 1964, pp. 19–25.

Piglia, Ricardo. *Formas breves*. Anagrama, 2013.

Podlubne, Judith. "Sur 1942: El 'Desgravio a Borges' o el doble juego del reconocimiento." *Variaciones Borges*, vol. 27, 2009, pp. 43–66.

Rivera, Jorge B. "Borges, ficha 57.323." *Acerca de Borges: Ensayos de poética, política y literatura comparada*, Editorial de Belgrano. Edited by Jorge Dubatti, 1999, pp. 27–41.

Rodríguez Monegal, Emir. *Borges, una biografía literaria*. Fondo de Cultura Económica, 1987.

Rosato, Laura, and Germán Álvarez. *Borges, libros y lecturas*. Biblioteca Nacional, 2017.

Rosato, Laura, and Germán Álvarez. *Borges el mismo, otro. Una lógica simbólica: Manuscritos de Jorge Luis Borges en la Biblioteca Nacional*. Biblioteca Nacional, 2016.

Rosato, Laura, and Germán Álvarez. "Colección Jorge Luis Borges de la Biblioteca Nacional: una hipótesis de trabajo." *Variaciones Borges*, vol. 46, 2018, pp. 77–91.

Saítta, Sylvia. "De este lado de la verja: Jorge Luis Borges y los usos del periodismo moderno." *Variaciones Borges*, vol. 9, 2000, pp. 74–83.

Sarlo, Beatriz. *Borges, un escritor en las orillas*. Ariel, 1992.

Sarlo, Beatriz. "Lector esquivo." *Borges lector, Biblioteca Nacional*. Edited by Rosato Laura and Germán Álvarez, 2011, pp. 7–11.

Vaccaro, Alejandro. *Borges: vida y literatura*. Edhasa, 2006.

Woodall, James. *La vida de Jorge Luis Borges: El hombre en el espejo del libro*. Gedisa, 1998.

PART II

REPRESENTATIVE WORKS

CHAPTER 8

ORALITY AND LITERACY IN BORGES

Two Manuscripts of "Del culto de los libros"
[On the Cult of Books]

DANIEL BALDERSTON

ONE of the most important essays in *Otras inquisiciones* [*Other Inquisitions*] (1952) is "Del culto de los libros," first published in *La Nación* on July 8, 1951 (Figure 8.1). This famous discussion of what Borges calls the "sacred" nature of books begins and ends with Mallarmé's phrase "Tout, au monde, existe pour aboutir à un livre,"[1] which Borges wittingly contrasts with an excerpt from Shaw's *Caesar and Cleopatra* about the library of Alexandria: "Theodotus. 'What is burning there is the memory of mankind.' Caesar. 'A shameful memory. Let it burn'" (Act II). The defense of literature that opens with these two quotations then moves from Pythagoras and Plato and Clement of Alexandria[2] to the Bible and the Qur'an, from Al-Ghazali to Scholem, Sérouya, and Deussen on the Kabbalah, to Bacon and Browne, and then to Bloy and Mallarmé: around the world in three or four pages. In this chapter, after a brief discussion of the essay itself, I then move to an analysis of the extant manuscripts, which will show how much research and synthesis Borges did for a newspaper article, but also the ways in which it was probably an intervention in debates about Argentine culture, particularly heated at that moment of the Peronist decade.

Perhaps the most notable passage in "Del culto" is a quotation from Book Six of Augustine's *Confessions*, which Borges signals as culturally important because it announces the move from reading aloud (with its reminiscences of the oral culture of Homer and of the peripatetic philosophers) to silent reading. From Plato he derives a skepticism about writing against oral teaching, and, of course, he shares Plato's admiration for Socrates's skills as an oral teacher.[3] He also works in a good deal of information on Greek literature and philosophy, with his main source being H. R. Rose's *A Handbook*

FIGURE 8.1 "Del culto de los libros" in *La Nación*, 8 July 1951.

Source: Courtesy of the Biblioteca Nacional Mariano Moreno.

of Greek Literature.[4] Passing from orality to literacy, he notes what Augustine says of his teacher, Ambrose, who was then the bishop of Milan:

> As he read, his eyes scanned the pages and his heart searched out the meaning, but his voice and tongue were silent. Often, when we were present (and he never forbade entry to anyone, nor was it the custom for a visitor to be announced), we saw him reading quietly in that way and never in any other. After sitting silent for a long time (for who would dare to impose a burden on one so engrossed?) we would depart, thinking that in the small time that he had to himself to refresh his mind, free from the noise of other people's troubles, he preferred not to be distracted by something else; that, perhaps, he was afraid lest some listener following it with great interest might ask him about some more obscure passage which he was reading—and then it would be necessary to dedicate time to this task, he would read fewer volumes than he desired. However, it was quite possible that the more correct reason for his silent reading was for the sake of keeping his voice, which, in his case, was easily made hoarse. Anyhow, whatever his purpose was in doing this, this man had a good reason for doing it. (133–34)[5]

This memorable scene, which Borges had already alluded to in "La supersticiosa ética del lector" [The Superstitious Ethics of the Reader] twenty years earlier[6] is used here to describe the central place of reading, and of books, in history. Like Aeschylus's introduction of the second actor or Snorre Sturluson's celebration of the bravery of the English enemy, it serves as a secret turning point in human history. These secret points, he claims in "El pudor de la historia" [The Modesty of History] (published a little bit later, in March 1952), are more significant than the great battles and loud proclamations that take up so much of our memory of the past. In the later sections of the essay, he notes what Bacon and Browne have to say about the relations between two books, the Bible and the Book of Nature. He then concludes with Thomas Carlyle's and Léon Bloy's reflections on history as a book which is continuously written and in which we ourselves will be written (Carlyle) and as a liturgical text, the meaning of which is hidden from us (Bloy).

ORALITY AND LITERACY IN BORGES 137

There is also considerable attention in the essay to Jewish and Islamic traditions of reading and writing. On the Kabbalah he quotes Gershom Scholem, Henri Sérouya,[7] Erich Bischoff,[8] and Paul Deussen[9] paying particular attention to their comments on the role of letters and numbers in the Creation, according to the *Sefer Yetzirah*. From Scholem, he quotes from *Major Trends in Jewish Mysticism*, the series of lectures that Scholem gave in England after World War II (Figure 8.2):

> The existence of speculative Gnostic tendencies in the immediate neighborhood of Merkabah mysticism has its parallel in the writings grouped together under the name of *Maaseh Bershith*. These include a document—the *Sefer Yetzirah* or Book of Creation—which represents a theoretical approach to the problems of cosmology and cosmogony. The text probably includes interpolations made at a later period, but its connection with the Merkabah literature is fairly evident, at least as regards terminology and style. Written probably between the third and the sixth century, it is distinguished by its brevity; even the most comprehensive of the various editions does not exceed sixteen hundred words. Historically, it represents the earliest extant speculative text written in the Hebrew language. (75)

On the following page, also referenced by Borges, he adds,

> After the author has analysed the function of the *Sefiroth* in his cosmogony, or rather hinted at the solution in some more or less oracular statements, he goes on to explain the function of the letters in creation: "[God] drew them, hewed them, combined them, weighed them, interchanged them, and through them produced the whole creation and everything that is destined to be created." He then proceeds to discuss, or rather to unveil, the secret meaning of each letter in the three realms of creation known to him: man, the world of the stars and planets, and the rhythmic flow of time through the course of the year. (76)

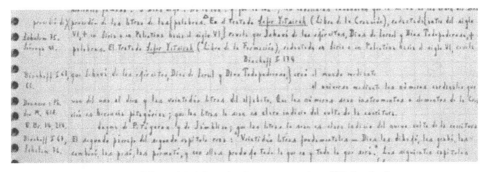

FIGURE 8.2 Discussion of the Kabbalah in the first manuscript of "Del culto."
Source: Stephen O. Murray and Keelung Hong Special Collections, Michigan State Library, MSS 678_03, p. 3 in Borges's numbering, page 114 in the notebook. Reprinted with permission.

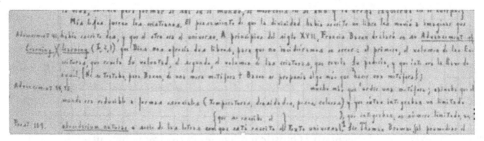

FIGURE 8.3 Discussion of Bacon in the first manuscript of "Del culto."
Source: Stephen O. Murray and Keelung Hong Special Collections, Michigan State Library, MSS 678_03, p. 3 in Borges's numbering, page 114 in the notebook. Reprinted with permission.

The Islamic sources include Asín Palacios in *Huellas del Islam*, a reference to Al-Ghazali (drawn at least in part from Asín Palacios), and a careful reading of the footnotes to George Sale's translation of the Qur'an (Figure 8.3).

Turning to the reference to Bacon's *Advancement of Learning* (the edition that Borges used also includes the *Novum Organum*), we find,

> For as it were neither easy nor useful to discover the form of a sound that shall make a word, since words, by the composition and transposition of letters are infinite; but practicable, easy and useful to discover the form of a sound expressing a single letter, or by what collision or application of the organs of the voice, it was made; and as these forms of letters being known, we are thence directly led to inquire the forms of words: so, to inquire the form of an oak, a lion, gold, water, or air, were at present vain; but to inquire the form of density, rarity, heat, cold, gravity, levity, and other schemes of matter and motions, which, like the letters of the alphabet, are few in number, yet make and support the essences and forms of all substances, is what we would endeavor after, as constituting and determining that part of metaphysics we are now upon. (95)[10]

Like the references to the commentators on the Kabbalah, this passage focuses on the economy of the letters of the alphabet, that are few, yet that can "make and support the essences and forms of all substances."

In the case of Sir Thomas Browne, the page numbers in the manuscript refer to pages 27 and 29 of Browne's *Religio Medici*. In particular, Borges engages with Browne's idea that "there are two books" and that "Nature hath made one World, and Art another. In brief, all things are artificial; for Nature is the Art of God." Borges notes a similar concern in Carlyle's essays, mentioning specifically the 1833 essay "Count Cagliostro: In Two Flights" (but the same idea is expressed in the famous essays "On History" and "On History Again," which immediately precede the Cagliostro essay in some editions of Carlyle's essays). Borges's exact phrase in the published version reads: "el escocés Carlyle, en diversos lugares de su labor y particularmente en el ensayo sobre Cagliostro, superó la conjetura de Bacon: estampó que la historia universal es una Escritura Sagrada que desciframos y escribimos inciertamente, y en la que también nos escriben" [the Scot

FIGURE 8.4 The four-page manuscript of "Del culto" in Cuaderno Avon.
Source: Stephen O. Murray and Keelung Hong Special Collections, Michigan State Library, MSS 678_03.
Reprinted with permission.

Carlyle, in various places in his books, particularly in the essay on Cagliostro, went beyond Bacon's hypothesis; he said that universal history was a Sacred Scripture that we decipher and write uncertainly, and in which we too are written] (*OC* II: 94; *SNF* 361), which I believe is a translation of the end of the 1833 essay "On History Again": "we might liken Universal History to a magic web.... History is the true Epic Poem, and universal Divine Scripture" (432). Carlyle refers to the place of Giuseppe Balsamo's or Cagliostro's confession in Rome to the Inquisition, which led to his imprisonment and death in 1793, in "the grand sacred Epos, or Bible of World-History; infinite in meaning as the Divine Mind it emblems; where he is wise that can read here a line and there a line" (24).[11] However, the phrase "universal history" appears in a number of other Carlyle essays, including "Early German Literature," the essays on Boswell's *Life of Johnson*, Diderot, and "On History Again," to cite just a few examples from one of the editions of Carlyle's essays that Borges consulted (which also, interestingly, included Emerson's essays, hence a possible explanation for Borges's edition of the essays of Carlyle and Emerson for volume 37 of the Clásicos Jackson in 1949).

Two manuscripts of this essay survive. The first extant manuscript (MSS 678_03) is in one of the notebooks that were acquired in 2019 by the Stephen O. Murray and Keelung Hong Special Collections Library at Michigan State University after the death of Donald Yates; it is typical of Borges manuscripts of this period, with intense writing and rewriting, many alternatives and insertions (above and below the line, in the left margin, and at the top of the pages), and important bibliographical notations in the left margin (and a few elsewhere, including in the body of the text) (Figure 8.4).

The second extant manuscript is a fair copy that Borges sent to *La Nación*, which was for sale several years ago in Buenos Aires; it is now held in Special Collections at the Hillman Library of the Universe of Pittsburgh (Figure 8.5). In what follows, I trace the process of writing in the Michigan State draft (i.e., the first of the two extant manuscripts).

The first draft of this essay is four pages long, but the second page is cut off after twenty lines. The first page does not have many bibliographical references besides the ones that ended up in the published text; the second has four; the third has an astonishing nineteen;

FIGURE 8.5 The four-page second draft of "Del culto," marked "Para La Nación."
Source: Special Collections, Hillman Library University of Pittsburgh. Reprinted with permission.

the fourth has eight. I have successfully identified most of the editions to which the page numbers in the manuscript refer, which gives us a good sense of how Borges read (and, of course, how he wrote, but that's a topic that I have already written a lot about).[12]

The third page of the manuscript, the one with the most notes in the left margin, includes references to the following: Miguel Asín Palacios's *Huellas del Islam* (1941), George Sale's translation of and commentary on the Qur'an,[13] Paul Deussen's *Die Philosophie des Mittelalters* (1915), Gershom Scholem's *Major Trends in Jewish Mysticism* (1941), Henri Sérouya's *La Kabbale* (1947), Erich Bischoff's *Die Elemente der Kabbalah* (1914), Francis Bacon's *The Advancement of Learning*,[14] Walter Frost's *Bacon und die Naturphilosophie* (1926), an article from the eleventh edition of the *Encyclopaedia Britannica* (more about that later), and Sir Thomas Browne's *Religio Medici* (Figure 8.6).[15] That said, I should note that Borges generally does not bother to write down the titles of the books or the editions used, so cracking his internal code is fairly arduous. The reference to Asín Palacios, for instance, is to his preface, in which he describes the contents of his book *Huellas del Islam* (1941); there the Spanish scholar argues that Islamic beliefs on the superiority of human beings to animals was based on neo-Platonic ideas "decorada con todas las galas de la imaginación oriental" [dressed up in the fashion of the Oriental imagination] (9). The reference immediately following this is to a footnote in George Sale's translation of the Qur'an, in which he translates the verse from the holy book, "Every age hath its book *of revelation*: God shall abolish and shall confirm *what he pleaseth*. With him is the original of the book." This is glossed in a footnote that reads: "Literally, *the mother of the book*; by which is meant *the preserved table*, from which all the written revelations which have been from time to time published to mankind, according to the several dispensations, are transcripts" (244).[16] That is followed by an avalanche of references to the Kabbalah, and then to Bacon and Browne. It is worth noting the precision of the references, over and over again: Borges carefully synthesizes ideas he has gleaned from his reading, mostly in German but also in French, Italian, and English (no Spanish sources here other than Asín Palacios). Just one example: the reference to Deussen's book on medieval philosophy is to page 418, on the *Sefer Yetzirah*, in which Deussen writes of the ways that the first ten numbers and the

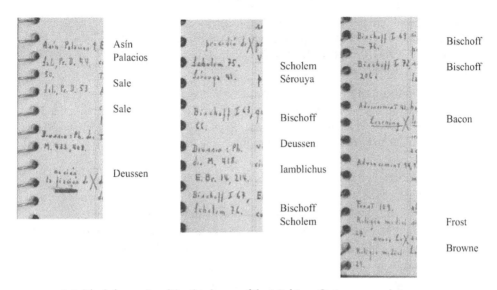

FIGURE 8.6 The left margin of the third page of the Michigan State manuscript.
Source: Stephen O. Murray and Keelung Hong Special Collections, Michigan State Library, MSS 678_03.
Reprinted with permission.

22 letters of the Hebrew alphabet are the creative forces through which God realizes his nature in the world; Deussen notes that these are fused with neo-Pythagorean ideas. The quotation from Scholem that immediately follows is the one already quoted about the Creator having shaped the world through combinations of letters. It is clear, then, that the essay is built around the quotations: in this first draft, the connections from one quotation to another are clear, while the commentaries on the quotations serve to lead to the next stage of the argument.

The manuscript contains references to four entries in the eleventh edition of the *Encyclopaedia Britannica*: manuscript,[17] punctuation,[18] Aristophanes of Byzantium,[19] and Iamblichus.[20] All of these have to do with questions of textual production, explicitly in the titles of the first two, and implicitly in the ones on Aristophanes of Byzantium and Iamblichus. There are also two Biblical references, both interesting in this context. The first is Matthew 7:6: "Do not give what is holy to dogs; and do not throw your pearls before swine, or they will trample them under foot and turn and maul you" (1256).[21] This reflection on the reception of wisdom is of course familiar to everyone who has taught. The other Biblical reference is to John 8:6: "They said this to test him, so they might have some charge to bring against him. Jesus bent down and wrote with his finger on the ground" (1895–96). Here Borges confirms the illustrious lineage of oral teachers who refused writing: Homer, Pythagoras,[22] Socrates, Jesus, Mohammed, and relates them, throughout the essay, with the world of learned commentators, weaving together orality and literacy.

A reference in the margin of the fourth page (one that does not make it into the final essay) is to Borges's own "Estudio preliminar" [Preliminary Study] to the Clásicos Jackson edition of the *Divina Commedia*. In that introduction, written just two years before, Borges writes,

142   DANIEL BALDERSTON

la comedia difiere de la tragedia por el lenguaje suelto y común y por el desenlace feliz. La etimología confirma esa distinción: comedia se deriva de *kome*, y quiere decir canto villano; tragedia de *trages*, y quiere decir canto cabrío, "por lo fétido y horrible del desenlace." (xii)

[comedy differs from tragedy due to its use of informal and ordinary language and because of the happy ending. The etymology confirms that distinction: comedy comes from *kome*, which means a common song; tragedy from *trages*, which means a goat song, "due to its fetid and horrible ending."]

On the fourth page of the manuscript there are cryptic references to "comedy," "tragedy," and to Boccacio as the source of the title *La Divina Commedia*; these make sense when they are viewed as cross-references to Borges's earlier introduction to Dante.

We can see, then, that Borges uses reference works to confirm quotations and ideas from his reading and that he is very precise in his notes about that checking. Bioy Casares writes in his diary: "Borges insiste siempre en comprobar las citas. Me sale del alma y estoy a punto de pensar que entorpece el trabajo con una manía personal o capricho. Casi infaliblemente la enciclopedia le da la razón: la consulta no fue inútil, alguna corrección introduciremos en nuestro texto o en nuestros conocimientos" [Borges always insists on checking quotations. I feel like protesting that he delays our work because of his personal manias or whims. Almost always the encyclopedia proves him right: checking it was not useless; we will make some correction in our text or in our knowledge] (*Borges* 924). Bioy is writing about a later period, after Borges went blind and could no longer do his own cross-checking; the marginalia of this essay shows the rigor with which Borges undertook this task when he could still see. Another example of his rigor: the texts mentioned in this essay follow a rough chronological order. He is interested in tracing in sequential fashion the various ideas he is discussing. This is not to imply causality or evolution, but it does show a close attention to what he calls the "diverse intonation" of an idea in the essay on Pascal's sphere.

An important example of "diverse intonation" is the quotation from Léon Bloy's book *L'Âme de Napoléon* (1912), identified in the manuscript as "*Sur* 66, 76" (Figure 8.7).

This refers to the 1940 publication in issue 66 of *Sur* of Borges's essay "El espejo de los enigmas" [The Mirror of Enigmas] (also included in the 1952 *Otras inquisiciones*), which

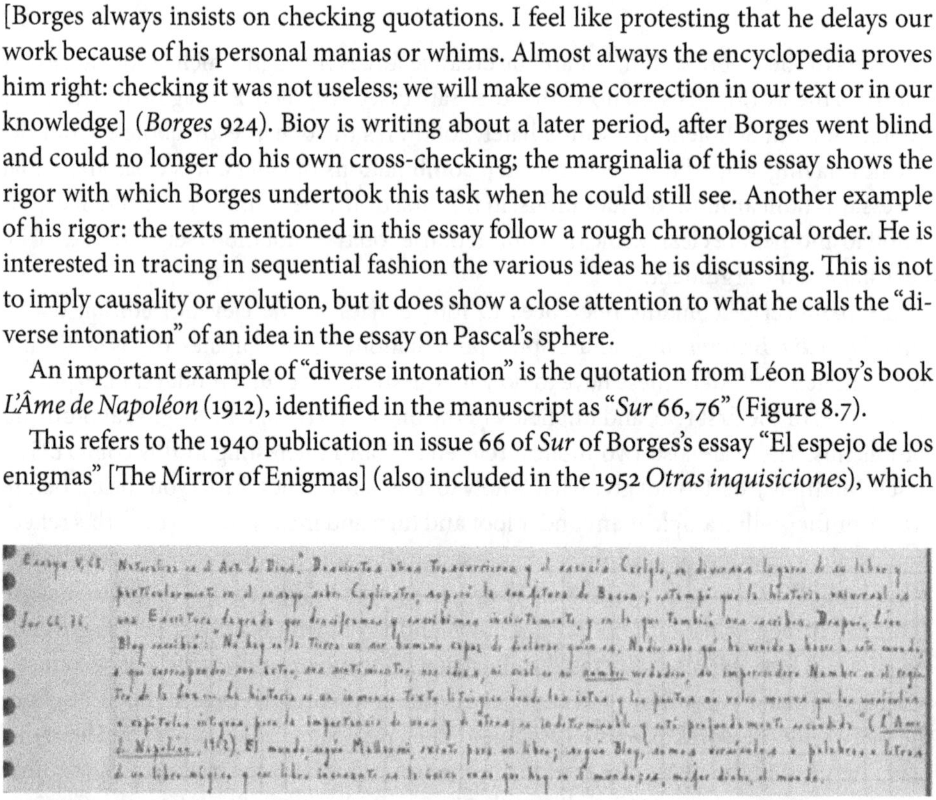

FIGURE 8.7 Fourth page of the Michigan State manuscript.

Source: Stephen O. Murray and Keelung Hong Special Collections, Michigan State Library, MSS 678_03.
Reprinted with permission.

ORALITY AND LITERACY IN BORGES   143

contains a translation of a key passage from Bloy's book on Napoleon, a reflection on human history.

> Il n'y a pas un être humain capable de dire ce qu'il est, avec certitude. Nul ne sait ce qu'il est venu faire en ce monde, à quoi correspondent ses actes, ses sentiments, ses pensées; qui sont ses plus proches parmi tous les hommes, ni quel est son *nom* véritable, son impérissable Nom dans le Registre de la Lumière. [. . .] L'Histoire est comme un immense Texte liturgique où les iotas et les points valent autant que des versets ou des chapitres entiers, mais l'importance des uns et des autres est indéterminable et profondément cachée. (18)

> [No human beings are capable of saying what they are with any certainty. They do not know what they came into the world to do, to whom their acts and feelings and thoughts belong; who they are closest to among other humans, now what is their true *name*, their enduring Name in the Registry of Light. . . . History is an immense liturgical Text in which the dots and strokes are as important as whole verses and chapters, but the importance of each is indeterminable / indeterminate and profoundly hidden.]

In "El espejo de los enigmas," this passage is translated in full (*OC* II: 99–100) except for the ellipsis marked here, which is a brief evocation of the figure of Napoleon as Emperor[23]; this is followed a half page later by an ironic commentary by Borges on whether Bloy could really have believed this idea of history as a liturgical text: "Es dudoso que el mundo tenga sentido; es más dudoso que tenga doble o triple sentido" [It is doubtful that the world has a meaning; it is even more doubtful that it has a double or triple meaning] (*OC* II: 100; *Labyrinths* 212). His final paragraph there reads: "*Ningún hombre sabe quién es*, afirmó Léon Bloy. Nadie como él para ilustrar esa ignorancia íntima" [*No man knows who he is*, affirmed Léon Bloy. No one could illustrate that intimate ignorance better than he] (*OC* II: 100; *Labyrinths* 212). Eleven years later he copies the quotation, but it leads him in an entirely different direction: "El mundo, según Mallarmé, existe para un libro; según Bloy somos versículos o palabras o letras de un libro sagrado, y ese libro incesante es la única cosa que hay en el mundo: es, mejor dicho, el mundo" [The world, according to Mallarmé, exists for a book; according to Bloy, we are the versicles or words or letters of a magic book, and that incessant book is the only thing in the world: more exactly, it is the world] (*OC* II: 94; *SNF* 363) (Figure 8.8).

He is returning to some of the same sources in 1951, but with a quite different thesis, one that connects with his other writings on history in 1951 and 1952, in which he expresses a sharp skepticism about pronouncements like Goethe's at Valmy ("Von hier und heute geht eine neue Epoche der Weltgeschichte aus, und ihr könnt sagen, ihr seid dabei gewesen" [A new epoch of world history is beginning here and now, and you can say you were there])[24] or, no doubt, those of Perón that were the soundtrack of the period when he was writing. His defense of books, and of reading, could be read in the context of slogans like "Alpargatas sí, libros no," a chant, said to originate in October 1945, that was used by Peronism's antagonists to argue that Peronism was anti-intellectual,[25] a position with which Borges sympathized. "Del culto de los libros,"

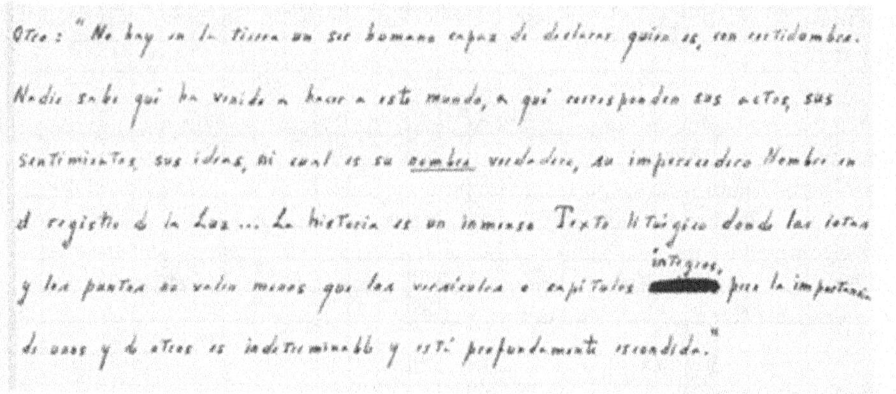

144 DANIEL BALDERSTON

FIGURE 8.8 Fifth page of the manuscript of "El espejo de los enigmas" (1940).

Source: Stephen O. Murray and Keelung Hong Special Collections Library, Michigan State, MSS678_17.
Reprinted with permission.

like "El escritor argentino y la tradición" [The Argentine Writer and Tradition] and "El pudor de la historia," is his intervention in these debates, although here he only hints at the political context. The quotation from Bloy here, that history is "un immense Texte liturgique où les iotas et les points valent autant que des versets ou des chapitres entiers, mais l'importance des uns et des autres est indéterminable et profondément cachée" is his careful hint.[26] The different intonation of a quotation that he had already translated in 1940 points to a changed context, one that he, as a man of letters, is anxious about.

Upside down at the top of the fourth page, the manuscript includes a reference to Schopenhauer's *Parerga und Paralipomena* that is not in the published text. Schopenhauer writes, in Borges's crabbed note,

> Die Werke sind die <u>Quintessenz</u> eines Geistes; sie werden daher, auch wenn er der größte ist, stets ungleich (incomparablemente) gehaltreicher sein als sein Umgang (trato) auch diesen in wesentlichen ersetzen—ja, ihn weit übertreffen

> [The works are the quintessence of a mind; and so even if a man has the greatest mind, his works will always be incomparably more valuable than his acquaintance. In essential points they will even replace and indeed far surpass]

Borges breaks off here because he has run out of space in the top right corner of the page, but the quotation in question continues as follows (Figure 8.9):

> und hinter sich lassen. Sogar die Schriften eines mittelmäßigen Kopfes können belehrend, lesenswert und unterhaltend sein, eben weil sie sein Quintessenz sind, das Resultat, die Frucht alles seines Denkens und Studierens; während sein Umgang uns nicht genügen kann. Daher kann man Bücher von Leuten lesen, an deren Umgang man kein Genügen finden würde, und deshalb wieder bringt hohe Geisteskultur uns allmählich dahin, fast nur noch an Büchern, nicht mehr an Menschen Unterhaltung zu finden.

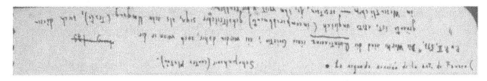

FIGURE 8.9 Fourth page of the Michigan State manuscript.

Source: Stephen O. Murray and Keelung Hong Special Collections, Michigan State Library, MSS 678_03. Reprinted with permission.

[this. Even the writings of a mediocre mind can be instructive, entertaining, and worth reading, just because they are his quintessence, the result and fruit of all his thought and study; whereas associating with him may not satisfy us. Thus we can read books by those in whose company we should find no pleasure; and so great mental culture gradually causes us to find entertainment almost entirely in books and no longer in people. ("On Reading," *Parerga and Paralipomena: Short Philosophical Essays* §296a)]

Here Borges includes a couple of notes on how to translate the German terms, in parenthesis: "trato" for "Umgang," "incomparablemente" for "ungleich." He tended to include such parenthetical translation notes when he was working on something for oral delivery. However, in this case, we don't have any record of his having given "Del culto de los libros" as a talk. The fair copy ends with the note in Borges's handwriting "Para La Nación," which implies that it was always intended for publication in written, not oral, form. Schopenhauer writes that "even the writings of a mediocre mind can be instructive, readable and entertaining" and that "one can read books with whom one would not find satisfaction in dealing with them" directly. Schopenhauer concludes this passage with the savage remark that this is why intellectual culture can bring us entertainment "almost exclusively in books and no longer in people." This is reminiscent, of course, of the equally savage close of "Tlön, Uqbar, Orbis Tertius," in which the narrator retreats from the nightmare of the world of 1947 (imagined from the nightmarish year 1940 when the story was written) into a Quevedian translation of Browne's *Urne Buriall*, which of course is a baroque masterpiece of a meditation on death (Figure 8.10).

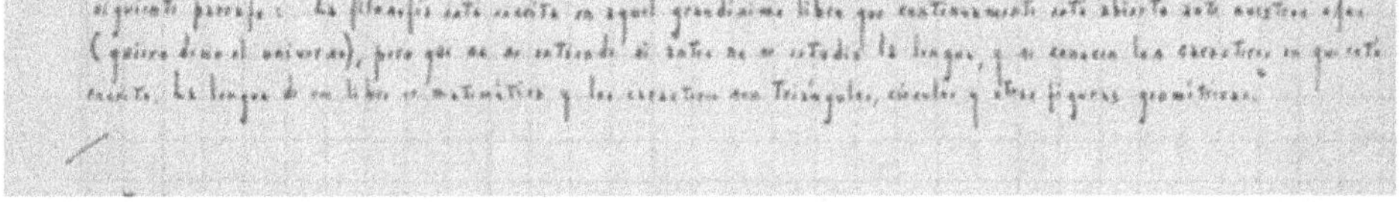

FIGURE 8.10 Fourth page of the Michigan State manuscript.

Source: Stephen O. Murray and Keelung Hong Special Collections, Michigan State Library, MSS 678_03. Reprinted with permission.

Another note that also does not make it into the published versions is a reference to Galileo Galilei's *Pensieri* in Antonio Favaro's edition. The quotation in question reads,

> La filosofia è scritta in questo grandissimo libro che continuamente ci sta aperto agli occhi (io dico l'universo) ma non si può intendere se prima non s'impara a intender la lingua, e conoscer i caratteri ne' quali è scritto. Egli è scritto in lingua matematica, e i caratteri son triangoli, cerchi, ed altre figure geometriche, senza i quali mezzi è impossibile a intenderne umanamente parola; senza questi è un aggirarsi vanamente per un oscuro laberinto.[27]

It is fascinating how wide-ranging Borges's reading is here, from a variety of commentaries on religious texts, to meditations on history and philosophy, to (as here) the meditations of an important scientist.

In his recent short introduction to Borges, published first in French in 2019 and then in English in 2021, Julio Premat writes,

> But more than the content of the catalog of this intimate library, what attracts our attention is the hyperbolic nature of it. . . . [T]he essay "On the Cult of Books" takes us on a journey through the history of the perception of books as sacred objects. Straight away, Borges compares Homer and *The Odyssey* to Mallarmé (considering them as belonging to different "theologies"); then Cervantes, Bernard Shaw, Pythagoras, Clement of Alexandria, the Gospel according to John, Saint Augustine, Lucian of Samosata, Flaubert, Henry James, James Joyce, the Koran, the Old Testament, the Jewish Cabalist tradition, Thomas Browne, Carlyle, and Léon Bloy are cited at random. The list only includes the names mentioned, but other references are most certainly implicit in this four- or five-page text. (119)

As we have seen, that list, which is certainly not "random," can, with the help of the manuscripts, be supplemented by other sources that Borges consulted: Theodor Gomperz on Pythagoras; the Gospel of Matthew; Vernon Bourke on Augustine; four articles from the eleventh edition of the *Encyclopaedia Britannica*; H. R. Rose on Greek literature; Miguel Asín Palacios on Al-Ghazali; George Sale as translator and annotator of the Koran; Gerschom Scholem, Henri Sérouya, Erich Bischoff, and Paul Deussen on the Kabbalah; Walter Frost on Bacon; Antonio Favaro on Galileo; and Arthur Schopenhauer on why it is better to read than to talk to people. All of this is crammed into four pages of a tightly written manuscript, then a bit more than three pages in the fair copy, and then four pages in the 1974 edition of the so-called complete works. This early exploration of the history of the book and the history of reading was written before both of those fields existed in their present forms. It is extravagantly bookish, yet at the same time manages to make the activity of reading a vital part of human life, first with the example of Saint Ambrose and then, implicitly, with the example of Borges himself, bringing together this dizzying display of his reading for an article in a newspaper in July of 1951. No doubt reading for him was (in 1940 and in 1951) an escape from what he considered a nightmarish reality, but no doubt that it was also a source of joy, of intellectual curiosity, and of private erudition shared (through the newspaper publication) with a broad reading public. It was also, as I hope to have shown, an intervention in what was then a very public debate about the shape of Argentine culture, one in which Borges would make his position explicit in his polemical talk "El escritor argentino y la tradición" just five months later, at the Colegio Libre de Estudios Superiores.

The pleasure of working on a text like this has been the uncovering of the precise sources and seeing the uses that Borges made of them. In this journey through the last three thousand years of human history, through oral and written cultures, through the meanders of intellectual debates, theology and philosophy, politics, through book history and the history of reading, Borges is quite a Virgil. His manuscripts bring to life his intellectual activity, making it possible to see pretty precisely what he was reading, thinking, and writing in 1951. "Del culto de los libros" holds a special place in his work as his most eloquent text on what he considered the "sacred" nature of books, one which enjoins us to read in depth. To read, that is, the way we can trace him reading in the Michigan State manuscript.

Notes

1. Mallarmé uses that phrase in "Le Livre, instrument spirituel" in *Variations sur un sujet/ Divagations* (1897). The English translation in *Selected Non-Fictions* reads: "The world exists to end up in a book" (359). In what follows, I quote from that translation.
2. The two references to Clement of Alexandria's *Stromata* have to do with the difference between the memory of speech and the possibilities of recovering ideas from written sources. He writes: "Some things I purposely omit, in the exercise of a wise selection, afraid to write what I guarded against speaking: not grudging—for that were wrong—but fearing for my readers, lest they should stumble by taking them in a wrong sense; and, as the proverb says, we should be found 'giving a sword to a child.'" In another section, he writes: "Both must therefore test themselves: the one, if he is qualified to speak and leave behind him written records; the other, if he is in a right state to hear and read.... For by teaching, one learns more; and in speaking, one is often a hearer along with his audience. For the teacher of him who speaks and of him who hears is one—who waters both the mind and the word." A central preoccupation in the text is the relation between oral speech and writing, particularly in the opening chapter on the utility of writing.
3. There are two references to Plato in the manuscript. The first, to the *Timaeus*, is Critias's reference to the accomplishments of Athens: "It's a story about the most magnificent thing our city has ever done an accomplishment that deserves to be known far better than any of her other accomplishments. But owing to the march of time and the fact that the men who accomplished it have perished, the story has not survived to the present" (1229). The second, to the *Phaedrus*, is from a discussion about a conversation between Thamus and Theuth in Egypt, in which Theuth claims that writing will improve human memory, whereas Thamus says that "it will introduce forgetfulness into the soul of those who learn it: they will not practice using their memory because they will put their trust in writing, which is external and depends on signs that belong to others, instead of trying to remember from the inside, completely on their own. You have not discovered a potion

148   DANIEL BALDERSTON

for remembering, but for reminding; you provide your students with the appearance of wisdom, not with its reality. Your invention will enable them to hear many things without being properly taught, and they will imagine that they have come to know much while for the most part they will know nothing" (551–52).

4. For instance, the information about Lucian of Samosata comes from Rose, who writes in his *Handbook*, "Some satirize contemporary life, as the violent attack *Against an ignorant book-buyer* and the savage picture of contemporary Roman society, *Concerning hired companions*, a Juvenalian account of the miseries of hangers-on of great houses" (420); Borges reminds himself that this reference is in a footnote: "AL PIE." A subsequent marginal reference to Rose concerns Zenodotos, the first director of the Library of Alexandria, as an early editor of the Homeric poems (388–89).

5. There is also a marginal reference that reads: "Bourke 34, 146." This refers to the following passages from Bourke's *Augustine's Quest of Wisdom*: "Years later, when he was listening to Ambrose (A.D. 384). Augustine tried very hard to conceive the nature of a spiritual substance, but he could not" (35 n. 19) and "Apart from the evidence of the *Retractations*, which places the treatise in the same period as the *De Doctrina Christiana*, there is internal evidence which points to the conclusion that part of the *Confessions* was written before Augustine heard of the death of St. Ambrose, that is, before the end of A.D. 397" (146).

6. "Ya hay lector callado de versos" [there are mute readers of verse] (*OC* I: 204–05; *SNF* 55).

7. Sérouya writes in *La Kabbale*: "le *Sefer Yetzirah* est plus ancien que l'Islam. Il ne connaît pas les points-voyelles qui, eux aussi, 'paraissent avoir été créés avant l'établissement de l'islamisme et qui trahissent tout au plus l'influence syriaque mais non arabe.'... En raison de ce qui le distingue de toute la littérature mystique du judaïsme de cette époque, le *Sefer Yerzirah* paraît avoir été écrit, selon Epstein et Isidore Loeb, en Palestine ou en Syrie, en tout cas dans le voisinage et sous l'influence directe de la gnose chrétienne et païenne" (41).

8. There are seven references to Bischoff's *Die Elemente der Kabbalah* (1913–1914; but I was able to consult a 1920 edition, which has the same pagination), one to pages 69–76, which is an index to a commentary on the Kabbalah. The most important reference is note 31 on pages 174 and 175: "'Jezirah' ist eigentlich nicht die 'Schöpfung (wie es meist übersetzt wird) im biblischen Sinne, d. h. die Hervorbringung der materiellen Welt, was vielmehr kabbalistisch mit 'Usijjah' bezeichnet wird, sondern die 'Formung' (Bildung) der dieser Welt zugrundeliegend den Wesenheiten mittels der 10 Zahlen und 22 Buchstabenprinzipien, so dass also die als derartig 'geformt' erwähnten Dinge (z. B. die drei Naturelemente Luft, Feuer, Wasser, seiner Himmel, Erde, Wind, die Sterne, [175] Sternbilder, Wochentage, Monate und Körperteile, eigentlich nicht die materiellen Erscheinungen, sondern deren übersinnliche Formen (Substrate, Dinge an sich, Ideen) bezeichnen. Daher wird im Texte unseres Buches das biblische Wort für '(materiell) Schaffen' ('bara') absichtlich vermieden und dafür stets 'jazar' (formen, bilden) gesagt."

9. Deussen writes in *Die Philosophie des Mittelalters*: "Das Buch Jezirah gibt sich nach dem Schlussabschnitt aus für eine dem Abraham durch Gott gewordene Offenbarung. Diese Offenbarung besteht in den '32 Wegen der Weisheit;, nämlich den 10 Grundzahlen und den 22 Buchstaben des hebräischen Alphabets, welche alle, analog den platonischen Ideen, als schaffende Kräfte erscheinen, durch welche Gott sein Wesen in der Welt verwirklicht. Hierbei aber sind, wie es scheint, zwei verschiedene Anschauungen mit einander verschmolzen, eine neupythagoreische, welche in den zehn Grundzahlen 1–10, und eine jüdische, welche in den 22 Buchstaben des hebräischen Alphabets die Prinzipien alles

Seienden erkennt.... Mit diesen neupythagoreischen Anschauungen ist es aber schwer zu vereinen...." (418).

10. Borges also refers to a commentator on Bacon, Walter Frost, who writes: "Hans Natge schliesst sich dieser von Heussler gegebenen Darlegung an. Das 'abecedarium naturae' bei Bacon, sagt er, bedeutet die Annahme einer bestimmten Anzahl von Urqualitäten" (109). See also Rosato and Álvarez, "Acerca de un ejemplar" (16).

11. See Bossche's comments on the Cagliostro essay: "Carlyle was probably drawn to the subject because, as he notes in his essay, his literary heroes Goethe and Schiller had both been fascinated by him. During his stay in Edinburgh Carlyle recorded in his journal that he had 'been exploring on all hands the foolish history of the quack Cagliostro: have read several Books about him; searching far and wide after him; learned, I ought to admit, almost nothing. Shall I *study* this enigma, then write my solution or no-solution'" (xlv).

12. Mariana DiCió and I began cracking the code to read the bibliographical marginalia when we prepared our critical edition of "La obra de Flaubert" from 1952, published in *Ensayos* (Balderston and Martín) in 2019; this has now become a central preoccupation of a team that I am working with on the Borges notebooks, some of whose work was featured in *Variaciones Borges* 52 (fall 2021), with more in issue 54 (fall 2022).

13. The Sale translation was originally published in 1734; Borges used an edition with an introduction by Edward Denison Ross, published by Frederick Warne, which is undated.

14. Borges used a 1900 edition of *The Advancement of Learning* and the *Novum Organum*, with an introduction by James Edward Creighton.

15. Borges used an anthology of Browne's writings edited by W. A. Greenhill (1926).

16. It is unclear in the edition that I have whether this footnote is by Sale or by the "most approved commentators," who edited his translation long after his death. There is also a reference to this issue in the manuscript "Místicos del Islam" that is at the Harry Ransom Center at the University of Texas (see Ubelaker Andrade and Karavar).

17. "In the early codices too it was a common practice to link letters together in monogrammatic form, such as the common verbal terminations *ur, unt*, and thus save space." "Rhetorical texts, such as the orations of Demosthenes and Cicero, and the text of the Bible, might be broken up into short clauses or sense-lines, apparently with the view of assisting reading aloud" (Thompson, "Manuscript" 622).

18. "In the earlier forms of writing the letters ran on continuously in lines; it was only by degrees that actual words were divided from one another by spacing within the line; then later came the distribution of words into sentences by means of points, and the introduction by Aldus Manutius in the 16th century of a regular system for these. The chief signs were inherited by the printers from the dots of the Greek grammarians, but often with altered meanings; thus the Greek interrogation mark (;) becomes the modern semicolon" ("Punctuation" 649).

19. "He introduced critical signs—except the obelus; punctuation, prosodiacal and accentual marks were probably already in use" (unsigned article, "Aristophanes of Alexandria," 2: 501).

20. Borges writes of Iamblichus ("Jámblico") that he believed, like Pythagoras, that numbers are instruments or elements of the creation. The article of the *Encyclopedia Britannica* to which the marginal reference points says: "We read of gods, angels, demons and heroes, of twelve heavenly gods whose number is increased to thirty-six or three hundred and sixty, and of seventy-two other gods proceeding from them, of twenty-one chiefs . . . and forty-two nature-gods . . . besides guardian divinities, of particular individuals and nations.

The world is thus peopled by a crowd of superhuman beings influencing natural events, possessing and communicating knowledge of the future, and not inaccessible to prayers and offerings" (Sobley, "Iamblichus" 214).

21. I am quoting from the Oxford Annotated Bible, not from the editions that Borges consulted. For the latter, see Lucas Adur, and for a full range of studies of Borges and the Bible, the book by Gonzalo Salvador and the one edited by Walsh and Twomey.

22. Borges's source on Pythagoras's refusal to write is Theodor Gomperz's *Griechische Denker*: "keine Zeile seiner Hand ist uns erhalten, ja es scheint nahezu ausgemacht, dass er sich des Behelfes schriftlicher Mittelung überhaupt nicht bedient und nur durch die Macht des Wortes und des Beispiels auf seine Umgebung gewirkt hat" (81).

23. He has left out a single sentence: "Empereur ou débardeur nul ne sait son fardeau ni sa couronne" (18). Bloy is ironic: no one knows whether his burden or his crown is that of an emperor or a longshoreman.

24. On the quotation from Goethe in "El pudor de la historia" [The Modesty of History] see *How Borges Wrote* (41–42).

25. There is much debate about Peronism's supposed anti-intellectualism. See for instance Javier de Navascués's *Alpargaratas contra libros*, which quotes Alicia Jurado as a witness to the crowd shouting this slogan as they passed on the street beneath her balcony (83). Also see the brief article by Victoria Chabrando and Ezequiel Adamowsky's *Historia de la clase media argentina*, which includes a commentary on this slogan. Another useful source on book production during the Peronist decade is Alejandra Giuliani's *Editores y política*.

26. This is related in the conclusion of the essay to the idea from Carlyle that "la historia universal es una Escritura Sagrada que desciframos y escribimos inciertamente y en la que también nos escriben" [universal history was a Sacred Scripture that we decipher and write uncertainly] (*OC* II: 94; *SNF* 361).

27. I am quoting from Giovanni Papini's edition of Galileo, p. 26. In *Selected Non-Fiction*, this passage is translated as follows: "Philosophy is written in that very large book that is continually opened before our eyes (I mean the universe), but which is not understood unless first one studies the language and knows the characters in which it is written. The language of that book is mathematical and the characters are triangles, circles, and other geometric figures" (361).

Works Cited

Adamovsky, Ezequiel. *Historia de la clase media argentina: apogeo y decadencia de una ilusión. 1919–2003*. Planeta, 2009.

Adur, Lucas. "Las biblias de Borges." *Variaciones Borges*, vol. 41, 2016, pp. 3–25.

"Aristophanes of Alexandria." [Unsigned article.] *Encyclopaedia Britannica*. Encyclopaedia Britannica Company, 1910, vol. 2, p. 501.

Asín Palacios, Miguel. *Huellas del Islam: Santo Tomás de Aquino, Turmeda, Pascal, San Juan de la Cruz*. Espasa-Calpe, 1941.

Augustine of Hippo. *Confessions*, translated by Vernon J. Bourke, Catholic University of America Press, 1953.

Bacon, Francis. *Advancement of Learning and Novum Organum*, introduction by James Edward Creighton. Colonial Press, 1900.

Bischoff, Erich. *Die Elemente der Kabbalah*. Übersetzungen, Erlauterungen, und Abhandlungen von Erich Bischoff. 2 vols. Hermann Barsdorf Verlag, [1913–1914] 1920. https://catalog.hat hitrust.org/Record/011987188.

Balderston, Daniel. *How Borges Wrote*. University of Virginia Press, 2018.

Bioy Casares, Adolfo. *Borges*, edited by Daniel Martino. Destino, 2006.

Bloy, Léon. *L'Âme de Napoléon*. [1912]. Norik ebooks, 2017.

Borges, Jorge Luis. "Del culto de los libros." *La Nación*. July 8, 1951. Second section, p. 1.

Borges, Jorge Luis. *Ensayos*, edited by Daniel Balderston and María Celeste Martín. Borges Center, 2019.

Borges, Jorge Luis. "El espejo de los enigmas." *Sur*, no. 66, 1940, pp. 74–77.

Borges, Jorge Luis. "Estudio preliminar." *La divina comedia*. Dante Alighieri. Clásicos Jackson, 1949, pp. ix–xxviii.

Borges, Jorge Luis. *Labyrinths: Selected Stories & Other Writings*, edited by Donald A. Yates and James E. Irby. New Directions, 1962.

Borges, Jorge Luis. *Obras completas*. 4 vols. Emecé, 1996.

Borges, Jorge Luis. *Selected Non-Fictions*, edited by Eliot Weinberger, translated by Esther Allen, Suzanne Jill Levine, and Eliot Weinberger. Viking, 1999.

Bourke, Vernon J. *Augustine's Quest of Wisdom: Life and Philosophy of the Bishop of Hippo*. Bruce Publishing Company, 1944.

Browne, Sir Thomas. *Religio Medici and Christian Morals*, edited by W. A. Greenhill. London: Macmillan, 1926.

Carlyle, Thomas. "Count Cagliostro: In Two Flights." 1833.

Carlyle, Thomas. *Historical Essays*, edited by Chris R. Vanden Bossche. Norman and Charlotte Strouse Edition of the Writings of Thomas Carlyle. University of California Press, 2003.

Chabrando, Victoria. "¿Alpargatas sí, libros no?" *Alfilo*. https://ffyh.unc.edu.ar/alfilo/alparga tas-si-libros-no/.

Clement of Alexandria. *Stromata*. https://www.newadvent.org/fathers/02101.htm

de Navascués, Javier. *Alpargatas contra libros: El escritor y las masas en la literatura del primer peronismo (1945–1955)*. Iberoamericana Vervuert, 2017.

Deussen, Paul. *Die Philosophie des Mittelalters*. F. A. Brockhaus, 1915.

Favaro, Antonio. *Galileo Galilei: Pensieri, motti e sentenzi*. [1907] Edizioni Nazionale delle opere, 1949.

Frost, Walter. *Bacon und die Naturphilosophie*. Verlag Ernst Reinhardt, 1927.

Giuliani, Alejandra. *Editores y política: Entre el mercado latinoamericano de libros y el primer peronismo (1938-1955)*. Tren en Movimiento, 2018.

Gomperz, Theodor. *Griechische Denker*. Verlag von Veit & Comp., 1895.

Karavar, Nesrin. "Místicos del Islam en los manuscritos inéditos de Jorge Luis Borges." *Variaciones Borges*, vol. 52, 2021, pp. 51–57.

The Koran: Translated into English from the Original Arabic, with Explanatory Notes from the Most Approved Commentators, translated by George Sale [1734], introduction by Edward Denison Ross. Frederick Warne and Co., n.d.

Mallarmé, Stéphane. "Le Livre, instrument spirituel." *Variations sur un sujet. Divagations*. Eugène Fasquelle éditeur, 1897, pp. 273–80.

The New Oxford Annotated Bible: New Revised Standard Version with the Apocrypha, edited by Michael D. Coogan, 4th ed. Oxford University Press, 2010.

Plato. *Complete Works*, edited by John M. Cooper. Hackett Publishing Company, 1997.

Premat, Julio. *Borges: An Introduction*, translated by Amanda Murphy. Vanderbilt University Press, 2021.

"Punctuation." [Unsigned article.] *Encyclopaedia Britannica*. Encyclopaedia Britannica Company, 1911, vol. 22, p. 649.

Rosato, Laura, and Germán Álvarez. "Acerca de un ejemplar de Sir Thomas Browne perteneciente a la biblioteca personal de Jorge Luis Borges: adelanteo del segundo volumen del libro *Borges, libros y lecturas*." *La Biblioteca*, no. 13, 2013, special issue "Cuestión Borges," pp. 66–90.

Rosato, Laura, and Germán Álvarez. *Borges, libros y lecturas*. Biblioteca Nacional, 2010.

Rose, H. R. *A Handbook of Greek Literature: From Homer to the Age of Lucian*, 3rd ed. Methuen, 1948.

Salvador, Gonzalo. *Borges y la Biblia*. Iberoamericana Vervuert, 2011.

Scholem, Gerschom. *Major Trends in Jewish Mysticism*. [1946] Schocken Books, 1995.

Schopenhauer, Arthur. "On Reading and Books." *Parerga and Paralipomena: Short Philosophical Essays*. Translated by E. F. J. Payne. Clarendon Press, 1974, vol. 2.

Schopenhauer, Arthur. *Parerga und Paralipomena*. http://www.buecherlei.de/fab/autor/sch/schopen2.htm.

Sérouya, Henri. *La Kabbale: Ses origines, sa psychologie mystique, sa métaphysique*. Grasset, 1947.

Sobley, William Ritchie. "Iamblichus." *Encyclopaedia Britannica*. Encyclopaedia Britannica Company, 1910, vol. 14, pp. 213–15.

Thompson, Edward Maude. "Manuscript." *Encyclopaedia Britannica*. Encyclopaedia Britannica Company, 1911, vol. 17, pp. 618–24.

Ubelaker Andrade, Max. *Borges Beyond the Visible*. Pennsylvania State University Press, 2019.

Walsh, Richard, and Jay Twomey, eds. *Borges and the Bible*. Sheffield Phoenix Press, 2015.

CHAPTER 9

THE 1920S POETRY OF JORGE LUIS BORGES

Remapping, Nostalgia, and Mythification

SEBASTIÁN HERNAIZ

ULTRAISMS

JORGE Luis Borges published his first poem on December 31, 1919, in the Spanish journal *Grecia*. Entitled "Himno del mar" [Hymn of the Sea], it was irrefutably inspired by enthusiasm for Walt Whitman, a highly regarded poet in Borges's reading during those years: Guillermo de Torre described Borges in 1925 as "arriving drunk on Whitman" (62). Emphatic in tone and word choice, sensual in its representation, the poem is an initiation that Borges would soon abandon, seduced down the paths of two experimental movements of the time: German Expressionism and Spanish Ultraism. Expressionism provided Borges an arsenal of possibilities and resources for finding a tone suitable for incorporating new social realities (the end of the Great War, the Russian Revolution) into his initial poetry—as can be found in poems such as "Trinchera" [Trench], "Rusia," or "Gesta maximalista" [Maximalist Achievement]. Yet, even then, these poems demonstrate characteristics of the trend that would mark his poetry and many of his theoretical and polemical writings in the coming years: Ultraism.

Borges's ultraist period had two phases: the first in Spain, the second in Buenos Aires. In Spain, Borges actively participated in ultraist literary circles; he wrote and published poems and essays in its literary journals (*Grecia, VLTRA*), defended ultraist aesthetics in literary polemics, and promoted the movement in manifestos and explanatory texts in a variety of media. Above all, the Spanish phase of Borges's ultraism is characterized by its explicitly avant-garde approach that actively confronted established aesthetic movements in Spain such as modernism, whose poetic devices the ultraists considered outdated and predictable (Anderson, Videla). Ultraist proponents published poems, prose, and manifestos, and participated in aesthetic debates while seeking to outline the premises of the "movement." Borges published essays debating with those whom he considered not to have "entendido una sola palabra de los poemas ultraístas" [understood a single word of ultraist poetry] (Borges, "Réplica"). The controversial nature of Borges's contributions seems to have been their primary purpose. In a letter to his close friend Jacobo Sureda, Borges highlighted the reception of one publication: "El *Manifiesto* y los poemas han provocado un escándalo mayúsculo. Una piara de fósiles, entre los cuales está Elviro Sanz, amenazan hasta ultimarnos a bastonazos" [The *Manifiesto* and the poems have provoked a major scandal. A pack of fossils, including Elviro Sanz, have even threatened to beat us to death] (*Cartas del fervor*). In another letter, Borges writes: "Alomar, Sureda y yo hemos hecho el *Manifiesto* que tú sabes y que provocó un asombro y un escándalo espléndidos" [Alomar, Sureda and I composed the *Manifiesto* you know about, which caused splendid shock and scandal] (*Textos recobrados* 108).

Borges lived in Europe between 1914 and 1921, primarily in Switzerland and Spain. In March 1921, he sailed back to Buenos Aires where he soon met other young writers and spread the tenets of ultraism, while continuing to send work to the various Spanish journals that promoted the new movement. From Buenos Aires, with quick enough turnaround to publish in the June 1921 issue of *VLTRA*, Borges sent the essay "Anatomía de mi 'Ultra'" [Anatomy of my "Ultra"], which evidences the campaign of renewal launched by Borges's own brand of *ultraismo* ("enunciaré las intenciones de mis esfuerzos líricos" [I will state the intentions of my lyrical efforts]). There were two devices, he wrote, upon which his poetic work relied: "rhythm and metaphor." With respect to rhythm, he would propose the use of free verse ("no encarcelado en los pentagramas de la métrica, sino ondulante, suelto, redimido, bruscamente truncado" [not imprisoned in the pentagrams of meter, but undulating, loose, liberated, abruptly truncated]). Regarding metaphor, in "Anatomía de mi 'Ultra,'" Borges synthesized a concept he would further develop in subsequent manifestos: "La metáfora: esa curva verbal que traza casi siempre entre dos puntos—espirituales—el camino más breve" [Metaphor: that verbal curve that almost always traces the shortest path between two *spiritual* points]. The principles of Borges's Buenos Aires phase of ultraism were quickly consolidated. On October 23, 1921, Borges published his first text in Buenos Aires. In *El Diario Español*, Manuel Machado had written about the young ultraists. Borges responded: "quiero rebatir los errores que verbenean en la antedicha exégesis y enunciar, breve y sencillamente, la significación del ultraísmo" [I want to refute the errors that riddle the aforementioned exegesis and outline, briefly and simply, the meaning of ultraism]. In this text, Borges added a local innovation to his usual style. If the still quite active practice of modernism was ultraism's target during Borges's Spanish phase, publishing in Buenos Aires, he would aim at the *sencillismo* movement: "en novecentistas y sencillistas, la música del verso—ese aglutinante que valoriza con tanta exorbitancia Manuel Machado—es el beleño que amodorra al lector" [in novecentistas and sencillistas, the music of the verse—that agglutinative so exorbitantly praised by Manuel Machado—is the nightshade that lulls the reader to sleep].

In the second half of 1921, Borges founded the "mural journal" *Prisma* in Buenos Aires, which swiftly reverberated among the city's literary circles, and the well-established journal *Nosotros* invited young ultraists to explain the innovation they were promoting. Borges then published an updated outline of his poetic creed, which by its very form of expressing rejection (*reducción, tachadura, abolición* [reduction, deletion, abolition]) revealed the movement's iconoclastic nature ("Ultraismo," *Nosotros*; cf. Balderston 46). Through his declarations, Borges synthesized a proposal that eventually would become synonymous with the ultraist movement: the production of suggestive metaphors and the composition of poems based on the synthetic alignment of images, as can be seen, for example, in the final verses of "Atardecer" [Dusk], the poem Borges would publish three months later in the second issue of *Prisma*: "La tarde maniatada / solo clama su queja en el ocaso / La mano jironada de un mendigo / esfuerza la congoja de la noche" [The hectic afternoon / only makes its complaint at sunset / The beggar's tattered hand / forces the anguish of the evening].

CORRESPONDENT

Though an ultraist based in Buenos Aires, throughout 1921, Borges still maintained close ties with Spain: he continued publishing regularly in *VLTRA* and began to work as an Argentine correspondent for a magazine based in Madrid. As he wrote in a letter to Sureda: "¿Te dije que me han nombrado corresponsal de *Cosmópolis*?" [Did I tell you that they made me a correspondent for *Cosmópolis*?] (*Textos recobrados* 147). After his seven years' absence from Argentina, the bases for the work he was soon to produce can be located in his correspondence for *Cosmópolis*. The texts Borges sent from Argentina to publish in Madrid in 1921 refined his aesthetic positions but also unveiled a doubly estranged perspective of Buenos Aires: a gaze that looked to the city to find subject matter for his writing, and the gaze of one who seeks to communicate to foreign readers that which was his own as a *porteño* [resident of Buenos Aires]. Between August and December 1921, Borges sent *Cosmópolis* the poem "Arrabal"; the essays "Crítica del paisaje" [Critique of Landscape], "Buenos Aires," and "La metáfora" [The Metaphor]; and the critical anthology *La lírica argentina contemporánea* [*Contemporary Argentine Poetry*]. Central to every piece, and for the first time in his work, was the question of how to represent Buenos Aires.

In "Buenos Aires" (*Cosmópolis*), one can see how the perception of the city emerges in *contrast*, as if placing it alongside the European cities he had recently visited and which the readers of *Cosmópolis* would recognize. That he anticipated a Spanish audience is made explicit in Borges's analysis of Buenos Aires's houses: "Estas casas de que hablo son la traducción, en cal y ladrillo, del ánimo de sus moradores, y expresan: Fatalismo. *No el fatalismo individualista y anárquico que se gasta en España*, sino el fatalismo vergonzante del criollo" [These houses to which I refer are the translation, in brick and mortar, of the spirit of their inhabitants, and they express: Fatalism. *Not the individualistic and anarchic fatalism that grinds away in Spain*, but the shameful fatalism of the criollo[1]] (*Textos recobrados* 107; my emphasis). This representation of the city coincides with the disenchanted view he conveys midyear to his friend Sureda in personal letters from the same dates: "Nos hemos anclado en Buenos Aires en un barrio geometral, serio y sosegado. (Casas de un piso, filas de plátanos otoñales que cubren sus ramas pobres con vendas de sol, tranvías, pentagramas telefónicos rayando el flaco y aguachirle azul del cielo, risas de niños en la calle . . .) Esto no nos entusiasma gran cosa" [We have taken anchor in Buenos Aires in a neighborhood that is geometrical, serious and composed. (Single-story houses, rows of autumnal plane trees whose poor branches are covered in mere patches of sun, trams, telephone wires scraping the thin and washed out (*aguachirle*[2]) blue of the sky, children's laughter in the street . . .) We are not exactly thrilled] (*Cartas* 198).

In the following dispatch to *Cosmópolis*, "La metáfora," Borges analyzed and refined the process that, during those same months, was the distinguishing feature of ultraism, which he defined "como una identificación voluntaria de dos o más conceptos distintos, con la finalidad de emociones" [as a willful identification of two or more different concepts, with the purpose of emotions]. At the end of the article, he asserted this aesthetic principle's dual locations in the unique wandering gaze of the ultraist correspondent in Buenos Aires: "Crítica es la anterior que enderezo en contra del aguachirlismo rimado que practican aquí en mi tierra, la Argentina, los lamentables 'sencillistas', y en pro del creacionismo y de la tendencia jubilosamente barroca que encarna Ramón Gómez de la Serna" [Criticism is the literary past that I lift up against the rhymed *aguachirlismo* practiced here in my land, Argentina, by the unfortunate "*sencillistas*," and in favor of *creacionismo* [creationism] and the jubilantly baroque trend embodied by Ramón Gómez de la Serna]. In the following issue of *Cosmópolis*, Borges's "La lírica argentina contemporánea" [Contemporary Argentine Poetry] took up previous arguments and described what—in a proclamation in *Prisma* that same month—Borges would denounce as the "nadería que es la literatura actual" [nothingness that is current literature]. It censures, for example, Rafael Alberto Arrieta ("indigencia de su facultad metafórica, casi no existen sus poemas" [poverty of his metaphorical faculty, his poems barely even exist]), Alfonsina Storni (of whose poems he said, "las encuentro cursilitas más bien. Son una cosa pueril, desdibujada, amarilleja, conseguida mediante el fácil barajeo de palabras baratamente románticas—flor, ninfa, amor, luna, pensión" [I find them rather trite. They are puerile, blurry, yellowing, created through the facile shuffling of cheaply romantic words—flower, nymph, love, moon, pension]), and Baldomero Fernández Moreno (whose poems "suelen faltar verdaderas intuiciones, en cuyo reemplazo campea, un confesionalismo anecdótico y gesticulante" [tend to lack any true intuitions, in whose place prevails an anecdotal and gesticulating confessionalism]).

Conceived for Spanish readers, filtered through an ultraist inclination, and written with the eyes of a correspondent recently arrived, in these collaborations, Borges was constructing the question of how to represent Buenos Aires. While lacking any will to celebrate the city and looking somewhat disdainfully upon it, in those collaborations with *Cosmópolis*, he nonetheless highlighted some of the features that he would later deploy, newly revalued, in *Fervor de Buenos Aires* [*Fervor of Buenos Aires*]. In sum: in 1921, Borges arrived in Argentina, renovated and promoted the importation of ultraism from Spain, and, at the same time, made Buenos Aires the subject of his writing and used his writing as a way to represent Buenos Aires, be it as dispatches to Spain or frank discussions with the dominant aesthetic trends in Argentina.

In confrontation with the "rhymed *aguachirlismo*" of the overly anecdotal *sencillista* poetry and modernism's residual meter, lexicon, and rhyme schemes, Borges dedicated 1922 to promoting ultraism and to writing and publishing poems, some—but not all—of which would be collected in *Fervor de Buenos Aires*: of the forty-six poems that comprise the first edition, the book included only a dozen that had been previously published. The entire book would be a platform for reckoning with his essay, "Buenos Aires," published in *Cosmópolis*.

READJUSTMENTS

In 1925, in the "Advertencias" [Reader Advisements] of *Inquisiciones* [*Inquisitions*], Borges would falsely state that the book's essay "Buenos Aires" was a rewriting of the same essay published in *Cosmópolis*, which "fue abreviatura de mi libro de versos y la compuse el novecientos veintiuno" [was an abbreviation of my book of verses and I composed it in nineteen twenty-one] (2). However, the 1925 version of "Buenos Aires" notably alters the judgments made in 1921. That year, the essay began by expressing contempt for the most common features of the city's landscape: "Ni de mañana ni al atardecer ni en la noche vemos realmente la ciudad (. . .) las etapas que acabo de enunciar son demasiado literarias para que en ellas pueda el paisaje gozar de vida propia" [Neither in the morning nor the afternoon nor at night do we really see the city (. . .) the times of day just listed are too literary for the cityscape to have its own life within them] (*Textos recobrados* 107). In 1925, however, the afternoon will be the prized moment of the day: "es a fuerza de tardes que la ciudad va entrando en nosotros" [it is by dint of the afternoons that the city begins to enter into us] (*Inquisiciones* 87). In 1921, the city's flat, grid-like layout, where "las líneas horizontales vencen las verticales" [the horizontal lines surpass the vertical ones], results in crossroads from where "se adivinan cuatro *correctos* horizontes" [one makes out four *correct* horizons] (*Textos recobrados* 107). In 1925, he elevated those *correct* streetcorners to thought-provoking and enriching conjectures: "Atraviesan cada encrucijada cuatro infinitos" [Four infinities traverse each crossroads] (*Inquisiciones* 88). If, in 1921, long distances were disdained ("Horizontes con esa lejanía exasperante que tienen las mangas de los gabanes" [Horizons with that exasperating length of overcoat sleeves]), in 1925 they were exalted ("nos hemos azorado a veces ante las interminables calles que cruzan nuestro camino" [we have been humbled at times by the interminable streets that cross our path]), as they allow one to experience "gigantescas puestas de sol que sublevan la hondura de la calle y apenas caben en el cielo" [gigantic sunsets that raise the streets from the depths and barely fit in the sky" (*Inquisiciones* 88). If in 1921 the city's outskirts were only the urban margins "que los verbalismos no mancharon aún" [not yet stained by words] ("Crítica del paisaje"), in 1925 they would be the means needed to truly see the sunsets: "Para que nuestros ojos sean flagelados por ellas en su entereza de pasión, hay que solicitar los *arrabales*[3]" [For our eyes to be flagellated by the sunsets in the entirety of their passion, we must make for the outskirts of the city] (*Inquisiciones* 88). If in the Buenos Aires of the 1925 essay "desfilan grandemente los ocasos" [sunsets parade grandly], in the 1921 version, most notable were "automóviles y vehementes anuncios de cigarrillos" [automobiles and vehement advertisements for cigarettes]. Finally, in both versions of the essay, Borges comments on "las casas" [the houses] and "las plazas" [the plazas or neighborhood squares], but while in 1921, the houses of Buenos Aires expressed "el fatalismo vergonzante del criollo que intenta hoy ser occidentalista y no puede" [the shameful fatalism of the *criollo* who today tries to be a Westerner and cannot], in 1925, they would still be a sign of fatalism, but a fatalism that is "burlón y criollo que informan el *Fausto* de Estanislao del Campo y aquellas estrofas del *Martín Fierro* que no humilla un prejuicio de barata doctrina liberal" [mocking and *criollo* and that informs Estanislao del Campo's *Fausto* and those stanzas of *Martín Fierro* not demeaned by a prejudice toward cheap liberal doctrine]. The city's plazas, are in fact the only aspect whose description does not vary between 1921 and 1925. Sunsets, horizons, corners, streets, sunsets, *arrabales*, houses and plazas: with praise and disdain that he would continue to rebalance, in his 1921 essay "Buenos Aires," written for Madrid's *Cosmópolis*, Borges found the subject of his first collection of poems. In the 1925 rewrite, he synthesized all the counterpoints to the 1921 essay that would be manifested in his first book of poetry: *Fervor de Buenos Aires* (1923). At the same time, he extended and reoriented the 1925 version of "Buenos Aires" toward the *criollismo* that would make its way into in his books *Luna de enfrente* [*Moon Across the Way*] and *El tamaño de mi esperanza* [*The Extent of My Hope*].

The poem "Benarés" published in *Fervor de Buenos Aires* in 1923 has surprised readers. In the notes of the "critical edition" of the *Obras completas* [*Complete Works*], for example, the reference to the Indian city of Varanasi (formerly known as Benares, and even earlier as Kashi) is attributed to Borges's youthful readings of Rudyard Kipling, yet the annotators mention their surprise: "it is strange, regardless, that he wrote about a city he had not visited" (100). A fragment of the aforementioned essay, "Buenos Aires" (1921), however, offers some answers regarding the relevance and meanings of the poem: "the times of day just listed" Borges had written in *Cosmópolis* referring to sunrise and sunset, "are too literary for the cityscape to have its own life within them. I am sure that the sunrise in Benares has the same meaning as sunrise in Madrid" (107). The assertion of equality between sunrises in the contrasting cities of Benares (in India, representing exoticism) and Madrid (home of the intended audience of the essay) was proposed in 1921 as an argument to reject poems that focused on "stages" (*etapas*) of the day such as sunrise or sunset. However, both such "stages" would become preferred moments when constructing the settings for poems in *Fervor*. Moreover, contradicting the poetic edicts of the 1921 essay, *Fervor de Buenos Aires* would include the poem "Benarés," where, through the use of ultraist imagery, Borges described an imaginary dawn: "juntamente amanece / en las persianas todas que miran al oriente / y la voz de un almuédano / que ya rezó el disperso rosario de los astros / apesadumbra desde su alta torre / la leve madrugada" [At the same time dawn breaks / on all shutters looking east / and the voice of the muezzin / who has already recited the disparate rosary of the stars / saddens from its high tower / the mild dawn" (*Fervor de Buenos Aires*; English translation based on "Benarés," *Selected Poems* 27).

DEMARCATIONS

In 1923, Borges published *Fervor de Buenos Aires*, which takes up, revises, and comes to terms with ongoing controversies (with modernism, with *sencillismo*) using the material outlined in "Buenos Aires" and the ultraist manifestos published between 1920 and 1922. While Borges's contemporaries (in 1923, in 1924) read it as the work of the young advocate of the new poetic movement, *Fervor* was not the ultraist book that more than one "member of the sect" might have expected. Fewer than two months after *Fervor* was published, one of its most attentive reviewers, Roberto Ortelli, wrote reproachfully: "Es realmente lamentable que Borges no haya publicado en este volumen, sus admirables versos que responden a esa novísima modalidad estética" [It is really lamentable that in this volume Borges did not publish those admirable verses of his that respond to that innovative aesthetic style] (62). While disenchanted, Ortelli astutely describes some of the characteristics of Borges's poetry collection that in fact do move it away from ultraist principles: "el anecdotismo, el desarrollo continuado con una hilación ininterrumpida, el prosaísmo y la mezquindad de metáforas e imágenes" [anecdotism, the continuous development of an uninterrupted thread, prosaicism and the paltriness of its metaphors and images] (63). Indeed, Borges's imagery was secondary to the writing methods that would allow him to create a concept that, when commenting on the title of first book of poems, he would define as "mi patria" [my homeland] (*Fervor de Buenos Aires*).

For the problematic Buenos Aires of 1921 to become Borges's "homeland" by 1923, the city had to undergo a conceptual remapping, which is powerfully evoked in the collection's opening poem, "Las calles" [The Streets]. This operation of remapping the city can initially be seen in his 1922 review of *Andamios interiores*, Mexican poet Manuel Maples Arce's book of stridentist poetry, which Borges describes as being "todo un contraste"—a contrast requiring the remapping of both urban and aesthetic terms:

> Permitir que la calle se vuelque de rondón en los versos—y no la dulce calle de arrabal, serenada de árboles y enternecida de ocaso, sino la otra, chillona, molestada de prisas y ajetreos—siempre antojóseme un empeño desapacible (. . .). Generoso de imágenes preclaras, el estilo de Maples Arce lo es también de adjetivos, cosa que no debemos confundir con el charro despliegue de epítetos gesteros que usan los de la tribu de Rubén.

> [Allowing the street to pour itself into the verses—and not the sweet street of the *arrabal*, serenaded by trees and softened by the sunset, but the other: shrill, perturbed by the hustle and bustle—always struck me as a disagreeable endeavor (. . .).

Generous in illustrious images, Maples Arce's style is also one of adjectives, which we should not confuse with the garish display of suggestive epithets used by those of Rubén's tribe]. ("Manuel Maples Arce" 4–5)

Remapping and adjectivization: these alone are the bases for creating *Fervor de Buenos Aires*'s opening poem. The system of inclusion and exclusion proposed in the poem from its opening lines ("no las calles enérgicas / . . . sino la dulce calle de arrabal" [not the energetic streets / . . . but the sweet street of the *arrabal*]) ushers the unpoetic city of 1921 into a system of evaluative oppositions upheld by hypallages, metonyms, and diminutives.

The peripheral snapshot of the city that is experienced through sensations—which in the first poem on the subject published by Borges, "Arrabal" (*Cosmópolis*, August 1921), were laden with negative estimations ("Mis pasos claudicaron / cuando iban a pisar el horizonte / *y caí* entre las casas / miedosas y humilladas" [My steps gave way / when they were about to set foot on the horizon / and *I fell* among the / fearful and humiliated houses])—is retaken and becomes the center of the poetic construction of the author, who in 1923 rewrote the verses of "Arrabal" in a tone of reconciliation ("Mis pasos claudicaron / cuando iban a pisar el horizonte / *y estuve* entre las casas / miedosas y humilladas" [when they were about to set foot on the horizon / and *I was* among the / fearful and humiliated houses]). Borges's remapping of the city is carried out through a long series of poems that evoke Buenos Aires's outskirts (*arrabales*) but also find its counterpoint in poems such as "Ciudad [City], which recovers those "vehementes anuncios de cigarrillos" [vehement advertisements for cigarettes] that "exasperated" the viewer in the essay "Buenos Aires" of 1921.

Present

In 1964, Guillermo de Torre would recall that when Borges published "su primer libro poético (*Fervor de Buenos Aires*), excluye, salvo una, todas las composiciones de estilo ultraísta (. . .) ante la pluralidad del universo, sustituye el 'fervor' por el espacio acotado de una ciudad; más exactamente, de unos barrios y un momento retrospectivo. *Vuelve a su infancia, y casi a la de su país, idealizando nostálgicamente lo entrevisto*" [his first book of poetry (*Fervor de Buenos Aires*), excludes, with just one exception, all ultraist compositions (. . .) facing the plurality of the universe, he substitutes "fervor" for the space surrounding the city; more precisely, a handful of neighborhoods and a specific time in the past. *He returns to his childhood, and practically that of his country as well, nostalgically idealizing what he glimpses*] (de Torre, "Para la prehistoria ultraísta" 458; my emphasis).

Yet, the city that becomes "endiosada" [deified] subject matter in *Fervor* is distinctly contemporary, even if the techniques used to represent it are not new. It does not rely on a precise topographical system but rather on indeterminate constructions, blurred into generalization by a meticulous imprecision in its composition (Pezzoni 81). The only four poems that break with the present tense construction of the remapped city are those dedicated to his ancestors, to the totalitarian caudillo Juan Manuel Rosas and to his childhood home. But in all four, the interest resides precisely with the current impacts those pasts have on the poetic subject's present moment: the figure of Rosas wars with the family memory that condemns him ("No sé si Rosas / fue sólo un ávido puñal como nuestros abuelos decían" [I do not know if / Rosas was merely an avid knife as our grandparents used to say]); with respect to his ancestors, he outlines how their memories reverberate in the present ("Hoy es orilla de tanta gloria el olvido" [Today he is as much the ripple of glory as oblivion]) ("Inscripción sepulcral: Para el conorel Don Isidro Suárez, mi bisabuelo") or long for a better future ("ruego al justo destino / aliste para ti toda la dicha / y que toda la inmortalidad sea contigo" [I ask fair destiny / to prepare for you all joy / and that all immortality be with you] ("Inscripción sepulcral: Para el coronel don Francisco Borges, mi abuelo"). As far as there is any "return to a childhood home," it is as part of an urban thematic device ("Después de muchos años de ausencia / busqué la casa primordial de la infancia" [After many years away / I sought out the primordial home of my childhood] begins "La vuelta") that allows for the contemplation and elevation of the reconceived parts of the city Borges loved. The poetic subject walks to the house he proposes as his childhood home and soon this return becomes part of the contemporary landscape, encoded in the "luna *nueva*" [*new* moon] that rises amidst the "palmera *pródiga*" [*prodigal* palm]: "advertí al desparramarse la tarde / la frágil luna nueva / que se arrimó al amparo benigno / de la palmera pródiga de hojas excelsas" [I noted as the afternoon drifted away / the fragile new moon / that crested under the benign shelter / of the prodigal palm of sublime fronds].

From the book's preface, Borges made clear: "*Sin miras a lo venidero ni añoranzas de lo que fue, mis versos quieren <u>ensalzar la actual visión porteña</u>, la sorpresa y la maravilla de los lugares que asumen mis caminatas*" [*Without looking at what is to come or longing for what was, my poems try <u>to lionize the current vision of Buenos Aires</u>, the surprise and marvel at the places to which my walks take me*" (*Fervor de Buenos Aires*; emphatic italics in the original, underline mine). And yet, it is commonplace among scholars of *Fervor* to indicate that the book represents a "past city," a city that Borges sought to evoke from his memory as a rejection of the contemporary one. Alicia Jurado, for example, proposed that upon returning to Buenos Aires, Borges "redescubre su ciudad en lo que ésta tiene de más pintoresco y *primitivo*: los barrios apartados, las sencillas casas" [rediscovers his city in its most picturesque and *primitive* facets: the remote neighborhoods, the simple houses] (33–34 [emphasis added]). Rafael Olea Franco, in his oft cited *El otro Borges. El primer Borges* [*The other Borges. The first Borges*] seeks to negate the "currency" of the text because it is filtered through the routes of Borges's personal strolls through the city. Partly following the work of Enrique Pezzoni, Olea Franco considers the setting of *Fervor* to be "una ciudad descrita por medio de elementos marginales que *más bien remiten al pasado*, por lo que resulta imposible reconocer en ella la imagen bonaerense moderna" [a city described by means of marginal aspects that *in large part refer to the past*, making it impossible to recognize the image of a modern Buenos Aires within it] (141; emphasis mine). Yet, the city through which the poetic subject moves, creating unity within the collection of poems, is a city in the present, a city that is characterized (through comparisons, series of images, and adjectives) as "esta numerosa urbe de Buenos Aires / asemejable en complicación a un ejército" [that numerous urb of Buenos Aires / comparable in its complication to an army] ("Amanecer"), whose center is characterized by "calles enérgicas / molestadas de prisas y ajetreos" [energetic streets / bothered by rushes and hurries] ("Las calles") and in whose thriving port, at night "Se apagaron los barcos / en el agua cuadrada de la dársena. / Las periódicas grúas relajan sus tendones. / Los mástiles se embotan en el cielo playo" [the boats' {lights} went out / in checkered water of the slip / The periodic cranes relax their tendons. / The masts are blunted in the low sky] ("Alba desdibujada"). Beatriz Sarlo, in her classic *Borges, un escritor en las orillas* [*Borges, a Writer on the Edge*], also repeats this commonplace: "Borges debía recordar lo olvidado de Buenos Aires en un momento en que eso olvidado comenzaba a desaparecer materialmente. Esta experiencia encuentra su tono poético: la nostalgia de *Fervor de Buenos Aires*" [Borges must have been remembering the forgotten aspects of Buenos Aires at a time when what was forgotten was beginning to materially disappear. This experience finds its poetic tone: the nostalgia of *Fervor de Buenos Aires*] (25). A curious affirmation if one takes into account the image of Buenos Aires that Borges had when he returned in 1921: disenchantment, as is clearly seen in his "Buenos Aires" essay in *Cosmópolis* (1921). Not long after arriving, he wrote to his ultraist friend Jacobo Sureda: "No me abandones en el destierro de la ciudad cuadriculada y de los jovencitos que hablan de la argentinidad (. . .) ¡Horror!" [Don't abandon me in my exile in this checkerboard city with its punk kids trying to talk about "Argentineness" (. . .) Horror!] (*Cartas* 194).

Regardless, Sarlo persisted in arguing, for example, when comparing him with the artist Xul Solar: "Xul no siente, como Borges, *nostalgia por la ciudad criolla que está desapareciendo*" [Xul does not feel, like Borges does, nostalgia for the *criolla* city that is disappearing] (30–31; emphasis mine). As if in passing, and apparently without noticing, Sarlo herself seemed to recognize a crucial problem in her argument: "A la fascinación de la calle céntrica (. . .) se opone la nostalgia de la calle de barrio, donde la ciudad se resiste a los estigmas de la modernidad, *aunque el barrio mismo haya sido un producto de la modernización urbana*" [On the one hand, there is the fascination with the downtown (. . .) On the other hand, there is the nostalgia for the neighborhood street, where the city resists the stigmas of modernity, *although the neighborhood itself may have been a product of urban modernization*] (33; emphasis mine). The elements of this contradiction were studied in detail by Adrián Gorelik, whose book, *La grilla y el parque*, explores how the design of the Buenos Aires street grid—that "checkerboard" that Borges derided in his letters and in *Cosmópolis* and came to revalue in *Fervor*—was a condition and a cause for the emergence of "barrios," which in turn was a direct consequence, of the process of modernization.

Gorelik, in a summary of his work specifically related to the study of Borges's work in the 1920s, synthesized, discussed, and roundly refuted readings such Sarlo's, though not

THE 1920S POETRY OF JORGE LUIS BORGES   163

mentioning her but explicitly highlighting and correcting the erroneous readings from other sources:

> La literatura sobre la presencia de Buenos Aires en el Borges de los años veinte ha enfatizado por lo general el intento, en buena medida nostálgico, de "fijar en imágenes durables el pasado de la ciudad" (Grau 20); la obra borgesiana habría buscado "restituir" el Buenos Aires de su infancia y, aun más atrás, sus restos criollos previos a la modernización que se desenvolvía sin pausa desde la década de 1880 (. . .) se insiste en que "Borges se inventa una ciudad a su medida" (Andreu), pero se desconocen las relaciones entre esa ciudad y las otras representaciones contemporáneas, y el modo en que entre todas disputan por una Buenos Aires "verdadera", con lo cual resulta imposible entender la originalidad y los efectos de la mirada borgesiana. ("El color del barrio" 36–37)

> [The literature on the presence of Buenos Aires in Borges of the 1920s has generally emphasized the largely nostalgic attempt to "focus on lasting images of the city's past" (Grau 20); Borges's work is held to have sought to "restore" the Buenos Aires of his childhood and, even further back, the remains of a *criollo* culture that existed prior to the modernization that had ceaselessly unfolded since the 1880s (. . .) There is an insistence that "Borges invents a city fitting his own expectations" (Andreu), but little is known about the relationships between that city and other representations at that time, or the ways in which they all contend for a "true" Buenos Aires, making it is impossible to understand the originality and the effects of the Borgesian gaze.]

Contrary to these readings, Gorelik interpreted the "operations" Borges carried out in the 1920s as "quite the opposite" ("El color del barrio" 36). As he writes in his book:

> A diferencia de la producción mitologizante de la bohemia literaria y tanguera, que construye un barrio de arquetipos necesariamente distanciados de la realidad urbana y social que ha estado moldeando el barrio, Borges produce un barrio mitológico a partir de la reunión y la potenciación poética de una serie de objetos existentes en el barrio real (. . .) esa referencialidad material, esta producción sobre elementos existentes, permite pensar que el barrio de Borges no sólo es un intento de "restitución" de un Buenos Aires anterior, como han interpretado algunas aproximaciones a las relaciones de su literatura con la ciudad: en su propio presente suburbano Borges encuentra el espacio donde combinar de modo típicamente vanguardista tradición y novedad. (*La grilla* 82)

> [Unlike the mythologizing production of bohemian literature and tango, which constructs a neighborhood of archetypes that, by necessity, are distanced from the urban and social reality that has actually shaped the neighborhood, Borges produces a mythological *barrio* through the combination and poetic deployment of a series of objects existing in the real *barrio* (. . .) that material referentiality, this production based upon truly existing elements, suggests that Borges's *barrio* is not merely an attempt to "restore" a previous Buenos Aires, as has been argued in some discussions of the relationship between his literature and the city: in his own current present on the city's outskirts, Borges finds the space where he can combine tradition and novelty in a typically avant-garde way.]

Thus, Sarlo's hypothesis characterizing *Fervor* as *nostalgic* to distinguish it from that of his contemporaries proves problematic: "Lo que, en los años veinte, era evidente para sus contemporáneos, se vuelve invisible en la poesía de Borges: Arlt o González Tuñón o Girondo no podían sino descubrir el movimiento de lo nuevo, Borges reconstruye aquello que está desapareciendo, que pertenece con mayor justicia a la memoria de otros y que, por eso mismo, sostiene la nostalgia" [What, in the 1920s, was evident to his contemporaries, becomes invisible in Borges's poetry: Arlt or González Tuñón or Girondo could not but discover the movement of the new, [but] Borges reconstructs what is disappearing, which belongs more justly to the memory of others and which, for that very reason, sustains nostalgia[4]] (51). The problem here can be seen in the fact that it was the port area, the city center, the historic parts of the city where tradition was developing, while what was *new* in Buenos Aires were precisely the unstable outskirt neighborhoods that were appearing—not disappearing—on the urban grid. This development becomes the subject of Borges's poems in *Fervor*:

> Siempre hay otros ocasos, otra gloria;
> yo siento el rendimiento del espejo
> que no descansa en una imagen sola.
> ¿Para qué esta porfía
> de clavar con dolor un claro verso
> de pie como una lanza sobre el tiempo
> si mi calle, mi casa,
> desdeñosas de plácemes verbales,
> me gritarán su novedad mañana?
> ("Vanilocuencia" 1923)

> [There are always other sunsets, other glory;
> I feel the output of the mirror
> that does not rest on a single image.
> Why this insistence
> on painfully nailing a clear verse
> by the foot, like a spear over time
> if my street, my house,
> disdainful of verbal pleasantries,
> will shout their news at me tomorrow?]

COMPADRITOS

In a detailed book on *Fervor*, Antonio Cajero Vázquez expanded this view of Borges's early poetry when he spoke of a "past-looking gaze" and conjectured that "los poemas en que Borges hace referencia a la ciudad, a sus calles y plazas (. . .) *constituyen un itinerario de finales del siglo XIX* (. . .) representan una búsqueda de la *ciudad perdida*" [the poems in which Borges refers to the city, its streets and squares (. . .) *constitute a late nineteenth century itinerary* (. . .) they represent a search for the *lost city*] (92; emphasis mine). From his perspective, the poetic subject of *Fervor*'s poems, "mientras se aleja del puerto, también *sufre un regreso en el tiempo. Busca y encuentra la imagen viva del recuerdo en el suburbio*" [as he moves away from the port, he also *undergoes a regression in time. He seeks and finds the living image of memory in the suburb*] (93; emphasis mine). Summarizing his perspective, Cajero explains: "La ciudad solitaria de *Fervor* no resulta extraña en lo absoluto: el joven Borges *simpatiza con la Buenos Aires de otro siglo y de ella apenas quedan unos cuantos compadritos*, las historias de los héroes familiares muertos y una actitud iconoclasta, pues prefirió un espacio semihabitado, previo al auge inmigratorio" [The solitary city of *Fervor* should not strike us as strange at all: the young Borges *identifies with the Buenos Aires of another century and from it there remain but a few compadritos*, stories of dead family heroes and an iconoclastic attitude, since he preferred a semi-inhabited space, existing prior to the immigration boom] (98–99; emphasis mine).

The "few *compadritos*" Cajero sees in *Fervor* are significant. It is likewise significant that Cajero's mode of reading—which adheres to the tendency of finding in *Fervor* a "Buenos Aires from another century"—should lead to glimpses of "a few *compadritos*" in *Fervor* given that such persons not only do not appear in the text, they are not even hinted at. In all of Borges's early work, the *compadrito* has but a sporadic and negative appearance. In 1924, the *compadrito* was considered, but precariously, as stemming "del poema que entrelazan los tangos" ("totalidad precaria, ruin, que contradice el pueblo en parodias y *que no sabe de otros personajes que el compadrito nostálgico*") [from the poem intertwined by tangos (precarious, vile totality, that contradicts the true people in parodies *and that knows no other characters than the nostalgic compadrito*)] ("Después de las imágenes" 23). In 1925, Borges associated the figure with the self-aggrandizing swagger inherent in the *lunfardo* issuing from the mouth of the "compadrito de la esquina" [streetcorner thug] ("El idioma infinito" 43). It would be only in 1926 that the figure of the turn-of-the-century *compadrito* would acquire notable prominence in Borges's texts, becoming a frequent reference from that year on: then *compadritos* will appear as founders of old-school tango ("El tamaño de mi esperanza") and they will be the "hombres de boca soez que se pasaban las horas detrás de un silbido o de un cigarrillo" [men whose foul mouths spent their hours behind a whistle or a cigarette] reverberating through the hypallage used to describe Palermo at the turn of the century: "El barrio era peleador en ese anteayer" [The *barrio* was a fighter back then] ("Carriego y el sentido del arrabal" 5).

Nonexistent in *Fervor* and even in *Luna de enfrente*, "compadritos" began to multiply in various prose essays in 1926; only in the summer of 1927 did the mythologized *compadrito* come onto the scene that Borges narrated in his foundational "Leyenda policial" [Police Legend]. The appearance of the old-time fighting *compadre* eventually became a synecdoche of Borges's push to renew *criollismo*. Reviving the *compadrito*, whose true existence dates back to the end of the nineteenth century, allowed him to distinguish the *arrabal* of the 1920s from Buenos Aires's outskirts at the end of the 1800s:

"Hablo de cuando el arrabal, rosado de tapias, era también relampagueado de acero; de cuando las provocativas milongas levantaban en la punta el nombre de un barrio; de cuando las patrias chicas eran fervor. Hablo del noventa y seis o noventa y siete y el tiempo es caminata dura de desandar" [I'm talking about when the *arrabal*, with its rose-colored walls, was also flashed with steel; of when provocative milongas raised high the name of a neighborhood; of when tiny homelands were the rage. I'm talking about ninety-six or ninety-seven and time is a difficult path to retrace] ("Leyenda policial" 4).

In Borges's poetry, the *compadrito* makes an appearance only at the end of 1926, in "Elegía de Palermo" [Elegy for Palermo] whose verses deploy a lexicon similar to that of "Leyenda policial" when describing this classic urban figure. Presenting the Palermo neighborhood as it was in the days of Evaristo Carriego, he wrote: "Esta es una elegía / que recuerda los taitas que se pasaban horas / empujando un silbido / o conversando un truco traicionero / en que una flor cruzada preludiaba cuchillos" [This is an elegy / that recalls the *taitas*[5] who spent hours / pushing out a whistle / or conversing a treacherous *truco* / in which a crossed flower preluded knives] (322).

Nostalgia

Toward the end of 1926, the poem does evoke, with the nostalgia typical of elegies, a city of the past ("Esta es una elegía / de cuando los portones de Palermo hacían sombra" [This is an elegy / from when the gates of Palermo cast a shadow] ("Elegía de Palermo" 22), populated by the *compadritos* who Borges defined in his essays as characteristic of the turn of the century. "Elegía de Palermo" also presents formal characteristics that distance it from the poems of *Fervor*, such as its heptasyllabic construction with a subtle system of linking rhymes, and with the seven-syllable line "Esta es una elegía" [This is an elegy] which anaphorically repeats five times in the first twenty lines.[6] These metrical features link it to the writing of other poems from those years—"el general Quiroga va en coche al muere" [General Quiroga Rides to His Death in a Carriage] (*Luna de enfrente*) and "La fundación mitológica de Buenos Aires" [The Mythological Founding of Buenos Aires] (*Nosotros*, 1926)—all composed of alexandrines with assonant rhymes. Borges explained these metric recurrences in the poem that closes *Luna de enfrente* ("versos de catorce" [verses of fourteen]) and justified them in his prologue: "La verdá es que no me interesa lo auditivo del verso y que me agradan todas las formas estróficas, siempre que no sean barulleras las rimas" [The truth is that I am not interested in the auditory aspects of poetry and that I enjoy all strophic forms, as long as the rhymes are not too sloppy] (6). The construction of a nostalgic poetic subject who evokes the past, which is clearly seen in "Elegía de Palermo" and which was already present in some poems in *Luna de enfrente*—but not in *Fervor*—was consolidated between 1925 and 1927. This can be seen if one compares three poems that share the same referent (the house on Calle Serrano where Borges spent his childhood) but were published in 1923, 1925, and 1927.

In "La vuelta" [The Return] (*Fervor de Buenos Aires*), a gaze is constructed in the present, sensitive but not nostalgic, which seeks the "casa primordial de la infancia" [primordial home of childhood]. This house is literally sought and touched[7]: "Mis manos han tanteado los árboles / como quien besa a un durmiente" [My hands have felt the trees / like someone who kisses a sleeper]. The poetic subject there finds the figure of the "luna nueva" [new moon], which appears "al amparo benigno / de la palmera pródiga" [under the benign shelter / of the prodigal palm tree], which plays into intuitions for the future ("cuánta quebradiza luna nueva / infundirá al jardín su dulcedumbre" [how many brittle new moons / will infuse the garden with their sweetness"]). With slight assonances that intertwine as it progresses, "La vuelta" is a poem in free verse, though with a few hendecasyllables, which, as stated in its preface, are frequently found in the book. The poem does not lack for comparisons, eloquent adjectives, or the unusual but effective images (habitual in this era of Borges's poetry) that exalt the scene: "cuánto heroico poniente / militará en la hondura de la calle" [how many heroic sunsets / will militate in the depths of the street].

From the very title of the poem, "a la calle Serrano" (*Luna de enfrente*), with its dedicatory tone, an intention of conveying nostalgia is made evident. It begins "Calle Serrano. / *Vos ya no sos la misma* de cuando el Centenario" [Calle Serrano. / You are no longer the same as in the time of the Centenary] and consolidates its nostalgic interpellation by replacing the present tense verbs at the beginning of poem with the past imperfect. Like "Elegía de Palermo," it is composed primarily of heptasyllables (with nearly half of the lines composed as the hemistichs of an alexandrine), which in turn foregrounds a line placed in the last third of the poem that consists solely of the adverb "Antes" [Before], strengthening the nostalgic gaze. This structure is accompanied by some more insistent assonant rhymes that reinforce the tone of the standard meter: for example, lines ending in *a-a* to link the words: fach*adas*, ros*adas*, guar*anga*, guit*arra*, *alma*, *casa*, and alegr*aban* (respectively, facades, pink, rude, guitar, soul, house, and cheered).

Finally, in "Versos con ademán de memoria" [Verses that gesture at memory] (published in the journal *Aurea* 1927, retitled "Fluencia natural del recuerdo" when included in *Cuaderno San Martín* that same year), with a more irregular meter—although not as systematically irregular as in *Fervor*—Borges privileged the alternation of eneasyllables with hendecasyllables and a complex and subtle network of assonances that leave only two verses without reflecting sounds. As the title indicates, remembrance is the principle that governs the images that accumulate in the poem in past tense enunciation, building upon the primary hendecasyllable "Recuerdo mío del jardín de casa" [Memory of mine of the garden of the house]. The tone of the poem is sustained through verbs in the past imperfect tense, which distance and establish the finality of the reality they describe, thereby invoking a longing tenderness ("parra firmamental de uva negra / los días de verano dormían a tu sombra" [heavenly vine of black grapes / the summer days slept in your shade]). Unlike the two previous poems, when recreating the era through an archetype, "Versos con ademán de memoria" actually references— though does not specifically name—the *compadrito* ("El almacén, hermano del *malevo*,

/ dominaba la esquina" [The bodega, brother to the *malevo* (ruffian), / dominated the corner]).

Between 1925 and 1926, Borges once again reconfigured the image of the city manifested in his poetry. If between the essay "Buenos Aires" (1921) and the publication of *Fervor* the city's treatment shifts due to a metaphorical remapping of its neighborhoods, between 1923 and 1926 there is—only now—a new shift toward a mythologized past which, through a series of lexical, rhetorical, and metrical devices, furnishes the poetic subject's gaze with nostalgic nuances. These devices tend to be associated with the *criollismo* that Borges principally defends in his essay collection *El tamaño de mi esperanza* (1926) and which are most notable in poems from *Luna de enfrente*. These devices include a *criollo* lexicon ("Como la estaca pampa bien metida en la pampa" [Like the pampa stake[8] well buried in the pampa]); an "apuesta lingüística para rescatar el habla criolla ('rosao', 'dualidá', 'ciudá')" [linguistic gambit to rescue *criollo* speech ("rosao" {rose-colored}, "dualidá" {duality}, "ciudá" {city})][9] (Blanco 151); and even the Argentine appropriation of the concept of *arrabal*.

RETROACTIVE

The first poem published in *Cosmópolis* in 1921 was entitled "Arrabal," but "arrabal" was not a word specific to Buenos Aires; rather, it belonged to "*ese intemporal, eterno español (ni de Castilla ni del Plata) que los diccionarios registran*" [that timeless, eternal Spanish (neither from Castilla nor the River Plate) recorded in dictionaries] (*Luna de enfrente* 8). The term was already extensively recorded in Spanish dictionaries (by 1780, it was already registered by the Real Academia Española), Quevedo had used it, and it would be geographically and chronologically universalized by Cansinos Assens in 1921: "*todas* las ciudades tienen un arrabal" [*all* cities have an *arrabal*] ("El arrabal en la literatura")—preceding Borges's publication of "Arrabal" in *Ultra* by four full months: "en las tardes de fiesta, en que los arrabales estarán cercanos" [on holiday afternoons, when the *arrabales* will be close] ("En primavera" [In spring]). One does not have to look hard in *Cosmópolis* to find the motif of city outskirts and descriptions of Madrid's *arrabales*; for example, in the review of the album *Arrabales*, published in the same issue as Borges's poem: "El alma sonora de los arrabales es la voz de los niños que juegan en el arroyo, la danza de la gitana, el paso del tocador de aristón, la melopea del ciego" [The sonorous soul of the *arrabales* is the voice of the children who play in the stream, the dance of the gypsy, the turn of the Ariston phonograph, the melopoeia of the blind man] (Vuillermoz 667). Borges himself used the term as well in October 1921 to refer to the outskirts of Madrid, when describing an outing to a brothel: "En los arrabales del mundo el amanecer monstruoso y endeble ronda como una falsedad" [In the *arrabales* of the world, the monstrous and feeble dawn haunts like a falsehood] ("Casa Elena" 2).

In those early years, Borges used the vernacular "arrabal," but the term "orillas" as a synonym for *arrabal* was recorded as a specifically Argentine usage in those years

(Segovia 251; *Pequeño Larousse* 679), and likewise "orillero," to name who lived there (Garzón 342). In 1923, Borges appealed to the urban as a device that allowed the poetic subject's gaze, viewing from the point of the "arrabales," to venerate the city. But at that time, they were still *arrabales*, not *orillas*. Only after *Fervor* would Borges incorporate the "voz las *orillas*" with a clear awareness of that term's temporal and expressive reverberations: "*Nadie dijo arrabal en esos antaños. La zona circular de pobreza que no era el centro, era las orillas*" [*Nobody said* arrabal *in those days. The sphere of poverty that was not the city center, was the orillas*] ("Leyenda policial" 4; emphasis mine). But when he incorporated this word, he also rewrote his past: the poem that closes the *Luna de enfrente*, frequently read as the standard of his poetic work, illuminates the reconceptualization made with respect to *Fervor*. There, for example, we read "I apunté la patriada que hacen los organitos / Acriollando gorriones a puro moler tangos" [And I pointed out the homeland made by the *organitos* / making *criollos* of the sparrows purely by playing tangos] or "Yo presentí la entraña de la voz *las orillas*" [I sensed the deep meaning of the word *orillas*] (*Luna de enfrente* 42).

However, this "standard," if it is taken as an interpretative lens for *Fervor*, is as potent as it is fallacious, and it is akin to the topical treatment of the *compadrito* discussed above, where some critics overdetermine this figure as somehow populating *Fervor de Buenos Aires*. In "versos de catorce," both the alexandrine "I apunté la patriada que hacen los organitos" [And I pointed out the homeland made by the *organitos*] as well as "Yo presentí la entraña de la voz *las orillas*" [I sensed the deep meaning of the word *orillas*] speak in the past tense of operations that, with this collection of poems, Borges was actually carrying out for the first time. And if until then he had called the peripheral areas of the city "arrabales" and not "orillas"—the move toward the use of *orillas* being a way of facing the poems toward the past—the presence of the *organito* [street organ] can be seen as complementary. In Carriego's writing, the street organ was collective and communal. In that of Borges, like the *compadrito* and the *orillas*, the *organito* would be, from his 1925 book *Inquisitions* on, a strategy for creating *criolledá* [creoleness], orthography reflective of traditional pronunciation. The line is forceful in associating writing— homeland—street organs, but this association is also newly typical of the *criollismo* of the *mid*-1920s and not of the times of *Fervor*, which did not include street organs of any kind. *Compadritos, orillas, organitos*: in *Luna de enfrente* the operations being carried out in the present are proposed as having unfolded in the past.

CONTEMPORARIES

In 1924, Luis Emilio Soto analyzed "El sentido poético de la ciudad moderna" [The poetic sense of the modern city] in *Fervor* according to Borges's redefinition of the city's urban topography (16–17), and in the magazine *Martín Fierro*, Evar Méndez described him as "Borges, un renovador" [Borges, a renovator] (9). In 1926, however, the novelty of the *criollista* project and the new inflections proposed by poems from *Luna de enfrente* changed the ways Borges was viewed by his contemporary readers: both in those who celebrated him and in those who opposed him. Ildefonso Pereda Valdés was among those in the first group; reading *Luna de enfrente*, he wrote:

> Su amor es mayor por el Buenos Aires que fue, que por el Buenos Aires que es (. . .) Borges es una ciudad, que requiere un Baedecker especial, escrito en un doble idioma: en criollo y en español (. . .) "El año cuarenta," cuadro de Figari transformado en música donde se encuentran expresiones frescas como una cachimba: "En carretas bajonas, detrás de bueyes bajo pértigo y yugo, iba el río a las casas." (108–09)

> [His love is greater for the Buenos Aires that was, than for the Buenos Aires that is (. . .) Borges is a city, which requires a special Baedecker travel guide, written in a double language: in Argentine Creole and in Spanish (. . .) "El año cuarenta," Figari's painting transformed into music in which one finds expressions as fresh as a pipe: "In low wagons, behind oxen under beam and yoke, the river went to the houses.]

But more eloquent in perceiving the ways in which Borges was read was the parody of his work created by some of his detractors.

Included in the May 1927 issue of *La Campana de Palo* was the "Nueva exposición de la actual poesía argentina" [New Anthology of Current Argentine Poetry] (5), in which Pedro Juan Vignale and César Tiempo anthologized a series of parodies. The poem "Rabón,"[10] signed by a fictitious Jorge Luis Borges, featured several of the novelties found in his *criollista*-era work. The parodic poem (five stanzas of alexandrines with assonant rhymes between the odd lines of each stanza) affects a traditional card game, "truco," among four "criollos" in a "boliche baqueano" [pathfinders' nightclub] Among the hallmarks of Borges's *criollista* style between 1925 and 1926 that are imitated in the parody are spelling that suggests *criollo* pronunciation ("La oscuridá del campo"); favored topics ("los ponientes" [sunsets], "los criollos," "el patio," "el truco" [Argentine card game]); the use of diminutives ("amontonaditos"); the use of images and comparisons ("la oscuridá del campo se aclaró en un envido" [the darkness of the field was clarified in a {truco} bid], "las caras (. . .) tirantes como cuerdas" [the faces (. . .) tight as ropes]; adjectives ("suspiro flaco," "un no quiero prudente," "soberbio, un siete bravo," "lindo fin"); the criollo lexicon of the card game *truco* ("la porotada," "al bueno," "siete bravo," "¡Quiero, maula!"); the exaggerated use of countryside lexicon ("cachaza de bolichero viejo," "palenque").

In *La Campana de Palo's* parody, the characteristics—obviously visible to his contemporaries—of the *criollo* Borges are accurately if unkindly synthesized. Perhaps between Pereda Valdés's celebration ("se encuentran expresiones frescas como una cachimba: 'En carretas bajonas, detrás de bueyes bajo pértigo y yugo'" [one finds expressions as fresh as a pipe: In low wagons, behind oxen under beam and yoke, the river went to the houses]) (5) and the verses falsely attributed to Borges ("Las caras de los criollos de puro preocupadas / Se pusieron de pronto tirantes como cuerdas" [The faces of the criollos out of pure preocupation / Suddenly became as tight as ropes]) (5), the interpretation coincides as much as the assessment differs.

MYTHOLOGICAL

By 1929, Borges moderated some of the devices that were parodied (he abandoned oral spelling and some rural terminology) but radicalized the way he took the imagination of the poetic subject into the past. After publishing *Luna de enfrente*, Borges had already begun projections for his next book, *Cuaderno San Martín*. Carlos García cited a letter to Guillermo de Torre dated December 31, 1925, where he describes the project as "una historia argentina versificada" [an Argentine history in verse] (128). That historical gaze will, however, lead to a mythologization of the past (of his childhood, of the past of his neighborhood, of the founding of Buenos Aires). In 1927, the project also included a topographical reorganization of the topics of his poems: "Estoy escribiendo otro libro *de versos porteños* (*digamos palermeros o villaalvearenses*, para que no suene ambicioso)" [I am writing another book of Buenos Aires poems (let's say Palermo or Villa Alvear poems, to not sound too ambitious)] ("Autobiografía" 6).

Borges's last book of poems of the 1920s opens with "La fundación mitológica de Buenos Aires," which culminates the movement that began in the remapped city of *Fervor*, was adjusted with the criollo nostalgia of *Luna* ("soy un hombre de ciudad, de barrio, de calle" [I am a man of the city, the barrio, the street]) (26), and which in 1929, dovetails with the imaginary founding of the city as plays out in the street block with which the poetic subject identifies in his biography[11]: "Fue en una manzana entera y en mi barrio: en Palermo" [It was in an entire block and in my neighborhood: in Palermo].

"La fundación mitológica" had already been published in 1926, with several variations (Lois 166–69). The most significant is the modification of the seventh stanza and the inclusion of a new eighth stanza, whose first verse would be "El *primer organito* salvaba el horizonte" [The first *organito* was saving the horizon]. In 1926, the seventh stanza was:

> Un almacén rosado como rubor de chica
> Brilló y en la trastienda lo inventaron al truco
> Y a la vuelta pusieron una marmolería
> Para surtir de lunas al espacio desnudo.

> [A general store as pink as a girl's blush
> Shone, and in the back room they invented truco
> And around the corner they put a stonemason's
> To supply the bare space with moons.]

172   SEBASTIÁN HERNAIZ

In 1929:

> Un almacén rosado *como revés de naipe*
> Brilló y en la trastienda conversaron un truco;
> El almacén rosado floreció en un *compadre*
> Ya *patrón de la esquina, ya resentido y duro.*
>
> [A pink general store *as the back of playing card*
> Shone bright and in the back there was talk of truco.
> The pink bodega flowered in a *compadre*
> Already *owner of the corner, already resentful and hardened.*]
> (emphasis mine)

Although he has moderated the "fraseología estridentemente autóctona" [stridently autochthonous phraseology] (Lois 168) and reduced orthographic innovations, in 1929, Borges seemed not to heed the criticism of the 1927 parody and not only kept the well-recognized *criollo* figures but also reinforced them. In the revised poem, the reference to *truco* replaces the romantic "girl's blush" and the figures of the bodega, the compadre, and the organito fuse together, in the mythical time proposed in the poem, all the *criollista* Borges's operations that we have reviewed.

The construction of the mythical time proposed in "La fundación mitológica," is a function of casting doubt upon the historical account, moving from its title, to the interrogative opening of the poem, and a resolution in its third stanza: "Lo cierto es" [The truth is]. This grammar of interrogating history and affirming its mythical reformulation is confirmed in the 1929 version of "Elegía de Palermo," which captures the intent of *Cuaderno San Martín* as a whole: "Yo digo que así fuiste en un día del tiempo" [I say that you were like this one day in time] ("Elegía de los portones" [Elegy of the Gates]). Here, the power of the affirmation that opens the line is attenuated by the indeterminacy of "one day in time," confirming the constitution of a mythologized time.

CONSOLIDATION

Around 1929, Borges's readers read him in the following way: in June, Carlos M. Grünberg reviewed *El idioma de los argentinos* [*The Language of Argentines*] in the magazine *La Vida Literaria* and noted: "El Buenos Aires de Borges es el Buenos Aires de ayer. No, pues, el que está construido delante de nuestros ojos, sino el que necesita ser reconstruido de espaldas al devenir" [Borges's Buenos Aires is the Buenos Aires of yesterday. Not, however, the one that is built before our eyes, but rather the one that must be rebuilt with its back to the future] (5). And in 1930, the magazine *Caras y Caretas* [*Faces and Masks*] included his caricature in Valdivia's running page "Nuestros escritores" [Our writers], with a brief comment: "Jorge Luis Borges es un crítico de espíritu poético.

THE 1920S POETRY OF JORGE LUIS BORGES 173

Evoca las cosas viejas, los matices desvanecidos de la vida porteña. Lo hace con un arte complicado: siempre con gusto personal" [Jorge Luis Borges is a critic with a poetic spirit. He evokes things of old, the faded nuances of Buenos Aires life. He does it with a complicated art: always to his personal taste] (65).

If a constant in Borges's three collections of poems is the question of time, the method of questioning that he adopts in each instance is different. If in *Fervor de Buenos Aires*, it is the present time that verse cannot capture; in *Luna de enfrente* it is nostalgia for the time that has passed; and in *Cuaderno San Martín*, it is the affirmation of the time that could have been.

NOTES

1. TN: In colonial terms, "criollo" was a person of Spanish descent who was born in the Americas and held an elite status just below that of the Spanish-born colonizer; with individual nations' independence, *criollo*, and *criollismo* took on culturally specific meanings as varied as each nation's amalgamation of peoples who preexisted the Spanish, were born to colonizers, were forcibly brought to the Americas as slaves, or eventually came pouring in as immigrant laborers. In Borges's context, un "criollo" is an Argentine whose cultural roots in Argentina are stronger than their ties to Europe. *Criollismo* is a literary movement that seeks to privilege Argentine cultural folklore.
2. TN: "Aguachirle" is an archaic Spanish term for watered-down or weak beverages, which Góngora used as an insult in his own literary feud with Lope de Vega in 1621: "Patos de la aguachirle castellana / que de su rudo origen fácil riega / y tal vez dulce inunda nuestra Vega." The term appears repeatedly in Borges's writing in 1921.
3. TN: Poor urbanizations outside the city proper, often translated as "slums," but better understood as an intermediate zone between the pampas and the city, where inhabitants still retain certain rural habits. As will be discussed, *arrabal* was a Spanish term of generalized usage, which Borges would eventually substitute with the particularly Argentine term *orillas* as he began shedding the Castilian acculturation of his teens in favor the *criollismo* that would define his twenties.
4. TN: Sarlo's published English translation of these lines varies some from her Spanish text, which was directly translated above: "What was evident to his contemporaries, becomes invisible in Borges's poetry of the 1920s. Two of his most eminent contemporaries, the novelist Arlt and the poet Girondo were fascinated by the movement of the new. . . . Instead, Borges reconstructs something which probably had not quite existed and which, for that very reason, could be transformed into nostalgia."
5. TN: The Argentine acception of "taita" is defined by the Real Academia Española (RAE) as: "Hombre que domina una actividad por lo general vinculada al folclore urbano" [Man who dominates an activity, generally related to urban folklore].
6. Mariela Blanco analyzed this change in tone as follows: "*Luna de enfrente* (1925), si bien continúa esta temática en la ponderación del paisaje porteño, se caracteriza por un tono más grandilocuente (. . .). Las metáforas al modo ultraísta del primer poemario se atemperan y aumenta el número de repeticiones." [*Luna de enfrente* (1925), while it continues the themes of pondering the landscape of Buenos Aires, is characterized by a more grandiloquent tone (. . .) The ultraist-style metaphors are tempered and the number of repetitions is increased] (145–46).

7. Horacio Coppola recalled: "Era interesante (su) gusto por la piel, por decir así, de Buenos Aires. Por ejemplo, paseando por un lugar por donde había un paredón, un paredón revocado y descascarado, hubo un momento en que Borges puso las manos así, y lo tanteó, así, como si fuera algo vivo" [It was interesting, his taste for the skin, so to speak, of Buenos Aires. For example, strolling through some place that had a wall, a neglected and peeling wall, there was moment when Borges put his hands like this, and felt it, like this, as if it were something living] ("Horacio Cóppola: testimonios," cited in Gorelik, *La grilla*, 82).

8. TN: With virtually nothing to tie their horses to in the vast expanses of the pampa, indigenous peoples and gauchos would tie them to bones or stakes and bury them horizontally in the ground or under rocks.

9. TN: In typical rural and working-class varieties of Spanish, including that of Buenos Aires and its environs, the "d" sound is often omitted from the ends of words and the past participle ending "-ado.".

10. We include the complete poem as it is not particularly well known:

Rabón

El boliche baqueano de todos los ponientes
Cantó un réquiem pampero al porrón de ginebra
En las cuatro gargantas se ahogó un suspiro flaco.
La cara de los criollos solivió una pena.

Los naipes, en la mesa, bien amontonaditos
El patrón, gringo zurdo, de mirón en el patio
Mirando con cachaza de bolichero viejo
A quién le tocaría empalmar con el gasto.

La oscuridá del campo se aclaró en un envido
Que frustró la cautela de un no quiero prudente
¡Como para agarrarlo con veintitrés de copas
Y un cabeceo de chúcaro mal sujeto al palenque!

Por fin, la porotada los avecinó al bueno
Nueve a nueve quedaron para la última vuelta.
Las caras de los criollos de puro preocupadas
Se pusieron de pronto tirantes como cuerdas.

La primera y segunda, mano a mano, de firme.
Luego se cortó el aire, soberbio, un siete bravo.
¡Retruco! ¡Quiero, maula! Y cayó como un bólido
—lindo fin para el truco del Juicio—¡As de Bastos!

11. Regarding autobiography, automythology, and self-portrait, see Lefere (18–38).

Works Cited

Anderson, Andrew A. *El momento ultraísta. Orígenes, fundación y lanzamiento de un movimiento de vanguardia*. Vervuert, 2017.

Balderston, Daniel. "Las sucesivas rupturas." *Innumerables relaciones*. Universidad Nacional del Litoral, 2010, pp. 42–57.

Blanco, Mariela. "La invención de la nación en los primeros poemarios de Borges." *Variaciones Borges*, vol. 17, no. 35, 2013, pp. 1–19.

Borges, Jorges Luis. "Anatomía de mi Ultra." *VLTRA* (Madrid), vol. 1, no. 11, May 20, 1921, p. 1.

Borges, Jorges Luis. "Apuntaciones críticas: La metáfora." *Cosmópolis* (Madrid), vol. 11, no. 35, November 1921, pp. 395–402.

Borges, Jorges Luis. "Arrabal." *Cosmópolis* (Madrid), vol. 10, no. 32, August 1921, p. 622.

Borges, Jorges Luis. "Atardecer." *Prisma*, vol. 2, no. 2, March 1922, p. 1.

Borges, Jorges Luis. "Autobiografía." *Martín Fierro*, vol. 4, no. 39, March 28, 1927, p. 6.

Borges, Jorges Luis. "Buenos Aires." *Cosmópolis* (Madrid), vol. 11, no. 34, October 1921, pp. 197–99.

Borges, Jorges Luis. "Carriego y el sentido del arrabal." *La Prensa*, April 24, 1926, p. 5.

Borges, Jorges Luis. *Cartas del fervor. Correspondencia con Maurice Abramowicz y Jacobo Sureda (1919-1928)*. Galaxia Gutemberg, 1999.

Borges, Jorges Luis. "Casa Elena (Hacia una estética del lupanar en España)." *VLTRA* (Madrid), no. 17, October 30, 1921, p. [2].

Borges, Jorges Luis. "Crítica del paisaje." *Cosmópolis* (Madrid), vol. 11, no. 34, October 1921, pp. 195–97.

Borges, Jorges Luis. *Cuaderno San Martín*. Editorial Proa, 1929.

Borges, Jorges Luis. "Después de las imágenes." *Proa* [segunda época], vol. 1, no. 5, 1924.

Borges, Jorges Luis. "Elegía de Palermo." *Nosotros*, vol. 54, no. 210, November 1926, pp. 22–23.

Borges, Jorges Luis. *El idioma de los argentinos*. Manuel Gleizer, 1928.

Borges, Jorges Luis. "El idioma infinito." *Proa* [segunda época], vol. 2, no. 12, July 1925, pp. 43–46.

Borges, Jorges Luis. "El tamaño de mi esperanza." *Valoraciones* (La Plata), vol. 3, no. 9, March 1926, pp. 222–24.

Borges, Jorges Luis. *El tamaño de mi esperanza*. Editorial Proa, 1926.

Borges, Jorges Luis. *Fervor de Buenos Aires*. Serantes, 1923.

Borges, Jorges Luis. *Inquisiciones*. Editorial Proa, 1925.

Borges, Jorges Luis. "La fundación mitológica de Buenos Aires." *Nosotros*, vol. 53, no. 204, May 1926, pp. 52–53.

Borges, Jorges Luis. "La lírica argentina contemporánea." *Cosmópolis* (Madrid), vol. 11, no. 36, 1921, pp. 640–51.

Borges, Jorges Luis. "Leyenda policial." *Martín Fierro*, vol. 4, no. 38, February 26, 1927, p. 4.

Borges, Jorges Luis. *Luna de enfrente*. Editorial Proa, 1925.

Borges, Jorges Luis. "Manuel Maples Arce. Andamios interiores." *Proa* [primera época], vol. 1, no. 2, 1922.

Borges, Jorges Luis. *Obras completas I (1923-1949)*. Edición crítica, anotada por Rolando Costa Picazo e Irma Zangara, Emecé Editores, 2009.

Borges, Jorges Luis. *Poemas (1922-1943)*. Editorial Losada, 1943.

Borges, Jorges Luis. "Proclama." *Prisma*, vol. 1, no. 1, 1921.

Borges, Jorges Luis. "Réplica." *La última hora*, October 19, 1920.

Borges, Jorges Luis. "Sobre el idioma de los argentinos." *La Prensa*, September 24, 1927.

Borges, Jorges Luis. *Textos recobrados (1919-1929)*. Emecé Editores, 2007.

Borges, Jorges Luis. "Ultraísmo." *El Diario Español*, October 23, 1921, p. 4.

Borges, Jorges Luis. "Ultraísmo." *Nosotros*, no. 151, 1921, pp. 466–71.

Cajero Vázquez, Antonio. *Palimpsestos del joven Borges*. El Colegio de San Luis, 2013.

Cansinos Assens, Rafael. "El arrabal en la literatura". *Variaciones Borges*, vol. 3, no. 8, [1924] 1999, pp. 30–35.

Cansinos Assens, Rafael. "En primavera." *VLTRA*, vol. 1, no. 7, April 1921.

de Torre, Guillermo. *Literaturas europeas de vanguardia*. Caro Raggio Editor, 1925.

de Torre, Guillermo. "Para la Prehistoria Ultraísta de Borges." *Hispania*, vol. 47, no. 3, 1964, pp. 457–63.

García, Carlos. *El joven Borges, poeta (1919–1930)*. Corregidor, 2000.

Garzón, Tobías. *Diccionario argentino*. Imprenta Elzeviriana de Borrás y Mestres, 1910.

Gorelik, Adrián. "El color del barrio. Mitología barrial y conflicto cultural en la Buenos Aires de los años veinte." *Variaciones Borges*, vol. 3, no. 8, 1999, pp. 36–68.

Gorelik, Adrián. *La grilla y el parque*. Universidad Nacional de Quilmes, [1998] 2017.

Grünberg, Carlos M. "Crítica de libros." *La Vida Literaria*, vol. 2, no. 11, June 1929, p. 5.

Helft, Nicolás. *Jorge Luis Borges. Bibliografía e índice*. Ediciones Biblioteca Nacional, 2013.

Jurado, Alicia. *Genio y figura de Jorge Luis Borges*. Eudeba, 1966.

Lefere, Robin. *Borges. Entre autorretrato y automitografía*. Gredos, 2005.

Lois, Elida. *Génesis de escritura y estudios culturales*. Edicial, 2001.

Méndez, Evar. "La nueva revista Proa." *Martín Fierro*, vol. 1, no. 8–9, September 6, 1924, p. 9.

"Nueva exposición de la actual poesía argentina." *La Campana de Palo*, vol. 3, no. 15, May 1927, p. 5.

Olea Franco, Rafael. *El otro Borges. El primer Borges*. Fondo de Cultura Económica, 1993.

Ortelli, Roberto. "Dos poetas de la nueva generación." *Inicial*, vol. 1, no. 1, October 1923, pp. 62–68.

Pequeño Larousse Ilustrado. Librería Larousse, 1912.

Pereda Valdés, Ildefonso. "Jorge Luis Borges, poeta de Buenos Aires." *Nosotros*, vol. 52, no. 200–11, January–February 1926, pp. 106–09.

Pezzoni, Enrique. *El texto y sus voces*. Editorial Sudamericana, 1986.

Segovia, Lisandro. *Diccionario de argentinismos, neologismos y barbarismos*. Coni Hermanos, 1911.

Sarlo, Beatriz. *Borges, un escritor en las orillas*. Seix Barral, [1993] 2003.

Soto, Luis Emilio. "El sentido poético de la ciudad moderna." *Proa* [segunda época], vol. 1, no. 1, 1924, pp. 11–20.

Valdivia, Víctor, "Nuestros escritores." *Caras y Caretas*, no. 1675, November 8, 1930.

Videla, Gloria. *El ultraísmo*. Gredos, 1963.

Vignale, Pedro, and César Tiempo. *Exposición de la actual poesía argentina (1922–1927)*. Minerva, 1927.

Vuillermoz, Emilie. "Un gran compositor español desconocido en España." *Cosmópolis*, vol. 10, no. 32, 1921, pp. 663–68.

CHAPTER 10

THE ART OF RECAPITULATION

The Early Essays (1920–1936)

NICOLÁS LUCERO

IN "Pierre Menard, autor del Quijote" [Pierre Menard, Author of the *Quixote*], the narrator reflects, with irony or scorn, that "es lícito ver en el *Quijote* 'final' una especie de palimpsesto, en el que deben traslucirse los rastros—tenues pero no indescifrables—de la 'previa' escritura de nuestro amigo" [it is legitimate to see the "final" Quixote as a kind of palimpsest, in which the traces—faint but not undecipherable—of our friend's "previous" text must shine through] (*OC* I: 450; *CF* 95). Ironically, because what should we understand by "previous" or "final" after Menard? What is "early," and what is "late"? Sardonically, because the narrator, who admires Menard with such a suspicious fervor, may in his heart hesitate (and laugh) about the very existence of his infinite drafts. It is a temptation to "reverse the labors" and read Borges's early essays as a palimpsest of his later, classic work. There may have been thousands of handwritten pages, and there are hundreds of published pages of his early prose, where traces of the later work are not unsubstantial or tenuous. It is not a matter of hints. There is a conspicuous recurrence of themes, aesthetic judgments, philosophical and literary discussions, epithets, images, and creative ways of reading; even whole paragraphs in the early essays will reappear in later pieces. Borges summarizes others' arguments and stories, abridges his own, resumes philosophical debates from earlier to later texts, continuously restates for the purposes of order or to introduce alternative hypotheses and objections. Recapitulation is a central device in the craft of the review, encyclopedic writing, and philosophical investigations. It serves an almost mechanical purpose in expository and argumentative genres; Borges seems to have made the most of it, taking it to another formal, metaphysical dimension.

Metaphysics and Imagination

"La nadería de la personalidad" [The Nothingness of Personality], published in the modernist little magazine *Proa* in 1922, is the first piece collected in the *Selected Non-Fictions* and likely the earliest Borges essay that English readers will encounter. They may be surprised by its solemn and emphatic overtones (at times prophetic, at times intensely confessional), the flamboyant words, the loose fragmentation of paragraphs, the absence of humor. It reads as an enthusiastic proclamation of his intention to "abatir la excepcional preeminencia que hoy suele adjudicarse al yo" [tear down the preeminence now awarded to the self] and "probar que la personalidad es una trasoñación, consentida por el engreimiento y el hábito, mas sin estribaderos metafísicos ni realidad entrañal" [prove that personality is a mirage maintained by conceit and custom, without metaphysical foundation or visceral reality], and "aplicar . . . a la literatura las consecuencias dimanantes de esas premisas" [apply to literature the consequences that issue from these premises] (*Inquisiciones* 93; *SNF* 3). The negative revelation that "no hay tal yo de conjunto" [There is no unifying self], which is coined and repeated as a motto, is matched by an exalted confidence in its liberating corollaries. It is a paradoxical text of beginnings that denounces vanity and the fallacy of self while inscribing the name of the author, equivocally, as "ese conjetural Jorge Luis Borges" [that conjectural Jorge Luis Borges] (*Inquisiciones* 94; *SNF* 4).

Less equivocal will be his loyalty to that vision. In fact, "La nadería de la personalidad" is a seminal concept in Borges's work and a good starting point to see how ideas are developed and realized in his literature. He grounds his aesthetic program in a philosophical inquiry in which he proceeds by cramming in examples. These illustrations are heterogeneous: quotes from a Kabbalist and from an early modern Spanish writer; the illumination by Schopenhauer that the I is "todos aquellos que dijeron yo durante ese tiempo" [all those who ever said I] (*Inquisiciones* 102; *SNF* 8); the questioning of the reader's illusion of continuity while gliding over the arguments made by the not less discontinuous writer; the narration of the crushing revelation that instants annihilate the past at the moment of saying goodbye to a beloved friend in Mallorca; a detailed pondering of the Buddhist precept that "Aquellas cosas de las cuales puedo advertir los principios y la postrimería, no son mi yo" [Those things of which I can perceive the beginning and the ends are not myself] (*Inquisiciones* 103; *SNF* 8); a celebration and a critique of Whitman's all-embracing "I," and the not less ambitious endeavor to found a new aesthetic program of the non-self. Starting from these very early essays, metaphysics and imagination, literature and philosophy are woven together so tightly that their boundaries blur. There is a consistent appeal to estrange readers' experiences and unsettle their habits of thought. Fond of philosophers like David Hume, Arthur Schopenhauer, and William James, who are thinkers and writers, Borges invites his reader to examine their ideas thoroughly and, equally thoroughly, to imagine their disquieting consequences. The purpose of philosophical investigations is to review "aclaraciones de la vida" [clarifications of life],

THE ART OF RECAPITULATION   179

he writes in "El cielo azul, es cielo y es azul" [The Blue Sky Is Sky and Is Blue] (*Textos recobrados 1*: 190). That same year he will publish an essay on Berkeley's idealism, "La encrucijada de Berkeley" [Berkeley at the Crossroads] to explain the chain of thoughts from which the fragmentary "La nadería de la personalidad" derives. In that essay, Borges exposes, refutes, and expands Berkeley's and Spencer's arguments extending the negation of the continuity of space to the negation of the continuity of conscience, self, and time. The metaphysical essays progress by persistent objection and imagination and by constant reformulation of ideas that spring from their development. He paraphrases for the purposes of clarity; at times his sentences reach an epigrammatic nature, which will echo his later essays and fictions: "Mejor dicho: todo está y nada es" [Better said: all appears in its contingency and nothing is essentially] (*Textos recobrados 1*: 192) condenses the vision of "El cielo azul, es cielo y es azul"; "La realidad es como esa imagen nuestra que surge en todos los espejos, simulacro que por nosotros existe, que con nosotros viene, gesticula y se va, pero en cuya busca basta ir, para dar siempre con él" [Reality is like that image of ourselves that comes out of every mirror, a simulacrum that exists because of us, comes with us, makes gestures and then leaves, but which can always be found if we go looking for it] caps Borges's discussion of Berkeley in 1922 (*Inquisiciones* 127).[1]

Borges's first critical essays started appearing as early as January 1920. They were brief expositions—occasionally manifestoes or defenses—of the ultraist avant-garde movement, which he had joined while living in Spain. He also contributed with his own poems and with short overviews and translations of German expressionist poets of the *Aktion* and *Sturm* movements. Back in Buenos Aires in 1921, he continued his relation to the avant-gardes by founding three little magazines and publishing poems, manifestoes, reviews of anthologies and books of poetry, translations, and essays, in periodical publications in Buenos Aires and Spain. Although his period of enthusiastic adhesion to the avant-gardes would be short, it played a significant role in his essayistic writing. Borges begins publishing in the middle of the effervescence of the new sensitivity and the theoretical discussions about art, form, and the renewal of perception. As he metaphorically puts it in "Al margen de la moderna estética" [At the Margin of Modern Aesthetics] in 1920, "esa floración brusca de metáforas" [that brusque flowering of metaphors] which seeks to "expresar la milenaria juventud de la vida" [express the millennial youth of life] (*Textos recobrados 1*: 37) will cause fascination in him, immediately followed by an urgent desire for a new rhetoric to investigate, verse by verse, in successive annotations, what a metaphor is, how it works, and, if it works, how (or when) it produces emotion in the reader. In the early "Anatomía de mi 'Ultra'" [Anatomy of my "Ultra"] (1921), his personal take on being "Ultra," he sketches his poetic plan of reversing the "proceso emotivo" [emotive process], from "emoción a la sensación, y de ésta a los agentes que la causaron" [emotion, to sensation to the agents that caused it], and centers it around the investigation of the metaphor (*Textos recobrados 1*: 118).

These essays on metaphor can be seen as the beginning of Borges as a microscopic reader, and the form of his essays will be shaped over time by the necessities of a syntax for that kind of poetic critical thinking. Unlike Paul Valéry, who is famous for his celebration of intelligence in poetry, Borges will commit to the idea that poetry and metaphors need to think with the "finalidad de emociones" [finality of emotions] (*Textos recobrados 1*: 141) as he proposes in his essay "La metáfora" [The Metaphor] in 1921, where the word "finalidad" stands for purpose but also for that appearance of irreversibility of that which has been achieved independently from any intention or reasoning. Borges will write on the brink of that irreducible contradiction, and the essay as the writing of reversing the emotive process will become the aesthetic experience itself—even when, in his 1933 "Elementos de preceptiva" [Elements of Rhetoric], he will change his critical view and surmise "la imposibilidad final de una estética" [the final impossibility of an aesthetics] (*Borges en* Sur 124). Several of his most accomplished fictions and essays written later, like "Historia del guerrero y de la cautiva" [Story of the Warrior and the Captive Maiden] and "La muralla y los libros" [The Wall and the Books], are motivated by an emotion and written as the investigation of its conjectural causes.

To the close reading of a stanza, a verse, a tone, Borges will bring a wide and often unexpected constellation of relations; the thrust of his inquiries, however, will be guided by a thorough examination of what he refers to as the "idiosincrasia de nuestras facultades" [idiosyncrasy of our faculties] (*Textos recobrados 1*: 141): visual and auditory imagination, memory (and its frailty), surprise, pleasure, expectation, understanding, boredom, fear, pleasure, disgust. There is an immense discrepancy between the clumsiness and imprecision of words and devices, and the swirl of sensations and emotions we experience. In "Examen de metáforas" [Examination of Metaphors] (1924), metaphors respond to a "urgencia poética" [poetic urgency] for which language "necesita troquelarse en figuras" [needs to mold itself into figures] (*Inquisiciones* 73). As befits an avant-garde writer, the word "rhetoric" has negative connotations for him, and his idiosyncratic formalism, which calls for a metaphysical slowdown, the need to pause and consider something thoroughly, systematically rejects sanctioned value and rigid conceptions of art and scoffs at the "poquedumbre de los elementos que componen la lírica" [scarcity of elements that compose lyric poetry]—a conclusion that he derives from an exercise in cataloguing types of metaphors (*Inquisiciones* 77).[2] Refutation drives his detailed consideration of poetry the same way it drives his expositions of philosophical disputes.

What is already perceptible in these early essays is what Sylvia Molloy defined as "a constant and honest disquisition on writing, his own writing, the writing of others" (4). The decision to read the dynamism of metaphors from any period, particularly the Spanish Baroque, alongside ultraísta verses, does not support the idea that there is nothing new under the sun, but rather that novelty is not a valid ground for judgment and, most importantly, that it is a futile way of reading. He discards tradition and the new sensitivity as categories that dispense of any verification. Although he will follow through on his analyses infinitesimally, the critical illuminations will often spring from a reductio ad absurdum that shows the disparity or the indifference between explanation and efficacy. He will particularly rejoice in metaphors that are identical, but one works and the other does not depending on the context; or two very dissimilar metaphors that, when examined attentively, are the same. By the time of his 1926 "La metáfora," collected in *El idioma de los argentinos* [*The Language of Argentines*] under the title "Otra vez la metáfora" [On Metaphor Once Again], the journey seems to reach an end, as Borges will consider that the precision of images and the "invención o hallazgo de pormenores significativos" [invention or finding of meaningful details] are much more capable of accomplishing emotions than metaphors, which are "una de tantas habilidades retóricas para conseguir énfasis" [one of many rhetorical skills to produce emphasis] (*El idioma* 52); metaphors are not a matter of invention—only a few can be created—but of varying contexts and unlimited skillful wording. In his 1933 essay, "Las Kenningar" [Kennings], on the Old Norse metaphorical compounds, the bewilderment will be caused, not by their ability to express but by the utterly formulaic conventionality of their use and the reader's realization of the irrevocable loss of that moment when words were uttered to name for the first time. At the end of "Otra vez la metáfora," the modern metaphor had been vindicated for the generic function it serves: "Cuando la vida nos asombra con inmerecidas penas o con inmerecidas venturas, metaforizamos casi instintivamente. Queremos no ser menos que el mundo, queremos ser tan desmesurados como él" [When life bewilders us with undeserved sorrows or undeserved fortunes, we metaphorize almost instinctively. We don't want to be less than the world, we want to be as overwhelming as the world] (*El idioma* 55).

In "An Autobiographical Essay" (1970), Borges will declare that "the productivity" of the 1920s "amazed" him and that he "only (felt) the remotest kinship with the work" of those years (159). Some of his *ficciones* of the 1940s, however, are unthinkable without the examination and conception of metaphors he developed in his early essays. "Siglos y siglos de idealismo no han dejado de influir en la realidad" [Century upon century of idealism could hardly have failed to influence reality] writes the conjectural Borges who narrates "Tlön, Uqbar, Orbis Tertius" (*OC* I: 439; *CF* 77). The "metódica producción" [methodic fabrication] of hrönir will crown Borges's long habit of scrutinizing metaphors and images in the 1920s (*OC* I: 439; *CF* 77). As it turns out, the idea and the imagination of the particulars of that story are tightly congruent with the metaphysical vision he had sketched in his earliest essay on the metaphor, in 1921, in which he had defined it as "subrayaduras de aspectos parcialísimos del sujeto que tratan hechos nuevos que se añaden al mundo" [emphases of extremely partial aspects of the subject which treat new facts that are added to the world] (*Textos recobrados 1*: 141).

KINDS OF HUMOR

It is also in his prose of the 1920s that Borges's humor becomes apparent, mostly in his biting epithets and in a few satirical replies and parodies written in collaboration for the avant-garde periodical *Martín Fierro*.[3] The quarrels of the avant-garde provide a favorable environment to exercise and hone the art of epithets, which are an occasion for a good fight and for memorable concise judgments. I illustrate this with two examples. In "Crítica del paisaje" [Critique of Landscape] [1921], against the nineteenth-century rhetoric of rural landscape, Borges attacks Italian Futurism as a continuation of the old aesthetics of representation. His argument against Futurism fits in a parenthesis: "Whitman mal traducido al italiano, instalación de luz eléctrica en la retórica" [Whitman poorly translated into Italian, electrical lighting installation in rhetoric] (*Textos recobrados 1*: 124). My second example comes from the already mentioned "Elementos de preceptiva" (1933). Borges will now defend the virtues of rhetoric so long as it is not vague and so long as it is oriented to explain the effect of words on the reader, not the author's insurmountable intentions. To discern his own approach from other critical theories, he mocks the Austrian philologist Leo Spitzer's stylistics. Borges sardonically writes that he leaves the [final] investigation of vague purposes "al Juicio Final—o al ascendente y rápido Spitzer, *que sube por los hilos capilares de las formas más características hasta las vivencias estéticas originales que las determinaron*" [to the Last Judgment—or to the ascending and hasty Spitzer, who *rises up through capillary threads from the most characteristic forms to the original aesthetic experiences that determined them*] (*Borges en* Sur 121, emphasis in the original). The epithet scornfully frames the quote in italics, distinguishes critical methods, and makes it hard for the reader to dissociate Spitzer from capillarity.

The potential of conceptual humor for invention, which will fully shine in the creativity of his readings and in the ideas and execution of his short stories, can be traced to Macedonio Fernández (1874–1952), who made humor an oblique method of philosophical thinking, and to Borges's early readings of Quevedo. In "Quevedo humorista" [Quevedo as Humorist] (1927), he identifies and reviews three kinds of humor. The first two, innuendos and puns, he dismisses as traditional. Puns are a case of association by sound, which he mistrusts and considers an invalid method of poetic thinking. It is the third kind of humor that excites him. He praises it as Quevedo's "íntimo reír" [intimate laughing] (not smiling), and names it "calaveradas de imaginación" [pranks of imagination] and, at some point, calls it "*ficción*" [fiction] (*Textos recobrados 1*: 348). In Quevedo's *La fortuna con seso y la hora de todos* [*Fortune in Her Wits, or, the Hour of All Men*] (posthumously published in 1650, most likely finished by 1635), Borges delights in how the "razonamiento de la incongruencia y el caos" [reasoning of incongruence and chaos] (349) opens up to rigorous invention. In an astonishing reading, he links *La hora de todos* to the ideation of stories in H. G. Wells, making Wells the precursor of Quevedo. Although he prefers Quevedo's to Wells's execution for matters of prose style, the details he shrewdly spots in *La hora de todos* are consistent with his remarks on circumstantial invention that he will illustrate with a summary of Wells's *The Invisible Man* (1897), in "La postulación de la realidad" [The Postulation of Reality] (1931).

Conceptual humor in Borges is linked to his understanding of genres, which will come to full prominence in the 1930s. The influence of Macedonio Fernández here is conspicuous. Everything Macedonio writes is a humoristic negative theory of what he writes: letters, greetings, stories, novels, characters, dialogues, conferences, radio broadcasts, prologues, epilogues, footnotes, jokes. There are glimpses of that in the early Borges, for example in the idea and the prose of the mural magazine *Prisma*. Contrary to the "shouting" and "gesticulating" manifestos he reviews, Borges and his friends in *Prisma* seize the possibility to joke and comment on its circulation (they were posted in the streets) and, thus, on the contradictions and vicissitudes of readership, democratization, and public space of an avant-garde little magazine, which aspired to intervene in the poetic foundation of Buenos Aires. The opening text of its second and final issue reads: "Por segunda vez, ante la numerosa indiferencia de los muchos, la voluntaria incomprensión de los pocos i el gozo espiritual de los únicos, alegramos con versos las paredes" [For a second time, before the numerous indifference of the majority, the voluntary misunderstanding of the few and the spiritual pleasure of the unique, we liven up the walls with verses] (*Textos recobrados 1*: 183).

Both strains of Borges's humor—the satirical epithet and the conceptual joke on genre—will converge in his 1933 "Arte de injuriar" [Art of Insult], collected in *Historia de la eternidad* [*A History of Eternity*]. He proceeds by analyzing examples he has cherished and gathered—one of the conditions of good insults is that they need to be memorable—including Paul Groussac's diatribes and "panegíricos turbios" [ambiguous eulogies] (*OC* I: 419; *SNF* 87), bully rhymes, passages from Shakespeare, Dr. Johnson, De Quincey, and Jonathan Swift's *Gulliver's Travels*, among others. The patently stated goal of the essay is to review the repertory of "handy" methods of insults and emphasize their regular patterns. However, the underlying question that runs throughout the article is not only how insults work but what they are, how they are the kernel of polemics and satire, how they change our feel of language. What defines insults is the fear of verbal retaliation and, consequently, the pressure on the aggressors (and their ultimate uncertainty) to come up with the exact string of words. As Borges writes in "El truco" [Truco] (1928) of the short sly rhymes said by players in that card game, which is popular in Río de la Plata: "Un yo distinto, un yo casi antepasado y vernáculo, enreda los proyectos del juego. El idioma es otro de golpe" [A different I, a vernacular and almost ancestral I, entangles the game plan. All of a sudden, language is different] (*El idioma* 28). Same with insults: underneath the detailed analysis of their game-like conventions lurks the atavistic "maldiciones mágicas de la ira" [curse of wrath]: "Es la reliquia de un inverosímil estado, en que las lesiones hechas al nombre caen sobre el poseedor" [It is the relic of an unlikely state in which the wounds inflicted upon the name fall upon the possessor] (*OC* I: 421; *SNF* 90). It is a matter of rhetoric that, driven by detailed examination, turns into a matter of metaphysics. The unrivaled example of an insult Borges will give is Colombian José María Vargas Vila's lapidation of the prominent Peruvian intellectual José Santos Chocano:

> [Esta] es la injuria más espléndida que conozco: injuria tanto más singular si consideramos que es el único roce de su autor con la literatura. "Los dioses no consintieron que Santos Chocano deshonrara el patíbulo, muriendo en él. Ahí está vivo, después de haber fatigado la infamia." Deshonrar el patíbulo. Fatigar la infamia. A fuerza de abstracciones ilustres, la fulminación descargada por Vargas Vila rehúsa cualquier trato con el paciente, y lo deja ileso, inverosímil, muy secundario y posiblemente inmortal. (*OC* I: 422–23)

> [(It) is the most splendid verbal abuse I know, an insult so much more extraordinary if we consider that it represents its author's only brush with literature: "The gods did not consent Santos Chocano to dishonor the gallows by dying there. He is still alive,

having exhausted infamy." Dishonoring the gallows, exhausting infamy. Vargas Vila's discharge of these illustrious abstractions refuses to treat its patient and leaves him untouched, unbelievable, quite unimportant, and possibly immortal.] (*SNF* 91)[4]

The encounter and the vivid memory of the insult, the lethal framing of the quote, the reflection he derives from Vargas Vila's wording, all of these are telling of Borges as an essayist. What Theodor Adorno writes about Valéry fits Borges well: "the person who knows about the work of art through his métier, the exacting work process," so thoroughly and immanently, that he "turns [that process] into theoretical insight, in that good universality that does not leave the particular out but rather preserves it" ("The Artist as Deputy" 100). It is the particulars that propel the movement of the essay. Borges's case is exemplary of this: the young ultraist poet and translator of expressionist poetry as a theorist of metaphor and images, the iracund polemicist and inventor of epithets as a theorist of the art of insult, the reviewer of films and novels as a theorist of verisimilitude and causality in fiction, the translator and examiner of words and contexts of meaning as a theorist of translation.

CRIOLLISMO: BORGES AT THE CROSSROADS

But humor is exercised in a voice, and, in the essays of the 1920s, Borges's chords are tensed by other more pressing urgencies. That decade was a period of conflicting cultural responses to the vertiginous process of immigration and urbanization that had dramatically changed Buenos Aires since the turn of the century. Tradition, modernization, and national language, in such a heterogeneous culture, were highly contested fields.[5] Borges did not avoid the polemics of his time, taking strong stances. Where this response is felt most imperatively, and intimately, is in his desire for a very personal Argentine voice that he envisioned as a peculiar and eccentric form of *criollismo*.

In *El tamaño de mi esperanza* [*The Extent of My Hope*] (1926), he encapsulates his stance in a sentence with two negations: "No quiero progresismo ni criollismo en la acepción corriente de esas palabras" [I do not want *progresismo* nor *criollismo* in the commonly understood senses of those words], "progresismo" being the desire to be "almost European" and "criollismo," a "palabra de nostalgia" [word of nostalgia] for the past (*El tamaño* 14). The meanings of "criollo" and "criollismo" were intensely disputed in the 1920s because they referred to a wide range of linguistic and cultural phenomena that emerged as a consequence of the waves of immigration. The term "criollos" denoted old Argentines who derived a sense of pride from not being newcomers; but it also alluded to a complex and dynamic process of identity formation by immigrants themselves, who, lacking a common tradition, would find it in a pop culture (melodramas, music, theater) and in versatile spoken varieties of Spanish where the folk "criollo" element, often overacted, played a decisive role. While the aesthetics of *criollismo* was often assertive of tradition, rural themes, and a compact national identity, Borges aimed to found his literature on more ambiguous, uncertain, and contentious grounds: a *criollismo* that would talk about the "mundo y del yo, de Dios y de la muerte" [world and the I, God and death], as he proclaims in "El tamaño de mi esperanza" (*El tamaño* 14); a *criollismo* that would be so constrained to the local, to an endearing and almost forgotten neighborhood, that it could not be appropriated by any generic feeling of national identity; a *criollismo* at the ever moving margins, away from the modern city and the *pampas*; a *criollismo* retrieved from the impossibility of fully speaking the spectral voices of the past; a *criollismo* that would defy that "progresismo" of "being almost European" that Borges would see as a sign of readers' superstition. A good part of that laborious process took place in the essays of the 1920s, as he sought to derive that idiosyncratic voice from his many reviews and disquisitions on nineteenth-century gauchesque poetry, folk verses, tango and milonga lyrics, colloquial and slang varieties spoken in Buenos Aires, and the poetry and narrative by contemporary Argentine and Uruguayan *criollista* writers.[6]

The self-effacing premises he sets out as his aesthetic program in "La nadería de la personalidad" go alongside a craze for differentiation and individuation in his poetic voice. Julio Premat defines this self-figuration of the young Borges as the aspiring poet of Buenos Aires as foundational and heroic (11–15). "Buenos Aires no ha recabado su inmortalización poética" [Buenos Aires has not yet attained its poetic immortality], writes Borges in "Después de las imágenes" [After Images] in 1924, and he goes on to identify two possible paths to follow: "el poema que entrelazan los tangos" [the total poem woven by the tangos] and "[el] genial y soslayado *Recienvenido* de Macedonio Fernández" [the oblique humor of *Papeles de Recienvenido* by Macedonio Fernández] (*Inquisiciones* 31; *SNF* 11). In the early essays, we can read Borges's pursuit of a personal poetic voice as if he were attempting to single it out by discerning divergent possibilities. Macedonio is invoked as a metaphysical conversationalist to emulate and, at the same time, is admired for being "ejercitado en el silencio" [exercised in silence] (*Textos recobrados 1:* 163), as Borges defines him in "La lírica argentina contemporánea" [Contemporary Argentine Poetry] (1921). Paradoxically, the trait of Macedonio that will stand out in Borges's early style is the propensity for audible abstract neologisms. Another aspirational voice for Borges is the prose of nineteenth-century writers (Esteban Echeverría, Domingo Faustino Sarmiento, Eduardo Wilde, Lucio V. Mansilla) who wrote as they spoke, in Argentine Spanish, without affectation; and yet, "hoy, esa naturalidad se gastó" [now that naturalness is worn out], he admits in "El idioma de los argentinos" [The Language of Argentines] (145–46). The ultimate point of reference will be the verbal austerity and clarity achieved by José Hernández's gauchesque poem *Martín Fierro* but that is an ideal model impossible to repeat since a rural poetics is equivalent to stagnation and nostalgia. Modes of humor, styles of conversation, disputes about *criollismo* and over the slangs and colloquial varieties of Spanish spoken in Buenos Aires: with all those factors, some of them so ghostly, how to come up with a voice through close listening and reading and not create some sort of Golem?

Although the search for a voice is primarily oriented to poetry, it will have an impact on Borges's essays, especially when he experiments with using a *criollista* voice to utter his *criollista* program. In those cases, inconsistencies of tone are not uncommon. In "Quejas de todo criollo" [Laments of Every Criollo] (1925), for example, his praise for the modesty, the irony, and the lack of verbiage and boastfulness of gauchesque verses clashes with his own lofty rhetoric: "Fracasa el criollo, pero se altiva y se insolenta la patria" [The criollo fails, but the motherland becomes proud and insolent] (*Inquisiciones* 145). The voice is discordant with the ear; the writing is often out of pitch with the tones he finds in his listening and reading. He will come to a solution when he gives up his search for an individualized Argentine voice for his lyric poetry and essays. The same features that he celebrates in *Martín Fierro* (stringency, the use of plain unstressed colloquial words that need to be heard and are capable of emotions, the emphasis on the precision of the image, tone, and syntax) will guide the revision of his first three books of poetry and the writing of the voices of characters and narrators in his short stories of *orilleros*. This new *narrative* strategy had been in *Martín Fierro* and the gauchesque genre all the time: to write like *the other* spoke. This will open Borges's process of writing, publishing, revising, rewriting, and republishing his first short story "Leyenda policial" [Police Legend] (1927), that will become "Hombres pelearon" [Men Fought] (1928), and later "Hombre de la esquina rosada" [Man on Pink Corner] (1935). He will come back to the stories of *orilleros* once and again over time, mediating the voice even further by retelling the stories he was told.

As for the essays on topics related to "criollismo," Borges will "resign himself" to be a critic. He will privilege nineteenth-century gauchesque, merging his previous essays and commentaries on Hilario Ascasubi, Estanislao del Campo, and José Hernández (later adding Antonio Lussich) into chronological overviews, a form of exposition that stems from the lectures or introductions when he will start delivering them (see Blanco chapter, in this volume). The final table of contents of *Discusión* [*Discussion*] in *Obras completas*, which begins with the lengthy overview "La poesía gauchesca" [Gauchesca Poetry] and includes the influential lecture "El escritor argentino y la tradición" [The Argentine Writer and Tradition] (1951) by the end of the book, before the miscellaneous section "Notas," suggests a retrospective closing balance of Borges's dealings with *criollismo*. But the most striking use of his expertise in reading all things "criollo" will be diverted and condensed in two essays, both published in 1928 and later appended as complementary pages of his book *Evaristo Carriego* (1930): the first on the card game "El truco," which I have already mentioned, and the second on the inscriptions on horse cart-wagons, originally published under the title "Séneca en las orillas" [Seneca at the Outskirts] in a little magazine. The latter is a "noticia" [report] in which Borges delights in reviewing over forty epigrammatic phrases he found on cart-wagons while walking in the streets of Buenos Aires and by the warehouses at the outskirts. He evaluates them, comments on their subgenres, on the circumstances when he read them, on the implied meanings of some word intonations, on the emotions caused by an occasional obscure inscription whose meaning stays secret. He relates the slowness and proverbial delays of the cart-wagons to the experience of reading them, as it were, in a standstill. Overall, the "noticia" feels like a reconciliation with literature and criticism: "Yo creía descreer de la literatura, y me he dejado aconsejar por la tentación de reunir estas partículas de ella"

[I once believed I disbelieved in literature, and now I have let myself be led astray by the temptation to collect some of its fragments] (*OC* I: 150; *Evaristo Carriego* 118).[7]

Borges decides that his first work of prose to be included in the *Obras completas* will be *Evaristo Carriego*, which can be regarded, adding omissions, as the recapitulation of his previous work until 1930. Besides "El truco" and "Séneca en las orillas" (retitled "Las inscripciones de los carros"), the third prose piece to make it into the *Obras completas* is the short prose "Sentirse en muerte" [Feeling in Death] (1928), which first appeared in his book *El idioma de los argentinos*. It is a personal narrative of a stroll in the outskirts in which he came upon an epiphany of eternity, reminiscent of his earlier realization of the nothingness of personality at the moment of a farewell to a friend in Mallorca. Borges will present "Sentirse en muerte" as a token of his metaphysical imaginations, *his* contribution to the "Historia de la eternidad" in 1936, and, once again, he will reprise it by attaching it at the end of the first article of "Nueva refutación del tiempo" [A New Refutation of Time] in 1944. In "Sentirse en muerte" there is a convergence of his wanderings in metaphysics, his flâneries in the *orillas* and the narration of an emotion, which he had set as the finality of his aesthetics in 1921.

As we are seeing, Borges's work undergoes a series of unattachments or "resignations" by the end of the 1920s. This is anticipated by the conclusion of his 1927 essay "Indagación de la palabra" [An Investigation of the Word]: "Que la resignación—virtud a que debemos resignarnos—sea con nosotros. Ella será nuestro destino: hacernos a la sintaxis, a su concatenación traicionera, a la imprecisión, a los talveces, a los demasiados énfasis, a los peros, al hemisferio de mentira y de sombra en nuestro decir" [May resignation—the virtue to which we must resign ourselves—be with us. It will be our destiny to mold ourselves to syntax, to its treacherous chain of events, to the imprecision, the maybes, the too many emphases, the buts, the hemisphere of lies and of darkness in our speech] (*El idioma* 24; *SNF* 39). *Evaristo Carriego* stands out as the synthesis of those renunciations. Borges will no longer aim to be the poet of Buenos Aires in a *criollista* voice and will accept to be its "biographer," as he goes from poetry to the mischievous syntax of prose, from the ambition of being a foundational hero to just becoming a bio-bibliographer of the first local poet who sang their beloved neighborhood. *Evaristo Carriego* is a strange artifact. Beatriz Sarlo prefers to think of it as a treatise and not a biography, and she compares it to an image of Tlön, a simulacrum not of the poet Evaristo Carriego but of Borges's work (*Borges, A Writer on the Edge* 23–25). Arguably, it is Borges's only book, in the sense of what we would call a thematic book, although it is hardly a conventional monograph.[8] For an essay that confesses to being more imaginary than documentary, there is a craving for rigorous documentation on the urban history of Buenos Aires and Palermo and on the slightest nuances and variations of the oral stories he collects. And yet the whole text is written like an image, threatened by absence. There is no direct witnessing of anything: the Palermo that Carriego sang was already fading away in 1908 when he published the poems that made him the first "espectador de nuestros barrios pobres" [observer of our poor neighborhoods] (*OC* I: 143; *Evaristo Carriego* 105). It is Borges's only book that contains chapters, but these chapters will grow in number and kind in later editions as he incorporates pieces that range from readers' letters providing additional information to essays on horsemen and the history of tango. It closes, like a summa, the 1920s, but continues, like a work in progress.

The beginning of the second chapter, "Una vida de Evaristo Carriego" [A Life of Evaristo Carriego], is felt throughout the text and, in its negativity, may be a good hint to the book's oddly splintered unity: "Que un individuo quiera despertar en otro individuo recuerdos que no pertenecieron más que a un tercero, es una paradoja evidente. Ejecutar con despreocupación esa paradoja, es la inocente voluntad de toda biografía" [That one person should wish to arouse in another memories relating only to a third person is an obvious paradox. To pursue this paradox is the harmless intention of all biography] (OC I: 113; Evaristo Carriego 51). This initial and memorable insight that shakes our habits of reading biographies calls for a new syntax for its execution.[9] Once again, Borges pauses to reconsider how our faculties work. It is all about the vacillations, dissonances, and joys of sharing memories through something as uncertain as an image. At some point in that chapter, the narration of a life of "Carriego" is resolved by juxtaposing two series. The first is the enumeration of the common "frecuencias" [frequencies] of living that "lo repiten infinitamente en nosotros, como si Carriego perdurara disperso en nuestros destinos, como si cada uno de nosotros fuera por unos segundos Carriego" [repeat him over and over in us, as if Carriego went on living in our lives, as if for a few seconds each one of us were Carriego] (OC I: 119; Evaristo Carriego 63). The second series, aligned back-to-back with the first, is complex: it starts by dismissing the images in which Carriego would have liked to have lived and goes on to enumerate the "borrosas imágenes . . . que defenderían su memoria: el patio que es ocasión de serenidad, rosa para los días, el fuego humilde de San Juan, revolcándose como un perro en mitad de la calle, la estaca de la carbonería, su bloque de apretada tiniebla, sus muchos leños, la mampara de fierro del conventillo, los hombres de la esquina rosada" [random images . . . that would preserve his memory: the patio, a place of serenity, a rose for one's days, a modest St. John's Night bonfire, wallowing like a dog in the middle of the street, the wood-and-coal merchant's sign, its compact heap of blackness, its stacks of wood, the iron door of a tenement house, the men lounging on pink street corners] (OC I: 119–20; Evaristo Carriego 63–64).[10] It is all about conjectural affinities between Carriego, Borges, and the reader. The ambiguity of the images is sustained by a constant disquisition of sameness and difference and by a detailed writing that always requests and craves the imagination of the reader.

SHIFTS AND RECAPS

Seen in retrospect, the publication of *Evaristo Carriego* is a turning point that signals Borges's will to forget the old essays, which paradoxically coincides with the form of the essay becoming his main literary exploration in the 1930s. The question arises as to why he suppressed the three first books of essays when compiling his *Obras completas* and never republished them again, whereas he revised his three early books of poetry by correcting, deleting some poems, and adding new ones.[11] In his 1969 prologue to *Fervor de Buenos Aires* [*Fervor of Buenos Aires*], he would confess that "aquel muchacho que en 1923 lo escribió ya era esencialmente—¿qué significa esencialmente?—el señor que ahora se resigna o corrige" [the young man who wrote it in 1923 already was essentially—what does essentially mean?—the man who now resigns himself or corrects] (*OC* I: 13). We can say of the young poet what the narrator says of Emma Zunz: "ya era [el] que sería" [(he) was already the person (he) was to become] (*OC* I: 564; *CF* 215). In the case of the essays of the 1920s, there are several reasons, both practical and aesthetic, that might have deterred him from revising them: the convoluted Baroque style; the *criollista*, messianic, or solemn overtones; changes in his critical judgments of poetry, but also some discontinuities in his own essayistic prose, which will become visible from the late 1920s. We may also conjecture that these early essays had not been achieved yet, that they were still in a state of becoming, and many of them would have a better afterlife as recapped and recycled in his writings of the 1930s and 1940s. Alan Pauls writes about Borges's change around the end of the 1920s: "He no longer thinks of writing something for the very first time, something that nobody has ever written before, but something that can be *read* twice" (18). Perhaps, the early essays were not to be *read* twice just yet.

Borges starts his 1927 "La fruición literaria" [Literary Pleasure] with a brief periodization of the stages of his literary experience: the lost paradise of childhood as an avid and trusting reader of fiction, the discovery of words and the friendship of poets, and, *now*, the risk of becoming a specialized critic and losing the ability to feel joy and surprise. For an essay on the pleasure of literature, this is an ominous beginning: the sequence goes from belief, to disbelief, to nostalgia, to remorse. "Literary fruition" does not work as a translation, but the English word captures a decisive idea on literary experience, one that recurs in the early essays: the delight caused by that which is "realized" (both achieved and found), the sheer material evidence of that which has come to fruition in reading. In the microscopic inquisitions of the 1920s, the thorough investigation of the word often leads to the conclusion that techniques do not explain aesthetic facts. Borges will still insist on this idea in "La supersticiosa ética del lector" [The Superstitious Ethics of the Reader] (1931) as well as in his quotes of Angelus Silesius ("Die Rose ist ohne Warum" [The rose is without why]) and James McNeill Whistler ("Art happens") in later interviews and prologues. However, as Sergio Pastormerlo has shown, this will no longer hold as Borges's core view as a critic in the 1930s (78–83). In his 1933 "Elementos de preceptiva," he writes, opposing Silesius: "yo afirmo que es imprescindible una tenaz conspiración de porqués para que la rosa sea rosa" [I state that a tenacious conspiration of reasons is indispensable for the rose to be a rose] (*Borges en* Sur 124). Borges had fully shared Benedetto Croce's disdain for technicalities and the idea that the experience of poetry is prior to all interpretation. In the 1930s, he will continue being a reader of details, but now against Croce, against "la identidad de lo estético y de lo expresivo" [the identical nature of the aesthetic and the expressive] (*OC* I: 217; *SNF* 59) as he abruptly abridges the Italian's *Aesthetics* in "La postulación de la realidad" (1931). He will now investigate the efficient method of genres, formulas, devices, conventions.

In the early 1930s, Borges will write his most influential essays on fiction and narration, "La postulación de la realidad" (1931) and "El arte narrativo y la magia" [Narrative Art and Magic] (1932). They examine verisimilitude and motivation in narrative as different from truth and causality in reality. The declared emphasis is on the artificiality of the procedure. The microscopic reading of the word, tones, and poetic experience of the essays of the 1920s will now continue in the detailed reading of narrative features. However, Borges modifies the quest. Before, he had sought to write a rhetoric from direct contemplation that would legislate a vast array of genres, from avant-garde witty vignettes to the confessional novel and contemporary occurrences of old poetic figures; it aimed at a unified aesthetic experience regardless of genre. Now he starts to read how genres transfigure language in such a powerful way that their workings can be read in surprising details, even in the dexterous choice of a pronoun in a line or verse.

In "La postulación de la realidad," Borges defends what he calls the classical procedure, which relies on a belief in the "virtud de cada uno de sus signos" [virtue of every single sign (of language)] (*OC* I: 217; *SNF* 59), and which can take three distinct forms: "notificación general de los hechos que importan" [a general notification of the important facts]; "imaginar una realidad más compleja que la declarada al lector y referir sus derivaciones y efectos" [imagining a more complex reality than the one declared to the reader and describing its derivation and results]; and "la invención circunstancial" [the invention of circumstances] (*OC* I: 219-20; *SNF* 59). In "El arte narrativo y la magia," against the "resultado incesante de incontrolables e infinitas operaciones" [endless, uncontrollable causes and effects] of reality, Borges claims for narrative the rigorous clarity of magic in which "profetizan los pormenores" [every lucid and determined detail is a prophecy] (*OC* I: 232; *SNF* 82). The inquiry has changed from how the poetic experience is achieved to how the strong appearance of factual truth is attained. It is openly about techniques, but is still grounded on a broader metaphysical examination of reality and truth. These literary essays are illuminations of the logic of fiction and the estrangement of readers' habits of dealing with truth and reality in the world. Borges never ceases to connect both realms, the world of signs and the world of experience. If some "notificación general" in narrative, for example, was effective but overtly imprecise, it might be explained by the hypothesis that "la imprecisión es tolerable o verosímil en la literatura, porque a ella propendemos siempre en la realidad" [imprecision is tolerable or plausible in literature because we almost always tend toward it in reality] (*OC* I: 218; *SNF* 61).[12] Borges's understanding of forms is posed, again, as a matter of honesty to experience against simulation. In "La aventura y el orden" [Adventure and Order] (1925), he had defined the classic method, the choice for order, in similar terms as he would explain in "La postulación de la realidad." In that earlier piece, he had mentioned Ben Jonson as one of the prototypes of the classic, having composed an autobiographical book made of translations and quotes (*OC* I: 217). There is an implicit communal reconciliation with the voices, joys, and sufferings of others in the classic method that goes hand in hand with the metaphysical negation of a unifying self in "La nadería de la personalidad."

Borges's discussions of the procedures of the novel are also revealing of noticeable shifts taking place in the form of his essays. They become more classic in many ways that are in line with his understanding of narrative art. In the essays of the 1930s, there is more confidence in the imagination and emotions that the reader will bring to the succinct communication of ideas of others, the implied corollaries in words and their prophetic power (in extensive quotes, in translations of quotes, in successive reformulations and illustrations of ideas) and in the sharing of surprising details, which create complicity in estrangement. Plain notification, inference of an underlying enigma, circumstantial invention, and prophetic details are also the methods of his concise essayistic creations. Parataxis often prevails; however, many other times Borges will comically exaggerate the devices of expository, argumentative, and narrative articulation: summaries, recaps, orderings, examples, conjectures, presentations, revisions, contradictory and forking hypotheses, refutation, footnotes, dramatization: "Lane tradujo contra Galland, Burton contra Lane; para entender a Burton hay que entender esa dinastía enemiga" [Lane translated against Galland, Burton against Lane; to understand Burton we must understand this hostile dynasty]—he introduces his work in "Los traductores de *Las 1001 Noches*" [The Translators of *The Thousand and One Nights*] (*OC* I: 397; *SNF* 92); or "El propósito de dar interés dramático a esta biografía de la eternidad me ha obligado a ciertas deformaciones: verbigracia, a resumir en cinco o seis nombres una gestación secular" [In the aim of adding dramatic interest to this biography of eternity I committed certain distortions, for instance, that of condensing into five or six names a step that took centuries] (*OC* I: 366; *SNF* 139n), a procedure he discloses in a note to "Historia de la eternidad," all for the purpose of clarity of exposition and amazement. Summaries of arguments, both of ideas and stories, may go comically unrestrained. For example, in "Las pesadillas y Franz Kafka" [Nightmares and Franz Kafka], an essay on the difficulties of writing dreams, Borges discusses the details of the narration of a dream in *The Prelude* by Wordsworth by summarizing a summary by De Quincey. He will then proceed to summarize Kakfa's "An Imperial Messenger," a story so brief and so devoid of circumstantial details that he jokes that he is summarizing what is already a summary (*Textos recobrados 2*: 100). His whole hypothesis of why Wordsworth fails and how Kafka achieves the truthful narration of a nightmare fully depends on the particulars he extracts from these summaries of summaries.

Borges's ideas on narrative art are coterminous with the onset of his fictions but also with his new strategies for writing his essays after the 1930s. Without a doubt, the essays collected in *Discusión* (1932) and *Historia de la eternidad* (1936) read more like the ones written in the 1940s and early '50s and then collected in *Otras inquisiciones* [*Other Inquisitions*] (1952) than those in the previous three suppressed books.[13] The inclusion of later pieces in the second edition of *Discusión* strengthens that resemblance. Neither the topics nor the procedures are strictly new, though—some procedures just become more prominent—and most of the metaphysical ideas, themes, and interests that will be the subject matter of his fictions and essays are scattered all over his writing in the 1920s. One brief example: John Wilkins's utopian language, which will be the topic of his

1942 "El lenguaje analítico de John Wilkins" [The Analytical Language of John Wilkins]: in 1928, in "El idioma de los argentinos," Borges summarizes and celebrates Wilkins's system as a "música silenciosa" [silent music] and uses it against the absurd lexical proliferation of Spanish dictionaries (*El idioma* 141).

By the turn of the decade, there is a major reconfiguration. We know that Borges worked in all jobs available to a writer: as editor, translator, anthologist, librarian, lecturer, founder of little magazines, director of literary supplements, writing prologues, introductions, literary and film reviews, short articles, longer feature articles, capsule biographies, notes, and even ads for a wide range of newspapers and magazines. These provided him with challenges, skills, and insight. What is also significant is that his essays will take the shape of some of those genres: the article to summarize and present an idea, its derivatives, and its revisions ("La perpetua carrera de Aquiles y la tortuga" [The Perpetual Race of Achilles and the Tortoise], "La doctrina de los ciclos" [The Doctrine of the Cycles]), the exposition of arguments around a theological speculation ("La duración del infierno" [The Duration of Hell]), the report of a theogony ("Una vindicación del falso Basílides" [The Defense of Basilides de False], "Una vindicación de la Cábala" [A Defense of the Kabbalah]), the report of a genre through the analysis of examples ("Las kenningar," "El arte de injuriar"), or the summary presentation of the rules of a genre ("Los laberintos policiales y Chesterton" [The Labyrinths of the Detective Story and Chesterton]). He will continue amassing piles of examples, as in 1922, or filling pages with information, but the constraints of exposition will favor a tighter condensation in paragraphs.

The role of the essays in the writing of Borges's fictions can hardly be exaggerated. This goes beyond the fact that many of his fictions or passages in them are written, stylized, or parodied as literary reviews, bibliographic memoirs, theological investigations, encyclopedia entries. The same relentless logic we see in the essays drives and pervades the order of his fictions: the plots usually progress and fork by conjectures; the narrator often comments on the story by summarizing conflicts, dissonances, and corollaries of what he is telling, or by pondering sameness and difference with a vast array of other stories and ideas. Because they require orderly plots and detailed execution, detective fiction and fantastic literature will be good matches with the logic of Borges's essayistic writing: they will reinforce each other and create composites in which the logic of the essays will affect narration thoroughly.

Readers can trace Borges's fictions back to a sequence of essays. Menard's "la subterránea, la interminablemente heroica" [subterranean, the interminably heroic production] is anticipated by his "visible" work, but also by "La fruición literaria" (there is a speculation on how time improves the meaning of a verse by Cervantes and comments on different possible interpretations of a verse from Aeschylus), "Indagación de la palabra" [An Investigation of the Word] (the first part consists of a reductio ad absurdum of an analysis, word by word, of the beginning of *Don Quijote* as if Borges, the critic, were aiming to write it from scratch, from pure reasoning), and a review of Paul Valéry's *Introduction à la poétique*, published in *El Hogar* in 1938, months before the writing of the fiction, in which the references to *Don Quijote* suggest the ideation of the story. The idea for "Funes el memorioso" [Funes the Memorious] is summarized at the beginning of a review on James Joyce's *Finnegans Wake*, titled "Fragmento sobre Joyce" [Fragment of Joyce], published in *Sur* in 1941. It can be related to a brief note on a few of Joyce's portmanteau words in "Joyce y los neologismos" [Joyce and Neologisms], published in *Sur* in 1939, and, even earlier, to the ambiguous praise of Joyce in a 1925 review of *Ulysses*, collected in *Inquisiciones*. The essays are not just the source of ideas on which Borges's fictions are founded, but, most significantly, it is where many of them start to be visualized even in their particulars of plot, images, rhythm, characters, and narrators. There are liminal passages in the essays where arguments transition from idea to "invención circunstancial" (*OC* I: 220). In "Fragmento sobre Joyce," for example, Funes springs up: "Nosotros, de un vistazo, percibimos tres copas en una mesa; Funes, todas las hojas y racimos que comprende una parra. Sabía las formas de las nubes australes del amanecer del treinta de abril de mil ochocientos ochenta y dos y podía compararlas en el recuerdo con las vetas de un libro en pasta española que manejó una vez en la infancia" [We, at first glance, perceive three glasses on a table; Funes, every leaf and grape on a vine. He knew the shapes of the southernmost clouds in the sunrise of April 30, 1882, and he could compare them in his memory to the veins in the stiff marbled binding of a book he once held in his hands during his childhood] (*Borges en Sur* 167; *SNF* 220). Ultimately, what Borges resumes in his fictions is the long habit of thinking and imagining rigorously in his essays.

If "Tlön, Uqbar, Orbis Tertius" may be regarded as Borges's most ambitious text, it is partially so because it is the most thorough and condensed recap of all his previous work: the many essays on the idealist dispute, on the metaphor and the image, on encyclopedias and mirrors, on conceptual humor and narrative art, on the Gnostics and translation. Recapitulation in his writing often acquires even a musical nature, akin to that moment Adorno highlights in *Beethoven*, in which memory pauses and the identity of the non-identical and the non-identity of the identical are reached (17). Exemplary of this is how Borges sequences and frames the iteration of the variations of the metaphor in "La esfera de Pascal" [Pascal's Sphere] or the expectation he creates when, comparing and contrasting it to Cervantes's text, the narrator introduces the revelatory evidence of Menard's fragment of part I chapter IX of *Don Quixote*.

After the extension he requested from God has been granted, Jaromir Hladik, the protagonist of "El milagro secreto" [The Secret Miracle], resumes his unfinished tragedy *Los enemigos* (*The Enemies*). The librarian in "La biblioteca de Babel" [The Library of Babel] wanders in hexagonal rooms; Hladik wanders in the stringent corridors of memory and hexameters, where circumstances impose on him "un afortunado rigor" [a providential strictness]: he picks the tragedy up again, redoes, strikes out words, cuts, condenses, expands, comes up with a last epithet (*OC* I: 512; *CF* 162). Those are Hladik's action verbs. In Borges's literature, recapitulation, a basic writing device, becomes an instrument and an adventure of order. Recapitulation does not tame infinity but provides a syntax in which that infinity can be postulated and achieved. That motion starts in his early essays, where readers can glimpse and share that literary experience of the infinite that Maurice Blanchot saw and defined so well (93), in the seemingly boundless library,

Notes

1. Daniel Balderston notes that it is easier to extract epigrams from Borges's essays written in the 1940s and 1950s than from his earlier writings, where it is harder to isolate phrases that would stand by themselves. ("Borges ensayista" 117–19). This is another sign of shifts in Borges's essayistic syntax at the end of the 1920s. Epigrammatic sentences like the one at the end of the essay on Berkeley or, for example, the aphoristic *ars poetica* in a one-liner in "Crítica del paisaje" [Critique of Landscape] (1921), "Lo marginal es lo más bello" [What is marginal is the most beautiful] (124), may become noticeable as a retrospective effect of reading his later work.

2. For a nuanced periodization and an insightful understanding of Borges as critic, see Pastormerlo. For the form of the essay in Borges, see Giordano whose idea of reading as "an evaluating experience" in Borges illuminates what is literary in his essays (37).

3. Alan Pauls underscores the importance of laughter as "context" for Borges's literature (153). This stands out in the satirical responses and parodies Borges wrote in the 1920s in collaboration with friends and will loom large in his later collaboration with Adolfo Bioy Casares as well as in the stylization of the overtly mordacious voice of the narrator in "Pierre Menard, autor del Quijote." Interestingly, in many of these satirical pieces, Borges rejoices in the types of Argentine slang and the two kinds of humor, puns and crass jokes, which he examines and discards for his own Argentine voice. A notable example is a reply to an article by Guillermo de Torre, in which the Spanish critic had stated the preeminence of Madrid as the intellectual "meridian" of the Spanish-speaking avant-gardes. Borges and Mastronardi responded in kind with a jocular rant written in a pastiche of Argentine slangs, under the threatening title "A un meridiano encontrao en una fiambrera" [To a Meridian Found in an Ice Box] (1927). "Fiambre" means "cold cuts" and is slang for "corpse"; "fiambrera," the container, is slang for "cemetery" or "morgue."

4. A typographical error haunts this passage in many editions: "inmortal" (immortal) often appears as "inmoral" (immoral).

5. Beatriz Sarlo's *Borges a Writer on the Edge* provides an accurate and comprehensive account of how Borges's poetics took shape in the cultural polemics of the 1920s and how his contentious and lucid positions contribute to our understanding of competing cultural responses to the rapid modernization of Buenos Aires at the time.

6. In the 1920s, Borges is an assiduous reader and critic of the literatures of the Río de la Plata. Graciela Montaldo suggests that his essays configure a fragmentary history of Argentine literature, which can be regarded as an alternative to Ricardo Rojas's monumental *Historia de la literatura argentina* (220). Exemplary of this is Borges's influential reading of the gauchesque genre, of which it can be said that it is a history he writes and on which he will be written by later critics, most notably by Josefina Ludmer and Julio Schvartzman.

7. In "Las inscripciones de los carros," Beatriz Sarlo finds Borges's answer to the challenge of inventing a poetics where *criollismo* would converge with the avant-garde. See "Borges: Tradition and the Avant-Garde."

8. Nora Benedict underscores the importance of *Evaristo Carriego*'s materiality as a book. She studies its meticulous production by the printer and typographer Francisco A. Colombo

and Borges's expectations about this, his first "longish" book on an Argentine topic (55–61). Benedict also analyzes the detailed passage on the physical aspects of a first book, with which Borges starts his critical essay on Carriego's *Misas herejes* [*Heretic Masses*] (18–19). That passage is a good example of the use of the detailed image in Borges, as if he was requesting the reader to imagine a first book before beginning the critical assessment of the poems.

9. Against a novelistic conception of the biography, Patricio Fontana sees *Evaristo Carriego* as a "distillate or extract," "a laconic modulation" that "seeks to elude or avert" . . . "the proliferation of facts presupposed by a life" (9).

10. Sylvia Molloy sees the biography in *Evaristo Carriego* as a "montage," in which "the narrator shatters the character, and identifies with him, fleetingly, through images that shape both the story and the narrator himself" (14).

11. Although less consequential than his decisions on what to keep in his *Obras completas*, the question may extend to Borges's criteria for what to include in his miscellaneous collections of essays among the many articles and reviews published in magazines and newspapers. Daniel Balderston has studied several tentative outlines for table of contents for *Inquisiciones, El tamaño de mi esperanza, El idioma de los argentinos*, and *Otras inquisiciones* that Borges jotted down on blank pages of books he was reading. Balderston concludes: "His own books are still in flux when he thinks about collecting texts for them; beginnings for Borges are terribly uncertain" (*How Borges Wrote* 76).

12. Sylvia Molloy highlights how Borges, in his postulations of reality, "engages in a playful counterpoint" between the text and that "*other* reality" that exceeds it. She sees "imprecision and selection" as a "differential supplement" that "attempts to incorporate the infinity of the world or its *specular* illusion into a finite model that is perpetually undermined" (62).

13. James Irby sees the first edition of *Discusión* in 1932 as *the* turning point in Borges's writing. He highlights a shift of topics "toward cosmology and theology" and a qualitative difference in what he calls, after Barthes, "the power of text," which was "already operative" in that collection (71–72).

Works Cited

Adorno, Theodor. "The Artist as Deputy." Notes to Literature, vol. 1. Translated by Sherry Weber Nicholsen. Columbia University Press, 1991, pp. 98–108.

Adorno, Theodor. *Beethoven: The Philosophy of Music*, translated by Edmund Jephcott. Polity Press, 1998.

Balderston, Daniel. "Borges ensayista." *Borges: realidades y simulacros*. Biblos, 2000, pp. 117–34.

Balderston, Daniel. *How Borges Wrote*. University of Virginia Press, 2018.

Benedict, Nora C. *Borges and the Literary Marketplace: How Editorial Practices Shaped Cosmopolitan Reading*. Yale University Press, 2021.

Blanchot, Maurice. "Literary Infinity: The Aleph." *The Book to Come*. Translated by Charlotte Mandell, Stanford University Press, 2003, pp. 93–96.

Borges, Jorge Luis. "An Autobiographical Essay." *The Aleph and Other Stories, 1933–1969*. Translated by Norman Thomas di Giovanni. E. P. Dutton, 1970, pp. 135–85.

Borges, Jorge Luis. *Borges en Sur. 1931–1980*. Emecé, 1999.

Borges, Jorge Luis. *Collected Fictions*, translated by Andrew Hurley. Penguin Books, 1998.

Borges, Jorge Luis. *El idioma de los argentinos*. Seix Barral, 1994.

Borges, Jorge Luis. *El tamaño de mi esperanza*. Seix Barral, 1993.

Borges, Jorge Luis. *Evaristo Carriego*, translated by Norman Thomas di Giovanni. E. P. Dutton, 1984.

Borges, Jorge Luis. *Inquisiciones*. Seix Barral, 1994.

Borges, Jorge Luis. *Obras completas*. 4 vols. Emecé, 1996.

Borges, Jorge Luis. *Selected Non-Fictions*, edited by Eliot Weinberger. Penguin, 1999.

Borges, Jorge Luis. *Textos recobrados 1 (1919–1929)*. Emecé, 2007.

Borges, Jorge Luis. *Textos recobrados 2 (1931–1955)*. Sudamericana, 2011.

Fontana, Patricio. "A Mode of Truth. Borges y la biografía en tres episodios." *Variaciones Borges*, vol. 47, 2019, pp. 3–24.

Giordano, Alberto. *Modos del ensayo. De Borges a Piglia*. Corrected and enlarged edition. Beatriz Viterbo Editora, 2005.

Irby, James. "Textual Series in *Discusión*." *Variaciones Borges*, vol. 31, 2011, pp. 71–81.

Ludmer, Josefina. *The Gaucho Genre. A Treatise on the Motherland*. Duke University Press, 2002.

Molloy, Sylvia. *Signs of Borges*. Duke University Press, 1994.

Montaldo, Graciela. "Borges: una vanguardia criolla." *Yrigoyen entre Borges y Arlt (1916–1930)*. Edited by Graciela Montaldo, Editorial Contrapunto, 1989, pp. 213–28.

Pastormerlo, Sergio. *Borges crítico*. Fondo de Cultura Económica, 2007.

Pauls, Alan. *El factor Borges*. Anagrama, 2004.

Premat, Julio. *Borges: An Introduction*, translated by Amanda Murphy, Vanderbilt University Press, 2021.

Sarlo, Beatriz. *Borges: A Writer on the Edge*. Verso, 1993.

Sarlo, Beatriz. "Borges: Tradition and the avant-garde." Borges Studies Online. Borges Center for Studies & Documentation, April 14, 2001. http://www.borges.pitt.edu/bsol/bsbt.php.

Schvartzman, Julio. *Letras gauchas*. Eterna Cadencia, 2013.

CHAPTER 11

INVENTING AUTHORS, IMAGINING BOOKS

An Invisible Literary History

JULIO PREMAT

AN EVENT

DESPITE Borges's own distrust of "events" in terms of literary history, the 1941 publication of his collection of short stories, [*El jardín de senderos que se bifurcan*] *The Garden of Forking Paths*, was undoubtedly one of them. Although the National Prize for Literature in Argentina was not awarded to him at the time—an honor he would not receive until 1956—those involved with the literary journal *Sur* sought to remedy that injustice through their own kind of recognition—an episode of polemical exchanges and literary assumptions that itself could have appeared in any of the multiple stories in *El jardín de senderos que se bifurcan* that parody institutional systems of evaluating literature (Podlubne). It was in *Sur* in 1942 that friend Adolfo Bioy Casares published a review suggestive of "an event," when he attributed to Borges a discovery ("las posibilidades literarias de la metafísica" [the literary possibilities of metaphysics]) and an invention (*"El jardín de senderos* que se bifurcan crea y satisface la necesidad de una literatura de la literatura y del pensamiento" [*The Garden of Forking Paths* both creates and satisfies the need for a literature about literature and about thought]) (56; my translations). Thus, the *event* can be understood both as a point of reference (creation) and, retrospectively, as the conditions that made this referentiality possible (as it corresponds to a necessity). Many years later, Italo Calvino, pointing to similar characteristics, asserted that Borges created the latest innovation to occur within literary genres: what he calls "Borgesian Fiction." This innovative fiction is characterized by a specific practice of erudition, most notably, in imaginary books and "potential literature"—or, as Bioy Casares had previously stated, by a literature about literature (51).

Borges devotes half of the carefully written "Prologue" introducing *El jardín de senderos que se bifurcan*'s eight stories, to presenting, among other keys to approaching his work, the imaginary books that are found in the collection. Such thoroughness underlines the importance this device had for him. I quote a fragment:

> Desvarío laborioso y empobrecedor el de componer vastos libros; el de explayar en quinientas páginas una idea cuya perfecta exposición oral cabe en pocos minutos. Mejor procedimiento es simular que esos libros ya existen y ofrecer un resumen, un comentario. Así procedió Carlyle en *Sartor Resartus*, así Butler en *The Fair Haven*; obras que tienen la imperfección de libros también, no menos tautológicos que los otros. Más razonable, más inepto, más haragán, he preferido la escritura de notas sobre libros imaginarios. Estas son "Tlön, Uqbar, Orbis Tertius"; el "Examen de la obra de Herbert Quain"; "El acercamiento a Almotásim." (*OC* I: 511)

> [It is a laborious madness and an impoverishing one, the madness of composing vast books—setting out in five hundred pages an idea that can be perfectly related orally in five minutes. The better way to go about it is to pretend that those books already exist, and offer a summary, a commentary on them. That was Carlyle's procedure in *Sartor Resartus*, Butler's in *The Fair Haven* though those works suffer under the imperfection that they themselves are books, and not a whit less tautological than the others. A more reasonable, inepter, and more lazy man, I have chosen to write notes on *imaginary* books. Those notes are "Tlön, Uqbar, Orbis Tertius"; "A Survey of the Works of Herbert Quain"; "The Approach to Al-Mu'tasim.] (*CF* 67)

Quite clearly, this is an agenda-setting affirmation, highlighting the contours of that groundbreaking "Borgesian Fiction" described by Bioy Casares and Calvino, which is also present in two other stories of the collection, "Pierre Menard, autor del Quijote" [Pierre Menard, Author of the *Quixote*] and "El jardín de senderos que se bifurcan."

This chapter will focus on the three stories in *El jardín de senderos que se bifurcan* that most explicitly engage with the dynamics of both inventing a book and inventing an author as a figure in literary history: "El acercamiento a Almotásim" [The Approach to Al-Mu'tasim], "Pierre Menard, autor del Quijote" and "Examen de la obra de Herbert Quain" [A Examination of the Work of Herbert Quain]. It should be noted, however, that this approach is repeated, if less explicitly, in almost all the collection's stories and within more traditional modalities of fantastic narrative, at times inspired by Kafka. The three texts chosen here are the most notable in terms of the "invention" and "discovery" of unprecedented forms of narration, although many elements carry through to other stories, either by referring to nonexistent books or by allegorizing the role of the writer (such as in "La biblioteca de Babel" [The Library of Babel] or "Las ruinas circulares" [The Circular Ruins].

Regardless, the magnitude of the intention and its ambition are undeniable: inventing a book or an author is to invent a world; it is to invent a literature, treat its reality as a given, and then comment upon it. Moreover, considering that at least two of those stories ("Pierre Menard . . ." and "Examen . . .") have been written as obituaries—to take that author's being dead for granted and evaluating his legacy for posterity—is to take a position on something finished, and in doing so, building fictions that tend to transform what has happened. In other words, to invent worlds, invent authors, is also to

THRESHOLDS FOR AN AUTHOR

One of the most visible techniques of the hypertextual and secondhand or "received" dimension of Borges's writing, so often pointed out, consists of combining recognizable narrative forms with essayistic writing conventions, such as those found in encyclopedic, academic and journalistic texts about literary history or reception (reviews, author biographies, obituaries, or fictitious quotes, often in English). Also very noticeable is the tendency to "introduce" or "frame" what is going to be written, thereby creating a complex system of paratexts, peritexts, prologues, and introductions to precede and accompany the texts themselves. I am of course referring to the interviews, the dedications, the footnotes, the epilogues, and a general compulsion to preface, present, orient, what we are going to read: introductions and hybrid genres are the most visible features of a specific "method." Noting this phenomenon, Michel Lafon concludes that Borges is undoubtedly "one of the most surprising paratextualists of all time. All of his work is inscribed, to some degree, within the framework of an expansive paratextuality" ("Pour une poétique"; my translation). The three texts discussed here are initial examples of both characteristics: certain types of essayistic conventions and more or less evident modalities of narrative prologues.

Then, again, Borges's choice of turning traditional forms of the essay into mechanisms for storytelling not only entails constantly centering thought in fiction and inextricably combining truth and invention; it also reveals an important step in the progressive transformation of his literary practices. The stories that Borges claimed, in one way or another, as his "first" ("El acercamiento a Almotásim" and "Pierre Menard . . .") expand upon the dominant forms of his writing in the 1930s: bibliographical inventions (*Historia universal de la infamia* [*A Universal History of Infamy*]), the lateral practice of biography (*Evaristo Carriego*), and his numerous reviews and literary biographies of contemporary authors (contributions in the magazines *El Hogar* [*The Home*] and *Sur*).

This is how "El acercamiento a Almotásim" bears the title of the novel whose *second* edition is reviewed in the story, while "Pierre Menard" and "Examen de la obra de Herbert Quian" are obituaries, both of which seek, after the deaths of the writers, to restore some justice to their texts, reevaluating or adding nuance to critiques by their contemporaries and, in so doing, deploying the main characteristics of those authors' writing. In all three, the nucleus of the plot (if you can call it that) is the program for each story's creation and the individual methods used to accomplish it.

These prologues or forewords include an indissoluble mixture of real and invented information, with a series of people's names, historical moments, publications, and publishers, which creates a verifiable literary and cultural history, in combination with fictional characters. The pact made with the reader is sealed in the pragmatic's pointing to the poetic as a way to justify the texts' existence, or to legitimize them within those genres that canonize, evaluate, and disseminate literature. In that sense, it is a fantasy-style technique that introduces fiction into a horizon considered real or, rather, that posits the disturbing fictional character of reality. Thus, the passage from "reality" to "fiction" occurring within these narrative frameworks points to an indeterminacy of the discourse that contradicts the rational and argumentative dimension of the essay genre. Something like a "fiction effect" is produced, as opposed to the referential effect: what is true, in Borges, seems false. This concerns, above all, a certain type of story considered factual: the "true" literary history.

The texts that frame the presentation of the works of these imaginary authors (Quain, Menard, Ali in "El acercamiento . . .") are a way of defining a fourth author, not only in the sense of an authorial voice but above all in a positioning of authorial knowledge— a relationship to the novel and to narrative procedures, an opinion on literary criticism and the circulation of texts. The three narrators do not hide their subjectivities or their close relationships with the subject: they are witnesses, friends, connoisseurs. They do not speak from a neutral institutional authority but in the first person. Then again, Menard's bibliography is a mocking compendium, among many other things, of Borgesian themes and procedures, just as at the end of "Herbert Quain," the narrator states that he "naively" took from Quain's last book, *Statements*, the plot of "*Las ruinas circulares, que es una de las narraciones del libro El jardín de senderos que se bifurcan*" [*The Circular Ruins*, which is one of the stories in the book *The Garden of Forking Paths*], that is, the very book we are reading (*OC* I: 557).

The author who would hide behind the narrator moves from reality (his name on the book cover) to being an imaginary voice, an imaginary author. Inventing another author (Pierre Menard, Herbert Quain, Mir Bahadur Ali) is a subterfuge to invent himself. Borges, the new Borges, creator of labyrinthine encyclopedic stories, emerges in those prefaces and is also created there as a narrator. As the procedure supposes a subtle method of self-creation, of establishing an affiliation and a series of models based on games about knowledge and displacements of authority, another account of the truth of history is outlined: the origin of Borges the writer.

Along with the procedures that give verisimilitude to the imaginary, the three stories (and in some cases their development) are present themselves as interventions that seek to restore truths, justify narrative preferences, critique techniques, and, in general, insert themselves into a present sort of literary life in a markedly controversial way. Thus, the narrator intends to "examine" and "discuss" the construction of "El acercamiento a Almotásim," by arguing that the "commendable literary practice" (*CF* 85) of the first edition is spoiled in the second (and criticizing in passing the ultimate modern novel, Joyce's *Ulysses*) due to its "insignificant" relationships with the past. There is a violence in his vision that is repeated in numerous judgments on Quain's literary production. For example, he finds that the "ejecución deficiente" [careless plotting] (*OC* I: 553; *CF* 108) of his first novel explains its failure; underlines "la vana y frígida pompa de ciertas descripciones del mar" [the hollow, frigid stiltedness of certain descriptions of the sea] (*OC* I: 462; *CF* 108); and opines that some of the nine stories included in *April March* are "indignos de Quain" [unworthy of Quain] (*OC* I: 463; *CF* 110) or are "afectados por bromas lánguidas y por pseudoprecisiones inútiles" [marred by pallid jokes and instances of pointless pseudoexactitude] (*OC* I: 463; *CF* 110). In Menard, there is an effort to "rectify" a truth, but made from a perspective of invective, accusation, and even ideological judgment (references to unforgivable omissions, fallacious catalogue, deplorable readers): two clearly defined sides oppose each other, Menard's authentic friends and *others*. It is a parodic representation—not disdainful of irony and caricature—of the literary media and its various modes of legitimation, judgment, and canonization (collectives, magazines, specialized journalism, editorials, controversies) (Alonso Estenoz). From this depiction emerges, in turn, a conception of the writer's life as a permanent confrontation (Pauls 27–46).

While these narrators position themselves as judges, since to reestablish literary value, one must first criticize an erroneous, insufficient, or partial reception, these "discussions" and "inquisitions" (to take up the titles of two books of essays by Borges) go further. Not only do they involve criticism and humor at the expense of the literati, they also express a reevaluation of the novel as a form, a theory of literary writing, and a certainty about the appropriate ways to write a story. Confrontation provides a space for delineating one's own positions on "asombro" or the experience of the unexpected in literature, on novelty and innovation, and on dialogues with works from the past. Thus, these stories function as an imaginary extension of the essays on the novel that are included in Borges's book *Discusión* [*Discussion*]. There, in texts originally published in the popular home journal *El Hogar*, he unpacks his variations upon, as well as many (often scathing) reviews of, contemporary novels.

THE DEMON OF PARALLELISMS

The invention of authors and books produces stories not only about writing but also about the evolution of texts, about their reception, and about the ways of negotiating with tradition and novelistic form. The narrators' evaluative and controversial positions presuppose some very specific journeys through the library. The most obvious device in this regard is the way in which these writers relate to the writers of the past. The first approach is always comparative: the new in the face of what has already been written— what Gérard Genette called Borges's "demon of parallelisms" (203). The ubiquitous phenomenon can be equated, to some extent, to the invention of writers and books themselves; the unreal referential effect does not point to reality but to the books that already exist in the library. It is through these books that the characteristics of the invented characters are defined.

Yet the biographical and psychological information about Alí, Menard, and Quain are but pointless details, because there is no life, no experience behind the works. The only information that matters when inventing authors or books is that which identifies similarities to existing texts in that panopticon that is the universal library. In an equally legendary way, Borges's writings imagine the invention of an author, the invention of a work, which entails creating affiliations, similarities, ruptures, constants: it is, in a way, to narrate. Thus, the similarities, the tracing of literary precursors, are the object of infinite variations, ranging from plausible to witty to absurd. Reading is less the perception of aesthetics and effects than the discovery of associations to what has already been written.

In all three stories, these kinds of associations abound. In "El acercamiento . . .," the list of names that reinforces the plausibility of the invented book or that function as jokes or witticisms is overwhelming. A review the narrator quotes and takes issue with argues that the novel is "a somewhat awkward combination" of allegorical Islamic poems and crime novels; another finds "la doble, inverosímil tutela de Wilkie Collins y del ilustre persa del siglo XII, Ferid Eddin Attar" [the dual, and implausible, influence of Wilkie Collins and the illustrious twelfth-century Persian poet, Ferid Eddin Attar] (*OC* I: 414; *CF* 82); yet another lists analogies to a Kipling story. Almost all the texts in Pierre Menard's "visible" bibliography are commentaries, rewritings, translations, or rearrangements that, in one way or another, refer to preexisting books. Throughout the rest of the story, books or authors that inspired Menard or which he reviled are constantly cited: references to *Salammbô*, Quevedo, Nietzsche, Bertrand Russell, Novalis, William James, Maurice Barrès, Rodríguez Larreta, Daudet, Shakespeare, Paul Valéry, and others situate the writer and his project. Influences and similarities, whether proposed by the narrator, by a random critic, or even by Herbert Quain himself, also abound in "Examen . . .": we are told that his books have been compared to "uno de Mrs. Agatha Christie y otros a los de Gertrude Stein" [one by Mrs. Agatha Christie and others to those by Gertrude Stein] or are "como las odas de Cowley" [like the odes of Cowley] (*OC* I: 461). Some dialogue is said to falter "entre la mera vanilocuencia de Bulwer-Lytton y los epigramas de Wilde o de Mr Philip Guedalla" [between the extremes of a hollow grandiloquence worthy of Bulwer-Lytton and epigrams and Wilde or Philip Guedalla (*CF* 110)]; and in evaluating his theatrical work, *The Secret Mirror*, "la crítica pronunció los nombres de Freud y de Julien Green" [critics spoke the names "Freud" and "Julien Greene"] (*OC* I: 464; *CF* 111).

These prolific citations evoke the history of literature, not only by pointing out constancies and repetitions but by emphasizing the dynamic of the influence wielded by the tomes enshrined in the inherited library and the dramatization of reading them. The precursor thus becomes a central theme and even a kind of founding mytheme. The gesture of clarifying desired or despised precursors is not unlike what could be called the "biographeme of influences," in which Macedonio Fernández and Evaristo Carriego occupy a foundational place, extended with other names, such as Schopenhauer, Coleridge, or Berkeley (Lafon, *Borges ou la réécriture* 81).

"El acercamiento . . .," the first text of this long series, deserves a more detailed discussion, given the variations found among the first editions (*Historia de la eternidad* [*A History of Eternity*] from 1936, *El jardín . . .* from 1941, *Ficciones* [*Fictions*] from 1944) before its standardization in what would be the definitive version, in the 1974 *Obras completas* [*Complete Works*]. The variations concern the end of the story and consist, precisely, of changing the literary references to accentuate similarities, heighten the incongruous effect of a simile, or simply to add more names and works to the list. Initially, the conclusion to the fictional book review makes reference to Eliot having pointed out a resemblance between "El acercamiento" and Daudet's *L'Arlésienne*, while the narrator closes the story by mentioning, in all humility, another resemblance that he perceives to Conrad's *Heart of Darkness* (*Historia de la eternidad* 114). As of 1941, Eliot definitively changes his mind, as he now refers to the "incompleta alegoría *The Faërie Queene*" [unfinished allegory *The Faërie Queene*] (*CF* 86) and, with the same humility, the narrator points to "un precursor lejano y posible: el cabalista de Jerusalén, Isaac Luria" [a distant, possible precursor: the Kabbalist Isaac Luria] (*CF* 86). In the prologue to *El jardín de senderos que se bifurcan*, Borges includes yet another coordinate: the parallelism that he reads in Henry James's 1901 novel, *The Sacred Fount*. Evidently, the texts Borges was reading in 1936 and 1941 led him to continue writing the story, correcting and expanding its effects.

Another change, which also points to bibliographic parallels, is the long explanatory footnote that appears at the end of the story in the first edition of *El jardín de senderos que se bifurcan* (1941: 48) and later in *Ficciones* (1944): in it, the plot of Farid ud-din Attar's *Conference of the Birds* is mentioned in the main text, as if to evaluate, after giving various scholarly references, its rather tenuous similarities to Alí's novel. The definitive edition of *Historia de la eternidad* as collected in the *Obras completas* maintains the rewriting of the ending (i.e., the transformations to the 1936 version), but the footnote disappears. With it diminishes the symmetrical effect of reality/fiction that points to literary themes or an interpretation of the story in terms of a crossroads where current writing faces off with the past. Without the footnote, "El acercamiento a Almotásim" seems to deal more with the theme of eternity, which is the place where the story begins and ends up including itself. To the contrary, the presence of the footnote extends the fiction of a literary history that is characteristic of all stories in *El jardín de senderos que se bifurcan*, a history that is neither truly historical nor totally invented.

This is because the footnote adds or emphasizes clues to interpreting the story, from the position of what could be considered a library search. There we read: "ésa y otras ambiguas analogías pueden significar la identidad del buscado y del buscador; pueden también significar que éste influye en aquél. Otro capítulo insinúa que Almotásim es el 'hindú' que el estudiante cree haber matado" [that and other ambiguous similarities may signal the identity of the seeker and the sought; they may also signal that the sought has already influenced the seeker. Another chapter suggests that Al-Mu'tasim is the "Hindu" that the law student thinks he murdered] (*OC* I: 418; *CF* 87). Read from the relationship between influencers and the influenced, we see that Al-Mu'tasim's specificity is blurred: the sought and the seeker are the same, or it is the seeker who influences the sought, or the search may even be for a precursor who has been murdered.

From the footnote, it is evident that the questions of influence, of the weight of past works upon the writing of the present, of the arduous relationship that is established with those literary figures made sacred through the force of tradition, are perhaps not alien to the initial plot and the "progresos del alma en el ascenso místico" [the progress of the soul in its ascent to mystical plenitude] (*OC* I: 415; *CF* 85) described in Alí's novel. In this way, his search could be understood as visible "a través de los delicados reflejos que [. . .] ha dejado" [by means of the delicate glimmerings or reflections the soul has left] (*OC* I: 416; *CF* 84) upon other people—in other words, his influence. In a smile, in a word, the presence can be perceived, all those having come into contact with Al-Mu'tasim being mere "mirrors" (i.e., incomplete repetitions) of a superior being, a model. Thus, the mystical search emblematizes a quest for perfection, unattainable for the modern writer. Through this spiritual device, then, one can see the relationship to those "great men" of literary history, whose aura permeates all who have come close to them. It is not surprising, then, that the last "mirror," the one closest to Al-Mu'tasim, his immediate predecessor, is a bookseller, a man of letters.

Noting similarities and influences is equivalent to writing; it is, in itself, a gesture of creation. If, as Piglia notes, erudition is a syntax of writing in Borges, this zigzagging pattern in the virtual space of what is written is also akin to the process of creation (*Crítica y fiction* 147). In this regard, one can consult Daniel Balderston's study of the procedure of bibliographic references and citations in Borges's writing process (21–49) and the publication of annotations Borges made in the books in his library (Rosato and Álvarez). This also leads to "installing laughter at the heart of thought," transforming, as Alan Pauls writes, "erudition into vertigo" (145; my translation). In this sense, the simultaneous attribution of dissimilar models or precursors for a work is a parodic and even comical distortion of reading, which is, as we know, the quintessential approach to writing in Borges. To narrate is to propose fanciful variants of literary history. In many other texts and places in Borges's work, we see similar operations at play.

Forms of Posterity

As can be seen, finding or repeating Al-Mu'tasim is arduous work, for which Alí, in literary terms, seems not to have the capacity: he gives into the "más burda de las tentaciones del arte: la de ser un genio" [that basest of art's temptations: the temptation to be a genius (*OC* I: 417; *CF* 86). He not only desires to approach and take refuge in Al-Mu'tasim's "resplendence" but also to match it. It is not enough to reflect the resplendence of the past to triumph. Fate for him is failure.

With other strategies and from another point of view, Quain's project is also a failure. His works "anhelan demasiado el asombro" [strive too greatly to astonish] (*OC* I: 461; *CF* 108), even though he never "considered himself a 'man of genius'" (*CF* 107) and often repeated his modest position toward creation: "No pertenezco al arte, sino a la mera historia del arte" [I belong not to art but to the history of art] (*OC* I: 461; *CF* 107). And even though the highest "pleasure literature can minister" is "the imagination," many are incapable of that happiness and must content themselves with "simulacra" (*CF* 111). Yet Quain's stories also establish an explicit relationship with art: a search for the "experimental" that does not prosper ("asombrarse de memoria es difícil" [being astonished by rote is difficult (*CF* 108)] (*OC* I: 461; *CF* 108), the narrator quips).

By comparison, Menard's extraordinary project seems more promising, although it remains unfinished. His work transforms the *Quixote*—the narrator perceiving Menard's influence even on pages of the *Quixote* that he did not write—altering the generational order: "es lícito ver en *el Quijote* 'final' una especie de palimpsesto, en el que deben traslucirse los rastros—tenues pero no indescifrables—de la 'previa' escritura de nuestro amigo" [it is legitimate to see the "final" Quixote as a kind of palimpsest, in which the traces—faint but not undecipherable—of our friend's "previous" text must shine through] (*OC* I: 450; *CF* 95). By altering how the text is read, the past is changed, and turns back upon itself. This leads not only to reversals in the chronology but, as I have been postulating, to attribution functioning as a means of creation, as a way of giving meaning to a text.

This device of theme and variations on erudition, citation, and fanciful attribution foregrounds a certain relationship with the past, with representations of historical time and with various conceptions about the advent of texts. The temporal location tends to be "after," most notably by using an obituary as a story's starting point (that of Pierre Menard, that of Herbert Quain). From the beginning, the use of vindicating or controversial obituaries implies the construction of a specific approach to the past that extends to many other levels.

"El acercamiento . . ." notes a consensus on the usefulness of drawing inspiration from the past: "Se entiende que es honroso que un libro actual derive de uno antiguo: ya que a nadie le gusta (como dijo Johnson) deber nada a sus contemporáneos" [It is generally understood that a modern-day book may honorably be based upon an older one, especially since, as Dr. Johnson observed, no man likes owing anything to his contemporaries] (*OC* I: 417; *CF* 86). The list of models is therefore a way of distinguishing oneself from the literature of one's time, which, if we agree with Piglia, implies a paradoxical form of vanguard and innovation. Parallelly, Quain disbelieves in the cult of the past: "Deploraba con sonriente sinceridad 'la servil y obstinada conservación de libros pretéritos'" [he deplored with smiling sincerity "the servile, stubborn preservation of past and bygone books"] (*OC* I: 461; *CF* 108) and disdained history ("No había, para él, disciplina inferior a la historia" [In his view, there was no lower discipline than history] [*OC* I: 461; *CF* 107]), not because the world was regressive, but rather "la manera de historiarlos" [the way the stories are told] (*OC* I: 462; *CF* 109), which allows for the infinite ramifications and possibilities of a past that thereby transform it.

Just as a formative and influential resplendence lies at the heart of "El acercamiento a Almotásim," "Pierre Menard . . ." in its turn includes a referential figure, but whose values and impacts are practically the opposite. Or, if not opposite, that have more to do with the final erasure of Al-Mu'tasim suggested in the footnote mentioned above ("identidad del buscado y del buscador" [identity of the seeker and the sought] and the hypothesis that "éste influye en aquél" [the sought has already influenced the seeker] (*OC* I: 418; *CF* 87). Those monuments to the past, those "strong authors" Harold Bloom exalts when describing influence, lack such impact upon Menard unless one takes into account the opinions the narrator attributes to him.

206   JULIO PREMAT

Indeed, Cervantes's *Quixote* would be for Menard a "contingent," "unnecessary" book, which could therefore be forgotten; to write his *Quixote* was to write on the basis of an "imprecisa imagen anterior de un libro no escrito" [the vague foreshadowing of a yet unwritten book] (*OC* I: 448; *CF* 92). In Menard's opinion, *the Quixote* is subject to "falling by the wayside" (*CF* 94); from an unavoidable monument to merely a "pleasant book," it inexplicably becomes "una ocasión de brindis patrióticos, de soberbia gramatical, de obscenas ediciones de lujo" [an occasion for patriotic toasts, grammatical arrogance, obscene deluxe editions] (*OC* I: 450; *CF* 94). Thus, Menard's project involves rewriting something that, in a way, is nonexistent or pointless. In any case, the model thus ceases to be a Great Work and Menard's position is made ambiguous: on the one hand, he rewrites a book from the past, but on the other hand, he insists that to be able to reinvent it, the text must be forgotten. This is the strategy to succeed in repeating a classic, which is, by definition, unrepeatable. The fabled book (Menard's) obscures the true one (Cervantes's). It also openly challenges the existence of a national literature based on hierarchies and texts organized into a literary history. The iconoclastic dimensions of Menard's project stand out not only because he is French but also because his project opposes the patriotic "glorification" of the creations of the past (Pastormerlo 95–102).

Hence, the logic of the succession of authors and texts, the chronological organization of the past, is placed on unstable ground—when not governed by the absurd. Menard denounces the "plebeyo placer del anacronismo o (lo que es peor) [. . .] la idea primaria de que todas las épocas son iguales o de que son distintas" [plebeian delight in anachronism or (what is worse) [. . .] the elementary idea that all times are the same, or that they are different] (*OC* I: 446; *CF* 90–91). With the relationship between a text and history framed as such, with its specific moment and conditions for possibility, an "epoch" is not a determinant but a convention. When interpreting a quote from Menard's *Quixote* ("*la verdad, cuya madre es la historia, émula del tiempo, depósito de las acciones, testigo de lo pasado, ejemplo y aviso de lo presente, advertencia de lo por venir*" [*truth, whose mother is history, rival of time, depository of deeds, witness of the past, exemplar and adviser to the present, and the future's counselor*] [*OC* I: 449, emphasis in the original; *CF* 94]), read in counterpoint to the exact same fragment by Cervantes, a certain concept of social history emerges that is not far removed from literary history. History is not "una indagación de la realidad" [*delving into* reality] but rather "su origen. La verdad histórica, para él no es lo que sucedió; es lo que juzgamos que sucedió" [the very fount of reality. Historical truth, for Menard, is not "what happened"; it is what we believe happened] (*OC* I: 449; *CF* 94, emphasis in the original). In any case, amnesia triumphs over the book itself: part of the project is "olvidar la historia de Europa" [to forget the history of Europe] (*OC* I: 447; *CF* 91) and thus (as far as Western culture is concerned) to forget literary history itself.

As can be seen, the three stories cultivate three allegories and three stances in positioning oneself toward the past: seeking the resplendence or reflection of something that is never found, and which ends up being the writer himself (Al-Mu'tasim); altering chronology, forgetting the past in order to rewrite it, and, in doing so, annulling, changing, or desecrating the precursor in some way (Menard); and breaking with the old by means of surprising devices, akin to the avant-garde (Quain). Each of them

INVENTING AUTHORS, IMAGINING BOOKS   207

inclines toward a specific position in terms of conceptualizing the creation of and relationship with the past, with a marked ambiguity between creating the new and repeating or disdaining the past.

Literary History at Stake

Found at every step in his work, the foundation for Borges's fertile and profuse variations on time, whether rooted in fantasy or philosophy, lies in the imaginary variations of our conventional story about the succession of texts and authors: literary history. In this regard, we might cite Borges's comments about conceptions of time from an essay in *Otras inquisiciones* [*Other Inquisitions*], "El tiempo y J.W. Dunne" [Time and J. W. Dunne]:

> Dunne, asombrosamente, supone que ya es nuestra la eternidad y que los sueños de cada noche lo corroboran. En ellos, según él, confluyen el pasado inmediato y el inmediato porvenir. En la vigilia recorremos a uniforme velocidad el tiempo sucesivo, en el sueño abarcamos una zona que puede ser vastísima. Soñar es coordinar los vistazos de esa contemplación y urdir con ellos una historia, o una serie de historias. Vemos la imagen de una esfinge y la de una botica e inventamos que una botica se convierte en esfinge. Al hombre que mañana conoceremos le ponemos la boca de una cara que nos miró antenoche . . . (Ya Schopenhauer escribió que la vida y los sueños eran hojas de un mismo libro, y que leerlas en orden es vivir; hojearlas, soñar). (OC II: 26)

> [Dunne, surprisingly, presumes that eternity already belongs to us, as corroborated by the dreams we have each night. In them, according to him, the immediate past and the immediate future intermingle. Awake, we pass through successive time at a uniform speed; in dreams we may span a vast zone. To dream is to orchestrate the objects we viewed while awake and to weave from them a story or series of stories. We see the image of a sphinx and the image of a drug store and then we invent a drug store that turns into a sphinx. We put the mouth of a face that looked at us the night before last on the man we shall meet tomorrow. (Schopenhauer wrote that life and dreams were pages from the same book and that to read them in their proper order was to live but to leaf through them was to dream.)] (*SNF* 219)

From these postulations, we can deduce three major characteristics that synthesize Borges's allegories of literary history: a history not lived but leafed through, a history not real but dreamed, a history not progressive but eternal.

LEAFING THROUGH A HISTORY

First, it should be noted that literary history is not located in what happened or what was published but in the specific ways of browsing through that history, a path that constantly transforms what has already been written and that endows the reader with unusual insight (in "Herbert Quain": "El lector de ese libro singular es más perspicaz que el *detective*" [The reader of this remarkable book, then, is more perspicacious than the detective] [*OC* I: 461; *CF* 108]). As in so many other aspects of Borges's vision of literature, the readers and their historical moment are central to establishing the meanings of the past (it has been said many times: his is a poetics of reading, not of writing) (Rodríguez Monegal). Or, if one prefers, the axis of literary history is the reader and not the ineluctable succession of generations, even when defining what constitutes a classic ("Sobre los clásicos" 1952). This position coincides with various theoretical developments of the twentieth century, which situated the historicity of texts within the ways they were read (Jauss 64), or appropriated (Chartier 271), in what Gadamer calls a "fusion of horizons" between the work and the receiver that redefines its temporality by superimposing past experiences and present concerns (Grondin).

Yet we are not dealing with an orderly and respectful reading but with a specific mode of reading: that "leafing through" (as in Schopenhauer's metaphor for experiencing time), browsing not in any chronological or thematic or any other arbitrarily imposed order, in a casual wandering, following a memory understood to be an adulterated resource, a nonhistorical montage of time (Didi-Huberman 35). Referring to the past through the zigzag movement of leafing through a text implies disordering the encyclopedia, altering the linear, disrupting orders and hierarchies, and making the anachronistic the norm. The inexorability of chronology, the constant looming awareness of having come after, of being previous writers' posterity, are called into question when the evolutionary vision of literature is transformed into a space of correspondences and repetitions. Here, the most unlikely encounters may take place in which no one precedes anyone, and no one has absolute authority or ownership over anything. It is the "reminiscent" present that Didi-Huberman writes of, in which clashes, ruptures, and reappearances of past times occur, intensifying (at least in Borges) the vision of literature as a heterochronic or malleable time system and reading as a journey made of discontinuities and duplications (10). The rewriting, the repetition, the varying tones of the same thus transform temporal form into a circular shape. Gérard Genette saw in Borges's allegorization of literature a kind of panopticon in which all works of all time would be present simultaneously: the Library of Babel is the nightmarish version of this fantasy. As Blanchot has affirmed, Borges finds the infinite in literature (116–18).

We are presented, then, with a history where one can skip from one century to another, from one author to another, from one cultural category to another, in a movement that inserts the fantastic into the historicity of the texts: the fantasy of being able to change the past, that the present can modify what has been inherited. For this implies, in accordance with Eliot's and Borges' takes on influence, that the act of writing displaces and transforms—when it does not simply invent—that very past that intervenes in the act of creation, as described in Borges's well-known essay "Kafka y sus precursores" [Kafka and his Precursors]. The past, in this sense, is a form of the present. Borges participates in a trend that parallels official literary histories, introducing anachronism and temporal alteration as ways of thinking about changes in works.

It follows that a literature without chronology is also a literature with other sorts of hierarchies, ones that are selected and erased, that dialogue with one another and repeat each other. This is what happens with Menard's *Quixote*, the manifestation *par excellence* of the implosion of established literary history: the displacement of a segment—but it is a foundational segment, a pillar—disrupts the entire subsequent chronological edifice. The relationship with existing models is not one of submission and imitation but one of creation. Here, the precursor prepares and nourishes the successor: literary history is no longer the story of a progressive exhaustion but rather that of elaboration and expansion in being and meaning (Schlanger 15).

Leafing through literary history authorizes false attributions (such as those proposed by the narrator of "Pierre Menard . . ."), aberrant parallelisms, the iconoclastic combination of prestigious and marginalized names, and the interrogation of inherited authority of literary history—but while staying within its purported limits (Molloy 188). To leaf through is also to selectively choose events, thereby constituting a different story each time. For Borges, this is the true nature of biography: depending on which facts of a life are selected, the meaning of that life will be different. It is not a rigid system or a coherent construction but rather a hypothesis, a possible outline, transgressive and functioning as the back room or guilty conscience of academic or encyclopedic literary histories. Fantastic literature already played that role in the face of nineteenth-century positivist scientific discourse.

A last note in this regard: leafing through literary history from the margins allows a twentieth-century Argentine to assimilate the great canonical story, to browse through it but also integrate himself into it from a unique stance: the story of an *orillero* or interloper on the outskirts of the metropolis (Sarlo). The insolence of this nonhierarchical appropriation is not unrelated, then, to the tension between the center and the periphery so often at play in Borges's work. It is consequently not surprising that the three fictional writers discussed in this chapter are in one way or another located on a periphery: Ali in India versus England, Menard in Nîmes versus Spain, Quain in Ireland versus England.

A DREAMT STORY

To posit a book as already written and consider its fictitious writer dead is to write another posterity; it is akin to writing history, understanding by *history* the story to which the writings of the past lend intelligibility. As occurs in the novel *Acercamiento a Almotásim* [*The Approach to Al-Mu'tasim*], there is a visible (and anonymous) protagonist and another "invisible protagonist," namely, Al-Mu'tasim—since the actions of the other characters are prompted by partial reflections of the "clarity" that emanates from him, the "clarity" that is Al-Mu'tasim himself. In any case, behind the apparent protagonist there is another protagonist, and behind the narrated story another story is suggested; it is available for the telling, comprised of multiple possibilities. In "Pierre Menard . . ." the operation is similar: we have the visible work "de fácil y breve enmueración" [easily and briefly enumerated] (*OC* I: 444; *CF* 88) and the other, invisible, consisting solely of his project to write the *Quixote*. The narrator deems this "la subterránea, la interminablemente heroica, la impar" [the subterranean, the interminably heroic production—the *oeuvre nonpareil*] (*OC* I: 446; *CF* 90), suggesting by contrast with the rest of Menard's bibliography that it is only the unknown, the unwritten, that merits such dithyrambic praise. There must exist, then, an "invisible" literary history, such as Menard's secret work, of which there are almost no tangible proofs but whose few traces are capable, in their repetition of the Cervantine text, of changing the meaning of an undisputed classic.

An invisible history tells the stories of books not yet written, aborted books, ideal books, thereby introducing unknown paths and overlooked options. In that history, the protagonists are perforce authors, real or nonexistent; as it progresses, the history unfolds, evokes and narrates what was not written, what can be imagined, a "potential literature" (Calvino): a history, then (and returning to Schopenhauer), that is dreamed. If in the world of Tlön any book, to be considered complete, must also contain its counterbook—the same seems to happen in Borges's writerly dynamic: every literary history must contain its counterstory.

Central, then, is the invention of books, authors, precursors, influences, traces, and effects. With this, Borges creates something like a family history of literature, in which the most recent progeny of an extensive lineage begins to dream up other alliances, other births, other family trees, other relationships, and, above all, other ancestors. At its height is the fantasy of "what if" we could write *Don Quixote* and reading "as if" *Don Quixote* were written by an early twentieth-century French symbolist poet. A principle underpinning Borges's family history of literary affiliations is what we could call a counterfactual story: a way of representing, of questioning, of understanding the past based on what did *not* happen. Counterfactual stories have been considered powerful tools for diverting the apparent fatalism of what has passed and the supposed unavoidability of what has been inherited, because they are capable of subverting the impression of continuity (Deleurmoz 123). Or, as Blanchot suggests (142–43), it could be said that literature is not a simple deception, but rather that it possesses the dangerous power of approximating the real due to its infinite possible variations upon the imaginary. Thus, in Borges, knowledge of literary history is engendered through fiction. Ultimately, this principle perceives literary history as a series of unnamed possibilities that is still being written for a reader-demiurge or a reader-god, capable of embracing multiplicity, as in the intrigue of Quain's *April March* ("infinitas historias, infinitamente ramificadas" [infinite stories, infinitely branching] (*OC* I: 463; *CF* 110)) or like the forks in "El jardín de senderos que se bifurcan."

It is then a question of presupposing or insinuating the existence of an alternative literary history, of a fiction of literary history, which is written around and about the very work one has begun to write. This nonacademic history of literature, this literary history of the writer, is a constant frequently commented upon in the literature of the twentieth century (Debaene), and which may have played, in a curious boomerang effect, an important role in the era's debates about the nature of literary history, in which Borges was often cited (Piglia, *Las tres vanguardias* 200).

Indeed, Borges's allegory makes visible the function of the library for an author at work: on their table, texts from different times, apparently irreconcilable genres and with divergent meanings manage to intersect, overlap, and interact. Literary history thus abandons institutional or pedagogical discourses and traditional canonizations to place itself on the side of creation and of the will of the writer as reader, undoing the apparent permanence of what has already happened. The past becomes active memory; it becomes an available text. Writing a work, becoming an author, not only implies transforming the past of literature but also opposing oneself, more or less explicitly, to the grand normative story that a linear, progressive, and harmonious literary history can represent: a story already written that must be destabilized to recover a past that has yet to occur and a future of freedom that can intervene in the act of creation.

An Eternal Story

Finally, we find an invisible literary history that prefigures and points to the utopian, the ideal or even the eternal (a literary history of eternity, a history that is eternal, which is to say, without history). Literature would be on the side of another temporality, that of an eternity glimpsed, desired, that of a revelation condemned not to occur (according to Borges's famous statement in "La muralla y los libros" [The Wall and the Books]). And taking up another title—at every step, in this alternative history there is examination of and judgment upon the past but also an "approach" that is postulated. It is not the sacred, not the revelation, not the supreme identity; it is the uncertain path toward them.

Regardless of how one feels about it, this approach also supposes if not the romantic belief in an absolute, then at least the search for something of that order, which is what is narrated in Al-Mu'tasim, a story first published precisely within the framework of the history of eternity. At this point, we could take the title of Borges's 1936 essay collection, *Historia de la eternidad* [*A History of Eternity*], with its internal paradox (history and eternity are opposites), as a way of describing or signifying a history of literature that contradicts the parameters of the historical. Literature has a history, and it is eternal. There must then be a discrepancy, an aporia, and an insurmountable gap between the two terms. History and literature would thus be incompatible, dramatizing an unsolvable conflict between social time and literary time that reaches its zenith in "El milagro secreto" [The Secret Miracle], a story whose protagonist, Hladík, is also an author, whose book is entitled, no less, *Vindicación de la eternidad* [*The Vindication of Eternity*].

The multiform frames and introductions that we discussed at the beginning of this chapter, the paratextual dimension of the entire work, then function as a constant promise of a writing to come. In this twice-removed literature, everything has been written, and everything, at the same time, is about to be written. Thus, posteriority (commentary, quotation, expansion, repetition, obituary) and origin are superimposed: always about to begin. Not only is there a transformation to the order in which books are inherited, but an imaginary situation is posited in which the beginning never stops beginning.

Imagining books without trying to write them both suggests and obscures a certain messianism. In this sense, Borges's work revives and transforms the tradition of the total text, whose modern emblem is *The Book* by Mallarmé. Inventing books and authors is a skeptical yet powerful representation of the quest for perfection, as defined by Starobinski: an elusive horizon that legitimizes writing without trying to reach it. The impossibility becomes the representation of a road that leads to nowhere; perfection is no longer found in the chimerical destination. Rather, it accompanies the narration of the process, the path, which leads to a hypothetical absolute. Indeed, in renouncing the aim to write perfect books, equivalent or superior to those of the past—the intention, the desires, the utopias underlying those creations are salvaged. Borges's work always deals, to some degree, with the hypothetical shadow of a writing that will not take place, thereby resolving, on an imaginary plane, the modern aporia of the impossible book.

Therefore, the invention of the author by the introduction, the prologue, by reading, by posterity, has to do with utopia, in the sense of a promise of a future work, as impossible as it is desired (Premat). This implies that the future is included in this fabulation of literary history and that this future is also in some way situated in the past: Borges's stories have often been cited to refer to a "model realism" that does foresee the future but multiplies the entities of the past, the ways things could have been (Marrero-Fente 216). Inventing another past is a gesture of temporary utopia, since by modifying what happened, a different future is projected, an uchronia is created.

That is, after all, the core of Borges's many fictions about the recognition and influence of what is to come; the constant discussion about posterity actualizes the existence of a future. Framed as such, we understand Borges's reflection on the effect literature will have in the future: "si me fuera otorgado leer cualquier página actual—ésta, por ejemplo—como la leerán el año 2000 yo sabría cómo será la literatura del año 2000" [if I were granted the possibility of reading any present-day page—this one, for example—as it will be read in the year two thousand I would know what the literature of the year two thousand will be like] (*OC* II: 125; *Labyrinths* 214). The outcome and crystallization of all this is present in Borges's publication of his *Obras completas* in 1974, that copious volume that transforms the approaches, the preambles, the promises, and the fragments that constituted his writings up to that point in one (total) book. Closing the mechanism defined in the stories studied here, and introducing the volume, Borges integrates an "Epilogue" (1143–45) that imagines the way in which a Chilean encyclopedia published a century later will give account of his person, his project, his texts.

CONCLUSION

One of the strongest features of Borges's work is his insistence on fervently praising that which is called the past and, at the same time, his obsession with making that past present: reactivating it, appropriating it, transforming it, and turning it into subversion and creation; a past that is rectified, invented, and instrumentalized in a dynamic of controversial incorporation into the present. The apparent contradiction between veneration and reinvention is instead an alternative definition of the relationship to tradition and with the story that leads us to recognize tradition as such: literary history. That story establishes a bridge between the shapeless mass of texts already written and those that are being written in the present—it is the way to make the past intelligible, to produce interpretations, to search for explanations, to discuss conclusions. Adorno affirmed: "The place to which the enigmatic character of art points can only be understood by means of mediation" (9; my translation). For Borges, the mediation of a rewritten literary history is, as we see, a central mechanism of legitimation for the work itself, which resolves the aporia of inheritance with its plenitude of historical memory, through obscuration, transformation, and transgression. And still, when identifying the operations of fictionalization or displacement of erudition to the realm of the imaginary in Borges, literary history must take a privileged place. Along with other stories and other interpretations of the world, literary history is a story and a means of explaining art (and, therefore, in Borgesian terms, human beings and the world), with which it is in constant dialogue.

In this sense, the function of literary history is akin to the rewriting and recuperation of the histories of philosophy and theology, because Borges's "entry into fiction" (or at least the conditions that allowed him to write his celebrated stories of the 1940s) was contingent upon changing the historicity of texts. It begins not by creating a grand work that fits into the usual categories but by redefining those categories; not writing a work, but rewriting, *sotto voce*, the entire system in which the work will be integrated. The act of writing, in Borges, is thus defined as a variation on lineages, relationships, and orders, such as those proposed, in terms of the primal proceedings of the human imagination, in a family history (Anzieu 217). It is defined, in this perspective, as an alteration of orders and successions, making the temporality of history a space for the unimagined, as variations on the theme proposed by fantastic literature. It is defined as, ultimately, an unattainable utopia of perfection and a utopian postulation about the existence of a form of the future.

To return to his 1965 article and to utopia, Gérard Genette, in his historical moment, associated the Borgesian conception of literature with a myth. Yet, this affirmation can be applied more broadly, not only to the "profound determination of thought," as Genette argues, but above all, to the story, as a narrative device that accounts for that which cannot be addressed conceptually. In any case, the term "myth" applied to this construction should warn us against the temptation to see in literature a closed and articulable theory of literary history. In a very evident way, Borges was obsessed with the great names of the past (as his many anthologies of the "great works" and the "great authors" can attest), as well as with the transcendence of posterity's judgment (though this merits discussion), and ultimately with the canon, originality, and value (Pastormerlo 141–45). It is also worth noting his assiduous efforts, both as a lecturer and as an instructor of literary history, particularly of English, in respecting chronological orders but with highly arbitrary subjectivity in his selection of works and literary periods (Perrone-Moisés; Vecchio). He was examining a fable, not a system of understanding, an imaginary story, not a reliable hypothesis. The programmatic, if any, can be found not so much in what is expounded (rewriting in Menard, formalism in Quain, supremacy of the book over the real in Tlön, desires to dominate time in Hladík), as in the procedure for doing so. The programmatic gesture is to free the past from the obstacles posed by historical monuments, from what has already been written; it is programmatic, not because of the different positions outlined in the texts of *El jardín de senderos que se bifurcan,* and in many others, but because of the gesture that makes the past a space for untaken routes.

Despite being invisible, despite reading what has not been written or leafing through pages in disorder, despite pointing to improbable eternities and unattainable chimeras, this literary history was thus operative; it acted and continues to act in the understanding of the historicity of literature. To some extent, Borges's approaches to influence had their own impact upon that institutional and hierarchical story that is literary history, functioning as what was repressed or forgotten by critics. It is no coincidence that the "theoretical avant-gardes" of the 1960s revived this aspect, in an understandable and, above all, French sort of misreading (Perrone-Moisés), or that in theories about hypertextual literature and the death of the book, critics see—in a vaguely caricaturesque way—Borges as a precursor of new text types—when not an inventor of the internet (Sasson-Henry).

Surely, this chapter, written in 2022, is subject to similar phenomena: a reading of certain aspects of Borges's work made from the perspective of the pressing concerns of the contemporary world about modes of narrating and making past events operational. For all this dialogues today with revisions of the ways the past is made current in a presentist world in which the past is desecrated and exalted: a debt is paid and an inheritance is perverted. This lends the past an operationality that satisfies the need for exchange with the dead, with the law of the progenitors, without submitting to them. The past is a value, but not an imposition. Together with Borges, one can be alive in the past, since from and with the past, something new can be written.

Works Cited

Adorno, T. W. *Théorie esthétique.* Klincksieck, 1995.
Alonso Estenoz, Alfredo. "Herbert Quain o la literatura como secreto." *Variaciones Borges,* vol. 23, 2007, pp. 51–67.
Anzieu, Didier. *Le corps de l'œuvre.* Gallimard, 1981.
Balderston, Daniel. *How Borges Wrote.* University of Virginia Press, 2018.
Bioy Casares, Adolfo, *"El jardín de senderos que se bifurcan"* (SUR año XII, número 92, mayo 1942 60). *Jorge Luis Borges,* edited by Jaime Alazraki. Taurus, 1976, pp. 56–60.
Blanchot, Maurice. *Le livre à venir.* Gallimard, 1959.
Borges, Jorge Luis. *Collected Fictions,* translated by Andrew Hurley. Penguin, 1999.
Borges, Jorge Luis. *Historia de la eternidad.* Viau y Zona, 1936.

Borges, Jorge Luis. *El jardín de senderos que se bifurcan*. Editorial Sur, 1941.

Borges, Jorge Luis. *Obras completas I*. Emecé Editores, 1974.

Borges, Jorge Luis. *Obras completas*. 4 vols. Emecé Editores, 1996.

Borges, Jorge Luis. *Selected Non-Fictions*, edited by Eliot Weinberger. Penguin, 1999.

Borges Jorge Luis, Donald A. Yates, and James E. Irby. *Labyrinths: Selected Stories & Other Writings*. New Directions, 1964.

Bloom, Harold. *The Anxiety of Influence: A Theory of Poetry*. Oxford University Press, 1973.

Calvino, Italo. *Six Memos for the Next Millennium*. Harvard University Press, 1988.

Chartier, Roger. *Au bord de la falaise: L'Histoire entre certitudes et inquiétude*. Albin Michel, 1998.

Debaene, Vincet, Jean-Louis Jeannelle, Marielle Macé, and Michel Murat. *L'histoire littéraire des écrivains*. Presses de l'Université Paris-Sorbonne, 2013.

Deluermoz, Quentin, and Pierre Singaravélou. *Pour une histoire des possibles. Analyses contrefactuelles et futurs non advenus*. Seuil, 2016.

Didi-Huberman, Georges. *Devant le temps. Histoire de l'art et anachronisme des images*. Minuit, 2000.

Genette, Gérard. "La utopía literaria." *Jorge Luis Borges*, edited by Jaime Alazraki. Taurus, 1976, pp. 203–10.

Grondin, Jean. "La fusión des horizons: La versión gadamérienne de l'*adæquatio rei et intellectus*?" *Archives de Philosophie*, vol. 68, no. 3, 2005, pp. 401–18.

Jauss, Hans Robert. *Pour une esthétique de la réception*. Gallimard, 1978.

Lafon, Michel. *Borges ou la réécriture*. Seuil, 1990.

Lafon, Michel. "Pour une poétique de la préface. Autour de *La Invención de Morel*." *Le Livre et l'Édition dans le monde hispanique, XVIe–XXe siècles. Pratiques et discours paratextuels*, Revue Tigre, Actes de Colloque international organisé par le Centre d'etudes et recherches hispaniques de l'Université Stendhal, 1992, pp. 303–10.

Marrero-Fente, Raúl. *Playas del árbol. Una visión trasatlántica de las literaturas hispánicas*. Huelga y Fierro, 2002.

Molloy, Sylvia. *Las letras de Borges*. Editorial Sudamericana, 1979.

Pastormerlo, Sergio. *Borges crítico*. FCE, 2007.

Pauls, Alan. *El factor Borges*. FCE, 2000.

Perrone-Moisès, Leyla. "L'histoire littéraire selon J.-L. Borges." *Histoires littéraires*, vol. 124, 2001, pp. 67–80.

Piglia, Ricardo. *Crítica y ficción*. Siglo XX, 1990.

Piglia, Ricardo. *Las tres vanguardias. Saer, Puig, Walsh*. Eterna Cadencia, 2016.

Podlubne, Judith. "*Sur* 1942: El 'Desagravio a Borges' o el doble juego del reconocimiento." *Variaciones Borges*, vol. 27, 2009, pp. 43–66.

Premat, Julio. "Borges utopista y los narradores del fin de siglo argentino." *Variaciones Borges*, vol. 50, 2020, pp. 149–65.

Rodríguez Monegal, Emir. *Borges: Hacia una lectura poética*. Guadarrama, 1976.

Rosato, Laura, and Germán Álvarez, eds. *Borges, libros y lecturas*. Ediciones Biblioteca Nacional, 2010.

Sarlo, Beatriz. *Borges, a Writer on the Edge*. Verso, 1993.

Sassón-Henry, Perla. *Borges 2.0: From Text to Virtual Worlds*. Peter Lang, 2007.

Schlanger, Judith. "Le précurseur." *Le Temps des œuvres. Mémoire et préfiguration*, edited by Jacques Neefs. Presses universitaires de Vincennes, 2001, pp. 13–27.

Starobinski, Jean. "La perfection, le chemin, l'origine." *Starobinski en mouvement*, edited by Murielle Gagnebin and Christine Savinel. Champ Vallon, 2001, pp. 167–97.

Vecchio, Diego. "Borges professeur: la bibliothèque du père et ses fantômes." *Critique*, vol. 4, 2007, pp. 239–49.

CHAPTER 12

KNIVES, VENDETTAS, BIFURCATIONS

Detective Fiction in Borges

JÚLIO PIMENTEL PINTO

[E]l cuento policial nada tiene que ver con la investigación policial, con las minucias de la toxicología o de la balística. Puede perjudicarlo todo exceso de verosimilitud, de realismo; trátase de un género artificial, como la pastoral o la fábula.

[(T)he detective story has nothing to do with police investigation, with the minutia of toxicology or ballistics. It can be marred by any excess of verisimilitude, or realism; this is an artificial genre, like the pastoral or the fable.]

—Jorge Luis Borges
Review of Manuel Peyrou's *La espada dormida* (1944)

SIX LAWS

THE paths connecting Borges to detective stories are multiple.

First, he was an enthusiastic reader of puzzle-solving and mystery stories. Edgar Allan Poe, whom Borges considered the uncontested inventor of the genre, was always behind his writing:

Poe fue un proyector de sombras múltiples. ¿Cuántas cosas surgen de Poe? . . . Derivan dos hechos que parecen muy lejanos y que sin embargo no lo son; son hechos afines. Deriva la idea de la literatura como un hecho intelectual y el relato policial. El primero—considerar la literatura como una operación de la mente, y no del espíritu—es muy importante. El otro es mínimo, a pesar de haber inspirado a grandes escritores. (*OC* IV: 190)

[Poe was caster of multiple shadows. How many things arise from Poe? . . . From him stem two facts that seem quite distant from one another and in fact are not; they are related. There comes the idea of literature as an intellectual feat and the detective story. The first—considering literature an operation of the mind, and not the spirit—is very important. The other is minimal, despite having inspired great writers.]

The mention of Poe links the advent of detective fiction to his recognition of the cerebralism that is inherent to literary creation—the axis upon which Borges rests his defense of detective fiction—and to the inauguration of a literary tradition to which he would ascribe.

Second, Borges wrote his own detective stories, individually and in collaboration with Adolfo Bioy Casares. Third, and equally as important, he was a scrupulous compiler, reviewer, and translator of detective fiction, making decisive contributions to the genre's dissemination in Argentina. Between May 1936 and May 1939, he wrote twenty-five reviews of detective fiction for the magazine *El Hogar* [*The Home*].[1] Additionally, together with Bioy, he published an anthology of the "best detective stories" (collected in two volumes and published in 1943 and 1951) and co-directed, from 1945 on, publisher Emecé's Séptimo Círculo collection, which sought to translate and circulate British analytical detective fiction.[2] Borges and Bioy chose the first 120 titles for the collection, which ended up including authors of other origins and even hard-boiled American crime fiction, whose realist leanings were not particularly appreciated by the series' organizers.

Borges's multiple levels of engagement with detective fiction was guided by certain "laws" of the genre, which he identified and discussed in two nearly identical texts in 1933 and 1935.[3] In these essays, the matrix created by Poe's and Borges's readings of G. K. Chesterton seems to stand out while at the same time taking care to emphasize "respect for the reader" as the basis for any mystery story.

The first law limits the number of characters to six and insists that by restricting the quantity of elements deployed the narrative avoids the text becoming too diffuse; it likewise ensures the force of the story and the progression of the detective's rigorous thought process—as well as the reader's. The two following laws expand on the same idea, but with variations: the second highlights the necessary "declaración de todos los términos del problema" [declaration of all of the terms of the problem], which is to say, all of the facts of the mystery should be made known to readers. The third is the "avara economía de los medios" [avaricious economy of means], in other words, the simplification of storylines and avoidance of any games of illusion.[4] For Borges, respecting these two postulates guarantees the "honesty" of a detective story and keeps relevant information from being "drowned out" or a distractive fact from being excessively highlighted (*Borges en* Sur 127–28; *SNF* 113). This emphasizes the text's commitment to the reader and the reading pact based both on the text's and the reader's belief in the rigorous analytical geometry of the genre.[5]

DETECTIVE FICTION IN BORGES   219

The fourth law affirms the "primacía del cómo sobre el quién" [priority of how over who], that is, of the crime and investigative strategy over the mere naming of the criminal. With the fifth law, "el pudor de la muerte" [reticence concerning death], Borges attacks "hard boiled" fiction by rejecting excessive violence and reiterating that "en la narración policial, . . . musas glaciales son la higiene, la falacia y el orden" [in the detective story . . . glacial muses are hygiene, fallacy and order].[6] In the sixth and last of the laws, he highlights the importance of precision and surprise in the dénouement and illustrates this in Chesterton: "Chesterton, siempre, realiza el *tour de force* de proponer una aclaración sobrenatural y de reemplazarla luego, sin pérdida, con otra de este mundo" [Chesterton always performs a tour de force by proposing a supernatural explanation and then replacing it, losing nothing, with one from this world] (*Borges en* Sur 128; *SNF* 114). The reference to Chesterton is no accident. Not only does Borges consider him to be Poe's primary heir, but the Borgesian laws of the genre fully coincide with the principles that Chesterton himself set out in 1925 in his essay "How to Write a Detective Story," which distinguishes detective fiction from any realistic endeavor and associates it with terms such as "fancy," "avowedly fictitious fiction," "artificial form of art," "toy," and "trick."[7] It is no coincidence that Borges publicized and endorsed these principles, making the guidelines for the genre the Englishman had established the basis for his own rules for detective fiction.

WITH BIOY

The primacy of the "how" over the "who" or "what" is also evident in the detective stories that Borges wrote in collaboration with Bioy. The texts are collected in five volumes and involve two pseudonyms. H. Bustos Domecq signs *Seis problemas para don Isidro Parodi* [*Six Problems for Mr. Isidro Parodi*] (1942) and *Dos fantasías memorables* [*Two Memorable Fantasies*] (1946); his disciple B. Suárez Lynch is the author of *Un modelo para la muerte* [*A Model for Death*] (1946). With their own names, Borges and Bioy also publish *El paraíso de los creyentes* [*The Paradise for Believers*] and *Los orilleros* [*The Hoodlums*] (1955)—screenplays that, stylistically, incorporate the logical rigor of the detective narrative (Oubiña 72)—as well as *Crónicas de Bustos Domecq* [*Chronicles of Bustos Domecq*] (1967) and *Nuevos cuentos de Bustos Domecq* [*New Tales of Bustos Domecq*] (1977).[8]

Seis problemas opens with a profile of Bustos Domecq signed by the "educadora, señorita Adelma Badoglio" [the schoolteacher Miss Adelma Badoglio] in which the fictional author lists the author's bio-bibliographical data; mentions his literary debut with a set of romantic, patriotic, and historical poems; and praises his turn toward the detective genre (*OCC* 13; *Six Problems* 159). That text is followed by the "Palabra liminar" [Foreword] of Gervasio Montenegro and the six short stories that relate the activities of don Isidro Parodi, a strange detective who solves cases from inside a jail cell.[9] In the foreword, Montenegro talks more about himself than the work, resorts to countless clichés, and belittles Bustos Domecq. A hybrid character and friend of the author, he sometimes acts as an involuntary support for Parodi's reason—the classic, often obtuse assistant who accompanies the analytical detective—and, on other occasions, he serves as his antipode: the one who relies on intuition and, because of this, lacks the rigor and reason needed to perform the detective's role. Although his discourse generally sounds ridiculous and empty, Montenegro defines Parodi's place and affiliation in the universe of detective narratives with unexpected precision:

> En sus cuentos no hay planos que olvidar ni horarios que confundir. Nos ahorra todo tropezón intermedio. Nuevo retoño de la tradición de Edgard Poë [sic], . . . se atiene a los momentos capitales de sus problemas: el planteo enigmático y la solución iluminadora. Meros títeres de la curiosidad, cuando no presionados por la policía, los personajes acuden en pitoresco tropel a la celda 273, ya proverbial. En la primer consulta exponen el misterio que los abruma; en la segunda, oyen la solución que pasma por igual a niños y ancianos. El autor, mediante un artificio no menos condensado que artístico, simplifica la prismática realidad y agolpa todos los laureles del caso en la única frente de Parodi. (OCC 16)[10]

> [In his stories there are no false trails or confusing timetables. He spares us all blind alleys. Offspring of the tradition of the tragic Edgar Allan Poe, our author concentrates on the main events in his cases—the statement of the problem and its illuminating solution. Mere puppets of curiosity—if not under direct pressure from the police—the characters gather in a colorful flock in the now legendary cell 273. On their first visit they put forward the mystery that troubles them; on their second they hear its solution, which astounds young and old alike. The author, whose skill is as compact as it is artistic, reduces elementary reality and heaps all the laurels of the case on the brow of Parodi alone.] (*Six Problems* 9)

The presentation highlights Poe's centrality to the text's origin and Bustos Domecq's ability to contrast reason with the uncertainties of the world, orderly investigation with the hustle and bustle of big cities, and the house (or, in this case, the cell in which the detective isolates himself to reflect) with the street (the crime scene). The aspects that Montenegro praises in Bustos Domecq's text are very close to Borges's laws: the reduced number of characters (not least because of the dimensions of the cell in which Parodi is imprisoned), the statement of all the terms of the problem (because of the impossibility of Parodi obtaining more elements than those offered to him by whomever brings him a crime to solve), the economy of means (expressed, for example, in Parodi's irritation with the wandering accounts of those who come to him and in his effort to reduce their long stories to bare essentials), the primacy of the how over the who (manifested in the concern to clarify the paths that led to the mystery, rather than the person responsible, who is usually already identified in the first account given to him), and the necessity and wonder of the solution. Montenegro also echoes Borges in his rejection of violence and adventure and even reproduces Borges's defense of reading as a determining element of the genre. No wonder he ends the prologue with an appeal to the reader: "Suena la hora del adiós. Hasta aquí, hemos marchado de la mano; ahora estás solo, frente al libro" [The time has come to say goodbye. To this point we have walked together; from here, face to face with the book, you are on your own] (*OCC* 19; *Six Problems* 13).

Dos fantasías memorables by Bustos Domecq and *Un modelo para la muerte* by Suárez Lynch, came out the same year. The two authors dialogue with one another and participate in the same fictitious intellectual circle (Parodi, "Una Argentina virtual" 53–143; Almeida 33–51). The first title, a brief work, is composed of two short stories: "El testigo" [The Witness] and "El signo" [The Sign]. *Un modelo* opens with a sardonic cast list of the characters in Isidro Parodi's stories and is characterized by the predominance of dialogue. *Crónicas de Bustos Domecq* and *Nuevos cuentos de Bustos Domecq* take up that satirical tone and also keep the majority of the characters from Don Isidro's first stories. *Crónicas* was originally composed of twelve texts, written in the early 1960s, to which were later added another five stories, a prologue, and twenty-one short texts. *Nuevos cuentos* collects stories written between the 1940s and 1960s and includes Borges and Bioy's most violent text: "La fiesta del monstruo" [The Monster's Party], a corrosive critique of Peronism.

Cristina Parodi, in her very thorough analysis of the collaboration between the two writers, points out that, despite the apparent differences in the volumes that were written together, there is an important unity between them, one provided by the "organización artística de una multiplicidad de voces individuales y sociales, de los más variados lenguajes, jergas y modos de hablar. . . . los personajes son de naturaleza puramente verbal y el resultado es un humorístico muestrario de los más diversos modos de hablar del Buenos Aires de su tiempo" [artistic organization of a multiplicity of individual and social voices, of the most varied lingos, argot and speech habits. . . . the characters are purely verbal in nature and the result is humorous cross section of the most diverse speech practices of the Buenos Aires of this era] (*Borges-Bioy en contexto* 7). The variety of discourses facilitates the primacy of "how" the story is told over "what" is told, and Buenos Aires, with its multiplicity of languages, functions as a microcosm through which paradigmatic figures of the city's daily life and intellectual milieu are moving. For Davi Arrigucci Jr., the polyphony of the stories and their ability to swerve between the chronicle and the short story allow for the incorporation of historical experience "através dos interstícios da própria linguagem que [a obra] desmonta com tanta comicidade" [through the interstices of language itself that the work so comically dismantles] (Arrigucci 154). This establishes a direct link between the detective as written in collaboration and the one who exists in the texts signed by Borges alone.

In (and Out of) the Dance Hall

In his individual work, Borges frequently visited and revisited the matrices of the detective story—in some cases explicitly; in others, as a kind of subterranean movement or ciphered game of quotations. Five short stories categorically illustrate the mutations and disparate itineraries of the Borgesian detective story: "Hombre de la esquina rosada" [Man on Pink Corner], "El jardín de senderos que se bifurcan" [The Garden of Forking

Paths], "Emma Zunz," "La muerte y la brújula" [Death and the Compass], and "Abenjacán el Bojarí, muerto en su laberinto" [Ibn Hakkan Al-Bokhari, Dead in his Labyrinth].

In the prologue to the first edition (1935) of *Historia universal de la infamia* [*A Universal History of Infamy*]—in which "Hombre de la esquina rosada" is included[11]—Borges emphasized that the stories collected in that volume "derivan, creo, de mis relecturas de Stevenson y de Chesterton y aun de los primeros films de von Sternberg y tal vez de cierta biografía de Evaristo Carriego" [stem, I believe, from my re-readings of Stevenson and Chesteron, and also from Sternberg's early films, and perhaps from a certain biography of Evaristo Carriego] (*OC* I: 289; *A Universal History* 13). Subsequently, he turns to "Hombre de la esquina rosada" to exemplify "certain tricks" he claims the stories "abuse": "las enumeraciones dispares, la brusca solución de continuidad, la reducción de la vida entera de un hombre a dos o tres escenas" [random enumerations, sudden shifts of continuity, and the paring down of a man's whole life to two or three scenes] (*OC* I: 289; *A Universal History* 13).

The story does indeed touch on the Stevensonian universe of adventures; it expresses strong visuality—the reader can easily imagine the movements of the characters and identify the editing strategies and the moments when the narrative is cut. The story takes place in the world of *compadritos* [thugs] found in *Evaristo Carriego*, a narrative biography Borges released five years earlier; it compiles lists and enumerations; it interrupts the narration to resume it from another perspective; it assumes the Borgesian principle of a life being ciphered in an event.

The three protagonists—Francisco Real, la Lujanera, and Rosendo Juárez—are the focus of the narrator, who seems to remain in the background, relatively passive. He tells the fictionalized story—beginning, "Parece cuento" [All this may seem made-up] (*OC* I 389; *A Universal History* 90)—to an interlocutor who is addressed as "sir," "gentlemen," and, finally, "Borges." The gauchesque prevails: everything takes place in a virile world marked by knife fights, the territorial hegemony of street toughs, the submission of women to local strongmen, and an ethic that presides over the group's internal relations. It is in this environment that Real challenges Juárez; it is there that Juárez refuses the confrontation and, as a result, loses to the rival gang leader both his command and his woman, la Lujanera, who even urges him to fight, but to no avail.[12]

Through visual and aural references,[13] the narrator details the movements of the dance hall, from the arrival of the neighborhood rivals to the tension of the imminent duel. Discreet, attentive, and observant, he dissolves into the crowd of extras. After the apparent resolution of the conflict, however, his hitherto precise account becomes vague: the reader only knows that the narrator leaves the ballroom, contemplates the beauty of the night, considers the whereabouts of Real and la Lujanera, and, three paragraphs later, returns to the dance.

The enigma is slow to appear: only in the last part of the story does news get out of Real's murder, which had been anticipated by the narrator's subtle observation that "Yo esperaba algo, pero no lo que sucedió" [I was on the lookout, but not for what happened] (*OC* I: 333; *A Universal History* 95). A stranger's having knifed the new strongman is reported by la Lujanera and the dying man himself, and even the police get involved. The narrator makes it clear, however, that no one wanted the intervention of the agents of law and order: in gaucho ethics, conflicts are resolved internally.

In "Hombre de la esquina rosada," which was written contemporaneously with his elaboration of the rules stipulated in "Leyes de la narración policial" [Laws of the Detective Story] and "Los laberintos policiales y Chesterton" [Detective Labyrinths and Chesterton] Borges maintains the basic structure of the detective story: crime, mystery, deciphering. One night came to define the life of the narrator—an unexpected protagonist[14] in a conflict that, in theory, did not concern him but which he had already hinted about at the beginning of the story.[15] His respect for the "modesty" of violence led him to interrupt the account of the space-time between his departure from the dance and his return to the dance hall, eliding the scene of the crime. He has thereby built in the surprise of the ending, in which the solution to the riddle is presented only to the listener of the story, the future author of the tale, and, of course, to the readers who follow along when the narrator looks at his own knife and, satisfied, realizes that "no quedaba ni um rastrito de sangue" [there wasn't the slightest trace of blood on it] (*OC* I: 334; *A Universal History* 98).

RIDDLES AND REASONING

"El jardín de senderos que se bifurcan"[16] also makes use of the narrative strategies of the detective story and respects the Borgesian laws of the genre, but adapts them to the purposes of the story, which overlaps and combines various enigmas and marks a movement that later became frequent in Borges: the description of the crime takes precedence over the details of the investigation.

As opposed to the local and gauchesque content of "Hombre de la esquina rosada," the plot of "El jardín de senderos que se bifurcan" is set during World War I. Like the 1935 story, it contains lists—reproducing the effort to enumerate—and deals with betrayals, traditions, and relationships between temporalities. It also features the contest between the Irish Captain Richard Madden, described as "a las órdenes de Inglaterra" [at the orders of the English] (*OC* I: 472; *CF* 119), and the Chinese spy Yu Tsun, who is working for Germany. The narration of the story by Tsun himself is preceded by a brief introduction, which, in addition to citing the basis from which Borges builds the tale—*A History of the World War*, by Liddell Hart—also reveals the origin of Yu Tsun's testimony. The spy survived the episode the story recounts, thereby contradicting the multiple instances in the plot when Tsun anticipates his imminent execution on the gallows: he managed to write his own story.

The duel between Madden and Tsun is not about knives; it is about riddles and reasoning. Tsun takes on the role of the criminal and constructs the mystery that Madden, his pursuer and player of the role of the classic detective, must decipher. Eager to pass on information to his German superior that is essential to the war's progress, Yu Tsun ciphers the information into the action itself, indicating, with the name of the man he kills, the location where the British have built their new artillery park.

Tsun succeeds in his endeavor: "Abominablemente he vencido: he comunicado a Berlín el secreto nombre de la ciudad que deben atacar. Ayer la bombardearon; lo leí en los mismos periódicos que propusieron a Inglaterra el enigma de que el sabio sinólogo Stephen Albert muriera asesinado por un desconocido, Yu Tsun. El Jefe ha descifrado ese enigma" [I have most abhorrently triumphed: I have communicated to Berlin the secret name of the city to be attacked. Yesterday it was bombed—I read about it in the same newspapers that posed to all of England the enigma of the murder of the eminent Sinologist Stephen Albert by a stranger, Yu Tsun. The Leader solved the riddle] (*OC* I: 480; *CF* 127–28). In other words, Tsun covers up one enigma—the one he deciphered and was duty bound to transmit—with another enigma, that of the murder he committed. Prison and a death sentence are, for him, the least he could pay for defeating Madden in the duel of reasoning.

The mirroring between the Irishman Madden and the Chinese Tsun is obvious: they are foreigners in the service of the powers at war; they play a dangerous game of chess, in which anticipation or delay in identifying the opponent's next move can determine the success or failure of the action (Yu Tsun is always a few minutes ahead of Madden, and it is this interval that allows him to triumph); both recognize and respect their opponent—or perhaps they recognize and respect their opponent's rational capacity, knowing that the game's very existence derives from the commitment and involvement of the participants. In Borges, however, no detective story is pure or straightforward: if "Hombre de la esquina rosada" is slow to offer the enigma, "El jardín de senderos que se bifurcan" is full of duplicities right from the title and recognizes the plurality of mysteries surrounding each successive mystery. The primary enigma is that of time, of the tortuous relationships between the multiple temporalities. The second is that of the labyrinth, an enigma in itself, into which every book and every reading sends us. The reader is called on to feel active and multiple and, like the victim Stephen Albert, led to assume various positions: sometimes he follows Tsun's saga curiously, sometimes he looks for a connection between the real events of World War I and the strange episode narrated in the Chinese man's story, sometimes he wonders whether Tsun's action was traitorous or heroic—a recurring theme in Borges, who always emphasized the porousness between these two positions. This same reader discovers that there is no definitive answer: the ambiguities and the "infinitas series de tiempos, en una red creciente y vertiginosa de tiempos divergentes, convergentes y paralelos" [infinite series of times, a growing, dizzying web of divergent, convergent and parallel times] (*OC* I: 479; *CF* 127) reinforce Borges's conviction that inventiveness and rational calculation always prevail in fiction.

Unbelievable but True

"Emma Zunz"[17] is one of the rare Borges stories whose protagonist is a woman—a woman for whom men "inspiraban, aún, un temor casi patológico" [still inspired . . . an almost pathological fear] (*OC* I: 565; *CF* 216). It is also a story in which—in an equally

DETECTIVE FICTION IN BORGES   225

unusual manner for Borges—there appear sex, violence, and callousness in the face of blood, breaking some of Borges's own laws for detective fiction. This callousness, which is not central to the plot, serves to reiterate a greater horror—one that Emma Zunz brings from the past, that she avenges in the present, and which, in the future of the story, will be difficult to remember and recount:

> Referir con alguna realidad los hechos de esa tarde sería difícil y quizá improcedente. Un atributo de lo infernal es la irrealidad, un atributo que parece mitigar sus terrores y que los agrava tal vez. ¿Cómo hacer verosímil una acción en la que casi no creyó quien la ejecutaba, cómo recuperar ese breve caos que hoy la memoria de Emma Zunz repudia y confunde? (*OC* I: 565)

> [To recount with some degree of reality the events of that evening would be difficult and perhaps inappropriate. One characteristic of hell is its unreality, which might be thought to mitigate hell's terrors but perhaps makes them all the worse. How to make plausible an act in which even she who was to commit it scarcely believed? How to recover those brief hours of chaos that Emma Zunz's memory today repudiates and confuses?] (*CF* 217)

In a manner similar to "Hombre de la esquina rosada" and "El jardín de senderos que se bifurcan," in "Emma Zunz" the Borgesian dilemma of time imposes itself, as does the subversion of the traditional dynamics of the crime narrative. The protagonist combines different temporalities: the past accusation against her father, which forced him to distance himself from Emma, and the secret he keeps about who is really responsible for the "desfalco del cajero" [the embezzlement of funds by the teller]; the present of the action, concentrated in three practically sleepless days; and the sense of timelessness she experiences during the planning and execution of the murder: "Los hechos graves están fuera del tempo, ya porque en ellos el pasado inmediato queda como tronchado del porvenir, ya porque no parecen consecutivas las partes que los forman" [The most solemn of events are outside of time—whether because in them, the most solemn of events, the immediate past is severed, as it were, from the future or because the elements that compose those events seem not to be consecutive] (*OC* I: 566; *CF* 217).

Ricardo Piglia summarizes the story with three concepts: "equivalencias, sustituciones, un nombre por otro" [equivalences, substitutions, one name for another] (Piglia, *Los diarios* 393) and reveals the multiplicity of enigmas that burrow their way through "Emma Zunz." After all, in addition to the death of the miserly, hypocritical, and lonely Aaron Loewenthal, other secrets persist, concealed by the game of masquerades and the exchanges planned by the protagonist: the reportedly false accusation against Emanuel Zunz, from whose name comes that of his daughter (Emanuel/Emma),[18] but which is changed after his escape and exile in Brazil, connoting the loss of the family bond; Emma's deception of Loewenthal, who treats her as an informant; the identity of the person who has sex with her; the inverted use of the revolver which, from being Loewenthal's instrument of defense, comes to be the weapon that kills him.

The game of equivalences and substitutions reaches its climax at the end of the story, when the omniscient narrator, in a turn typical of Borges, proposes a philosophical reflection—which is also a judgment of the protagonist's actions—about the complexity and ambiguity of what we assume to be true or false: "La historia era increíble, en efecto, pero se impuso a todos, porque sustancialmente era cierta. Verdadero era el tono de Emma Zunz, verdadero el pudor, verdadero el odio. Verdadero también era el ultraje que había padecido; sólo eran falsas las circunstancias, la hora y uno o dos nombres propios" [The story was unbelievable, yes—and yet it convinced everyone, because in substance, it was true. Emma Zunz's tone of voice was real, her shame was real, her hatred was real. The outrage that had been done to her was real, as well; all that was false were the circumstances, the time, and one or two proper names] (*OC* I: 568; *CF* 219). The "incredible" becomes credible because it is supported by truths internal to the plot, truths that are not supported by the real referent but by the process of signification produced through the protagonist's account of the crime.

Beatriz Sarlo highlights the partial appropriation of the logic of the crime narrative in the short story, noting that the traces of the plan and its execution prevail but no other clues remain (she tears up the letter informing her of her father's death and the money the sailor left her for their brief sexual encounter), nor are there made explicit any "pormenores que darían sustancia a la resolución de Emma" [details that substantiate Emma's resolution] (Sarlo 233): her confidence in her father's innocence; Loewenthal's moral accountability for her father's suicide; the evocations of her mother's suffering with "la cosa horrible" [the horrible thing] she finds sex to be; and the connection between the workers' strike and the opportunity to deceive Loewenthal and carry out her revenge.

Commenting on the ending of the story, Sarlo also notes that "en la economía borgesiana, los actos y los seres cobran, ante los ojos de Dios, una independencia relativa de sus existencias mundanas" [in the Borgesian economy, actions and beings take on, before the eyes of God, a relative independence from their mundane existences] (Sarlo 232). The same could be said about the general way in which Borges uses the detective: in the story of Emma Zunz's revenge—just as in the narration of "Hombre de la esquina rosada" and the path that leads Tsun to the place where he meets and kills Albert—there are bifurcations, ellipses, and detours that allow for a relative independence from the rules of the genre, including the criminal playing the role of the victim, which open up space for the genre's subversion.

GAME OF DOUBLES

"Subversion of the genre" is the expression Cristina Parodi (1999) uses to define one of Borges's most direct incursions into the detective narrative: "La muerte y la brújula."[19] There are the basic elements of a detective story: the imaginative detective and his realistic assistant, the intricate plot involving the crimes, the atmosphere of mystery and expectation, the logic of the investigation in contrast to the trivialities of everyday life, the games of signs, the triumph of reason. The mirroring between criminal and detective is taken to the extreme and generates an effect of almost total identification between them.[20]

Certain traits of Borges's unique handling of the detective genre are also evident. The story is self-referential and hides local traits under French titles.[21] As with "Hombre de la esquina rosada," "El jardín de senderos que se bifurcan," and "Emma Zunz," the reader receives, right from the start, encrypted information about the solution to the mystery. Ambiguities, duplicities, and role-swapping characterize Erik Lönnrot's investigation into a series of events that he attributes to the criminal Red Scharlach. The detective is ambiguous: he had, the narrator explains, "temeraria perspicacia . . . se creía un puro razonador, un Auguste Dupin, pero algo de aventurero había en él y hasta de tahur" [reckless perspicacity. . . . He thought of himself as a reasoning machine, an Auguste Dupin, but there was something of the adventurer in him, even something of the gambler] (*OC* I: 499; *CF* 147).

Everything in the story is reversed: the simplistic and prosaic view of the assistant is correct while the detective's genius is fanciful. Secluded and isolated, Lönnrot disregards the concrete conditions of the crimes and comes up with solely theoretical explanations; secondary characters in the story, such as the Jewish journalist and the narrator himself, mock the detective's arrogant serenity and wild imagination as he insists on applying the rational geometry that characterizes analytical detective fiction to the urban layout of Buenos Aires. His ultimate solution is inventive and unreal, an unreality that proves fatal: the expected meeting with Scharlach in the last pages of the story confirms the path suggested by the clues the detective found, leading readers to realize these had been false, the criminal having lured Lönnrot into a trap to carry out his promised revenge.

The end of the story holds more surprises for the reader and confirms that, in the game of doubles, deception prevails: it is the murderer who explains the crime, not the investigator; the crime to be deciphered is not the one that took place in the past (or, at the beginning of the text) but the one committed in the last sentence of the story. Borges also transposes his constant concern with reading and ways of approaching the literary text to the world of detective stories: Lönnrot confuses his role with that of a reader, and the main surprise of the outcome comes above all from realizing that he is not the only reader, not even the best one (Parodi, "Borges y la subversion" 89–90).

In "La muerte y la brújula," two of Borges's laws receive special attention: "la declaración de todos los términos del problema" [the declaration of all of the terms of the problem] and "la necesidad y maravilla de la solución" [the need for and surprise by the solution], precisely those that dictate the relationship between text and reader. The subversion in the short story means that the statement, frequent in detective fiction, that the detective "reads the criminal's text" is not just a metaphor (Parodi "Borges y la subversion" 88) and can even be equated with literary criticism.[22] Borges himself, moreover, was the kind of reader that Lönnrot and Scharlach, each in their own way, represent: he carried out transactions with his readings, surpassed them, betrayed them, rewrote them. And so he recreated the work of fictionalization from the matrices of the policeman.

ORTHODOX AND SUBVERSIVE

If "Hombre de la esquina rosada," "El jardín de senderos que se bifurcan," "Emma Zunz," and "La muerte y la brújula" follow the rules for detective fiction in order to subvert them, "Abenjacán el Bojarí, muerto en su laberinto"[23] is the most orthodox of the mysteries Borges wrote.[24] Perhaps this orthodoxy is aided by the fact that the story's writing coincides chronologically with several of Borges' lectures on the genre.[25] The short story does, however, contain traces of the Borgesian practice of transmuting the foundations of the genre. The plot, which at first seems simple, unfolds on two levels. On the most immediate level, it is the summer of 1914, and two friends are conversing while walking toward the center of an impressive circular labyrinth. Dunraven tells Unwin the story of an event that took place about a quarter of a century ago. At the deepest level of the tale, the story being narrated takes place: Ibn-Hakam, a terrible tyrant, is dethroned and flees with the cowardly Said, his cousin and former vizier, a slave, and many riches. Dunraven details the events in which, in the midst of his escape, Ibn-Hakam is led by ambition to kill his cousin; he stabs Said in his sleep and orders his slave to obliterate the dead man's face. He then dreams of the promise of revenge by Said's ghost and, terrified, flees to build the labyrinth where he hides, protected by his slave and a lion. Dunraven's tale ends with him proposing the mystery announced in story's the title: Ibn-Hakam murdered in his labyrinth.

The only possible solution to the enigma is fantastic: the dead cousin seems to have taken his revenge by breaking into the insolvable labyrinth; killing the tyrant, the slave, and the lion in the same way Ibn-Hakam had murdered him; mutilating their faces, and thus fulfilling the promise he had made in Ibn-Hakam's terrible dream. The narrator himself attests to the strangeness of the events: "Al cabo de los años las circunstancias de su muerte siguen obscuras. . . . En primer lugar, esa casa es un laberinto. En segundo lugar, la vigilaban un esclavo y un león. En tercer lugar, se desvaneció el tesoro secreto. En cuarto lugar, el asesino estaba muerto cuando el asesinato ocurrió" [Even after all these years, the circumstances of his death are still not entirely clear. . . . First, that house up there is a labyrinth. Second, a slave and a lion had stood guard over it. Third, a secret treasure disappeared. . . . Fourth, the murderer was already dead by the time the murder took place] (*OC* I: 600; *CF* 255).

As often happens in Chesterton's detective stories, and as Borges highlighted in his laws for the genre, a supernatural solution is proposed (the murder committed by a dead man) and then replaced by a rational explanation. In "Abenjacán el Bojarí, muerto en su laberinto," the person responsible for the turn toward logic is Unwin, who opposes Dunraven's fascination with the "multiplication of mysteries." He turns to Poe and the motif of crimes committed in locked rooms (which frequently appears in detective stories and is analogous to the case of Ibn-Hakam, whose labyrinth serves as a locked door) to defend the argument that all enigmas should be simple and straightforward.

In the story, Unwin emulates the figure of the reader: initially passive and described as "docile." He grows throughout the unfolding of the story, questions his friend's fascination with the supernatural causes of the crime, and theorizes about the detective genre. At the end of the account of Ibn-Hakam's adventures and to Dunraven's rhetorical question, "¿No es inexplicable esta historia?" [Quite an inexplicable story, don't you think?], Unwin curtly responds: "No sé si es explicable o inexplicable. Sé que es mentira" [I don't know whether it is explicable or inexplicable. I know it's a bloody lie] (*OC* I: 603; *CF* 259). The harsh reaction provokes an argument between the friends, followed by Unwin's apology and their arrival at the center of the labyrinth, where they spend the night. Upon awakening—light overtaking the night, reason replacing beliefs—Unwin proposes a new solution to the riddle, one consisting of reflections on set theory, allegorical recourse to myths, greed, cowardice, resentment, revenge: a purely logical solution that replaces Dunraven's supernatural conclusion. He, in turn, "versado en obras policiales" [who had read a great many detective novels] (*OC* I: 604; *CF* 260), finds, disappointedly, that "la solución del misterio siempre es inferior al misterio" [the solution to a mystery was always a good deal less interesting than the mystery itself] (*OC* I: 604; *CF* 260) because the solution eliminates any appeal to the divine and reveals itself instead to be mere sleight of hand.

Still, he accepts the outcome proposed by Unwin, justifying himself with a critical argument: "Tales metamorfosis, me dirás, son clásicos artificios del género, son verdaderas convenciones cuya observación exige el lector" [Such metamorphoses, you will tell me, are classic artifices of the genre—conventions the reader insists must be followed] (*OC* I: 600–06; *CF* 262). Even when resorting to the orthodoxy of the detective model in "Abenjacán el Bojarí, muerto en su laberinto," Borges does not abandon his subversive stance: he transforms the confrontation between the tyrant and the vizier into a dispute between two friends about their conceptions of detective narrative. In this way, he reaffirms his position on the rules of the genre—above all because it is the reader, even as a character in the plot, who sets the course of mystery stories.

The Aesthetic Fact

Let us repeat: Borges's relationship to detective storytelling has always been multiple. He was a reader, an anthologist, a legislator, an editor, and author of individual and collaborative stories. These approaches were heterodox, but his understanding of the genre remained consistent. A cultivator of Poe's matrix for storytelling and a follower of Chesterton's guidelines, Borges held fast to his commitment to rigor, artificiality, and the cerebralism of all enigmas.

In his detective stories, facts are reordered and reconstructed and hypotheses are presented without anything being hidden from the reader's gaze. The genre's traditional narrative strategies are also present: the search for clues, the rational basis for deciphering them, the recognition of different voices and perspectives, the combination of data, and the linking of past and present, synthesizing them in narrative form.

Fidelity to the operation of reason did not prevent Borges's usual repertoire and themes from abounding in his detective stories and essays on the genre. His enigmas focus on time, involve duplicities and variations in positions and names, feature revenge and duels with knives, reconcile local and universal content, cipher a person's life in a single event, include erroneous attributions, indulge in satire, privilege the place of the reader and their modes of reading, combine fiction with criticism and history, and reveal how every path contains forks. They are unusual detective stories and have porous boundaries. They are evidence of Borges's belief that the narrative strategies for detective fiction extend beyond any genre boundary, and they are essential for guiding literary practice.

At the end of "La muralla y los libros," [The Wall and the Books],[26] an account whose explanation seems impossible and any verisimilitude improbable, Borges attests that the strange case of the Chinese monarch who ordered the destruction of all books—thereby dissolving the past—and the construction of the impressive wall may not have its explanation in reality, strictly within the two hyperbolic and contradictory actions.

> Generalizando el caso anterior, podríamos inferir que todas las *formas* tienen su virtud en sí mismas y no en un 'contenido' conjetural. Esto concordaría con la tesis de Benedetto Croce: ya Pater, en 1877, afirmó que todas las artes aspiran a la condición de la música, que no es otra cosa que forma. La música, los estados de felicidad, la mitología, las caras trabajadas por el tiempo, ciertos crepúsculos y ciertos lugares, quieren decirnos algo, o algo dijeron que no hubiéramos debido perder, o están por decir algo; esta inminencia de una revelación, que no se produce, es, quizá, el hecho estético. (*OC* II: 12–13)

> [Generalizing, we might infer that *all* forms have virtue in themselves and not in an imagined "content." That would support the theory of Benedetto Croce; by 1877, Pater had already stated that all of the arts aspire to resemble music, which is nothing but form. Music, states of happiness, mythology, faces worn by time, certain twilights and certain places, all want to tell us something, or have told us something we shouldn't have lost, or are about to tell us something; that imminence of a revelation as yet unproduced is, perhaps, the aesthetic fact.] (*SNF* 344)

I do not think Borges would be opposed to detective fiction being placed on the list of arts that "aspiran a la condición de la música, que no es otra cosa que forma" [aspire to resemble music, which is nothing but form]. Beyond the specific content, each of his mystery stories shows that the long-awaited final revelation is not just about a murderer's name or the way he commits his crime: what it exposes is the characterization of a genre, one whose dynamics are both respected and subverted. Or even more: it is a theory of fiction, a synthesis of Poe and Borges in the belief that literature is an intellectual, artificial, and imaginative construction of the world.

Notes

1. "Un enemigo del escritor argentino 'lo injurió por contribuir a la delincuencia juvenil de la nación, patrocinando edición de novelas policiales'. Borges, Sócrates del siglo XX, aparece como 'corruptor de menores': efectos inusitados pero imaginables en la múltiple industria crítica borgesiana" [An enemy of the Argentine writer, 'he was reviled for contributing to the nation's juvenile delinquency, endorsing the publication of detective novels'. Borges, the Socrates of the 20th century, is represented as a 'corrupter of minors': unusual but imaginable effects in the many branches of the critical industry built on Borges] (Brescia 146–47).

2. El Séptimo Círculo (The Seventh Circle) was contemporary with other collections that promoted detective fiction in Argentina, but it had some peculiar features: the sophisticated name expressed in the title, taking from Dante "las pautas de la novela-problema" [the standards for the problem-novel] and the selection of works based on "las novedades de las editoriales londinenses y neoyorkinas más conspicuas y las recomendaciones de *The Times Literary Supplement*" [new releases from the most conspicuous London and New York publishers and recommendations from *The Times Literary Supplement*] (Lafforgue and Rivera 17).

3. "Leyes de la narración policial" was published in *Hoy Argentina* (April 1–2, 1933); "Los laberintos policiales y Chesterton" in July 1935, in *Sur* (*Borges en* Sur 126–29). In April 1942, also in *Sur*, Borges returned to the subject when he reviewed Roger Caillois's *Le roman policier*, provoking controversy and a response from Caillois. After criticizing the Frenchman's work, Borges concludes: "Mediocre o pésimo, el relato policial no prescinde nunca de un principio, de una trama y de un desenlace. Interjecciones y opiniones agotan la literatura de nuestro tiempo; el relato policial representa un orden y la obligación de inventar" [Mediocre or terrible, the detective story never dispenses with a beginning, a plot and a resolution. Interjections and opinions exhaust the literature of our time; the detective story represents an order and the obligation to invent] (*Borges en* Sur 250).

4. Borges uses the example of Sherlock Holmes to illustrate disregard for the law of the "avara economía de los medios" [avaricious economy of means]. Although he went so far as to praise the "vitality" of Holmes as compared to Auguste Dupin, Borges considered Conan Doyle "un escritor de segundo orden" [a second-rate writer] (*OCC* 849). In manuscripts, Borges likens Conan Doyle to the "raíces platónicas de la teoría de la inspiración, en oposición a teorías de la composición poética como un trabajo de la razón" [Platonic roots of the theory of inspiration, as opposed to theories of poetic composition as an intellectual task] (Lizalde 218).

5. In "El cuento policial," a lecture given in June 1978, Borges proposed the hypothesis that, more than a genre, Poe founded a specific type of reader, the reader of detective fiction who "está lleno de sospechas, porque el lector de novelas policiales es un lector que lee con incredulidad, con suspicacias, una suspicacia especial" [is full of doubt, for the reader of detective novels reads with incredulity and suspicions, or rather, with one particular suspicion] (*OC IV*: 190; *SNF* 492).

6. Despite his proclaimed rejection of the hard-boiled, Borges employs the subgenre's resources and strategies in stories such as "El muerto" [The Dead Man], first published in *Sur* (November 1946) and later incorporated into *El Aleph* (Benedict 144).

7. The essay was originally published in *G. K's Weekly* (October 17, 1925). See also "A Defence of Detective Stories" (*The Defendant*, 1901), "Errors About Detective Stories" (*Illustrated London News*, August 28, 1920), "The Ideal Detective Story" (*Illustrated London News*,

October 25, 1930), available at https://www.chesterton.org/category/discover-chesterton/chestertons-selected-works/the-detective/

8. Regarding the history of collaboration between Borges and Bioy, see Lafon and Peeters 199–217; Schwartz 107–08.

9. The first two adventures of don Isidro appeared in *Sur* (January and March 1942), before the book was published in December of the same year. There is a variation in genre caused by Parodi's imprisonment: "Ao invés da solução externa de um delito cometido num quarto fechado, eis, saída de um quarto fechado, a solução de uma série de delitos cometidos fora" [Inversely to an external solution to a crime committed in a closed room, here, coming from a closed room, is the solution to a series of crimes committed outside a closed room] (Eco 155).

10. Montenegro became a regular character in Bioy and Borges's stories: in addition to this prologue, he appears in four short stories in the same book, in *Un modelo para la muerte* and in *Crónicas de Bustos Domecq*, which he also prefaces.

11. A first version of "Hombre de la esquina rosada" came out under the title "Hombres de las orillas," signed with the name Francisco Bustos, in *Crítica. Revista Multicolor de los Sábados*. n. 6, Buenos Aires, September 9, 1933. The plot is based on an argument that had already appeared in "Leyenda policial," published in the journal *Martín Fierro* in 1927, and, in 1928, included in the essay collection *El idioma de los argentinos* [*The Language of Argentines*] (126–28) with the title "Hombres pelearon." "Hombre de la esquina rosada" is also associated with later short stories by Borges: "El desafío" [The Challenge], written in 1952 and included in *Evaristo Carriego* starting with the edition released in 1955, and "Historia de Rosendo Juárez," which was included in *El informe de Brodie* [*Doctor Brodie's Report*] and tells the story of "Hombre de la esquina rosada" from the perspective of Juárez. It is also possible to relate the story to writings by Hilario Ascasubi (Spagnuolo 57) and with *The Gangs of New York*, by Herbert Asbury, listed in the "Índice de las fuentes" "List of Sources] in *Historia universal de la infamia* as the basis for the book's story "El provedor de iniquidades Monk Eastman" (Balderston, "Borges and the Gangs" 27).

12. An interesting parallel to the gesture of la Lujanera, who hands Juárez the knife and demands that he fight, appears in the ending of the 1953 story "El Sur" [The South], which was included in *Ficciones* as of the 1956 edition, in which an old gaucho throws a dagger at the protagonist Dahlmann so that he can fight a duel. The reactions of Dahlmann and Juárez, however, are opposite.

13. For example, the mixing of "placero insolente de ruedas coloradas" [flashy red-wheeled buggy] (*OC* I: 329; *A Universal History* 90) with the dances and music from the dance hall. The passage exemplifies the contrast in Borges of red ("symbolic value of the immediate reality") with pink ("a reflection of reality many years later, attenuated by memory so abstract for the one who participated in it and tells it so it will be heard" (Bedford 222).

14. The tale emphasizes the heroic status of the three protagonists and the reaffirmation of the myth of courage as the principle of manly action (Gallo 86).

15. Also in "La muerte y la brújula," from *Ficciones*, the first paragraph of the story cryptically foreshadows its ending.

16. "El jardín de senderos que se bifurcan" originally came out in 1941 as the last of eight stories in the collection *El jardín de senderos que se bifurcan*, which, combined with *Artificios*, composed *Ficciones* as of 1944.

17. "Emma Zunz" was originally published in *Sur* (September 1948) and was later incorporated into *El Aleph*.

18. Maier has developed an interesting theory about the choice and impact of the names used in this story (80). Briceño analyses the strategies of the *melodrama* in "Emma Zunz" (Briceño 138).

19. A first version of "La muerte y la brújula" was published in *Sur* (May 1942). It was republished in the anthology *Los mejores cuentos policiales* [*The Best Detective Stories*] (edited by Borges and Bioy) and, as of 1944, was included in *Ficciones*.

20. In an interview at the end of the 1970s, Borges highlighted the identification, in the story, between detective and criminal: "Ese es un lindo cuento policial. Pero yo tengo que reescribir ese cuento. Para que se entienda que el 'detective' ya sabe que la muerte lo espera, al fin. No sé si he recalcado eso. Pero si no, queda como un tonto el detective. Sería mejor que él ya supiera todo eso, ya que el otro es él, ya que el que lo mata es él" [It is a nice detective story. But I have to rewrite that story. So that it is clear that the 'detective' already knows that death awaits him, in the end. I don't know if I have emphasized that. But if not, the detective seems like an idiot. It would be better if he already knew all of that, since the other is him, since the one who kills him is himself] (*Borges el memorioso* 229). Irwin, Balderston, and other critics debate the choice of the names of the story's protagonists as a mirroring device (Irwin 30; Balderston, "Fundaciones míticas" 126–27).

21. In the lecture "El escritor argentino y la tradición" [The Argentine Writer and Tradition] (1953), Borges discusses his writing of "La muerte y la brújula" and his concern with downplaying the characteristics of Buenos Aires's outskirts and in mixing gauchesque material with European referents, creating a story that was simultaneously Argentine and cosmopolitan (*OC* I: 267). In toning down the environment in which the plot takes place, there is a refusal of the realism so often associated with the detective genre, which also manifests itself in Borges's review of *La espada dormida*, by M. Peyrou, published in *Sur* (May 1945) (Fernández Vega 31–33).

22. "Scharlach y Lönnrot (esto es, el criminoso y el detective) son dos modos de leer. Dos tipos de lector que están enfrentados. El lector como criminal, que usa los textos en su beneficio y hace de ellos un uso desviado, funciona como un hermeneuta salvaje. . . . Podríamos pensar a la crítica literaria como un ejercicio de ese tipo de lectura criminal. Se lee un libro contra otro lector. Se lee la lectura enemiga. El libro es un objeto transaccional, una superficie donde se desplazan las interpretaciones" [Scharlach and Lönnrot (that is, the criminal and the detective) are two modes of reading. Two types of reader are at odds with one another. The reader as criminal, who uses texts to his advantage and makes a deviant use of them, functions as a savage hermeneut. . . . We could think of literary criticism as an exercise of this type of criminal reading. One reads a book against another reader. One reads the enemy's reading. The book is a transactional object, a surface where interpretations are displaced] (Piglia, *El último lector* 35).

23. "Abenjacán el Bojarí, muerto en su laberinto" was originally published in *Sur* (August 1951) and included in *El Aleph* as of the second edition of the book, released in 1952.

24. "'El jardín de senderos que se bifurcan' y 'La muerte y la brújula', textos que Borges reconoce como policiales, son los que más atención crítica han recibido. Pero es en 'Abenjacán' . . . donde Borges al parecer quiso condensar y problematizar al mismo tiempo las operaciones que había venido realizando con la narrativa policial durante más de quince años" ['El jardín de senderos que se bifurcan' and 'La muerte y la brújula,' texts that Borges recognizes as detective stories, have received the most critical attention. But it is in 'Abenjacán' . . . where Borges seems to have wanted to both condense and problematize the techniques he had been deploying with detective narrative over the last fifteen years] (Brescia 149).

25. Balderston notes that "Varias conferencias en 1949 versan sobre lo policial: sobre Poe el 30 de marzo en el Colegio Libre de Estudios Superiores, y sobre lo policial en Tucumán el 9 de octubre y en Bahía Blanca el 5 de noviembre. Está entrando en tema cuando bosqueja 'Abenjacán el Bojarí', lo más cercano que escribió al cuento policial clásico" [Several lectures in 1949 deal with the detective genre: on Poe on March 30 at the Colegio Libre de Estudios Superiores, and on detective fiction in Tucumán on October 9 and in Bahía Blanca on November 5. He is warming to his theme when he sketches "Ibn-Hakam al-Bokhari, Murdered in His Labyrinth," the closest thing he ever wrote to the classic police story] (Balderston, *Lo marginal* 70).

26. "La muralla y los libros" was first published in *La Nación*, October 22, 1950, and was included in *Otras inquisiciones* [*Other Inquisitions*] in 1952.

WORKS CITED

Almeida, Iván. "*Seis problemas para Don Isidro Parodi* y la teologia literária de Borges." *Variaciones Borges*, vol. 6, 1998, pp. 33–51.

Arrigucci Jr., Davi. *O guardador de segredos*. Companhia das Letras, 2010.

Balderston, Daniel. "Borges and *The Gangs of New York.*" *Variaciones Borges*, vol. 16, 2003, pp. 27–33.

Balderston, Daniel. "Fundaciones míticas en 'La muerte y la brújula.'" *Variaciones Borges*, vol. 2, 1996, pp. 125–36.

Balderston, Daniel. *Lo marginal es lo más bello: Borges en sus manuscritos*. Eudeba, 2022.

Bedford, D. "Clasicismo, trama y el hecho estético en el cuento 'There are more things' de Borges." *Variaciones Borges*, vol. 10, 2000, pp. 215–26.

Benedict, Nora C. "La novela negra en Borges: una aproximación nueva a 'El muerto.'" *Variaciones Borges*, vol. 39, 2015, pp. 143–58.

Borges, Jorge Luis. *A Universal History of Infamy*, translated by Norman Thomas di Giovanni. E. P. Dutton, 1979.

Borges, Jorge Luis. *Borges el memorioso. Conversaciones de Jorge Luis Borges con Antonio Carrizo*. Fondo de Cultura Económica, 1982.

Borges, Jorge Luis. *Borges en Sur, 1931–1980*. Emecé, 1999.

Borges, Jorge Luis. *Collected Fictions*, edited and translated by Andrew Hurley. Penguin, 1998.

Borges, Jorge Luis. *El idioma de los argentinos*. Seix Barral, 1997.

Borges, Jorge Luis. *Obras completas*. Emecé, 1974.

Borges, Jorge Luis. *Obras completas*. 4 vols. Emecé, 1996.

Borges, Jorge Luis. *Obras completas en colaboración*. Emecé, 1979.

Borges, Jorge Luis. *Selected Non-Fictions*, edited by Eliot Weinberger, translated by Esther Allen, Suzanne Jill Levine, and Eliot Weinberger. Penguin, 1999.

Borges, Jorge Luis, and Adolfo Bioy Casares, eds. *Los mejores cuentos policiales*. Emecé, 1943.

Borges, Jorge Luis, and Adolfo Bioy Casares *Six Problems for Don Isidro Parodi*, translated by Norman Thomas di Giovanni. E. P. Dutton, 1980.

Brescia, Pablo A. J. "De policía y ladrones: Abenjacán, Borges y la teoría del cuento." *Variaciones Borges*, vol. 10, 2000, pp. 145–66.

Briceño, Ximena. "El crimen para la venganza: 'Emma Zunz' en el borde del melodrama." *Variaciones Borges*, vol. 25, 2008, pp. 137–53.

Eco, Umberto. *Sobre os espelhos e outros ensaios*. Nova Fronteira, 1989.

Fernández Vega, J. "Una campaña estética. Borges y la narrativa policial." *Variaciones Borges*, vol. 1, 1996, pp. 27–66.

Gallo, Marta. "*Historia universal de la infamia*: una lectura en clave épica." *Variaciones Borges*, vol. 11, 2001, pp. 81–101.

Irwin, John. *The Mystery to a Solution. Poe, Borges and the Analytic Detective Story.* Johns Hopkins University Press, 1994.

Lafforgue, Jorge, and Jorge B. Rivera. *Asesinos de papel: ensayos sobre narrativa policial.* Colihue, 1996.

Lafon, Michel, and Benoît Peeters. *Escribir em colaboración: historias de duos de escritores.* Beatriz Viterbo, 2008.

Lizalde, Ornela. "Los grandes escritores no crean mitos. Borges habla sobre Conan Doyle." *Variaciones Borges*, vol. 52, 2021, pp. 197–222.

Maier, Linda S. "What's in a name? Nomenclature and the case of Borges' 'Emma Zunz.'" *Variaciones Borges*, vol. 14, 2002, pp. 79–87.

Parodi, Cristina. *Borges-Bioy en contexto: una lectura guiada de H. Bustos Domecq y B. Suárez Lynch.* Borges Center, 2018.

Parodi, Cristina. "Borges y la subversión del modelo policial." *Borges: desesperaciones aparentes y consuelos secretos.* Edited by Rafael Olea Franco, El Colégio de México, 1999, pp. 1–17.

Piglia, Ricardo. *El último lector.* Anagrama, 2005.

Piglia, Ricardo. *Los diarios de Emilio Renzi.* Vol. II. *Los años felices.* Anagrama, 2016.

Parodi, Cristina. "Una Argentina virtual. El universo intelectual de Honorio Bustos Domecq." *Variaciones Borges*, vol. 6, 1998, pp. 53–143.

Oubiña, David. "*Monstruorum Artifex*. Borges, Hugo Santiago y la teratologia urbana de *Invasión*." *Variaciones Borges*, vol. 8, 1999, pp. 69–81.

Sarlo, Beatriz. "El saber del cuerpo. A propósito de 'Emma Zunz.'" *Variaciones Borges*, vol. 7, 1999, pp. 231–47.

Schwartz, J., ed. *Borges Babilônico.* Companhia das Letras, 2017.

Spagnuolo, Marta. "Ascasubi, Borges y La Lujanera." *Variaciones Borges*, vol. 16, 2003, pp. 57–68.

CHAPTER 13

BORGES, ANTHOLOGIZER OF THE FANTASTIC

EMRON ESPLIN

WE might call Jorge Luis Borges the great disseminator of the fantastic in the twentieth century. Although arguments about what constitutes the fantastic continue today (is it a genre, a mode, something else?), there is little debate that Borges propagated fantastic literature throughout his career. Between 1936 and 1940, Borges published three pieces—"El acercamiento a Almotásim" [The Approach to Al-Mu'tasim], "Pierre Menard, autor del Quijote" [Pierre Menard, author of the Quixote], and "Tlön, Uqbar, Orbis Tertius"—that his friend and perennial collaborator Adolfo Bioy Casares claimed formed "un nuevo género literario, que participa del ensayo y de la ficción" [a new literary genre that is part essay and part fiction], listing the third story under the label "fantasías metafísicas" [metaphysical fantasies] (13).[1] Borges published several more fantastic stories in the face of national and regional realism throughout the 1940s; he wrote other stories in this mode in the 1970s even while taking a more realist turn; he lectured on the fantastic to national and international audiences alike from the 1940s through the 1980s; and he mentioned the fantastic in articles as early as the 1920s and in prologues as late as the 1980s.

Perhaps Borges's most profound effect on the spread of fantastic literature, however, came through his work as an anthologizer and editor. Borges developed several anthologies of fantastic literature throughout his career, beginning with the highly influential *Antología de la literatura fantástica* [*Anthology of Fantastic Literature*] in 1940 with Silvina Ocampo and Bioy Casares. He directed and edited the literary magazine *Los Anales de Buenos Aires* [*The Annals of Buenos Aires*], which published many works of fantastic literature during its short but influential run from 1946 to 1948. Much later, in the 1970s and 1980s, he served as the literary voice behind two multivolume libraries or book series that included fantastic texts—*La Biblioteca di Babele/La Biblioteca de Babel* [*The Library of Babel*] and *Biblioteca personal* [*Personal Library*]. In short, Borges disseminated fantastic literature both by writing it himself (and in collaboration) and by rewriting it. For André Lefevere, rewriting consists of several literary activities that exist outside, but simultaneously enrich, what we typically call the authoring of literary texts—including translating texts, anthologizing works, and creating literary history and criticism (6–7). Lefevere sees rewriting as "the hidden motor behind literary evolution and the creation of canons and paradigms"; he claims that "[i]f a work of literature is not rewritten in one way or another, it is not likely to survive its date of publication by many years or even many months," and he invites scholars to "seriously and comprehensively" examine "the power of these rewriters" and "the various ways in which they tend to exercise it" (14).

In the field of Borges scholarship, the analysis of Borges as a rewriter of texts is well underway in terms of his work as a literary critic and his efforts as a translator.[2] However, surprisingly little work, with the exception of Nora Benedict's recent *Borges and the Literary Marketplace*, has been written on Borges as an anthologizer and editor of texts.[3] This chapter takes up Lefevere's invitation to analyze the works of rewriters by engaging with the concept of the anthology to demonstrate how Borges's work as an anthologizer and editor of the fantastic both perpetuates and elevates the genre, introducing the fantastic to new readers while simultaneously raising its status from low- to highbrow by connecting it to his own erudite reputation. In doing so, Borges helps to create a local fantastic literary market—a space where he, his friends, and other authors in his wake can publish their own works of the fantastic—which eventually vaults both Argentine and Latin American letters onto the global stage.[4]

This chapter begins with a brief discussion of the power of the anthology as an organizing apparatus and as a creator of literary canons and tastes and with an explanation of why Borges is an ideal subject for anthology studies. It then unpacks the term "fantastic" as both problematic and slippery for Borges scholars. Finally, the greater part of the chapter offers a chronological examination of Borges's major anthological projects dealing with the fantastic.

Studying Anthologies

Many writers and editors have created anthologies, but until the past few decades, few scholars have paid critical attention to the process.[5] Between the late 1980s and early 2000s, academics in both Spanish- and English-language literary studies began to openly examine the power of the anthology in the formation of literary canons, and both conversations have continued into the twenty-first century.[6] While these two disciplinary approaches to anthology studies have remained isolated from one another, they have raised similar critiques. For example, both Daniel Balderston ("Introduction" ix) and Jeffrey Di Leo (*On Anthologies* 9) comment on the ubiquity of anthologies in the literature classroom and wonder why they are not studied more by scholars of literature and literary history since they are major tools in the creation of literary canons and cultures. Following the invitations of Balderston, Di Leo, and others, critics in both fields have begun to examine the difficult decisions anthologizers make, the limits of space, the power of inclusion or exclusion, and the effects of juxtaposing works (and authors) alongside one another. Tellingly, Borges commented on many of these same issues in book reviews and in the prologues to anthologies that he co-created.[7] In short, we should consider him a precursor to yet another field of study—that of the anthology—which would not emerge until many decades after his musings.[8]

Anthologizers and editors—part of a group Leah Price calls "professional mediators" (10)—make difficult decisions, and their choices have real power to include, to recuperate, to challenge, to reify, to exclude, and to ostracize. Borges commented on this issue of space and the problems it creates in the prologue he wrote for the *Antología poética argentina* [*Anthology of Argentine Poetry*], the second anthology he coedited with Ocampo and Bioy Casares, claiming that the reader of an anthology of contemporary literature "inevitablemente denunciará pecados de omisión y de comisión" [will inevitably denounce sins of omission and of commission] (7). These decisions to include or exclude, regardless of the possible outcry of the reader that Borges laments, end up serving as de facto value judgments. The anthology protects what the anthologizer decides to include while "ignora[ndo]" [ignoring] or "borra[ndo]" [erasing] what she omits (Achugar 55–56).[9] This ontology of exclusion which, at its core, allows the anthologizer to create a usable product—a representative but certainly not infinite book—puts the chosen texts on a published pedestal while relegating the omitted texts to oblivion.

Anthologizers and editors are also creators of order; they decide what goes where, and the juxtapositions they create alter how texts are read. Borges saw the textual mixture created in an anthology as "el encanto peculiar de las antologías" [the strange charm of anthologies] and felt that placing different works side by side could create a positive experience that was not inherent to any of the texts on their own ("The Albatross" 219).[10] In a manner similar to the theory of influence that Borges crafted in his lecture on Hawthorne and in his famous essay on Kafka, texts affect one another by influencing or changing how readers interpret them.[11] Anthologizers and editors also affect specific readers because both the intended reader and the actual reader for a given piece change depending on the venue or vehicle through which the anthologizer presents the piece.

Such editorial choices affect individual readers, and they also create canons. Scholarship that pays attention to the anthologization process sets out to examine the work of these literary mediators and to investigate how their choices—everything from textual inclusion to exclusion, textual order, usage of instructive and/or biographical headnotes, insertion of explanatory footnotes, addition of paratextual material, and more—create literary traditions and affect both writers and readers of the anthologized texts. Borges makes a compelling case study in this field because he was both an author and a literary mediator, both a writer and a rewriter. And, on the side of the rewriter, Borges was performing quadruple duty. In his mediator role, he acted as critic, translator, anthologizer, and editor. He was constantly curating, framing, and organizing his and other authors' texts for both limited and mass consumption. He re-created local, regional, and (eventually) global literary tastes, and he reshaped the literary systems of Argentina and the broader Spanish-speaking world.[12] And, a significant amount of his curatorial work revolved around the idea of the fantastic.

The Trouble with Definitions

In the latter third of the twentieth century, literary and cultural critics codified and theorized the fantastic—from Tzvetan Todorov's structuralist thought of the 1970s to various thinkers of the 1990s and early 2000s who juxtapose fantastic literature with magical realism, science fiction, fantasy, fairy tales, and so on. Since most discussions of the fantastic after 1970 refer to Todorov's study, whether the critics agree with his analysis or not, his book makes for a good starting point when trying to define the fantastic. In his *Introduction à la littérature fantastique* [*The Fantastic: A Structural Approach to a Literary Genre*], Todorov describes the fantastic as "that hesitation experienced by a person who knows only the laws of nature, confronting an apparently supernatural event" while living "[i]n a world which is indeed our world, the one we know" (25). This moment of doubt is key for Todorov's understanding of the fantastic, and for him, the fantastic only lasts as long as "the duration of this uncertainty" (25). If a character or narrator (and the reader, following suit) chooses to believe or disbelieve the supernatural event, Todorov argues that the narrative leaves the fantastic behind and becomes either "the uncanny" or "the marvelous" (25). For Todorov, the fantastic is fairly rare in literature because the story or novel must end in character doubt or hesitation. This is somewhat limiting and, indeed, odd for the author of a book whose title, in translation, claims that the fantastic is "a literary genre."

Later critics, particularly Amaryll Beatrice Chanady and Julio Rodríguez-Luis, take Todorov as a starting point but suggest that the fantastic can still exist in a text that appears realistic but is interrupted by the supernatural, even if the hesitation or doubt faced by the character or narrator in question comes to an end within the text. Chanady sees the fantastic as "a mode" that can occur in various genres or subgenres of literature (1–2). Character doubt or hesitation is still key for Chanady as she differentiates between the fantastic and magical realism—the latter, for Chanady, contains no doubt on the part of the characters or narrators when supernatural happenings occur—but she allows texts in which the character eventually has to acknowledge that the supernatural is real to remain fantastic (69). In short, Todorov's "fantastic-marvelous" qualifies for Chanady as fantastic while his "fantastic-uncanny" does not. For Rodríguez-Luis, both of Todorov's subgenres remain fantastic; he argues that neither the shift in the character's worldview nor a rational explaining away of the supernatural erase the hesitation or doubt that surfaces in this type of story when the supernatural enters (112). Defining the fantastic this way still clearly delineates it from fairy tales, science fiction, fantasy, and magical realism while also allowing for a story like "El Aleph"—or for several supernatural stories by nineteenth-century authors like Edgar Allan Poe—to remain fantastic.

This discussion is certainly helpful for readers of supernatural literature after Todorov, but it faces two problems for the readers of this chapter. First, not all critics agree with Todorov's taxonomy.[13] Second, and more important for our current purposes, Borges did not understand the fantastic in these terms. In fact, Borges somewhat famously refused to define the fantastic. Instead, he repeatedly listed "procedimientos" [procedures or methods] or "temas" [themes] of the fantastic and then offered lists of stories to serve as examples of these themes, but sometimes the stories he chose did not even illustrate the particular themes with which he paired them.[14]

Borges came closest to defining the term in a talk that he gave on the fantastic on April 7, 1967, at the Escuela Camillo y Adriano Olivetti by suggesting that the only limits to the fantastic were the limits of human imagination. In this lecture, Borges repeated what he did in all of his talks on the fantastic—he named several "temas" of the fantastic (in this case, seven) and then offered various examples from literature to try to demonstrate the themes in action. In this particular lecture, the seven themes were "la transformación" [transformation/metamorphosis], "la confusion de lo onírico con lo real" [confusion between dream and reality], "el hombre invisible" [the invisible man], "los juegos con el tiempo" [games with time], "la presencia de seres sobrenaturales entre los hombres" [the presence of supernatural beings among men], "el doble" [the double], and the "idea de acciones paralelas" [idea of parallel actions] (*La literatura fantástica* 6–18).[15] What is different in this talk is that Borges opens with a juxtaposition between realism and the fantastic that seems to allow for more than these seven themes: "[d]e un lado, tenemos la literatura realista, la literatura que trata de situaciones más o menos comunes en la humanidad, y del otro la literatura fantástica, que no tiene otro límite que las posibilidades de la imaginación" [on the one side, we have realist literature, literature about situations that are more or less common in humanity, on the other, fantastic literature, that has no other limit than the possibilities of the imagination] (5). Immediately, however, Borges limits his own description of the fantastic by saying that its "temas [...] no son ilimitados; son unos pocos" [themes (...) are not infinite; they are very few], and he finishes the lecture by reminding his audience of what he sees as the finite number of fantastic themes (5, 19).

Even in this lecture's contradiction, these words are helpful when trying to grasp what Borges means by the fantastic. Its themes might be limited, but it is unabashedly imaginative. The fantastic, for Borges, is anti-realism, not because it cuts against "reality" but because it cuts against so-called realistic literature, a mundane approach to literature that pretends to be about the real even though it is, at its core, literary artifice. Borges's anthologizing and editing projects of fantastic literature allow for various types of stories that resist realist literature, some that clearly fit within his repeated themes of the fantastic and some that do not, some that contain supernatural elements and some that openly avoid them. By anthologizing the fantastic, Borges praises literature that challenges what he often called the newer or younger literature that was realism ("Coloquio" 25). So while Todorov claims that the fantastic is rare, Borges almost universalizes it by casting the fantastic as literature that does not pretend to be "realistic" (or, in the case of some of his own fictional works that read like literary criticism, as literature that *openly pretends* to be, and thus critiques, realism). In anthologizing the fantastic, he brings this type of literature to the forefront of both local and global traditions that had, over the past several decades, canonized and codified a realist approach.

Antología de la literatura fantástica (1940; 1965)

Borges's first foray into anthologizing the fantastic was his most well-known and most impactful. In late December 1940, Editorial Sudamericana released the *Antologia de la literatura fantástica*, edited by Borges, Silvina Ocampo, and Bioy Casares. This anthology provided its initial audience with fifty-four selections (the second edition, also examined below, includes seventy-five) that challenged the realist orthodoxy of Argentina's contemporary literary system and placed works by Borges and several of his fellow Argentines in the company of both ancient and modern writers of fantastic fiction. As Bioy Casares explains in the "Postdata" to the prologue of the second edition, he, Silvina Ocampo, and Borges compiled the first edition as a sort of "panacea" for "novelas psicológicas" [psychological novels] that abound in pages but lack problem or plot (14).

Bioy Casares famously states in the prologue to the first edition that the anthologizers have followed "un criterio hedónico" [a hedonic criterion] when creating this anthology, but the book's contents reveal more than what satisfies the trio's tastes when reading for pleasure (14); what they include and exclude creates a mini-canon of fantastic literature for their readers, and their organizing principles reveal who or what they consider fantastic, sometimes in strange contrast to what Borges or Bioy Casares said elsewhere. The first edition of the *Antología* contains some very old texts (see the entries from Chuang Tzu and Petronius), but it favors the nineteenth and early twentieth centuries and arrives at the very year the anthology was published by including Borges's "Tlön, Uqbar, Orbis Tertius." The selections are usually from Western literary traditions, with the exception of three Chinese entries and one excerpt from *Las 1001 noches* [*The 1001 Nights*],[16] and, apart from four or five women, the rest of the authors are male.[17] In short, in this anthology the fantastic can be old, but it is mostly new and is probably written by a European man.

Parsing the contents even more, at both national and linguistic levels, we see that the *Antología* casts the fantastic as a mode dominated by the English language with healthy representation from both French and Spanish (mostly Argentine) but surprisingly little German.[18] The book values British literature above all others (only three of the English-language entries are from the United States), which makes sense when we consider Bioy Casares's claim in the prologue that the fantastic becomes a "género más o menos definido [. . .] en el siglo XIX y en el idioma inglés" [genre more or less defined [. . .] in the nineteenth century and in the English language] coupled with Borges's well-documented Anglophilia (7). The inclusion of seven French entries might foretell the success that Borges's own fantastic literature will find in France in the 1950s. Perhaps the number of French selections also demonstrates a shift in the French language since six of the seven entries are from the nineteenth and twentieth centuries, well after the 1782 French composition of William Beckford's *Vathek*, a text whose "indefinidos horrores" [undefined horrors], Borges wrote, worked better in English than in "el francés del siglo XVIII" [eighteenth-century French] (*OC* II: 133).

The near exclusion of German texts in this anthology is shocking, especially considering Borges's thoughts on the German literary tradition. In "Los traductores de *Las*

1001 Noches" [*The Translators of The 1001 Nights*], Borges argues that "Alemania posee una literatura fantástica—mejor dicho, sólo posee una literatura fantástica" [Germany possesses a literature of the fantastic—rather, it possesses *only* a literature of the fantastic] (*OC* 1: 412, *SNF* 108). Yet this tradition of the fantastic, which Borges claims to thoroughly appreciate, only appears in two selections from Kafka. The *Antología* does contain a short entry from Gustav Weil and another brief selection from Richard Wilhelm, but both of these entries show their authors bringing Eastern stories into the German tradition.[19] The famous Bohemian author Franz Kafka, a known favorite of Borges, makes up almost all of the German-language representation in the *Antología* via his "Josefine, die Sängerin oder Das Volk der Mäuse," which is rendered as "Josefina la cantora o El pueblo de los ratones" [Josephine the Singer, or the Mouse Folk], and his parable-like "Vor dem Gesetz," which appears as "Ante la ley" [Before the Law]. E. T. A. Hoffmann, conversely, does not appear in this anthology, and although his absence feels strange, it is intentional since Bioy Casares notes in the prologue that the organizers have excluded him and a handful of other authors "[d]eliberadamente" [deliberately] (15).

The collection's treatment of German-language texts might serve as a microcosm for the organizers' overall views on the fantastic. Juxtaposing Kafka's double appearance with the absence of any works by Hoffmann or other German writers like him shows the anthologizers' preference for a certain type of fantastic. Their fantastic may cause but does not require fear, and it may include but does not require the supernatural. Indeed, by excluding Hoffmann and asking Kafka to represent all of German-language fantastic fiction, Borges, Bioy Casares, and Ocampo demonstrate a clear preference for the very type of fantastic fiction that they also write—the type of fantastic fiction that is, in the words that Borges uses to praise the plot of Bioy Casares's novel *La invención de Morel* [*The Invention of Morel*], "fantástico pero no sobrenatural" [fantastic but not supernatural] (*OC* IV: 29).

The *Antología*'s coverage of Spanish-language literature follows this same proclivity, and it also announces Argentina as a contemporary hotbed for the production of fantastic fiction. The anthologizers' preference for what Bioy Casares calls "fantasías metafísicas" [metaphysical fantasies] (13) in the prologue is most easily visible in Borges's "Tlön," but their inclusion of Leopoldo Lugones's "Los caballos de Abdera" [The Horses of Abdera] also shows a willingness to allow for the supernatural in the fantastic. Of the eleven entries from Spanish-language authors, almost all of them come from or are connected to Argentina. Six pieces are by Argentine writers (Borges, Santiago Dabove, Macedonio Fernández, Leopoldo Lugones, Manuel Peyrou, and Arturo Cancela/Pilar de Lusarreta); two are by a Spanish writer who spent the last three decades of his life in Argentina (Ramón Gómez de la Serna); one is by the Chilean writer María Luisa Bombal whose literary career began in Buenos Aires; and only two entries are from Spanish writers without connections to Argentina's capital (Don Juan Manuel and José Zorrilla).[20] Tellingly, apart from Bombal's work, the book includes no works from other Spanish American or broader Latin American writers.[21] The *Antología* casts the Spanish-language fantastic as a primarily Argentine and an overwhelmingly twentieth-century phenomenon. The collection simultaneously brings fantastic literature from the margins to the center of serious literary study and shifts Argentine letters, within the pages of its covers, from a peripheral standing in world literature to a position of shared power with the influential literary traditions of Britain and France.[22]

In 1965, Editorial Sudamericana released an expanded second edition of the *Antología* with seventy-five texts, and this edition has been reprinted time and again well into the twenty-first century. The second edition, although it reprints the vast majority of the fifty-four pieces from the first edition while adding more than twenty others, is structured in a more controlled manner than the first edition. The 1940 edition contains no clear ordering of the included texts—the texts do not appear in chronological, geographical, alphabetical, or any other specific order; multiple texts by the same author do not appear together; and Bioy Casares does not overtly point toward any organizing apparatus in the prologue. Balderston argues that this edition follows "un orden menos obvio, donde ciertos nexos temáticos [. . .] definen los diversos ámbitos de lo fantástico que interesan a los antólogos" [a less obvious order, where certain thematic connections define the diverse spheres of the fantastic that interested the anthologizers] (218). The 1965 edition tames the supposed chaos and the subtle thematic structure of its precursor through the mundane organization of texts in alphabetical order by the last name of the author, with multiple texts by the same writer appearing in succession.[23] The second edition does, however, maintain the central importance of Argentina's authors of the fantastic. All six Argentine selections from the 1940 edition remain, along with eight new entries (including one from Ocampo, one from Bioy Casares, and a cowritten piece by Borges and Delia Ingenieros), for a total of fourteen Argentine pieces. The percentage of Argentine representation in the overall anthology rises from just over 11% to more than 18% percent, and the Argentine pieces make up three-quarters of the Spanish-language selections, reaffirming the importance of the fantastic in the local literary tradition and highlighting the growth of fantastic literature in Argentina during the quarter of a century between the two editions.[24]

The influence of the *Antología* on twentieth-century literature in Argentina, in Spanish America, and in the Spanish-speaking world cannot be overstated. The second edition (with all of its reprintings) reaches more readers, but the first edition—with what Balderston calls its "carácter didáctico—hasta evangélico" [didactic—even evangelical—character] toward the fantastic (217)—changed Argentine and Spanish American literature, influencing Argentine writers who were later included in the second edition (for example, Julio Cortázar and Juan Rodolfo Wilcock) and creating the space for nonrealist literature that would soon be filled by the so-called Boom. Critics and historians of twentieth-century literature have overwhelmingly praised the *Antología* as a key text in Argentine letters and Spanish American literary history. For example, Balderston claims that it "define un hito en la historia de la literatura argentina" [establishes a landmark in the history of Argentine literature] and that the "proyecto es uno de los más importantes en la narrativa rioplatense del siglo XX" [project is one of the most important in River Plate fiction of the twentieth century] (217, 227).[25] Its anthologizers held similarly high opinions of the project. Bioy Casares recalled the evenings in which they worked together on the *Antología* as some of the "mejores momentos de [su] vida" [best days of

[his] life] (*Borges* 29). Borges, typically his own greatest critic, told Bioy Casares in 1968 that "Aun prescindiendo de sus textos argentinos, nuestra Antología [de la literatura] fantástica es una de las obras capitales de la literatura argentina" [Even without its Argentine texts, our *Antología de la literatura fantástica* is one of the seminal works of Argentine literature], and in 1977, he went even further, claiming that the "Antología [e]s el mejor libro del mundo" [is the best book in the world] (1220, 1512). This anthology, with all of its influence, takes the fantastic seriously and places several of Argentina's writers of fantastic fiction in great company. And, it is only the first in a group of collaborative projects in which Borges redeems this type of literature.

Los Anales de Buenos Aires (1946–1948)

Borges's next anthological project of the fantastic came in the form of a monthly literary journal: *Los Anales de Buenos Aires*.[26] Although the publication was relatively short-lived—twenty-three issues in just over two years—compared to some of Borges's anthologies, which were republished for decades, its impact on the reception of the fantastic in Argentina should not be underestimated. Borges directed the magazine—under the titles of "director" or "asesor" [consultant]—beginning with its third issue, and he included the works of several of his close friends and other acquaintances (including Bioy Casares, Silvina Ocampo, Manuel Peyrou, Santiago Dabove, and Ezequiel Martínez Estrada), his own essays and stories, and works that he cowrote with Bioy Casares under the pen name B. Lynch Davis or anonymously. While not a journal dedicated solely to the fantastic, the amount of fantastic fiction and the diversity of the authors published in this journal demonstrate both the power of the *Antología* only six years after its initial publication (Borges, Dabove, and Peyrou each appear several times in *Los Anales*, although not all of their entries are fantastic) and the connection between this magazine and the growing reputation of other Argentine writers of the fantastic (Silvina Ocampo, Bioy Casares, Cortázar, and Wilcock all publish in *Los Anales* and are then included in the 1965 expansion of the *Antología*). Along with these Argentine voices, Borges also includes his favorite detective writer who delves into the fantastic—Chesterton—several times and publishes one piece by Kafka. While his previous anthologies took fantastic and detective fiction seriously, they did so in the popular literary marketplace. *Los Anales* also embraces these nonrealist genres, but it does so in a highbrow venue aimed at the literary elite. Taking the *Antología*, *Los mejores cuentos policiales* [*The Best Detective Stories*], and *Los Anales de Buenos Aires* together shows how, during the 1940s, Borges simultaneously popularizes the fantastic for a broad swath of local and regional readers and elevates the fantastic to a form of high literature.

Without disparaging any of the journal's other fantastic stories, especially Borges's own "El Zahir" and "El inmortal" [The immortal]—*Los Anales* can be considered a milestone in the anthologization of fantastic literature for launching Julio Cortázar's literary career. Borges accepted and published Cortázar's famous tale of the fantastic "Casa tomada" [House Taken Over] in December 1946, and, many years later, he celebrated the fact that he had been an "instrumento" [instrument] in bringing forth Cortázar's first published short story (*OC* IV: 551). Then, in August–September 1947, the magazine published Cortázar's "Bestiario" [Bestiary], and in December of that same year, Borges included Cortázar's short play "Los reyes" [The Kings]—a response to Borges's own "La casa de Asterión" [The House of Asterion], which had been published in *Los Anales* just six months earlier—in the penultimate issue of journal.[27] Cortázar's corpus of short fiction offers the strongest and most impactful examples of the fantastic in the Argentine literary tradition apart from Borges's own fantastic catalogue, and *Los Anales* keeps the two in good company. This journal serves as a powerful reminder of Borges's role in popularizing and elevating the fantastic, both as a writer and as an editor—as a creator of literature and as a co-creator of the reputation of another iconic Argentine writer.

Cuentos breves y extraordinarios Extraordinary Tales (1955)

In 1955, Borges and Bioy Casares released a strange anthology with Editorial Raigal—strange in its repetition and its apparent role as an intermediary between the 1940 and 1965 editions of the *Antología* as well as in its subject matter. As the title suggests, one of the primary requirements for inclusion in this anthology appears to be length. Of the ninety-three entries, the majority of the stories are less than a full page in length and only four span more than three pages. The extraordinary nature of many of these pieces fits within Borges and Bioy Casares's parameters for the fantastic, as seen in the anthology's repetition of several authors (and even exact pieces) that Borges, Ocampo, and Bioy Casares included in the first or second editions of the *Antología*, or both.[28]

While the total number of pieces included is higher than either edition of the *Antología*, the table of contents feels familiar for readers who know either edition of the more famous anthology. The following authors appear with pieces different from those in the *Antología* (either first or second edition): David-Neel, Chesterton, Kafka (three times, with one entry—"El silencio de las sirenas" [The Silence of the Sirens]—having appeared in *Los Anales*), Peyrou, Ocampo, Dabove, Poe, Swedenborg, and Bioy Casares. Borges and Bioy also include in *Cuentos breves* several pieces from the first edition of the *Antología* that would also appear in the second: a dream about a butterfly from Chuang Tzu, "La secta del loto blanco" [The Sect of the White Lotus] by Wilhelm, an excerpt from Zorrilla's *Don Juan Tenorio*, and "Final para un cuento fantástico" [Climax for a Ghost Story] by I. A. Ireland. Finally, there are also pieces in *Cuentos breves* that were not in the first edition of the *Antología* in 1940 but that would appear in the 1965 edition: "El encuentro" [The Encounter] from the Tang dynasty, Jean Cocteau's "El gesto de la muerte" [Death's Gesture], Martin Buber's "El descuido" [The Oversight], G. Willoughby-Meade's "Los ciervos celestiales" [The Celestial Stag], and Borges/Delia Ingenieros's "Odín."[29] In short, this anthology appears to act as a bridge between the two editions of the *Antología* in two ways. First, as Borges and Bioy Casares mention in the "Nota preliminar" [Preliminary Note], it more openly includes "las antiguas y generosas fuentes orientales" [the ancient and generous sources of the orient] (7) in

246   EMRON ESPLIN

comparison with the first edition of the *Antología*. Second, it reifies the fantastic reputations of many authors included in one or both versions of the *Antología*.

Manual de zoología fantástica (1957) and *El libro de seres imaginarios* [*The Book of Imaginary Beings*] (1967)

Borges collaborated on another project of the fantastic in 1957 when he released, with Margarita Guerrero, the *Manual de zoología fantástica*. Unlike his previous anthologies of the fantastic that gather published materials, this book takes an encyclopedic approach—offering entries about eighty-two fantastical animals in alphabetical order, describing the creatures and noting where they have appeared in myth, scripture, and literature in various cultures throughout time. In the book's prologue, Borges and Guerrero analyze the experience a child has when visiting a zoo for the first time and then juxtapose the animals of nature with the creatures of the human imagination, and they end up arguing that "la zoología de los sueños es más pobre que la zoología" *de Dios* [the zoology of dreams is sparser than the zoology of God] (8). They present contradictory perspectives on the size of a fantastic zoology, at one point arguing that while the number of fantastic creatures should be limitless, it is not in actual practice, and at another point recognizing the limits of the offerings in their book since the "tema que aborda[n] es infinito" [theme that (they) address is infinite] (9).

In 1967, the pair released an expanded version of this book under the new title *El libro de los seres imaginarios*. This version contains a new prologue that elides the juxtaposition between the animals found on the earth and those found in the human imagination, and it avoids the contradiction of the first prologue by suggesting that the topic of fantastic creatures is limitless and that future editions will contain even more entries (10), just as this one adds thirty-three entries to the previous book's eighty-two. This prologue also openly acknowledges the book's encyclopedic function by stating that the book is not designed for "lectura consecutiva" [consecutive reading] (10).

These two fantastic catalogues are inherently different from the previous anthologies of the fantastic that Borges and his friends had created because they are not plot driven. The *Antología*, *Los Anales de Buenos Aires*, and *Cuentos breves* are all, even in their differences, narrative projects. With the exception of *Los Anales*, these previous projects are "readers" that invite their audience to follow micro-, short-, and medium-length texts through the problems and solutions that each text offers. These two later works, contrastingly, serve as reference books that lead the reader toward other texts about the included creatures. Even with this core difference, however, Borges and Guerrero accomplish the same overarching goal that Borges fulfilled with his previous approaches to the fantastic—an open challenge to realist literature. Borges and Guerrero take the fantastic seriously enough to catalogue numerous fantastical creatures, describe them, and then send their readers out to find them in the literary landscape. Creating this type of encyclopedic work of the fantastic parodies realism in a way similar to the playful manner that Borges approaches encyclopedias in his own fantastic fiction, especially "Tlön," revealing the artificial nature of so-called realism.

This chapter has argued that Jorge Luis Borges promulgated fantastic literature as a rewriter of fantastic texts, specifically as an anthologizer and editor of works of the fantastic. It has explored the anthological projects and practices that spanned the majority of his career.[30] The same message, throughout the decades and regardless of the shifting collaborators, rings out. Borges reads what he prefers, he anthologizes what he likes, and he favors fantastic literature over realism. Since each of the endeavors was collaborative, we could question the specific focus on Borges rather than on one or more of his collaborators. Bioy Casares, for example, collaborated time and again with Borges and also published his own fantastic works. The chapter focuses on Borges specifically because he is the common denominator in all of these projects; he is the connector who helped his various colleagues bring forth several anthologies, a literary journal, and two libraries/series that all focused on the fantastic. From the 1940s through the 1980s, he packaged, prepared, and distributed the fantastic to his readers through a consistent approach and with a determination to provide his audience with enjoyable literature that challenged the realist genres that he saw as recent, artificial, and, in a word, pleasureless.

In short, Borges was the unparalleled propagator of the fantastic in the twentieth century. Perhaps the easiest way to see the impact of his anthological work with the fantastic is simply to compare how Argentine literature and the broader Spanish American literary tradition were seen from the outside before Borges's career and afterward. Both the national (Argentine) and the regional traditions received little attention in Europe and the United States in the early twentieth century; they were studied by native Spanish speakers and serious students of the Spanish language and/or by specialists who dedicated their careers to the region, but they were certainly not popular. Now, both Argentine literature and broader Spanish American letters fill a significant spot on the map of world literature, and several authors from the nation and the region are read and enjoyed in translation in languages beyond Spanish—especially English, French, and German. This shift certainly has something to do with the alleged Latin American Boom—a movement that Borges heavily influenced and which took place in his wake—and a movement that, for better or for worse, revolved around literatures of the fantastic and the so-called magical realism. It also has much to do with Borges's own world fame during the latter third of his life. Finally, Borges himself recognized the effect his career had had on the fantastic, stating as much in a 1985 conversation with Osvaldo Ferrari in which he laughs and says "yo soy uno de los culpables" [I am one of the culprits] for what Ferrari called "el renacimiento de la literatura fantástica en la Argentina" [the rebirth of fantastic literature in Argentina] (34). As an author, coauthor, literary critic, public speaker, translator, editor, and anthologizer of the mode, he did more than any other writer or literary mediator to perpetuate the fantastic, and his own growing reputation simultaneously raised the literature that he read for pleasure to a level of serious study that it had not previously obtained.

Notes

1. Unless otherwise noted, all translations are my own.
2. For work on Borges's translations, see Kristal, Waisman, Leone, and a pair of chapters in *Borges's Poe* (Esplin 67–80 and 81–100).
3. See "Borges as Editor and Anthologist" (ch. 4) in which Benedict analyzes several of Borges's anthological projects from 1930 through 1951 to show how he changes Argentine literature and "shap[es] cosmopolitan literature throughout Latin America" (184). The one Borges anthology that does seem to attract broader scholarly emphasis as an anthology is Borges's coedited *Antología de la literatura fantástica*. See Olea Franco, Balderston, and Louis for compelling readings about the anthologization process of Borges and his colleagues, and Esplin, "A Century of Terror, Ratiocination, and the Supernatural," for Borges's anthologization efforts with Poe.
4. María Teresa Gramuglio argues that Borges and Bioy Casares "crea[n] las condiciones de recepción de sus propios textos" [create the conditions of reception of their own texts] by anthologizing fantastic and detective fiction (288). Also see María de los Ángeles Mascioto (129).
5. In everyday usage, people often interchange the terms "anthology," "collection," and "text-book." My use of "anthology" follows Odber de Baubeta's succinct definition: "an anthology is defined as a compilation of self-standing poems or short stories, deliberately selected and organized in such a way as to serve the editor's purpose" (34).
6. On the Spanish side, see Beatriz González Stephan, *La historiografía literaria del liberalismo hispano-americano del siglo XIX*, Hugo Achugar, "El poder de la antología/La antología del poder," and Daniel Balderston, "Introduction," *The Latin American Short Story: An Annotated Guide to Anthologies and Criticism*. On the English side, see Alan Golding, *From Outlaw to Classic: Canons in American Poetry*, a double issue of the journal *symplokē* in 2000 (edited by Jeffrey Di Leo); Barbara Korte, Ralf Schneider, and Stefanie Lethbridge, editors, *Anthologies of British Poetry*; Jeffrey Di Leo, editor, *On Anthologies*; and a handful of well-placed monographs and articles in the early 2000s—including those by Price, Ferry, Csicsila, and Lauter. Odber de Baubeta's work on anthologies in Portugal is also important for this growing field.
7. Alfonso Reyes—Borges's friend, Mexican diplomat, and well-established man of letters—also theorized the anthology in the 1930s ("Teoría de la antología" [Theory of the Anthology]) and shared several of the concerns that Borges offered in the late 1930s and early 1940s.
8. I say "another" because scholars in various disciplines—from quantum mechanics to post-modern literature, from neuroscience to translation studies, and from linguistics to the creation of the Internet—see different works by Borges as foundational to, or precursory of, their own fields of study.
9. See similar ideas in Kilcup (113).
10. See Benedict (121). I would argue that certain juxtapositions can also be jarring.
11. Apart from the actual juxtaposition of texts, the framing of each author whose work is included in any anthology also changes the reader's experience with a text. For example, as Benedict argues, the authorial descriptions that Borges includes or excludes in his anthological projects "tell us a great deal about Borges's larger project of enhancing reading habits in Latin America" (122).
12. While this chapter focuses on how Borges's anthologies of the fantastic reshape local and global literary tastes, Benedict makes a similar argument around all of Borges's anthology

and editing work from 1930 to 1951. She creates a compelling case for how Borges's "impeccably edited anthologies and volumes of collected literature, in conjunction with his extensive reviews of foreign authors and books, change both what people read and how people read" (8).

13. Ana María Barrenechea offers an important Latin American rejoinder to Todorov's theorization. She recognizes the value of Todorov's schematic and appreciates his clarity ("Ensayo" 391), but she openly challenges his reliance on "duda" [doubt] and focuses, instead, on "la problematización" [the problematic] that occurs when supernatural and natural events occur in the same text ("Ensayo" 392–93; "La literatura fantástica" 47). Also see Bessière and Rodríguez Monegal for examples of approaches to the fantastic that fundamentally differ from those of Todorov and others who rely on the concept of character/reader hesitation.

14. For more details on Borges's lectures on the fantastic and his resistance to offering a clear definition of the term, see Esplin, *Borges's Poe* (124–25 and 193–94, nn. 6–10), Svensson, and Colman Serra. The *Antología* does contain a prologue, but it was signed by Bioy Casares rather than Borges, and it also fails to *define* the fantastic. Bioy does, like Borges, offer several *técnica[s]* and examples (8–14).

15. This list of seven is very similar to the lists that Borges offered in lectures throughout the Southern Cone, in Europe, and in Canada, although not verbatim. See Passos and Svensson.

16. Bioy Casares acknowledges the existence of a tradition of the fantastic in Chinese literature, calling the Chinese, "tal vez los primeros especialistas en el género" [perhaps the first specialists in the genre] ("Prólogo" 7).

17. The *Antología* contains two entries by Alexandra David-Neel, one by María Luisa Bombal, one by May Sinclair, and an entry cowritten by Pilar de Lusarreta. It also includes a text, "Los ganadores de la mañana" [The Old Man], which the anthologizers attribute to Holloway Horn. See Zavala Medina for a fascinating interpretation of Bioy Casares, Ocampo, and Borges's playful misattributions in the *Antología*, including the biographical note on Horn ("Tres notas" 183–84).

18. Benedict offers a useful table that helps to visualize these national preferences (152).

19. Borges praises Weil's translation of *Las 1001 noches* in "Los traductores" (*OC* 1: 410), but he still wishes that someone, perhaps "un Kafka," would translate *The Nights* in a way that takes advantage of Germany's *unheimlichkeit* (*OC* 1: 412).

20. The Goméz de la Serna entries were published before his move to Argentina. The Bombal story, however, comes from her time in Argentina.

21. This lacuna is not due to a lack of available fantastic material from other Latin American countries. Oscar Hahn's *Fundadores del cuento fantástico* compiles several fantastic stories from the nineteenth century that would have been available to Borges, Ocampo, and Bioy Casares—as were the tales of the Brazilian writer Machado de Assis. Both Borges and Bioy Casares were also well aware of the fantastic fiction of the *ríoplatense* writer Horacio Quiroga, although Borges was always quite critical of his work.

22. Apart from their overall decision to anthologize fantastic literature and their specific choices about which authors to include and which to exclude, the anthologizers of the *Antología* make several other important decisions, including their willingness to print both stand-alone pieces and excerpts of larger works and their choice to usually divide longer works from one another with the inclusion of one to several very short pieces. However, as Benedict claims, some of their choices—the "lack of chronological, alphabetical, or even

250 EMRON ESPLIN

geographical organization" and their tendency to fill every blank spot on each page rather than allowing shorter texts to exist on their own pages—detract from the reading experience and are "reminiscent more of a miscellany than an anthology" (149).

23. It is impossible to tell if the anthologizers made these changes or if someone at Editorial Sudamericana brought about this "reordering." We do know, however, that the anthologizers picked the new texts since Bioy Casares implies as much in the "Postdata" (13).

24. Bombal's story from the 1940 edition does not appear in the 1965 version, but a work by the Mexican author Elena Garro does. The four works by Spaniards also reappear.

25. For further praise of the *Antología* along these lines, see Zavala Medina (*Borges* 352), Olea Franco (257), and Reeve (250).

26. Between the *Antología* and *Los Anales de Buenos Aires*, Borges and Bioy Casares coedited the influential anthology *Los mejores cuentos policiales* [*The Best Detective Stories*]. Due to a lack of space, I will not examine this anthology here even though it demonstrates Borges's tendency to discuss detective fiction in terms of the fantastic.

27. For more on Borges and Cortázar's literary relationship, see *Borges's Poe* (156–58).

28. Recycling pieces Borges had previously anthologized elsewhere was a common move for Borges, Ocampo, and Bioy Casares. See Mascioto (128–29).

29. *Cuentos breves* also includes Borges's "Los dos reyes y los dos laberintos" [The Two Kings and the Two Labyrinths] with a slightly altered title, although Borges and Bioy Casares attribute the story to Richard Burton.

30. In the 1970s and 1980s, Borges continued to anthologize the fantastic by curating two multivolume book series or "libraries" that incorporated fantastic literature—*La Biblioteca di Babele* and *Biblioteca personal*. Both series merit further analysis.

WORKS CITED

Achugar, Hugo. "El poder de la antología/La antología del poder." *Cuadernos de Marcha*, vol. 46, 1989, pp. 55–63.

Balderston, Daniel. "De la *Antología de la literatura fantástica* y sus alrededores." *El oficio se afirma*, edited by Sylvia Saítta, Emece, 2004, pp. 217–27.

Balderston, Daniel. "Introduction." *The Latin American Short Story: An Annotated Guide to Anthologies and Criticism*, compiled and edited by Daniel Balderston. Greenwood, 1992, pp. ix–xx.

Barrenechea, Ana María. "Ensayo de una tipología de la literatura fantástica (A propósito de la literatura hispanoamericana)." *Revista Iberoamericana*, vol. 38, no. 80, 1972, pp. 391–403.

Barrenechea, Ana María. "La literatura fantástica: Función de los códigos socioculturales en la constitución de un género." *El espacio crítico en el discurso literario*. Kapelusz, 1985, pp. 43–54.

Benedict, Nora C. *Borges and the Literary Marketplace: How Editorial Practices Shaped Cosmopolitan Reading*. Yale University Press, 2021.

Bessière, Irène. *Le récit fantastique*. Larousse, 1974.

Bioy Casares, Adolfo. *Borges*, edited by Daniel Martino. Destino, 2006.

Bioy Casares, Adolfo. "Postdata." *Antología de la literatura fantástica*. 1965, 2nd ed. Edited by Jorge Luis Borges, Silvina Ocampo, and Adolfo Bioy Casares. Editorial Sudamericana, 1998, pp. 13–15.

Bioy Casares, Adolfo. "Prólogo." *Antología de la literatura fantástica*. Edited by Jorge Luis Borges, Silvina Ocampo, and Adolfo Bioy Casares. Editorial Sudamericana, 1940, pp. 7–15.

Borges, Jorge Luis. "The Albatross Book of Living Prose." *Textos cautivos: Ensayos y reseñas en El Hogar (1936–1939)*. Tusquets Editores, 1986, pp. 219–20.

Borges, Jorge Luis. "Coloquio con Borges." *Literatura fantástica*. Ediciones Siruela, 1985, pp. 13–36.

Borges, Jorge Luis. *La literatura fantástica*. Ediciones Culturales Olivetti, 1967.

Borges, Jorge Luis. "Modos de G. K. Chesterton." *Borges en Sur: 1931–1980*. Emecé, 1999, pp. 18–23.

Borges, Jorge Luis. *Obras completas*. 1996, 4 vols. Emecé, 1996.

Borges, Jorge Luis. "Prólogo." *Antología poetica argentina*. Edited by Jorge Luis Borges, Silvina Ocampo, and Adolfo Bioy Casares. Editorial Sudamericana, 1941, pp. 7–11.

Borges, Jorge Luis. *Selected Non-Fictions*, edited by Eliot Weinberger, translated by Weinberger, Esther Allen, and Suzanne Jill Levine. Penguin, 1999.

Borges, Jorge Luis, and Roberto Alifano. "La literatura policial: Poe y Chesterton." *Conversaciones con Jorge Luis Borges*. Editorial Atlántida, 1984, pp. 11–18.

Borges, Jorge Luis, and Adolfo Bioy Casares. "Nota preliminar." *Cuentos breves y extraordinarios*. Santiago Rueda, 1967, p. 7.

Borges, Jorge Luis, and Adolfo Bioy Casares, eds. *Cuentos breves y extraordinarios*. 1955. Santiago Rueda, 1967.

Borges, Jorge Luis, and Osvaldo Ferrari. "Literatura fantástica y ciencia ficción." *Reencuentro: Diálogos inéditos*. Sudamericana, 1999, pp. 33–36.

Borges, Jorge Luis, and Margarita Guerrero. "Prólogo." *El libro de los seres imaginarios*. 1967. Bruguera, 1979, pp. 9–10.

Borges, Jorge Luis, and Margarita Guerrero. "Prólogo." *Manual de zoología fantástica*. Fondo de Cultura Económica, 1957, pp. 7–9.

Borges, Jorge Luis, and Margarita Guerrero, eds. *El libro de los seres imaginarios*. 1967. Bruguera, 1979.

Borges, Jorge Luis, and Margarita Guerrero, eds. *Manual de zoología fantástica*. Fondo de Cultura Económica, 1957.

Borges, Jorge Luis, Silvina Ocampo, and Adolfo Bioy Casares, eds. *Antología de la literatura fantástica*. Editorial Sudamericana, 1940.

Borges, Jorge Luis, Silvina Ocampo, and Adolfo Bioy Casares, eds. *Antología de la literatura fantástica*. 2nd ed. Editorial Sudamericana, 1965.

Chanady, Amaryll Beatrice. *Magical Realism and the Fantastic: Resolved Versus Unresolved Antinomy*. Garland, 1985.

Colman Serra, Rocío. "Variaciones sobre lo fantástico en tres conferencias de Borges." *Variaciones Borges*, vol. 42, 2016, pp. 87–96.

Csicsila, Joseph. *Canons by Consensus: Critical Trends and American Literature Anthologies*. University of Alabama Press, 2004.

Di Leo, Jeffrey R., ed. *Anthologies*. Spec. issue of *symplokē*, vol. 8, nos. 1–2, 2000.

Di Leo, Jeffrey R., ed. *On Anthologies: Politics and Pedagogy*. University of Nebraska Press, 2004.

Esplin, Emron. *Borges's Poe: The Influence and Reinvention of Edgar Allan Poe in Spanish America*. University of Georgia Press, 2016.

Esplin, Emron. "A Century of Terror, Ratiocination, and the Supernatural: Poe's Fiction in Argentina from Carlos Olivera to Julio Cortázar." *Anthologizing Poe: Editions, Translations, and (Trans)National Canons.* Edited by Emron Esplin and Margarida Vale de Gato. Lehigh University Press, 2020, pp. 325–49.

Ferry, Anne. *Tradition and the Individual Poem: An Inquiry into Anthologies.* Stanford University Press, 2001.

Golding, Alan C. *From Outlaw to Classic: Canons in American Poetry.* University of Wisconsin Press, 1995.

González Stephan, Beatriz. *La historiografía literaria del liberalismo hispano-americano del siglo XIX.* Casa de las Américas, 1987.

Gramuglio, María Teresa. *Nacionalismo y cosmopolitismo en la literatura argentina.* Editorial Municipal de Rosario, 2013.

Hahn, Óscar. *Fundadores del cuento fantástico hispanoamericano.* Editorial Andrés Bello, 1998.

Kilcup, Karen L. "The Poetry and Prose of Recovery Work." *On Anthologies: Politics and Pedagogy.* Edited by Jeffrey R. Di Leo. University of Nebraska Press, 2004, pp. 112–38.

Korte, Barbara, Ralf Schneider, and Stefanie Lethbridge, eds. *Anthologies of British Poetry: Critical Perspectives from Literary and Cultural Studies.* Rodopi, 2000.

Kristal, Efraín. *Invisible Work: Borges and Translation.* Vanderbilt University Press, 2002.

Lauter, Paul. "Taking Anthologies Seriously." *Melus*, vol. 8, nos. 3–4, 2004, pp. 19–39.

Lefevere, André. *Translating Literature: Practice and Theory in a Comparative Literature Context.* MLA, 1992.

Leone, Leah. "A Translation of His Own: Borges and *A Room of One's Own.*" *Woolf Studies Annual*, vol. 15, 2009, pp. 47–66.

Leone, Leah. "Voice Distortion: Character Narration in Borges's Translation of Herman Melville's *Bartleby.*" *Variaciones Borges*, vol. 31, 2011, pp. 137–59.

Louis, Annick. "Definiendo un género. La *Antología de la literatura fantástica* de Silvina Ocampo, Adolfo Bioy Casares y Jorge Luis Borges." *Nueva Revista de Filología Hispánica*, vol. 2, 2001, pp. 409–37.

Mascioto, María de los Ángeles. "Literatura fantástica entre el diario *Crítica* y la Editorial Sudamericana: Políticas editoriales, materialidad de los textos y modos de escritura." *Revista Chilena de Literatura*, vol. 93, 2016, pp. 127– 53.

"Los mejores asesinatos de la literatura." *La Nación*, https://www.lanacion.com.ar/cultura/los-mejores-asesinatos-de-la-literatura-nid487962/. Accessed Apr. 2003.

"Nota del editor." *Biblioteca personal (prólogos)*, by Jorge Luis Borges, Alianza, 1988, pp. i–ii.

Odber de Baubeta, Patricia Anne. *The Anthology in Portugal. A New Approach to the History of Portuguese Literature in the Twentieth Century.* Peter Lang, 2007.

Olea Franco, Rafael. "Borges y la *Antología de la literatura fantástica.*" *Variaciones Borges*, vol. 22, 2006, pp. 253–78.

Passos, Carlos A. "Sobre 'La literatura fantástica,' disertó ayer Jorge Luis Borges." *El País* [Montevideo], September 3, 1949, p. 4.

Price, Leah. *The Anthology and the Rise of the Novel: From Richardson to George Eliot.* Cambridge University Press, 2000.

Reeve, Richard. "Los cuentos de Carlos Fuentes: de la fantasía al neorrealismo." *El cuento hispanoamericano ante la crítica.* Edited by Enrique Pupo-Walker. Editorial Castalia, 1973, pp. 249–63.

Reyes, Alfonso. "Teoría de la antología." 1930. *Obras completas de Alfonso Reyes*, vol. 14. Fondo de Cultura Económica, 1962, pp. 137–41.

Rodríguez-Luis, Julio. *The Contemporary Praxis of the Fantastic: Borges and Cortázar.* Garland, 1991.

Rodríguez Monegal, Emir. "Borges: Una teoría de la literatura fantástica." *Revista Iberoamericana*, vol. 4, no. 95, 1976, pp. 177–89.

Svensson, Anna. "Borges en Gotemburgo: Sobre su conferencia 'La Literatura Fantástica' y sus contactos con el Instituto Iberoamericano." *Anales* [Nueva Época], vol. 11, 2008, pp. 25–47. *University of Gothenburg*, http://hdl.handle.net/2077/10436.

Todorov, Tzvetan. *The Fantastic: A Structural Approach to a Literary Genre* translated by Richard Howard. Cornell University Press, 1975.

Todorov, Tzvetan. *Introduction à la littérature fantastique*. Éditions du Seuil, 1970.

Waisman, Sergio. *Borges and Translation: The Irreverence of the Periphery*. Bucknell University Press, 2005.

Zavala Medina, Daniel. *Borges en la conformación de la* Antología de la literatura fantástica. Universidad Autónoma de San Luis Potosi, 2012.

Zavala Medina, Daniel. "Tres notas de presentación tergiversadas en la *Antología de la literatura fantástica*." *Variaciones Borges*, vol. 27, 2009, pp. 175–86.

CHAPTER 14

ANTHOLOGIES OF THE SELF

Borges's Self-Figuration Process between 1935 and 1960

SEBASTIÁN URLI

IN a review of Borges's first compilation of his own poems, *Poemas (1922–1943)* [*Dreamtigers*], reviewer E. F. praises Borges's lyrical works as those of a writer who has not published nor written much but whose poems have an unmistakable tone, a very distinguishable accent: "Es el acento 'ciudadano' el decirnos cómo son los patios de sus casas y el cielo que a ellos se asoma" [It's the city intonation, the way the poems tell us about the patios in the houses and the sky above them] (242).[1] Aside from describing some of the recurrent elements of Borges's first books of poetry, E. F. notices that this collection includes five new poems along with some rewritings of his former work. The reviewer concludes their critique with a personal opinion about these modifications: "nos atrevemos a decir que algunas de estas modificaciones . . . al dar al poema un acento de mayor generalidad, le quitan, por ello mismo, ciertas esquinas de localismos y color que, a nuestro parecer, le iban muy bien" [we venture to say that some of these modifications . . . by giving the poem a more general vibe, deprive it of some local color and expressions, that, in our opinion, suited it well] (243). Whatever specific local color elements E. F. is referring to (the text doesn't provide any particular examples), it is worth noting that the review, almost contemporary to the publication of the first of the poetic compilations of his own work that Borges publishes in the 1940s and 1950s, captures one of the two significant procedures that he will put into practice in those years and well into the 1960s: on the one hand, the lexical and syntactical transformation of some of the poems, and, on the other, the self-figuration, the construction of a literary persona that will dominate the poetry published from *El hacedor* (1960) to *Los conjurados* [*The Conspirators*] (1985).

These poetic compilations operate as an experimental threshold, a productive liminal space that resonates with Borges's writing process (Balderston, *How Borges Wrote*) and his other publishing activities from that time, such as the creation of different anthologies[2] or the editorial project Destiempo.[3]

Borges's poetical work, however, has not always been well received. Some critics regard it as very inferior in quality to the short stories of *Ficciones* [*Fictions*] (1944) or *El Aleph* [*The Aleph*] (1949), or even the essays of *Otras inquisiciones* [*Other Inquisitions*] (1952) (Lihn; Muschietti). Others describe it as mere repetition, a toned-down version of the ideas developed in those other books. Muschietti, for instance, compares Borges's first three books of poetry with Alfonsina Storni's final works and concludes that her style is much more experimental, more aligned with the avant-garde aesthetics of the instant photographic image than Borges's poems of the time (23, 26).[4]

In an interview with Pedro Lastra, Chilean poet Enrique Lihn praises Borges by saying that his works have anticipated some of the most important theoretical enquiries of the École Practique des Hautes Etudes in France and have also challenged two or three generations of Latin American authors by having the same effect on them that a flea does in a person's eardrum or a splinter in a finger. However, when discussing his poetical works, he goes so far as to say that they owe their fame to the quality of his short stories and essays and their readers' inability to understand poetry (65). Lihn also suggests that most of Borges's poems from the 1960s, '70s, and '80s can be "translated" to prose without losing much nuance in the process, a sign, for Lihn, of their poor quality. However, he also stresses that Borges is the producer of a commodity ("mercancía") that is valued for its effects, for its final effect: "sorprende a su lector ganándole la partida con una última jugada imprevisible aunque enteramente verosimilizada por el respeto a las reglas del juego" [he surprises his reader by winning the game with an unpredictable yet entirely credible hand, credible because it respects the rules of the game] (69). Although Lihn is referring to Borges's short stories and essays here and not his poems, it is worth noting that the self-figuration process that Borges develops in his later poetry, his interest in portraying a poetic persona named "Borges" through the portraits of friends, family members, and other writers, works along the same lines as the final effect described by Lihn: the reader keeps finding the poetic persona "Borges" in very unexpected places and in close connection with very unexpected poets—and all within the limitations of some very canonical, or even conservative, metric rules.

Last, for Héctor Libertella, Borges's signature operates as a copyright rubric, the literary marketing brand "de una obra virtual (cómo llamarla, ¿ilegible? ¿Macedonio Fernández?) que ha interrumpido su proliferación sintáctica para coagularse o mostrarse como Borges©" [of a virtual project (how should we call: illegible? Macedonio Fernández?) which has interrupted its own syntactic proliferation to end up coagulating or showing itself as Borges©] (*La librería* 77). And that rubric, or brand, should be read as a symptom of a writer who is no longer capable of affecting the Argentine canon (Libertella associates this via Borges with Macedonio Fernández). On the contrary, the only task left for this writer, for this rubric or signature, is to create a nostalgia of his own disease. As Libertella puts it: "de tanto exhibir su ideología universalista, la firma 'Borges' se hace así el síntoma de una enfermedad literaria irreal, pero deseada: la oscuridad nacionalista, el idiolecto" [by constantly exhibiting its universalist ideology, the 'Borges' signature thus becomes the symptom of an unreal, yet desired, literary disease: the nationalist darkness, the idiolect] ("Borges" 708).

This is why, for Libertella, we can no longer read Borges's signature without that nostalgic feeling of something that could have been disruptive and ended up becoming "Literature."[5]

Although I agree with Muschietti's and Lihn's descriptions of Borges's lexical and strophic choices as not being innovative or challenging with regard to what they do to language and to the Latin American poetic tradition (Borges is certainly not Vallejo nor Blanca Varela, and he criticized the work of important poets such as Oliverio Girondo and Alejandra Pizarnik), I believe that his self-figuration process does not consist of solely repeating his own rubric as Literature, as Libertella suggests, nor of writing as if he were someone else. On the contrary it consists of making everyone else (including God, in a short piece called "Everything and Nothing") talk as if they were "Borges," as if they had the same philosophical inquiries as his narrators or the voice that thinks in his essays. As I will show, Borges's poetic compilations of the 1940s and '50s and his rewritings of his first three books of poetry signal the beginning of this complex self-figuration process. And if Borges's short stories and essays constitute the core momentum of his innovative ideas (i.e., reading and translating as creative writing practices, the arbitrariness of classification systems, the ways in which narrative causality is or should be constructed, etc.), his later poetry constitutes the arena in which the self-figuration process will become the most visible procedure and a very radical one indeed.

In the sections that follow, I first briefly describe the contents of the three poetry collections from the 1940s and '50s.[6] I then detail several specific changes that occur in *Fervor de Buenos Aires* [*Fervor of Buenos Aires*] from its original publication in 1923 to its inclusion in the poetic anthology of 1958 as a way to understand the first strategies of self-figuration. Finally, in the last two sections of this chapter, I analyze two poems that Borges added at the end of these compilations that were later included in *El otro, el mismo* [*The Other, The Same*] (1964): "Insomnio" [Insomnia] and "Baltasar Gracián."

POEMAS: THREE DIFFERENT COMPILATIONS

Poemas (1922–1943), published by Editorial Losada in 1943, collected and rewrote many of the poems from Borges's first books of poetry (*Fervor de Buenos Aires, Luna de enfrente* [*Moon Across the Way*], *Cuaderno San Martín* [*San Martín Notebook*]) and added several new compositions. Almost ten years later Emecé published a new collection of poems, *Poemas, 1923–1953*, in 1954, which also served as the second volume of the *Obras completas*. This work follows the same structure of the previous volume, but it eliminates some poems from the 1920s and adds new ones in the final section. Finally, in 1958, a new edition of this second volume of the *Obras completas* appeared in Buenos Aires with a slightly altered title (*Poemas, 1923–1958*). Once again, the structure remains the same. Although no additional poems were added from *Fervor, Luna de enfrente*, or *Cuaderno San Martín*, the rewritings continued, and new poems were added to the final section. In the 1943 edition, these additional poems included: "Prose poems for I. J.," "Insomnio," "La noche cíclica" [The Cyclical Night], "Del infierno y del cielo" [Of Heaven and Hell], and "Poema conjetural" [Conjectural Poem]. In the 1954 edition, he kept these new poems, changed the title of "Prose poems for I. J." to "Two English Poems," and added some newer compositions: "Poema del cuarto elemento" [Poem of the Fourth Element], "A un poeta menor de la Antología" [To a Minor Poet of the Anthology], "Página para recordar al coronel Suárez, vencedor en Junín" [A Page to Remember Colonel Suárez, Victor at Junín], and "Mateo XXV, 30" [Matthew, XXV, 30]. Finally, in the 1958 edition, he kept all these poems but added some newer ones: "Una brújula" [A Compass], "Una llave en Salónica" [A Key in Salonica], "Un poeta del siglo XIII" [A Poet of the Thirteenth Century], "Un soldado de Urbina" [A Soldier of Urbina], "Límites" [Limits], "Baltasar Gracián," "Un sajón" [A Saxon], "El Golem" [The Golem], and "El tango" [Tango].

Besides the fact that most of these poems later form a part of either *El otro, el mismo* (1964) or *Elogio de la sombra* [*In Praise of Darkness*] (1969), it is worth noting that Borges changed not only the order of certain poems in these three collections, but also some of the titles. In a few radical cases, he eliminated entire poems from the works, as is the case of "Llamarada" [Flare] from *Fervor de Buenos Aires*.[7] This poem, the only one written in the form of poetic prose, is a good example of some of the changes that Borges imposes on his earlier poems.[8] Here we find a poetic voice that walks close to a flame and begins to reflect on its philosophical significance and the effects that it produces on the immediate surroundings and on his own feelings. This is a typical procedure of the self-figuration process in the first three books of the 1920s: a poetic voice that defines himself either by evoking his close friends and ancestors (the great-grandfather for instance)[9] or by describing the impressions and thoughts that the streets, the sunrises and sunsets, and the margins of the city produced in him. Take the last part of the poem, for example:

> Espoleados—deseando deslumbrarnos y perdernos en las culminaciones carnales— en la crucifixión de cuerpos tremantes—(y pienso—que tal vez no es otra cosa la vida—que el ascua de una hoguera muerta hace siglos—que el último eco de una voz fenecida—que arrojó el acaso a esta tierra—algo lejano a los dos cauces del espacio y del tiempo)—Y la llama se hunde en el gran crepúsculo enfermo—que en girones desgarran los grises vientos. (*Fervor* w/p)

> [Spurred—desiring to surprise and lose us in the carnal culminations—in the crucifixion of trembling bodies—(and I think—that maybe life isn't anything else—than the ashes of a bonfire that died out centuries ago—than the last echo of a disappeared voice—that chance threw at this earth—something distant from the two channels of space and time)—And the flame sinks into the great disk twilight—that gray winds tear apart][10]

Here we find a poetic voice defined by the act of thinking about the echoes of things long gone in the context of a sunset described as a "sick twilight." I mention this example since Borges abandons the reference to sex in "culminaciones carnales" [carnal culminations] and its associations with lexical words that connote religious feelings such as "crucifixión de cuerpos tremantes" [crufixion of trembling bodies] in the anthologies of the 1940s and '50s and in his later poetry. In fact, in *Fervor*, we find multiple references to God and to the soul, yet he eliminated or transformed these references into more philosophical or abstract concepts in later publications. To give another brief example, in the poem "Un patio" we read: "Hoy que está crespo el cielo / dirá la agorería que ha muerto un angelito. / Patio, cielo encauzado. / El patio es la ventana / por donde Dios mira las almas" [Today that the sky is tortuous / the divination will say that a little angel has died. / Patio, channeled heaven. / The patio is the window / from where God observes the souls] (*Fervor* n.p.). In the version of "Un patio" in the collection from 1943 we read: "Patio, cielo encauzado. / El patio es el declive / por el cual se derrama el cielo en la casa" [Patio heaven's watercourse. / The patio is the slope / down which the sky flows into the house] (24; *Selected Poems* 15). All of the divine references (God, the little angel, and the soul) have been removed. Something similar happens with the use of words that denote violence, sickness, or fragmentation. In "Llamarada" the image of the "crepúsculo" [twilight] as a sick entity that is being attacked and dismembered by gray winds is certainly not a lexical nor a literary choice that Borges will use in many poems after the 1960s.[11] Finally, it is worth noting that most of the changes that Borges instituted reflect either the omission of some relative pronouns and conjunctions (as a way to "clean up" the cadence of a poem or improve its flow) or the use of archaisms, regionalisms, or words that he initially preferred because of their etymology, their history. These words will then be transformed into more neutral or common Spanish ones.[12]

It is important to note, however, that in addition to these changes in lexical choices, the self-figuration process still responds to a poetic voice that is constantly thinking and being affected by what he perceives in the margins of the streets. As I show in the next two sections, Borges will explore and finally discard the use of extreme bodily driven lexical choices to create his poetic persona in order to gradually move to the creation of a poetic voice called "Borges" (with more open references to his real life) and to the incessant portrait of himself in the depiction of other artists and thinkers.

The Road Not Taken?: The Case of "Insomnio"

In the last section of the three anthologies from the 1940s and '50s, Borges added the poem "Insomnio." Originally published in December of 1936, in the journal *Sur*, and later incorporated as the opening poem of *El otro, el mismo* (1964), "Insomnio" is one of Borges's most intriguing poems. For starters, once it appeared in *Sur* it was never rewritten, as many of the poems published in the 1920s and 1930s were. In fact, the version published in *Sur* is identical to the version in the 1958 collection, as well as the version in *El otro, el mismo* and in the different reprints of the *Obras completas*.

It is true, however, that there is a poem called "Insomnio" that Borges published in the journal *Grecia* (1920) and that was later republished in *Textos recobrados*. In this poem, we do find some of the same ideas regarding the lack of sleep that can still be felt in the 1936 poem. However, most of the images and phrases that appear in the verses of the poem published in *Grecia* are not found in the poem published in *Sur*. This makes me think that we are dealing with two different poems with different sources and manuscripts. To give just a few examples of these images and phrases from the poem published in *Grecia*: "Y en el cráneo sigue vibrando esta lamentable llama de alcohol que no quiere apagarse" [and in the skull this pathetic and endless flare of alcohol is still vibrating]; "La ventana sintetiza el gesto solitario del farol" [the window summarized the lonely gesture of the street lamp].[13] Curiously enough, the violence of some of these images seems to anticipate Girondo's poetry from the 1920s.[14]

If we consider Balderston's and Cajero Vázquez's work on Borges's manuscripts and on *Fervor*, the fact that not a single comma has been modified in a poem that was written, according to the date at the end of the page (which reads Adrogué 1936), is significant because it puts this composition much closer to the poems that Borges will publish in the 1960s, '70s, and '80s than to the ones from his three previous collections. What is more, the fact the Borges chose it as the opening poem for *El otro, el mismo* suggests its connection to a tension between something that remains and something that is lost, a tension that, as we shall see, takes the shape of a complex self-figuration practice in which the portrait of other writers is gradually invaded by a figure named "Borges."

Another reason why "Insomnio" is a rare case in Borges's work is that it received praise from writers and critics who previously lacked interest in his poetry. In his famous four classes on Borges's essays and short stories from the 1940s, '50s, and '60s, Ricardo Piglia suggests that "Insomnio" was an incredible poem, probably Borges's most accomplished one.[15] Even Muschietti, when quoting some of the few poetic images that she considered interesting in Borges's poetry, makes use of "Insomnio" (33). In this light, the poem is seen as a kind of exception, a path that Borges could have taken instead of opting for a classical approach to rhythm, imagery, and metrics.

Indeed, if we take a closer look at the poem, the first stanza opens with a visceral image of the night: "de encorvados tirantes de enorme fierro tiene que ser la noche" [of curved suspenders of enormous iron must the night be] (*OC* II: 237). Here we find that only a gigantic structure of iron straps can hold all the nasty things that the eyes of the poetic voice have seen throughout the day and are forced to keep seeing in the absence of sleep. The second stanza goes even further because the connection between "las muchas cosas que mis abarrotados ojos han visto" [the many things that my overwhelmed eyes have seen] (*OC* II: 237) is linked explicitly with the body's fatigue after all of the activities of the day: "Mi cuerpo ha fatigado los niveles, las temperaturas, las luces: / [. . .] en un banquete de hombres que se aborrecen, / en el filo mellado de los suburbios / [. . .] en la noche repleta donde abundan el caballo y el hombre" [My body has exhausted the levels, the temperatures, the lights: / in a feast full of men that hate each other, / in the toothless edge of the suburbs / (. . .) in the cram-full night where man and horse abound] (*OC* II: 237). It is not surprising, then, that the third stanza brings together the night and the body while also adding the philosophical tone of someone who is trying to understand simultaneously a physical sensation and some abstract concept related to it: "El universo de esta noche tiene la vastedad / del olvido y la precisión de la fiebre" [Tonight's universe has the vastness / of oblivion and the precision of fever] (*OC* II: 237). The juxtaposition of the vastness of oblivion and the precise painful experience of bodily fever, a juxtaposition that rests in an enjambement (as if the complete assimilation of the two realms wasn't completely possible yet close enough), sums up all the elements that the poem will explore. On the one hand, the pain of the body that is deprived of sleep, its most immediate decay and the hallucinations that took over the night. On the other, a meditation on more abstract topics such as death, nothingness, and identity.

This way of structuring a poem is not completely unique to "Insomnio." In fact, the combination of personal references to his family members with a poetic voice that identifies himself as "Borges" and a tone of constant philosophical meditation would become a common trend in the poems that Borges published from the 1960s onward. The difference, however, is that "Insomnio" does not include autobiographical traits (biographemes)[16] or a poetic voice easily identified as "Borges," but rather the presence of the body and the effects that the lack of sleep generates both in the flesh but also in the thoughts about death and immortality and in the perception of the suburbs that the poetic voice has. For example, when describing his body, the poetic voice mentions "los rumbos minuciosos de la muerte en las caries dentales" [the thorough paths of death in dental cavities] and later depicts the suburbs in the south as "leguas de pampa basurera y obscena, leguas de execración" [miles of trashy and obscene plains, miles of execration] that are full of "lotes anegadizos, ranchos en montón como perros, charcos de plata fétida" [flooded plots of land, ranches that pullulate like dogs, puddles of fetid silver] and of "alambre, terraplenes, papeles muertos, sobras de Buenos Aires" [wire, embankments, dead papers, the leftovers of Buenos Aires] (*OC* II: 238). And if this place is presented through the lenses of ugliness and putrefaction, something similar happens with the subject who speaks in the poem, who goes as far as stating that he is "el aborrecible centinela de esas colocaciones inmóviles" [the loathsome sentinel of these still settings] (*OC* II: 238). The end of the poem, however, is probably the most compelling part because the poetic voice accepts that this "inevitable realidad de fierro y de barro" [inevitable reality of iron and mud] will cut through the indifference of every human being (whether they are dead or alive it does not matter) and will condemn them to a horrible vigil that is worse than the corruption of the body previously mentioned (*OC* II: 238). However, besides this never-ending condemnation that makes of insomnia a kind of new and twisted form of immortality, the poem does not end with a universalization of the experience of insomnia. The last two verses, probably the most lyrical ones, take us back to the poetic voice and its personal situation.

> Toscas nubes color borra de vino infamarán el cielo;
> amanecerá en mis párpados apretados. (*OC* II: 238)
>
> [Tough clouds the color of wine's dregs will offend the sky,
> It will be morning in my tight eyelids.]

If Borges had written the poem later—in his sixties or seventies—these last two lines would not have been there. The poem would have finished either with a specific biographeme, with the explicit identification of the poetic voice with Borges (or with a portrait of another writer who talks like Borges), or with a tone more like the one in the second-to-last stanza: a philosophical reflection that takes insomnia away from the specific decay of a body and transforms it into a reflection about immortality. However, in the poem, we find a lot of images that connect to a semantic field that connotes violence, ugliness, and fragmentation. The image of the clouds that closes the poem is a perfect example of those three semantic connotations. The clouds are tough, they are like "borra" [dregs], or what is left at the bottom of a wine bottle or glass, and they offend and disrespect the sky with their presence. This is not a common lexical choice for Borges, certainly not a common one for a poem that will continue to appear as the opening composition in one of the most iconic collections of the 1960s. But, as I argue, the image of the clouds is not alone in its mission to defamiliarize our perception as readers of poetry in general and of Borges's poetry in particular. The lexical choices, indeed, are bold and rare. In fact, of the 319 words that make up the poem, 171 are nouns, adjectives, verbs, or adverbs. And of those 171 words, there are at least 37 that appear fewer than fifteen times in Borges's complete works, with many of them appearing fewer than 10 times and some only appearing in this poem.[17] To give some examples, the words "revienten" [burst] and "desfonden" [bilge] only appear in this poem and the same occurs with "dentales" [dental] and "insoportablemente" [unbearable] (at least as an adverb). "Abarrotados" [crowded/overwhelmed] (in the plural) only appears in the poem and in the singular two other times, one of them in "Funes, el memorioso" [Funes, the Memorious] and also in relation to the lack of sleep. It does appear two more times in "Tlön, Uqbar, Orbis Tertius" but as a verb. And something similar happens with "niveles" [levels]: in plural, it only appears in "Insomnio," and, in singular, it appears three other times and fewer that ten times as "desnivel" [inclination] or "nivelar" [level]. Many of these words relate to the semantic ideas of fragmentation, violence, and ugliness: "despedazado" [torn into pieces] appears seven times in masculine and three in feminine; the combination of "mellado" [toothless] and "filo" [edge of a knife] only appears one more time in the complete works, in the poem "Un cuchillo en el norte" [A Blade in the Northside] in *Para las seis cuerdas* [*For Six Strings*] (1965); "calurosa" [warm] only appears in this poem; "caries" [cavities] only three times and, one of those times, is once again in "Funes"; "circulación" [circulation] only appears six times but only twice in relation to bodily fluid: in this poem and in the famous long sentence from "El Aleph"; "execración" [execration], "crapulosa" [crapulous], and "colocaciones" [settings] appeared in the poem and only one more time each; and "basurera" [trashy] as an adjective only in "Insomnio"; "fétida" [fetid] only three times, and "alambres" [wires] only twice, the second case being the poem "Calle con almacén rosado" [Street with a Pink Corner Store] from *Luna de enfrente*; "sobras" [leftovers] appears a total of four times and "borra" as a noun only in this poem.

Although there might be other explanations regarding the specific use of some of these words, "Insomnio" constitutes a path that Borges could have taken, a path in which free verse and the descriptions of the body are in constant tension with the philosophical tone and the analysis of abstract ideas.[18] However, in one of the other poems that he added at the end of the 1958 compilation of his previous poetry collections, dedicated to Baltasar Gracián, Borges will put into practice a different strategy, one that will eliminate any lexical choices linked to fluids or the decaying of the body or to the feelings associated with them and that will become the central force of his later work: the portrait of the other as a continuation of the figure "Borges."

Quevedo, Gracián, and the Self-Figuration Process of the Late Poetry

With the publication of *El hacedor* in 1960, Borges's self-figuration practice becomes the most prominent feature of his work, especially his poetry. In fact, *El hacedor* operates as the book that synthetizes some of Borges's most famous themes (doubling of identity, limits and possibilities of our categorization of the world through classification systems, theories of reading and narrative causality, etc.). But it adds to them a constant practice of portraying the self through the portrait of other writers, family members, and literary characters.[19] From the 1960s onward, then, instead of making a reference to a specific sunset or marginal street or to a grandfather who has the same name as Borges's military relative, the poetic voice of the poems will speak as if Borges were acting like someone else or, in many cases, as other writers speaking as themselves but sounding like "Borges" or having some of his personal cultural obsessions. For instance, in the inscription to Lugones that opens *El hacedor* we find the possibility of being no one to being everyone, which also appears in the "Poema de los dones" [Poem of the Gifts] where Borges and Groussac seem to fuse themselves into one person. More extreme, however, is the case of "Everything and Nothing" where we find an imaginary dialogue between Shakespeare and God in which both seem to share some of Borges's pantheistic interests.

In other cases, we have a poetic voice that clearly assumes the identity or persona "Borges," but it does so by apostrophizing a friend and by reflecting on some aspects of the writing process. This is the case in poems such as "Epílogo," [Epilogue], from *La cifra* [*The Limit*] (1981), where the apostrophe has the name of Francisco Luis Bernárdez, one of Borges's friends during his year as a collaborator in the journal *Martín Fierro*. In this case, the self-figuration is based on the fact that they both shared similar literary interests at some point in their careers.

Finally, in some poems, the relationship that the voice establishes between portrait and death constitutes one of the most iconic forms of Borges's self-figuration. And this is mainly for two complementary reasons. On the one hand, as Premat has shown, this relationship works as a way of controlling the image of a dead man that Borges presents to his readers as himself. But, on the other hand, this control functions as a threshold between the impossibility of saying or representing what we tend to associate with death and the need, in order to counter that impossibility, to fictionalize the moment of death. As Mills-Court has analyzed in her book on epitaphs and the tension between presence and representation in some English poets,

> The death of presence leaves a ghost-like trace that is not quite nothingness. The act of representation bears the doubleness of an epitaphic gesture. Like an inscription on a cenotaph, it proclaims death and an empty core, but that emptiness is of a peculiar sort: the emptiness of a nothing that seems, somehow, to signify something. It is the nothingness of a haunting. (13)

Mills-Court explores this oscillation between presence and representation to show that, in lyric poetry, it is not easy to privilege one over the other. Every presence or manifestation that is included in a discourse becomes a representation, the epitome of which is to assert that for the impossibility of representing, we, in fact, need a discourse that "shows" or at least postulates that impossibility. But representation cannot be prioritized either because, as Mills-Court suggests, there is always a detail or excess that cannot convey an articulated or specific meaning but which is still acting there in the inscription or in the cenotaph as a presence.

In this vein, one of the most radical examples of this type of self-figuration is found in "Baltasar Gracián," a poem that Borges included in the collected *Poemas* (1958) and some years later in *El otro, el mismo* (1964). In this case, the writer that Borges used as a point of departure for his self-figuration process is clearly identified: first, in the title of the poem; then in the first quatrain in a more elusive yet still deductible fashion: "Laberintos, retruécanos, emblemas, / helada y laboriosa nadería, / fue para *este jesuita* la poesía, / reducida por él a estratagemas" [Labyrinths, symbols, all the tricks of language, / a cold and overintricate nothingness / that, *for this Jesuit*, was poetry, / reduced by him to verbal stratagem] (*OC* II: 259, emphasis added; *SP* 185). And, finally, in the sixth stanza: "Su destino ulterior no está en la historia; / librado a las mudanzas de la impura / tumba el polvo que ayer fue su figura, / el alma de Gracián entró en la gloria" [His later destiny is not recorded. / The dust that formed him finally delivered / to the corrosive changes of the tomb, / the soul of Gracián entered into glory] (*OC* II: 259; *SP* 185). This last use of the name, however, is very important because it appears at the same moment in which the poetic voice is describing Gracián's death. This is an important detail because it delineates a separation between those biographical traits that could potentially be verified in a historical document or a biography of Gracián from those other moments that are part of a speculative realm, a realm that is addressed in the last part of the poem. In the seventh stanza, the poetic voice seems to consider a different hypothesis regarding Gracián's encounter with God and his behavior in front of Him (he may have cried or felt that he wasted his life), but he quickly decides to drop the hypothesis and propose a new more radical interpretation: after dying, Gracián did not reach salvation, he did not encounter God, but rather kept creating riddles with the aid of different rhetorical procedures, similar to the ones we can find in his books.

The fact that Gracián's portrait reaches its culmination in the stanzas that described his death and the possible outcomes of it foregrounds the impossibility of representation that death entails, an impossibility that oscillates between showing and representing. Or, to put it differently, it signals that to talk about death (and identity) always implies some kind of distance or deviation and, above all, a contradiction. By linking a name (the epitome of identity and identification) with death, this poem brings us back to the tension analyzed by Mills-Court: an emptiness that we try to represent by creating an illusionary portrait and the constant returning to that emptiness.[20] In that process, in the tension between a void and the illusion of a presence, the poetic voice of Borges's poem creates a space in which he controls not only Gracián's portrait as a writer but, mainly, the speculative realm of his after-death punishment. Why is that so? Why doesn't the poem end with Gracián's death in the sixth stanza? Why is it so important for the poetic voice of the poem to control a realm of this other figure that he is trying to describe in his portrait and of which nothing can be said?

One possible answer is that the last stanzas are not used as a continuation of the portrait displayed in the previous ones. On the contrary, they are used to underline and manipulate an "otherness" that is different from the self. By trying to control the narrative around Gracián's death, Borges's poetic voice is diminishing, or avoiding, its radical otherness and, by extension, is invading the portrait with his own image. We now read Gracián as a prolongation of Borges even if he is depicted in a negative light. A second possibility, one that does not necessarily exclude the previous one, would be to treat those conjectures about Gracián's after-life as parodies, as caricatures. And this is not a small detail if we consider that in the "Prologue" to the 1954 edition of *Historia universal de la infamia* [*A Universal History of Infamy*] Borges writes: "Yo diría que barroco es aquel estilo que deliberadamente agota (o quiere agotar) sus posibilidades y que linda con su propia caricatura. [. . .] yo diría que es barroca la etapa final de todo arte, cuando éste exhibe y dilapida sus medios" [I would define the baroque as that style that deliberately exhausts (or tries to exhaust) its own possibilities and that borders on self-caricature. . . . I would venture to say that the baroque is the final stage in all art when art flaunts and squanders its resources] (*OC* II: 291; *A Universal History* 4).[21] How should we read this definition if we put it side by side with the poem? And how should we read the parodic elements that it displays?

On the one hand, the definition of the Baroque as a terminal stage of a specific artistic practice seems to be linked to an excess of rhetorical devices, something that is clearly mentioned throughout the poem as a negative and unnecessary "quality" of Gracián's work. In this sense, Borges seems to be making fun of the Baroque obsession with excessive ornamentation. However, and as is usually the case with Borges's jokes (think of "Pierre Menard, autor del Quijote" [Pierre Menard, Author of the *Quixote*] or "El arte de injuriar" [The Art of Insult]), they also operate as a way of multiplying and enhancing narrative possibilities and procedures. If, in the case of "El idioma analítico de John Wilkins" [The Analytical Language of John Wilkins], the fact of ignoring what the universe is does not prevent the use and enumeration of different theories that try

ANTHOLOGIES OF THE SELF 265

to explain it, in the poem about Gracián the impossibility of knowing what happened to him after his death, far from dissuading the self-figuration process of the poetic voice, enhances it.[22] And instead of accepting the impossibility of trespassing or manipulating the "otherness of the other," the poetic voice of Borges's poem uses it as an aesthetic and figurative opportunity and as a means to control his own image as a writer and, in some cases, even that of a dead man.

The anthologies of the 1940s and '50s, then, either by modifying some verses and poems from the first three poetry collections or by adding new and almost unique ones, function as a threshold that allows us to see that even though some of the self-figuration procedures were already present in the '20s they only become central later in the '60s. These anthologies also allow us to better rethink and understand Borges's self-figuration process and encourage us to explore roads less taken by him, such as the lexical and metaphorical choices of "Insomnio."

NOTES

1. Unless stated differently, all translations into English are mine.
2. Regarding the *Antología poética argentina* [*Anthology of Argentine Poetry*], see Morales. For an analysis of Borges's role in the creation of different collaborative anthologies and edited collections in the 1930s and '40s, see Benedict (121–84) and Adur.
3. With regards to the editorial project *Destiempo,* see Mascioto (64) and Benedict (238–71).
4. Muschietti adds that Borges's later poetry takes the form of static stanzas such as neo-classical quartets, milongas, and baroque sonnets (23) and, thus, ends up functioning as a literary museum: it is full of battles, gods, monuments, marble statues, and anachronistic lexical choices that emulate Lugones and Almafuerte, as if Borges would have preferred a dead language over a more contemporary and transformative one (24).
5. For more on Libertella's complex ideas about Borges, see Urli ("Libertella y Borges").
6. I will not analyze the lexical or syntactic variations in detail here. See Scarano and Sassi, Balderston (*How Borges Wrote* and *Lo marginal es lo más bello*) and Cajero Vázquez.
7. See Cajero Vázquez, Contreras Bustamante, García, Hernaiz, Shaw, and Videla de Rivero for more on the publication history of *Fervor de Buenos Aires* as well as for details on the poems' variants.
8. For a detailed study of Borges's rewriting choices for his early books of poetry, see Scarano and Sassi.
9. See Balderston (*Lo marginal es lo más bello*) for a detailed study of two manuscripts of the poem "Página para recordar al coronel Suárez, vencedor en Junín," published in 1953 in *Sur* and dedicated to the figure of his maternal great-grandfather.
10. Translation by Daniel Balderston.
11. See Cajero Vázquez (50–52) for more on Borges's lexical choices in the first edition of *Fervor.*
12. To give just one example, in the poem "Barrio reconquistado," the first verse of the first edition reads "Nadie justipreció la belleza" [No one appraised the beauty] (*Fervor* w/p) while in the 1943 edition we find "nadie percibió la belleza" [Nobody perceived the beauty]

(25). It is possible to assume that in the case of "Llamarada" words like "espoleados" [spurred],"culminaciones" [culminations], "tremantes" [trembling], and "fenecida" [deceased] would have probably changed if Borges hadn't eliminated the poem entirely.

13. Other examples include "Apergaminado y plausible film cinemático" [A looking like parchment and plausible cinematic film]; "Cómo me ahorcan las cuerdas del horizonte" [How the horizon's strings strangle me]; "¿Llueve? ¿Qué morfina inyectarán a las calles esas agujas?" [Is it raining? What kind of morphine are those needles injecting to the streets?]; "Los días son todos de papel azul bien cortaditos por la misma tijera / sobre el agujero inexistente del Cosmos" [all days are made of the same blue paper cut by the same scissor / over the inexistent hole of the Cosmos]; "El sol ventilador vertiginoso tumba los caserones" [The sun like a vertiginous fan brings down the mansions] (*Textos recobrados* 74–75).

14. The original poem was published on *Grecia* (September 15, 1920) on page 9. A digitized version of the journal can be browsed at Hemeroteca Digital, part of the Biblioteca Nacional de España.

15. The classes were broadcasted by the TV Pública Argentina [Argentine National Public Channel] in 2013 and are available on YouTube. See TV Pública.

16. For this term I am following Roland Barthes, who describes its importance in the preface of his book *Sade, Fourier, Loyola* (8–9).

17. In addition to using the print version of the *Obras completas*, I also have them as two searchable PDFs. I used the search tool in the Adobe PDF system to look for specific words (and their derivatives), and I listed how many times they appeared in the complete works and where. Although the technique is not as precise as a formal mathematical statistic, it gives a general idea of the importance of the lexical choices made by Borges in this poem.

18. "Insomnio" is not the only poem that can be read as an example of a road not taken. The "Two English Poems" can be read in the same light since they were written in the same period, 1934, and have been included in the poetic compilations of the 1940s and '50s. Due to space, I won't analyze them here, but it is important to note that, in them, we also found some abstract philosophical meditations on love linked to the body, autobiographical traits, and a vulnerability in the tone that is not very common in Borges. However, they are not as radical in their use of lexical words that connote ugliness, fragmentation, or decay. For a study of these poems and their manuscripts, including a third English Poem that was never published, see Balderston ("Borges in Love") and Borges (*Poemas y prosas breves*).

19. See Lefere, Alonso Estenoz, Premat (*Héroes*), Molloy, Pezzoni, and Urli ("'De un yo plural'") for more on this complex ambivalence toward the use of autobiographical traits and the fictionalization of other writer's biographies.

20. In a similar note, Paul de Man has written, "can we not suggest, with equal justice, that the autobiographical project may itself produce and determine the life and that whatever the writer does is in fact governed by the technical demands of self-portraiture and thus determined, in all its aspects, by the resources of his medium?" (69).

21. Borges's explanation is longer, and it coincidentally includes a reference to Gracián (*OC* II: 291).

22. For a detailed analysis of Borges's comments on Gracián, see Pellicer.

Works Cited

Adur, Lucas. "El antólogo como autor. Sobre algunas antologías preparadas por Borges y Bioy." *Antologías argentinas. Intervenciones sobre el canon y emergencias del imaginario.* Compiled by María Amelia Arancet Ruda, Teseo, 2017, pp. 23–61.

Alonso Estenoz, Alfredo. *Los límites del texto: Autoría y autoridad en Borges.* Verbum, 2013.

Balderston, Daniel. "Borges in Love." *Variaciones Borges,* vol. 45, 2018, pp. 131–51.

Balderston, Daniel. *How Borges Wrote.* University of Virginia Press, 2018.

Balderston, Daniel. *Lo marginal es lo más bello.* Eudeba, 2022.

Barthes, Roland. *Sade, Fourier, Loyola,* translated by Richard Miller. John Hopkins University Press, 1997.

Benedict, Nora C. *Borges and the Literary Marketplace. How Editorial Practices Shaped Cosmopolitan Reading.* Yale University Press, 2021.

Borges, Jorge Luis. *Fervor de Buenos Aires.* 1923. Alberto Casares, n.d.

Borges, Jorge Luis. *Obras completas.* 4 vols. Emecé, 1996.

Borges, Jorge Luis. *Poemas [1922–1943].* Losada, 1943.

Borges, Jorge Luis. *Poemas 1922–1953.* Emecé, 1954.

Borges, Jorge Luis. *Poemas 1922–1958.* Emecé, 1958.

Borges, Jorge Luis. *Poemas y prosas breves,* edited by Daniel Balderston and Celeste Marín. Borges Center, 2018.

Borges, Jorge Luis. *Selected Poems,* edited by Alexander Coleman. Penguin, 1999.

Borges, Jorge Luis. *Textos recobrados (1919–1929).* Emecé, 2007.

Borges, Jorge Luis. *A Universal History of Iniquity,* translated by Andrew Hurley. Penguin, 2004.

Cajero Vázquez, Antonio. *Palimpsestos del joven Borges: Escritura y reescrituras de Fervor de Buenos Aires.* El Colegio de San Luis, 2013.

Contreras Bustamente, Marta. "La escritura de Borges en *Fervor de Buenos Aires* y *El Hacedor.*" *Acta literaria,* no. 25, 2000. http://dx.doi.org/10.4067/S0717-68482000002500003.

de Man, Paul. *The Rhetoric of Romanticism.* Columbia University Press, 1984, pp. 67–81.

E. F., "Rev. of Jorge Luis Borges, Poemas [1922–1943]." *Revista Hispánica Moderna,* vol. 11, no. 3/4 (July–Octover 1945), pp. 242–43.

García, Carlos. "La edición 'princeps' de 'Fervor de Buenos Aires.'" *Variaciones Borges,* vol. 4, 1997, pp. 177–210.

Hernaiz, Sebastián. "Borges y sus editores: itinerarios de *Fervor de Buenos Aires* (1923–1977)." *Orbis Tertius,* vol. 20, no. 22, 2016, pp. 10–20.

Lefere, Robin. *Borges, entre autorretrato y automitografía.* Gredos, 2006.

Lihn, Enrique, and Pedro Lastra. "Borges: gran poeta y mediocre versificador." *Inti: Revista de literatura hispánica,* vol. 1, no. 8, 1978, pp. 62–74.

Libertella, Héctor. "Borges: Literatura y Patografía en la Argentina." *Revista Iberoamericana,* vol. 49, no. 125, 1983, pp. 707–15.

Libertella, Héctor. *La librería argentina.* Alción, 2003.

Mascioto, María de los Ángeles. "Borges editor." *Anclajes,* vol. 22, no. 2, 2018, pp. 57–68.

Mills-Courts, Karen. *Poetry as Epitaph.* Louisiana State University Press, 1990.

Molloy, Sylvia. "Cita y autofiguración en la obra de Borges." *Las letras de Borges y otros ensayos.* Beatriz Viterbo, 1999, pp. 227–236.

Morales, Jesús Eduardo. "La 'Antología poética argentina' de 1941 en el canon lírico." *Variaciones Borges,* vol. 42, 2016, pp. 97–119.

Muschietti, Delfina. "Borges y Storni: la vanguardia en disputa." *Hispamérica*, vol. 32, no. 95, 2003, pp. 21–44.

Pellicer, Rosa. "Borges, lector de Gracián: 'Laberintos, retruécanos, emblemas.'" *Boletín de la Fundación Federico García Lorca*, nos. 29–30, 2001, pp. 229–45.

Pezzoni, Enrique. "*Fervor de Buenos Aires*: Autobiografía y autorretrato." *El texto y sus voces*. Eterna Cadencia, 2009, pp. 79–110.

Premat, Julio. "A impulsos de la sangre germánica: Usos y paradojas del origen." *Variaciones Borges*, vol. 39, 2015, pp. 23–49.

Premat, Julio. *Héroes sin atributos*. Fondo de Cultura Económica, 2009.

Scarano, Tommaso, and Manuela Sassi. *Concordanze per lemma dell'opera in versi di J. L. Borges*. Mauro Baroni, 1992.

Shaw, Donald L. "Borges's Tinkerings: Concerning the Evolution of 'Calle desconocida' ('Fervor de Buenos Aires')." *Revista Hispánica Moderna*, vol. 56, no. 2, 2003, pp. 327–40.

TV Pública Argentina. "Borges por Piglia." *YouTube*, September 14, 2013, https://www.youtube.com/watch?v=pKW7okGH_6I.

Urli, Sebastián. "'De un yo plural y de una sola sombra': Autofiguración y retrato en *El hacedor*." *Cuadernos LIRICO*, vol. 12, 2015. OpenEdition Journals, https://doi.org/10.4000/lirico.1978.

Urli, Sebastián. "Libertella y Borges, o las patografías de Menard." *Letras*, no. 81, 2020, pp. 225–44.

Videla de Rivero, Gloria. "El sentido de las variantes textuales en dos ediciones de *Fervor de Buenos Aires* de Jorge Luis Borges." *Revista Chilena de Literatura*, vol. 23, 1984, pp. 67–78.

CHAPTER 15

....

THE MIDDLE ESSAYS
AND REVIEWS

....

DARDO SCAVINO

INTRODUCTION

JORGE Luis Borges's essays revolve around three concepts he adopted in the early 1930s and continued to use until his final days, though under a variety of names: figuration, prefiguration, and transfiguration. At times he called them superstition, omen, and echo; other times modesty, precursor, and repetition. While in the pages of his book *Discusión* [*Discussion*] (1932), these concepts did not exceed the limits of "narrative art," in the essays of *Otras inquisiciones* [*Other Inquisitions*] (1952) and in other later texts, this trilogy would gradually assume a metaphysical status resulting from an ever-widening understanding of writing, which, according to Borges, is a part of the world but is also its totality. That is, writing is the world itself. Time, memory, and personal and universal history would become dimensions of writing: anything that figures among the things of the world is, in fact, a *thing*—a discreet transfiguration of something that has already happened and an enigmatic prefiguration of something yet to come.

FIGURATIONS

In a 1946 article on H. G. Wells, Borges asserted that "la obra que perdura es siempre capaz de una infinita y plástica ambigüedad; es todo para todos, como el Apóstol; es un espejo que declara los rasgos del lector y también un mapa del mundo" [Work that endures is always capable of an infinite and plastic ambiguity; it is all things for all men, like the Apostle; it is a mirror that reflects the reader's own traits and it is also a map of the world] (*OC* II: 76; *Borges: A Reader* 172). The apostle in question was, of course, Paul of Tarsus, who had become "Jewish with the Jews," "weak with the weak," and "everything to everyone, to save everyone" during his evangelical wanderings (1 Corinthians 9: 20–22). A philosopher such as Alain Badiou would argue that if the word of Paul was adopted by Jews and pagans alike, it was because he advanced a universal truth, something that was the same for all peoples, as would be the case with any physical or mathematical principle (*Saint Paul* 15). For Borges, however, this universality is not linked to the univocality of the truth but to the equivocality of what is written. The numerous divisions of the Christian church seem to confirm this: from Catholics to the Orthodox, from the Armenians and the Copts to the various Protestant sects, all—although they disagree with each other—see themselves reflected in the mirror of that "infinite and plastic ambiguity" of Paul's correspondence and consider his letters to be the most reliable map for orienting themselves in the world. That passage from the Epistle to the Corinthians would become a recurring element in *Otras inquisiciones,* and Borges would locate it again in a letter by Bernard Shaw: "Yo comprendo todo y a todos y soy nada y soy nadie" [I understand everything and everyone, and nobody and nothing] (*OC* II: 127). Like Shakespeare in his time, Borges writes "de esa nada (tan comparable a la de Dios antes de crear el mundo, tan comparable a la divinidad primordial que otro irlandés, Juan Escoto Erígena, llamó *Nihil*), Bernard Shaw edujo casi innumerables personas, o *dramatis personae*" [From that nothingness (so comparable to the nothingness of God before He created the world, so comparable to the primordial divinity that another Irishman, Johannes Scotus Erigena, called *Nihil*), Bernard Shaw educed almost innumerable persons, or dramatis personae] (*OC* II: 127; *Other Inquisitions* 164). One of the British playwright's celebrated critics, William Hazlitt, asserted that Shakespeare "se parecía a todos los hombres, salvo en lo de parecerse a todos los hombres. Íntimamente no era nada, pero era todo lo que son los demás, o lo que pueden ser" [was just like any other man, but that he was unlike other men. He was nothing in himself, but he was all that others were, or that could become] (*OC* II: 116; *SNF* 342). Like the God of negative theology, the work of William Shakespeare had room for all possible variants of humanity, because all humanity's variations were recognized in the work of William Shakespeare. Like Spinoza's substance, his writing contained all the virtual attributes of the human, precisely because it had been, and would continue to be, subject to the most widely varied interpretations.

Borges was not unaware that, with his vindication of the equivocations of writing, with his defense of its figurative, symbolic, elliptical, ambivalent nature, he was trespassing into a debate that dates to the dawn of European philosophy. In a passage from the *Phaedrus*, a fictionalized Socrates had narrated "una fábula egipcia contra la escritura" [an Egyptian fable against writing] and compared books with "figuras pintadas 'que parecen vivas, pero no contestan una palabra a las preguntas que les hacen'" [painted figures "that seem to be alive, but do not answer a word to the questions they are asked"] (*OC* II: 91; *SNF* 358). Socrates then evoked an Egyptian god, Thoth, whom the Greeks called Hermes and to whom they credited the invention of hieroglyphic writing. Tradition ascribes to another Hermes, calling himself Trismegistus, the voluminous *Corpus hermeticum* of the third century CE, "en cuyas páginas estaban escritas todas las cosas" [on whose pages all things were written] (*OC* II: 14; *SNF* 351).

THE MIDDLE ESSAYS AND REVIEWS   271

Borges then conjectures that Plato invented the philosophical dialogue "para atenuar o eliminar" [to alleviate or eliminate] (*OC* II: 91; *SNF* 358) the silence of books, although he continued to distrust those "painted figures" likely to fall into the hands of readers who would misrepresent or misunderstand them.

Borges himself supposed that, existing as writing, any book maintains an "infinite dialogue" with its various readers. The words *amica silentia lunae*, Borges explained in his "Nota sobre (hacia) Bernard Shaw" [A Note on (toward) Bernard Shaw], "significaban ahora la luna íntima, silenciosa y luciente," but in the *Aeneid*, they alluded to "interlunio, la oscuridad que permitió a los griegos entrar en la ciudadela de Troya" [Now the words *amica silentia lunae* mean 'the intimate, silent, and shining moon,' and in the *Aeneid* they meant 'the interlunar period, the darkness that permitted the Greeks to enter the citadel of Troy'] (*OC* II: 125; *Other Inquisitions* 163).[1] Literature "no es agotable, por la suficiente y simple razón de que un solo libro no lo es" [is not exhaustible, for the sufficient and simple reason that a single book is not] (*OC* II: 125; *Other Inquisitions* 163). That "infinite dialogue" is but a variant of that "infinite and plastic ambiguity" of writing, and for this reason, Borges estimated that if he were able to know how his texts would be read in the year two thousand, "sabría cómo será la literatura del año 2000" [he would know what literature would be like in the year 2000] (*OC* II: 125; *Other Inquisitions* 163). For Plato, any oral exchange was preferable to the most precise writing because the interlocutors would be able to answer any questions and thus avoid the misrepresentation of their concepts. Socrates describes writing as the "orphan" of its author, its "muteness" lending itself to the most extravagant misunderstandings or, as Beatriz Sarlo notes: to the most diverse "versions" and "perversions" (93). When Borges asserts that a book is an "infinite dialogue" with readers, he is suggesting the opposite of Plato's argument: that "muteness" does not prevent him from answering questions, because his answers will be the echoes of the beliefs, presuppositions, or values of his readers. What for Plato was an imperfection of writing becomes for Borges its primary virtue, thus opening not only fiction but also the Latin American essay to, as Daniel Balderston says, "the tentative" and "personal," "traits uncharacteristic of this genre" (576).

In a 1978 conference entitled "El libro" [The Book], Borges would compare the "infinite and plastic ambiguity" of writing with the fate of the fragments composed by the obscure Heraclitus of Ephesus. This philosopher had maintained that "nadie baja dos veces al mismo río" [no one goes down the same river twice],[2] although he forgot to add that we ourselves "somos no menos fluidos como el río" [are no less fluid than the river] and that we likewise change between one current and another (*OC* IV: 171). "Cada vez que leemos un libro, el libro ha cambiado, la connotación de las palabras es otra" [Each time we read a book, the book has changed, the connotation of the words is different] (*OC* IV: 171). This transformation takes place *a fortiori* between different readers: the *Hamlet* read by Coleridge, by Goethe or by Bradley is not the same play, just as happens in Argentina when *Martín Fierro* is read by Leopoldo Lugones, by Ricardo Rojas, or by Ezequiel Martínez Estrada. Borges would recall a few years later, in his lecture "La poesía" [On Poetry], that according to John Scotus Eriugena, the Holy Scriptures contained "un número infinito de sentidos y la comparó con el plumaje tornasolado del pavo real" [an infinite number of meanings and he compared it to the innumerable colors in peacock's tail]. He then evoked a Spanish Kabbalist who explained how "Dios hizo la Escritura para cada uno de los hombres de Israel y por consiguiente hay tantas Biblias como lectores de la Biblia" [God made Writing for each of the men of Israel and therefore there are as many Bibles as there are readers of the Bible] (*OC* III: 254).

In a 1938 review of Paul Valéry's *Introduction à la poétique*—in which he briefly anticipated Pierre Menard's undertaking—Borges explained this phenomenon through a verse by Cervantes: "¡Vive Dios, que me espanta esta grandeza!" [I vow to God, this greatness frightens me!] (*OC* IV: 368).[3] As the verb *espantar* was synonymous with *asombrar* [to astonish] in the seventeenth century and *asustar* [to frighten] in the twentieth, this verse had undergone a transformation comparable to that of Heraclitus's river. The signifier remains the same; what is signified does not. Borges even assumed that "el tiempo y sus incomprensiones y distracciones colaboran con el poeta muerto" [time and its misunderstandings and distractions collaborate with the dead poet] (*OC* IV: 368), and for this reason Menard's *Quixote* would also be better, in his opinion (or at least in that of his narrator), than Cervantes's. Opposing Plato, Borges thought that avoiding distortions was both impossible and undesirable, because, akin to biology, literary creation (and even nonliterary creation) resulted from the various errors of interpretation or translation that have generated "mutations."

Thus, everything occurs as if Borges were remembering the primitive meaning of the verbs *mutate* and *change* as they allude to the exchanging of two elements with comparable values. It is enough for any author to release their writing into the world: readers will enact the permutations or the interpretations. Seventeenth-century readers exchanged *espantar* for *asombrar* [to astonish], while those of the twentieth century, transacted *espantar* for *asustar* [to frighten]. In consequence, Borges lamented that Nathaniel Hawthorne had "damaged" some of his narratives with "el deseo puritano de hacer de cada imaginación una fábula" [the Puritan desire to make a fable out of each imagining] an aesthetic error that "lo inducía a agregarles moralidades y a veces a falsearlas y deformarlas" [induced him to add morals and sometimes to falsify and deform them] (*OC* II: 51; *Other Inquisitions* 51). In a sketch from 1836, Hawthorne imagines the plot of a snake lodged in a man's stomach and fed by him, despite the torments it inflicted on the man for many years. Borges argues it would have been enough simply to present this idea, and Hawthorne would have bequeathed us a formidable story. But overwhelmed by the weight of his Puritan ancestors, the North American felt compelled to "reveal" the meaning of the parable: "Podría ser un emblema de la envidia o de otra malvada pasión" [It could be type of envy or some other evil passion] (*OC* II: 51; *Other Inquisitions* 51). The same occurred with his story *Earth's Holocaust*, another parable "que estuvo a punto de ser magistral" [that was close to masterful], but which Hawthorne marred with his Calvinist sermons on the innate depravity of Adam's descendants (*OC* II: 56). This moralizing interrupted the "infinite and plastic ambiguity" of his writing and kept it from becoming "all things for all people": "En Hawthorne, siempre la visión germinal era verdadera; lo falso, lo eventualmente falso, son las moralidades que agregaba en el último párrafo o los personajes que ideaba, que armaba, para representarla" [In

THE MIDDLE ESSAYS AND REVIEWS   273

Hawthorne, the germinal vision was always true; what is false, what is ultimately false, are the moralities he added in the last paragraph or the characters he conceived, or assembled, in order to represent that vision] (*OC* II: 59; *Other Inquisitions* 60). Around that same time, Scottish author Thomas Carlyle was making similar gaffes. In his *Saga of Harald the Tyrant*, Snorri Sturluson wrote that on the eve of a battle south of York, King Harold of England offered his brother Tostig a third of his domain in exchange for fighting alongside him, despite Tostig's having betrayed him to the Norwegian invaders. For the Viking ruler, on the other hand, he reserved "seis pies de tierra inglesa y, ya que era tan alto, uno más" [six feet of English soil and since he is so tall, one more] (*OC* II:133; *Other Inquisitions* 169). Carlyle "desbarata con una desdichada adición" [spoils . . . with an unfortunate addition] (*OC* II: 134n1; *Other Inquisitions* 169) the modest verbal economy of this ingenious reply by adding "*for a grave.*"

In a similar vein, Borges asserts that readers would do just as well to ignore that, with his couplet, "Su tumba son de Flandes las campañas / y su epitafio la sangrienta Luna" [His tomb is from Flanders the campaigns / and his epitaph the bloody Moon], Francisco de Quevedo was alluding to the red sigil of the Ottomans' standards (*OC* II: 42). "Estos versos deben su riqueza a su ambigüedad" [These verses owe their richness to their ambiguity] (*OC* III: 259) declared the Argentine, paraphrasing his essay in *Otras inquisiciones*: "La grandeza de Quevedo es verbal. Juzgarlo un filósofo, un teólogo o (como sugiere Aureliano Fernández Guerra) un hombre de Estado es un error que pueden consentir los títulos de sus obras, no el contenido" [The greatness in Quevedo is verbal. Judging him a philosopher, a theologian or (as Aureliano Fernández Guerra suggests) a statesman is an error that the titles of his works might allow, but not their content] (*OC* II: 39). As was the case with Hawthorne or Wells, Quevedo's texts do not owe their enduring fame to their political doctrine, or to their Catholic zeal, but to the prodigious ambiguity of their writing. And if Quevedo did not achieve the same glory as others, it was due, according to Borges, to the fact that he had not succeeded in landing upon a symbol "que se apodere de la imaginación de la gente" [that captures the popular imagination] (*OC* II: 38; *Other Inquisitions* 36), that is, a symbol "plastic" enough to become a "map" of our worlds and a "mirror" of our features.

We find a similar argument in a lecture added to the second edition of *Discusión*, published contemporarily with *Otras inquisiciones*: "El escritor argentino y la tradición" [The Argentine Writer and Tradition]. Borges dedicated this conference to demonstrating that, by merely by being inspired by the speech of rural laborers, gauchesque poetry is not indisputably more Argentine than other literary trends. He uses a poem by Enrique Banchs to prove this argument:

> El sol en los tejados
> y en las ventanas brilla. Ruiseñores
> quieren decir que están enamorados.(*OC* I: 269)

> [The sun glints on the tiled roofs
> and on the windows. Nightingales
> mean to say they are in love.](*SNF* 423)

These verses seem less Argentine than a few gauchesque octosyllables about ranches and thrushes. In the outskirts of Buenos Aires, Borges observed in his lecture, "no hay tejados sino azoteas" [there are no tiled roofs, there are flat terrace roofs] (*OC* I: 269; *SNF* 423) and the nightingale is a bird of Greek and Germanic tradition. Borges asserted, however, "que en el manejo de estas imágenes convencionales, en esos tejados y en esos ruiseñores anómalos, no estarán desde luego la arquitectura ni la ornitología argentinas, pero están el pudor argentino, la reticencia argentina" [that in the use of these conventional images, and these incongruous tiled roofs and nightingales, although neither the architecture nor the ornithology is Argentine, there is the Argentine reserve, the Argentine reticence] (*OC* I: 269; *SNF* 423) because "al hablar de esa mujer que lo había dejado y había dejado vacío el mundo para él" [in speaking of a woman who left him and left the world empty for him] (*OC* I: 269; *SNF* 423) Banchs turned to those figures. Attributing that reticence to Argentines, of course, was a ruse of Borges's: at that time, national literature had to reflect the "spirit of a people," and this spirit was found, for a Lugones or a Rojas, in the "gaucho epic" with its cult of courage and its assumption of a rural lexicon, when in reality, Borges replies, the characteristic of the Argentine soul would be modesty and reluctance to expose intimacy, and Banchs's poetry, written by an Argentine, and directed to Argentines, perfectly reflects that national psychology. Yet one needs only to read a contemporary essay such as "El pudor de la historia" [The Modesty of History] to see that Borges attributes that same reticence to an English monarch and an Icelandic writer. Because the question of modesty, for him, was not ethnic or psychological but rather rhetorical: the use of tropes that silence the very subject they discuss—tropes that figure, or frame the subject and, for that very reason, disfigure it, to the point that the readers can fill in those ambiguous hints with different content. The "floating signifiers" (Lévi-Strauss XLIX) that philosophy has always tried to conjure—defining their words or turning them into concepts with a fixed meaning—are the favorite food of literary texts: "La música, los estados de felicidad, la mitología, las caras trabajadas por el tiempo, ciertos crepúsculos y ciertos lugares," Borges wrote, "quieren decirnos algo, o algo dijeron que no hubiéramos debido perder, o están por decir algo; esta inminencia de una revelación, que no se produce, es quizá el hecho estético" [Music, states of happiness, mythology, faces worn by time, certain twilights and certain places, all want to tell us something, or have told us something we shouldn't have lost, or are about to tell us something; that imminence of a revelation as yet unproduced is, perhaps, the aesthetic fact] (*OC* II: 13; *SNF* 346).

PREFIGURATIONS

Something becomes an "aesthetic fact," from Borges's perspective, when it assumes the status of a signifier whose meaning is suspended: we know it means something, but we are not exactly sure what; we know that "it wants to tell us something," but we do completely understand it, like Quevedo's "sangrienta Luna." When a philosopher defines a

THE MIDDLE ESSAYS AND REVIEWS   275

given word and turns it into a concept, he tries, as Plato did, to prevent future readers from interpreting it in any other way. In a utopian effort, philosophy seeks to exorcise misunderstandings. Literature, on the contrary, multiplies them and, in consequence, assumes the ineluctable historicity of meanings. Philosophy is the friend of necessity— literature, of contingency. And that is why Borges finds examples of this historicization in messianic writings, as occurs, once again, with the first Epistle to the Corinthians. We live, according to Paul, in that "imminence of revelation": "Ahora vemos como a través de un espejo, en oscuridad; mas entonces *veremos* cara a cara" [Now we see through a mirror, in darkness; but then *we shall see* face to face] (*OC* II: 98; *Other Inquisitions* 126 [emphasis in original]). For the ascetic Apostle, these enigmatic mirrors were the various figures in the Old Testament who prefigured Christ. This meant that the events referred to by the Holy Scriptures belonged to two registers: the first, real, with its respective material causes and consequences; the second, symbolic, with its actors who unconsciously perform "un drama secreto, determinado y premeditado por Dios" [a secret drama, determined and premeditated by God] (*OC* II: 98; *Other Inquisitions* 125). When they acted, the various characters of the Old Testament did not just bequeath material consequences (such as building the ark with which Noah saved the animals from the Flood); they also performed a vast symbolic drama that secretly foreshadowed events to come (the construction of the ark prefigures the construction of the Church with which Christ will save believers from the Final Judgment).

Theologians like Irenaeus of Lyon or Augustine of Hippo would turn this "typological" interpretation of the Old Testament into an exegetical tradition that more than one modern writer would perpetuate in their essays and narratives. John Donne, in the *Biathanatos*, only cared about Samson as the "emblem of Christ" because

> En el Antiguo Testamento no hay héroe que no haya sido promovido a esa autoridad: para san Pablo, Adán es la figura del que había de venir; para san Agustín, Abel representa la muerte del Salvador, y su hermano Seth, la resurrección; para Quevedo, "prodigioso diseño fue Job de Cristo." (*OC* II: 79)

> [There is not a hero in the Old Testament who has not been promoted to this authority: for St. Paul, Adam is the figure of He who was to come; for St. Augustine, Abel represents the death of the Savior, and his brother Seth the resurrection; for Quevedo, Job was a "prodigious design" for Christ.] (*SNF* 335)

These characters are the "precursors" of Christ because their stories vaguely prophesy the life and passion of the Redeemer, although that significance is only revealed to us retrospectively from the New Testament. Or to put it in Borges's terms: Jesus "created" his precursors, and in the same way that Noah or Moses had been the "precursors" of the crucified Christ, Zeno of Elea or Hawthorne were Kafka's "enigmatic mirrors":

> La circunstancia, la extraña circunstancia, de percibir en un cuento de Hawthorne, redactado a principios del siglo XIX, el sabor mismo de los cuentos de Kafka, que trabajó a principios del siglo XX, no debe hacernos olvidar que el sabor de Kafka ha

sido creado, ha sido determinado, por Kafka. "Wakefield" prefigura a Franz Kafka, pero este modifica, y afina, la lectura de "Wakefield." (*OC* II: 55–56)

[The circumstance, the strange circumstance, of perceiving a story written by Hawthorne at the beginning of the nineteenth century the same quality that distinguishes the stories Kafka wrote at the beginning of the twentieth must not cause us to forget that Hawthorne's particular quality has been created, or determined, by Kafka. "Wakefield" prefigures Franz Kafka. But Kafka modifies and refines the reading of "Wakefield."] (*Other Inquisitions* 56–57)

The verb *espantar* becomes the equivalent of *asustar* [to frighten] when the twentieth century arrives; Moses prefigures Jesus when Paul writes his missives; Samson's "suicide" prophesies the crucifixion of the Nazarene in Donne's *Biathanatos*; William Beckford's *Vathek* "pronostica, siquiera de modo rudimentario, los satánicos esplendores de Thomas de Quincey y de Poe, de Charles Baudelaire y de Huysmans" [prognosticates, at least in a rudimentary away, the satanic splendors of Thomas De Quincy and Poe, of Charles Baudelaire and Huysmans] (*OC* II: 109; *Other Inquisitions* 140); Wakefield and Bartleby obscurely foreshadow K. and Gregor Samsa, although the significance of this foreshadowing is only revealed after reading *The Metamorphosis* and *The Trial*. Thomas Carlyle or Léon Bloy extended this typological exegesis to the totality of history, both conceiving it as a vast "texto litúrgico donde las iotas y los puntos no valen menos que los versículos o capítulos íntegros," although "la importancia de unos y de otros" is, for the moment, "indeterminable" and "profundamente escondida" [an immense liturgical text, where the eyes and the periods are not worth less than the versicles or whole chapters, but the importance of both is undeterminable and is profoundly hidden] (*OC* II: 94; *SNF* 362). Thus, in *L'Âme de Napoleon*, Bloy dedicates himself to "descifrar el símbolo Napoleón, considerado como *precursor* de otro héroe—hombre y simbólico también—que está oculto en el porvenir" [to decipher the symbol of *Napoleon*, considered as the *precursor* of another hero—a man and a symbol—who is hidden in the future] (*OC* II: 99; *Other Inquisitions* 127). These "enigmatic mirrors," these modest or reticent symbols, these secret messages whose meaning is just about to be revealed, correspond to the equivocation of the "aesthetic fact" from Borges's perspective. These "enigmatic mirrors" are signifiers awaiting a revelation that will come in the form of another signifier: although he is a flesh and blood historical figure, Napoleon's life is an extensive liturgy, a detailed ritual in which each action, each gesture, each word has a figurative or symbolic value that heralds the advent of another historical character, man and symbol both, in the same way that Julius Caesar, according to Bloy, had been a secret prefiguration of the French emperor.

This theory of human acts seems to preclude the existence of "free will," and Borges addressed this thorny question in a review of a book by Martin Davidson, *The Free Will Controversy*. That he decided to include this particular text in the second edition of *Discusión*, of the many brief reviews he wrote for *Sur* during those years, suggests the importance he attributed to this very problem. Davidson pointed out that the oldest form of determinism was "judicial astrology." For the Stoics, individuals were subject to the "influjos de los planetas" [influences of the planets] and this had allowed them to devise their theory of "omens": "formando un todo el universo" [forming the universe a whole], Borges writes, "cada una de las partes prefigura (siquiera de un modo secreto) la historia de las otras" [each part prefigures (even if in a secret way) the history of the others] so that, for Seneca, "todo cuanto ocurre es un signo de algo que ocurrirá" [everything that happens is a sign of something that will happen] (*OC* I: 282). The world is ordered in such a way, Cicero explained, "que a determinados acontecimientos, preceden determinadas señales que suministran las entrañas de las aves, los rayos, los prodigios, los astros, los sueños y los furores proféticos" [that certain signs supplied by the guts of birds, lighting bolts, prodigies, stars, dreams, and poetic bursts precede certain events] (*OC* I: 282). These omens were, from Borges's perspective, a primitive superstition, but good stories obeyed their logic. "Todo, entre los mortales" [Everything in the world of the mortals], explained the Roman narrator of one of the stories included in *El Aleph*, "tiene el valor de lo irrecuperable y de lo azaroso," "entre los Inmortales, en cambio, cada acto (y cada pensamiento) es el eco de otros que en el pasado lo antecedieron, sin principio visible, o el fiel presagio de otros que en el futuro lo repetirán hasta el vértigo" [has the value of the irrecoverable and contingent. Among the Immortals, on the other hand, every act (every thought) is the echo of others that preceded it in the past, with no visible beginning, and the faithful presage of others that will repeat it in the future, *ad vertiginem*] (*OC* I: 541–42; *CF* 192). "No hay cosa que no esté como perdida entre infatigables espejos," he concluded, and "nada puede ocurrir una sola vez, nada es preciosamente precario" [There is nothing that is not lost between indefatigable mirrors, he concluded, and nothing can happen just once, nothing is preciously precarious] (*OC* I: 542). It is enough to substitute the terms *mortal* and *immortal* for *real* and *symbolic* to understand the self-referential value of this passage from "El inmortal" [The Immortal].

In a 1932 essay, "El arte narrativo y la magia" [Narrative Art and Magic] Borges argued that this fabric of omens "es impertinente o inútil en el asiático desorden del mundo real, no así en la novela que debe ser un juego preciso de vigilancias, ecos y afinidades" [is out of place or pointless in the overwhelming disorder of the real world, but not in a novel, which should be a rigorous scheme of attentions, echoes, and affinities] (*OC* I: 231; *SNF* 81). At that time, Borges did not base his poetics on the providentialist theses of St. Paul or Léon Bloy, or on the Stoic doctrine of Seneca and Cicero, but upon English anthropologist James Frazer's *The Golden Bough*, and his famous theory of sympathy and contagion—or metaphor and metonym—as the primary axes of "primitive" thought. "Los hechiceros de la Australia Central se infieren una herida en el antebrazo que hace correr la sangre, para que el cielo imitativo o coherente se desangre en lluvia también" [medicine men in central Australia inflict a wound on their forearms to shed blood so that the imitative or consistent sky will shed rain] (*OC* I: 230; *SNF* 80), while many kinds of witches torment a wax or cloth doll to cause the individual it represents to suffer, or they perform some ritual with the hair, nails, or any garment belonging to the victim. Actions and gestures are "effective signs," as Duns Scotus called them: acts and words that do not merely evoke something but also provoke it and, for that very reason, predict it. Regarding Chesterton's meticulous fictions, Borges recalled a story that began with an "Indian" who killed his fellow tribesman by throwing a dagger at him and ended with the scene of an Englishman who murdered his friend by stabbing him with an arrow. The "cuchillo volador" [flying knife], Borges explained, prefigures the "flecha que se deja empuñar" [a plunged arrow] and this "proyección ulterior" [subsequent projection] of an episode, these temporary "echoes" that we could describe as "rimas narrativas" [narrative rhymes] characterize any good fiction, including "buenos films" [good films] (*OC* I: 231; *SNF* 81). Two decades later, Borges himself would write a story that began by evoking the death of a soldier, Francisco Flores, "lanceado por indios de Catriel" [speared by the Indians under Catriel] (*OC* I: 524; *CF* 175 [translation modified]), and concluded with his grandson, the librarian Juan Dahlmann, about to be stabbed to death in an anachronistic duel with a ranch hand "de rasgos achinados y torpes" [the young thug with an Indian-looking face] (an episode that Dahlmann may be dreaming while dying in a Buenos Aires hospital) (*OC* I: 528; *CF* 179). In "La muralla y los libros" [The Wall and the Books], Borges attributes to the emperor Shih Huang Ti a similar thought about historical repetitions: "Los hombres aman el pasado" he thinks, "y contra ese amor nada puedo, ni pueden mis verdugos, pero alguna vez habrá un hombre que sienta como yo, y ese destruirá mi muralla, como yo he destruido los libros, y ese borrará mi memoria y será mi sombra y mi espejo y no lo sabrá" [Men love the past and against that love there is nothing that I nor my executioners can do, but someday there will be a man who feels as I do, and he will destroy my wall, as I have destroyed the books, and he will erase my memory and will be my shadow and my mirror and will not know it] (*OC* II: 12; *SNF* 345).

There is no doubt that building the wall took decades of effort by hundreds of thousands of workers. But Borges was less interested in the material aspect of the work than in its symbolic aspect. "La muralla y los libros" was an essay devoted to speculating about the multiple meanings of that colossal building. "Acaso la muralla fue una metáfora," writes Borges, "acaso Shih Huang Ti condenó a quienes adoraban el pasado a una obra tan vasta como el pasado, tan torpe y tan inútil" [Perhaps the wall was a metaphor; perhaps Shih Huang Ti condemned those who adored the past to a work as vast as the past, as stupid and as useless] (*OC* II: 14; *SNF* 345). Like Noah's ark or Napoleon's military campaigns, human actions are symbolic writings addressed to a reader or theatrical performances addressed to a spectator. The Persian poet Omar Khayyam thought that "la historia del mundo es una representación que Dios, el numeroso Dios de los panteístas, planea, representa y contempla, para distraer su eternidad" [the history of the world is a representation of God, the numerous God of the pantheists, plans, represents, and contemplates to entertain his eternity] (*OC* II: 48). But in Borges's literature, that spectator is not necessarily divine. Each of the historical characters repeats, or imitates, some other character from the past, and their performance is directed, quite theatrically, toward a third party. Fighting a duel in the Pampas, Juan Dahlmann was reiterating his criollo military grandfather, but this performance, this identification, was directed toward the gaze of his German grandfather; we consequently cannot decide, at the beginning of the story, if the "antepasado romántico, o de muerte romántica" [romantic ancestor, or that of a romantic death] (*OC* I: 524; *CF* 174) mentioned by the narrator is the man of action or the man of letters (Scavino 23). For Borges, something similar could be seen with the Nazi sympathizers in Argentina. They "played" at being Vikings, Tartars, Spanish conquistadors, gauchos, or Indians (*OC* II: 106), but this dramatic plagiarism was aimed at the "romantic" gaze of Westerners (and perhaps Borges did not realize that, by posing this theory, he was paraphrasing Marx's *18th Brumaire*: history repeats itself because its actors need to imitate the characters of the past, as seen when the French revolutionaries of 1789 adopted the rhetoric and poses of Roman republicans). This kind of gaze that is fascinated with "barbarie enérgica" [vigorous brutality] (*OC* II: 106) was also held by Argentine nationalists: paradoxically, says Borges, they regarded gauchos and the rural world from the mystifying perspective of the foreigner or the tourist. For Borges, there was only one difference between European fascists and those Argentines, a difference that local nationalists failed to understand: while the Nazis' ideal hero was the soldier who fought in service to the Reich, the popular hero of the Argentine is Martín Fierro, Juan Moreira, or Hormiga Negra, that is, "el hombre solo que pelea con la partida" [the lone man who fights against the group] (*OC* II: 37; *SNF* 310) or against the representatives of the State. Whether they act, create, build, or fight, historical or literary characters are writing, or leaving meaningful impressions, for the person who eventually interprets them. When it comes to humans, the historical world is also governed by that "juego preciso de vigilancias, ecos y afinidades" [a rigorous scheme of attentions, echoes, and affinities] because human actions not only have a material effect but also a symbolic one (*OC* I: 231; *SNF* 81).

TRANSFIGURATIONS

No interpretation exhausts the meanings of a "symbol," declared Borges in 1937 when discussing the "parables" of his much-admired H. G. Wells, which he compares with the famous riddle attributed by Sophocles to the Sphinx: "¿Cuál es el animal que tiene cuatro pies en el alba, dos al mediodía, y tres en la tarde?" [What animal has four legs in the morning, two at noon, and three in the evening?] (*OC* I: 275). We immediately perceive that the answer, *human beings*, "es inferior al mágico animal que deja entrever la pregunta y a la asimilación del hombre a ese monstruo y de setenta años a un día y del bastón de los ancianos a un tercer pie" [is as inferior to the magical animal that is glimpsed in the question as an ordinary man is to that changeable monster, seventy years to one day, and an old man's staff to a third foot?] (*OC* I: 275). Something similar occurs in Borges's "La secta del Fénix" [The Sect of the Phoenix] where he creates a myth of a guild that is adept in an enigmatic ritual: we soon realize that this sect is all of humankind, and the secret ceremony, coitus—but the solution to this riddle is equally inferior to the mysterious liturgy proposed by the myth. The same happens, he believes, with the symbols that tradition has bequeathed us. In direct opposition to the ultraist poet he once was, for whom the creation of metaphors and symbols was the apex of poetry, the mature Borges understands that "el número de fábulas o de metáforas de que es capaz la imaginación de los hombres es limitado, pero que esas contadas invenciones pueden ser todo para todos, como el Apóstol" [the number of fables or metaphors of which men's imagination is capable is limited, but that these few inventions can be all things for all men, like the Apostle] (*OC* II: 153; *Other Inquisitions* 201). When Borges asserts that the same text assumes different meanings according to readerly purpose, he is simply maintaining that the same text, or even the same word, has different equivalents and that every reader will propose different substitutions depending on the times, the countries and even personal sensibilities, as was the case with the verb *espantar* in the seventeenth [to astonish] and twentieth [to frighten] centuries or with the name *Moses* from the first century onward. Hadn't he and Bioy Casares turned Juan Manuel de Rosas into a "precursor" of Juan Domingo Perón when they wrote "La fiesta del monstruo" [The Monster's Party]? And hadn't Léon Bloy made Julius Caesar a precursor of Napoleon Bonaparte? Borges and Bioy Casares thought that Rosas was a tyrant but also a symbol charged with announcing yet another tyrant, "hombre y simbólico también" [man and symbolic also], hidden in the future, though Rosas only became a "precursor" to Perón when the former rose to power—in other words, when, retrospectively, the copy "created" the original.

Making the "Historia de los ecos de un nombre" [A History of the Echoes of a Name] implied, for Borges, looking for the substitutions that different readers might propose for the same floating signifier, for example: *I Am That I Am* (Exodus 3:14). Universal history could then be understood as "la historia de unas cuantas metáforas" [the history of a few metaphors]—a few mutations or permutations—as occurs with his famous "La esfera de Pascal" [Pascal's Sphere] (*OC* II: 14; *SNF* 351). This sphere was *being* for Parmenides; *divinity* for Plato; the *universe* for Bruno; *nature* in Pascal. And if, in the texts of Bruno the Nolan, the infinity of this sphere like the "rotura de las bóvedas estelares" [breaking of the stellar vaults], seventy years later "no quedaba un reflejo de ese fervor y los hombres se sintieron perdidos en el tiempo y el espacio" [not even a glimmer of that fervor remained, and men felt lost in time and space] (*OC* II: 15; *SNF* 352). Pascal's *Pensées* do not interpret this infinite sphere as a metaphor for the liberation of humankind but rather as "un laberinto y un abismo" [a labyrinth and an abyss] (*OC* II: 16; *SNF* 353). Each one of the interpretations of that "sphere" was the "echo of a name" handed down to us by that reservoir of signifiers that is the archive or the library—in other words, the past. The history of thought or culture is not the invention of new metaphors, as the young collaborator in *Proa* or *Martín Fierro* once thought, but the history of new interpretations of some age-old concepts: "Empezaré la historia de las letras americanas con la historia de una metáfora; mejor dicho, con algunos ejemplos de esa metáfora" [I shall begin the history of American literature with the history of a metaphor; or rather, with some examples of that metaphor] (*OC* II: 48; *Other Inquisitions* 49).

In the same way that no amount of interpretation can exhaust the possibilities of a symbol, literature, in general, "no es agotable, por la suficiente razón de que un solo libro no lo es" [is not exhaustible, for the sufficient and simple reason that a single book is not] given that "una literatura difiere de otra, ulterior o anterior, menos por el texto que

THE MIDDLE ESSAYS AND REVIEWS 281

por la manera de ser leída" [one literature differs from another, either before or after it, not so much because of the text as for the manner in which it is read] (*OC* II: 125; *Other Inquisitions* 163). "La biblioteca de Babel" [The Library of Babel] was a masterful illustration of this theory, responding to Kurd Lasswitz, the German scientist who had calculated the dimensions of a library that would record "todas las posibles combinaciones de los veintitantos símbolos ortográficos" [all possible combinations of the twenty-two orthographic symbols] (*OC* I: 467; *CF* 115). In the prologue to *Ficciones* [*Fictions*] (1944), the Argentine acknowledged that he had written "La biblioteca de Babel" [The Library of Babel] after reading the German mathematician's story "The Universal Library," but suggested that they both had drawn from a common source: the atomist Leucippus of Miletus. In his treatise *On Generation and Corruption*, Aristotle evoked an analogy proposed by this Ionian philosopher: just as "Tragedy and Comedy are both composed of the same letters," the various entities of the universe are composed of multiple combinations of the same atoms (and thus the decomposition of bodies is nothing more than the dissolution of a specific association of elements) (trans. Joachim). Lucretius would subsequently declare: "Thus easier 'tis to hold that many things / Have primal bodies in common (as we see / The single letters common to many words)" and so "thou must confess each verse, each word / From one another differs both in sense / And ring of sound—so much the elements / Can bring about by change of order alone" (trans. Leonard). Borges would go on to say that the flower the protagonist of *The Time Machine* brought back from the future was composed of atoms that "ahora ocupan otros lugares y no se combinaron aún" [not yet assembled, now occupy other spaces] (*OC* II: 18; *SNF* 241). And although it is highly unlikely, nothing prevents those same atoms from ever combining to make up the "same" flower. The expression *amica silentia lunae* has eighteen letters and two spaces, meaning there are 2.43×10^{18} possible combinations (or, if one prefers, 2.43 followed by eighteen zeroes). Were someone to make every possible combination of these letters and spaces at a rate of one per second, it would take them over a century. But were there a device to speed up this monotonous task, one would obtain this same expression sooner or later, without having to turn to the Muse to explain its emergence. It would appear, upon returning, and it is to this reappearance that Borges refers when he recalls the ancient concept of circular time.

Nevertheless, both Lasswitz and Borges point out that most of the books in that "universal library" possess no meaning at all, as in the mere succession of letters of the alphabet or random variations in the letters of word that could possibly create an anagram. Only in a few rare cases do these letters combine in such a way that we, their readers, recognize meaningful segments, for the simple reason that the letters do not, in themselves, signify. Unlike signifiers, letters cannot be translated. When we move from one alphabet to another, they are transliterated. Letters remain identical to themselves no matter where they are placed in a combination (in AB and BA, the A remains the same letter). The meanings of the linguistic signs change according to their positions: In Spanish, the sound /a/ means "feminine" when placed at the end of the adjective *roja* [*red*]; it creates the "third person singular" when placed at the end of the verb *canta* [*sing*], it signifies "negation" when placed at the beginning of the adjective *asocial*, but also creates "verbalization" as in *acobardar* [to cow] or *aleccionar* [*to instruct*]. To devise his analytical language, John Wilkins must assign some value to the letters of the alphabet according to their position in a sequence. Thus *a* means animal, *ab* mammal, *abo* carnivore, and so on (*OC* II: 85). For them to assume that value, Wilkins had to propose a table of equivalences, and for his language to be universal, those equivalences would have to be accepted by all humans and remain unchanged over the centuries. In natural languages, the dictionary never stops changing, as happened, we have seen, with the word *espantar* or with the name *Moses*.

Unlike letters, signifiers are never identical to themselves: even when we utter those letters and consequently make them speak, they do not tell us what they mean, and interpreters supplant this "muteness of books" with other signifiers (*astonish/frighten, Moses/Jesus, blood/rain, Julius Caesar/Napoleon, Rosas/Perón*). For Borges, letters belong to the domain of identities; signifiers, to the domain of equivalencies. The letter combination ABCD is identical to the combination ABCD and differs from XYZA, even though the letter A is the same in both cases. Something similar occurs with the oxygen atom, whether it occurs in a water molecule (H_2O) or in carbon dioxide (CO_2). And this identity of the letters does not change over the centuries. The signifier *espantar,* on the other hand, was equivalent to *astonishing* in Quevedo's poems, but this equivalence changed when Spanish speakers began to use it to mean *frighten,* so that, although the word seems the same, it is not: the *espantar* of the seventeenth century does not have the same value as the *espantar* of the twentieth century. The letters are repeated in the same order; the signifiers they repeat are different. If Pierre Menard had wanted to write a *Quixote* that signified the same thing as Cervantes's *Quixote,* he would have had to write another text, that is, a totally different combination of letters, and Borges suggests that he would have had to speak of "estaciones de aprovisionamiento de nafta" [gas stations] instead of inns and taverns (*OC* II:45). Heraclitus's axiom is an adequate metaphor about the meaning of books but not about combinations of letters: the water of that river is always the same because, between two splashes, the water molecule continues to be composed of the same combination of atoms: H_2O. And that is why the image of the Pythagorean or Buddhist reincarnation, to which Borges refers in an essay on the link between the poet Omar Khayyam and his English translator, Edward FitzGerald, alludes to this "tránsito del alma por muchos cuerpos" [soul's passage through many bodies] (*OC* II:68; *SNF* 368) and does not correspond to the repetition of the same combination of letters or atoms but to an equivalence of signifieds: a translation or a gloss repeats what one text says, but does so in other terms. Like reincarnation, historical repetition is, in this case, a transfiguration.

At the beginning of his *Introducción a la literatura norteamericana* [*Introduction to North American Literature*], Borges attributes to George Berkeley the old topic of *translatio imperii,* which, in fact, goes back as far as Saint Augustine and which Marsilius of Padua addressed in a famous treatise: *De translatione imperii.* Berkeley asserted that "los imperios, como el sol, van de oriente a occidente" [Westward the Course of Empire takes its Way] (*Introducción* 5), so that history would come to an end with the emergence of the last great empire on the planet: the United States. Inspired by this same concept,

Sarmiento had reached a very similar conclusion in his *Viajes* (40). In Borges's readings, however, *translatio* acquires the meaning of transfer, but also of transit, transfiguration, and translation. As Jaime Concha (471) suggested, Borges would read "universal history" as if it were a literary history made of readings and rewritings, while de Toro (191) extended the concept of *translatio* to a whole set of semiotic operations amongst which translation, recoding and rereading stand out. This *translatio*, therefore, concerns signifiers and not letters, translation and not transliteration (Sylvia Molloy's essay *Las letras de Borges* alludes in this regard to writing in its condition of signifier).

Kafka does not create his precursors on the level of signifiers but of signifieds. The past bequeaths us its written traces or its "enigmatic mirrors," and the present proposes, in the manner of Paul of Tarsus, new equivalents, that is, new significations. The idea of a past created retrospectively was already present in Borges's 1929 poem, "Fundación mitológica de Buenos Aires" [The Mythological Founding of Buenos Aires] and the author often explained this phenomenon by recalling chapter IX of *The Analysis of Mind* in which Bertrand Russell proposed the *experimentum mentis* of a planet "creado hace pocos minutos, provisto de una humanidad que 'recuerda' un pasado ilusorio" [created only moments ago, filled with human beings who "remember" an illusory past] (*OC* I: 437 n.1; *CF* 74). Borges would again evoke Russell's conjecture in a passage from "Tlön, Uqbar, Orbis Tertius" with respect to *hrönir*, those objects that individuals believe they find but actually create with their minds: "La metódica elaboración de *hrönir* (dice el onceno tomo) ha prestado servicios prodigiosos a los arqueólogos. Ha permitido interrogar y hasta modificar el pasado, que ahora no es menos plástico y menos dócil que el porvenir" [the systematic production of *hrönir* (says Volume Eleven) has been of invaluable aid to archaeologists, making it possible not only to interrogate but even to modify the past, which is now no less plastic, no less malleable than the future] (*OC* I: 439–40; *CF* 77–78). This "plasticity" of the past resembles the "plasticity" of writings that are subject to many interpretations. And this is no accident: for Borges, as for any historian, the past is preserved in an archive comprised of documents as "plastic," as "modest," and as "mute" as any other writing: "es un espejo que declara los rasgos del lector y también un mapa del mundo" [it is a mirror that reflects the reader's own traits and it is also a map of the world] (*OC* II: 76; *Other Inquisitions* 91). Thus begins the first essay of *Otras inquisiciones*: the Chinese emperor Shih Huang Ti ordered the wall to be built and the burning of all books that predated him to thereby abolish history, or, in other words, to abolish the past.

Borges recalls P. H. Gosse who, to reconcile creationism and Darwinism, imagined that God created Adam and the various species that preceded that first *homo sapiens* at the same time; he recalls Piero Damiani, the theologian who suggested that God, because of his omnipotence, possessed the ability to transform the past (*OC* II: 28); he also evokes Oscar Wilde for whom "arrepentirse de un acto es modificar el pasado" [to repent of an action is to modify the past] (*OC* II: 70; *SNF* 315), and frequently refers to George Berkeley for whom that past can become a dream that we are having in the present. But these metaphysical speculations, which provided him with premises for his fantastic narratives, only assume the value of truth in reference to the universe of writing: Wakefield or Bartleby are, for us, two *hrönir* induced by reading Kafka, while the title *Martín Fierro* brings together a succession of different *hrönir*, such as those "found" by Lugones, Rojas, and Martínez Estrada. J. W. Dunne was not incorrect, then, when he declared in *Nothing Dies* that we knew eternity from the moment in which the past and the future became nothing more than dimensions of the present (*OC* II: 24). Shih Huang Ti need not have burned all the books: it would have been enough for his scholars to re-interpret them, much as Coleridge, Goethe, and Bradley would create, or exhume, their various *hrönir* of *Hamlet*. History, after all, is not only the succession of human acts and thoughts that leave written traces: it is also the succession of interpretations of those traces, interpretations that continually "modify the past" like the repentant in Wilde. In an etymological sense, these interpretations are also *interloans* or permutations of signifiers. History exists because of modesty, or because the enigmatic documen-tary traces left by human actions and thoughts are subject to countless equivalencies. If these traces abandoned their reticence, if they said everything, omitting nothing, there would be no need to interpret them, and historians would merely uncover, rather than interpret, the documents bequeathed to us by the past. History exists, then, for the same reason that there is literature: because signifiers, modest or laconic, si-lence their meanings, and because the signification of these elements is only unveiled when they come back around: transfigured, translated, or revealed. History exists be-cause the past endures in writings and because those writings and that past never stop metamorphosing with each new reading.

CONCLUSION

When something is "everything for everyone," it becomes a sacred entity: a part of that whole that is, paradoxically, the totality itself at the same time. A "map of the world," Borges would say, remembering an example from Josiah Royce:

> Imaginemos que una porción del suelo de Inglaterra ha sido nivelada perfectamente y que en ella traza un cartógrafo un mapa de Inglaterra. La obra es perfecta; no hay detalle del suelo de Inglaterra, por diminuto que sea, que no esté registrado en el mapa; todo tiene ahí su correspondencia. Ese mapa, en tal caso, debe contener un mapa del mapa; que debe contener un mapa del mapa del mapa, y así hasta lo infinito. (*OC* II: 47)

> [Let us suppose that a portion of the surface of England is very perfectly leveled and is then devoted to the production of a precise map of England. The work is perfect; there is not a single detail of the surface of England, however small it may be, that is not registered on the map; everything has its connection. That map, in such a case, should contain a map of the map, which should contain a map of the map of the map, and so on without limit.]

Some years after Royce, Bertrand Russell would attempt to resolve the paradox posed by this map. It had to be considered, in his opinion, as an anomalous or exceptional element, as if, despite being on English soil, it was not part of England. Something similar is found in Epimenides's paradox: if I admit that "everything I say is a lie," I cannot include this confession in the list of my statements. In effect, from time immemorial, this exceptional element, this part elevated to the dignity of the whole, is that which is sacred.

There is no coincidence in Borges evoking Royce's paradox in "Del culto de los libros" [On the Cult of Books]. Like Plato, the pagans mistrusted writing, regarding it merely as a silent substitute for orality. Our modern cult of books, he explained, begins with the religions that have a sacred script: Judaism, Christianity, and Islam. And this writing is sacred because it is part of the world, one more thing among others that became its "map" and, for this very reason, became something separate, something different from other things: something sacred. If we find book burning scandalous, it is because "un libro, cualquier libro, es para nosotros un objeto sagrado" [a book, any book, is for us a sacred object] (*OC* II: 91; *SNF* 358). The sacrilege does not reside, of course, in the mere disappearance of the material object but in the suppression of what is written. Study of the sacred, for Borges, does not consist of understanding what a particular text means but rather how writing works in general, for to understand the function of writing is to understand the function of the world and of history. According to Bloy, Borges said, "somos versículos o palabras o letras de un libro mágico, y ese libro incesante es la única cosa que hay en el mundo: es, mejor dicho, el mundo" [we are the versicles or words or letters of a magic book, and that incessant book is the only thing in the world: more exactly, it is the world] (*OC* II:94; *SNF* 362). And is this not precisely what Heidegger proposed as a definition of metaphysical discourse? Metaphysics is characterized by elevating an entity to the dignity of being: the idea, God, the will, the conscience, and so on. A contemporary of Heidegger and Wittgenstein—a contemporary of *the linguistic turn*—Borges identified being and writing. As the inhabitants of Tlön believed, metaphysics is a branch of literature, not only because Berkeley or Leibniz provided Borges with excellent premises for his speculative fictions, but also, and above all, because from their point of view, there was no difference between metaphysics and poetry.

Notes

1. Cf. Silvio Mattoni's chapter in this volume.
2. Any English translation of Borges's text not accompanied by a citation is owed to the absence of any existing English publication and is the work of the present translator.
3. Cervantes's line was, in fact, "Voto a Dios que me espanta esta grandeza."

Works Cited

Aristotle. *On Generation and Corruption*, translated by H. H. Joachim. Internet Classics Archive, http://classics.mit.edu/Aristotle/gener_corr.mb.txt. Accessed January 11, 2023.
Badiou, Alain. *Saint Paul. La fondation de l'universalisme*. PUF, 1997.

Balderston, Daniel. "Borges ensayista." *El siglo de Borges*. Edited by Alfonso de Toro, Vervuert, 1999, vol. 1, pp. 565–77.

Borges, Jorge Luis. *Obras completas*. 4 vols. Emecé, 1996.

Borges, Jorge Luis, and Esther Zemborain. *Introducción a la literatura norteamericana*. Alianza, 1996.

Concha, Jaime. "El Aleph: Borges y la historia." *Revista Iberoamericana*, vol. 49, nos. 123–124, 1983, pp. 471–85.

de Toro, Alfonso. "Jorge Luis Borges: *Translatio* e Historia." *In memoriam Jorge Luis Borges*. Edited by Rafael Olea Franco, Colegio de México, 2006, pp. 191–236.

de Toro, Alfonso, ed. *Jorge Luis Borges: Translación e Historia*. Georg Olms Verlag, 2010.

Lévi-Strauss, Claude. "Introduction à l'œuvre de M. Mauss." *Sociologie et anthropologie*. Edited by Marcel Mauss, PUF, 1950, pp. IX–LII.

Lucretius. *On the Nature of Things*, translated by William Ellery Leonard. E. P. Dutton, 1916. http://www.perseus.tufts.edu/hopper/text?doc=Perseus:abo:phi,0550,001:1:797.

Molloy, Sylvia. *Las letras de Borges y otros ensayos*. Beatriz Viterbo, 1999.

Sarlo, Beatriz. *Un escritor en las orillas*. Ariel, 1998.

Sarmiento, Domingo Faustino. *Viajes en Europa, África y América*. Julio Belin, 1851.

Scavino, Dardo. "El autor y su musa." *Cuadernos Lirico*, no. 1, 2006, pp. 13–31.

CHAPTER 16

VIRGIL'S KEEPSAKES

Memory and Oblivion in Poetic Form

SILVIO MATTONI

IN the prologue to *La rosa profunda* [*The Insightful Rose*] (1975), Borges writes that every verse must fulfill two duties: "comunicar un hecho preciso y tocarnos físicamente, como la cercanía del mar" [communicate a precise evento and touch us physically, like the closeness of the sea] (*OC* III: 77). He then uses a line from Virgil as an example: "*Sunt lacrimae rerum et mentem mortalia tangunt*" (*Aeneid*, I, 462), which could be translated as: "They are tears of things and mortality touches your mind," or, given the context: "They are tears for past things and those mortal ones affect your spirit." Translators highly trained in philology tend to paraphrase, straying rather far from the physical, condensed aspect of the verse. Javier de Echave-Sustaeta thus interprets the line: "Aquí también hay lágrimas para las desventuras, / la breve vida humana lancina el corazón" [Here too are there tears for misadventures, / the brief human life lancinates the heart], causing simple things to become contaminated with the ill-fated aspect of sorrow, and "mortal things" or mortality in general to function as a commentary on human life, notably, with a mere touch being forceful enough to tear a wound (Virgil 1997: 154). Another Spanish translator, Rafael Fontán Barreiro, offers: "Lágrimas hay para las penas y tocan el corazón las cosas de los hombres" [There are tears for sorrows and the heart is touched by things of men], reiterating his colleague's emphasis on the sadness of first things, but here maintaining the physical simplicity of the verb that touches mortal affairs, despite adding "men" for context (Virgil 1990: 19). Borges does not note where in the *Aeneid* the verse is found; he is interested in its truth and its rhythm. But the emotion it communicated for him would be that of memory: something suddenly, materially awakens the memory of the fleeing Trojans and moves them. They have just arrived on the shores of Carthage not knowing how they will be received. The city is being fortified. Aeneas seems to compare the joy of those who built its walls with the ruins he has left behind. Then he enters a temple constructed on the order of Queen Dido and there sees the combatants of Troy painted on its walls; it is then that he says to one of his companions "*Sunt lacrimae rerum et mentem mortalia tangunt*" (*Aeneid*, I, 462). The paintings recall the glory and misfortune of his city: Aeneas then knows that he will be welcome. He is given over to tears remembering past events, and Virgil, to the ekphrasis of those paintings that recalls Homer's *Odyssey*. It is worth noting that the scene more generally recalls Ulysses' tears when he hears, in the court of the Phaeacians, the lines of song describing the Trojan War. In both cases, paintings and verses are talismans of a memory suddenly recalled and whose details touch the soul of the person remembering. For this reason, in a number of poems, Borges lists objects that hold a vestige of memory, even while poems, as a physical fact, can fulfill that function themselves.

In the short story that gives Borges's book *El hacedor* [*Dreamtigers*] (1960) its name, Homer, the first quintessential poet, whose figure is sunken in myth, encounters "los goces de la memoria" [the pleasures of memory] (*OC* II: 159; *CF* 292) and manages to recover some of the memories that stand out against the hazy background of his blindness. More than duels to the death, love, stories which, once heard, must be captured in hexameters never to be forgotten, what matters here is the act of remembering. Before constructing his world of verses about stories that may have already existed—impressions, sensations occupied the poet's mind, touched him too physically. But losing his sight would provide the poet a different way to touch, one that originates by descending into his memory, to "sacar de aquel vértigo el recuerdo perdido" [draw up from that vertigo the lost remembrance], whose content is less important than its appearance, shining like coins in the rain (*OC* II: 159; *CF* 293). Only then would he be able to compose "Odiseas e Ilíadas" [Odysseys and Iliads] without sensorially experiencing the descent into memory with anything but his words, which emerge, are forged, and shine like coins. In this descent, not a single impression or anticipation can be found, nor does the rhythm of the verse elicit an image, not even in the writer's footsteps as he descends "a la última sombra" [into his last darkness] (*OC* II: 160; *CF* 293). The images, the stories that are retrieved from memory—which not only include impressions, unique sensations, but also the words that were repeated and which name these images and feelings (that which what is heard can at times take on the form of a memory)—, all would be transformed into objects that cannot so easily sink into oblivion. Thereby, these poetic figures or scenes would become what, fifteen years later, Borges would call "Talismans": books, things loved because they were gifts, "Líneas de Virgilio y de Frost. / La voz de Macedonio Fernández" [Lines of Virgil and Frost. / The voice of Macedonio Fernández] (*OC* III: 111; *SP* II: 365). Yet these substitutes for remembrance, even if they allow the fixed form of a memory to be shaped around them, cannot avoid the indescribable and final moment when the person remembering must face his own disappearance, "la sombra que no puedo nombrar" [the dark I cannot name] (*OC* III: 111; *SP* II: 365).

If we were to think mythologically, we know what success Orpheus had in descending to search after a beloved memory. But although, in the end, his beloved dissolves like a mirage, Orpheus comes away from his search with his poem, which does not completely disappear. The price, perhaps, is that he himself must become the poem, cease his endless remembering to establish the formal limits of memory, like a floating head reciting verses in a river that always repeats itself.

In *La cifra* [*The Limit*] (1981), another poem is also titled "El hacedor," but it does not retell the origin of an epic; it is not about Homer but addresses a more humble task: how to write—using the matter of memory, literature, things, and moments—poems that cannot be lost. In hendecasyllables, that verse form so appreciated for its both baroque and modernist sound, but which here might have an echo of the variable emphases from the more extensive hexameter, the poet gives himself over to turning his images and words into what he calls "el verso incorruptible" [the incorruptible lines] (*OC* III: 309; *SP* II: 443). Yet this belief in immortality through literature, viewed from the twilight age of a life, is continually belied because tangible memory descends into the body, into that recurrence that will, by definition, become corrupted. As a formal sign of negated immortality, the poem ends by breaking with the previous twenty-seven hendecasyllables, in their impersonal enumeration, and deploying a seven-syllable, interrupted line, which is further altered by the parenthesis: "Y (es mi deber) salvarme" [And (this is my duty) save myself] (*OC* III: 309; *SP* II: 443), as if, in a way, the goal of the poem was to deny personal death, or at least redeem it. Poetry, or literature, would thus assume Horace's classic personal justification: the "verso incorruptible" would be an avatar of the monument more lasting than bronze.

In the final poem of Book III of the *Odes*, which definitively completed the set, Horace affirmed his posthumous success: *Exegi monumentum aere perennius* ("I have built a monument more lasting than bronze.")[1] The work will not be corrupted, undermined by countless ages or the flight of time—at least while the rites of Rome lasted, which, in Horace's time, seemed eternal. History's confirmation of Horace's poem, however, may owe less to the rhythmic consistency of its originality than to the same random fortune affecting any monument. Both the pyramids in his ode (*regalique situ pyramidum altius*) and the minor Asclepiadean that it imported from Greek lyricism are present there in their same places, but time has changed their meaning: neither immortality nor the Latin language belong in the speech of the present.

Borges is thereby able to think of impossible memories, of forgotten poets or lost languages, as in the poem titled "A un poeta menor de 1899" [To a Minor Poet of 1899], in *El otro, el mismo* [*The Other, The Same*] (1964). An interpellation is made with the poet, whose claim to make eternal a given moment, some intense point of a life, is destined to fail—or rather achieves its goal, but in being eternally forgotten. Given that oblivion must prevail in the end—if an entire language can cease to exist, then every writer can necessarily be forgotten. Yet their achievements existed and perhaps continue to exist, even in oblivion: "No sé si lo lograste ni siquiera, / vago hermano mayor, si has existido" [I do not know if ever you succeeded / Nor, vague elder brother, if you existed] (*OC* II: 278; *SP* II: 205). And in the same year the poet was born who is now writing a sonnet about oblivion, the other may have been writing "el extraño verso" [strange verse], trying to capture in words the light, the colors of a moment (*OC* II: 278; *SP* II: 205). The poem concludes in a supplication lifted to that very nonexistence: "quiero que el olvido / restituya a los días tu ligera / sombra" [(I) want oblivion / To restore your fleeting shade to the days], because in that communication to the forgotten, in that figure from another century, in that image dedicated to the useless task of a lost verse is inscribed the possibility of remembering the afternoon, both the other's and one's own (*OC* II: 278; *SP* II: 205).

Horace also imbued his immodest description of poetry with an idea of survival. If the poems are not forgotten, their author, that individual claiming "I" in each line of that immaterial monument, will not be so either. Thus he wrote: *Non omnis moriar multaque pars mei / vitabit Libitinam* ("I shall not wholly die; and a great part of me shall escape Libitina [the grave]"). Within those verses, in whose isosyllabism some philologists locate the remote ancestor of the Romance languages' hendecasyllable verse form, a part of the poet resides—an important part. And the following verse clarifies that the poem is not about a being's simple division into matter and spirit because only a body can avoid the dominion of Libitina, goddess of corpses, patroness of funeral rites. "Not wholly dying" would be, in a way, not to completely surrender to the fate of the body. Horace thereby establishes the contrast between the poem in its incorruptibility and the body— the entity that is corruptible par excellence.

Borges, while at times imagining the incorruptibility of certain literary objects, such as the poems of Homer, seems rather to dispute this declaration of personal survival. The "hacedor" composes the stories that will forever be repeated, but he himself surrenders to oblivion or his name is lost among the shadows cast by the poems. And if Homer's existence is debated within philology, especially within Romance Studies, the imagined life of Horace can also be reduced to the vestige of a given collection of poetry. The duty to rescue the day or the evening, to capture the moment, rhythmically pronouncing his imperative: *carpe diem*, does not necessarily imply Horace's success in escaping total death.

Thus, in his *sphragis*, instead of begging the muse for the definitive, immortal acceptance, Horace ends his ode: *Sume superbiam / Quaesitam meritis et mihi Delphica / lauro cinge volens, Melpomene, comam* ("Melpomene, assume that pride which your merits have acquired, and willingly crown my hair with the Delphic laurel"). The poet's greatest pride would be the acceptance of death. If anything remains of a life, even without becoming material for a book, it will be so similar to its physical vestige as to be indistinguishable. The body gives itself to the written prayer, which is not addressed to anyone and could be read, perhaps, by anyone.

In *Elogio de la sombra* [*In Praise of Darkness*] (1969), we find Borges' response to Horace's arrogance in the short prose piece "Una oración" [A Prayer]. It begins with allusions to prayer, the timeless "Our Father," but declares the intention of it being a personal prayer, said on a specific day in 1969. The long opening paragraph is proposed as a series of denials; nothing is requested: facts cannot be changed, and forgiveness provides relief only to the one who grants it. Finally, since one cannot give what he does not have—courage, hope, or willingness to learn—the first conclusion is expressed as a series of wishes: "Quiero ser recordado menos como poeta que como amigo" [I want to be remembered less as a poet than as a friend] (*OC* II: 392; *CF* 339). It would, however, be a friendship indivisible from books, the closeness of a friend who compels one to read, to share some verses that they have found and loved. The justice and lucidity that are then mentioned also seem to be the attributes of a critic, a friend who can communicate that desire to read. Yet an abrupt sentence separates itself from the rest of the poem: "Quiero morir del todo; quiero morir con este compañero, mi cuerpo" [I want to die completely; I want to die with this body, my companion] (*OC* II: 392; *CF* 339). Given the evidence of time, which has refuted Horace, reducing him to the rank of a mere thing, a book—one cannot assert that death is not complete, even desirable. Being a poet from a language and a country now lost, subject to chance encounters, to seemingly inexorable oblivion would not be true survival because it would lack friendship. But there is a paradox in the prayer, between "ser recordado" [being remembered] and "morir del todo" [dying completely], that can be found in its imprint, the addressee of the act of writing. To whom or what is the prayer addressed? To whomever reads it, of course, not to some unlikely entity exempt from time. Therefore, the poet's writing undercuts the desire it expresses. He does not give in to the temptation to leave no traces. Even when one no longer believes, with Horace's ingenuous arrogance, in the immortality of works, the relativity of that desire can still be found in the vestiges of memory, the possibility of friendship, the gift of what one does not have (for one who is dead has nothing to give). If what is given "as a friend" is the love of literature, the impressions it made—writings can age, be forgotten, and then be recovered through history, but they remain part of the writer. It is not, as Horace boasted "a great part of me," but a small part, the desire, as Borges writes, for "una sinceridad más que humana" [a sincerity that is more than human] that does not disappear entirely (*OC* II: 392; *CF* 339).

In 1976, in one of *La moneda de hierro*'s [*The Iron Coin*] many sonnets, the idea of complete death resurfaces. The poem "A mi padre" [To My Father] begins with this verse: "Tú quisiste morir enteramente" [You wished to die entirely and for good] (*OC* III: 141; *SP* II: 381).[2] It is a death interpreted as a peaceful, almost happy ending, "sonriente y ciego" [smiling and blind] (*OC* III: 141; *SP* II: 381). Even as the father, in his son's memory, is still explaining to him the archetypes of ancient philosophy, the son knows his father expected nothing beyond the cessation of the body, the interruption of a memory. Thus, the father also wanted to die completely in the sense of resisting the desire to produce a work into which he would have deposited a part of himself. Reading and reflection fueled his entire life, but his attempts at writing were minimal. And, then again, perhaps the father did not die "entirely" because he passed on to the son something akin to hope: the desire to write. His death would thus never be complete because a part of the deceased permanently marks the memory of the son. Still, the greater part, contrary to what Horace boasted, must disappear. In effect, the depthless memory, objects, voices, recollections of a moment that cannot fit within the simple verbal enumeration of all it contains is lost with the body. The voice of Macedonio, for example, heard by father and son, perhaps with different intensities, is a memory comparable to the page of a book, to a verse that persists and returns, to something touched many times and kept in a drawer in a room; but its materiality, not its evocation in a poem or a dialogue, will be erased with the body. In a work, then, in what is written, even in the memorable form of a perfectly crafted verse, the greater part of the writer cannot be recovered; one is left with but the fragments of an inaccessible totality. In any case, each fragment of memory may also reveal the trace of someone else. The blind father, smiling because he

292   SILVIO MATTONI

dies almost entirely, will keep returning, in a way, in the name and the poem of the son who remembers his father's passing.

Then again, in that tide that covers and uncovers recollections or words, memory can usher forth fragments that had been overlooked: dreams, repeated days, illustrations one might have seen in a childhood book: "La memoria / me concede esta lámina de un libro / cuyo color y cuyo idioma ignoro" [Memory / has given me this image in a book / whose color and language I ignore] (*OC* III: 188). Rather than a sea, where remembrances float and may eventually reach a shore, in the poem entitled "El grabado" [The Engraving], from *Historia de la noche* [*History of the Night*] (1977) memory can also be a palace, or a complex of "cóncavas grutas" [concave caves] (*OC* III: 188). There, around every corner, lies the hideous material of nightmares, which exists in the same space as any ordinary day, but also there can be found the memory of calm, the possibility of thought, "la razón y su ejercicio" [reason and its practice], writes Borges. The return of sumptuous memories, the heavenly side of memory, transforms the cave into a library and the inhospitable tide into fresh water, with simple things that stop time or reverse it: "La tersura del ébano invariable / O—luna y sombra—el oro de Virgilio" [The smoothness of unchanging ebony / Or—moon and shadow—the gold of Virgil] (*OC* III: 188). And yet, the gold in the poem cannot make up for what was lost. It is like a talisman against death, a consolation whose material is easily transfixed into an image, an *ersatz* of the body in the very process of disappearing: the operation of memory has the same fluidity, the same fleetingness as life.

Memory, in other words, is comprised of a lost part. At times what is missing may be the greater part of a lifetime, but, at others, it may be a part that is found, which stands out in relief against oblivion, and which can sometimes recover in the enduring space of poetry even more lost parts: those who died, those who lived nearby, those who made their marks in books and those who did not. In the poem dedicated upon the death of his friend, "Manuel Peyrou," Borges commemorates "la amistad genial" [fantastic friendship], their shared tastes and readings, but above all, he highlights the presence of an individual: "Yo lo he visto" [I saw him] (*OC* III: 195); his literature is also praised, "fábulas que el tiempo / no dejará caer" [tales that time / will not let fall] (*OC* III: 195). In that manner of living on, preserved in part in Peyrou's writing, the friend is evoked in the poem, not his image or his work, but rather his lasting presence. Though the poem is in part an elegy for his dead friend, what it conveys is not a complete farewell. In the rhythm of the poem, which conveys the affection felt for so many years, that part of his friend that does not die is treasured: "Llanamente / Hemos hablado de un querido amigo / Que no puede morir. Que no se ha muerto" [Plainly / We have spoken about a dear friend / Who cannot die. Who has not died] (*OC* III: 195). That same concept of incomplete oblivion, of memory partially triumphing, even celebrating the heroism of its own foreseeable defeat, can be applied to yet another subject: Borges himself. He persists, that part of him that writes himself into his work; it is the body that dies, the dear companion who absents himself.

Borges has written many texts that interrogate this process, at times ironically. In "Límites" [Limits] from *El otro, el mismo*, the enumeration of lost things, of all the details that will be forgotten (and yet which the poem paradoxically revives), conjures up a vast compilation of experiences and readings, a "rumor de multitudes que se alejan" [turbulent murmur of crowds milling and fading away] that then "son lo que me ha querido y olvidado; / Espacio y tiempo y Borges ya me dejan" [they are all I have been loved by; / Space, time, and Borges now are leaving me] (*OC* II: 258; *SP* II: 183). Borges's own name is included in the category of lost things, like books, like important moments, and joins the crowd in its slow march toward oblivion. Yet neither is the inexorability of the loss absolute, even from the perspectives that locate the source of one's gaze upon the world—from a place, a time period, a name given at a specific moment in time. The limits of what is lost stand out against the contours of what is partially recovered, this being the very subject of the poem: the potential revivals of memory. Even more ironically, the poem "G. A. Bürger" from *Historia de la noche*, proposes the fiction of a contemporary figure based on the eighteenth-century German poet Gottfried August Bürger who nevertheless lives next to the plains, in a city that can only be Buenos Aires, named in clef, "la ciudad junto al río inmóvil" [the city beside the unmoving river] referring to the title of a novel Borges publicly disparaged, written by contemporary novelist.[3] The erstwhile narrator of the poem feels greatly affected by "las cosas que le sucedieron a Bürger" [the things that happened to Bürger], which are fairly common for most people or which are unique but not exceptional, like hearing the voices of dead poets, like writing poems (*OC* III: 191). The closing of the piece seems to suggest that Bürger, who is alone, writing in Buenos Aires, is also composing a few verses, the poem "G. A. Bürger," in a book by Borges in that same "now." Against all hope of recollection, "sabía que el presente no es otra cosa / que una partícula fugaz del pasado / y que estamos hechos de olvido" [I knew that the present was not anything else / but a fleeting particle from the past / and that we are made of oblivion] (*OC* III: 191); however, he "lima unos versos" [refines some verses], builds a thing with material that is only partly physical, where the present can again be recognized in its novelty. The task seems useless, the past seems to annul the present; still the poem is being written in the hopes of becoming a shining speck of gold for others to discover and in whose words they might find the friendly shadows of their own lives yet to come.

It is not a contradiction to state, on the one hand, that there is an enduring friendship, a possibility of life returning from the past, a verse read so often that it has become engraved upon the memory despite the rushing multitude of forgotten verses, and on the other, to assert that oblivion is the goal for every poem. Although poetry, once written, exists as a thing, even when lost amid books, among the anthologies that have forgotten it, that *thing* still existed once and, as a remnant, endures. Memory then, like moments of revelation in literature, is not a sum of treasured objects but a subtraction, a retrieval from the stream of oblivion. And physically writing down a recollection, with its rhythm and its phrasing, modifies the flowing course of oblivion; writing affords memory a landmark, a point on which to focus: the fleeting moment taken out of time. But fleetingness can only be read by other fleeting beings. Memory, ephemeral or forgettable, is an emblem of death. Thus, if there existed such a thing as immortality, always repeated and empty, it could not read the written movement of a life, which summons the remains of the past awaiting the finality of memory and of the body. Something is enciphered in the writing that always awaits the arrival of the other.

Though Virgil, for example, has died—as have his epoch, his language, and his memory—he remains a possibility for experience: an hexameter, a place where it was learned, its deciphering, its memorization with the exhilaration of finding that shining remnant which lasted far longer than a mortal body ever could. Someone, with a fleeting and limited memory, once felt the physical contact of the verse, its conceptual truth inseparable from its rhythmic effect; someone may have spied the gold of its meaning, indistinguishable from the lunar shadow of its cadence. In "La cifra," a poem from the eponymous book (1981), a line from the *Aeneid* returns once again: "La amistad silenciosa de la luna / (cito mal a Virgilio) te acompaña" [The silent friendship of the moon / (I am quoting Virgil badly) accompanies you] (*OC* III: 337). The *cifra*,[4] or figure, being counted includes the number of times the poem's addressee contemplated the moon, an emblem of literature for millennia while also present in poetry's most recent antecedents; both are equally distant from the poet's memory of symbolism or modernism among other imprecise historical classifications. But the count does not yet end because the forgetting of each contemplation or each distracted glimpse of that evening light renews its discovery. Every night, without speaking a word, one can feel the moon's silent friendship; and, what is more, in the past, which is never static, though there may be a literal number of times one may contemplate the moon in a lifetime, that quantity keeps shifting, the number is always lost. The number will stop increasing when it is the last moon for the person who remembers it, he who silently counts out his eleven-syllable verses to denote another, less fleeting silence in the sky. For Virgil's verse is placed in a passage that announces death, the destruction of a city, of friends who were previously remembered in the scene of Aeneas' sorrow, when memories of those events turned to tears and the mortality of all beings weighed so heavily on his mind. The actual verse reads: *a Tenedo tacitae per amica silentia lunae* (*Aeneid* II 255; Virgil 1990: 29). Here, the Greek ships advanced silently through the night, capitalizing on the horse already within the city walls, while all the Trojans slept. And the ships advance with that "silent friendship of the moon," complicit in the coming destruction, so indifferent to mortal beings that it can have no allies. That same friendship then, a last glimpse before a peaceful death, is elicited through the line, "en un jardín o un patio que son polvo" [in a garden or a courtyard that are dust], because Troy is the end, the cipher of every life (*OC* III: 337). Yet, what was is still remembered: even ruin is a thing repeated in images and in verses. And in the words spoken *hic et nunc* through the action of remembering, the present, aware of its destiny, receives its own affirmation.

In another poem, "The Thing I Am," which references Shakespeare, Borges translates: "Soy la cosa que soy" [I am the thing that I am] (*OC* III: 197). It thereby alludes to the time of the present and to its connection to memory, which also unfolds in the memories of a body, of a certain name, and in history and literature. The forgetting of one's own name becomes the memory of all others, ciphered in the name and in those who no longer have one: "Soy su memoria, pero soy el otro" [I am their memory, but also someone else] (*OC* III: 196). In the *thing* that utters its memory is inscribed the past, or what remains of it, as that past exists in the form of voices that are able to rescue the precision of a world. For this thing that forgets its singular name to thereby be anyone and everyone, to become the speaker of many poems, the character of the dream, that reader of hexameters, may perhaps wish to "salvar un orbe que huye / Del fuego y de las aguas de la Ira / Con un poco de Fedro y de Virgilio" [save a world that flees / From the water and the first of the Wrath to come / armed with a few tags of Phaedrus and Virgil] (*OC* III: 196). In Borges's endnote on Shakespeare's quote, one glimpses an almost theological sketch of that *thing*, as relating to a divinity that is at the same time both man and the absolute:

> Parolles, personaje subalterno de *All's Well That Ends Well*, sufre una humillación. Súbitamente lo ilumina la luz de Shakespeare y dice las palabras:
>
> > *Captain I'll be no more;*
> > *But I will eat and drink, and sleep as soft*
> > *As captain shall. Simply the thing I am*
> > *Shall make me live.*
>
> En el verso penúltimo se oye el eco del tremendo nombre Soy El Que Soy, que en la versión inglesa se lee *I am that I am*. (Buber entiende que se trata de una evasiva del Señor urdida para no entregar su verdadero y secreto nombre a Moisés.) Swift, en las vísperas de su muerte, erraba loco y solo de habitación en habitación, repitiendo *I am that I am*. Como el Creador, la criatura es lo que es, siquiera de manera adjetiva. (*OC* III: 203)
>
> [Parolles, a minor character in *All's Well That Ends Well*, endures a humiliation. Suddenly he is illuminated by Shakespeare's light and speaks the words,
>
> > *Captain I'll be no more;*
> > *But I will eat and drink, and sleep as soft*
> > *As captain shall. Simply the thing I am*
> > *Shall make me live.*
>
> In the next-to last line can be heard an echo of the tremendous name *I am that I am*. (It is Buber's understanding that we have here a cunning evasion by the Lord so as not to reveal His true and secret name to Moses.) Swift, on the eve of his death, wandered from room to room, mad and solitary, saying over and over, *I am that I am*. Like the Creator, the creature is what he is, although with attributes.] (Borges, "The Thing I Am")

It is not unironic that the belief in an absolute being assumes the aspect of madness, the loss of the name and the rationality by which a subject recognizes itself; according to the first line of the poem: "He olvidado mi nombre. No soy Borges" [I have forgotten my name. I am not Borges] (*OC* III: 196). This is underscored by the reference to Swift wandering through the house repeating "*I am that I am*" (*OC* III: 203). It is an irony present when a Shakespeare character states: *Simply the thing I am / Shall make me* ("Sencillamente esta cosa que soy / me hará vivir"). The name Parolles, who plays a minor, almost picaresque character in *All's Well That Ends Well*, in fact means "words."

Thus, phrases that accumulate and that are suddenly, as Borges says, illuminated by Shakespeare's light, find their expression. The English line, though, is less baroque than Borges's translation, which is literal where many Spanish versions prefer to paraphrase, using a relative construction to avoid the noun *cosa* [*thing*]. With Shakespeare, we will hear the word "thing" in other works—from the mouth of Desdemona, for example (*Othello*, Act II, scene 1), who argues: *I am not merry, but I do beguile / The thing I am, by seeming otherwise*. In this case, no longer being oneself does not allow the possibility of being any- or everyone. Rather, being a thing implies appearance and the possibility of both portraying oneself and of being seen in different ways. Parolles, to the contrary, with his rhythmic words illuminated in the felicitous expression, offers Borges an expansion of memory—not of records or history or its monuments, but the tacit experience of every speaker. "The thing I am" is rescued from oblivion's fire under the protection of the poetry of Phaedrus, who was, in his turn, a character; of Virgil, who wrote and who was for another, Dante, a remembered friend—as he was for others, like Borges, now nameless, just part of a memorable friendship. Only in the words of a minor character in a comedy is this faith in language as salvation affirmed as a possible future of memory. Only the act of writing, which is having read and having loved what was read, will give life to the thing one is.

It is not only a matter of personal salvation, proudly defeating death in the style of Horace, but also of a possibility extended to that innumerable world of readings, conversations, and moments: entire cities whose rumblings can be heard in certain books, like Carthage and Troy in Virgil's poem. More skeptically, given the refutation of literary immortality we have seen in other Borges poems, salvation can also be found in the feelings that imprint themselves upon given words, phrases, verses, from a specific day or the days that a body has accumulated over a lifetime. Of course, if that life belonged to a friend who shared in the writer's own life, it becomes a story, joining the series of other stories that memory constructs against the backdrop of forgotten repetitions, infusing with intimacy what would otherwise be an enumeration of arbitrary details.

There is also something to be found in the negative space, the impossible elegy of a life not lived, registering what could have been possible, what only poetry can transform from a lost future into a relic. Thus, "En memoria de Angélica" [In Memory of Angélica], from *La rosa profunda* (1975), dedicated to a great-niece who died when just a few years old, emphatically proclaims the vast space of what is possible when what is real is suddenly annulled: "Cuántas posibles vidas se habrán ido / En esta pobre y diminuta muerte" [How many possible lives will have gone / with this unfortunate and tiny death] (*OC* III: 108). Considering how she will not be limited by the specific details of an adult life, like a flower unknowingly sinking in water, in Borges's metaphor,[5] the writer wonders about his own end, which will be the exact opposite. "Cuando yo muera morirá un pasado" [When I die a past will die], he observes, comparing his place in individual time with the future of the girl, which has been "arrasado por los astros" [pulled down from the stars] (*OC* III: 108). However, the opposition is false. And the poem will reveal the potential identification between the old man and the girl, between the one who remembers and that lamented flower who opened inside the impossible, in oblivion: "Yo, como ella, muero de infinitos / Destinos que el azar no me depara" [I, like her, die of infinite / destinies that fate does not afford me] (*OC* III: 108). The writer looks for other lives in the past, remembers myths and books, yearns to learn languages no longer spoken; she, too, becomes a memory, for her loved ones, for the poem that honors her, tears for things that do not fulfill their destiny—but, on the brief inscription on a marble tomb and in the books already written, history accumulates: that enumeration that dilutes individual acts, never to be repeated, into a series of vain repetitions.

And yet, repetition itself, that ever-returning time of oblivion, does not fail to serve as the possibility of a memory: the poem extracts its material from time. As with Virgil, through fragments, through found music and meaning, it survives. Everything seems to repeat itself, sinking into peaceful oblivion, but suddenly, as occurs in Borges's "Heráclito" [Heraclitus], one is struck by a persistent verse. On the banks of a silent river (in Borges's hypallage), that first philosopher, Heraclitus (to whom the term "philosopher" was still unknown), would pronounce his well-known axiom about the impossibility of repetition, where no one steps into the same river twice. This of course includes his own future commentary: not only does the river change and flow, but he himself "es un río y una fuga" [is a river and an escape] (*OC* III: 156). Therefore, it is impossible to recall, to recover what once happened, even as his phrase continues to repeat that same impossibility throughout the unrepeatable course of history. Then, changing tack, the poem describes the phrase once it has been printed, deployed in books and in languages of other times, and it is found to be written by a single name, Heraclitus, who "no sabe griego" [does not know Greek], who "no tiene ayer ni ahora" [does not have yesterday nor the present], and who goes on to think of what is irretrievable that yet persists, and on what he misses. Heraclitus in his river is in fact just Borges on a stay abroad: "Un hombre que entreteje endecasílabos / Para no pensar tanto en Buenos Aires / Y en los rostros queridos. Uno falta" [A man who weaves together hendecasyllables / So as not to think too much about Buenos Aires / And in the faces of loved ones. One is missing] (*OC* III: 156). You cannot return to the same river, the Greek philosopher thought, but in Spanish verse, the essential, unreachable city returns where those beloved faces are found from which is missing the one that harries the poet's thoughts like something mortal for which tears are better left unshed. Thus, Virgil's tears for the glorious things that have been lost are intertwined in verses to avoid just one thing: his stark definition of madness, that which it is impossible to forget. On the edge of the river, which, at the beginning of the story, was indistinct from the image of time, the writer seems to forget and lose himself. But even if he forgets his own name, the language, the rhythm return it back to the same shore.

There is an ambivalence between the happiness of memories, in certain Borges poems, and the condemnation of remembering, of repeating, in others. Only in the memory of someone else, who perhaps did not write or wrote to be forgotten, can poetic justice be found, literally speaking. In the poem "Epílogo" [Epilogue], dedicated to the death of a poet and friend, a meeting is recalled that neither realized would be their last. Their encounter served to summarize the long years that had elapsed since their youth, when the

298   SILVIO MATTONI

young men sought out the secret of Buenos Aires, shared a taste for a particular type of literature and an enthusiasm for novelty that itself was old as time. Within the sentences "digo que has muerto. Yo también he muerto" [I say that you died. I have also died], the caesura separating the two hemistichs of the verse is the distance between the other and the self, which the poem tries to overcome through memory (*OC* III: 302). The rhythm allows the poet, in his thoughts, closeness to the absent other. Borges calls him "brother" when stating one last wish, that he might add a happy epilogue to his friend's "estudioso libro" [studious book], which reads: "ojalá compartieras esta vana / tarde conmigo, inexplicablemente" [I wish you would share this pointless / afternoon with me, inexplicably], just as they once shared an ingenuous adherence to a poetic meter, shared books, shared nostalgia for the intensity of beginnings (*OC* III: 302).

The friendship thus forged by poems that accompany the two for a lifetime can also be found, at times with the constancy of a memorable fantasy, in the reappearance of that first poet who endeavored to write something that would permeate the ages and languages without his signature. One can explore nearly the entirety of Borges's work tracking more or less explicit allusions, versions, and references to Virgil which hide or display themselves in his poetry and prose. This was in fact carried out by Spanish philologist Francisco García Jurado in a uniquely detective-like fashion. Among the quotes partially modified by Borges, he pointed out a fragment of the *Eclogue III*, which reads: *Iovis omnia plena* (Virgil 2004 70). In a prologue he wrote for a Spanish edition of the *Aeneid*, Borges, mingling the poems in his memory, would translate the line: "Todas las cosas están llenas de Júpiter" [All things are full of Jupiter] (*OC* IV: 521). García Jurado writes:

> No se trata de un verso citado al azar dentro del apretado compendio virgiliano. Precisamente, lo encontramos en un poema dedicado a Sherlock Holmes, dentro de *Los conjurados* (libro tardío donde abunda el recuerdo de Virgilio), abriendo un verso del propio Borges y con notable alteración del orden de las palabras: "(*Omnia sunt plena Jovis*. De análoga manera / diremos de aquel justo que da nombre a los versos / que su inconstante sombra recorre los diversos / dominios en que ha sido parcelada la esfera.)" (293; *OC* III: 470).

> [This is not some verse quoted at random from Virgil's dense compendium. Indeed, we find it in a poem dedicated to Sherlock Holmes, in *Los conjurados* (a late book in which references to Virgil abound), opening Borges's own poem and with a notable alteration in word order: "(*Omnia sunt plena Jovis*. And likewise / of that just man who gave his name to verse / we say inconstant shadow rules diverse / dominions where the sphere is sliced like pies.)"] (Borges, "Sherlock Holmes" 216)

García Jurado points out that Borges added the verb and that he seems to give the Latin a more traditional Spanish syntax. But in the parentheses is also enciphered the name of the only poet who cannot be forgotten, the friendly rhythm that always accompanies him, inconstant yet ubiquitous, suggesting the enigma could be translated: "All things are full of Virgil." Even the dreams of the unnamed shadow appeal to its music, to the memory of verses that disperse without ever getting lost: "*quantum lenta solent inter viburna cupressi,*" quotes the dreaming Borges, also in *Los conjurados* (*OC* III: 485). It is verse 25 of *Eclogue I*, describing Rome, which "Above all other cities rears her head / As cypress above pliant osier towers" (trans. Rhoades 391). In his dream, Borges sees a Roman wolf that announces his death. But in the same funereal dream, he can still remember that the adjective *lenta* applied to *viburna* does not suggest movement, but rather a quality of those bushes, supple, yielding, lacking the height, the firmness of the Roman cypress. Virgil's quote does not fail to allude to *The Aeneid*, since it is there that he discusses where true dreams come from and from where mere simulacra. The most frequently remembered of Virgil's lines—the one that Borges transcribes in the prologue to *El hacedor*, which consists of an imaginary visit to a dead poet (*Ibant obscuri sola sub nocte*)—describes the passage of Sibyl and Aeneas on their march to the Underworld. So, too, advances Borges, holding a book dedicated Leopoldo Lugones, a master lost in the memory of "sana teoría" [clean-limbed theory], which is also a hypallage (*OC* II: 157; *CF* 291). The encounter is impossible, like the embrace of Aeneas who thrice tries to grab hold of the body of his dead father, dissolved into an image and into words. "Pero mañana yo también habré muerto" [but tomorrow I too will be dead], Borges writes, "y se confundirán nuestros tiempos y la cronología se perderá en un orbe de símbolos y de algún modo será justo afirmar que yo le he traído este libro y que usted lo ha aceptado" [and our times will run together and chronology will melt into an orb of symbols, and somehow it will be true to say that I have brought you this book and that you have accepted it] (*OC* II: 157; *CF* 291). At some point, a reader, a rememberer of some remarkable verse, will be able to unite, in the studious light of their lamp, the names of the two poets. Soon thereafter, in "Un lector," published in *Elogio de la sombra*, Borges will recognize himself as a reader, since reading is the act that can give meaning to the encounters that, little by little, have drawn a line, a series of intensities in life's imagined fluidity. He writes: "Mis noches están llenas de Virgilio" [My nights are full of Virgil] (*OC* II: 394). Despite the forgetfulness that chips away at the continuity of books, that erodes his command of Latin—merely having known it, having thought he knew it once "es una posesión, porque el olvido / es una de las formas de la memoria" [is a possession, because forgetting / is a form of memory] (*OC* II: 394). And somehow, in a manner analogous to other languages, a forgotten language continues to express "la pasión del lenguaje" [the passion of language] in its strange devolution of syllables and accents, in its amassing of arguments, in the possibility of speaking the elusive, unrepeatable instant, through that repeated succession of words that is a line of poetry (*OC* II: 394). Another reader will then be able to feel the unexpected passion communicated by a book, ignited by the friendship of someone who happens to be absent, like a light piercing the slow diffusion of chronology.

Notes

1. A complete analysis of this ode, with Spanish translations and metric studies, can be seen in Villaseñor Cuspinera.

2. In *Poemas y prosas breves*, Balderston and Martín published a hitherto unpublished 1938 poem of the same title, written soon after the death of Jorge Guillermo Borges. It is considerably more melodramatic and sentimental than the 1976 version, although a few lines, including this one, reappear in the later poem.
3. The reference here is to Eduardo Mallea's *La ciudad junto al río inmóvil* (Sur, 1936).
4. The English translation for Borges's poem "La cifra," as published in Viking's *Selected Poems* is "The Limit." The choice is surely due to the Spanish "cifra" and English "cipher" being false cognates in nearly every acceptation. In Spanish, like the French "chiffre," "cifra" can simply be a numerical "digit" or "figure," but it can also mean "sum" or, more closely to English, "code."
5. Borges writes: "Con esta flor un porvenir ha muerto / En las aguas que ignoran" (*OC* III: 108). While the metaphor of the flower lends itself to an allegorical understanding of those "waters" that destroyed a life that had just begun, a fact outside the poem suggests its literal reading. On November 24, 1974, Adolfo Bioy Casares noted in his diary: "Come en casa Borges. Murió Angélica, una hijita de su sobrino Luis, de cinco años, ahogada en una pileta" [I ate at Borges's place. Angélica died, his nephew Luis's little girl, just five years old, drowned in a swimming pool] (1492).

Works Cited

Bioy Casares, Adolfo. *Borges*. Destino, 2006.

Borges, Jorge Luis. *Collected Fictions*, translated by Andrew Hurley. Penguin, 1998.

Borges, Jorge Luis. *Obras completas*. Emecé, 1996. 4 vols.

Borges, Jorge Luis. *Poemas y prosas breves*, edited by Daniel Balderston y María Celeste Martín. Borges Center, 2018.

Borges, Jorge Luis. *Selected Poems*. *Volume 2*, translated by Alexander Coleman. Penguin, 1999.

Borges, Jorge Luis. "Sherlock Holmes," translated by Willis Barnstone. *Semiotica*, vol. 79, no. 3/4, 1990, pp. 213–16.

Borges, Jorge Luis. "The Thing I Am," translated by Robert Mezey. *Paris Review*, vol. 125, 1992, https://www.theparisreview.org/poetry/2004/the-thing-i-am-jorge-luis-borges.

García Jurado, Francisco. "'Todas las cosas que merecen lágrimas.' Borges, traductor de Virgilio." *Studi Ispanici*, no. 35, 2010, pp. 291–309.

Mallea, Eduardo. *La ciudad junto al río inmóvil*. Sur, 1936.

Villaseñor Cuspinera, Patricia. "Metro y sintaxis en Horacio (asclepiadeos menores *kata stichon*)." *Nova Tellus. Revista Semestral del Centro de Estudios Clásicos*, vol. 11, 1993, pp. 63–87.

Virgil. *Eneida*. Edición bilingüe, Introducción y traducción de Rafael Fontán Barreiro. Alianza, 1990.

Virgil. *Eneida*. Introduction by Vicente Cristóbal and translation by Javier de Echave-Sustaeta. Gredos, 1997.

Virgil. *Bucólicas*. Introducción, traducción y notas de Pablo Ingberg. Editorial Losada, 2004.

Virgil. *The Aeneid, The Georgics, The Eclogues*, translated into English verse by James Rhoades. Oxford University Press, 1921.

CHAPTER 17

BORGES'S SELF-FIGURATION PROCESS IN THE LATE FICTION (1970–1983)

EVELYN FISHBURN

THIS chapter discusses different aspects of Borges's self-figuration in his late fiction, a subject that has not received much attention hitherto. Its central aim is to discover what new levels of interpretation are revealed by this approach as distinct from one based on direct recollection in biographical or autobiographical accounts with its attendant belief in causality. This is not to minimize the importance of biographies as an informative source of study, and the present essay owes much to Edwin Williamson's and Emir Rodríguez Monegal's informative works. My purpose, however, is not to seek authorial endorsement but rather to focus on the subjectivity of associations linked to the author in his literary persona—his *textual* figurations—and assess their presence and role in the fiction. In this chapter, the "self" is understood as a plural and open-ended concept as opposed to a monolithic entity and "self-figuration" as a term relating primarily to the portrayal of oneself by oneself. In the case of Borges, this can be a direct reference but is more often an opaque representation using transposed clues that are purposely and misleadingly disguised. These are biographical details, momentary snippets that operate on the lines of "biographemes," the term coined to relate to the minimal unit of biographical discourse. Its relevance to my argument is that these biographemes do not pretend to be *ex ungue leonem* building blocks of a totality but instead relate to representations that remain fragmentary, without pretension to being representative of a totality. Roland Barthes compares the biographeme to a photograph, a momentary representation, the illustration of a detail, but not necessarily emblematic of its subject (the subject of the photo). The difference, however, is not simply one of size but also of intent: if a biography recounts a destiny, a biographeme can travel outside any destiny or trigger the fantasy of a direct contact with reality. In this sense, it may be considered a metaphorical bridge between reality and fiction.[1]

Regarding Borges's overall use of biographical associations, it has often been observed that he enmeshes his own history with that of his ancestors and, through them, with his place in the story of Argentina's national and cultural identity. A different tactic relates to other authors with whom he ostensibly identifies either by endowing them with his own characteristics (biographemes) or vice-versa. These are some of the particularities that invite the question of whether and the extent to which, if at all, this self-figuration is authentic or is itself a subterfuge to mask greater unknowable complexities (c.f.: Brant) This is the position that underlies my discussion of the collections published from 1970 onward, namely, *El informe de Brodie* [*Doctor Brodie's Report*] (1970), *El libro de arena* [*The Book of Sand*] (1975), and *La memoria de Shakespeare* [*Shakespeare's Memory*] (1983). These works appeared nearly twenty years after the publication of *Ficciones* [*Fictions*] (1944) and *El Aleph* (1949)—both of which led to his worldwide. The reason given for this was his failing eyesight, which caused him to rely on memory and dictation, so that when he eventually returned to writing fiction he created less complicated plots and adopted a narrative style based on aural aesthetics rather than the visual effect of handwriting. The aim of this article is to offer an in-depth study of this change in direction as manifest in some carefully selected stories and to consider the presence and effect of this new age-related condition in the late fiction imaginatively and in the spirit in which it was written.

EL INFORME DE BRODIE (1970)

This collection marked a turning point in the direction of Borges's fiction, as he himself explicitly, though not necessarily reliably, claimed in the Foreword: "ahora, cumplidos los setenta, creo haber encontrado mi voz" [now that I am seventy years old I think I have found my own voice], in plain tales written in a realist style (*OC* II: 400; *CF* 346). One might infer from this declaration that these new stories will be simpler, or at least more straightforward than his earlier works, but Borges's elaboration of his terms of reference, his definition of what is "plain" or "realistic" in literature, casts doubt on this contention. Contrary to expectation, he implies that a plain text is more complex than an intricate one and is only to be attempted by an experienced writer "ya avanzada [en] edad" [in his [sic] advanced years]; he further undermines the accepted notion of realism as a transparent reproduction of reality by calling it no menos convencional que los otros" [a genre no less convention-ridden than all the others] (*OC* II: 400; *CF* 346).

The same can be said about another principal component of realism: the notion of identity. It is important to stress that a distinguishing feature of this collection is the unmissable yet often overlooked fact that the eleven tales that comprise it are framed in a first-person introduction in which a named or easily identifiable Borges-like figure presents himself as the teller of the tales about to be told or, in most of cases, retold. These are mainly violent tales of duplicity, rivalry, and *machista* bravado, themes whose associations to the Borges-myth are familiar and entirely plausible. Though the actual name "Borges" appears only once, he is unquestionably the first-person narrator interpellated in each story.

Clues in *El informe de Brodie*, which point to the "real Borges" or rather to the constructed Borges-myth, are copious. They consist mainly of details about his family, such as mentioning a cousin named Lafinur (in "El encuentro" [The Encounter]); the "quinta" [country house] in Adrogué in which he and his family spent summer vacations (in "El otro duelo" [The Other Duel]); a free-thinking father and a strictly observant Catholic mother ("El evangelio según Marcos" [The Gospel According to Mark]); and Godel, an old school friend ("Juan Muraña"). I have chosen "Juan Muraña" as an example of the interpretative potential that a passing reference to a Borges-related association may engender. The frame story reads almost like an extract from Borges's "Autobiographical Essay," which lends credence to the alleged encounter between "Borges" and the core story's narrator, the fictional Trápani: "Yo iba a Morón; Trápani, que estaba junto a la ventanilla, me llamó por mi nombre. Tardé en reconocerlo; habían pasado tantos años desde que compartimos el mismo banco en una escuela de la calle Thames. Roberto Godel lo recordará" [I was taking the train to Morón; Trápani, who was sitting beside the window, spoke to me by name. It took me a moment to recognize him; so many years had gone by since we shared a bench in that school on Calle Thames. (Roberto Godel will recall that.)] (*OC* II: 420; *CF* 370). Godel is not mentioned again, but a connection has been established. The bench allegedly shared with the fictional Trápani alludes to an incident cited by Williamson where he refers to a trauma suffered by Borges during childhood, when Godel, the only other middle-class boy in the rough local school which they both attended, was sent away to another school and Borges was left to deal with the taunts and derision of his classmates on his own (46). These details are not present in the story and the reference appears entirely gratuitous; many sensitive readings of the story are possible without recourse to it and yet no allusion in Borges is ever gratuitous, as I have argued elsewhere.

In the core story, the fictional Trápani tells the story of his aunt, a shy, reclusive old woman, the widow of the famed Muraña of the title, who was being threatened with eviction by her landlord, a man called Luchessi. When one morning the latter is found knifed, Muraña's ways of dealing with any affront is recalled by the narrator in a haunting dream, but Luchessi's killer is never found. The explanation offered is that the old aunt, emboldened by the memory of her heroic late husband, adopted his persona and his knife. The point being made is that, in the narrative, she does not simply use the murder weapon but *becomes* it. It is the knife that enacts the revenge: "La daga era Muraña, era el muerto que ella seguía adorando" [The dagger was Muraña, it was the dead man she went on loving] (*OC* II: 423; *CF* 374). It is not easy to link this to Godel and yet the allusion remains, gnawingly present. I argue that the old, confused, threatened woman reflects the eleven-year-old abandoned schoolboy and that the tale is symbolic of his fear and the burden of his defense. There were many displays of daggers and other tokens of the cult of courage in Borges's home, and I cite the story's fanciful elaboration of this biographical snippet as a notable example of the workings of a biographeme.[2] The dagger in "Juan Muraña" acquires a supernatural quality and leads to a reading of the story as a metaphor for the fear felt by his abandonment by Roberto Godel and the old aunt's eventual triumph as symbolic of Borges's unexpressed longing for a worthy solution. The autobiographical details in this story have not been noticed hitherto, but

I hope to have shown how they allow for unexpected revelation regarding the different ways in which Borges inscribes himself in his fiction.

A strong autobiographical link underpins the plot and writing of the collection's opening story, "La intrusa" [The Intruder], the tale of two brothers, known as rough and pugnacious to others but very close between themselves. When one brings a prostitute to live with them, jealousy sets in though not over the girl but of each other. To end this conflict the older brother kills her and when he confesses what he has done, the two embrace, now linked by an even stronger bond, "la mujer tristemente sacrificada y la obligación de olvidarla" [the woman grievously sacrificed and the obligation to forget her] (*OC* II: 404; *CF* 531). The story has been richly interpreted in its sexual and cultural complexity. To begin, the verse stated in the epigraph, 2 Kings 1:26, does not exist in the King James version of the Bible since the first chapter of the second book of the Kings has only 18 verses and not 26, but the quotation can be found in the second book of Samuel, also known as Kings in the Hebrew Bible. It reads "I am distressed for thee, my brother: very pleasant hast thou been to me: thy love to me was wonderful, passing the love of women." The question arising is why Borges chose to camouflage this passage in such a way. Is this simply a teasing trick or is there a more profound motivation? The topic of Borges's sexuality exceeds the scope of this chapter in its vastness and complexity, but, in terms of self-inscription, it is noteworthy that when Estela Canto, a close friend and one-time confidante of Borges, suggested to him the possibility of a homoerotic reading, he was outraged and stated categorically that there was no such implication whatsoever in the love of the two brothers (Canto 230).

Canto's testimony needs to be assessed in the context of her amorous involvement with Borges and of his mother's strong disapproval of it, but her insinuation of autobiographical undertones regarding an enclosed mother and son bond, ready to sacrifice an intruding love interest, is based on her personal knowledge (Williamson 359–60). This suggests the plausibility of two opposing yet linked interpretations of the story: one, that Borges might be projecting himself as the perpetrator of the crime in compliance with his mother's wishes, or, alternatively, as its victim, identifying himself with the silenced sacrificial lamb. Both relate to a childhood incident in Geneva when the young Borges was forced to have sex with a woman also "known" to his father.[3]

Regarding the cult of violence in the story, Borges confesses that it was influenced by his interest in Old Norse literature: "Cuando lo escribí intenté proceder como los autores de las sagas islandesas. Las tuve como ejemplo" [When I wrote it I meant to emulate the writers of Icelandic sagas. I had them as an example] (Hadis 62).[4] He refers, presumably, to the importance of the cult of courage and to its use in this fiction, where he establishes a link between these legendary heroic warriors and the "compadritos" [thugs] of his native Buenos Aires.[5] These are interpretative matters regarding the plot: what is known is that when Borges had difficulties in ending the story he asked for his mother's help. As has been mentioned, because of his increasing blindness, Borges no longer wrote his stories but dictated them, mostly to his mother. At the time of creating "La intrusa," he recalls that when he came to the point when the older brother tells the younger one that he has knifed the woman, he could not find the right wording to finish the story. He turned to his mother for help, and she duly gave him the ending. Borges relates the incident as follows: "She gave me those words, and for a moment *she became, somehow, one of the characters in the story* and believed in the story, as if it had actually taken place" (Barnstone 104, emphasis added). This biographical gloss adds a touch of the fantastic to the writing of the story, enriching the strong biographical links present in its contents as well as in its telling.

"La señora mayor" [The Elderly Lady], placed in the middle of the collection, is a story permeated with echoes and resonances of Borges's life and family history, specifically regarding those ancestors who were heroes of the Wars of Independence. The Señora de Jáuregui, the eponymous "señora mayor," is about to celebrate her hundredth birthday. Living in somewhat straitened circumstances, not poor but not in as grand a manner, she is portrayed as the daughter of an illustrious father, Colonel Mariano Rubio. The gradual demise of her faculties is sympathetically observed and a certain parallel can be drawn between the dwindling of her mental faculties and that of the family fortunes. Her memories are stuck in a mythified past, for she lived firm in her belief in the values of her traditional Hispanic Catholic upbringing. "Seguía abominando de Artigas, de Rosas y de Urquiza" [She still abominated Artigas, Rosas and Urquiza], rulers who had been important in her youth, and clung to the way streets were called then and insisted in talking of "orientales" [Easterners] the term used in colonial times for "uruguayos" (*OC* II: 424; *CF* 377). As is pointed out in the story, she did not do so out of affectation but, because she never left home, she remained unaware of the changes that her native city underwent and this was her only frame of reference.

There is not much written about this story, but Williamson (361–62, 417) presents an authoritative argument about its biographical connections, alleging that its main character is modeled on Borges's mother, Leonor Acevedo, but the values upheld by her—a distinct pride in her patrician inheritance—also reflect those of his two grandmothers, Leonor Acevedo's mother, Leonor Suárez, and Fanny Haslam. The publication of *Memorias de Leonor Acevedo de Borges* (Hadis 2021) supports this claim. For example, Borges recalls an amusing vignette that illustrates his mother's general attitude: "Se hablaba de historia argentina y mi madre dijo: yo soy la historia argentina. Ella honraba a sus mayores" [We were talking about Argentina's history and my mother said: I am the history of Argentina] (Hadis 109). And yet there is a surprisingly forthright outburst from Doña Leonor in these recorded memoirs, expressing annoyance at so much family glorification: "harta ya de tantos elogios un día me dije: 'Ojalá mi abuelo hubiera sido zapatero'" [tired of so much praise, one day she told me: If only my grandfather had been a cobbler] (Hadis 12). This anecdote sheds light on the telling of "La señora mayor," allowing for the speculation that Borges reacted to this pride in the family's ancestral past with a sense of identification, responsibility, awe, and, ultimately, like his mother in the previous reference, a burden.

There are several passages in this story that relate to the process of Borges's self-figuration. For instance, the fictional Colonel Rubio fought in Chacabuco, at the defeat of Cancha Rayada, at Maipú, and, two years later, at Arequipa, as did Borges's ancestor, Colonel Isidoro Suárez, whose actions in the Wars of Independence played a pivotal role in the defeat of the Spanish army.[6] The story mentions that he and Olavarría exchanged swords: this was a romantic custom among generals, and Borges recalls specifically that his grandfather had exchanged swords, though with another general (General Mansilla), on the eve of a battle in the Paraguayan war (Borges, *Veinticinco Agosto* 86). The fictional Rubio also overlaps with the legend of General San Martín, an iconic figure in Argentine history who crossed the Andes and fought in the same battles as Rubio is said to have fought. Rubio and San Martín coincide in being remembered as noble generals who self-lessly stepped down in favor of Simón Bolívar because San Martín believed Bolívar to be more favorably placed to secure victory against the Spaniards. This idea is held as dogma in Argentine history, which adds to the irony of the way it is recast here as relating to Venezuelans: "Siempre envidiosos de nuestras glorias, los venezolanos atribuyeron esta victoria al general Simón Bolívar, pero el observador imparcial, el historiador argentino, no se deja embaucar y sabe muy bien que sus laureles corresponden al coronel Mariano Rubio" [Always envious of our Argentine glories, the Venezuelans have attributed that victory to General Simón Bolívar, but the impartial observer, the *Argentine* historian, is not so easily taken in; he knows full well that the laurels won there belong to Colonel Mariano Rubio] (*OC* II: 424; *CF* 375).[7] Rubio is a first-born child, was made inspector of poultry and rabbits, and was a frequent visitor to the National Library, all of which are biographical snippets that link him to Borges directly and not through his ancestors. My point here is to argue for a certain fluidity in how Borges inscribes himself in the late fiction, sometimes in oblique reference to his ancestors and sometimes to himself. As a social commentary, the story offers a clearly critical stance concerning the hypoc-risy of the past and of the present, but this is modulated by a warm feeling of nostalgia, as in the narrator's recollection: "Me acuerdo de un olor a cosas guardadas" [I recall the odor of things locked away] (*OC* II: 425; *CF* 376). Similarly, a gloss on the elderly lady's straitened circumstances, judges that "la pobreza de ayer era menos pobre que la que ahora nos depara la industria. También las fortunas eran menores" [the poverty of yes-terday was less squalid than the one we purchase with our industry today. Fortunes were smaller then as well] (*OC* II: 425; *CF* 376).

"La señora mayor" is one of the few Borges stories in which a female character's history and her thoughts and memories are the main focus of the narrative, which is indirectly told by a (Borges-like) narrator.[8] This opens the way for the implication that her fate is seen as no less decisive in the construction of the nation than the contribution of her male relatives, thereby subtly and implicitly undermining the patriarchal assumptions that underlie the cult of courage in the rest of this collection. By showing another side of the picture, "La señora mayor" recasts the values of Borges's assumed self-figuration. Borges's biographer and close friend María Esther Vázquez commented on the irony that someone as shy and as inclined to self-effacement should have inscribed him-self so often in his writing. This last idea is particularly apposite to his coded presence throughout *El informe de Brodie*. Most relevant for the present discussion is the shift from Borges's accepted self-effacement as a given to an appreciation of his subtle, recon-dite opposite, his coded self-inscription.

EL LIBRO DE ARENA

El libro de arena consists of thirteen stories, in which, as in *El informe de Brodie*, there is a first-person narrator but not the same thematic consistency. These stories evolve around several themes which revisit Borges's well-known preoccupations but now with greater emphasis on storytelling, using fewer erudite allusions and clearer and more accessible plot lines though, in the words of Rodríguez Monegal, some are "unabashedly fantastic" (461). An added feature of the collection is a fascination with Norse mythologies, the hovering presence of death, and, quite unusually in Borges's fiction, love. Borges lived, from childhood onward, in the certain knowledge of his predestined blindness, which may be why these late fictions are marked, to an even greater extent than those in *El informe de Brodie*, by a deepening emotional intensity in which nostalgia plays a prominent role. They revisit earlier topics now recollected from the wider perspective of the aged narrator, where the topic of memory itself is the object of analysis and discussion. Concentrating on three autobiographically significant stories from *El libro de arena*, I examine different angles from which the author inscribes himself in the narrative.

"El otro" [The Other] is the first story in *El libro de arena*. It is about an encounter between a seventy-year-old "Borges" sitting on a bench by the Charles River in Boston in 1969, and his younger self sitting at the other end of what purports to be the same bench by the river Rhône in Geneva in 1918. The following dialogue encapsulates the dilemma of the different time and place in which the story is set:

> —En tal caso—le dije resueltamente—usted se llama Jorge Luis Borges. Yo también soy Jorge Luis Borges. Estamos en 1969, en la ciudad de Cambridge.
>
> —No—me respondió con mi propia voz un poco lejana.
>
> Al cabo de un tiempo insistió:
>
> —Yo estoy aquí en Ginebra, en un banco, a unos pasos del Ródano. (*OC* III: 11–13)

> ["In that case," I resolutely said to him, "your name is Jorge Luis Borges. I too am Jorge Luis Borges. We are in 1969, in the city of Cambridge."
>
> "No," he answered in my own slightly distant voice, "I am here in Geneva, on a bench, a few steps from the Rhône."] (*CF* 412)

This story is of crucial relevance to the topic under discussion in that it deals with an essential element of Borges's self-figuration, a perception of its dual or multiple nature and even of its illusory essence. In what has become to be regarded as a seminal text, "Borges y yo" [Borges and I], the Borges figure is split into the historic person called Borges and the mythical persona created by his literary fame and attendant adulation. The two, person and persona, exist simultaneously: their difference is not resolved but dissolved in that they become one indistinguishable self. In "El otro," however, the confrontation differs in that it is presented diachronically, set in two disparate time sequences. The interplay between them is maintained throughout the story and becomes its mainstay. The details that are chosen by the two contenders to confirm their identity are of particular interest in so far as they repeat and perpetuate stock features in biographical and autobiographical accounts. Statements presented by either the older or the younger Borges as proof of their inside knowledge take the form of references to his literary works and repeat some of his more idiosyncratic opinions. For example, the allusion to *Los himnos rojos* [*Red Anthems*] relates to a collection of poems in praise of the Russian Revolution whose utopian ideas and violent imagery he later repudiated; the discussion of metaphor ties in with the already mentioned views in *Doctor Brodie's Report*; in 1966 he published, in collaboration with María Esther Vázquez, *Literaturas germánicas medievales* [*Medieval Germanic Literature*] (it includes a section on Scandinavian literatures)[9]; the flower in the fantasy by Coleridge alludes to his essay "La flor de Coleridge" [Coleridge's Flower] (*OC* II: 17–19); the predictions concerning Jichlinski, a friend from his Geneva years, are correct, as is the mention of the Geneva restaurant, "*the Crocodile*"; the self-parodic remark about not being surprised if the teaching of Latin were to be replaced by Guaraní accords with the reactionary views expressed in "El duelo" [The Duel] where Guaraní is referred to as "un utensilio casero" [a household implement], whose meaning I read as useful to ladies in Corrientes for communicating with their servants. The younger man's predictions regarding the older writer's future publications bear the hallmark of Borges's famed self-mockery: too many books, poetry admired more by himself than others, writing fantastic stories, teaching "like your father," a remark slyly intended as an indirect criticism of his father's failure as a writer (Cf. the saying "those who can, do; those who can't, teach").

There are other works of literature mentioned which are inconclusive of the identity of the speaker because they could have been read and left their mark on either of them, but there is one cultural allusion cited by the older man that the younger one admits that he could not have written or memorized because he himself had not come across it by 1918 (Shaw 172). The implication of this is that it could not be the younger one dreaming the older. This is a line by Victor Hugo, "L'hydre-univers tordant son corps écaillé d'astres" whose cryptic meaning is that the universe is wondrously alive and that God exists everywhere, just as we exist in all our former and future selves.[10] The implied parallel between ourselves and God to argue a unified sense of self is a significant new facet in Borges's self-figuration but, bearing in mind Borges's known skepticism about any absolutist notion, not a defining one. Rather, it can be fruitfully construed as an ironic inconsistency in Borges's self-figuration as underlying all these recollections.

Another argument presented as decisive in deciding whether it is the older man recalling his younger self or the younger imagining his future self relates to the recollection of a dated dollar bill from the year 1964, which would make its discussion in 1918 impossible. There is a vast critical literature on this issue but what is relevant in the present context is that, according to the *données* of the story, dollar bills are not dated individually but according to series and the date when the series was issued. This accepted fact is pivotal in the narrative, which ends in the voice of the younger man, and from his perspective: "El otro me soñó, pero no me soñó rigurosamente. Soñó, ahora lo entiendo, la imposible fecha en el dólar" [The other man dreamed me, but did not dream me *rigorously*—he dreamed, I now realize, the *impossible date* on that dollar bill] (*OC* III: 16; *CF* 417, second emphasis added).[11] And so the confusion lives on.

A brief interchange regarding Walt Whitman's self-figuration offers a most revealing insight regarding Borges's own self-figuration through that of another author. Voiced by one of his alternating personae, it alludes to Whitman's recollection of a night when he had been truly happy and the lapidary observation that "Si Whitman la ha cantado . . . es porque la deseaba y no sucedió. El poema gana si adivinamos que es la manifestación de un anhelo, no la historia de un hecho" [Whitman sang of that night, . . . it's because it never happened. The poem gains in greatness if we sense that it is the expression of a desire, a longing, rather than the narration of an event] (*OC* III: 15; *CF* 416). This idea is an enlightening insinuation that what appears to be an authentic self-portrayal may be the subterfuge for an unfulfilled desire: "Luego está también aquella parte de mi vida que yo no he tenido y que hubiera querido tener" [and then there is that part of my life that I haven't had and that I would have liked to have had] (qtd. in Rojas 75).[12]

"Ulrica" [Ulrikke] is the story of a brief encounter between two strangers, one, a university professor from Colombia named Javier Otálora, and the other, a mysterious Norwegian woman, Ulrikke (her surname is not given). They meet by chance one evening at an inn in the city of York where they both happen to be staying for the night on their way in different directions. Otálora, whose first-person account this is, falls in love immediately with Ulrikke, though not much occurs between them that evening. On the following morning they meet again and decide to go out for a walk together, downriver. He now kisses her, and she rejects him gently but firmly, promising to make love to him that evening. They meet again at the same inn and sexual intercourse finally takes place: he possesses her, or rather possesses her image: "Como la arena se iba el tiempo. Secular en la sombra fluyó el amor y poseí por primera y última vez la imagen de Ulrica" [Like sand, time sifted away. Ancient in the dimness flowed love, and for the first and last time, I possessed the image of Ulrikke] (*OC* III: 19; *CF* 421). This is the only Borges story in which the act of love is extensively imagined and consummated, albeit in dream form.[13]

Borges inscribes himself prominently in this story, both directly through overt statements and the inclusion of many recondite autobiographical details (Williamson 397–98) and indirectly through a series of aphorisms associated with his persona. Borges has chosen "Ulrikke" as one of his favorite stories, and while this is a claim he has made elsewhere ("El Sur" [The South], "La intrusa") there is a ring of truth here in that it deals with a very personal and persistent preoccupation: the attainment of love as an (im)possibility. Like all epigraphs, the one heading this story acts as a gateway to its meaning. It is a quotation from a Norse epic, the *Volsunga Saga*, whose translation reads: "He takes the sword Gram and lays it between them." This is a reference to Sigurd placing his sword between himself and his former lover, Brynhild, to ensure his chastity given that she is now betrothed to someone else and is prohibited to him. The epigraph emphasizes the connotation of the sword as an instrument of power, armed conflict, and, ultimately, of prohibition; given the numerous swords displayed in Borges's home honoring their military ancestors, the quoted inscription has been interpreted as an allusion to Borges's sexual and emotional difficulties, whether by self-imposition or fear of his mother (Williamson 399). According to the Saga, the lovers' (incestuous) union is finally consummated in the grave, and Borges's choice of this epigraph to be placed as an inscription on his tomb is telling in terms of self-projection.

The story was conceived by Borges during a trip with Maria Kodama to Iceland, and he told her that the character of Ulrica was based on her. However, by making her Norwegian, he added a dimension to her portrayal, turning her into the prototype of the northern European woman—proud, noble, and unattainable—and, as such, symbolic of Borges's long, complex love. The identification of Otálora with Borges is more straightforward. As an aged university professor from the University of the Andes in Bogotá, he resembles Borges who, in 1956, was awarded the title of Doctor Honoris Causa from the University of Cuyo (at the foot of the Andes). Otálora's visit to York is in tune with Borges's trip to Great Britain in 1964 and in particular to his short stay in the city of York. Further indirect traces of Borges's self-inscription can be found in some of Otálora's aphorisms, which are interpolated in the story. For example, "Mi relato será fiel a la realidad o, en todo caso, a mi recuerdo personal de la realidad, lo cual es lo mismo" [My story will be faithful to reality, or at least to *my personal recollection of reality, which is the same thing*] (*OC* III: 17; *CF* 418, emphasis added). This sentence foregrounds the solipsism of his view of fiction as a guided dream yet clashes with another comment by the narrator: "La frase quería ser ingeniosa y adiviné que no era la primera vez que la pronunciaba. Supe después que no era característica de ella, pero lo que decimos no siempre se parece a nosotros" [The pronouncement was an attempt at wit, and I sensed this wasn't the first time she'd voiced it. I later learned that it was not like her—*but what we say is not always like us*] (*OC* III: 17; *CF* 418, emphasis added).

The lines "¿Qué es ser colombiano?" [What is 'being Colombian'?] and "—No sé— le respondí—. Es un acto de fe" ["I'm not sure," I replied. "It's an act of faith"] recalls Borges's many anti-nationalist pronouncements, while "Para un hombre célibe entrado en años, el ofrecido amor es un don que ya no se espera. El milagro tiene derecho a imponer condiciones" [For a celibate, middle-aged man, proffered love is a gift that one no longer hopes to find. *The miracle has a right to impose conditions*] has an unmissable Borges-like nostalgic ring, and the reference to "condiciones" [conditions] and to a girl who, in his youth, had denied him her love, is a likely allusion to his many frustrated love affairs (*OC* III: 18; *CF* 419–20, emphasis added). Reflecting the inscription, love is accompanied by death and the story ends with the impending danger of death: "—En estas tierras —dije—, piensan que quien está por morir prevé lo futuro. —Y yo estoy por morir —dijo ella." ["In these lands," I said, "people think that a person who's soon to die can see the future." "And I'm about to die," she said] (*OC* III: 19; *CF* 420). The purpose of the foregoing discussion is to argue the increased emotional intensity and personal involvement in the late fiction. The intellectual or philosophical complexities of "Emma Zunz" have given way, here, to a story about passion, desire, and fear.

"El Congreso" [The Congress] is Borges's longest story and one which he thought about for much of his creative life, from about the early 1940s until its first publication in 1971. It is the realization of an idea conceived in early life and presented from the vantage point of old age. Borges spoke of it as being "perhaps the most autobiographical," an obvious reference to the longevity of its gestation but also and pertinently, to the narrator, Alejandro Ferri's, who has many points in common with "Borges." Ferri is the founder and mastermind of the Congress, an ambitious project to include all mankind and its history, and is also the perpetrator of its destruction when he realizes the impossibility of the task because the Universe is essentially irreducible. I confine my discussion of Borges's self-projection here to a series of paratextual comments followed by an examination of one or two representative biographemes in the core text.

When Borges gave an ironic resumé of his life and writings in an invited talk at the University of Wisconsin-Milwaukee, he singled out "El Congreso" with ambivalent praise as "perhaps the best story I have ever written. Though critics have not been too fond of it" (Leone 215). He expands on this opinion in a famed interview with María Esther Vázquez, where he recalls a criticism of the story as "un libro inútil" [a useless book] because it is already included in his previous work, a sort of resumé of his *opera omnia*. But the author disagrees, pointing out that "El Congreso" differs from the rest by uniquely portraying something that was intended as a failure—the annihilation of all that constituted the Congress—to be seen ultimately as a success. The metaphysical significance of this success-in-failure is the illustration that the universe is irreducible, but a more prosaic understanding would note that annihilation is not total because although everything is burned and members of the Congress disperse, one remnant of the Congress escaped the flames, namely the eponymous self-reflective story we are now reading. A recondite association which has not be seen so far, but which may be justified considering Borges's increasing reference to Norse mythology in the late fiction, is to "Ragnarök," the Scandinavian myth of the Twilight of the Gods, according to which, after a great conflagration, the world will be renewed.[14] I cite this as one of the many literary writings by Borges which are reflected in the story and which add to its being "the most autobiographical" of his fictions.

The foregoing is a subtle understanding of the autobiographical nature of "El Congreso"; more blatantly obvious are the many references that suggest Ferri as an alter ego of Borges. The interchangeability between the two is often teasingly misleading, but at times the divergences become more meaningful. The similarity of the narrator's age and Borges's, his arrival in Buenos Aires in 1899 (the year Borges was born), and giving classes to small numbers of students are all known details that I suggest instill a sense of security in the reader; "no me casé" [I never married] and "estoy solo" [I am alone] are inexact yet an interesting take on his relationship with his mother (*OC* III: 20; *CF* 422); "un síntoma inequívoco es el hecho de que no me interesan o sorprenden las novedades, acaso porque advierto que nada esencialmente nuevo hay en ellas y que no pasan de ser tímidas variaciones" [one unequivocal sign is that I find novelty neither interesting nor surprising, perhaps because I see nothing essentially new in it] are familiar thoughts regarding a change of direction in his late fiction (*OC* III: 20; *CF* 422). This is taken further with the words "Cuando era joven, me atraían los atardeceres, los arrabales y la desdicha; ahora, las mañanas del centro y la serenidad. Ya no juego a ser Hamlet" [When I was young, I was drawn to sunsets, slums, and misfortune; now it is to mornings in the heart of the city and tranquility. I no longer play at being Hamlet] (*OC* III: 20; *CF* 422). On this change in his aesthetics, he commented "I am no longer that writer" (Carrizo 237). As a final example of a controversial self-inscription, I quote "El curioso puede exhumar, en algún oscuro anaquel de la Biblioteca Nacional de la calle México, un ejemplar de mi *Breve examen del idioma analítico de John Wilkins*, obra que exigiría otra edición, siquiera para corregir o atenuar sus muchos errores" [The curious reader may exhume, from some obscure shelf in the National Library on Calle México, a copy of my book *A Brief Examination of the Analytical Language of John Wilkins*, a work which ought to be republished if only to correct or mitigate its many errors] (*OC* III: 20; *CF* 422). This lengthy extract justifies the many oblique allusions it enables. The title refers not to a book but to a seminal essay on the epistemological limitations in understanding the universe; the exact wording is "El idioma analítico de John Wilkins" [The Analytical Language of John Wilkins]. In this fictional essay, Borges caricatures the attempts to offer a linguistic form as equivalent to reality: "notoriamente no hay clasificación del universe que no sea arbitaria y conjectural. La razón es muy simple: no sabemos qué cosa es el universo" [obviously there is no classification of the universe that is not arbitrary and speculative. The reason is quite simple: we do not know what the universe is] (*OC* II: 86; *SNF* 231), which is a clear reformulation of the gist of "El Congreso." The laconic statement which follows, "obra que exigiría otra edición, siquiera para corregir o atenuar sus muchos errores" [a work which ought to be republished if only to correct or mitigate its many errors] is in line with the revelation that Borges corrected and rewrote indefatigably, as shown in Daniel Balderston's *How Borges Wrote* (*OC* III: 20; *CF* 422). The tease concludes with the dismissive declaration by the Borges-like Ferri regarding the Borges Director of the National Library: "Nunca he querido conocerlo" [I have never wished to meet him] (*OC* III: 20; *CF* 423). This twist in the perspective of the narrative epitomizes the deliberate unreliability in Borges's self-figuration whereby a fictional persona that doubles up into itself becomes the framing component of the story.

La memoria de Shakespeare

Published in 1983, *La memoria de Shakespeare* is Borges's last and shortest collection of fiction. It consists of four stories each told by a Borges-like aged, vulnerable figure as narrator. One, "Tigres azules" [Blue Tigers], is a fictionalization of Borges's well-known fear of tigers and tells the story of a man's intuition that the nightmare objects of his dream may be emblematic of his own existence; another, "La rosa de Paracelso" [The Rose of Paracelsus], is about a renowned elderly magician who can no longer perform his miracles for anyone but himself. The association between magician and fabulist need not be argued. In the section that follows, I discuss the first and last story of the collection.

"Veinticinco de Agosto, 1983" [August 25, 1983] is a variation of "El otro," told from the vantage point of the older man but not primarily in confrontation with another self but with death. The narrator, at the time of telling the story, is sixty-one years old and the story is about an imagined meeting with his eighty-four-year-old self. In conversation with each other, they recall many incidents from "their" youth and in particular memories of a planned suicide. Vázquez remembers Borges dictating this story to her and recalls that, in real life, he had decided to commit suicide and set the date for this on his thirty-fifth birthday, but when it came to it, he was too cowardly to do so. The shame of this stayed with him forever, and the story gains by being read from this perspective. In contrast to "El otro," the two Borges figures here do not stand in opposition to each other for they know that "la verdad es que somos dos y somos uno" [the truth is that we are two yet we are one] (*OC* III: 376; *CF* 491). They consider the intimacy of death, not from an abstract intellectual point of view, but as an authentic life experience, imagined with pathos and rare tenderness, with "una especie de dulzura y de alivio, que no he sentido nunca" [a sort of sweetness and relief (I've) never felt before] (*OC* III: 378; *CF* 492). However, they still recoil at the thought of touching each other, and, what is more, with the impunity that the knowledge of imminent death gives them, they vent feelings of mutual hatred, which turn out to be self-hatred: "Aborrezco tu cara, que es mi caricatura, aborrezco tu voz, que es mi remedo, aborrezco tu sintaxis patética, que es la mía" [I loathe your face, which is a caricature of mine, I loathe your voice, which is a mockery of mine, I loathe your pathetic syntax, which is my own] (*OC* III: 378; *CF* 492). The vehemence of this unanticipated outburst of hatred adds a distinctive layer to the palimpsestic assemblage of Borges's self-figuration, valuable in that it is not a fantasy of desired alternatives to the self but of the horror thereof. A literary-based aspect in this story is Borges's auto-figuration in a *projected* book that lists all the main known themes in the *existing* fiction: "los laberintos, los cuchillos, el hombre que se cree una imagen, el reflejo que se cree verdadero" [the labyrinths, the knives, the man who thinks an image, the reflection that thinks it's real], and so on (*OC* III: 377; *CF* 491). Ironically, the author was considered "no ser Borges y de haber repetido lo exterior del modelo" [not actually being Borges yet mirroring all the outward appearances of the original" (*CF* 492). And I suggest that this sentence mirrors all that has been argued so far—self-projections that are outward appearances of an elusive and possibly absent center.

"La memoria de Shakespeare" is the title of Borges's last fiction in his eponymous last and shortest collection. The story's narrator is the fictional character Hermann Soergel, a Shakespeare scholar, who unexpectedly is offered the gift of the Bard's memory, which he accepts. He is delighted at the thought/possibility of "being Shakespeare," but when the new memory takes over and destroys his own, he deplores its loss and longs to be himself once more. The title, particularly in the original Spanish, means both "what Shakespeare remembers" and "how Shakespeare is remembered," a questioning that is placed in the general context of the working and significance of memory. To what extent is memory a reflection of the self or its constituent? How does it function, and what are its limitations? This is defined by the narrator as "La memoria del hombre no es una suma; es un desorden de posibilidades indefinidas" [A man's memory is not a summation; it is the chaos of vague possibilities] (*OC* III: 395; *CF* 513). The story is an exploration of these vague possibilities: one, the possibility of willing oneself into another self;

another, regarding its cost, namely the destruction of one's self by this abandonment. A further vague possibility is the author's imagination of himself as his fictional character.

Borges's self-inscription in the character of Soergel is subtle yet convincing: bookish, a lover of Shakespeare, fascinated by the English language and its verbal music, an allusion to memorized readings from Chaucer to Plutarch, an article referencing "the versions of Homer," a thinly disguised rewording of Borges' essay title, "Las versiones homéricas" [The Homeric Versions]. One could also mention his sexual initiation with a mature woman, his half-blindness, or his tone—at once self-deprecating and assured. A teasing addition is the boasting comment that his book on Shakespeare's chronology was translated into several languages "incluso el castellano" [*including Spanish*] (*OC* III: 391; *CF* 508, emphasis added). And finally, in the inescapably Borgesian plaintive tone of the Postscriptum: "P.S. 1924 —Ya soy un hombre entre los hombres. En la vigilia soy el profesor emérito Hermann Soergel, que manejo un fichero y que redacto trivialidades eruditas" [P.S. (1924)—I am now a man among men. In my waking hours I am Professor Emeritus Hermann Soergel; I putter about the card catalogue and compose erudite trivialities] (*OC* III: 397; *CF* 515). The literary and biographical references are familiar but not so the pathos of their recollection.

The story is perhaps unique in its assertion of the existence of the individual self, not only as a fact but as something precious and quintessential. This realization comes to the protagonist through the memory of a saying by Spinoza, "Todas las cosas quieren perseverar en su ser . . . La piedra quiere ser una piedra, el tigre un tigre, yo quería volver a ser Hermann Soergel" [the wish of all things . . . is to continue being what they are. The stone wishes to be stone, the tiger, tiger—and I wanted to be Hermann Sörgel again] (*OC* III: 396; *CF* 514). Two observations spring to mind: one, this idea is a teasing contradiction of a (Buddhist) notion often argued by Borges, the "nothingness of personality," and, two, that this sentence about "uniqueness" is itself nearly a verbatim repetition. I refer to its mention in "Borges y yo." This idea of an essential concept of a unique self in this last fiction is an ironic example of the intensely diversified and complex process of self-figuration noted so far.

Borges's presence in his fiction has so far been studied mainly from the perspective of biographies written about him, including his own essay, as authoritative and meaningful points of comparison—the author as explanation of the work. The originality of this investigation is that it considers Borges mainly as a fabulist and consequently departs from the fiction itself to study the fictionalization of the "Borges" figure as the subject of the narrative. It looks at the method with which the author weaves biographical snippets, or biographemes, into a story and assesses the effect of this on the interpretative possibilities of the story. A significant finding is that every single one of the late fictions has a first-person narrator. There is a trajectory in how this manifests itself which ranges from the detached narrators in *El informe de Brodie* who often tell a story told and retold by another, to the increasingly emotional involvement in the later ones. According to Borges's own claim, these characters are all different manifestations of himself, as he robustly states here: "I've never created a character. It's always me, subtly disguised. . . . I'm always myself, irreparably, incurably, myself" (de la Fuente 36). The interest of this avowal lies, as I hope to have shown, in the detailed particularity of these "disguises" and the joy that their awareness brings to an appreciation of Borges's late fiction.

NOTES

1. See Urli, chapter 14.
2. See Michael Greenberg.
3. This incident will be discussed more fully in the context of "El otro" [The Other].
4. All unattributed translations are my own.
5. Old Norse becomes a more prominent feature in *El libro de arena*.
6. Borges recalls the memory of Isidoro Suárez in three poems.
7. The story "Guayaquil" in *El informe de Brodie* draws on this rivalry. See Balderston, *Out of Context* (115–31).
8. Two other key stories with female protagonists are "Emma Zunz" and "Ulrica."
9. This is a reedition of the early work that Borges published with Delia Ingenieros (*Antiguas literaturas germánicas* [1951]).
10. See Ali Shehzad Zaidi for a discussion of this idea (189–90).
11. Dollar bills are not dated according to when they were issued, but they do carry the date of the series to which they belong.
12. For a longer discussion of Borges and this Whitman poem, see Balderston, "The Fecal Dialectic."
13. For a more detailed discussion, see Alice E. H. Petersen and Ana María Hurtado.
14. There is a short piece called "Ragnarök" in *El hacedor* [*Dreamtigers*].

WORKS CITED

Balderston, Daniel. *How Borges Wrote*. University of Virginia Press, 2018.
Balderston, Daniel. *Out of Context: Historical Reference and the Representation of Reality in Borges*. Duke University Press, 1993.
Balderston, Daniel. "The Fecal Dialectic: Homosexual Panic and the Origin of Writing in Borges." *¿Entiendes? Queer Readings, Hispanic Writings*. Edited by Emilie L. Bergmann and Paul Julian Smith. Duke University Press, 1995, pp. 29–45.
Barnstone, Willis, ed. *Borges at Eighty: Conversations*. University of Indiana Press, 1982.
Borges, Jorge Luis. *Collected Fictions*, translated by Andrew Hurley. Penguin, 1999.
Borges, Jorge Luis. *Obras completas*. 4 vols. Emecé, 1996.
Borges, Jorge Luis. *Selected Non-Fiction, 1922–1986*, edited by Eliot Weinberger. Penguin, 2000.
Borges, Jorge Luis. *Veinticinco Agosto 1983 y otros cuentos*. Siruela, 1983.
Borges, Jorge Luis, and María Esther Vázquez. *Literaturas germánicas medievales*. Falbo, 1965 (first published as *Antiguas literatura germánicas*, con la colaboración de Delia Ingenieros, *Fondo de cultura económica*, 1951).
Brant, Herbert J. "Dreams and Death: Borges's *El libro de arena*." *ispanófila*, vol. 107, 1993, pp. 71–86.
Canto, Estela. *Borges a contraluz*. Espasa Calpe, 1989.
Carrizo, Antonio. *Borges el memorioso. Conversaciones de Jorge Luis Borges con Antonio Carrizo*. Fondo de Cultura Económica, 1982.

de la Fuente, Ariel. *Borges, Desire, and Sex*. Liverpool University Press, 2018.

Greenberg, Michael. "The Daggers of Jorge Luis Borges." *The New York Review*, January 9, 2014. https://www-nybooks-com.libproxy.ucl.ac.uk/articles/2014/01/09/daggers-jorge-luis-borges/.

Hadis, Martin. *Memorias de Leonor Acevedo*. Editorial Claridad, 2021.

Hadis, Martin. *Siete Guerreros Nortumbrios*. Emecé, 2012.

Hurtado, Ana María. "Ulrica o El enamorado y la Muerte. A propósito de un cuento de Jorge Luis Borges." *Trópico Absoluto*, May 19, 2016, https://tropicoabsoluto.com/2019/05/19/ulrica-o-el-enamorado-y-la-muerte-a-proposito-de-un-cuento-de-jorge-luis-borges/.

Leone, Leah. "A Chain of Endless Tigers: Borges at the University of Wisconsin-Milwaukee, April 9, 1976." *Variaciones Borges*, vol. 40, 2015, pp. 205–24.

Petersen, Alice E. H. "Borges's 'Ulrike': Signature of a Literary Life." *Studies in Short Fictions*, vol. 33, 1996, pp. 325–31.

Rodríguez Monegal, Emir. *Jorge Luis Borges: A Literary Biography*. Dutton, 1978.

Rojas, Santiago. "El desdoblamiento creador-personaje en Borges: Usos y efectos de creación." *Confluencias*, vol. 11, no. 1, 1995, pp. 75–88.

Shaw, Donald. *Borges' Narrative Strategy*. Francis Cairns, 1992.

Shehzad Zaidi, Ali. "The Overlooked Library in Borges's 'El otro.' " *Variaciones Borges*, vol. 31, 2011, pp. 181–97.

Williamson, Edwin. *Borges: A Life*. Viking, 2004.

PART III

COLLABORATION

CHAPTER 18

THE BUSTOS DOMECQ CYCLE

Going With and Against the Flow

MARIANO GARCÍA

> With friends, even what is boring is fun.
>
> —Adolfo Bioy Casares, *Wilcock*

FIVE years after their introduction at Victoria Ocampo's house, the productive intellectual relationship between Adolfo Bioy Casares and Jorge Luis Borges began in 1936, in one rather disconcerting way and another fairly predictable one. The disconcerting start to their work together is the notorious advertising brochure the two created for La Martona fermented milk, a product from the Casares' pioneering family dairy business (Martona was the nickname for Marta Casares, daughter of Vicente Casares and mother of the writer). Bioy Casares discussed the episode in his *Memorias,* and it has been analyzed in detail by Cristina Parodi ("Borges") and Nora Benedict, who point out Silvina Ocampo's overlooked presence as the illustrator of the mildly ironic image on the cover of the brochure (this trinity of "father," "son," and "holy spirit"—Silvina—would reappear in many other literary adventures). The predictable aspect of the duo, already fairly well-known, is the common theme that fueled their respective interests at the time and, in turn, fueled the writers' literary relationship: utopia (Levine 137–62).

These two disparate occurrences may well be apt symbols for characterizing certain aspects of Bioy Casares's and Borges's shared writing: the background of the writerly lineage and a shared literary genealogy.[1] While the collaboration to market fermented milk, with its ridiculous and even scatological basis,[2] demystifies any possible attribution of solemnity to that scriptural beginning, their rigorous theoretical and practical considerations of utopia reveal not only common interests but also the early desire to profile a certain type of reader and a certain canon. Advertising and the literary canon would thus converge in the inexhaustible work of both writers (Silvina Ocampo's discreet presence often included) in magazines, anthologies, and the collection of crime fiction novels, El Séptimo Círculo, for Emecé Editores.

The advertising brochure thus established some carnivalesque guidelines and some common ground (which would soon become the "orbis tertius") where the friends could put aside the strong sense of decorum that marked their social lives and their fictions— for they now had a mask, still somewhat blurred, of a third man who was coming into being. For readers of Bustos Domecq, the marketing brochure's fictionalized biography of a real scientist (Elías or Élie Metchnikoff) and the historical and geographical exoticism in its descriptions of the strange societies that consume fermented milk are recognizable to those accustomed to the pair's tongue-in-cheek, intellectual approach to an absurd topic.

With respect to the utopian atmosphere of their relationship in those years, it is tied to Borges's and Bioy Casares's active defense of fantastic literature. In his review of Bioy Casares's novella, *La estatua casera* (1936), Borges admonished the young author's surrealist dalliances but, at the same time, prescribed, for Bioy and for Argentine literature in general, a healthy diet of fantasy. He acknowledged, however, that in his exhaustive explorations of literary utopias, a very "articulado y orgánico" [articulated and organic] set of texts, there was indeed little fantasy to be found (*Borges en* Sur 130). Utopia would continue to be a theme explored by both writers, becoming, one might say, an emblem of the literary foundations of their relationship. Bioy appeared as a character in Borges's "Tlön, Uqbar, Orbis Tertius" in 1940. Likewise, in Bioy's own publication that same year, *La invención de Morel* (with its famous prologue by Borges), this first of his island novels (like the following one, *Plan de evasión* [1945]), dialogues with the utopian tradition while also problematizing it. To a great extent, both Borges and Bioy identify utopia with the world of letters and specifically with literature of imagination—as opposed to the less attractive pretensions of literature that sought to reflect reality (Premat).

Bioy's two novels dialogue with Borges in their positing utopia as heterotopia, that is, they are neither completely utopian nor completely dystopian. The very term "*orbis tertius*" alludes to the historic and often fanciful cartographies of our planet such as the *orbis terrae* or *orbis terrarum*, or even to Russian mystic Piotr Ouspensky's *Tertium organum* (1912), making it a third term: the negation of and prevailing over space and time. Indeed, Ouspensky's book, a refutation of Aristotle's *Organon* and his *principium tertii exclusi* (Principle of the Excluded Third), took as its starting point the reflections on the fourth dimension published by Charles Howard Hinton, a mathematician who is mentioned in "Tlön . . ." and other Borgesian texts.[3] But the writers' collaboration was itself an "obra tercera" ("third world" or "third work") (Levine 139), a strange region that sought to confront "los límites caseros de la sátira" [the domestic limits of satire] (*Borges in* Sur 130) that Borges criticized in the utopian tradition.

Between these two well-known foundations of Borges's and Bioy Casares's relationship, a somewhat less commented aspect often slips by. If we are to trust the Bioy Casares memoir, the same week they spent in the country writing the advertising brochure, they also tried writing an "enumerative sonnet" and sketched out a crime story Borges had thought up. The three extant pages of the tale's plot show "literally two-handed" writing (Martino 275) and pose a kind of utopian reductio ad absurdum: Dr. Preetorius, a "vasto caballero holandés" [vast Dutch gentleman] (Bioy Casares, cited in Martino 225), acquires

THE BUSTOS DOMECQ CYCLE   321

an island in the countryside south of Buenos Aires (which is rumored to hide a treasure) to demolish its old ranch and in its place build a youth retreat he would call El Recreo. Every fifteen days, Preetorius travels to "Lanús Oeste, a los bajos de Berazategui, a Villa Luro, a las curtiembres de Campana, a los alrededores de los gasómetros y las quemas" [Lanús Oeste, to the lowlands of Berazategui, to Villa Luro, to the tanneries of Campana, to the outskirts among the gasometers and the garbage dumps] (Bioy Casares, cited in Martino 226). In other words, he was traveling to working-class, immigrant-dense areas in the southwest of Buenos Aires province (similar to the area favored by Bustos Domecq) to recruit children to the retreat. The intrigue would begin when Preetorius was found dead, pierced by the lance of a famous cacique, to the consternation of his students, who swear revenge. Though just hinted at in the three notebook pages found among Bioy's papers at Rincón Viejo in 1990—Preetorius bringing the children "animales vistosos" [amazing animals] and "paquetes rectangulares envueltos en papel madera" [rectangular packages wrapped in kraft paper] (Bioy Casares, cited in Martino 226) —we know (based solely on what Bioy has told others) that the intention was turn Preetorius into a kind of philanthropic assassin who killed children by force of compulsory games and music at all hours.[4] Such a ridiculous crime being the narrative trigger and occurring within the framework of a paradox may very well be the seed from which grew the authors' shared detective fiction series (*Seis problemas para don Isidro Parodi* [*Six Problems for Mr. Isidro Parodi*] [1942]; *Un modelo para la muerte* [*A Model for Death*] [1946]), while the attempted sonnet (of which Bioy only remembered the line "los molinos, los ángeles, las eles") foreshadows the evolution of *Crónicas de Bustos Domecq* [*Chronicles of Bustos Domecq*] (1967). As for the ubiquitous name of the doctor, although Cristina Parodi offers an exhaustive panorama of possibilities that includes the speculations of other critics (*Borges-Bioy en contexto* 283), we might also consider, due to his mixture of comedy and terror, the infernal Doctor Pretorius who appears in James Whale's 1935 film *Bride of Frankenstein*, which came out in Argentina just a year before this initial collaboration.

Perhaps, more than the myth of Prometheus modernized by Mary Shelley, we might consider another myth, that of Pygmalion, when contemplating the extent to which Borges shaped Bioy Casares's style (or indeed shaped the man himself as a writer). Regarding their famous first meeting at Victoria Ocampo's house in 1932,[5] Bioy recalls that he spoke to Borges about his admiration for Azorín's descriptions and style.

> Me parece recordar que sobre el estilo de Azorín Borges murmuró algo acerca de la simplicidad y las frases cortas y que yo advertí, con un poco de sorpresa, que no era dicho elogiosamente. (Siempre tuve por virtud la simplicidad, aunque no siempre la practiqué.) Argumenté que las frases cortas permitían que lo descrito se viera aisladamente, como una piedra engarzada. . . . Volví a decir que todo se notaba distintamente y, si no me equivoco, Borges acotó, como para sí mismo: "También las frases cortas". No me atrevía a confesarle que el ritmo de las frases cortas me gustaba (*Bioy Casares a la hora de escribir* 118–19).

> [I seem to remember that, about Azorín's style, Borges murmured something about simplicity and short sentences, and that I noticed, somewhat surprised, that it had not been said in praise. (I always held simplicity as a virtue, although I did not always

practice it.) I argued that short sentences allowed what was being described to be seen in isolation, like a set stone. . . . I said again that everything was perceived in a different way and, if I'm not mistaken, Borges added, as if to himself: "Also the short sentences." I did not dare to confess that I liked the rhythm of the short sentences.]

It is difficult to reconcile Bioy Casares's taste for simplicity with the imminent adventure of Bustos Domecq. For Borges, who aspired to the clarity of a transparent style,[6] short sentences, apparently, did not necessarily equate to simplicity or clarity. Something of this attitude would later be found in the *Crónicas*, in reference to Loomis's synthetic art. But, before continuing, something more must be said regarding Borges's 1936 critique of Bioy Casares's *La estatua casera* in *Sur*.

This book (inexplicably omitted, along with the 1929 book *Prólogo*, from the bibliography of the *Obra completa* edited by Daniel Martino) betrays the presence of Silvina Ocampo not only in the cover art, but, essentially, in its style. The novella features a type of writing that deliberately blends fantasy with everyday experience, attempting—in this case—a not entirely successful imitation of the surrealist tone found in writings by Silvina Ocampo, whose singular voice would forcefully break onto the literary scene just a year later with *Viaje olvidado* (1937). Throughout the 1930s, Bioy Casares vacillated in his style and imitated other writers' voices, seeking his own: first that of his future wife and, shortly afterward, that of Borges (García, "La voz ajena" 80–82). He does not seem particularly sure in his conception of literature, as evidenced by the defense he attempts in "Sobre la técnica de los cuentos fantásticos" [On the technique of fantastic tales], included in *La estatua casera* and which he repeats in the rather muddled prologue to the *Antología de la literatura fantástica* [*Anthology of Fantastic Literature*] (1940) four years later, now with the obvious veneer of Borgesian stylistics (Louis 413–15). However, in the perpetual game of concessions and resistance that marked his relationship with Borges, here, a slight deviation from the "absolute" opinion of his great mentor can be glimpsed: Borges had already expressed his disagreement on the value of explaining the outcome of fantastic tales, which Bioy Casares had raised in his essay included in *La estatua casera* (*Borges en* Sur, 130–31). Yet Bioy would persist in emphasizing plot elucidation in the *Antología de la literatura fantástica*—and we all know the extremely long explanation with which *La invención de Morel* concludes. The fact is that most of Bioy Casares's fictions are inscribed not so much in what we understand to be fantastic literature as in the traditions of the gothic novel and the classic detective story, where a supernatural manifestation is displaced by the introduction of a rational clue that eliminates ambiguity, usually through a lengthy final explanation (Rivera 130). What in Borges can be left to unfathomable metaphysics, in Bioy needs justification. The opposition of these tendencies is what seems to inspire Bustos Domecq's joint writing.

However, the common ground, the *orbis tertius*, is achieved through their sharing and enjoying work with literature. It is the terrain of their anthologies, the detective collection, and the magazines *Destiempo* and *Los Anales de Buenos Aires* [*The Annals of Buenos Aires*].[7] Crime novels are quite obviously related to *Seis problemas* and *Un modelo*.

The discontinuous structure of the Bustos Domecq/Suárez Lynch cycle exhibits a disorienting asymmetry that begins with its mutable authorial attributions and, especially, with its erratic classification as a genre. The name of H(onorio) Bustos Domecq, who opens the series and of whom a "silhouette" is presented, is only used in the first two titles, *Seis problemas para don Isidro Parodi* and *Dos fantasías memorables* [*Two Memorable Fantasies*], while the name of B(enito) Suárez Lynch, purported disciple of Bustos Domecq, apart from the texts of "Museo," would only grace *Un modelo para la muerte*. The double surnames in both cases refer to respective ancestors of the authors. The film scripts published in 1955, however, were published with the friends' real names, as were *Crónicas de Bustos Domecq* (1967) and *Nuevos cuentos de Bustos Domecq* [*New Tales of Bustos Domecq*] (1977), where the former "author" had been subsumed into the title (Aguilar). It is worth remembering, though, that the use of pseudonyms remained a regular practice for Bioy Casares, who signed his *17 disparos contra lo porvenir* (1933) as Martín Sacastrú and the *Breve diccionario del argentino exquisito* (1971) as Javier Miranda.

These disconcerting deviations have a no less disconcerting correlate in their refusal to conform even minimally to reader expectations of genre. If the first book in the group, *Seis problemas para don Isidro Parodi*, is presented as the beginning of what would clearly be a serial publication, with the next title, *Dos fantasías memorables*, the authorship of Bustos Domecq is maintained, but the book deals not with detective cases but rather with supernatural events related to worlds of the *Libro del cielo y el infierno* [*Book of Heaven and Hell*]. Moreover, the imprisoned detective, Isidro Parodi, is not present in the second book but returns for *Un modelo para la muerte*; here, however, the author is no longer Bustos Domecq but Suárez Lynch. What could have motivated these changes? If it is true, as so often has been said, that the authors' collaborative writing was for the pure pleasure of working together, it is not so clear what was meant by these sudden changes of course other than the fear of getting bored repeating the same scheme. A review of the anthologies, magazines and the Séptimo Círculo collection can reveal a certain amount of whimsy and idiosyncrasy but also the awareness of and responsibility for operating in an intellectual field that they themselves (Borges in particular) had helped shape. Fiction writing as a duo, on the other hand, seems subject to somewhat darker designs that cannot be motivated by mere caprice.

Seis problemas para don Isidro Parodi from its outset weaves a complex para-thematic fabric whose warp and weft would progressively loosen, without disappearing entirely, in the titles that follow. The book would come to display a baroqueness that could not but progress toward a *manierismo* whose logic would eventually be inverted when finally arriving, with the *Crónicas*, at a critique of mannerism—understood as stylistic exaggeration due to excess or to absence. The profusion thus begins in *Seis problemas* with a "silhouette" of the unknown Bustos Domecq written by an "educator," which facilitates the dual objectives of outlining a humorous biography of the alleged author (a procedure that is taken up and described in more detail in the aforementioned *Crónicas*) and employing the mawkish, pedantic tones typical of Argentine school teachers of the time (and which Manuel Puig would recreate in "Diario de Esther, 1947" from his 1968 novel, *La traición de Rita Hayworth*). This abbreviated biography is followed by the introductory foreword of another pompous individual, Gervasio Montenegro, who also shows up in *Un modelo para la muerte* and *Nuevos cuentos de Bustos Domecq*. This prologue, however, already contains footnotes signed "HBD," yet Bustos Domecq's would not be the only interventions: occasionally the characters add notes themselves, creating Macedonio Fernández's noted "mareo del yo" [vertigo of the self] (214), which Borges addressed in his essay "Magias parciales del *Quijote*" [Partial Enchantments of the *Quixote*]. To the paratexts must also be added the profusion of quotes, epigraphs, and dedications not always attributable to the internal play of fictional characters and authors (for example, is it Bustos Domecq who dedicates one of the stories to Pope, or is it Borges and Bioy?) and for whose elucidation Parodi has offered us a treasure trove of keys that allow us to update an author–reader pact that has grown obscure over time and which, in fact, must not have been very clear even at the time of publication (*Borges-Bioy en contexto*).

In *Seis problemas para don Isidro Parodi*, the purported author, Honorio Bustos Domecq, narrates the various cases that the eponymous elderly barber[8]—imprisoned for a crime he did not commit—solves from behind bars. The "limited detective" takes up a detective tradition already present in characters such as M. P. Shiel's Prince Zalewski (a self-confined opium addict) or Ernest Bramah's Max Carrados (who is blind). Each story is a different case, following the same set-up: one or more visitors—compromised in a murder—visit Parodi's cell to tell their perspective of what happened. Each character who visits Don Isidro (not generally considered great practice for police) is an excuse to accumulate clichés, class markers, idiolects, fanciful turns, "al vesre" speech,[9] and general ugliness occasionally reaching extremes unheard of at the time. Overall, *Seis problemas* heralded a degree of colloquialism hitherto unpublished in Argentine literature, with the exceptions of gauchesque poetry and the orality of the *generación del 80*. Bustos Domecq's usages, nevertheless, are not limited to the exotic ostentation of rural speech, much less to the delicate register of fin de siècle dandies.

Within a fairly brief time, Parodi finds the answer, revealing an amazing capacity for interpretation that allows him to select, from within the cumbersome monologues, the few details necessary for solving the case. From the gallery of grotesque, cowardly, affected, or simply stupid characters, the *criollo* Isidro Parodi is the sober counterpoint, being the only character who is not a parody of anything. He is instead a paradigm of the detective, a perceptive reader of signs who deduces through logic and who knows how to retain the essentials of speeches that are loaded with "noise." Bioy's tendency for long explanations is clinched in just two or three short sentences in which Isidro Parodi solves and clears the case. Readers, for their part, must resignedly assume that the verbal pyrotechnics have distracted them enough not to retain any of the clues with which Isidro Parodi solves each case.

Four years later, the stories that comprise *Dos fantasías memorables* already present a change of course. There, a narrator named Mascarenhas addresses a certain Lumbeira, who limits himself to listening, in an elocutive situation similar to that of Don Isidro Parodi, but without then cleanly closing the case. Here we are not dealing with murders but with visions of a religious nature. These are announced by the book's title, a reference to the William Blake prose poem, "A Memorable Fancy," included in his *Marriage of Heaven and Hell* (1789–1790), which itself parodies Swedenborg's "memorable relations" in *Heaven and Its Wonders and Hell* published in Latin in 1758 (Parodi, *Borges-Bioy en contexto* 139). Apart from the motley language, which in this case imitates rural speech mixed with *cocoliche*,[10] the structure is different. Continuity is barely hinted at despite the attribution of authorship to Bustos Domecq and the reappearance of characters such as Carbone, Fainberg, and Bonfanti. In "El testigo" [The Witness], the grotesque vision of the Trinity in a basement—later demolished—on Belgrano Avenue (an echo of "El Aleph") is preceded by a scatological episode featuring pigs (a very recurrent animal throughout the series). Upon seeing the impossible ugliness of the divine monster, a girl dies, but there is no crime.

"El signo" [The Sign] presents an even more radical conjunction by extending the supernatural vision to the story of a publisher of antique pornographic and erotic books (*The Perfumed Garden, The Kama Sutra, The Hermaphrodite*) as well as invented ones (*Las capotas melancólicas*, a book found in Bioy Casares's *Plan de evasión* [Parodi, *Borges-Bioy en contexto* 159]). There is also mention of Oportet & Haereses, an apocryphal publishing house under whose name were published *Dos fantasías memorables*, *Un modelo para la muerte*, and *Nueva refutación del tiempo* by Borges. The name of the publisher alludes to a phrase from Paul to the Corinthians regarding heresy.[11] The usefulness of heresy and its ambiguous juxtapositions (which Borges will later develop spectacularly with "Los teólogos" [The Theologians]) is cryptically referenced by mention of the "Archbishop of Benevento," Giovanni della Casa, an author of licentious poems who inaugurated the Catholic Church's index of prohibited books (Parodi, *Borges-Bioy en contexto* 160). Yet the fact that Oportet & Haereses's publication claims value in heresy offers a clue about the authors' intention: not only are the visions impious in the sense of their ugliness; they also seem to negate or interrogate the idea of literature as necessarily being a vision of beauty. As for the second vision itself—a procession of foods that ascends to the zenith—the divine is diluted with the base material of these plebeian victuals, among which sneaks in a sexual allusion to female genitalia, the "empanadas con flecos," in a kind of surrealist mise en scène in spite of itself (Parodi, *Borges-Bioy en contexto* 162). These jarring empanadas in a Rabelaisian catalog of foods reproduce the sacrilegious strategy of combining celestial visions with excrement, base foods, and female genitalia. Just as Borges considered the allegorical procession at the end of Dante's *Purgatorio* "de una complicada fealdad" [of a complicated ugliness], *Dos fantasías memorables* seems to deepen their experimental interest in presenting ugliness without the support or justification of allegory and playing with it as literary heresy (*OC* II: 370).

Un modelo para la muerte returns us to the recognizable universe of Isidro Parodi, although this time the book is authored by Benito Suárez Lynch, a disciple of Bustos Domecq, who refers to him in the prologue as "mi joven amigo" [my young friend], "el novato" [the novice], "el mamón" [the suckling babe or mama's boy or sucker], or "el catecúmeno" [the recently baptized], possibly a humorous reflection upon the

Borges-Bioy relationship. While the slight stylistic differences from the previous titles do not appear sufficient to justify the change of "author," this change may ironically play with the "influence" that the older writer imposes on the disciple, whose writing is almost indistinguishable from his mentor. Borges and Bioy considered this their worst collection, "la decadencia de Bustos Domecq" [the decadence of Bustos Domecq] (Bioy Casares, *Borges* 706). However, it is fair to say that despite the "jokes about jokes about other jokes," the "ridiculous humor," and the "darkness" (Parodi, *Borges-Bioy en contexto* 165), which made the authors doubt the advisability of republishing it, there is nothing in *Un modelo para la muerte* that is exceptionally inconsistent with the first publication, except for the fact that the book contains just one case to be solved. While the plot is thus more extensively developed, this actually makes the book less convincing, the stylistic technique of baroque orality mentioned above being unsustainable over a longer text, as compared to the stories. The most outstanding mark of continuity with the previous text is the reappearance of characters—possibly the highest stakes for this installment in the series—a fact that is reflected in the *dramatis personae*, which, in the manner of (the reviled) Agatha Christie's novels, precedes the narration.

The greatest difference between *Un modelo para la muerte* and its "model," *Seis problemas*, resides in the dénouement, where Isidro Parodi does not clarify the mystery with his lucid deductions and the clear language that the reader appreciates, but instead receives it in a letter that explains the conclusion in the same overwrought style used by the rest of the characters. Indeed, from the prologue, Suárez Lynch is criticized: "Se ha permitido caricatos, ha cargado las tintas" [he has gone overboard into caricatures, he has laid it on thick]; later there is mention of "su versión, más o menos caricatural y deforme, del crimen de San Isidro" [his more or less caricaturized and deformed version of the San Isidro crime], "de la cacofonía y del caos" [of the cacophony and the chaos], and the torrential prose accumulates phrases in French, in Italian, as well as various mocking imitations of peninsular Castilian (or something that attempts to pass as such) (*OCC* 147, 158, 185):

> . . . hogaño se manifiesta henchida y pujante, alzaprimando a machamartillo el pendón de la fabla de Indias, y aporreando con fiera tozudez a galiparlistas noveleros y a casticistas añejados en el perimido remedo de Cervantes, de Tirso, de Ortega y de tantos otros maestros de una cháchara mortecina. (*OCC* 157)

> [. . . today it manifests itself swollen and thriving, hoisting with grave conviction the standard of the fable of the Indies, and with fierce obstinacy beating Gallophile novelists and aged Castilian purists into the outdated imitation of Cervantes, Tirso, Ortega and so many other masters of decrepit prattle.]

> Quienes azacanadamente regruñen que es de novacheleros el afán de sopalancar y engreír la novísima parla indocastellana, muy a las claras patentizan su mustia condición de antañones, cuando no de pilongos y desmarridos. (*OCC* 184)

> [Those who assiduously grumble that the zeal for elevating and indulging the latest Indocastillian speech is the stuff of *novacheleros*, very clearly show their musty condition of being geriatrics, when not infirm and wilted.]

As the Frogman character sums it up at the end of the fourth section, this text is the closest thing to "un libro-misterio que estaba en idioma que ni Dios pescaba ni diome" [a book-mystery that was in a language that not even God could understand the half of], though at least it captures a kind of sustained mockery of the kind of Spanish purism from which Borges had sought to distance himself even from his first publications in Argentina, and of which Bioy was wary, seeing it embodied in the figure of his, for him, unpleasant sister-in-law (*OCC* 179).[12] Here the excess points less to the grotesqueness of the story, as found in *Dos fantasías*, than to that of language.

Between *Un modelo para la muerte* and *Crónicas* spans a period of two decades, interrupted solely by the "serious" film scripts *Los orilleros* [*The Hoodlums*] and *El paraíso de los creyentes* [*The Paradise for Believers*] (1955), which fall within the authors' well-known views on what was, by then, the already distant world of *malevos* and *compadritos*. This joint contribution could be said to illuminate both authors' interests in this history of which, more than traces or imprints, only relics remain. The misleading nostalgic look on the character of Julio Morales in *Los orilleros*, when recounting an episode from his youth, structures the story in a series of flashbacks that contrast the noisy present—trucks with loudspeakers presumably playing the Peronist anthem—against an end of the nineteenth century presented as a remote world (very much in harmony with what Bioy's father recounts in his 1958 memoire, *Antes del novecientos*) (*OCC* 201). The figure of Fermín Soriano is somewhat more complex than a mere picturesque *compadrito*, as the authors themselves testify in the prologue and as evidenced by the scene in which he tortures and kills a cat in front of Elena (*OCC* 199, 223). Beyond its legendary aura, which Borges himself helped to create, the representation of the *compadritos* repeatedly reveals the critical nuances Bioy dealt with a year earlier in *El sueño de los héroes* (Grieco y Bavio and Veda 253; García "Reformulation").[13] While these scripts aroused little interest in the local film scene (the filming of *Los orilleros* would only occur twenty years later under the direction of the relatively unknown Ricardo Luna),[14] Borges's and Bioy's shared interest in cinema would bear much more recognized fruit in their collaboration with the director Hugo Santiago: *Invasión* [*Invasion*] (1969)—with which they return to dystopian spheres—and *Les Autres* (1974) perhaps demonstrate their autonomy to be a product of film; they wrote them together with the director and were not concerned about publishing them. It is worth mentioning that *Los orilleros* and *El paraíso de los creyentes* carry their literary weight: more than anything, they are a book. The films made with Santiago, however, belong to the cinematographic universe in their own right while possessing a "hybrid, trans-genre, unsituatable, disturbing" aspect that is far from the "deliberate, effective and conscious" writing of their other collaborations (Lafon and Peeters 213).

Crónicas de Bustos Domecq represents the most striking deviation of the series. The authors return to the writer from Pujato, in Santa Fe province, now with their own names on the book cover, as would happen with the next and last volume of their collaboration. In this installment, we are far from murders or supernatural visions: the crimes in question are perpetrated against the arts, where "tontos son admirados por otros tontos" [fools are admired by other fools] (Bioy Casares, *Borges* 990). With a fairly controlled language, *legible* as opposed to his previous baroque orality, the voice of Bustos Domecq only occasionally seems to dissolve into that of the pompous Gervasio Montenegro when describing modern or avant-garde works that constitute, in several of the twenty-one cases, parodies of Borges himself. The use of plagiarism in "Homenaje a César Paladión" [Homage to César Paladión] is an (even greater!) reductio ad absurdum of Pierre Menard's procedure; "Una tarde con Ramón Bonavena" [An Afternoon with Ramón Bonavena] plays with the problem of mimesis and representation that Borges had been taking on since the time of "La postulación de la realidad" [The Postulation of Reality] (1932); "Naturalismo al día" [*Naturalism of the Day*] refers to the life-scale, 1:1 map published in the "Museo" section (*Los Anales de Buenos Aires* 3) recovered by Borges for the similarly titled section of *El Hacedor* [*Dreamtigers*] (1960); the chaotic enumeration of "El gremialista" [The Union Member] recalls the famous Chinese encyclopedia of "El idioma analítico de John Wilkins" [The Analytical Language of John Wilkins]. All these stories, in general, refer us to those false bibliographic notes so characteristic of Borges's work and which would be elevated in literature by Juan Rodolfo Wilcock with his *La sinagoga degli iconoclasti* (1972), *Lo stereoscopio dei solitari* (1972), and *Il libro dei mostri* (1978). Abstract painting and sculpture receive their share of scorn in "Un pincel nuestro: Tafas" [A Paint Brush of Our Own: Tafas] and "El ojo selectivo" [The Selective Eye] as does cuisine in "Un arte abstracto" [An Abstract Art] (where the aforementioned Doctor Preetorius makes an appearance), architecture in "Eclosiona un arte" [An Art Hatches] (with echoes of Macedonio Fernández's absurd inventions during his campaign for president of Argentina), theater in "El teatro universal" [Universal Theater], sartorial arts in two texts entitled "Vestuario" [Wardrobe], and, finally, history in "Un enfoque flamante" [A Brilliant Point of View], where what we know today as "post-truth" is presented as a ridiculous joke. The general subject under attack with *Crónicas* are art's mechanisms of synthesis and its aspiration to austerity. In this sense, the book confirms the authors' baroque posture in its brilliant (it is the most satisfactory book of the entire collaboration) but, again, somewhat dark realization of its intentions. We might view the distribution of the authors' collaborations in the following way: Borges contributes his famous theories and Bioy laughs at them, according to what he himself has confessed: "Yo soy un escritor satírico. Me place reírme de lo que más quiero, quizá en un secreto afán de sentir que ese amor es desinteresado, puro" [I am a satirical writer. It pleases me to laugh at what I love most, perhaps in a secret desire to feel that this love is disinterested, pure] (*Memorias* 67). Although the obvious target of the attack is "contemporary art," the parody directly touches Borgesian creations. Perhaps it was a way of putting a stop to the already hypertrophied baroque style of *Un modelo para la muerte*, even if the revision and miniaturization of the great Borgesian moments are themselves still baroque.

The *Nuevos cuentos de Bustos Domecq*, the last avatar of the series, was published in 1977, although the texts that comprise it were written between the 1940s and 1960s, a fact that is betrayed in the disjointed stylistic and creative cohesion of the collection. The series remains loosely articulated through the recurring characters, although here they are mostly minor, and there is a general dispersion with respect to the dramatic unity and setting present in *Seis problemas* and *Un modelo*. In "Penumbra y pompa" [Shadow and Celebration] we learn that Isidro Parodi has regained his freedom, and thus, without further emphasis, the conclusion of the cycle seems to be announced. The volume's quite gruesome humor finds its paradigm in the already legendary "La fiesta del monstruo"

[The Monster's Party] (written in 1947), which radiates its *tremendismo* to the rest of the stories and largely outshines them.

Both the title of the first story, "Una amistad hasta la muerte" [A Lifelong Friendship], as well as the epigraph of "La fiesta del monstruo" and the mention of José Hernández in "La forma de la gloria" ultimately inscribe the Bustos Domecq cycle in the political tradition of pamphlets and of gauchesque poetry by invoking the names of Eduardo Gutiérrez, Hilario Ascasubi, and the author of *Martín Fierro*. In the light of that tradition, defined by its cryptic lexicon that highlighted local color and an oral syntax that recreated the speech of the gaucho as imagined by the men of letters who imitated it, the extravagances and mannerisms of the Borges-Bioy cycle seek to position themselves within a tradition and a genealogy of which the Bustos Domecq cycle is a deformed, motley reflection, only occasionally marked by political struggle. The use of the foreign voice, however, is part of a broader and older tradition than that of the Argentine *gauchesque*. Let us consider, for example, the case of Giuseppe Baretti, an Italian critic very close to Dr. Johnson who, following in the footsteps of publications such as the *Spectator*, created a fictitious character, a soldier of extremely low extraction from under whose mask idiomatic barbarities were lavished (Wellek 166), or in the much closer and contemporary Carlos Warnes, a writer and journalist who, like Borges, spent time writing for the newspaper *Crítica*, and who would offer a concentrate of idiomatic aberrations from the hand of his very famous character César Bruto.

In any case, Bustos Domecq's swan song poses a darker atmosphere than that of its beginning, a movement from a certain spirit of social satire to a bitter and even misanthropic sarcasm. The characters, among whom not even Parodi or Bustos Domecq are spared, are revealed as scoundrels, the crimes end up being petty, the tone disenchanted. This may be connected in part with the spirit of negating the changes in the country, which was present from the beginning, but also with the very exhaustion of the process and the collaboration, a scheme that could no longer give more of itself and had reached its climax with the *Crónicas*.

Despite the history of their friendship and the productive results just discussed, the personalities of the two writers reveal significant differences. The orality in writing pursued by each is one of these differences. Borges experimented with oral register in his early writings, but he moved away from the strict imitation of speech to seek instead an abstraction of its various forms (Balderston). Bioy Casares, on the other hand, after the more bookish beginnings of his career, points to a simple imitation of a certain middle-class type of Argentine speech, which is evidenced in his many and unsuccessful attempts at writing theater. With respect to their choices in reading, Borges was a very broad and curious reader until his definitive blindness, while Bioy Casares was a more selective, limited reader, with a relatively narrower view of literature; one who, throughout his life, repeated comments on the same books with hardly any variations and was very unenthusiastic when encountering novelty (compared to Borges, Bioy did not exactly stand out as a literary critic). Being the great diarist that he was, what do stand out are his readings of diaries, memoirs, and writings on the self—a field apparently foreign to Borges.[15] In terms of style, Borges is a fan of irony, eventually of allegory, but not exactly of satire or caricature, while Bioy is (*Memorias* 67–68). These differences may have required an extreme negotiation, which is sanctioned in a stylistic relaxation—jokes, rudeness, the grotesque—that could operate in both the contemporary atmosphere and the tradition of universal literature. The tendency toward depth in Borges wrangles with the immediacy or, frankly, the superficiality in Bioy. It appears we could consider this the concession of the teacher to the student after having schooled him during the "utopian" period. Thus, Borges would accept Bioy's rather crude humor (especially in the caricatures of society people, which were quite infrequent in Borges) as well as his tendency toward the grotesque. This search for internal balance constitutes the tension and the strangeness of Bustos Domecq and his avatars, hypnotic artifacts of a hidden, secret, but indisputable influence on Argentine literature.

Notes

1. Pride in their ancestors is a class trait common to both authors that is reflected in their process of choosing pseudonyms. To this we must add the fact that both men's fathers, Jorge Guillermo Borges and Adolfo Bioy, wrote notable books: *El caudillo* (1921) and *La senda* (2015, posthumous), and *Antes del novecientos* (1958) and *Años de mocedad* (1963), respectively. If Borges Sr. aspired, through an elaborate style, to an allegorical and didactic literature that at times approached Macedonio Fernández, Adolfo Bioy's books constituted a luminous and joyful evocation of his childhood and adolescence whose highlights include descriptions of rural life and *criollo* speech as well as memories of Buenos Aires and Europe at the turn of the century.
2. Fermented milk's contribution to intestinal regularity appears sublimated in Silvina Ocampo's cover art, a drawing in the form of ethereal doves against the background of womanly hips. The text of the brochure, meanwhile, abounds in "intestinal putrefaction" and "gastric poisoning." See Benedict 97 and Parodi, "Borges": 265–68.
3. A prologue to Hinton's *Scientific Romances*, the essays "La cuarta dimensión" [The Fourth Dimension], "Fragmento sobre Joyce" [A Fragment on Joyce], and the review "Edward Kasner and James Newman," the stories "El milagro secreto" [The Secret Miracle] and "*There are more things*," and, finally, a prologue to Maeterlink's *The Intelligence of Flowers* (Helft).
4. Bioy Casares offered this evocation for the 1964 issue of *L'Herne* dedicated to Borges, later collected as "Libros y amistad" [Books and Friendship] in *La otra aventura* (1968); he would repeat the anecdote with some variations in a talk with the members of Félix della Paolera's literary workshop (115–16) and textually in his *Memorias* (76–78).
5. This is the year that Bioy Casares usually gives when recalling that anecdote. Daniel Martino, however, proposes the end of 1931 as the date of the meeting (*ABC de Adolfo Bioy Casares* 282).
6. Borges frequently associated good writing with clarity or "transparency." In his prologue to the Spanish translation of Gide's *Les Faux-monnayeurs*, for example, he states that the French writer, after having used "el dialecto ornamental de los simbolistas" [the ornamental dialect of the symbolists"] in his early work, "siempre fue fiel, después, a la buena tradición de la claridad" [was always faithful, later on, to the good tradition of clarity] (Borges, *Biblioteca personal* 27). Better known is his definition of José Bianco's style: "Como el cristal o como el aire, el estilo de Bianco es invisible" [Like glass or like air, Bianco's style is invisible], to indicate a classic style that does not interfere between text and reader (Bianco 9). Like Gide and like Bioy, Borges also had his youthful baroque excesses, which he later partially abjured.

7. For the history of the texts in the "Museum" section in the magazines *Destiempo* and *Los Anales de Buenos Aires* [*The Annals of Buenos Aires*] signed by B. Suárez Lynch, see Mariela Blanco.

8. On this curious character and his story, see Pitlevnik.

9. A colloquial lower-class mode of speech in which the syllables of certain words are inverted, a classic example being *tango = gotán*.

10. An Italian-Spanish hybrid spoken by Italian immigrants, especially in Greater Buenos Aires, during periods of mass immigration (1880s–1920s) with many words still present in informal speech.

11. "*Nam oportet et haereses esse*" (1 Cor 11:19).

12. In a diary entry for July 24, 1961, for example, Bioy wrote: "Victoria lee un discurso que empieza con una de esas fealdades tan de su cuño: «Hace la friolera de treinta y cinco años que conozco a Borges»" [Victoria reads a speech that begins with one of those ugly assertions so typical of her: 'I have known Borges for a whopping thirty-five years'] (*Borges* 734).

13. Bioy affirms that his collaboration in *Los orilleros* was limited to running behind Borges (*Borges* 49).

14. In argentine cinema Ricardo Luna was best known as choreographer, actor and also as screenwriter for some of Leopoldo Torre Nilsson's films. *Los orilleros* was the only film he directed.

15. The writing of a diary seems to condemn its author to a certain self-limitation caused by the need to contain the details of reality—and literature—so that they do not overwhelm the space of a regular journal entry. In this way, we see that Bioy copies fragments of letters in his diary or vice versa; that he repeats his opinion about a book verbatim, sometimes decades later' and that, overall, he surrenders to an *economic and synthetic* version of reality that allowed him to manage and write about it daily.

WORKS CITED

Aguilar, Gonzalo. "La disolución del arte (sobre *Crónicas de Bustos Domecq*)." *Variaciones Borges*, no. 49, 2020, pp. 33–48.

Balderston, Daniel. *El precursor velado: R. L. Stevenson en la obra de Borges*. Sudamericana, 1982.

Benedict, Nora. "(In)visible Collaborations between *los hermanos* Borges and *los* Bioy." *Variaciones Borges*, no. 49, 2020, pp. 89–116.

Bianco, José. *Ficción y reflexión. Una antología de sus textos*. FCE, 1988.

Bioy, Adolfo. *Años de mocedad (recuerdos)*. Nuevo Cabildo, 1963.

Bioy, Adolfo. *Antes del novecientos (recuerdos)*. Nuevo Cabildo, 1952.

Bioy Casares, Adolfo. *Bioy Casares a la hora de escribir*, edited by Esther Cross and Félix della Paolera. Tusquets, 1988.

Bioy Casares, Adolfo. *Borges*, edited by Daniel Martino. Destino, 2006.

Bioy Casares, Adolfo. *La estatua casera*. Jacarandá, 1936.

Bioy Casares, Adolfo. *La otra aventura*. Emecé, 2004.

Bioy Casares, Adolfo. *Memorias. Infancia, adolescencia y cómo se hace un escritor*. Tusquets, 1994.

Bioy Casares, Adolfo. *Obra completa I (1940–1958)*, edited by de Daniel Martino. Emecé, 2012.

Bioy Casares, Adolfo. *Wilcock*, edited by de Daniel Martino. Emecé, 2021.

Blanco, Mariela. "Las piezas de 'Museo' de B. Suárez Lynch." *Variaciones Borges*, no. 49, 2020, pp. 117–41.

Borges, Jorge Guillermo. *El caudillo.* Mansalva, 2009.

Borges, Jorge Guillermo. *La senda,* edited by María Julia Rossi and Daniel Balderston. Borges Center, 2015.

Borges, Jorge Luis. *Biblioteca personal (prólogos).* Alianza, 1988.

Borges, Jorge Luis. *Borges en* Sur. *1931–1980.* Emecé, 1999.

Borges, Jorge Luis. *Obras completas.* Emecé, 1974.

Borges, Jorge Luis. *Obras completas en colaboración.* Emecé, 1979.

Borges, Jorge Luis. *Obras completas II. 1975–1985.* Emecé, 1989.

Fernandez, Macedonio. *Museo de la Novela de la Eterna, Obras completas, Tomo VI.* Corregidor. 1975.

Helft, Nicolás. *Jorge Luis Borges. Bibliografía e índice.* Ediciones Biblioteca Nacional, 2013.

García, Mariano. "La voz ajena. Bioy Casares como lexicógrafo y antólogo." *Texturas. Estudios interdisciplinarios sobre el discurso,* no. 14, 2014, pp. 79–90.

García, Mariano. "Reformulación de lo heroico borgeano en la obra de Adolfo Bioy Casares." *Gramma,* no. 48, 2011, pp. 108–21.

Grieco y Bavio, Alfredo, and Miguel Vedda. "Nueva refutación del coraje. La destrucción del 'mito criollo' en la obra de Adolfo Bioy Casares." *Homenaje a Adolfo Bioy Casares.* Edited by Alfonso De Toro and Susanna Regazzoni. Vervuert, 2002, pp. 251–67.

Lafon, Michel, and Benoît Peeters. *Escribir en colaboración. Historias de dúos de escritores.* Beatriz Viterbo, 2008.

Levine, Suzanne Jill. *Guía de Bioy Casares.* Fundamentos, 1982.

Louis, Annick. "Definiendo un género. La *Antología de la literatura fantástica* de Silvina Ocampo, Adolfo Bioy Casares y Jorge Luis Borges." *Nueva Revista de Filología Hispánica,* vol. 49, no. 2, 2001, pp. 409–37.

Martino, Daniel. *ABC de Adolfo Bioy Casares.* Ediciones de la Universidad, 1991.

Parodi, Cristina. *Borges-Bioy en contexto. Una lectura guiada de H. Bustos Domecq y B. Suárez Lynch.* Borges Center, 2018.

Parodi, Cristina. "Borges, Bioy y el arte de hacer literatura con leche cuajada." *Reescrituras,* edited by Luis Rodríguez-Carranza and Marilene Nagle. Rodopi, 2004, pp. 259–72.

Pitlevnik, Leonardo. "Celda 273, Penitenciaría Nacional." *Variaciones Borges,* no. 49, 2020, pp. 143–62.

Premat, Julio. "Borges utopista y los narradores del fin de siglo argentino." *Variaciones Borges,* no. 50, 2020, pp. 149–65.

Rivera, Jorge B. "Lo arquetípico en la narrativa argentina del 40." *Ficciones argentinas. Antología de lecturas críticas.* Norma, 2004, pp. 125–52.

Wellek, René. *Historia de la crítica moderna (1750-1950). Tomo I. La segunda mitad del siglo XVIII.* Gredos, 1959.

CHAPTER 19

....

JORGE LUIS BORGES AND THE INTERVIEW AS THEATER

....

CODY C. HANSON

JORGE Luis Borges is among the most well-known and thoroughly researched authors of the Spanish language. Countless critics have meticulously analyzed his short stories, poems, and essays. His prodigious literary production spans many genres, including biography, detective fiction, essay, poetry, screenplay, short story, and story essay, and features works authored both individually and collaboratively, yet this versatile writer never composed a dramatic work (or a novel).[1] In fact, from time to time Borges voiced his aversion toward writing novels, but on at least one occasion manifested his intent to write a play ("Borges una vez más" 12; Cruz 2; Geneson 252; Gilio 44; Milleret 71; Vargas Llosa, "Fictions" 1329; Zito Lema 46).[2] Since this desire never materialized, however, L. Howard Quackenbush speculates the Argentine author may have been a "frustrated dramatist" whose story "El milagro secreto" [The Secret Miracle] is best read as a hybrid *cuento-drama* (77–78). Yet beyond this sole example, it would appear that Borges deliberately avoided experimenting with theater in his fiction. Tellingly, perhaps, Borges was well versed in the works of numerous playwrights but did not particularly enjoy attending the theater (Childress and McNair 32; Cruz 2; Quackenbush 77; Scott 106). Quackenbush's observation on the *cuento-drama* emphasizes what critics have long recognized: hybrid or blended genres are characteristic of Borges and that makes it difficult to fix his works within the limits of any particular category (Vargas Llosa, "Fictions" 1332). Indeed, Borges rejects the conventional structures and confines of literary genres and forges his own unique creative outlets. He imitates, parodies, and mixes traditional genres and invents new ones, including his ingenious blending of the standard essay and the short story (Stark 12). His expertise in transgenre literature, coupled with his propensity for innovation, reveals an ability to create new and divergent theatrical forms.

One genre that has great potential for literary experimentation is the interview. Critics laud Borges's original literary production and his unique style, but few have considered the contributions he made by granting hundreds of interviews throughout his life, particularly after he went blind. Borges used the medium as a rich autobiographical narrative and took advantage of its performative qualities to create literary-filled interlocutions, which significantly add to our understanding of his life and work. Naturally, the tension between biographical and fictional selves is not new in Borges. This motif plays out beautifully in "Borges y yo" [Borges and I] and is what motivates the narrator "Borges" to confess that he goes on living so that his other persona can weave literary texts that justify his existence (*OC* II: 186). While the interview genre may call for a more factual performance, its specific circumstances and contexts create a space where that performance can be reconceptualized and reinterpreted. Indeed, the interview cultivates a site-specific performance and may even become a space where literature and theater occur (Birch and Tompkins 1; Pearson and Shanks 23). This chapter argues that in Borges's hands, the interview ceases to be a mere journalistic endeavor and becomes a type of dramatic production. In fact, Borges's interviews are a hybridized genre similar to his fictional works. Through his engagement with the ubiquitous interview genre, Borges becomes a prolific interviewee-dramatist whose "theatrical works" have been hiding in plain sight as his published interviews.

Interviews are the product of an exchange between individuals and so their very nature invites dramatic performance and interpretation. Indeed, one playwright has noted that "drama *is* dialogue" (Ionesco, *Notes* 177). In point of fact, Roberto Alifano asserts that in interviews Borges is "a master of dialogue" whose oral and written voices "share the same imaginative ideas—profound and beautiful in their expression" (*Twenty-Four Conversations* xiv). A brilliant interview with Borges by James Irby at the University of Texas at Austin in 1961 also captures Borges's charisma as an interviewee. Fernando Sorrentino likewise observes that in interviews, Borges "is a courteous, easy-going gentleman who verifies no quotations, who does not look back to correct mistakes, who pretends to have a poor memory; he is not the terse Jorge Luis Borges of the printed page, that Borges who calculates and measures each comma and each parenthesis" (xv). Borges undoubtedly creates and embellishes in both his interviews and his traditional literary works. Consider, for instance, how it is widely known that Borges was an expert in English language and literature, yet, in an interview with Willis Barnstone, Borges poetically and antithetically confessed: "I myself first read *Don Quijote* in English. It was one of those books in my father's library, a room from which I may never have come out. Later when I read Cervantes in Spanish I felt I was reading an uncertain translation from English" (49). This surprising comment is not true—the edition he refers to, published by Garnier Hermanos in Paris, was in Spanish. But it is also ironic because it privileges Borges's fascination with the English language and echoes his idea that context determines one's relation to a literary work, as illustrated in his fictional account of Pierre Menard's attempt to rewrite the *Quixote* by becoming Cervantes ("Pierre Menard" 447). Borges's remark on English and Cervantes also suggests that, like "La biblioteca de Babel" [The Library of Babel], circularity and repetition are inevitable given an infinite amount of time and space (465–71). This example demonstrates that Borges possesses the ability to create oral texts as enigmatic and captivating as his written fictions.

The modern understanding of the interview as a journalistic inquiry whose purpose is to produce "statements or facts for publication" comes from nineteenth-century

American English and carries with it the original connotation of a "face to face" meeting or "formal conference" of "great persons" ("Interview"). The interview genre, therefore, tends to be a serious endeavor that aspires to factual and historical fidelity (Lasky 63). Indeed, readers of interviews generally anticipate straightforward and honest responses to earnest questions. Ted Lyon observes that the public even considers literary interviews to be thoughtful events "where sober utterances allow us insight into a writer's mind and works [. . .]. In creative literature we have come to look down on the author's presence as too intrusive. In the interview, however, we expect her/him to be there, strongly present, and we expect her/him to be truthful and honest with us" ("Jorge Luis Borges" 78). Unlike the fictional narrator found in literary works, people generally suppose the interview has a nonfictional narrator who accurately reveals their genuine self and work. In fact, Jean Royer goes so far as to affirm the two main sources of literary information are criticism and the interview (122). Many readers anticipate an authentic account that provides insight into the interviewee's life and work.

While interviews with authors do produce valuable statements for publication, many of which are insightful and trustworthy, their primary appeal has more than a touch of fiction. While the ostensible intent of interviews is to establish fact, Ronald Christ asserts that they "allude to data while being about the real business of creating character" ("An Interview" 114). The character the interview creates, however, may not always be as straightforward and factual as anticipated, and may increase the differences between the narrated and actual selves (Arnold 569). Writers, in particular, tend to be acutely aware of their ability to create fiction in the interview and take advantage of the genre "to compose a self which turns out to be remarkably like the selves they invent in their work" (Arkin 13, 18). Similar to traditional literary texts, authors may use the interview to reveal a story while hiding behind a fictitious narrator. Indeed, the literary interview is a dramatic performance akin to what John Rodden terms a "docudrama" because it combines biographical, fictional, and theatrical elements (16–17). The literary interview, therefore, is a hybrid form whose aesthetic qualities approach existing literary genres and even fiction itself (Masschelein et al. 39). Bruce Bawer thus cynically concludes that literary interviews are primarily entertainment (429). When literary actors exploit the interview's stylistic elements, the genre's factual and journalistic significance recede behind a fictional foreground.

A handful of scholars have devoted critical attention to the numerous interviews Borges granted throughout his life. Chief among them are dual studies by Ted Lyon that identify the literary qualities of Borges's interviews. In the first, Lyon explores how Borges used humor and the "put-on" to play creatively and comically in the interview ("Put-on" 58). In the second, he postulates that Borges regularly controlled the interview more directly than the interviewer did and thus turned the medium into a literary genre and a personal art form ("Jorge Luis Borges" 75). Likewise, Daisi Vogel argues it is possible to think of Borges's interviews as a late form of his essays because they are filled with aesthetic and philosophical experimentation (14, 262). My previous study continues in the vein of these critics to claim that the performative aspects of Borges's interviews make them subjective texts much like his other fictional works (Hanson 254).

Indeed, in interviews Borges frequently delivers a rich fictional performance as complex as his traditional literary works, and thus makes it routinely difficult to separate performance from fact. In his analysis of the interviews, Antonio Munir Hachemi Guerrero uses a distinct approach to examine Borges's voice as both a part of his literary work and his biography. He applies Leonor Arfuch's notion of biographical space to examine how Borges capitalized on the interview genre to project a certain autobiographical image of himself and concludes that the Argentine author was hyperconscious of the fact that others would interpret his literary works through his words (Hachemi Guerrero 182, 201). The present study considers Borges's interviews to be a literary performance that are best understood as theatrical performances akin to Readers Theater and the Theater of the Absurd.

Although Borges never wrote an official play, Quackenbush identifies dramatic qualities and connections that open up the possibility of reading "El milagro secreto" as the theatrical expression of Borges's frustrated inner playwright. In fact, Borges admits that he included drama in the story as a way to write a play that he would not produce otherwise (Burgin 25). Borges's tragedy, as revealed in narrative form, recounts the dramatic tale of a Czech writer named Jaromir Hladík who the invading Nazis arrest in 1939 on suspicion of being Jewish. Condemned to die by firing squad, Hladík laments the quality of his professional literary work and concludes his only path to redemption and "vindication in eternity" is by finally composing his play *Los enemigos* [*The Enemies*]. For Hladík, the "secret miracle" transpires when God suspends time between the fatal shot and his inevitable execution, thereby granting the frustrated writer the time needed to finish his masterpiece (*OC* I: 510, 512). Quackenbush notes that Hladík's hope for immortality represents humanity's common struggle with death and corresponds to "Borges' search for eternal life through the medium of dramatic creation" (79). He further argues that the story's theatricality is the result of Hladík's incomplete tragedy and Borges's suppressed play as intercalated intertextual dramas; the preeminence of the dramatic through parallel imagery, universal name types, and dream states that telescope into each other; intertextual interrelationships between characters and authors; the juxtaposition of the terms tragedy and tragicomedy at each end of the story; Hladík's tragic destiny; the metaphysical interwoven plot; and the story's circular layers of metatheater (80–85). Reading "El milagro secreto" as theater, as a hybrid story-drama, and as the product of Borges's dramatic expression, reveals a highly capable and innovative author who willingly pushed the limits of genre to create fresh literary works. It also suggests Borges is willing to take advantage of the characteristics of other genres to create theater.

Readers Theater is the dramatic declamation of the written word and possesses distinct characteristics as a unique theatrical genre that bears semblance to the interview. In fact, Readers Theater and the literary interview both developed contemporaneously as new phenomena in the middle of the twentieth century and were primed for experimentation and imaginative techniques (Bawer 422; Coger and White 19). In its most basic arrangement, Readers Theater involves two performers with individual roles who engage in presenting a literary work through oral interpretation (Kleinau and Kleinau

238). These readers face each other while seated on stage holding a script and establish eye contact in what Leslie Coger and Melvin White term "Onstage Focus" (46, 51). They largely preserve their own identity rather than "become" a character from the work, since their function is to cultivate the power of literary suggestion through vivid oral and visual cues (Brooks et al. 226). The creative reading that they deliver produces "mental images of characters enacting a scene that exists primarily in the minds of the participants" (Coger and White 9). Indeed, this type of theater creates meaning through imagination rather than literal representation and evokes analysis and action as an antithesis to dramatic escapism (Brecht 136; Kleinau and McHughes 5–6). Most importantly, Readers Theater strives to cultivate a closer and more personal relationship between performer and audience (Coger and White 19). The physical delivery and introspective interpretation of Readers Theater also make it an apt metaphor for reading the interview as drama.

The interview normally follows the same basic format as Readers Theater. It presents a dialogical performance in which at least two individuals (interviewer and interviewee) interact while presenting a scripted work that an audience (reader or viewer) interprets (Lyon, "Jorge Luis Borges" 76–77). In formal interviews participants are typically seated facing each other and maintain regular eye contact. Furthermore, televised or live interviews may occur on stage before an audience. Like an actor in a play, the interviewee is the lead character because they are the focus of the interviewer's attention and use the setting to project their own identity through meaningful oral and visual expression. Although the interview dialogue may be "fluid" and "serendipitous," the interviewer generally follows a list of predetermined questions, and the interviewee may deliver rehearsed, memorized responses (Bawer 421; Knoblauch 177). So although the interview may feel highly contrived and arranged, especially after editorial revisions, participants should feel as if they are engaged in a joint production (Christ, "An Interview" 112; Lasky 63). The notion of a joint production recalls the collaborative nature of theater. Indeed, the interview relies on formulaic dialogue with repeated themes and variations on similar conversations that is analogous to different productions of the same play. The remarkable similarities between the traditional interview format and Readers Theater set the stage for viewing Borges's interviews as a type of theatrical performance.

One interview that harks back to Readers Theater is the markedly scripted dialogue that occurred between Borges and Germinal Nogués on a leisurely Sunday in 1979. In this conversation, interviewer Nogués reiterated a series of inquiries inspired by the famous Proust Questionnaire and interviewee Borges dedicated himself to delivering creative responses steeped in literariness. The Proust Questionnaire provides the framework for a series of ubiquitous questions that frequently stimulate conversation in modern interviews and in popular culture (Carter 1–2). This type of interview involves light-minded inquiries devoid of follow through and depth, but which proponents claim may reveal the interviewee's psyche (Servat 11). Indeed, the survey's voguish acceptance and lack of depth causes one critic to deride its "pedestrian" questions while applauding the respondents' "ingenious answers" (Kindley 18–21). This assessment also applies to the Nogués interview in that, like Proust, Borges responds brilliantly to a

338   CODY C. HANSON

sequence of seemingly trivial questions. As expected, the questionnaire-inspired interrogation begins with a noncontextualized inquiry that sets the stage for a lively exchange
of words:

NOGUÉS: ¿Cuál considera usted el colmo de la infelicidad?
BORGES: Ya que vamos a jugar, juguemos a este juego. Sobre la pregunta, le diré que
           podría depender de las circunstancias o de personas; claro que es muy
           difícil . . . (145)
[NOGUÉS: What do you consider the culmination of unhappiness?
BORGES: Since we are going to play, let's play this game. Regarding the question, I
           would say that it depends on the circumstances or the person; of course it is
           very difficult . . .][3]

This initial interchange between interviewer and interviewee illustrates the characteristics that the conversation shares with Readers Theater. It involves two individuals
who maintain their own identity and perform their respective roles while absorbed in a
give-and-take of words. The conversation begins with the interviewer reading a scripted
question and the interviewee signaling his intent to participate in the proposed literary
game. Borges's response confirms his intention to engage in the ridiculous exercise for
which he has been cast by delivering a spirited dialogue worthy of a theatrical performance while also recognizing that he must act within the limits set by the questionnaire.
His answers reveal a fascinating character who is willing to engage in a witty dialogue
that is full of allusion and embroidered fact. Moreover, the interviewer unexpectedly
turns the initial question on its head by framing the inquiry in the negative rather than
the anticipated positive as recorded in the Proust Questionnaire (Proust). This playful
substitution recalls the survey's origins as an amusement of the fin de siècle, paving the
way for interpreting the interview as a disparate collection of questions that provoke
a bidirectional, comical colloquy reminiscent of the back-and-forth banter typical of
Absurdist Theater (Kindley 23). The interaction between interviewer and interviewee
thus presents a literary-like work through a carefully executed dialogical oral encounter.
    While this interview can be viewed as Readers Theater due to its formulaic narra-
tive structure, Borges's shrewd rejoinders provide the groundwork for reading that theater as an exercise in nonsensical futility and as a scene from the Theater of the Absurd.
In the alternating raillery between the interviewer and interviewee that follows, Borges
takes advantage of the survey's frivolous inquiries to cultivate humor and to amplify the
performative theatricality of the episode by turning to his familiar literary habit of self-
deprecation. Indeed, an innovative characteristic of Borges's fictional prose is "his original concept of a personal, self-conscious often self-effacing narrator" (Lyon, "Borges"
363). Borges channels this same self-aware, self-derogating, quasi-literary persona while
delivering his lines in the Nogués interview. Consider the telling exchange that arises in
what could be considered the final act of the interview:

NOGUÉS: ¿Qué es lo que más le gusta soñar con los ojos abiertos?
BORGES: Con escribir un libro que realmente me justifique.
NOGUÉS: ¿Cuál sería para usted la mayor desdicha?

BORGES:	Perder la integridad mental que no tengo.
NOGUÉS:	¿Cuál es su color favorito?
BORGES:	El amarillo, el único que la ceguera me ha dejado.[. . .]
NOGUÉS:	¿Cuál es el pájaro que más le gusta?
BORGES:	No tengo preferencias ornitológicas. (148)
[NOGUÉS:	What do you most like to daydream about?
BORGES:	Writing a book that actually justifies me.
NOGUÉS:	For you, what would be the greatest misfortune?
BORGES:	To lose the mental integrity that I don't have.
NOGUÉS:	What is your favorite color?
BORGES:	Yellow, the only color blindness has left me.[. . .]
NOGUÉS:	What is your favorite bird?
BORGES:	I don't have ornithological preferences.]

In this segment of the conversation, Borges sandwiches a readily verifiable pronouncement about his color perception between evasive intellectual jargon and self-deprecating but demonstrably false personal assertions. He coyly blends fact, diversion, and humor to deliver the lines of a purposefully modest and elusive character. Borges's witty retorts confuse the traditional limits between fact and fiction, history and literature, and leave the reader wondering whether the Borges present in the dramatic interview can be trusted to convey accurate details. Just as footnotes and cited works in Borges's standard prose serve to bog down and distract the reader, his clever and self-effacing repartees in the interview blur the line between objective reality and pure fiction. Indeed, Borges often spoke pragmatically about his blindness and how the color yellow was the last to leave him (Fermosel 11; Christ, "Jorge Luis Borges" 127). As well, his prodigious memory and mastery of diverse subjects are on full display in numerous interviews (Burgin vii–xii). Yet as this portion of the interview shows, he purposely avoids candid answers with pedantic expression, absurd incongruous self-effacement, and wordplay, which cause the reader to question the historical reality presented in the interview. Although Borges's artistic ripostes may not reveal authentic fact or feeling, they do raise the curtain on reading the interview as a theatrical production and spotlight its absurdist tendencies.

Interviews with Borges also parody absurdist dialogue through the art of evasion and denial. Borges commonly gains control of the conversation by avoiding sincere responses to questions, which disorients and confuses his interviewer. In one particularly entertaining and honest interview report from 1946, for example, Estela Canto narrates how Borges took advantage of her ignorance, uncertainty, and lack of preparation by also adopting a naïve identity in response to her inquires:

—¿Qué opina del existencialismo?
—¿Qué es eso? —nos pregunta Borges. Pasamos un momento embarazoso: nosotros tampoco sabíamos nada del existencialismo, y habíamos contado con Borges para enterarnos. Rápidamente nos escapamos por la tangente con otra pregunta:
—¿Qué opina de la literatura francesa de la resistencia?
—¿Es que existe esa literatura? —nos contesta Borges. Evidentemente no quiere decirnos nada. Estamos tentados de decirle que, en algunos sectores, esta literatura

es casi tan popular como la de las novelas policiales, pero prudentemente guardamos silencio (363)

[—What do you think about existentialism?

—What is that? —Borges asks. We felt embarrassed: we likewise knew nothing about existentialism and had counted on Borges to explain it to us. We quickly escaped through a tangent on another question:

—What do you think about French resistance literature?

—Does that type of literature exist? —Borges replies. Evidently he does not want to tell us anything. We are tempted to say that, in some places, this literature is almost as popular as detective fiction, but prudently we keep silent]

In her narrated reflection on Borges's replies, Canto seems to recognize that Borges expresses some level of willful, unforthcoming disregard for her queries while also not quite grasping the extent of his playful deception. She further admits Borges's replies change the course of the interview and oblige her to ask different questions. Borges manifests his wit by responding with questions that cast doubt on the topics his interviewer wishes to explore. Although one can only speculate as to why Borges would avoid these questions, what is evident is the satirical and caricatured sensation his responses produce (Canto 361). He effectively lampoons his interviewer and makes light of her line of questioning in order to influence the course of the conversation. His artful evasion of superficial conversation frustrates his interviewer's attempt to make sense of a complicated and confusing world. Borges feigns ignorance on topics with which he is intimately familiar and as a result creates a dialogue that emphasizes incomprehensibility and absurdity.

Dialogue in the Theater of the Absurd includes amusing and illogical conversations about the identity of others in order to make dramatic statements about the everchanging human condition. In fact, the guiding philosophy behind the absurdity that gives this theater its name is the existential crisis one endures when confronting the prospect that life has no significance or purpose (Blocker 1). Take, for example, the conversations Vladimir and Estragon have as they endlessly wait for Godot in Samuel Beckett's famous play. They pass time by discussing Godot's identity and unsuccessfully attempting to resolve who he is. In fact, Vladimir, who purportedly knows Godot, is unable to identify him confidently and so the pair's crosstalk articulates feelings of uncertainty and repeated disappointment (Beckett 14, 50; Esslin 24–26). En attendant Godot [Waiting for Godot] (1952) thus dramatizes the insignificance of time when life is not stretched out through accomplishment or purpose (Blocker 171). The characters' mindless discussion parodies meaningful dialogue and devalues it as a vehicle for conceptual thought and for understanding others (Beckett 16; Esslin 64). This dialogue calls attention to the elusiveness of human existence and challenges the reality of personality and individuality (Esslin 53).

Conversations identifying individuals in the Theater of the Absurd utilize ridiculous and senseless expressions full of wordplay and cyclical interlocution to convey the bewilderment one experiences when faced with a meaningless world. They employ clichés and nonsequiturs to create confusion, to break down logical communication, and to reveal poignant truths. Eugène Ionesco's play *La Cantatrice chauve* [*The Bald Soprano*] (1950), for instance, contains several excellent examples of bizarre persiflage on the identity of others. The play begins with an anecdote about Bobby Watson, who is identified simultaneously as a man and a woman, dead and alive, beautiful and ugly, large and small (11–13). Bobby Watson's fluid identity in the conversation indicates that they cannot be named reliably, thereby subverting and destabilizing the basic referential principles of language and signification. The episode demonstrates that proper nouns can slip semantically and assume different identities or functions (Issacharoff 273). It further illustrates the chaotic processes through which communication and language occur (Elsky 360). The play employs a grotesque reversal of familiar situations to show how banal and mechanical speech can be (Dukore 177). A prime example is the dialogue that transpires when Mr. and Mrs. Martin meet. The couple initiates a highly tedious and mundane exchange full of ludicrous coincidences that ironically lead them to discover that they are intimately acquainted, not only from the train but also from their marriage and bedroom (15–18). While this conversation of discovery includes nonsensical and clichéd dialogue that highlights a humanity caught in endless, hopeless, and meaningless action, it also affirms profound truths about relationships. It turns everyday phrases into something strange and irrational to show that people who are intimately acquainted may not truly know each other and that couples may grow apart until they no longer recognize one another (Elsky 358). Dialogue satirizes the banality of the characters' lives and makes it a game that only possesses the meaning one bestows upon it.

Borges frequently avoids commenting on his contemporaries by dissimulating knowledge of them and their work and by evoking similar conversational strategies as those employed in the Theater of the Absurd. In his narrated account of a 1969 interview, Selden Rodman records his surprise about Borges's self-purported ignorance of famous Spanish American writers: "I asked him whether he admired César Vallejo's poetry. 'Vallejo? Never heard of him.' I couldn't believe my ears. 'García Márquez's fiction?' I ventured. 'Never heard of him either'" (13). When Rodman followed up with Borges a couple of years later and called out the ruse, Borges good-naturedly continued the farce (29). Borges manipulates everyday language and ordinary topics to frustrate the line of questioning and to guise the scenario in absurdity. Ensuing occasions confirm Borges's familiarity with García Márquez's work, and, on occasion, he even wryly mused that *Cien años de soledad* [*One Hundred Years of Solitude*] "tiene cincuenta años de más" [was fifty years too long], suggesting that he had purposely dissimulated awareness of the Colombian novelist in the Rodman interview (Alifano, *El humor* 15; Biguenet and Whalen 8; Carrizo 80; Conde 189; Garramuño 93; Neustadt).[4] Borges's hesitancy to speak about his contemporaries is not likely due to a lack of confidence in Rodman (the pair knew each other well and had developed a rapport), but rather due to a preference for other types of conversations (Burgin viii–ix; Christ, "An Interview" 116–17). Rodman does not speculate as to why Borges would deny knowledge of Spanish

American authors, but he does observe that "Borges's whole personality changes" when discussing English or American literature (13–14). Indeed, Borges is capable of giving page-long responses and speaking in a way that shifts the discussion to his preferred topics.[5] Moreover, Borges observed that he preceded García Márquez as a writer and was not aware of or affected by him (Cortínez 19). Borges reacted similarly when questioned about Horacio Quiroga; at times ignoring, acknowledging, complementing, or criticizing the Uruguayan ("Borges entre malevos"; Estrázulas 36; Garramuño 94; Olaso 109). Feigning ignorance of well-known public figures was one of Borges's favorite evasive techniques that allowed him to gain control of the interview (Lyon, "Put-on" 62). Borges's purposeful obfuscation of other famous writers creates situations where he and his interviewers talk past each other and in circles, resulting in ridiculous dialogue that evokes the playful inconclusive identity discourse at the heart of Absurdist Theater.

Borges's expressed hesitation with the names of his literary counterparts deflates their importance and permits him to sidestep skillfully a bland conversation in favor of exchanges he finds more engaging. One particularly masterful example of Borges's artistic ability to redirect interviews occurs when Irma Cairoli relates Vargas Llosa's observation that Borges conceives of literature through abstract, intellectual ideas rather than through narrative action. Borges's lengthy reply dissembles awareness of his fellow critic's identity while confirming the accuracy of the observation with an anecdote about John Milton's *Paradise Regained*. In his rambling remarks, the Argentine corroborates the Peruvian's premise that for Borges, motivation takes precedence over action. Once Borges concludes his musings on Milton, he preemptively deflects potential discussion on the famed Andean novelist and gains control of the conversation by posing a question to his interviewer:

BORGES: [. . .] de modo que creo que Vargas Llosa, ¿se llama así? ¿Cito bien el nombre?
CAIROLI: Sí, Vargas Llosa, el novelista peruano.
BORGES: Porque yo no conocía el nombre. Tiene razón en lo que dice. Además Óscar Wilde ya dijo que todos los acontecimientos de la historia empiezan en la mente. (122)
[BORGES: [. . .] so I believe that Vargas Llosa, is that the name? Am I citing the right name?
CAIROLI: Yes, Vargas Llosa, the Peruvian novelist.
BORGES: Because I didn't know the name. He is right in what he says. Furthermore Oscar Wilde has said that all historical events begin in the mind.]

This expressed hesitation with the name of a literary counterpart allows Borges to eschew potentially polemical pronouncements about a famous personality that is likely familiar to all involved. The lack of a straightforward response about Vargas Llosa means the conversation briefly adopts a simplistic air that exemplifies the back-and-forth banter typical of absurdist characters who supposedly are unaware of the identity of others. One might simply contend Borges was unfamiliar with Vargas Llosa or did not clearly hear the name, yet, in his response Borges accurately repeats the Peruvian's name before claiming he did not know it.[6] Throughout this interview, he also freely cites dozens of other writers and literary works with remarkable familiarity and detail. Indeed, Borges possessed an impressive ability to recall names and literary minutiae with ease, and that ability is evidence of his prodigious memory (Burgin vii–xii; Estrázulas 32). Moreover, when asked about Vargas Llosa in a different interview from the same year, Borges confidently characterized the novelist's writing as having a political bent (Garramuño 93). By temporarily engaging in a rote dialogue about Vargas Llosa's identity, Borges is able to shift what could have become a trite conversation into a more intellectually stimulating address on his favorite subjects. In fact, Borges's absurd assertion allows him to wrest control from his interviewer, and by posing his own question, the interviewee effectively becomes the interviewer. Borges's circumlocutory response permits him to steer the conversation toward his preferred topics and to dodge potentially controversial commentary on his contemporary.

In most interviews, Borges willingly spoke at length on his areas of expertise and interest but preferred to avoid going on record about political and social topics. In a December 1973 interview with the Mexican newspaper *Excélsior*, for example, Borges lamented how reporters had unrelentingly questioned him on politics, the Nobel Prize, and Boom writers before he began pleading: "Pregúnteme de literatura, por favor. Yo soy un escritor, ¿por qué no me hacen preguntas sobre literatura o filosofía? Desgraciadamente, es de lo único que sé hablar" [Ask me about literature, please. I am a writer so why don't you ask me about literature or philosophy? Unfortunately, I don't know how to talk about anything else] (Solares 2). Borges deemed his opinions on current events to be inconsequential in comparison to what he had to offer on literature and philosophy. As a result, Borges took questions outside his purview as an invitation to take the interview in a dramatic direction.

Interviews with Borges often delve into the absurd when interviewers structure their line of questioning around controversial and sensitive issues. A case in point occurred in April 1973 when journalists Andrés Oppenheimer and Jorge Lafforgue tried to press Borges into a polemical political debate shortly after elections that led to Juan Perón's return from exile. They doggedly pursued Borges's record on numerous provocative topics, but instead of successfully cornering the literary master into giving straightforward answers, he distracted and deflected with preposterous declarations. The following fragments from the interview highlight its dramatic dialogue and confrontational tone. The interview begins with questions on Argentina's elections:

OPPENHEIMER AND LAFFORGUE: —¿Qué opinión le merece la situación política del país?
BORGES: Yo abandonaría la Argentina, pero mi madre está muy, muy enferma. (56)
[OPPENHEIMER AND LAFFORGUE: —What is your opinion on the political situation of the country?
BORGES: I would leave Argentina, but my mother is very, very sick.]

While pressing Borges on his critical view of the Peronist government, the interview continues:

OPPENHEIMER AND LAFFORGUE: —¿A qué atribuye, entonces, el hecho de que más de seis millones de argentinos lo hayan votado?
BORGES: La mayoría de la gente es tonta. (56)
[OPPENHEIMER AND LAFFORGUE: —So then, to what do you attribute the fact that more than six million Argentines have voted for him?
BORGES: The majority of people are foolish.]

Borges likewise avoids clear answers when asked about Boom writers:

OPPENHEIMER AND LAFFORGUE: —Muchos críticos han hecho notar la influencia de sus cuentos sobre los de Cortázar.
BORGES: —Yo supongo que los de él serán mejores. Bueno, no seamos pesimistas. (57)
[OPPENHEIMER AND LAFFORGUE: —Many critics have noted the influence your stories have on Cortázar's stories.
BORGES: —I suppose his are better. Well, let's not be pessimists.]

In response to a line of questioning on the Conquest and violence against Argentina's indigenous population, Borges interjects:

¿por qué insisten tanto en un tema tan exótico como el de los indios? ¡Ustedes parecen bolivianos! (58)

[Why do you insist on a topic as exotic as the Indians? You both sound like Bolivians!]

Finally, when challenged on his elitism and snobbish admiration of Great Britain, Borges dryly contests:

—¿Y qué tiene que ver? Los ingleses también hicieron mucho mal al mundo. Por ejemplo, lo han llenado de estupideces como el fútbol. (59)

[—And what does that have to do with anything? The English have also greatly harmed the world. For example, they have filled it with stupidities like soccer.]

Oppenheimer and Lafforgue structure their interview around controversial topics, perhaps intending to provoke Borges or hoping to uncover his genuine opinion. While they do get him on record on a number of contentious subjects, Borges's statements succeed in stymieing the interview and allow him to avoid topics he finds distasteful and problematic. Borges manipulates his interlocutors with inflammatory interjections and thereby avoids being forthcoming about his true feelings. In fact, the interview concludes with Borges explicitly stating that his unbridled statements are purposely ironic and that his interviewers take him too seriously (Oppenheimer and Lafforgue

59). Along these lines, Salvador Elizondo maintains that those who criticize Borges's political opinions do so because they cannot comprehend the irony that permeates his literature and politics (Molachino and Mejía Prieto 54). Additionally, Vargas Llosa argues that Borges's primary deficiency is his ethnocentric limitations but forgivingly concludes they do not distract from his work because they affirm his humanity as an imperfect individual ("Fictions" 1333). In this interview Oppenheimer and Lafforgue do not seem to grasp that Borges is feeding them absurd declarations that likely have more literary than literal value. Indeed, the nuances in Borges's ironic opinions and in his fictional works seem to be lost on his interviewers. They avoid engaging in Borges's inflammatory comments and instead continue the interrogation while trying to stay on top of the interview. Through their inquiries, Oppenheimer and Lafforgue unwittingly collaborate with Borges in writing a highly literary text that stars Borges as the protagonist and features drama, emotion, and doubt.

Although Borges was weary of political discussion in interviews, from time to time he did express its absurdity through humorous wordplay. Borges was particularly unapologetic about his antagonism toward the Perón regime and expressed that frustration in interviews. The Barnstone interview that began this chapter contains a prime example. In that friendly and relaxed conversation, Borges artistically mused:

> Now we have had that *cornudo* (cuckold) Perón. The only battle he ever fought was to try to rename the city of La Plata for his wife Evita, and he even failed at that. He wanted to call it *La Puta* (The Whore) in her honor but wouldn't accept the compromise of *La Pluta*. After all, in Argentina (silver country) La Pluta—a silver prostitute—is quite fine. (53)

Borges contemptuously criticizes Perón's government and satirically derides its actions with ironic pessimism by recalling that the City of La Plata was briefly known as Eva Perón City in the 1950s. His amusing play on words consists of an intentional spoonerism in which he transposes the city's name with a pejorative term that he relates to the etymology of Argentina. He further disparages Juan and Eva Perón through parallel identities as a cuckold and a whore to highlight his perception of their incompetency. Borges also introduced wordplay and was similarly frank with his political opinions in an interview with the Chilean educational magazine *Presencia*. After speaking at length about the threats facing democracy in Latin America, for example, Borges states he prefers the term "Sudamérica" [South America] due to his perception that the continent "se viene literalmente abajo" [is literally going south] ("Diálogo"). Borges's amusing use of language and play on words emphasizes the challenges facing the region and highlight the absurdity he felt at the time of Perón's return to power. These comments demonstrate that dialogue in interviews can express the bewilderment one experiences when faced with the task of creating meaning out of repeated, frustrating, and senseless events. *Presencia* thus rightfully characterizes conversations with Borges as more than interviews because they "constituyen documentos históricos y literarios" [constitute historical and literary documents] ("Diálogo"). Interviews with Borges use dramatic literary dialogue to reveal historical realities that might otherwise remain unexplained and unanalyzed.

Jorge Luis Borges was a highly capable writer and public intellectual who took advantage of the interview genre to create dramatic dialogues as complex and as literary as his traditional fictions. In these dialogues, just as in his fiction, different versions of Borges appear. In fact, Adolfo Bioy Casares, Borges's dear friend and frequent collaborator, recalls that during a photography session Borges once whispered, "Qué raro que toda persona tenga pequeñas reproducciones de sí mismo. Son como los repuestos de sí que tenía en su tumba el faraón" [It's strange that people carry around small effigies of themselves. They are like the spare parts Pharaoh had for himself in his tomb] (20). Like photographs, interviews with Borges record him in different settings and contain unique representations of who he is. Moreover, photographs, interviews, and theater are all staged, have fixed backgrounds and poses, and are not easily reproducible. Although some might consider interviews to be historical documents, interviews with Borges have performative qualities and are best understood as theatrical dialogues that share similarities with Readers Theater and the Theater of the Absurd. The formulaic structure of the interview recalls Readers Theater due to its physical format and its scripted dialogue filled with prewritten questions and repeated variations of common themes. Borges's lively repartees introduce humor and entertainment into the interview and raise the curtain on a subtext that emphasizes the absurd.[7] Indeed, Borges often strays into a nonsensical performance through evasion, humor, self-deprecation, pretend ignorance, identity confusion, and wordplay. Milton Fornaro recognizes that Borges delivers artistic interview dialogues that parallel his fictional texts: "responde lo que se le antoja. Inventa datos y cifras, inclusive nombres, finge no recordar títulos de libros célebres, y de pronto salta-suelta el recitado fiel y monótono de un largo poema casi desconocido" [he answers whatever he wants. He invents details and numbers, including names, pretends to forget the titles of celebrated books, and without notice jumps into the faithful and monotonous recital of a long, obscure poem] (103). Borges skillfully and playfully uses the interview genre as a personal art form. He chooses how to respond to questions and thus influences the writing of the interview script. He embellishes conversations with fictionalized names, figures, and other data. In the interview, Borges manipulates memory to suit his needs by temporarily "forgetting" acclaimed literary knowledge or by brandishing his ability to memorize. In a quintessential final act, Borges expertly turns an otherwise serious endeavor into a type of dramatized performance.

Notes

1 David Oubiña comments that Hugo Santiago said that the Borges-Bioy film scripts included dialogues that were impossible to use in the films he adapted from them (140–44).
2 The 9th edition of the *MLA Handbook* (2021) advises that interviews be cited by listing the interviewee as author, while the interviewer is noted as having conducted the interview (336). In this chapter, I reference nearly 30 interviews with Borges and in every case the work lists the interviewer as the author, while Borges is often referenced in the title. In order

to avoid the confusion that would result by citing these interviews under Borges's name, and in keeping with *MLA* guidelines to "cite a work under the name recorded on the work itself" (115, 108–09), I cite the interviews with the interviewers' names. I acknowledge the interview is a collaborative work and, as this chapter shows, Borges (co)authors every interview text.

3   All translations from the original Spanish to English are my own.

4   Borges was similarly dismissive when asked about Manuel Puig, claiming to have never read him while asserting *Boquitas pintadas* was "rubbish" (Scott 106).

5   For examples of Borges's preferred topics, see any one of the several collections of conversations between Jorge Luis Borges and Osvaldo Ferrari.

6   Vargas Llosa had interviewed Borges in his apartment on Maipú in 1963 for a Peruvian newspaper. He is said to have commented on the modest size of the apartment and on the leaks from the ceiling. Borges is then reported as having told Bioy that he had been visited by a Peruvian journalist who should have been a real estate agent. The entire exchange may be apocryphal, but there are numerous references to it in newspaper articles, including by Vargas Llosa, who talks about his interviews with Borges in *Medio siglo con Borges*.

7   On humor in Borges, see Fishburn, Alifano, and de Costa.

WORKS CITED

Alifano, Roberto. *El humor de Borges*. Ediciones de Urraca, 1996.

—. *Twenty-Four Conversations with Borges: Including a Selection of Poems*. Translated by Nicomedes Suárez Araúz, Lascaux, 1984.

Arkin, Stephen. "Composing the Self: The Literary Interview as Form." *International Journal of Oral History*, vol. 4, no. 1, 1983, pp. 12–18.

Arnold, Whitney. "The Secret Subject: Michel Foucault, *Death and the Labyrinth*, and the Interview as Genre." *Criticism*, vol. 54, no. 4, 2012, pp. 567–81. https://doi.org/10.1353/crt.2012.0029.

Barnstone, Willis. "With Borges in Buenos Aires." *Denver Quarterly*, vol. 15, no. 1, 1980, pp. 48–57.

Bawer, Bruce. "Talk Show: The Rise of the Literary Interview." *The American Scholar*, vol. 57, no. 3, 1988, pp. 421–29.

Biguenet, John, and Tom Whalen. "An Interview with Jorge Luis Borges." *New Orleans Review*, vol. 9, no. 2, 1982, pp. 5–14.

Beckett, Samuel. *Waiting for Godot: Tragicomedy in 2 Acts*. Translated by Samuel Beckett, Grove, 1977. Vol. 20 of *The Collected Works of Samuel Beckett*.

Bioy Casares, Adolfo. "Fragmentos de una larga conversación entre amigos." In *Borges*, edited by Nicolás Cócaro, Fundación Banco de Boston, 1987, pp. 19–22.

Birch, Anna, and Joanne Tompkins, eds. *Performing Site-Specific Theatre: Politics, Place, Practice*. Palgrave Macmillan, 2012.

Blocker, H. Gene. *The Metaphysics of Absurdity*. UP of America, 1979.

"Borges entre malevos." *Así: La luna y el mundo en sus manos*, vol. 13, no. 608, May 30, 1975, n.p.

Borges, Jorge Luis. *Obras completas*. 4 vols. Emecé, 1996.

"Borges una vez más." In *El otro Borges: Entrevistas (1960–1986)*, edited by Fernando Mateo, Equis Ediciones, 1997, pp. 11–16.

Brecht, Bertolt. *Brecht on Theatre: The Development of an Aesthetic*. Translated by John Willett, Hill & Wang, 1992.

Brooks, Keith, Robert C. Henderhan, and Alan Billings. "A Philosophy on Readers Theatre." In *Readers Theatre Handbook: A Dramatic Approach to Literature*, by Leslie Coger and Melvin White, Scott, Foresman, 1967, pp. 225–29.

Burgin, Richard, ed. *Jorge Luis Borges: Conversations*. UP of Mississippi, 1998.

Cairoli, Irma. "Algunos viven obsesionados." In *El otro Borges: Entrevistas (1960–1986)*, edited by Fernando Mateo, Equis Ediciones, 1997, pp. 119–26.

Canto, Estela. "Entrevista con Jorge Luis Borges." In *Textos recobrados (1931–1955)*, by Jorge Luis Borges, Emecé, 2001, pp. 361–64.

Carrizo, Antonio. *Borges el memorioso: Conversaciones de Jorge Luis Borges con Antonio Carrizo*. Fondo de Cultura Económica, 1982.

Carter, Graydon, ed. *Vanity Fair's Proust Questionnaire: 101 Luminaries Ponder Love, Death, Happiness, and the Meaning of Life*. Rodale, 2009.

Childress, Mark, and Charles C. McNair, Jr. "The Dark Riddle of Jorge Luis Borges." *Saturday Review*, March-April 1983, pp. 32–34. *UNZ Review: An Alternative Media Selection*, https://www.unz.com/print/SaturdayRev-1983apr-00032/.

Christ, Ronald. "An Interview on Interviews." *Literary Research Newsletter*, vol. 2, no. 3, 1977, pp. 111–24.

—. "Jorge Luis Borges: An Interview." *Paris Review*, no. 40, 1967, pp. 116–64.

Coger, Leslie Irene, and Melvin R. White. *Readers Theatre Handbook: A Dramatic Approach to Literature*, Scott, Foresman, 1967.

Conde, Perfecto. "Borges: 'Yo no merezco el Nobel.' " In *El otro Borges: Entrevistas (1960–1986)*, edited by Fernando Mateo, Equis Ediciones, 1997, pp. 185–92.

Cortínez, Carlos, ed. *Simply a Man of Letters: Panel Discussions and Paper from the Proceedings of a Symposium on Jorge Luis Borges at the University of Maine at Orono*. University of Maine at Orono Press, 1982.

Costa, René de. *El humor en Borges*. Cátedra, 1999.

Cruz, Jorge. "Mis libros." *La Nación* [Buenos Aires], April 28, 1985, sección 4a, pp. 1–2.

"Diálogo con Jorge Luis Borges." *Presencia*, [Instituto de Servicio Educacional de Chile], no. 8, July-August 1985.

Dukore, Bernard F. "The Theater of Ionesco: A Union of Form and Substance." *Educational Theatre Journal*, vol. 13, no. 3, 1961, pp. 174–81.

Elsky, Julia. "Rethinking Ionesco's Absurd: *The Bald Soprano* in the Interlingual Context of Vichy and Postwar France." *PMLA*, vol. 133, no. 2, 2018, pp. 347–63.

Esslin, Martin. *The Theatre of the Absurd*. Revised Updated ed., Eyre Methuen, 1974.

Estrázulas, Enrique. "Borges y los orientales." In *Borges: Dos palabras antes de morir y otras entrevistas*, edited by Fernando Mateo, LC Editor, 1994, pp. 21–42.

Fermosel, José Luis A. "El premio Cervantes para Borges: 'Una generosa equivocación.' " *Pájaro de Fuego*, vol. 3, no. 22, February 1980, pp. 8–13.

Fishburn, Evelyn. "Humor Strategies in Borges's Fiction." In *Hidden Pleasures of Borges's Fiction*. Borges Center, 2015, pp. 147–61.

Fornaro, Milton. "El otro, el mismo Borges." In *Borges: Obra y personaje*, edited by Washington Benavides et al., Acali, 1978, pp. 103–14.

Garramuño, Carlos A. "La vigilia con los ojos abiertos." In *El otro Borges: Entrevistas (1960–1986)*, edited by Fernando Mateo, Equis Ediciones, 1997, pp. 75–105.

Geneson, Paul. "Interview with Jorge Luis Borges." *Michigan Quarterly Review*, vol. 16, 1977, pp. 243–55.

Gilio, María Ester. "Jorge Luis Borges: 'yo querría ser el hombre invisible.'" *Crisis*, no. 13, May 1974, pp. 40–47.

Hachemi Guerrero, Antonio Munir. "Borges en disputa: las entrevistas de Jorge Luis Borges." *Variaciones Borges*, no. 40, 2015, pp. 181–204.

Hanson, Cody. "Jorge Luis Borges Performing the Interview." *Variaciones Borges*, no. 36, 2013, pp. 251–70.

Ionesco, Eugène. *The Bald Soprano. Four Plays*. Translated by Donald M. Allen, Grove, 1958, pp. 7–42.

—. *Notes and Counter Notes: Writings on Theatre*. Translated by Donald Watson, Grove, 1964.

"Interview." *The Compact Edition of the Oxford English Dictionary: Complete Text Reproduced Micrographically*, vol. 1, 1971.

Irby, James E. "Encuentro con Borges." In *Encuentro con Borges*, by James Irby, Napoleón Murat, and Carlos Peralta, Galerna, 1968, pp. 7–54.

Issacharoff, Michael. "Bobby Watson and the Philosophy of Language." *French Studies*, vol. 46, no. 3, 1992, pp. 272–79.

Kindley, Evan. *Questionnaire*. Bloomsbury Academic, 2016. Object Lessons.

Kleinau, Marion L., and Marvin D. Kleinau. "Scene Location in Readers Theatre: Static or Dynamic?" In *Readers Theatre Handbook: A Dramatic Approach to Literature*, by Leslie Coger and Melvin White, Scott, Foresman, 1967, pp. 238–46.

Kleinau, Marion L., and Janet Larsen McHughes. *Theatres for Literature: A Practical Aesthetics for Group Interpretation*. Alfred, 1980.

Knoblauch, C. H. "A Response to Gary Olson's Interview with Paulo Freire." In *(Inter)views: Cross-Disciplinary Perspectives on Rhetoric and Literacy*, edited by Gary A. Olson and Irene Gale, Southern Illinois UP, 1991, pp. 177–83.

Lasky, Melvin J. "The Art of the Interview or, the Difficulties of Asking a Question & Getting an Answer." *Encounter*, vol. 72, no. 3, 1989, pp. 61–64.

Lyon, Thomas E. [Ted]. "Borges and the (Somewhat) Personal Narrator." *Modern Fiction Studies*, vol. 19, no. 3, 1973, pp. 363–72.

—. "Jorge Luis Borges and the Interview as Literary Genre." *Latin American Literary Review*, vol. 22, no. 44, 1994, pp. 74–89.

—. "Put-on by Borges: The Interview as Play." *Confluencia*, vol. 10, no. 1, 1994, pp. 57–66.

Masschelein, Anneleen, Christophe Meurée, David Martens, and Stéphanie Vanasten. "The Literary Interview: Toward a Poetics of a Hybrid Genre." *Poetics Today*, vol. 35, no. 1–2, 2014, pp. 1–49. *Duke UP*, https://doi.org/10.1215/03335372-2648368.s.

Milleret, Jean de. *Entrevistas con Jorge Luis Borges*. Translated by Gabriel Rodríguez, Monte Ávila, 1970.

Molachino, Justo R., and Jorge Mejía Prieto. *En torno a Borges*. Hachette, 1983.

Neustadt, Bernardo. "¿Un nuevo Borges?" Revista Extra, vol. 16, no. 187, 1981. *Sitio oficial de Bernardo Neustadt 2007*, https://web.archive.org/web/20080222060545/http://www.berna rdoneustadt.org/contenido_458.htm.

Nogués, Germinal. "Frente a Jorge Luis Borges: El Cuestionario Proust." In *El otro Borges: Entrevistas (1960–1986)*, edited by Fernando Mateo, Equis Ediciones, Equis Ediciones, 1997, pp. 145–49.

Olaso, Ezequiel de. "El arte de la conversación." In *El otro Borges: Entrevistas (1960–1986)*, edited by Fernando Mateo, Equis Ediciones, Equis Ediciones, 1997, pp. 107–17.

Oppenheimer, Andres, and Jorge Lafforgue. "El pensamiento vivo de Jorge Luis Borges." *Siete Días* [Buenos Aires], April 29, 1973, pp. 54–59.

Oubiña, David. "El espectador corto de vista: Borges y el cine." *Variaciones Borges*, vol. 24, 2007, pp. 133–52.

Pearson, Mike, and Michael Shanks. *Theatre/Archaeology*. Routledge, 2001.

Proust, Marcel. "Les questionnaires de Marcel Proust." *The Kolb-Proust Archive for Research*, Rare Book & Document Library, University of Illinois Library, 2017, www.library.illinois.edu/rbx/kolbproust/proust/qst/#confess.

Quackenbush, L. Howard. "Borges' Tragedy." *Hispanófila*, no. 92, 1988, pp. 77–86.

Rodden, John. *Performing the Literary Interview: How Writers Craft Their Public Selves*. U of Nebraska P, 2001.

Rodman, Seldon. *Tongues of Fallen Angels*. New Directions, 1974.

Royer, Jean. "De l'entretien." *Études françaises*, vol. 22, no. 3, 1986, pp. 117–24.

Scott, Ann. "Interview: Perón is a Second Rater." In *El mapa del imperio: del escritorio de Manuel Puig al campo intelectual*, edited by Julia G. Romero, Ediciones Al Margen, 2009, pp. 105–107.

Servat, Henry-Jean. "A Question of Marcel Proust. Introduction." In *The Proust Questionnaire*. Translated by Anne Rubin, Assouline, 2005, pp. 9–14.

Solares, Ignacio. "Borges: 'he renunciado a las bondades del cielo.'" *Diorama de la cultura, Excélsior* [México D.F.], December 9, 1973, pp. 1–5.

Sorrentino, Fernando. *Seven Conversations with Jorge Luis Borges*. Translated by Clark M. Zlotchew, Whitston, 1982.

Stark, John. "Borges and His Precursors." *Latin American Literary Review*, vol. 2, no. 4, 1974, pp. 9–15.

Vargas Llosa, Mario. "The Fictions of Borges." *Third World Quarterly*, vol. 10, no. 3, 1988, pp. 1325–33.

—. *Medio siglo con Borges*. Alfaguara, 2020.

Vogel, Daisi. *Borges e a entrevista: Performances do escritor e da literatura na cena midiatizada*, edited by Nelson Rolim de Moura, Editora Insular, 2009.

Zito Lema, Vicente. "Jorge Luis Borges y su último libro: 'El congreso que yo soñé.'" In *El otro Borges: Entrevistas (1960–1986)*, edited by Fernando Mateo, Equis Ediciones, 1997, pp. 39–48.

CHAPTER 20

BORGES AND THE CREATIVE ECONOMY OF THE APOCRYPHAL

ALFREDO ALONSO ESTENOZ

IN one of the several conversations he had with his friend Adolfo Bioy Casares on the subject of Oscar Wilde, Borges observed, "Wilde escribió: 'Meredith is a prose Browning: and, of course, so is Browning'. Toda la gracia está en *of course*" [Wilde wrote: "Meredith is a prose Browning: and, of course, so is Browning." All the humor is in that *of course*] (302). A footnote by the editor of Bioy Casares's diaries, Daniel Martino, clarifies: "La frase original de Wilde no incluye *of course*" [Wilde's original phrase does not include *of course*] (302). Borges adds a variation to an ingenious sentence from one of his favorite writers and considers his own contribution the best part of the phrase.[1]

Why would Borges do something like this? The conversation was a private one, held at Bioy Casares's house, where Borges dined almost every evening over the course of several decades. Was he trying to amuse or fool Bioy Casares? Did he consider the original phrase inferior, from a literary point of view, if it did not include "of course"? Borges knew Wilde's observation very well: he had transcribed it in his notes for a series of talks on the Irish writer he gave in 1950, and later in Bioy Casares's diary he quotes the sentence again, this time respecting the original wording.

This anecdote illustrates one of Borges's uses of apocryphal references, whether they consist of short quotations or longer texts: when the original source seemed to him insufficient or defective from a literary viewpoint, he would modify it, sometimes slightly, to achieve the desired effect. A more significant example, thoroughly examined by Iván Almeida, is found in one of Borges's favorite passages: Snorri Sturluson's account of the Battle of Stamford Bridge, which took place in 1066. Borges transcribed on several occasions the dialogue between the main antagonists of the battle, King Harold Godwinson of England and his brother Tostig, who had formed an alliance with the Norwegian King Harald Hardrada. Harold offers a pardon and a third of his kingdom to Tostig, who in turn asks what Harold would give to his ally, the Norwegian King, for having helped him. "Le dará seis pies de tierra inglesa y, ya que es tan alto, uno más" [He will give him six feet of English soil, and, since he is so tall, one more], was, according to Borges, the Anglo-Saxon king's answer (*OC* II:133). Nowhere in the Icelandic original or in the English and German translations does the offer consist of six feet. The original clearly says seven, with Roman numerals, and all the translations, except Borges's, repeat this number (Almeida, "Goethe" 15). The instant association of six feet with the grave may have driven Borges to alter the original. A six-foot man is considered tall; seven feet of ground seems to be enough to bury him. More than that may sound like a fantastic intrusion at the center of a narrative that Borges regarded as a paradigm of understated realism.[2]

This chapter is an attempt to classify and analyze Borges's multiple uses of the apocryphal in his fiction and his critical work. The analysis will mostly include examples from his writings but also from his life story, questioning his account of how his literary career came to be. Among other purposes, Borges employed apocrypha and pseudepigrapha as literary mechanisms that challenge notions of authorship, originality, and literary canon.

Apocrypha: A Brief History

The concept of "apocrypha" originated in Judaism and was applied to books that were excluded from the canon; the same word would later extend to Christian writings. Etymologically, the word, from the Greek *apókryphos*, means hidden. Initially, then, apocrypha designated texts that were hidden from the public for containing a knowledge that went against orthodoxy or for propagating esoteric teachings, although the Greek term itself began to be used much later. Apocrypha is sometimes confused with pseudepigrapha, which designated books whose writing was attributed to biblical figures or other authors, such as the *Apocalypse of Abraham* or *Biblical Antiquities*. In contemporary literary discussions, the adjectives "apocryphal" and "pseudepigraphal" often appear without a clear distinction between them. They have come to designate books—as well as phrases and events—of dubious authorship or existence, but also texts falsely attributed to real or fictional authors. The terms may refer to writings that attempt to pass as authentic (like Avellaneda's *Don Quixote*)[3] and others where the authors employ these concepts as literary devices.

In a religious context, the existence of apocrypha that were once read as authentic calls into question the notions of authorship, textual authority, and divine revelation. The final text of the Hebrew Bible took centuries to be established, but once it was finalized, around the middle of the second century, no other books were included on account— among other reasons—of their recent composition. The criteria for determining which texts belong to the canon and which ones are excluded may seem, from the perspective of the present, well established, but the fact that they were ultimately decided through human intervention shows the problematic nature of canon formation. This fact must have appealed to Borges beyond its religious significance. If a group of men (like the secret society that conceived of the *First Encyclopedia of Tlön*) is to decide what constitutes the word of God and what does not, what can be expected from the writings of mere mortals—literary authors?

Borges was clearly aware of the original meaning of apocrypha. In his foreword to a Spanish edition of the noncanonical Gospels, he wrote: "La palabra apócrifo ahora vale por falsificado o por falso; su primer sentido era oculto. Los textos apócrifos eran los vedados al vulgo, los de lectura sólo permitida a unos pocos" [The word apocryphal means falsified or false today; its first meaning was hidden. Apocryphal texts were those banned from the common people and which only a few were allowed to read] (*OC* IV:452). The entry "Apocrypha" in the eleventh edition of the *Encyclopedia Britannica*, one of Borges's favorite sources of information and research, addresses this meaning and explains how the term evolved throughout history. Among the Jews, it was once believed that such texts were destined only for the wisest of men. The reasons for such a restriction may reside in the notion that they disrupted orthodoxy, and only scholars who possessed the right education could engage with them. Several Jewish apocryphal texts, particularly the apocalyptic ones that proliferated around the turn of the common era, and other Christian texts that were later labeled heretical, were the ordinary literature of early Christians. In a first stage in its evolution, the term was even laudatory, referring to a knowledge that was only accessible to a few; in a second period, the term came to signify texts that "were excluded from the public use of the Church." Finally, as the Christian canonical texts were established, apocryphal writings acquired the meaning of "false, spurious, bad, heretical" (Charles 176).

THE APOCRYPHAL IN BORGES

One of the first instances in which the word "apocryphal" appears in Borges's work is his 1930 biography of the Argentinian poet Evaristo Carriego. Its meaning here corresponds to false or falsified, but its connotations go beyond that. Borges writes that tango, the best-known genre of Argentine popular music, produces on his compatriots the same effect that Oscar Wilde observed about music in general: "After playing Chopin," wrote Wilde, "I feel as if I had been weeping over sins that I had never committed, and mourning over tragedies that were not my own. Music always seems to me to produce that effect. It creates for one a past of which one has been ignorant, and fills one with a sense of sorrows that have been hidden from one's tears" (1175). Borges paraphrases the passage as follows: "En un diálogo de Oscar Wilde se lee que la música nos revela un pasado personal que hasta ese momento ignorábamos y nos mueve a lamentar desventuras que no nos ocurrieron y culpas que no cometimos" [We read in one of Oscar Wilde's conversations that music reveals to each us a personal past which until then we were unaware of, moving us to lament misfortunes we never suffered and to feel guilt for acts we never committed] (*OC* I:162; *Evaristo Carriego* 136). He then adds: "de mí confesaré que no suelo oír *El Marne* o *Don Juan* sin recordar con precisión un pasado apócrifo, a la vez estoico y orgiástico, en el que he desafiado y peleado para caer al fin, silencioso, en un oscuro duelo a cuchillo" [For myself, I confess I cannot hear *El Marne* or *Don Juan* without remembering exactly such an apocryphal past, at one and the same time stoic and orgiastic, in which I have thrown down the challenged and, in silence, met my end in an obscure knife fight] (*OC* I:162; *Evaristo Carriego* 136).

This is Borges at one of his most typical moments: he remembers a past that did not exist, an alternative history, but he remembers it *exactly* ("con precisión" in the Spanish original). The effect tango produces in him is not merely personal—it also involves aspects of national identity. "Tal vez," the text continues, "la misión del tango sea ésa: dar a los argentinos la certidumbre de haber sido valientes, de haber cumplido ya con las exigencias del valor y el honor" [Perhaps that is tango's mission: to give Argentines the conviction of having had a brave past, of having fulfilled the demands of bravery and honor] (*OC* I:162; *Evaristo Carriego* 136). Tango functions here as an element of national identity, but the past it seems to reveal, and which would unite his fellow citizens in a common sentiment, never actually existed; it is false. The paradox of Borges's view resides in that the construction of a national project is an endeavor that usually focuses on the future. In this case, the illusory past created by tango is something every Argentine is supposed to aspire to: being courageous and honorable. It embodies a desire to be better, while Borges's phrase implies that up until that moment, Argentines had not yet behaved according to that ideal. The aspiration is, at the same time, rescued from a sense of the past that is false, created by a musical genre that idealizes a nonexistent reality. In the same way that people tend to romanticize the past as a symptom of a discontent with the present, tango would offer Argentineans a certain comfort, by giving them a false sense of having accomplished something that may never come to fruition. Borges was clearly aware of the human tendency to idealize the past as a means of escaping a distressing reality, usually by considering the past a happier time, when the present is threatening or uncertain.[4]

In this instance, the sense of apocryphal as falsified allows for two interpretations. On the one hand, it expresses a distorted view of national identity, a "memory" of events that never occurred, implying that national identity is often based on events that are actually imagined. They were invented, manipulated, or falsified to fit a narrative that satisfies the needs of a particular moment in history. When Borges quotes Wilde's sentence many years later, he alters the original wording, condensing its meaning and adding another dimension of his own: "la música nos revela un pasado desconocido y acaso real" [music reveals to us a previously unknown and perhaps real past] (*OC* II:70). The fact that this past may be real is absent in the original phrase, but it serves Borges's purpose in a more suitable manner.

Two short stories from Borges's *Ficciones* [*Fictions*] (1944) illustrate another sense of the term "apocrypha." "Tlön, Uqbar, Orbis Tertius" offers an example that is closer to the original meaning of the word: the existence of a hidden text—or of a hidden truth which readers tend to miss even though the text itself is accessible to anyone. The word "apocryphal" does not appear explicitly in "Tlön," but, as we shall see later, it is fundamental to the story's structure and understanding. At the beginning, the narrator and protagonist "Borges" recounts how he and his friend "Bioy Casares" were discussing the composition of "una novela en primera persona, cuyo narrador omitiera o desfigurara los hechos e incurriera en diversas contradicciones, que permitieran a unos pocos lectores—a muy pocos lectores—la adivinación de una realidad atroz o banal" [a first-person novel whose narrator would omit or distort the facts and engage in various contradictions which would allow a few of the book's readers—a very few—to discover a terrible or banal reality] (*OC* I:431). The existence of a hidden text or meaning is connected here to the notion of attentive reading. This intentional misleading—a practice that the detective novel usually engages in—is an attempt to rescue the activity of reading as one that requires close attention.

In "Examen de la obra de Herbert Quian" [Examination of the Works of Herbert Quain], a play by the minor writer whose name gives the story its title becomes successful because the public misinterpreted it as a "Freudian comedy." Quain had published several books before, but they all enjoyed poor critical and public reception due to the circumstances in which they appeared. Psychoanalysis was a popular trend at the time and offered Quain an experience he had never enjoyed before: literary success, even though it was based on a misreading. After his brief brush with fame, Quain decides to take revenge on his audience and publishes a book that deliberately manipulates the plots to mislead his inattentive readers. The "true" meaning of his work, the one that stays hidden, remains visible only to a selected few, among whom we can count the narrator and apologist. Although these two examples could be interpreted as an illustration of Borges's elitist and antidemocratic views regarding literature and the literary market, they also point to a conception of reading as quite distinct from consumption. The book, according to these two short stories, is not another commodity in a world saturated with merchandise and information. The reader should proceed like a detective, discarding false leads.

That a piece of writing or an historical event is apocryphal does not mean that it is lacking in values or wisdom. "Un hecho falso puede ser esencialmente cierto" [a false fact can be essentially true], Borges wrote in "Nota sobre Walt Whitman" [Note on Walt Whitman] (*OC* I: 252). "Es fama que Enrique I de Inglaterra no volvió a sonreír después de la muerte de su hijo; el hecho, quizá falso, puede ser verdadero como símbolo del abatimiento del rey" [A false event could be true in its essence. It is said that Henry I of England never smiled again after his son's death. This may be false as a fact, but not as a symbol of the King's sorrow] (*OC* I:252). This way of interpreting the apocryphal offers an insight into Borges's own plays with reality and his alterations of it. The intention may be benign or more aesthetically pleasing, but it nonetheless constitutes a manipulation. Some fabricated or distorted phrases and events tend to resonate with people in a profound manner because they correspond to their expectations and offer a simplified view of more complex occurrences.

Borges himself practiced the alteration and manipulation of stories and texts. If we are to believe him, his first book of short stories, *Historia universal de la infamia* [*A Universal History of Infamy*] (1935), is nothing but "el irresponsable juego de un tímido que se animó a escribir cuentos y que se distrajo en falsear tergiversar (sin justificación estética alguna) historias ajenas" [the irresponsible sport of a shy sort of man who could not bring himself to write short stories, and so amused himself by changing and distorting (sometimes without aesthetic justification) the stories of other men] (*OC* I:391; *Fictions* 4), according to the preface that Borges added to the 1954 edition. In fact, this book has never been considered by some critics as Borges's first work of fiction, given the nature of most of its stories. He did not invent the characters or the plots, taking them instead from well-known sources and declaring explicitly the procedures he employed in the book's composition at the end of the volume. The question of how much Borges recreated his sources has been the object of study for many decades. If we were to believe him, we can accept the fact that these "exercises"—as he called them— were a sort of warm-up, a learning endeavor that made possible the abundant creativity his work took on a few years later. Rewriting well-known tales prepared him to become the author of *Ficciones* and *El Aleph*.

However, as Daniel Balderston has pointed out, "[e]ach of the stories of the book, however closely based on the source material, contains a few sharp scenes that are not to be found in the source" ("Borges" 28). Borges emphasized visual aspects or those "circumstantial details" that, according to his article "El arte narrativo y la magia" [Narrative Art and Magic] (1932), have the purpose of revealing an entire world without needing to explain or describe too many details. The question then arises as to how intentional—how apocryphal—these distortions could be. Appropriating other people's stories served Borges as a learning exercise, helped him erase the limits between source materials and his own inventions, contributing to the creation of one of the most ambitious works of the twentieth century. In some of these stories, Borges's intervention is the one remembered the most. An example appears in the new edition of *The Gangs of New York*, the 1927 book by Herbert Asbury which served as the inspiration for Borges's "El proveedor de iniquidades Monk Eastman" [Monk Eastman, Purveyor of Iniquities], included in *Historia universal de la infamia*. When Martin Scorsese's adaptation of the work premiered in 2002, the book was reissued. The cover announced that the foreword to the new edition was authored by Borges. The text, of course, was not apocryphal, but presenting it as the foreword to the book that inspired Borges was. The original source of the story and Borges's version have turned a full circle: the fact that he recreated a character from the book has, with time, lent a greater legitimacy to it.

On another level, the apocrypha are connected to Borges's ideas about originality and personal expression, as shown in the short story "El inmortal" [The Immortal] (*El Aleph* 1949). It begins with a comment by an unnamed narrator, who introduces himself as editor and translator and explains that the events the reader is about to encounter constitute a literal translation of an English manuscript found inside a volume of Alexander Pope's *Iliad*. The text in question is an account written by a Roman soldier, Marcus Flaminius Rufus (later known also as Joseph Cartaphilus), on how he found the river whose waters make humans immortal, met Homer, and participated in several historical events until he recovered his mortality. The short story's postscript, written by the editor who introduced the manuscript, summarizes the reactions to the publication, detailing one of them: the book *A Coat of Many Colors* by one Nahum Cordovero, who considers the text to be apocryphal due to the many "intrusiones, o hurtos" [interpolations, or thefts] (*OC* I:544). By these he means the many Homer quotes that appear throughout the manuscript, but also other references. Cartaphilus himself had brought the reader's attention to most of Homer's references. When he revised the manuscript a year after finishing the first draft, he noticed "algo falso" [a certain falseness] in its pages (*OC* I:542). Cartaphilus first explains it as an abuse of circumstantial details but later finds a more "private and inward" reason: in his story, the experiences of two men are mixed. Homer had been so fundamental in his life that he lost the ability to distinguish his own experiences from those of the Greek poet.

In his argument, Cordovero quotes several examples of similar literary procedures: the Greek and Roman *centos* (poems composed using lines from other poets, mainly from Homer) and techniques displayed by T. S. Eliot and George Moore, among others. According to this critic, the proof that the text is apocryphal resides in the fact that the author has taken fragments from many other writers without acknowledging his debt. The "editor" disagrees. After living for centuries, he argues, Cartaphilus has experienced all emotions and thoughts a human being is capable of. Therefore, he can express his own thoughts and feelings using other writers' words. Cartaphilus does not possess memories anymore but only words, which are often confused with those of others in his mind.[5]

The apocryphal nature of the text, according to Cordovero, is recognizable in the manuscript on account of the high number of unacknowledged references. The resulting product could not have been authentic or conceived by a single author because it is composed of fragments of other people's words. However, as some critics have pointed out, Cordovero himself has fallen victim to the same method he denounced. His commentary is about a hundred pages long. Fishburn and Hughes observe that one hundred, a *cento*, suggests his book has been composed also in the manner of the patchwork Greek and Roman compositions (52). Therefore, not even the critic can escape the impersonal, patchwork-like nature of the literary work.

The choice of a character's name is never casual for Borges. The last name Cordovero reminds us of the famous sixteenth-century cabalist Moses ben Jacob Cordovero. He is mostly known for his attempts at systematizing the Kabbalah and at solving the contradictions in one of the main books of Jewish mysticism, the *Zohar*, the thirteenth-century work by Spanish rabbi Moses de León. Cordovero defended the idea that the entirety of the *Zohar* is the work of a single author. The *Zohar* itself is a well-known example of pseudepigrapha, since Moses de León presented it as the transcription of a manuscript in his possession written by the second-century Rabbi Shimon bar Yochai, one of the greatest sages of Judaism. Even though current scholarship agrees that the Castilian rabbi wrote most of the book,[6] displaying the classic technique of attributing a text to an ancient authority, two of its books are still debated: *Tikkunei Zohar* and *Ra'ya Mehemna* are considered later additions. Cordovero, the cabalist, tried to reconcile these two parts and attribute them to de León as well. Since he conceived them "to be by the same author, he felt constrained to harmonize their different and at times even opposing conceptions" (Ben-Shlomo 220). It is not a coincidence, then, that a defender of textual unity, of single authorship, has lent his name to someone who proceeded, unsuccessfully, in a similar manner.

The confluence of Greek and Jewish thinking at the opening and the end of "El inmortal" adds another dimension to the story. It begins with one of the most famous proverbs attributed to King Solomon: "There is no new thing upon the earth." But Borges does not cite it directly from the Bible—he quotes Francis Bacon, who writes: "So that as Plato had an imagination, that all knowledge was but remembrance; so Solomon giveth his sentence, that all novelty is but oblivion" (*OC* I:533). The story questions the emphasis on originality by pointing to the similarities between two authors who belonged to different worlds but who nonetheless arrived at the same conclusion. When the narrator argues that there is no improper or deceitful appropriation of other texts, that every person should be capable of arriving at all thoughts, concepts like attribution, plagiarism, apocrypha, and pseudepigrapha lose their relevance.

HIDDEN CLUES AND MEANINGS

The concept of apocrypha is not only explicitly expressed in some of Borges's writings—as we have seen—he also employs it as a literary device. In his analysis of a series of suspicious quotations in Borges's work (the passage from Snorri Sturlusson is an example), Iván Almeida concludes that the apocryphal may function as a mechanism to bring attention to other parts of a given text, or to hide a passage that would reveal a more profound interpretation. In this manner, Borges establishes a game with his readers in which the "real" or "secret" meaning may be found somewhere else. He offers clues, but they often mislead the reader, who must remain attentive to other clues and find their true purpose. Sometimes a misquotation, a reference to the wrong page or chapter, might become the key to understanding a text.[7]

In the short story "La secta del Fénix" [The Cult of the Phoenix], also from *Ficciones* (1944), we find an example of this intricate game of displacements. When the narrator notes that, for the members of the sect, anything—even a poem to the sea—could be perceived as an allusion to the Secret, he quotes a Latin maxim: "*Orbis terrarum est speculum Ludi* reza un adagio apócrifo que Du Cange registró en su Glosario" [*Orbis terrarum est speculum Ludi*, goes an apocryphal saying reported by Du Cange in his *Glossary*] (*OC* I:522; *Fictions* 173). The phrase comes from an authoritative source: the French scholar Charles du Fresne, seigneur du Cange (1610–88). His best-known works are *Glossarium mediae et infimae latinitatis*, an encyclopedia of medieval Latin, and a similar dictionary of Greek.[8] The phrase means "The world is a mirror of a game," but, given the structure of Latin grammar, it could also be read as "The games are a mirror of the world." From the way the narrator introduces the maxim, one may infer that Du Cange was the unwitting victim of a hoax and included it in his *Glossarium* without suspecting its questionable origins. Either the quote is attributed to someone who never

BORGES AND THE CREATIVE ECONOMY OF THE APOCRYPHAL   359

said it, or its true author remains unknown. However, we may excuse Du Cange for this oversight because the phrase does not actually appear in his glossary. It is also not found in any of the search engines that Latinists routinely use. Everything suggests that Borges invented the maxim and attributed it to a well-known authority. In doing so, he called attention to the apocryphal nature of the saying but did so indirectly: someone else— not him—had invented it, and Du Cange fell for it. The game is twofold: the apocryphal nature of the phrase is revealed, but its actual origin becomes clear only after the reader has done the additional work.[9]

The maxim fits perfectly not only the moral of the story but also an idea that is central to Borges's work: games as reflections of a deeper and more complex structure, as mirrors of life. His favorite instance is perhaps the story of the enemy commanding officers who play chess while their respective armies clash in the battlefield.[10] When one of the opponents capitulates, his army is defeated. In "La lotería en Babilonia" [The Lottery in Babylon], the game of lottery chance becomes a metaphor for the randomness of life itself. In "La secta del Fénix," the members of the sect also engage in a game of sorts. As the narrator observes, "El rito constituye el Secreto" [The ritual is, in fact, the Secret] (*OC* I:522; *Fictions* 172). On the one hand, we can think of the ritual as a game, as a simplified representation or reflection of a more complex reality or belief; on the other, as the narrator asserts, everything in the universe can be interpreted as a reference to the Secret (i.e., the ritual). The two possible readings of the Latin phrase summarize the essence of the cult. However, this essence is disguised by the narrator: first, by presenting it in Latin; second, by attributing it to someone else and hinting at the original source as apocryphal. Borges hides a key phrase by using Latin and by giving falsified leads. This, however, is not only the *modus operandi* that "a shy sort of man" would employ to disguise his own contributions. By pointing out that the phrase is apocryphal, Borges calls attention to himself: he is able to express not only a fundamental concept in his work in Latin, but also one of competing with high authorities in the field. All this is accomplished in "a game of shifting mirrors," to quote the subtitle of another fictitious book, the novel *The Approach to Al-mu'tasim*, the subject of the short story of the same title.

In probably the most compelling essay on Borges's use of the apocryphal, Almeida argues that for Borges "[l]os espejos repiten y multiplican sin substituir. Lo apócrifo, en cambio, substituye y estiliza sin multiplicar" [Mirrors repeat and multiply without replacing. The apocryphal, on the other hand, replaces and refines the style without multiplying] ("Celebración" 183). Almeida comes to this conclusion from his analysis of "Tlön, Uqbar, Orbis Tertius," and the threat mirrors exert on the two main characters while they discuss the novel that would be accessible to only a few readers. In fact, what triggers the entire action of the story is the quote that the character Bioy Casares attributes to a heresiarch from Tlön: "los espejos y la cópula son abominables porque multiplican el número de los hombres" [mirrors and copulation are abominable, for they multiply the number of mankind] (*OC* I:431; *Fictions* 68). When Bioy Casares finds the original phrase in his copy of the apocryphal *American Cyclopedia*, the narrator points out that it was "formulada en palabras casi idénticas a las repetidas por él, aunque—tal vez—literariamente inferiores" [formulated in words almost identical to those Bioy had quoted, though from a literary point of view perhaps inferior] (*OC* I:431; *Fictions* 69). Thus, the phrase is refined by Bioy Casares, distilled to its essence.[11]

The apocryphal, continues Almeida, "está estrechamente relacionado con la economía de condensación y desplazamiento propia de los tropos" [is closely connected with the economy of condensation and displacement that characterize literary tropes] ("Celebración" 184). Why do we need to read a forty-volume encyclopedia on a fictional planet when we can just read a fourteen-page review—the short story itself—of the eleventh volume of such an exhausting work? Why, Borges himself asked, in the prologue to *El jardín de senderos que se bifurcan* [*The Garden of Forking Paths*], take five hundred pages to develop an idea whose simple exposition could fit in a few?[12] The method of writing short stories that mimic book reviews is an essential creative mechanism in Borges. It allowed him to produce some of his most distinctive short stories: "Tlön, Uqbar, Orbis Tertius," "El acercamiento a Almotásim" [The Approach to Al-Mu'tasim], and "Examen de la obra de Herbert Quian," to mention a few. It cannot be stated with absolute certainty that when these texts first appeared in the journal *Sur*, Borges intended to deceive his readers in passing as authentic book reviews texts that were the product of his imagination. But it is said that at least some of his readers fell for the trick: Bioy Casares himself may have believed the novel that the narrator "reviews" in "El acercamiento a Almotásim" was real and visited an English bookstore in Buenos Aires to order it. That Borges played purposely with the blurring of boundaries between literary genres is obvious in his work. He would publish a short story under a section of a book titled "Dos notas" [Two Notes], the other one being his short essay in the art of insult (*Historia de la eternidad*).

There is in Borges—at least, initially—a desire to confuse his readers as to what exactly they were confronting: a fictional work, a review of an existing book, an authentic quote, a reference to an historical character. He may have intentionally intended to challenge the notion of literary genre—a concept he defined less by a text's intrinsic characteristics than by the way it is read. However, all these complicated games lead to questions about the nature of fiction. In his short stories, Borges does not pretend to pass a fictional creation as the recounting of a real event. But he suggests that despite the fictional nature of a text, the ideas, characters, and emotions it contains, their meaning is as real as anything else. This is what Almeida calls "la ontología doblemente apócrifa que constituye toda ficción" [the twice-apocryphal ontology of every fiction] ("Celebración" 203). A dream may have the same relationship to reality as a fiction, but even a dream must follow its own intrinsic rules. A more liberating procedure would be to imagine that we are dreaming. This is how Borges establishes the difference between simulating a book that already exists (and offering a summary of it, as Carlyle in *Sartor Resartus* and Butler in *The Fair Haven* do) and imagining a book. The first method produces books that are "no less tautological" than the simulated ones; the other one results in works that can incur in contradictions without the need of rationalizing or explaining them. Like an apocryphal past, these books can be imagined at will.

A final example of how Borges put to the work the creative possibilities of the apocryphal can be found in "La otra muerte" [The Other Death], a short story from *El Aleph*.

As in every fictional creation, the narrator of "La otra muerte" employs several artifices to make us believe in the reality of his main character: he has made us identify with Pedro Damián's struggle to redeem his past of cowardice. When the protagonist finally redeems himself, the narrator confesses that Damián may not have existed after all, and that the plot of the story was suggested by a passage in the theologian Pier Damiani's book *De Divina Omnipotentia*. In that treatise, the author argues that God may undo or correct the past if a person deserves such a redemption. Pedro Damián's fate is similar: through his actions he prepares himself to relive his past and dies as a courageous man in the Battle of Masoller. His action causes a correction in the timeline the narrator also lives in. The memories of some of the people who knew Pedro Damián experience a transformation, and they now remember him as a brave man, dying in combat forty years before. Another man who had a closer relationship with him dies suddenly because he preserved too many details of Damián's life. The narrator considers for a moment that he may also perish for having found out the truth and exposed it. But then, he finds comfort in the speculation that he may have invented the character and all the events after reading Damiani's book.

Having convinced us the latter is the case, the narrator adds a final paragraph: "¡Pobre Damián! La muerte lo llevó a los veinte años en una triste guerra ignorada y en una batalla casera, pero consiguió lo que anhelaba su corazón, y tardó mucho en conseguirlo, y acaso no hay mayores felicidades" [Poor Damián! Death took him at twenty in a sad, forgotten war and in a minor battle. He managed to achieve his heart's desire, and even though it took him a long time, perhaps there is no greater happiness] (*OC* I:575). The fact that Pedro Damián might not have existed does not prevent the narrator from commiserating about his destiny, nor does it prevent us as readers from experiencing a similar sentiment. The narrator has thus staged a complex *mise en abyme*: his account begins with his attempt at writing a story (Damián's heroism at the Battle of Masoller) that becomes another story (Damián's cowardice and further redemption). This would have been a complete narrative arc. But the narrator adds another layer at the end: it is possible that the existence of Damián is apocryphal and that the events related in the story never took place. Borges again alludes to the nature of fiction, showing the complex interconnections between reading and writing, between philosophical ideas and the development of a captivating narrative. What Damián's apocryphal life story communicates is not less true because the character—as happens in every fiction--did not actually exist, not even within the fictional realm of the story.

An (Occasional) Apocryphal Life Story

The confession at the end of "The Other Death"—that the main character may have never existed and the story was suggested in its entirety by the narrator's reading of Pier Damiani—could be applied to the ways in which Borges constructed himself as an author and refined his own personal story through the years. This process is filled with dubious anecdotes that he repeated as legitimate. His "Autobiographical Essay," written in English in collaboration with Norman Thomas di Giovanni and published originally in *The New Yorker* in 1970, contains several of them. The most notorious is probably his account of having read *Don Quixote* for the first time in English; later, when he read the Spanish original, he supposedly deemed it a bad translation. However, when Borges described the physical characteristics of the book he presumably read, the description corresponds to the Spanish edition published in 1882 by the French printer Garnier, which never printed *Don Quixote* in English. Borges repeated this false recollection on several occasions and corrected himself on others. It seems the anecdote fluctuated between real and false depending on the audience he was presenting to: when speaking to an English-speaking public, he would mention reading *Don Quixote* in English.[13] On one occasion, however, before a Spanish-speaking audience, he stated unequivocally that he had never read *Don Quixote* in English.[14] Rafael Olea Franco adds another level to this anecdote: "Además, quienes repiten esta anécdota sin hurgar en su sentido, se olvidan de la ironía típica del autor, ya que este pudo haber querido reelaborar la broma, cierta o falsa, que se le adjudica a Byron, quien dijo que había leído a Shakespeare primero en italiano" [Moreover, those who repeat this anecdote without delving into its meaning are ignoring the author's characteristic irony, since he might have wanted to retell the joke, true or false, attributed to Byron, who said he first read Shakespeare in Italian] (50). Borges's "joke" has proliferated, creating other possibilities: he *might* have quoted a Byron phrase that *may not* be real either. The apocryphal has engendered its own gravitational field.

Another telling story concerns how Borges learned German. According to him, he started with a book of Henrich Heine, a German Bible, and an English-German dictionary.[15] However, as Alejandro Vaccaro has demonstrated, Borges took several years of German at the Collège Calvin in Geneva where he was living with his family in the 1910s: "Sus notas en estas materias [latín y alemán] eran razonables para un estudiante que acababa de ser transplantado de otro continente" [His grades in these subjects (Latin and German) were good for a student who had just been transplanted from another continent] (87). The examples could be multiplied: his reading of the *Divine Comedy* (using just a bilingual edition while traveling to and from work on the tram) and how he wrote his first short story, "Pierre Menard, autor del *Quixote*" [Pierre Menard, author of the Quixote] (as an attempt to test if he had not lost his creative capacities after a head surgery).

All these falsehoods, distortions, and re-elaborations point to a constant self-fashioning, to a refining of his personal evolution as a writer. An apocryphal fact, Borges pointed out, could contain a truth deeper than what happened. It is not a coincidence that many of the public's favorite anecdotes about Borges are taken from distortions he put forward himself. In a way, they fulfill the expectation of what is considered typically Borges. These manipulations may have never served a disingenuous goal: probably Borges did not fool anyone with them. But the question arises as to whether they fit his life story in a more harmonious manner, the narrative he wanted to present about himself when his global fame became apparent. As Borges himself understood, when the past is rewritten, reinterpreted, it becomes more perfect, so perfect that it becomes apocryphal.[16]

Apocryphal Borges

With his many uses of the apocrypha, Borges stimulated the creative potential of this concept in Latin American literature. Consequently, texts attributed to him circulated even when he was still alive, and writers conceived of works that employed practices that were similar to the ones in his fiction. Several of these works aim to pay tribute to his work or to parody it. With a few exceptions, these texts did not pretend to pass as authentic.[17] Such are the cases of Pablo Katchadjian's *El Aleph engordado* [*The Fattened— or Extended—Aleph*] (2009), a work that adds around 5,600 words to Borges's original short story, and *El hacedor (de Borges). Remake* (2011) by Agustín Fernández Mallo, where the author takes Borges's *El hacedor*, preserves the titles of the original poems and the book's structure, and writes his own. Both works were the subject of legal battles initiated by the Borges Estate. Katchadjian won a trial for plagiarism against him, but Fernández Mallo's book was withdrawn from circulation, even though it contains fewer of Borges's words than *El Aleph engordado*. It is certainly paradoxical that the work of a writer who was very critical of authorship and even defended plagiarism became enmeshed in legal battles over works that were tributes or used his creative methods.

However, another paradox emerges when reading works that make Borges's words proliferate in a way. Given that Borges, in accordance with Almeida, used the apocryphal to display an aesthetics of verbal economy, what can be said of works that attempt to multiply his work, to make his words proliferate? Do they constitute a valuable homage or are they following the tradition of attempting to create more Borges, more Borgesian literature?

Some texts, on the other hand, have circulated with the intention of passing as written by Borges. The most successful of them is undoubtedly the poem "Instantes" [Moments], which appeared in the prestigious Mexican journal *Plural* in 1989, three years after Borges's passing, and was reproduced in other journals.[18] The Mexican writer Elena Poniatowska even quoted it in an interview with Borges, in which she supposedly read the poem to him, and Borges said nothing while listening to words he never wrote. The incident, though, does not lack a "Borgesian" feeling to it. The authenticity of Poniatowska's interview has been questioned due to its many inconsistencies: if she did in fact interview Borges, she took some liberties during the editing process.[19] What exposed this fact was the apocryphal poem "Instantes" she added later, when the interview was reprinted in the second edition of a volume on Borges in Mexico (the book was taken out of circulation due to this oversight). The apocryphal poem served to expose the partially apocryphal interview. It involuntarily acted as a misquotation that called attention to another part of the text, or, in this case, the longer text in which it appeared.

Other texts have continued the tradition. Probably the most widely circulated in recent years is a poem entitled, in one of its versions, "Con el tiempo uno aprende" [With Time One Learns]. Instead of appearing in a reputable magazine, this poem has been spreading mainly on social media, where one can find countless attributions to Borges and other authors. The nature of the medium, with its emphasis on sharing and reposting, makes it easier for apocryphal creations to circulate at greater speeds and without any critical filter. Given the propensity of the social networks to propagate unconfirmed facts and outright lies, it should not be surprising that texts of this nature will continue to appear and circulate, even though it is less likely that cultural and academic journals will be easily deceived by these practices.

Conclusion

The apocryphal—the existence and the creation of texts and stories of false or dubious authenticity—afforded Borges numerous creative possibilities. As is well known, he explicitly declared his tendency to "estimar las ideas religiosas o filosóficas por su valor estético y aun por lo que encierran de singular y de maravilloso" [evaluate religious or philosophical ideas on the basis of their aesthetic worth and even for what is singular and marvelous about them] in his epilogue to his essay collection *Otras inquisiciones* (1952) (*OC* II:153; *Other Inquisitions* 189). If religion and philosophy provided Borges with abundant concepts and ideas that he transformed into groundbreaking stories (Pier Damiani's *De Divina Omnipotentia* is a wonderful example), the apocryphal, on the other hand, allowed him to examine the nature of fiction. It also enabled him to question a series of notions that have traditionally accompanied literary and artistic work: authorship, originality, canon formation, and the definition of literary genres. In some of the essential areas of Borges's work, the games with the apocryphal became a metaphor for literary invention.

Although it would be pretentious to establish a hierarchy of the creative procedures Borges employed in his work, his interest in the apocryphal should not be understated. It offered him ample possibilities, as both a creative mechanism and a critical tool. Throughout his literary career, Borges displayed a tendency to distrust authority, literary and otherwise. The apocryphal is one of the ways in which he carried out an irreverent, radical reading of literary traditions. It should come as no surprise that he felt attracted to apocryphal texts, stories, and characters, particularly the ones that challenged established knowledge and orthodoxy.

Borges opened the creative potential of the apocryphal for other generations of Latin American writers, such as Julio Cortázar and Roberto Bolaño, who utilized similar procedures in their work. In his 1951 talk "El escritor argentino y la tradición" [The Argentine Writer and Tradition], Borges celebrated the Latin American writers' advanced position with respect to Western literary tradition: the ability to treat this tradition with irreverence. His treatment of the apocryphal was one the ways in which

NOTES

1. English translations that do not come from a printed edition of Borges's works are mine.

2. In the same article, Almeida proves that Borges's favorite Goethe quote, "Lo cercano se aleja" [What is near becomes far], is also an alteration of the original, this time as a sort of revenge on Goethe, whose fame and literary significance Borges considered unmerited ("Goethe" 20–22).

3. *El Quijote de Avellaneda* [*Avellaneda's Don Quixote*] is the title given to a novel published in 1614 that pretended to be the account of Don Quixote's third journey. The name of the real author remains unknown, but it is clear that the novel intended to discredit some of the more irreverent ideas that Cervantes put forth in his work. The publication of this apocryphal Quijote exerted a considerable influence on the writing process of the second volume, which Cervantes was working on at the time. Throughout the second part of *Don Quijote*, published in 1615, the narrator as well as the characters claim ownership of the story and attack Avellaneda's work as misinformed and false. Maybe it was Cervantes himself who opened the possibility that others might write about his character, when in the first pages of the novel, employing a narrative device aimed to making his story more believable, mentioned that "there is some difference of opinion [on Quixote's actual name] among the authors who write on the subject" (*Don Quixote* pt. I, ch. 1). When other authors did write on the subject, Cervantes claimed exclusive authorship immediately.

4. Almeida mentions this aspect as well, accompanied by the following Borges quote: "Nuestra época es, a la vez, implacable, desesperada y sentimental; es inevitable que nos distraigamos con la evocación y con la cariñosa falsificación de épocas pretéritas" [Our time is, at the same time, implacable, desperate, and sentimental; it is inevitable that we distract ourselves with the invocation and the affectionate falsification of past times] (*Textos* 232).

5. The story concludes with a reference that sums up this perspective: Cartaphilus is left only with "palabras desplazadas y mutiladas, palabras de otros" [words, words taken out of place and mutilated, words from other men] (*OC* I:544; *Fictions* 195). Balderston argues that this ending is a reference to Joseph Conrad's words in the preface to *The Nigger of the "Narcissus"* and this is "quizás el acto consumado del arte de Borges: 'la apología del plagio plagiada de un autor predilecto'" [perhaps the consummated act of Borges's art: "an apology of plagiarism that he plagiarized from a favorite author"] (*El precursor* 171).

6. Abraham Zacuto, the great fifteenth-century astronomer whose charts were used by Christopher Columbus in his sailing to the West, mentions the account of Isaac of Acre, who went to Valladolid to meet de León and ask him in person if bar Yochai's manuscript was real. De León confirmed this, but on his way to Ávila, where the manuscript was stored, he died. His widow informed Acre that De León had confessed to her: "If I would say that I wrote this book from my own mind, no one would take notice of the work and I would not receive any gifts for it" (qtd. in Zacuto). Later, Joseph Abulafia Todros told Acre he had tested de León's claim by telling him he had lost a chapter of the *Zohar*. De León gave him another copy that presented only "one change in the use of language and a few small details" (Zacuto). However, Rabbi ha-Levi affirmed this test was not conclusive: de León may have already made another copy of the book.

7. Another proof of Borges's interests in the relationship between what is hidden and what is revealed could be found in his 1949 short story "El Zahir." According to Fishburn and Hughes, Zahir is "Arabic for 'visible,' 'manifest': one of the attributes of Allah mentioned in the Koran (57:3): 'He is the First and the Last, the Manifest (*zahir*), and the Hidden (*batim*).' The dichotomy between *zahir* and *batim* is reflected in the two ways of interpreting the Koran: whereas *zahir* is based upon a purely literal reading of the text, *batim* seeks more hidden or esoteric meanings" (214).

8. According to the *Encyclopedia Britannica* entry on Du Cange, "he attempted to develop a historical perspective on the two languages; i.e., he tried to distinguish the medieval Latin and Greek vocabularies from their classical counterparts. Moreover, because he illustrated from documents and primary sources not only the words but also the matters described by the words, the two books are more like encyclopaedias than dictionaries. The works were of epic scale and virtually unprecedented in their fields; the recent reprints attest to the continuing value of his scholarship as a forerunner of modern historical linguistics" ("Charles du Fresne . . .").

9. I want to thank my colleague Dan Davis for having helped me with the meaning of the phrase and the (fruitless) search for a phrase that might resemble Borges's attribution.

10. One version of the story appears in *Cuentos breves y extraordinarios* (1955), which he coedited with Bioy Casares.

11. A previous version of the phrase as quoted in the *American Cyclopedia*, the one Bioy Casares improved upon, appeared in Borges's 1935 story "El tintorero enmascarado Hákim de Merv" (*Historia universal de la infamia, OC* I:327).

12. For more on these ideas, see chapter 11 (Premat, this volume).

13. In a 1976 interview with Willis Barnstone, he repeated this version (138–39). This "fluctuation from real to false" is also in the Tom Castro story from *Historia universal de la infamia*. The text concludes with a mention of the talks Castro gave after his release from prison for having impersonated Roger Charles Tichborne. In those talks, "declaraba su inocencia o afirmaba su culpa. Su modestia y su anhelo de agradar eran tan duraderos que muchas noches comenzó por defensa y acabó por confesión, siempre al servicio de las inclinaciones del público" [he declared his innocence and confessed his guilt. His modesty and his desire to please remained with him such that many nights he would begin by defending himself and end up confessing to it all, depending on his audience's desires] (*OC* I:305). Borges was probably not trying to please his public, but he did like to include amusing and surprising facts and stories in his talks.

14. "No, jamás he dicho eso, además, no lo he leído en inglés. No puedo imaginármelo en inglés tampoco, es inconcebible para mí. . . . Uno de los primeros libros que yo leí fue el Quijote. Y lo recuerdo desde luego en castellano, ya que hay tantas frases que yo aprendí de memoria" [No, I have never said that; moreover, I have never read it in English. I cannot imagine it in English, it's inconceivable to me. . . . One of the first books I read was *Don Quixote*. And I remember it in Spanish of course, since there are so many phrases I learned by heart] ("Jorge Luis Borges. Coloquio" 28).

15. In his interview with María Esther Vázquez, Borges says: "El vocabulario de Heine en sus obras iniciales es deliberadamente sencillo; una vez que conocí las palabras *Nachtigall, Herz, liebe, Nacht, trauer, geliebte* . . . me di cuenta de que podía prescindir del diccionario y seguí leyendo, de modo que llegué por esa vía a dominar la lengua espléndida de la música de los versos de Heine" [In his first works, Heine's vocabulary is deliberately simple; once I learned the words *Nachtigall, Herz, liebe, Nacht, trauer, geliebte* . . . I realized

I could manage without the dictionary and kept reading. And that's how I got to master the splendid musical language of Heine's poetry] (46).

16. Almeida also observes this fact and offers Borges's reading of T. F. Powys: "Es de ascendencia ilustre, ya que entre las personas de su sangre están John Donne y William Cowper. (No hablo de ciertos príncipes de Gales, tan antiguos que ya son legendarios, tan legendarios que más bien son apócrifos)" [He comes from a distinguished ancestry, since among his blood relatives are John Donne and William Cowper. (I will not mention certain Princes of Wales, so old they are legendary, so legendary they are rather apocryphal)] ("T. F. Powys" 358).

17. One notable exception is the case of the Salvadoran writer Álvaro Menen Desleal, who published a supposed letter by Borges in his 1963 book *Cuentos breves y maravillosos*, the title already being a close resemblance to Borges and Bioy Casares's (*Cuentos breves y extraordinarios*, 1955). In Bioy Casares's diary there is an amusing passage in which Borges seems genuinely to question if he actually wrote the letter. See Parodi and Almeida.

18. For a thorough analysis of the poem, its history, and its reception, see Almeida, "Jorge Luis Borges, autor del poema 'Instantes.'"

19. Poniatowska included the interview in her book *Todo México* (1990) and dated it 1976, a year Borges had not visited Mexico. The original version was published in a Mexican magazine in 1973 and did not include questions that are in the (hypothetical) 1976 version. For the second edition of *Borges y México* (1999, 2012), the editor Miguel Capistrán took the interview from the 1990 book, which already included the reference to "Instantes."

WORKS CITED

Almeida, Iván. "Celebración del apócrifo." *Variaciones Borges*, vol. 15, 2003, pp. 181–206.

Almeida, Iván. "Goethe y la trastienda de la historia." *Variaciones Borges*, vol. 34, 2012, pp. 3–25.

Almeida, Iván. "Jorge Luis Borges, autor del poema 'Instantes.'" *Variaciones Borges*, vol. 10, 2000, pp. 227–46.

Balderston, Daniel. "Borges and *The Gangs of New York*." *Variaciones Borges*, vol. 16, 2003, pp. 27–33.

Balderston, Daniel. *El precursor velado. R. L. Stevenson en la obra de Borges*. Editorial Sudamericana, 1985.

Barnstone, Willis. "With Borges in Buenos Aires." *Jorge Luis Borges: Conversations*. Edited by Richard Burgin. University Press of Mississippi, 1998, pp. 38–48.

Ben-Shlomo, Joseph. "Cordovero, Moses ben Jacob." *Encyclopaedia Judaica*. Edited by Michael Berenbaum and Fred Skolnik, 2nd ed., vol. 5. Macmillan Reference USA, 2007, pp. 220–21.

Bioy Casares, Adolfo. *Borges*, edited by Daniel Martino. Destino, 2006.

Borges, Jorge Luis. "An Autobiographical Essay." *The Aleph and Other Stories, 1933-1969*. E.P. Dutton, 1970, pp. 203–60.

Borges, Jorge Luis. *Collected Fictions*, translated by Andrew Hurley. Viking, 1998.

Borges, Jorge Luis. *Evaristo Carriego. A Book about Old-time Buenos Aires*, translated by Norman Thomas di Giovanni. E.P. Dutton, 1984.

Borges, Jorge Luis. *Obras completas*. Emecé Editores, 1996. 4 vols.

Borges, Jorge Luis. *Other Inquisitions. 1937–1952*, translated by Ruth L. C. Simms. U of Texas P, 1964.

Borges, Jorge Luis. *Textos recobrados (1931–1955)*. Emecé Editores, 2001.

Capistrán, Miguel, ed. *Borges y México*. Plaza y Janés, 1999.

Cervantes, Miguel de. *Don Quixote*, translated by Henry Edward Watts. D. Appleton and Company, 1899.

"Charles du Fresne, seigneur du Cange." *Britannica Academic: Encyclopædia Britannica*, July 20, 1998.

Charles, Robert Henry. "Apocryphal Literature." *Encyclopedia Britannica*, 1911. e-book ed.

Conrad, Joseph. *The Nigger of the "Narcissus."* Harper & Brothers, 1951.

Fishburn, Evelyn, and Psiche Hughes. *A Dictionary of Borges*. Revised edition. Duckworth, 1990.

"Jorge Luis Borges. Coloquio." *Literatura fantástica*. Ediciones Siruela, 1985, pp. 13–36.

Olea Franco, Rafael. "El otro, el mismo: Borges y la (auto)biografía." *Jorge Luis Borges: Viajes y tiempos de un escritor a través de culturas y sistemas*. Edited by Margherita Cannavacciuolo, Alice Favaro, and Susanna Regazzoni. Georg Olms Verlag, 2018, pp. 43–58.

Parodi, Cristina, and Iván Almeida. "Celebración del plagio. La línea Menard Paladión Desleal." *Variaciones Borges*, vol. 49, 2020, pp. 10–31.

Vaccaro, Alejandro. *Georgie (1899–1930)*. Editorial Proa, 1996.

Vázquez, María Esther. *Borges, sus días y su tiempo*. Javier Vergara Editor, 1984.

Wilde, Oscar. *Collected Works*. Barnes and Noble, 2006.

Zacuto, Abraham. *The Book of Lineage; or, Sefer Yohassin*, edited by Israel Shamir. Zacuto Foundation, 2005.

PART IV

RECEPTION

IN LITERATURE

CHAPTER 21

A HISTORY OF BORGES'S RECEPTION IN ARGENTINA

SERGIO PASTORMERLO

BORGES began his career as a writer at the same time Ricardo Rojas published his *Historia de la literatura argentina* (1917–1922). From the very beginning, Rojas's four-volume oeuvre elicited jokes about its "monumental" dimensions. Even more notable was Rojas, in the "Introduction," having dedicated a few pages to a question he did not think superfluous: Did Argentine literature exist? As of 1913, Rojas had been the nation's first professor in its first university program dedicated to Argentine Literature. That same year, *Martín Fierro* had been defined as Argentina's national epic poem in a canonization effort Rojas made alongside Leopoldo Lugones. These were the years of what was called the "cultural nationalism of the Centenary," of the May 1810 Revolution. Moreover, Rojas created the Instituto de Literatura Argentina (1923) and directed the first academic publishing series ("Biblioteca Argentina" [1915–1928]) intended to inaugurate, with the support of philology, the region's literary canon. It was clear that the "national literature" proposed by the Generation of 1837, but whose founding was constantly put off for future realization, was finally coming to fruition. As of the 1880s, there was a general consensus that Argentina should complement its visible material progress with a compensatory cultural ("spiritual") development.

In the first few years of the twentieth century, the generation before Borges's (Ricardo Rojas, Manuel Gálvez, Roberto Giusti) had begun defining itself as the first generation of professional writers. The cohort prior to that of Rojas had been the generation of Spanish American modernists, what Manual Ugarte called "the failed generation,"[1] as these writers were compelled to depart for Paris or Madrid in search of the literary milieu their countries lacked.[2] Borges's generation, though it had been preceded by two or three self-proclaimed "new literary generations," understood that Argentine literature in fact began with them. "What have we Argentines accomplished?" Borges asked in 1926, and responded, after a quick historical inventory from which he salvaged just a few names: "pienso que el lector estará de acuerdo conmigo si afirmo la esencial pobreza de nuestro hacer" [I think the reader will agree with me if I affirm the essential poverty of our production] ("El tamaño" 6–7). The avant-garde rupture with tradition thus faced the disappointing challenge of confronting a preceding tradition that was as brief as it was weak. Borges's trajectory, and the history of his reception, take this as his point of departure: Borges began creating Argentine literature when that literature itself was just beginning.

At the start of the 1920s, Buenos Aires's incipient literary life still revolved around the long-standing journal *Nosotros* (1907–1943), directed by Roberto Giusti and Alfredo Bianchi. *Nosotros* had a hospitable policy of bringing together writers from diverse trends and generations. It was understood that such a reduced literary environment, surrounded by a society that was hostile or indifferent to letters, demanded the participation of all. In 1923, the journal also tried to incorporate the youngest writers by organizing an "Encuesta sobre la nueva generación literaria" [Survey about the new literary generation] which, despite its good intentions, would fail to successfully register the avant-garde storm that was brewing. *Prisma* (1921–1922), *Proa* (first era: 1922–1923; second era: 1924–1926), *Inicial* (1923–1926), and *Martín Fierro* (1924–1927) stand out among the many journals of the "new sensibility" that proliferated over the course of the decade. The most important was *Martín Fierro*, the journal that used new forms of mass publicity to eventually sell nearly 20,000 copies per issue. "Martinfierrismo" and "vanguardismo" would eventually become synonymous. At the same time, a literary left was beginning to take shape around its own journals.[3] To the rupture with the past, which basically came down to writing against Leopoldo Lugones, was added the confrontation between *martinfierrismo* and *boedismo*. The polemic between Florida and Boedo was not merely a publicity stunt (as those in the Florida group alleged), but a real opposition between two camps in a literary field that were already different enough to create foundational tensions. As Roberto Arlt wrote in *El Mundo* in 1932: "Se es de Boedo o se es de Florida. Se está con los trabajadores o con los niños bien. El dilema es simple, claro, y lo entienden todos" [You're either from Boedo or from Florida. You're with the workers or the rich kids. The choice is simple, clear, and everybody understands it] (108).

Borges, from the very beginning, participated actively in the intense literary sociability of the young avant-garde writers of the 1920s. With his friends he founded and directed his own journals. He collaborated in all the journals historically associated with *martinfierrismo*. He took the prerogative to represent, in Argentina, Ultraism from Spain. Though eight years younger than his primary rival at the time, Oliverio Girondo, the author of *Martín Fierro*'s manifesto, he precociously inserted himself into Buenos Aires's avant-garde with the mural journal *Prisma* (1921) and his first book of poems, *Fervor de Buenos Aires* [*Fervor of Buenos Aires*] (1923). At any rate, the differences in literary, cultural, and social capital that divided the Florida and Boedo groups were multiplied in Borges as an individual. He brought surprising renovations from Europe, such as German Expressionism. He spoke Spanish, English, and French and had learned a considerable amount of German and Latin. Within just a few years he published three books of poetry and three of essays. Borges's visibility, and the recognition that goes along with it, could not be immediate. But from here begins a long history of increasing recognition by his peers that is challenging to chronicle.

The period in which Borges was primarily recognized among his Argentine peers becomes exceptionally prolonged if one takes a retrospective point of view, as does Mario Vargas Llosa. For Vargas Llosa, who met the Argentine in an interview in 1963, during the years when his canonization was finalizing, Borges was the rare example of a great writer who had not been recognized (in the mass media or internationally) until he was over sixty years old and his oeuvre had been completed. Borges had his beginnings in a world of cultural vanguards that, while taking advantage of new forms of advertising, maintained a certain indifference or opposition to a publishing market that was otherwise quite different from that of the Latin American Boom. In 1923, Borges had distributed his *Fervor de Buenos Aires* in the pockets of coats hanging in the publishing offices of *Nosotros*; in 1936, several months after its debut, just forty-seven copies of *Historia de la eternidad* [*A History of Eternity*] had sold: anecdotes such as these were fundamentally true. The young Borges published in major newspapers such as *La Prensa* (as of 1926) and *Crítica* (1933–1934), as well as in the mass-market home magazine *El Hogar* [*The Home*] (1936–1939), but without conforming to the broad audiences of these periodicals. Borges did not want to be a bad but successful writer, like Manuel Gálvez, but rather a good, prestigious, but failed writer, like Leopoldo Lugones. Josefina Ludmer has suggested that one can trace the process of Argentina's literary autonomy in Borges's personal trajectory: between 1930 and 1960, Borges brought to fruition the literary actualization that had begun so parsimoniously in the Río de la Plata in the 1880s.

As the avant-garde was international, Borges's visibility and recognition, early on, were also amplified beyond local reception. Journals of the 1920s such as *Proa* or *Martín Fierro*, sought to bring together and promote young Spanish American writers. In 1926, Borges collaborated with Peruvian Alberto Hidalgo and Chilean Vicente Huidobro on the *Índice de la nueva poesía americana*, one of three anthologies of young avant-garde writers published in Buenos Aires in that decade. Here Borges wrote about the *estridentismo* of Mexican poet Maples Arce and about the avant-garde nativism of Uruguayans Pedro Leandro Ipuche and Fernán Silva Valdés. Even more important, in the early 1920s, were his ties to Spain, which would soon be so thoroughly forgotten. Borges brought *Fervor de Buenos Aires* to Madrid on his second stay in Europe (1923–1924), and Ramón Gómez de la Serna reviewed it in the *Revista de Occidente* (1924). Borges was first introduced to France by Valery Larbaud ("Sur Borges" 1925), a friend of Ricardo Güiraldes. A few years later, two other writers living in France would discover Borges, the Franco-Argentine Néstor Ibarra (1930) and Pierre Drieu La Rochelle (1933), but their contributions would only have immediate effects in Buenos Aires, not in Paris.

Megáfono was the first magazine to give Borges his own section (1933). The second was *Sur* (1942) and the third was *Ciudad* (1955).[4] This series is heterogenous because *Megáfono* and *Ciudad* were ephemeral publications, very minor in comparison with Victoria Ocampo's journal. Still, the beginning of this series was significant. *Megáfono*'s dossier, "Discusión sobre Jorge Luis Borges" [Discussion about Jorge Luis Borges] already referred to the classic Borges of *Discusión* [*Discussion*] (1932), so different from the first Borges. The dossier was preceded by Drieu La Rochelle's text that ended by assuring readers that Borges was "worth the trip" ("*Borges vaut le voyage*"). And while almost all of the articles were favorable, it was also here that some of the most common criticisms of Borges's work first appeared: his writing was too intellectual, was not "human," was not "national"—reproaches that would follow him for the next fifty years.[5] Thus began the story of Borges's detractors, so illustrative of the drawn out stages in his process of canonization: years later, Adolfo Prieto's *Borges y la nueva generación*, the first book ever published about Borges, would solely be aimed at negating the value of his work.

The founding of *Sur* (1931–1970) had established a new scene, one different from *Nosotros*, which was losing its monopoly and beginning its long decline, but it also differed from the youthful *martinfierrismo* of the previous decade. *Sur* partially continued its avant-garde approach but in a less festive, less immature way. Created within the framework of Victoria Ocampo's (1890–1979) relationships with travelers such as Waldo Frank and José Ortega y Gasset, the journal brought together a new elite of foreign and Argentine writers. Borges, who belonged to the inner circle of *Sur* from the very start, began being "Borges" after the new turn his work would take around 1930. Even though the survey in *Megáfono* was based on *Discusión*, it still gravitated around the as-yet-undefined image of the first Borges (avant-garde and anti–avant-garde, nationalism and anti-nationalism). The classic Borges who emerged in the decade of 1930 was the Borges of *Sur*: on the pages of Victoria Ocampo's journal, pleased to liken themselves to those of the *Nouvelle Revue Française*, Borges published his essay on "El arte narrativo y la magia" [Narrative Art and Magic] (initially published in a little magazine in Azul), his film reviews, and his articles about the crime fiction genre. In *Sur*, in 1939, appeared "Pierre Menard, autor del Quijote" [Pierre Menard, Author of the *Quixote*] and "La biblioteca total" [The Total Library]; in 1940, "Tlön, Uqbar, Orbis Tertius." As of 1933, *Sur* also had its own publishing house; under its colophon Borges would publish the books *El jardín de senderos que se bifurcan* [*The Garden of Forking Paths*] (1941), *Ficciones* [*Fictions*] (1944), and *Otras inquisiciones* [*Other Inquisitions*] (1952).

In Argentina, two literary awards emerged around 1920: the career-defining National Prize, whose award amounts were very high, and the Municipal Prize, whose payout was more modest and aimed at younger writers. Borges, who up to that point had won a second Municipal Prize in 1928, submitted *El jardín de senderos que se bifurcan* for the 1939–1941 award cycle. The story, later recalled in "El Aleph," is well known. The prize was awarded to *Cancha larga. Novela del campo argentino* (1939). The difference between Acevedo Díaz's traditionalist novel and Borges's surprising book of short stories seemed almost too great to be possible. The "Desagravio a Borges" [Reparation to Borges] published in *Sur* in July 1942[6]—a completely unprecedented episode that remains unique in all of Argentina's literary history—would only be complete in 1944, when the Sociedad Argentina de Escritores (SADE) created the "Gran Premio de Honor" solely to award *Ficciones*.[7]

Among the five writers on the National Prize jury who were taken to task in *Sur*'s call for amends was Roberto Giusti, the director of *Nosotros*, who promptly responded with an unsigned letter from the editor, calling Borges's recent writing a "literatura deshumanizada, de alambique; más aun, de oscuro y arbitrario juego cere-bral" [dehumanized, opaque literature; what's more, a dark and arbitrary mind game] (1942). He certainly did not lack respect for Borges's "conocida personalidad literaria" [renowned literary personality] and admitted that the book was written "con admirable pericia artística en una prosa de notable precisión y elegancia" [with admirable artistic expertise in a prose notable for its precision and elegance]. The note concluded as follows:

> Si el jurado entendió que no podía ofrecer al pueblo argentino, en esta hora del mundo, con el galardón de la mayor recompensa nacional, una obra exótica y de decadencia que oscila, respondiendo a ciertas desviadas tendencias de la literatura inglesa contemporánea, entre el cuento fantástico, la jactanciosa erudición recóndita y la narración policial; oscura hasta resultar a veces tenebrosa para cualquier lector, aun para el más culto (excluimos a posibles iniciados en la nueva magia)—juzgamos que hizo bien. . . . Lo más curioso, como índice de la confusión de ideas en que se vive actualmente, es la adhesión a este libro de algunos paladines de la literatura proletaria. Están lucidos si pretenden que el pueblo se sienta interpretado en esta misteriosa alquimia literaria de cenáculo y guste de ella. (116)

> [If the jury recognized that it could not, at this moment in time, present to the Argentine people as the winner of nation's major book award an exotic, decadent work that, in response to certain deviant tendencies in contemporary English litera-ture, swings between fantastic narrative, swaggering, recondite erudition and crime fiction; dark, at times to the point of becoming murky for any reader, even the most cultured (we omit possible insiders in the new magic)—we judge that it did well. . . . What is most curious, as an indicator of the confusion of ideas that currently reigns, is the following this book has with some supporters of proletarian literature. They are clearheaded if they imagine that the people feel interpreted in this mysterious lit-erary alchemy of elitism and like it.]

The editorial about the national prize was preceded by another, shorter note signed by *boedista* Álvaro Yunque regarding the death of Roberto Arlt, who had just died. The journal *Conducta. Al servicio del pueblo*, a venue for the Teatro del Pueblo run by Leónidas Barletta, also a *boedista*, dedicated an issue to Arlt.[8] In its conflict with *Sur* and SADE, *Nosotros* responded with arguments that were unabashedly *boedistas* and even seemed to dare to teach literary ideology to the very writers from Boedo. *Nosotros* closed in 1943, after the death of Alfredo Bianchi, Giusti's generous codirector and partner. With the military coup of 1943, a period that as of 1945 would come to be called the "Década infame" [Infamous Decade] for its succession of military dictatorships and un-disguised electoral fraud—begun with the overthrow of Hipólito Yrigoyen in 1930—was coming to a close.

Nosotros said that Borges's writing was anti-national and anti-popular but also de-fined it as a literature for "insiders." Who were the "insiders" at this time? Surely one of them, perhaps the first of them, was Néstor Ibarra. Also, possibly José Bianco, chief editor at *Sur* since 1938, and other younger writers, such as Ernesto Sábato and Julio Cortázar, who had yet to publish their first books. What goes without question is that, up until 1942, and for many years thereafter, no one wrote about Borges as Bioy Casares did with his review of *El jardín de senderos que se bifurcan*, printed in *Sur* just before it published the "Desagravio." It was taken for granted that Borges was a writers' writer, that he was doing something truly unprecedented and that those who understood it best were involved in *Sur* and *La Nación*—the traditional newspaper founded by Bartolomé Mitre where Borges began collaborating in 1940 with one of his essays against European totalitarian regimes.[9] While reaching the peak of his recognition among his peers, all of the attention he received did not dispel the aura of being a secret writer whose literature was aimed at "unos pocos lectores—a muy pocos lectores—" ("Tlön" 30) [a few readers—a very few readers—].[10]

The singular intimacy between Borges and Bioy Casares, which began in the early 1930s, put Bioy in a situation reminiscent of Borges's joke about detectives in crime mysteries: "El investigador descifra el problema porque el autor le revela confidencialmente la solución" [The detective solves the puzzle because the author confidentially reveals him the solution] ("Howard Haycraft" 67). In 1942, Borges and Bioy also published their first Bustos Domecq collaboration, *Seis problemas para don Isidro Parodi* [*Six Problems for Mr. Isidro Parodi*]. Thus began a collaboration uninterested in being understood by even the writers closest to them. The humor in Borges and Bioy multiplied to the point of saturation in texts overwhelmed by gags in every single sentence. Their game consisted of publishing stories that, if not written for the people, were not directly aimed at their friends at *Sur* either. And, at the same time, something was starting to happen among certain readers, especially those born ten or fifteen years before Borges (José Bianco, Ernesto Sábato, Julio Cortázar, Adolfo Bioy Casares), which confirmed his limited but at the same time excessive influence: no longer was it just a few, as suggested by the articles in the "Desagravio," who were writing like Borges. One of the most notable cases was the young Ernesto Sábato, who would come to occupy the mass media's role of "great Argentine writer" made vacant after Borges's death.

Borges was not always kind to his admirers. In his 1937 essay, "Las 'nuevas generaciones' literarias" [The "New Literary Generations"], he wrote,

> Leo en las respetuosas páginas de una revista joven (porque los jóvenes, ahora, son respetuosos y optan por los prestigios de la urbanidad, no por los del martirio): "La nueva generación, o heroica, como también se la llama, cumplió plenamente su cometido: arrasó con la Bastilla de los prejuicios literarios, imponiendo a la consideración de achacosos simbolistas nuevas ideas estéticas. . . ." Esa generación impositiva, arrasadora y cumplidora es la mía: he sido, pues, calificado, siquiera colectivamente, de héroe. (97)

> [In the respectful pages of a young literary journal (because young people nowadays are respectful and prefer the prestige of urbanity over that of martyrdom): "The new generation, or heroic generation as it is also called, fully achieved its goal: it razed the Bastille of literary prejudice, forcing ailing symbolists to consider new aesthetic ideas. . . ." This forceful, razing, committed generation is my own: For I have been deemed, collectively no less, its hero.]

Borges never lost the aggressive humor, begun in his early years in the avant-garde, as the ethos guiding the literary social exchanges he published—face to face, the rules were quite different. To the self-styled "novísima generación" who celebrated the avant-garde of the previous "nueva generación" with excessive enthusiasm, Borges responded with sarcasm, garnering all of his most cynical memories of *martinfierrismo* and undercutting every attempt at homage. If Américo Castro, in 1941, approved of his style, Borges leaned on this authorization to mercilessly criticize that of the Spanish philologist. If Roger Caillois, in 1942, deigned to write about the history of the crime fiction genre in France, Borges took issue, as always, with his most disdainful brevity: "La conjetura de Caillois no es errónea; entiendo que es inepta, inverificable" [Caillois's conjecture is not wrong; I understand that it is inept, unverifiable] (vol. 12, no. 92, p. 73). Years later it could be said, all jokes aside, that Borges was an invention of Caillois. Borges's reception in France unquestionably modified his reception in Argentina. But, as Sylvia Molloy has observed, Borges does not appear to have been anxious to ensure the dissemination of his writings in Paris. Borges's translations into French[11] took place unhurriedly throughout the 1940s, in a slow process that would eventually culminate in the long-delayed[12] publication of *Fictions* (1951) in Gallimard's new collection, "La Croix du Sud."

Throughout the 1950s in Buenos Aires, there occurred what would later come to be known as a "modernization of literary criticism." In truth, it was a modernization of academic literary criticism, which was beginning to overtake the tradition of criticism that had been practiced up until then by writers in the region.[13] *Contorno* (1953–1959) was the journal most emblematic of this process. Some of the young scholars involved in the cultural journal, such as David Viñas, Noé Jitrik, and Adolfo Prieto, would come to be the professors of a new generation of critics who emerged in the 1970s (Josefina Ludmer, Nicolás Rosa, Beatriz Sarlo, María Teresa Gramuglio) and who would advance the renovation begun with *Contorno* in journals such as *Los Libros* (1969–1976), *Literal* (1973–1977), and *Punto de Vista* (1978–2008). The first issue of *Contorno* opened with an article by Juan José Sebreli, "Los 'martinfierristas': su tiempo y el nuestro" [The 'martinfierristas': their time and ours], in which the new generation of the 1950s defined itself, skipping the intermediate generation, in opposition to the youth of the 1920s. *Contorno* believed in the Sartre of *Qu'est-ce que la littérature* (1948), chose essayist Ezequiel Martínez Estrada as its patron forebear and initiated the importation of new flavors of Parisian literary culture that happened to be precisely the kinds Borges least esteemed. In 1956, Emir Rodríguez Monegal called them the "Parricide" Generation.

In 1954, Adolfo Prieto published *Borges y la nueva generación*, a short text of some ninety pages. While Prieto's academic gestures clashed with the more colloquial, editorial, or even pamphleteering tones taken by other members of *Contorno*, the book was, as the title suggests, as much about the author and his group or generation as it was about Borges. Prieto compared Borges's criticism against that of Martínez Estrada and challenged Borges with "Sartre's doctrine" of committed writing (*Borges* 20). It was the first book about Borges, which implied even a modest act of canonization, but it was also a book in whose pages the importance of his literature was negated. The young Prieto's primary and quite insistent argument denounced the complete imbalance between his prestige as a writer and the value of his work: Borges was "un gran literato sin literatura" [a literary genius with no literature] (*Borges* 84). Prieto organized his analysis into three sections: critical essays, poetry, and short stories. Of these three sections, he was especially interested in the first, which, in 1953, he had published as a preview in the journal *Centro*, the venue of the Centro de Estudiantes and a precursor to *Contorno*.[14] Let us recall, once again, the well-known story: while *Contorno*, inspired by *Les Temps Modernes*, scorned Borges, Sartre's and Simone de Beauvoir's journal celebrated him.[15]

Contorno not only took on the Peronist government for its intervention in the nation's universities, but also *Sur* and *La Nación* for their liberalism. The journal dedicated its second issue to Roberto Arlt, its fourth to Martínez Estrada, and its fifth to the history of the Argentine novel. After the 1955 "Revolución Libertadora," the military coup that ended Perón's second presidency, literature gave way to politics. In 1956, contemporaneous to the Borges/Martínez Estrada debate, *Contorno* dedicated another of its issues to Peronism with contributions notable for their equanimity and understanding. In their issue on Arlt, who, ten years after his death, was experiencing his own slow canonization, David Viñas argued that the author of *El juguete rabioso* [*The Furious Toy*] belonged neither to the communists nor the avant-garde, in an appropriation of his image that successfully divorced him from the incipient intellectual leftism of Boedo. In its issue on Peronism, *Contorno* included a brief review of "La fiesta del monstruo" [The Monster's Party], which had been published in the Uruguayan weekly *Marcha* (1955). Apart from this, in the pages of *Contorno*, Borges was most conspicuous for his absence.

In addition to their political differences, Borges (*Sur*) and *Contorno* also—and perhaps especially—differed in literary subject matter. For Borges, dealing with Argentine literature had been an obligation he had to meet with professionalism and resignation. A critic should be aware of what was being published in his country and produce reviews of new work on a fairly regular basis. With the exception of the 1920s, Borges did not extend this obligation to other Spanish American national literatures, which he considered too similar across the board. Borges's anti-nationalism appeared backwards in *Contorno*, which focused on the Argentine literary tradition and interpreted it as the political history of a national project born with the Romanticism of the generation of 1837. David Viñas's influential book, *Literatura argentina y realidad política* (1964), would synopsize and complete *Contorno*'s project.

In the meantime, in that same decade, the 1950s, Borges's ultimate canonization was beginning to take shape. Critics and university professors such as Emir Rodríguez Monegal (as of 1947), Juan Carlos Ghiano (1948), Raimundo Lida (1951), Ana María Barrenechea (1953), and Enrique Anderson Imbert (1953) began publishing their first studies of Borges in Buenos Aires, Montevideo, Madrid, and Mexico City, which would go on to be reproduced in college instruction. Borges's criticism was now reaching a level of specificity and academic legitimacy reserved for canonized writers (Herminia Brumana, "Borges conferencista" 1952; María Rosa Lida de Malkiel, "Contribución al estudio de las fuentes de Jorge Luis Borges" 1952). Emecé Editores began publication of his complete works (1953–1960) in nine volumes. In 1955, the journal *Ciudad* (2–3) dedicated a section to him that included, in addition to five thoughtful articles (one of them entitled "Borges and His Detractors"), a first bibliography prepared by José Luis Ríos Patrón and Horacio Jorge Becco. The first books on Borges were also published (Prieto 1954; Tamayo y Ruiz Díaz 1955; Ríos Patrón 1955; Barrenechea 1957; César Fernández Moreno 1957; Gutiérrez Girardot 1959).

The history of the translations of his books had begun in France in 1951 or 1952, with the translation of *Ficciones* by Ibarra and Verdevoye. The first translation into English, in 1962, was presented by a French writer, André Maurois. The first translations into Italian and German circulated in 1955 and 1961, respectively. It was France, where translations of Borges's classic writings (*Ficciones, El Aleph, Otras Inquisiciones*) were produced more quickly and with greater continuity, that truly achieved the historic mission of disseminating the Argentine's work abroad. Then again, in the 1960s, it began to be clear that Borges's writing had certain affinities with the latest vanguard, the *Nouveau Roman*, based this time on the novel, and consequently bore affinities with *Nouvelle Critique* as well, France's critical vanguard. Maurice Blanchot (1958), Gérard Genette (1964), Jean Ricardou (1964), Pierre Macherey (1966), and Michel Foucault (1966) had written about Borges. To these and other names of authors who, in academia, would become required reading for generations to come, Borges's name would be included in a long process that culminated around 1980.

"Qué raro que nosotros seamos oficialistas" [How weird that we are the establishment] Borges would say to Bioy in June 1957. The Revolución Libertadora undoubtedly came to transform the role Borges held in Argentina's public imagination. From the risks of being an opposition writer during Peronism, Borges moved onto the risks (presaged in an early article about Capdevila) of being considered "cómplice de la fealdad de los edificios públicos, de la tristeza de los domingos y de las estatuas" [an accomplice to the ugliness of public buildings, the sadness of Sundays and of statues] and being assimilated into the "siempre deplorable 'orden de las cosas' que es urgente abolir" [ever deplorable 'order of things' that must urgently be abolished] (Borges, "Arturo Capdevila" 6). The various appointments and recognitions immediately following the 1955 coup d'état (the directorship of the National Library, the post as Professor of British and North American Literature at the College of Philosophy and Letters, the National Prize for Literature) combined the dangers of literary canonization with those of being an official, establishment writer. As the new director of the National Library, Borges obtained a modicum of visibility outside the world of intellectuals and academics. It was around this time that he published "Borges y yo" [Borges and I] (1957). After the fall of Perón, the military dictatorship's repression of Peronism, now become a lost cause, and the need to take stock of the history of Perón's undeniable popularity, caused realignments not only in politics (like the internal schisms within the Unión Cívica Radical and the Socialist Party) but among intellectuals as well. In a 1956 interview, Martínez Estrada went so far as to call Borges a "turiferario a sueldo" [paid mouthpiece]. Borges responded with "Una efusión de Ezequiel Martínez Estrada." This debate was followed shortly thereafter by another with Ernesto Sábato.

Once begun, the process of Borges's ultimate canonization did naught but expand and actualize ever more quickly. In the 1960s, the first biographies began to appear;

the Formentor Prize (1961) consolidated his international recognition, and Borges finally began to travel again. He visited the United States for the first time in 1961, and, in 1963, returned to Europe, where he had not set foot since 1924. Interviews began to proliferate, and, in the 1970s, shifted from newspapers and books to television. Borges, who, after long delays, had started becoming an internationally celebrated writer, was now becoming, in a matter of just a few years, a celebrity.[16] In the 1980s, Borges reached a point of mass media saturation. As José Sazbón would write in 1982, with respect to the oral Borges of interviews, conferences, and statements: "Borges quiere ser *inmolado*. Borges, de un modo oscuro, colabora con los inevitables interlocutores que lo trivializarán" [Borges wants to be *sacrificed*. Borges, in a dark way, collaborates with those interlocutors who will inevitably trivialize him] (24).

Around 1980, however, there was still a reckoning to be had between Borges and the critical tradition begun with *Contorno*. Noé Jitrik's 1981 "Sentimientos complejos sobre Borges" [Complicated Feelings about Borges] is exemplary of this historical moment.[17] It was a long, autobiographical article in which Jitrik weighed his early enchantments with Borges's texts against his unsalvageable political distance: Borges had never been on "our side" (191). Jitrik also remembered, among so many stories, having laughed at an interview Borges gave Gudiño Kieffer in *La Nación* (1974): "Borges hacía trizas todos los intentos de Gudiño para encaminarlo al 'bien'; Gudiño decía: 'El *Che Guevara*, héroe latinoamericano' y Borges acotaba, distraídamente: 'Guevara, Guevara: es un apellido mendocino, ¿no es cierto?" [Borges tore Gudiño's every attempt to guide him toward 'correctness' to shreds; Gudiño would say, '*Che Guevara*, the Latin American hero,' and Borges would distractedly retort: 'Guevara, Guevara: that's a last name from Mendoza, right?'] (181). At that point, Borges had already signed the petition denouncing the disappearances committed by the latest military dictatorship (1976–1983), which was still in power. Jitrik could not make peace with Borges: he was still undecided. He also said that Borges was the inheritor of Macedonio Fernández and that he had betrayed this inheritance ever since he had celebrated the fascist Leopoldo Lugones and had called Macedonio a bad writer. Later, Jitrik edited the *Historia crítica de la literatura argentina* (1999–2015); of its twelve volumes, only two were dedicated to individual authors: Domingo F. Sarmiento in the nineteenth century and Macedonio Fernández in the twentieth.

That long-standing indecision (what to do with the "great reactionary writer"?) was no longer present, however, in the article Ricardo Piglia published in *Punto de Vista* in 1979, "Ideología y ficción en Borges"—which should be read alongside "Roberto Arlt: una crítica de la economía literaria," published in *Los Libros* in 1973. There began a new way of writing about Borges which, despite deploying the Marxist pastiche popular at the time, seemed to go back to to Bioy Casares's 1942 review of *El jardín de senderos que se bifurcan* in its willingness to understand him. Piglia, a writer and a critic, as Borges was, believed the Argentine literary canon of the twentieth century should center around Borges and Arlt. And with his classes and critical and fictional writings, he managed to make this idea stick. Borges was the writer who had grown up among the limitless English books in his father's library, and Arlt, as he himself related in the episode of *El juguete rabioso* when three boys burgle a school library, had entered literature by less legitimate means. For Piglia, it was worthwhile to uphold this tension (as Borges had maintained tension between *criollismo* and cosmopolitism), which in turn made Argentine literary history more interesting.

Los Libros and *Literal* were journals too removed from the time-worn world inhabited by Borges, who studied ancient languages and Germanic literatures while intellectual vanguards and revolutionary dreams were proliferating around him. *Los Libros* featured a large photograph of Borges on the cover of its tenth issue, August 1970, in which he let them publish a previously unpublished story, "El otro duelo" [The Other Duel]. Not much more interaction occurred. Like *Contorno*, it shifted from literature to politics as Argentina's political situation became increasingly dire. *Punto de Vista*, however, took it upon itself to revise *Contorno*'s history and, at the same time, reread Borges. As Beatriz Sarlo wrote in 1981, "Es notorio que *Contorno* no pudo leer a Borges. . . . Sería un gesto anacrónico complacerse hoy en una especie de fácil escándalo retrospectivo" [It is well known that *Contorno* could not read Borges. . . . It would be an anachronic gesture to enjoy today a kind of easy retrospective scandal] (7). The studies of Borges, *Sur*, and Victoria Ocampo that Sarlo and Gramuglio began publishing in the early 1980s opened new lines of discussion with less radical political concerns. Thus began, quite late, an extraordinary production of critical texts that were finally reconciled with Borges, which would continue through last two decades of the twentieth century.

In the end, Argentina had to admit that, except to his own compatriots, Borges was much more than a peripheral or provincial "national literature." And that this literature was, to a great extent, whatever Borges had been making of it since the 1920s. In 1992, Beatriz Sarlo gave four lectures at Cambridge which later became the book *Jorge Luis Borges: A Writer on the Edge* (1993), translated into Spanish three years later. Sarlo said these lectures had taught her that "la imagen de Borges es más potente que la de la literatura argentina" [the image of Borges is stronger than that of Argentine literature]. She added: "Como sea, las conferencias en la Universidad de Cambridge me enseñaron esto (que debería haber sabido antes)" [In any case, the lectures at the University of Cambridge taught me this (which I should have known long before)] (*Jorge Luis Borges* 8–9). To the intellectual left seeking to distance itself from the kinds of nationalisms exalted during the Falklands/Malvinas War (1982), Borges became a welcome and legible alternative. The impossible hopes of "El escritor argentino y la tradición" [The Argentine Writer and Tradition] (1951) were starting to come true.[18] Borges died in June 1986, just a few months after which his *Textos cautivos* was published, initiating the recovery of Borges's less accessible and least remembered texts. Over the course of the 1990s, this editorial process ramped up, recuperating unpublished texts, and undoing the drastic work the elder Borges had undertaken since the 1950s to reduce his complete works to just a limited, discerning selection.[19] Graciela Montaldo hardly exaggerated when expressing her surprise at "la capacidad que ha tenido Borges de rehacer su obra, *post mortem*, y empezar a escribir, en los 90, un corpus completamente nuevo y crear, por tanto, un nuevo autor" [the capacity that Borges has had to remake his ouevre, *post mortem*, and to begin writing, in the '90s, a completely new corpus, thereby creating a new author] (7).

Notes

1. "Voy a hablar de una generación malograda, de una generación vencida" [I am going to speak on a failed generation, of a vanquished generation] (Ugarte 11).
2. In fact, there was another forgotten generation that preceded the modernists, one consisting of young writers of 1880s (Martín García Mérou, Benigno Lugones, Carlos Olivera). They were the first to call themselves a "new literary generation." They tried to launch the invention of literary life based on the Parisian tales of bohemian life found in Murger and Champfleury. The myth of bohemia, so present in the foundation of the following two generations, was no longer active in Borges's generation.
3. *Los Pensadores* (1922–1926), *Extrema Izquierda* (1924), *Claridad* (1926–1941).
4. María Luisa Bastos included these three publications in her notable study about Borges's reception in Argentina (1974). The book was a revised version of her doctoral thesis, *Trayectoria de la crítica argentina ante la obra de Jorge Luis Borges, 1923–1960*, Universidad Nacional de La Plata, 1970.
5. I refer in particular to the disdainful response from the very young Enrique Anderson Imbert and the virulent judgment of Ramón Doll (1933), who responded to the survey from the journal *Letras*. The first edition of *Discusión* began with "Nuestras imposibilidades" [Our Impossibilities], an essay about "los caracteres más inmediatamente afligentes de los argentinos" [the most immediately distressing Argentine characters]. Borges decided to exclude it from the following editions.
6. Twenty-one writers took part in the "Desagravio," in the following order: Eduardo Mallea, Francisco Romero, Luis Emilio Soto, Patricio Canto, Pedro Henríquez Ureña, Alfredo González Garaño, Amado Alonso, Eduardo González Lanuza, Aníbal Sánchez Reulet, Gloria Alcorta, Samuel Eichelbaum, Adolfo Bioy Casares, Ángel Rosenblat, José Bianco, Enrique Anderson Imbert, Adán Diehl, Carlos Mastronardi, Enrique Amorim, Ernesto Sábato, Manuel Peyrou, and Bernardo Canal Feijóo.
7. In the following years it would be received by Ricardo Rojas (1945), Eduardo Mallea (1946), Ezequiel Martínez Estrada (1947), Arturo Capdevila (1948), Baldomero Fernández Moreno (1949), and Victoria Ocampo (1950).
8. Around this same time, Waldo Frank was declared persona non grata by the Argentine government and survived an assassination attempt condemned by intellectuals from across the political spectrum.
9. "Algunos pareceres de Nietzsche" [Some of Nietzsche's Views] (1940).
10. "Bioy Casares había cenado conmigo esa noche y nos demoró una vasta polémica sobre la ejecución de una novela en primera persona, cuyo narrador omitiera o desfigurara los hechos e incurriera en diversas contradicciones, que permitieran a unos pocos lectores—a muy pocos lectores—la adivinación de una realidad atroz o banal" [Bioy Casares had come to dinner at my house that evening, and we lost all track of time in a vast debate over the way one might go about composing a first-person novel whose narrator would omit or distort things and engage in all sorts of contradictions, so that a few of the book's readers—a very few—might divine the horrifying or banal truth] (*OC* I: 431; *CF* 68).
11. In 1936, *La Revue Argentine* published a translation of the essay "Paul Groussac," from *Discusión*; Borges was but one of many Argentine writers translated for that journal (Paris, 1934–1945), directed by Octavio González Roura. The series of initial translations of Borges's texts into French had a more significant start in 1939, with "L'approche du caché" [El acercamiento a Almotásim ()], Néstor Ibarra's translation published in *Mesures* (Paris, 1935–1940). Between 1941 and 1947, Roger Caillois headed the journal *Lettres françaises*,

A HISTORY OF BORGES'S RECEPTION IN ARGENTINA   385

funded by Victoria Ocampo and published by Sur; there, in 1944, he published Ibarra's translation "Assyriennes" ("La loterie de Babylone" and "La bibliothèque de Babel"). "Les ruines circulaires," translated by Verdevoye, was published in *Confluences* (2e série, Paris, 1945–1948) in 1946. In 1947, "Fictions" [Tlön, Uqbar, Orbis Tertius], also translated by Verdevoye, appeared in *La Licorne* (Paris, 1947–1948), a journal run by the Uruguayan writer Susana Soca. Caillois's translation, "Histoire du guerrier et de la captive," was published in *Les Cahiers de la Pléiade* (Paris, 1946–1952) in 1949.

12. "Once back in Paris, in 1946, Caillois would task Paul Verdevoye with translating *Ficciones* for Gallimard publishing house, and has one of the stories from the collection, 'Las ruinas circulares' published in *Confluence*, a journal Caillois directs. The publication of *Fictions* was inexplicably delayed until 1952" (Bastos 135). Bastos seemed to know that the book, printed at the end of 1951, was put into circulation at the beginning of the following year.

13. *Borges y la nueva generación* (1954) was less a book written against Borgesian literature—a kind of culminating point in the history of readings against Borges (Lafforgue)—than it was a dispute about the legitimizing protocols of literary criticism (Pastormerlo, *Borges* 189–97).

14. Adolfo Prieto, "Borges y el ensayo crítico" (1953).

15. The first text about Borges in *Les Temps Modernes* was an article by René Étiemble (1952).

16. See Casale O'Ryan.

17. Originally published in the newspaper *Unomásuno* (Mexico City, May 23, 1981) as well as in an issue of *Les Temps Modernes* (420–21, July-August 1981) dedicated to "Argentine entre populisme et militarisme" and coordinated by David Viñas and César Fernández Moreno. In 2011, the National Library in Buenos Aires published a thoughtful and accessible edition in Spanish of this issue of Sartre's journal, from which the citations above are taken.

18. The talk "El escritor argentino y la tradición" was first presented in December 1951. It was first published in magazine form in 1953, in *Cursos y conferencias* in 1955, then included in the second edition of *Discusión* in 1957. See Balderston for a detailed analysis of the six pages of manuscript notes for the 1951 oral presentation.

19. See Pastormelo, "Borges contra Borges."

Works Cited

Arlt, Roberto. "Peñas de artistas en Boedo." *Aguafuertes porteñas: cultura y política*. Losada, 1994, pp. 107–13.

"El atentado contra Waldo Frank." *Nosotros*, no. 76, julio 1942, p. 118.

Balderston, Daniel. *How Borges Wrote*. University of Virginia Press, 2018.

Bastos, María Luisa. *Borges ante la crítica argentina, 1923-1960*. Hispamérica, 1974.

Bioy Casares, Adolfo. *Borges*, edición de Daniel Martino. Destino, 2006.

Bioy Casares, Adolfo. "Jorge Luis Borges: *El jardín de senderos que se bifurcan*." *Sur*, no. 92, May 1942, pp. 60–65.

Borges, Jorge Luis. "Algunos pareceres de Nietzsche." *La Nación*, February 16, 1940a.

Borges, Jorge Luis. "Américo Castro. *La peculiaridad lingüística rioplatense y su sentido histórico*." *Sur*, no. 86, November 1941, pp. 66–70.

Borges, Jorge Luis. "Arturo Capdevila. *Tierra mía*." *Crítica, Revista multicolor de los sábados*, vol. 2, no. 54, August 18, 1934, p. 6.

Borges, Jorge Luis. "Assyriennes" ("La loterie de Babylone" y "La bibliothèque de Babel"). *Lettres françaises*, no. 14, October 1, 1944, pp. 9–26.

Borges, Jorge Luis. "Borges y yo." *La Biblioteca* (2a época), no. 1, 1957, pp. 117–18.

Borges, Jorge Luis. "El tamaño de mi esperanza." *El tamaño de mi Esperanza*. Editorial Proa, 1926, pp. 6–7.

Borges, Jorge Luis. "Fictions" ("Tlön, Uqbar, Orbis Tertius"). *La Licorne*, no. 1, March 1947, pp. 13–26.

Borges, Jorge Luis. "Histoire du guerrier et de la captive." *Les Cahiers de la Pléiade*, no. 8, 1949, pp. 159–64.

Borges, Jorge Luis. "Howard Haycraft. *Murder for pleasure*." *Sur*, no. 107, September 1943, pp. 66–67.

Borges, Jorge Luis. "L'approche du caché." *Mesures*, no. 2, April 15, 1939, pp. 115–22.

Borges, Jorge Luis. "Las 'nuevas generaciones' literarias." *Textos cautivos. Ensayos y reseñas en "El Hogar" (1936–1939)*. Tusquets, 1986, pp. 97–100.

Borges, Jorge Luis. "Les ruines circulaires." *Confluences* (2ᵉ série), no. 11, April 1946, pp. 131–36.

Borges, Jorge Luis. *Obras completas*. 4 vols. Emecé, 1996.

Borges, Jorge Luis. "Observación final." *Sur*, no. 92, May 1942, pp. 72–73.

Borges, Jorge Luis. "Paul Groussac." *La Revue Argentine*, no. 13, 1936, pp. 33–36.

Borges, Jorge Luis. "Tlön, Uqbar, Orbis Tertius." *Sur*, no. 68, May 1940, pp. 30–46.

Borges, Jorge Luis. "Una efusión de Ezequiel Martínez Estrada." *Sur*, no. 242, September–October 1956, pp. 52–53.

Casale O'Ryan, Mariana. *The Making of Jorge Luis Borges as a Cultural Icon*. Modern Humanities Research Association, 2014.

"Desagravio a Borges." *Sur*, no. 94, July 1942, pp. 7–34.

Doll, Ramón. "Discusiones con Borges, una encuesta." *Letras*, no. 1, September 1933, pp. 3–13.

Drieu La Rochelle, Pierre. "Discusión sobre Jorge Luis Borges." *Megáfono*, no. 11, August 1933, p. 13.

"Nuestra encuesta sobre la nueva generación literaria." *Nosotros*, no. 168–172, May–September 1923.

Étiemble, René. "Un homme à tuer: Jorge Luis Borges, cosmopolite." *Les Temps Modernes*, no. 83, July–August 1952, pp. 512–26.

[Giusti, Roberto]. "Los Premios Nacionales de Literatura." *Nosotros*, no. 76, July 1942, pp. 114–16.

Gómez de la Serna, Ramón. "El fervor de Buenos Aires." *Revista de Occidente*, no. 4, April–June 1924, pp. 123–27.

Gramuglio, María Teresa. "Bioy, Borges y *Sur*. Diálogos y duelos." *Punto de Vista*, no. 34, July–September 1989, pp. 11–16.

Gramuglio, María Teresa. "*Sur*: constitución del grupo y proyecto cultural." *Punto de Vista*, no. 17, April–July 1983, pp. 7–9.

Gramuglio, María Teresa. "*Sur* en la década del treinta: una revista política." *Punto de Vista*, no. 28, November 1986, pp. 32–39.

Ibarra, Néstor. *La nueva poesía argentina. Ensayo crítico sobre el ultraísmo, 1921–1929*. Imprenta Vda. de Molinari, 1930.

Jitrik, Noé. "Sentimientos complejos sobre Borges." *Tiempos modernos. Argentina entre populismo y militarismo*. Edited by David Viñas, César Fernández Moreno, Sebastián Scolnik, and Horacio Nieva. Biblioteca Nacional, 2011, pp. 177–98.

Lafforgue, Martín. *Antiborges*. Vergara, 1999.

Larbaud, Valéry. "Sur Borges." *La Revue Européenne*, año 3, t. VI, no. 34, 1925, pp. 66–70.

Ludmer, Josefina. "¿Cómo salir de Borges." *Jorge Luis Borges. Intervenciones sobre pensamiento y literatura*. Edited by William Rowe et al. Paidós, 2000, pp. 292–94.

Ludmer, Josefina. *El cuerpo del delito. Un manual.* Perfil, 1999.

Martínez Estrada, Ezequiel. "Grandeza y miseria de los escritores." *Propósitos*, no. 135–137, June 26 and July 10, 1956. Interview.

Molloy, Sylvia. *La diffusion de la littérature en France au XXe siècle.* Presses Universitaires de France, 1972.

Montaldo, Graciela. "Borges, Aira y la literatura para multitudes." *Boletín del Centro de Estudios de Teoría y Crítica Literaria*, no. 6, October 1998, pp. 7–17.

Pastormerlo, Sergio. "Borges contra Borges. Sobre las reediciones de textos olvidados." *Punto de Vista*, no. 75, April 2003, pp. 21–24.

Pastormerlo, Sergio. *Borges crítico.* Fondo de Cultura Económica, 2007.

Piglia, Ricardo. "Ideología y ficción en Borges." *Punto de Vista*, no. 5, March 1979, pp. 3–6.

Piglia, Ricardo. "Roberto Arlt: una crítica de la economía literaria." *Los Libros*, no. 29, March–April 1973, pp. 22–27.

Prieto, Adolfo. "Borges y el ensayo crítico." *Centro. Revista del Centro de Estudiantes de Filosofía y Letras*, no. 7, December 1953, pp. 9–19.

Prieto, Adolfo. *Borges y la nueva generación.* Letras Universitarias, 1954.

Rodríguez Monegal, Emir. *El juicio de los parricidas. La nueva generación argentina y sus maestros.* Deucalión, 1956.

Rojas, Ricardo. "Introducción." *La literatura argentina. Ensayo filosófico sobre la evolución de la literatura en el Plata*, v. 1, Librería "La Facultad," 1917, pp. 36–38. 4 vols.

Sanromán, V. [Ismael Viñas]. "La fiesta del monstruo." *Contorno*, no. 7/8, July 1956, p. 50.

Sarlo, Beatriz. "Borges en *Sur*: un episodio del formalismo criollo." *Punto de Vista*, no. 16, November 1982, pp. 3–6.

Sarlo, Beatriz. "Borges y la literatura argentina." *Punto de Vista*, no. 34, July–September 1989, pp. 6–10.

Sarlo, Beatriz. "Los dos ojos de *Contorno*." *Punto de Vista*, no. 13, November 1981, pp. 3–8.

Sarlo, Beatriz. *Jorge Luis Borges. A Writer on the Edge.* Verso, 1993.

Sarlo, Beatriz. "La perspectiva americana en los primeros años de *Sur*." *Punto de Vista*, no. 17, April–July 1983, pp. 10–12.

Sarlo, Beatriz. "Sobre la vanguardia, Borges y el criollismo." *Punto de Vista*, no. 11, March–June 1981, pp. 3–8.

Sarlo, Beatriz. "Victoria Ocampo: la mujer-sabia." *Una modernidad periférica: Buenos Aires 1920 y 1930*, Ediciones Nueva Visión, 1988, pp. 85–93.

Sazbón, José. "Borges declara." *Espacios*, no. 6, October–November 1987 [1982], pp. 23–25.

Sebreli, Juan José. "Los 'martinfierristas': su tiempo y el nuestro." *Contorno*, no. 1, November 1953, p. 1.

Ugarte, Manuel. *Escritores iberoamericanos de 1900.* Vértice, 1947.

Vargas Llosa, Mario. "Entrevista online de Leila Guerriero a Mario Vargas Llosa con motivo de la publicación de *Medio siglo con Borges*," June 30, 2020, https://www.youtube.com/watch?v=khzjXJEFWPY.

Yunque, Álvaro. "Roberto Arlt." *Nosotros*, no. 76, July 1942, pp. 113–14.

CHAPTER 22

BORGES AND THE CRUCIBLE OF AESTHETIC AUTONOMY IN LATIN AMERICA

HÉCTOR HOYOS

IN Argentina, the influential 1920s tussle between Jorge Luis Borges's Florida and Roberto Arlt's Boedo literary groups—simply put, between affluent aesthetes and socially engaged contenders—has ramifications that continue to this day. But what about the rest of Latin America? This chapter addresses this question in salient instances from across the region, particularly more or less local debates on aesthetic autonomy. Borges and his phantasmatic Other reemerge time and again as symbols, imaginary interlocutors, leverage points, or even floating signifiers. In Latin America, to be Borgesian or anti-Borgesian always means something, although this meaning may shift across different epochs and national contexts. Given the mature Borges's long-standing, outspoken anti-populism, it is easy to assume that his enduring function would be to resurface as either class enemy or role model. While these are certainly forces at play, the case is more complex.

The sections below, followed by a short general conclusion, consider two major periods. The first spans the author's increasing prominence, through the turbulent years following the Cuban Revolution in 1959, to his death in 1986, up to the world-defining geopolitical shift of 1989. The second considers the disruptive onset of neoliberalism, a period best reflected in the Chilean Roberto Bolaño and his contemporaries' emblematic appropriation. Cold War politics followed by globalization—processes that bleed into each other—shape the conditions of possibility for art in the region.

A word about the framework. Aesthetic autonomy is a notoriously thorny subject. Even seemingly explicit pronouncements are complicated by context and *mise en abyme*. Consider Oscar Wilde ruminating on *l'art pour l'art*—particularly the independence of art from moral constraints—while living a scandalous fin-de-siècle life or Rubén Darío capturing the affordances and inanity of pure form in his mordant *modernista* short story "El rey burgués" [The Bourgeois King] (1888). Borges's interventions are no less fraught, in his own words or through his characters, whether it's casting a Nazi concentration camp commandant in "Deutsches requiem" (1946) or remarking during an interview, having just landed in Madrid from Buenos Aires in September of 1976—that is, traveling to a recently restored democracy from a budding military dictatorship—that "democracy is a superstition, based on statistics" (Samaniego). Many different positions on aesthetic autonomy can reasonably be attributed to Borges or derived from his works. He was openly anti-fascist in the 1940s and anti-communist after a brief youthful period of enthusiasm for Bolshevism just after the Russian Revolution, but also sought to transcend the politics of his day in his fiction. A multifarious Latin American reception reflects this.

This much is certain: Borges did not see literature as a means to emancipation. (Enlightenment, entertainment, and edification, surely.) Because so much of the region's literature did, and because so many intellectuals saw this as part of their mission, he was often at odds. At the same time, as the Peruvian critic Efraín Kristal has recently shown with a counterintuitive interpretation of "Tlön, Uqbar, Orbis Tertius" (1940) as an allegory of the rise of Nazism, it is a false dichotomy to think that, in Borges, the choice was between fantasy or history. Per Kristal, in crafting the former, the Argentine engaged with the latter, for instance by defying genre conventions that relied on xenophobia and nationalism in retellings of World War I. It holds for Borges what Theodor Adorno remarked in 1970 apropos the Irish playwright Samuel Beckett, his fellow 1961 Formentor Prize awardee: "In all art that is still possible, social critique must be raised to the level of form, to the point that it wipes out all manifestly social content [*Inhalt*]" (250). Often removed from the laborious, formal, historically inflected analysis that Adorno and Kristal engage in, generations of Latin American writers and intellectuals had to face a puzzling author whose reactionary *boutades*, genre-bending characters, and brazen high-art values all seemed to spell out conflicting views about aesthetic autonomy.

A DIVISIVE CLASSIC

The Cuban critic Roberto Fernández Retamar did not mince words in his 1971 essay "Calibán" when he described Borges as "the typical colonial writer, who represents among us a social class that has lost its strength" (69–70).[1] The charge was laced with ad hominem accusations having to do with the author's positions regarding the Bay of Pigs invasion (which he endorsed), U.S. president Richard Nixon (to whom he is said to have dedicated a book), and the French revolutionary intellectual Régis Debray (whose execution he advocated). Although Fernández Retamar would later mollify his views, especially in the epilogue to the *Páginas escogidas* of Borges published in 1988 by Casa de las Américas, the piece is highly informative of the Latin Americanist animus surrounding Borges. "Calibán" claims that the Argentine is the natural continuation of his countryman Domingo Faustino Sarmiento's Eurocentric ideology, including the founding father's inveterate racism; his writerly act (*acto de escritura*) is a readerly act (*acto de lectura*) and, as a corollary, this relatively submissive stance signals his colonial condition; he is truly of the New World, that is, *americano*; there is no split between the writer and the pundit; and he is unequivocally important, despite all disagreement. These claims serve as coordinates to read the Latin American reception of the period.

The first of these stances speaks to the interface between Argentine nationalism and Latin Americanist grand narratives. Sarmiento's 1845 *Facundo* was a major work across a region that was still finding its footing in postcolonial times. Its dichotomy of civilization versus barbarism, embracing of a liberal ideal of progress, as well as its deep-seated rejection of what it held as the atavistic, Hispanic, criminal ethos of the gaucho informed Latin American modernity. By aligning Borges with Sarmiento, Fernández Retamar was flattening the intricate intertextuality that Borges had established with Sarmiento and gauchesque literature at large, including the more favorable takes on the social type to be found in José Hernández's *Martín Fierro* (1872) or Ricardo Güiraldes's *Don Segundo Sombra* (1926). Indeed, this was the pretext of Borges's masterful short story "El Sur" [The South] from 1953—the year Fidel and a cadre of revolutionaries led an armed attack on the Moncada Barracks—in which Juan Dahlmann, a man of letters, may or may not join in a knife fight at the end. And what was the Cuban Revolution if not men of letters taking arms? There is a latent antipathy between the Guevarista ideal of the New Man and Borges's irresolute, metaphysical tales. The Cuban intellectual is merely trying to pin it down.

For Fernández Retamar, to posit Borges as a new Sarmiento is to posit himself as a new Martí. In "Nuestra América" (1891), the celebrated "Cuba's Apostle" had memorably declared "No hay batalla entre la civilización y la barbarie, sino entre la falsa erudición y la naturaleza" [The struggle is not between civilization and barbarism, but rather between false erudition and nature] (28). Martí's *hombre natural* rejects imported books; he is the autochthonous mestizo who has vanquished the exotic criollo. With these lines drawn, bookish Borges clearly falls under false erudition and White creole exoticism. "Calibán" is intended as an interpretative overview of the current state of Latin American culture and a takedown of the profound, colonial reasons for its underappreciation on the world stage. However, Borges, a Latin American and an Argentine no less than Ernesto Che Guevara, is the darling of European readers. And so Fernández Retamar finds himself in the awkward situation of having to both include and disavow him. The path not taken would have been to separate the man from his work, a position articulated among others by the Uruguayan writer Mario Benedetti, who had described Borges in 1967 as a writer "exceptionally gifted for intellectual speculation and utterly damaged for the appreciation [captación] of reality" (qtd. in Ortega 1977: 266). But a de facto member of a Cuban nomenklatura that successfully leveraged cultural politics into politics *tout court* cannot just dismiss the public statements of a major literary author. Instead, in an exercise of Jamesonian cognitive mapping *avant la lettre*, Fernández Retamar sees them as points in a broader conspiracy that engulfs the writing itself.

This explains the emphasis in declaring Borges *americano* and important. Both are unnecessary, underhanded concessions, as if Fernández Retamar and Casa de las Américas were brokers of all things worthy of note in the New World. Fredric Jameson, in his own foreword to the English edition of *Caliban and Other Essays* (1989), will similarly describe Havana as an "alternate capital" of the Americas and of the Caribbean world (ix). The conservative, libertarian figure of Borges is a threat to this imagined leftist geocultural order. Too close to the Old World and too far from Toussaint Louverture or Fidel Castro's radical Caribbean, Borges's brand of cosmopolitanism must be, to riff on a familiar adjective, abominable. There is also a missed opportunity here. Exceptionalizing Borges forecloses appreciating the continuities at opposite ends of the political spectrum. For instance, the thematization of the encounter of city and country folk extends beyond the fabled Argentine gauchos into Brazilian *gaúchos*, Chilean *huasos*, Colombian-Venezuelan *llaneros*, and even Cuban *guajiros*.[2] These are all idealized, more or less racialized popular social types that may complicate accounts of "the people" as a unified political subject or the role of the intelligentsia in conjuring them and it.

On the other hand, a piercing 1981 essay by the late critic Jean Franco supports the idea of salvaging Latin Americanist utopianism from Borges and extricating him from his contemporaries. It is worth citing at length:

> For Neruda and García Márquez, community (whether nation, class, or family) is productive of resistance to economic and to cultural domination. Liberation therefore must be national, social and cultural. Borges, in contrast, attaches no value to community since, for him, "reality" belongs only to the level of individual perceptions. His social philosophy (if such it can be called) is purely pragmatic. . . . [He] acknowledges that there are nations with national characteristics but speaks as if international politics were conducted as duels to gain respect. (55–56)

Note how Franco also establishes a link between the writing itself, peppered with duels, traitors, and heroes, and the public statements. Several of Borges's characters, among them Juan Dahlmann, are titillated by the heroic past of their nation. They gloss over unsavory episodes such as Sarmiento, turned statesman, presiding over the genocide of the nomadic gaucho. By contrast, when evoking similar iniquities throughout the continent, Neruda and García Márquez, like Fernández Retamar, fall closer to outrage.

Of course, there are commonalities between Neruda and Borges as poets—both take after Whitman—or between García Márquez and Borges as prose writers—both are fascinated by the topic of memory, say. Moreover, it is clear that Borges influenced the younger García Márquez, for all their differences and petty disputes, some the fodder of journalistic sensationalism.[3] However, the rift surrounding the key concept of community is so significant that, for Franco, this merits situating them in opposite camps. The conflict of reading Borges *as* Latin American literature or *against* it is laid bare. Ditto for seeing him as part of the Boom, an unprecedented publishing phenomenon that, ironically, stemmed in part from the world attention-grabbing qualities of the Cuban Revolution. In 1966, casting a wide net, the Argentine-U.S. journalist and writer Luis Harss saw Borges as part of the Boom, alongside the Guatemalan Miguel Ángel Asturias and the Brazilian João Guimarães Rosa. In 1972, the Chilean novelist and essayist José

Donoso situated Borges in the "proto-Boom" (91). Some saw Borges simply as the Boom's Other. More forcefully, Fernández Retamar calls the Argentine writer, alongside the Mexican diplomat-novelist Carlos Fuentes, "un intelectual de la anti-América" [an intellectual from anti-América] (87).

Recall the claim that Borges's readerly prose is colonial. Some of this has to do with an undertone of machismo in "Calibán." It's the time for action, not words, or at least for writing, goddammit, not quoting. Borges is the antipode of the committed intellectual, a disintegration of arms and letters. And yet, is there not a kernel of truth here? "Apart from a few philology professors who receive a salary for this, there is no other kind of human being who truly knows European literature *in toto*: the colonial subject" (Fernández Retamar 70). Fernández Retamar chooses not to draw a troubling inference: that Latin America's colonial condition is a creative opportunity. Borges, instead of ignoring this, builds upon it, as Beatriz Sarlo would suggest in 1993. In his 2017 study, Robin Fiddian will go further, claiming counterintuitively that Borges's writing constitutes "a prototype of postcolonial literature and theory," ultimately having much in common with Fernández Retamar and Leopoldo Zea (189). But, at this juncture, the origin story and the futurity of the Cuban Revolution is at stake. Borges's constant evocation of traditions much longer than the foundational moments of 1810, 1898, or 1959 relativizes "Latin America" as a concept in time, let alone one with revolutionary Cuba at its forefront. The longue durée of Borges's imagination is an existential threat. To boot, just as Borges favored "Banda Oriental" over "Uruguay," he used "South America" where others would use "Latin America." Meanwhile, Fidel Castro, in "Palabras a los intelectuales" (1961), leveraging freedom of expression against the Revolution's right to exist, famously decrees: "dentro de la Revolución, todo; contra la Revolución, nada" [within the Revolution, everything; against the Revolution, nothing]. A work like *Ficciones* [*Fictions*] (1944) presents a vision of aesthetic autonomy from the verboten Outside.

Crucially, the tropology of Prospero, Ariel, and Caliban—drawn from Shakespeare's *The Tempest* (1611)—breaks down with a writer who in some ways matches all three characters: the bookish master, the sparky spirit, the misfit who learns the colonizer's language the better to curse him with it. (In this male-centric account, Miranda and Sycorax are not in the picture.) For present purposes, rather than dwell on the blind spots of the 1971 essay, it is useful to see it as a lightning rod for the troubled animosity and admiration that were the hallmarks of Borges's Latin American reception for many decades, easily forgotten amid today's near-universal acclaim.[4] This is no historical quirk. Extrapolating, one can see here burning questions about the role of the intellectual, the teleology of Latin American history, the place of the region's culture on the world stage, the role of class origins in shaping art and thought, colonial legacies, elective affinities, literary constellations, and originality writ large.

Elsewhere in the continent, the situation is similar. The country outside Argentina with the longest engagement with Borges is, well, "la Banda Oriental" [the Eastern Bank]. Emir Rodríguez Monegal, first from Montevideo and later from his perches in Paris and at Yale, was instrumental in the writer's canonization. (Fernández Retamar bemoans the critic's "pesantez profesoral" 81.) The lucid Marxist critic Ángel Rama was openly antagonistic, declaring in 1959 that he always militated against *borgismo* and incidentally against Borges (qtd. in Rocca 38). Reportedly, the Argentine writer reciprocated in kind, boycotting a 1961 conference that the Uruguayan critic was to hold at the Biblioteca Nacional in Buenos Aires. Rama accused the librarian, not unreasonably, of "McCarthyism." The philosopher and art critic Juan Fló also wrote against Borges while courting him as part of the jury of a literary award. Meanwhile, Borges weighed in on matters of cultural relevance in the neighboring country, for instance, dismissing Horacio Quiroga for writing "what Kipling or Poe had already written much better" (Rocca 16). Although cultural magazines traveled on both sides of the River Plate, Uruguayan media vastly ignored Borges through the 1940s (Volonté), until *Marcha* enshrined him by lambasting him in the 1960s. At that point, the literati and the general public were enthralled, as elsewhere in Latin America. Apocryphal poems were sold in public transportation, while recognized bona fide poets—namely Ida Vitale, Washington Benavídez, Jorge Arbeleche, and Jorge Arias—imagined hypothetical encounters and conversations with Borges in their verses well into the 1990s (Lago 83–98).

In Colombia and Perú, Borges was met with unbridled enthusiasm. Despite the tense Cold War politics and internal strife in both countries, the author's greatness and standing above the fray seemed all but a fait accompli even during the rocky Sixties. Whether due to a general aloofness of the cultural elites or their alignment with Borges's hemispheric politics, the author visited Colombia rather unpolemically in 1963, 1965, and 1978; Perú for a short layover, in transit from Bogotá, in 1963, then formally in 1965 and 1978, along the same route. Already a celebrity writer and something of a traveling circus, he pleased the crowds with allusions to local authors—José Eustasio Rivera, José Asunción Silva, Miguel Antonio Caro, José María Eguren, and César Vallejo—that tipped the scales of canon formation (Batalla). He also wove in allusions from his own work and personal myth, for instance the role that his great-grandfather Manuel Isidoro Suárez (1799–1846) played in the decisive independence Battle of Junín, northwest from Lima, or, eventually, in his much discussed short story "Ulrica" [Ulrikke], from *El libro de arena* [*The Book of Sand*] (1975), where the protagonist, a Colombian professor, remarks in passing that to be Colombian is "un acto de fe" [an act of faith] (*OC* III: 18). The phrase would gain a life of its own in the country as a ready-made device for national soul-searching.

Similarly, anecdotes about his mercurial presence abound, including an unlikely afternoon in December 1963, at Gloria Valencia de Castaño and Álvaro Castaño Castillo's genteel *finca* in the outskirts of Bogotá. On that occasion—alongside his mother, Leonor Acevedo de Borges—the writer socialized with dignitaries including the Cartagenero poet-scholar Ramón de Zubiría, the Argentine art critic-novelist Marta Traba, and, perhaps uncharacteristically, the Mexican *ranchera* singer Chavela Vargas (García Estrada and López Bermúdez; Rincón). HJCK, the Castaños' cultural enterprise, bore the motto "el mundo en Bogotá, una emisora para la inmensa minoría" [the world in Bogotá, a radio station for the immense minority]. Aptly, such social gatherings show Borges as a key player in the region whenever negotiations of rooted cosmopolitanism and minority–majority culture are at stake.

In Brazil, this occurs before, during, and after the 1964–1985 military regime. The *modernista* pope Mário de Andrade celebrated Borges, alongside *martinfierristas* Girondo, Güiraldes et al, as early as 1927 (Schwartz and Araújo 121). The Argentine's silence over the master Machado de Assis was a source of national concern. In that respect, the ambition of worldliness that Mariano Siskind dubbed in 2014 "cosmopolitan desire" begot, rather, cosmopolitan jealousy. Symbolically, but also symptomatically, Borges received a first edition of Euclides da Cunha's *Os sertões* during his two-day, televised celebrity tour in São Paulo in 1984. This was only his second visit to the country, having been there in 1970 to receive a book biennale award endowed with a whopping $25,000 USD. In Borges's writings, Brazil is an exotic place, more distant from the River Plate than it actually is. Such exoticism, coupled with the casual racism of a man of his time and social background, complicate his Brazilian reception and role in local debates on the autonomy of art. Critic Luiz Costa Lima, not a leftist by any stretch of the imagination, claimed in his tour-de-force post-dictatorship essay *O fingidor e o censor* (1988) that "[Borges's] monism of the fictional is just as authoritarian and controlling as any other" (268). More recently, Marcelo Mendes de Souza, building on Harvard scholar Bruno Carvalho (2008), finds a dichotomy in Borges between backwardness and blackness, on the one hand, and universalism and whiteness, on the other (2021). Per that account, Brazil, and its racialized subjects, are Borges's irrational Other. Despite such serious reservations, Borges's standing in the country has barely budged (Schwartz).

In Mexico, Borges's proximity to Alfonso Reyes, the unchallenged master of Mexican letters since the 1920s until his death in 1959, cemented his reputation (Barili). Since the 1940s, so did the admiration of then-emerging Guadalajara-based writers who would turn out to be literary giants—with Juan José Arreola and Juan Rulfo among them—as well as important cultural brokers such as Antonio Alatorre, the editor of several prominent literary magazines throughout a long, prolific career (Olea Franco 19). In a context where cultural nationalism and the *novela de la revolución mexicana* were ubiquitous, Borges's playfully intellectual games came as a welcome respite. In 1958, still a teenager at the time, José Emilio Pacheco published short stories in Borges's style under the telltale titles "La sangre de Medusa" and "La noche del inmortal." In 1964, the *Revista Mexicana de Literatura* published a special issue on the author. For his part, the eminent poet and essayist Octavio Paz celebrated Borges, though Borges never quite reciprocated. By the turn of the century, Carlos Fuentes, Margo Glantz, Elena Poniatowska, Enrique Krauze, and many others had all written essays on the author. In 1999, Pacheco capped forty-odd years of engagement with Borges with a book-length study of an Argentine author that was, by then, a Mexican classic beyond dispute.

Disputes—there had been plenty along the way, including the familiar condemnation of the author's alleged escapism, notably in Jaime García Terrés's contrarian articles for *Revista de la Universidad de México* in 1956 and 1962 (159–60). But the most memorable entailed a botched speaking tour in 1976, the year of Borges's infamous public acceptance of Pinochet's *honoris causa*. Under the Partido Revolucionario Institucional, Mexico had broken off diplomatic relations with the Chilean dictatorship and taken in thousands of Chilean exiles. As a result, despite having attained the fateful Alfonso Reyes literary award in 1973, his invitation was rescinded (Deschamps in Capistrán). It merits further study how the figure of Borges may have contributed to the disidentification of state-subsidized Mexican intellectuals with the post-revolutionary state. Borges's heroic cult of the past, particularly his representation of seismic political transformations and social contradictions as duels of honor, in some ways jibes with national doctrine. His anti-populism, clearly, does not. It is telling that, in his score-settling obituary essay, Octavio Paz criticizes Borges for singing the praises of the defenders of the Alamo: "my patriotic zeal did not allow me to appreciate the heroic bravery of those men; he could not see the siege of El Álamo as an episode in an unjust war" (28). A reader from the Left might hear this as "you say tomato, I say tomato." Paz doubles down, chiding Borges in absentia for mistaking mere bravery for true heroism.

Speaking of Pinochet, Borges's reception in Chile is deserving of several volumes. The unavoidable punctum is September 21, 1976, a couple of weeks after the democracy-as-superstition Madrid trip. On that day, the de facto head of state conferred the honorary degree ex officio at Universidad de Chile *and* a car bomb took the life of Orlando Letelier, deposed president Salvador Allende's cabinet member, in Washington DC. It would take years of declassified documents and judicial inquiries to establish the responsibility of the Chilean secret police, especially Manuel Contreras and US operative Michael Townley, but it took no leap of the imagination to hypothesize that Pinochet was behind the assassination. Borges was the dictator's unwitting alibi, a diversionary tactic in the public eye. For many, that day the author became a beacon of aesthetic heteronomy.

Not for all—Borges went back to Chile the following year to celebrate María Luisa Bombal. Sara Vial recounts being in one of Valparaíso's charming elevators against a backdrop of fluttering seagulls with Borges, Bombal, María Kodama, Enrique Lafourcade, Carlos León, Enrique Gómez-Correa, and María Isabel Aldunate. For their part, *engagé* writers in Chile both decried Borges and wrote extensively about him, including volumes by critic Grínor Rojo and novelist essayist Volodia Teitelboim. Philosopher Victor Farías, who had famously revealed Heidegger's Nazi sympathies, builds on the 1983 visit of Borges to Ernst Jünger in West Germany to claim that both writers display a "poetics of aggression," particularly one where "a new aristocracy emerges from struggle [el acto de lucha]." For Farías, there was something troubling about Borges's *violentismo*, that is, his fascination with knife-wielding ways.

The most extreme Chilean reaction came from noted polemicist Eduardo Labarca. In the cover of the first—recalled—edition of his idiosyncratic collection *El enigma de los módulos* (2011), Labarca can be seen taking a literal piss on Borges's tombstone in Geneva. (The photo was staged.) Less crass, but no less conflicted about the Argentine's legacy, Roberto Bolaño made it his life's work to investigate the sinister contiguity of belles lettres and power epitomized in such indelible images as a blind Borges reaching out into the darkness to shake Jorge Rafael Videla's or Augusto Pinochet's hand. Fittingly, Bolaño approached the topic by revisiting motifs employed by Borges, as I now turn to analyze.

GLOBAL MONSTERS

Michael Townley, one of the men who assassinated Letelier the day of Borges's *horroris causa*, was married to Mariana Callejas, a Chilean author and secret police agent herself. Bolaño's *Nocturno de Chile* [*By Night in Chile*] (2000; 2003), fictionalizes the couple as Jimmy Thompson and María Canales—an ingenue, unlike Callejas. The characters organize literary evenings in the upper floors of their residence while the basement serves as a clandestine torture center. Reportedly, so did the real-life pair. The narrator points at their uncanny house and remarks: "así se hace literatura" (147). One interpretation of this open-ended deixis is that literature is only so removed from utter violence, an indictment that would surely extend to Borges. (Callejas once attended a dinner party for Borges hosted by Lafourcade [Gómez]). Another, putting more weight on the "así," speaks to the affordances of literary characters as distorted mirrors through which literary conceits may reflect upon the world. This interpretation, too, points at the Argentine author, particularly the oft-cited passage in "Tlön, Uqbar, Orbis Tertius" where "los espejos y la cópula son abominables, porque multiplican el número de los hombres" [mirrors and copulation are abominable, for they multiply the number of mankind] (*OC* I: 431; *CF* 69). Throughout his literary career, Borges crafted a veritable poetics of mirrors, abounding in aliases and distortions that have a profound impact on the imagination of later authors and their understanding of aesthetic autonomy—in Bolaño's case, heteronomy.

The Townley-Thompson or Callejas-Canales derivations originate in *Historia universal de la infamia* [*A Universal History of Infamy*] (1935), one of the many works in which Borges depicted infamous characters, a lifelong fascination of his. Bolaño politicized and actualized the master's trope. His most sustained engagement is *La literatura nazi en América* [*Nazi Literature in the Americas*] (1996; 2008), a series of short bio-bibliographical entries that insinuate a fascist conspiracy across the lives and oeuvres of imaginary, variously fascist women and men of letters throughout the continent. The volume is a Borgesian teratology, complete with an "Epilogue for Monsters," clearly inspired by *Historia universal*'s "Etcétera" final section. In an effort to subsume and make a travesty of Borges within his fictional word, Bolaño will feature one of his female characters, Edelmira Thompson de Mendiluce, a composite *grande dame* modeled on Mariquita Sánchez de Thompson and Victoria Ocampo, penning a chapbook called "Fervor." The tongue-in-cheek allusion to Borges's disavowed *criollista* masterpiece, *Fervor de Buenos Aires* [*Fervor of Buenos Aires*] (1923), makes light of the author, but also insinuates that there is something sinister about the nationalist, racist overtones of criollismo. This position is not unlike Fernández Retamar's.

Additionally, Bolaño exacerbates the mirror motif, abandoning one-to-one correspondences between imaginary characters and actual authors, thematizing abominable multiplication itself. Case in point, an entry describes "Cosmogonía del Nuevo Orden," an epic poem written by Jesús Fernández-Gómez, a Colombian volunteer in the

Wehrmacht during World War II. The poem juxtaposes the story of a Germanic warrior who must slay a dragon with the story of a South American student who must prove his worth. There are parallel dreams: the warrior dies, the student is blinded by "a cascade of mirrors." Note the similarity with Borges's "La flor de Coleridge" [Coleridge's Flower] (1952): blindness here is the flower, that is, the evidence that carries over from the dream into vigil. Blindness itself could be regarded as a synecdoche for Borges. But then, in a triple *mise en abyme*, the character Fernández-Gómez dies—like his epic poem's character's dreamed character. Borges was fond of *reductio ad absurdum*; Bolaño, of its corresponding *amplificatio*. At a symbolic level, these antics allow Bolaño to complicate the story of Borges's outspoken anti-Nazism, rather than positioning him as the absent Ur-father of generations of writers with fascist proclivities. Bolaño renders Borges's legacy as a nightmare.

The conceit of describing an absent poem takes after "El Aleph" (1949), where Carlos Argentino Daneri, frenemy of "Borges" the character, writes a sappy poem called "La Tierra," a double entendre for Land and Planet. The irony is that Daneri, from his last name onward, stands for criollismo, while "Borges" stands for cosmopolitanism. In this remarkable short story, the tension between the local and the global is explored to its ultimate consequences, including in the bewildering title object, found in a corner of a soon-to-be demolished house on Garay Street, "Sí, el lugar donde están, sin confundirse, todos los lugares del orbe, vistos desde todos los ángulos" [the place where, without admixture or confusion, all the places of the world, seen from every angle, coexist] (*OC* I: 623; *CF* 281). Bolaño takes note. "Cosmogonía del Nuevo Orden" presents a paradoxical fantasy where a hyperlocal ideology, a blood-and-soil ethos, gets globalized. Call it cosmopolitan racism. The disturbing rise of the alt-right around the world suggests that such positions are less untenable than one may hope. Bolaño anticipates this, probing *avant la lettre* in contemporary political fabrications, by channeling Borges. Like other writers, he borrows from the Argentine to make sense of an increasingly interconnected, often beleaguered, world. It is one where the left versus right camps of the Cold War are both ever-present and insufficient. The role of literature vis-à-vis the political must be thought anew. In this vein, Borges is less a source for answers than for persistent interrogation.

Similarly, the acerbic Colombian satirist Fernando Vallejo revisits the Aleph motif in *La Virgen de los sicarios* (1994), about an aging grammarian who falls in love with underage hitmen in Pablo Escobar's Medellín. There is an undercurrent of brooding eroticism in Borges's original tale, as the rival authors vie in mourning the object of their affection, Beatriz Viterbo. The found object displaces and condenses their fascination. In 1919, Sigmund Freud reported on a curious, frequent clinical finding among "neurotic men": "what they find uncanny [unhomely] [in female genitals] is actually the entrance to man's old 'home,' the place where everyone once lived" (151). Viterbo, vagina: psychoanalytically, "El Aleph" is a heterosexual fantasy about staring into this particular abyss, a cipher for what is both strange and familiar. The iterating letter "v" in the original brings the force of the signifier to bear on this interpretation: "vi el populoso mar, vi el alba y la tarde, vi las muchedumbres de América, vi una plateada telaraña. . . . "

[I saw the populous sea, saw dawn and dusk, saw the multitudes of the Americas, saw a silvery spiderweb. . . .] (*OC* I: 625; *CF* 283). In Vallejo's homosexual poetics, the love triangle of two men of letters and an elusive (dead) woman becomes that of a well-off man of letters, a slum assassin, and an agonizing city. The phrase resurfaces in connection to the shantytowns, transformed: "Vi al subir los 'graneros', esas tienduchas donde venden yucas y plátanos, enrejados ¿para que no les roben la miseria? Vi las canchas de fútbol voladas sobre los rodaderos. Vi el laberinto de las calles y las empinadas escaleras" [On the way up I saw the 'graneros,' those dirty little mini marts where they sell yuccas and plantains, behind bars. Is it so nobody can make off with their misery? I saw the football pitches sticking out over the precipices. I saw the maze of streets and the steep steps] (86, 93). The haughty narrator, an exile returned, evokes this topsy-turvy world not to pique the Borges reader, but to exacerbate contradictions between the local and the global, high and popular culture. At a time of national commotion—the novel is published a mere six months after Escobar was felled on the rooftops—Vallejo's perversely Borgesian antics mobilize the power of literary language against the ideological entrapments of both heteropatriarchy and the so-called War on Drugs.

Another author from Medellín, Héctor Abad Faciolince, has literally made headlines with allusions to Borges. Very much at loggerheads with Vallejo, Abad Faciolince involved Borges in a protracted attention-grabbing mytheme that is every bit as revealing of post-1989 sensibilities as Fernández Retamar was of post-1959. In an age where personal identity, authenticity, and memory often take center stage, Abad Faciolince's *El olvido que seremos* (2006)—since widely translated and disseminated, adapted into a 2020 feature film by the Spanish director Fernando Trueba and a 2021 graphic novel by the Catalan artist Tyto Alba—takes its title from an apocryphal Borges verse. The verse, and the sonnet that contains it, are inscribed onto the tombstone of the author's father, Héctor Abad Gómez, a left-of-center medical practitioner, human rights activist, and writer (Bernal). In the book, a fictionalized memoir, Abad Faciolince finds the sonnet in Abad Gómez's pocket on the day that assassins cut his life short, in 1987. The misattribution and the real mourning and paramilitary violence behind it quickly turned to clickbait, coinciding with the rise of social media (Ortiz-Ospina). Mainstream media all over Latin America also took up the sensational story: Could this be a hoax? Abad Faciolince doubled down in an article for *Letras Libres* in 2009, chastising those who suspected him of seeking fame by association while pointing out that the initials on his father's tombstone, JLB, "are the same as Borges's" (16).[5] He also mentions having requested an expert opinion from Daniel Balderston, co-editor of the present volume, as if reaching out to "an internationally acclaimed oncologist" (18).

It may appear that, at some point, this saga has little to do with Borges, who truly neither penned nor dictated such lines. However, the generative power of the Argentine's oeuvre and its hold on the imagination of Latin American readers and writers to this day is laid bare. One likely explanation is that, at the time, the Abad family simply assumed the sonnet was Borges's. Carving a poem into stone in the Campos de Paz cemetery, on a rolling hillside of the city, would be going to too much trouble—or derangement—for a willful deception. Abad Gómez probably mistook a parody by an erudite enfant terrible *bugueño* writer, Harold Alvarado Tenorio, for the real thing. (He would not have, presumably, had he seen the slapstick engravings in Alvarado Tenorio's 1972 *Pensamientos de un hombre llegado el invierno* that nonsensically depict "Borges en Bicicleta," followed by Dorges and Forges, all riding a bike, in a postmodernist undoing of the force of the signifier.) Hoping against all hope that the sonnet is Borges's is more about the desire to bring the literal father back to life than it is about the desire to be taken in by the literary father. Contemporary celebrity culture, rife with scandals and peccadilloes, focuses on the latter, possibly because the former, for all the mainstream iterations of the Abad story, continues to be too hard to stomach. The epitaph that was to provide closure is an invitation for philological hounding and creative reappropriations, including a 2011 novelistic elaboration by the Argentine writer Jaime Correas with the none-too-subtle title *Los falsificadores de Borges*. These are more palatable options than facing open wounds much greater than one particularly relatable and charismatic, if truncated, father-son relationship.

Abad Faciolince ventriloquizes Borges to vindicate a right to play, even mischief, in the face of tragedy and philological propriety. This amounts to a stance on aesthetic autonomy. Awkwardly situating himself in a continuum that goes from desecration to sacralization, he borrows from the Argentine's *specie aeterni* mode, at its most sentimental, for consolation. His successful tear-jerker provides readers and audiences a chance to mourn and cry, be it over a country's decades-long civil war or over the general passing of the older generations. Such flattening of historical specificity takes Borges too closely at his word: "un hombre es todos los hombres" [a man is all men]. As a widely read op-ed writer for several media, Abad Faciolince leverages respectability and gravitas, vaguely derived from the Borges affair, to forward a humanist, conciliatory take on Colombian politics. Abad Gómez wrote a book about tolerance; his son channeled righteous rage into a similar agenda.

Fernando Vallejo would not have any of it: neither the Borges game, nor the pathetic appeal. In 2020, he quit his own op-ed post at *El Espectador* over an unpublished, scathing critique of Abad Faciolince entitled "El huerfanito" [the little orphan]. The piece, a primer of ad hominem mockery, made its way into social media (*Malsalvaje*). More than three decades since the assassination, yet contemporary with its memorialization, Vallejo does not find it too soon to call Abad Gómez a coward while also chiding his son for producing watered-down imitations of such works as his own *La Virgen de los sicarios* or *El desbarrancadero*. He also cries wolf over the Borges bit.

> Dice el huerfanito que la frase "El olvido que seremos" es de Borges. No creo. Borges era un anglizado más bien sordo, por razón de su ceguera, a la propiedad o casticidad de la lengua española. No tenía el sentido de sus ritmos, de sus sonoridades, de sus evocaciones. Pero eso sí: una frase tan pendeja como esa él no la escribió. ¡La escribió el huerfanito!

> [The little orphan says that Borges wrote the phrase "The oblivion we shall be." I don't think so. Borges was an anglicized man who was rather deaf, on account of his blindness, to the propriety or Castilianness of the Spanish language. He had no sense of

its rhythm, sonorities, or evocations. No matter: a phrase as puny as that he did not write. The little orphan did!]

The cantankerous, combative grammarian presents a different take on aesthetic autonomy here and elsewhere. Rather than bank on Borges's standing to ambiguously build his own, he decries Borges the better to get at Abad Faciolince, positing himself as the superior, most Castilian stylist. Vallejo defends his right not to be a humanist (though he might call himself an animalist) and forecloses a backdoor return to traditional family values in the wake of the Colombian civil war. The time for rage is far from over, he seems to say, the time to fight fire with fire. Note how both Vallejo and Abad Faciolince tiptoe around de facto limits of aesthetic autonomy, be they libel, plagiarism, or censorship. Their controversy, with all its ugly undertones, is reminiscent of the contradictory roles Borges played in different camps during the Cold War, except the terrain now is affect.

I have argued elsewhere that post-1989 Latin American authors turn to Borges's *Aleph* to reflect on the global condition and resituate themselves in world literature. Several multimedia transnational successes that greatly expand the reach of fiction, namely Barbet Schroeder's 2000 film adaptation of *La Virgen de los sicarios*, Trueba's above-mentioned 2020 adaptation of *El olvido que seremos*, or the various theatrical adaptations of Roberto Bolaño's *2666* (2008), suggest as much. It is easy to miss how the originating books do not just take after the Colombian–Mexican iconicity of the War on Drugs, but after Borges.

Nods to the Argentine master are no guarantee for transnational dissemination or enduring critical acclaim, however. Additional works by Latin American authors who reimagine Borges, with vastly differing levels of impact, would also include the Brazilian Luís Fernando Veríssimo's *Borges e os orangotangos eternos* (2000), a cleverly delirious whodunnit; and *bogotano* Hugo Chaparro Valderrama's *Los elogios de la tribu* (2018), an imaginary biography of a Borges-like character, Ricardo Torres, whose fiendish widow threatens to sue. There is similarly a flurry of works that exceed the scope of this chapter, addressed elsewhere in this reader, such as the Spaniard Agustín Fernández Mallo's *El hacedor (de Borges), Remake* (2011), whose giveaway title is equal parts opportunism and homage, or a rich Argentine tradition ranging from the contemporary classic César Aira to the lesser-known Susy Shock, whose poetry collection *Realidades* (2021) riffs off *Ficciones*, or Belén Gache with her hypertextual, cy-borgesian writing (Marún 2022). In some of these cases, other than a penchant for all things meta, name-dropping, and self-seriousness, Borges appears, symptomatically, to challenge copyright in an age where the market is all-encompassing or, alternatively, to invoke a higher tradition at a time of immanence and information overflow.

It is fair to say that, although Borges's stylistic and thematic innovations impact in one way or another most, if not all, ensuing Latin American literature, authors who openly thematize this tend to be men. Several possible, somewhat complementary explanations come to mind. Perhaps Bloom's anxiety of influence trends male; women authors, despite the current boom, are disappointingly still a minority (Martínez 2023);

there is a masculinist streak in Borges worth revisiting; contemporary writing is overall more amicable to Carverian realism than to Borgesian fantasy; bookishness is being redefined; women authors have relative freedom from the yoke of the father—case in point, Mariana Enríquez's affinities largely bypass Borges via Silvina Ocampo and H. P. Lovecraft. To boot, the line between the woman of letters and the muse types tends to blur, not just in Borges or Latin America, complicating literary historiographical accounts such as the present one.

Conclusions: A Post-Autonomous Future?

Nomos in "autonomy" is about custom or law; autonomy is self-regulation. Absolute aesthetic autonomy is as impossible as movement without friction; absolute heteronomy is as impossible, or at least as unverifiable, as perfect determinism (a fitting paradox for a Borges tale). Aesthetic autonomy is not just relative, however, but subject to historicization, as the preceding sections suggest.

An informed speculation about the role that Borges may continue to play in Latin American literature could consider two positions by distinguished Argentine Latin Americanists. Josefina Ludmer remarked in 2007 that the era of the autonomy of art is over, which renders debates about engaged versus pure art or leftist versus rightist literature moot because "everything cultural (and literary) is economic and everything economic is cultural (and literary)" (238). For his part, Juan Pablo Dabove pointed out in 2008 that, from a certain moment on, literary disputes do not so much involve Borges or his legacy but happen *in* Borges. Taken together, these two pronouncements put Borges in a pickle. If Borges, a darling of general readership and critics alike, *is* the market, then writers will continue to hope against all hope for an outside.

In Latin America, this might happen by excising Argentina, identified with Borges by force of synecdoche. Such a regrettable outcome would ignore complex, long-standing interdependencies between nation and continent (see Sarmiento, above). Foreseeably, emerging figures, faced with the ever-increasingly interwoven categories of market and canon, will continue to be hostile to Borges when resisting such status quo (Fló 1978), or, on the contrary, be all the more amicable to him, when embracing it (Soto 2015). There are pitfalls in either path. In any case, reading Borges as a Latin American contingency, at a time when the author is already a global necessity, furthers reception into cocreation.

Notes

1. Translations from sources in languages other than English will be my own unless otherwise specified.

2. For a heuristic "Mineiro-Argentine" methodology that builds a bridge between *jagunços* in Guimarães Rosa and *orilleros* in Borges, see Campos.
3. In one emblematic interview, the Colombian author playfully declares the Argentine "completamente insustancial" [lacking in substance] (Ortega 10–11).
4. For a granular account of Borges's reception in Cuba, including the pre-1959 connection with Virgilio Piñera and the post-1988 détente with Fernández Retamar, see Alonso Estenoz.
5. The sonnet in question was published in *Variaciones Borges* in 2006 ("Cinco sonetos") with the help of Harold Alvarado Tenorio and William Ospina.

WORKS CITED

Abad Faciolince, Héctor. *El olvido que seremos*. Planeta, 2005.

Abad Faciolince, Héctor. *Oblivion: A Memoir*, translated by Anne McLean. Farrar, Straus and Giroux, 2010.

Abad Faciolince, Héctor. "Un poema en el bolsillo." *Letras Libres*, August 2009, pp. 16–25.

Abad Faciolince, Héctor, and Tyto Alba. *El olvido que seremos*. Salamandra Graphic, 2021.

Abad Gómez, Héctor. *Manual de tolerancia*. Secretaría de Educación y Cultura de Antioquia, 1988.

Adorno, Theodor W. *Aesthetic Theory*. University of Minnesota Press, 1997.

Alonso Estenoz, Alfredo. *Borges en Cuba: Estudio de su recepción*. Borges Center, 2017.

Alvarado Tenorio, Harold. *Pensamientos de un hombre llegado el invierno*. Piraña, 1972.

Barili, Amelia. *Jorge Luis Borges y Alfonso Reyes: La cuestión de la identidad del escritor latinoamericano*. Fondo de Cultura Económica, 1999.

Batalla, Carlos. "¿Qué hizo Jorge Luis Borges en Lima en 1965?" *El Comercio*, April 26, 2019. https://elcomercio.pe/180-anos-diario-el-comercio-2019/historias/hizo-jorge-luis-bor ges-lima-1965-noticia-629135-noticia/.

Bernal, Diego. "Homenaje floral al médico Héctor Abad Gómez, precursor de la Facultad Nacional de Salud Pública en Colombia." *Red iberoamericana de cementerios patrimoniales*, 2020. https://redcementeriospatrimoniales.blogspot.com/2020/09/homenaje-floral-al-medico-hector-abad.html.

Bolaño, Roberto. *By Night in Chile*, translated by Chris Andrews. New Directions, 2003.

Bolaño, Roberto. *La literatura nazi en América*. Seix Barral, 1996.

Bolaño, Roberto. *Nazi Literature in the Americas*, translated by Chris Andrews. New Directions, 2008.

Bolaño, Roberto. *Nocturno de Chile*. Anagrama, 2000.

Bolaño, Roberto, and Àlex Rigola. *2666*. Teatre Lliure, 2008.

Borges, Jorge Luis. *Collected Fictions*, translated by Andrew Hurley. Penguin, 1999.

Borges, Jorge Luis. *Obras completas*. 4 vols. Emecé, 1996.

Campos, Vera Mascarenha de. *Borges & Guimarães: Na esquina rosada do Grande Sertão*. Perspectiva, 1988.

Capistrán, Miguel, ed. *Borges y México*. Plaza & Janés México, 1999.

Carvalho, Bruno. "Charting Brazil in Borges." *Variaciones Borges*, no. 25, 2008, pp. 79–100.

Castro, Fidel. "Palabras a los intelectuales." *Política cultural de la Revolución Cubana: documentos*. Editorial de Ciencias Sociales, 1977, pp. 3–48.

Chaparro Valderrama, Hugo. *Los elogios de la tribu*. Seix Barral, 2018.

"Cinco sonetos." *Variaciones Borges*, no. 22, 2006, pp. 289–91.

Correas, Jaime. *Los falsificadores de Borges*. Alfaguara, 2011.

Costa Lima, Luiz. *The Dark Side of Reason: Fictionality and Power*. Stanford University Press, 1992.

Dabove, Juan Pablo, ed. *Jorge Luis Borges: Políticas de la literatura*. Instituto Internacional de Literatura Iberoamericana. University of Pittsburgh Press, 2008.

Deschamps, Eduardo. "La entrega del Premio Alfonso Reyes." *Borges y México*. Edited by Miguel Capistrán, Plaza & Janes México, 1999, pp. 83–85.

Donoso, José. *Historia personal del 'boom'. Nueva edición con Apéndice del autor seguido de El 'boom' doméstico por María Pilar Serrano*. Sudamericana/Planeta, 1984.

Farías, Victor. "Borges-Jünger: La poética de la agresión." *Hoy*, no. 686, September 10–16, 1990, pp. 41–44.

Fernández Mallo, Agustín. *El hacedor (de Borges), remake*. Alfaguara, 2011.

Fernández Retamar, Roberto. *Caliban and Other Essays*, translated by Edward Baker, foreword by Fredric Jameson. University of Minnesota Press, 1989.

Fernández Retamar, Roberto. *Todo Calibán*. Callejón, 2003.

Fiddian, Robin W. *Postcolonial Borges: Argument and Artistry*. Oxford University Press, 2017.

Fló, Juan, ed. *Contra Borges*. Editorial Galerna, 1978.

Franco, Jean. "The Utopia of a Tired Man: Jorge Luis Borges." *Social Text*, vol. 2, no. 4, 1981, pp. 52–78.

Freud, Sigmund. *The Uncanny*, translated by David McLintock. Penguin, 2003.

García Estrada, Rodrigo, and Andrés López Bermúdez. "El otro Borges en Colombia (extractos literarios)." *El Espectador*, July 21, 2020. https://www.elespectador.com/el-magazin-cultural/el-otro-borges-en-colombia-extractos-literarios-article/.

García Terrés, Jaime. *Obra completa*. Fondo de Cultura Económica, 2000.

Gómez Bravo, Andrés. "Ha habido un aprovechamiento de la historia del taller de Lo Curro." *La Tercera*, November 6, 2010, p. 84. http://www.bibliotecanacionaldigital.gob.cl/coleccio nes/BND/00/RC/RC0240591.pdf.

Güiraldes, Ricardo. *Don Segundo Sombra*. Editorial Proa, 1926.

Harss, Luis. *Los nuestros*. Editorial Sudamericana, 1966.

Hernández, José. *El gaucho Martín Fierro*. Imprenta de la Pampa, 1872.

"Homenaje a Jorge Luis Borges." *Revista Mexicana de Literatura*, Special issue, nos. 4–5, May-June, 1964.

Kristal, Efraín. "Jorge Luis Borges y las guerras mundiales." *Letral*, no. 21, 2009, pp. 160–82, https://revistaseug.ugr.es/index.php/letral/article/view/8104.

Labarca, Eduardo. *El enigma de los módulos*. Catalonia, 2011.

Lago, Sylvia. "Borges en cuatro poetas uruguayos." *Actas de las jornadas: Borges y el Uruguay*. Edited by Sylvia Lago and Alicia Torres, University of the Republic Press, 2001, pp. 83–98.

Ludmer, Josefina. *Aquí América Latina: Una especulación*. Eterna Cadencia, 2010.

Ludmer, Josefina. "Literaturas postautónomas." *Ciberletras*, no. 17, July 2007, pp. 236–44.

Martí, José. *Nuestra América*. Biblioteca Ayacucho, 1977.

Martínez, Luciano. "Políticas de lectura: Escritoras, escrituras y crítica literaria." *Revista Iberoamericana*, vol. 89, no. 282–283, January 2023, pp. 19–66, https://doi.org/10.3828/revi sta.2023.89.282-283.19.

Marún, Gioconda. "De la literatura impresa a la digital: Borges en las obras de Belén Gache." *Revista de la Academia Norteamericana de la Lengua*, vol. 9, nos. 17–18, 2022, pp. 255–66.

Olea Franco, Rafael. "Sobre la percepción de Borges en México." *Jorge Luis Borges: Perspectivas críticas, ensayos inéditos*. Edited by Pol Povic Karic and Fidel Chávez Pérez, Porrúa, 2016, pp. 13–38.

Ortega, Carlos. "Gabriel García Márquez. Su clave: la sinceridad." *El Comercio Gráfico Lima*, Sunday, September 10, 1967, pp. 10–11.

Ortega, Julio. "Borges y la cultura hispanoamericana." *40 Inquisiciones sobre Borges*, special issue edited by Alfredo A. Roggiano and Emir Rodríguez Monegal. *Revista Iberoamericana*, vol. XLIII, nos. 100–101, July–December 1977, pp. 257–68.

Ortiz-Ospina, Esteban. "The Rise of Social Media." *Our World in Data*, March 2019. https://our worldindata.org/rise-of-social-media.

Pacheco, José Emilio. *Jorge Luis Borges*. Ediciones Era, 1999.

Pacheco, José Emilio. *La sangre de medusa, y otros cuentos marginales*. Ediciones Era, 2014.

Paz, Octavio. "El arquero, la flecha y el blanco." *Vuelta*, no. 117, 1986, pp. 26–29.

Rincón, Juan Camilo. *Ser colombiano es un acto de fe: Historias de Jorge Luis Borges y Colombia*. Libros & Letras, 2014.

Rocca, Pablo. *El Uruguay de Borges: Borges y los uruguayos (1925–1974)*. Linardi y Risso, 2002.

Sarlo, Beatriz. *Jorge Luis Borges, a Writer on the Edge*. Verso, 1993.

Samaniego, Fernando. "La democracia es una superstición." *El País*, September 7, 1976, https://elpais.com/diario/1976/09/08/cultura/210981602_850215.html.

Sarmiento, Domingo Faustino. *Facundo: Civilización y barbarie*. Espasa-Calpe, 1845.

Schroeder, Barbet, director. *La Virgen de los sicarios*. Vertigo Films, 2000.

Schwartz, Jorge, ed. *Borges no Brasil*. Editora UNESP, 2001.

Schwartz, Jorge, and Maria Carolina de Araújo, eds. *Borges Babilônico: Uma Enciclopédia*. Companhia das Letras, 2017.

Shock, Susy. *Realidades*. Muchas Nueces, 2021.

Siskind, Mariano. *Cosmopolitan Desires: Global Modernity and World Literature in Latin America*. Northwestern University Press, 2014.

Soto, Ángel, ed. *Borges, Paz, Vargas Llosa: Literatura y libertad en Latinoamérica*, with prologue by Carlos Alberto Montaner. Unión Editorial, 2015.

Souza, Marcelo Mendes de. "Unoriginal Opinions of an Original Man: Jorge Luis Borges's Views on Race and Brazilian People in His Conversations with Adolfo Bioy Casares and His Literary Works." *Latin American Research Review*, vol. 56, no. 3, September 2021, pp. 668–78. https://doi.org/10.25222/larr.1073.

Trueba, Fernando, director. *El olvido que seremos*. Cohen Media Group, 2020.

Vallejo, Fernando. *El desbarrancadero*. Debolsillo, 2001.

Vallejo, Fernando. "El huerfanito." *Malsavaje*, April 20, 2020. https://malsalvaje.com/2020/04/29/fernando-vallejo-hector-abad.

Vallejo, Fernando. *La Virgen de los sicarios*. Alfaguara, 1994.

Vallejo, Fernando. *Our Lady of the Assassins*, translated by Paul Hammond. Serpent's Tail, 2001.

Vallejo, Fernando. "El huerfanito." *Malsavaje*, April 20, 2020. https://malsalvaje.com/2020/04/29/fernando-vallejo-hector-abad.

Verissimo, Luis Fernando. *Borges e os orangotangos eternos*. Companhia das Letras, 2000.

Vial, Sara. "Con Borges en un ascensor de Valparaíso." *El Mercurio*, March 20, 1996. http://www.bibliotecanacionaldigital.gob.cl/visor/BND:173022.

CHAPTER 23

BORGES'S RECEPTION IN EUROPE AND THE USA

EDWIN WILLIAMSON

"I am an invention of Roger Caillois," Borges liked to say, and there was a kernel of truth in this self-deprecating joke, for Caillois, a prominent French intellectual living in Buenos Aires during World War II, would be instrumental in bringing Borges to the attention of the literary world in postwar Paris, thereby opening the door to his eventual emergence as a world-class writer. For the previous twenty years or so, Borges had been almost completely unknown outside Latin America, which at the time was regarded as a remote backwater of Western culture. In his native Argentina, he was a controversial and divisive figure. He had been the leader of the Buenos Aires avant-garde in the 1920s and a passionate advocate of a progressive form of urban-centered cultural nationalism, but, in the 1930s, he found himself marginalized for his denunciation of both fascism and communism. Nationalists of right and left condemned his idiosyncratic essays and fantastic stories for being too abstruse and detached from political and social realities. His outspoken defense of individual liberty would make him a notorious opponent of the authoritarian regime of Juan Domingo Perón (1946–1955). These ideological conflicts prevented an appreciation of the quality and significance of his writing in his native land. Without the agency of foreign critics, scholars, translators, and publishers in Europe and the United States he would probably never have been acclaimed as one of the great writers of the twentieth century.

Despite Caillois's "discovery" of Borges in the mid-1940s, it would take a long time before the Argentine's peculiar genius was recognized abroad. But, in the course of the 1960s, this obscure writer from a far-off country would rise to an astonishing peak of international renown and influence. Obviously, there is not enough space here for a full account of this extraordinary trajectory; I offer instead an overview of what I regard as the most significant stages in that process, focusing principally on France, where the earliest lines of interpretation were established, and the United States, where this approach was further developed and where the power of the media helped to spread his reputation to the rest of the world.

On his return to Paris from Argentina after the war, Caillois became a reader and editorial adviser at the publishing house Gallimard, where he founded "La Croix du Sud," a series dedicated to publishing translations of Latin American fiction; all but one translations of Borges's works until 1964 would be published in this series. Caillois commissioned a translation of *Ficciones* [*Fictions*] from Néstor Ibarra and Paul Verdevoye which appeared as *Fictions* in 1951. In 1953, Caillois brought out his own translation of four stories—"Historia del guerrero y de la cautiva" [The Story of the Warrior and the Captive], "El inmortal" [The Immortal], "La escritura del dios" [The Writing of the God], and "La busca de Averroes" [Averroes's Search]—for which he chose the title *Labyrinthes*. In 1955, Jean-Paul Sartre, then editor of the journal *Les Temps Modernes*, published several essays by Borges in advance of Gallimard's publication in 1957 of *Otras inquisiciones* [*Other Inquisitions*], translated by Paul and Sylvia Bénichou with the title *Enquêtes*; that same year a translation of "El Aleph" appeared in Sartre's journal. Caillois and Laure Guille published translations of *Historia universal de la infamia* [*A Universal History of Infamy*] and *Historia de la eternidad* [*A History of Eternity*] (Éditions du Rocher, 1958). By the end of the decade, therefore, the French literary world had access to *Ficciones*, several major stories from *El Aleph*, *Historia universal de la infamia*, and two collections of his essays, *Historia de la eternidad* and *Otras inquisiciones*.[1]

Caillois and his fellow translators Ibarra and Bénichou wrote the first critical evaluations, playing down the "local color" of Borges's stories to avoid his being dismissed as a mere Latin American by French readers. Ibarra's preface to *Fictions* all but erased his national identity: "Hispano-anglo-portugais d'origine, élevé en Suisse, fixé depuis longtemps à Buenos-Aires où il naquit en 1899, personne n'a moins de patrie que Jorge Luis Borges . . . Borges est un homme de lettres européen qui serait à sa place à Londres, à Paris aussi" [Of Hispano-Anglo-Portuguese origin, brought up in Switzerland, settled for many years in Buenos Aires, where he was born in 1899, no one could be less rooted in a country than Jorge Luis Borges. . . . Borges is a European man of letters who would feel at home in London as well as Paris] (Ibarra 7).[2] Instead, they stressed his use of fantasy to explore metaphysical themes. Caillois's choice of *Labyrinthes* as the title for his anthology would indelibly stamp the labyrinth—an intellectual labyrinth, of course, because of its "symétries abstraites presque vertigineuses" [abstract and almost dizzying symmetries] (Caillois 10)—as the hallmark of Borges's imagination. These early French translations of the 1950s brought Borges to the attention of the novelist Alain Robbe-Grillet, an advocate of the *nouveau roman* associated with writers who were reacting at the time against the politically committed literature that was prevalent after the war. The "new novelists" challenged the assumption that plot and character should reflect lived experience, and this chimed with Borges's long-held skepticism about psychological realism, as Robbe-Grillet noted in his review of *La invención de Morel*, a novel by Adolfo Bioy Casares, a friend and disciple of Borges, which he later included in his book *Pour un nouveau roman* (1963) [*Towards a New Novel*].

The critical reception of the Argentine author in France would be shaped to a considerable extent by the novelist Maurice Blanchot. In a 1959 essay, "L'infini littéraire: L'Aleph," he argued that we normally ascribe a finite character to the world so that its boundaries may allow us to take our bearings and live our lives. Fiction purports to hold up a mirror to this well-defined world but in fact this representation is deceptive inasmuch as the world is not delimited but boundless. Borges's fiction, in contrast, makes us feel "l'approche d'une étrange puissance, neutre et impersonelle" [the proximity of a strange force, neutral and impersonal], for it exposes us to a sense of a boundless world, to a "labyrinthe de la lumière" [labyrinth of light], that far exceeds our desire for understanding (Blanchot 141). Thus, for instance, in "Pierre Menard, autor del Quijote" [Pierre Menard, Author of the *Quixote*] Borges plays with the "memorable absurdity" of a writer being able to reproduce an earlier text with absolute precision; were this "double parfait" [perfect double] to be achieved, it would negate originality: "l'original est effacé, et même l'origine" [the original is effaced, and even the origin] (Blanchot 142), in which case a literary text would not, in principle, have a unique author but a multitude of possible authors, for the essence of literature is not the individual writer but literature itself. And so, if a book were capable of reflecting the world as it truly is—infinite and limitless—it could not have a beginning or an end but would have to take the form of a spherical volume written by everyone and in which they would themselves be written: it would be equivalent to Borges's Aleph, "le prodigieux, l'abominable" [the prodigious, the abominable] (Blanchot 142).

In Italy a translation of *Ficciones* by Franco Lucentini was published by Einaudi in 1955, with the title *La biblioteca di Babele*. It had a transformative impact on three writers who would come to be counted among the most important in postwar Italy: Italo Calvino, an editor at Einaudi at the time; Leonardo Sciascia, one of the book's first reviewers; and Umberto Eco. "All three absorbed him then," writes Robert S. C. Gordon, "and over the following 30 years (and more for Eco) into their reflections on literature and into their works of literature" (262). Borges's influence contributed to the turning away from the neorealism which had been dominant in Italian literature and film since the war.

> He inspired an intense dialogue with many of the most creatively interesting and intellectually sophisticated writers of modern Italy. The depth of interaction has led one critic to talk of a "Borges function" in modern Italian literature. . . . His influence in Italy was both deep and wide, pluriform and multi-dimensional. Many highly important writers absorbed Borgesian elements in many different ways, often mediated through other writers and models. (Gordon 262)

In Germany, Carl Hanser Verlag published *Labyrinthe* (1959), a selection of stories from *Ficciones* and *El Aleph*, translated by Karl August Horst, Eva Hesse, Wolfgang Luchting, and Liselotte Reger, but the anthology received mixed reviews from influential critics and passed largely unremarked. More translations followed, mostly anthologies of uneven quality by many different hands and from various publishers, reaching a peak in the 1980s, notably with Carl Hanser Verlag's project for a "complete works" in eleven volumes, which was, alas, "in part a [bibliographic] disaster" (Bollinger 226). Still, as Borges's fame spread throughout Europe, he would eventually gain admirers and wider visibility in Germany: "A second peak can be seen at the beginning of this century, which is marked by a second comprehensive edition of Borges's work [from Carl Hanser Verlag] as well as a wave of publications investigating broader themes in his writing" (Köhler-Busch 137).

Spain was still too absorbed by problems following its civil war to take much notice of Spanish American literature, but, in 1960, Carlos Barral, a partner at Seix Barral of Barcelona, had the idea of creating an International Publishers' Prize for an author "of any nationality whose existing body of work, will in the view of the jury, have a lasting influence on the development of modern literature" (Rodríguez Monegal, *Jorge Luis Borges* 443). The winner would receive $10,000 and have a book translated and published in each of six countries by Seix Barral, Gallimard, Einaudi, Rowohlt of Germany, Weidenfeld and Nicolson of London, and Grove Press of New York. In May of the following year, six national committees comprising writers, critics, and academics were convened at the Hotel Formentor in Mallorca. Two favorites emerged: Samuel Beckett and Borges. The British, Americans, and Germans preferred Beckett but the French, Spanish, and Italians favored Borges. To break the deadlock, the Americans proposed Henry Miller, but this late bid was thrown out. It was Roger Caillois's final intervention that swung it for Borges—it was agreed to split the prize between him and Samuel Beckett.[3]

Meanwhile, in the early 1950s Borges himself was at a low ebb in Buenos Aires, making a precarious living from teaching and lecturing, having resigned his post as an assistant in a municipal library over a suspect promotion after Perón's election as president in 1946. He was outraged and depressed by Perón's restriction of free speech and promotion of an inward-looking nationalist ideology, but the publication of the French translation of his *Ficciones* in 1951 was an encouraging sign of recognition abroad at a time when a feverish atmosphere was being whipped up by the Peronists in the run-up to the presidential elections due in November. The writer Betina Edelberg recalled driving Borges to Ezeiza airport to pick up a copy sent from Paris, and, when he held the book in trembling hands, his joy was "impossible to describe" (Williamson, *Borges* 316). After this wonderful boost to his morale, and only a month following Perón's landslide victory, he gave a public lecture on "El escritor argentino y la tradición" [The Argentine Writer and Tradition], arguing that Argentine writers should not feel constrained by a national "tradition" defined by the state: they were heirs to the whole of Western culture and were free to write on whatever subject they chose. But, otherwise, he endured a catalogue of woes in the 1950s: the loss of his already weak sight, failures with several women, and bitter public disputes over his support for the generals who overthrew Perón in 1955. Creatively, he had reached a dead end: he wrote no fiction after 1953, only some poetry and short prose reflections on the failure of his literary ambitions (later collected in *El hacedor* [*Dreamtigers*]). But then, in May 1961, he received a telephone call informing him that he had won a prize he had never heard of—the International Publishers' Prize. At first, he thought it was a joke, but he was later to claim that "as a consequence of that prize my books mushroomed overnight throughout the Western world" (Borges, "An Autobiographical Essay" 254). In fact, it would take another decade for his reputation to become established in Europe and the United States.

The prize stimulated further interest in Borges in France. Michel Foucault prefaced his vastly influential *The Order of Things* (1966) with an anecdote that neatly illustrates why Borges caught the attention of French intellectuals: "This book first arose out of a passage in Borges, out of the laughter that shattered, as I read it, all the familiar landmarks of my thought" (Foucault xv). The passage was from the essay "El idioma analítico de John Wilkins" [The Analytical Language of John Wilkins] describing "cierta enciclopedia china" [a certain Chinese encyclopedia] which classified animals according to criteria that made absolutely no sense to the rational Western mind (*OC* II: 85; *SNF* 231). Foucault found it unsettling because it undermined the standard conception of knowledge as a progressive accumulation of objective truths about the world. This Borges-induced uneasiness led him to develop a relativizing history of the principles which underpinned the various ways of organizing knowledge in different periods and places. The French title of Foucault's book, *Les mots et les choses* [*Words and Things*] encapsulated a fundamental premise of the new thinking: there was no intrinsic connection between words and things because language generated meaning through the operation of its own internal rules rather than by reference to the external world. Since words had no secure anchorage in objective reality, they could not describe things in absolute and universally valid terms. Knowledge, therefore, was a "construct" of the mind, mediated through *discours* [discourse] and *écriture* [writing], terms employed by French theorists in anthropology, philosophy, sociology, political science, psychoanalysis, history, and literary studies.

The prime vehicle for disseminating these emerging theories was the journal *Tel Quel*, founded in 1960. In "Le langage à l'infini," Michel Foucault adapted Blanchot's "infini littéraire" to language, which he represented as an impersonal "Discourse" [capital D in the original] whose purpose was, like Scheherazade's in *The 1001 Nights*, to overcome "the black wall of death" by "reduplicating" itself endlessly in mirror-like works of literature, much like Borges's Library of Babel whose infinite abundance of books contained language in every possible variation of sense and non-sense and "reduplicated" itself periodically in the limitless course of time. Another notable contributor to *Tel Quel* was Gérard Genette, whose version of Blanchot's "infini littéraire" was to become influential in Borges studies: since meaning was subjectively determined by each and every reader, as Pierre Menard's "rewriting" of *Don Quijote* had implicitly shown, a text was susceptible to an infinity of interpretations. A reader therefore became a kind of author who "rewrote" the text in the very act of reading it.

Thus, "Pierre Menard, autor del Quijote" [Pierre Menard, Author of the *Quixote*] was taken, by and large, as the paradigm of Borges's putative theory of literature. Shades of "Pierre Menard" can be found in Julia Kristeva, for whom a text was not a piece of original writing but a web of intertextual relations, and also in Jacques Derrida's deconstruction, which discounted the "presence" of an author in a literary text because of the indefinite "deferral" of a fixed meaning due to the inherent instability of language. Above all, "Pierre Menard" was an apt illustration of Roland Barthes' essay "The Death of the Author," who was replaced by an *écriture* that erased the author's personal voice within a text, freeing readers to determine its meaning for themselves.[4]

The image of Borges created in France was that of a cosmopolitan writer absorbed in a hermetic world of books, one who wrote tales of metaphysical fantasy as well as provocative essays predicated on a notion of literature, in the words of Gérard Genette, "comme une espace homogène et réversible où les particularités individuelles et les préséances chronologiques n'ont pas cours, . . . [et] qui fait de la littérature universelle une vaste création anonyme où chaque auteur n'est que l'incarnation fortuite d'un Ésprit intemporel et impersonnel" [as a homogeneous and reversible space where individual particularities and succession in time are not relevant, . . . (and) which conceives of universal literature as a vast anonymous creation in which an individual author is no more than the fortuitous incarnation of a timeless and impersonal Mind] (Genette 125). And yet, somewhat paradoxically, several essays by writers associated with the *nouveau roman* and *Tel Quel* appeared alongside interviews, letters, reminiscences, unpublished texts, photographs, and other personal documents, in a volume produced by the publishing house *L'Herne* in 1964 celebrating Borges as an author of particular genius. France, however, was no longer the cultural powerhouse it once had been, and it would require two further developments to propel Borges finally to worldwide glory—the influence of French literary theory in US universities and his exposure to the powerful US media.

Interest in Borges in the United States was still mostly confined to specialists in Latin American literature and their students. The semester he spent in 1961, as a visiting professor in the Spanish department at the University of Texas at Austin, would produce in due course translations of *El hacedor* (1964) and *Otras inquisiciones* (1967) by the University of Texas Press. But the real impetus for his rise to fame was the publication of two collections in 1962: Anthony Kerrigan's translation of *Ficciones* (the Spanish title was retained) by Grove Press, the US representative for the International Publishers' Prize, and a selection of fiction and essays with the title *Labyrinths*, translated by Donald Yates and James E. Irby from New Directions. These two niche publishers of experimental modern fiction were based in New York and known to literary editors of major newspapers and magazines, thanks to whom reviews began to appear in *The New Yorker*, *The New York Times Book Review*, *The New York Review of Books*, *The Atlantic Monthly*, and similar publications.[5]

One of the earliest critical appraisals of Borges was "A Modern Master" by Paul de Man, who would become a leading light of the "Yale School" of deconstructionists. The *ficciones* were not based on "an actual experience" but on an "intellectual proposition," their subject being how to create a style (Alazraki 57). At the center of the stories "always stands an act of infamy" (57), a theme linked with the "duplicity" of the writer, who "presents the invented form as if it possessed the attributes of reality" (58). As "prototypes of the writer," Borges's characters committed "misdeeds like plagiarism, impersonation, in which someone pretends to be what he is not" (57), for the artist had "to wear the mask of the villain in order to create a style" (56), which was why Borges's "mirror-world" was haunted by shades of terror and violence (60).

In "The Author as Librarian," John Updike observed that Borges's essays possessed a "sealed" quality: "They are structured like mazes and, like mirrors, they reflect back and forth on one another" (Alazraki 66). From his "immense reading" he had distilled a "fervent narrowness": "The same parables, the same quotations recur" (66). "His ideas border on delusions; the dark hints—of a cult of books, of a cabbalistic unity hidden in history—that he so studiously develops are special to the corrupt light of libraries and might vanish outdoors" (67). Alfred Kazin wrote of "a wholly and obsessively mental world, of a lack of great experiences, of any deep sexual concern" (Alazraki 129). John Ashbery described his art as "a closed one, self-contained, pre-determined, the work of a metaphysical Fabergé" (Alazraki 96). George Steiner admired the "arch learning," "his love of charade and high intellectual slapstick" (Alazraki 121, 123). "Borges builds an anti-world, a perfectly coherent space in which his mind can conjure at will," but his fictions were like "autistic dreams" (120, 118).

The affinity with Kafka was generally acknowledged, and also to a degree with Nabokov, but reviewers were often puzzled by the sheer oddity of Borges's imagination and, conscious of his love of English literature, they tried to place him on the Anglo-American literary map. Was he a modernist like Joyce, Faulkner, Lawrence, or Woolf? If anything, he seemed to hark back to the Victorians or Edwardians, but it was strange that he admired writers like Stevenson, Chesterton, Kipling, Wells, and Shaw, who were generally considered marginal to the canon of modern literature. Or maybe, as Alfred Kazin suggested, he was more akin to nineteenth-century American writers since his characters seemed "burdened, like the solitary figures in so much American fiction, by the incongruence of their existence in an unfathomable land" (Alazraki 129). All the same, Steiner thought he presented an alternative to "the loud graffiti of erotic and political emancipation that currently pass for fiction and poetry" (Alazraki 124). Updike wondered whether his "narrative innovations" might not point "the way out of the dead-end narcissism and downright trashiness of present American fiction" (Alazraki 62).

It was the novelist John Barth who found Borges a place on the Anglo-American map as a forerunner of the "postmodernism" of his own experimental generation, among them Thomas Pynchon, Don DeLillo, William Gass, Kurt Vonnegut, and Donald Barthelme, writers who believed that the modern novel had run out of steam and resorted to irony, parody, pastiche, and self-reflexive trickery to subvert the authority implicit in their own fiction. Barth claimed in "The Literature of Exhaustion," that in "an age of ultimacies" (Alazraki 85) Borges had found a new way of dealing with the "exhaustion of certain possibilities" (83), as in "Pierre Menard, Author of the *Quixote*" where, by treating a known work with ironic intent, "he confronts an intellectual dead end and employs it against itself to accomplish new human work" (87). In "The Politics of Self-Parody," Richard Poirier also described Borges in postmodernist terms as a writer who made "the formal properties of fiction into the subject matter of fiction" (Alazraki 99). However, this "self-parody," which "makes fun of itself *as it goes along*" (emphasis in original 96) provided an escape from "the [realistic and rationalistic] trap" in which literature found itself, for "insofar as they are available for discussion, life, reality, or history only exist as discourse"; thus, "to talk or to write is to fictionalize" (97). "Borges himself cannot be located in most of his writing . . . he is a writer with no center, playing off, one against the other, all those elements in his work which aspire to centrality" (107).

American postmodernism overlapped with French critical theory, which was making inroads in US universities at this time, and Borges's fiction would increasingly be studied through the terminology and concepts of poststructuralism: the "death of the author," the "decentered subject," "rewriting," "intertextuality," the arbitrariness of language, the limitations of rationality, the "constructed" nature of knowledge, and so on.

An invitation from Harvard University to spend the academic year 1967–1968 as the Charles Eliot Norton Professor of Poetry gave a decisive boost to Borges's reputation. His lectures made him "the literary hero of Cambridge": "Famous writers like Robert Lowell, Robert Fitzgerald, Yves Bonnefoy, John Updike and Bernard Malamud attended his lectures and lined up to meet him. John Barth said Borges was the man 'who had succeeded Joyce and Kafka'" (Burgin 14).

While at Harvard he met a thirty-four-year-old translator, Norman Thomas di Giovanni, with whom he established a remarkable partnership, allowing the American a free hand in dealing with English-language publishers and agreeing to equal shares of the royalties from translations undertaken together. Di Giovanni secured a contract for a poetry anthology which Delacorte Press would publish as *Selected Poems (1923–1967)*. The New York publisher E. P. Dutton offered a multibook contract for whichever works remained free of copyright and also commissioned a new anthology with the title *The Aleph and Other Stories*. Di Giovanni's masterstroke was a lucrative deal with *The New Yorker* to submit poems and stories on an occasional basis.

At first Borges did not fare well in the United Kingdom. Weidenfeld & Nicolson had shared with Grove Press the costs of translating *Ficciones*, but its publication in 1962 failed to attract much attention. When he arrived in the United Kingdom for a lecture tour in 1963, his reception by the literary establishment could be summed up in Philip Larkin's derisive query to a journalist: "Who is Jorge Luis Borges?" It did not exactly help either that he had chosen as the subject of his lecture *The Gaucho Martín Fierro*, an Argentine classic which was altogether unknown in Britain. In Edinburgh, for instance, an audience was raised by persuading the local Spanish Circle to hold a special meeting. The honorary secretary dutifully recorded afterwards: "Prof. Borges, himself no mean literary writer, was obviously carried away by his subject and spoke at some length without notes, as he is almost blind" (qtd. in Williamson, *Borges* 349).

Still, the fame he was garnering in the United States did eventually filter through to the United Kingdom, and, by the end of the 1960s, *Labyrinths*, the anthology by Yates and Irby published in Britain by Penguin, had achieved cult status with a mostly youthful readership. What's more, Borges had been referenced in films by famous French "New Wave" directors like Jacques Rivette, Jean-Luc Godard, and Alain Resnais, and, in 1970, he would become even more "hip" thanks to two new films: Bernardo Bertolucci's *La strategia del ragno* [*The Spider's Stratagem*], was inspired by "Tema del traidor y del héroe" [Theme of the Traitor and the Hero] and acclaimed at the Venice and New York film festivals; Nicolas Roeg and Donald Cammell's *Performance*, starring Mick Jagger of the Rolling Stones, explored themes dear to Borges like the labyrinth, the double, and the enigma of personal identity, albeit weirdly transposed to a world of sex, drugs, and rock and roll. Playing a decadent rock star in a crumbling Notting Hill mansion,

Jagger quotes from "Tlön, Uqbar, Orbis Tertius" and "El Sur" [The South]; a photograph of Borges appears twice on the jacket of *A Personal Anthology*; and his image flashes on screen as Jagger is shot by a gangster played by James Fox. It was not to everyone's taste: a critic for *The New York Times* attacked its "mindless pretension" and complained that "even that great writer, Jorge Luis Borges, is dragged into the cesspool" (qtd. in Williamson, *Borges* 396–97).

In March 1971, he returned to the United States for yet another round of award ceremonies, talks, and readings at venues packed to overflowing with enthusiastic audiences. He then traveled to England to be invested with an honorary doctorate at Oxford, following which he gave four lectures at the Institute of Contemporary Arts in London that were a resounding triumph: after the first lecture the organizers had to move the series to Central Hall at Westminster to cope with the demand for seats. The Argentine press reveled in the acclaim Borges was receiving—he had been given a standing ovation, it was reported, by "an audience of London hippies," "hairy, disheveled, wildly enthusiastic young people" (qtd. in Williamson, *Borges* 396).

Despite the clamor of success, Borges had not published a new story in sixteen years, but, in April 1969, he began to dictate "El encuentro" [The Encounter], which di Giovanni translated and sent to *The New Yorker*. Nine more stories were added over the next year to form a new collection, which appeared as *El informe de Brodie* [*Doctor Brodie's Report*] in late 1970. It did not live up to expectations: reviewers were dismayed at the absence of metaphysics and fantasy, and, when the English translation was published by Dutton in 1972, the reception was much the same. The image that had been "made in France" seemed to have been betrayed by the man himself. But the fact was that Borges disagreed with his characterization as a cerebral writer inhabiting a kind of impersonal literary utopia.

The Paris Review: Some readers have found that rather like some of the newer French writers. Is that your intention?

BORGES: No. (*Sadly*) If that has happened, it is out of mere clumsiness. Because I have felt them very deeply. I have felt my stories so deeply that I have told them, well, using strange symbols so that people might not find out that they were all more or less autobiographical. The stories were about myself, my personal experiences. (Christ 155)

Such declarations, however, cut no ice with foreign theorists and critics, for the poststructuralists rejected the figure of "the author," while American critics generally scorned the "intentional fallacy," the supposedly simplistic belief that the aim of interpretation was to get at an author's intentions.

Yet, much as he relished his international renown, Borges valued his creative autonomy and integrity above all. Even at the pinnacle of his fame, he had the nerve to publish a book of stories that possessed few if any of the qualities that were earning his *ficciones* the huge acclaim he was currently enjoying. In the Foreword to *El informe de Brodie* he explained that his new stories were "realistas" [realistic] and "directos" [direct], and shared "ciertas afinidades íntimas" [certain secret affinities] (*OC* II: 399; *CF* 346). And, indeed, the collection "presents a very harsh critique of the various hierarchies that make up Argentina," examining "with equal harshness the upper classes, the working classes, and the gauchos and cattle-drovers" (Echavarría 148, 157). There was self-critique, too. In "Historia de Rosendo Juárez" [The Story from Rosendo Juárez], a favorite trope is undone when the eponymous *cuchillero,* a character in a Borges story from the 1930s, explains why he threw away his knife rather than accept a challenge to a duel. Other stories signal a distaste for the patrician superiority affected by his own family, whose ancestors included some figures who were important in the early years of the Republic. "La señora mayor" [The Old Lady] clings to the memory of her illustrious military forebear to keep the riff-raff of modern Buenos Aires at bay. In "Guayaquil," a patrician historian yields to his rival, a Jewish immigrant, the coveted honor of undertaking work on correspondence between the great South American Liberators Simón Bolívar and José de San Martín.

In *El informe de Brodie* Borges allowed readers a glimpse of the autobiographical dimension of his fiction through a subtle disclosure of his growing estrangement from the values of his own family and society. It may be no coincidence that the day after delivering the *Brodie* manuscript to his Argentine editor, he began to dictate "An Autobiographical Essay" (in English), which di Giovanni sent off to *The New Yorker* and later included in *The Aleph and Other Stories.* But Borges was growing tired of publishers' deadlines and translating with di Giovanni; his mind was on other things: on September 19, 1971, he published a poem in the newspaper *La Nación,* in which he declared: "Una sola mujer es tu cuidado, / igual a las demás, pero que es ella" [A woman is all that matters to you / one who is no different from the others, except that it is she] (Borges, *El oro de los tigres* 87). A few months later, he abruptly dismissed di Giovanni. Their partnership had produced *The Book of Imaginary Beings* (1969), *The Aleph and Other Stories, 1933–1969* (1970), and *Brodie's Report* (1972), all published by E. P. Dutton, as well as *Selected Poems, 1923–1967* (1972) for Delacorte Press.

Borges's reaction to the worsening violence and disorder in Argentina would do great damage to his image in Europe and America. When a second Peronist government was overthrown by the armed forces in 1976, his declarations of support for the military junta, together with endorsements of General Augusto Pinochet's brutal dictatorship in Chile, would earn him a reputation as a political reactionary that he would never quite live down. It ended his hopes of winning the Nobel Prize: his candidacy would be repeatedly opposed by a veteran member of the prize committee. In 1980, the Spanish literary establishment snubbed him by having this giant of world literature share the Cervantes Prize, the premier award in Hispanic letters, with a minor poet, Gerardo Diego. In 1983, he was decorated by the President of France with the Légion d'Honneur and signed up by Gallimard for their Pléiade series, a distinction which placed him in the company of the great writers of France. And yet, after a lecture at the Collège de France, attended by Michel Foucault and other luminaries, he was accused by a member of the audience of living in "an ivory tower." Borges replied: "I am very aware of what is happening in my country and in the world. And I have proved it—I criticized Perón in his time and now the generals and their government" (qtd. in Williamson, *Borges* 459–60). In fact, he had denounced the 1982 Malvinas-Falklands war with Britain and condemned the armed forces for their atrocities during the earlier guerrilla insurgency. Yet outside Argentina there was little awareness of his record as a public intellectual or of the principles underlying his apparently erratic political allegiances.[6]

Still, the Anglophone world's ingrained interest in literary biography would prove difficult to ignore. Glimmers are evident already among the early reviewers. Updike suspected that Borges's "textual diagrams" could be "ciphers for concealed emotions" (Alazraki 67) and pointed to "major obscurities," such as "his religious concerns and his affective life," and especially "physical love," which seemed to be "something remote, like an ancient religion" (70). George Steiner regretted the dearth of women in his fiction, other than as "blurred objects of men's fantasies or recollections" (Alazraki 122), as well as the absence of "a matrix of society" (123). Poirier felt he was "too little concerned with the glory of the human presence within the wastes of time" (Alazraki 107). The philosophical speculations, which had attracted so much theoretical work on the I "impersonality" of literary creation in France, suggested existential disquiet to some. John Barth compared Borges to Menelaus lost "in the larger labyrinth of the world" and seeking to arrive at "his 'true' self"; but the "aptest image for Borges" was that of "Theseus in the Cretan labyrinth," whose ultimate goal was to "go straight through the maze to the accomplishment of his work"; this was "a heroic enterprise, with salvation as its object" (Alazraki 92). George Steiner saw this quest for salvation in a mystical vein: we are surrounded by a "limitless network of significance" which Borges connected ultimately to the Aleph, "the final word . . . that is the name of God" (Alazraki 121). Paul de Man gave it a tragic sense: the creation of style was "an attempt at immortality" but "this attempt was bound to fail" (Alazraki 61). A "final confrontation [with God] throws its darkening shadow over Borges's entire work," for "with [God's] appearance the life of poetry comes to an end"; even so, "Borges refuses to give up his poetic predicament for a leap into faith" (61). John Updike put these stirrings of biographical curiosity in a nutshell by wondering about "the sense of life that drives [Borges] from unequivocal philosophical and critical assertion to the essential ambiguity of fiction" (Alazraki 72).

It was a French psychoanalyst, Didier Anzieu, who first attempted a searching biographical study, drawing on Freud, Lacan, and Melanie Klein and based on the "Autobiographical Essay" and on an analysis of major stories. Borges's bilingualism had produced in childhood a psychic disarray and sense of bodily fragmentation due to his separation from his Spanish-speaking mother and subjection to the English "code" of his father and English grandmother, a conflict which created a desire to recover the all-enveloping security of the primal bond with mother. This Oedipal struggle was inscribed in his writing: his psychic confusion was represented by metaphors like the labyrinth and the mirror, while tropes of the quest for a key to the universe, such as the Aleph and the Zahir, reflected the unconscious goal of reconciling the warring linguistic codes in coherent and unified literary forms.

Anzieu's interpretation was substantially expanded by the Uruguayan scholar, Emir Rodríguez Monegal, in his *Jorge Luis Borges. A Literary Biography* (1978). Before his appointment in 1969 to a professorship at Yale, Rodríguez Monegal had lived in Paris, where he had absorbed the poststructuralism of *Tel Quel*, as a consequence of which his role was informed by the Genette-inspired notion of "the reader as writer." He conceived the project as "a tacit pact" with Borges: he would write "the biography of the literary *oeuvre* called Borges," but whereas Borges had had to split himself into the narrator and protagonist of his "Autobiographical Essay," his own task was "simpler": "I had only to create the perspective of a third literary persona (the reader)" (Rodríguez Monegal, *Jorge Luis Borges* 478). His "main sources would not just be the usual biographical data but the texts themselves: texts authored by Borges alone as well as texts authored with the help of relatives, friends, collaborators, interviewers, critics, and even enemies" (Rodríguez Monegal, *Jorge Luis Borges* 478). The result would be "a commentary on and an extension of" the "Autobiographical Essay," for he "aspired to write on the interstices and margins left by [Borges's] own account" (Rodríguez Monegal, *Jorge Luis Borges* 478).

For Borges's psychological travails, Rodríguez Monegal turned to Anzieu's psycho-analytic interpretation, which he wanted to place in a broader context: "What is still to be done is to attempt to integrate that interpretation in the larger context of Borges' personal myth as it is presented both in the writing of his works and in the writing of his life—that is, in the writing of his literary (auto)biography" (Rodríguez Monegal, "Borges" 49). Borges's "personal myth" was rooted in an Oedipal conflict in which English culture, associated with his free-thinking father and English grandmother, was perceived to be superior to Hispanic culture, associated with mother's narrow-minded Catholicism and the alleged ignorance of her Argentine family. Rodríguez Monegal, however, refrained from delving too deeply into Borges's private life to avoid embarrassing his friend, though he did hint at sexual problems and at certain delib-erate omissions and misrepresentations in the "Autobiographical Essay." The biography came out eight years before its subject's death, so this precluded coverage of the late work, the controversial relationship with María Kodama, the disillusionment caused by Argentina's terrible crises, and the disputes resulting from his will and burial in Geneva.

The process of contextualization was substantially advanced by Daniel Balderston's landmark study, *Out of Context: Historical Reference and the Representation of Reality in Borges* (1993), which challenged Borges's reputation as an author of self-referring stories which bore little relation to the world outside the text. "The critical consensus had been that he was an 'escapist' writer," but this consensus was "profoundly mistaken" (Balderston 13). Through a detailed examination of seven stories from *Ficciones*, *El Aleph*, and *El informe de Brodie*, Balderston demonstrated that Borges's "writing is in-timately marked by the experience of twentieth-century Argentine history and politics, by life in Europe during World War I and just after" (15). This important book opened up new pathways for research and remains enormously influential.

A considerable obstacle to further contextualization was the muddled chronology of Borges's publications. He kept adding new, and sometimes older, texts to later editions of his books, and he continually revised the poems of his youth, even omit-ting a good number from successive editions of his *Obras completas*. In the case of the three collections of essays published in the 1920s, he refused to have them reprinted in his lifetime. The confusion was worse in translation: it was not until the publication of the two volumes in Gallimard's Pléiade series (1993, 1999) that a chronological overview of his output became available in French. Things were worse in English because of the diversity of publishers and translators, their preference for anthologies, the neglect of his poetry, and disputes over translation rights. As a result, Borges's career appeared to be full of gaps and surprising turning-points. Why did he conceal or disguise so much of his youthful writing? Why had he (supposedly) abandoned poetry after 1929? Why did he cease publishing new stories in 1953 and turn to poetry once more? And why did the stories in *El informe de Brodie* show few, if any, of the metaphysical qualities of his earlier *Ficciones*? The question of how to relate the Borges who claimed to write "about myself, my personal experiences" (Christ, *The Paris Review*) to the author celebrated for his postmodernist fictions became even more pressing with the publication in 1989 of Estela Canto's memoir of their tormented relationship, which laid bare his troubles with women stemming from conflicts within the family. In the 1990s, the re-edition of the proscribed books of youthful essays and the publication in book form of a good number of his uncollected writings for magazines and the press offered more insights into the evolution of his ideas and beliefs.

A comprehensive and detailed contextualization of the full span of Borges's life and work, based on extensive research on primary sources, was Edwin Williamson's *Borges, A Life* (2004). Instead of the reclusive sage oblivious of the world beyond his bookish imagination, Borges was portrayed as a combative public intellectual imbued with a profound sense of Argentine history.[7] His inner conflicts were addressed, not through psychoanalytic theory, but by reading his master-symbols (e.g., library, mirror, labyrinth, sword, dagger, tiger, rose) as a poetic code that, when placed in a sufficiently meticulous biographical context, could yield fresh insights into the emotional "subsoil" of his writing, as conditioned by personal experience over time.[8]

Paul de Man had written that "to understand the full complexity" of Borges's artistic personality one would have to follow his "enterprise from the start and see it as the unfolding of a poetic destiny" (61). *Borges, A Life* developed a closely documented interpretation of this "unfolding" based on Borges's assertion: "From the time I was a boy it was tacitly understood that I had to fulfil the literary destiny that circumstances had denied my father . . . I was expected to be a writer" (Borges, "Autobiographical Essay" 211). The burden of this expectation aroused a desire to overcome his sense of "la nadería de la personalidad" [the nothingness of personality] (the title he gave to a youthful essay), by writing a work that would confirm the uniqueness of the self: "Ya he escrito más de un libro para poder escribir, acaso, una página. *La página justificativa, la que sea abreviatura de mi destino*" [I have already written more than one book in order to write, perhaps, one page. *The page that justifies me, that summarizes my destiny*] (*El tamaño de mi esperanza* 116; *SNF* 27, emphasis added).[9] But in order to discover his unique self through his writing he needed the inspiration of a muse, for not only would love of another person dissipate "la nadería de la personalidad," it would— as imagined in texts like "El Aleph" and "El Zahir"—reveal one's true relation to the world: "Para el amor no satisfecho / el mundo es misterio, / un misterio que el amor satisfecho / parece comprender" [The world is a mystery / for love unsatisfied, / a mystery which satisfied love / appears to understand] (qtd. in Borges, *El idioma de los argentinos* [121]). His writing, therefore, was intimately bound up with his difficulties in love and sex, hence the pivotal impact of a failed romance in the 1920s with his protégée, the poet Norah Lange, who suddenly deserted him for a hated rival.[10] This emotional disaster was compounded by the failure of his *criollismo* (the progressive, democratic form of cultural nationalism he had championed in the 1920s), due to the rise of proto-fascist *nacionalismo*, and this double blow would change the expressionist, "romantic" young poet into the reticent, solipsistic "classical" writer who produced the *ficciones*.[11]

The desire to fulfill his literary destiny still haunted him in middle age. In "El milagro secreto" [The Secret Miracle], a Jewish writer (or at least a writer interested in Judaism), believing that his unfinished play could "rescatar (de manera simbólica) lo fundamental de su vida" [rescue (albeit symbolically) what was fundamental to his life], asks God to spare him from a Nazi firing squad long enough to complete this work, "que puede justificarme y justificarte" [which can justify me and justify Thee as well] (*OC* I: 511; *CF* 160, 161). But Borges himself kept being rejected by what he called "una cadena de mujeres" [a chain of women] (Bioy Casares 991). His confidant Bioy Casares wrote in his diary: "Refiere Borges las desdichas de su amor romántico, las vicisitudes, los análisis, las conjeturas" [Borges tells me about the misfortunes of his love-life, the ups-and-downs, the analyses, the conjectures] (Bioy Casares 996), and noted: "habla de su *trágico destino repetido* y de que por una fatalidad siempre aparece un hombre y se las quita" [He talks about his *recurrent tragic destiny* and about how, by some perverse fate, a man always appears and takes them away from him] (Bioy Casares 963, emphasis added).[12] Far from arriving at an understanding of "the mystery of the world" through the love of a muse, Borges felt ever more estranged from his homeland as he witnessed its inexorable slide into such violence and economic chaos that he could no longer make sense of Argentine history. His final relationship with María Kodama offered some relief from this mounting distress and brought about further changes in his literary ideas and practice.

I have argued that Borges owes his status as a world-class writer to his reception in Europe and the United States. His enormous influence was due to two factors, both fortuitous. In the first place, his work became known at a time when a younger generation of European and American writers were looking to break away from various kinds of social and psychological realism. Borges, moreover, was—supremely—a "writers' writer," not just for his prodigious bookishness and unceasing explorations of the nature and purpose of literary creation, but also for his liberating inventiveness with narrative form—he rehabilitated fantasy as a resource for the modern writer; favored modes of storytelling more ancient than the novel; blurred high and low genres by infusing thrillers, science fiction, and detective stories with philosophical and existential concerns; and even brought scholarly essays, book reviews, and footnotes within the bounds of fiction. Second, his *ficciones* and essays struck a chord with intellectuals when a critique of Enlightenment rationalism happened to be under way in France. The new theories of poststructuralism and deconstruction then crossed the Atlantic and melded with American postmodernism, providing fertile ground for his enthusiastic reception in the Global North.

Borges's selective appropriation by foreign elites, however, resulted in his being perceived as a deracinated writer wholly absorbed in the life of the mind, for whom literary creation was a form of "rewriting" that excluded the possibility of originality. But, as Balderston argued: "The recovery of the 'context' . . . is a necessary stage in the interpretation of the text, yet speaking of it is necessarily transgressive, a 'return of the repressed'" (16). Easily the most "transgressive," and therefore the most "repressed," of all forms of contextualization is the biographical approach, owing to poststructuralist attacks on the "author" and the Anglo-American aversion to "the intentional fallacy" (Wimsatt and Beardsley). Although Borges studies have come a long way since he was described as "a European man of letters who would feel at home in London as well as Paris," his own understanding of what he was about as a writer has not been sufficiently taken into account, and his actual literary ideas and practices, and especially their evolution, have succumbed to theories superimposed on his texts by critics and scholars. (For example, the French theorists failed to notice that "Pierre Menard" was a bitter satire, rather than a justification of the "death of the author.") Although the myriad subtleties of invention cannot, of course, be reduced to context, a biographical approach can shed light on the formation and growth of Borges's artistic personality. As the story "El otro" [The Other] so poignantly reveals, the Borges of 1918 was quite different from the Borges of 1968.

Virginia Woolf's famous image for the mysterious connection between fiction and life applies to Borges, too.

> Fiction is like a spider's web, attached ever so lightly perhaps, but still attached, to life at all four corners. . . . When the web is pulled askew, hooked up at the edge, torn in the middle, one remembers that these webs are not spun in mid-air by incorporeal creatures, but are the work of suffering human beings, and are attached to grossly material things, like health and money and the houses we live in. (41–42)

Borges needs to be released from the ivory tower in which he has been incarcerated and restored to historical reality, to the trials and tribulations of living in this world. At the height of his fame, he insisted that "en mis cuentos hay emoción. No puede escribirse sin emoción" [There is emotion in my stories. It isn't possible to write without emotion] (Bioy Casares 766–67). By his own reckoning even his most cerebral fictions were fueled by emotion. On receiving a prize for *Ficciones* in 1945, he declared that he had been "alimentado de azarosos venenos"—"de sombra, de amargura, de frustración, de inacabables tardes inútiles y de olvido" [nourished on dangerous poisons—darkness, bitterness, frustration, interminable useless evenings, and neglect] (*Borges en* Sur 300–02). I would contend that the astonishing originality and power of his writing were due to his genius for inventing metaphysical fantasies, philosophical tales, and pseudo-erudite essays that served as vehicles for his all-too-real desolation and angst. The

420 EDWIN WILLIAMSON

integration of the three contexts—"cosmopolitan," Argentine, and biographical—would give us a fuller, truer measure of his stature as one of the great writers of the twentieth century.

Notes

1. See Wijnterp (89–147) for a publication history of the first translations into French.
2. All translations of quotations into English in this chapter are my own, unless otherwise indicated within the main text, thus: (*CF*) for *Collected Fictions*; (*SNF*) for *Selected Non-Fiction*; (Borges 1970) for "An Autobiographical Essay."
3. My account is based on Barral (Williamson, *Borges* 273–75).
4. Barthes himself was less interested in Borges than some of his French contemporaries. For more on this line of thought, see Cámpora.
5. See Wijnterp (263–323) for a publication history of the first translations into English.
6. For more on Borges's reception in Argentina, see Pastormerlo; for his global reception, see Hoyos, Corwin, and Scholz, all in this volume.
7. See an overview of this aspect of his life in Williamson ("Borges as a Public Intellectual").
8. For an example of how certain master-symbols are articulated in this "poetic code," see Williamson ("Borges's Libraries").
9. See Williamson ("Borges's Libraries") for a condensed analysis of Borges's dialectic between the self and the non-self.
10. See Williamson (*Borges* 149–74), for this pivotal experience.
11. The distinction between "romantic" and the "classical" authors was crucial for Borges's evolution toward the invention of his *ficciones*. See Williamson ("Borges in Context" 209–10, 212–13).
12. For the friendship of Borges and Bioy Casares, see Williamson ("Borges y Bioy" 30–37).

Works Cited

Alazraki, Jaime, ed. *Critical Essays on Jorge Luis Borges*. G. K. Hall, 1987.

Anzieu, Didier. "Le corps et le code dans les contes de J. L. Borges." *Nouvelle Revue de Psychanalyse*, no. 3, Printemps 1971, Gallimard, pp. 177–205.

Ashbery, John. "A Game with Shifting Mirrors." *Critical Essays on Jorge Luis Borges*. Edited by Jaime Alazraki.` G. K. Hall, 1987, pp. 93–95.

Balderston, Daniel. *Out of Context: Historical Reference and the Representation of Reality in Borges*. Duke University Press, 1993.

Barral, Carlos. *Los años sin excusa. Memorias*, vol. 2. Barral, 1978.

Barth, John. "The Literature of Exhaustion." *Critical Essays on Jorge Luis Borges*. Edited by Jaime Alazraki. G. K. Hall, 1987, pp. 83–92.

Barthes, Roland. "The Death of the Author." *Image-Music-Text*. Edited and translated by Stephen Heath. Hill and Wang, 1977, pp. 142–48.

Bioy Casares, Adolfo. *Borges*, edited by Daniel Martino. Destino, 2006.

Blanchot, Maurice. "L'infini littéraire: L'Aleph." *Le livre à venir*. Gallimard, 1959, pp. 130–34.

Bollinger, Rosemarie. "Borges en Alemania." *Cuadernos Hispanoamericanos*, nos. 505–507, 1992, pp. 221–28.

Borges, Jorge Luis. "An Autobiographical Essay." *The Aleph and Other Stories, 1933–1969*. Edited and translated by Norman Thomas di Giovanni in collaboration with the author. E.P. Dutton, 1970. (See also, *Critical Essays on Jorge Luis Borges*. Edited by Jaime Alazraki. G. K. Hall, 1987, pp. 21–55.)

Borges, Jorge Luis. *A Personal Anthology*. Edited and with a Foreword by Anthony Kerrigan. Grove Press, 1967.

Borges, Jorge Luis. *Borges en* Sur, *1931–1980*. Emecé, 1999.

Borges, Jorge Luis. *Collected Fictions*, translated by Andrew Hurley. Viking Penguin, 1998.

Borges, Jorge Luis. *El oro de los tigres*. Emecé, 1972.

Borges, Jorge Luis. *El tamaño de mi esperanza/El idioma de los argentinos*. [1926/1928] Debolsillo, 2012.

Borges, Jorge Luis. *Obras completas*. 4 vols. Emecé, 1996.

Borges, Jorge Luis. *Selected Non-Fictions*, edited by Eliot Weinberger. Viking Penguin, 1998.

Burgin, Richard. *Conversations with Borges*. Holt, Reinhart, and Winston, 1969.

Cahiers de L'Herne: Jorge Luis Borges. L'Herne, 1964.

Caillois, Roger, ed. and transl. *Jorge Luis Borges: Labyrinthes*. Gallimard, 1953.

Cámpora, Magdalena. "¿Y Borges? Sobre un desinterés de Barthes." *Variaciones Borges*, vol. 36, 2013, pp. 53–63.

Canto, Estela. *Borges a contraluz*. Espasa-Calpe, 1989.

Christ, Ronald. "The Art of Fiction XXXIX: Jorge Luis Borges: An Interview." *The Paris Review*, no. 40, Winter-Spring, 1967, pp. 116–64.

de Man, Paul. "A Modern Master." *Critical Essays on Jorge Luis Borges*. Edited by Jaime Alazraki. G. K. Hall, 1987, pp. 55–62.

Echavarría, Arturo. "*Brodie's Report*." Williamson, 2013, pp. 146–59.

Foucault, Michel. "Le langage à l'infini." *Tel Quel*, 15, 1963, pp. 44–53.

Foucault, Michel. *The Order of Things*, anonymous translator. Routledge, 1989.

Genette, Gérard. "L'utopie littéraire." *Figures: essais*. Seuil, 1966, pp. 123–32.

Gordon, Robert S. C. "Borges in Italy." *Jorge Luis Borges in Context*. Edited by Robin Fiddian, Cambridge University Press, 2021, pp. 259–66.

Ibarra, Néstor. "Préface." *Jorge Luis Borges: Fictions*, translated by Néstor Ibarra and Paul Verdevoye. Gallimard, 1951.

Kazin, Alfred. "Meeting Borges." *Critical Essays on Jorge Luis Borges*. Edited by Jaime Alazraki. G. K. Hall, 1987, pp. 127–30.

Köhler-Busch, Madelon. "The Reception of Borges in Germany: A Timeline of Translations." *Moenia*, 14, 2008, pp. 137–44.

Larkin, Philip. Interviewed by Robert Phillips. *The Paris Review*, no. 30, 1982, https://www.the parisreview.org/interviews/3153/the-art-of-poetry-no-30-philip-larkin.

Poirier, Richard. "The Politics of Self-Parody." *Critical Essays on Jorge Luis Borges*. Edited by Jaime Alazraki. G. K. Hall, 1987, pp. 96–107.

Robbe-Grillet, Alain. *Pour un nouveau roman*. Minuit, 1963, p. 9.

Rodríguez Monegal, Emir. "Borges, the Reader." *Diacritics*, 4, Winter 1974, pp. 41–49.

Rodríguez Monegal, Emir. *Jorge Luis Borges: A Literary Biography*. E. P. Dutton, 1978.

Steiner, George. "Tigers in the Mirror." *Critical Essays on Jorge Luis Borges*. Edited by Jaime Alazraki. G. K. Hall, 1987, pp. 116–24.

Updike, John. "The Author as Librarian." *Critical Essays on Jorge Luis Borges*. Edited by Jaime Alazraki. G. K. Hall, 1987, pp. 62–76.

Williamson, Edwin. *Borges, A Life*. Viking, 2004.

Williamson, Edwin. "Borges in Context: The Autobiographical Dimension." *The Cambridge Companion to Jorge Luis Borges*. Edited by Edwin Williamson. Cambridge University Press, 2013, pp. 209–10, 212–13.

Williamson, Edwin. "Borges as a Public Intellectual: The Challenges of Building a Post-Colonial Nation." *Literaturwissenschaftliches Jahrbuch*, vol. 63, no. 1, 2022. pp. 177–203.

Williamson, Edwin. "Borges's Libraries." *Libraries in Literature*. Edited by Alice Crawford and Robert Crawford, Oxford University Press, 2022, pp. 196–208. [Spanish version: "Las bibliotecas de Borges." *Letras Libres*, vol. 261, 2023, pp. 31–37.]

Williamson, Edwin. "Borges y Bioy: una amistad entre biombos." *Letras Libres*, vol. 81, 2008, pp. 30–37.

Williamson, Edwin. *The Cambridge Companion to Jorge Luis Borges*. Cambridge University Press, 2013.

Wijnterp, Lies. *Making Borges: The Reception of Borges's Work in France and the US*. PhD thesis, Radboud University, 2015.

Wimsatt, William, and Monroe Beardsley. "The Intentional Fallacy." *The Sewanee Review*, vol. 54, no. 3, 1946, pp. 468–88. Later included in Wimsatt, Willam. *The Verbal Icon: Studies in the Meaning of Poetry*. University of Michigan Press, 1954.

Woolf, Virginia. *A Room of One's Own*. Houghton Mifflin Harcourt, 1989.

CHAPTER 24

BORGES IN THE EASTERN BLOC

LÁSZLÓ SCHOLZ

THE historic dynamic of the center versus periphery model has received significant attention from scholars with respect to certain directions of influence: Darío in Paris, Moholy-Nagy in Berlin, Eisenstein in New York. But what we know about the relationship between periphery and periphery is much more limited. In general, it has been restricted to anecdotal evidence about efforts that seemed fairly inevitable and motivated by personal contact or political occurrences and, after a brief period, ended up dissolving into the vast domain of the center. Yet there are other cases that produce a series of variants on this history that alter traditional bipolar relationships and nuance the concept of "center" itself.

"RUSIA" [RUSSIA] AND "MAÑANA" [TOMORROW]: THE FIRST BORGES TEXTS TRANSLATED INTO ANOTHER LANGUAGE

Before the news media created the "Socialist Bloc" or "Eastern Bloc," an expression coined as a result of World War II, the vast territory between Germany and Russia was divided into Central and Eastern Europe. Central Europe was comprised of countries such as Czechoslovakia, Hungary, and Poland, which, having been part of the Austro-Hungarian Empire, were culturally closer to Western Europe. The Eastern Bloc was a much larger and more heterogeneous expanse, with a significant number of languages,[1] religions, and traditions. Borges first appeared in *Mitteleuropa* in 1921, when the literary journal *Ma*, having relocated to Vienna, published a "verse version" of Borges's poem "Rusia" in Hungarian, making it the very first translation of any Borges text (Barbeira

424   LÁSZLÓ SCHOLZ

33). How did "Rusia" end up in a Hungarian journal? The original had been published in Spain, but, from there, it is equally possible that poem was given to Lajos Kassák, the director of *Ma*, by Guillermo de Torre or that it arrived with Tadeusz Peiper, a key figure in the Polish avant-garde whose travels from Spain to Warsaw around this time also took him through Vienna. However it happened, a Borges poem appeared in the Hungarian journal *Ma* on September 15, 1921, in Vienna, and in excellent company, given the texts by Moholy-Nagy, Arp, and Mayakovsky also featured in the issue.

This phenomenon occurred again a few months later in another country in the region: in February 1922, his poem "Mañana" was published in Polish in an ephemeral journal, *Nowa Sztuka*, out of Warsaw. The translator was the aforementioned Tadeusz Peiper, who presented a selection of "Spanish" poets for an issue. Alongside Peiper's presentation of "Luis Borges" were Vicente Huidobro, "Juan" Rivas Panedas, Humberto Rivas, Guillermo de Torre, Ernesto López Parra, and Rafael Lasso de la Vega. In other Central European countries, we also find unpredictable traces of Borges. In Czechoslovakia, for example, in 1926, the journal *Host*, translated some lines of "Anatomía de mi Ultra" [Anatomy of My Ultra] and mentions the poems "Gesta maximalista" [Maximalist Achievement] and "Rusia" (Černý, "O španělském Ultraismu" 46–47). Two years later, Jiří Mašek published a brief note in *Rozpravy Aventina*, the journal associated with a Czech publishing house, in which he reviews Borges's earliest works and cites a few lines of "Rusia" (144). In 1930, Václav Černý himself would publish an article about "Spain's newest young poets and poetry" in *Literární noviny* and translate a few verses of "Rusia" and "Calle desconocida" [Unknown Street] and two complete poems, "Remordimiento por cualquier muerte" [Remorse for Any Death] and "Amorosa anticipación" [Anticipation of Love] ("Nejmladší španělská poezie" 6).

This first relationship between avant-garde poets from Latin America and Central Europe is indicative in the sense that Argentina and Hungary or Poland do not meet directly in Buenos Aires or Budapest or Krakow but halfway in the Western center and that in their contact, ideology is a decisive factor. In this era, Borges professed some "Red" positions; Kassák, for example, was forced to flee Hungary after the fall of the Republic of Councils (*Räterepublik*) for expressing similar political ideals. They also share an attitude typical in the peripheries: interest in exploring and introducing the most recent trends of the West into their own cultural environment. Borges writes and translates texts, for example, about the English avant-garde, which were little known in the Hispanophone world; Peiper, upon returning to his homeland, founded an entire avant-garde movement in Krakow; Kassák, for his part, included dozens of Western European authors in his journal between 1916 and 1925.

CHANGE OF CENTER

After their first fortuitous encounter within the Western center, Argentina and *Mitteleuropa* would grow distant for the next three decades and, with the end of World

War II, remain separated for another thirty years. The Iron Curtain closed Eastern Europe off, forcing its complete dependence on Moscow as cultural center for the next forty-five years. What system came to govern the realm of literary institutions that made publishing Borges an impossibility in the Communist Bloc? For the publication and translation of books, as with every other area of life, a central plan controlled by the Party and its respective professional and regional bodies had been designed. In every country, a State Institution was created (e.g., the General Office of Books and Publishing) which organized and supervised the entire process of book production from presses, the provision of paper, distribution, bookstores, and pricing to the selection of which books to publish. A very limited number of publishing houses were founded—all of them part of the State (in the prewar years, by way of example, in 1938, Hungary had some one hundred publishing houses [Bart 48] and during the socialist era only just over twenty)— and each was assigned a unique thematic and genre profile as well as a director who had the full confidence of the Party. Text selection for publication was based on ideological criteria that was doubly enforced: publishers obligatorily practiced self-censorship and, facing any doubts, could consult the General Office or ask a local literary critic who was in the know about the most recent ideological trends in Moscow. In Russia, censorship grew to imperial dimensions as an institution with regional branches, private libraries, and access to Western media. There were a few basic classifications a text had to overcome to be considered for translation. In Hungary, for example, they were known as the "TTT," which in English would translate to "Prohibited, Permitted, Patronized" (Bart 33). The reasons a text might be rejected were primarily based on its political content: for many years nothing considered anti-Socialist or anti-Soviet could be published, but the use of slang, sexual and racial issues, and avant-garde formal experimentation were also disapproved of.

Literary translation still played a key role in the literary polysystem of the Bloc because, on the one hand, in this polyglot region, it constituted a cultural space with a long tradition that could not be suppressed, and, on the other, translations could fill the void left by all the national works that had been eliminated. One look at the statistics for translated works reveals the political manipulation. In Hungary, for example, between 1945 and 1978, translations generally constituted about 45 percent of all published literary works; during the years of confiscation of private property (1949–1950), the figure rose to 48.5–56 percent. A similar increase could be seen in 1957 and 1958, when, with 55 percent of all published texts being translations from abroad, an attempt was made to defuse the tension that had remained after the failed revolution of 1956 (Bart 64–65).

Amid all the tribulations that befell Eastern Europe's postwar countries, there was one element that proved favorable for Borges's reception in the following decades: those of the nations of *Mitteleuropa* that had been part of the eastern zone of the West continued to uphold that legacy in the westernmost region of the Eastern Bloc. Both by tacit approval of the new center and by rights acquired through violent confrontations against that power (1956 in Budapest, 1968 in Prague, 1980 in Warsaw), these countries' peripheral situations fomented dual orientations toward opposing centers allowing them to continue their relationships with the West to some extent while continuing to abide by Moscow's Eastern directives. The history of Borges's reception in the region can be traced along a path of progressive Westernization led by the Western peripheries of the Bloc until the collapse of the Eastern system in 1989–1991.

As was to be expected, appearances of translations of Borges in the 1950s were very limited in the region. In fact, until Stalin's death (1953) and Khrushchev's well-known political "Thaw" (1954), not a single text by the Argentine author was published. It was Poland and Hungary that broke the ice. Falling back on the solution it had used in 1921, Hungary published some stories by Borges in literary magazines resulting from Hungarian emigrations to the Western world. "A halott" ("El muerto" [The Dead Man]) appeared in 1952 in Buenos Aires, then in 1955, in Munich, as did five stories in *Irodalmi Újság*, which continued to appear in Vienna, Paris, and London between 1958 and 1964 (Kiss and Scholz 598, 613). Who were the translators? Renowned postwar emigrants. The first two texts were signed by Szabolcs Vajay, an eminent historian and genealogist considered persona non grata in Hungary during the socialist years; publications in London were probably the work of Béla Szász, a journalist and politician who fled the country in 1957; both had lived in Argentina for several years. During the same period, Poland's attitude was resolute and daring in founding the cult of Borges that would continue to grow over the following years. Between 1955 and 1960, no fewer than sixteen texts from *Fervor de Buenos Aires* [*Fervor of Buenos Aires*], *Historia universal de la infamia* [*A Universal History of Infamy*], and *El Aleph* were printed in national magazines—works that were not yet being read in many parts of Europe (Łazicki 71–72). Borges's repeated appearances in émigré journals did not cease altogether in the decades that followed. Among them we can mention several Borges poems that were included in the Munich-based journal *Suchasnist* translated into Ukrainian (Orlova 100–01) and various texts published in translation in Polish émigré journals circulating in London and Paris (Łazicki 14).

The Thaw and the Weapons of the Weak

The real thaw, however, occurred only in the 1960s, with the relaxing of strictures from the previous decade and the international opening brought by Khrushchev. While there was a turn toward capitalism and a certain Westernization of cultural institutions, we should also remember that the Formentor Prize was awarded to Borges in the same year the Berlin Wall was built. Most relevant for the publication of foreign authors during this time was the new awareness and consolidation of interdependence at all levels among the peripheries and the center. The image Haraszti uses in the foreword to *The Velvet Prison* for the creators of the socialist era suggests the "mutual embrace" of censors and artists alike who "diligently and cheerfully cultivate the gardens of art together" (5–7). There were naturally some scandals, for example in Poland, where on more than one occasion, Borges enthusiasts surreptitiously removed pages censored by the State, replacing them with the original text (Sobol-Jurczykowski 199). In principle, Borges's works were blacklisted on ideological grounds, but there was a degree of tolerance for certain tricks editors used to be able to publish at least some of his works; these are the so-called "weapons of the weak," to use James E. Scott's famous formulation, to which most publishers resorted throughout the Bloc.

The first ploy for publishing any author not tolerated by the authorities for ideological or aesthetic reasons was to include them in an anthology. These collections were very popular and had surprisingly large print runs that were promoted for their value in cultural dissemination. Indeed, the idea to publish classic authors in major collections for popular readers dates back to initial projects led by Gorky during the Russian revolution. The themes, formats, and selections varied significantly, but they all included a certain percentage of texts that had not appeared in individual books. Thus was published in Hungarian in 1967, forty-four years after it appeared in Spanish, "Ismeretlen utca" ("Calle desconocida") from *Fervor de Buenos Aires*, which declared "que toda casa es un candelabro / donde las vidas de los hombres arden / como velas aisladas, / que todo inmediato paso nuestro / camina sobre Gólgotas" [that every house is a branching candlestick / where the lives of men burn / like single candles, / that each haphazard step we take / treads on Golgothas] (*SP* 11). This vision of the world presented independently would not have met with approval by any ideologist or socialist censor, but, as part of an anthology, the text "passed" without problem. That same year, "Delia Elena San Marco" was published in a purely popular collection, as the title itself indicates: *Szerelmes ezüst kalendárium* [*Silver Calendar of Love*] which contained 365 love poems written by individual poets; among so many names, Borges surely did not attract the attention of any censor, but he would have liked, I think, being a link in such a circular silver chain that year. Borges also appears in a Czech anthology of science fiction, a genre that would later be used quite frequently in the Bloc for related purposes. The 1962 volume *Laberynt* compiled by Robert Abernathy contained texts by Bradbury, Padgett, Heinlein, Robinson, and Borges's "La biblioteca de Babel" [The Library of Babel], among others. In Bulgaria, "Kraglita razvalini" ("Las ruinas circulares" [The Circular Ruins]) was included in a collection of Latin American fantastic literature published in Plovdiv in 1979. In Romania, a similar selection was printed in July 1966, in the magazine *Viața Românească*, which included Borges's "El Aleph," a number of national authors, and two established figures of the speculative genre, the Soviet Union's Valentina Juravliova and US science fiction writer Ray Bradbury. In Zagreb in 1968, "La lotería en Babilonia" [The Lottery in Babylon], translated into Serbian by Antun Šoljan, was included in a collection entitled *100 odabranih novela svjetske književnosti* [*One Hundred Stories of World Literature*]. In late 1960s and 1970s, the anthology trick was deployed again: Polish editors publishing five collections, Hungarians publishing three, and always with titles that were as general as possible (e.g., *Égtájak, Ewokacje* [*The Four Winds, Evocations*]), so that they could include authors from anywhere in the world.

Yet how did this method work in the case of Borges when dealing with explicitly Latin American selections from the twentieth century? Many times, Borges was simply not included, or, when he was, editors resorted to another trick: adding "clarifying" paratexts such as a title, subtitle, prologue, or biographical note to deter any ideological misunderstanding or aesthetic "misinterpretation." In Budapest in April 1963, a selection of three texts by Borges, Juan Rulfo, and H. Téllez, respectively, was published in the magazine *Nagyvilág*, under the title "South American Storytellers," concealing ideological and aesthetic differences within an expansive geographical category. Although the biographical information did not specify the original date, the following comment was added to "Hombre de la esquina rosada" [Man on Pink Corner], Borges's first text published in the People's Republic of Hungary: "Despite the fact that Borges is characterized by cosmopolitanism (in his work, realism intermixes with mystical elements), international critics consider him one of the most important figures in Latin American literature" (639). When "El Sur" [The South] was translated into Hungarian in 1969, it required the following interpretation: "This multi-layered text seems to highlight the idea that from the real, we want to pass into dreams, and from dreams to the real, but our destiny is to suffer in both places: refuge means suffering, subjection means suffering. But its deepest meaning is that idle dreams are ruinous, as are hesitant acts" (319).

The paratext can also reveal surprising lapses in censorship. "El milagro secreto" [The Secret Miracle] was published in Slovak in an anthology in 1969, something hard to believe given the references that appear in the text from its first lines: Prague in March 1939, tanks, a protagonist possibly of Jewish blood, the translator of *Sepher Yezirach*, the author of an unfinished tragedy called *The Enemies*. However, the biographical note written by translator Vladimír Oleríny describes Borges in superlatives as a renovator of the continent's literature who forged an original unity of literary genres and undoubtedly surpassed the borders of Latin America. How could the publication of that story and that commentary be justified just a few months after the invasion of Prague by Soviet troops? In fact, although Czechoslovakia was occupied in August 1968, the new pro-Soviet regime was not consolidated until the early 1970s, and editors took advantage of the brief interregnum to audaciously uphold the spirit of the Prague Spring.

That same decade, "La escritura del dios" [The Writing of the God] was published in Romania in a Hungarian literary magazine with Italian illustrations and a very brief biographical note. On the same page, below Borges's text, as a kind of counterbalance, was a review of an academic reader published under the title *Introducere în literatura Americii latine* [*Introduction to Latin American Literature*] by Francisc Păcurariu (1965), a Romanian diplomat and writer. The reviewer quotes Miguel Ángel Asturias, who wrote the prologue to the text, to emphasize that literature allows readers to learn, for example, "the laborious efforts of our peoples, students, women, urban and peasant masses" (7). The reviewer then goes on to state that the favored trend in twentieth-century literature is realism and that the great figures of Latin America profess revolutionary ideas of the peasantry, and have anti-imperialist aspirations and, not infrequently, socialist consciousnesses. Closing, with a wink to the reader, the reviewer says what he had set out to communicate: "This is obviously not the only way to organically unite narrative and socialist ideology" (7).

What happened a year later must have been a joke, one very appropriate to Borges at that, by the translator or the editors. The true story cannot be devised from the legends of the time, but the May 1964 issue of the Hungarian magazine *Nagyvilág* printed a text with the title *Mindörökre* [*Until Eternity*], in which the translator introduced a

Borges manuscript sent to him by a friend abroad. It begins like this: "Paloma effortlessly hopped over the mud wall of the chicken pen, landing right on the rocky part, like she used to do as a child. The goat also tends to slip around there, that's why folks keep saying that 'it should be covered with some stones'—but they never do it" (662). The work receives paratextual commentary in a biographical note as follows: "The story that we have published—its original title is *Lacos* (sic) *indisolubles*—was sent to the translator in handwritten form from Argentina; in contrast to the mystical inclinations of the writer, one notices in this instance a social realist sensibility" (800). Two months later, a rectification of the apocryphal account appeared in Issue 7 of the journal: "we informed the author and the editor in Buenos Aires of the text's publication. To our surprise, they replied that the story we published is not the work of the prominent author. We will do everything possible to explore the reason for this misunderstanding or mystification" (1119).

The most important channel for accessing authors who were not aligned with Soviet ideology was undoubtedly literary magazines. From today's perspective, Moscow's system was impressive: a guiding body was created at the center, the famous journal *Inostrannaia Literatura* [*Foreign Literature*], which had several antecedents that functioned similarly in the previous decades. The journal had several "branches" in each member country which separated world literature from national writing and always operated under political control. The obvious top-down structure, however, did not lead to total dependence. In fact, if we review the list of authors and texts published in the national capitals of the Bloc, it immediately becomes clear that a large number of texts by a given writer only appeared during certain periods and, above all, only in certain countries of the East. With this arrangement, the magazines fulfilled multiple functions in the hands of the politicians; beyond representing the official line, they contained a heavy dose of "the forbidden" for their intellectual readers, sometimes producing "daring" issues in an attempt to prove the freedom of the foreign press and the continuity of the previously established tradition of literary translations. No doubt there was a certain "tug-of-war" between center and periphery, but various national branches built a "buffer" with room to introduce more individual solutions as long as basic ideological principles were left unquestioned. Decisions were in the hands of journal editors who were well versed in the methods of ideological self-monitoring and regarded the center as an institution only for consultation. The data we have from the period of Khrushchev's Thaw (1955–1964) make an eloquent case on its own: while for Western authors, only 20 percent of translations overlap between the Soviet Union and Hungary, more than 55 percent of the texts rendered into Hungarian did not appear in the central Russian journal during that same period (Takács 58).

Let us take as an example the rather dramatic initial path taken by the Hungarian journal *Nagyvilág* from the moment of its foundation in 1956. The first issue was intended to be released in January, bringing a certain anti-Stalinist spirit to literary life, but the only issue to come out that year appeared only in October, a few days before the 23rd: the beginning of the armed conflict with the Soviet troops. The issue reflects the culmination of the turbulent months during which the writers' association played a decisive role. The introduction was written by none other than György Lukács himself, who had taken an active part in the "counterrevolutionary" events, for which he was later expelled from the country for a few months. In the October introduction, "Magyar irodalom—Világirodalom" [Hungarian Literature—World Literature] he noted that "The 20th Congress put an end to the dogmatic leadership and bureaucratic, sectarian management of literature. Neither writers nor readers will, in the future, be regarded as children to be minded, but rather as adults who are fully aware of their responsibility" (5). The list of authors included in the first issue paints a more than balanced picture: authors from the Bloc appeared alongside Dylan Thomas, Thomas Mann, Valery Larbaud, Graham Greene, Giosuè Carducci, Bertolt Brecht, Boris Pasternak, and Ernest Hemingway. Their texts were accompanied by essays dealing with topics such as the status of Russian and Italian publications, the reading habits of young workers in the country, dilemmas faced by the GDR when considering the future after Stalin, the historical avant-garde, and, to everyone's great surprise (who could travel to the West in those years?), memoirs of trips to Paris and Amsterdam. Was there to be any mention of Latin America? As hard as it is to believe, just a single poem by Ecuadorian Eugenio Moreno Heredia was included. The second issue came out only in April 1957, with an introduction entitled "After the Storm" which, despite the repressive crisis in the country, essentially just reaffirmed the plans outlined in the first issue because "literature that refuses inspiration, lessons, experiences of common beauty, is threatened to remain dry, dehumanized, discolored, monotonous" (Kardos 4). In other words, the journal, with not a few writers in jail or living as refugees in some Western country, did not change course from the 1956 issue; instead of adapting to the hardline politics of the moment, it presented a second issue quite similar to the first, a strategy that surely must have been approved and monitored.

Which Spanish and Latin American authors appeared in 1957 and in the following years? The journal did not follow the Moscow core of *Inostrannaia Literatura*, which from the start had paid more attention to developing countries, publishing fifty-four Latin American authors, while the Hungarian magazine presented only twenty-two and only six of whom coincided with the Soviet selection. The editors of *Nagyvilág* opted—probably more out of ignorance than conscious selection—for classic or canonized poets of the Hispanic world such as Darío, Jiménez, A. Machado, and little-known writers such as Serafín J. García Correa (Uruguay), Jorge Calvetti (Argentina), Alejandro Peralta (Peru), and Eglé Malheiros and Gilka Machado (Brazil). The scenario would change with the entrance of Cuba into the Eastern Bloc in 1959: soon texts by Nicolás Guillén were published in the magazine, among them the essay "Kuba, 1959" [Cuba, 1959]. And where is Borges? The only mention resulted from the journal becoming apprised of the Formentor Prize, perhaps because of Beckett, but in its brief note about Borges sharing the award, they mistakenly state he was "Mexican."

In Romania, there was a similar magazine called *Secolul 20* [*Twentieth Century*], founded in 1961, which undoubtedly played a leading role in the introduction of Borges's works in the country. At first it was published quarterly at nearly the length of a book and with a print run of two thousand copies, yet it was one of the most financially stable journals. Why? Because the editorial staff followed the contemporary Soviet model for the internal organization of artistic institutions: the magazine was a publication of the writers' association, but its management was in the hands of individuals trusted by the state. The government provided them with a budget and a larger staff, which, as of 1968, even acquired a state employee–like status, with well-defined rights and responsibilities. It was, in fact, a company financed by the state for cultural purposes and controlled according to ideological criteria (Macrea-Toma 93–105). Borges arrived on this scene only in 1967, but, over the course of five years, he appeared no fewer than nine times, occupying important sections of the magazine. Issue 9 of that year included a lengthy section on Mircea Eliade followed by a mini-anthology of eight essential Borges texts, complete with an interview fragment and essays by Victoria Ocampo and Stafan Augustin Doinas. An equally enriching selection was published two years later in issue 6 (1969), which placed Borges between a section of previously unpublished texts by critic and theorist George Călinescu and a chapter from the Romanian translation of Faulkner's *The Sound and the Fury*. From Borges's oeuvre, five poems and six fictions from a variety of his books were included. The selection was completed with several essays on Borges by well-known international figures from outside the Bloc, namely Ema Risso Platero, Maurice Nadeau, Jean Cassou, and Pietro Citati; the issue also included an excerpt from Leonor Acevedo de Borges's biography, copies of some manuscript pages, and photos of the author. We do not detect any political tension or social conflict in the country (regarding neither Paris, nor the 1968 invasion of Czechoslovakia by its "brother countries," as member states of the Bloc were usually called by Moscow) nor does there appear to be any ideological censure of Borges, as seen elsewhere. The text introducing the Argentine author is carefully thought out and written from a broad comparativist perspective meant to appeal to readers anywhere in the world. Thus, the trick worked: since it proved impossible to publish Borges's books, copious thematic issues were printed in the most important literary magazine in Romania.

It was to be expected that, beyond the methods applied to publish a bit more of Borges in the 1960s, editors and publishers would take advantage of the unforeseen enlargement of the Bloc in 1961 with a Spanish-speaking country, Cuba. This expectation did not come to fruition, however—not for lack of Borges's influence on the island during the pre-revolutionary era (Virgilio Piñera's collaboration with Borges, for example, or his influence on the ideation of Cintio Vitier and the *Orígenes* group) but because of the obvious prohibition dictated by the Castro regime. A few tributes were initially organized in venues such as *Lunes de Revolución* and *Revolución*, and some repercussions could be detected years later among a group involved with the cultural journal *Caimán Barbudo*, but Borges's work made its way to the island in one lone anthology, *Páginas escogidas*, which was only published in 1988—barely a year before the collapse of the Bloc. Its appearance was due to one of many last-minute maneuvers carried out by Roberto Fernández Retamar, who had visited the writer in Buenos Aires in 1985 (Alonso Estenoz 10–11, 127). In both his role as Director of Casa de las Américas and as ideological advisor to the Bloc, his recommendation was the same: to delay publication until the author's death, in which Borges failed to oblige. It speaks volumes that Borges had more of a presence in pre-revolutionary Cuba than during the long decades of socialism; even in the Soviet Union Borges received more attention than in Communist Cuba. The literary importance of Cuba for the Bloc would manifest itself in another way: in the unprecedented increase in the translation of its authors into the languages of Eastern Europe. There was of course a preference for propagating Cuba's revolutionary vision and its social realist aesthetics, but there was room for more than a few works of the island's history, folklore, and essays. Even more striking, in the opposite direction, from periphery to periphery, was the importance of the translations into Spanish of an enormous number of works from the Eastern Bloc: it is no exaggeration to call the process, in Puñales-Alpízar's terms, a Spanish-language "socialist literary boom," which, as she notes, was "supported and financed by the State" (35).

INDIVIDUAL VOLUMES

Given the increase in Borges's translations in magazines in the 1960s, it was to be expected that this opening would continue in the following years and that the publication of Borges's own books would finally become a reality. The order in which they appeared sheds light on how the principle of "divide and conquer" was applied throughout the region. The first hints came from the southeastern part of the Bloc, Yugoslavia, which was no great surprise considering the country's ambiguous status: as a Socialist Federative Republic it was considered a non-aligned state, but with obvious ties to the Eastern Bloc. In 1963, *Maštarije* was published in Belgrade as part of a series called *Metamorfoze*; the volume contained no less than three unabridged books (*El jardín de senderos que se bifurcan* [*The Garden of Forking Paths*], *Ficciones* [*Fictions*], and *Historia universal de la infamia*) in Serbian, including all of the prefaces. That format would reach the so-called socialist camp only decades later, as would the kind of literary introduction in which Miodrag Pavlović mentioned the idea that "there already exists somewhere the encyclopedia of the world with the past and the future already described" (12), which was not exactly the concept of history promulgated in the Bloc. The second case arose in Czechoslovakia in 1969, at the height of the post-traumatic period after the invasion of Prague, with the surprising appearance of *Artefakty* containing *Fictions* and *The Aleph*. Needless to say, after this unexpected "grace period," Borges's further publications in Czech were postponed for many years. Not so in the rest of the Bloc, where, soon, more and more freedom was extended, allowing translation and dissemination of entire books by the Argentine author. We do not know the details regarding the coordination of the project, but the publication of four important books by Borges in a single year—1972—in four countries (Estonia, Hungary, Poland, and Romania), makes clear the political message issuing from the center: the leash has begun to slacken. As for the Estonian edition of *Hargnevate teede aed: novellid* [*The Garden of Forking Paths*], we are struck by the fact that, while there were no books by Borges translated into Russian until the following decade, he was allowed to be published far from the center, in a minor state, such as the Estonian Soviet Socialist Republic. In Romania, on the contrary, an excellent selection of nine texts was printed in *Moartea și busola* [*Death and the Compass*], prefaced and translated by Darie Novaceanu; the prize the book was awarded undoubtedly indicated a certain acceptance of Borges already present in the literary polysystem. In Hungary, a selection of short stories was published under the title *Körkörörös romok* [*The Circular Ruins*] by the publishing house Kozmosz, whose very popular associated magazine, *Galaktika*, published, among other cheap paperbacks, huge print runs of science fiction books with covers very similar to those of sci-fi magazines of the time. It is striking that the selection contains "El acercamiento a Almotásim" [The Approach to Al-Mu'tasim], "La intrusa" [The Intruder], and twenty-two stories from *Ficciones* and *El Aleph*. Of the latter are omitted, for example, "Tres versiones de Judas" [Three Versions of Judas] and "Deutsches Requiem," something understandable if the goal was merely to avoid any unwanted ideological associations; but the choice to exclude "Tlön, Uqbar, Orbis Tertius," "La muerte y la brújula" [Death and the Compass], or "El Zahir" is difficult to explain. Reading the epilogue of the Hungarian edition, we can grasp the difficulty the editors had in proving that Borges was a science fiction author. Making an aesthetic-ideological leap, the essayist sought support in ambiguous phrases such as "Of course Borges does not appear to be a science fiction writer, even if his great admirer, the classic author of the genre Stanislaw Lem, says that 'he has spent years trying to reach the area where the works of Argentine's best writer were born'" (223); referencing Lem went without question, and he was a writer from a "brother country." Even more indicative is the list of Borges's canonized precursors named in the epilogue, including, among others, Renan, Kafka, Swift, Poe, and finally to E. T. A Hoffmann—and it is at this point that the inevitable, sanctifying name is inserted—"whose mysterious stories Marx, reader of a great number of works on economy and history, leafed through so eagerly; but as *an active rest*" (233, emphasis in the original).

With the approval apparently granted to Borges in 1972, his presence in the Bloc was consolidated throughout the decade. Poland was again at the forefront, publishing no fewer than seven books and over two hundred Borges texts. An interesting innovation was the 1978 publication in Romania of a selection of fiction, *A titokban végbe ment csoda* [*The Secret Miracle*], by Kriterion Publishing House (Bucharest) in Hungarian, the language of the country's minority community. In the same year, *Brodiova zpráva* [*Brodie's Report*] was published. In 1979, the first translation of Borges's work into Bulgarian, "Kraglite razvalini" ("Las ruinas circulares") appeared in an anthology of Latin American fantasy stories translated by Anna Zlatkova. The author's presence is also reflected in the formation of several writers' groups who seem to be, and often declare themselves so, "Borgesian." We find important traces in Poland and Romania-Transylvania, but the greatest effect undoubtedly occurred in Serbia, creating a trend in "Borgesian prose" (Freixa Terradas 262). Among these we can note, for example, Milorad Pavić, famous creator of the *Jázaro Dictionary*, and, above all, the international stature of Danilo Kiš, who in his *Anatomy Lesson* declared nothing less than that narrative art could be categorized as "pre-Borges and post-Borges" (Kiš 53, my translation).

434   LÁSZLÓ SCHOLZ

FINALLY, THE CENTER

Seeing this ever-expanding panorama of publications, magazines, translations, and influences in the Bloc, one cannot help but wonder when Borges's work actually arrived in Russia, the country of his youthful "red" dreams. At the center of the Socialist empire, he was all but ignored until the 1980s. There were a few attempts to introduce him to the Russian reading public; deploying the tricks cited above, he was included in a 1975 anthology of Latin American poetry, volume 170 of a gigantic collection, with the poems "Las calles" [The Streets], "A una moneda" [To a Coin], and "Límites" [Limits]. He was published randomly in member countries of the Soviet Union, for example, *Kunstükid* [*Artifices*] printed in Estonia in 1976. Such silence could not be explained as simple ignorance; Borges's name had appeared in a Russian encyclopedia as early as 1962 (Odnopozova 142). The fact is that, for decades, in the Soviet ideological landscape, interest in Latin America was limited to countries and artists who were explicitly sympathetic to the Soviet system; in fact, preference was always given to representatives of countries that had waged their own revolutions (Mexico, Bolivia, Brazil, and, of course, Cuba). This principle was evident from the first selection of Latin American authors published in the 1957 inaugural issue of *Inostrannaia Literatura*, the guidepost venue of literary policy, which included poems by Pablo Neruda, Nicolás Guillén, Carlos Augusto León, Juan Gonzalo Rose, Matilde Espinosa de Pérez, Eugenio Moreno Heredia, and Eladio Romero. Suffice it to say that four of these writers were awarded some variant of the Stalin/Lenin Prize or World Peace Council Prize. It was well known that the Argentine author's youthful enthusiasm for revolutionary Russia disappeared forever in 1921; subsequently, in the press, he expressed more than a few anti-Soviet remarks, consistently refused invitations from the Eastern Bloc countries (Odnopozova 100), and even in his critical work paid little attention to Russian history, cinema, and classical literature. The censors evidently saw no reason to end the silence until the 1980s. Despite the sophisticated systems designed to control books, an atmosphere of constant insecurity surrounded both the process and the criteria of publishing decisions. Tomas Venclova, a poet and translator from Lithuania, recounts that when he contacted a literary magazine in his country in the 1970s to offer them the translations of four Borges stories, the first thing the editor-in-chief asked him was "Doesn't that Borges by any chance have an anti-Soviet tendency?" And the response was: "Well, it is not so much that he would be an enemy of the Soviet system; he just does not like the *solar* system" (Venclova 61).[2] The conversation ended with the editor asking for more time to decide, since it was very complicated for him to find and peruse the corresponding blacklists. Ultimately, the decision was a yes and a no: the magazine published two of the four proposed Borges texts.

Excepting three Borges poems ("A una moneda," "Las calles," and "Límites"), published in a 1975 anthology, Borges only came out of the shadows in Russia during the crisis of the 1980s; with a decades-long delay, the Moscow center finally began following the publication routines of its "brother countries." Initially, he appeared in two anthologies, then had his debut in two stand-alone volumes where he was lauded as an author of major significance. Borges's first introduction to Soviet Russia was the authorized inclusion—though under genuinely tragicomic circumstances—of "El jardín de senderos que se bifurcan" [The Garden of Forking Paths] in an anthology of Argentine short stories. After several years of preparation, a large publishing house (Khudozhestvennaia Literatura) was about to publish the anthology when the inclusion of Borges's story was detected by the state. As editor Ella Braginskaia later told us, a Party meeting was called without delay and it was decided that "Borges, our ideological enemy, should be taken out and his name should never be mentioned!" (Odnopozova 148) and his text was subsequently removed from the volume. However, Argentine Alfredo Varela, winner of the Lenin Peace Prize, happened to be in Moscow—a writer who was more popular in the Eastern Bloc than in his homeland for *El río oscuro* [*The Dark River*], which had been translated into several languages in the 1950s. Reportedly due to his intervention, the decision was reconsidered and Borges's story was authorized for the 1981 volume, but on the condition that "Blues en la noche" [Blues in the Night] by Varela's Jewish compatriot, Germán Rozenmacher, be removed. A year later, a selection of more than forty poems by Borges was included in an anthology *Iz sovremennoi argentinskoi poezii* [*On Contemporary Argentine Poetry*] by Progress publishing house (97–132). Borges's true arrival in the Soviet Union would come soon thereafter: in 1984, two representative volumes of his narrative were released by important publishers: *Iug: rasskazy* [*The South: Stories*] and *Proza ranih let* [*Prose from Other Times*]. In light of the prologue and an alleged anniversary speech that appeared contemporaneously in the magazine *Latinskaia Amerika* [*Latin America*], in 1984, translator and scholar I. A. Teteryan compared, in a very diplomatic way, the figures of Borges, Juan Carlos Onetti, and Julio Cortázar and was finally able to explicitly state the truth that had been silenced for forty-some years: that in reality Borges, the first, the eldest, was indeed the founder of the new Latin American narrative (Teteryan 123–34). This was the price paid for the colossal delay in the center—Borges was presented as the post-facto grandfather of the *Boom*'s child prodigies who had been in vogue in Russia for years.

ON THE ROCKY PATH TO LIBERTY

But why introduce Borges to the Russian public precisely in the mid-1980s? Varela's ad hoc intervention, the uneven role of censorship, and the skill of Russian critics are all details that attract our attention today, but, from a political perspective permitted us decades later, it is evident that Moscow was abandoning the project of the Eastern Bloc after the Polish crisis (Solidarity, 1980–1981). This trend became manifestly apparent with the rise of Gorbachev, his *glasnost* and *perestroika*, and, above all, with his meeting in Reykjavik with Reagan, which would lead to the dissolution of the Bloc in 1989–1991. In our case, the data on Borges's translations in the region speak for themselves:

the previous limitations disappeared, and the doors were opened wide for Borges in the 1980s. In Bulgaria, two volumes were published after the Russian compilations of 1984. In Poland, five individual books and more than 110 short texts were printed, and, in Hungary, five volumes and nearly one hundred texts were published in magazines and anthologies. In the following decade, the socioeconomic phenomenon we saw at the end of the 1940s was repeated, but in the opposite direction: the state publishing houses were re-privatized, socialist annual and five-year plans were annulled, and the free-market book publishing trade was created. Aesthetic criteria for selecting works to be published were no longer disguised by the "weapons of the weak," but rather came to depend on private support and national and international cultural funds. Under the new circumstances, Borges's presence as a classic author was consolidated and remains so to this day. He is understood to be a cultural figure who deserves ongoing attention and special treatment, a sign of which can be seen in the continuous appearance of new collections of his "complete" works. Assembled either by genre or chronologically, formats vary from country to country; in Hungary, for example, a first edition (1998–2000) came out in five volumes, in Romania in three (1999–2000), in the Czech Republic in six (2009–2013), in Russia in variety of formats since 1994. His texts have been included in secondary school and, naturally, university curricula, and it is quite striking that more and more theoretical and critical approaches to his work are being released; that texts such as Fernando Sorrentino's *Siete diálogos con Jorge Luis Borges* or Guillermo Martínez's *Borges y la matemática* or Edwin Williamson's *Borges: A Life* are being translated; and that numerous theses and monographs by researchers in the former Soviet Union and Eastern Bloc continue to be published, such as those by A. Housková (2018), S. Łazicki (2009), and G. Szabó (2000). Awaiting Borges in the future is the well-established aesthetic-intellectual capital of young translators ready to continue the work of the first generation. In the 1960s, due to the obvious influence of Cuba, Hispanic Studies departments were founded in the leading universities of the Eastern Bloc, expanding the number of well-trained literary scholars available to create new and updated versions. The number of translators who contributed Borges's texts to their respective countries is impressive: to date both Poland and Hungary have more than fifty translators of Borges.

In view of the Eastern Bloc's collapse in 1989–1991, let us return to the initial theme: the options for literary relations among peripheral countries. The encounters between the Spanish-American world and *Mitteleuropa* during the 1920s avant-garde were isolated and primarily dependent upon personal and ideological motivations. From 1945 onward, we find a new construct that established contacts between an Eastern center and a larger bloc of Central and Eastern European countries. The relationship at the level of literary translations was governed mainly by political and ideological criteria. In the case of Latin America, Moscow asserted a concept that aimed, on the one hand, at political openness toward developing peoples and, on the other hand, at possessing a double-edged cultural tool to form and, at the same time, influence "educated" citizens through literature, a concept it inherited from post-revolutionary Russia. Considering only the quantitative dimension of its projects, literary translations reached a very high level both between the center and its peripheries and among the peripheries themselves.

Borges made an incursion into this context with an ideology that went counter to the norm and, in some four decades, went from total obscurity and prohibition to becoming a best-seller in the region. His entry became a reality largely due to the countries of *Mitteleuropa*, former peripheries of the West who were the main drivers in the process of introducing his texts into the Bloc and eventually leading them to the very center, which had remained untouched by Borges until the early 1980s. *Mitteleuropa* truly embodied the adage often observed with respect to its history, that it obeyed but did not comply, maintaining its cultural orientation toward the West to the degree Eastern political power permitted it. The triumph of Borges's work was foreseeable as early as the 1980s, coming to be canonized in publications that are continually exerting influence on new generations. The delay in reaching such a point seems even longer if we compare Borges's reception in France with Russia or Cuba, but the European average was closer to what we observe in the two Germanies: in the Federal Republic, *Labyrinthe* came out in 1959; in the GDR, *Erzählungen* was printed in 1975. Against expectations, this lag was not compensated for after Cuba's accession to the Eastern Bloc; on the contrary, the island was locked in a ban for decades. Among other factors, it was because of this delay that the Argentine author was frequently catalogued according to fashionable criteria or trends either as a science fiction writer or as representative of the supposed "magical realism" of the *Boom*. From today's perspective there is nothing to regret. Gaps are generally unavoidable, and, as we have seen, publishers took advantage of these labels to be able to publish at least some of Borges's texts. Let us take it rather as an ironic twist of fate that befell a writer who dedicated his life and work to unraveling Time. And let us ask ourselves the following question: What fate would have befallen and how many millions of copies would Borges have sold in the Eastern Bloc if, in the 1950s, Moscow had read "El escritor argentino y la tradición" [The Argentine Writer and Tradition] instead of his press statements?

NOTES

1. Given the extreme variety of sources and languages that this topic required, I received the generous help of my Hispanist colleagues Mirjana Polić Bobić, Barbara Ďurčová, Anna Housková, Bojana Kovačević Petrović, Adriána Koželová, Sylwester Łazicki, Zalán Serestély, Anna Zlatkova, and Maja Zovko, as well as a number of librarians in Budapest, Oberlin, Riga, Tallin, and Zagreb. Sarolta Tóthpál, a doctoral student in Slavic philology at Eötvös Loránd University, helped me decipher and transcribe many key Slavic texts (with all of their consonants).
2. These last words came from Ostap Bender, a popular character by the famous Soviet-era satirists Ilf and Petrov.

438   LÁSZLÓ SCHOLZ

WORKS CITED

Borges's Works Translated in Magazines and Anthologies in the Eastern Bloc

Borges, Jorge Luis. "A una moneda." In Russian: "Moneta." *Poezia Latinskoi Ameriki* [Latin American Poetry]. Khudozhestvennaia Literatura, 1975, p. 90.

Borges, Jorge Luis. "Amorosa anticipación." In Czech: "Nejmladší španělská poezie" [Young Spanish Poetry]. *Literární noviny*, vol. 5, no. 13, 1930, p. 6.

Borges, Jorge Luis. "Anatomía de mi 'Ultra." In Czech: "O španělském Ultraismu" [On Spanish Ultraísmo]. *Host*, vol. 6, no. 2, 1926, pp. 46–47.

Borges, Jorge Luis. "Calle desconocida." In Czech: *Literární noviny*, vol. 5, no. 13, 1930, p. 6. In Hungarian: "Ismeretlen utca." Franyó, Zoltán. *Lírai világtájak: válogatott műfordítások* [Lyric Regions of the World: Selected Translations]. Európa, 1967, p. 433. The original lines are in *Obras completas*, Emecé, 1996, I: 20.

Borges, Jorge Luis. "Delia Elena San Marco." In Hungarian: *Szerelmes ezüst kalendárium* [A Silver Calendar of Love]. Kozmosz Könyvek, 1967, pp. 442–43.

Borges, Jorge Luis. "El Aleph." In Romanian: "Aleful." *Viața Românească*, vol. 19, no. 7, pp. 77–83.

Borges, Jorge Luis. "El jardín de senderos que se bifurcan." In Russian: *Argentinskie rasskazy* [Argentine short stories]. Khudozhestvennaia Literatura, 1981, pp. 28–38.

Borges, Jorge Luis. "El milagro secreto." In Slovak: *Dni a noci Latinskej Ameriky* [Days and Nights in Latin America]. Edited by Y. Moretič. SPKK, 1969, pp. 363–69.

Borges, Jorge Luis. "El muerto." In Hungarian: *Argentin dekameron: szemelvények* [Argentine Decameron: Fragments]. Délamerikai magyarság, 1952, pp. 61–66.

Borges, Jorge Luis. "El Sur." In Hungarian: "Dél." *Nagyvilág*, vol. 14, no. 2, 1969, pp. 215–18, 319.

Borges, Jorge Luis. "Gesta maximalista." In Czech: "O španělském Ultraismu" [Sobre el ultraísmo español]. *Host*, vol. 6, no. 2, 1926, pp. 46–47.

Borges, Jorge Luis. "Hombre de la esquina rosada." In Hungarian: "A szögletes arcú ember." *Nagyvilág*, vol. 8, no. 4, 1963, pp. 487–91, 639.

Borges, Jorge Luis. "La biblioteca de Babel." In Czech: "Bábelská knihovna." Edited by A. Hoffmeister. *Laberynt* [Labyrinth]. Státni nakladateslství krásné literarury a umění, 1962, pp. 233–40.

Borges, Jorge Luis. "La escritura del dios." In Hungarian: "Isten írása." *Utunk*, vol. 20, no. 41, 1965, p. 7.

Borges, Jorge Luis. "La lotería de Babilonia." In Serbian: "Babilonska lutrija." *100 odabranih novela svjetske književnosti* [100 Short Stories of World Crisis]. Stvarnost, 1968, pp. 211–13.

Borges, Jorge Luis. "Las calles." In Russian: "Ulicy Buenos-Airesa" [Calles de Buenos Aires]. *Poezia Latinskoi Ameriki* [Latin American Poetry]. Khudozhestvennaia Literatura, 1975, p. 89.

Borges, Jorge Luis. "Las ruinas circulares." In Bulgarian: "Kraglite razvalini." Translated by A. Zlatkova. *Latinoamerikanska fantastika* [Latin American Fantastic Literature]. Jristo G. Danov, 1979, pp. 427–32.

Borges, Jorge Luis. "Límites." In Russian: "Predeli." *Poezia Latinskoi Ameriki* [Latin American Poetry]. Khudozhestvennaia Literatura, 1975, p. 90.

Borges, Jorge Luis. "Mañana." In Polish: "Poranek." *Nowa Sztuka*, no. 2, 1922, p. 10.

Borges, Jorge Luis. "Mindörökre" [Forever]. An apocryphal work in Hungarian: *Nagyvilág*, no. 5, 1964, pp. 662–69, 800 and no. 7, 1964, p. 1119.

Borges, Jorge Luis. "Remordimiento por cualquier muerte." In Czech: *Literární noviny*, vol. 5, no. 13, p. 6.

Borges, Jorge Luis. "Rusia." In Hungarian: "Oroszország." *Ma*, vol. 6, no. 9, 1921, p. 122. In Czech: *Rozpravy Aventina*, no. 11–12, 1928, p. 144; *Literární noviny*, vol. 5, 1930, n. 13, p. 6.

Books That Include Individual Volumes of Selections of Borges

A titokban végbe ment csoda [*The Secret Miracle*]. Kriterion Könyvkiadó, 1978.

Artefakty [*Artifices*]. Odeon, 1969.

Brodiova zpráva [*Brodie's Report*]. Odeon, 1978.

Hargnevate teede aed: novellid [*The Garden of Forking Paths: Storie*]. Perioodika, 1972.

Iug: rasskazy [*The South: Stories*]. Izvestia, 1984.

Iz sovremennoi argentinskoi poezii [*Of Contemporary Argentine Poetry*]. Progress, 1982.

Körkörös romok [*The Circular Ruins*]. Kozmosz Könyvek. 1972.

Kraglite razvalini [*The Circular Ruins*]. Jristo G. Danov, 1979.

Kunstükid [*Artifices*]. Perioodika, 1976.

Maštarije [*Fictions*]. Nolit, 1963.

Moartea și busola [*Death and the Compass*]. Univers, 1972.

Páginas escogidas [*Selected Writings*]. Ed. and intro. Roberto Fernández Retamar. Ediciones Casa de las Américas, 1988.

Proza ranih let [*Prose of Different Periods*]. Raduga, 1984.

Secondary Bibliography

Alonso Estenoz, Alfredo. *Borges en Cuba*. Borges Center, 2017.

Barbeira, Candelaria. "Variaciones sobre el poema 'Rusia.'" *Variaciones Borges*, no. 38, 2014, pp. 29–46.

Bart, István. *Világirodalom és könyvkiadás a Kádár-korszakban* [World Literature and the Publication of Books in the Kádár Era]. Scholastica, 2000.

Černý, Václav. "O španělském Ultraismu" [On Spanish Ultraísmo]. *Host*, vol. 6, no. 2, 1926, pp. 46–47.

Černý, Václav. "Nejmladší španělská poezie" [On Young Spanish Poetry]. *Literární noviny*, vol. 5, no. 13, 1930, p. 6.

Ďurčová, Barbara. *K špecifikám prekladu prozaických textov jorgeho luisa borgesa do slovenčiny* [On the Peculiarities of translation in Borges's prose]. Univerzita komenského v Bratislave, 2015.

Freixa Terradas, Paul. "Jorge Luis Borges en Danilo Kiš o la lección intertextual" [Jorge Luis Borges in Danilo Kiš or a lesson on intertextuality]. *Konteksty Kultury*, vol. 13, no. 3, pp. 260–70.

Guillén, Nicolás. "Kuba, 1959" [Cuba, 1959]. *Nagyvilág*, no. 7, 1959, pp. 1050–53.

Haraszti, Miklós. *The Velvet Prison: Artists Under State Socialism*. Tauris, 1988.

Housková, Anna. *Nekonečný Borges* [Infinite Borges]. Triáda, 2018.

Kardos, László. "Vihar után" [After the storm]. *Nagyvilág*, vol. 2, no. 1, 1957, pp. 4–5.

Kiš, Danilo. *Cas anatomije* [The Anatomy Lesson]. 1978.

Kiss, Ildikó, and Scholz, László. "Borges magyarul. 1921–2021" [Borges in Hungarian. 1920–2021]. Borges, Jorge Luis. *A végtelen életrajza* [Biography of the Infinite]. Jelenkor, 2021, pp. 591–620.

Łazicki, Sylwster. *Borgesowskie wersje, czyli traktat o translatorskiej niekompetencji* [Versions of Borges: Essay on the incompetence of translation]. Poznań: MA dissertation, 2009.

Lukács, György. "Magyar irodalom—világirodalom" [Hungarian literature—world literature]. *Nagyvilág*, vol. 1, no. 1, 1956, pp. 3–5.

Macrea-Toma, Ioana. "Írói intézmények a Román államszocializmusban" [Writers' institutions in socialist Romania]. *Múltunk*, no. 1, 2011, pp. 78–125.

Mašek, Jiří. "Tři nejzajímavější postavy mladé literární generace španěské" [The three most interesting figures in the young literature of Spain]. *Rozpravy Aventina*, no.11–12, 1928, p. 144.

Odnopozova, Dina. *Russian-Argentine Literary Exchanges*. Dissertation. Yale University, 2013.

Orlova, Iryna. "Borges in Ukraine: The Reception of Borges's Works in Ukrainian Translation." *Variaciones Borges*, no. 37, 2016, pp. 97–114.

Păcurariu, Francisc. *Introducere în literatura Americii latine* [Introduction to Latin American Literature]. Pentru Literatura Universala, 1965.

Puñales–Alpízar, Damaris. "Geopolíticas de la traducción en la Cuba soviética: de la estética marxista al *boom* literario socialista" [Geopolitics of translation in Soviet Cuba: From Marxist aesthetics to socialist literary *boom*]. *Revista de Letras*. UNESP, vol. 57, no. 2, 2017, pp. 34–52.

Sobol-Jurczykowski, Andrzej. "La recepción de la obra de Jorge Luis Borges en Polonia" [Reception of Jorge Luis Borges in Poland]. *Variaciones Borges*, no. 16, 2003, pp. 198–201.

Szabó, Gábor. *Hiány és jelenlét: Borges-értelmezések* [Absence and presence: Interpretations of Borges]. Messzelátó, 2000.

Takács, Róbert. "Szovjet és magyar nyitás a kultúrában Nyugat felé 1953–1964" [The Soviet and Hungarian opening to the West in 1953-1964]. *Múltunk*, no. 3, 2015, pp. 30–68.

Teteryan, I. A. "Vmesto iubileinoi rechi" [Instead of an anniversary]. *Latinskaia Amerika*, October 1984, pp. 123–34.

Venclova, Tomas. "USSR: Stages of Censorship." *Index on Censorship*, vol. 7, no. 4, 1978, pp. 61–62.

CHAPTER 25

···

BORGES AND THE FORMATION OF THE LITERARY GLOBAL SOUTH

···

JAY CORWIN

A signature characteristic of Borges's aesthetic innovation is his incorporation of older texts and their themes into his fiction. Some of the pieces he reworks into his writing were written in classical antiquity and others in languages in the modern era. Certain Old World texts that Borges melded into his fiction also surface in his essays and may be key to a deeper understanding of *Ficciones* [*Fictions*] and *El Aleph*. Contemporary writers from the Global South have been cognizant of this, engaging under the influences of Borges's aesthetic renovations of literature. However, certain critics, guided by politics and disadvantaged by translations and partial readings, have misinterpreted Borges's use of texts from the Middle East and South Asia. Despite such misinterpretations, some exceptional writers have acculturated patterns set in Borges's works, forming a literary dialogue with the Argentine writer. For the purposes of this chapter, I focus exclusively on Borges's literary influences on a few well-considered, representative writers from the Old World Global South, exclusive of political or sociological inferences.

The term "Global South" emerged from the sphere of politics rather than the study of literature. As replacement nomenclature for outmoded or condescending terms such as "third world," the Global South refers to zones of varying degrees of development without strict regard for hemispheres or regional borders. Its boundaries tend to follow the Brandt Line, devised by and named after Willy Brandt in the early 1980s, and used largely by sociologists after Antonio Gramsci (Lees). Discussing the origin of the term, Nour Dados and Raewynn Connell note that "Gramsci explored the difficulties southern peasants and northern workers faced in forging an alliance with one another. In Italian social thought, most later treatments of the 'North-South differential' addressed only variations in economic development" (12). Dados and Connell further cite Edward Said and Gayatri Chakravorty Spivak as authorities on the postcolonial question, while acknowledging "African American and Chicana/o scholars" of the 1990s

(12). One of the consequences of applying terms such as "Global South" to literary history is that purely aesthetic questions may become subordinated to politics. To avoid that and other unintended difficulties, the term is used here only to indicate the geographic origins of major pieces of writing and of contemporary literary figures whose works show the influence of Borges.

Borges's use of themes and motifs from historical and literary pieces is well-documented. This includes writings from the Near East, South Asia, and China which provide deeper layers of meaning in *Ficciones* and *El Aleph*. Despite clichéd pronouncements on the topic, Borges's use of literature and imagery from large sections of the planet is comparable to the imaginative Aleph in Carlos Argentino Daneri's basement in the story of the same name. In "Borges en el mundo, el mundo en Borges," Daniel Balderston notes that "Borges, sin embargo, es una presencia incómoda sobre la literatura mundial: descree del todo en su existencia, pero parece conocerla mejor que nadie" [Borges, however, is an uncomfortable presence in world literature: he does not believe at all in its existence, but seems to know it better than anyone] (11). Borges's essays comment on old texts while his stories appropriate elements of them. A result of his ensuing literary fame is that his stories have become almost inseparable from his literary acculturations, as I will show.

Among sacred texts Borges drew from, the Qur'an is clearly quoted, while the Pentateuch and the Avesta are referenced *sotto voce*. Examples of text from the Qur'an can be found in "La busca de Averroes" [Averroes' Search] in *El Aleph*, and in the mysterious epigraph to "El milagro secreto" [The Secret Miracle] in *Ficciones*. The Hebrew Pentateuch is much less obvious but appears in references in "La muerte y la brújula" [Death and the Compass] to the tetragrammaton, the four-letter unpronounceable name of God. The Decalogue, introduced in Exodus and repeated in Deuteronomy, is recited in the infractions of it in "Emma Zunz." At the start of the story Emma receives a letter of nine or ten lines from someone whose name she cannot pronounce, "Fein" or "Fain." This recalls the tetragrammaton and its uncertain pronunciation. The story begins with a violation of the Sabbath, hidden in the exact date (January 14, 1922 was a Saturday), a clever concealment of Emma's infraction of the decalogue by working on that day. This is followed by covetousness, dishonoring of parents, theft, adultery, idolatry, false witness, and murder. In fact, in the final scene, Emma commits adultery, bears false witness, and commits murder all on the Sabbath (Corwin, " 'Emma Zunz' " 150). The redoubling of crimes and infractions against the decalogue become obvious, as even the photograph of 1920s matinée idol Milton Sills suggests idolatry, hidden beneath a veneer of detective fiction. The real detective work is for the reader to discover how this story relates to the first letter of the Hebrew *abjad*, its origins, and its allegorical mirror in the myth of the Minotaur of Crete (Corwin, " 'Emma Zunz' " 159).

The unmentioned text behind "Las ruinas circulares" [The Circular Ruins] is the Avesta, the fragmentary sacred book of Zoroastrianism. That text is also inferred in suggestions of heresy (the historic character may have been accused of secretly retaining Zoroastrian beliefs) in the title character of "El tintorero enmascarado Hákim de Merv" [The Masked Dyer, Hakim of Merv] from *Historia universal de la infamia* [A Universal

History of Infamy]. That story's character is taken from several scant historical accounts. His imposture is reflected in the name of Smerdis in "Tlön, Uqbar, Orbis Tertius," first mentioned in Herodotus's *Histories*, and as Bardiya on the earlier Behistun inscription. Bardiya, or Smerdis, was a magus who ruled Persia for several weeks while pretending to be Gaumata, the brother of Darius the Great. In the word "zend" in "Las ruinas circulares," the Avesta has its closest direct reference, as "Zend" was mistakenly used to mean the long dead language of the Gathas of Zarathustra, now known as Avestan. Other texts in these stories are much more frequently cited, such as *The Thousand and One Nights*, an Arabic translation of the lost Middle Persian *Hazar Afsana*. This source is mentioned by Borges in *Siete Noches*, and it is also known to Iranologists, as noted in the *Encyclopaedia Iranica*: "The most ancient testimony to the existence of a collection of tales bearing this title is given by Masʿūdī" (d. 345/956; see *Morūj* IV, p. 90; ed. Pellat, sec. 1416). He refers to work full of untrue stories translated from Persian, Sanskrit, and Greek, including the "book entitled *Hazār afsāna*, or the thousand tales, because a tale is called in Persian *afsāna*" (Pellat).

There are further tenuous references to the Avesta in "El acercamiento a Almotásim" [The Approach to Al-Muʾtasim]. That story, along with "Las ruinas circulares," contains images of structures sacred to Zoroastrianism: the former includes a Tower of Silence, and the latter, Fire Temples, some of which is indicated by Mac Williams (2008). The question of the purity of the magus's Avestan in "Las ruinas circulares" suggests that the tale's time frame is either Seleucid, Arsacid, or early Sassanid, although it is a deliberate anachronism as Avestan was already long dead by the Seleucid era. Conversely, "El acercamiento a Almotásim" is very clearly set in early twentieth-century Mumbai and thereafter in other regions of India, with direct references to Parsees and their means of disposal of human remains, all relevant to the Avesta. Also attached to the text is a note suggesting the plot of the story stems from Attar of Nishapur's eleventh-century epic poem, "Conference of the Birds." Other stories such as "La lotería en Babilonia" [The Lottery in Babylonia] may refer to the Achaemenid lingua franca, Aramaic, through the mention of the first three letters of its *abjad*, and by extension its Semitic sister language, Hebrew, whose *abjads* are also the source of the title of *El Aleph*. While unrelated to the Indo-European Avestan, it further underscores the breadth of influence of Persian history and literature in *Ficciones* and *El Aleph*.

In one of Borges's signature pieces, "El jardín de senderos que se bifurcan" [The Garden of Forking Paths], the eighteenth-century *Hong Lou Meng* (*The Dream of the Red Chamber*) is unveiled. As Balderston notes, it serves as a bibliographical marker indicating Borges's recycling of a character from that novel, a student named Yu Tsun ("The Labyrinth of Trenches Without Any Plan" 42), and as part of Borges's device of adding layers of fiction and mirroring a work of fiction within a work of fiction. In short, the novel at the center of the story is a reflection of its eighteenth-century Chinese model. *Hong Lou Meng*, which was written in vernacular Chinese, is often cited as a lexicographer's source for standardization of the modern Mandarin language, or *Putonghua*. Haiqing Sun introduces her study on Borges's uses of the novel as it deserves: "Cao Xueqin's *Hong Lou Meng* (*Dream of the Red Chamber*) represents the highest achievement of the classical narrative during the

444   JAY CORWIN

Ming-Qing period of China. Studies of the text have long become an important subject for scholars worldwide" (Sun 15). After juxtaposing Borges's impressions of both the *Hong Lou Meng* and *The Thousand and One Nights* in his essays and their appearances in "El jardín de senderos que se bifurcan," Sun proceeds to demonstrate three correlations in the story to "The Garden of Total Vision" in the *Hong Lou Meng*. Furthermore, Sun notes "the universal and encyclopedic image that these scholars figure for *Hong Lou Meng* is also the image that Borges uses to depict what he believes to be great literature in his story: '*El jardín de senderos que se bifurcan* es una imagen incompleta, pero no falsa, del universo'" [*The Garden of Forking Paths* is an incomplete, but not false, image of the universe] (Sun 25).

Such careful attention paid by Borges to important texts from regions of the Global South may only have piqued the interest of writers who saw their sacred and secular texts embedded in his most important writing. Their writings, in turn, have become responses in a form of literary dialogue. This point is made most starkly in the comparative criticism of Astrid Møller-Olsen. In her lyrical essay, "Sounding the Dream," the critic discusses the rewriting of "El jardín de senderos que se bifurcan" in contemporary Chinese novelist Can Xue's fictionalized interpretation of that piece. This is prefaced by a comment in "Nueva refutación del tiempo" [A New Refutation of Time], in which the Argentine author and critic homes in on fourth-century BCE Chinese philosopher Zhuangzi's parable of a man who falls asleep and dreams he is a butterfly, waking to wonder if he is a butterfly dreaming that he is a man. Møller-Olsen notes that both "Borges's re-narration of the Chuang Tzu and Can Xue's fictionalized interpretation of Borges are literary works in their own right as well as direct responses to other texts" (469). Møller-Olsen observes that Can Xue's writing is not just inspired directly by Borges but is a veritable response to Borges's thoughtful observation of a piece of writing that is sacred to Chinese letters and especially to Taoism.[1] More directly it is a literary dialogue initiated by Borges and enjoined by Can Xue, the pen name of Den Xiaohua, perhaps contemporary China's best-known avant-garde writer. The essay that Møller-Olsen refers to is written in Chinese and is contained in a collection of essays by the author, *Interpretation of Borges*. There is a single translation into English undertaken by Can Xue herself that allows readers from the outside world a glimpse of her prose, and it is precisely her rewriting of "El jardín de senderos que se bifurcan." The interpretation begins with the self-explanatory title, followed by a cast of characters as follows:

> "I" – The artist who broke into the labyrinth
> Albert – Another "I" who had accomplished myself, or the old "I"
> Capt. Madden – Death
> The Superior – Destiny
> Ts'ui Pên – A forerunner of Artists, who represented art history (Xue)

Can Xue's rewriting of Borges as an interpretation extends beyond the limits of other writers' engagement with Borges. By offering an interpretation as a rewriting, Can Xue repeats a pattern suggestive of "Pierre Menard, autor del Quijote" [Pierre Menard, Author of the *Quixote*], while at the same moment engaging with themes of mirrors,

Chinese boxes, and the ever-present labyrinth, absorbing each character into a central "I." At the end of this piece Can Xue writes,

> The old artist wrote in a letter: 'I leave to several futures (not to all) my garden of forking paths.' These words emphasized the infiniteness of time, which is the same thing as emphasizing that imagination is above everything, and it is able to build infinite labyrinths. So during the writing my great-grandfather found the channels to infiniteness and eternity. The book in his imagination can never be finished—in the book he creates many times and many futures, and this time is always expanding, forking. Every outcome happens, and every choice is chosen. So the layers of the novel are very rich, and the intersections dazzle one's eyes.

Borges's imprint may also be found on contemporary Arabic literature, as Aida O. Azouqa suggests, discussing the use and origins of geometric shapes in the late Gamal al-Ghitani's (1945–2015) *Pyramid Texts* (1994). Azouqa proposes that: "In Borges's fiction, the setting invariably relies on images of infinitude in the form of labyrinths and labyrinthine structures. These geometric structures could be a library, a city, a jungle, or any other form that suggests infinity" (6). She proceeds to note that al-Ghitani uses the obvious culturally relevant pyramid for the same purpose: "*Pyramid Texts* leans towards the Borges canon. Clarifying its fictional concerns and its intertextuality with the Borges canon, the present study attempts to open up *Pyramid Texts* for other scholars to begin where this study ends" (Azouqa 7). The patterns she examines in several of al-Ghitani's texts show particular affinities with Borges's stories. One example is in "Annihilation," whose protagonist is a young polyglot who aspires to be an artist but disappears, voided by light. Azouqa compares the character, a descendant of notable ancestors whose histories are found in texts, to the portrait of Ibn Rushd in "La busca de Averroes," although through her description one might find further, more direct associations in "Funes el memorioso" [Funes the Memorious], especially as the character is a young male with an unusual talent who vanishes from physical existence but not from the memory of the author. Azouqa recalls that al-Ghitani stated in an interview that he sought inspiration in the works of Western novelists, though how Western or which writers he meant are not revealed. However, it is possible that Azouqa is correct in affirming that the Egyptian novelist's sources of inspiration included Borges.[2]

A more obvious and literal dialogue between Borges and a contemporary Arabic writer can be found in Nobel laureate Naguib Mahfouz's *Arabian Nights and Days* (1979). Mahfouz's novel retells the epic of Shahrazad and Shahryar and the series of stories in different settings. Summarized well by Abdalhadi Nimer Abdalqader Abu Jweid,

> In *Arabian Nights and Days*, characters' names and their positions are the same as those of *The Arabian Nights*. As such, Mahfouz's reading of *The Arabian Nights* influences his writing style because he chooses to begin where *The Arabian Nights* ends. Being so, he reformulates the characterizations of *The Arabian Nights* for allegorical purposes. This is true in the Mahfouzian borrowing some of *The Arabian*

Nights' characters, notably, Shahryar, Shahrazad, Dunyazad, Nur Al-Din, Alaeddin, and Sindbad. (95)

Remarking further on the question of Borges's presence in the work, Rodica Grigore notes that

> Despite all appearances, the same is true of the novel *A Thousand and One Nights and Days* (1982), which, although on its first level of meaning emphasizes the importance of the Arabic tradition of the famous collection of texts gathered under the title *The Thousand and One Nights*, manages to say something essential not only about the role and importance of stories in a world marked by violence, as Borges does in *Historia universal de la infamia*, but also about how people manage—or fail—to adapt to new, often historically-determined realities. Of course, all this is exposed through the narrative reactualization of the situation familiar to anyone who has read *The Thousand and One Nights* that imposes the Arabic tradition on the frame story. (Grigore 219–20; my translation)

In short, the temptation to view Borges's imprint on this work is inevitable. Even though the extant Arabic translations are culturally relevant to Egypt, writing on the theme after Borges opens itself to suggestions of his influence. As Mahfouz retains the Pahlavi-era Persian names of the main characters of the original frame story, he acknowledges the pre-Islamic Persian origins of the piece. And the act of rewriting such a famous work associated with Borges would bring Pierre Menard to the minds of all contemporary readers.

Iranian literati discovered Borges through the 1965 translations of *Labyrinths* and *The Aleph*, undertaken and published quietly by Ahmad Mir'ala'i (1942–1995). Mir'ala'i had a master's degree in English literature from the University of Leeds and was active in literary circles in Isfahan until his suspicious death in 1995. His literary circle included novelist Hushang Golshiri (1938–2000), little known outside of the Persian-speaking world but among the most highly regarded modern novelists in the Persian language, as suggested by the annual literary prize that bears his name.[3] Of Golshiri, Arta Khakpour notes: "Although best known for his groundbreaking novel *Shazdeh Ehtejab* (*Prince Ehtejab*), and the controversial film based upon it (which precipitated Golshiri's arrest for its supposedly anti-monarchical content), it was Golshiri's short stories in the *Jong* (a literary journal he edited) era that first established him as Iranian fiction's preeminent opponent of mimetic realism in the generation after Hedayat" (Khakpour 452). The reference is to Sadeq Hedayat's unusual novel, *The Blind Owl* (*Būf-e kūr*, 1936) that seems to follow its narrator down a path of obsession and madness, always returning to the same image of a man and a woman. It is here, however, that Khakpour (and he is certainly not alone, as several studies available in Persian suggest) begins to express the arrival of Borges into Isfahan's literary scene, timely in that Persian avant-garde writers were moving from established boundaries of fiction: "One issue after the publication of Sadeqi's story, *Jong* introduced Jorge Luis Borges to the Iranian reader, through Ahmad Mir Alai's translation of 'Circular Ruins' (translated as 'Viraneh-ha-ye modavvar'). Mir

BORGES AND THE FORMATION OF THE LITERARY GLOBAL SOUTH   447

Ala'i also published his translations of 'The Aleph' and 'The Gospel According to Mark' in *Jong* 9" (Khakpour 456). The point which Khakpour summarizes next is of great importance because it solidifies the impression Borges's fiction made on later Persian fiction: "*Jong's* translation of this story is significant both for the way Borges' experiment with ontological paradoxes was reminiscent of modern Persian literature's earliest exposure to the same, namely the words of Hedayat, as well as for the way these devices would be incorporated into the later fiction of writers like Golshiri himself" (456). An unintentional irony occurs because "Las ruinas circulares" was translated into Persian from English rather than Spanish. Khakpour's summary states that it "involves a sorcerer consumed with the task of dreaming a full manifested human being into existence" (456). Borges's original Spanish refers to the dreamer with the word "mago" (i.e., a magus rather than a sorcerer), a point of reference which, along with the dreamer's language (Avestan) places the story culturally within Achaemenid or Sassanid Persia (Corwin, "Borges" 29). Because the text debuted in modern Persian second-hand via an early translation into English, a relevant cultural reference was lost to Iranian writers because of an imprecise translation of a key term used in the original, a consequence of the inaccessibility of Spanish to Iranian writers of that era.

These oversights that result from reading Borges in translation or from partial readings of his oeuvre can be found in an essay by Shaahin Pishbin, who bemoans that

> From a tradition that spans a millennium, [Borges] only repeatedly discusses the two poets Omar Khayyam and 'Attar, and cynics may justifiably complain that his discursive instrumentalization of these thinkers reproduces stereotypes of the Orient as essentially mystical and ancient. We are inevitably left wondering what Borges might have made of the *Shahnameh's* epic blending of history and legend, of the widespread bibliomancy of Hafiz's *Divan*, or of Nima Yushij and Persian literature's decisive turn towards modernism which occurred in his own lifetime. (226)

It is precisely the *Shahnameh* from which Borges draws the ending of "Las ruinas circulares," arguably one of his best-known stories. The passage of the magus through fire, unscathed, recycles the ordeal of Siyâvash, who must pass through fire to prove his innocence of an accusation of seduction by his stepmother (Corwin, "Borges" 31). The purity of the magus's Avestan, uncontaminated by Greek, is a subtle hint in the same direction, as the *Shahnameh* is often noted for the extreme paucity of Arabic borrowings in its sixty thousand couplets. Ferdowsi, author of the *Shahnameh*, is mentioned in a line in "El Zahir" and in an essay, "Nota sobre Walt Whitman" [Note on Walt Whitman] (*OC* I: 591, 249). The word "diván" appears in "El jardín de senderos que se bifurcan," which may be a clue laid for careful readers engaged in analysis (*OC* I: 476). Borges more than once mentions Edward Granville Browne's *A Literary History of Persia*. These points underscore the need for good criticism to engage in a whole reading of Borges rather than to sift through scattered or cursory readings. Subtlety defines Borges; therefore, oversights such as these, which are likely to emerge from under-reading Borges and overlooking available criticism, become intolerable.

Along the same lines, Ian Almond notes that "For Borges, the *Thousand and One Nights* and the story of al-Mokanna obviously have one thing in common: Islam" (446). Borges's noted readings suggest that these two texts have something very different in common: Persia, since both works derive from Persian cultural patrimony, the first being a set of tales around a pre-Islamic Pahlavi-era Persian frame story, and the second from a slimly recorded account of historical imposture. The parallel that Almond misses in the Al-Mokanna story is Smerdis (or Bardiya as he was known in Persian) the impostor, the only historical character which fictionalized versions of Borges and Bioy Casares can find in the apocryphal encyclopedia entry they locate on a place called "Uqbar." Almond's relegation of Persian identity (and history) into a neat but erroneous category of "Islamic Culture" fails to recognize Borges's focus on Persia's distinctive history, including and especially its pre-Islamic origins and identity. This becomes more evident as one reads more of Borges and the books that he cites. Here the author (Almond) misunderstands Borges's intentions, which undermines his effort to shed light on the Argentine writer's subject. Early in his essay, Almond poses the following questions: "Is there anything different about Borges, *écrivain préféré* of Derrida and Foucault, which distinguishes his representation of Islamic Culture from the standard Romantic or Late Victorian responses he appears to be familiar with? Or is Borges, for all the novelty of his Argentinian perspective (writing, as one fellow Argentine puts it, "from the edge of the West" [Sarlo 5]), just another bemused European writing about the Oriental Other?" (435–36). The answer to that may come from yet another Argentine writer, Estela Canto: "del mismo modo, los argentinos se sentían superiores a los otros sudamericanos por no tener sangre negra o india en sus venas. Lo cierto es que la tenían—no mucha, no conspicua—, pero los mitos son más tenaces que las estadísticas" [in the same way, Argentinians felt superior to other South Americans because they had no black or Indian blood in their veins. They certainly did have it—not much, and not conspicuous—but myths are more tenacious than statistics] (36). Almond's bibliography is entirely in English, meaning his work was not informed by Borges's original texts or by major scholarship available only in Spanish. His insistent and somewhat awkward misclassification of Persia's literature and its history parallels his incomplete and erroneous views of Borges and Argentina as Western.

Similarly, Almond attempts to reduce Borges's mirror motif to a nineteenth-century style Orientalist fantasy, referring to it condescendingly as "magic mirrors" (445). The mirror appears in "El tintorero enmascarado Hákim de Merv" and returns in subsequent writings in relation to a single phrase in that piece, regarding its monstrousness and comparison to paternity. "Tlön, Uqbar, Orbis Tertius" and "Emma Zunz" see a return of the motif, but neither one has anything to do with the subject of Islam, and both are conveniently disregarded by the critic. The objectionable motifs envisaged by Almond of an Orientalist's fantasy are noted as follows: "The landscapes of these stories are dressed abundantly with a wealth of familiar Oriental images: emirs, visors, deserts, scimitars, turbans, and camels" (441). As Almond limits his arguments to stories set in a questionable all-encompassing "Islamic Culture" his notions of the bad sort of Orientalism in Borges's writings are compressed, even though Borges's projections of

BORGES AND THE FORMATION OF THE LITERARY GLOBAL SOUTH   449

Persia begin with imagery and references to history, language, and beliefs that predate the advent of Islam by over a thousand years.

Iran's mirror may be India before partition, as Vedic Sanskrit, Avestan, and Old Persian evolved, respectively, into Hindi and Urdu, Pashto, and Farsi. Borges was well aware of this, having read Percy Sykes's *A History of Persia*, which he twice refers to in *Historia universal de la infamia* (*OC* I: 324, 329). Modern Persian, a prestige language of India, left its mark on major North Indian languages, especially Hindi and Urdu. Another major cultural moment in Indian history was the arrival of Parsees a thousand years ago, bringing Zoroastrianism and the Avestan language with them, marked by the tower of silence of Bombay in "El acercamiento a Almotásim," and the fire temples in "Las ruinas circulares." That India's best-known novelists writing in English would embrace the words or techniques of Borges should be of little surprise then, given the place of India in Borges's writings. Kiran Desai, born in Delhi, uses a Borges poem, "Jactancia de quietud" [Boast of Quietness], as an epigraph in her Man Booker award-winning novel, *The Inheritance of Loss* (2006), one of her only two (so far) published novels. Her more famous mother, Anita Desai, begins her collection of novellas titled *The Artist of Disappearance* (2011) with the first line of Borges's poem, "Everness." While there have not been any essays yet devoted to aesthetic assimilations of Borges's techniques by either Kiran or Anita Desai, Daniela Fargione notes that both pieces share a theme of oblivion and devotes some time to explaining it. How much of that can be conclusively viewed as the influence of Borges is yet to be proposed, although the presence of his poetry is not debatable. Perhaps the best-known or most notorious of contemporary Indian novelists who writes primarily in English is Salman Rushdie. The Ayatollah Khomeini's famous *fatwa* against Rushdie after the publication of *The Satanic Verses* (1988) turned his into a household name. On the matter of his exposure to Borges's writing, Rushdie mentions in an interview in *The Guardian*, in 2018, that "I can think of books that made little explosions in my mind, showing me literary possibilities I hadn't dreamed of until I read them. James Joyce's *Ulysses* was one such book. Jorge Luis Borges's *Fictions* (*Ficciones*) was another, and three stories from that collection, 'Death and the Compass,' 'Funes the Memorious' and 'The Garden of Forking Paths' have never left me, and still help me to think about what I'm doing, or might do, or should never try to do" (Rushdie). The most evident so far of Rushdie's ventures into literary paradigms set by Borges may be *Quichotte* (2019). His modernization and rewriting of *Don Quixote* was quickly followed by a succession of reviews published in different periodicals and newspapers, many of which eagerly point to Borges in the background. In Kolkata's *Telegraph*, Deeptanil Ray begins his review with Borges: " 'The Quixote,' as Jorge Luis Borges read in the literary notes of a certain Pierre Menard, once and another true author of the œuvré [sic] non-pareil, 'was first and foremost a pleasant book. . . .' *Quichotte* is not. Pertinacious in its mockery of the 'Age of Anything-Can-Happen', *Quichotte* misses out on the simple and essential pleasure triggered by the good old Quixote—the pleasure of reading as true adventure while reality morphs into strangeness in a mad, unreal world" (Ray). As it would appear, both Rushdie and the author of the unfavorable review share a predilection for Borges. A review from another Indian journal, *Scroll.in*, published a much more favorable review of the same novel, with a section titled "Kafka, Borges, Greene" that notes "Another influential echo is the famous Borges short story in which twentieth century French writer Pierre Menard rewrites some chapters of *Don Quixote* 'which coincided—word for word and line for line—with those of Miguel de Cervantes.' This is Borges's manner of pointing out how history and context are inseparable from meaning" (Sipahimalani). In a manner of speaking, both Ray and Sipahimalani subordinate Rushdie to Borges, in the subtle suggestion that it is no longer possible for a writer to model a novel on *Don Quixote* without comparison to Borges while also inferring subtextually that it is *de rigueur* for reviewers to be aware of Borges and ever vigilant of his imprint on other writers.[4]

Perhaps the best-known novelist, essayist, and scholar from sub-Saharan Africa is J. M. Coetzee. His personal affinity for Borges is well-documented, particularly through his own essays. In *Stranger Shores*, Coetzee comments with remarkable ease (not remarkable for a worthy Nobel laureate) about the fiction and essays of Borges, and finally about the difficulties of translation, including some of his disappointment in Borges's collaboration with Norman Thomas di Giovanni in altering descriptions in their English translation. Andrew Hurley's later translations are the final subject of his essay: "If there is one general weakness, it is that Hurley's feel for the level of formality of English words is not always reliable" (Coetzee 150). From there Coetzee remarks on alterations made by Hurley that go beyond a translator's license: "Hurley also performs a disturbing revision of his own. In 'The Circular Ruins,' a story about a male generative power and male birth, Borges writes 'A todo padre le interesan los hijos que ha procreado.' 'Every father feels concern for the sons he has procreated'. Hurley translates this, 'Every parent feels concern for the children he has procreated'" (Coetzee 150). What surfaces from this essay is Coetzee's attention to minute detail in his readings of Borges and that he has read in the original after having learned Spanish well enough to distinguish register and timbre in that language, an obvious, monumental advantage. In this regard, Coetzee goes far beyond the realm of the norm, in which critics might pluck a piece of translated fruit with which to garnish an essay, missing perhaps the deepest meanings implicit in the text. Fernando Galván in "Coetzee versus Menard or the Making of a Writer" identifies particulars:

> In my view, 'Pierre Menard, autor del *Quijote*' (Borges 1989a, 444–50) must have been in the back of his mind when he alluded to 'rewriting another novel . . . or . . . making that rewriting into the subject of your own writing'. Coetzee—this is my principal contention in this essay—was reading Borges in the previous years, while in the US, and before his return to South Africa in 1971; in fact, he mentioned Borges explicitly in those 1973 notes, as he made reference to the book in which 'Pierre Menard' was included, i.e., *El jardín de senderos que se bifurcan* (1941), cited in English as 'The Garden of the Forking Paths'. (Attwell 2015, 84) (176–77).

Galván has devoted a great deal of time to studying the traces of Borges in Coetzee's writing. In contrast to others who may not have employed Borges's particular literary devices, Galván notes Coetzee's particular embrace of the one used in "Pierre Menard, autor del Quijote," as follows:

> In *The Childhood of Jesus*, the 'Menard device' is so obvious that the whole novel takes place in a strange and fantastic place where characters have Spanish names and speak Spanish. It is not La Mancha, true enough, but a country of refugees where the book that boy protagonist, David, reads and from which he learns to read is none other than *Don Quixote*. But curiously enough, when the question of who wrote that book arises, the answer is not Cervantes but 'Benengeli'. ("Borges, Cervantes and Coetzee" 10).

Noteworthy writing after Borges in the Global South ranges from the subtly mimetic to the dialogic, evident in the work of writers from Africa, the Middle East, India, and China. Writers who in recent times reworked classic texts such as *The Thousand and One Nights* and *Don Quixote* have had their fiction scoured for points of convergence with Borges. The figure of Borges looms large over the reception of *The Thousand and One Nights*; similarly, in the case of *Don Quixote*, the matter of rewriting the novel that surfaced in "Pierre Menard, autor del Quijote" has inspired various writers' attempts to do just that. The results are to be found in criticism of Coetzee's *The Childhood of Jesus*, Rushdie's *Quichotte*, and Mahfouz's *Arabian Nights and Days*. Can Xue does not attempt to conceal the influence of Borges on her fiction and criticism, but rather engages directly with Borges, rewriting neither *The Thousand and One Nights* nor *Don Quixote*, but "El jardín de senderos que se bifurcan," conscious of the Argentine author's compact rewriting of the *Hong Lou Meng* in that story and of his readings of Zhuangzi. Well-versed literary critics in India were quick to note that Rushdie's fiction was at least partially under the spell of Borges. Those less familiar with the breadth of Borges's readings may also have missed the literary engagement between him and some of the finest writers from the Global South, as well as some of the major literary jewels he drew from in his stories. The same has not been true of exceptional writers. Few works of Hushang Golshiri have been translated into other languages, and only scant literary criticism from modern Iran has been translated, although several critics contend that Borges influenced Golshiri's later work. Whether all comparisons made are entirely plausible or not will be the subject of further debate. That stated, it is beyond contention that Borges's treatment of national literary treasures from the Middle East, South Asia, and East Asia has sparked responses from writers from the Global South.

NOTES

1. For more on Borges and Chinese literature, see Yu.
2. Other writers in Arabic who have a close relation to Borges are the Moroccan novelists Tahar Ben Jalloun and Abdelfattah Kilito. The latter has written several essays on Borges in French.
3. On Golshiri and Persian literature more generally, see José Darío Martínez Milantchi.

4. Another Rushdie text that is a tacit tribute to Borges is the 1995 novel *The Moor's Last Sigh*, in which the first sentence of one of the chapters is an unmarked quotation of the first line of "La escritura del dios" [The Writing of the God].

WORKS CITED

Almond, Ian. "Borges the Post-Orientalist: Images of Islam from the Edge of the West." *MFS Modern Fiction Studies*, vol. 50, no. 2, 2004, pp. 435–39.

Azouqa, Aida O. "Gamāl Al-Ghīṭānī's 'Pyramid Texts' and the Fiction of Jorge Luis Borges: A Comparative Study." *Journal of Arabic Literature*, vol. 42, no. 1, 2011, pp. 1–28.

Balderston, Daniel. "Borges en el mundo, el mundo en Borges." *Revista Chilena de Literatura*, no. 96, 2017, pp. 55–66.

Balderston, Daniel. "'The Labyrinth of Trenches Without Any Plan' in 'El jardín de senderos que se bifurcan.'" *Out of Context: Historical Reference and the Representation of Reality in Borges*. Duke University Press, 1993, pp. 39–55.

Borges, Jorge Luis. *Obras completas*. 4 vols. Emecé, 1996.

Canto, Estela. *Borges a contraluz*. Espasa-Calpe, 1989.

Coetzee, J. M. *Stranger Shores: Literary Essays, 1986–1999*. Viking, 2001.

Corwin, Jay. "Borges, the Magi and Persian Histories." *Variaciones Borges*, vol. 41, 2016, pp. 27–40.

Corwin, Jay. "'Emma Zunz' in the Mirror and the Labyrinth." *Theory in Action*, vol. 13, no. 4, 2020, pp. 148–59.

Dados, Nour, and Raewynn Connell. "The Global South." *Contexts*, vol. 11, no. 1, 2012, pp. 12–13.

Galván, Fernando. "Borges, Cervantes and Coetzee, or the Fictionalisation of the author." *European Journal of English Studies*, vol. 20, no. 2, 2016, pp. 179–91.

Galván, Fernando. "Coetzee *versus* Menard, or the Making of a Writer." *Romance Studies*, vol. 39, no. 2–3, 2021, pp. 175–87.

Grigore, Rodica. "Istorie, memorie și ficțiune în proza lui Naghib Mahfuz." *Meridianele prozei*. Editura Casa Cărții de Știință, 2013, pp. 219–23.

Jweid, Abdalhadi N A Abu. "Naguib Mahfouz's Arabian Nights and Days: The Allegorical Sequel of The Arabian Nights." *Studies in Literature and Language*, vol. 21, no. 2, 2020, pp. 91–100.

Khakpour, Arta. "Beyond the One-World Frame of Fiction: The Breakdown of Reality in Hushang Golshiri's Stories." *Iranian Studies*, vol. 49, no. 3, 2021, pp. 451–69.

Lees, Nicholas. "The Brandt Line After Forty Years: The More North–South Relations Change, the More They Stay the Same?" *Review of International Studies*, vol. 47, no. 1, 2021, pp. 85–106.

Møller-Olsen, A. "Sounding the Dream: Crosscultural Reverberations between Can Xue and Jorge Luis Borges." *Canadian Review of Comparative Literature*, vol. 47, no. 4, 2020, pp. 463–79.

Pellat, Ch. "ALF LAYLA WA LAYLA." *Encyclopædia Iranica*, http://www.iranicaonline.org/articles/alf-layla-wa-layla.

Pishbin, Shaahin. "Borges and Persian Literature." *Jorge Luis Borges in Context*. Edited by Robin Fiddian. Cambridge University Press, 2020, pp. 219–27.

Ray, Deeptanil. "Salman Rushdie's *Quichotte* Is Not a Pleasant Book." *The Telegraph*, November 11, 2019. https://www.telegraphindia.com/culture/books/salman-rushdie-s-quichotte-is-not-a-pleasant-book/cid/1717617.

Rushdie, Salman. "Salman Rushdie: 'I Couldn't Finish Middlemarch. I Know, I Know. I'll Try Again.'" *The Guardian*, January 26, 2018. https://www.theguardian.com/books/2018/jan/26/salman-rushdie-the-books-that-changed-me.

Sipahimalani, Sanjay. "With His Next Novel, Salman Rushdie Joins an Illustrious Line of Those Who Rewrote 'Don Quijote.'" *Scroll.in*, April 13, 2019. https://scroll.in/article/919737/with-his-next-novel-salman-rushdie-joins-an-illustrious-line-of-those-who-rewrote-don-quixote.

Sun, Haiqing. "'Hong Lou Meng' in Jorge Luis Borges's Narrative." *Variaciones Borges*, vol. 22, 2006, pp. 15–33.

Williams, Mac. "Zoroastrian and Zurvanite Symbolism in 'Las ruinas circulares.'" *Variaciones Borges*, vol. 25, 2008, 115–35.

Xue, Can. "An Interpretation of 'The Garden of Forking Paths' by Jorge Luis Borges." http://web.mit.edu/ccw/can-xue/files/CanXue-Borges.pdf.

Yu, Lou. "Borges en China (1949–2017)." *Variaciones Borges*, vol. 45, 2018, pp. 5–22.

IN OTHER FIELDS

CHAPTER 26

"NUEVA REFUTACIÓN DEL TIEMPO" [A NEW REFUTATION OF TIME] AND THE PORTRAYAL OF AN IRONIC FATE

MARINA MARTÍN

IN THE LIBRARY'S FORKING PATHS

PERHAPS the best way to address an intricate subject like this requires accepting a realistic and humble approach. There is every reason to tread carefully. Dwelling in Borges's erudition no doubt adds a significant challenge to the one already posed by the enigma par excellence of time. As a result, perplexities keep rising, but they also yield horizons of interpretation that enrich our vision, if only to further plunge us into deeper levels of questioning.

Jorge Luis Borges's legendary erudition unfolds endlessly around the subject of *time* in all of his writings, regardless of their literary genre. And this is done in such a way that different disciplines are invited to participate in debates held throughout history. Philosophers, theologians, mathematicians, literary critics, and linguists, among others, are frequently summoned to a discussion in his pages. For good reason, Daniel Balderston does not hesitate to emphasize in *How Borges Wrote* the labyrinthine nature of Borges's writings with countless allusions "to works well and little known, in many languages and on diverse subjects" (3). The same can be said about his manuscripts. In fact, as Balderston remarks, the profusion of bibliographical references in the left margins is one of the "most notable features" in manuscripts of essays or lectures (21). Indeed, that tendency portrays a natural habit rooted in a persistent devotion to libraries. Those of us who have had the chance to examine some of Borges's manuscripts have seen that feature emerge invariably from them. Such is the case with the notes and lecture papers focusing on David Hume that I was able to examine.[1] Gathered in one of Borges's Avon notebooks at the Michigan State University (MSU) Library, these manuscripts go beyond the author's intention to deliver a humble and basic introduction to Hume's doctrine, or, as he himself puts it: "una lección—elemental porque yo no podría dar otra—de metafísica" [a rudimentary lesson on metaphysics—since I would not be able to do otherwise] (13). Yet although concise, those handwritten pages do not fall short of rich and stimulating challenges. Patiently marked in the margins, numerous references to ancient and contemporary works featuring epistemological, philosophical, and theological debates held throughout history sketch multiple forking paths. Among them, the explicit reference to "Nueva refutación del tiempo" confirms Borges's commitment to the *esse est percipi* principle, along with his support for the arguments discussed in that essay. And he does so in a brief and witty manner by recreating imaginary dialogues among Locke, Berkeley, and Hume and having them develop the epistemological tenets they share.[2] We therefore reencounter a line of thought that not only plays a fundamental role in "Nueva refutación del tiempo" but also lies at the heart of memorable stories, such as "El milagro secret" [The Secret Miracle], or "Funes, el memorioso" [Funes, the Memorious], for instance. Be it fiction or essays, prose or verse, the subject of time reappears, bringing along an interplay with questions regarding memory and identity or mind and language as related themes. Although essential and going beyond the scope of the present study, these intertwined themes—with their own subdivisions and network of implications—bear the spirit of a library.

"Time Is a River That Sweeps Me Along, but I Am the River"

πάντα ῥεῖ. Borges's interest in the enigma of time is remarkable. There is no doubt it runs with persistence throughout his lifelong devotion to metaphysics. Time flowing from past to future or from future to past, both directions being equally probable and unverifiable. Time moving backward or forward in an infinite manner . . . or just the opposite, as eternity: "the lucid and simultaneous possession of all instants of time" (*SNF* 219). The list of riddles goes on, revealing inherent difficulties in each conceptual version. How can each person's experience of time synchronize with the general time in mathematics? How can an individual go through different perceptions of time, as shown in "El milagro secreto"? If time is a mental process, how can it be shared? And, finally, to crown it all, Zeno's refutation of movement, leaving disarmed opposing arguments. Borges often recreates with fondness the simplicity and power of this ancient jewel: "*Es imposible que en ochocientos años de tiempo transcurra un plazo de catorce minutos, porque antes es obligatorio que hayan pasado siete, y antes de siete, tres minutos y medio, y antes de tres y medio, un minute y tres cuartos y así infinitamente, de manera que los catorce minutos nunca se cumplen"* [*It is impossible for fourteen minutes to elapse in eight hundred years of time, because first seven minutes must pass, and before seven, three and a half, and before three and a half, one and three-quarters, and so on infinitely*] (*OC* I:354; *SNF* 124; emphasis in the original). We might as well recall at this point the humorous question—or rather masterful blow—that Borges raises at the end of "La perpetua carrera de Aquiles y la tortuga" [The Perpetual Race of Achilles and the Tortoise]: "¿Tocar a nuestro concepto del universo, por ese pedacito de tiniebla griega?" [Would this bit of Greek obscurity affect our concept of the universe?] (*OC* I:248; *SNF* 47).

The *infinite* marks Borges's entire writings, revealing his growing fascination to explore it in metaphysics, theology, and even mathematics—disciplines most dear to him. Already present in his early writings, time and the infinite stand out in *Discusión* [*Discussion*], particularly in "The Perpetual Race of Achilles and the Tortoise" and the later "Los avatares de la tortuga" [Avatars of the Tortoise], both memorable essays on Zeno's paradoxes—a favorite theme in his works. In 1936, featured as the meeting point of theological and philosophical debates, the subject of time guides "Historia de la eternidad" [A History of Eternity]. Originally written in two Sol de Mayo notebooks in 1934, under the title "Historia Aeternitatis," this essay foreshadows "Nueva refutación del tiempo" not just in the subject matter, but also in the inclusion of the 1928 charismatic text "Sentirse en muerte" [Feeling in Death].[3]

The essay's ironic title, Historia de la eternidad, tacitly intends to share with readers the appeal and reception that the concept of eternity had over the years. With touches of humor, Borges then traces the versions of an image that, far from being intelligible, is enriched over time by disputes and perplexities. And it is certainly a plan that he takes up again with great skill in essays like "La esfera de Pascal" [Pascal's Sphere], "El tiempo y J. W. Dunne" [Time and J. W. Dunne], and "La creación y P. H. Gosse" [The Creation and P. H. Gosse], included in *Otras inquisiciones* [*Other Inquisitions*] (1952).

Time is for us a pressing topic, and "acaso el más vital" [perhaps the most vital] problem of metaphysics, Borges claims in "Historia de la eternidad" (*OC* I: 353; *SNF* 123). Seven years later, in 1941, he corroborates with no hint of hesitation in "The Creation and P. H. Gosse" that it is the *central* problem of metaphysics. Finally, when composing "Nueva refutación del tiempo" in 1946, he confirms his previous position but also elaborates a stunning image of the concept. Profoundly paradoxical in nature, this image depicts human life's ironic fate: "El tiempo es la sustancia de que estoy hecho. El tiempo es un río que me arrebata, pero yo soy el río; es un tigre que me destroza, pero yo soy el tigre; es un fuego que me consume, pero yo soy el fuego" [Time is the substance of which I am made. Time is a river that sweeps me along, but I am the river; it is a tiger that mangles me, but I am the tiger; it is a fire that consumes me, but I am the fire] (*OC*: II: 148–49; *SNF* 332).

There is hardly any room for indifference when reading those words at the end of the essay. Might a hint of despair be detected here? Perhaps. Yet since courage and endurance are prevalent values over anguish or fear in Borges's fiction, it should be no surprise that he concludes his reflections with a note of stoic acceptance. Most importantly, the use of powerful metaphors gives readers no other discernment than wonder and no other conclusion to cast into the mythical *Know Thyself.*

SAPERE AUDE

Building on Hume's doctrine in "Nueva refutación del tiempo," or illustrating its twofold character through a network of subtle references in "Tlön, Uqbar, Orbis Tertius," Borges sheds light on the nature and limits of skepticism. What can we know, and how far can our doubts be pushed? How far, in turn, can our language go? Hume, the vast scholarship on his doctrine, and philosophers like Mauthner come into play here. According to T. H. Huxley, quoted at the beginning of this central essay, the three questions considered by Kant to be the major targets of philosophy (i.e., "What can I know, what ought I do, and what may I hope?") *resolve* themselves in the long run into the first, since philosophy fundamentally "is the answer to the question, What can I know?" (48).

For Huxley, Kant's *Kritik der reinen Vernunft* and Hume's *Treatise of Human Nature* basically aim at developing a "critical philosophy" that limits knowledge to the world of phenomena revealed by experience. This approach would at least have the merit to restrict errors over any lofty truth claims. However, the confident and rigorous method that Hume applied to experience had ironically led him to a deep awareness of reason's limitations, arriving at the disintegrated scenario of perceptions that Borges describes when carrying the *esse est percipi* principle further. Following the spirit of Ockham's razor, the application of a brief and apparently harmless formula had nevertheless revealed unsettling consequences. Borges quotes passages from both Berkeley's *Principles of Human Knowledge* and Hume's *Treatise* to help his readers penetrate "ese inestable mundo mental" [this unstable world of the mind] (*OC* II: 139; *SNF* 321). We are invited to picture a world of evanescent impressions, without matter or spirit, neither objective nor subjective; a world with no space, just made of time, progressively dissolving into "un laberinto infatigable, un caos, un sueño" [an inexhaustible labyrinth, a chaos, a dream] (*OC* II: 129; *SNF* 321).

No other case seems to describe Hume's own experience. In the "Conclusion" of Book I of his *Treatise,* he admits finding "nothing but doubt and ignorance" when turning "my eye inward" (172). A similar mood is reported in the "Appendix," when he declares to find himself involved "in such a labyrinth, that, I must confess, I neither know how to correct my former opinions, nor how to render them consistent" (399). But, despite the anguished tone that can at times be detected in his words, the skeptical outlook of his doctrine hardly ever falls into dark melancholy. Sooner or later, a sense of balance, acceptance, and subtle humor pervades his writings. These features are especially present in his *reply* to Berkeley, and in his posthumous *Dialogues Concerning Natural Religion* (1979), a work in which the tacit role of irony is fundamental. Borges shares and praises this spirit, as the manuscripts in the Avon notebook show: "Hume

"NUEVA REFUTACIÓN DEL TIEMPO" 461

parece ignorar o desdeñar las posibilidades patéticas de la doctrina escéptica; muchos entenderán que esa falta de patetismo es una pobreza. Yo no lo entiendo así; yo miro con nostalgia esa moderación tan civilizada, de la que nuestro siglo está desterrada—quizá definitivamente" [Hume seems to ignore or disdain the pathetic possibilities involved in the skeptical doctrine; many may view as a shortcoming that lack of drama. I don't think so. I look with nostalgia on such civilized moderation, absent from our time—perhaps forever] (MSU Avon notebook).

Such reflections help us understand that Borges's own skepticism aligns with Hume's doctrine. Far from being a mere affinity, the adoption of both Hume's skepticism and naturalism represents the very heart of Borges's *reply* to his own refutation and ultimately sheds light on his decision to embrace Schopenhauer's *Weltanschauung*.

A Lifetime Devoted to Metaphysics

"Nueva refutación del tiempo" is perhaps one of Borges's most important writings.[4] It is composed of two similar studies. The first one, version (A), was written in 1944; the second one, version (B), in 1946, since he felt the need to revisit the subject. We can imagine the interest and care he invested in the elaboration of this essay—being the analysis of time—as he states in the "Nota preliminar," "indócil" [unyielding] in nature. And, for that reason, also precious. In fact, he could be seen in this case as emulating the spirit of his own character, Pierre Menard, in pursuing an unreachable, quixotic goal. Indeed, Borges makes his intentions very clear from the start, letting a self-addressed irony take place by declaring that his essay is nothing but "el débil artificio de un argentino extraviado en la metafísica" [the feeble artifice of an Argentine adrift on a sea of metaphysics] (*OC* II: 135; *SNF* 317). Yet often in his writings the use of humor, parodic devices, metaphors, and/or references intertwined with a network of implications turn into epistemological strategies that enable philosophical discernment. This is the case with his fiction and essays. And it is perhaps one of Borges's most remarkable skills. Patiently crafted fictions that turn into cognitive strategies, such as "Tlön," as well as the analysis of texts quoted in "Nueva refutación" end up questioning the refusal to see any sort of philosophical contribution in his writings.[5]

If *irony* touches "Historia de la eternidad" in the very title, that approach is reinforced in "Nueva refutación" to the point of becoming a central motif. Here, Borges's mature voice warns readers from the start. Yes, the title is meant to be a joke: it is "un ejemplo del monstruo que los lógicos han denominado *contradictio in adjecto*" [an example of that monster called a *contradictio in adjecto* by logicians], for if we say that a refutation of time is *new* or *old*, we are recognizing "un predicado de índole temporal, que instaura la noción que el sujeto quiere destruir" [a temporal predicate that restores the very notion the subject intends to destroy] (*OC* II: 135; *SNF* 317–18). But it is more than a joke. It is meant to portray a condition rooted in an internal disparity. Although time is the substance of human life and is unavoidably present in language, it is ultimately a reality subject to a refutation that—borrowing Hume's reply to Berkeley—"admits of no answer and produces no conviction" (Hume, *Enquires:* 155). No matter how sound the arguments advanced against common *assumptions* may be, they will have no effect in life whatsoever. The arguments used to question the external world, the self, and time will have no bearing; those illusions will nevertheless be taken as *real* when reason yields to the force of nature and language. By the same token, analysis and logic cannot disappear either, and arguments sooner or later will be applied further on to experience. Borges takes that path and, rather than presenting readers with the comfort of familiar grounds and solutions, he embraces the impasse of a paradoxical fate.

Berkeley's doctrine and Hume's skepticism are fundamental to fully appreciate the philosophical issues involved in both "Nueva refutación" and in "Tlön." If the former is wholly immersed in analysis and rich quotations from those philosophers, the latter turns fiction into a cognitive artifact, anticipating contemporary debates on language.[6] Those philosophers' doctrines create an impact that expands throughout his writings. Essays such as "La encrucijada de Berkeley" [Berkeley's Crossroads] and "La nadería de la personalidad" [The Nothingness of Personality] (*Inquisiciones*, 1925) already endorse refutations of the external world and the self, this time drawing from "endless discussions with Father" on idealism and with his admired Macedonio Fernández who held strong affinities with Hume (Rodríguez Monegal 170).[7]

As is well known, Borges's interest in the British cultural tradition is nurtured in his family upbringing. He himself admits to being raised in a house with a fenced garden in Buenos Aires but growing up in the shelter of a library of "unlimited English volumes" (*OC* I: 101), his father's books. And he does not merely read Berkeley and Hume with interest; he shares their beliefs, adopts their epistemological arguments, and incorporates them into his fiction. Most importantly, in "Nueva refutación" he claims to have deducted "la consecuencia inevitable de su doctrina" [the inevitable consequence of their doctrine] (*OC* II: 135; *SNF* 317).

From the very start, a move of that kind needs to be handled, analyzed, and performed within the field of philosophy. Yet, in an interview with the journal *Philosophy and Literature*, in 1976, he denies any philosophical value to his works, declaring that his thinking had been done by Berkeley, Hume, Schopenhauer, and Mauthner, since he was "simply a man of letters" (339). The same declaration was made in 1969, when, in the Foreword to Ronald Christ's *The Narrow Act*, he states that, far from being a thinker or a moralist, he is "simply a man of letters who turns his own perplexities and that respected system of philosophy into the forms of literature" (ix). That type of self-portrait has become legendary.[8] There is no reason to mistrust his words, but it is equally valid to hold that an essay like "Nueva refutación" adds another dimension to his writings.

Bringing the *esse est percipi* principle to its full extent is a perfectly legitimate move, despite its consequences. And Borges is determined to do so. From the start, he frames his decision with a humorous note, claiming that if his refutation had been published in the eighteenth century, it might have been included in the scholarship devoted to Hume, "y acaso hubiera merecido una línea de Huxley o de Kemp Smith" [or at least mentioned by Huxley or Kemp Smith] (*OC* II: 135; *SNF* 317). Jokes aside, there is no doubt that

Borges not only worked at length on Berkeley and Hume but also extended his interest to their commentators. This is particularly evident in the MSU manuscripts where Huxley's study is a valued source of information and biographical data.[9] And "Nueva refutación" corroborates such interest with the significant inclusion of Kemp Smith since this critic represents a turning point in the vast scholarship on Hume and plays no small part in the present essay.

Kemp Smith sheds light on Hume's naturalism and questions the exclusive portrayal of his doctrine in negative terms.[10] Borges shares this view and imaginatively expands the implications in his fiction. The interplay between skepticism and naturalism sets the limits for both, involving a twofold philosophical position that, as Richard Popkin elaborates in his studies, disables pyrrhonism.[11] The duplicity in the essay "Borges y yo" [Borges and I], or in *El otro, el mismo* [*The Other, the Same*] is not foreign to the present topic. Skepticism and naturalism coexist in the ambiguity of a position that incorporates them both, and "Nueva refutación" builds exactly on it: "En el decurso de una vida consagrada a las letras . . . he divisado o presentido una refutación del tiempo de la que yo mismo descreo, pero que suele visitarme en las noches y en el fatigado crepúsculo, con ilusoria fuerza de axioma" [In the course of a life dedicated to belles-lettres . . . I have glimpsed or foreseen a refutation of time, one in which I myself do not believe, but which tends to visit me at night and in the hours of the weary twilight with the illusory force of a truism] (*OC* II: 137; *SNF* 318). An observation of this kind opens again the scenario to Hume's *reply* to Berkeley, so significant in Borges's writings and so embedded in his own position.

Time, the only postulate left untouched by British empiricism, turns into a chimera once the immaterialist principle is brought to its ultimate consequences: "Negados el espíritu y la materia, que son continuidades, negado también el espacio, no sé qué derecho tenemos a esa continuidad que es el tiempo" [If we deny matter and spirit, which are continuities, and if we also deny space, I do not know what right we have to the continuity that is time] (*OC* II: 139; *SNF* 321). The application of Berkeley's principle leaves no room for doubt. Its clarity has the force of an axiom . . . but cannot *convince*. Zeno's magic seems to be at work here. And so is the perplexity it raises.

Hume genuinely admired Berkeley. However, he viewed the writings of that "ingenious author" as "the best lessons of scepticism" (Hume, *Enquires* 155). Here is his reply: "[Berkeley] professes, however . . . to have composed his book against the sceptics as well as against atheists and free-thinkers. But that all his arguments, though otherwise intended, are, in reality, merely skeptical, appears from this, *that they admit of no answer and produce no conviction*" (155). The use of italics for emphasis here is not accidental. It's Hume's own; he truly meant it. Yet critics have often overlooked the significance of this passage, perhaps because it appears *discreetly* in a footnote of Section XII, entitled "Of the Academical or Sceptical Philosophy," in his first *Enquiry*. Borges, however, honors that observation. Furthermore, he places its impact at the heart of his own skepticism.

Balderston refers to the celebration of the marginal or peripheral as being "essential to Borges's work" (3). This is the case here. In the same way that the adoption of a *clean* principle comes along with sweeping consequences, now a footnote's brief observation generates a position that achieves a protagonist role. In the opening paragraph of "La postulación de la realidad" [A Postulation of Reality], published in 1931, Borges praises Hume's reply for being both "educada y mortal" [polite and deadly] (OC I: 217). In "Tlön," the passage emerges as an essential part of this fiction's epistemology.[12] In the MSU manuscripts, it reappears as a cryptic and isolated quotation. Finally, in "Nueva refutación del tiempo," Borges pays full tribute to the passage, mapping the irony in Berkeley's doctrine and acknowledging its impeccable logic as much as its complete unfeasibility: "Tal es, en las palabras de su inventor, la doctrina idealista. Comprenderla es fácil; lo difícil es pensar dentro de su límite" [Such is, in the words of its inventor, the idealist doctrine. To understand it is easy; the difficulty lies in thinking within its limitations] (OC II: 138; SNF 320).

The Berkeleyan principle admits no refutation, yet its logic opens a disturbing scenario. Hume himself did not hide his concern when personal identity had to be dismantled.[13] No matter how many times a detailed scrutiny of perceptions could be performed, the outcome would remain the same: "When I turn my reflection on *myself*, I never can perceive this *self* without some one or more perceptions; nor can I ever perceive any thing but the perceptions" (*Treatise* 399). Borges transfers this very scrutiny to the analysis of time: "Admitido el argumento idealista, entiendo que es posible—tal vez, inevitable—ir más lejos" [Once the idealist argument is accepted, I believe that it is possible—perhaps inevitable—to go further] (OC II: 139; SNF 321).

If every idea comes from a preceding impression, where is the specific impression supporting the idea of *succession*? There is no such simple, individual entity; there is no trace of its existence. Once we argue that there is no matter beyond each individual perception, and no self beyond each mental state, we could equally maintain that there is no time beyond each instant: "tampoco el tiempo existirá fuera de cada instante presente" [neither then must time exist outside each present moment] (OC II: 146; SNF 329).[14] The application of the immaterialist principle here seems to be a perfectly valid move. Understood as succession, as the vast temporal *series* taken for granted by the idealist doctrine, time vanishes. Borges has followed both Berkeley and Hume and has arrived at a most unusual scenario, one that happens to be our own mental world.

Having to declare that we are nothing but a *bundle* or *collection* of different perceptions succeeding each other rapidly "in a perpetual flux and movement," as Hume did in T 1. 4. 6, takes courage (*Treatise* 165). Borges adopts this logic and moves on, acknowledging the novelty of his approach and claiming that his thesis is as ancient as Zeno's arrow. If we believe with Berkeley that time is the succession of ideas in the mind, or support Hume in thinking that it is composed of indivisible moments, where then does each moment start or end? If beliefs in the external world and in the self are both bold and senseless assumptions, it is not less illogical to assume that those perceptions bear limits in their limitless succession, or, as Borges states, "una serie cuyo principio es tan inconcebible como su fin" [in a series whose beginning is as inconceivable as its end] (OC II: 139; SNF 321). The impossibility to distinguish or separate in each moment its apparent yesterday from its apparent today is enough to disintegrate it. In other words, time is "a delusion" (SNF 325).

That Magic Artifice: Eternity

If Borges's interest in time can be traced through his entire career, the refutation he envisions usually comes along in a subtle and cryptic manner. Already prefigured in early poems from *Fervor de Buenos Aires* [*Fervor of Buenos Aires*] (1923) and in the intriguing "Sentirse en muerte" (1928), both tendencies somehow touch his entire writings, as indicated in the 1944 version of "Nueva refutación."

Within Borges's writings, "Sentirse en muerte" stands out for defying all kinds of literary genres and schemes. This famous text narrating a casual anecdote must have been linked to a memorable experience. It was first published in *El idioma de los argentinos* [*The Language of Argentines*] (1928), then included in the fourth section of "Historia de la eternidad" (in the 1936 volume of the same name), and finally inserted in section II of "Nueva refutación" (1944 version). Despite the sparks of humor and the moderate tone used, we know that Borges struggled to find the right words to express a deeply personal and unusual experience. Balderston's studies of the manuscript shed light on the text. His findings reveal significant differences in the composition of the manuscript since the writing here is "quick and irregular, as if he started jotting down ideas" to grasp something that is "hard to narrate" (52). The manuscript would then come closer to poetry than to prose, seizing the inspiration in rapid strokes, as if it were evoking "the surrealists' automatic writing" (55). Most certainly, the discourse at times becomes cryptic, even paradoxical when trying to express something that transcends language. In fact, Borges's introductory remarks to the text in "Nueva refutación" refer specifically to linguistic barriers: "Todo lenguaje es de índole sucesiva; no es hábil para razonar lo eterno, lo intemporal" [All language is of a successive nature; it does not lend itself to reasoning on eternal, intemporal matters] (*OC* II: 142; *SNF* 324). And the intention here is to record an experience that can neither be named nor understood; it can at most be described in conflicting terms, as "evanescent and ecstatic" (*SNF* 324).

The use of a hesitant tone to evoke a seemingly trivial yet unforgettable experience, such as an evening walk, does not exclude humor either when trying to downplay its significance. However, we learn that such a trifling event—"fruslería"—is related to "a scene and its word, a word I had said before but had not fully experienced until that night" (qtd. in Balderston 59). The contrast between *naming* and *living* collapses in the encounter of a timeless experience. Pointing to one of Borges's recurrent themes, this confession brings up the different approaches between realism and nominalism. Yet, pushing nominalism further into the refutation of time, Borges finds in both Schopenhauer and Plotinus the key to reconcile the contrast: "Por la dialéctica de Berkeley y de Hume he arribado al dictamen de Schopenhauer" [Via the dialectic of Berkeley and Hume, I have arrived at Schopenhauer's dictum] (*OC* II: 148; *SNF* 331). Keats's nightingale would then symbolically embody both the universal and the individual.[15] And identity would be the ultimate reference challenging language and time.

466 MARINA MARTÍN

Borges also moves away from any kind of grand stance when introducing "Sentirse en muerte" in earlier editions. That is the case with "Historia de la eternidad," where the preliminary remarks added to the text take the lead of a humorous, even satirical tone in the report of a personal and godless portrayal of eternity. However, an evaluation of the text, as Balderston's study suggests, gradually discloses an intimate and even *poetic* account of an experience lived at the heart of an unusual moment. There is no reason to question the authenticity of his remarks: "Me sentí muerto, me sentí percibidor abstracto del mundo. . . . No creí, no, haber remontado las presuntivas aguas del Tiempo; más bien me sospeché poseedor del sentido reticente o ausente de la inconceibible palabras *eternidad*" [I felt dead, I felt I was an abstract perceiver of the world. . . . No, I did not believe I had traversed the presumed waters of Time; rather I suspected that I possessed the reticent or absent meaning of the inconceivable word *eternity*] (*OC* II: 143; *SNF* 325). And there is no reason to take his remarks as trivial either, especially when considering the impact of this anecdote on Borges's life.

Is "Sentirse en muerte" reporting a mystical experience? This is not clear since the whole text moves away from any type of clichéd terminology. Instead, Borges refers in the closing paragraph to an "emotional anecdote" brought about by a glimpse of an idea and admits his inability to put into writing "a real moment of ecstasy and the possible insinuation of eternity" (*SNF* 326). Be it an insight, a glimpse, or an insinuation lived with full involvement, Borges seems to be dealing, in any case, with an idea that questions succession, the inherent nature of language.[16]

For theologians, eternity is a divine attribute that features the simultaneous and lucid possession of all instants of time. For Borges, that description is simply inconceivable, yet fascinating, since it turns into both a source of inspiration in his fiction and a periodic motif in his collection of essays, especially in *Historia de la eternidad* and *Otras inquisiciones*. If theologians throughout history understand eternity not as a mechanical aggregation of past, present, and future events but rather as their *simultaneous* presence, such an idea is for Borges inexplicable since its nature ultimately defies logic as much as language. For Hume, the simultaneous coexistence of instants of time doesn't make sense either, and he claims that it is utterly absurd: "the year 1737 cannot concur with the present year 1738, every moment must be distinct from, and posterior or antecedent to another" (*Treatise* 26). For him, succession of one instant after another is the essence of time. But, as we know, Borges challenges this conception, too. And, going further, he insists that eternity understood as a simultaneous totality is no less incomprehensible than time understood as succession. Both concepts would ultimately fall under the realm of fantastic literature. In other words: "Negar la eternidad, suponer la vasta aniquiliación de los años cargados de ciudades, de ríos y de júbilos, no es menos increíble que imaginar su total salvamento" [To deny eternity, to suppose the vast annihilation of the years freighted with cities, rivers, and jubilations, is no less incredible than to imagine their total salvation] (*OC* I: 364; *SNF* 136).

Although cryptic, new layers of refutation can still be found in Borges's writings. The next move is to challenge the concept of eternity as portrayed by one of the most

"NUEVA REFUTACIÓN DEL TIEMPO"   467

captivating motifs in his pages: cyclical time and/or variants of the doctrine of the Eternal Return. And, most certainly, this refutation is already announced in poems from *Fervor de Buenos Aires* (1923), in "Sentirse en muerte" (1928), and in "El truco," a reflection on a card game included in *Evaristo Carriego* (1930).[17] We will not find in these texts elaborated arguments, as fashioned in "Nueva refutación" through quotations from Berkeley and Hume, but rather brief hints as if we were filling in the missing pieces of a puzzle. Yet, built on allusion techniques and a network of implications, the open nature of those writings enables a poetic reading.

In "Nueva refutación," Borges explicitly declares that two arguments led him to question time: Berkeley's idealism and Leibniz's principle of Indiscernibles. The former is addressed to refute time as succession, as an infinite sequence; the latter aims at refuting the infinite repetition of a limited series/sequence. In this case, Borges uses Leibniz's principle to challenge the very notion of repetition when appealing to the repetition of two identical entities.

Borges uses the "truco" card game metaphorically to illustrate his claim that time is a fiction. Card permutations, despite reaching gigantic numbers, are nonetheless limited; given enough time, these same permutations keep cropping up to the extent that the card players themselves are not only repeating hands that had already come up in the past, but, as Borges suggests, they themselves are a repetition of former players because, they *are*, in fact, the former players. And these, according to pantheistic idealism, in the end turn into just one player that encompasses them all. Same instances, same games; Borges insists: How is it they differ? "Postulada esa igualdad" [Having postulated such an identity], Borges writes, "cabe preguntar: Esos instantes que coinciden ¿no son el mismo? ¿No me basta *un solo término repetido* para desbaratar y confundir la historia del mundo, para denunciar que no hay tal historia" [we may well ask: Are not those coinciding moments identical? Is not *one single repeated term* enough to disrupt and confound the history of the world, to reveal that there is no such history?] (*OC* II: 147; *SNF* 330). Even if we accept the infinite repetition of identical cycles or world histories, how is it that two completely identical series differ? "¿qué significa el hecho de que atravesamos el ciclo trece mil quinientos catorce" [What does it mean that we are going through the thirteen thousand five hundred and fourteenth cycle], he continues, "y no el primero de la serie o el número trescientos veintidós con el exponente dos mil" [and not the first in the series or number three hundred twenty-two to the two thousandth power?] (*OC* I: 391; *SNF* 122). What does this truly mean? Borges adds the following conclusion: "Nada, para la prática—lo cual no daña al pensador. Nada, para la inteligencia—lo cual ya es grave" [Nothing in practice—which is no impairment to the thinker. Nothing for the intellect—which is serious indeed] (*OC* I: 391; *SNF* 122).[18]

The presence of Leibniz's philosophy in Borges's fiction is subtle and powerful, especially in relation to the *Praedicatum inest subjecto* principle and the Identity of Indiscernibles. The story "Pierre Menard, author del Quijote" (1939) bears this trace with wit, opening venues of interpretations in both literary criticism and philosophy. In "Nueva refutación," Borges fully supports the Identity of Indiscernibles principle and uses Leibniz's argument to refute the idea of identical repetitions as portrayed by the doctrine of the cycles.

In a letter to Arnauld, Leibniz makes his first principle—*Praedicatum inest subjecto*—clear, stating that the predicate "is somehow included in the subject": "la notion du predicate est comprise en quelque façon dans celle du sujet" (G II 56).[19] And this is so for every true affirmative proposition, whether necessary or contingent, universal or particular. In this case, a perfect knowledge of the subject would enable us to deduce all its predicates (i.e., past, present, future, necessary or contingent) since they are all comprised in it.

The Identity of Indiscernibles is expressly deduced from the analytic character of all true propositions and can stand in the history of philosophy as a solid and clear principle. Leibniz's classic formulation states "qu'il n'est pas vray que deux substances se ressemblent entièrement, et soyent differentes *solo numero*" [it is not true that two substances resemble each other completely and differ only in number] (G IV 433).[20] In other words, if two things share all properties, they are identical, or $(\forall F)(Fx \leftrightarrow Fy) \rightarrow x = y$.

It would make no sense to assume that A and B are two indiscernible substances and think that A would differ from B exactly as B would differ from A. We would be saying that they are different but without a difference. "And as regards space and time, Leibniz always endeavoured to reduce them to attributes of the substances *in* them," Bertrand Russell remarks (14, emphasis added). Consequently, there must be "an internal principle of distinction," for places and times are distinguished by means of things, and *not vice versa* (G V 213). Let us then observe that Leibniz holds on to the idea that certain kinds of properties do *not* count as difference-making properties, such as *spatio-temporal properties*. Only intrinsic differences count to determine diversity. The refutation of both time and space can be understood under those lines, ultimately pointing to the immutable present as the only conceivable form of existence.

Bertrand Russell praises Leibniz's logical rigor as clear evidence of his philosophical excellence, but he also believes that the *Monadology* is "a kind of fantastic fairy tale" (xiii). Borges would agree. And so would the fictitious Tlönians for whom metaphysics is within their skeptical outlook, no more, yet no less, than a branch of fantastic literature. Beyond truth, then, there seems to be a path to beauty and wonder in the midst of an illusion that consumes and shapes human life: Time.

NOTES

1. My gratitude to the *Borges Center*, especially to Daniel Balderston, for making this possible.
2. See my study "Notas sobre David Hume" in *Variaciones Borges*.
3. Balderston studies the manuscript of "Historia de la eternidad" and views "Nueva refutación del tiempo" as a continuation of the reflections elaborated in that former essay (198–203).
4. "Nueva refutación del tiempo" is referred to as "Nueva refutación" from now on.

"NUEVA REFUTACIÓN DEL TIEMPO" 469

5. Fictions like "Tlön, Uqbar, Orbis Tertius," "Funes, el memorioso," or "Pierre Menard, autor del Quijote" [Pierre Menard, Author of the *Quixote*], for instance, illustrate this case from epistemological standpoints, or from topics related to time and identity.

6. The volume *Hume: A Re-evaluation* gathers essays centering on meaning as one of Hume's most important philosophical discoveries. This scholarship trend is in tune with strategic mechanisms of intertextuality found in Borges's fiction. D. Livingston, for instance, claims that the Humean epistemology offers "a critical reflection on the language of common life" (10). Stories like "Tlön" anticipate similar scholarship through the emphasis placed on language.

7. Borrowing significantly from Hume's refutation of the self, the essay "La nadería de la personalidad" was first published in 1922, in *Proa*. The manuscript is held at the Hillman Library Special Collections (University of Pittsburgh).

8. Borges revisits this image in "Simply a Man of Letters," included in the proceedings of a Symposium held at the University of Maine.

9. Huxley is also mentioned in the essay "El tiempo y J. W. Dunne" in relation to the subject of personal identity.

10. Kemp Smith is also a Kant scholar. His translation of Kant's first *Kritik*, *A Critique of Pure Reason*, is a classic, and his studies present interesting insights into the nature of idealism in both Hume and Kant. See his article "The Naturalism of David Hume."

11. His article "David Hume: His Pyrrhonism and His Critique of Pyrrhonism" elaborates in depth the skeptical position presented in Section XII of *An Enquiry Concerning Human Understanding*.

12. The passage reads: "Hume notó para siempre que los argumentos de Berkeley no admiten la menor réplica y no causan la menor convicción. Ese dictamen es del todo verídico en su aplicación a la tierra, del todo falso en Tlön" [Hume noted once and for all that Berkeley's arguments admit no reply and produce no conviction. That pronouncement is entirely true when applied to earth, and entirely false in Tlön] (*OC* II: 435).

13. The fact that he omitted treatment of the subject in his first *Enquiry* has generated a great deal of speculation among his commentators.

14. For Berkeley, time "is the succession of ideas in our minds" (87). For Hume, time (i.e., succession) "must be compos'd of indivisible moments" succeeding one another, and, for that reason, "none of them, however contiguous, can ever be coexistent" (26). For Borges, both space and time are challenged on the same grounds: "Negar la coexistencia no es menos argudo que negar la sucesión" [To deny coexistence is no less difficult than to deny succession] (*OC* II: 140; *SNF* 322).

15. This topic is succinctly elaborated in "El ruiseñor de Keats" [Keats's Nightingale] (*Otras inquisiciones*).

16. Language "no es hábil para razonar . . . lo intemporal" [does not lend itself to reasoning on intemporal matters] (*OC* II: 142; *SNF* 324). See also Section I of "Historia de la eternidad."

17. Borges mentions two poems: "Inscripción en cualquier sepulcro" and "El truco."

18. This essay is entitled "La doctrina de los ciclos" [The Doctrine of the Cycles] (*Historia de la eternidad*).

19. *Die Philosophischen Schriften*: Referred to as G.

20. Another classic formulation is found in a letter to Samuel Clarke: "J'en infère entre autres conséquences, qu'il n'y a point dans la nature deux êtres réels absolus indiscernables" (G VII 393). Russell translates: "There are not in nature two indiscernible real absolute beings" (54).

Works Cited

Balderston, Daniel. *How Borges Wrote*. University of Virginia Press, 2018.

Berkeley, George. *A Treatise Concerning the Principles of Human Knowledge*. Open Court, 1913.

Borges, Jorge Luis. *Selected Non-Fictions*, edited by Eliot Weinberger, translated by Eliot Weinberger, Esther Allen, and Suzanne Jill Levine. Viking, 1999.

Borges, Jorge Luis. *Obras completas*. 4 vols. Emecé, 1996.

Borges, Jorge Luis. "Davd Hume." *Cuaderno Avon*. Special Collections Library, Michigan State University, MSU 678_04. 9–14.

Borges, Jorge Luis. *Inquisiciones*. Proa, 1925.

Borges, Jorge Luis. "La nadería de la personalidad." Proa, 1922.

Borges, Jorge Luis. "Simply a Man of Letters." *Simply a Man of Letters*. Edited by Carlos Cortínez. Panel discussions and papers from the proceedings of a symposium on Jorge Luis Borges. University of Maine at Orono Press, 1982, pp. 1–24.

Borges, Jorge Luis. "An Interview with Jorge Luis Borges." *Philosophy and Literature*, vol. 3, 1977, pp. 337–41.

Borges, Jorge Luis. "Foreword." *The Narrow Act: Borges' Art of Allusion*. Edited by Ronald Christ. New York University Press, 1969, pp. ix–x.

Christ, Ronald. *The Narrow Act: Borges' Art of Allusion*. New York University Press, 1969.

Hume, David. *A Treatise of Human Nature*, edited by David F. and Mary J. Norton. Oxford University Press, 2004.

Hume, David. *Enquiries Concerning Human Understanding and Concerning the Principles of Morals*, edited by P. H. Nidditch. Clarendon Press, 2002.

Huxley, T. H. *Hume*. Cambridge University Press, 2011.

Kemp Smith, Norman. "The Naturalism of Hume." *Mind*, vol. 14, 1905, pp. 149–73.

Leibniz, Gottfried Wilhelm. *Die Philosophischen Schriften*. Weidmann, 1890. 7 vols.

Livingston, D. W. "Hume's Historical Theory of Meaning." *Hume: A Re-evaluation*. Edited by Donald W. Livingston and James T King, Fordham University Press, 1976, pp. 213–38.

Martín, Marina. "Notas sobre David Hume." *Variaciones Borges*, vol. 52, 2021, pp. 59–81.

Popkin, Richard. "David Hume: His Pyrrhonism and His Critique of Pyrrhonism." *Philosophical Quarterly*, vol. 1, 1951, pp. 385–407.

Rodríguez Monegal, Emir. *Jorge Luis Borges: A Literary Biography*. Dutton, 1978.

Russell, Bertrand. *A Critical Exposition of the Philosophy of Leibniz*. George Allen & Unwin, 1958.

CHAPTER 27

···

BORGES AND POSTCOLONIAL STUDIES

Toward the Universal and Back

···

GUIDO HERZOVICH

It may seem unsurprising that Borges has been hailed as a sort of postcolonial literary hero, for among writers who lived and worked in more or less peripheral regions and languages he has enjoyed a unique position in the Western canon. However, the fact that he had been singularly unburdened to act as a sort of representative of his country or culture of origin—unlike many other peripheral writers who garnered worldwide visibility—made his incorporation into postcolonial debates rather polemical at first. In 1992, when the US scholar Edna Aizenberg proposed him as a "postcolonial precursor," Borges was both the least expected and the unbeatable figure to weaponize. More recently, Robin Fiddian's *Postcolonial Borges* (2017) showcases the breadth of scholarship that was produced in that crossover in a quarter of a century and suggests the waters have grown calmer.

Aizenberg's point of departure was the frequent references to Borges by French and American philosophers and theorists—among them Michel Foucault, Gérard Genette, Jacques Derrida, and Harold Bloom—as well as scholars of the postmodern cultural turn, who saw Borges's oeuvre as a collection of postmodern forms and concerns. "It can be argued that Postmodernism is the first literary code that originated in America and influenced European literature," Dutch scholar Douwe Fokkema wrote in 1984, oblivious of Rubén Darío's "Modernismo," "with the possibility that the writer who contributed more than anyone else to the invention and acceptance of the new code is Jorge Luis Borges" (38).[1] "'Logical growth' turned this speculation into an indisputable truth," Emil Volek joked: "In 1991, following Fokkema's suggestion from a decade earlier, Alfonso de Toro categorically declares: 'Borges's *Ficciones* initiates postmodernity'" (72).[2] Volek, with the benefit of hindsight, added that a postcolonial Borges inevitably had to follow suit. "What is forgotten" in postmodern discussions of Borges,

Aizenberg protested, "is the peripheric, ex-centric position" of the author, or the "Latin American condition of the texts" (21). In the case of Fokkema, a brief claim in the very last paragraph indicated that "part of Latin America" shared "a particular way and view of life, common in the Western world" (55) which could be "linked" to the postmodernist "code," but his discussing it as such "code" made origin in fact irrelevant beyond questions of precedence and literary influence.

The alleged neglect that Aizenberg protested may be traced back to the inaugural French reception of Borges in the 1950s, where it was often explicitly claimed that he was in no meaningful way an Argentine or Latin American writer (Wijnterp 104–12).[3] His friend and translator Néstor Ibarra famously said as much in a preface to the first book-length French translation of Borges (Gallimard's *Fictions* in 1951): "nobody has less of a fatherland than Jorge Luis Borges. He should be understood only in himself, not in relation to a country, or to a continent, or to a culture he does not belong to nor represent in any way" (Borges, *Fictions* 7). Toward the end of the same paragraph, having no fatherland and representing no one made it possible for him to be "a European man of letters, who would be at home in London, or even in Paris, or at least, more generally, at the *Nouvelle Revue Française*" (7). This is unsurprising, since being European, like being "universal," is to be geographically unmarked.

This European introduction continued previous Argentine debates, where the issue of contention was whether Borges could represent a path forward for national literature as a whole—a customary way for assessing a writer's standing at the time. Ibarra's preface was at once a precedent for subsequent metropolitan attitudes. French critic René Étiemble, writing in Jean-Paul Sartre's *Les Temps Modernes* in 1952, praised in Borges "la perfection de l'esprit cosmopolite" [the perfection of the cosmopolitan spirit] (qtd. in Wijnterp 203). Just as Foucault reported in *Les mots et les choses* a most spontaneous and inspiring laughter while reading about an incongruous Chinese encyclopedia in "El idioma analítico de John Wilkins" [The Analytical Language of John Wilkins], critics of postmodernist literature perceived or acknowledged no essential alterity in reading Borges. They thus misjudged, according to Aizenberg, the historical reality to which his work was a "correlative":

> The "postmodern" characteristic of Latin American and Borgesian literature enthusiastically embraced by U.S. and European critics—self-reflexivity, indeterminacy, carnivalization, decanonization, intertextuality, pastiche, hybridity, the problematizing of time and space and a historical and fictional narration—are primarily a correlative of a colonized history and an uncohered identity, of incomplete modernity and uneven cultural development, rather than postindustrialization and mass culture. Their uncritical incorporation into a metropolitan repertoire indicates that the centering impulse of a 'decentered' postmodernism is far from gone. (21)

Her postcolonial claim was therefore presented as a reparatory measure against an expropriation, for Borges's alleged "cosmopolitanism" or "universalism" had been used as a subterfuge. This was more explicit in a 2003 article by US-based Uruguayan scholar Mabel Moraña:

> Foremost critics like Paul de Man and Michel Foucault, Harold Bloom, Gérard Genette and Italo Calvino, developed on the basis of Borges—not to say at his expense—the timeless image of the great allegorist of the mythologies that hold Modern Occidentalism in place, seeing only in some cases that of its most implacable and paradoxical deconstructor. In that self-reflexive reading, they sacrificed precisely the most singular feature of Borges's thought: that of an alterity that situates him in the outskirts [*arrabales*]—more than the margins or the periphery—of great systems, thus understanding his creations as emerging *despite* their unwavering River Plate condition, and not precisely because of it. (103)

Moraña's tone is characteristic of postcolonial demands, but perhaps overly mortified in the case of Borges. After all, his alleged contemporaneity with Europe—a long-standing ambition among Latin American *letrados* and intellectuals—has been cause for pride for legions of the region's critics. For dramatic effect we may illustrate this fact with Walter Mignolo's writings from the 1970s, densely imbued with (post)structuralist jargon and semiotic concerns, where any idea of a "correlation" between Borges's *écriture* and any non-universal "reality" was programmatically rejected: "Every time we write 'Borges,' we think not of the personality bearing that name, but of the six letters used as a codifying notation for certain texts" (Mignolo and Aguilar Mora 187; see also Mignolo, "Emergencia"). Mignolo, an Argentine philosopher who completed his doctoral studies in semiotics in France and then pursued a career in the United States, went on to become an important figure and critic in and of the Latin American postcolonial field since the 1990s, in fact rejecting the concept and advocating for "decoloniality" instead (Bhambra).

Aizenberg claimed that the proliferation of metropolitan references to "Pierre Menard, autor del Quijote" [Pierre Menard, Author of the *Quixote*] or "Kafka y sus precursores" [Kafka and His Precursors], while "El escritor argentino y la tradición" [The Argentine Writer and Tradition] was rarely mentioned, was a symptom that those critics were actively avoiding "the postcolonial implications" of Borges's work (21). The latter essay was Borges's postcolonial manifesto, whose topics and tropes brought him closer to writers from former colonies of Africa or Asia and explained why he was a "postcolonial master" to writers as distant—or perhaps as essentially similar—as Palestinian Anton Shammas, Indian Salman Rushdie, Moroccan Tahar Ben Jelloun, or Argentine Sergio Chejfec (Aizenberg 24).[4] Tradition itself was one of those topics, since it probed a more uncertain concept in Borges than in T. S. Eliot's "Tradition and the Individual Talent," an intertext of the essay's title. "Nowhere in his discussion does Eliot interrogate what tradition is for the English writer," while in Borges it requires "a great deal more probing [. . .] as well as heterogeneity in describing it and subversiveness in treating it," allegedly because of Argentina's postcolonial condition (Aizenberg 22). Another element was the relation between orality and writing, which Borges discussed in *gauchesca* [gauchesque] poetry and was equally "at the heart of literary-critical discourse in Africa" (Aizenberg 22). Aizenberg credited Jewish thought, also understood as subaltern tradition, for Borges's interest in the intertextual nature of all writing or the subtle interplay between faithfulness and transgression in textual commentary. Remarkably, she made no mention of the essay's most ostensible target, cultural nationalism, or its original context—when it was offered as a talk, in an openly anti-Peronist private institution in Buenos Aires, only a month after nationalist leader Juan Domingo Perón got reelected with more than 63% of the popular vote.

The vindication of this essay proved timely. Since the 1990s, "El escritor argentino y la tradición" has not only become an important text within Borges's body of work—key to contemporary interpretations of his literature—but one that also gets cited in wider discussions of postcolonial and world literature. Argentine Beatriz Sarlo's *Borges, un escritor en las orillas* [*Borges, A Writer on the Edge*], first presented as guest lectures in Cambridge in 1992, found inspiration in the essay for its title and key contentions, such that Borges's positioning at the southern "edge" of metropolitan culture is central to understanding not only his singularity but also his success. In 2003, a colloquium was devoted to "El escritor argentino y la tradición" in France, followed by an edited volume where it was claimed that "more than fifty years later," the essay "not only remains relevant but has overcome the limits of its original geographic and historical context" (Attala 10). Indeed, it has been used as a jumping-off point for discussions of cultural appropriation regarding Moroccans in France (Brozgal), "national literatures in the age of globalization" (Hassan), for teaching world literature (Damrosch), or even for reclaiming the Goethean idea of *Weltliteratur* in the Yugoslav context (Mijatović), to name a few examples. In these instances, the essay is generally invoked as a critique of efforts to define an identity or a project for national literatures, as a vindication of literary freedom to appropriate (usually dominant) forms or themes, or as a foregrounding of "today's global span of literature" (Damrosch 392). In 2013 Daniel Balderston asserted that it was "Borges's most famous essay" ("Detalles" 9).[5]

It is interesting to observe, however, that until the 1980s, this was not the case—not even in Argentina. Although widely available in Spanish, English, or French, "El escritor argentino y la tradición" was infrequently cited. Only those who rejected it seemed persuaded by its explanatory power. This was partly for the reasons that Aizenberg and Moraña observed: the interests of Borges's exegetes lay elsewhere, in his short stories for the most part, in the eloquence of the figures by which he tackled the dissonances between *Les mots et les choses*—in his "labyrinths."

As for critics who were inclined to "postcolonial" concerns like cultural "dependency" or "underdevelopment," during the Cold War—which coincided with a period of unprecedented visibility for Latin American literature—they were looking elsewhere for cues. In Cuban Roberto Fernández Retamar's famous *Calibán* (1971), Borges features prominently as a sort of postcolonial villain, for he "is not a European writer; there is no European writer like Borges," but a "typical colonial" one (28). In 1982, foremost Uruguayan critic Ángel Rama, briefly in exile in the United States—before his visa application got rejected on political grounds—, was still relying on Étiemble to deny Borges's literature of a "transcultural" nature. His "bold positioning in a cosmopolitan and universal perspective" placed him outside the framework of "transculturation," which Rama regarded as the only literary strategy capable of a *mestizaje* of sorts between modernizing foreign tendencies and deep-rooted inland traditions. He instead celebrated writers like Juan Rulfo or José María Arguedas (Rama 52).

"El escritor argentino y la tradición" briefly received serious critical attention in Argentina in its first years of circulation. It did not get taken up by the growing number of Borges enthusiasts but instead by young, middle-class, university-trained critics who set out to bring his reputation down. Children of poor immigrants who leaned left-liberal or left, tangibly influenced by Sartre's *What is Literature?*, these critics were neither Peronist nor nationalist; they did not stand up to defend any of the sources for a national tradition that Borges debunked—gauchesque poetry and Spanish literature—nor were they moved in their responses by identitarian concerns about national literature or the legitimate materials for Argentine writers to elaborate on it.

The aspects of the essay they rejected may in fact seem almost untraceable to us, a striking indication of profound changes in cultural dynamics since the 1950s, as well as in Borges himself as a cultural figure. In Juan José Sebreli's "El escritor argentino y su público" (1953) or Adolfo Prieto's introduction to his *Borges y la nueva generación* (1954), a primary objection is that Borges, by undermining the collective nature of literary tradition, surreptitiously unties literary writing and community-building. Diminishing literature's role toward social cohesion entailed a more general weakening of literature's stake in the nation's fate, while those critics remained attached to an idea of literature as a collective project with an impact on the country's sovereign role and international standing.[6] A model of cultural practice whose claim to success, according to Borges, was in having allowed a certain number of Jews and Irishmen to innovate within a cultural tradition that obliterated the collective quality of their alleged difference, had little appeal for someone like Prieto, who conceived of "a tradition of culture as a form of collective living" (24). As such, the essay's final plea seemed to him impossibly overwritten by capitulation, even in its phrasing: "Creo que si *nos abandonamos* a ese sueño voluntario que se llama la creación artística, seremos argentinos y seremos, también, buenos o tolerables escritores" [I believe that if we lose ourselves in the voluntary dream called artistic creation, we will be Argentine and we will be, as well, good or adequate writers] (274, emphasis added; *SNF* 427).

It is nonetheless this final plea which has made the essay's postcolonial and especially world literary appeal, rather than its rebuttal of specific "solutions" to the "problem" of a peripheral or postcolonial national tradition. For Borges's argument to appear "indisputable for us, to this day" (Contreras 209), general divestment of the "pseudoproblem" of tradition has been key. The idea that an artist's accomplishments depend partly on the wealth and strength of their tradition, and that their contribution to it is an important part of their worth, seems antiquated today, but well into the twentieth century it was fairly common. Néstor Ibarra's 1951 presentation is telling: for Borges to be "at home" at the *Nouvelle Revue Française* (*NRF*), he had to be "a European man of letters," thus deprived of a place in another tradition (7).

We may thus speak of a general weakening of the paradigm of tradition, brought about by aesthetic and infrastructural transformations. This is apparent in the changing ideas of one of Borges's most influential contemporaries in the realm of art theory. In 1948, Argentine art critic and curator Jorge Romero Brest (1905–1989), also an anti-Peronist intellectual who taught at the Colegio Libre where Borges delivered the essay, claimed that the history of Argentine art was nothing but a series of failed imports. He urged a "return to what we are": "to start off from those forms and topics that are naturally deep-rooted in most of us, in order to refine and dignify them gradually" (16). In the 1960s, however, he became a proponent of neo-avant-garde experiences, asserting that the dematerialization of art would do away with global inequalities among national traditions: a by-product of time-honored ways of doing and making, those traditions were embedded in the artifacts themselves, thus it would be unprofitable or even impossible to pass them on. Success, Romero Brest asserted, would be with those who shattered "rigid inherited mindsets in all fields" (*Arte* 19). "Our lack of tradition won't be for naught. That most regrettable dearth has become an advantage, which now makes it easy for us to cross the Rubicon" (Romero Brest, "Conciencia" 117).

The internationalization of the circulation of books and literature throughout the twentieth century, and especially since the 1950s, is intimately related to these transformations. Borges's first global readership was made possible by the Formentor Prize he shared with Samuel Beckett in 1961, as a function not only of prestige but of availability, since it was awarded by a consortium of some of the most sophisticated literary publishers in Europe and the United States, who translated and released his work simultaneously in numerous countries and languages. "As a consequence of that prize, my books mushroomed overnight throughout the western world" (Borges, "Autobiographical" 254). Since then, infrastructures for the international dissemination of literature have continued to expand, diversify, and accelerate, making it a lot easier for Latin American writers to be translated and published not only in Europe and the US but elsewhere as well, although this rarely happens without a first step into global visibility via English or French.

"In the days of *Don Quixote*," Robert Escarpit observed in 1965, "it took fifty years for a book to circulate throughout Europe, whereas now books are commonly translated within a year of their original publication" (108). Today, the influx of peripheral literature into American and European markets is not so much a consequence of capitalist globalization as we tend to think of it—monopolistic transnational publishers—than of a more piecemeal combination of small to medium local publishers; public or private aids to translation; young(ish) translators often residing where living costs are lower; and a precarious network of literary festivals, universities, and awards. As is the case with literary fiction generally, while the number of translated titles have risen, average print runs have dropped.

Postcolonial and world literary perspectives are also an effort to tackle these changes, made increasingly visible by the diversification of the faculty and the student body in many metropolitan universities.[7] In 1992, when Edna Aizenberg hailed Borges as a "postcolonial precursor," the term was fairly widespread—so that she felt no need to define it—but it was not as institutionalized in books, journals, and conferences as it is today. As it is well known, the regional and disciplinary scope of postcolonial studies greatly exceeds (and initially often excluded) Latin American literature. A contemporary to the processes of decolonization and nation-building in Asia and Africa, it was chiefly associated with South Asian- and Middle-Eastern-born scholars from top American universities like Homi Bhabha, Gayatri Spivak, or Edward Said, whose *Orientalism* (1978) is often mentioned as a foundational work. The "offspring of a tense marriage between anti-imperial critique and metropolitan privilege" (Coronil 225), the postcolonial is centrally a project to critique and deconstruct the colonizer's gaze in cultural and knowledge production, under the persuasion that the latter has always been an important component of colonial power.

Postcolonial studies is originally both indebted and a contribution to poststructuralist theory, thus equally a product of the debates about the closure of modernity beginning in the 1960s. In the case of literary studies, however, it has generally pushed for geopolitical and ethical concerns to be brought into literary analysis, thus colliding historically with the emerging field of cultural studies to puncture the immanency of form encouraged by (post)structuralism. Some scholars in the field have more recently voiced an inverse complaint, that extra-literary concerns have pushed away the analysis of form almost entirely (Park Sorensen 3).

In the 1990s, debates around Latin America's place in the framework and/or the field of the postcolonial gathered steam. Some Latin Americanists initially resisted being towed behind a concept seemingly conceived for vastly different colonial experiences (Klor de Alva). In retrospect, resistance seems an important part of the remarkable trail of writing that ensued, whose productivity for rethinking the region's history and culture, at least from the perspective of metropolitan institutions, is hard to deny. A broad understanding of the term postcolonial, and of the meaning of the prefix "post," has become widely accepted. "I do not understand 'postcolonial' to be a moment when colonialisms have been overcome, but from a perspective that is critical of their legacies," Walter Mignolo wrote in 1995. "In that sense, I understand 'postcolonial' like other scholars understand 'postmodern,' as a moment of criticism of the legacies of modernity. 'Postcolonial' theories, as a consequence, would be critical responses to modernity from the periphery. In other words, a postcolonial perspective in the face of modernity and postmodernity, two sides of the same cube" (Mignolo, "Occidentalización" 29; see also Fiddian, "Locating the Object" and Bhambra). It is then easy to see why, as Emil Volek remarked, the transition from postmodern to postcolonial readings of Borges was rather smooth in conceptual terms, since he was already seen as a critic of modernity.

But his relocation to the margins, sometimes appearing as the return home of a captive of the White man, is not without irony. His demand for universality from the periphery, as expressed in an essay that allegedly strived to set South American writers free from the national in order to partake in a tradition that he described indistinctly as European or universal, has been used against the "universalist" readings of his work. To that end, some postcolonial critics, as we saw above, finding that Foucault or Fokkema

478   GUIDO HERZOVICH

understood Borges as speaking of a shared "reality" of some sort, proceeded to other both Borges and Latin American reality.

Beatriz Sarlo's book is explicit in this respect. While it clearly shares some of the concerns of postcolonial perspectives, it does not see Borges's Euro-American reception as an expropriation but as a measure of his fair-and-square success. While traveling in England she found Borges's books in the "ancient and modern classics" section of all bookstores. She notes, however, that unlike his shelfmates Dickens or Baudelaire, Borges "is stronger than Argentine literature itself, more powerful than the cultural tradition to which he belongs": "Borges's reputation in the world has cleansed him of nationality" (*Borges: A Writer* 1).

> But such a reading, however well justified, implies both recognition and loss, because Borges has gained what he always considered to be his—the right of Latin Americans to work within all traditions. He has also lost, albeit partially, something that he considered to be an essential part of his world: his links with River Plate cultural traditions and with nineteenth-century Argentina. (Sarlo, *Borges: A Writer* 2)

For Aizenberg, the postcolonial "correlative" of Borges's literature was very abstract: a colonized history, a fragmented identity, an incomplete modernity, and an uneven cultural development. "In her eagerness to canonize Borges as the precursor of postcolonial fiction in several continents" (Fiddian, *Postcolonial Borges* x), Aizenberg made no effort to define the cultural space where he wrote in any specificity. Sarlo, conversely, set off from the view that "there is no writer in Argentine literature more Argentine than Borges" (3). She opposed her claim to the tenets of a "narrow cultural nationalism, which denounced Borges in the 1940s and 1950s"—now "weakened, perhaps terminally" (Sarlo, *Borges: A Writer* 3). It was "in his exploration of how great literature can be written in a culturally marginal nation" where his Argentine condition lay, an exploration that allowed him "to invent a strategy for Argentine literature" (Sarlo, *Borges: A Writer* 3): "From the edge of the West, Borges achieves a literature that is related to foreign literature but not in any subordinate way" (Sarlo, *Borges: A Writer* 5). The wording is stronger in the Spanish-language version of the book: "Desde un margen, Borges logra que su literatura dialogue de igual a igual con la literatura occidental. Hace del margen una estética" [From a margin, Borges succeeds in putting his literature in dialogue with Western literature on an equal standing. He creates an aesthetics out of the margin] (n.p.). The commanding presence of "El escritor argentino y la tradición" is transparent.

Of course, Borges can embody an "aesthetics of the margin" as a function of having conquered the center, and of being read first from "universal," then from postcolonial and world-literary perspectives. In the 1950s, those emerging middle-class critics who contested "El escritor argentino y la tradición" could not see Borges as a postcolonial subject writing from a position of geopolitical marginality; to them, he was the most accomplished representative of the country's cultural elite. His call for appropriating the whole of the "universal tradition" sounded to their ears less as a claim to a right than as a challenge, for the required skills and access were unevenly distributed. As for Sarlo's assertion that Borges's literary achievement is in not subordinating himself to Western literature, it seems less a statement about the singularity of his work than about her findings in English bookstores.

Likewise, Borges's "strategy for Argentine literature," which many critics have read in recent decades through the terms of "El escritor argentino y la tradición," is primarily backed by his extraordinary global success. It is thus primarily a "strategy" to fulfill a time-honored ambition among *letrados* and intellectuals in Latin America and other peripheral Western countries, that of recognition in Europe and the US. Postcolonial scholars have often disavowed this postcolonial desire, stating that Latin American cultures "do not require an altar of consecration nor do they need to measure their distance from European models," in the words of Mabel Moraña (qtd. in Gramuglio 368). This kind of "proud declaration of self-sufficiency," as Argentine scholar María Teresa Gramuglio has observed, often comes from Latin American scholars based in the US (368).

The other paramount postcolonial ambition, traditionally seen with metropolitan recognition as essential to the cultural emancipation of a "young" nation, was that of defining the identity of the national culture. It was precisely the ideology of tradition that kept together these elements, making national identity a requisite of international visibility. "El escritor argentino y la tradición" operates within this compound, discrediting the former element in the name of the latter.

In that sense, Borges's 1951 proposal and some of its contemporary rebuttals were insightful in their assessments of the transformations of the cultural dynamics at the time and up through the present. Literature's role in the national project diminished, weakening literature as a national project. While central concerns of the ideology of tradition like representativity and authenticity—key problems in Borges's essay for that very reason—have in no way disappeared from cultural discussion, they have all but lost their national character, and also to a large extent, despite their seemingly collective nature, a communitarian one—burdening and vitalizing individual experience. As the transformation of cultures and infrastructures made the cosmopolitan promise of *Weltliteratur* seem attainable in an unprecedented way, and the privileged focus on individual appropriation—that Borges's essay validates in his praise of irreverence—makes it more difficult to see form as ever oppressive; it is the structural character of geopolitical inequality that tends to fade from view.

Reading his essay through a poststructuralist fascination with deviance and *détournement*, Borges's appropriations of world literatures, and his irreverence toward established limits and hierarchies, have been posited not only as a key to his singularity but also as a viable "strategy" for the emancipation of postcolonial literatures. These contemporary readings of his aesthetic politics, so antithetical to Fernández Retamar's or Rama's, are perhaps in line with a preference for nonconfrontational forms of subaltern resistance in academic discussion since the 1980s. Sarlo's work is also explicit in this respect, apologizing in the name of "we left-wing Latin American intellectuals" who "have been too slow to recognize" that "[against] all forms of fanaticism, Borges's work offers the ideal of tolerance" (*Borges: A Writer* 5)—"tolerance" being a key term in postdictatorship Argentina.

In this light, Borges's irreverence can be seen as a "weapon of the weak" strategy, to use US anthropologist James C. Scott's famous term from 1985 (i.e., a literary form of resistance that owns its subalternity in order to unavowedly disavow it). "Most subordinate classes are, after all, far less interested in changing the larger structures of the state and the law than in what Hobsbawm has appropriately called 'working the system . . . to their minimum disadvantage' " (Scott xv). Ultimately, an "aesthetics of the margin" befits a time when it is hard to imagine a politics of literature but from a position of marginality.

Notes

1. Aizenberg also mentions Barth (1984) and McHale (1987).
2. See Alfonso de Toro (1995, 2002).
3. For more on Borges's reception in France, see the chapter by Bosteels in this volume.
4. See the chapter by Corwin in this volume.
5. See also Balderston's "Borges in the World, the World in Borges" and *How Borges Wrote* (112–28).
6. In the fin-de-siècle formulation of Miguel Cané, this project read like this: "Good literature means culture, progress, civilization" (59).
7. From 1976 to 2016, the percentage of "white" university students in the US dropped from 83 to 57% (Menand).

Works Cited

Aizenberg, Edna. "Borges, Postcolonial Precursor." *World Literature Today*, vol. 66, no. 1, 1992, pp. 21–26.

Attala, Daniel, et al. *L'écrivain argentin et la tradition*. Presses Universitaires de Rennes, 2004.

Balderston, Daniel. "Borges in the World, the World in Borges." *A Companion to World Literature*, vol. 5b. Edited by Ken Seigneurie et al. Wiley Blackwell, 2019, pp. 3179–88.

Balderston, Daniel. "Detalles circunstanciales: sobre dos borradores de 'El escritor argentino y la tradición.'" *Cuadernos LIRICO*, no. 9, 2020. http://lirico.revues.org/1111.

Balderston, Daniel. *How Borges Wrote*. University of Virginia Press, 2018.

Barth, John. *The Friday Book: Essays and Other Nonfiction*. Putnam, 1984.

Bhambra, Gurminder K. "Postcolonial and decolonial dialogues." *Postcolonial Studies*, vol. 17, no. 2, 2014, pp. 115–21.

Borges, Jorge Luis. "An Autobiographical Essay." *The Aleph and Other Stories, 1933–1969*. Edited and translated by Norman Thomas di Giovanni. Jonathan Cape, 1971.

Borges, Jorge Luis. *Fictions*. Translated by Paul Verdevoye and Néstor Ibarra. Gallimard, 1951.

Borges, Jorge Luis. *Obras completas*. 4 vols. Emecé, 1996.

Brozgal, Lia. "Hostages of Authenticity. Paul Smaïl, Azouz Begag, and the Invention of the Beur Author." *French Forum*, vol. 34, no. 2, 2009, pp. 113–30.

Cané, Miguel. *Prosa ligera*. Moen, 1903.

Contreras, Sandra. "Breves intervenciones con Sarmiento (A propósito de 'Historias de jinetes')." *Variaciones Borges*, no. 9, 2000, pp. 202–10.

Coronil, Fernando. "Latin American Postcolonial Studies and Global Decolonization." *The Cambridge Companion to Postcolonial Studies*. Edited by Neil Lazarus. Cambridge University Press, 2004, pp. 221–40.

Damrosch, David. *World Literature in Theory*. John Wiley & Sons, 2014.

Escarpit, Robert. *The Book Revolution*. UNESCO, 1966.

Fernández Retamar, Roberto. *Todo Calibán*. CLACSO, 2004.

Fiddian, Robin. "Locating the Object, Mapping the Field: The Place of the Cultures of Latin America and Lusophone Africa in Postcolonial Studies." *Postcolonial Perspectives on Latin American and Lusophone Cultures*. Edited by Robin Fiddian. Liverpool University Press, 2000, pp. 1–26.

Fiddian, Robin. *Postcolonial Borges. Argument & Artistry*. Oxford University Press, 2017.

Fokkema, Douwe. *Literary History, Modernism, and Postmodernism*. John Benjamins, 1987.

Gramuglio, María Teresa. "El cosmopolitismo de las literaturas periféricas." *Nacionalismo y cosmopolitismo en la literatura argentina*. Editorial Municipal de Rosario, 2013.

Hassan, Ihab. "Janglican: National Literatures in the Age of Globalization. Philosophy and Literature." *Philosophy and Literature*, vol. 34, no. 2, 2010, pp. 271–80.

Klor de Alva, J. Jorge. "Colonialism and Post Colonialism as (Latin) American Mirage." *Colonial Latin American Review*, vol. I, no. 1–2, 1992, pp. 3–23.

McHale, Brian. *Postmodernist Fiction*. Routledge, 1987.

Menand, Louis. "The Changing Meaning of Affirmative Action." *The New Yorker*, January 20, 2020, https://www.newyorker.com/magazine/2020/01/20/have-we-outgrown-the-need-for-affirmative-action.

Mignolo, Walter. "Emergencia, Espacio, 'Mundos Posibles': Las Propuestas Epistemológicas de Jorge L. Borges." *Revista Iberoamericana*, vol. 43, no. 100–101, 1977, pp. 357–80.

Mignolo, Walter. "Occidentalización, imperialismo, globalización: herencias coloniales y teorías postcoloniales." *Revista Iberoamericana*, vol. 41, no. 170–171, 1995, pp. 27–40.

Mignolo, Walter, and Jorge Aguilar Mora. "Borges, el libro y la escritura." *Cahiers du monde hispanique et luso-brésilien*, no. 17, 1971, pp. 187–94.

Mijatović, Aleksandar. *Temporalities of Post-Yugoslav Literature: The Politics of Time*. Lexington Books, 2020.

Moraña, Mabel. "Borges y yo. Primera reflexión sobre 'El etnógrafo." *Crítica impura*. Edited by Carlos Jáuregui and Juan Pablo Dabove. Iberoamericana Vervuert, 2004, pp. 102–22.

Park Sorensen, Eli. *Postcolonial Studies and the Literary. Theory, Interpretation and the Novel*. Palgrave, 2010.

Prieto, Adolfo. *Borges y la nueva generación*. Letras Universitarias, 1954.

Rama, Ángel. *Transculturación narrativa en América Latina*. Siglo XXI, 2004.

Romero Brest, Jorge. " 'Conciencia de imagen' y 'conciencia de imaginar' en el proceso del arte argentino." *Escritos de vanguardia*. Edited by Inés Katzenstein. MoMA, Fundación Proa, Fundación Espigas, 2007, pp. 111–17.

Romero Brest, Jorge. "El arte argentino y el arte universal." *Ver y Estimar*, no. 1, 1948, pp. 4–16.

Romero Brest, Jorge. *Arte en la Argentina. Últimas décadas*. Paidós, 1969.

Said, Edward. *Orientalism*. Pantheon, 1978.

Sarlo, Beatriz. *Borges, A Writer on the Edge*. Verso, 1993.

Sarlo, Beatriz. *Borges, un escritor en las orillas*. Ariel, 1995.

Scott, James C. *Weapons of the Weak: Everyday Forms of Peasant Resistance*. Yale University Press, 1985.

Sebreli, Juan José. "El escritor argentino y su público." *Centro*, no. 7, 1953, pp. 24–29.

Toro, Alfonso de. "Jorge Luis Borges: The Periphery at the Center/The Periphery as Center/ The Center of the Periphery: Postcolonialism and Postmodernity." *Borges and Margins: Post-Colonialism and Post-Modernism*. Edited by Fernando de Toro and Alfonso de Toro. Vervuert, 1995, pp. 11–45.

Toro, Alfonso de. "The Foundations of Western Through in the Twentieth and Twenty-First Centuries: The Postmodern and the Postcolonial Discourse in Jorge Luis Borges." *Semiotica*, vol. 140, 2002, pp. 67–94.

Volek, Emir. "Jorge Luis Borges, precursor postcolonial y otros cuentos de la prehistoria de la posmodernidad." *Estudios*, vol. 5, no. 10, 1997, pp. 67–78.

Wijnterp, Lies. *Making Borges. The Early Reception of Jorge Luis Borges's Work in France and the United States*. PhD diss., Radboud University, Radboud Repository. https://repository.ubn. ru.nl/handle/2066/150648.

CHAPTER 28

BORGES IN FRENCH THEORY

BRUNO BOSTEELS

A DARK PRECURSOR?

STARTING in the early 1960s, after sharing the Formentor Prize with Samuel Beckett in 1961 and having a volume of the *Cahiers de l'Herne* devoted to him in 1964, Jorge Luis Borges quickly became a celebrity among French thinkers. This led the author half-jokingly to approve of Jean de Milleret's observation, in a set of interviews published in 1967, that "it was the French who first discovered you" (17). Not just writers and critics such as Maurice Blanchot or Pierre Macherey, filmmakers such as Jean-Luc Godard, or novelists such as Alain Robbe-Grillet, but also philosophers such as Gilles Deleuze, Jacques Derrida, Jean-François Lyotard, and Philippe Lacoue-Labarthe; historians such as Michel Foucault; analysts such as Jacques Lacan, Félix Guattari, Didier Anzieu, and René Major; sociologists and cultural theorists such as Jean Baudrillard and Louis Marin; or semiologists such as Julia Kristeva, all had recourse at one point or another to ideas from the Argentine writer. In addition to the appeal of Borges's style, two lines of affinity facilitated this confluence of interests: the shared critique of the subjectivity of "man," or of the human at the center of the discourse of the modern human sciences, and the critique of language as "mimesis," the imitation or representation of the real. A small number of Borges's texts thus allow several French thinkers to push all the presuppositions behind the twin topics of language and subjectivity to their logical extreme, where they reveal themselves to be fundamentally inconsistent, unfounded, or based on the absence of a common ground. Together with writers such as Lewis Carroll, James Joyce, and Jean Genet, Borges in this sense emerges as a "dark precursor," to use one of Deleuze's concepts, of a postfoundational (or what later would be called postmodern) approach to the central tenets of Western thought. In fact, the Deleuzian concept of the "dark precursor" in *Difference and Repetition* may itself have been influenced by the strange temporal loop of Borges's "Kafka y sus precursores" [Kafka and His Precursors], according to which authors somehow come before their own precursors, whose recognizability they help create in retrospect (Deleuze, *Différence* 156–58 and *Difference* 119–20; Borges, *OC II*: 88–90).

By now, the broad influence of Borges's writing on French intellectual and artistic circles is well documented.[1] Conceptually, however, the elective affinity between the Argentinean writer's literature and thought and the central obsessions of French theory and philosophy may well be based on a profound misunderstanding. Already the way in which Deleuze in the late 1960s connects Borges's writing to a logic of the simulacrum, setting up an argument that Jean Baudrillard in the 1970s and 1980s would twist and turn even further in the direction of a logic of full-blown simulation, suggests a different understanding of language and, by extension, a new conception of subjectivity or personhood. This conception no longer would be based on the impossible ideals of language as the mimetic representation or imitation of the real, nor would there have to be a stable human essence hidden behind the persona or mask of one's public appearance. Borges himself views language in terms of its efficacy for guiding us through a world of true appearances, while the sense of self comes to be defined as little more than the effect of a logical urgency. In this sense, at least in their critical or deconstructive mode, French theory and philosophy target metaphysical definitions of language and subjectivity that to a large extent are foreign to Borges's own convictions. Such definitions may provide the Argentine writer with fodder for some of his best-known thought experiments and paradoxes, but by no means do they exhaust his own views on the symbolic efficacy of language or on the logical inevitability of a certain subject-effect.

As a matter of fact, the Argentine's own theoretical and philosophical commitments favored a tradition that, especially after World War II, would become anathema to the whole Parisian intellectual scene, namely, the tradition of New England pragmatism—frequently dismissed in offhand remarks as a philosophy that would correspond merely to the "American way of life" in which truth would be reduced to the "cash-value" of "what works" (James, *Pragmatism* 53, 80). Thus, what would come to be known in the Anglophone world as "French theory," by giving right of entrance to Borges in some of its most significant texts, may have been welcoming into its midst the uncanny force of a Trojan horse. When Derrida or Foucault cited Borges with such enthusiasm in some of their most pivotal early statements, little did they know that they were opening the door to someone for whom Plato, Berkeley, or Leibniz may have been aesthetically more pleasing, but ethically speaking none was superior to the American pragmatist. "Para un criterio estético, los universos de otras filosofías pueden ser superios (el mismo James, en la cuarta conferencia de este volumen, habla de 'la música monismo'); éticamente, es superior el de William James" [From an aesthetic point of view, the universes of other philosophers may be superior (James himself, in the fourth conference of the present volume, speaks of 'the music of monism'); ethically, that of William James is superior], Borges writes in 1945 in a "Nota preliminar" [Preliminary Note] to the Argentinean translation of James's *Pragmatism*: Es el único, acaso, en el que los hombres tienen algo que hacer" [His is the only world, perhaps, in which human beings have something to do] (*Textos recobrados* 221). For someone known for his self-ascribed "escepticismo escencial" [essential skepticism], as Borges calls it in the Epilogue to *Otras inquisiciones* [*Other Inquisitions*], this is a rare and exceptional statement of ethical and philosophical commitment, one that we ignore at the risk of losing out on a crucial dimension of the author's own thinking (*OC* II: 153).

The pragmatist slant behind Borges's way of thinking places the critic before a difficult decision. It could mean that his French readers were simply wrong or at least one-sighted—caught unaware of Borges's own philosophical loyalties. Or, inversely, it could mean that there is a secret impulse toward a form of pragmatism—a way of conceiving of truth as a creative process that involves a doing or a making—behind the work of some of the major exponents of French theory and philosophy.

A New Style of Thought

With his most canonical "fictions" and "inquisitions" having been translated in France in the 1950s under the auspices of the prestigious publishing house of Gallimard, Borges appeals to French thinkers above all for his unique style of thinking and writing. This style concerns the execution as much as the conception of language and literature, in short stories or fictions that are often narrativized thought experiments and essays or inquiries that turn ideas and paradoxes into so many proto-narratives. Mimicry seems to be inevitable in this regard. As Lacoue-Labarthe, inspired by "*Ragnarök*" from *El hacedor* [*Dreamtigers*], wrote in a dream-like essay-fiction from 1965–1966 that he would revisit in 2007 shortly before his death: "But have I not wanted (rather desired, which is the only word that is apt here), obscurely, to write Borges's books, just as I almost dreamed his dream?" (42).

On one hand, Borges's ideas and practices allow a redefinition of the autonomous space of the modern literary. From Maurice Blanchot's brief chapter on "Literary Infinity: The Aleph" in his 1959 collection *The Book to Come*, via Michel Foucault's 1963 "Language to Infinity" in the journal *Tel Quel*, to Gérard Genette's "Literature According to Borges" in the 1964 *Cahier de l'Herne*, Borges is made part of a pantheon of modern writers and thinkers that includes Stéphane Mallarmé on a par with G. W. F. Hegel. In fact, the Argentine allows us to understand the former's quest for the infinite Book as the ultimate truth of the latter's speculative journey toward the Absolute. "I suspect Borges of having acquired the infinite from literature. This is not to suggest that he has only a calm knowledge of it drawn from literary works, but to assert that the very experience of literature is perhaps fundamentally close to the paradoxes and sophisms of what Hegel, to distance it, called the evil infinite," Blanchot concludes. "The truth of literature might be in the error of the infinite" (*Le livre* 130; *The Book* 93).[2] What Hegel disqualifies as the "evil," "spurious," or "bad" infinity, in other words, might well name the truth of the literary, emblematized in the Aleph.

Borges's style of writing, in its avowed fictionality and artificiality, would be a prefiguration of the book to come, understood less as a physical object than as a virtual space for experimenting with the totality as text and the world as library. Literature in this utopian view, as Genette and Foucault would elaborate, is the work of a single impersonal author, repeated if not recreated by every reader, and language becomes an infinite space of dispersal, the endless reduplication in the alphabetic writing of the West of what is always already doubled in speech, to keep death at a distance. "A work of language is the body of language crossed by death to open this infinite space where doubles reverberate," Foucault suggests, invoking Borges's "El milagro secreto" [The Secret Miracle] and "La biblioteca de Babel" [The Library of Babel] as possible sites for an investigation into the being of language that redoubles itself as if in a mirror, placed in the face of death. "And the forms of this superimposition, essential to the construction of any work, can undoubtedly only be deciphered in these adjacent, fragile, and slightly monstrous figures where a division into two signals itself; their exact listing and classification, the establishment of the laws that govern their functioning or transformations, could well lead to a formal ontology of literature" (Foucault, "Le langage" 47; "Afterword" 93). One year later, in an "Afterword" to *The Temptation of Saint Anthony*, Foucault once again places Borges in the select company of modern writers of whom Gustave Flaubert might have been the precursor: "In writing *The Temptation*, Flaubert produced the first literary work whose exclusive domain is that of books: following Flaubert, Stéphane Mallarmé and his *Le Livre* become possible, then James Joyce, Raymond Roussel, Franz Kafka, Ezra Pound, Jorge Luis Borges. The library is on fire" ("Un 'fantastique'" 12; "Afterword" 107).[3]

Borges's fictions and inquisitions, on the other hand, open the possibility of writing philosophy in a new style. "The time is coming when it will hardly be possible to write a book of philosophy as it has been done for so long: 'Ah! the old style . . . ,'" Deleuze exclaims in the Preface to his 1968 book *Difference and Repetition*. And it is once again Pierre Menard who leads the way toward a new philosophical style: "Borges, we know, excelled in recounting imaginary books. But he goes further when he considers a real book, such as *Don Quixote*, as though it were an imaginary book, itself reproduced by an imaginary author, Pierre Menard, who in turn he considers to be real. In this case, the most exact, the most strict repetition has as its correlate the maximum of difference" (*Différence* 4–5; *Difference* xxi–xxii).

During a few years, in the mid to late 1960s, some of the most famous French thinkers thus repeatedly have recourse to stories and ideas from the Argentine writer, as if he were a dark precursor of the various philosophies of difference. "On this question of the game of repetition and difference as governed by the death instinct, no one has gone further than Borges, throughout his astonishing work," Deleuze concludes (*Différence* 152–53; *Difference* 116), before quoting from "El jardín de senderos que se bifurcan" [The Garden of Forking Paths], one of his favorite short stories that the French philosopher would revisit the following year in *The Logic of Sense*, together with fictions such as "La muerte y la brújula" [Death and the Compass] and "La lotería en Babilonia" [The Lottery of Babylon] (Deleuze, *Logique* 77–78, 139, 210; *Logic* 61–62, 114, 176; see also Gardes de Fernández).

In "Violence and Metaphysics," an essay from 1963–1964 on Emmanuel Levinas subsequently included in the 1967 volume *Writing and Difference*, Jacques Derrida explains why Borges's approach to the history of Western philosophy might be so appealing. Discussing the sun as a central metaphor for truth, Derrida comments that "if language (except when it names being *itself* or nothing: almost never) is elementally metaphorical, Borges is correct: 'Perhaps universal history is but the history of several metaphors,'" and a few lines further down he adds: "If all languages combat within it, *modifying only the same metaphor* and choosing the *best* light, Borges, several pages later, is correct again: 'Perhaps universal history is but the history of the diverse *intonation* of several metaphors'" (*L'Écriture* 137; *Writing* 114, Derrida's emphasis; *OC* II: 14–16). For Derrida, in effect, the history of Western metaphysics has been dominated by a limited series of names and metaphors: light/darkness, day/night, speech/writing, center/margin, presence/absence, reason/madness, and so on. As he reiterates in what is perhaps his most anthologized essay, "Structure, Sign, and Play in the Discourse of the Human Sciences," this time without explicitly having to mention "La esfera de Pascal" [Pascal's Sphere] from which he took the previous two quotes: "Successively, and in a regulated fashion, the center receives different forms or names. The history of metaphysics like the history of the West, is the history of these metaphors and metonymies" (*L'Éscriture* 410–11; *Writing* 353). Thanks to his attention to the different intonations of such metaphors, Borges for a brief while attracted the attention of Derrida. "He seduced me," the main thinker of deconstruction would recall in a conversation with Borges's best-known biographer Emir Rodríguez Monegal two decades later while visiting Yale (*Writing* 121).[4]

In the reception of Borges, there are two concept-metaphors that might sum up the Argentine's seductive influence on French theory and philosophy from the 1960s until the 1980s, on the cusp between structuralism and poststructuralism and between the modern and the postmodern. On the one hand, the critique of language can be appreciated through the different intonations of the metaphor of the impossible or useless map that coincides with the territory; on the other, the critique of "man" or of the subject at the center of the human sciences leads to renewed appreciations of the notion of its monstrous other, lurking at the margins of Western metaphysics.

And yet we will also begin to observe a growing dissatisfaction and even a certain rejection of Borges's works and ideas among these French readers who previously had been among his most fervent admirers. Derrida in *Dissemination* will still use two epigraphs from Borges, bracketing a third one from Joyce, at the center of his long essay on "Plato's Pharmacy," originally published in 1968 in the journal *Tel Quel* (Derrida *Dissémination*: 104–05; *Dissemination* 84–85). But already in his seminar from 1964–1965 on *Heidegger: The Question of Being and History*, the French thinker had pointed out the insufficiency of the Borgesian idea from "La esfera de Pascal" [Pascal's Sphere], insofar as the task of philosophy or of thought must also include a destruction or deconstruction of the structure of metaphoricity itself, "for it is not only a matter of substituting one metaphor for another without knowing it: that is what has always happened throughout history, that universal history that Borges says is perhaps only the history of a few metaphors or of various inflections of a few metaphors"; only Heidegger's thinking of being allows us perhaps to denounce the movement of metaphor itself by making it appear as such: "One can perhaps call thinking and the thinking of being (the thinking of being as the horizon and the appeal of an impossible non-metaphorical thought) what calls for such a gesture of de-metaphorization" (*Heidegger: La question* 278–89; *Heidegger: The Question* 190). For such a gesture, even the vast universe of Borges's ideas would no longer suffice according to Derrida.

Similarly, while Deleuze still invokes Borges's image of "the labyrinth which is composed of a single straight line" from "La muerte y la brújula" as one of "Four Poetic Formulas Which Might Summarize the Kantian Philosophy" in the Preface written for the English translation of *Kant's Critical Philosophy: The Contest of Faculties* (Deleuze, "Preface" vii–xiii; *OC* I: 507), and while he will return once more to "El jardín de senderos que se bifurcan" in his discussion of compossible worlds in *The Fold: Leibniz and the Baroque* (Deleuze, *Le Pli* 83–84; *The Fold* 62–63), by contrast in *A Thousand Plateaus*, coauthored with Guattari, he prefers to point out Borges's failed or botched projects. "Jorge Luis Borges, an author renowned for his excess of culture," Deleuze and Guattari now write, "botched at least two books, only the titles of which are nice: first, *A Universal History of Infamy*, because he did not see the sorcerer's fundamental distinction between deception and treason (becoming-animal are there from the start, on the treason side); second, his *Manual de zoología fantástica*, where he not only adopts a composite and bland image of myth but also eliminates all of the problems of the pack and the corresponding becoming-animal of the human being" (*Mille Plateaux* 295; *A Thousand Plateaus* 241).[5] Here, again, it would fall on others to continue what remained insufficiently elaborated in Borges's work.

Finally, as if to confirm Deleuze and Guattari's change of heart, Foucault after the 1960s would go on to make only vague allusions to Borges's work in some of his titles, as in his 1977 essay "The Lives of Infamous Men," and just as a decade later his English translator would opt to publish Foucault's 1963 book *Raymond Roussel* under the ultra-Borgesian title of *Death and the Labyrinth*. Since the days of his contributions to *Tel Quel*, however, Foucault had long abandoned his dreams of an ontology of literature and with them his fascination with the Argentine writer so crucial for his 1966 magnum opus *The Order of Things: An Archaeology of the Human Sciences*.

A TERATOLOGY OF THE HUMAN SCIENCES

Few readers will ignore how Foucault opens *The Order of Things* with a reference to how his book has its origin in the laughter that stirred him upon reading the absurd classification of animals in a Chinese encyclopedia quoted in "El idioma analítico de John Wilkins" [The Analytical Language of John Wilkins] from *Otras inquisiciones* (*OC* II: 85–86). Foucault calls this list "monstrous," not so much because it would contain fantastic monsters of the kind that populate Borges's *El libro de los seres imaginarios* [Book of Imaginary Beings] but rather because it takes away the very ground on which such disparate beings might fit together. "The quality of monstrosity here does not affect any real body, nor does it produce modifications of any kind in the bestiary of the imagination; it does not lurk in the depths of any strange power," Foucault observes. "The monstrous quality that runs through Borges's enumeration consists, on the contrary, in the fact that the common ground on which such meetings are possible has itself been destroyed" (*Les mots* 7; *The Order* xvi).

Foucault's Preface is meant not only to explain the book's origin and method but also to serve as a threshold to announce a discourse that would no longer be trapped in the figure of "man" as both the transcendental subject and the empirical object of "human sciences" such as biology, political economy, and philology. We know that this modern discursive order, based on the empirico-transcendental redoubling of "man," constitutes the main target of Foucault's antihumanist impetus—one he shares with other French thinkers in the second half of the 1960s, such as Derrida or Louis Althusser. Prior to this modern order centered on the human, Foucault describes, first, the Renaissance, for which knowledge was based on a fundamental order of resemblance between the earthly and the heavenly; and, second, what in French is called the "classical age," governed by the ideal of knowledge as a mathematical table or taxonomy. Now, interestingly, for the abrupt and mysterious transitions between these three epistemic orders, Foucault has recourse to examples taken from the Spanish-speaking world. Georges Canguilhem speaks in this regard of Foucault's "*espagnolisme*," a form of Orientalist Hispanophilia ("The Death" 72). Thus, *Don Quixote* (1605; 1615) would mark the end of the Renaissance and the beginning of the classical age as the relations of similitude break down between words and things and the knight-errant wanders off between the world of letters and the real; Velázquez's *Las Meninas* (1656) would present a complete table or *tableau* of the order of representation of the classical age, with a lacuna waiting to be filled by the sovereignty of "man" of the modern age to take the place of the absent monarch standing before the Spanish painter; and the classification of animals in Borges's Chinese encyclopedia would announce a discourse after and beyond the modern, based on the dispersal of language devoid of a human center. If Foucault's three thresholds move back in time from Borges to Velázquez to Cervantes, appearing in reverse order from the historical transitions from the Renaissance to the classical age to the modern era, we can conclude that the Preface to *The Order of Things* announces the imminent end of modernity and offers a glimpse into a posthumanist and postmodern future.

Only by virtue of a paradoxical reversal can Borges's "unthinkable space" or "non-place" (*non-lieu*) constitute what Foucault in the book's opening line calls the "place of birth" (*lieu de naissance*) of his archaeological "inquiry" or "inquisition" (*enquête*, incidentally the same term used in French to translate *inquisición* as in Borges's *Other Inquisitions*). As an analysis of "the pure [or naked, *nue*] experience of order and of its modes of being," Foucault's archaeological project emerges out of the "wonderment" caused by the Argentine's apocryphal taxonomy, which discloses "the stark [naked, *nue*] impossibility of thinking *that*" (*Les mots* 7; *The Order* xv). By nestling his own discourse in the "interstitial blanks" of our modern order of things, Foucault grounds his archaeology of the human sciences in nothing less than the "monstrosity" of Borges's classification.

No doubt unaware of the Argentine's repeated desire to reconstruct something like a "teratological museum," as he puts it in "Sobre el doblaje" [On Dubbing] (*OC* I: 283)[6], elsewhere in *The Order of Things* Foucault thematizes the importance of teratology—the science or discourse of monsters—for the construction of knowledge of the living. In "Monsters and Fossils," he explains how positive facts and monstrosities paradoxically go together during the classical age. Classifications of forms of life and their evolution often carry with them "the necessity of introducing monsters into the scheme—forming the background noise, as it were, the endless murmur of nature," Foucault states; in fact, as one eighteenth-century scientist remarks: "It is only, perhaps, by dint of producing monstrous beings that nature succeeds in producing beings of greater regularity and with a more symmetrical structure," which to the archaeologist signals that "the proliferation of monsters without a future is necessary to enable us to work down again from the continuum, through a temporal series, to the table" (*Les mots* 168–69; *The Order* 155–56). Applied to Foucault's own classification of epistemic structures, this means that *The Order of Things* provides us with a key to understanding the necessity of Borges's "monstrous" invention for the archaeologist to work his way down to the "table" of modern knowledge about the living, speaking, and laboring human being.

In his most theoretical work, *The Archaeology of Knowledge*, Foucault will recognize that it is perhaps impossible to situate his own discourse with respect to the modern human sciences. In the book's opening pages, he writes "I have tried to define this blank space from which I speak, and which is slowly taking shape in a discourse that I still feel to be so precarious, and so unsure," but even toward the end of the book Foucault's archaeology remains marked by a profound uncertainty, in that "for the moment, and as far ahead as I can see, my discourse, far from determining the locus in which it speaks, is avoiding the ground on which it could find support" (*L'archéologie* 27, 267; *Archaeology* 17, 205). This does not mean that Foucault would be conceding the failure of his archaeological method. Rather, if we compare such alleged confessions in *The Archaeology of Knowledge* to the prefatory remarks about Borges in *The Order of Things*, we must conclude that, in both cases, Foucault is at pains to formulate an unusual theory of language and interpretation, one that no longer seeks support in any stable "ground" or "foundation" whatsoever. None of the subsequent works seeks to compensate for this absence of a "common locus" by providing his discourse with a stable point of view from where to speak.

Even in his genealogical works Foucault will continue to work from within a teratological perspective. Aside from Borges, this is a strategy he also may have learned from his mentor Canguilhem who, in *The Normal and the Pathological*, insists on "the possibility and even the obligation of enhancing the knowledge of normal formations by using knowledge about monstrous formations" (31). Thus, in Foucault's later essay, "The Life of Infamous Men," infamy marks the place where knowledge and power reciprocally reinforce one another to define not only what is true or false in an epistemological sense, but also what is normal or abominable—worthy of fame or infamy—in an ethical and political sense, a topic that Kristeva would revisit three years later in light of Borges's *Historia universal de la infamia* [*A Universal History of Infamy*] in a brief section of her *Powers of Horror: An Essay on Abjection* (*Pouvoirs* 31–33; *Powers* 23–25). Similarly, in his 1974–1975 lecture course at the Collège de France, published as *Abnormal*, Foucault shows how the notion of a "human monster" is juridical as well as moral, defining a place where forms of knowledge and forces of power combine to mold the subject's body: "The monster is the limit, both the point at which law is overturned and the exception that is found only in extreme cases. The monster combines the impossible and the forbidden" (*Les anormaux*

51; *Abnormal* 56). Perhaps, then, the science of monsters is a more likely candidate than the study of literature for becoming the third "counter-science" announced in *The Order of Things*, after ethnology and psychoanalysis, to wake us up from our anthropological slumber. It is from the study of abnormal, infamous, and monstrous cases that Foucault wishes to contest the normal formations of knowledge and power. Instead of a theory of pure language or an ontology of literature, teratology is this more general counter-science that Foucault hopes will break the spell of our humanism and our anthropologism. Whether in the fields of epistemology, ontology, or ideology, monstrosity is this positive force of alterity that is the necessary and constitutive outside lying beneath and beyond all identity. It is the region of the impossible and the forbidden, of that which is yet unthinkable, but which summons the archaeologist and the genealogist to chart the rules and norms that define what is normal and true at a given moment and, in so doing, clear a path for new and as yet unheard types of thinking. Foucault is not alone in this. In "Sign, Structure, and Play in the Discourse of the Human Sciences," Derrida, too, ends on a teratological note to imagine a form of thinking that does not continue to give different names and metaphors to the truth at the center of the structure. "Here there is a kind of question, let us call it historical, whose *conception, formation, gestations*, and *labor* we are only catching a glimpse of today," Derrida writes, also thinking of "those who, in a society from which I do not exclude myself, turn their eyes away when faced by the as yet unnamable which is proclaiming itself and which can do so, as is necessary whenever a birth is in the offing, only under the species of the nonspecies, in the formless, mute, infant, and terrifying forms of monstrosity" (*L'Éscriture* 428; *Writing* 370).

A MISREADING OF MAPS

If the figure of monstrosity helps French theorists and philosophers imagine a posthumanist thought to come, the different intonations of the metaphor of the map allow them to dismantle the system of mimetology that runs through Western metaphysics from Plato onward and, if Lacoue-Labarthe is correct, reaches all the way to Martin Heidegger.

Readers in France and elsewhere who refer to "the Borges map" often fail to mention any specific texts, but of about a dozen cartographic references in the Argentine's work they seem to have in mind above all "Del rigor en la ciencia" [On Exactitude in Science], a prose piece from *El hacedor* (*OC* II: 225) and, to a lesser extent, the example of a map within a map within a map, and so on, quoted from the American philosopher Josiah Royce's *The World and the Individual* in "Magias parciales del *Quijote*" [Partial Enchantments of the *Quixote*] from *Otras inquisiciones* (*OC* II: 45–47). The paradoxes of mimesis enacted in these two cases should not be conflated: the first narrativizes the paradox of complete mimesis, which leads to a useless form of tautological perfection, whereas the second discusses the very different paradox of self-referential mimesis, which leads to an aporetic form of abyssal embedding. Borges thus puts a double check on the project of mapping a totality. Whenever the map *is* the territory, cartography is useless or, in any case, without value as a sign. Yet no sooner do cartographers abandon the futile ideal of representation on a scale of 1:1 than the rigor of an exact map implodes into infinity and the dream of total mimesis becomes a self-destructive nightmare.

French theory and philosophy will exploit these twin reductions to the absurd of cartographic representation to question the foundations of the logic of mimesis that has been at the heart of Western metaphysics ever since Plato engaged in an age-old polemic with poets and painters in the *Republic*. Allowing for a similar ambivalence between fascination and condemnation, Borges's approach takes what appears to be the utopian premise behind mimetic representation and pushes it to its logical extreme, where it turns out to be either impossible or undesirable. As Marin writes in a luminous chapter titled "The Utopia of the Map" in his 1973 treatise *Utopics: Spatial Play*, Borges's "Del rigor en la ciencia," which itself coincides word for word with a citation attributed to a seventeenth-century author named Suárez Miranda, may well embody the ideal of the utopian text as such. To be sure, already in his *Écrits* published in 1966, in a footnote to his "Seminar on 'The Purloined Letter,'" Lacan had mentioned the "semiological utopia" of John Wilkins, through which Borges "harmonizes so well with the phylum of my subject matter" ("La Séminaire" 23 n. 1; *Écrits* 47 n. 8); and, in the same year, Genette would reissue his article on Borges under the title "The Literary Utopia" (1966). But now Marin shows the critical and even deconstructive potential of Borges's utopia of the map of the Empire that coincides with the Empire: "In its singularity this text may reveal the crucial experience of the utopia of every text, a play of levels and surfaces joining together and breaking apart to articulate 'possible meaning'; there is play in the movement because a surface of identities making any difference between Empire and its Map indiscernible" (*Utopiques* 295; *Utopics* 236). In fact, the completion of the perfect map of the Empire is only one moment in Borges's short parable, overcome when subsequent generations realize the uselessness of such cartographic zeal and, not without impiety, allow the map to fall to ruins in the deserts of the West, inhabited by beggars and animals. "The desecrating movement of time reveals the useless passion involved in this creation of simulacra, no matter how exact or scientific it is," Marin remarks. "The utopic *work* is not only contained in constructing that double or representation in the form of a simulacrum that enables a city or society to imagine itself as different from itself and as containing a reversed image of itself. The work of utopia also consists in its *ruin*, in its deconstruction" (*Utopiques* 293; *Utopics* 234, translation modified). Borges's parable hinges on a temporal sequence of different stages in the interrogation of mimetic representation, scaling upward toward the perfect map and downward into the ruination of the utopic impulse itself.

Following a structure common to a great many of his "fictions" and "inquisitions," the minimal narrativization of Borges's thought experiment in "Del rigor en la ciencia" in fact involves at least three moments or stages: first, the postulate of the utopian ideal of perfect adequacy or resemblance between map and territory; then, the moment of the practical realization of this premise; finally, the aftermath as a moment of

BORGES IN FRENCH THEORY   493

disillusionment or acceptance of the status quo.[7] Depending on the mood, the latter define the different intonations of the metaphor of the perfect map and its refutation or deconstruction by way of a reduction to the absurd: in some instances, the affective tonality tends toward pessimistic resignation, while in others the tone is one of jubilant affirmation of our condition as mortal animals who remain bound to the irrefutable play of time, difference, and finitude.

With respect to the critique or deconstruction of mimesis, a first conclusion to be drawn from Borges's parable would be to accept, if not also to celebrate, the fact that representation is possible not despite but thanks to a minimal difference between word and thing, signifier and signified. "A perfect imitation is no longer an imitation. If one eliminates the tiny difference that, in separating the imitator from the imitated, by that very fact refers to it, one would render the imitator absolutely different: the imitator would become another being no longer referring to the imitated," Derrida writes in "Plato's Pharmacy": "Imitation does not correspond to its essence, is not what it is—imitation—unless it is in some way at fault or rather in default. It is bad by nature. It is only good insofar as it is bad. Since (de)fault is inscribed within it, it has no nature; nothing is properly its own" (*Dissémination* 173–74; *Dissemination* 139). Such an acknowledgment of the inevitable distance at the heart of representation, though, continues to rely on all the fundamental oppositions of mimetic reasoning in the West: idea and image, model and copy, essence and appearance, the original and its double, and so on. Only now such oppositions become dislocated from within by an uncontrollable force of alterity. But what if Borges's map also puts the reader on a different track? What if the logic of language and interpretation in the meantime has moved away from the play between the real and its imaginary representation or mimetic reduplication? What if, in the digital age, the map becomes a simulacrum without any real territory as its referent? A map capable of simulating rather than imitating the territory? Such are the rhetorical questions that are answered in the affirmative in the reading of Borges's map as a full-blown simulation that would become popularized in the work of Baudrillard.

Already in the late 1960s, the logic of the simulacrum had become an obsession of French thought. In *The Logic of Sense* and *Dissemination*, Deleuze and Derrida would mobilize this logic as a reversal or dislocation of Platonism, considered the foundation of philosophy in the West. Plato's dialectical method for them consists above all in the division not just between an Idea and its copy or imitation, but rather between two forms of imitation, or two types of repetition—one "good" and the other of the "bad" type—depending on whether what is imitated or repeated, the original model or paradigm, is the truth typical of the thing itself. "We are now in a better position to define the totality of the Platonic motivation: it has to do with selecting among the pretenders, distinguishing good and bad copies or, rather, copies (always well-founded) and simulacra (always engulfed in dissimilarity)," Deleuze writes in "Plato and the Simulacrum," one of the appendices to *The Logic of Sense*: "It is a question of assuring the triumph of the copies over the simulacra, of repressing simulacra, keeping them completely submerged, preventing them from climbing to the surface, and 'insinuating themselves' everywhere" (*Logique* 296; *Logic* 256–57). However, no sooner do we enter a degraded world of copies of copies, like a labyrinth of mirrors infinitely reflecting one another, than there are only simulacra, without an original referent at the level of being. Respectively using Carroll and Mallarmé, but also Michel Tournier and Philippe Sollers, as exemplary forms of modern writing that disassemble this whole ontological and dialectical machine, whether Plato's or Hegel's, Deleuze thus speaks of "the revenge of simulacra" that for him represents a complete "reversal of Platonism" (*Logique* 302; *Logic* 262), while Derrida in "The Double Session" from *Dissemination* analyzes "the simulacrum of Platonism or Hegelianism" that, as in the case of Mallarmé's mime, produces a "displacement without reversal of Platonism and its heritage": "Copy of a copy, a simulacrum that simulates the Platonic simulacrum—the Platonic copy of a copy as well as the Hegelian curtain—have lost here the lure of the present referent and thus find themselves lost for dialectics and ontology, lost for absolute knowledge" (*Dissémination* 255, 260, 270; *Dissemination* 207, 211, 219). In this view, modern art and writing would stage the radical undoing of the whole philosophical tradition with its endless quest for a clean cut to divide truth from opinion, essence from appearance, model from copy, and the original from its fake double, phantasm, or simulacrum.

To this relatively ahistorical discussion of the logic of simulacra in French theory and philosophy, Baudrillard adds an important element of historicity. Pointing in the direction of social and technological changes that have revolutionized our capacities for representation since the discovery of coding and computers, among other artifacts, in a chapter from his *Symbolic Exchange and Death* the French sociologist distinguishes three orders of simulacra since the Renaissance, which roughly correspond to Foucault's periodization in *The Order of Things*, except for the addition of what we now would call the postmodern age: (1) the order of *counterfeits*, dominant throughout the classical age; (2) the order of *(re)production* typical of the industrial age; and (3) the order of *simulation* that would characterize our current code-governed age (*L'Échange symbolique* 77; *Symbolic Exchange* 50). While Borges is not mentioned by name, his map would mark the passage into this third stage, where the real becomes hyperreal and simulacra give way to simulation: "The coefficient of reality is proportionate to the reserve of the imaginary that gives it its specific weight. This is true of terrestrial as well as space exploration: when there is no more virgin, and hence available to the imaginary, territory, when the map covers the whole territory, something like the reality principle disappears," Baudrillard claims about this epochal transformation, "which is equivalent to the derealisation of human space, or its reversal into a hyperreality of simulation" (*L'Échange symbolique* 115 n. 1; *Symbolic Exchange* 86 n. 9).

Three years later, however, in a text called "The Precession of Simulacra" also taken up in his *Simulacra and Simulations*, Baudrillard offers a brief self-criticism of his interpretation of Borges's map. "If once we were able to view the Borges fable in which the cartographers of the Empire draw up a map so detailed that it ends up covering the territory exactly," he writes on this occasion, "as the most beautiful allegory of simulation, this fable has now come full circle for us, and possesses nothing but the discrete charm of second-order simulacra" ("La précession" 3; *Simulacres* 9; *Simulacra* 1). Baudrillard still defines simulation in terms of genetic and digital coding typical of the postmodern age, but Borges's parable no longer serves as an exemplary instance of such third-order simulacra because it remains based on the metaphysical opposition between map and territory, between imitator and imitated, or between the real and the imaginary. Thus, in a later chapter of *Simulacra and Simulation*, Baudrillard similarly concludes with a rebuttal of his older interpretation: "Gone even the Borgesian Utopia, of the map coextensive with the territory and doubling it in its entirety: today the simulacrum no longer goes by way of the double and of duplication, but by way of genetic miniaturization," he now writes: "End of representation and implosion, there also, of the whole space in an infinitesimal memory, which forgets nothing, and which belongs to no one. Simulation of an immanent, increasingly dense, irreversible order, one that is potentially saturated and that will never again witness the liberating explosion" (*Simulacres* 108; *Simulacra* 71).[8]

Does this mean that the only alternative to the order of mimetic reason in the West is a world of pure simulation, devoid of any promise of liberation? Can Borges be said to participate, unknown to himself, in this giddy kind of active nihilism that is so common among postmodern thinkers in France? Or does his adherence to a minimal difference between map and territory promise an explosive revenge of the world of simulacra over and against all Platonist or Hegelian metaphysics?

To answer these questions, we should remember that the most famous philosopher of the postmodern cites "Del rigor en la ciencia" as an expression of the collapse of the last attempt to legitimize the pursuit of science in the current era. Thus, if in *The Postmodern Condition*, originally produced in 1979 as a report on the state of the sciences titled *The Problems of Knowledge in the Most Developed Industrial Countries*, Lyotard defines postmodernity as the incredulity toward all modern grand narratives of enlightenment, revolution, or emancipation since 1789, Borges's parable would illustrate how the last remaining principle for the legitimation of scientific work—that is, the principle of performativity based on a minimal input for a maximal output—also leads to a necessary failure or dead end: "A layman's version of the de facto impossibility of ever achieving a complete measure of any given state of a system is provided in a note by Borges," he writes, before offering a paraphrase that he admits to being partly unfaithful: "An emperor wishes to have a perfectly accurate map of the empire made. The project leads the country to ruin—the entire population devotes all its energy to cartography" (*Les Problèmes* 78, 116 n. 191; *The Postmodern Condition* 55). Similarly, in 1985, as part of a major exhibition of art and thought called *Les Immatériaux* that Lyotard helped curate, a voice recording of "Del rigor de la ciencia" would play together with Baudrillard's "The Precession of Simulacra," among other texts, on the soundtrack that visitors would hear on their personal headphones as they strolled through the galleries of the Centre Georges Pompidou, also known as Beaubourg, in Paris.

Earlier in his career, however, Lyotard had recourse to another of Borges's stories, the entry on "Animales de los espejos" [Animals That Live in the Mirror] from *El libro de los seres imaginarios* coauthored with Margarita Guerrero (*OCC* II: 132–33). Here the mirror replaces the map as a more conventional metaphor to imagine the operations of mimetic representation or reflection—with the image already appearing in Book X of Plato's *Republic* (596c–e) to condemn painters and ultimately poets for being imitators and impostors who merely hold a mirror to the world. In Borges's account, we once again can distinguish three different moments in the interrogation of mimetic reason: first, a bygone era in ancient China when creatures would be able effortlessly to come and go through the looking glass; second, the moment the Yellow Emperor forced the mirror creatures back inside the mirror, obliging them to be nothing more than faithful reflections; and, finally, the premonition that there may come a moment when the reflections will take revenge and come back to do battle with the people standing on this side of the glass pane. Each of these moments in Borges's story fascinates Lyotard, but especially the promise contained in the first and the last. In an essay published in 1973 and subsequently included in his book *The Assassination of Experience by Painting—Monory*, on the French painter Jacques Monory whose work is often associated with hyperrealism, Lyotard reads the story as the promise of a "libidinal economy" in which the world is loosened from the perspective of a sovereign subject standing over a set of passive reflections and instead becomes an open battlefield of force and power, with the mirror as a momentary stasis to be overflown again in the future with a barrage of figures that will break with all the metaphysical oppositions between the real and the imaginary. "In assuming the autonomy of the mirror creatures, Borges is not proposing a meditation on the isomorphism and the heteromorphism of what represents and what is represented—something that has been done a thousand times since part I of Plato's *Parmenides*; he imagines these beings as forces, and this bar as a barrier," Lyotard comments. "The existence of the subject depends only on this dividing wall, on enslaving the fluid and lethal powers, repressed from the other side, to the function of representing the subject. Representation is thus assumed to be an energetic set-up, whose ruin would be that of the subject and of power" (*L'Assassinat* 12–13; *The Assassination* 90–91).

The anxiety behind these imperial projects would be the same, whether in setting up the barrier of the mirror against the flow of energy or in outlining a perfect map of the empire. "It wants to eliminate every partial pulsion, it wants to immobilize the body," Lyotard writes in his *Libidinal Economy*: "Such is the anxiety of the emperor of whom Borges speaks, who desired a map of the empire so exact that it had to cover the whole territory in every aspect and therefore duplicate its scale exactly, to such an extent that the monarch's subjects spent so much time and used up so much energy in putting the finishing touches to it and maintaining it that the empire 'itself' fell to more and more ruin as its cartographic blueprint became more and more perfect" (*Économie libidinale* 257; *Libidinal Economy* 215).

Finally, bringing together the critique or deconstruction of the human subject with the ruin of mimetic representation, the revolt of the mirror creatures would sum up the greatest promise of Borges's literature for French theory and philosophy. It should come as no surprise, therefore, that, in 1990, a selection of Baudrillard's writings would be published in English under the title of *The Revenge of the Crystal*, or that the French sociologist in the concluding chapter "The Revenge of the Mirror People" from his 1995 book *The Perfect Crime* would once more revisit Borges's entry from *El libro de los seres imaginarios*.[9]

A Maker in Disguise

Even when they imagine multiple reversals or displacements, all these interpretations take as their point of departure metaphysical definitions of the subject and of representation that may not be compatible with some of Borges's own theoretical positions—always more indebted to an Anglophone tradition that runs the gamut from Hume's empiricism to James's pragmatism than to the canon of Western metaphysics from Plato to Hegel. The metaphor of language as a map, to give but one example, receives a strikingly different interpretation in one of Borges's earliest "inquisitions," which no longer bears much resemblance to the old Platonic framework of models, copies, and simulacra:

> Lo que nombramos sustantivo no es sino abreviatura de adjetivos y su falaz probabilidad, muchas veces. En lugar de contar frío, filoso, hiriente, inquebrantable, brillador, puntiagudo, enunciamos puñal; en sustitución de ausencia de sol y progresión de sombra, decimos que anochece. Nadie negará que esa nomenclatura es un grandioso alivio de nuestra cotidianidad. Pero su fin es tercamente práctico: es un prolijo mapa que nos orienta por las apariencias, es un santo y seña utilísimo que nuestra fantasía merecerá olvidar alguna vez. ("Examen de metáforas" 65–66)
>
> [What we call a noun is nothing but an abbreviation of adjectives and, often, their fallacious probability. Instead of saying cold, hurting, unbreakable, shining, sharp-pointed, we state dagger; to substitute the absence of the sun and the progression of shadow, we say that it darkens. Nobody will deny that this nomenclature is a grandiose relief for our everyday life. Yet their aim is stubbornly practical: it is a prolix map that steers us through appearances, it is a most useful sign that our fantasy will at some point deserve to forget.]

This description of language as "a prolix map that steers us through appearances," as I have tried to show elsewhere, constitutes a subtle paraphrase of James's view about the practical role of concepts and percepts. "Concepts not only guide us over the map of life, but we *revalue* life by their use," the New England pragmatist writes in his unfinished *Some Problems of Philosophy*: "They steer us practically every day, and provide an immense map of relations among the elements of things, which, though not now, yet on some possible future occasion, may help to steer us practically" (71, 73; see Bosteels, "El fin" and "The Truth"). Contrary to the view of language as a mimetic reflection in need of a vengeful reversal or utopian ruination, a pragmatist outlook allows Borges to envision a world in which language continues to grow alongside a changing reality: "Language is an efficacious ordering of this enigmatic abundance of the world" ("Examen" 65).

None of Borges's famous French readers seems to have been aware of the Argentine's pragmatist inclinations, and, even if they were, few of them would have been interested in further exploring such a connection. Only Deleuze and Guattari might have been pleased to discover the proximity between Borges and James—an author whom Deleuze at the end of his life had no qualms placing on a par with Marx, with pragmatism representing for the mass of immigrants in the New World what Marxism meant for the proletariat in Europe. "One cannot understand pragmatism if one sees in it a summary philosophical theory fabricated by the Americans," Deleuze wrote: "By contrast, one understands the novelty of American thinking when one sees in pragmatism one of the attempts to transform the world, and to think a new world, a new man insofar as they *make themselves*" (*Critique* 110; *Essays* 86, trans. modified). If we were to connect this view to Borges's appreciation of James's ethical superiority, we might also begin to understand a hidden pragmatist tendency in contemporary French theory and philosophy.

As Borges suggested in his "Nota preliminar" to *Pragmatism*, it would be a question of grasping how both truth and fiction are made: the result of a making or doing that seeks to keep on growing together with a world that is likewise constantly in the making. Only in this creative sense could Borges's map be said to entail "a cartographic activity which engenders the territory to which it refers," as Guattari proposes in *Molecular Revolution* (*La Révolution* 52 n. 1; see also *L'Inconscient* 234 n. 28). In fact, though his name is more frequently associated with notions of "inoperativity" or "unworking" (i.e., *désœuvrement* in French), even Blanchot may have recognized this practical side of Borges's writing when he suggested that "we should conclude that at work [*à l'œuvre*] in the world is not only the ability to make [*faire*], but that great ability to feign [*feindre*], to trick and deceive, of which every work of fiction is the product, all the more so if this ability stays concealed in it"; in this sense, as Blanchot adds, "*Fictions, Artifices* risk being the most honest names that literature can be given" (*Le livre* 132; *The Book* 94). Last, Borges himself insists in one of his interviews with Milleret that the title of *El hacedor*, translated as *L'Auteur* in French, is best understood as *The Maker* in English, since such is the source from where Borges took his original title: "In England in the Middle Ages, this word would be applied to the poet, which itself derives from the Greek *poiein*: making, creating. There exists a very beautiful Scottish poem from the Middle Ages, titled *Lament for the Makers*, by William Dunbar, where the *makers* are the dead poets" (77). Could it be that his French readers, focused as they were on unworking the metaphysics of the West, lost sight of this element of making in Borges's work? Or should we perhaps revisit some of these same texts of French theory and philosophy in search of the pragmatist poet-maker concealed in them like a Trojan horse?

NOTES

1. See Alazraki, Alonso, Block de Behar, Bosteels, Flamand, Foster, González Echevarría, Lafon, Molloy, Rodríguez Monegal, Selnes, and Wood.
2. See Attala and Collin.
3. See also O'Sullivan and Roger.
4. See also González Echevarría and Toro.
5. See also Deleuze 1986: 102 n. 3; 1988: 145 n.3.
6. See Bosteels 1995: 52–114.
7. See Peters.
8. See also Baudrillard's interpretation of "La lotería en Babilonia" [The Lottery of Babylon] as a "simulation of the social by the game" in 1979: 205–09; 2001: 150–53; and Gane.
9. See Almeida.

Works Cited

Alazraki, Jaime. "Borges and the New Critical Idiom." *Borges and his Successors*. Edited by Edna Aizenberg. University of Missouri Press, 1990, pp. 105–06.

Almeida, Iván. "Borges à la carte (tres citas de Baudrillard)." *Variaciones Borges*, no. 25, 2008, pp. 25–51.

Alonso, Carlos. "Borges y la teoría." *MLN*, vol. 120, no. 2, 2005, pp. 437–56.

Anzieu, Didier. "Le corps et le code dans les contes de J. L. Borges." *Lieux du corps. Nouvelle Revue de Psychanalyse*, vol. 3, 1971, pp. 177–205.

Attala, Daniel. "Magias parciales de Macedonio o del Borges de Blanchot al Borges de Genette." *Borges-Francia*. Edited by Magdalena Cámpora and Javier Roberto González. Pontificia Universidad Católica Argentina, 2011, pp, 119–30.

Baudrillard, Jean. *De la seduction*. Galilée, 1979.

Baudrillard, Jean. *For a Critique of the Political Economy of the Sign*, translated by Charles Levin. Telos Press, 1981.

Baudrillard, Jean. "La précession des simulacres." *Traverses*, vol. 10, 1978, pp. 3–37.

Baudrillard, Jean. "La revanche du peuple des miroirs." *Le Crime parfait*. Galilée, 1995, pp. 203–04.

Baudrillard, Jean. *L'Échange symbolique et la mort.*Gallimard, 1975.

Baudrillard, Jean. *Pour une critique de l'économie politique du signe*. Gallimard, 1972.

Baudrillard, Jean. *The Revenge of the Crystal: Selected Writings on the Modern Object and Its Destiny, 1968-1983*, edited by Paul Foss and Julian Pefanis. Pluto Press, 1990.

Baudrillard, Jean. "The Revenge of the Mirror People." *The Perfect Crime*. Translated by Chris Turner. Verso, 1996, pp. 148–49.

Baudrillard, Jean. *Seduction*, translated by Brian Singer. New World Perspectives, 2001.

Baudrillard, Jean. *Simulacra and Simulation*, translated by Sheila Faria Glaser. University of Michigan Press, 2011.

Baudrillard, Jean. *Simulacres et simulation*. Galilée, 1981.

Baudrillard, Jean. *Symbolic Exchange and Death*, translated by Iain Hamilton Grant. Sage, 1993.

Blanchot, Maurice. *The Book to Come*, translated by Charlotte Mandell. Stanford University Press, 2003.

Blanchot, Maurice. *Le livre à venir*. Gallimard, 1959.

Block de Behar, Lisa. *Al margen de Borges*. Siglo XXI, 1987.

Borges, Jorge Luis. "Examen de metáforas." *Inquisiciones*. Seix Barral, 1993, pp. 71–81.

Borges, Jorge Luis. *Obras completas*. 4 vols. Emecé, 1996.

Borges, Jorge Luis. *Obras completas en colaboración*. 2 vols. Emecé, 1972.

Borges, Jorge Luis. *Textos recobrados (1931-1955)*. Emecé, 2001.

Bosteels, Bruno. *After Borges: Literary Criticism and Critical Theory*. University of Pennsylvania, PhD dissertation, 1995.

Bosteels, Bruno."El fin de la eternidad: En torno al pragmatismo de Jorge Luis Borges." *Federico García Lorca et Cetera: Estudios sobre las literaturas hispánicas en honor de Christian De Paepe*. Edited by Nicole Delbecque, Nadie Lie, and Brigitte Adriaensen. Leuven University Press, 2003, pp. 435–44.

Bosteels, Bruno. "A Misreading of Maps: The Politics of Cartography in Marxism and Poststructuralism." *Signs of Change: Premodern, Modern, Postmodern*. Edited by Stephen Barker. State University of New York Press, 1996, pp. 109–38.

Bosteels, Bruno. "Monstrosity and the Postmodern: Michel Foucault's Approach to Jorge Luis Borges." *Literature and Society: Centers and Margins*. Edited by García, Kaplan, Lechner, et al., Department of Spanish and Portuguese. Columbia University Press, 1994, pp. 9–20.

Bosteels, Bruno. "The Truth Is in the Making: Borges and Pragmatism." *The Romanic Review*, vol. 98, nos. 2–3, 2007, pp. 135–51.

Canguilhem, George. "The Death of Man, or Exhaustion of the Cogito?" *The Cambridge Companion to Foucault*. Edited by Gary Gutting. Cambridge University Press, pp. 71–91.

Canguilhem, George. *The Normal and the Pathological*, translated by Carolyn R. Fawcett and Robert S. Cohen. Zone, 1991.

Collin, Françoise. "The Third Tiger; or, From Blanchot to Borges." *Borges and His Successors: The Borgesian Impact on Literature and the Arts*. Edited by Edna Aizenberg. University of Missouri Press, 1990, pp. 80–95.

Deleuze, Gilles. *Critique et clinique*. Minuit, 1993.

Deleuze, Gilles. *Différence et répétition*. PUF, 1968.

Deleuze, Gilles. *Difference and Repetition*, translated by Paul Patton. Columbia University Press, 1994.

Deleuze, Gilles. *Essays Critical and Clinical*, translated by Daniel W. Smith and Michael A. Greco. Verso, 1997.

Deleuze, Gilles. *The Fold: Leibniz and the Baroque*, translated by Tom Conley. University of Minnesota Press, 1993.

Deleuze, Gilles. *Foucault*. Minuit, 1986.

Deleuze, Gilles. *Foucault*, translated by Seán Hand. University of Minnesota Press, 1988.

Deleuze, Gilles. *Le Pli: Leibniz et le baroque*. Minuit, 1988.

Deleuze, Gilles. *The Logic of Sense*, translated by Mark Lester with Charles Stivale; edited by Constantin V. Boundas. Columbia University Press, 1990.

Deleuze, Gilles. *Logique du sens*. Minuit, 1969.

Deleuze, Gilles. "Preface: On Four Poetic Formulas Which Might Summarize the Kantian Philosophy." *Kant's Critical Philosophy: The Doctrine of Faculties*. Translated by Hugh Tomlinson and Barbara Habberjam. Athlone Press, 1984, pp. vii–xiii.

Deleuze, Gilles, and Félix Guattari. *Mille Plateaux: Capitalisme et schizophrénie*. Minuit, 1980.

Deleuze, Gilles, and Félix Guattari. *A Thousand Plateaus: Capitalism and Schizophrenia*, translated by Brian Massumi. University of Minnesota Press, 1987.

Derrida, Jacques. *Dissemination*, translated by Barbara Johnson. University of Chicago Press, 1981.

Derrida, Jacques. *Heidegger: La question de l'Être et l'Histoire. Cours de l'ENS-Ulm 1964–1965*, edited by Thomas Dutoit with the assistance of Marguerite Derrida. Galilée, 2013.

Derrida, Jacques. *Heidegger: The Question of Being and History*, translated by Geoffrey Bennington. University of Chicago Press, 2016.

Derrida, Jacques. *La Dissémination*. Seuil, 1972.

Derrida, Jacques. *L'Écriture et la différence*. Seuil, 1967.

Derrida, Jacques. *Writing and Difference*, translated by Alan Bass. University of Chicago Press, 1978.

Flamand, Éric. *Le Nom et le savoir: Abrégé de culture borgésienne*. 2nd ed. Noël Blandin, 1987.

Foster, David W. "Borges and Structuralism: Toward an Implied Poetics." *Modern Fiction Studies*, vol. 19, no. 3, 1973, pp. 341–51.

Foucault, Michel. *Abnormal: Lectures at the Collège de France 1974–1975*, edited by Valerio Marchetti and Antonella Salomoni. General Editors François Ewald and Alessandro

Fontana. English Series Editor Arnold I. Davidson. Translated by Graham Burchell. Verso, 2003.

Foucault, Michel. "Afterword to *The Temptation of Saint Anthony*." Translated by Donald F. Brouchard and Sherry Simon. *Aesthetics, Method, and Epistemology*. Edited by James D. Faubion. *Essential Works of Michel Foucault*. Vol. 2. The New Press, 1998, pp. 103–22.

Foucault, Michel. *The Archaeology of Knowledge and The Discourse on Language*, translated by Alan M. Sheridan Smith. Pantheon, 1972.

Foucault, Michel. *Death and the Labyrinth: The World of Raymond Roussel*, translated by Charles Ruas. Athlone Press, 1986.

Foucault, Michel. *L'archéologie du savoir*. Gallimard, 1969.

Foucault, Michel. "La Vie des hommes infâmes." *Les Cahiers du Chemin*, vol. 29, 1977, pp. 12–29.

Foucault, Michel. "Le langage à l'infini." *Tel Quel*, vol. 15, Fall 1963, pp. 44–53.

Foucault, Michel. *Les anormaux. Cours au Collège de France (1974-1975)*, edited by Valerio Marchetti and Antonella Salomoni. General Editors François Ewald and Alessandro Fontana. Gallimard, 1999.

Foucault, Michel. *Les mots et les choses: Une archéologie des sciences humaines*. Gallimard, 1966.

Foucault, Michel. "Lives of Infamous Men." *Essential Works of Michel Foucault 1954-1984*. Edited by Paul Rabinow. Vol. III. *Power*. Edited by James D. Faubion, translated by Robert Hurley et al. New Press, 2000, pp. 157–75.

Foucault, Michel. "Nachwort." *Gustave Flaubert: Die Versuchung des Heiligen Antonius*. Insel Verlag, 1964, pp. 217–51.

Foucault, Michel. *The Order of Things: An Archaeology of the Human Sciences*, translated by Alan M. Sheridan Smith. Vintage, 1973.

Foucault, Michel. *Raymond Roussel*. Gallimard, 1963.

Foucault, Michel. "Un 'fantastique' de bibliothèque." *Cahiers de la Compagnie Madeleine Renaud-Jean-Louis Barrault*, vol. 59, 1967, pp. 7–30.

Gane, Mike. "Borges." *Baudrillard's Bestiary*. Routledge, 1991, pp. 19–25.

Gardes de Fernández, Roxana. "La lógica de Deleuze y el universo borgeano." *Borges-Francia*. Edited by Magdalena Cámpora and Javier Roberto González. Pontificia Universidad Católica Argentina, 2011, pp. 329–38.

Genette, Gérard. "La littérature selon Borges." *Cahiers de l'Herne Jorge Luis Borges*. Edited by Dominique de Roux and Jean de Milleret. L'Herne, 1964, pp. 323–27.

Genette, Gérard. "L'utopie littéraire." *Figures*. Seuil, 1966, pp. 123–32.

González Echevarría, Roberto. "BdeORridaGES (Borges y Derrida)." *Isla a su vuelo fugitiva: Ensayos críticos sobre literatura hispanoamericana*. Porrúa Turanzas, 1983, pp. 205–15.

González Echevarría, Roberto. "Borges and Derrida." *Jorge Luis Borges*. Edited by Harold Bloom. Chelsea House, 1986, pp. 227–34.

Guattari, Félix. *La Révolution moléculaire*. Recherches, 1977.

Guattari, Félix. *L'Inconscient machinique: Essais de schizo-analyse*. Recherches, 1979.

James, William. *Pragmatism, a New Name for Some Old Ways of Thinking: Popular Lectures on Philosophy*. American Theological Library Association Historical Monographs, 1907.

James, William. *Some Problems of Philosophy; A Beginning of an Introduction to Philosophy*. Greenwood Press, 1911, 1968.

Kristeva, Julia. *Pouvoirs de l'horreur: Essai sur l'abjection*. Seuil, 1980.

Kristeva, Julia. *Powers of Horror: An Essay on Abjection*, translated by Leon S. Roudiez. Columbia University Press, 1982.

Lacan, Jacques. Écrits. Trans. Bruce Fink. New York: W. W. Norton, 2006.

Lacan, Jacques. "Le Séminaire sur 'La lettre volée.'" *Écrits*. Seuil, 1966, pp. 11–61.

Lyotard, Jean-François. *The Assassination of Experience by Painting—Monory/ L'Assassinat de l'expérience par la peinture—Monory*, edited by Sarah Wilson; translated by Rachel Bowlby. Black Dog, 1998.

Lacoue-Labarthe, Philippe. *Préface à La disparition*. Christian Bourgois, 2009.

Lafon, Michel. "Borges y Francia, Francia y Borges." *Borges-Francia*. Edited by Magdalena Cámpora and Javier Roberto González. Pontificia Universidad Católica Argentina, 2011, pp. 21–34.

Lyotard, Jean-François. "Contribution des tableaux de Jacques Monory à l'intelligence de l'économie politique libidinale du capitalisme dans son rapport avec le dispositif pictural et inversement." *Figurations: 1960–1973*. Union Générale d'Editions, 1973.

Lyotard, Jean-François. *Économie libidinale*. Minuit, 1974.

Lyotard, Jean-François. *L'Assassinat de l'expérience par la peinture, Monory*. Le Castor Astral, 1984.

Lyotard, Jean-François. *Les Problèmes du savoir dans les sociétés industrielles les plus. La Condition postmoderne: Rapport sur le savoir*. Minuit, 1979.

Lyotard, Jean-François. *Libidinal Economy*, translated by Iain Hamilton Grant. Indiana University Press, 1993.

Lyotard, Jean-François. *The Postmodern Condition: A Report on Knowledge*, translated by Geoff Bennington and Brian Massumi. University of Minnesota Press, 1984.

Macherey, Pierre. "Borges et le récit fictif." *Les Temps Modernes*, no. 236, January 1966, pp. 1309–16.

Major, René. "La mort, l'immortel et l'autre." *Cahiers Confrontation*, vol. 7, 1982, pp. 79–84.

Marin, Louis. *Utopics: Spatial Play*, translated by Robert A. Vollrath. Humanities Books, 1984.

Marin, Louis. *Utopiques: Jeux d'espaces*. Minuit, 1973.

Molloy, Sylvia. "Jorge Luis Borges." *La Diffusion de la littérature hispano-américaine en France au XXème siècle*. PUF, 1972, pp. 194–247.

O'Sullivan, Gerry. "The Library Is On Fire: Intertextuality in Borges and Foucault." *Borges and His Successors: The Borgesian Impact on Literature and the Arts*. Edited by Edna Aizenberg, University of Missouri Press, 1990, pp. 109–21.

Peters, John Durham. "Resemblance Made Absolutely Exact: Borges and Royce on Maps and Media." *Variaciones Borges*, vol. 25, 2008, pp. 1–23.

Rodríguez Monegal, Emir. "Borges and Derrida: Apothecaries," translated by Paul Budofsky and Edna Aizenberg. *Borges and His Successors: The Borgesian Impact on Literature and the Arts*. Edited by Edna Aizenberg, University of Missouri Press, 1990, pp. 128–38.

Rodríguez Monegal, Emir. "Borges/De Man/Derrida/Bloom: La desconstrucción 'avant et après la letter.'" *Diseminario: La desconstrucción otro descubrimiento de América*. XYZ Editores, 1987, pp. 119–23.

Rodríguez Monegal, Emir. "Borges y Derrida: Boticarios." *Maldoror*, vol. 20, 1985, pp. 123–32.

Rodríguez Monegal, Emir. "Borges y la 'nouvelle Critique.'" *Borges: Hacia una lectura poética*. Guadarrama, 1976, pp. 95–120.

Roger, Julien. "Genette, el otro de Borges." *Borges-Francia*. Edited by Magdalena Cámpora and Javier Roberto González. Pontificia Universidad Católica Argentina, 2011, pp. 109–18.

Selnes, Gisles. "Fiction at the Frontiers of Narrative: Borges and Structuralism Revisited." *Variaciones Borges*, vol. 16, 2003, pp. 79–96.

Toro, Alfonso de. "Borges/Derrida/Foucault." *Jorge Luis Borges: Pensamiento y saber en el siglo XX*. Edited by Alfonso de Toro y Fernando de Toro, Vervuert, 1999, pp. 139–63.

Wood, Michael. "Borges and Theory." *The Cambridge Companion to Jorge Luis Borges*. Edited by Edwin Williamson. Cambridge University Press, 2013, pp. 29–42.

CHAPTER 29

BORGES, GENDER, AND SEXUALITY

AMY KAMINSKY

WITH his dearth of attention to women characters, his apparent lack of interest in conventional character development, and his purported squeamishness around issues of sexuality, Borges does not particularly invite feminist and queer analyses of his work. Consequently, when I first approached the idea underlying this chapter, the notion that Borges's writing might have contributed directly to gender and sexuality studies, I smiled ruefully at the apparent futility of the project. Gender and sexuality seem to be kind of beside the point.

Borges was famously conservative and conventional in his few pronouncements on sexuality, and although he was a self-declared feminist, he appears to have been content with standard constructs of gender. Nor, in his writing, does he seem particularly concerned either with human psychology or with sociopolitical questions. But he is such a compelling writer that queer and feminist critics still want to engage with him, and because they have done so primarily in the context of his stories, that is where this chapter finds its focus. Because Borges himself rarely questions patriarchal heteronormativity, even as he discombobulates time, history, and the very grounds of what we want to think of as reality, his work provides access to the cultural givens of gender and sexuality for scholars to examine. Borges may be primarily concerned with time, space, literature, and other matters of mind, but the mind comes attached to a body that just won't go away, and Borges's apparently unexamined assumptions about bodies provides ample material for scholars concerned with gender and sexuality.

As one might deduce from my use of the adjectives "feminist" and "queer," I understand gender and sexuality studies to be modified by the silent but essential adjective, "critical." These fields, which overlap and inform each other but are by no means coterminous, are liberatory practices, interventions into cultural norms that perpetuate inequality and perform oppression. They are also interdisciplinary, though my primary focus here is on work by scholars of literature. However, the rethinking of gender and sexuality in and through Borges occurs in nonscholarly spaces as well.

It is a mistake to try to police the borders of feminist and LGBTQ studies, but their underlying worldview is that the dominant culture is both masculinist and heteronormative at best, misogynist and homophobic at worst, and that literary texts, like all cultural products, bear the mark of this power dynamic. Feminist and queer scholars are judgmental, assessing, explicitly or implicitly, the extent to which any text reproduces homophobia and/or the objectification of women, or, conversely, interrogates gendered constructs and promotes an openness and acceptance, even a celebration, of women's subjectivity and/or of sexual transgression. Feminist and queer criticism are necessarily inflected by other markers of differentiated power, and the best of them are attentive to those differences, including, but not limited to, coloniality and race, taking as a central project the analysis of such dynamics as a means of interrupting them. It should go without saying (but my saying it is a good indicator otherwise) that not all discussions of gender are feminist and not all analyses of transgressive sexuality are queer.

In its earliest stages, feminist criticism focused largely on representations of women in literature written by men; feminist criticism of Borges largely falls into this category by default. Subsequently, attention shifted to include gender as a symbolic system that maps onto and intersects with a range of differences. For its part, early queer criticism tended more toward getting familiar figures out of the closet and finding moments of queerness in canonical writers, thus the speculations concerning a writer's sexuality. A few critics, bridging feminist and queer theory, engage with Borges's representation and production of conventional masculinity.[1] What we have come to call toxic masculinity is rife in Borges's gaucho and *compadrito* stories, but most of the critical work addresses it only indirectly or in passing (sometimes conflating it with masculinity *tout court*) and rarely grapples with it in any theoretical way.

Because of their insistence on corporeality and their refusal to abstract the text from the cultural, historical soup in which it is steeped, and of which it is a productive part, feminist and queer critics have afforded biography an important place in their approach to literary analysis. Many commentators have linked Borges's famously tentative approach to textualized sex to assumptions about the writer's sexual life. Max Ubelaker Andrade is among those who engage the problematics of sexuality in "Emma Zunz" and "La intrusa" [The Intruder] through Borges's own experience as gleaned from both primary and secondary sources. Phillip Swanson gestures vaguely toward a consensus about Borges and sex (*"by all accounts* Borges was sexually timid" [85; emphasis added]), as does Efraín Kristal, who notes "his purported sexual inadequacies," using an adjective that suggests Kristal himself may be remaining agnostic on the subject (161). Edwin Williamson, on the other hand, gets very specific, citing Borges's close friend and collaborator as his source of knowledge on the subject: "Bioy surmised that [Borges's] relationships were invariably 'platonic' because he thought of sex as 'dirty'" (217). Others note a therapist's diagnosis of Borges's impotence or play psychoanalyst themselves in linking a reportedly disastrous encounter with a sex worker when he was nineteen to sexual squeamishness, or hint at an unhealthy relationship with his mother. Some remark on his body dysphoria and his history of unsuccessful relationships with women, all in the service of accounting for his dyspeptic attitude to sexuality in general.

Although attention to the embodied, historically situated, culturally marked, and gendered writer is one of the grounds of feminist criticism, and even though I believe that gossip is an essential mechanism of knowledge transmission, especially among the disempowered, stories of Borges's sexual inadequacies are, in many cases, more prurient than enlightening. Psiche Hughes, herself writing biographically about his work, even contends that explorations of Borges's emotional life and speculation about his repressed homosexuality are "ultimately irrelevant" (36). I would not go quite so far. Although she may be right about sexual speculations that simply exhibit kneejerk homophobia, when the recovery of queer moments in history, biography, and textuality serve as a scaffolding on which to build a sturdy edifice of queer-positive scholarship, or when, as in Daniel Balderston's "The Fecal Dialectic," it is analyzed in terms both of Borges's own grappling with homosexuality in his writing and of the critical reception grounded in sexual gossip, it is another matter altogether.

Ariel de la Fuente describes his reading of Borges as biographical but claims that it is unique because he proposes "a different relationship between his sexual biography and his literary experience [. . . showing] that Borges's sexuality was the point of departure for parts of his oeuvre and uncovers a history of Borges as "a curious and ardent reader of erotic literature" (206). He goes on to contest the conventional notion that instances of desire and sex are rare in Borges's work. But apart from his position that one needs to pay attention to sex and sexuality in any consideration of cultural production, which he shares with feminist and queer critics, de la Fuente does not engage in the critical analysis of conventional constructions of sexuality that is the hallmark of feminist and queer scholarship, nor is he in conversation with queer theory more generally. His book does, however, provide a considerable amount of biographical and historical information around issues of sexuality. Others, notable among them Balderston and Herbert J. Brant, have tangled more fruitfully with Borges's own homophobia, especially in light of apparently queer moments in his writing.[2]

As most Borges scholars who address gender and sexuality have noted, women characters are few and far between in his stories. Two that stand out as exceptions, Juliana Burgos of "La intrusa" and the eponymous Emma Zunz, both title characters, offer readers a way into a critique of cultural constructions of gender and sexuality, displaced homoeroticism, the extreme objectification of women, and female rebellion and vindication. There are few moments when Borges proposes a woman protagonist, and it is telling that critics who wish to talk about women's subjectivity in his work choose overwhelmingly to discuss "Emma Zunz," in which Borges relies overtly on the conventions of sexuality, specifically here the virgin/whore dichotomy, according to which it is unthinkable that the hypervirginal subject could deploy the practices of prostitution. Equally fruitful for critical readings around women's subjectivity is the investigation of its radical absence in "La intrusa." Borgesian inversion both depends on those tropes and has the power to subvert them, tempting the reader with what might be suggestions of Emma's latent lesbianism (as Balderston suggests) or a glimpse of Juliana's subjectivity that is as thrilling as a flash of ankle on an otherwise completely covered body. Fewer critics engage with "El duelo" [The Duel], in which the central characters are women artists, or "Ulrica" [Ulrikke], in which the protagonist is a desiring sexual subject. It is possible, as well, that the captive woman in "Historia del guerrero y de la cautiva" [Story of the Warrior and the Captive] chooses to stay with her indigenous husband for reasons that include her own sexual satisfaction, but that conjecture is only barely hinted at in the story. In any case, the captive woman and Ulrica are both outsiders, one reduced (in the story's own terms) to savagery and the other rarefied by her cosmopolitanism. For the most part, Borges's women characters are either chaste middle-class women or acquiescing underclass objects used to satisfy male desire. As Sharon Magnarelli points out, Borges never creates maternal figures, nor does he forge any symbolic links between femininity and fecundity, differentiating his writing from much of male-authored Latin American literature. Rather, his sexualized female figures are linked to passion, violence, and death, most often as objects of sacrifice. In this light, it is clear why Brant and others discuss "El muerto" [The Dead Man] in which the unnamed red-headed woman is just another of the alpha male's possessions, as a companion piece to "La intrusa." As tokens of desire of men in competition, both characters serve to exemplify the extreme objectification of women and the undercurrent of homosexual desire in a homosocial, misogynist milieu. The red hair that marks them both is a sign not of their own lust but of the passion they are meant to evoke in the men who claim them.

Even before "La intrusa" was written, Estela Canto, to whom Borges recounted the outlines of the plot as he was formulating the narrative, found the story shocking. Maybe, she muses, it was because the woman seemed to be so utterly an object. What she said to him, though, was that it looked like a homosexual story to her. Nonplussed, Borges demurred. This is where most critics leave Canto's memory of the writing of "La intrusa," but what follows is at least as intriguing. Canto reports that after much struggle Borges finally wrote the story, but he was having trouble with the ending. She reports that it was his mother, the formidable Leonor Acevedo, who suggested he kill off Juliana, and Canto deduces that for Borges, the story was, subconsciously, about his relationship with his mother, who inevitably came between her son and any woman who might have taken him away from her (120–21). Her allusion to the familiar trope relating homosexuality to the overbearing mother figure, neatly meshing sexism and homophobia, is more than a little problematic, but still we can name Canto as the first of many people intrigued by the nature of the desire of the two brothers who share Juliana. Their readings range from homophobic (Lima) through heteronormative (de la Fuente) to queer (Brant and Balderston). The text also lends itself to discussions of masculinity (Biron), representations of women (Carter), structural sexism (Fare), women's subjectivity (Reiss), the conundrum of homosociality (Johnson), and the symbolic and structural functions of the sign, "woman" (Magnarelli).

As Sharon Magnarelli suggests, the symbolic system in which Borges operates offers fertile ground for probing culturally constructed gender. Like her, Bella Brodzki, Bernard McGuirk, and Mark Frisch all use Borges as a way to get at the intersection of feminist and deconstructionist theory. Brodzki's reading of "Emma Zunz" illuminates a key productive tension in feminist criticism of the 1980s and 1990s between an antiessentialist approach to understanding the protagonist's limited range of action in a male-dominated society and the deployment of essentialized sexual difference in deconstructing unconscious structures of language and power. Bernard McGuirk uses Borges to make an argument that a nonessentialist approach to reading the story is more useful than reading it through theories of écriture féminine, even as the latter "highlights and problematizes the inadequacy of notions of individual subjectivity, personal morality, the propriety of a name, or even the 'nature' of woman" (201–02). Like Brodzki, McGuirk implicitly argues that Borges's work helps further discussions of competing feminist critical approaches. Alex McVey, on the other hand, dismisses the issue of women's oppression altogether, following Baudrillard, for whom "the feminine" is the crucial source of symbolic power in the struggle against "phallic rationality."

Mark Frisch's examination of what Borges brings to our understanding of postmodernism and feminism includes the rather astonishing claim that Borges's work forwarded the project of feminism. Even more astonishingly, perhaps, he makes a convincing case. Frisch notes that Borges considered himself a feminist, reminding his reader that he translated Virginia Woolf's *Orlando* and *A Room of One's Own*.[3] He thereby provides us a clue to reading "El duelo," which, though sometimes noted in discussions of Borges and gender, is rarely discussed with much complexity.

Despite his professed dislike of *A Room of One's Own*, with "El duelo" Borges seems to have taken up its challenge to write about women's relationships with each other in the context of their own professions. Woolf's "Chloe liked Olivia. They shared a laboratory together" may well have emerged in Borges as the two women painters who were construed as each other's rivals but whose relationship went far deeper. In "El duelo" Borges, uncharacteristically, questions normative femininity, undermining and ridiculing the narrow-minded sexism of the cultural arbitrators of gender.

Commentaries on "El duelo" have dutifully attended to the purported—but in fact very slippery and unconvincing—rivalry between Clara Glencairn and Marta Pizarro, the two women artists who are at its center. Clara, capable of both female friendship and of appreciating other women's talent ("capaz de apreciar el ingenio de los otros y aun de las otras" [she did appreciate the wit of others—even of other women] [*OC* II: 429; *Doctor Brodie's Report* 35–36]) becomes an artist following her friend's lead, choosing the same art form but a different expression within that form. Marta is a figurative painter; Clara chooses abstraction. Carefully positioned to represent one strain in the history of twentieth-century painting, Marta and Clara complete, as well as compete with, each other. Neither is appreciated or understood; the provincial art world of Buenos Aires alternately tolerates them, uses them, and ignores them. Clara, at least, finds this neglect liberating, and each woman depends on the other as a source of inspiration. Strikingly, the death of one ends the creative life of the other. When Clara dies, Marta stops painting.

To my knowledge, the double meaning of the story's title has not been addressed. Readers have followed the overt references to the duelo as duel, but I have not seen a consideration of "duelo" as "grief" or "mourning" in relation to this narrative. Profoundly marking the end of the story, Marta's grief at Clara's death doubles back to make the rest of the story about an intense relationship between the two characters that goes beyond mere rivalry, and that has precious little to do with the masculine-tinged violence of the sort of duel that is meant to end in a death that returns honor to or confers prestige upon the winner.[4] Those who observe Marta and Clara, including the narrator, follow the cultural script that sees women in relation to each other only as rivals, but their relationship is nourishing and productive for both of them. Marta's grief at the loss of her friend is real.

"El duelo" is perhaps the single Borges story that passes the Bechdel test. Begun as a joke in the comic strip *Dykes to Watch Out For* by graphic novelist and playwright Alison Bechdel, the Bechdel test assesses a narrative on three criteria: are there at least two women? Do they talk to each other? Do they talk about something other than a man? Perhaps because it so resoundingly passes the Bechdel test, "El duelo" has caught the attention of some scholars writing about gender, but it has not been nearly as well studied as "La intrusa" or "Emma Zunz." I believe that is largely because the story is in some sense illegible. The cultural grooves into which Borges so deftly pours his other fictions are simply not available for telling the story of these two women.

The narrator of "El duelo" announces these difficulties from the outset: The story "should" take place in Boston or London (where first-wave feminism flourished), but instead it happens in Buenos Aires.[5] It properly needs to be a novel, preferably by Henry James, but it is recounted by a narrator who eschews the long form. Most importantly, Clara and Marta are simply not the sort of women about whom stories are typically written. Marta is known in society as the sister of the lively, flamboyant, sexually desirable Nélida Sara who functions primarily to demonstrate what a heroine ought to look like. In contrast, the two actual protagonists defy expectations. Marta's unconventional choice to paint seriously does not fit into any familiar narrative, and Clara has been a dutiful wife who subordinated her desires to her husband's until his death. As such she is narratively uninteresting. To press the point home, Borges describes Clara as a tall, lively, redhead, but any passion that might signify has nothing to do with the desire evoked by the objectified underclass women of "La intrusa" or "El muerto." When Clara dies, her obituary is not about her as an individual but as a shining representative of genteel womanhood. There is really no model for telling this story of women's friendship, love, and mutual professional admiration and support, of a rivalry that is a collaboration. Moreover, Borges imbues "El duelo" with deliberate tentativeness: "perhaps" the true rivalry was between Clara and Marta's sister (429); Clara's decision to become a painter "might have been" motivated by Marta's example (429); "some" considered Marta's portrait of Clara her best work (432). It is as if this narrative is so new that nothing in it can be stated with certainty.

This story of women in relation to each other, to creativity, and to a life of work, where men are peripheral, may be Borges's most revolutionary fiction. Borges writes of the women's mutual passion for art and of their love for each other, as well as of the mutual influence and reciprocity in their work, Clara painting both "against" and "for" Marta. He also brings attention to the invisibility of their art and the unintelligibility of their relationship. Their "duel" was not only "intimate"; Borges describes it oxymoronically as carried out by them in "perfect loyalty" to each other:

La vida exige una pasión. Ambas mujeres la encontraron en la pintura o, mejor dicho, en la relación que aquélla les impuso. Clara Glencairn pintaba contra Marta y de algún modo para Marta; cada una era juez de su rival y el solitario público. En esas telas, que ya nadie miraba, creo advertir, como era inevitable, un influjo recíproco. Es importante no olvidar que las dos se querían y que en el curso de aquel íntimo duelo obraron con perfecta lealtad.

Fue por aquellos años que Marta, que ya no era tan joven, rechazó una oferta de matrimonio; sólo le interesaba su batalla. (*OC* II: 432)

[Life demands a passion. Both women found it in painting, or rather, in the relationship imposed on them by painting. Clara Glencairn painted against Marta and in a sense for Marta; each of them was her rival's judge and only public. In their pictures, which even then no one ever looked at, I think I observe—as was unavoidable—a mutual influence. Clara's sunset glows found their way into Marta Pizarro's patios, and Marta's fondness for straight lines simplified the ornateness of Clara's final stage. It is important to remember that the two women were genuinely fond of each other and that in the course of their intimate duel they behaved toward one another with perfect loyalty.

It was during those years that Marta, who by then was no longer so young, rejected a marriage proposal. All that interested her was her battle.] (*Doctor Brodie's Report* 40)[6]

With his evocation of Henry James's *The Bostonians* at the outset, and the impenetrable, multifaceted intimacy he evokes between his protagonists, it is hard to imagine Borges writing a more lesbian text than this one. But he remains coy: the last line of "El duelo" reads "La historia que se movió en la sombra acaba en la sombra" [The story that made its way in darkness ends in darkness] (*OC* II: 433; *Doctor Brodie's Report* 41).

If "El duelo" rehearses the difficulty in telling a story of women's friendship, "La historia del guerrero y de la cautiva" cements its impossibility with a variation on the Bechdel test that we might call the Borges impediment, in which at least two women are brought together in the text but are denied the opportunity of engaging with each other. In "Historia del guerrero y de la cautiva," the captive and the grandmother, both British, cross paths in rural Argentina, but they cannot communicate. Each has been constrained in the life she can lead. The same people who keep the captive alive and teach her to survive are those who murdered her birth family. The narrator's British grandmother is removed to a frontier outpost by a husband, a military officer representing and maintaining the original violence that took the land (and many of the lives) of the indigenous people embraced by the captive. Each woman is conscripted to one side of that conflict, and, importantly, each of them embraces the side that has claimed her. The narrator's grandmother is distressed by the other woman's descent into savagery and her choice to remain there; the reader may feel the same about the grandmother's acceptance of her own situation. In any case, the violent history that separates them—we can call it patriarchal—makes even language between them impossible. Although both women have experienced radical estrangement, they are rendered incapable of sharing it with each other, no less to make a coherent story out of it for themselves.

Other scenarios in which Borges gestures momentarily toward a connection between women only to foreclose upon it include the brief scene in "La intrusa" when Eduardo brings a new woman home, thinking to distract his desire for Juliana with a woman of his own. The introduction of the second woman into the household brings anything but the desired equilibrium, however. It interrupts the mutual relationship between Eduardo and Cristián carried out through Juliana, and it also threatens to displace Juliana's attention to the men with its offer of proximity to another similarly situated woman, who might serve as a companion and interlocutor. The woman no sooner makes an appearance than she is dispatched from the house and from the narrative.

"Emma Zunz" also includes a brief reference to a potential relationship among women, but the glimpse of Emma's friendship with Elsa Urstein and Perla Kronfuss remains just that. It is not folded into the narrative, and it only gestures toward other possibilities for Emma. Even so, Balderston suggests their active social life and Emma's aversion to men might be read from a lesbian perspective. Unlike the woman Eduardo brings home in "La intrusa," whose presence threatens the household's precarious equilibrium and must be disposed of, Emma's social life gestures toward the world of women's clubs, sport, and movie theaters that Emma, a modern working girl, already moves in. In both stories, however, opening up a narrative space for interactions among women threatens foundational norms, whether of narrative itself or of male homosocial relationships; and in these stories that opening is quickly slammed shut.

Analyses of "Emma Zunz" create a space for still another subset of feminist (and to a lesser extent queer) approaches to Borges in which Jewishness is an important site of inquiry. The characters in "Emma Zunz" move in secular spaces, but their names mark them as Ashkenazi Jews. Even so, Josefina Ludmer raises the question of whether or not Emma Zunz is really Jewish, and Alfred MacAdam wonders if hers is in fact a Jewish story. For many critics, though, Emma's Jewishness is a key aspect of both her character and her story, and Latin American Jewish feminist criticism finds Borges particularly fascinating. Edna Aizenburg examines the echoes of Jewish mysticism in her erudite analysis of the feminine aspect of the divine in "Emma Zunz," and others attend to secular meanings of Jewishness and gender in that text. Implicit in Erin Graff Zivin's exploration of the confluence of money and prostitution as tropes of transaction linked to Jewishness in the story, for example, is a critique of sexism and antisemitism. Bernard McGuirk reconfigures midrash as deconstruction in his (also sociopolitical and psychoanalytical) feminist reading of "Emma Zunz." Donna Fitzgerald's feminist postcolonial reading of "La intrusa" weaves an analysis of the historical and cultural meanings of Judaism and Jewishness into a rich consideration of multiple forms of marginalization and exclusion. These four very distinct approaches to Jewishness, gender, and Borges suggest how resonant this convergence is.

If Borges has moments where he expresses sympathy with feminist ideas, the same cannot be said for any overt sign of an appreciation of queer male sexuality, which tends to emerge either as the return of the repressed or the occasional homophobic remark. Brant and Balderston, for example, typically read across the current of Borges's homophobia to find moments of queer desire—or its suppression—in his work. Balderston finds the moment when Borges ventures out with homoerotic fascination only to retreat like a startled crustacean into his gorgeous shell. "The Fecal Dialectic: Homosexual Panic and the Origin of Writing" is a feat of both critical detective work and thoughtful analysis whose importance can be discerned in the number of times it has been reprinted. As his title clearly states, Balderston locates the very origin of Borges's writing in homosexual panic. Balderston examines what he calls Borges's "phobic treatment" of homoeroticism in "La intrusa," of course, but he also finds quieter queer moments in such stories as "La biblioteca de Babel" [The Library of Babel], "La forma de la espada" [The Form of the Sword], and "La secta del Fénix" [The Sect of the Phoenix] and in essays on Walt Whitman and Oscar Wilde. Similarly, Brant teases out the queer undercurrents of "La forma de la espada" and explores homoerotic desire triangulated through a woman in "El muerto" and "La intrusa."[7]

Even when his writing is not the object of analysis, Borges often appears as an oblique presence in the work of critical sexuality scholars. Paul Julian Smith, in his discussion of Federico García Lorca in *The Body Hispanic,* notes Foucault's reference to Borges at the beginning of *Les mots et les choses.* Foucault informs Smith on Lorca, and Foucault is (queerly) informed by Borges, who provides pleasure and humor in the form of disruption of Western epistemological system. Borges also lurks at the margins but undergirds the center of the 1998 volume, *Hispanisms and Homosexualities,* where the editors evoke him on the essential act of rereading to disrupt and unsettle as the fundamental proposal of their volume:

> "The notion of a *definitive* text," Borges writes memorably, "belongs to religion or to fatigue." It is against such notions of the definitive—be it a text, a field of knowledge, an academic discipline, or even a national identity—that the essays in this volume work. Ours was not, to be sure, the only destabilizing move possible: it was the one that we, as queer critics, chose to effect. Hispanism—that particular construction of Hispanism [as defensive, exclusionary, and needless to say as a heteronormative monolith]—was begging, one might say, to be queered. (Molloy and McKee xi; emphasis in the original)

Borges himself is not one of the writers their contributors choose to reread in this destabilization project (his name turns up again twice, marginally, in two of the chapters). Moreover, I feel safe in asserting that the queering of Hispanism was not what Borges was thinking about when he wrote disdaining the idea of the definitive text. But Borges's literary iconoclasm, or at least destabilization, resonates with a queer literary project, and we may count his refusal of conventional expectations as one of Borges's important contributions to a literary and cultural analysis that defies propriety, redirects the gaze, and takes on the very Marquess of Queensberry.

Balderston also grazes Borges in his collection of essays, *Los caminos del afecto,* relying on Borges for an epistemological framework to resolve the conundrum of awakening memories in someone when the experience attached to those memories were someone else's; Borges claims that it is the condition of any biography (20). Later in that study, Balderston cites Borges on what it means for a text to be a classic, and in a gesture we see in him elsewhere, he recognizes that Borges might not be in complete accord with the use to which his observations were being put: "no sé qué hubiera opinado Borges" [I don't know what Borges would have thought] (211).

Conversely, we find traces of queer content in Borges criticism, most remarkably in Balderston's work and in that of another leading Borges scholar, Sylvia Molloy, who, like Balderston, is also a central figure in the establishment of Latin American LGBTQ scholarship. For the most part both Molloy and Balderston either write about Borges *or* about queer (and in Molloy's case, feminist) literary issues. With a few important exceptions, the two lines of scholarly work run on more or less parallel tracks, with occasional moments of subtle convergence. Molloy's reading of Borges and Baudelaire, for example, is not an overtly queer reading, yet it is streaked with traces of queer estrangement. And when Molloy names her scholar-self in "Mock Heroics," I believe that she speaks for both herself and others in considering the complexity of a scholar's identity:

> But there is always more than one hyphen: intellectual practices, my own included, are the product of many intersections. The identification papers issued to me as an Argentine national working in the US say that I am a French-trained/comparatist; that I am an Argentine Latin Americanist; that I am a novelist; that I have written on Latin American autobiography but also (and also?) on Borges, a committed challenger of the first person; that I am a feminist critic; that I am a queer scholar. (1072–73)

Molloy proposes and implicitly champions "the idea that there may be more than one story being told in any critical fiction or scholarly exercise" (1073). It is not incidental that both Molloy and Balderston write in one way or another about learning to read with Borges. We, together with them, can credit Borges with demanding a new kind of reading, a new kind of attention that positioned them to help invent and legitimate Hispanophone LGBTQ criticism.

Feminist Borges scholars also examine nonconvergence and tangentiality in their works. Dalia Wassner, who directs the Project on Latin American Jewish and Gender Studies at Brandeis, writes about gender and power, but not in Borges, and in Beatriz Sarlo's *Jorge Luis Borges: A Writer on the Edge*, questions of gender burst forth only at the end of a marvelous disquisition, as if always lurking but never finding a way to emerge until *boom!* they blast through out of an apparent nowhere. In Sarlo, it happens on the penultimate page of the book, in a wonderfully subtle disentangling of Borges's relation to language, his dance of inclusion and exclusion of Argentineity in his famously careful lexicon. Sarlo's observation, that only those fully immersed in and protected by their social and economic status could participate fully in the renovation of language and aesthetics of the avant garde, is redolent of Borges's sexual anxiety coded as textual, around a vocabulary of prostitution. Her interest here is ostensibly Borges's daring creation of a literary language that is (also) *criollo*, but after gesturing toward linguistic sexual anxiety, she also chooses to ignore its referentiality, until the penultimate paragraph of the book, in which she notes that Borges's lexicon consists of "a corpus of words with blurred contours, and expression," criollo but not *lunfardo*, "familiar and masculine, never vulgar or plebeian" (136).

What are we to make of this bizarre chiasmus, the "familiar and masculine" set in oblique motion against the "vulgar or plebeian"? Sarlo's essays in this book have all been about disentangling apparent contradictions in Borges, but here she inserts a whole new direction for reading him, leaving us with a clue in the form of a negative analogy ("masculine and familiar, never vulgar or plebeian") that is more puzzling than clarifying. Where did the question of masculinity come from, so suddenly, hanging like Pauline at the edge of a cliff with no subsequent episode for her rescue?

Like these critics, Edgardo Cozarinsky works on wobbly parallel tracks: some of his fiction and some of his films engage with transgressive sexuality; some are about Jews in Argentina and on the anomie of the post-Holocaust diaspora; as a cultural critic he has written about Borges, most notably in *Borges en/y/sobre cine*.[8] From time to time, Borges brushes up against sexuality in Cozarinsky's writing. His very brief discussion of Carlos Hugo Christensen's film version of "La intrusa," which he dismisses for its ham-handed depiction of the brothers' desire for each other, is one such place. More rarely do the two come together with Jewishness, but they do in Cozarinsky's erudite introduction to his delightful collection of gossipy anecdotes, *Nuevo museo del chisme*, which includes a discussion of Borges's approach to narrative. The subject of so much sexual gossip himself, Borges appears in the body of Cozarinsky's book only as the source of an amusing anecdote about Alberto Gerchunoff's circumcised penis.

With Cozarinsky, who is a writer, filmmaker, Borges enthusiast, and cultural critic, we come to a consideration of Borges's impact in the production and circulation of constructs of gender and sexuality as they are received and refashioned by other artists and writers. However, it is not as mere source material but as a point of departure for considering the problematics of gendered power relations and transgressive sexuality that Borges has had his most exhilarating effect among other artists.

Filmmaker Leandro Katz takes the Emma Zunz story as a site from which to explore gender, power, and the constraints that the medium imposes on the female subject as well as on narrative itself. In *Splits,* an experimental short film that radically reinvents the Borges story, Katz disassembles and reconfigures phallogocentric and phalloscopic constructions of woman. Katz splits the screen, splits the single female figure of the story into two, and desynchronizes the voiceover narration from what appears on the screen. Kaja Silverman argues that by misaligning the female voice and body *Splits* succeeds in freeing the female subject from the confines of conventional narrative constraints. *Splits,* she argues, "exposes the complicity of classic cinema in the construction and maintenance of sexual difference, and awakens in the viewer/listener the desire for something else" (68).

Similarly, Natalie Bookchin's pioneering artist game, "The Intruder," brings together narrative, visual art, and the form of the video game itself to critique the masculinist world of video gaming. Positioning the viewer/player within the narrative, which can only proceed if the viewer plays the game, "The Intruder" centers around the humiliation and murder of the female figure. "The Intruder" is not simply a retelling of "La intrusa" in another genre, but is, rather, a transformative piece of activist art. Bookchin uses the overt misogyny of the story and the interactive nature of the game both to lay bare the violently misogynistic nature of video games and to implicate the player in them. In order to make the story move forward, the player must engage in a series of games based on classic video games that increasingly require acquiescence to and performance of violence against the woman figure. Bookchin's work catches the player in a vise; the pleasure of playing the games is itself rewarded the pleasure of the narrative that is the prize for completing each level of the game, and both pleasures are bound up with producing the woman's pain.

Estela Pereda performs a similar act of visual confrontation in her canvas, "Si la querés, usala" [If You Want Her, Use Her], included in a traveling exhibit of paintings inspired by Borges's work. Referencing perhaps the most chilling moment in "La intrusa," Pereda depicts the naked, prone body of a woman in icy colors, lightly overlaid with a geometrical grid, the viewer positioned at her feet. The visual representation of the woman being offered up to the viewer presages Juliana Burgos's death at the end of the story, conflating her dehumanization with her murder. The title, quoting Cristián's invitation to his brother to make use of Juliana, hails the reader into the painting as well, as the intended consumer of the inert body on the canvas. The famous line is utterly dismissive: its brevity alone suggests an afterthought, something trivial that might not even be of particular interest. The painting is an altogether devastating indictment of patriarchal brutality, occasioned by Borges.

Escrito sobre Borges, Josefina Delgado's compilation of fourteen short stories inspired by Borges, contains three feminist and queer narratives that overwrite "La intrusa." In Luisa Valenzuela's brief rendition, two sisters share a single man whom they ultimately kill, bury, and forget. Marta Mercader imagines a series of women narrators who guard and transmit the story sympathetically, highlighting Juliana's suffering and rescuing her from the matter-of-fact tone of the original. Mercader's Cristián kills Juliana because she confronts him with his desire for his brother, bringing the story of internalized homophobia full circle. Eduardo Gudiño Kieffer, on the other hand, keeps the Juliana figure alive and kills off the men. His retelling is a delightful mash-up of "La intrusa," and "Emma Zunz," in which Emma/Juliana sets up the brothers (now urban toughs living in a hotel called Esquina Rosada), kills them both, and is never suspected of the crime. Following an impulse much like Katz's in *Splits,* Alicia Steimberg gives Emma Zunz control of her narrative in "La ventana de Emma" [Emma's Window], making her the narrator of her own story and even dividing Emma in two at the end. Steimberg's Emma is accompanied more robustly by her women friends, and she calls Borges out by name to correct some of the details in his version of her story.

Responding to Magnarelli's claim that gender is not an important feature of Borges's work, Bella Brodzki points out that "Emma Zunz" could not have been about a male character. It is equally true, however, that his male-centered stories could not have been populated by women characters. The cultural givens of gender and sexuality generally provide a translucent wash that fixes his stories to the canvas, making the stories legible. The rabbi who dies at the beginning of "La muerte y la brújula" [Death and the Compass] had to have been a man—there were no women rabbis at the time. Borges's *compadritos*, gauchos, and warriors all rely on unmarked masculinity; if they were women (or nonbinary subjects, for that matter), the smooth line of the old story of gender would be interrupted by a new one that would simply get in the way of the play of ideas and of language. That is precisely what some of the authors writing in homage to Borges propose. Several of the stories in *Escrito sobre Borges* transpose gender, not always happily. "La mujer de Elimelec" [The Woman of Elimelec], Angélica Gorodischer's retelling of Funes strips the main character of her own name even before the text traps her in suffocating memory. Unlike her male counterpart, Gorodischer's Irene only suffers from the ability to remember everything. An urban housemaid and factory worker to his rural gaucho, she is paralyzed by the knowledge that inhabits her mind in the wake of an industrial accident, whereas her male counterpart seeks knowledge and is enriched and ennobled by his prodigious memory.

The final story in Delgado's collection, Luisa Valenzuela's "El otro libro" [The Other Book], is about a book, found by the narrator's friend in a forbidden library, that contains the original versions of Borges's stories. Rewritten with male protagonists, the stories now support the project of masculine hegemony that silences, surveils, and isolates women; the book of women's stories is so dangerous to the patriarchy that it burns the narrator's hands. Visual artist Laura Delgado takes some of that stolen power back in her reconfiguration of Borges's "El otro" [The Other]. In Borges's version otherness resides, benignly, in his own younger self. Delgado's mixed media image, "La otra," portrays a seated young girl, face covered by her hand, before her child-like drawing of a female figure. Mirta Kupferminc, who also rethinks Borges's through visual art, has created a playful, marginal cast of often strangely gendered humanoid characters some of whom blend markers of femininity like breasts, waistlines, and long hair with nonhuman features.[9] These figures, which tend toward joy and disruption, appear in many of her works, and they populate several of the images in *Borges y la Cábala: Senderos del Verbo*, an artist's book that Kupferminc co-created with Sául Sosnowski. Although gender is not a theme of *Borges y la Cábala*, it is one of the commonplaces Kupferminc defies with these characters. *Borges y la Cábala* is not *about* gender, just as the perpetuation of heteronormative gender difference is not Borges's conscious project. Nevertheless, Borges has inspired such revisions of his work. And just as he has provoked analyses of gender and sexuality among scholarly readers, Borges has challenged feminist and queer artists, filmmakers, and writers to participate in the fundamental work of defamiliarizing representations that reify a phallocentric, heteronormative view of the world.

NOTES

1. Various critics have discussed Borges's few representations of women, as well as his approaches to masculinity. See, for instance, Piñeyro, Aizenberg, Mattalía, Brant, and McGuirk.

2. See Balderston, "The Fecal Dialectic" and *Borges, realidades y simulacros*; and Brant, "The Mark of the Phallus."
3. On Borges's translations of Woolf, see Leone.
4. I do not think that mere coincidence accounts for the placement of "El duelo" in *El informe de Brodie* [*Doctor Brodie's Report*] immediately before "El otro duelo" [The Other Duel], which indeed takes up the conventional masculine duel.
5. The narrator (and very possibly Borges himself) was apparently unaware of the lively feminist activity in Buenos Aires, and indeed throughout Latin America, at the time.
6. The astute reader will note that Di Giovanni's translation includes a sentence, absent from the original, reinforcing the artists' mutual influence.
7. Borges famously hated the film *A intrusa* for its overt reference to the brothers' incestuous homoerotic desire.
8. See Aguilar's chapter in this volume, and also Aguilar and Jelicié, *Borges va al cine*.
9. Although she is best known for her Holocaust postmemory art, Kupferminc has also produced a considerable body of feminist work.

Works Cited

Aguilar, Gonzalo, and Emiliano Jelicié. *Borges va al cine*. Libraria, 2013.
Aizenberg, Edna. "Emma Zunz: A Kabbalistic Heroine in Borges's Fiction." *Studies in American Jewish Literature (1981–)*, vol. 3, 1983, pp. 223–35.
Altamiranda, Daniel. "Jorge Luis Borges." *Latin American Writers on Gay and Lesbian Themes: A Bio-Critical Sourcebook*. Edited by David William Foster. Greenwood Press, 1994, pp. 72–83.
Balderston, Daniel. *Borges, realidades y simulacros*. Editorial Biblos, 2000.
Balderston, Daniel. *Los caminos del afecto*. Instituto Caro y Cuervo, 2015.
Balderston, Daniel. "La 'dialéctica fecal': pánico homosexual y el origen de la escritura en Borges." *Borges: realidades y simulacros*. Editorial Biblos, 2000, pp. 59–75.
Balderston, Daniel. "La 'dialéctica fecal': pánico homosexual y el origen de la escritura en Borges." *Desde el armario: disidencia genérico-sexual en la literatura argentina*. Edited by José Maristany, Editorial de la Universidad Nacional de La Plata, 2019, pp. 35–54.
Balderston, Daniel. "'The Fecal Dialectic': Homosexual Panic and the Origin of Writing in Borges." *¿Entiendes: Queer Readings, Hispanic Writings*. Edited by Emilie L. Bergman and Paul Julian Smith. Duke University Press, 1995, pp. 29–45.
Biron, Rebecca. "Telling Secrets of Brotherly Love." *Murder and Masculinity: Violent Fictions of Twentieth-Century Latin America*. Vanderbilt University Press, 2000, pp. 30–48
Bookchin, Natalie. "The Intruder." *Frontiers*, vol. 26, no. 1, 2005, pp. 43–46.
Borges, Jorge Luis. *Doctor Brodie's Report*, translated by Norman Thomas di Giovanni. E. P. Dutton, 1972.
Borges, Jorge Luis. *Obras completas*. 4 vols. Emecé Editores, 1996.
Brant, Herbert J. "The Mark of the Phallus: Homoerotic Desire in Borges' 'La forma de la espada.'" *Chasqui*, vol. 25, no. 1, 1996, pp. 25–28.
Brant, Herbert J. "The Queer Use of Communal Women in Borges' 'El muerto' y 'La intrusa.'" *Hispanófila*, no. 135, 1999, pp. 37–50.
Brodzki, Bella. "'She was unable not to think': Borges' 'Emma Zunz' and the Female Subject." *MLN*, vol. 100, no. 2, 1985, pp. 330–47.

Canto, Estela. *Borges a contraluz*. Espasa-Calpe, 1989.

Carter, E. D. "Women in the Short Stories of Jorge Luis Borges." *Pacific Coast Philology*, no. 14, 1979, pp. 13–19.

Cozarinsky, Edgardo. *Borges en/y/sobre cine*. Fundamentos, 1980.

Cozarinsky, Edgardo. *Nuevo museo del chisme*. La Bestia Equilátera, 2014.

Delgado, Josefina, ed. *Escrito sobre Borges: 14 escritores le rinden homenaje*. Planeta, 1999.

Fare, Gustavo. "Borges's Women in Film." *Chasqui*, vo. 34, no. 2, 2005, pp. 166–75.

Fitzgerald, Donna. "Borges, Woman, and Postcolonial History." *Romance Studies*, vol. 24, no. 3, 2006, pp. 227–39.

Frisch, Mark. *You Might Be Able to Get There from Here: Reconsidering Borges and the Postmodern*. Fairleigh Dickinson University Press, 2004.

Fuente, Ariel de la. *Borges, Desire, and Sex*. Liverpool University Press, 2018.

Gorodischer, Angélica. "La mujer de Elimelec." *Escrito sobre Borges*. Edited by Josefina Delgado, 1999, pp. 61–74.

Graff Zivin, Erin. "Transacciones judías y discursos promiscuous en "Emma Zunz." *Variaciones Borges*, vol. 22, 2006, pp. 191–99.

Gudiño Kieffer, Eduardo. "La intrusa." *Escrito sobre Borges*. Edited by Josefina Delgado, 1999, pp. 87–98.

Hughes, Psiche. "Love in the Abstract: The Role of Women in Borges' Literary World." *Chasqui*, vol. 8, no. 3, 1979, pp. 34–43.

Johnson, David E. "Talking to Ourselves, Over Her (Dead) Body: On Heidegger, Borges, and Seeing the Other." *The New Centennial Review*, vol. 11, no. 1, 2011, pp. 143–60.

Kieffer, Eduardo Gudiño. "La intrusa." *Escrito sobre Borges*. Edited by Josefina Delgado, 1999, pp. 87–98.

Kristal, Efraín. "*The Book of Sand* and *Shakespeare's Memory*." *The Cambridge Companion to Jorge Luis Borges*. Edited by Edwin Williamson. Cambridge University Press, 2013, pp. 160–71.

Leone, Leah. "A Translation of His Own: Borges and *A Room of One's Own*." *Woolf Studies Annual*, vol. 15, 2009, pp. 47–66.

Lima, Robert. "Coitus Interruptus: Sexual Transubstantiality in the Works of Jorge Luis Borges." *Modern Fiction Studies*, vol. 19, no. 3, 1973, pp. 407–17.

Ludmer, Josefina. *El cuerpo del delito: un manual*. Eterna Cadencia, 1999.

MacAdam, Alfred. "Emma Zunz, Revisited." *The Romanic Review*, vol. 98, no. 23, 2007, pp. 237–48.

Magnarelli, Sharon. "Literature and Desire: Women in the Fiction of Jorge Luis Borges." *Revista/Review Interamericana*, vol. 13, nos. 1–4, 1983, pp. 138–49.

Mattalía, Sonia. "Borges: Historias de amor y de odio." *Reescrituras*, edited by Luz Rodríguez Carranza and Marilene Nagle. Rodopi, 2004, pp. 177–91.

McGuirk, Bernard. "Z/Z: On *midrash* and *écriture féminine* in Jorge Luis Borges' 'Emma Zunz.'" *Latin American Literature: Symptom, Risks, and Strategies of Post-Structuralist Criticism*. Routledge, 1997, pp. 185–206.

McVey, Alex. "Baudrillard: Toward New Readings of Borges and Sexuality." *International Journal of Baudrillard Studies*, vol. 9, no. 1, 2012. https://baudrillardstudies.ubishops.ca/baudrillard-toward-new-readings-of-borges-and-sexuality/#content.

Mercader, Marta. "Los intrusos." *Escrito sobre Borges*. Edited by Josefina Delgado. Planeta, 1999, pp. 135–46.

Molloy, Sylvia. "'Flâneries' Textuales: Borges, Benjamin y Baudelaire." *Variaciones Borges*, no. 8, 1999, pp. 16–29.

Molloy, Sylvia. "Mock Heroics and Personal Markings." *PMLA*, vol. 111, no. 5, 1996, pp. 1072–75.

Molloy, Sylvia, and Robert McKee Irwin, eds. *Hispanisms and Homosexualities*. Duke University Press, 1998.

Piñeyro, Juan Carlos. Ficcionalidad e ideología en trece relatos de Jorge Luis Borges. Department of Spanish and Portuguese, Stockholm University, 2000.

Reiss, May-Ann. "Dearth and Duality: Borges' Female Fictional Characters." *Revista de Estudios Hispánicos*, vol. 17, 1990, pp. 281–90.

Sarlo, Beatriz. "Decir y no decir: Erotismo y represión en tres escritoras argentinas." *Escribir en los bordes: Congreso Internacional de Literatura Femenina Latinoamericana*. Edited by Carmen Berenguer, et al. Editorial Cuarto Propio, 1990, pp. 127–69.

Sarlo, Beatriz. *Jorge Luis Borges: A Writer on the Edge*, edited by John King. Verso Books, 2006.

Silverman, Kaja. "'Splits': Changing the Fantasmatic scene." *Revista de Estudios Hispánicos*, vol. 22, no. 3, 1988, pp. 65–85.

Smith, Paul Julian. *The Body Hispanic*. Oxford University Press, 1989.

Steimberg, Alicia. "La ventana de Emma." *Escrito sobre Borges*. Edited by Josefina Delgado. Planeta, 1999, pp. 183–90.

Swanson, Philip. "Borges and Popular Culture." *The Cambridge Companion to Jorge Luis Borges*. Edited by Edwin Williamson. Cambridge University Press, 2013, pp. 81–95.

Ubelaker Andrade, Max. *Borges Beyond the Visible*. Penn State University Press, 2020.

Valenzuela, Luisa. "El otro libro." *Escrito sobre Borges*. Edited by Josefina Delgado. Planeta, 1999, pp. 191–98.

Wassner, Dalia. "The Salience and Pervasiveness of the Literary Figure of the Jew in Latin America: From Sor Juana Inés de la Cruz to Jorge Luis Borges." *Latin American Research Review*, vol. 54, no. 2, 2019, pp. 398–412.

Williamson, Edwin, ed. *The Cambridge Companion to Jorge Luis Borges*. Cambridge University Press, 2013.

Woolf, Virginia. *A Room of One's Own*. Hogarth Press, 1929.

Films

A intrusa. Directed by Carlos Hugo Christensen. Carlos Hugo Christensen Produções Cinematográficas, 1979.

Splits. Directed by Leandro Katz. USA, 1978.

Artworks

Delgado, Laura. "La otra." *Painting Borges: Philosophy Interpreting Art Interpreting Literature*, by Jorge J. E. Gracia, SUNY Press, 2012.

Kupferminc, Mirta, and Saúl Sosnowski, *Borges y la Cábala: Senderos del Verbo*. Artist's Book, 2006.

Pereda, Estela. "Si la querés usala." Jorge G.E. Gracia. *Painting Borges: Philosophy Interpreting Art Interpreting Literature*. SUNY Buffalo, 2012.

Natalie Bookchin. "The Intruder." USA, 1999.

CHAPTER 30

XUL SOLAR AND JORGE LUIS BORGES IN THE *REVISTA MULTICOLOR DE LOS SÁBADOS* [*MULTICOLOR SATURDAY MAGAZINE*]

PATRICIA M. ARTUNDO

INTRODUCTION

IN 1940, the Argentine artist Alejandro Xul Solar (1887–1963) had an exhibition at the Asociación Amigos del Arte. It consisted of a set of twenty-five paintings, mostly watercolors, among which were *Tlaloc* (*Dios Lluvi de México*) (1923) and *San Montes lejos* (1938). It was on this occasion that Jorge Luis Borges bought one his friend's paintings and that, as Miguel de Torre tells it, Xul Solar, "de yapa le regaló una" [he threw in another one as a gift] (*Un día de Borges* 13). Many years later, in a lecture on Xul Solar, Borges would recall,

> uno de los primeros sueldos que cobré, que fue un sueldo de 300 pesos, [. . .] pensé: "Yo tengo que hacer algo por Xul." Entonces le compré un cuadro, le pregunté cuánto costaba y él me dijo: "Bueno, yo había pensado en 100 pesos, pero voy a hacerle precio de amigo, de modo que voy a cobrarle 50, no más", y luego, como tenía remordimientos él me regaló otro cuadro mucho más grande, muy lindo también. ("Mis recuerdos" 49).

> [one of the first checks I received, which was for a salary of 300 pesos, . . . I thought: "I have to do something for Xul," so I bought a painting from him, I asked him how much it cost and he told me: "Well, I was thinking about 100 pesos, but I am going to give you the price for a friend, so I am going to charge you just 50," and then, because he felt bad, he gave me another painting that was much bigger, very nice too.]

Following this recollection, we can deduce that the work Borges purchased was *Tlaloc* (26 × 32.5 cm) and the one he received as a "bonus" was *San Montes lejos* (31 × 47 cm). Curiously, the price he noted for the painting was considerably lower than the one Xul had offered more than ten years prior, when he exhibited it in 1929 (Artundo, "Un artista y su obra"). The one hundred pesos, reduced to just fifty, is a symbolic price that reveals what little interest the artist had in the sale of his works but also his need for one of them to remain in the hands of his friend.

When Borges became the owner of those paintings, they exited the public space of exhibition and entered the private sphere, that "austero dormitorio-escritorio-biblioteca" [austere bedroom-office-library] of the apartment at 994 Maipú Street (Torre, *Un día de Borges* 72). Borges kept the works for a little more than forty years, and, although we do not know the reasons why he parted with them, we do have more or less precise dates in which they did: *Tlaloc* in 1982, and *San Montes lejos* in 1985, passed into the keeping of galleries or entered auctions (Xul Solar et al. I: 234–35, 337).

In a way, this chapter explains the reason *Tlaloc* got into Borges's hands and reconstructs the context in which his interest in the painting may have originated with a few books in Xul's personal library, kept in his house at 1214 Laprida Street. As we shall see, two of those books became source-texts, one for Borges's 1926 article in *La Prensa*, "Cuentos del Turquestán" [Stories from Turkestan] and the other for a translation by Xul in the *Revista Multicolor de los Sábados* [*Multicolor Saturday Magazine*], "Cuentos del Amazonas, de los mosetenes y guarayús: primeros historias que se oyeron en este continente" from 1933.

Although discussion of *San Montes lejos* may appear to move us away from our main subject, it is worthwhile to dwell on this watercolor to better understand the artist's attraction for the writer.[1] We think of Xul as an unclassifiable figure within Argentine modern art, as represented in the 1940s. *San Montes lejos* is a painting we might consider the expression of a particular interiority as it engages with its visionary being— landscapes whose meaning he must have explained to his friend during those years, as Borges recalled that all "los cuadros de él eran fantásticos; pero él me dijo que no, que eran realistas, que él no había inventado nada, que él pintaba lo que él veía en el otro mundo, en los estados de éxtasis, que eran cuadros realistas del otro mundo simplemente, que él no se jactaba de otra cosa" [his paintings were fantastic; but he told me that no, they were realistic, that he had not invented anything, that he painted what he saw in the other world, in states of ecstasy, that they were simply realistic paintings of the other world, that he didn't purport to paint anything else] ("Mis recuerdos" 49–50).

For this dialogue to take place between the two, there had to be a friendship that allowed Xul to open the doors to his inner self. Borges was undoubtedly one of the few (if not the only) friends of the artist who had full access to that world. He was also the only friend who insistently, for more than twenty years following Xul's death in 1963, defended him and sought to give him a place alongside visionaries of other times, be it San Juan de la Cruz or William Blake (Borges, *Jorge L. Borges*).

The other point to emphasize is the distinction between the realistic and the fantastic, especially if we take into account that the time period Borges is referring to in his recollections of Xul—the end of the 1930s and the beginning of the following decade—is when he, together with Silvina Ocampo and Adolfo Bioy Casares, was publishing the *Antología de la literatura fantástica* [*Anthology of Fantastic Literature*] (1940).[2] Xul's response to the writer should be understood in that context: his painting is not fantastic, but, on the contrary, it is realistic, for what it represented was a physical record of his visions, what he saw in his exploration of higher worlds (Artundo, "Primera historia").

Borges provided another recollection of his friend, his prologue for Xul's exhibition at the Samos Gallery in 1949. It was the first time that the artist's catalog had a prologue, in this case, requested by a friend. It is a brief but dense text, in which Borges refers to his paintings as "documentos del mundo ultraterreno, del mundo metafísico en que los dioses toman las formas de la imaginación que los sueña" [documents of the other-worldly realm, of the metaphysical world in which the gods take the forms of the imagination that dreams them] ("Prólogo" 3). This definition of a metaphysical world linked to a visionary experience, which Borges ascribed to Swedenborg and Blake, but also to other Buddhist, Islamic, and Christian mystics, is at the heart of some the anthologies he organized, such as *Libro delle visioni* (1980) or even his collaboration with Adolfo Bioy Casares, *Libro del cielo y del infierno* [*Book of Heaven and Hell*] (1960).

But, in 1949, Borges's position on contemporary art also went beyond his friend; he writes in the prologue: "El gusto de nuestro tiempo vacila entre el mero agrado lineal, la transcripción emotiva y el realismo con brocha gorda" [The taste of our times vacillates between mere linear appeal, emotive transcription and broad-brush realism] (Borges, "Prólogo" 4). This synthesis of some of the main trends in Argentine art[3] and his somewhat out-of-place critique within Xul's prologue were instrumental to his purpose: to lodge a complaint, not only because he personally did not like that type of art, but also that art's politics. In this regard, the "mero agrado lineal" [mere linear appeal] refers to none other than the concrete art that had burst onto the local scene, in 1944, with the journal *Arturo*, which, from that point on and among various artist collectives, had a strong public presence not only in terms of exhibitions, but also in Buenos Aires's art journals, not to mention with the Argentine Communist Party. The "transcripción emotiva" [emotive transcription] referred to painting whose object was the representation of everyday life, including portraits and still-lifes, works occasionally charged with emotion, which were nevertheless anecdotal and easily deciphered. Undoubtedly, "el realismo con brocha gorda" [broad-brush realism] alluded to the New Realism movement headed by Antonio Berni, who was downgraded, in Borges's description, to a wall painter. He was directly criticizing mural painting, as it was manifested through the activity of the Taller de Arte Mural—comprised of Berni, Lino Enea Spilimbergo, Juan Carlos Castagnino, Demetrio Urruchúa, and Manuel Colmeiro, all of them committed to the local Communist Party—which was responsible for the paintings at the Buenos Aires shopping center Galerías Pacífico (1946). It should be recalled here that those two extremes within which Borges located Xul had been discussed just shortly prior by his sister Norah (under the pseudonym Manuel Pinedo) in the pages of *Los Anales de Buenos Aires* [*The Annals of Buenos Aires*]—although from a different standpoint that

522 PATRICIA M. ARTUNDO

positively assessed both of her experiences at the first exhibition of the Asociación Arte Concreto-Invención and a permanent exhibit of contemporary Argentine artists (51).

In any case, it is evident that the writer knew the ins and outs of the art of his time very well and understood the place that Xul had in the context of contemporary Argentine art. Throughout his life, Borges was aware of the art world—whether informed by Norah or his brother-in-law Guillermo de Torre who, by the late 1940s, had been publishing art criticism for more than twenty years.[4] We must also consider the publishing spaces in which Borges was active, such as the journal *Sur*—not to mention other spaces committed to the anti-fascist struggle, such as *Argentina Libre*—in which art criticism had a specific function, with debates and surveys about art not only with de Torre, but also with other figures such as Attilio Rossi.

The prologue and its contents occupy a particular place in Borges's critical production; in fact, it opens an inquiry into art rarely seen in his work to that point. Between 1951 and 1983, Borges wrote nine prologues dedicated to artists[5] and went on to discuss drawings, paintings, sculptures, and photographs. While some of these prologues, such as those dedicated to Rossi or Aldo Sessa, reveal friendship or familiarity with the artist's purpose, others seem more the result of an agreement. Some underlying interest is present, and they constitute spaces for proposing writing strategies and conceptual developments. In the case of the prologue dedicated to Xul, his words create a very particular feeling and reveal a personal commitment. Though presented as a visionary painter, Xul was, as Borges makes clear, many other things as well: "versado en todas las disciplinas, curioso de todos los arcanos, padre de escrituras, de lenguajes, de utopías, de mitologías, huésped de infiernos y de cielos, autor panajedrecista y astrólogo, perfecto en la indulgente ironía y en la generosa amistad, Xul Solar es uno de los acontecimientos más singulares de nuestra época" [versed in all disciplines, curious about all arcane topics, the father of writings, of languages, of utopias, of mythologies, the host of hells and of heavens, creator of panchess and an astrologer, perfect in indulgent irony and generous friendship, Xul Solar is one of the most singular events of our time] ("Prólogo" 3).

The prologue also marks a turning point in Borges's reflections on Xul, which, from early in his writing career, had led him to mention his friend at different times, whether in the context of language and its possibilities outside of academic norms, or duodecimal numbering, or the detective story. This was the first time he dedicated a text so completely to Xul, and while he never stopped referring to him, this kind public valorization of his work would only appear in Borges's writing again after 1965.[6] It is worth noting here that no other writer or artist friend of Borges received so much consideration in his writing, even mentors such as Rafael Cansinos Assens or Macedonio Fernández, for whose work he also penned prologues. In each of the four public talks Borges is known to have given on Xul Solar, he revived, one by one, the authors and works the two of them had enjoyed together: Chuang Tzu, G. K. Chesterton, Andrew Lang, Swinburne, Becher, Hölderlin, and Kipling, as well as the *I Ching*, the Cabala, Gnosticism, the "Heroic Fragment of Finnsburh," and fairy tales, not to mention Swedenborg and Blake.

In 1980, at the start of the last lecture he dedicated to the artist, given the "vértigo de todo aquello infinito" [vertigo of all that is infinite] that he caused for Borges, he reflected,

> Yo hablo de Xul y pienso en una imagen, no sé si es de Conrad, no sé si es mía, total qué importa las imágenes son las mismas, y es esta: es la de un navegante que atraviesa el mar y ve una línea, quizá una claridad y entonces piensa: esa claridad es el África, o es Asia o América. Y piensa que detrás de esa claridad, que esa vaga línea que él descifra apenas en el horizonte, que detrás de esa vaga claridad, de esa muy vaga línea, hay un continente y en ese continente hay religiones, dinastías, ciudades, selvas, desiertos, hay muchas cosas, pero que a él le toca ver simplemente esa línea. Y ahora yo siento que en este momento soy ese navegante. Yo tengo que hablar de ese gran continente, de este vasto país con sus imperios y su historia y sus mitologías y su botánica y su zoología, todo eso que fue Xul Solar. (Borges, "Recuerdos" 54–55)

> [I speak of Xul and I think of an image, I don't know if it is Conrad's, I don't know if it's mine, what does it matter, the images are the same, and it is this: there is a seafarer who crosses the sea and sees a line, perhaps a light and then he thinks: that light is Africa, or Asia or America. And he thinks that behind that light, that vague line that he can just make out on the horizon, that behind that vague light, behind that very vague line, there is a continent and on that continent there are religions, dynasties, cities, jungles, deserts, there are many things, but that he only gets to see that line. And now I feel that at this moment I am that seafarer. I have to speak of that great continent, of this vast country with its empires and its history and its mythologies and its botany and its zoology, all of that which was Xul Solar.]

In a way, the work we present in the rest of this chapter is a part of that vast geography with which Borges was confronted. And what defines that space is a library, Xul's personal library, with all the ramifications that derive from this understanding.

Our Theme

Proposing a reading of Xul Solar's presence in the *Revista Multicolor de los Sábados* (RMS) leads us, without a doubt, to one of its editors, Borges.[7] We know that, by the early 1930s, Xul had illustrated two of Borges's books, *El tamaño de mi esperanza* [*The Extent of My Hope*] (1926) and *El idioma de los argentinos* [*The Language of Argentines*] (1928) with his sketches, thus beginning the first of several collaborations that would find him working as an illustrator in several of Borges's publishing ventures (Xul Solar et al. II: 84–87, 91–93, 97–99).

One might expect that in a publication such as the RMS, in which no text went without illustration, Xul would have taken on the role of illustrator even if he hadn't stood out as a graphic artist in Argentina's classic publications of the 1920s, such as the newspaper *Martín Fierro* (1924–1927) and the second phase of the journal *Proa* (1924–1926) (though he made an advertising poster for the journal, it was never used) (Xul Solar et al. I: 279; II: 141). Likewise, it was evident that any image Xul might propose would differ greatly from whatever was offered by the illustrators brought in to work on the new supplement. Trained through their work on previous publications, they were familiar with journalistic practices and the variety of styles in their illustrations shared visual unity through the use of color. Thus, the famed "multicolor illustration" announced at the time the cultural supplement was launched helped create close connections between text and image while at the same time functioning as a unifying element in terms of the visuality of the supplement as a whole (Mascioto 61–67).

Xul Solar's participation in the RMS speaks to two personalities who had interests in common, shared readings and who now appeared committed to the same project. But, on this point, and recalling that their presence was not always explicit, we also respect Annick Louis's warning given more than two decades ago about the danger of attributing certain texts published in the RMS to specific individuals on the basis of assumptions or reasoning that may lead to erroneous conclusions ("Instrucciones"). Therefore, and in objective terms, our starting point is some of the books that were in Xul's library. These are objects that, as such, are sometimes included in other sets and collections; some bear personal or other types of marks, and others are mentioned in personal accounts that allow us to correctly associate the books with Xul and Borges. All of which leads us to think of them as part of a shared library held in a physical and private space, the artist's home.

Borges always emphasized the exceptional character of that library, and, in his conversations with Adolfo Bioy Casares, in his lectures on Xul, and in his constant references to the artist, he mentioned it more than once. Thus, in 1963, a little less than a month after Xul's death, Borges recalled that his friend had "una biblioteca prodigiosa: colecciones de cuentos de hadas de todos los países, en alemán, Historia de las religiones; la *Historia de la Filosofía* de Deussen; libros sobre el origen del lenguaje; un libro sobre los *tartans* de Escocia, que le gustaba mucho. Él, es claro, los perfeccionaba" [a prodigious library: collections of fairy tales from every country, in German, History of Religions; Deussen's *History of Philosophy*; books on the origin of language; a book on the *Tartans* of Scotland, which he liked very much. He, of course, perfected them] (Bioy Casares 874). He also remembered Xul's mastery of English and German, and the hours he had spent "en su casa, en la calle Laprida 1214, en esa espléndida biblioteca, quizás una de las mejores bibliotecas que yo he visto en mi vida, con libros en todos los idiomas" [at his house, at 1214 Laprida Street, in that splendid library, perhaps one of the best libraries I have ever seen in my life, with books in every language] (Borges, "Recuerdos" 54). It is no exaggeration to say that there was no library like Xul's in Buenos Aires in the 1920s. By 1930, the artist's library appeared to be defined mainly by the books that had entered it prior to his departure to Europe in 1912, and by then it had the profile of a personal library, stored in a cabinet and preserved by his father, although today we do not know how it was arranged. The books he acquired during his twelve years in Europe (1912–1924) were also added to the library, in particular, a set acquired in Munich and Stuttgart between 1921 and 1923.[8]

Xul's library at the time was "prodigiosa" [prodigious], "espléndida" [splendid], as well as "versátil y deleitable" [versatile and delightful] (Borges, "Laprida" 76), and, from a very early date, the friendship between the two seems to have been forged around it. In one of his articles published in the Buenos Aires newspaper *La Prensa*, "Cuentos del Turquestán," Borges wrote up Gustav Jungbauer's book, *Märchen aus Turkestan und Tibet* [Tales from *Turkestan and Tibet*] (1923).[9] The title was abbreviated and presented in Spanish as "Cuentos del Turquestán," a practice—that of translating authors' names and book titles—that he would continue for quite some time when working on texts of literary dissemination such as this.[10]

To introduce his topic, Borges gave a brief summary of the origin of these tales from Turkestan:

> Fueron contados en el Norte, tierra de espaciada llanura, alrededor de fogatas de bosta de camello que arden en los campamentos Kirghises; fueron contados en el Sur, tierra de arrozales y acequias, por cuenteras profesionales en los bazares, entre la atención redonda y gustadora de los oyentes; fueron traducidos primero al ruso, por Ostrumof, y de allí al alemán, por el doctor Gustavo Jungbauer; fueron publicados en Jena el año 23, y, finalmente, después de esos conventilleos étnicogeográficos del destino, cayó un ejemplar en mi casa, fácilmente el único en la ciudad. ("Cuentos" 260)

> [They were told in the North, land of wide-open plains, around campfires of camel dung burning in the Kirghiz camps; they were told in the South, land of rice fields and irrigation ditches, by professional storytellers in the bazaars, amidst the rapt and delighted attention of the listeners; they were translated first into Russian, by Ostrumof, and from there into German, by Dr. Gustav Jungbauer; they were published in Jena in 1923, and, finally, following all of destiny's ethno-geographical gossip, a copy landed at my house, easily the only one in the city.]

This opening statement underscores the exceptional nature of the book in his hands: somewhere between amazed and astonished, he could hardly believe that there was not a single additional copy in all of Buenos Aires. That book's specific provenance was not mentioned, yet it was the same as another text he mentions in the article, written by an ethnologist he calls Teodoro Guillermo Danzel, that concerned pre-Columbian Mexican mythology. While he does not identify Theodor Wilhelm Danzel's 1922 book, *Mexiko II. Kultur und Leben im alten Mexiko,* by name, it is as exceptional as Jungbauer's in having also come from Xul's library. In mentioning *Mexiko*, Borges sought to foreground the beliefs of various indigenous peoples for whom magic infuses certain rites, where the marvelous and the everyday are intertwined. Several scholars have already noted the importance of "Tales of Turkestan" to Borges's 1932 essay in *Sur* "El arte narrativo y la magia" [Narrative Art and Magic] (Brescia 142–44; Balderston 82–83). Consequently, it is perhaps unsurprising that the painting Xul gave his friend in 1940 was *Tlaloc* (1923), whose iconography was taken directly from an illustration in volume I of *Mexiko*: "Tlaloc, der Regengott" (Xul Solar et al. 1: 234).

A consideration of the young writer's tone is worthwhile as he describes himself reading *Märchen aus Turkestan und Tibet* in Xul's library: "Lo leí casi de un tirón, adjudicándole, sin duda, escenarios falsos: cosa que no me preocupa, porque es de cuentos fabulosos el libro, y cada versión nueva es un nuevo mito. Que un argentino hable (y aun escriba) sobre la versión alemana de la traducción rusa de unos cuentos imaginados en el Turquestán, ya es magia superior la de esos cuentos" [I read it almost in a single sitting, doubtlessly attributing false scenes to it: this doesn't worry me, because it is a book of fabulous tales, and each new version is a new myth. That an Argentine should speak (much less write) about the German version of the Russian translation of some stories dreamed up in Turkestan is already more magical than that contained in the stories themselves] ("Cuentos" 260). This last sentence is especially notable because it models the author putting into practice a concept that he had been theorizing about in *La Prensa* just weeks prior: in his essay "Las dos maneras de traducir" [Two Ways to Translate], Borges discussed the concept of textual versions and their validity without regard for the original. In the case of "Tales from Turkestan," he is citing a process in which the stories went from oral tradition, to being captured in written format in Russian by Orthodox missionary and Orientalist scholar Nikolai Petrovich Ostroumov (*Skaski Sartov* [*Tales of the Saratovs*], 1906), which became, according to Jungbauer, the main source for his German versions of the tales. Indeed, stories one to fifteen were based on the Russian missionary's translations, including "Der reiche Atametoi," a story Borges highlighted in his review. But most important is that the Argentine also added his own version, placing himself in that same line of transmission. His version, marked by orality, sought to recreate in written form, in a newspaper article, the mode of communicating those tales of Turkestan.

A similar process underlies Xul's first contribution to RMS: "Cuentos del Amazonas, de los mosetenes y guarayús: primeros historias que se oyeron en este continente" signed "versión de Alejandro Schulz" (Schulz [Xul Solar] 1933), which was recovered and attributed to the artist by Jorge B. Rivera (1976). Notably, Xul's full name was Oscar Agustín Alejandro Schulz Solari, so the "pseudonym" is an abbreviated form. This choice, if not his own decision, must at least have been agreed upon with Borges. Still, it is unlikely that, in 1933, anyone could have identified him: since deciding upon his name in 1920 (*Jorge L. Borges* 43–44, note 72), his public contributions (published texts and exhibition catalogs) were signed Xul Solar, or in some cases Alejandro Xul Solar or A. Xul Solar. What's more, personal accounts of the time always refer to Xul Solar.

With respect to calling the text a "versión de Alejandro Schulz" [version by Alejandro Schulz], we should consider other variables that relate to his name and which, although in a different way, also link him to Borges. In 1935, when composing *Historia universal de la infamia* [*A Universal History of Infamy*], Borges was working on the basis of those stories published in RMS (Louis, *Jorge Luis Borges*). Our interest here is in "El tintorero enmascarado Hakim de Merv" [The Masked Dyer Hakim de Merv] (called "El rostro del profeta" [The Face of the Prophet] in the RMS), because in the "Índice de fuentes," Borges lists one of the story's sources as "*Die Vernichtung der Rose. Nach dem arabischen Urtext* übertragen von Alexander Schulz, Leipzig, 1927" (*OC* I: 409). As the name Alexander Schulz has since been identified as Xul (Di Giovanni 10), there is no doubt that the book is being attributed to him. But thinking about this attribution in the context of this chapter, there are some points worth clarifying. First, scholars have repeatedly pointed out that the book in question does not exist; it is apocryphal, and, consequently, its author is part of that fiction. But why attribute it to Xul Solar? We might recall that the artist's grandfather was named Alexander Schulz, and this leads us to Borges's practice of choosing pseudonyms derived from the names of his and his collaborators' ancestors. In this case, however, we would be correct in assuming that the pseudonym is a translation of Xul's name into German (Postigo 110). However, we saw that Alejandro Schulz was not the name by which Xul was known, but it *is* the name of an author to whom the Spanish version of the "Cuentos del Amazonas" is attributed in issue two of RMS. Given Borges manner of naming him, and by assigning his friend the role of translator, he appears to give Xul the ability to render an Arabic text into German just as Enno Littmann and Max Henning had done. Their translations of *The Thousand and One Nights* were cited as sources in Borges's essay 1936 "Los traductores de las *1001 noches*" [The Translators of *The 1001 Nights*] (a first version of which appeared in issues of the RMS in February and March 1934), and it appears that he used their citations as a reference for formatting "Alexander Schulz's" credit for the translation of *Die Vernichtung der Rose*.

When closely reading the *History of Infamy* story in its two versions ("El rostro del profeta"/"El tintorero enmascarado"), there are other elements that bring us back to Borges's review of "Cuentos del Turquestán": the Prophet's being located in Turkestan; or the name of the engineer Andrusov—which surely refers to the famous Russian geologist and paleontologist Nikolai I. Andrusoff, who explored the Black Sea, which in turn brings to mind the Russian missionary "Ostrumof" (Ostroumov). Yet, when editing the story for publication in 1935, Borges exchanged the mention of the Kama Shastra Society (clearly linked to Richard Francis Burton) for the nonexistent Morgenländisches Archiv (Oriental Archive), reinforcing his recognition of Xul. Let us remember his library with its considerable number of books dedicated to different countries and regions of the East, not to mention the first edition of Max Henning's eight-volume *Tausend und eine Nacht*. Consequently, Borges effects the transposition of an Indian cultural society to a German archive specialized in the Orient, and, while not stated explicitly, it is Alexander Schulz who provides a new version of the codex, recovered from the original text (which had been lost), suggesting the previous version had been apocryphal.

Although we again encounter the concept of versions, the lack of transparency with the author's name leads us not only to the question of authorship when a text is translated into another language, but also to considerations of the particular language into which it is translated. In 1934—around the same time unsigned translations of various Kipling stories had started appearing in the newpaper's supplement, RMS—*Crítica* featured a review entitled "Hablan los libros: *Genghis Khan, Emperor of All Men*" signed by Fulano de Tal, which we attribute to Xul based on Borges's testimony (*Jorge L. Borges* 45).

The book in question (preserved today in the artist's library) was Harold Lamb's *Genghis Khan: Emperor of All Men* (translation published in the *Revista de Occidente*,

1928). Although we do not know for certain why Borges asked his friend to review a book that had already been out for six years, he likely wanted to make sure Xul was in a position to write a text that might be included in an issue of RMS. At that time, Xul's language was *Neocriollo*—an artificial language, on which he had begun to work around 1918–1920. While it initially fused Spanish and Portuguese and involved mechanisms of agglutination, phonetization, and the use of *criollo* oral forms (Schwartz 39; Pagni 55–57), he progressively added roots from other languages, including French, German, Greek, Latin, and Sanskrit. In his various writings, *neocriollo* appears in constant transformation, though it followed specific phono-morphological, orthographic, and grammatical rules (Nelson 28–29). This process of transformation meant that, by the mid-1930s, Xul's writing was practically illegible and had lost the initial transparency that made it comprehensible to the two large blocks of Latin American readers; in some cases, it had to be translated to be understood. Thus, in 1934, when writing his text for *Crítica*, Xul had to stick to one motto: write in Spanish, not *neocriollo*.

With respect to how "Cuentos del Amazonas" was signed, this was not the first time Xul had played with the concept of "version": as early as 1927 he translated a selection of aphorisms by Christian Morgenstern, taken from the latter's book *Stufen: Eine Entwickelung in Aphorismen und Tagebuch-Notizen*, with the title "Algunos piensos cortos de Cristián Morgenstern" in "versión de Xul Solar." Published in *Martín Fierro*, he seems to have worked on this translation closely with the newspaper's editor, Evar Méndez (Morgenstern 9). In the published version, one can recognize the attenuation of *neocriollo* features that had been present in one of the two known previous versions, a typewritten text (Pagni 57). Then, too, he was working with a book acquired in Germany, and the choice of the term *version* brings us closer in time to discussions that Xul and Borges may have had regarding the problematics of translation and texts moving to another language.

As far as the RMS is concerned, the "versión de Alejandro Schulz," which was indeed in Spanish and not *neocriollo*, orients us to a specific place: as a version, "Cuentos del Amazonas" refers to another text whose origin is not indicated and remains unknown. As its own version, Xul's text positions itself above its source: the book by German ethnologist Theodor Koch-Grünberg (1872–1924), *Indianermärchen aus Südamerika* [*Tales of South American Indians*] (1920), also found in Xul's library. Like *Märchen aus Turkestan und Tibet*, *Indianermärchen* is part of the Die Märchen der Weltliteratur [Folk Tales from World Literature] series. Both books were part of what Borges had recognized as the profile of his friend's library. And although there were other collections of folktales in his library, Die Märchen der Weltliteratur was the most widely represented (eleven books from the collection). As indicated in the copy of *Indianermärchen* (347–50), this series included the Deutscher Märchen [German Tales], then the Europäische Märchen [European Tales], followed by the Außereuropäische Märchen [Non-European Tales], and finally Die Märchen der primitiven Völker [Tales of Primitive Peoples]. Within these categories, Xul had the Nordic, Finnish, and Russian tales from Europe; among the non-European, he had tales from India, the Caucasus, and Jungbauer's text on Turkestan and Tibet; and among the "primitive" tales, he owned the volumes dedicated to Malaysia, Australia, New Guinea and Fiji, and Africa. Taken as a whole, this collection can be related to other encyclopedic books in Xul's library in their attempts to codify the knowledge of the world, such as *Die Sitten der Völker* (1914), edited by Georg Buschan, or *Die Wunder der Welt* (1912–1913), by Ernst Hesse-Wartegg.

With all this in mind, the question is: Why choose Koch-Grünberg's book to publish a selection of short stories in the RMS? If we consider that, in each of its issues, the supplement was advertised as being "the most widely circulated in South America," the choice seems obvious—these were stories that were collected in South America. Yet there is another point to consider: of the three stories translated—"Das Augenspiel" [The Game of the Eyes], "Die Pfeilketten" [The Chain of Arrows], and "Der große Schlange" [The Great Serpent]—the first two had similar tales among North American native peoples, as Koch-Grünberg made clear in his explanatory notes (322, 335). This relationship sheds interesting light on the subtitle given these tales in the RMS: "first stories to be heard on this continent," which foregrounded the orality of the narration and, at the same time, defined a particular space: the American continent.[11] The other thing to consider is the character of this compilation, which Koch-Grünberg points out in his prologue:

> Es ist ein buntes Material, das in diesem Bändchen zusammengestellt ist. Schöpfungs- und Heroensagen, die zum Teil wohl aus Naturmythen entstanden sind, wechseln mit einfachen Märchen, Tierfabeln und humoristischen Erzählungen. Zauberei und Verwandlungen mannigfacher Art spielen darin eine Rolle. (Indianermärchen [iv])

> [There is a colorfully varied collection of material in this small volume. Sagas of creation and heroes, some of which probably originated with nature myths, alternate with simple fairy tales, animal fables, and humorous stories. Magic and transformations of various kinds play a part in it].[12]

He then elaborates on the following point:

> Indessen geben die folgenden Erzählungen beim Lesen nur einen matten Abglanz ihrer urwüchsigen Schönheit. Man muß die Leute hören, wie sie am Lagerfeuer ihre Stammesgeschichten erzählen, auf die sie so stolz sind, wie sich ihre Darstellung häufig zu dramatischem Schwung erhebt. ([iv])

> [Yet, when the following stories are read, they give only a faint reflection of their primal beauty. One must hear the people telling their tribal stories around the campfire, of which they are so proud, to perceive how their interpretation often rises to a dramatic vividness].

It is this characterization that seems to make these stories suitable for publication in the RMS, sharing with *Märchen aus Turkestan und Tibet* their orality and strong communicative charges. These, in other words, are the aspects that were of interest to Borges (as he himself has told us) as editor of the supplement and which must have had an active role in his choosing to publish them. The other point to consider is that the *Revista Multicolor de los Sábados* was directed toward the entire family as its intended audience, as indicated by an illustration in the main body of *Crítica* announcing the launch of RMS in 1933: the stories had an adaptability in their readings that allowed them to reach the nuclear family of father, mother, and children. However, the stories occupied only the bottom third of page four of the supplement, and they were arranged in a confusing manner. There are two small, unsigned illustrations: on the right, occupying half the column is a crab and a jaguar, two protagonists from "Das Augenspiel" [El juego de los ojos (The Game of the Eyes)]; the image on the left seems to correspond to "Die Pfeilketten" [La cadena de flechas (The Chain of Arrows)], possibly representing Abaangui and one of his sons. While the two images seem intended to function as illustrations of the narratives, their locations within other stories causes them to lose part of their efficacy.

This situation seems due to a somewhat careless layout, which resulted in there being no title printed for the first story, "El juego de los ojos," nor a subtitle indicating its origin, as was included with the other two: "La cadena de flechas (De los guarayús, guaraníes del este boliviano)" [The Chain of Arrows (From the Guarayu, Guaranis from Eastern Bolivia)] and "La gran serpiente (Leyenda mosetene. Norte de Bolivia)" [The great serpent (Mosetene Legend. Northern Bolivia)]. The specifications in these two subtitles were taken from Koch-Grünberg's foreword and his explanatory notes. In the case of "Das Augenspiel" [El juego de los ojos], the ethnologist had taken the narrative from his own book, volume II of *Vom Roroima zum Orinoco -Mythen und Legenden der Taulipang und Arekuna Indianer* (1924 [1916]), the very book whose chapters dedicated to the hero Makunaíma launched the key book for Brazilian modernism, Mário de Andrade's *Macunaíma* (1928), which also could be found in Xul's library (López).

However, in its transformation from the 1916 to the 1924 edition, "Die Augenspiel" lost its subtitle ("*Krabe, Jaguar und Vater des Trahíra-Fisches*" [The Crab, Jaguar, and Father of the Trahíra Fish]) and the information about its origin "*Erzählt vom Taulipáng Mayūluaípu*" [Told by the Taulipang Mayūluaípu] (132). In an attempt to make the book easier to read, some language that had originally appeared in footnotes was incorporated into the text. For example, in the 1916 version, "*Die Krabbe schickte ihre Augen nach dem See Palauá*" [The crab sent its eyes to Lake Palauá] had the footnote "*Im Urtext:* paluá-kupe = *Meeres-see.* Palauá, parauá = *Meer*" [In the original text: paluá-kupe = sea-lake. Palauá, parauá = sea] (132); in *Indianermärchen* this was simply rendered "*Die Krabbe schickte ihre Augen nach dem Meeressee*" [The crab sent his eyes to the sea-lake] (131). The new edition of the story had lost the critical apparatus created through its interlinear translation, which had included the explanation or gloss of names and words. As we shall see, this had some consequences for Xul's version. The modifications that resulted from the re-edition have to do with a distinguishing feature of all of the books included in Die Märchen der Weltliteratur collections: each of its volumes was entrusted to a specialist; they were not solely aimed at professional and academic readers, but also to those merely interested in the subject matter (Crane 329). This is, in fact, what made it possible for the young Borges to marvel at *Märchen aus Turkestan und Tibet* in 1926, and it is this that set Xul on his path to translating the stories. He not only owned those books, he also had a command of the language, thanks to his Baltic German father, which he had perfected during his two-year stay in Germany. Thus, he seemed the most likely person to provide a version of the stories.

We do not know if there was any editing work by Borges on Xul's translation prior to its publication, but it seems probable. But whenever we consider collaborative work between Borges and Xul, we cannot ignore the writers' shared interest in the various processes involved in creating books such as this (Reiter 199). To this end, the ethnologist worked from rich and varied multilingual sources, which he lists at the end of the book—texts in Spanish, Portuguese, French, English, German, and Swedish by authors such as Alexander von Humboldt, Alcide D'Orbigny, Couto de Magalhães, William Brett, José Barbosa Rodriguez, Karl von Steinen, Rudolf Lenz, João Capistrano de Abreu, Feliciano de Oliveira, Eurt Nimuendajú-Unkel, Erland Nordenskiöld, and Walter E. Roth. As Sabine Reiter points out, this selection of 117 stories contained tales from over thirty indigenous groups, representing different linguistic families found in Bolivia, Brazil, British Guyana, Chile, and Surinam (208).

It was now Xul's turn to provide his own take on the stories from this extensive series and to make them comprehensible to the readers of the literary supplement—a new version that omitted the name of Koch-Grünberg, who had, of course, provided his own version; he was not the author of those stories, but one more link in the chain that stretched from their origin to us. Hence, the statement about the origin of the tales and their collective authorship was realized in the title "Cuentos del Amazonas" [Tales from the Amazon]. Some of the sources that Koch-Grünberg had used were known to Xul. This was the case for "Die Pfeilketten" [La cadena de flechas (The Chain of Arrows)], a tale whose source the German ethnologist listed as José Cardús's book, *Las misiones franciscanas* (1899) [The Franciscan Missions]; in Germany, Xul had also acquired Erland Nordenskiöld's *Indianer und Weisse in Nordostbolivien* [Indians and Whites in the Bolivian Northeast], which, also based on the Spanish missionary's texts, included the same myth (158). Thus, in their own ways Xul, and surely also Borges, were aware of the German author's path to *Indianermärchen aus Südamerika*.

In describing the novel points of contact Koch-Grünberg's book afforded between the South and North American versions of the tales, in a 1921 book review, folklorist Thomas F. Crane summarized the plot of "Die augenspiel" as a

> story in which a crab sent its eyes to the sea, and then recalled them. A jaguar was watching the crab, and wanted to see the trick. The crab sends its eyes, and only the empty sockets are left. Then the eyes are recalled. The jaguar insists on having its own eyes sent. The crab sends them and recalls them. The second time a fish swallows them. The jaguar tries to kill the crab, but it jumps into the water and escapes. A king vulture anoints the jaguar's eye-sockets with sap of a tree, and cures him. Since then the jaguar kills animals for the vulture to eat. (330)

Likewise, regarding "Die Pfeilketten" he noted, "Abaangui, the grandfather of the Guarayu, had two sons. One day each of them shot an arrow toward heaven, so that it stuck fast in the heavenly vault. Then each shot a second arrow into the first, and so

532   PATRICIA M. ARTUNDO

on until two arrow-chains reached from heaven to earth. On these they climbed to heaven and remain there changed into sun and moon" (330). The other story, "Die große Schlange," tells the story of a couple who adopt a worm who will only feed on the hearts of birds, animals, and finally, human beings. The worm, Ñoko, grows inordinately fast and his father must kill more and more beings to feed him, to the point of causing an entire village to disappear; finally, the father is discovered and killed. Ñoko, who is a great serpent by this time, climbs to the heavens and stays there, but then comes down to search for his father. On finding him dead, the serpent enwraps the entire village with his body and kills its inhabitants; he and his father become men, and Ñoko is transformed into the Milky Way.

What did Xul's work consist of? First, it is clear that he did not opt for a literal translation; second, some of his decisions reflect his own work on language, the *neocriollo* he had begun creating around 1918–1920. In particular, there is an Argentine creolization of the Spanish, colloquial language is used over formal or even literary expressions, and certain words are even expressed phonetically. There is also interesting word choice, particularly with terms that have corresponding word in Spanish but which, due to regional pragmatics, modify the meaning of what they translate.

In "Die Augenspiel" [El juego de los ojos (The Game of the Eyes)] for example, the German term "*Schwager*" is translated as *cuñado* in Spanish [brother-in-law], but this term has another meaning in several Spanish American countries, where "cuñado" or "cuñada" is, according to the Real Academia Española "an affectionate formula for addressing friends" (online, my translation).[13] This creates a certain strangeness in the jaguar's relationship with the other two protagonists, when he addresses the crab, for example, in these terms: " '¡Eh!' Le preguntó: '¿qué dices ahí, cuñado?' " ['Eh!' He asked him: 'What are you saying there, *cuñado*?']. The tone, moreover, reveals that the orality Koch-Grünberg sought to include in his retellings of the tales runs through Xul's versions as well. In translating *der Vater des Trahíra-Fisches* [the father of the Trahíra fish], he used "Tata Tararira"—not "padre" but "tata," an affectionate, yet respectful term for addressing a father, which was appropriate within the narrative for naming the fish. What's more, "tata" was used in a similar way among the Guarani and Quechua (Granada 370). In other instances, Xul eliminated certain names for which he had no translation. For example, "Aimalá-pódole, *der Vater des Trahíra-Fisches*," was rendered merely as "Tata Tararira." Thus we find a case where Koch-Grünberg eliminated the footnote from the 1920 version of the story that would have made clear to Xul that "aimalá, aimará *ist ein großer Raubfisch: Macrodon Trahira*" [aimalá, aimará is a large predatory fish: Macrodon Trahira] (*Mythen* 132). In other cases, the translator opted for phonetization, thus the *Jatahy-Baumes* would become the "Yatahí tree," and the *kaikusäschimpipö* tree, would be the *caicusashimpipo*; the digraph "ch" was eliminated as its sound is reflected in the German pronunciation of "sh," as Xul would have known (Borges, *Jorge L. Borges* 43–44). In "Die große Schlange" [La gran serpiente (The Great Serpent)], *Grashalm* [blade of grass], is rendered as "yuyo," a Quichua term widely used in Argentina and other South American countries; and instead of "großeren Teller," [larger plate or dish], he opts for "botijo," which encapsulates the image conveyed by a "potbellied jug" (RAE 183).

If orality and colloquialism are the dominant registers in Xul's version, it is clear that this form of expression seeks to recover the stories' history as oral tales, just as Koch-Grünberg himself had attempted. In any case, at this point, we should ask ourselves what impact, if any, resulted from the publication of these stories. Initially, there was no continuity, in fact, it would be an entire year before Xul contributed any translations again, this time with a few of Rudyard Kipling's *Just So Stories* (1902). These tales, despite the distance that separates them, have points of contact with those collected in *Indianermärchen aus Südamerika* (Artundo "Borges").

Some time after the publication of "Cuentos del Amazonas," Borges confessed in his review of *Chinese Fairy Tales and Folk Tales* that, "Pocos géneros literarios suelen ser más tediosos que el cuento de hadas, salvo, naturalmente, la fábula. (La inocencia y la irresponsabilidad de los animales determinan su encanto; rebajarlos a instrumentos de la moral, como lo hacen Esopo y La Fontaine, me parece una aberración.)" [Few literary genres tend to be more tedious than the fairy tale, except, of course, the fable. (The innocence and irresponsibility of animals is what makes them so charming; to reduce them to instruments of morality, as Aesop and La Fontaine do, seems to me an aberration)] (204). This statement comes as a surprise when considering his approach to the tales of Turkestan and Tibet or to indigenous Amerindian stories. His negation was likely a tactic that allowed him to make an argument about what he saw as different in the stories coming from China as opposed to those from European (or from Arabian) tales. We can understand his criticism as revealing Borges's interest in stories that are told outside of the European world, as Die Märchen der Weltliteratur [The Fairytales of World Literature] classified them, in particular those selected for the RMS. "Die große Schlange" [La gran serpiente (The Great Serpent)] describes the interaction between humans and other beings; "Die Augenspiel" [El juego de los ojos (The Game of the Eyes)] is a fable in which animals interact with each other; and "Die Pfeilketten" [La cadena de flechas (The Chain of Arrows)] recounts the creation of the world (the Sun and the Moon). None is governed by moral criteria, nor do they offer judgment of the facts narrated; others take a perspective on the origin of the universe from an enriched cosmogony; the creation myths demonstrate the transformations all beings undergo, and all of the tales are surprising in offering a type of narrative that differs from those of Europe. Finally, while we do not intend to suggest that Xul thought everything that we know Borges did, the topics we have discussed here were very likely the subject of their conversations. Therefore, the choice of Theodor Koch-Grünberg's book and the selection of stories to be published in the RMS is far from a spontaneous contribution on Xul's part. It is a direct consequence of themes and readings the two friends discussed and of Borges's specific interest in certain types of popular narratives that left their mark on the *Revista Multicolor de los Sábados*.

Notes

1. Emir Rodríguez Monegal was the first to draw attention to this point, although this interest was addressed directly in terms of influence (*Jorge Luis Borges* 217).
2. For more on Borges and the fantastic, see Esplin in this volume.
3. See Rossi "Aquellos años 40," 2007, for more on the major trends in Argentine art of the 1940s.
4. From an early age, Borges showed an interest in art, and his relationship to it not only lasted over time, but is complex and can be the object of a number of different readings. With respect to the many sketches in his manuscripts and occasionally his letters, see Balderston, "Borges, Portrait of an Unexpected Artist."
5. These were Attilio Rossi (1951), Gustavo Thorlichen (1958), Emilio Pettoruti (1962), Pablo Lameiro (1965), Juan Carlos Faggioli (1966), Carlos Páez Vilaró (1971), Aldo Sessa (1976), Norah Borges (1978), and Santiago Cogorno (1983). Except for those dedicated to Rossi and Norah, the remaining ones were reproduced in *El círculo secreto* (2003).
6. See *Jorge L. Borges recuerda a Xul Solar: prólogos y conferencias, 1949–1980*, edited by Patricia M. Artundo, Buenos Aires: Fundación Internacional Jorge Luis Borges, 2013.
7. For more on Borges and the RMS, see Saítta in this volume.
8. In 1964, a fire caused by a wood stove in the living room of Xul's house resulted in the loss of a large part of these books since the majority of books related to his stay in Europe was kept in that very room. For a first reconstruction of the books purchased in Germany, see Fischler.
9. *Märchen aus Turkestan und Tibet* was also the writer's first contact with the Simurgh, that amazing bird that encompassed other birds (Balderston, "De cómo Borges" 79–80).
10. For more on Borges's translation of proper names, see Willson in this volume.
11. Many cultures understand there to be just five continents: Europe, Asia, Africa, Oceania, and America. Most texts referring to "América" are designating North, Central, and South America—though the term is often used reflexively to denote Spanish America.
12. The original Spanish translations of this and the following quote were by Carlos García, in Hamburg, for whose help I am grateful. I also thank Edgardo Krebs, who supported the development of this research.
13. The closest English equivalent would be calling a friend "brother" or "sister" or a derivation such as "bro," "bruv," "sis," etc.

Works Cited

Artundo, Patricia M. "Borges, Kipling y Xul Solar: intervenciones y apropiaciones en la *Revista Multicolor de los Sábados*," *H-Art. Revista de Historia, Teoría y Crítica de Arte*. Edited by María Amalia García and Silvia Dolinko. *Las revistas como fragmento de los procesos del arte moderno en América Latina: perspectivas contemporáneas*, mayo-agosto 2023, n. 14, 2023. https://doi.org/10.25025/hart14.2023.04.

Artundo, Patricia M. "Primera historia de un diario mágico." Alejandro Xul Solar, *Los San Signos: Xul Solar y el I Ching*. Translated by Daniel E. Nelson, edited by Patricia M. Artundo, El hilo de Ariadna, Fundación Pan Klub, 2012, pp. 103–24.

Artundo, Patricia M. "Un artista y su obra: Xul Solar, mercado de arte y coleccionismo entre 1925 y 1963." Paper presented at the conference *Jornada sobre coleccionismo en la Argentina*. Universidad de Palermo, 2005.

Balderston, Daniel. "Borges, Portrait of an Unexpected Artist." *What's In a Name? A Collection of Articles, Reminiscences, Poetry and Prose That Defines the Life of a Man, Donald A. Yates*. Edited by Andrea Labinger and Joanne Yates. MSU Libraries, 2018, 229–49.

Balderston, Daniel. "De cómo Borges llegó a los cuentos del Turquestán y qué encontró en ellos." *Variaciones Borges*, vol. 53, 2022, pp. 75–85.

Bioy Casares, Adolfo. *Borges*, edited by Daniel Martino. Destino, 2006.

Borges, Jorge Luis. "Chinese Fairy Tales and Folk Tales," translated by Wolfram Eberhard. *Textos cautivos: ensayos y reseñas en "El Hogar": 1936–1939*. Edited by Enrique Sacerio-Garí and Emir Rodríguez Monegal, Tusquets, 1986, pp. 204–05.

Borges, Jorge Luis. "Cuentos del Turquestán." *Textos recobrados (1919–1929)*. Emecé, 1926, pp. 260–63.

Borges, Jorge Luis. *El círculo secreto: prólogos y notas*. Emecé, 2003.

Borges, Jorge Luis. "El rostro del profeta." *Revista Multicolor de los Sábados*, January 24, 1934, p. 6.

Borges, Jorge Luis. "El tintorero enmascarado Hákim de Merv." *Obras completas*. Emecé, 1996, pp. 324–28.

Borges, Jorge Luis. "El tintorero enmascarado Hákim de Merv." En *Historia universal de la infamia. Obras completas: 1923–1972*. Emecé, 1935, pp. 324–28.

Borges, Jorge Luis. *Jorge L. Borges recuerda a Xul Solar: prólogos y conferencias, 1949–1980*, organized by Patricia M. Artundo. Fundación Pan Klub – Fundación Internacional Jorge Luis Borges, 2013.

Borges, Jorge Luis. "Laprida 1214." *Jorge L. Borges recuerda a Xul Solar*, pp. 75–76.

Borges, Jorge Luis. "Las dos maneras de traducir." *Textos recobrados (1919–1929)*. Emecé, 2007, pp. 256–9.

Borges, Jorge Luis. "*Los traductores de las 1001 noches.*" *Obras completas*. Vol. 1. Emecé, 1996, pp. 397–413.

Borges, Jorge Luis. "Mis recuerdos sobre Xul Solar, pintor argentino de lo desconocido." *Jorge L. Borges recuerda a Xul Solar: prólogos y conferencias, 1949–1980*, organizado por Patricia M. Artundo, Fundación Pan Klub—Fundación Internacional Jorge Luis Borges, 2013, pp. 33–51.

Borges, Jorge Luis. *Obras completas (1923–1949)*, anotada por Tolando Costa Picazo e Irma Zangara. Emecé, 2009.

Borges, Jorge Luis. "Prólogo galería Samos. Muestra Xul Solar." *Jorge L. Borges recuerda a Xul Solar: prólogos y conferencias, 1949–1980*, organized by Patricia M. Artundo. Fundación Pan Klub – Fundación Internacional Jorge Luis Borges, 2013, pp. 3–4.

Borges, Jorge Luis. "Recuerdos de mi amigo Xul Solar." *Jorge L. Borges recuerda a Xul Solar: prólogos y conferencias, 1949–1980*, organizado por Patricia M. Artundo. Fundación Pan Klub—Fundación Internacional Jorge Luis Borges, 2013, pp. 52–74.

Brescia, Pablo A. J. "Los (h)usos de la literatura fantástica: notas sobre Borges." *Escritos*, vol. 21 (January–June), 2000, pp. 141–53.

Crane, T. F. [Review of *Indianermärchen aus Südamerika* de Theodor Koch-Grünberg]. *The Journal of American Folklore*, 133 (July–September), 1921, pp. 329–32. https://doi.org/10.2307/535160.

Crítica. 1933. ["Announcement of the *Revista Argentina Multicolor*"]. *Crítica. Revista Multicolor de los Sábados, 1933–1934*. Edited by Nicolás Helft, Fondo Nacional de las Artes, 1999.

Danzel, Theodor Wilhelm. *Mexiko II. Textteil: Kultur und Leben im alten Mexiko; Bildteil: Mexikanische Plastik.* Folkwang-Verlag, 1922. https://archive.org/details/mexiko0002unse.

Di Giovanni, Norman T. "Borges' Infamy: A Chronology and a Guide." *Review: Literature and Arts of the Americas*, vol. 7, no. 8, 1973, pp. 5–12. https://doi.org/10.1080/08905767308593746.

Fischler, Graciela Viviana. *Xul Solar: 2 años, 229 libros.* Undergraduate thesis. Universidad de Palermo, Facultad de Humanidades y Ciencias Sociales, 2009.

Fulano de Tal [Alejandro Xul Solar]. "Hablan los libros: *Genghis Khan, Emperador de todos los hombres.*" *Crítica*, August 9, 1934, p. 8.

Granada, Daniel. *Vocabulario rioplatense razonado.* Imprenta Rural, 1890. https://archive.org/details/vocabularioriploogranuoft.

Jungbauer, Gustav. *Märchen aus Turkestan und Tibet.* Eugen Diederichs Verlag, 1922. https://archive.org/details/marchenausturkestanundtibet/.

Koch-Grünberg, Theodor. *Indianermärchen aus Südamerika.* Eugen Diederichs Verlag, 1920. https://archive.org/details/indianermarchenaussudamerika.

Koch-Grünberg, Theodor. *Mythen und Legenden der Taulipang- und Arekuna- Indianer.* Vol. 2 de *Vom Roroima zum Orinoco.* Strecker und Schröder, 1924 [1916]. https://archive.org/details/bub_br_1918_01011120.

Louis, Annick. "Instrucciones para buscar a Borges en la *Revista Multicolor de los Sábados.*" *Variaciones Borges*, vol. 5, 1998, pp. 246–64. https://www.jstor.org/stable/24879528.

Louis, Annick. *Jorge Luis Borges: œuvre et manœuvres.* L'Harmattan, 1997.

Louis, Annick. "Silvina Ocampo et *La antología de la literatura fantástica*: Le fantastique argentin: Silvina Ocampo, Julio Cortazar, América." *Cahiers du CRICCAL*, vol. 17, 1997, pp. 256–89.

Mascioto, María de los Ángeles. *Nuevos modos de escritura en la* Revista Multicolor de los Sábados *(1933–1934).* Doctoral dissertation. Universidad Nacional de La Plata. Facultad de Humanidades y Ciencias de la Educación, 2019. https://www.memoria.fahce.unlp.edu.ar/tesis/te.1526/te.1526.pdf.

Morgenstern, Christian. "Algunos piensos cortos de Cristián Morgenstern, versión de Xul Solar." *Martín Fierro. Periódico quincenal de arte y crítica libre*, vol. 41, 1927, p. 9.

Nordenskiöld, Erland. *Indianer und Weisse in Nordostbolivien.* Strecker und Schröder, 2012. http://www.archive.org/details/indianerundweissoonord.

Pagni, Andrea. "Xul Solar en dos escenas de traducción." *Latinoamérica entre lenguajes y lenguas.* Edited by Mónica Marinone and Gabriela Tineo, EUDEM, 2017, pp. 45–74.

Pinedo, Manuel [Norah Borges]. "Los frescos de la Galería Pacífico." *Los Anales de Buenos Aires*, no. 8, 1946, pp. 57–58.

Pinedo, Manuel [Norah Borges]. "Primera exposición de la Asociación Arte Concreto-Invención." *Los Anales de Buenos Aires*, no. 4, 1946, p. 51.

Postigo, Ximena. "La obra de Xul en la historia de Hákim de Merv, 'Tlön, Uqbar, Orbis Tertius' y otras ficciones reales." *Variaciones Borges*, vol. 28, 2009, pp, 107–25. https://www.borges.pitt.edu/sites/default/files/8%20Postigo.pdf.

Reiter, Sabine. "Die Übersetzung der Kashinawa-Mythen in Theodor Koch-Grünbergs *Indianermärchen aus Südamerika* [The translation of the myths of the Cashinahua people in Theodor Koch-Grünberg´s *Indianermärchen aus Südamerika*]." *Pandaemonium*, vol. 37, 2019, pp. 199–230. http://dx.doi.org/10.11606/1982-88372237199.

Real Academia Española (RAE). *Diccionario de la lengua española.* Real Academia Española, 1925.

Real Academia Española (RAE). *Diccionario de la lengua española.* 23rd ed., [online version 23.5]. https://dle.rae.es

Rivera, Jorge B. "Tres leyendas aborígenes en versiones de Alejandro Schulz-Xul Solar." In "Los juegos de un tímido: Borges en el suplemento de *Crítica*. Sus escritos," *Crisis*, vol. 38, 1976, pp. 24–25.

Rodríguez Monegal, Emir. *Jorge Luis Borges: A Literary Biography*. E. P. Dutton, 1978.

Rossi, Cristina. "Aquellos años 40." *Expotrastiendas, 4ª Feria de Arte en Argentina.*, Expotrastiendas, 2007, pp. 17–33.

Schwartz, Jorge. " 'Silabas las Estrellas compongan': Xul y el neocriollo." *Xul Solar: visiones y revelaciones*, Malba – Coleccion Costantini, Pinacoteca do Estado de São Paulo, 2005, pp. 35–47.

Schulz, Alejandro [Xul Solar, Alejandro]. "Cuentos del Amazonas, de los mosetenes y guarayús: primeras historias que se oyeron en este continente." *Revista Multicolor de los Sábados*, vol. 2, 1933, p. 4.

Torre Borges, Miguel de. *Nosotros, los Borges: apuntes de familia*. Colección de Poesía "Juan Ramón Jiménez," Universidad de Huelva, 2005.

Torre Borges, Miguel de. *Un día de Borges*. Editorial Mate, 2013.

Xul Solar, Alejandro. *Entrevistas, artículos y textos inéditos*, edited by Patricia M. Artundo, Corregidor, 2005.

Xul Solar, Alejandro, Patricia M. Artundo, Candelaria Artundo, and María Sofía Frigerio. *Xul Solar: Catálogo razonado: obra completa*. 2 vols. Fundación Pan Klub, 2016.

Xul Solar, Alejandro. *Los San Signos: Xul Solar y el I Ching*, traducción de Daniel E. Nelson, edición al cuidado de Patricia M. Artundo. El hilo de Ariadna/ Fundación Pan Klub, 2012, pp. 21–72.

CHAPTER 31

....

BORGES, BEWITCHED
BY FILM

....

GONZALO AGUILAR

NEARLY every text by Jorge Luis Borges deals with literature. He wrote very little about painting, almost nothing about music, and his mentions of dance or sculpture are very rare. However, and despite his eventual sight loss, there was one art form—to which he dedicated numerous pages—that clearly fascinated Borges: film.[1] What is more, even after going blind, Borges, who was not in the habit of going to concerts, much less to art shows, did keep going to movies. What was so fascinating to him about the world of cinema? When he began collaborating with the cultural journal *Sur*, why did he head up the film criticism department?[2] What led him to write film scripts with his friend Bioy Casares, even though they knew the possibility of their ever making it to the screen was practically null? And why, after going blind, did he go to see *West Side Story* nearly twenty times, go to see *Citizen Kane* one last time, or enjoy, accompanied by Maria Kodama, a film by Ingmar Bergman?

Nearly all critics agree that Borges found a narrative mode in film, and particularly those narrative genres that interested him when he first started writing fiction. In other words, this discovery came at the point at which he abandoned poetry (he did not publish any books of poetry between 1929 and 1960) and began writing the stories that would form part of the *Historia universal de la infamia* [*A Universal History of Infamy*] (1935). According to that book's prologue, its stories were derived from his "relecturas de Stevenson y de Chesterton y aun de los films de von Sternberg" [rereadings of Stevenson and Chesterton, [even] from the first films of von Sternberg] (*OC* I: 289; *CF* 3). Those are the same years in which he began to run, alongside Ulises Petit de Murat, the *Revista Multicolor de los Sábados* [*Multicolor Saturday Magazine*] published by the newspaper *Crítica* (1933–1934), and also began collaborating with the popular home journal *El Hogar* [*The Home*] and in the more elite cultural journal *Sur*.[3] All these facts place Borges's passion for film within a much larger constellation of inquiries not only into questions of narrative but also into the relationship between art and the masses. This is evidenced both by his interest in seeing movies (which were aimed at the masses) and in his choosing to work in popular media such as *Crítica* or *El Hogar* (and in *Sur* by selecting the journal's film criticism department for his area of contribution). Borges participated, as did many other writers, in the post-vanguard climate of the 1930s, which left poetic experimentation behind to focus instead on new settings of public space where film, magazines, and radio—as well as the masses who determined those entities' political leanings—posed new challenges to artists and intellectuals. It was as if the question Borges asked in the prologue to his third book of essays—"¿Mediante qué procesos psicológicos entendemos una oración?" [Through which psychological processes do we understand a sentence?]—had been moved from poetry (and the instantaneity of metaphor) and asked instead of narrative and its modes of unfolding successively in time before the eyes of the reader or viewer (*El idioma de los argentinos* 9). As if in these narrations of new mass media practices—above all cinema and journalism—the new shapes that literature, societies, and individuals would eventually acquire were being defined. For Borges, film was undoubtedly a narrative laboratory, but one in which filmmakers could play with new modes of understanding—and narrating—societies' destinies in a very turbulent decade.

Borges felt especially inclined toward directors who knew how to tell stories, like Sternberg or Lubitsch, and he abhorred those who attempted to elevate their artistic status by focusing on the aesthetics of imagery (his primary critique of Orson Welles's *Citizen Kane* was its "pedantry" in privileging aesthetic contemplation over enjoyment of the narrative or, in other words, the fact that its preciousness is at times so overwhelming that it affects the flow of the plot). Thus, when the Buenos Aires Cine Club, founded by Horacio Coppola, Jorge Romero Brest, and José Luis Romero in 1929, praised Sergei Eisenstein's *October* or Carl Theodor Dreyer's *Joan of Arc*, Borges dissented because, for him—as he would appreciatively declare much later—film was a bastard art form:

> Hay numerosos films —*El martirio de Juana de Arco* sigue siendo el espejo y el arquetipo de ese adulado error— que no pasan de meras antologías fotográficas; acaso no hay un solo film europeo que no sufra de imágenes inservibles . . . *La fuga* [de Saslavsky], en cambio, fluye límpidamente como los films americanos. (*Borges en Sur* 191)
>
> [There are numerous films—*The Passion of Joan of Arc* remains the mirror and the archetype of this highly praised error—that are nothing more than photo albums; there may not be a single European film that does not suffer from pointless images . . . *La fuga* [by Saslavsky], on the contrary, flows limpidly like American films.]

For Borges, film's unique ability is not to reach the status of visual art, taking inspiration from painting or seeking aesthetic contemplation, but rather in revealing ways to wield the diverse possibilities of narrative (Jelicié 18–23). Cinema's popular narratives entertain and, at the same time, present ethical dilemmas that demand political solutions. A laboratory for pondering the challenges of the age—film held Borges under its spell his entire life.

DESTINIES

Borges's first text about the *septième art*, entitled "El cinematógrafo, el biógrafo" [The Cinematographer, The Biographer], was published in the newspaper *La Prensa* on April 28, 1929, and, as the title suggests, it dealt with the two ways of naming this new art form. The word "cinematographer" evokes movement (kinos), the root of which carries an avant-garde element that Borges despised. He writes ironically of the "pasmo burgués ante las diabluras que hacen las máquinas" [bourgeois panic over the devilry done by machines], possibly aiming at Maples Arce or Oliverio Girondo (*Textos recobrados 1*: 382). Borges prefers the second term, "biographer," because cinema "nos descubre destinos, es el presentador de almas al alma" [reveals to us destinies; it is the herald of souls to the soul] (*Textos recobrados 1*: 382). In addition to reflecting on the sequential character of narrative (so different from that of poetry), Borges also muses on how the community and the masses play out in the destiny of the individual ("souls" and "soul"). That each story in *Historia universal de la infamia* focuses on just one character and that his/her name features prominently in each title was no casual choice. Destiny is social, but it is incarnated by individuals. In "El cinematógrafo, el biógrafo," Borges names as "authors" of the films not the directors but rather the actor-characters: Charlie Chaplin ("fine Jewish *compadrito*"), Emil Jannings, and George Bancroft. What happens to them and the ways that they react in kind define the aesthetic and dramatic dimension of the narrative situation. In these characters, Borges found a revival of the epic, which had been absent from literature or which literature had perhaps abandoned. In a 1984 interview, he commented "I believe Hollywood—for commercial reasons naturally— saved the epic at a time at which the poets had forgotten that poetry began with the epic [...], this was saved by the westerns" (Ferrari 191). In this way, Borges redefined the epic which, in his opinion, had been revived with the advent of cinema but which no longer related, as Hegel would have it, to the action of the State or to the organic totality of the community or "the life of a nation." The focus instead was on the heroic actions of the individual who, by threatening the ties that bind a community, strengthened those ties.

Bill Harrigan, the killer from *A Universal History of Infamy*, is "esmirriado, chúcaro, soez" [scrawny, quick-tempered, and foulmouthed] (*CF* 31), a frontiersman half cowboy, half *compadrito*, but whose death causes such jubilation in the community, it is as if a fraternity were founded over his cadaver. What Bill Harrigan (better known as Billy the Kid) does is affirm an individuality (despite its infamy) and destroy an element of communal ideology which, from that point on, would be the target of Borges's criticism: *uniformity*. Narrative opens space for deliberation, conjecture, and inquiry. The sense of the epic cannot be relegated to a sole heroic instance (be it that of the State or the nation); rather, it resides in the diversity of the individuals who offer their various points of view.

In his review of *Citizen Kane*, Borges maintained that the film has two plots: one is of "una imbecilidad casi banal" [pointlessly banal] (*SNF* 258) and refers to the discovery that a childhood sled is the only worthwhile memory that a millionaire still has. The second plotline is "muy superior" [far superior]: "El tema (a la vez metafísico y policial, a la vez psicológico y alegórico) es la investigación del alma secreta de un hombre, a través de las obras que ha construido, de las palabras que ha pronunciado, de los muchos destinos que ha roto" [A kind of metaphysical detective story, its subject (both psychological and allegorical) is the investigation of a man's inner self, through the works he has wrought, the words he has spoken, the many lives he has ruined] (*SNF* 259). While the first plotline is dead-ended and obvious, the second, with its disconnected fragments "nos invita a combinarlos y a reconstruirlo" [invites us to combine them and reconstruct him] (*SNF* 259). The community is not created through the epic action of an individual but rather in the diversity of interpretations of that act.

Mass Entertainment

A lingering misconception about Borges's literature is the belief that his antipathy toward Peronism (not to mention his friendship and closeness with certain elite writers) made him an anti-popular writer. From the point of view of sales, there are few writers who have been more popular and international than Borges.[4] He knew, as Rubén Darío would say, that "without fail" he had to move toward the masses,[5] and the pedagogical impetus of his work can be seen in conferences, news articles, translations, school visits, and the creation of anthologies. The experience of film during the 1930s and the beginning of the 1940s came to pose a question about how the passions of the masses function and about those functions' political and cultural clout. It is therefore not surprising that such questions arose in his literary pedagogy. As early as in "El cinematógrafo, el biógrafo," both narrative and political critiques are implied in his observation that German film seems unaware that the masses are much less than the individual person. With the growing visibility of the masses, stories should not lose sight of individual destiny for, by virtue of contrast and discordance, it is through individual action that one discovers the form in which a community may fight against its obstacles and adversities (thus betrayal, as found in "The Theme of the Traitor and the Hero," is one of the most powerful means for consolidating national or collective identities). Film is central to the arguments of Borges's most political texts because it is in audiences' reactions to a film that one can locate the multiplicity of interactions produced by this chemistry between society and the individual. "Nuestras imposibilidades" [Our impossibilities], written in 1931, ends with a critique of the "conservative government" (the dictatorship of Uriburu) after analyzing public reactions to the "foreigners" in *Hallelujah* (King Vidor, 1929) and the destiny of Bull Weed, the protagonist of *Underworld* (Joseph von Sternberg, 1927). Viewers' scorn represented the failure of the Borgesian epic that imagines an identification with the vanquished or, rather, with whomever had the courage to confront an adverse situation. More important than the fact of one's failure is the heroic action she/he takes, even if it is "useless and clumsy" as is that of Bull Weed. In the movie houses of Buenos Aires, however, this man—be it Sternberg's gangster or Vidor's African American—is humiliated. Here Borges comes close to a psychology of the masses akin to that of Ortega y Gasset or Ezequiel Martinez Estrella, which he practices reticently (later he would exclude "Our Impossibilities" from newer editions of *Discusión* [*Discussion*]). But what cinema gives him is the possibility of seeing audiences' reactions—something that with literature had been merely hypothetical.

Of course, outside the cinema, on the streets, there were mass demonstrations—two of which would have major impacts on Borges. The first occurred when Borges came out to celebrate the fall of Nazism. In "Anotación al 23 de Agosto de 1944" [A Comment on August 23, 1944], Borges discovered "que una emoción colectiva puede no ser innoble" [that a collective emotion can, in fact, not be ignoble] (*OC* II: 105). The second was when the masses poured in the streets to demand the liberation of Peron. In an oblique or tacit way, Borges referred to the explosion of Peronism in his "Nuestro pobre individualismo" [Our Poor Individualism], one of his most withering political texts. Here he returned to the theme of "Our Impossibilities" (one can note the similarity between the two titles) but now without local references, even though the essay was published in the journal *Sur* in July 1946, one month after Peron's assumption of the presidency.

In addition to foregrounding his disagreement with Hegel about the precise function of the State, the essay demonstrates what Borges believed the relationships between narrative and politics to be and the importance that cinema had in creating them. "Los films elaborados en Hollywood" [Films made in Hollywood] serve to give a political explication of the Argentine context: while North American films place obedience to the law above friendship, in Spanish America, the opposite is true (here Borges pointed to two literary examples: Don Quijote and Martin Fierro) (*OC* II: 36; *SNF* 309). And although Hollywood films suggest a *rich* individualism that can be contrasted with the *poor* individualism of Argentinians, perhaps the presence of a government that moves against liberty—according to Borges's vision—makes that individualism fertile for dissidence. One of cinema's major pedagogical functions resides in the possibility of evaluating diverse communicative situations. While in a democratic and liberal society, individualism is supported by the law, in an authoritarian society, its function is to question the application of the law: "el individualismo argentino, acaso inútil o perjudicial hasta ahora, encontrará justificación y deberes" [Argentine individualism, though perhaps useless or harmful until now, will find its justifications and its duties] (*OC* II: 37; *SNF* 309). In film, Borges found a possible articulation between the power of narrative (which is experienced by large audiences) and individual liberties. It is therefore no coincidence that, in keeping with his project of the 1930s (to use mass media as a narrative experimentation lab), in the following years, Borges would write several screenplays, dreaming of getting them into the cinemas and out to the public.

BORGES, SCREENWRITER

Borges was not only interested in cinema as a spectator and critic; he was also the writer of various screenplays in collaboration with Adolfo Bioy Casares and participated in the adaptation of his short stories into film. Through Bioy Casares's diary, we learn about their method of working together:

> **Viernes 10 al sábado, 25 de febrero [1950].** En Pardo, Borges llegó aquí el viernes 10, con Estela Canto. Hasta el domingo trabajamos en el resumen de un argumento para un film, *El paraíso de los creyentes* (que habíamos comenzado en Buenos Aires, uno o dos años antes). El domingo a la tarde, después del té, empezamos a escribir el libreto. Nos propusimos escribir once páginas por día; en los primeros días superamos ampliamente esa medida; el lunes 20 habíamos concluido el trabajo (noventa y siete páginas). (47)

> **[Friday the 10th to Saturday the 25th of February (1950).** In Pardo, Borges got here on Friday the 10th with Estela Canto. Until Sunday we worked on the outline of a plot for a film, *The Paradise of Believers*' (that we had begun in Buenos Aires a year or two ago). Sunday afternoon, after tea, we began writing the script. We proposed writing eleven pages a day; in the first days we amply exceeded that number; by Monday the 20th we had finished the work (ninety-seven pages).]

Borges's efforts at screenwriting were almost all unfortunate: *El paraíso de los creyentes* [*The Paradise of Believers*] and *Los orilleros* [*The Hoodlums*] were written at the beginning of the 1950s, and only the latter film made it to the cinema—more than thirty years later and in a very deficient version (Borges refused to attend the debut). Blame for these failures need not fall exclusively on the director. The understanding of film that informed Borges's original scripts in the 1950s lacked awareness of fundamental transformations in recent years (neorealism for one, but also about changes in dialogue, in the subjectivity of characters, and in the temporal organization of the narrative), which can be noted in his collaboration with Torre Nilsson—the director who launched modernist film in Argentina—in the adaptation of his story "Emma Zunz."

In 1954, "Emma Zunz" made it to the silver screen with the title *Días de odio* [*Days of Hate*]. More than telling a story of vengeance, Torre Nilsson was interested in "la historia de una soledad, en contraposición con un medio" [the story of an isolation, in counterpoint to a medium] (Couselo 144). If the film was very well done and original for the time, it was also marred by the addition of scenes not based on the story (it had first been considered for an episode within a full-length film). Borges, who did not agree in the choice of story, provided, among other, things the character of the "cripple" Rovituso, a villain with a creole hat and an affected, outmoded way of speaking ("depongo mi peligrosidad," "chanchada de bulto," "se arma cada trifulca"). Then again, on her solitary journey, Emma encounters Rovituso, who mentions a certain Morales, a character whose name coincides with the protagonist of the screenplay *Los creyentes* [*The Believers*], which Borges had just completed with Bioy Casares. In other words, all signs

544 GONZALO AGUILAR

point to Borges having contributed a sequence that ended up being comically out of step with the film. The shots of the factory, the detailed observation of the women working, and Emma's solitary wanderings are Torre Nilsson's contributions, which dialogue with contemporary films (Rossellini's *Europa 51*, for instance) but which violently contrasted with Borges's concept of cinema, which had been acquired taking in films released twenty years prior. "Los films que recordamos con más emoción, los de Sternberg, los de Lubitsch" [The films we remember with most emotion, those by Sternberg, those by Lubitsch] as he writes in the prologue to *Los orilleros* (*Los orilleros/El Paraíso de los creyentes* 7). Even though Borges hated the film, Bioy Casares had a very different experience, which he captured in his diary:

> Al principio yo pensaba: "El film nacional por excelencia: trivial, mecánico, tonto. Este muchacho no sabe dirigir." Después, insensiblemente, sin advertir el cambio, fui interesándome y, hacia el fin, tuve la impresión de haber visto una historia patética, extraordinaria, misteriosa y gobernada por un terrible destino. (89)

> [At first I thought: "The Argentine film par excellence: trivial, mechanical, stupid. This kid doesn't know how to direct." Afterward, unbelievably, without even recognizing the change, I started getting interested and, toward the end, I had the impression of having seen heart-breaking, extraordinary and mysterious story, governed by a terrible destiny.]

Borges's intervention in the adaptation reveals that, even if his view of narrative processes in film were insightful and dynamic, it was deficient in the composition of dialogue and in the very style that newer film that already had been left behind. It would take the arrival of a director like Hugo Santiago at the end of the 1960s, who had a very clear idea of film and mise en scène, to make a script by Borges and Bioy Casares be more than a mere antiquated diversion. Santiago approached them with an original idea, thereby avoiding the adaptation of a preexisting story, which would oblige the authors to come up with ill-fitting digressions. The concept of *Invasion* (1969) was very simple: an imaginary city (Aquilea) is invaded by men in white. A group of residents (dressed in black) headed by Don Porfirio (played by the musician Juan Carlos Paz) and Julián (Lautaro Murúa) organizes the resistance. Despite their courage, the original residents are ultimately defeated and nearly all of them die. The only survivors are Don Porfirio and Julián's partner, Irene (Olga Zubarry), who decided to reorganize the city's youth to take up the fight again (the last words of the film fall to the character of Lito Cruz who, bearing his weapon, says: "now it is our turn, but we will have to do it another way").

In the face of the political terror imposed by the men in white, Don Porfirio's group counters with the affective ties of friendship and the bravery of common men. The warring groups are, in effect, two different ways of understanding modernity: the merely instrumental versus one that incorporates the traces of the past. This divergence will be clearly seen in the maps of both groups: while the maps of the anonymous men in white are exact, mechanical, and abstract, only representing quantitative as opposed to qualitative gradations, Don Porfirio's map is artisanal and inventive and focuses more on the identities of the places (houses, street corners) more than on the representation of empty space (its similarities to Buenos Aires strengthen the allegorical character of Aquilea). While the allegory can be read politically, the equivalencies *Invasion* presents are not nearly as transparent as those other films of the period.

Both group solidarity and individual bravery characterize Don Porfirio's group: the most cowardly (Irala) offers up his life in an act of bravery. The gallant Lebendiger, in the moment he learns that a woman has betrayed him and that he is about to die, confesses, "now I can satisfy a curiosity that has always nagged at me: whether or not I am brave. It looks like I am." To the contrary, another of them, Cachorro,[6] hides in a cinema to watch a B-grade Western (Edward Killy's 1941 *Along the Rio Grande*). While he may have enjoyed the film, when the lights go up, he is found dead. The loud noises, the gunshots, and the hoofbeats heard on screen contrast with Cachorro's isolation and his silent death. Through this scene, we find an understanding of the epic that film can create both in the order of the imagination (the desire of the character to die a hero) and in its aloof and austere reality (his silent death to which the audience is indifferent). As in Borges's story "El Sur" [The South], the individual destiny of the character unfolds in an imaginary heroic death: this fantasy that film can deliver is what fascinated the writer.

With respect to context, *Invasion* offers a narrative at odds with the political cinema that had begun to dominate Latin American film. It was shot at the same time as *La hora de los hornos*, a militant film by Fernando Solanas and *Liberación* film group. A political reading of the film is thus inevitable, as is a consideration of how Santiago brings up to date Borges's cinematic legacy. For example, aesthetic pleasure (essential to the director's vision for mise en scène) is a tacit rejection of the political urgency presented by militant films (Aguilar 85). With the use of diverse genres (fantasy, noir, western), *Invasion* portrays the functioning of a group in which each individual is discovering her/his destiny. They do not fight for ideals (as in political films) but rather to protect their modest lifestyles from the brutal interference of the men in white (an incarnation of the impersonality of the modern State?). In an allegory that never hands the viewer a specific frame of reference or a clear code of equivalencies, and which does not refer to realities but rather to tentative, artificial, and arbitrary orders marked by deliberation and ambiguity, the open format of *Invasion* allows for the play of interpretations. Here the viewer is not obliged to act as a militant ("every spectator is a coward or a traitor" according to the Frantz Fanon quote cited in *La hora de los hornos*). Once again, in Borges, the narration is evidence of his aesthetic, ethical, political, and life choices.

The Flesh

There is another motive for Borges's passion for cinema which, while secondary, is not less important: like no other aesthetic experience, cinema offered him physical closeness to women who, at his side, could whisper to him what was happening on the screen. According to Estela Canto in *Borges a contraluz*, "el modesto cargo [en la biblioteca público] lo humillaba secretamente, pero le dejaba las mañanas libres, el horario no era demasiado estricto y podía disponer de un poco de dinero de bolsillo para invitar a sus amigas a comer e ir al cine. Esto y las librerías eran sus únicos gastos—literalmente" [his modest post (at the public library) secretly humiliated him, but it did leave his mornings open, the schedule wasn't too strict and it gave him a little pocket money to be able to invite his female friends to go out to eat and go see a movie. This and bookstores were his only expenses—literally] (37). This economic investment in books and movies reveals Borges's pleasures and the connection he made between seeing movies and spending time with his female friends, or "amigas" (note that Canto does not mention his "amigos"). When Borges goes blind, this practice is not lost but rather intensifies: in the darkened movie theater, the women's voices mediated between what was seen on the screen and his imagination.

The physical and erotic experience of the cinema did have some unfortunate effects for Borges, especially with respect to the adaptations of his stories. One of the habitual criteria for deciding whether to take a story to the screen was the presence of women, given the sexual attraction of female stars. It is perhaps thus no coincidence that the first Borges story to make it to the screen was "Emma Zunz." This is one of the few stories with a female protagonist, and it is perhaps the only story that directly references the sexual act (the "horrible thing" in the narrator's words). Leopoldo Torre Nilsson would not be governed by strictures of film for spectacle's sake (his goal was to make a "story of a solitude"), but filming the scene in which Emma goes to bed with the sailor from the Nordstjärnan to carry out her vengeance implied an erotic connotation unheard of in film from this era. The sexual encounter between Emma and the sailor is not produced by love, or for pleasure or money, but for vengeance. The ellipsis from the act and the shot of Emma half naked tearing up the money ("En la mesa de luz," the story reads, "estaba el dinero que había dejado el hombre: Emma se incorporó y lo rompió como antes había roto la carta" [On the night table was the money the man had left. Emma sat up and tore into shreds, as she had torn up the letter a short time before]) (*OC* I: 566; *CF* 217) revealed the point to which even the most literal and chaste adaptation, translated into visual terms, could take the story to unexpected (and undoubtedly uncomfortable) places for Borges.

The audacity of *Días de odio* can also be seen in the publicity that accompanied its debut. In the film's advertisement poster (fig. 31.1), Elisa Christian Galvé as Emma is depicted in a slip, sitting on a bed and putting on her pantyhose after being deflowered by the sailor (in the film, the shot is more closed, but evidently the designer wanted to attract a masculine audience with the promise of a few erotic scenes).[7] Borges, who had spent a number of evenings out with Leopoldo Torre Nilsson and Beatriz Guido, refused to attend the opening.[8] The erotic reverberation that his female friends' physical closeness might have on him in the movie theater acquired a physicality on screen that offended his modesty. Time and again, as with the poster for *Días de odio*, female nudity—a common theme in film—brought out Borges's true colors:

> Borges: "Yo pensaba bien de [Isaac] Aisemberg, el sobrino del capitán Wolberg." Bioy Casares: "Yo también." Borges: "También de René Mugica."[9] Bioy Casares: "A ese no lo conozco." Borges: "¿Sabés lo que me han propuesto? Hacer un film erótico con 'La

FIGURE 31.1 *Días de odio*, film's advertisement poster designed by Oscar Venturi.
Source: CINE.AR PLAY (https://play.cine.ar/INCAA/produccion/177).

intrusa'. Entonces no comprenden el cuento." Después de una pausa, en el colmo de la indignación, exclama: "¡Quieren mostrar a la protagonista desnuda en el baño! Qué porquería: mujeres desnudas en el baño." Para Borges el sexo es sucio. Por mucho tiempo me dejé engañar, porque entendía que lo excluía, en literatura, por ser un expediente fácil, socorrido y un poco necio. No; esa burla oculta, con alguna vergüenza de que lo tomen por mojigato, un violento rechazo. La obscenidad le parece una culpa atroz: *puta* no es la mujer que cobra, sino la que se acuesta." (Bioy Casares 1458–59)

[Borges: I used to think well of (Isaac) Aisemberg, Captain Wolberg's nephew. Bioy Casares: "Me too." Borges: "Also of René Mugica." Bioy Casares: "I don't know him." Borges: "Do you know what they proposed to me? Making an erotic film with 'La intrusa' ['The Intruder']. So, they don't understand the story." After a pause, at the height of indignation, he exclaims: "They want to show the protagonist naked in the bath! What garbage: naked women in the bath." Sex is dirty for Borges. For a long time, I let him fool me, because I believed he excluded it, in literature, for being a

548   GONZALO AGUILAR

facile, shallow and fairly annoying crutch. No; that scorn hides, with some shame that he might be taken for a prig, a violent rejection. Obscenity to him is an atrocious sin: *a whore* isn't a woman who charges money, but who has sex at all.]

Bioy Casares's solemn judgment comes from experience: Borges's relationship with Mugica, a director whom he appreciated (*Hombre de la esquina rosada* is one of the few adaptations that he praised) ended abruptly when Borges found out that Mugica had considered Isabel Sarli to play the role of Juliana (Peña 38).[10] This resistance to the physicality portrayed in film reached exasperating extremes when, in 1980, Carlos Hugo Christensen's *La intrusa* debuted at the height of the military dictatorship. A director of the so-called golden age of Argentinian cinema, Christensen left Argentina at the beginning of 1950 as a dissident of Peronism and continued his career in Venezuela and Brazil. In 1967, *O menino e o vento* [*The Boy and the Wind*] debuted, an interesting film that went against the grain of the political cinema being produced at that time, and which audaciously represented homosexual desire. After that film, Christensen worked in commercial film until making *La intrusa*, where he again took up the issue of homosexuality with nothing less than Borges's story and Astor Piazzola's music.

By including, after the opening titles, the complete Bible passage of a verse only numerically referenced in "La intrusa" (2 Kings 1:26),[11] it is evident that Christensen sought to make manifest what in Borges's story was merely hinted at: that the brothers' crime was related to homosexual desire.[12] What the writer invites as a veiled reading in Christensen acquires a literal sense, illustrated through explicit sex scenes.

The controversy began when the Argentine Film Rating Organization (Ente de Calificación Cinematográfica), which was charged with film censorship, forced the director to make various cuts. In the magazine *Somos*, Christensen wrote an opinion piece entitled "No a la censura" [No to Censorship]. In response came another article entitled "Sí a la censura" [Yes to Censorship] written by none other than Jorge Luis Borges. In it, he justified himself: "Yo no trato de ser obsceno, de escribir y pensar en forma decorosa" [I do not seek to be obscene, but to write and think decorously] (*Textos recobrados* 3: 267). A lover of paradoxes, Borges tended to propose an aesthetic resolution to a moral dilemma. Here, for instance, censorship is good because it improves art, stimulates authors' ingenuity, and leads them to avoid obvious references and scandalous scenes. But in addition to questions of morality, *La intrusa* raises a political problem: Borges always sustained that the State should not interfere with individual rights. In the case of *La intrusa*, in affirming that "when it comes to pornography, the application of censorship is good," he justifies the invasive role of the State when dealing with issues of obscenity or modesty. It is as if in cinema, where Borges had found (or thought himself to have found) a resurrection of the epic that was free from intrusion of the State, and which privileged the heroism of the individual when facing adversity, he also found the extent and limits of his modesty, or as Bioy Casares says, his "priggishness." Film allowed Borges to share in a sense of community and, at the same time, to reaffirm another sense more singularly his own: he could observe the masses' passion for narrative but also how these passions could be too carnal.

NOTES

1. Many of the arguments made in this chapter have their origin in the collaborative work I undertook with Emiliano Jelicié when we wrote *Borges va al cine* [Borges Goes to the Movies] in 2010.

2. While Borges did publish a variety of articles in *Sur*, from number 3 (Winter, 1931) until 1945, he wrote about film (the last of these notes is "Sobre el doblaje" [On dubbing]). In the double issue retrospective *Sur* dedicated to film (1974, 334–35), they republished his essays as well as an extensive interview he gave to Carlos Burone (see Borges, *Borges en* Sur).

3. In keeping with his habit of adopting positions that were eccentric or that clashed with the dominant opinion (as he did with the Buenos Aires Cine Club), Borges wrote about movies in *Sur* (a journal aimed at the elite intellectual reader) and about literature in *Revista Multicolor de los Sábados* from the popular newspaper, *Crítica*. *Crítica's* film section was assigned to Néstor Ibarra, who wrote about Ernst Lubitsch (issue 1), Joseph von Sternberg (3), King Vidor (10), and Robert Mamoulian (53).

4. During the last Argentine dictatorship (1976–1983), years during which Borges's canonization was moving apace, Ricardo Wulicher produced the film *Borges para millones* [Borges for Millions] (1978), in which the writer participated actively. Time has proved the title not to be an exaggeration: while Borges was widely read around the world at the time of the film (though in Argentina he faced major political critique), today his books sell in the millions every year.

5. Graciela Montaldo makes this kind of comparison between Borges and Rubén Darío (95ff).

6. Cachorro can be translated from Spanish as *puppy* or *cub*.

7. Oscar Venturi created two posters for the film. The first is consistent with the melodramas and romantic films of the period, depicting Christian Galvé fainting in a man's arms. The other, seen here, erotically suggests the moments just after sex.

8. Borges never stopped publicly expressing his contempt for *Días de odio* despite maintaining good personal relationships with Torre Nilsson and with Beatriz Guido. From Bioy Casares's diary, we can infer that Borges saw *El secuestrador* [The Kidnapper] ("some realism, like the one by Torre Nilsson and Beatriz Guido [in which a pig eats a child] could be called unreal realism") (502) and *La mano en la trampa* [Hand in the Trap] (731), both by Torre Nilsson. In the story "La hermana de Eloísa" [Eloisa's Sister], which Borges wrote in collaboration with Maria Luisa Levinson (at the same time *Días de odio* was being produced), Torre Nilsson is mentioned: "Ponderé sus dotes de actriz; me dijo que Torre Nilson le había ofrecido un papel en una película. Esta eventualidad, lo confieso, no dejó de alarmarme." [Let me ponder her acting skills; she told me Torre Nilson had offered her a role in a film. This possibility, I confess, I found eminently alarming.]

9. René Mugica directed *Hombre de la esquina rosada* [Streetcorner Man] in 1962, with a screenplay by Isaac Aisemberg, Joaquín Gómez Bas, and Carlos Adén. The lead was played by Francisco Petrone, Borges's favorite actor, and the writer was on set while the movie was being filmed.

10. Isabel Sarli was an Argentine beauty queen (a semifinalist for Miss Universe in 1955), discovered and seduced by film director Armando Bó, whose erotic films made her an international sex symbol. She was the first woman ever to appear nude in an Argentine film.

11. This reference is to The Septuagint—the Greek translation of the Old Testament—which divides the text into four books of Kings, as opposed to the Hebrew Bible's division

of the text into two books of Kings two books and of Samuel. An English translation of the passage reads: "I am grieved for thee, my brother Jonathan; thou wast very lovely to me; thy love to me was wonderful beyond the love of women" (trans. Sir Lancelot C. L. Brenton, 1851).

12. There are several hypotheses about whether this famous Bible passage actually refers to homosexuality and whether or not it can be applied to the brothers (possible interpretations Borges must have been aware of). In a rare interview with Osvaldo Ferrari, Borges roundly rejected it: "Ahora, como el concepto de amistad ha sido, contaminado, bueno, por la sodomía ¿no?, yo pensé: *para que nadie pueda sospechar eso,* voy a hacer que esos dos hombres sean hermanos" [Now, since the concept of friendship has been, contaminated, well, by sodomy, no? I thought: to ensure no one suspects that, I am going to make these two men brothers] (Ferrari 236). Daniel Balderston takes an approach to the story that affirms the "credibility" of a coded homosexual reading ("The 'Fecal Dialectic' " 36).

WORKS CITED

Aguilar, Gonzalo. "La salvación por la violencia: *Invasión* y *La hora de los hornos.*" *Episodios cosmopolitas en la cultura argentina.* Santiago Arcos Editor, 2009, pp. 85–120.

Balderston, Daniel. "The 'Fecal Dialectic': Homosexual Panic and the Origin of Writing in Borges." *¿Entiendes?: Queer Readings, Hispanic Writings.* Edited by Emilie L. Bergmann and Paul Julian Smith. Duke University Press, 1995, pp. 29–46.

Bioy Casares, Adolfo. *Borges.* Destino, 2006.

Borges, Jorge Luis. *Borges en Sur (1931–1980).* Emecé, 1999.

Borges, Jorge Luis. *El idioma de los argentinos.* Seix Barral, 1994.

Borges, Jorge Luis. *Obras completas.* 4 vols. Emecé, 1996.

Borges, Jorge Luis. *Textos recobrados 1 (1919–1929).* Emecé, 1997.

Borges, Jorge Luis. *Textos recobrados 3 (1956–1986).* Emecé, 2003.

Borges, Jorge Luis, and Adolfo Bioy Casares. *Los orilleros/El Paraíso de los creyentes.* Editorial Losada, 1983.

Canto, Estela. *Borges a contraluz.* Espasa Calpe, 1989.

Couselo, Jorge Miguel, comp. *Torre Nilsson por Torre Nilsson.* Fraterna, 1985.

Cozarinsky, Edgardo. *Borges y el cine.* Sur, 1974.

Ferrari, Osvaldo. *Borges en diálogo. Conversaciones de Jorge Luis Borges con Osvaldo Ferrari.* Grijalbo, 1985.

Ferrari, Osvaldo, and Jorge Luis Borges. *En diálogo II.* Siglo XXI, 2005.

Hegel, G. W. F. *Estética – Tomo II.* Editorial Losada, 2008.

Jelicié, Emiliano, and Gonzalo Aguilar. *Borges va al cine.* Libraria, 2010.

Montaldo, Graciela. *Zonas ciegas. Populismos y experimentos culturales en Argentina.* Fondo de Cultura Económica, 2010.

Peña, Fernando. *René Mugica.* Centro Editor de América Latina, 1993.

Films Cited

Along the Río Grande (Spanish: *A través de Río Grande*). Directed by Edward Killy, 1941.

Borges para millones. Directed by Ricardo Wulicher, 1978.

Citizen Kane (Spanish: *El ciudadano*). Directed by Orson Welles, 1941.

Días de odio. Directed by Leopoldo Torre Nilsson, 1954.

Europa '51. Directed by Roberto Rossellini, 1952.

Hallelujah. Directed by King Vidor, 1929.

La hora de los hornos. Directed by Fernando Ezequiel Solanas, 1968.

Invasión. Directed by Hugo Santiago, 1969.

Los orilleros. Directed Ricardo Luna, 1975.

Underworld (Spanish: *La ley del hampa*). Directed by Josef von Sternberg, 1927.

West Side Story (Spanish: *Amor sin barreras*). Directed by Robert Wise, 1961.

CHAPTER 32

··

POLITICAL THEORY AND BORGES'S WORK

··

ALEJANDRA M. SALINAS

INTRODUCTION

JORGE Luis Borges disliked politics, understood as partisan activities, the activity of governing, and the imposition of national boundaries or cultural identities, at least in later periods (*OC* III: 3:506). However, political events such as wars, conquests, assassinations, and colonization inspired him to write world-renowned stories, articles, and poetry. His texts also touch on political concepts such as liberty, democracy, and patriotism. As the list illustrates, Borges was not an intellectual who retreated into his private world but someone who took interest in local and global affairs and chose to give literary form to the political. That said, Borges's approach to politics was not guided by the need to comply with any social function or agenda. He found it "absurdo que el arte sea un departamento de la política" [absurd for art to be a department of politics] (*OC* IV: 403). For him, art should be free from political commitments mainly because of the unintended consequences of human actions, that is, a committed art more often than not fails to produce the desired effects. Kipling and Swift are a case in point since they were guided by a political purpose, but their fame is entirely alien to that purpose. Kipling was (mis)judged by his political opinions and not by the quality of his art (*OC* IV: 271, 496), and Swift wanted to write a diatribe against humanity, but *Gulliver's Travels* ended up becoming a classic of children's literature (*OC* I: 273).

In defense of the autonomy of art, Borges limits himself to using many of the political preoccupations for the sake of artistic creation and aesthetic purposes only. He addresses the nature, benefits, and perils of politics by drawing multiple connections including moral, social, and psychological aspects, and in this regard, he proceeds in the manner of political theorists (Klosko). In particular, his texts show concern with free political orders and the threats and challenges they undergo. Scholars have pointed out that "any political philosophy that fails to conceptualize the threat of state authoritarianism and the centrality of private life and individual freedom to human emancipation provides a haven for despots and fanatics" (Bowles and Gintis 31). Borges shares such warnings and invokes the defense of individual liberty against nationalist and revolutionary causes and against totalitarianism of diverse signs. Political interference and violence are associated with social disorder, ignorance, and submission and are ultimately conducive to State oppression and domination. Borges's literary treatment of the wars of conquest and revolution, the spirit of patriotism, and the spread of nationalism and populism are the main aspects to be highlighted in this matter.

In light of the preceding paragraphs, the objective is to address in a general and synthetic way how the political inspired Borges to write about (1) conflictive or undesirable political worlds, (2) foundational historical deeds, and (3) political ideals and utopias. The analysis will be mainly textual; that is, it will not provide much detail on the historical-intellectual context or on his biographical data or interviews.

CONFLICTIVE POLITICAL WORLDS

For Judith Shklar, human history shows that the institution of the State tends to inflict physical or psychological harm on individuals, thus giving rise to a fear of cruelty, arbitrariness, fanaticism, and disorder. As such, she argues for a type of liberalism that seeks to prevent and denounce the political practices that generate fear. During World War II, Borges employs the term "barbarism" to refer to the cruelty imposed by Nazis (*OC* I: 473; *OC* II: 106). More broadly, the noun relates to anyone devoted to the use of violence or war as a means to advance political ends (*OC* I: 193–97; *OC* II: 121).

Why and how does barbarism emerge? One of Borges's best-known fictions that helps to address this question is "Tlön, Uqbar, Orbis Tertius" (1940), a tale about a planet marked by unrestrained liberty in an "articulado" [articulated], "armoniosa" [harmonious], and "simétrico" [symmetrical], environment (*OC* I: 431–33). There we find institutions—such as schools, prisons, and religions—that are not the object of confrontation or strife or subject to the concentration of power by any one group. Tlön is a society that contrasts with the reality of war. Indeed, toward the end of the text, we read: "Encantada por su rigor, la humanidad olvida y torna a olvidar que es un rigor de ajedrecistas, no de ángeles" [Spellbound by Tlön's rigor, humanity has forgotten, and continues to forget, that it is the rigor of chess masters, not of angels] (*OC* I: 443). The sentence is an allusion to the mistake of assuming that any person or group can successfully arrange the lives of others according to political designs imposed from above. Worst, the rigor becomes outright cruelty when political attempts are carried out with barbaric means that annihilate art and life itself. In "El milagro secreto" [The Secret Miracle] a writer struggles to finish his work before being shot by the Nazis.

Borges's crudest and most direct story inspired by Nazism is "Deutsches Requiem" (*OC* I: 576–81) in which a German officer is to be executed for the crimes he committed in a concentration camp. On the night prior to his execution, the man justifies to himself the need to sacrifice individual lives at the altar of racism. In speaking to the ideas of the officer, Borges chooses to enhance the philosophical rather than the factual tone of the story, in a similar approach to social theorists. In totalitarian ideologies, they argue, war is "the eternal shape of higher human existence [and] some mystical entity orders man to behave morally, that is, to renounce his selfishness for the advantage of a higher, nobler, and more powerful being, society" (Mises 140–43). Thus the primacy of the collective, and the submission of the individual to society, is typical of totalitarian systems of governance (Gentile 90–91).

Borges sees Nazism as a futile attempt to destroy the fact of human diversity: "El nazismo adolece de irrealidad, como los infiernos de Erígena. Es inhabitable; los hombres sólo pueden morir por él, mentir por él, matar y ensangrentar por él" [Nazism suffers from unreality, like Erigena's hells. It is uninhabitable; men can only die for it, lie for it, kill and wound for it] (OC II: 105–06). The target attacked by the German imperialists and their followers is the order of liberty, as a writer Borges sometimes admired, Leopoldo Lugones, alerts while reporting from Europe during World War I. Lugones first spoke of the "Germanophiles," a noun later adopted by Borges to denounce those who thought that Hitler was a "varón providencial cuyos infatigables discursos predican la extinción de todos los charlatanes y demagogos, y cuyas bombas incendiarias, no mitigadas por palabreras declaraciones de guerra, anuncian desde el firmamento la ruina de los imperialismos rapaces" [a providential man whose tireless speeches preach the extinction of all charlatans and demagogues, and whose firebombs, not mitigated by wordy declarations of war, announce from the sky the ruin of the rapacious imperialisms] (OC IV: 441–43).

When World War II was over, Borges's attention shifted from the international to the national arena. In February 1946, the military caudillo, nationalist, and populist Juan D. Perón became president of Argentina. The context was far less dramatic, but the writer's tone is no less emphatic. A few years into the new regime, he writes to a friend: "The dictatorship has us accustomed to times of barbarism. Now is the time to praise Rosas, Hittler [sic], Mussolini [. . .] it is a time of ignorance that hurts the Homeland" (qtd. in Benedict 93). Borges's worries about the reinstantiation of political threats to liberty animate the essay "Nuestro pobre individualismo" [Our Poor Individualism], published in July 1946, where he writes: "El más urgente de los problemas de nuestra época [. . .] es la gradual intromisión del Estado en los actos del individuo" [The most urgent of the problems of our time (. . .) is the gradual meddling of the State in the acts of the individual] (OC II: 37). Borges hoped that Argentine individualism—anchored in a distrust of political authority—would make a contribution to the world by promising "un mínimo de gobierno" [a minimal government] (OC II: 37). The manuscript to the essay is accompanied by a revealing drawing by the writer, which is entitled "die Hydra der Dikator." The figure is inspired by the mythical Hydra of Lerna, and it contains a multiheaded monster that includes the faces of Evita (the wife of Perón and the main head of the monster), Rosas, Perón, Marx, Hitler, and Mussolini (Borges, Ensayos 32–33).[1]

Another text where a political order becomes conflictive to the point of oppression is "La lotería en Babilonia" [The Lottery in Babylon], a story "no es del todo inocente de simbolismo" [not wholly innocent of symbolism] (*OC* I: 429). Borges does not mention if it is a political symbol of the ongoing world war or if it alludes to Argentine political history. One element allows for this latter reading: it is "un país vertiginoso" [a dizzying country] (*OC* I: 456). But there are also institutions common to all societies: prisons, a judicial system, class differences, and social strife. There are decision-making mechanisms as well, which are made the object of social disputes, and we are explicitly told that the majority ends by imposing their will on others. At some point, the agency in charge assumes all public powers and the monopoly of the interpretation of its history, which is not subject to publicity, controversy, or discussion. The fact that the "Compañía" [Company] has the sum of public power and it is not subject to contestation indicates that Babylon is not a democracy, nor is it a description of the forces of the free market (cf. Dapía 159–64). Rather, the agency's political modus operandi resembles that of authoritarian and totalitarian regimes built upon a torpid society.

The opposite situation is that of a proactive society, and it is found in "El hombre en el umbral" [The Man in the Threshold]. Located in colonial India, Glencairn is an oppressive British ruler who suddenly disappears amid an apparent general indifference. From an old poor man lying on the threshold of a shabby house, the reader learns that a previous tyrant had been taken to a trial by the people and sentenced to death. In the end, we find out that Glencairn has also been executed in that manner; the people have rebelled once again against a tyrant. The circumstances of the popular rebellion merits a political philosophical reflection in reading the story. For Locke, power is delegated to the rulers; should they act illegitimately, the people are entitled to rebel, remove, and even alter the form of government: "Where-ever law ends, tyranny begins" (Locke §202). Locke's view is inscribed in a natural rights theory, which we can also associate with the text under analysis, where one line speaks metaphorically of a type of universality proper of natural rights theories: "Una casa no puede diferir de otra: lo que importa es saber si está edificada en el infierno o en el cielo" [One house is like another, what matters is if it is built in heaven or in hell] (*OC* I: 615). The metaphor of the house could represent individuals but also societies and political organizations, and both individual and collective actions are evaluated on the basis of an ethical or normative criterion of universal scope, thus establishing "moral absolutes" and a concern about the injustice of colonialism (Balderston, *Out of Context* 104–05; Balderston, "Liminares" 36).

A more subtle and different version of an ethical criterion is latent in the story "La forma de la espada" [The Shape of the Sword]. John Vincent Moon is an Irish communist who leaves behind his European past marked by revolutionary violence and ideology: "Había cursado con fervor y con vanidad casi todas las páginas de no sé qué manual comunista; el materialismo dialéctico le servía para cegar cualquier discusión" [He had studied with fervor and vanity almost all the pages of I don't know what communist manual; dialectical materialism served to blind any discussion] (*OC* I: 492).[2] Exiled in Brazil and then in Uruguay, Moon becomes a businessman and, more importantly, a person who longs to reveal the historical truth and take responsibility for past crimes, a revelation that comes at the very end of the story. Unlike Babylon and colonial India, there are no collective bodies to judge Moon's past crimes; it is his personal decision to seek judgment and punishment. This voluntary decision, which entails integrity and will, attests to Borges's confidence in the human capacities to operate individually in the political arena.[3]

The exact opposite of Moon's decision is found in "Tema del traidor y del héroe" [Theme of the Traitor and the Hero], where the dark of politics carries the day. Revolutionary leader Kilpatrick is a secret traitor who is killed by a comrade but presented as a hero to preserve public respect for and engagement with the cause. The staging is discovered by a relative years later, who nonetheless keeps the shameful secret in order to save the family's reputation. The treason and the lie thus trump moral integrity and historical truth.

Besides revolutions, political conflict in Borges is often tied to assassinations (as in "Avelino Arredondo", see below) and duels, as in "El soborno" [The Bribe]. "El soborno" narrates a "duel" between two professors in the context of university politics where the conflict of interest is resolved with civility by following the rules of the academic game. In contrast, a verbal "duel" between two caudillos, the protagonists in nineteenth-century civil strifes, remains unresolved since they fail to agree on the evaluation of their past actions (*OC* II: 169–70). In any case, assassinations and executions are far more numerous than political duels in Borges's work. The killing of political leaders is a recurrent event in human history, as illustrated in the poems about the eternal death of the king ("Los ecos" [The Echoes]), the fatal death of Caesar ("La trama" [The Plot]), and the execution of Charles I ("Una mañana de 1649" [One morning in 1649]): "sabe que hoy va a la Muerte, no al olvido / y que es un rey. La ejecución lo espera; / la mañana es atroz y verdadera" [today he goes to death, not to oblivion / he is a king. Execution awaits him / the morning is atrocious and true] (*OC* II: 321). The short text "In memoriam J.F.K." focuses not on the victims but on the instruments that have been used to kill political leaders and concludes with an apocalyptic tone: "será muchas cosas que hoy ni siquiera imaginamos y que podrán concluir con los hombres y con su prodigioso y frágil destino" [It will be many things that today we do not even imagine and that will be able to end with men and with their prodigious and fragile destiny] (*OC* II: 231). But assassinations are also instigated by rulers ("Parábola del palacio" [Parable of the palace]) and, more generally, by anyone interested in eliminating adversaries ("El disco" [The Disk]). Underlying the motives of all these crimes seems to be always the corruptive influence of power, and in particular of absolute power, as warned by Lord Acton (Dalberg).

One last aspect in this ongoing analysis relates to the geographical location of political conflicts. The latter tend to be persistent in the countries of South America, a region included in the category "un país oprimido y tenaz" [an oppressed and tenacious country] (*OC* I: 496). The causes of this situation are tied to the failures of its political class, to the point that in the Hell imagined by Swedenborg, the reprobate "viven entregados a la política, en el sentido más sudamericano de la palabra; es decir, viven para conspirar, mentir e imponerse" [they live dedicated to politics, in the most South American sense of the word; that is, they live to conspire, lie and impose themselves] (*OC* IV: 146). Thus,

POLITICAL HISTORY, BETWEEN PATRIOTISM AND NATIONALISM

the history of Latin America is subject to a "doloroso y común destino" [a painful and common fate], that of dictatorships (*OC* IV: 81).

For some authors, patriotism and nationalism are opposed political visions: while the former is aligned with republican values, the latter fights diversity and may even support despotic regimes (Viroli). For others, patriotic loyalty is limited to those who share an identity "around a sense of common good," tied to the history of the community and its institutions (MacIntyre 6). However, when that allegiance is too strong, patriotism may turn into "virulent nationalism" (Taylor 203–05). Thus, the dynamics of national identity oscillate between respect and pride in the shared history, language, religion, artistic styles, and so on, and hostility toward those who do not belong to that culture (Miller 532, 543).

As evidenced in his stories, essays, and poems, Borges's literary pieces are aligned with the spirit of patriotism, not with the ideas of nationalists. His arguments against nationalism are mainly based on his opposition to monolithic cultural models. A national culture is at its best, Borges argues in "El escritor argentino y la tradición" [The Argentine writer and tradition], when it is in contact with foreign cultures and when it freely receives and transforms those influences (*OC* I: :267–74). In rejecting foreign influences, nationalism can only interfere in the creative task of individuals, an interference that is yet another aspect of "un Estado infinitamente molesto" [an infinitely annoying State] (*OC* II: 37). On the contrary, for the patriotic attitude, the homeland must not be reduced to what the State (and the nationalists) pretends it to be. It is up to a diverse, open, and socially mobile society to decide the profile of cultural identity, and this affirmation takes into account the past, the present, and the future generations (*Textos recobrados* 3: 154–55).

In relation to the image or conceptualization of his homeland, Borges writes in "Oda compuesta en 1960" [Ode composed in 1960]:

> No sabemos
> cómo eres para Dios en el viviente
> seno de los eternos arquetipos,
> pero por ese rostro vislumbrado
> vivimos y morimos y anhelamos,
> oh inseparable y misteriosa patria
>
> [We do not know
> how you are for God in the living
> bosom of the eternal archetypes,
> but for that glimpsed face
> we live and die and yearn
> oh inseparable and mysterious homeland.]

These lines in the poem have been associated with the tradition of idealism and read as "conspiratorial," in that we would live in a world "engineered by a higher power" (Díaz 13). However, the jump from metaphysics to politics seems unwarranted in such an interpretation, given that the use of archetypes as ideal and eternal models in Borges reflects only psychological and philosophical considerations, not practical political implications (Salinas, *Arquetipos* 129–35). The Patria is mysterious, precisely because the manifold realities that conform to it exceed our cognitive capacities to define it.

Along similar lines, "Oda escrita en 1966" [Ode written in 1966] calls attention to the collaborative and voluntary nature of creating an identity for the Patria. One important line in the poem reads: "Nadie es la patria, pero todos debemos / ser dignos del antiguo juramento" [No one is the homeland, but we all must be / worthy of the old oath] (*OC* II: 316–17). Published twelve days after a military coup d'état, Borges may be referring to the Preamble of the 1853 Argentine Constitution, which was largely inspired in the classical liberal thought of Alberdi (2014). The Preamble reads: "to secure the blessings of liberty to ourselves, to our posterity, and to all men of the world who wish to dwell on Argentine soil." This is clearly not a nationalist view but a call to populate the country and to rule it freely. The origins of this republican oath can be traced back to the wars of independence, a time that gives Borges both pride and nostalgia for those liberating fights and epic battles (*OC* III: 121). Thus, the invocation of military prowess for the sake of the homeland permeates many of his texts. To quote a few lines:

> Se acabaron los valientes
> y no han dejado semilla.
> ¿Dónde están los que salieron
> a liberar las naciones
> o afrontaron en el Sur
> las lanzas de los malones? (*OC* II: 335)

> [The brave ones are gone
> and they left us without seed
> Where are the ones that went out
> to liberate the nations
> or faced in the South
> the spears of the *malones*?]

> Es la Patria. Mis mayores
> la sirvieron con largas proscripciones,
> con penurias, con hambre, con batallas,
> [...]
> No soy aquellas sombras tutelares
> que honré con versos que no olvida el tiempo. (*OC* III: 104)

> [It is the Homeland. My elders
> served it with long bans
> with hardships, with hunger, with battles,
> (...)
> I am not those tutelary shadows
> which I honored with verses that time does not forget.]

Borges's choice of patriotic courage as a topic also marks his most famous poem, "Poema conjetural" [Conjectural Poem]. Published exactly one month after a military coup d'état, the text is presented as a clash between civilization and barbarism in the Argentine plains. Laprida, a man of letters and books, is killed by caudillo militias, directly reflecting the opposition between the rule of law and violent politics. "Vencen los bárbaros" [the barbarians win], Laprida thinks, though he finds joy in facing his death with courage (*OC* II: 245).

In terms of its impact on the political system, the year 1943 would become a political watershed since the coup brought nationalists and fascists to power, it led to the gradual weakening of liberal republican institutions, and it so configured the national political landscape of the next decades. By the 1970s, instability had proven to be already a permanent trait of Argentine politics. It is in that context that the topic of courage in the service of a patriotic cause reemerges in "Avelino Arredondo" (1975), a story based on a dramatic event that took place in Uruguay in 1897. The protagonist is a student of law who plans and executes the assassination of President Idiarte Borda to put an end to the cronyism and factionalism of the party in power. Claiming to have acted alone, he is convicted of the crime and imprisoned. Arredondo has a patriotic motivation, a sense that the common good—to use Taylor's words—was better served by eliminating factionalism in his country. Despite his confusion about the legitimacy of the means employed, the young man acts courageously in the pursuit of that end. Although Borges does not condone political assassination (*OC* IV: 73), one may wonder if he imagined Arredondo's decision as one way out of chronic political instability.

LIBERTY, DEMOCRACY, AND POPULISM

Borges finds in political theories and ideas strong literary stimuli (*OC* III: 77). What should a good political order be, and how is it preserved? What may be desirable standards or ideals for particular regimes or policies? Are the responses to these questions valid universally, or are they limited to a particular society and time? What are the threats and challenges of the political order? For Borges, a good political order is an anarchist one: "Creo, como el tranquilo anarquista Spencer, que uno de nuestros máximos males, acaso el máximo, es la preponderancia del Estado sobre el individuo . . . El individuo es real; los Estados son abstracciones de las que abusan los políticos, con o sin uniforme" [I believe, like the calm anarchist Spencer, that one of our maximum evils, perhaps the maximum, is the preponderance of the State over the individual. (. . .) The individual is real; the States are abstractions abused by politicians, with or without uniform] (*Textos recobrados 3*: 305–06). He hoped that "con el tiempo mereceremos que no haya gobiernos" [someday we will deserve not to have governments] (*OC* II: 399), a hope inherited from his father, who had told him to "take a good look at soldiers, uniforms, barracks, flags, churches, priests, and butcher shops, since all these things were about to disappear" (Borges, *Autobiography* 136, 138).[4]

The idea of an evolution toward a stateless society inspired "Utopía de un hombre que está cansado" [A Weary Man's Utopia], "the most honest and most melancholic piece" in *El libro de arena* [*The Book of Sand*] (*OC* III: 72). In the future human society depicted in the story, individuals no longer complain about oppression, scarcity, or injustice. Contrary to Babylon, with its suffocating climate, it is a scenery of self-sufficient individuals, governments have disappeared, the human species speaks one language, and liberty and peace prevail. In contrast, the world of the past is marked by triviality and robbery, and ruled by bureaucratic politicians:

> El planeta estaba poblado de espectros colectivos, el Canadá, el Brasil, el Congo Suizo y el Mercado Común. Casi nadie sabía la historia previa de esos entes platónicos, pero sí los más ínfimos pormenores del último congreso de pedagogos, la inminente ruptura de relaciones y los mensajes que los presidentes mandaban, elaborados por el secretario del secretario con la prudente imprecisión que era propia del género. (*OC* III: 54)

> [The planet was populated by collective specters, Canada, Brazil, the Swiss [sic] Congo, and the Common Market. Almost no one knew the previous history of these Platonic entities, but they did know the minute details of the last congress of pedagogues, the imminent rupture of relations, and the messages that the presidents sent, prepared by the secretary of the secretary with the prudent imprecision that was typical of the genre.]

Borges's utopia joins most utopian views in which "things are not quite what they should be, and [. . .] improvement is possible" (Tower Sargent 572–76). The text speaks to a type of liberal anarchism where the social order is based on individual freedom and voluntary associations, one that rejects the legitimacy of the State (Long 217). Borges's liberal anarchist society is the result of the fact that gradually and consciously the people find State services useless. In this regard, the author aligns with the theory of Herbert Spencer, for whom social evolution consists of the enlargement of the spheres of individual freedom and the gradual extinction of force and compulsion. Additionally, Spencer hoped for a future society where materialism is left behind (Long 221), and Borges's utopia is also austere to the point of the ascetic, absent the capitalist processes of mass production and excess consumerism.[5]

Another text to be read in conjunction with "Utopía" is one inspired by the Swiss political agreement. "Los conjurados" [The Conspirators] are people who "han tomado la extraña resolución de ser razonables" [have made the odd decision to be reasonable] and "han resuelto olvidar sus diferencias y acentuar sus afinidades" [have resolved to forget their differences and accentuate their affinities] (*OC* III: 501). The success of the Swiss case turns them into the archetype of tolerance and of peaceful coexistence, as imagined in the utopian world of the future. Yet, as we know, reasonable political agreements are hard to come by. A story that deals with one case of such failure is Borges's longest fiction, "El Congreso" [The Congress], in which a group plans to form "un Congreso del Mundo que representaría a todos los hombres de todas las naciones [lo que era] como fijar el número exacto de los arquetipos platónicos, enigma que ha atareado durante siglos la perplejidad de los pensadores" [a World Congress that would represent all men of all nations [which was] like fixing the exact number of Platonic archetypes, an enigma that has perplexed thinkers for centuries] (*OC* III: 23–24). The implementation of this ambitious idea fails, and the leader orders his followers to burn all the books when he realizes so. This ending is just another instantiation of what according to Borges is a recurrent political pretension: "Quemar libros y erigir fortificaciones es tarea común de los príncipes" [Burning books and erecting fortifications are the usual occupations of princes] (*OC* II: 11). Both tasks are associated with political projects that always fail: "El propósito de abolir el pasado ya ocurrió en el pasado y—paradójicamente—es una de las pruebas de que el pasado no se puede abolir. El pasado es indestructible; tarde o temprano vuelven todas las cosas, y una de las cosas que vuelven es el proyecto de abolir el pasado" [The purpose of abolishing the past has already occurred in the past and—paradoxically—it is one of the proofs that the past cannot be abolished. The past is indestructible; sooner or later all things return, and one of the things that return is the project of abolishing the past] (*OC* II: 58).

Besides reflecting his liberal anarchist sympathies, "Utopía" and "El Congreso" reflect Borges's late attitude, a weariness of the turmoil triggered by the political instabilities in his country. In justifying his incorporation to the Conservative Party, he observes that "es indudablemente el único que no puede despertar fanatismos" [it is undoubtedly the only one that cannot arouse fanaticisms] (*OC* III: 505–06). From a theoretical angle, Borges's conservatism is much like Oakeshott's demeaning view of the masses: masses are invented by leaders and become submissive, and popular government is the "authority of mere numbers," moved by feelings rather than thoughts (Oakeshott 373–74, 432). Of course, other conservatives prefer not to speak of masses or fanatics but of the ordinary person who is proudly seen as "the foundation of democracy" and capable of being proactive and even courageous (Churchill 64). For quite a long time Borges's writings were closer to Oakeshott's ideas than to Churchill's.

This was not always so. A younger Borges showed enthusiasm for the Russian Revolution and its appeal to universal brotherhood, as evident in various poems written in 1920 and 1921 ("Rusia," "Trinchera," "Gesta maximalista," and "Guardia roja"). He also supported the presidencies of Hipólito Yrigoyen, a leader with the local, popular, and austere tone that attracted Borges during the 1920s (Balderston, *Borges* 142). And, along the same lines, he praises the civic qualities of the people in admiration of Whitman's democratic call (*OC* I: 208; *OC* IV: 157), and he prefers Emerson's faith in the capacity of the common man over elitism (*OC* IV: 39–40). Yet, an older Borges appears to take a Carlylean turn when he explicitly rejects democracy: "Tal vez me sea perdonado añadir que descreo de la democracia, ese curioso abuso de la estadística" [Perhaps I can be forgiven if I add that I do not believe in democracy, that curious abuse of statistics] (*OC* III: 122). How to explain this change of mind?

In the 1970s, the violent turn of political events led Borges to criticize the Argentinian democratic experience and democracy at large. He eventually came to the conclusion that, despite its shortcomings and derailments, democracy had proven to be a better political regime when compared to the alternatives. The systematic human rights violations during the last military dictatorship in Argentina were a hard lesson for Borges to learn, as evidenced in a few media pieces published shortly after the return to democracy where he expresses his surprise, regret, and concern about those tragic years (Salinas, *Liberty* 107–09). In the end, Borges realized that his anarchist political utopia could only be possible in a democracy, and in this regard, his "anarchistic vision comes much closer to pluralistic, democratic models of government than to monistic, authoritarian ones" (Frisch 135).[6] In rejecting democracy Borges was, however, far from Carlyle, whom he saw defending the idea of "la entrega incondicional del poder a hombres fuertes y silenciosos" [the unconditional surrender of power to strong and silent men], since he found it conducive to "el servilismo, el temor, la brutalidad, la indigencia mental y la delación" [servility, fear, brutality, mental indigence and denunciation] (*OC* IV: 39). If he dismisses the masses, he also distances himself from the possibility that anyone can emerge from among the elites as a decent leader without becoming a strong, charismatic ruler in a unipersonal regime.

The type of demagogic regime Borges has in mind is what contemporary theorists call populism. Borges's reaction to mass democracy can be understood with the tools of the populist theory itself, as advanced by Ernesto Laclau. For one, populist theory replaces individualism with collectivism, dismantles the limited State, and promotes a permanent social antagonism. Second, it seeks to undermine the principles that nourished modern liberal democracies: individual liberty, procedural justice, and equality before the law. Third, it weakens republican institutions by proposing the adoption of strong, unlimited, and unaccountable regimes. This hegemonic view is accompanied by a hegemonic language as well, one that speaks only to one sector of the population—the underdogs, the excluded—as the sole subject of political attention. The populist theory also emphasizes the importance of sentiments in political discourse, which works at a double level: as the construction of solidarity and love between the leader and the people and as expression of resentment against their alleged antagonists (Laclau 57, 116).

Populist ideas and regimes were the objects of denunciation on the part of Borges. In times of Perón, he complained to his audience: "Dictatorships foster oppression; dictatorships foster servitude; dictatorships foster cruelty; more abominable is the fact that they foster idiocy. Hotel clerks mumbling orders, effigies of caudillos, prearranged 'long live's' and 'down with's,' walls embellished with names, unanimous ceremonies, mere discipline substituting for lucidity" ("Déle déle" speech, 1946, qtd. in Rodríguez Monegal et al. 66). Borges ironically criticizes the effects of populism on the people and calls into question the alleged solidarity and love between the leader and the people in a short piece dealing with a fraud committed after the death of Evita, when a swindler arrives in town to collect funds in memory of the late first lady ("El simulacro" [The Sham]). The conclusion to the story speaks directly to his opinion about the populist regime in Argentina: "tampoco Perón era Perón ni Eva era Eva sino desconocidos o anónimos (cuyo nombre secreto y cuyo rostro verdadero ignoramos) que figuraron, para el crédulo amor de los arrabales, una crasa mitología" [Neither Perón was Perón nor Eva was Eva but strangers or anonymous (whose secret name and whose true face we do not know) who invented, for the credulous love of the suburbs, a crass mythology] (*OC* II: 167).[7]

Conclusion

Borges took inspiration from the political realm to write many of his greatest pieces, including "La lotería en Babilonia," "Deutsches Requiem," "Poema conjetural," "El Congreso," "Utopía de un hombre que está cansado," "Avelino Arredondo," "Nuestro pobre individualismo," and "El escritor argentino y la tradición." This chapter presented a brief analysis of Borges's approach to the political. First, it showed how the writer deals with and criticizes violence or oppression in the form of racial imperialism, communist revolutions, and political assassination. Second, it called attention to Borges's treatment of foundational historical deeds, and his eulogy of the spirit of patriotism in the service of the republic against the claims of nationalism. Third, the chapter highlighted Borges's political ideal or utopia as a framework that allows people to live unoppressed, and it pointed out the basis of his opposition to populist theories and regimes on the grounds that they challenge the core of his liberal anarchist beliefs.

Upon receiving the Cervantes Prize, Borges stated that his hero was not Don Quixote but Alonso Quijano, the Spanish nobleman who "after reading about Brittany, France, and the great Rome, embarked on the task of 'being a champion' and 'restoring justice to a corrupt world'" ("Discurso"). Faced with cruel or stupid political projects implemented throughout the twentieth century, Borges found in the dream of Alonso Quijano inspiration to channel his literary imagination toward more idealist and better political goals. His is not the closed universe of nationalism (cf. Díaz 17), or a private world created to escape from reality (cf. Vargas Llosa 1331). Nor is it a postmodern work marked by nothingness (cf. Rodríguez Monegal et al. 69). Quite to the contrary, Borges's is a literary political utopia marked by tolerance, cosmopolitanism, and liberty.

Acknowledgments

This chapter is based on and expands the arguments presented in Salinas (2017).

Notes

1. The manuscript is housed in the Albert and Shirley Small Special Collections Library, University of Virginia (MSS 10155-ae). See Benedict (95–100) for a detailed analysis of the drawing, and Balderston ("Revelando las falacias del nacionalismo") for a reading of the manuscript and the essay that highlights the contrast between Borges's defense of individualism and his rejection of Peronism.
2. Borges is surely referring to Karl Marx and Friedrich Engels, *The Manifesto of the Communist Party* (1848), the "manual" of revolutionary Marxists.
3. For a contrast between the notions of a strong political individual and the limitations and fallibility of artistic and epistemic capacities in the texts of Borges, see Salinas (*Liberty* ch. 1).

4. For his father's ideas, see Jorge Guillermo Borges (2015) and Salinas ("En la senda intelectual de los Borges").
5. I thank the editors for calling my attention to Rosa, who argues that Borges's anarchism takes inspiration from the context of his father's generation, "marked by the last battles of Argentine anarchism" at the beginning of the twentieth century (80–81). However, I think Spencer's influence is stronger than the local anarchists, and it is distinct from them because it defends individualism and private property. Although Borges is mostly uninterested in property, see "Pedro Salvadores" [1970, in *OC* II: 372–73] for a story about a victim of political persecution that translates to the loss of liberty, dignity, and property.
6. Furthermore, democratic principles have been seen as the logical development of the idea of individual rights, including the right to self-government (De Ruggiero 370–80).
7. For further analysis of Peronism, see Salinas (*Liberty* 105–07). On Borges and Peronism, see, among others, Balderston, "Revelando las falacias del nacionalismo"; Williamson; Rodríguez Monegal et al.; González 181–99, and Bell-Villada 270–74.

WORKS CITED

Alberdi, Juan Bautista. *Basis and Starting Points for the Political Organization of the Argentine Republic* [1852], *Liberal Thought in Argentina, 1837–1940*, translated by Ian Barnett, edited by N. Botana and E. Gallo. Liberty Fund, 2014, pp. 115–76.

Argentina. *Constitution of the Argentine Nation*, http://www.biblioteca.jus.gov.ar/argentina-constitution.pdf.

Balderston, Daniel. *Borges, realidades y simulacros*. Biblos, 2000.

Balderston, Daniel. "Liminares: Sobre el manuscrito de 'El hombre en el umbral.'" *Hispamérica*, vol. 41, no. 122, 2012, pp. 27–36.

Balderston, Daniel. *Out of Context: Historical Reference and the Representation of Reality in Borges*. Duke University Press, 1993.

Balderston, Daniel. "Revelando las falacias del nacionalismo: de 'Viejo hábito argentino' a 'Nuestro pobre individualismo.'" *Variaciones Borges*, vol. 46, 2018, pp. 135–54.

Bell-Villada, Gene. *Borges and His Fiction: A Guide to His Mind and Art, Revised Edition*. University of Texas Press, 1999.

Benedict, Nora C. "Censorship and Political Allegory in Jorge Luis Borges's 'Viejo hábito argentino.'" *Bulletin of Hispanic Studies*, vol. 96, no. 1, 2019, pp. 87–105.

Borges, Jorge Luis. "Discurso de Aceptación del Premio Cervantes," 1979. http://biblio3.url. edu.gt/Discursos/03.pdf.

Borges, Jorge Luis. *Ensayos*, edited by Daniel Balderston and María Celeste Martín. Borges Center, 2019.

Borges, Jorge Luis. *Obras completas*. 4 vols. Emecé Editores, 1996.

Borges, Jorge Luis. *Textos recobrados 1 (1919–1929)*. Emecé Editores, 1997.

Borges, Jorge Luis. *Textos recobrados 3 (1956–1986)*. Emecé Editores, 2003.

Borges, Jorge Luis, and Norman Thomas di Giovanni. *The Aleph and Other Stories 1933–1969, together with Commentaries and An Autobiographical Essay*. Bantam Books, 1971.

Bowles, Samuel, and Herbert Gintis. *Democracy and Capitalism: Property, Community and the Contradictions of Modern Social Thought*. Basic Books, 1986.

Churchill, Winston. *Churchill by Himself: The Definitive Collection of Quotations*, edited by Richard Langworth. Public Affairs, 2008.

D'Agostino, Fred, and Gerald F. Gaus, eds. *The Routledge Companion to Social and Political Philosophy*. Routledge, 2013.

De Ruggiero, Guido. *The History of European Liberalism*. Beacon Press, 1959.

Dalberg, John E. E. [Lord Acton]. "Letter of April 5, 1887." *Acton-Creighton Correspondence*, 1887. *Online Library of Liberty*, http://oll.libertyfund.org/titles/2254.

Dapía, Silvia G. *Jorge Luis Borges, Post-Analytic Philosophy, and Representation*. Routledge, 2016.

Díaz, Hernán. *Borges between History and Eternity*. Continuum, 2012.

Frisch, Mark. *You Might Be Able to Get There from Here: Reconsidering Borges and the Postmodern*. Fairleigh Dickinson University Press, 2004.

Gentile, Emilio. "Total and Totalitarian Ideologies." *The Oxford Handbook of Political Ideologies*. Edited by Michael Freeden, Lyman Tower Sargent, and Marc Stears. Oxford University Press, 2013, pp. 80–99.

González, José Eduardo. *Jorge Luis Borges and the Politics of Form*. Garland, 1998.

Klosko, George, ed. *The Oxford Handbook of the History of Political Philosophy*. Oxford University Press, 2011.

Laclau, Ernesto. *On Populist Reason*. Verso, 2005.

Locke, John. *The Second Treatise of Government*, edited by Thomas Peardon. The Liberal Arts P, 1954.

Long, Roderick. "Anarchism." *The Routledge Companion to Social and Political Philosophy*. Edited by Fred D'Agostino and Gerald F. Gaus. Routledge, 2013, pp. 217–30.

Lugones, Leopoldo. *Mi beligerancia*. Otero y García, 1917. *Internet Archive*, https://archive.org/stream/mibeligeranciaoolugo#page/8/mode/2up.

MacIntyre, Alasdair. "Is Patriotism a Virtue?" The Lindley Lecture. University of Kansas, March 26, 1984, https://mirror.explodie.org/Is%20Patriotism%20a%20Virtue-1984.pdf.

Matravers, Derek, and Jonathan Pike. *Debates in Contemporary Political Philosophy: An Anthology*. Routledge/The Open University 2003.

Miller, David. "Nationalism." *Debates in Contemporary Political Philosophy: An Anthology*. Edited by Derek Matravers and Jonathan Pike. Routledge/The Open University, 2003, pp. 529–53.

Mises, Ludwig von. *Omnipotent Government. The Rise of the Total State and Total War* (1944). Liberty Fund/Mises Institute, 2010.

Oakeshott, Michael. *Rationalism in Politics and Other Essays*. Foreword by Timothy Fuller. Liberty Fund, 1991.

Rodríguez Monegal, Emir, Enrico Mario Santí, and Carlos J. Alonso. "Borges and Politics." *Diacritics*, vol. 8, no. 4, 1978, pp. 55–69.

Rosa, Luis Othoniel. *Comienzos para una estética anarquista. Borges con Macedonio*. Editorial Cuarto Propio, 2016.

Salinas, Alejandra M. "Los arquetipos en Borges: clasificación y análisis." *Variaciones Borges*, vol. 50, 2020, pp. 127–48.

Salinas, Alejandra M. *Liberty, Individuality, and Democracy in Jorge Luis Borges*. Lexington Books, 2017.

Salinas, Alejandra M. "En la senda intelectual de los Borges." *Variaciones Borges*, vol. 45, 2018, pp. 99–117.

Shklar, Judith. *Political Thought and Political Thinkers*. University of Chicago Press, 1998.

Taylor, Charles. "Cross-Purposes: The Liberal-Communitarian Debate." *Debates in Contemporary Political Philosophy: An Anthology*. Edited by Derek Matravers and Jonathan Pike. Routledge/The Open University, 2003, pp. 195–218.

Tower Sargent, Lyman. "Authority & Utopia: Utopianism in Political Thought." *Polity*, vol. 14, no. 4, 1982, pp. 565–84.

Trepanier, Lee, ed. *Cosmopolitanism in the Age of Globalization: Citizens without States.* University Press of Kentucky, 2011.

Vargas Llosa, Mario. "The Fictions of Borges." *Third World Quarterly*, vol. 10, no. 3, 1988, pp. 1325–33.

Viroli, Maurizio. *For Love of Country: An Essay on Patriotism and Nationalism.* Clarendon Press, 1997.

Williamson, Edwin. "Borges against Peron: A Contextual Approach to 'El Fin.'" *The Romanic Review*, vol. 10, no. 2–3, 2007, pp. 275–96.

CHAPTER 33

BIRD, SCHEDULE, NAME

On Some Media in Borges

JOHN DURHAM PETERS

"Otra declara que la Compañía es omnipotente, pero que solo influye en cosas minúsculas: en el grito de un pájaro, en los matices de la herrumbre y del polvo, en los entresueños del alba." [Another declares that the company is omnipotent but only exercises its influence in minute things: in the cry of a bird, in the nuances of rust and dust, in the dream-states of dawn.]

— Jorge Luis Borges, "La lotería en Babilonia"
(*OC* I: 460)

BIRD

Two hundred years ago Thomas De Quincey (142) opened a now famous essay thus: "From my boyish days I had always felt a great perplexity on one point in *Macbeth*. It was this: the knocking at the gate, which succeeds to the murder of Duncan, produced to my feelings an effect for which I never could account. The effect was, that it reflected back upon the murder a peculiar awfulness and a depth of solemnity; yet, however obstinately I endeavored with my understanding to comprehend this, for many years I never could see *why* it should produce such an effect."

De Quincey found his answer in the return of the quotidian world. His brilliant solution portends two centuries of critical thought about how minute realistic touches produce large aesthetic effects. The knocking wakes *Macbeth*'s spectators from the spell in murderous fantasyland into which they had briefly swooned: "the human has made its reflux upon the fiendish; the pulses of life are beginning to beat again; and the reestablishment of the goings-on of the world in which we live, first makes us profoundly sensible of the awful parenthesis that had suspended them" (De Quincey 147). Everyday reality interrupts; the Man from Porlock breaks the reverie by pounding on the door.

568   JOHN DURHAM PETERS

I have always felt a similar perplexity about the cry of a bird at the moment just before detective Erik Lönnrot is killed in "La muerte y la brújula" [Death and the Compass]: "Ya era de noche; desde el polvoriento jardín subió el grito inútil de un pájaro" [It was already night; from the dusty garden rose the useless cry of a bird] (*OC* I: 507).[1] For both Borges and Shakespeare, the haunting effect lies partly in the difficulty of identifying the author or place of the sound. "Knock, knock. Never at quiet. What are you?" asks the exasperated night watchman in *Macbeth* after Macduff's repeated knocking (2.3.15). There are nocturnal birds in *Macbeth* as well: "The obscure bird / Clamored the livelong night" (2.3.55–56). Even in daylight, birds are typically "obscure" since you often hear them without seeing them; they call up the primal and uncanny "acousmatic" scene of a voice without a body, a sound without a source (Kane).

Birds, like media, abound in Borges, and yet De Quincey's answer doesn't help us altogether. For one thing, Borges's timing is different from Shakespeare's: the bird cries *before* the death. De Quincey thought the knocking reflected *back* upon the murder. For another, he found in the knocking the return of *the human* element. We cannot say such a thing about a member of an avian (alien) species. Should we take its cry as a comment? Does the bird's cry participate in some larger cosmic scheme or does it simply signal the coming of the night? How could a nonlinguistic vocalization bear meaning at all? Like the knocking at the gate, the cry portends things to come, but unlike the knocking, there is no implied human agent. Though the night and the cry are structurally peripheral to the plot, they are more than mere setting. By what right do random and nonhuman bystanders enter the drama—even if their role is announced to be pointless? What role does circumstance play in the weightiest matters of life and death? In short, what role has the environment in interpretation?

"La busca de Averroes" [Averroes's Search] raises the question of the meaningfulness of nature. During a conversation of learned Muslim men in twelfth-century Spain, whose parry-and-thrust of philosophical opinion Borges makes as sparkly as Plato's *Symposium*, one scholar states that he has heard of gardens of roses in India that spell out the characters of the Shahada, Islam's profession of faith. This over-the-top claim presents an immediate problem: believe it and you risk being hoodwinked, deny it and you risk being accused of lacking faith. Someone suavely comes up with a Solomonic solution, quoting the verse from the Qur'an that states that God knows everything. Averroes, the hero of the story (whose name incidentally includes *ave*, bird—if we can even use the word *incidentally* in this inquiry), pipes up in his rationalist way, saying that it is easier to believe there was an error in reporting the observation than that the earth has roses that spell out the Shahadah. In this he sounds a bit like G. K. Chesterton's Father Brown (a character Borges admired), a man of faith who goes around relieving people of their credulity. Another symposiast reports the legend of a tree whose fruits consisted of green birds. Averroes administers the coup de grâce: "Además, los frutos y los pájaros pertenecen al mundo natural, pero la escritura es un arte. Pasar de hojas a pájaros es más fácil que de rosas a letras" [Moreover, fruits and birds belong to the natural world, but writing is an art. To go from leaves to birds is easier than from roses to letters] (*OC* I: 584). This point is quickly rebutted by another scholar who gives the orthodox view that writing is not simply a technique but part of creation itself: since the Qur'an predated and lent its structure to the world, writing is already nature. Averroes immediately thinks of Plato's forms—the Qur'an as the *Idea* of Creation—but remains silent, knowing his companions wouldn't understand.

In "Del culto de los libros" [On the Cult of Books], Borges quotes Sir Thomas Browne that God created two books, the Bible and Nature, "that universal and publick Manuscript." "Nature and letters seem to have a natural antipathy," wrote Virginia Woolf in *Orlando*, a novel that Borges translated in 1937 (8). Friedrich Kittler, the leading media theorist of the past fifty years, liked to quote Freud's flat declaration: "There are no letters in nature" (39). Which is it? The Book of Nature or Book against Nature? This antinomy is both Averroes's and ours. It is a metaphysical oscillation that Borges often arrived at. If the universe is overseen by a divine mind, then the cry could be meaningful as a mournful witness that nothing can be done to prevent the death, as a helpless partner in the tragedy and pathos. From this monistic or theistic point of view, the nature-culture (rose-letter) distinction would be the product of a narrowly human-centered outlook. But if art and nature are mutually distinct, then the bird's cry could be said to be useless because it is purely coincidental, a happenstance simultaneity. But calling it useless is still meaningful. (Making a bird's cry worthy of any adjective is itself a claim to meaning.) Few things are of deeper significance than nature's indifference to human affairs. After a loved one's death we feel most intensely the drawing away of "el incesante y vasto universo" [the unceasing and vast universe] (*OC* I: 617). If the universe is indeed a blank to our concerns, that information is of the utmost moral and metaphysical interest.

Chance happenings fill up retrospectively with meaning. Today's randomness is tomorrow's destiny. Recollection turns accident into fate. What Sergei Eisenstein said of film editing applies to life in general: "two film pieces of any kind, placed together, inevitably combine into a new concept, a new quality, arising out of that juxtaposition" (4). In the southern hemisphere of Tlön, mere simultaneity can even determine ideal objects, such as audiovisual montages: "objetos compuestos de dos términos, uno de carácter visual y otro auditivo: el color del naciente y el remoto grito de un pájaro" [objects composed of two terms, one with a visual and the other with an auditory character: the color of the rising sun and the distant cry of a bird] (*OC* I: 435). Does the uncanny effect in "La muerte y la brújula" stem from mere simultaneity? Or is the unaccountable connection itself the uncanny effect? Is the cry an authorial flourish or even a potentially corny bit of soundtrack? We all know the creepy effect of a footfall on a stair or the sound of a window closing in a scary movie; we also know how tired those tropes can become. (For my part, I do not find the bird's cry tired.) The effect lies partly in the arousal of an interpretive quandary: the vexingly indeterminate role played by circumstantial detail.

Birds, of course, have long served as omens and warnings, as obscure signals from the divinities whose interpretation requires reading of that which is not written in letters. The bird's cry also is rich with inescapable resonance: it echoes three important bird cries in European literature. The singular cry of the bird in "La muerte y la brújula" is reminiscent of Edgar Allan Poe's raven and its unitary toll chimes with the finality of *Nevermore*. And yet, Lönnrot's bravado and banter about the prospect of reincarnation hints of the many lives of John Keats's nightingale, with its intertemporal sound across the ages. But the most important bird cry in the canon must be the cock that crowed at Peter's denial of Christ. This episode has been analyzed brilliantly by Erich Auerbach (40–49), who, with Borges and two other B-names, Walter Benjamin and Roland Barthes, was one of the twentieth century's great thinkers on realistic effects. The story is well known: Jesus is arrested by an armed militia and his right-hand man, Peter, warily follows him into the palace by night, risking detection as a member of the inner circle. Warming himself at a fire he sputters denials to suspicious bystanders, having quickly forgotten Jesus's warning (or statement of fact, prophecy, or even implied command?) that he would deny him thrice before dawn. According to the Gospel of Luke, after Peter's third denial, "while he was yet speaking," the cock crows, Jesus turns and looks at him across the crowded palace (22.60). Peter remembers his pledge and goes outside to weep bitterly while Jesus is roughed up by his captors.

All three synoptic Gospels have the cock cry immediately after the third denial, but Luke narrates with especial crispness of pace and action, using the Greek grammatical form of the genitive absolute to link parallel events. You can easily imagine the camerawork, the montage of cuts from cock to Peter to Jesus to Peter to guards. What role does the rooster play in this heterogeneous company of human, deity, bird, and ruffians? Was Jesus's prophecy a kind of augury or avian divination? Or did Jesus use some kind of remote control to trigger the bird at the precise right moment? Did his foreknowledge predict the perfect synchronization of the two events? Did he, as author of Creation, have as much command over the bird as Borges, author of "Death and the Compass"? Or was he simply forecasting a likely outcome, knowing the predictability of Peter's behavior and the likely cry of a rooster in the morning after an all-night trial? Is the evangelist, writing his Gospel decades later, embellishing for effect? Even if Peter's denial and cock's cry were a mere splice of two otherwise autonomous events, they are forever after yoked. What could be more ordinary than a rooster crying at dawn? Yet what could be more momentous than human failure at the hour of divine peril, the cock tolling the meridian of sacred time? The horizontal movement from center stage to apparent sideshow intensifies the drama by showing its grander scope: even the animals take part in the turning of the world. A nonhuman element serves as the pivot on which everything else turns. Random shriek into the void or divine predestination: it's meaningful either way.

Borges, by the way, directly retooled the ornithomancy of the Passion narrative in "El evangelio según Marcos" [The Gospel According to Mark]. The last thing the victim hears before being hauled off to the cross is a bird: "Un pájaro gritó; pensó: Es un jilguero" [A bird shrieked; he thought: it's a goldfinch] (*OC* IV: 448). I'd like to know what is at stake in the choice of a goldfinch, a bird with a complex song and local habitation and name, rather than rooster or raven!

Borges uses circumambient but apparently irrelevant details to great effect in "El milagro secreto" [The Secret Miracle]. Jaromir Hladik, a Czech-Jewish author who has been rounded up and sentenced to death by the Nazis, stews in prison awaiting his doom. A bit of puffery in a publisher's catalog made him sound important to the authorities: "two or three adjectives in Gothic script" sealed his fate. (Such momentous details lie, however, purely within the realm of letters rather than roses.) Reflecting that since reality never matches anticipation, Hladik sets out to imagine every possible way his murder could occur in order to prevent them from ever happening: "con lógica perversa infirió que prever un detalle circunstancial es impedir que éste suceda" [with perverse logic he inferred that to foresee a circumstantial detail is to prevent it from happening] (*OC* I: 509). In the end, his shooting by firing squad takes place amid details so banal that his faith in the omnipotence of thoughts never could have conjured them: a raindrop lands on his cheek, and though the day is turning cloudy, a bee casts a shadow on a courtyard tile. These weathery bits of circumstance are both so real and so ordinary that their odds of being selected from an infinite enumeration of possibilities are infinitesimal. They show the mute doings of atmosphere—rain, sun, cloud, insect, architecture. The arbitrary details of setting deepen the poignancy in their indifference to murder.

Just how rigorously should we read circumstantial details when we know both that they might be random and that their randomness might have its meaning? Lönnrot's hermeneutically hyperactive reading strategy led him into the trap. If we overread the bird's cry, we risk the same fate. Yet if we ignore it, we miss the bird's unstable collaboration in the story's climax. One thinks of Kierkegaard's oscillating antinomy: "Marry, and you will regret it. Do not marry, and you will also regret it. Marry or do not marry, you will regret it either way" (39). In Spanish perhaps the best term for this uncertain correspondence between center and periphery, drama and surrounding, plot and happenstance, is "medio ambiente" [environment]. We might translate that term literally as media that surround, or to be more specific, as environing media (Wickberg and Gärdebo).

Schedule

"El jardín de senderos que se bifurcan" [The Garden of Forking Paths] features a bird. Yu Tsun, a Chinese spy working for Germany in England in 1916, flings himself on his bed and stares out the window in a quandary. He knows his opposite number, Captain Richard Madden, is closing in on him; he also knows the secret name of the location of a new British artillery park in France. He does not know how to give his chief in Berlin the strategic intel within the narrow slice of time before he is caught. Through the window he sees a bird and slips into a brief reverie: "Un pájaro rayó el cielo gris y ciegamente lo traduje en un aeroplano y a ese aeroplano en muchos (en el cielo francés) aniquilando el parque de artillería con bombas verticales" [a bird scratched the gray sky and blindly I translated it into an airplane and this airplane into many (in the French sky) annihilating the artillery park with vertical bombs] (*OC* I: 473). Yu Tsun's mental cross-cut from Staffordshire (a region in which Borges's English grandmother was born) to the Somme covers a lot more ground than Jesus looking across the Pretorium to Peter. In modernity, the means for circumambient perception have greatly multiplied. Birds montage into airplanes. The radius and speed of possible connection across space have expanded enormously.

Media, in other words, that span space and time are one mark of the modern world, and they abound in Borges's texts. One of his few poetic attempts in English, for instance, creates an imaginary triangle between the Argentine pampas, New York, and London through the BBC and sound recording: "In a lonely *estancia* on the plains I hear through the radio the clocks of London; in a gramophone record the men of Harlem are forever swearing and a man of Harlem is forever singing and praying. dying" (qtd. in Balderston, "Borges in Love" 149). The literary blowhard Carlos Argentino Daneri lists the accoutrements of modern man in "El Aleph": telephones, telegraphs, phonographs, wireless equipment, cinematographs, magic lanterns, glossaries, schedules, digests, and bulletins. It's a curious list, a mix of new and old, audiovisual and print media, but Daneri's point is something like the disappearance of distance: "Observó que para un hombre así facultado el acto de viajar era inútil; nuestro siglo xx había trasformado la fábula de Mahoma y de la montaña; las montañas, ahora, convergían sobre el moderno Mahoma" [He observed that for a man thus equipped, the act of traveling was pointless; this our twentieth century had switched the fable of Muhammad and the mountain: now the mountains converged upon the modern Muhammad] (*OC* I: 618). We should not take Daneri's trite observation—almost everyone in the nineteenth century noted "the annihilation of space and time" caused by steam and electricity—as speaking for Borges on media. The media Borges investigated were rarely flashy newfangled ones; they were old and everlastingly mysterious—maps, mirrors, compasses, encyclopedias, libraries, names, and lists.

Modern media are better seen in Borges less as content than as form—in his art of time and space itself. Media are often literally the medium of his texts. He is a film director of carefully timed and spaced plots as well as an architect of infinite databases. Consider again "The Garden of Forking Paths." Borges's love of the cinema and his active role as a film critic are well known, as are the cinematic features of this story (among many others) (Aguilar and Jelicié). This story is a taut thriller blending the genres of suspense, detection, and espionage. Though it may owe remote affiliation to Poe, it is thoroughly Hitchcockian. Borges favorably reviewed Hitchcock's *The 39 Steps* (1935), and this film has striking similarities with "El jardín de senderos que se bifurcan." (Borges panned Hitchcock's *Sabotage* [1936] for selling out the Conrad novel on which it was based, so I am not suggesting a slavish admiration.) The plot of *The 39 Steps*, like that of the story, turns on how to communicate top-secret military information involving aerial weaponry—in this case, an aircraft with a silent engine—that exists only in a single person's mind—in this case, a character Borges appreciated named "Mr. Memory," who is tempting to see (in some ways) as a forerunner of Funes el memorioso. (The theme of military secrets held in fragile vessels also appears in Hitchcock's *Foreign Correspondent* [1940], in which only two people know by heart the critical clause 27 of a European Peace Treaty. Borges could have seen it before publishing the story in 1941.)

Consider more parallels between *The 39 Steps* and "El jardín de senderos que se bifurcan." Both film and story concern Europe-wide military conflict and take place in Britain but away from London. Both involve a cameo by the author: about seven minutes into the film Hitchcock appears as a littering pedestrian, and we might take the young man on the train reading Tacitus as Borges (Balderston, *Out of Context* 51–52). Both film and story involve a case of the wrong man or at least an atrocious substitution. In the film, the wrong man, Richard Hannay, is suspected of being the spy. In the story, the wrong man, Stephen Albert, is killed. (He is the right man to send the message, but the wrong man in every other possible way.) Yu Tsun's reverie of bird turning into plane is not just a surreal association: it is structurally similar to one of the most famous cuts in the film, and perhaps all cinema. Hitchcock shows a woman screaming upon discovering a murder, but we do not hear her: we hear a train whistle and then see the train on which Hannay is escaping emerging from a tunnel. Mouth morphs into tunnel, woman morphs into train, cry morphs into whistle, bird morphs into plane, living creatures morph into modernity's high-speed travel machines. (A small allegory of how cinema transports its spectators!) Both film and story involve a harrowing chase on trains; in the film we see the feet of the pursuers from the window of the departing train slowing down as they just barely miss boarding it, and in the story, Yu Tsun, crouching down, away from the window, sees Richard Madden at the edge of the platform, having tried to catch the train in vain. In both, the protagonist arrives at a professor's house after a harried chase where they engage in dialogue before one of them ends up shooting the other. And what is the topic of the dialogue? The professor in the film is the actual spy and ends up half-apologizing to Hannay: "I'm afraid I've been guilty of leading you down the garden path. Or should it be up? I never can remember." "It seems to be the wrong garden, alright," says Hannay. This exchange about horticultural crisscrossing is minimal compared to that between Yu Tsun and Albert, but there it is in plain sight. QED.

In a twist worthy of both auteurs, film theorists now refer to Hitchcock's "forking path plots" (Mohr 73). Johan Grimonprez's film, *Double Take* (2009), also fuses Borges and Hitchcock. The snake bites its tail.

Classical Hollywood cinema depends on telephones, newspapers, trains, radio, clocks, and more to structure its plots, and in both *The 39 Steps* and "El jardín de senderos que se bifurcan," phones and news are crucial narrative devices. In the film, newspapers splash the supposed spy's face far and wide. Hannay learns from the newspaper that he is the target of a manhunt and the front page betrays him to his fellow passengers in a train compartment. As he spots a partly covered newspaper on the table of the lonely and beautiful wife of the stern and abusive Scotch crofter who briefly offers him refuge, he engages in absurdist comic maneuvering trying to keep her from seeing the headline. The paper broadcasts the message to everyone but aims to finger a single individual; its content and matter enter into person-to-person interactions. (Hannay keeps overhearing updates about the manhunt in snippets of conversation.) Yu Tsun, in turn, engages in a structurally inverted détournement of mass address: he uses the newspaper as a telephone, a point-to-point medium. In a classic Borgesian task, he has to communicate a secret name. But in order to encrypt a message to his chief in Berlin, he needs another kind of medium, one that Daneri perhaps should have added to his list: "La guía telefónica me dio el nombre de la única persona capaz de transmitir la noticia"

574   JOHN DURHAM PETERS

[The telephone book gave me the name of the only person capable of sending the news] (*OC* I: 473).

This seems to be the only telephone book in Borges's corpus, but it is hardly the only monstrous compilation. As a genre, the phone book descends from directories of elite families, such as the *Almanach de Gotha*, the go-to source for sorting out Europe's royal lineages. In 1916, the phone book would have also been a bourgeois genre; it is clear that Stephen Albert's treasures are more than cultural. (As late as the 1930s, a public opinion poll went horribly off the rails in predicting the US presidential election: by relying on telephone surveys, the *Literary Digest* overcounted Republicans [i.e. people who could afford phones]. In using a phone book to choose his victim, Yu Tsun exempted the working class.) "By 1914," we learn from an online history of British Telecom, "the phone book was the largest single printing contract in the UK, with a million and a half phone books being printed each year" ("The New Style Phone Book"). Such a book, presumably a regional or local edition, should have been ready to hand for Yu Tsun. The telephone book is a kind of panoptic societyscape, a survey in a single glance of a population of citizens listed in alphabetical order. Every phone book is a kind of false Aleph that offers a point through which to see the whole in its dizzying arbitrary totality. As a genre of instant summary, the phone book belongs next to Benedict Anderson's newspaper and novel, census and map, as an agent of imagined community, of "horizontal comradeship" (7). Yu Tsun engages in a kind of pinpoint targeting in picking out Stephen Albert's name from the vast multitude of the phone book just as he depends on his chief to pick out the signal of Albert's name amid the fog and noise of war/newspapers, who will then order the precision bombing of the artillery park in Albert.

The phone book is an all-at-once compilation. It is a database compressing facts in time and space. It both locates needles in haystacks and is out of date as soon as it is printed, a network of live and dead links. The compilation of many data points and trajectories is equally true of the train schedule, which plays a crucial role in "El jardín de senderos que se bifurcan." As Yu Tsun calculates his mission, he relies on the schedule's temporal precision. He knows how much time he has, down to the minute: "sin esa diferencia preciosa que el horario de trenes me deparaba, yo estaría en la cárcel, o muerto" [without this precious difference that the train schedule was offering me, I would be in jail or dead] (*OC* I: 474).

Strangely for a story whose subject is the multitudinous possibilities of time, some of Borges's US-American translators can seem indifferent to its temporal media. Early on in the story, Yu Tsun looks out his window: "En la ventana estaban los tejados de siempre y el sol nublado de las seis" [In the window were the roofs of always and the cloudy sun of six o'clock] (*OC* I: 472). Andrew Hurley misses the poetry of the line, and Donald Yates does a little better, but this contrast of always (and architecture) with clock (and weather—*el tiempo*) anticipates the discussion of different thicknesses of time in the garden itself. Yu Tsun beholds both *chronos* and *kairos* out his window. Even more oddly, both translators ignore the train schedule. Yates omits the line entirely and Hurley renders it as "the precious hour that the trains had given me," absorbing schedule (*horario*) into hour (*hora*), but also obliterating the critical medium. Perhaps the omission reflects an automotive culture lacking reliable railway infrastructure; Borges's French and German translators certainly do not miss it, noting the *horaire des trains* and *Fahrplan*. (The translation by Helen Temple and Ruthven Todd does not miss it.)

The train schedule is a key medium of modernity. The first public version was published in the UK in 1839 and Thomas Cook published a Europe-wide guide to train times in 1873, thus opening a bookselling empire still based in train stations. The timetable's job is to coordinate simultaneity. It synchronizes different points of space and time into a database. As Peter Galison notes, "Train lines had altered the experience of time across Europe and North America; more than that, for an ever growing portion of the population, railroad schedules had come to define time, to instantiate synchronicity" (125). If there could be such a thing as the "hic-stans" mocked by Thomas Hobbes in an epigraph to "El Aleph," it would be the train schedule. There are essential industrial reasons for the central coordination of railroad arrivals and departures: without it there would be hideous accidents (Beniger 213–25). The train, coupled with the telegraph and the clock, gave us the standard time of time zones and erased the ancient custom of local times set by the noon-moment of the shortest shadow (Carey 223–27). Little wonder that the train has been such a fertile subject for film directors: like cinema itself the train schedule is a logistical, carefully edited coordination of space, time, and material (human and otherwise) (Virilio). Like the phone book it is another false Aleph, an all-seeing compilation that allows a eusynoptic, often hard to read, overview of a grid or network (Esbester).The train schedule was a crucial imaginative instrument for Albert Einstein's discovery of special relativity, a model for thinking about the problem of distant simultaneity (Galison). It provides the suspenseful pace and structure of "El jardín de senderos que se bifurcan" just as the transportation grid, and its eventual comic breakdown (as Hannay traipses through car and moor, handcuffed to a woman, having escaped from the Professor), structures *The 39 Steps*. The edited and sometimes surreal integration of space and time is a precondition of modern life, cinema, and Borges's texts.

Apparently nobody thought (to quote Albert) that the phone book, train schedule, and labyrinth were a single object. Such compilations are themselves gardens of forking paths, compendia of parallel times, places, and trajectories. The number of possible itineraries is not infinite but is unimaginably large (Bloch). Such labyrinthine texts, if read like a standard novel, might appear to be "un acervo indeciso de borradores contradictorios" [a wavering heap of contradictory drafts] (*OC* I: 476). The path of one trip/chapter may utterly contradict that of another. The garden of Ts'ui Pên is as much a timetable as "El jardín de senderos que se bifurcan." We read Borges poorly if we miss the central place of logistical media (Peters, *The Marvelous Clouds* 37–38).

The train schedule and the phone book return us to "La muerte y la brújula." This story is also exquisitely structured by telephone, typewriter, newspaper, calendar, compass, and map, and, like its inspiration in Poe's "Mystery of Marie Rogêt" published exactly one century prior, it simulates an entire metropolis through paper media—and mathematics. The bird's cry is only the last, and perhaps the most easy to overlook, of a series of events whose timing invites scrutiny. Its emotional effect owes partly to its raising of an essential modern question: the meaning of synchronization. Like Yu Tsun's montage of bird to plane or his computation of the trip by means of a printed table, the bird evokes a horizontal imagination of simultaneities. Its cry is the cry of the *medio ambiente*.

NAME

If any two events "inevitably" combine into a new quality, as Eisenstein says, what gives them an emotional integrity free from the suspicion of fakery or arbitrary pasting? This is also Emma Zunz's question. Upon receiving a letter bringing news of her father's likely suicide, she plots revenge against the man, her factory boss Aaron Loewenthal, who she believes to be guilty of the embezzlement that her father was ruinously blamed for. Posing as a prostitute, she loses her virginity to a sailor and then calls Loewenthal, promising insider information on a potential strike at the factory. When they meet, she shoots him, and gets off scot-free, as her testimony convinces everyone that he raped her and she killed him in self-defense. Like a realist author, she looked for persuasive circumstantial details. The way to pull off the performance was to experience the precise outrages of which she would testify. "¿Cómo hacer verosímil una acción en la que casi no creyó quien la ejecutaba?" [How to make plausible an act in which even she who was to commit it scarcely believed?] (*OC* I: 565; *CF* 217, trans. Hurley). She mined trauma for authenticity, as if echoing the ancient belief that torture renders testimony honest by stilling the capacity to fabricate (duBois). To portray emotions powerfully to others, she had to feel them herself. She would not have otherwise known how to feign violation in every vocal tremor or stuttering sob. In creating the conditions inwardly that would compel others, Emma Zunz was, in short, a method actor.

She was also the editor of a trick film that she passed off as a documentary. The film critic André Bazin, another great realist thinker starting with B, proposed this aesthetic principle: "Quand l'essentiel d'un événement est dépendant d'une présence simultanée de deux ou plusieurs facteurs de l'action, le montage est interdit" [Whenever the essence of an event is dependent on the simultaneous presence of two or more agents editing is prohibited] (59). A film, he says, about a lioness stalking a child who innocently walked off with her cub might cross-cut between shots of the lioness and the child, but for a fully stupefying emotional burst and eruption of reality, the camera has to provide a single undoctored shot of them both in the same frame. Once we see this shot, all the previous parallel shots retroactively take on fresh force: they were not just concocted in the editing booth. Juxtaposition loses its whiff of fakery. Editing, we might say, is banned when bearing witness. Bazin seems to have been thinking especially of documentary, a film genre that claims testimonial validity. Emma Zunz's affidavit passed as a documentary, and no one could detect the edit, the substitution of the crude sailor for miserly Loewenthal. There never was a single shot of Loewenthal raping her. Her montage of the sailor and Loewenthal had the emotional dynamism that Eisenstein called for but lacked the ontological witness Bazin craved.

Emma Zunz got away with murder—but at what price? As in "El jardín de senderos que se bifurcan," we are left gnawingly unclear if the right target was hit or should even have been hit at all (though Loewenthal is hardly as sympathetic a character as Albert). We never know for sure if he was guilty, and she never got to deliver her rehearsed accusation or see his anticipated *anagnorisis*. The narrator concludes laconically, noting that though unbelievable, her story "sustancialmente era cierta. Verdadero era el tono de Emma Zunz, verdadero el pudor, verdadero el odio. Verdadero también era el ultraje que había padecido; sólo eran falsas las circunstancias, la hora y uno o dos nombres propios" [was substantially certain. Real was the tone of Emma Zunz, real the shame, real the hate. Also real was the outrage she had suffered; the only false things were the circumstances, the timing, and one or two proper names] (*OC* I: 568).

One or two proper names! Names cause a lot of mischief in Borges, and critics have noted "Emma Zunz's onomastic intricacies" (Maier, a critic whose name appears in the story itself). Take the scene where Emma Zunz signs in at the women's club where she will swim with her friends. Of all the words in any language, proper names probably demand the most intense daily repetition and inspection: "Se inscribieron; tuvo que repetir y deletrear su nombre y su apellido; tuvo que festejar las bromas vulgares que comentan la revisación" [They registered; she had to repeat and spell out her first and last name.] (*OC* I: 565). The final clause is tricky. Hurley translates: "She had to applaud the vulgar jokes that accompanied the struggle to get it correct." Yates: "she had to respond to the vulgar jokes that accompanied the medical exam." Nothing about her name seems to suggest double entendres, so it is unclear what is going on. Daniel Balderston suggests it could be (in 1922) a modesty check on their swim suits or even an exam to see if they are having their periods.

If the latter is true, this suggests another resonance. Could the *pileta* (swimming pool) be a sort of *mikvah*, the ritual purifying bath after menstruation for Jewish women? Emma Zunz has been compared to Judith, a Jewish widow who, according to the Book of Judith, seduced and beheaded the Assyrian general Holofernes to defend her people (de la Fuente 175–78). Yet "Emma Zunz" might even be better read as a structural permutation of the story of David and Bathsheba (2 Sam. 11). David, lounging in the palace instead of fighting in the ongoing war, voyeuristically spots beautiful Bathsheba emerging naked from the *mikvah* across the way. He finds out who she is, sends for her, has sex with her, and she becomes pregnant. He calls her husband Uriah home from battle, hoping to get him to sleep with her and thus pass as the father, but in his Spartan valor (perhaps shaming David) Uriah refuses to go near her while his men suffer in the field. After several failed attempts to arrange a tryst between the couple, David sends Uriah back into battle to die, carrying a letter to his commander that orders his death. As in "Emma Zunz," a letter triggers a death. In both narratives, the man killed is the one who did *not* have sex with the woman. (Borges's psychobiographers unfortunately might flock to this fact.) David, like the sailor, is the violator, but he is also like Emma in blaming—and killing—the substitute. Emma is like Bathsheba in being sexually

578   JOHN DURHAM PETERS

used but like David in shifting blame for its consequences (in fact, onto someone she blames for shifting blame). Emma's substitution successfully conceals her crime; not so David, whose family and empire start to crumble. David covers his sexual violation with murder; Emma uses hers to justify murder.

Yu Tsun picked a name out of a phone book; Emma Zunz switched the name of the perpetrator. In a telephone book, railroad schedule, or film editing booth, time is suspended. The "user" (that druggie word!) has nonlinear access to all data. The side-by-side spatial arrangement of items allows their manipulation outside linear time. Storage media allow for intervention into the flow of time—pauses, cuts, reversals, slow motion, and time lapse (Winkler). A phone book, dictionary, encyclopedia, or train schedule lets you open to S or Z as fast as you can to A or B (parallel processing). You have random access, the liberty to jump in and out, to spirit between points in space without worrying about the intervening distance. The codex format of these compilations saves you from having to travel successively as you would with a scroll (serial processing). All entries are equally available. They are, in other words, simultaneous. Alpha is as accessible as Omega. Or maybe we should say Aleph, in whose structure "todos ocuparon un mismo punto, sin supersición y sin transparencia" [all occupied the same point, without overlapping and without transparency] (*OC* I: 625). In playing with inscription media you are briefly safe from the scythe of unidirectional time.

But your personal lifetime clock never stops ticking. With media, memory, imagination, and books we live in a random-access universe. With our lives we do not. Time only goes in one direction. Even if history is a garden of forking paths each life is—to use Yu Tsun's term for his regret—"innumerable." Reversible media; irreversible life: such is our fate. The phone book, train schedule, or garden offers many paths; our life only offers one. We are back to the antinomy of interpretation. We never know if Loewenthal got what he deserved or if Yu Tsun's chief inferred the secret name from the newspaper—which announced both the murder and the bombing on the same day, thus making us wonder about even the military value of the murder as a signal. Getting the sequence right is indeed a matter of life and death: which is why the line about everything being correct except "the timing and one or two proper names" cannot be taken as a nihilistic benediction. It is, rather, a deeply ethical sense for the particular.

The indefiniteness, or rather the precision, of the phrase "one or two proper names" is a gut punch. (The "one or two" marks an infinite difference and its mathematical ethics deserves deeper inquiry.) It could mean simply Loewenthal and the sailor of unknown name. But it could also be pointing to the antinomy of absolute freedom of choice and strict determination of fate that plays out in the proper name. Though arbitrary at the point of christening, a name can lock in thereafter with barnacle-like stubbornness (Peters, "The Curious Power"). Yu Tsun, like novelists going back as far as Henry Fielding (Watt 17–19), plucked a name out of a list; the mark of a good name for a character is that it feels both arbitrary enough to be real and suggestive enough to fit the character. The whole plot of Thomas Hardy's *Tess of the d'Urbervilles* turns on a name randomly picked out of a directory of aristocratic names—with absurdly tragic ramifications. A name may seem as random as the cry of a bird, but once it has been given, the universe changes and its pathway takes on determinacy. At the point of thumbing the phone book, Yu Tsun could have easily lit upon another Albert (a not uncommon name). Once he is on the train, the degrees of freedom shrink. The Nazi authorities picked out Hladík's name from a catalog. Giving a name may be free, but having one can mean a destiny. Ask Stephen Albert or Jaromir Hladík.

Names, we imagine, are unique identifiers. And yet they are not. (There is no such thing as a unique name.) Philosophers of a certain bent, mostly English, have railed against this condition from the seventeenth century onward. They sought names that could be single-minded in reference and requiring no disambiguation. (Proper names have been a challenge to search engines.) For a system of nomenclature to be clear and distinct, as Borges said of John Wilkins, we would first need to know everything that exists. Such could exist only in a Laplacean universe where every particle and its motion could be known in the past, present, and future. And yet, "No sabemos qué cosa es el universo" [We do not know what the universe is] (*OC* II: 86). We do not know what the universe is because we do not know the future. Names are as subject to history and context as chapter 38 of Part One of the *Quijote* (*OC* I: 448–49). *Adolf* meant something different before Hitler, *Isis* something different after the Islamic state. Names are updatable. Semantically fuzzy names are the price we pay for a dynamic universe; they witness that we still have something to do with its fate.

Stephen Albert's name was certainly not what analytic philosophers call a "rigid designator." The name's fuzzy semantics referred at least to a man, a city, an artillery park, a Belgian king and a British prince, and a thinker who used the railroad schedule to imagine time as a relativistic garden of forking paths, Albert Einstein. (Luckily for Yu Tsun the name of the target was Albert and not, say, Foucaucourt or Longueval). In fact, Albert seems to have been named "Corbie" in another version of the story (Rabinowitz 179, 184). "Ningún nombre sabe quién es" [No name knows who it is] (*OC* II: 100). Translators typically take this as *hombre*, rendering "no man knows who he is" but *nombre* is more interesting; we should follow Borges in his precision. A proper name is identical neither with its object nor itself. Kafka is and is not Kafka (*OC* II: 89). Borges is and is not Borges (*OC* II: 186). The proper name is the prime example of Hegel's principle that identity is the identity of identity and nonidentity (Taylor 14, 23). Names are inhomogeneous gatherings. Their contents can shift sideways. The old wisdom about protecting the value of your name underscores the exquisite sensitivity of names to their environment. Thus names are like databases, railroad schedules, and narratives that pair a bird's cry and a death. Every name is a collection of circumstances. And every name is the transsubstantiation of the arbitrary into the necessary. These two qualities show that names follow a similar logic to circumstantial details like a bird cry or databases like a train schedule.

Many of the stories analyzed here, including *Macbeth* and Peter's denial, concern a murder—several of a Jewish victim. Death activates the desire to know why. Like sex, it is a great hermeneutic incitement. Details surrounding a death can't help but become part of the event. We intuit that the dead won't hear the birds or see the bee's shadow again. We are left behind as their proxies. From their point of view, there is nothing circumstantial in this world. Even the smallest thing is of infinite worth. What price they would pay for one more chance at life. We need the dead to tell us how precious every last, arbitrary thing is.

Circumstantial details show a cosmos full of parts we could not have expected to belong together. The metaphysical tickling of the tension between the apparent freedom of the now and the confinement of the *will have been* is the office of the bird's cry. In an almost Hegelian way, it shows essence and accident belonging together. The merest happenstance becomes the objective correlative of a death. The arbitrariness of the bird's cry, its obvious nonnecessity, the fact that another item could have just as easily been drawn from the author's database, tempts us with dreams of freely leaping out of our mortal momentum into a simultaneous path. This minuscule touch reveals the clash between multiple futures we fantasize and the strait gate of the now that we must pass through. The cry of the bird reveals a garden of many paths in which we can only ever choose one. It shows the cosmos as the *medio ambiente*. Its doctrine is the necessity of contingency. And it testifies that every shard of this world will be infinitely dear when we are dead.

What De Quincey (148) said of Shakespeare is also true of Borges: "the further we press in our discoveries, the more we shall see proofs of design and self-supporting arrangement where the careless eye had seen nothing but accident!" It is also, perhaps, true of the universe. Or of mind—which might or might not be the same thing.

ACKNOWLEDGMENTS

Thanks to Gonzalo Aguilar, Dudley Andrew, Dan Balderston, and Adam Wickberg for advice and feedback.

NOTE

1. Throughout, I provide my own plain translation unless the translator is identified.

WORKS CITED

Aguilar, Gonzalo, and Emiliano Jelicié. *Borges va al cine*. Libraria, 2010.

Anderson, Benedict. *Imagined Communities*. Rev. ed. Verso, 2006.

Auerbach, Erich. *Mimesis: The Representation of Reality in Western Literature*, translated by Willard Trask. Princeton University Press, 1974.

Balderston, Daniel. "Borges in Love." *Variaciones Borges*, vol. 45, 2018, pp. 131–51.

Balderston, Daniel. *Out of Context: Historical Reference and the Representation of Reality in Borges*. Duke University Press, 1993.

Barthes, Roland. "L'effet de réel." *Communications*, vol. 11, 1968, pp. 84–89.

Bazin, André. *Qu'est-ce que le cinéma?* Cerf, 1981.

Beniger, James R. *The Control Revolution*. Harvard University Press, 1986.

Benjamin, Walter. "The Storyteller." *Illuminations*. Translated by Harry Zohn, edited by Hannah Arendt. Schocken, 1969, pp. 83–109.

Bloch, William Goldbloom. *The Unimaginable Mathematics of Borges' Library of Babel*. Oxford University Press, 2008.

Borges, Jorge Luis. *Collected Fictions*. Translated by Andrew Hurley. Penguin, 1997.

Borges, Jorge Luis. *Obras completas*. 4 vols. Emecé, 1996.

Carey, James W. "Ideology and Technology: The Case of the Telegraph." *Communication as Culture*. Unwin Hyman, 1989, pp. 201–30.

De Quincey, Thomas. "On the Knocking on the Gate in *Macbeth*." Confessions of an English Opium Eater. Walter Scott, 1886 [1823], pp. 142–48.

duBois, Page. *Torture and Truth*. Routledge, 1991.

Eisenstein, Sergei. *The Film Sense*. Translated by Jay Leyda. Harcourt Brace, 1947.

Esbester, Mike. "Nineteenth-Century Timetables and the History of Reading," *Book History*, vol. 12, 2009, pp. 156–85.

De la Fuente, Ariel. *Borges, Desire, and Sex*. Liverpool University Press, 2018.

Galison, Peter. *Einstein's Clocks, Poincaré's Maps*. Norton, 2003.

Kane, Brian. *Sound Unseen: Acousmatic Sound in Theory and Practice*. Oxford University Press, 2014.

Kierkegaard, Søren. *Either/Or*, vol. 1, edited by Howard V. Hong and Edna H. Hong. Princeton University Press, 1987.

Kittler, Friedrich. *Aufschreibesysteme 1800·1900*. 3rd ed. Wilhelm Fink, 1995.

Maier, Linda S. "What's in a Name? Nomenclature and the Case of Borges' 'Emma Zunz,'" *Variaciones Borges*, vol. 14, 2002, pp. 79–86.

Mohr, Hans-Urlich. "Hitchcock's Plotting." *Reassessing the Hitchcock Touch*. Edited by Wieland Schwanebeck. Palgrave Macmillan, 2017, pp. 59–76.

"New Style Phone Book Trialled in Cornwall." *Cornish Times*, June 8, 2021.

Peters, John Durham. "The Curious Power of Names." *Sartoniana*, vol. 3, 2018, pp. 263–81, https://www.sartonchair.ugent.be/file/292.

Peters, John Durham. *The Marvelous Clouds*. University of Chicago Press, 2015.

Rabinowitz, Paula. "'The Abysmal Problem of Time': Dubbing Borges's Garden." *Cy-Borges: Memories of the Posthuman in the Work of Jorge Luis Borges*. Edited by Ivan Callus and Stefan Herbrechter. Bucknell University Press, 2009, pp. 178–97.

Taylor, Charles. *Hegel and Modern Society*. Cambridge University Press, 1979.

Virilio, Paul. *War and Cinema*, translated by Patrick Camiller. Verso, 1989.

Watt, Ian. *The Rise of the Novel*. University of California Press, 1957.

Wickberg, Adam, and Johan Gärdebo. "Where Humans and the Planetary Conflate—An Introduction to Environing Media." *Humanities*, vol. 9, no. 3, 2020, pp. 65–78.

Winkler, Hartmut. "The Geometry of Time" (2009), https://homepages.uni-paderborn.de/winkler/Winkler--Geometry-of-Time.pdf.

Woolf, Virginia. *Orlando*. Vintage, 2016 [1928].

CHAPTER 34

MIRROR. LENS. PUZZLEBOX. METAPHOR.

WILLIAM GOLDBLOOM BLOCH

> I wonder, have I lived a skeleton's life,
> As a questioner about reality,
> A countryman of all the bones of the world?
>
> —Wallace Stevens, *First Warmth* (1947)

JORGE Luis Borges was neither a mathematician nor a scientist. However, one need not have formal training or a university-granted certification to make inductive inferences about the world as does a scientist, nor to wrestle with the logic and implications of the ideas of mathematics. Borges skipped the traditional paths into the *Weltanschauung* of science: memorizing lexicons and taxonomies, formulae, and tables; mastering machine- and tool-driven skills in laboratories; and then writing tedious, careful reports of results of experiments. (I may have made this sound dull, but these are the cornerstones and hallmarks of sound science, thus the portal to the joys of discovery.) He also forewent the dreary time-worn methods of mastering mathematics: correctly implementing computing algorithms, successfully isolating the variable x, rehashing geometric proofs, and manipulating trigonometric identities that only lightly touch our shared reality. (Being able to successfully complete these often onerous tasks is a prerequisite to having the wherewithal to open the door to the abstracted worlds of higher mathematics and make one's way into a universe of wonder.) Side-stepping this necessary mundanity allowed Borges, the autodidact, to be instead moved by the bones of the ideas; to read widely and deeply, for example, on the meaning of infinity in the macroscopic and microscopic; to consider the factorial growth of combinatorial possibilities; to ponder recursion; and then, as his means of exploring the untouchable abstract, to engage his imagination in concert with his powers of analysis.

In his essays, Borges grapples as a philosopher with enigmatic abstractions, musing and testing his cascades of ideas against the thoughts that engendered them. In his short stories, he transubstantiates the ideas into mirrors, lenses, puzzle boxes, and ultimately, metaphors for his readers. *Mirrors*, of the tension between the universe of ideas and the hopelessness of our ability to grasp the deep structures of reality. *Lenses*, into the nature of divine-seeming patterns, the meanings of infinite time and infinite space, and the way that the human intellect is overwhelmed by unlimited vastness. *Puzzle boxes*, intricately crafted, beautifully fitted stories with astonishing premises and outcomes, ensnaring those parts of us that resonate with Bach's fugues, jigsaw puzzles, sudoku, crosswords, detective stories, bonsai trees, Russian lacquer iconography, Swiss watches, scrimshaw, haiku, and origami. Finally, and most importantly for scientists and mathematicians, his stories reverse the flow of *metaphor* in modern languages. Since at least the Cubists, some literary wordsmiths and artists have mined modern science and mathematics for words, phrases, and concepts to inform their work and spark their ideas. Borges's short stories, in contrast, invested with wonder and crafted with precision, provide frameworks and scaffolds for scientists and mathematicians to explain their work to others and to themselves.

I'll address each of these notions after a few explanations and caveats. First, I am a mathematician, not a scientist, and naturally I speak only for myself in these matters. One may imagine, say, a biologist whose perspective diverges from mine. More than that, my preferred areas are dynamical systems—chaos and fractals—and low-dimensional topology; an algebraist, logician, or number theorist might find different lessons in Borges's stories and essays. Also, by nature I'm more Platonist than Aristotelian: I believe that humans discover truth in the universe rather than impose a series of paradigmatic models on a barely compliant unknowable reality. Next, as I led with, and as much as we might wish it otherwise, Borges was neither a mathematician nor a scientist; he made no direct contributions to these disciplines. For example, for an investigation demonstrating the non-connection between the quantum physics ideas of the "multiverse" or "many worlds" hypothesis and "El jardín de senderos que se bifurcan" [The Garden of Forking Paths], see Rojo, *Contra Gargett* and others of a similar outlook, I am unconvinced by arguments that Borges "presciently anticipates developments in contemporary physics and scientific thought" (79). One could just as well, and perhaps with greater justification, note that the Pre-socratics or Aristotle appear to have anticipated most modern scientific thought.

Borges was an avid and eclectic reader, an autodidact who read, among other topics, about current developments in science, mathematics, philosophy, and logic. Thus I am sympathetic to Egginton's careful exposition of the convergence of Borges's thought with Kant's idealism and some notions of modern physics. Egginton notes that Borges moved toward a Kantian perspective and thus a description of consciousness and reality that doesn't disagree with certain aspects of quantum mechanics. This, to me, signals Borges's modernity without overextending the reach of his insights.[1]

Consequently, in lieu of applications of a theoretical apparatus accompanied by textual exemplars, the remainder of this essay unfolds via a series of *gedankenexperiments*, "thought experiments," an approach to science with a long history, starting with Zeno musing about races between tortoises and hares. Historians of science attribute another famous *gedankenexperiment* to Galileo; it is believed that he didn't actually drop balls from the Leaning Tower of Pisa to confirm that balls of different weights fall at the same velocity. A profound example is due to Albert Einstein, who wrote that the genesis of his theory of special relativity occurred when he was sixteen years old, when he imagined racing a beam of light and wondered what the beam would look like if he caught up to it.[2]

Philosophers of science have developed sophisticated analyses of how *gedanken-experiments* fit into the entanglements between ideas and the world and how to interpret them vis-à-vis physical experiments and derivations from axioms. For the purposes of this work, it is sufficient to see a *gedankenexperiment* as being an imagined scenario taking place in a model of the world of the senses in order to connect us more tangibly to that world.

Since I am convinced that Borges neither directly affected science or mathematics, nor that he presciently foresaw modern developments, I am taking the approach of crafting thought experiments that illuminate the effect that reading his stories has on practitioners of science, technology, engineering, and mathematics: all the STEM fields. The first step to set up the *gedankenexperiments* is to create an idealized model of such a practitioner. After that, the model is used to understand some of the ways Borges's stories affect practitioners, thence by extension the STEM fields. In what follows, I use the term "practitioner" as shorthand to denote anyone devoting a significant amount of time to STEM-based activities.

> "No precisa erigir un laberinto, cuando el universo ya lo es"
>
> [There's no need to build a labyrinth when the entire universe is one.]
> —Jorge Luis Borges, "Abenjacán el Bojarí, muerto en su laberinto"
> [Ibn Hakam al Bokhari, Murdered in His Labyrinth] (*OC* I: 604)"

The "entire universe" cannot be encompassed by human intellect. Even thin wedges or small corners of the universe are impossible to grasp; a physical or intellectual model, at least, has the possibility of comprehension. Key elements and notable traits of what is being examined are built into models so that theories may be bounced off of the models and tested against them. The argument of this chapter is that while Borges did not directly affect the trajectories of the STEM disciplines, he has had, and continues to have, a powerful and abiding effect on practitioners who read and admire his works, particularly his fictions. Although, as a mathematician, I desire an a priori proof of my claims, the nature of the argument instead demands an a posteriori scientific approach, in which, as described above, the best that may be hoped for is testing ideas on models and the plausibility granted by a measure of explanatory power.

In this enterprise of grafting a scientific process onto literary theory, in the consequent ad hoc construction of a model of a practitioner, I am painfully aware that the plural of "anecdote" is not "scientific data." Furthermore, as someone who teaches introductory statistics and advanced probability, I find it hard to believe in the results of small-sample surveys. Meaning: I have not run a survey regarding the attitudes of practitioners toward their work or themselves in reference to Borges. Even were I able to do so, it is wise to cultivate a healthy skepticism regarding surveys in general and, in most contexts, an equal skepticism toward small samples. Researchers in the social sciences publish their findings, but the past few decades have taught us that meaningful results are hard to reproduce.

So, what follows, like Borges's stories, is not science in its full statistical rigor. A good chunk of it is based on practitioners I know or have heard speak, writings I've read, and those practitioners I've learned about via the swirls and eddies of scuttle-butt washing around the internet. These massed impressions are as reliable, I think, as a randomized small-sample survey; perhaps even more so. Thus, for the upcoming *gedankenexperiments*, I have in mind practitioners who to greater or lesser extents share traits with the model practitioners described below.

Toward this end: when thinking of a practitioner, many people's minds spring to a surpassing genius. Some are easily identifiable by only one name, akin to a pop star, such as Newton, Einstein, and Feynman; Copernicus, Gödel, and Curie. Some have been overlooked or, worse, deliberately obscured during their lifetimes, before finding—cold comfort—a measure of belated historical acknowledgment. (Examples include Emmy Noether [mathematics], Rosalind Franklin [chemistry and biology], Admiral Grace Hopper [computer science], and Chien-Shiung Wu [physics].)

However, those gifted with piercing insight, an indefatigable work ethic, and a kind of historical luck that combine together to lead to the production of ideas and techniques that echo through the ages comprise a tiny smattering of all practitioners. Most must settle for making small contributions that interest only experts exploring similar arcane, complex, convoluted, and generally inaccessible constellations of ideas. William Thurston, a Fields Medal winner, likens important progress in mathematics to a low-scoring soccer game. For long periods, there are scrums of players, clouds of dust, the ball moving back-and-forth up-and-down the field, and people dashing around chaotically, like particles pinging around in random Brownian motion.[3] Yet, without that ongoing ferment of activity, it would be impossible for the ball to move forward enough for the often-startling sequence of plays, seeming inevitable in retrospect, to occur in which a player emerges from the pack and scores. (As I've grown older and the prospect of scoring a significant goal looks ever more unlikely, I've found it comforting to believe that my part of the ongoing ferment are my sporadic small breakthroughs, my minor contributions, and my helping to inspire young people to learn mathematics.)

Given that almost all practitioners are fermenters in the scrum rather than break-through goal-scorers, what are some reasonable characteristics with which to imbue a model of them? Let us build a bare-bones model by imagining what a practitioner does and what sorts of mental and emotional states are likely to follow from that work.

THE MODEL PRACTITIONER

Modern practitioners in STEM fields might be students who are embedded in labs, or immersing themselves in the ideas of their predecessors, or taking first steps toward their own small breakthroughs. They might be early-career practitioners, working at balancing a love of their discipline with the desire to live a rich and rewarding life. Research, and the hope of a breakthrough, may feed these desires, but perhaps they love teaching or want human relationships within and outside of the STEM community. Perhaps they crave the arts, the mastery of beloved hobbies, the disciplines of exercise, a giving-back to humanity, or other meaning-making activities. They might be middle- or late-career practitioners who have mastered the intricacies of their subjects but now must make choices about how to spend chunks and dollops of increasingly limited and precious time.

At all stages of their careers, practitioners confront difficulties within their fields of study. The ideas might be complex. The amount of material required to master or to gain insight into a particular issue might grow downward and backward from the point of inquiry into a geometrically increasing pyramid of sources, definitions, or prior experiments. The technical difficulty required to gain one more decimal place of accuracy and precision might require extensive and expensive retooling of hardware or, perhaps worse, a complete recoding of the software. Figuring out how to make the charge in a battery last a little longer or how to make the central processing unit of a computer run a little faster might be the outcome of months or years of work from teams of hundreds of practitioners working in concert. Regardless of which category a particular practitioner falls into, there are daily struggles en route to far-off, possibly unobtainable, goals.

Gedankenexperiment I: The Mirror

For the first experiment, picture the practitioner succumbing to an overwhelming feeling of drowning in the sheer immensity of data and information that has accumulated in the past few decades, a product of the explosive population growth of STEM practitioners and the ease of promulgating and publishing.

It might be the Sisyphean nature of pushing against the bounds of personal ignorance, striving to extend a little bit further a justifiable, reproducible new fact of our universe. It might be that, in endeavoring to follow in the footsteps of a colleague or predecessor, the material has become so subtle, so deep, and so convoluted, that the fatigue is hard to fathom, let alone live through. It might be that their thoughts and experiments, which once looked to be leading in a promising direction, either collapse into irremediable wrongness or, infuriatingly, become circular.

It is easy to fall into despair when confronted by the existential crisis of one's inadequacy in the face of ineffectual intellectual probings into understanding the universe. (These feelings are not unique to practitioners!) What is one to do? How best can a practitioner feel understood or find consolation?

The act of reading many of Borges's short stories serves as a salve by virtue of being a *Mirror*. Consider, for example, the Librarian, the ostensible narrator of "La biblioteca de Babel" [The Library of Babel], who has been contending for decades with the death of meaning of the books in the Library and the banality of the life-work of the librarians.

As with practitioners, the work of endeavoring to understand the vast collections of symbols in the books follows in the wake of intermittent, incremental progress over centuries of effort by librarians. Bit by bit, nibble by gnaw, a picture—unseen, even in contour—bursts into startling visibility after a final breakthrough using combinatorial mathematics: the Library is total, and every book is equivalent to any other book. The librarians' excitement and subsequent despair following this breakthrough are familiar to many practitioners. Understanding has been achieved! But the epiphany is, paradoxically, the opposite of what has been hoped for.

Another example: the detective or inspector Erik Lönnrot, the protagonist of "La muerte y la brújula" [Death and the Compass], believes he has found a pattern that explains a series of crimes. He is not wrong, but the pattern wasn't the one he expected, nor was the conclusion the one he hoped for. His dismay is piercing, as is his demise. Again, this is a feeling painfully familiar to many practitioners—that, when put together, what seemed to be a sought-after pattern laden with explanatory power, a set of ideas aligning perfectly, turns out to be untenable: The hypothesis is false, unsalvageable.

Another example: in "El libro de arena" [The Book of Sand], the narrator "Borges" is shown a book by a Bible salesman that appears to have infinitely many pages. The narrator trades for it, becomes obsessed with it, and it metamorphoses into a perpetual source of despondence: How can a mortal mind grapple with infinite cascades of information? Especially if the information is unorganized? Torn between madness and melancholy, at least the narrator stays sane.

A final example for this thought experiment: in "Tema del traidor y del héroe" [Theme of the Traitor and the Hero], Borges imagines a narrator whose great-grandfather was assassinated in the struggle for Irish independence. But as the narrator looks at the details, a pattern emerges, one that binds the great-grandfather as well as the great-grandson. The narrator is paralyzed by, then made melancholy by, then finds a reconciliation with his certainty that the pattern extends through history and will continue to do so.

For many of the stories, a labyrinth, literal or symbolic, befuddles or traps, or a universe of information overwhelms the agonist. Patterns emerge that are false, paradoxical, or token a vastly larger archetype, of which the initially perceived pattern is an impoverished, skewed embodiment. As with the Librarian, the characters might reach a new understanding and accept their inability to ultimately find a "true" pattern that fits the greater reality. Or, as with Lönnrot in "La muerte y la brújula," the realization of the unnatural origin of the pattern might be coincident with his untimely death. Or, as in "Tema del traidor y del héroe," it might lead to all three.

In Borgesian parlance, a mirror doubles the universe. It distorts. A mirror also allows readers to see themselves reflected in the work and empathize their way into a doubling of who they are and what they are undergoing via an osmosis into what the characters are undergoing. Practitioners may use Borges's stories as this kind of a mirror and, by being reflected, both be deeper in their experience and be taken out of it. Although twinned mirrors may reflect infinitely, the pattern may be broken—or, via a rigorous geometric reduction, the pattern converges to a point.

GEDANKENEXPERIMENT II: THE LENS

For the second thought experiment, as a specific example of the lensing effect, imagine an idealized practitioner working on building a reflexive understanding of the intricacies of Georg Cantor's theory of transfinite numbers.[4] Cantor's exploration of these "beyond the finite" numbers began with a search to find, then classify, the *transcendental numbers*, a collection of real numbers with special properties and an evocative name. It took laborious years, and, as a byproduct that turned into the main avenue of his research, Cantor founded both Set Theory and a classification system for transfinite numbers. Learning these theories means working with precise—if bloodless—definitions, and logical—if fleshless—scaffoldings. It is incumbent on the practitioner to make meaning from the definitions and their consequences. Mathematics students, speculative astrophysicists pondering infinite universes and quantum multiverses, cosmologists considering black holes, and even philosophers working on Nietzsche's Theory of Eternal Recurrence benefit from a deep understanding of Cantor's theories.

Borges had a particular interest in things growing infinitely large or becoming infinitesimally small, often while evoking or even encompassing the totality of the universe. He read and reread Bertrand Russell's use of Cantor to address Zeno's paradoxes. In stories such as "La biblioteca de Babel" and, in a different way, "El libro de arena" and "El Aleph," Borges's writings reify aspects of Cantor's theories.

In "La biblioteca de Babel," Borges has the old Librarian's plaintive, resigned note outline the combinatorial immensity of the collection of all books of a certain size and length, written in an alphabet of twenty-five symbols, including a blank space. Critically, for the idealized practitioner reading the short story, the Librarian-narrator details an incremental, steady increase in the astrophysical and philosophical understandings of the Babelian universe in which they find themselves. The plot hinges on understanding the exponential power of combinatorial selection with replacement. The twenty-five alphanumeric symbols, tiny atoms of construction, combine to form all thoughts and descriptions that are able to be inscribed in writing. The number of possibilities circumscribes a vast, yet finite, integer distinct from $\aleph_0$, Cantor's first transfinite number. At the end of the story, the Librarian raises the possibility that although the number of books is finite, the order might recur infinitely, setting up a palpable, fluid tension between an incomprehensibly large finite number and the smallest infinite number. Anyone striving to understand Cantor's theories is provided a substantive, poetic example, loaded with peripheral meanings, helping the practitioner to peer into the first level of transfinity.

In "El libro de arena," Borges takes some of these ideas from "La biblioteca de Babel," especially those encapsulated in the Librarian's final footnote, and compresses the entire Library of Babel, plus illustrations, into one handheld book. Again, Borges takes ideas in the orbit of infinity and tangibly embeds them into a plangent story. A reader encounters the notions of infinitesimally thin pages and (at least) countably infinitely many pages. Again, Borges invites readers to sharpen their focus on the interplay between the exceedingly small and the infinitely large.

How might these abstractions play out in our world and in our imaginations, limited as they are? Some critics believe that the Book of Sand is meant to signify Cantor's second transfinite number, denoted by $\aleph_1$, an infinitely larger magnitude of infinity than that indicated by $\aleph_0$, the first transfinite number. (The number $\aleph_1$ is typically understood as the magnitude of the irrational numbers, as compared with $\aleph_0$, which quantifies the rationals.) If we think of Borges's stories as microscopes, the Book of Sand turns the focusing knob another revolution, letting us look deeper into Cantor's theory.

In "El Aleph," the narrator "Borges" is led to a "Cask of Amontillado"-esque basement by Carlos Argentino Daneri, a character whom he detests and has no reason to trust. There, after lying down and looking up at the nineteenth step and the faint outlines of the closed trapdoor, the narrator "Borges" encounters the Aleph, a point-source of all conceivable visual perspectives throughout the spacetime continuum. Borges the writer has established another scenario in which a narrator confronts an overwhelming, literally unspeakable, "all-ness" of the universe, one that is concretely perceivable within an atomistic point-discontinuity. Similar to "El libro de arena," focusing attention on the Aleph zooms in on a question of practical value for a practitioner. What is the magnitude of viewpoints in the Aleph? Are there a finite number of sightlines and scenes? $\aleph_0$? $\aleph_1$?

A caution about this thought experiment. Expansively viewing an image or scenario and ruminating about it is (obviously) different from actually living in that situation. A sharply focused image of an idea is distinct from a workable understanding of it. The picture, the instance, is one example stemming from the idea. It is a lens that allows us to zoom into the idea. Playing with the ideas, toying with the ideas, working with the ideas; then, educing consequences, following false trails until the realization that they are wrong; and developing one's own examples and counterexamples that bring the limits of the idea into sharp relief: this is how an idea is learned by practitioners in STEM disciplines, not merely seen and appreciated. By analogy, enjoying listening to a piece of music is distinct from being able to play the notes correctly on an instrument. That, in turn, is different still from being able to find the music in the piece and bring it out, likely playing with others, so that a listener also hears the inherent musicality.

In many respects, it's simpler for a practitioner wishing to understand Cantor's theories to think about subsets of the real numbers and spaces of functions, but although those are sufficient objects with which to exercise the analytic imagination, they are not much for the poetic imagination to work upon. Borges's stories capture the imagination while simultaneously inspiring it. For many lovers of Borges's stories, while the lyrical precision of his prose may simply waft the reader's consciousness along, a sustained, focused attention is rewarded with insights outside the bounds of his prose.

GEDANKENEXPERIMENT III:
THE PUZZLE BOX

In some of the preceding paragraphs, I've given one practitioner's sense of what the art and *technē* of doing mathematics is like. From my forays into different sciences, I believe that there are direct analogues to the pencil or chalk work: the inferences made from data collection via observation or experiment point to the axioms of reality. Let us dig deeper into the psyche of an idealized practitioner. When not conducting experiments, running statistical tests on data, pondering consequences or origins of ideas held to be true, what sorts of things are particularly engaging?

A short answer is "puzzle boxes." I have in mind those ingeniously constructed wooden boxes which require a complex, unintuitive series of moves to open. That culmination—that grand opening—triggers a dopamine surge. For lovers of Borges's works, for readers of these essays, there is a part of our minds that lightly runs its figurative fingers over incised runes, that unties knots, that curves along with arabesques, that feels each string plucked pizzicato, then predicts the next note, thus filling in the pattern and building an internal model of what our senses are telling us. A certain kind of complexity is, paradoxically, relaxing. Soothing.

There is a particular delight in the coalescing of the unknown into either the already known, or, wonderfully, into the newly known. Finding order in chaos; hearing a musical motif in jackhammering; abruptly seeing both the forest and the trees; and, in a gestalt vision overlaying all that, adding in the hard-earned scientific knowledge of (continuing the metaphor of forest and trees) botany and agriculture, is irrefutably finding a *there* unmistakably *there*. Handling facts, theories, observations, and imaginative concepts bubbling up from within is an ongoing juggling act. Keeping aware of the different levels, being conscious of that process, then conscious of being conscious, then knowing that an unconscious flow state is perhaps even more desirable: walking a high wire over an implausible safety net.

Some such people look for these kinds of complexities outside of their practices. Borges's stories are more than a balm for this kind of mind, attracting its attention and providing material for mental play. Borges's stories comprise a self-referential, intertextual collection of fantastically detailed fractal-edged literary jigsaw pieces to turn round and round then assemble.

There isn't a logical syllogism that allows a straight line to be drawn between "enjoyment of Borgesian stories" and "enjoyment of the practices of STEM," yet there is a strong correlation. If this is plausible and a reasonable case has been built, then it follows that Borges's stories have a salutary effect on the psyche of practitioners. Both respite and inspiration, both an exhaling and an inhaling: unlike Gertrude Stein's Oakland, there is a there there. Juggling and walking high wires are mentally taxing pursuits that may eventually, with an appropriate level of mastery, become fulfilling and energizing. Even then, breaks are welcome, and, for some practitioners, addictive pursuits do not disengage, then re-engage the brain in a way that builds the positive feedback cycle required by sustained STEM-work.

> "Hablar es incurrir en tautologías... Tú, que me lees, ¿estás seguro de entender mi lenguaje?"
>
> [To speak is to fall into tautologies. . . . You who read me, are you sure you understand my language?]
> —Jorge Luis Borges, "La biblioteca de Babel" (*OC* I: 470)

The first three *gedankenexperiments* are intended to explicate broad aspects of the relationship between Borges's stories and an idealized practitioner's mind, such as I understand that interaction in myself and as I've learned about that relationship from many conversations with the scientists, engineers, and mathematicians over four decades. A critic might point out that my interlocutors constitute the polar opposite of a random and independent sample, and I concede the point. My rejoinder is that the outcome of this exercise is not finding, say, confidence intervals for population proportions of STEM practitioners nor is it to lay an unassailable foundation of axioms upon which to build a theory of the interactions of Borges's stories with readers. Professionally, I'm used to proving things and explaining my perspectives on universal, eternal mathematical truths to my colleagues (occasionally) and my students (daily). It comes hard to me instead to argue persuasively for a perspective that isn't precisely derivable.

By contrast, the final *gedankenexperiment* can be put on a firmer footing. Rather than seeking to grab hold of subjective experiences occurring while reading the work of Borges, a determined team of researchers could count factually the number of times practitioners cite Borges in their papers, if they make use of his imagery in explaining their work. The team might also engage practitioners known to have read Borges in discussions of their specialties and areas of research and quantify how often the practitioners used one of his stories in explaining the ideas of their research. In contrast to the prior thought experiments, this last one is functionally falsifiable, hence satisfying Karl Popper's basic scientific criterion for hypotheses.[5]

GEDANKENEXPERIMENT IV: THE METAPHOR

For the final thought experiment, let us suppose the model practitioner is wishing to describe their work or an aspect of their work to a non-practitioner or a non-specialist. It's a cliché in movies and other media to have a brilliant practitioner fail at explaining a complex idea by spouting incoherent streams of technobabble. The "joke" often lands— painfully. It's hard to explain any set of delicate, complex ideas in terms that don't devolve to the field's specialized argot.

One way forward is using the poetic, rhetorical devices of evocative imagery, simile, and metaphor. Borges's stories are a rich lode to mine of deep ideas embedded in memorable stories. In classrooms, at cocktail parties, in essays for general readers, it is a wonderful tool to deploy: the Borges reference.

For example, in *Body of Secrets*, although not precisely a practitioner, the journalist James Bamford uses "La biblioteca de Babel" as a metaphor to describe the National Security Agency of the United States:

> But in 2001, the light of the outside world was pushed even further away as construction continued on one more high fence stretching for miles around the entire city. By then Crypto City had become an avatar of Jorge Luis Borges' "Library of Babel," a place where the collection of information is both infinite and monstrous, where all the world's knowledge is stored, but every word is maddeningly scrambled in an

unbreakable code. In this "labyrinth of letters," Borges wrote, "there are leagues of sense cacophonies, verbal jumbles and incoherences." (527)

More generally, since Borges instantiated deep philosophic, mathematical, and scientific ideas in his work, practitioners may correspondingly find an abundance of Borgesian references to use to convey the bones of their work.

Here follows a small, necessarily incomplete, biased by my expertise list of correspondences or correlations between Borges's stories and practitioners' ideas.
For mathematics:

- "La biblioteca de Babel" is a jumping-off point for (at the very least) combinatorics and topology.
- "El libro de arena" opens a set of paths into discussions of Set Theory, as well as the relationship between the continuum and the real numbers.
- "La muerte y la brújula" invokes at the end one of Zeno's paradoxes of motion and thus also the notions of infinite sums.
- "El Aleph" opens a door to Cantor's theory of transfinite numbers and Differentiable Manifold Theory.
- "El disco" [The Disk] bridges a gap between Gottfried Leibniz's and Abraham Robinson's senses of infinitesimals and geometry.
- "Del rigor en la ciencia" [On Exactitude in Science] enhances explanations of injective functions and Brouwer's Fixed Point Theorem.
- "La lotería en Babilonia" [The Lottery in Babylon] may be seen as encoding ideas from dynamical systems or game theoretic concepts of multiplayer games evolving over time.

For computer science:

- "Las ruinas circulares" [The Circular Ruins] is a poignant model of recursion.
- "Funes el memorioso" [Funes the Memorious] illustrates difficulties in naming and retention of data.

For physics:

- "El jardín de senderos que se bifurcan" is a parsimonious, yet poetically rich, way to visualize the hypothetical incessant quantum forkings of the multiverse.

The class of metaphors to mine for communication are less concrete, but they flesh out the pattern under excavation. Practitioners may follow diverse paths toward conclusions, naming ideas, categorizing and cataloguing effects, and making hypotheses and conjectures. The form of these explorations, often guided by intuition built on experience and combined with the sensing of faint signals hiding in noisy data, can be hard to explain to a "civilian"—a non-practitioner.

Many of Borges's stories have, at their core, a *missing* core whose effects are exerted gravitationally on the characters and their milieus, a kind of a space-time curvature that the protagonists seek via tracing influences from a quiet susurration or small vibration to a larger distortion of the story's reality. A few examples of this phenomenon found in *Ficciones* are in the stories "Tlön, Uqbar, Orbis Tertius"; "El acercamiento a Almotásim" [The Approach to Al-Mu'tasim]; "Pierre Menard, autor del Quijote" [Pierre Menard, Author of the *Quixote*]; and, "Examen de la obra de Herbert Quain" [An Examination of the Work of Herbert Quain]. Perhaps most of Borges's stories have an explicit search for a missing center or centrality. (These are complemented by those in which the hapless protagonist wishes the inverse: to forget a truth or a focal point, as exemplified in the stories "El libro de arena," "El Zahir," "El Aleph," and "El disco.")

Two brief speculations end this section. First, aside from their content, I offer a structural reason why Borges's stories are amenable to being used as metaphors by practitioners and others. While some of the stories explicitly are parables or extended metaphors, on a sentence-by-sentence basis Borges deploys few similes or metaphors. His stories often read as learned essays or summaries of journalistic fact-finding. That they encroach, with a stealthy inevitability, upon the miraculous without resorting to the use of poetic devices strikes me as a deliberate strategy on Borges's part. (I reread *Ficciones* [*Fictions*] with this question in mind. My inexpert tally had it that several stories used five such poetic devices, a few used three or four, some used one or two, and for three of them, I counted none.) Second, to drift further from solid facts: perhaps using parts of a metaphor-laden tale as a metaphor would dilute the impact. The doubling property of a metaphor using another metaphor might shuttle meaning and impact away from the ideas a practitioner—or really, anyone—wished to impart.

AFTER THE *GEDANKENEXPERIMENT*: WHAT MAY BE INFERRED?

For practitioners, the act of reading Borges's stories may induce a number of powerful effects. The model has built the case that the stories, via an empathic identification, act as a balm for practitioners feeling overwhelmed or in despair. Some of the stories also serve as a lens, allowing practitioners to, via Borges's own explorations, look deeper into the ideas and substructures of their fields of inquiry. For all readers inclined to analytic thought work, the stories may function as involuted puzzle boxes, ornate and tactile. The baroque figurations engender relaxation by giving the mind a work of art, rather than the overwhelming workings of the universe, to focus on. Finally, many of the stories, created by Borges as he played with the STEM ideas of his time, may be used by practitioners to explain aspects of their work, rich metaphors to express substantive—yet chilly—ideas.

Furthermore, this work has been a deliberate attempt to demonstrate how practitioners approach problems or think their ways into theories. (Again, this kind of process is not unique to practitioners!) I have not stated the ideas of this piece as a hypothesis to test; instead, with the active help of you, the reader, a plausible model was constructed. Together, based on our readings of Borges's stories and our intuitive senses of the minds, the routines, and the psychologies of practitioners, we imagined the stories' effects on practitioners. By participating in the process, we gained insight and, were we to push further, might generate hypotheses to rigorously support or disprove.

Finally, although practitioners are ably blazing new trails into the unknown, there are forces, inspired perhaps by cynicism or a different kind of fervor, that seek to undermine knowledge-motivated projects. These forces seem to argue implicitly or explicitly for more and better technology but less knowledge and understanding—a position antithetical to most practitioners. It is as if a dark, acidic cloud is corroding a pillar upholding one of the grand projects of humanity.

By contrast, along with his manifold other interests, Borges was entranced by mathematics, logic, thinking, philosophy, and science. As one of my colleagues in the humanities reminded me, Borges had an affinity for the purity of ideas, for the range and power of hypotheses, and for the capture and then crystallization of faint ideas into something so much more than their surface senses suggest. A practitioner reading Borges ineluctably feels the finding of a kindred spirit: someone who appreciates science, logic, thinking, and mathematics; someone who is using these ideas to delineate and demarcate the amorphous boundaries of humanity's questing consciousness. It is easy to take delight in that. Many nights, it is enough to take delight in that.

NOTES

1. See Egginton, and also chapter 9 in Bloch for a discussion on books Borges was known to have read.
2. See Einstein for the original quote and Norton for a thorough analysis of its implications.
3. See Thurston for the details of the metaphor.
4. See Cantor for the mathematical details.
5. See Popper.

WORKS CITED

Bamford, James. *Body of Secrets: Anatomy of the Ultra-Secret National Security Agency*. Anchor Books, 2002.

Bloch, William Goldbloom. *The Unimaginable Mathematics of Jorge Luis Borges' Library of Babel*. Oxford University Press, 2008.

Borges, Jorge Luis. *The Aleph and Other Stories, 1933–1969*, edited by Norman Thomas di Giovanni. Dutton, 1978.

Borges, Jorge Luis. *The Book of Sand*, translated by Norman Thomas di Giovanni. Dutton, 1977.

Borges, Jorge Luis. *Collected Fictions*, translated by Andrew Hurley. Penguin Classics, 1999.

Borges, Jorge Luis. *Ficciones*, edited by Anthony Kerrigan. Grove Press, 1962.

Borges, Jorge Luis. *Obras completas*. 4 vols. Emecé, 1996.

Cantor, Georg. *Contributions to the Founding of the Theory of Transfinite Numbers*, translated by Philip Jourdain. Dover Publications, 1955.

Egginton, William. "Three Versions of Divisibility: Borges, Kant, and the Quantum." *Thinking with Borges*. Edited by William Egginton and David Johnson. The Davies Group, 2009, pp. 49–68.

Einstein, Albert. *Autobiographical Notes*, reprinted by LaSalle and Chicago. Open Court, 1979.

Gargett, Adrian. "Symmetry of Death." *Variaciones Borges*, vol. 13, 2002, pp. 79–97.

Norton, John. "Chasing the Light: Einstein's Most Famous Thought Experiment." *Thought Experiments in Philosophy, Science, and the Arts*. Edited by Mélanie Frappier et al. Routledge, 2013, pp. 123–40.

Popper, Karl. *The Logic of Scientific Discovery*. Routledge, 2002.

Rojo, Alberto. "The Garden of the Forking Worlds: Borges and Quantum Mechanics." *Oakland University Journal*, vol. 9, 2005, pp. 69–78.

Stevens, Wallace. *The Palm at the End of the Mind: Selected Poems and a Play*. Vintage Books, 1990.

Thurston, William. "On Proof and Progress in Mathematics." *Bulletin of the American Mathematical Society*, vol. 30, no. 2, 1994, pp. 161–77.

CHAPTER 35

FAITHFULNESS AND BETRAYAL

Community, Legitimacy, and Identity in Stories by Jorge Luis Borges

LEONARDO PITLEVNIK

THE MEANING OF BETRAYAL

IN several of his fictions, Borges presents plots of betrayal, where victims become indistinguishable from victimizers, where the damage caused by betrayal affects the traitor as much or more than the person betrayed. Disloyalty is reflected upon from a variety of perspectives. Based on the way betrayal is narrated in each story, it can be difficult to escape the pull of a faithless act that, simultaneously, can constitute a redemptive action. In this chapter, I analyze the representation of betrayal in several Borges texts.[1] I expound upon the different ways in which treason is perceived; its relationship to the community that is allegedly injured by betrayal; and the ways in which the state regulates, sanctions, or even rewards the act of informing on members of one's community. I begin with the biblical figure Judas, who, in the West, can be considered the traitor par excellence and to whom Borges dedicated a famous story. From there I turn to others of his texts in which the figure of the traitor occupies a central space and becomes an axis for reflecting on identity and belonging. Betrayal is projected, at least as Borges sees it, onto his own family tree. I then mention other ways in which betrayal appears in Borges's writings about translation and about the impact of tradition upon literary creation. In both cases, we can appreciate the ambivalent reconsideration of a presumably detestable act, which comes to define a deeper kind of fidelity—betrayals which, burdened under the negative connotations of the term, are, in truth, a priceless commitment to one's own identity.

From there, I will show how the questions raised in reading these texts become amplified when contextualized within various communities. I will try to expound, from outside Borges's fictions—though in constant reference to them—upon the ways in which we try to give meaning to the betrayal of a group, a community, or an individual by someone who always belonged: Which loyalties and betrayals do we nurture and which do we punish? What does the indefinite and porous nature of the term "traitor" imply when it comes to making meaning, offering a reward, or sentencing punishment? I will then deal with loyalty as a value, even when it conflicts with legality. Based on scenes from the stories presented here, I will demonstrate how certain meanings are replicated when betrayal becomes an instrument of the state when it believes itself to be in danger. This chapter is, in short, an inquiry about the meaning we assign to loyalty and betrayal, the way it shows up in Borges's stories, and the ambivalence it also reveals within the communities in which we live.

Versions of Judas

One of the foundational stories of Western culture occurs during Passover, when Jesus is betrayed by Judas. The Gospels provide no reason for his betrayal, except for John, who suggests that Satan must have taken hold of the apostle's body. As a result of this story, Judas has become Western culture's purest representative of betrayal. In fact, in Spanish, the word "*judas*" is synonymous with "traitor." With the exception of a brief period among Cainite Gnostics during the second century CE, the figure of Judas—from antiquity to the seventeenth century—embodied the antithesis of all things good; the ugliness, the infamy of his betrayal became one of the main sources from which anti-Semitism drew its wrath (Burnet 119, 214). Along with Brutus and Cassius, he is deemed one of the eternal inhabitants of the ninth circle of hell.

But with the Enlightenment (and even earlier, with certain debates held during the Reformation), the discourse surrounding Judas began to change (Burnet 215). Although the horrific image of the traitor prevailed, religious interpreters sought to find explanations, to imagine him in his humanity. They speculated that his betrayal may have been motivated by his desire to accelerate the world's salvation. Perhaps, inspired by Passover, which commemorates the end of Jewish subjugation and slavery to the Egyptians, he sought to ignite a revolution against the Roman occupation (Ehrmann 164). Borges, in "Tres versiones de Judas" [Three Versions of Judas], went even further. Elaborated by fictionalized theologian Nils Runeberg, the first version of Judas that Borges discusses interprets the apostle's betrayal to be a sacrifice. In acknowledgment of the divine character of his master, Judas tried to imitate Jesus's sacrifice on an earthly scale: if God became man, Judas would reflect this degradation by sinking to infamy. According to the second version, Judas is an ascetic who, by lowering himself to betraying Jesus, renounces all happiness. The third version holds that, for the redemption of humankind, God had to become flesh in the form of the lowest possible being, one who would be hated for all of eternity. Judas is, then, the true son of God (*OC* I: 514–17).

Even without the assumption of this divine role, in a scene that has been set for the crucifixion (as Borges had already described in "El *Biathanathos*" [*Biathanathos*]), Judas is—unquestionably—a central player in creating that outcome. As Borges writes, "antes que Adán fuera formado del polvo de la tierra, antes que el firmamento separara las aguas de las aguas, el Padre ya sabía que el Hijo había de morir en la cruz y, para teatro de esa muerte futura, creó la tierra y los cielos" [before Adam was formed from the dust of the earth, before the firmament separated the waters from the waters, the Father knew that the Son was to die on the cross and, as the theater of this future death, created the heavens and the earth] (*OC* II: 84; *SNF* 335). One of the central scenes of that theater was the kiss and the handover of Jesus to Roman authorities.

The other apostles also understand they may be instruments of a plan that exceeds them because, when Jesus announces the coming betrayal, they accept that any of them could be the traitor. Each one asks, "Surely not I, Lord?" as if they believe a role could have been assigned to them independently of what decisions they may make personally (*New Oxford Annotated Bible*, Matthew 26:22). In Luke, we read that "Then they began to ask one another which one of them it could be who would do this" (*New Oxford Annotated Bible*, Luke 22:23). Then, after Jesus tells Judas "Do quickly what you are going to do" and the apostle leaves, Christ exclaims "Now the Son of Man has been glorified, and God has been glorified in him" (*New Oxford Annotated Bible*, John 13:27 and 13:31). It is not a bitter thought, then, that glory appears when betrayal begins. If the Son of God must die because it has been so decreed, "Judas's act, both impossible and sacrilegious, is revealed to be necessary and desired by God" (Burnet 24).

MORE BETRAYALS IN BORGES'S STORIES

Other texts by Borges again focus on betrayal, even expressly or tacitly taking the figure of Judas as a model or reference. In stories such as "Tema del traidor y del héroe" [The Theme of the Traitor and the Hero] or "El indigno" [The Unworthy], betrayal is inscribed in the very title. Disloyalty is the axis of "La forma de la espada" [The Shape of the Sword], "Historia del guerrero y de la cautiva" [Story of the Warrior and the Captive Maiden], and "Biografía de Tadeo Isidoro Cruz" [A Biography of Tadeo Isidoro Cruz (1829–1874)] among several variations on betrayals, conspiracies, and deaths that can be found in others of his texts.[2]

Perhaps Borges's 1935 review and commentary in the magazine *Sur* of John Ford's film, *The Informer,* can be considered an antecedent of these stories (*Borges en* Sur, 179–81). It is hard to imagine this film did not radiate into "Tema del traidor y del héroe" and "La forma de la espada." Set in Ireland, in 1922, the film revolves around former Irish Republican Army (IRA) member Nolan's betrayal of his benefactor, Frankie, a leader in the revolutionary movement against English occupation. Nolan, like Judas, goes to the police to inform them of Frankie's whereabouts in exchange for a reward he then squanders that same night. With his information, the police find and kill the revolutionary leader. Nolan's betrayal is later revealed in a trial that the IRA members conduct clandestinely in a Dublin basement cellar; the verdict is his death sentence. In "Tema del traidor y del héroe," a traitor, Fergus Kilpatrick, is discovered by a character named, no less, Nolan. It takes place in Ireland and a revolutionary trial is held to establish Kilpatrick's guilt and condemn him to death. "La forma de la espada," like the story in the film, takes place in 1922, and it, too, tells the story of a person who betrays the Irish revolutionary who saved him and who, because of this betrayal, ends up being executed by English soldiers.

The figure of Judas clearly seeps into these accounts. In "La forma de la espada," we read that "no es injusto que una desobediencia en un jardín contamine al género humano" [it is not unfair that a single act of disobedience in a garden should contaminate all humanity] (*OC* I: 493; *CF* 141), in reference to the garden of Gethsemane (McGrady 144–45). The account refers directly to the Gospels by subsequently asserting that "por eso no es injusto que la crucifixión de un solo judío baste para salvarlo [al ser humano]" [that is why it is not unfair that a single Jew's crucifixion should be enough to save it] (*OC* I: 493; *CF* 141). Moon, the character who informs on his protector, "cobró los dineros de judas y huyó al Brasil" [was paid his Judas silver and he ran off to Brazil] (*OC* I: 494; *CF* 142). With the bounty, he must have bought the ranch (*campo*) called "La Colorada," likely another biblical reference, since, in the Book of Acts, Judas is said to have acquired the "Campo de sangre" [Field of Blood] with the money obtained by his betrayal (*New Oxford Annotated Bible*, Acts 1:19). In "Tema del traidor y del héroe," as in the version of Judas, both nouns combine within a single character who is both traitor and hero.

In "El indigno," another of Borges's fictions of betrayal, the narrator claims to remember the story of an old bookseller, Santiago Fischbein, who told him that, when he was still a boy, he had betrayed the leader of a gang of criminals who had previously placed their trust in him. Francisco Ferrari is the name of the man who is subsequently murdered by the police and portrayed in the newspapers. Fischbein's act made the dead man the hero he had never been. The character mirrors Judas in that he is a Jew who betrays his leader on a Friday. The name of the story corresponds to the adjective Borges assigns to the apostle in "Tres versiones de Judas," who thought himself unworthy of goodness. Fischbein betrays a "guapo" god, as Fishburn calls him, also relating the bookseller to Judas (404–05).[3] As in the Gospels, "El indigno" also fails to provide explanations for the Judas figure's betrayal.[4] And, although Ferrari's death was a possible outcome, it is not entirely clear that the character was seeking this when he informed on him to the police—which is consistent with certain readings of the gospel as to whether Judas was aware of what his act would bring about.[5]

The actions of Moon, Kilpatrick, and Fischbein, in the three stories just mentioned, regardless of what effect repentance, time, or amends might later have, are acts of betrayal that harm those who trusted them. Sometimes the person betrayed represents the homeland, a revolutionary movement, or a band of thieves. In other stories, however, breaking an existing commitment and moving to the enemy's side are not portrayed negatively, as can be seen in "Historia del guerrero y de la cautiva" and "Biografía de Tadeo Isidoro Cruz." In both, betrayal represents a commitment more integral and more profound than the consciousness of duty previously held, which the protagonists abandon. There is no repentance or attempt at amends, but strength in standing in and with one's decision. To think of it in a logic of faithfulness and betrayal, the characters are faithful to themselves. Betrayal, conversely, would be to keep abiding by a loyalty lacking content, a loyalty to a mere empty shell.

"Historia del guerrero y de la cautiva" describes the warrior Droctulft's decision to go over to the side of Ravenna, the city he and his fellow Lombards have under siege. The text notes that "no fue un traidor (los traidores no suelen inspirar epitafios piadosos); fue un iluminado, un converso" [Droctulft was not a traitor; traitors seldom inspire reverential epitaphs. He was an illuminatus, a convert] (*OC* I: 558; *CF* 209). In the second story, when Cruz, a troop commander, abandons his men and turns on them, Borges describes it as the moment when a man "sabe para siempre quién es" [knows forever who he is] (*OC* I: 562; *CF* 213) or, in the sense of the story's epigraph, where he discovers his original face.[6] His act is the abandonment of an identity that had been imposed on him. If there has been a betrayal, it came before, in believing oneself united to Lombard ideals or to those of a corrupt justice system persecuting the gaucho.

Of course, in Droctulft's case, the Lombards, at least initially, "culparon al tránsfuga" [heaped blame upon the turncoat] (*OC* I: 558; *CF* 209).[7] In the case of Cruz, other critics have reviled the act that Borges finds sincere. For Ezequiel Martínez Estrada, for example, Cruz is simply a traitor waiting to see which way the wind blows before switching sides, a despicable man who abandons his subordinates in favor of the enemy. For him, Cruz "carece de conciencia moral" [lacks moral conscience], and his character is made tragic, above all, because he pulls Martín Fierro down with him (Martinez Estrada 85–90). For Martínez Estrada, the commitment to the troop summoned to kill Fierro is more binding than the commitment arising from Cruz recognizing in Martín Fierro an equal. In these terms, if Cruz had acted as Sergeant Chirino did with Moreira, there would have been no "part two" to the Argentine epic poem, *Martín Fierro*.[8]

A FAMILY LEGACY

In Borges, the game of loyalties and disloyalties seems to have been part of a legacy issuing from one of his grandfathers to whom he dedicated five poems and made several references in an assortment of texts. Killed in the battle of La Verde, during the Mitre uprising against Avellaneda in 1874, Colonel Francisco Borges found himself divided between his loyalty to the outgoing president of the republic, as a soldier in the army, and his personal adherence to Mitre, who took up arms against the elected government. Once the outgoing president left the presidency, he separated from his troops and participated in the uprising against the new president, Nicolás Avellaneda, whose electoral win he believed to be fraudulent. This dubious timing, for novelist Eduardo Gutiérrez, who was critical of the colonel, made those on Mitre's side see him as a traitor (36). Yet Colonel Borges was likewise viewed with suspicion by the opposing forces and by the newspapers of the time (Donato 305).[9] For the colonel, as a military man, had executed others for that very betrayal of the outgoing president.[10] In other words, remaining faithful to his word earned Francisco Borges the nickname of traitor. This small personal tragedy of conflicting loyalties comes to a close when Colonel Borges, with the battle almost over, galloped to find the bullets that ended his life.[11] Borges's great-grandfather, Isidoro Suárez, was also accused of conspiring against his commander, Simón Bolívar, and was consequently expelled from Peru (Balderston, "Digamos Irlanda" 106). Borges also dedicates a poem to him and refers to him in several of his prose pieces.

As his own inheritance, Borges bears both ancestors' names.[12] To close the family saga, in another text, he refers to himself as an intellectual traitor when, in "Las Kenningar" [The Kenning], he mentions Snorri Sturluson, a medieval Icelandic poet, a traitor to the Icelanders and to the Norwegians to whom he had promised to hand over Icelandic terrain. Borges writes that Sturluson was, perhaps "un hombre desgarrado hasta el escándalo por sucesivas y contrarias lealtades" [a man torn up by the scandal of successive and opposing loyalties], a description that seems to fit with that of his grandfather (*OC* I: 371, n. 1). Then, in a footnote to the essay, he adds, "Dura palabra es traidor.... En el orden intelectual, sé de dos ejemplos: el de Francisco Luis Bernárdez, el mío" [Traitor is a harsh word.... In the intellectual realm, I know of two examples: that of Francisco Luis Bernárdez and my own] (*OC* I: 371, n. 1). He is alluding to his and Bernárdez's abandonment of the Ultraist poetic movement, whose manifesto Borges had signed a few years before. He thus compares himself to that poet who had offered his people to the enemy, although the Argentine's case is somewhat less momentous for having merely left behind a poetic movement.

In addition to his grandfather's era, in the second half of the nineteenth century, it was common for political adversaries to label one another "traitors." Many of the names gracing Argentine cities and street signs belong to founding politicians who either called their political opponents traitors or were called so in turn. One need merely read the controversies in which Domingo Faustino Sarmiento, Juan Bautista Alberdi, Bartolomé Mitre, or José Hernández were involved. Apparently, during Colonel Francisco Borges's era, "traitor" was an aspersion used readily in the face of any political disagreement.

Several decades later, in the years in which his grandson wrote and published an important part of his work, accusations of betrayal were frequently lobbed across a political field to which Borges was no stranger. Perón and his wife, Eva, often used the term in their speeches.[13] Words such as "*cipayo*" or "*vendepatria*" were used interchangeably with the word "traitor."[14] Law 13985, passed in 1950, defined as treason and punished with imprisonment anyone who by any means "deprima el espíritu público causando un daño a la Nación" [depresses the public spirit causing harm to the Nation].[15]

Borges presents his famous lecture "El escritor argentino y la tradición" [The Argentine Writer and Tradition] in this context. Published as an essay soon thereafter, the text can be conceived as a response to nationalist writers and to a governmental discourse that made *argentinidad* (Argentineness) a supreme value (Balderston, *El método* 118–30). This rhetoric made it very easy to plaster anyone who failed to uphold specific notions about national interest with the labels of foreignizer, *cipayo*, or traitor. A possible reading of this text, whose depth elevates it above the discussion of the moment, could be as a plea for self-defense, an explanation of why writing as he did was not traitorous.[16]

As for the political context, after the abrupt end of the Peronist period, the appellation changes sides. In 1958, after what was called the "Revolución libertadora" [Liberating Revolution], which Borges enthusiastically supported, a broad, general amnesty was issued. But the Court of Justice denied Perón exoneration because it was unthinkable to pardon someone accused of betraying the nation.[17] The justice that Perón would deny his enemies years later in his brief return to power thus mirrored the amnesty that the courts had denied him.[18] In Bioy's diary, *Borges*, entries compiled during those years reveal Borges's own uses of the term "traitor," some of which refer to political figures of the time (421, 851, 917).[19]

Betrayal or Perdition

When writing about translation, Borges uses the same criteria he applies to the Lombard warrior Droctulft or to Sergeant Cruz. To be unfaithful to the source text is an act of conscience, a valuable addition. Over the years, it is along these lines he interrogated the *traduttore-traditore* binary. For Borges, the assertion that translation betrays the original is mere superstition. To the contrary, it is by no means traitorous to make another's text one's own and thereby make it say other, more interesting things than does the original (Borges, "Word-Music and Translation" 43–76). An original can even be unfaithful to its translation.[20]

The same frame for analysis can be observed with respect to issues writers encounter in the face of tradition. Believing in the enduring presence of an identity forged by our predecessors that can be maintained through rites and symbols is often accompanied by the idea that one who turns their back on tradition betrays their community, devaluing and endangering this link between past and present.[21] Just as a translation is not unfaithful to an original text when embellishing or improving it, neither should we consider it a betrayal to create something new from tradition. The only thing that can be done with a received legacy, Borges says, is to modify it; fidelity, ultimately, is being faithful to oneself. One either sustains a tradition because it is part of who one is and thus impossible to uninhabit, or one leaves it behind because it no longer expresses what it once did for others.[22] To reject tradition purely to denigrate it is as spurious as holding fast to it out of some pointless overestimation of inertia.

The concept of two lineages in conflict—which, after Piglia's seminal article, "Ideología y ficción en Borges" (1979), became a central approach to interpreting Borges's work—long contained the idea of a bond, which, by virtue of the tension within it, enacts a writer's belonging to tradition. If origins are in conflict, it is because they present inheriting writers with different paths. It is the inheritors of tradition who can retrace these paths to suit their own destinations, who, from one or more existing traditions, can create their own. Those writers, however, who are unable to detach themselves or decide to sink under that sense of belonging to the past, are lost. This idea can also be traced in some of Borges's stories; in "Guayaquil," for example, the protagonist's ancestry prevents him from traveling in search of Bolívar's documents that he so desires to have in his hands (*OC* II: 438–43). The translator who improves does not betray, nor does the artist or writer who descends from a given tradition and then renews it.

WHEREFORE BETRAYAL?

Judas, or Nolan in the movie *The Informer*, receives cash in exchange for the information provided. Yet that money seems to have been an excuse, a false pretense. Regarding this aspect of the film, Borges writes: "Admiro la escena del delator que despilfarra sus treinta dineros por la triple necesidad de aturdirse, de sobornar a los terribles amigos que son tal vez sus jueces y que serán al fin sus verdugos, y de verse libre de esos billetes que lo están infamando" [I appreciated the scene where the informer wastes his thirty coins on the triple need to numb himself, to bribe those terrible friends who may likely be his judges and will, in the end, be his executioners, and to simply be rid of cash that indicts him] (*Borges en* Sur 180). According to one version of the Gospel, the repentant Judas returned the thirty coins, throwing them into the Sanctuary (Matthew 27:3). The only thing the traitors do with the money they gain by their betrayal is part with it. In cases like these, it is worth asking why we are so prone to say that the traitors sold their friends out for money, when the facts clearly seem to suggest otherwise.[23]

As for the acts that constitute betrayal, we can differentiate between those that involve abandoning one's previous beliefs and those actions that also entail intentional harm of those previously considered "one's own." The latter form of betrayal can have several variants: going over to the enemy's side or providing the enemy useful information are just two. Actions that involve abandoning the people or ideals to which one previously belonged or adhered to can only be considered betrayal when viewed through the expectations of others. Yet a mere departure, however innocuous it may seem, can be experienced as treachery by the group. The more intense a bond, particularly if a group understands its existence to be contingent upon it, the more its abandonment is understood as an attack. Refusal is resignified as treason. A closed community, or one that perceives itself in danger, tends to view those who abandon it as traitors.[24]

In "La forma de la espada," Borges broadens the scope of betrayal to something more than informing for, handing someone over to, or going over oneself to the enemy: disobedience itself becomes part of the definition.[25] In fact, the parallel that "Historia del guerrero y de la cautiva" draws between Droctulft and the captive Englishwoman reveals the Lombard fighting against those he used to command, while the captive seems only to reiterate it, not so much in attacking those who used to be "her own," but in refusing to continue recognizing herself in them. Betrayal is not only acting with harmful intent; it is also turning one's back, despising, denying.[26]

Modernity seems to have reduced the violence of our reactions to such acts. Abundant literature warning against betrayal of homeland or king, laws imposing penances designed to cause enormous suffering, public executions and humiliating punishments that extended even to a traitor's children have ceased to be common in much of the West. Political discussions, at least for the time being, have abandoned the constant rhetoric of treason to defame one's opponent. Yet this does not prevent such language from reappearing when a community or group feels threatened. Perceiving a risk, imagined or real, can turn the fear of being betrayed into existential panic, becoming enmeshed with fears for the very survival of the community (Margalit 67). The label of "traitor" can be overused to the point of being emptied of all content. This consequence, more intentionally than accidentally, allows a dissident to be branded as such regardless of what they actually do (Margalit 178–79). If we consider the punishment that awaits traitors, this accusation facilitates their elimination. It is not the traitor who puts the community at risk, but the community that needs the traitor to ensure loyalty within the group. The traitor, then, is not a figure who comes on the scene to weaken the state, but a creation by the state itself, with the purpose or the fantasy of strengthening it. In terms of criminal prosecution, as will be seen ahead, it is striking that the cultivation of the paid informant has a privileged place, precisely in those cases of crimes which are imagined to place the entire community in danger—those against which entire societies tend to consider themselves at war: the war on drugs, the war on terror, the relentless fight against alleged organized crime.

INFORMANTS, LEGALITY, AND CRIME

Judas takes action so that the Roman state will carry out a trial, pass sentence, and condemn a man who, according to the rules of occupation, is considered guilty. Seen from this perspective, Judas, Fischbein, Moon, and Kilpatrick were informers working on behalf of the state (Roman, Argentine, British). In the case of "El indigno," even though the police agent obtains useful information, his reaction upon taking Fischbein's statement is one of contempt. After asking Fischbein if he thinks he is a good citizen, he advises the young man to be careful. "Vos sabés lo que les espera a los batintines" [You know what happens to squealers] (*OC* II: 408; *CF* 356) an officer tells him.[27] In a similar vein, it has been noted that, in Sicily, police officers, criminals, and everyday inhabitants used to consider reporting crime to the authorities to be a morally dubious act (Rakopoulos 170). Margalit notes that those who work as informants for an occupying force are equally despised by those with whom they collaborate (198). Contempt is what Moon demands from whomever hears his story of betrayal. "La traición aplace, mas no el que la hace" [betrayal gives an upper hand, but never to the traitorous man] as an old popular saying goes.

The Argentine Constitution envisages treason to the homeland as the act of those who take up arms against it or join the nation's enemies by giving them aid and assistance

(Constitution, Arts. 29 and 119). It extends the concept to those who grant the entirety of public power to a single person, subjecting the lives and rights of others to that person's will. It equates this domestic act to collaborating with the enemy. Some provincial constitutions, more in tune with modernity, have reformulated the bases for treason; Córdoba, for example, qualifies those who rise up against it as "infames traidores al orden constitucional" [infamous traitors to the constitutional order] (Provincial Constitution, Art. 17). Although more reasonable (and perhaps, precisely for this reason), the rule loses some of its epic diatribe. The term "patria" has a much bloodier history than does "constitutional order," at least rhetorically.

In other venues, the laws in Argentina uphold the value of loyalty even when it does not expressly go hand in hand with legality. Thus, for example, cover-ups are not punishable when they are owed to certain family or emotional ties. A person who helps a friend to evade justice or to hide the evidence of a crime is not punishable by law. Indeed, several procedural codes prohibit, with few exceptions, reporting on or testifying against close relatives, while certain treacherous crimes are considered more serious. A type of premeditated homicide, for example, is understood to be murder by betrayal, once punishable by the death penalty and today punished with life imprisonment.

If, as mentioned earlier, we extend the concept of treason to disobedience, the meaning expands to any breach of a pact, even the mythical social contract. Thus, breaking a rule that is understood to be a basic norm of coexistence becomes treason to the extent that, as is often mentioned in criminal law, it implies a failure to meet the expectations that had been legitimately placed on the person who has harmed another or the community. Some of the most important theoretical currents in criminal law that emerged at the end of the past century rely on the concept of fidelity to the law, or lack thereof, to justify punishment (Jakobs 81). We punish those who are not faithful to the law, or, in other words, those who betray it.

Incentivized Informers

The state, in its turn, does promote certain betrayals when they are useful to it. Although it is a tactic with a long history, reliance on incentivized informers is used above all to prosecute crimes in which the state, as noted earlier, sees its own functioning as compromised and believes itself incapable of dealing with organizations that are sophisticated, strongly tied within the social fabric, or excessively violent (Ferrajoli 682). Such is the case with the mafia, drug trafficking, or terrorism. There is a wide array of incentives offered to informants: sentence reduction, new addresses, new identities, special protection, or payment. The names given to those who provide information under these conditions have also been varied: witness for the crown, criminal informant, confidential human source, paid informer, effective collaborator, snitch, *pentito*, *supergrass*.

In the eighteenth century, Beccaría questioned this practice; in his opinion, it was a sign of the law's weakness to call for help upon those who had broken it (246–47).

Bentham, to the contrary, although regarding it as a last resort, defended the practice of incentivizing informants, pointing out that it was an enticement for inhibiting criminal associations. For him, treason and disloyalty are dishonorable within relationships that do not cause harm, but not when they serve the security of society: "From the violation of engagements among criminals, what evil can be apprehended?" (106). Discussions surrounding the use of incentivized informants continue to be of considerable relevance, with general support from the state and marked opposition from some sectors of academia. Main criticisms of the practice have been that negotiating with those who commit crimes highlights the crisis in which the criminal justice system finds itself and the inability of the state to fulfill an essential function. It is said that it requires that the search for the truth undergo a negotiation whose value has yet to be proved and which depends on the spurious interests of those involved. Furthermore, it violates constitutional guarantees.[28] In its favor, proponents have cited that it is useful for putting an end to excessively harmful criminal structures; they argue that the deployment of incentivized informants does not reveal the weakness of the state but rather its strength in adopting more sophisticated forms of investigation. Proponents hold that the risks involved in incentivized informing can be neutralized by applying appropriate norms for evaluating the potential impact of an informant's contribution with respect to the likelihood of its usefulness in a criminal investigation as well as its symbolic value, insofar as it recognizes the authority of the state over the informer's bond of criminal complicity (Musco 38).

The efficiency of incentivized informing has also been in question. Some analysts attribute little value to past usage of paid informants in the fight against terrorism in Italy on the grounds that the armed organizations had already begun their decline and that this, in fact, was the reason for their disappearance (Musco 38–39; Tak 5). The credibility of those who provide incriminating data under these conditions has also been in question, as has the fact that, in practice, the weakness of the information that agents receive through this process often ends up derailing many investigations (Tak 6). Citing the European Court of Human Rights, Isabel Sánchez García de Paz points out that information obtained through private informants may be the product of manipulation, personal interests, or desires for revenge (24).

In the effort to sustain these types of criminal investigations, the state resorts to different terms meant to highlight the moral value of the denunciations they elicit to fight crime. Those who provide information are called, in Argentina, for example, "*arrepentidos*" [repentants], creating the illusion that the informant has taken a critical stance against their previous criminal actions, when the motives for informing are in fact quite varied.[29] Finally, a kind of contagion seems to infect the very investigative practices that require incentivized informing. It is not only an issue of what happens to those who provide the information, but also to the investigators who are immersed in an economy of information that is linked to crime; ultimately, they can come under question for devising negotiations that often respond to political design, the pursuit of extrajudicial purposes, or an attack on political opponents.[30] If the criticisms are accurate, the state ends up implementing a weapon of dubious utility, one that jeopardizes

FAITHFULNESS AND BETRAYAL   607

the core values of a democratic community and creates more problems than solutions. Regardless, incentivized information continues to seduce those who believe it more efficient in the prosecution of crime. In fact, in Argentina, it has gradually started being used to prosecute other crimes, thereby risking contamination of the criminal justice system as a whole.

DISLOYALTY AND COMMUNITY

Bonds with others and community ties cannot be built without a minimum of trust. When we consider sectors that are in conflict, there is consistently a need to trust the person next to you, someone who is on the same side. Even if they are different in almost every other aspect, what each individual projects onto to other group members is the same. Thinking in terms of investigating crime, a police officer, for example, trusts the other officers on patrol, just as the members of the gang that the police may be confronting trust the gang member next to them. Each member knows that they depend on the others within their group, regardless of the values we assign to what they are fighting for. Therein lies Martínez Estrada's criticism of Sergeant Cruz.

Those whose tactics are based on undermining the enemy's confidence in their peers corrode their own sense of trust as well. Betrayal affects the confidence one has in others and reflects a devalued image of the person who has been betrayed.[31] Disloyalty reframes the relationship whose value the betrayer reveals to be negligible.

A physical trait, a tradition, a way of speaking—all constitute the kinds of signs by which groups recognize what unites or differentiates them. Such ethnic and cultural qualities take on additional relevance in contexts of conflict or violence. In such situations, if we assume that among those who can pronounce a shibboleth there are individuals who secretly share and defend the interests of the enemy, the very categorization of shibboleth becomes not only insufficient, but also dangerous for the person who uses it because it unleashes a sort of autoimmune process.[32] An act or image that portrays itself as a part equivalent to the whole is, in truth, an element that allows the whole to be breached. While the labyrinthine network of informers and traitors with the roles of criminals and police intermixing appears to be the product of films and detective novels, it is in fact becoming a common backdrop for certain criminal justice issues, for example, trying to bring down drug traffickers.[33]

THE PERSISTENCE OF BETRAYAL

One could draw a line from the beginning of Borges's fictional production to his very last stories and constantly traverse issues of conflicting loyalties, as happens between "Hombre de la esquina rosada" [Streetcorner Man] and "Historia de Rosendo Juárez"

[The Story from Rosendo Juárez]. The second story, published thirty-five years after the first, is in fact the narration of the Cruz-like moment experienced by Juárez, the "Pegador," a character from the first story; it is his explanation for refusing to fight Francisco Real, the "Corralero," that fateful night in Julia's saloon. Juárez explains that, like Cruz, he stopped recognizing himself as the person whom he had been up until that instant. At that point, he saw himself—in his terms—as a fool looking for a fight and he felt ashamed, disgusted that even two animals might kill one another in such a way.

Given its quantity and frequency, we can see the attraction that betrayal exerts upon Borges's work. When, in another text, he selects a scene for the universal plot that will be reiterated forever, he chooses the Ides of March, where Caesar is taken by Brutus's dagger. This death is repeated in the gaucho stabbed by his godson who does not realize he is dying "para que se repita una escena" [so that a scene can be repeated] (*OC* II: 171). Cassius, one of Caesar's murderers, expressly refers to this cyclical reiteration: "How many ages hence / Shall this our lofty scene be acted over / In states unborn and accents yet unknown!" and then adds "So oft as that shall be, / So often shall the knot of us be called / The men that gave their country liberty" (Shakespeare, *Julius Caesar* from The Folger Shakespeare). Again, treason and homeland are reunited, as if one could not exist without the other.

That homeland or that state, while today less inclined to indulge in an epic of betrayals and loyalties, still deploys this drama in its anti-crime discourse. At times, it is used theoretically: crime as a betrayal of the community's expectations; at others, in limited application to specific practices—when that rhetoric seeks to move betrayal into the realm of repentance, when the breaking of a pact that intentionally harms the community is a form of reconversion in the style of Droctulft or Cruz. Yet, although it resorts to a moral discourse, this rhetoric of betrayal ultimately turns morals into something negotiable, into a weapon that can also wound the person wielding it. Called upon to combat what is believed to be an evil, betrayal runs the risk of destroying all involved.

An inflexible and difficult word is "traitor," Borges says when he applies the term to himself. Also difficult, perhaps, because of the polysemic nature the word has within his stories. "Traitor" can be assigned a meaning that differs from protagonists' or readers' traditional usage of the word. After all, as Otto Dietrich zur Linde reflects in "Deutsches Requiem" while awaiting his execution for Nazi war crimes: in the secret continuity of history, Arminius did not realize that in plotting against the very Romans who had given him citizenship, he made himself the precursor of the German Empire, nor did Luther, in translating the Bible into German, realize he was thereby forging the People that would one day destroy the Bible forever. Such occurred with Borges's grandfather, the colonel who, trapped between opposing loyalties, faced his fate on the plains of the pampa. Betrayal is the accursed act which, in its performance, also enacts its opposite. It may be too complicated to definitively state what we are faithful to, what exactly we betray, or what the meaning is of an act that, for over two thousand years now, has had a proper name. According to the third version, Judas, his betrayal, the quintessential infamy, is the act of salvation precisely because of its abominable character.

FAITHFULNESS AND BETRAYAL 609

NOTES

1. My thanks to José Nesis for his reading and critique of the initial versions of this chapter, and to Ana Pitlevnik for her assistance in the final edition of the text.
2. "El muerto" [The Dead Man] is the story of a betrayal that backfires, "La espera" [The Wait] is a kind of rewriting (Balderston, *El método* 116–17). "Tres versiones de Judas" has already been mentioned. The theme of betrayal also appears in "Avelino Arredondo." In "La secta de los treinta" [The Sect of the Thirty], Borges again takes up questions of Judas and Christ, as paired characters, central actors in the tragedy of the Cross (*OC* III: 38–40).
3. In Argentina, the term "guapo," rather than signifying "handsome," as it does in most of the Hispanophone world, is more often used as a noun whose usage issues from tango and signifies someone who is a big shot, a streetwise tough, a neighborhood's local strongman.
4. This parallel between Fischbein and Judas has been noted by other authors as well (Kellerman 663–70; Attala 119–40).
5. According to Hamilton, Judas repents, returns the money, and confesses his sin, thereby completing what was presaged in Numbers 5:6–7. In the Gospel of Matthew, this act does not stop the wheel that has already begun to turn. His repentance and sacrifice are taken as evidence of his possible salvation (Hamilton 433).
6. Ehrman discusses how the concept of a single act determining one's entire life can be understood differently, in the way that a specific act defines a person "toward the outside." That is, not in terms of the construction of their self-perception but in terms of the way they are perceived by others. A person's life can be hidden or disappear behind a single defining incident that renders all other information about their history irrelevant. This is what happens with Judas and his betrayal. He mentions other examples: Nixon's was Watergate, John Wilkes Booth's was Lincoln's assassination (Ehrman 153).
7. The story then goes on to tell how, in time, the Lombards themselves did same: they became Italians. This process can be read in relation to another historic figure often deemed a traitor: Malinche, the woman who, after being sold as a slave among the Mayans and then given as a gift to the Spanish, provides Cortez invaluable information for his conquest of Mexico. Todorov points out that, although despised as a traitor, she can be seen as the symbol of the *mestizaje*, of cultures that first heralded the modern Mexican state and, more broadly, the symbol of all of us who coexist in diverse languages and cultures. La Malinche "glorifies intermixing to the detriment of purity" (109).
8. Moreira, unlike Fierro, dies when stabbed through by the bayonet of the sergeant who has come to detain him. Borges, who has referred to Moreira in several instances, narrates the moment of the bandit's death in "La noche de los dones" (*OC* III: 41–44).
9. Balderston notes a certain parallel between Gutiérrez's characters, whom he calls "amigos leales y concienzudos" [loyal and thoughtful friends] who were obsessed with walking their talk, and the figure of Francisco Borges ("Dichos y hechos" 49).
10. In 2020, an unpublished text by Borges dedicated to Silvano Acosta was released in which he refers to the execution of a deserter by order of his grandfather, Colonel Borges.
11. It mentions that, dressed in white, already defeated, he advanced toward those taking aim at him—an act that could not but end in his death. His grandson writes: "Lo dejo en el caballo, en esa hora / Crepuscular en que buscó la muerte" [I leave him on his horse, at that twilight hour / in which he looked for death] and, he continues, "Avanza por el campo la blancura / Del caballo y del poncho. La paciente / Muerte acecha, en los rifles. Tristemente / Francisco Borges va por la llanura" [Whiteness sweeps across the field / From the horse

and the poncho. The patient / death lies in wait in the rifles. Sadly / Francisco Borges goes toward the plain] (*OC* II: 206). The idea of suicide easily points to Judas's fate.

12. His full name was Jorge Francisco Isidoro Luis Borges. Perhaps it no accident that the name by which he is known (Jorge Luis), conceals the two names of his ancestors.

13. The first television broadcast in Argentina was a speech by Eva Perón from the Plaza de Mayo on October 17, 1951; the so-called Day of Loyalty. Among other references to treason and to enemies of the people, the nation, and Perón, she said guards must stay at their posts: "Es necesario que cada uno de los trabajadores argentinos vigile y que no duerma, porque los enemigos trabajan en la sombra de la traición y a veces se esconde detrás de una sonrisa o de una mano tendida" [It is necessary for every Argentine worker to be vigilant and not to sleep, because enemies work in the shadow of betrayal and sometimes hide behind a smile or an outstretched hand]. See https://www.youtube.com/watch?v=cMrV m7j4nzU&ab_channel=CasaRosada-Rep%C3%BAblicaArgentina.

14. "*Cipayo*" or "Sepoy" in English, derives from Persian and came to be used to refer to Indian soldiers serving under British, Portuguese, and French colonial governments during the eighteenth and nineteenth centuries. In Argentina, the term was used, like "*vendepatria*" or "country-seller/sell-out," as a slur against people whose actions are seen to benefit foreign interests, particularly those of the United States and Britain.

15. *Boletín Oficial de la República Argentina del 16/10/1950*, no. 16757, 1. Available at http://servicios.infoleg.gob.ar/infolegInternet/verNorma.do;jsessionid=D316D00619D2B2340 79B47FB4087C243?id=198297.

16. Almost in response to his own self-recrimination for having abandoned Ultraism.

17. Decreed July 25, 1960 (Fallos 247: 387).

18. Perón's intervention can easily be found online in which he states: "Al enemigo, ni justicia" [For the enemy, not even justice] (https://www.youtube.com/watch?v=WDh9M9aty4U). Also, when explaining how to distinguish between comrades, enemies, and traitors: "quien no lucha contra el enemigo ni por la causa del pueblo, es un traidor" [whoever fails to fight against the enemy or for the cause of the people is a traitor]; see https://www.yout ube.com/watch?v=MtudOaHPH-k.

19. Silvina Ocampo and Juan Rodolfo Wilcock published a play in verse about ancient Rome called *Los Traidores* [*The Traitors*] in 1956 (Bioy 256).

20. In this sense, see "Las versiones homéricas" [The Homeric Versions], "Los traductores de las Mil y una noches" [The Translators of the Thousand and One Nights], and "Sobre el 'Vathek' de William Beckford" [On William Beckford's "Vathek"].

21. Premat has pointed out that, in Borges's work, tradition, which becomes a choice on the part of those who inherit it, is a construction of the creator, a personal artifact that, in certain instances, allows access to creativity (10).

22. Hence his assertion: "o ser argentino es una fatalidad y en ese caso lo seremos de cualquier modo, o ser argentino es una mera afectación, una máscara. Creo que si nos abandonamos a ese sueño voluntario que se llama la creación artística, seremos argentinos y seremos, también, buenos o tolerables escritores" [it is either our inevitable destiny to be Argentine, in which case we will be Argentine whatever we do, or being Argentine is a mere affectation, a mask. I believe that if we lose ourselves in the voluntary dream called artistic creation, we will be Argentine and we will be, as well, good or adequate writers] (*OC* I: 273–74; *SNF* 427).

23. Regarding the causes of betrayal, Borges imagines the monologue of another historic figure, Hengist Cyning, whom Borges makes say the following: "Yo sé que a mis espaldas / me tildan de traidor los britanos, / pero yo he sido fiel a mi valentía" [I know that behind

my back / the British brand me as a traitor, / but I have been faithful to my bravery] (*OC* II: 281). Money, power, bravery, and revenge could represent those other, stronger loyalties that identify others believed to be traitors.

24. Similar to Margalit, 176–77, 185.

25. Though here again there is a twist. In reality, when Judas runs to betray Jesus, he is in fact obeying him (John 13:27).

26. Unlike Judas, Peter does not cause harm with the three denials Jesus foretold. But this could be comprehended within a broad understanding of betrayal. At the same time Jesus announced Judas's betrayal, he also predicted Peter's three negations.

27. In Roberto Arlt's *El juguete rabioso,* the same contempt is felt by the engineer character toward the person who warns him of an impending crime against him. The character who brought him the information says: "comprendí todo el desprecio que me arrojaba a la cara" [I understood all of the contempt he threw in my face] (Arlt 192).

28. For a more complete analysis, see Ferrajoli, who cites a number of classic authors (Filangieri, Diderot, among others) in analyzing the negative impact of these kinds of strategies on criminal justice in places assumed to be governed under the rule of law (606).

29. Bonner reports that, during the period he studies, only one out of a total of twenty-seven informants used by the United Kingdom in Ireland was a true ideological convert, while all the others gave information for personal gain, such as sentence reduction and other benefits. Some of them even informed on others to eliminate opponents and move up in the criminal organization (31).

30. Musco mentions a case in which the district prosecutor of Messina investigated his counterpart in Reggio Calabria, the same prosecutor of Reggio Calabria investigated the district prosecutor of Messina, and both were investigated by prosecutors in Catania.

31. In the tango song "La traición" (1929), whose lyrics were written by Juan Villada and sung by Corsini (one of Borges's favorite singers and, like him, a backer of Yrigoyen in the 1928 elections), a former "Don Juan" sings of "La traición de oreja a oreja / para siempre me marcó" [Betrayal from ear to ear / has marked me forever], which has made him the laughing stock of the neighborhood, teased by "hasta los pibes" [even children]. Available at https://www.youtube.com/watch?v=3cIYbOTPz54). It is not unreasonable to consider some connection between this lyric and the scar marking El Inglés's face in "Tema del traidor y del héroe."

32. According to the biblical episode (Judges 12:4–6) after a battle, to recognize their enemies, the Gileadites made strangers say this word aloud, the pronunciation indicating whether or not they belonged to their group. Those who mispronounced "Shibboleth" were immediately killed.

33. For more on the issues resulting from the intermingling of police and crime organizations, see Auyero and Sobering (97–134).

WORKS CITED

Arlt, Roberto. *El juguete rabioso.* Espasa Calpe, 1993.

Attala, Daniel. "Conjeturas sobre una omisión deliberada: una lectura de 'El indigno.'" *Variaciones Borges,* vol. 44, 2017, pp. 119–40.

Auyero, Javier, and Katherine Sobering. *Entre Narcos y policías. Las relaciones clandestinas entre el Estado y el delito, y su impacto violento en la vida de las personas.* Siglo XXI, 2021.

Balderston, Daniel. "Dichos y hechos. Gutiérrez y la nostalgia de la aventura." *Borges, realidades y simulacros*. Biblos, 2000, pp. 39–58.

Balderston, Daniel. "Digamos Irlanda, Digamos 1824. Para repensar la historia en Borges." *Innumerables relaciones: cómo leer con Borges*. Universidad Nacional del Litoral, 2010, pp. 102–18.

Balderston, Daniel. *El método Borges*, translated by Ernesto Montequin. Ampersand, 2021.

Beccaria, César. *De los delitos y de las penas*, translated by Juan Antonio de las Casas Madrid. Universidad Carlos III, 2015.

Bentham, Jeremy. *The Rationale of Reward*, edited by John and H. L. Hunt, 1825.

Bioy Casares, Adolfo. *Borges*. Destino, 2006.

Bonner, David. "Combating Terrorism: Supergrass Trials in Northern Ireland." *The Modern Law Review*, vol. 51, no. 1, 1988, pp. 23–53.

Borges, Jorge Luis. *Borges en Sur, 1931–1980*. Emecé, 1999.

Borges, Jorge Luis. *Collected Fictions*, translated by Andrew Hurley. Viking, 1998.

Borges, Jorge Luis. *Obras Completas*. 4 vols. Emecé, 1996.

Borges, Jorge Luis. *Selected Non-Fictions*, edited by E. Weinberger, translated by Weinberger, Esther Allen and Suzanne Jill Levine. Viking, 1999.

Borges, Jorge Luis. "Word-Music and Translation." *This Craft of the Verse*. Harvard University Press, 2000, pp. 57–76.

Burnet, Regis. *El evangelio de la traición. Una biografía de Judas*, translated by Horacio Pons. Edhasa, 2011.

Donato, Elena. "Dos balas de remington todas las mañanas." *La Biblioteca, Cuestión Borges*, no. 13. Edicion Biblioteca Nacional, 2013.

Ehrman, Bart. *The Lost Gospel of Judas Iscariot: A New Look at Betrayer and Betrayed*. Oxford University Press, 2008.

Ferrajoli, Luigi. *Derecho y Razón*, translated by Andres Ibañez. Trotta, 1995.

Fishburn, Evelyn. "Borges, Cabbala and 'Creative misreading.'" *Ibero-Amerikanisches Archiv*, vol. 14, no. 4, 1988, pp. 401–18.

Gutierrez, Eduardo. *Croquis y siluetas militares*. Igon Editores, 1886.

Hamilton, C. S. "The Death of Judas in Matthew: Matthew 27:9 Reconsidered." *Journal of Biblical Literature*, vol. 137, no. 2, 2018, pp. 419–37.

Jakobs, Günter. *Derecho penal. Parte general. Fundamentos y teoría de la pena*, translated by Joaquín Cuello Contreras and José Luis Serrano González de Murillo, 2nd ed. Marcial Pons, 1997.

Kellerman, Owen L. "Borges y El informe de Brodie: Juego de Voces." *Revista Iberoamericana* vol. 38, no. 82, 1972, pp. 663–70.

Margalit, Avishai. *On Betrayal*. Harvard University Press, 2017.

Martínez Estrada, Ezequiel. *Muerte y transfiguración de Martín Fierro. Ensayo de interpretación de la vida argentina*, segunda edición corregida, vol. I. Fondo de Cultura Económica, 1958.

McGrady, Donald. "Prefiguration, Narrative Transgression and Eternal Return in Borges' 'La forma de la espada.'" *Revista Canadiense de Estudios Hispánicos*, vol. 12, no. 1, 1987, pp. 141–49.

Musco, Enzo. "Los colaboradores de la justicia entre el "penitismo" y la calumnia. Problemas y perspectivas." *Revista Penal*, no. 2, Tirant Lo Blanch, 1998, pp. 35–47.

The New Oxford Annotated Bible: New Revised Standard Version with the Apocrypha. Oxford University Press, 2010.

Piglia, Ricardo. "Ideología y ficción en Borges." *Punto de Vista*, vol. 2, no. 5, Buenos Aires, 1979, pp. 3–6.

Piglia, Ricardo. *Respiración artificial*. Editorial Sudamericana, 1990.

Premat, Julio. "Borges: tradición, traición, trangresión." *Variaciones Borges*, vol. 21, 2006, pp. 9–21.

Rakopoulos, Theodoros. "The Social Life of Mafia Confession Between Talk and Silence in Sicily." *Current Anthropology*, vol. 59, no. 2, 2018, pp. 167–77.

Sánchez García de Paz, Isabel. "El coimputado que colabora con la Justicia penal." *Revista Electrónica de Ciencia Penal y Criminología*, no. 7, 2005, pp. 05:1–05:33.

Shakespeare, William. "The Tragedy of Julius Caesar." *The Folger Shakespeare*. Edited by Barbara Mowat and Paul Werstine, Folger Shakespeare Library, April 17, 2023, https://folger-main-site-assets. s3.amazonaws.com/uploads/2022/11/julius-caesar_PDF_FolgerShakespeare.pdf.

Tak, Peter J. P. "Deals with Criminals: Supergrasses, Crown Witnesses and Pentiti." *European Journal of Crime Criminal Law and Criminal Justice*, 1997, pp. 2–26.

Todorov, Tzvetan. *La conquista de América: el problema del otro*, translated by Flora Botton Burlá. Siglo XXI, 2003.

Court Findings

Corte Suprema de Justicia de la Nación Fallo. "Perón, Juan Domingo y otros." Fallos 247:387, July 25, 1960.

Statutes

Constitución de la Nación Argentina. Boletín Oficial de la Nación, August 23, 1994, No. 27959, 1–8. https://www.argentina.gob.ar/normativa/nacional/ley-24430-804/texto.

Constitución de la provincia de Córdoba. September 14, 2001. http://www.saij.gob. ar/0-local-cordoba-constitucion-provincia-cordoba-lp0000000-2001-09-14/ 123456789-0abc-defg-000-00000vorpyel.

Ley 13985. Boletín Oficial de la Nación, October 16, 1950, No. 16757, 1. http://servicios.infoleg. gob.ar/infolegInternet/verNorma.do;jsessionid=D316D00619D2B234079B47FB4087C 243?id=198297.

Videos

Casa rosada. Discurso de Eva Duarte en la primera transmisión de Televisión argentina. https://www.youtube.com/watch?v=cMrVm7j4nzU.

Juan Domingo Perón:. "To the friend, everything; to the enemy, no justice." Interview conducted in June/July 1973. https://www.youtube.com/watch?v=WDh9M9aty4U.

Juan Domingo Perón (1971). Compañeros, Enemigos y Traidores. https://www.youtube.com/ watch?v=MtudOaHPH-k.

La traición. Ignacio Corsini, Tango (1929). https://www.youtube.com/watch?v=3cIYbOTPz54.

INDEX

For the benefit of digital users, indexed terms that span two pages (e.g., 52–53) may, on occasion, appear on only one of those pages.

Tables and figures are indicated by an italic *t* and *f* following the page number.

The 39 Steps (Hitchcock), 572–74, 575

Abad Faciolince, Héctor, 398–400
Abad Gómez, Héctor, 398–99
Abadi, Marcelo, 104
"Abenjacán el Bojarí, muerto en su laberinto" ("Ibn-Ḥakam al-Bokhari, Murdered in His Labyrinth," Borges), 221–22, 228–29, 233n.23, 234n.25, 584
Abramowicz, Maurice, 6–7
"El acercamiento a Almotásim" ("The Approach to Al-Mu'tasim," Borges)
apocryphal texts, 360
The Avesta, 443
Eastern Bloc translations of, 432–33
engagement with imaginary books in, 198–202, 209–10
as fantastic literature, 236
footnotes in, 203–4, 205
tower of silence in, 449–50
variations between editions of, 202–3
Acevedo, Isidoro, 5–6, 7–8, 63–64
Acevedo Suárez de Borges, Leonor
arrest (1948) of, xxiii, 102
Borges's correspondence with, 100
Buenos Aires home of, 7–8, 106–7
death of, xxv, 7–8
family background of, 5
religious beliefs of, 6, 416
Adorno, Theodor, 184, 193, 212–13, 389
The Aeneid (Virgil), 271, 287–88, 294, 298–99
Aizenberg, Edna, 471–72, 473–74, 510
"A la calle Serrano" (Borges), 167
Alatorre, Antonio, 394

Alba, Tyto, 398
"Alba desdibujada" (Borges), 161–62
Alegría, Fernando, 86
El Aleph (*The Aleph*, book, Borges)
Borges's global reputation, 302
as canonical Borges text, xv*t*
Global South authors influenced by, 442
Latin American literature's place in global literature, 400
publication (1949) of, xxiii, 117
The Qur'an, 442
translations in Eastern Bloc countries of, 426, 432–33
"El Aleph" ("The Aleph," story, Borges)
absent poem described in, 397
as canonical Borges text, xv*t*
French translation of, 406
imaginary texts in, 417–18
mathematics, 592
modern technology in, 572
Persian translation of, 446–47
publication (1945) of, 116
stationary in, 119–20
transfinite numbers in, 589
word choices in, 261
El Aleph engordado (*The Fattened Aleph*, Katchadjian), 363
Alexander, Francisco, 85, 87–91
All's Well That Ends Well (Shakespeare), 295–96
"Al margen de la moderna estética" ("At the Margin of Modern Aesthetics," Borges), 179

616   INDEX

Almeida, Iván, xviii, 351–52, 358, 359–60, 363,
    365n.2, 365n.4, 367n.16
Almond, Ian, 448–49
Althusser, Louis, 489
Alvarado Tenorio, Harold, 398–99
"Amanecer" (Borges), 161–62
Ambrose, 135–36, 146–47
"A mi padre" ("To My Father," Borges),
    130n.3, 291–92
"Una amistad hasta la muerte" (Borges and
    Bioy Casares), 329
Amorim, Enrique, xxii, 8, 44–45, 376n.6
Los Anales de Buenos Aires magazine
    Borges's direction of, xxiii, 4, 44–45, 106,
        236–37, 244
    cessation of publication (1948) of, xxiii
    editorial vision at, 44–45, 106
    fantastic literature, 236–37, 244–45
    Xul Solar, 44–45, 521–22
"Anatomía de mi 'Ultra'" ("Anatomy of My
    Ultra," Borges), 154, 179, 424
Anderson Imbert, Enrique, 376n.5, 380–81
Andrade, Mário de, 394, 530
"El Ángel de la Guarda en Avellaneda"
    ("The Guardian Angel in Avellaneda,"
    Borges), 63–64
"Animales de los espejos" ("Animals That Live
    in the Mirror," Borges), 495–96
Annie Hall (Allen), xvi
"Annihilation" (al-Ghitani), 445
"Anotación al 23 de agosto de 1944" ("A
    Comment on August 23, 1944,"
    Borges), 542
Ansolabehere, Pablo, 104–5, 109–10
Antiguas literaturas germánicas (Ancient
    Germanic Literatures, Borges and
    Ingenieros), xxiii, 110
Antología de la literatura fantástica
    (Anthology of Fantastic Literature,
    Borges, Bioy Casares, and Ocampo),
    xxiii, 76–77, 241–44, 322
Antología personal (A Personal Anthology,
    Borges), xxiv, 125–26
Antología poética argentina (Anthology of
    Argentine Poetry, Borges, Bioy Casares,
    and Ocampo), xxiii, 21–22, 238
Anzieu, Didier, 415–16, 483
Aparicio, Frances, 73–74

apocryphal texts
    attempts to pass as authentic, 352
    The Bible, 353
    Christianity, 352
    condensing and displacement in, 360
    deeper truth offered as a benefit of, 362–63
    elusiveness of Borges, 14
    hidden clues, 358–59
    Judaism, 352, 353
    social media, 364
Apollinaire, Guillaume, 55t
Arabian Nights and Days (Mahfouz), 445–
    46, 451
The Archaeology of Knowledge (Foucault), 490
Arfuch, Leonor, 335–36
Argentina
    constitution in, 558, 604–5
    coup (1943) in, 559
    coup (1976) in, 414–15
    "Década infame" (1930-1943) in, 377
    Generation of 1837 in, 373, 380
    Malvinas War (1982), 383, 414–15
    middle-class reading public in, 18–20
    oratory's role in the culture of, 104–5
    public education system in, 19–20
    publishing industry in, 19–20
    "Revolución Libertadora" (1955) in, 124,
        380, 381, 602
Argentina Libre magazine, 522
Argentine Film Rating Organization, 548
Argentine Writers Association (ADEA), 108
Arguedas, José María, 474–75
Aristophanes of Byzantium, 141, 141n.19
Aristotle, 73, 280–81, 320, 583
Arlt, Roberto, 21, 37–38, 164, 173n.4, 374, 377,
    380, 382–83, 388, 611n.27
"Arrabal" (Borges), 155, 160, 168
Arreola, Juan José, 394
Arrieta, Rafael Alberto, 156
Arrigucci Jr., Davi, 221
"El arte de injuriar" ("Art of Insult," Borges),
    21–22, 183, 192, 264–65
"El arte narrativo y la magia" ("Narrative Art
    and Magic," Borges), 190, 277–78, 356,
    376, 520
Artefakty (literary volume in
    Czechoslovakia), 432–33
Asbury, Herbert, 232n.11, 356

INDEX   617

"Ascendencia escandinava de Flaubert"
    ("Flaubert's Scandinavian ancestry,"
    Borges), 24–25
Ashbery, John, 410–11
Ashford, Daisy, 54
Así magazine, 47–49
Asín Palacios, Miguel, 138, 140–41,
    146–47
Asociación Argentina de Cultura Inglesa,
    xxiii, 97, 108
*Aspectos de la literatura gauchesca (Aspects
    of Gauchesque Literature*, Borges),
    xxiii, 125–26
Astete Millán, Elsa, xxv, 7–8, 47–48
Asturias, Miguel Ángel, 391–92, 428
"Atardecer" ("Dusk," Borges), 154–55
Atlas (Borges), xxvi, 127
Attar, Ferid Eddin, 202, 203
Auerbach, Erich, 569–70
Augustine of Hippo, 135–36, 136n.5, 146–47,
    275, 282–83
"A una moneda" ("To a Coin,"
    Borges), 434
"A un poeta menor de 1899" ("To a Minor Poet
    of 1899," Borges), 289–90
"A un poeta menor de la Antología" ("To
    a Minor Poet of the Anthology,"
    Borges), 256–57
"Die Augenspiel" ("The Game of Eyes," Koch-
    Grünberg), 530–33
"An Autobiographical Essay" (Borges)
    The Aleph, 414
    on Borges's finances, 16–17
    on Borges's productivity during the
        1920s, 181
    on Borges's tenure at Miguel Cané
        Municipal Library, 124
    dubious anecdotes passed off as legitimate
        in, 361–62
    errors and embellishments in, 4
    on *Historia universal de la
        infamia*, 42–43
    on library of Borges's father, 18–19
    on *Martín Fierro* journal, 40
    narrator and protagonist in, 415–16
    on *Prisma* magazine, 34–35
Les autres (film script written by Borges and
    Bioy Casares), xxv, 327

"Los avatares de la tortuga ("Avatars of the
    Tortoise," Borges), 120–21, 459
"Avelino Arredondo" (Borges), 556, 559, 563
"La aventura y el orden" ("Adventure and
    Order," Borges), 190
The Avesta, 442–43
Azouqa, Aida O., 445

Bacon, Francis, 135, 136, 138–41, 138f, 146–
    47, 358
Badiou, Alain, 269–70
Balderston, Daniel
    on anthologies and university
        education, 237–38
    *Antología de la literatura
        fantástica*, 243–44
    on Borges and the "world outside the text,"
        416, 419
    on Borges's allusive writing style, 457–58
    on Borges's apocryphal texts, 356
    on Borges's lecture preparation, 109
    on Borges's notetaking, 17
    on Borges's place in world literature, 442
    on Borges's process of citation, 204
    on Borges's re-writing process, 311–12
    on Borges's sexuality and homophobia,
        505–6, 510–11
    on Borges's storage of his notebooks, 16–17
    on Borges's working drafts, xviii, 15
    on "La lotería en Babilonia," 118–19
    on "the marginal" in Borges's works, 463–64
"Baltasar Gracián" (Borges), 256–57, 263–65
Banchs, Enrique, 273–74
Un barbare en Asie (Michaux), 80–85, 82f, 83f
Baretti, Giuseppe, 329
Barletta, Leónidas, 377
Barral, Carlos, 408
Barrenechea, Ana María, 249n.13, 380–81
"Barrio reconquistado" (Borges), 265–66n.12
Barth, John, 411–12, 415
Barthes, Roland, 301, 409, 569–70
Baudrillard, Jean, 483–84, 493–95, 496, 506–7
Bawer, Bruce, 335
Bazin, André, 576–77
Beccaria, César, 605–6
Becco, Horacio Jorge, 380–81
Bechdel, Alison, 508, 509
Beckett, Samuel, xxiv, 85, 340, 408, 476

618 INDEX

Beckford, William, 241, 276
Bello, Andrés, 61–62
Benedetti, Mario, 390
Benedict, Nora, 237, 248n.11, 248–49n.12, 249–50n.22, 319
Bénichou, Paul and Sylvia, 406
Benjamin, Walter, 569–70
Bentham, Jeremy, 605–6
Berkeley, George
    Borges influenced by philosophy of, 462, 463–64, 465
    Borges's imaginary dialogues involving, 457–58
    Hume, 460–62, 463
    idealism, 466–67
    on negation of the continuity of consciousness, 178–79
    on the past as a dream in the present, 283–84
    on time and continuity, 463, 464, 469n.14
    translatio imperii, 282–83
    on unstable world of mind, 460
Bernárdez, Francisco Luis, 39–40, 55t, 111n.7, 130–31n.7, 262, 601
"Bernares" (Borges), 153
Berni, Antonio, 86–87, 521–22
Bertolucci, Bernardo, 412–13
"Bestiario" ("Bestiary," Cortázar), 244–45
Bhabha, Homi, 476–77
Bianchi, Alfredo, 374, 377
Bianco, José, xvii, 43, 330n.6, 377–78
"La biblioteca de Babel" ("The Library of Babel," Borges)
    biblical tradition, 118
    Body of Secrets, 591–92
    Borges's work at Miguel Cané Library, 117–18, 130
    bowdlerizations of, xvii–xviii
    as canonical Borges text, 117
    engagement with imaginary works in, 198
    as fantastic literature, 236–37
    final lines of, 128
    Kafka, 117–19
    "La biblioteca total," 117
    Lasswitz, 280–81
    librarian's wanderings in, 193–94
    mathematics, 592

narrator in, 586–87
publication (1941) of, 117
queer criticism, 510
on tautologies, 590
transfinite numbers in, 588
La Biblioteca magazine (National Library of Argentina), xxiv, 46–47, 126–27
Biblioteca Miguel Cané. *See* Miguel Cané Municipal Library
"La biblioteca total" ("The Total Library," Borges), 116–17, 376
"Biografía de Tadeo Isidoro Cruz" ("A Biography of Tadeo Isidoro Cruz," Borges), 116, 598, 599–600
Bioy, Adolfo, 330n.1
Bioy Casares, Adolfo
    advertising work for fermented milk, 319–20
    Antología de la literatura fantástica, xxiii, 76–77, 236–37, 241, 242–45
    Antología poética argentina, xxiii
    Borges biography written by, 5
    on Borges's appointment to National Library directorship, 124–25
    Borges's detective fiction stories co-written by, xxiii, 76–77, 218, 244, 250n.26, 319–30, 378
    Borges's first meeting with, xxii, 321
    Borges's reviews of the works of, 322
    on Borges's sex life, 546–48
    Cuentos breves y extraordinarios, 245–46
    Destiempo magazine, xxii, 43–44, 322
    diary of, xix, 16, 29n.11, 142, 329–30
    El jardín de senderos que se bifurcan, 121
    on friendship and fun, 319
    Los Anales de Buenos Aires magazine, 244
Bischoff, Erich, 137, 137n.8, 140, 146–47
Blake, William, 324–25, 520–21, 522
Blanchot, Maurice, 193–94, 210, 381, 406–7, 409, 483, 485, 498
Blanco, Mariela, xiv, 44–45
Bloom, Harold, 205, 400–1, 471–72, 473
Bloy, Léon
    Borges's championing of, 24, 120
    "Del culto de los libros," 135, 136, 142–44, 146
    Napoleon, 142–44, 279–80

reflections on continuous writing of history by, 136

typological exegesis of history, 276–78

Body of Secrets (Bamford), 591–92

Boedo group, 36–37, 41–42, 102, 374–75, 377, 388

Bolaño, Roberto, 364–65, 388, 395–97, 400

Bolívar, Simón, 305–6, 413–14, 600–1

Bolshevik Revolution (1917), 4, 6–7, 153, 307–8, 427, 561

Bombal, María Luisa, 242–43, 395

Bookchin, Natalie, 513–14

Borges, Francisco ("Frank"), 5

Borges, Francisco Isidoro, 5–6, 600–1

Borges, Jorge Guillermo (father of Borges)
  atheism of, 3
  blindness of, 7–8
  books written by, 5–6, 330n.1
  childhood of, 5
  death of, xxii, 116
  law studies of, 7–8
  library of, 18–19
  political beliefs of, 5
  translation work by, 5

Borges, Jorge Luis
  Argentine literature's place in world literature, 247
  atheism of, 6
  on biographical writing, 3–4
  birth of, xxi
  blindness of, xiv, 4, 13, 16, 85, 98, 99, 124–25, 126, 142, 329–30, 339, 396–97, 408
  British cultural tradition, 462
  Buenos Aires home of, 7–8
  childhood of, 8–10
  death of, xxvi, 7–8, 383, 388
  education of, xxi, 4, 6–7
  English language, 6, 374–75
  finances of, 8, 16–17
  Formentor Prize (1961) awarded to, xxiv, 85, 381–82, 408, 426–27, 430, 476, 483
  French language, 6–7, 20–21, 381
  German language, 4, 6–7, 9–10, 362, 374–75
  marriages and divorces of, 47–49
  Municipal Prize won by, 376
  nervous breakdown (1918-1919) of, 6–7

Perón opposed by, 102, 122–23, 343–44, 345–46, 405, 414–15, 541–42, 554, 562

pseudonyms of, 42–43, 44, 219

psychotherapy with Kohan-Miller, xxiii, 97–98, 99

ultraísta movement, xxi, 6–7, 34–36, 37–38

Borges, oral (Borges), xxvi, 110

Borges en El Hogar collection, 8

Borges en Sur collection, 8

Borges Haslam, Leonor Fanny ("Norah")
  Argentine art world, 522
  arrest and imprisonment (1948) of, xxiii, 102
  birth of, xxi
  Editorial Proa, 54
  education of, 6–7
  Fervor de Buenos Aires, 62
  Luna de enfrente, 62
  marriage to Guillermo de Torre, xxii, 6–7
  Prisma magazine, 34
  religious beliefs of, 6
  ultraísta movement, 6–7

"Borges y yo" ("Borges and I," Borges), 9–10, 46, 307–8, 314, 333–34, 463

Botana, Natalio, 40–41

Bourke, Vernon, 136n.5, 146–47

Bouvard et Pécuchet (Flaubert), 25–28, 30n.17

Bradbury, Ray, 427

Braginskaia, Ella, 434–35

Brandán Caraffa, Alfredo, 36–37

Brant, Herbert J., 505–6, 510–11

Brazil, 390–91, 394, 434, 560

Breve antología anglosajona (*Brief Anglosaxon Anthology*, Borges), xxvi

Bride of Frankenstein (Whale), 320–21

Brodzki, Bella, 506–7, 514–15

Browne, Thomas, 59–61, 135, 136, 138–39, 140–41, 145, 146, 569

Brumana, Herminia, 380–81

Buber, Martin, 245–46, 295

Buenos Aires (Argentina)
  bookstores in, 18–19
  compadritos, 165
  criollismo, 61–62, 163
  grid-like layout of, 157–58
  literary life during 1930s in, 76
  public library network in, 18–19, 115

"Buenos Aires" (Borges), 155–56, 157–58, 161–62

Buenos Aires Cine Club, 539

Bulgaria, 427, 433, 435–36

"La busca de Averroes" ("Averroes's Search," Borges), 73, 406, 442, 445, 568–69

Cahiers de L'Herne (book), xxiv, 85

Caillois, Roger, 231n.3, 379, 379nn.11–12, 405–6, 408

Cairoli, Irma, 342

Cajero Vázquez, Antonio, 164–65, 259

"Calibán" (Fernández Retamar), 389–90, 392, 474–75

Călinescu, George, 430–31

"Calle con almacén rosado" ("Street with a Pink Corner Store," Borges), 61–62, 261

"Calle desconocida" ("Unknown Street," Borges), 424, 427

Callejas, Mariana, 396

"Las calles" ("The Streets," Borges), 159–60, 161–62, 434

Calvino, Italo, 197, 198, 210, 407, 473

Cammell, Donald, 412–13

Cámpora, Héctor, 129

Canal Feijóo, Bernardo, 107–8, 376n.6

Canguilhem, Georges, 489, 490–91

Cansinos Asséns, Rafael, 34, 54, 61, 168, 522

Canto, Estela
  on Argentines' views of other South Americans, 448
  on Borges and film, 545–46
  on Borges's finances, 107
  Borges's interview (1946) with, 339–40
  on Borges's public lectures, 98–99
  on Borges's sexuality, 97–98
  "La intrusa," 304, 506

Cantor, Georg, 587–89, 592

Can Xue, 444–45, 451

Carlyle, Thomas
  on biography, 3–4
  Borges's critiques of, 272–73
  Cagliostro, 138–39, 139n.11
  democracy rejected by, 561
  imaginary books in the works of, 198
  reflections on continuous writing of history by, 136
  summary of books by, 360
  typological exegesis of history, 276

Caro, Andrés, 55t

Caro, Miguel Antonio, 393

Carriego, Evaristo, 5–6, 92n.3, 169. *See also Evaristo Carriego* (Borges)

Carroll, Lewis, 483, 493–94

Casares, Marta, 319

"La casa de Asterión" ("The House of Asterion," Borges), 44–45, 244–45

"Casa tomada" ("House Taken Over," Cortázar), 244–45

Casella, Edgardo, 37–38

Cassirer, Ernst, 121

Castaño, Gloria Valencia de, 393

Castaño Castillo, Álvaro, 390

Castro, Américo, 80–81, 379

Castro, Fidel, 390–91, 392, 431–32

Catelli, Nora, 74

El caudillo (Jorge Guillermo Borges), 5

Centro journal, 379–80

Černý, Václav, 424

Certeau, Michel de, 13

Cervantes, Miguel de. *See Don Quixote* (Cervantes)

Chanady, Amaryll Beatrice, 239

Chaparro Valderrama, Hugo, 400

Chesterton, G. K.
  Borges's championing of, 41–42, 74, 222, 522
  Borges's fictional works influenced by, 128, 411
  Borges's frequent re-reading of, 24
  Cuentos breves y extraordinarios, 245–46
  on the death of the novel, 27–28
  detective fiction, 218–19, 229
  Father Brown character in stories of, 568–69
  Los Anales de Buenos Aires magazine, 244

Chien-Shiung Wu, 585

The Childhood of Jesus (Coetzee), 451

Chile, 394–95, 414–15

Christ, Ronald, 335, 462

Christian Galvé, Elisa, 546

Christensen, Carlos Hugo, 513

Cicero, 109–10, 121, 276–78

"El cielo azul, es cielo y es azul" ("The Blue Sky Is Sky and Is Blue," Borges), 178–79

Cien años de soledad (*One Hundred Years of Solitude*, García Márquez), 341–42

La cifra (*The Limit*, Borges, book), xxvi, 262, 289

"La cifra" ("The Limit," Borges, poem), 294

cinema and Borges
Borges's blindness, 545–46
film as mass entertainment, 541–42
screenplays written by Borges, 542–45
women's accompaniment of Borges in audience, 545–48
See also specific films

"El cinematógrafo, el biógrafo" ("The Cinematographer, The Biographer," Borges), 540, 542

Citizen Kane (Welles), 538, 539, 540–41

"Ciudad" (Borges), 160

Ciudad magazine, 375–76, 380–81

Clemente, José Edmundo, xvii, 45, 126

Cocteau, Jean, 245–46

Coetzee, J. M., 450–51

Colegio Libre de Estudios Superiores (CLES; Colegio Libre)
Borges's lectures at, xxiii, 15, 98–99, 100–1, 104–7, 108, 110
Peronist regime's closure of, 104, 105

Coleridge, Samuel Taylor, 65, 202, 283–84, 307–8

Collins, Wilkie, 202

Colombia, 393, 397–98

El compadrito (*The Thug*, edited by Borges and Silvina Bullrich), xxiii

"Composición escrita en un ejemplar de la Gesta de Beowulf" (Borges), 46

Conducta journal, 377

Los conjurados (*The Conspirators*, Borges), xxvi, 254, 298–99, 560–61

"Con el tiempo uno aprende" (apocryphal Borges poem), 364

"El congreso" ("The Congress," Borges), 127–28, 310–12, 560–61, 563

Connell, Raewynn, 441–42

Conrad, Joseph, 76, 202–3, 365n.5, 523, 572

Conservative Party (Argentina), 561

Contorno journal, 379–80, 382–83

Contreras, Manuel, 395

Córdova Iturburu, Cayetano, 41–42

Cordovero, Moses ben Jacob, 357–58

Correas, Jaime, 398–99

Cortázar, Julio, 243–45, 344, 364–65, 377–78, 434–35

"Cosmogonía del Nuevo Orden" (Fernández-Gómez), 396–97

Cosmópolis newspaper, 155–56, 157

Costa Lima, Luiz, 394

Cozarinsky, Edgardo, 513

Crane, Thomas F., 531

"La creación y P. H. Gosse" ("Creation and P. H. Gosse," Borges), 121, 459

crime fiction. *See* detective fiction

criollismo
compadritos, 166
Cuaderno San Martín, 63
definition of "criollo," 184–85
El tamaño de mi esperanza, 62–63, 157–58, 168, 184–85
Fervor de Buenos Aires, 66–69
Inquisiciones, 59–61
as language of Buenos Aires, 61–62, 163
Luna de enfrente, 61–62, 157–58, 168, 169–70
parodies of, 170–71, 172
racism, 396

"Crítica del paisaje" ("Critique of Landscape," Borges), 155, 157–58, 181–82, 194n.1

Crítica newspaper, 7–8, 19–20, 39, 375

Croce, Benedetto, 189, 230

Crónicas de Bustos Domecq (*Chronicles of Bustos Domecq*, Borges and Bioy Casares), 219, 221, 320–21, 322, 323–24, 327–28

Cuaderno San Martín (*San Martín Notebook*, Borges)
annotations in, 63–64
on books and language, 52
criollismo, 63
layout and editorial decisions regarding, 65, 68f
origins of the title of, 63–64, 66f
publication (1929) of, xxii, 52, 59–61, 59t, 63

Cuba
Bay of Pigs invasion (1961) in, 389–90
Borges publications in, 431–32
Eastern Bloc countries, 431–32, 435–36
revolution (1959) in, 388, 390, 392
"Un cuchillo en el norte" ("A Blade in the Northside," Borges), 261

622 INDEX

Cuentos breves y extraordinarios
(*Extraordinary Tales,* edited by Borges
and Bioy Casares), xxiv, 41–42, 245–47
"Cuentos del Amazonas" ("Tales from the
Amazon," Xul Solar), 520, 526–27, 528–29,
531, 533
"Cuentos del Turquestán" ("Stories from
Turkestan," Borges), 520, 525, 527
Czechoslovakia, 423–24, 425–26, 428, 430–
31, 432–33
Czech Republic, 435–36

Dabove, César, 46
Dabove, Juan Pablo, 401
Dabove, Santiago, 242–43, 244, 245–46
Da Cunha, Euclides, 77–78, 394
Dados, Nour, 441–42
Damiani, Piero, 121, 283–84, 360–61, 364
Darío, Rubén, 34, 35, 54, 388–89, 423, 430, 471–
72, 541–42
Daudet, Alphonse, 202–3
Davidson, Martin, 276–77
Debray, Régis, 389–90
Degiovanni, Fernando, 105
De la Fuente, Ariel, 505, 506
De La Guardia, Alfredo, 80–81
Del Campo, Estanislao, 62–63, 157–58, 186–87
"Del culto de los libros" ("On the Cult of
Books," Borges)
Bacon, 135, 136, 138*f*, 138–41, 146–47
on the Bible and nature, 569
books as sacred objects in, 146
Kabbalah, 135, 137*f*, 137, 137n.8, 140–
41, 146–47
on letters and creation, 137–38, 140–41
Mallarmé, 135, 143
Michigan State manuscript of, 139*f*, 139–47,
141*f*, 142*f*, 145*f*
publication in *La Nación* (1951) of, 135, 136*f*
The Qur'an, 135, 138, 140–41
on reading *versus* talking with others, 144–
45, 146–47
Royce's paradox, 285
on silent reading, 135–36
University of Pittsburgh manuscript,
139, 140*f*
"Dele, dele" (Borges), 122–23

De León, Moses, 357–58, 365n.6
Deleuze, Gilles, 483–84, 486, 488, 493–
94, 497–98
Delgado, Josefina, 514, 515
"Delia Elena San Marco" (Borges), 46, 427
della Casa, Giovanni, 325
"Del rigor en la ciencia" ("On Rigor in
Science," Borges), 14, 491–93, 495, 592
Del Vando Villar, Isaac, 34
De Man, Paul, 266n.20, 410, 415, 417–18, 473
De Quincey, Thomas, 9–10, 24, 44–45, 183, 191,
276, 567–68, 580
De Rougemont, Denis, 80–81
Derrida, Jacques
antihumanism, 489
on Borges's approach to Western
philosophy, 486–87
Borges's influence on, 483, 484
deconstruction, 409
on imitation and essence, 493
Pascal's sphere, 487
postmodernism, 471–72
simulacra, 493–94
on thinking that decenters
metaphors, 486
"Desagravio a Borges" ("Reparation to
Borges," *Sur* magazine), 122, 376, 376n.6,
377–78
Desai, Anita, 449–50
Desai, Kiran, 449–50
"Después de las imágenes" ("After Images,"
Borges), 59–61, 165, 185
Destiempo magazine, xxii, 43–44, 80–81,
254, 322
detective fiction
Borges's "laws" of, 218–19, 220–21, 227–29
Chesterton, 218–19, 229
Poe, 217–18, 220–21, 228–29
verisimilitude, 217
See also specific stories
de Ortiz Basualdo, Sara, 44, 106
de Toro, Alfonso, 282–83, 471–72
de Torre, Guillermo
art criticism by, 522
on Borges and Whitman, 153
editorial work by, 6–7
on *Fervor de Buenos Aires,* 160

Norah Borges's marriage to, xxii, 6–7
Prisma magazine, 34, 35
"Rusia," 423–24
Sur magazine, 43
Deussen, Paul, 121, 135, 137, 137n.9, 140–41, 146–47, 524
"Deutsches requiem" (Borges), 116, 388–89, 432–33, 553–54, 563, 608
De Zubiría, Ramón, 393
"Diálogo de muertos" (Borges), 46
Días de odio (*Days of Hate*, film by Torre Nilson), xxiv, 543–44, 546–48, 547*f*, 549n.8
Díaz, José Pedro, xxiii, 95–96
Diego, Gerardo, xxvi, 414–15
di Giovanni, Norman Thomas, 4, 16–17, 412, 413, 414, 450
Di Leo, Jeffrey, 237–38
"El disco," ("The Disk," Borges), 556, 592–93
Discusión (*Discussion,* Borges)
Borges's additions to subsequent editions of, xvii–xviii
Flaubert lectures reprinted in, 24–25
the infinite in, 459
publication (1932) of, xxii, 191–92
reviews of, 375–76
Divina Commedia (*The Divine Comedy,* Dante), 18–19, 141, 142, 362
"La doctrina de los ciclos" ("The Doctrine of the Cycles," Borges), 192
Doinas, Stafan Augustin, 430–31
Dólar, Mladen, 96–97
Donne, John, 275–76, 367n.16
Donoso, José, 391–92
Don Quixote (Cervantes)
Borges's reading of, 4, 74, 334
end of The Renaissance, 489
friendship in, 542
"Indagación de la palabra," 192–93
Quichotte, 449–50, 451
transitions of the text through reading of, 13–14
See also "Pierre Menard, autor del Quijote" (Borges)
Dos fantasías memorables (*Two Memorable Fantasies,* Borges and Bioy Casares), xxiii, 219, 221, 323, 324–25, 327

"Las dos maneras de traducir" ("The Two Ways of Translating," Borges), 73, 526
Drieu La Rochelle, Pierre, 375–76
du Cange, Seigneur Charles du Fresne, 358–59, 366n.8
"El duelo" ("The Duel," Borges), 307–8, 505–6, 507–9, 516n.4
Dunbar, William, 498
Dunne, J. W., 207, 283–84
Duns Scotus, John, 277–78
"La duración del infierno" ("The Duration of Hell," Borges), 192
Durand, Pascal, 74–75

Eastern Bloc
anthologies featuring prohibited authors in, 427
censorship, 424–25, 426–27
collapse of Communism (1989-1991), 436–37
Cuba, 431–32, 435–36
definition of, 423–24
literary magazines as means of accessing non-Communist authors in, 429
literary translations in, 425
Soviet hegemony in, 424–25, 428
"Thaw" after 1954 in, 426–27, 429
violent confrontations against Soviet forces, 425–26
East Germany, 437
Echave-Sustaeta, Javier de, 287–88
Echeverría, Esteban, 103, 185
Eco, Umberto, xiii, 232n.9, 407
"Los ecos" ("The Echoes," Borges), 556
Edelberg, Betina, 408
Editorial Proa
Borges, 59–63
Cuadernos del Plata series, 57–58, 59*t*, 60, 60*fb*, 60*fc*, 63
editorial philosophy, 53
founding (1924) of, 53
list of titles produced (1925-1927), 55*t*
marketing, 58
Martin Fierro, 53, 54, 57
Méndez, 53–54, 57–59, 63, 70
physical production and design of books, 53–58, 56*fa*, 56*fb*, 60*fa*, 60*fb*, 60*fc*, 61, 63, 66–69, 70
See also Proa magazine

624   INDEX

Egginton, William, 583–84
Eguren, José María, 393
Einstein, Albert, 575, 579, 583–84, 585
Eisenstein, Sergei, 423, 539, 569, 576–77
"Elegía de Palermo" ("Elegy for Palermo," Borges), 166, 172
"Elementos de preceptiva" ("Elements of Rhetoric," Borges), 179–80, 181–82, 189
Eliade, Mircea, 430–31
Eliot, T. S., 23, 202–3, 208, 357, 473–74
Elizondo, Salvador, 344–45
Elogio de la sombra (*In Praise of Darkness*, Borges), xxv, 85, 257, 290–91, 298–99
Emerson, Ralph Waldo, 16, 28, 138–39, 561
"Emma Zunz" (Borges)
    Días de odio as film adaptation of, xxiv, 543–44, 546–48, 547f, 549n.8
    dilemma of time in, 225
    female characters in, 224–25, 505–7, 510–11, 513, 514–15
    feminist and queer responses to, 514
    intellectual complexities of, 310
    Jewish characters in, 510, 577–78
    mirrors in, 448–49
    murder trial in, 576–77
    names in, 577, 578
    The Pentateuch, 442
    reading depicted in, 19
    sexuality, 504
    violence in, 224–25
En attendant Godot (*Waiting for Godot*, Beckett), 340
"En memoria de Angélica" ("In Memory of Angélica," Borges), 296–97
"La encrucijada de Berkeley" ("Berkeley at the Crossroads," Borges), 178–79, 462
"El encuentro" ("The Encounter," Borges), 245–46, 303, 413
Enríquez, Mariana, 400–1
"Epílogo" ("Epilogue," Borges), 262, 297–98
Erfjord, Estela, 5
Erro, Carlos, 103
Escarpit, Robert, 476
Escrito sobre Borges (Delgado), 514–15
"El escritor argentino y la tradición" ("The Argentine Writer and Tradition," Borges)
    on Argentines' modesty, 106–7

as canonical Borges text, xiv–xv, xvt
on gauchesque poetry, 273
lecture that served as basis for, 104–6, 408
on national culture, 557
nationalism critiqued in, 105–6
Peronism, 143–44, 601–2
postcolonial studies, 474–75, 478–79
reissuing (1953 and 1955) of, 125–26
on treating tradition with irreverence, 364–65
"La escritura del dios" ("The Writing of the God," Borges), 406, 428
"La esfera de Pascal" ("Pascal's Sphere," Borges), 193, 280, 459, 486–87
"El espejo de los enigmas" ("The Mirror of Enigmas," Borges), 142–43, 144f
"La espera" ("The Wait," Borges), 19, 130–31n.7
La estatua casera (Bioy Casares), 320, 322
Estonia, 432–33, 434
"Estudio preliminar" (Borges), 141
Étiemble, René, 472, 474–75
"El Evangelio según Marcos" ("The Gospel According to Mark," Borges), 6, 13–14, 19, 303, 447, 570
Evaristo Carriego (Borges)
    apocryphal Wilde texts, 353–54
    on biography, 3
    criollismo, 186–88
    cyclical time, 466–67
    format of, 187–88
    as "lateral biography," 199
    preface in later edition discussing Borges's childhood in, 8–10
    publication (1930) of, xxii, 68t, 69fa
    on tango and national identity, 354
"Everness" (Borges), 449–50
"Everything and Nothing" (Borges), 256, 262
"Examen de la obra de Herbert Quian" ("The Examination of the Works of Herbert Quain," Borges)
    apocryphal texts, 360
    as chronicle of failure, 204
    cult of past rejected in, 205
    engagement with imaginary books in, 198–99, 200–2, 210
    misleading of inattentive readers, 355
    as obituary, 199, 205
    readers' establishment of meaning in, 207–8

"Examen de metáforas" ("Examination of Metaphors," Borges), 180, 497

Facundo (Sarmiento), 390
Falcón, Alejandrina, 85–86
Falklands War (1982), 383, 414–15
fantastic literature
  anti-realism, 240
  Borges's seven themes of, 240
  character doubt, 239
  explanation of outcomes in, 322
  magical realism, 239, 247, 437
  Todorov, 239–40
Fargione, Daniela, 449–50
Farías, Victor, 395
Farrell, Edelmiro, 101–2, 122
Faulkner, William, 74, 80, 86, 91, 411, 430–31
Felipe, León, 85, 87–88
feminist criticism of Borges, 504, 506–10, 513–15
Fernández, Macedonio
  as Borges mentor, 5–6
  Borges's prologues for works by, 522
  Destiempo magazine, 44
  Editorial Proa, 59*t*, 60*fb*
  humor, 182–83, 185
  "vertigo of the self," 323–24
Fernández-Gómez, Jesús, 396–97
Fernández Mallo, Agustín, 363, 400
Fernández Moreno, Baldomero, 156
Fernández Retamar, Roberto, 389–90, 391–93, 431–32, 474–75, 479
Ferrari, Osvaldo, 247, 550n.12
Fervor de Buenos Aires (Borges)
  avant-garde, 374–75
  "Benares," 158–59
  Borges's articles in *Cosmópolis*, 156–57
  criollismo, 66–69
  design of, 62
  Eastern Bloc translations of, 426, 427
  eternity, 465
  Inquisiciones, 59–61
  "Insomnio," 259
  La literatura nazi en América, 396
  "Las calles," 159–60
  Obras completas, xvii

present *versus* past city in, 161–62, 164–65
  prologue to reissued edition of, 85
  publication (1923) of, xxi, 7
  reissuing (1969) of, 188–89
  return to childhood home, 160–61
  reviews of, 375
  Rosas, 160–61
  ultraísmo movement, 159, 160
Ficciones (*Fictions*, Borges)
  aesthetic autonomy, 392
  Borges's additions to subsequent editions of, xvii–xviii
  Borges's global reputation, 302
  as canonical Borges text, xv*t*
  Eastern Bloc translations of, 432–33
  editorial decisions regarding texts to include in, xvii–xviii
  French translation of, 406
  Global South authors influenced by, 442, 449–50
  Italian translation of, 407
  literary prizes for, xxiii, 376
  postmodernism, 471–72
  prologue in, 280–81
  publication (1944) of, xxiii
  Verdevoye's translation into French of, xxiii
Fiddian, Robin, 392, 471
"La fiesta del monstruo" ("The Monster's Party," Borges and Bioy Casares), 19–20, 126, 221, 279–80, 328–29, 380
film. *See* cinema and Borges
Fitzgerald, Donna, 510
FitzGerald, Edward, 5, 282
Flaubert, Gustave
  Borges's lectures (1952) regarding, 22–23, 24–28
  Borges's literary allusions to, 24
  death of the novel, 27–28
  dreaming in the works of, 25–26, 28
  Proust, 22–23
  temporality, 25, 27, 28
  Thibaudet, 22–23
"Flaubert y su destino ejemplar" ("Flaubert and His Exemplary Destiny," Borges), 24–25
Fló, Juan, 392–93

"La flor de Coleridge" ("Coleridge's Flower," Borges), 307–8, 396–97
Florida group, 36–37, 38–39, 374–75, 388
"Fluencia natural del recuerdo" (Borges), 167–68
Fokkema, Douwe, 471–72, 477–78
Fontán Barreiro, Rafael, 287–88
Ford, John, 598–99
"La forma de la espada" ("Form of the Sword," Borges), 510–11, 555–56, 598–99, 603
Fornaro, Milton, 346
Foucault, Michel
  antihumanism, 489
  Borges's influence on, 409, 483, 484, 485, 488
  classification systems of, 489–90
  "El idioma analítico de John Wilkins," 472, 488
  on the "human monster," 490–91
  on literature and the single impersonal author, 485–86
  Nouvelle Critique, 381
  Occidentalism, 473
  postcolonial studies, 477–78
  postmodernism, 471–72
  queer theory, 511
  Tel Quel journal, 409
"Fragmento sobre Joyce" ("Fragment on Joyce," Borges), 192–93
France, Borges's reception in, 405–7, 409, 411–12, 418–19
Franco, Jean, 391–92
Frank, Waldo, 376, 377n.8
Franklin, Rosalind, 585
Frazer, James, 277–78
French theory
  deconstruction, 484, 493, 496
  map reading, 491–96
  mimesis, 492–93
  postmodernism, 495
  pragmatism, 484–85, 497–98
  question of Borges's Argentine identity, 472
  semiotics, 492
  simulacra, 484, 493–95
Freud, Sigmund, 397–98, 569
Frías, Carlos, xvii
Frisch, Mark, 506–7

Frost, Walter, 138n.10, 140, 146–47
"La fruición literaria" ("Literary Joy," Borges), 23–24, 27, 189, 192–93
Fuentes, Carlos, 391–92, 394
"La fundación mitológica de Buenos Aires" ("The Mythological Founding of Buenos Aires," Borges), 63, 166, 171–72, 283
"Funes el memorioso" ("Funes the Memorious," Borges), 192–93, 261, 445, 457–58, 572, 592
Futurism, 181–82

"G. A. Bürger" (Borges), 292–93
Gache, Belén, 400
Galaktika magazine, 432–33
Galileo Galilei, 146, 146n.27, 583–84
Galison, Peter, 575
Gallardo, Jorge Emilio, 47
Galtier, Lysandro, 87
Galván, Fernando, 450–51
Gálvez, Manuel, 76, 373–74, 375
García, Carlos, 171
García, Héctor Ricardo, 47–48
García Jurado, Francisco, 298–99
García Lorca, Federico, 80–81, 511
García Márquez, Gabriel, 341–42, 391–92
Gardel, Carlos, 41–42
Gargatagli, Marietta, 74
gedankenexperiments (thought experiments)
  idealized models of STEM practitioners, 584–86
  lenses, 587–89
  metaphors, 591–93
  mirrors, 586–87
  puzzle boxes, 589–91
gender and sexuality
  "Bechdel test," 508, 509
  Borges's conservative pronouncements on, 503
  Borges's homophobia, 505, 510–11
  Borges's sexual life, 417–18, 504–5, 512–13, 546–48
  "El duelo," 505–6, 507–9, 516n.4
  "Emma Zunz," 505–7, 510–11, 513, 514–15
  feminist criticism of Borges, 504, 506–10, 513–15
  "La intrusa," 505–6, 508, 510, 513–14

LGBTQ studies, 504, 512
queer criticism of Borges, 504, 505–
6, 510–12
"El general Quiroga va en coche al muere"
("General Quiroga Rides to His Death in
a Carriage," Borges), 166
Generation of 1837, 373, 380
Genet, Jean, 483
Genette, Gérard
on authorship and the "tireless impersonal
mind," 410
on Borges and simultaneity of all works of
literature, 208
on Borges's "demon of parallelisms," 201
on literature and myth, 213–14
on literature and the single impersonal
author, 485–86
Nouvelle Critique, 381
Occidentalism, 473
postmodernism, 471–72
semiotics, 492
Tel Quel journal, 409
Gerchunoff, Alberto, 41–42, 100, 513
German Expressionism, 73–74, 153, 374–75
Germany, Borges's reception in, 407–8
"Gesta maximalista" ("Bolshevik Epic,"
Borges), 153, 424, 561
Al-Ghazali, 135, 138, 146–47
Ghiano, Juan Carlos, 46, 380–81
al-Ghitani, Gamal, 445
Ginzburg, Carlo, 20–21
Girondo, Oliverio
Borges's criticism of the poetry of, 256
Editorial Proa, 53, 55t, 57–58
Martín Fierro journal, 38–39, 374–75
Giusti, Roberto, 121, 373–74, 376–77
Glantz, Margo, 394
Glinoer, Anthony, 74–75
Global South
Borges influenced by literature from, 441
Borges's influence in, 444, 445–47,
449–51
"Brandt Line," 441–42
definition of, 441–42
postcolonialism, 441–42
Godard, Jean-Luc, 412–13, 483
Godel, Roberto, 6–7, 303–4

Goethe, Johann Wolfgang von, 143–44, 283–
84, 365n.2
Golshiri, Hushang, 446–47, 451
Gómez de la Serna, Ramón, 37–38, 44–45, 54,
156, 242–43, 375
Gomperz, Theodor, 141n.22, 146–47
González Lanuza, Eduardo, 34–35, 36–37,
39, 59–61, 376n.6
González Tuñón, Enrique, 41–42, 164
Gorbachev, Mikhail, 435–36
Gordon, Robert S. C., 407
Gorelik, Adrián, 162–63
Gorky, Maxim, 427
Gorodischer, Angélica, 514–15
Gospels
John, 141, 597
Luke, 569–70, 598
Mark, 6, 13–14, 19, 303, 447, 570
Matthew, 141, 146–47, 598, 603, 609n.5
Gosse, Edmund, 121
Gosse, P. H., 121, 283–84, 459
"El grabado" ("The Engraving," Borges), 292
Gramsci, Antonio, 441–42
Gramuglio, María Teresa, 76, 379, 383
Granville Browne, Edward, 447
Grecia magazine, 34, 153–54
Grigore, Rodica, 446
Grimonprez, Johan, 573
"Die große Schlange" ("The Great Serpent,"
Koch-Grünberg), 529, 531–32, 533
Groussac, Paul, xxiv, 100, 120, 126, 130n.2,
183, 262
Grünberg, Carlos M., 172–73
Guattari, Félix, 483, 488, 497–98
"Guayaquil" (Borges), 413–14, 602–3
Gudiño Kieffer, Eduardo, 382, 514
Guerrero, Margarita, xxiv, 85, 246–47,
495–96
Guevara, Andrés, 41–42
Guevara, Ernesto "Che," 382, 390
Güida, Pascual, 41–42
Guido, Beatriz, 546, 549n.8
Guillén, Nicolás, 430, 434
Guillot Muñoz, Gervasio, 96
Guimarães Rosa, João, 391–92
Güiraldes, Ricardo, 36–38, 40, 53, 54, 55t, 58,
59t, 60fa, 390, 394

628 INDEX

El hacedor (*Dreamtigers*, Borges)
captive in, 15–16
"El hacedor" story in, 288
Lugones, 126–27
prologue of, 298–99
publication (1960) of, xxiv, 46–47, 68*t*, 69*fd*, 254
self-figuration, 262
El hacedor (de Borges), Remake (Fernández Mallo), 363, 400
Hachemi Guerrero, Antonio Munir, 335–36
Hadis, Martín, 5–6, 305
Haedo, Esther, 8
Hallelujah (Vidor), 541–42
Haraszti, Miklós, 426–27
Hardy, Thomas, 578–79
Harss, Luis, 391–92
Haslam de Borges, Frances ("Fanny," paternal grandmother of Borges), xxii, 5, 7, 305
Hawthorne, Nathaniel, 238, 272–73, 275–76
Hazar Afsana, 442–43
Hazlitt, William, 269–70
Heard, Gerald, 121
Hedayat, Sadeq, 446–47
Hegel, G. W. F., 485, 493–94, 495, 497, 540, 542, 579
Heidegger, Martin, 395, 487, 491
Heine, Heinrich, 4, 362, 366–67n.15
Helmholtz, Hermann von, 120–21
Henning, Max, 526–27
Henríquez Ureña, Pedro, xxii, 110n.2, 376n.6
"Heráclito" ("Heraclitus," Borges), 297
Heraclitus, 271–72, 282, 297
Hernández, José, 37–38, 185–87, 329, 390, 601
Herrera Almada, Benigno, 97–98
Hesse, Eva, 407–8, 528–29
Hidalgo, Alberto, xxii, 375
"Himno del Mar" ("Hymn of the Sea," Borges), 34, 153
Hinton, Charles Howard, 320
Histoire de la littérature française de 1789 à nos jours (Thibaudet), 21–22
Historia de la eternidad (*History of Eternity*, Borges)
betrayal in, 598
commercial failure of, 375
definitive version of, 203

editorial decisions regarding texts to include in, xvii–xviii, 191–92
French translation of, 406
humor, 183, 466
ironic title of, 459, 461–62
nature of time, 466
paradoxical relation between history and eternity in, 211
publication (1936) of, xxii, 68*t*, 69*fb*, 76
Historia de la literatura argentina (Rojas), 373
Historia de la noche (*History of the Night*, Borges), xxvi, 292–93
"Historia del guerrero y de la cautiva" ("Story of the Warrior and the Captive," Borges), 6, 179–80, 406, 505–6, 509, 598, 599–600, 603
"Historia de los ecos de un nombre" ("A History of the Echoes of a Name," Borges), 280
"Historia de Rosendo Juárez" ("The Story from Rosendo Juárez," Borges), 413–14, 607–8
Historia universal de la infamia (*A Universal History of Iniquity*, Borges)
bibliographic inventions in, 199
Billy the Kid character in, 540
Borges on the writing of, 355–56
as canonical Borges text, xv*t*
Deleuze on, 488
Eastern Bloc translations of, 432–33
French translation of, 406
"infamous biographies," 4, 396
Kristeva, 490–91
Persian history, 449–50
prologue of, 222, 264
publication (1935) of, xxii, 42–43
single-character stories in, 540
Hitchcock, Alfred, 572–73
Hobsbawm, Eric, 480
Hoffmann, E. T. A., 241–42, 432–33
El Hogar magazine, 4, 16, 33, 40–41, 115, 218, 375, 538–39
"Hombre de la esquina rosada" ("Man on Pink Corner")
betrayal in, 607–8
compadritos, 222
detective story conventions, 222–23

Eastern Bloc translations of, 427–28
film version of, xxiv
gauchesque duel in, 222–23
"Leyenda policial" as predecessor of,
   38, 185–86
Revista Multicolor de los Sábados magazine's
   publication of, 42–43
Stevenson, 222
"El hombre en el umbral" ("The Man in the
   Threshold," Borges), 555
"Hombres pelearon" ("Men Fought," Borges),
   185–86, 232n.11
Homer, 135–36, 146, 287–88, 290, 356–57
*Hong Lou Meng (The Dream of the Red
   Chamber),* 443–44, 451
Hooper, Grace, 585
La hora de los hornos (Solanas), 545
Horace, 289–92, 296
Horst, Karl August, 407–8
"How to Write a Detective Story"
   (Chesterton), 219
Hughes, Psiche, 357, 505
Hugo, Victor, 308
Huidobro, Vicente, xxii, 375, 424
Hume, David
   Berkeley, 460–62, 463
   Borges influenced by philosophy of,
      462, 465
   Borges's imaginary dialogues
      involving, 457–58
   Borges's lecture notes on, 457–58
   on nature of time, 466
   personal identity, 464
   on reason's limits, 460–61
Hungary, 423–26, 427–28, 429–33, 435–36
Hurley, Andrew, 450, 574–75, 577
Hurtado, Leopoldo, 55t
Huxley, T. H., 460, 462–63

Iamblichus, 141, 141n.20
Ibarra, Néstor, 375, 377–78, 381, 406, 472,
   475
Idiarte Borda, Juan Bautista, 559
"El idioma analítico de John Wilkins" ("The
   Analytical Language of John Wilkins,"
   Borges), xvt, 191–92, 264–65, 311–12, 327–
   28, 409, 472, 488

*El idioma de los argentinos (The Language
   of Argentines,* Borges), xxii, 172–73,
   183, 191–92
"El idioma infinito" (Borges), 165
Ifor Evans, Benjamin, 21–22
"Indagación de la palabra" ("An Investigation
   of the Word," Borges), 187–88, 192–93
*Índice de la nueva poesía americana (Index
   of New American Poetry,* anthology),
   xxii, 375
"El indigno" ("The Unworthy," Borges), 21, 37–
   38, 598, 599–600, 604
El informe de Brodie (Borges)
   autobiographical elements of, 414
   departure from previous Borges work
      in, 416–17
   di Giovanni as translator by, 413
   Eastern Bloc translations of, 433
   editorial selections regarding, 37–38
   foreword to, 413–14
   narrators in, 314–15
   "plain tales" in, 302
   publication (1970) of, xxv
The Informer (Ford), 598–99, 603
Ingenieros, Delia, xxiii, 243, 245–46
Inicial magazine, 40, 374
"In Memoriam J. F. K." (Borges), 556
"El inmortal" ("The Immortal," Borges), 244–
   45, 276–77, 356–57, 358, 406
"Los inmortales" (Borges), 44–45
Inostrannaia Literatura journal (Soviet
   Union), 429–30, 434
Inquisiciones (Inquisitions, Borges)
   Borges's edits to, xvii
   "Buenos Aires," 157–58
   criollismo, 59–61
   essay format of, 59–61
   Fervor de Buenos Aires, 59–61
   omission from *Obras completas* of, xvii
   publication (1925) of, xxii, 52, 55t,
      56fa, 59–61
   ultraísta movement, 59–61
"Insomnio" ("Insomnia," Borges), 256–57,
   258–62, 265
"Instantes" (apocryphal Borges poem), 363
Instituto de Literatura Argentina, 373
"Intenciones" ("Intentions," Borges), 126–27

630 INDEX

interviews of Borges
    by Barnstone, 334
    by Cairoli, 342–43
    by Canto (1946), 339–40
    essays compared to, 335–36
    humor, 335–36, 339, 340, 341–42
    by Irby (1961), 334
    by Nogués, 337–38, 339
    by Oppenheimer and Lafforgue, 343–45
    political topics, 343–44
    Proust Questionnaire, 337–38
    Readers Theater, 336–38, 346
    by Rodman (1969), 341–42
    theatrical aspects of, 333–34, 336–37, 346
Introducción a la literatura inglesa
    (*Introduction to English Literature*,
    Borges and Vázquez), xxv
Introducción a la literatura norteamericana
    (*Introduction to North American*
    Literature, Borges and Zemborain de
    Torres), xxv, 282–83
"La intrusa" ("The Intruder," Borges)
    Borges's autobiographical links
      to, 304
    compadritos, 304–5
    digital game based on, 513–14
    Eastern Bloc translations of, 432–33
    female characters in, 505–6, 508, 510
    feminist and queer responses to, 513–14
    film version of, 513
    Jewish characters in, 510
    queer criticism, 510–11
    sexuality, 504
Invasión (Santiago), 327, 544–45
La invención de Morel (*The Invention of Morel*,
    Bioy Casares), 242, 320, 322, 406
Ionesco, Eugène, 334, 340–41
Ipuche, Pedro Leandro, 37–38, 95–96,
    170–71, 375
Iran, Borges's reception in, 446–47
Irby, James, xxiv, 334, 410, 412–13
Irenaeus of Lyon, 275
Irodalmi Újság journal, 426
Italy, Borges's reception in, 407
Iz sovremennoi argentinskoi poezii anthology
    (*On Contemporary Argentine*
    Poetry), 434–35

"Jactancia de quietud" ("Boast of Quietness,"
    Borges), 449–50
Jagger, Mick, 412–13
James, Henry, 146, 202–3, 508–9
James, William, 178–79, 202, 484, 497–98
Jameson, Fredric, 390–91
El jardín de senderos que se bifurcan (*The*
    Garden of Forking Paths, book, Borges)
    as canonical Borges text, xvt
    Eastern Bloc translations of, 432–33, 434–35
    editorial decisions regarding, xvii–xviii
    engagement with imaginary books in, 197–
      98, 200
    errors in, xvii–xviii
    Global South authors influenced by, 450
    National Literature Awards' ignoring of, 121,
      197, 376–77
    prologue to, 360
    publication (1941) of, xxiii, 117, 376
    reading depicted in, 19
    reviews of, 377–78
    See also specific stories
"El jardín de senderos que se bifurcan"
    ("The Garden of the Forking Paths,"
    story, Borges), 223–24, 443–44, 449–50,
    486, 488, 571, 572–74
    quantum physics, 583, 592
Jarkowski, Aníbal, xvi
Jauretche, Arturo, 87, 124
Jichlinski, Simon, 6–7, 307–8
Jitrik, Noé, 379, 382
John, Gospel of, 141, 597
Jonson, Ben, 190
Joyce, James, 59–61, 74, 192–93, 483
"Joyce y los neologismos" ("Joyce and
    Neologisms," Borges), 120–21, 192–93
Juan, Guillermo, 34, 35, 36
Juan Manuel, Infante de España, 242–43
"Juan Muraña" (Borges), 303–4
Judas Iscariot, 597–98, 599, 603, 604, 608
El juguete rabioso (Arlt), 21, 37–38, 380, 382–83,
    611n.27
Julius Casear (Shakespeare), 608
Jungbauer, Gustav, 525–26, 528–29
Jurado, Alicia, 122, 161–62
Juravliova, Valentina, 427
Jweid, Abdalhadi Nimer Abdalqader Abu, 445–46

INDEX 631

Kabbalah, 107–8, 135, 137, 137*f*, 137n.8, 140–41, 146–47, 357–58
Kafka, Franz
    Antología de la literatura fantástica, 241–42
    Borges's championing of, 44–45, 101–2, 191
    Borges's literary works influenced by, 117–19, 128, 130, 411
    Borges's translations of, 74
    creation of precursors by, 283
    Cuentos breves y extraordinarios, 245–46
    Flaubert, 27–28
    Hawthorne, 276
    Los Anales de Buenos Aires magazine, 244
"Kafka y sus precursores" ("Kafka and his Precursors," Borges), 23, 208, 473–74, 483
Kant, Immanuel, 460, 488, 583–84
Kassák, Lajos, 423–24
Katchadjian, Pablo, 363
Katz, Leandro, 513
Kazin, Alfred, 410–11
Keats, John, 465, 569–70
Las Kenningar (*The Kenning*, Borges), xxii, 180–81, 192, 601
Kerrigan, Anthony, 410
Khakpour, Arta, 446–47
Khrushchev, Nikita, 426–27, 429
Kierkegaard, Søren, 571
King, John, 43
Kipling, Rudyard
    Borges's championing of, 41–42, 74, 158–59, 202, 411, 522
    Editorial Proa, 54
    political purpose of writing of, 552
    Quiroga compared to, 392–93
    Revista Multicolor de los Sábados magazine, 527
    Xul Solar's translations of works by, 533
Kiš, Danilo, 433
Kittler, Friedrich, 569
Koch-Grünberg, Theodor, 528–33
Kodama, María, xxv, 310, 395, 416, 418, 538
Kohan-Miller, Miguel, xxiii, 97–98, 99
Kristal, Efraín, 73–74, 389, 504
Kristeva, Julia, 409, 483, 490–91
Kupferminc, Mirta, xvi, 515

Labarca, Eduardo, 395
"Los laberintos policiales y Chesterton" ("The Labyrinths of the Detective Story and Chesterton," Borges), 192, 223
Labyrinths (Borges), xxiv, 410, 412–13
Lacan, Jacques, 483, 492
Laclau, Ernesto, 562
Lacoue-Labarthe, Philippe, 483, 485, 491
Lafforgue, Jorge, 343–45
Lafon, Michel, 14, 16–17, 199
Lamarque, Nydia, 54–58, 55*t*
Lamb, Harold, 525
Lange, Norah, 36, 39, 55*t*, 59–61, 417–18
Lanuza, José Luis, 103
Laprida, Francisco Narciso de, 9–10
Larbaud, Valery, 37–38, 54, 375, 429–30
Larkin, Philip, 412
Lasswitz, Kurd, 117, 280–82
Lawrence, D. H., 44–45
Leaves of Grass (Whitman), 85–90, 88*f*, 89*f*, 91
"Un lector" ("A Reader," Borges), 13, 298–99
Lefevere, André, 236–37
Leibniz, Gottfried, 17–18, 285, 467–68, 484, 488, 592
Lem, Stanislaw, 432–33
El lenguaje de Buenos Aires (*The Language of Buenos Aires,* Borges and Clemente), xxiv
Letelier, Orlando, 395
Levingston, Roberto, 45–46
LeWitt, Sol, xvi
"Leyenda policial" ("Police Legend," Borges), 38, 165–66, 168–69, 185–86, 232n.11
"Leyes de la narración policial" (Borges), 223, 231n.3
LGBTQ scholarship, 504, 512
Libertella, Héctor, 255–56
Libra magazine, 40
El libro de arena (*The Book of Sand,* Borges)
    book with infinite number of pages in, 587
    Borges's National Library tenure, 127
    colonial identity, 393
    "El Otro," 9–10, 307–8
    Kafka, 128
    mathematics, 592
    publication (1975) of, xxv
    reading depicted in, 19
    transfinite numbers, 588–89

632   INDEX

Libro del cielo y del infierno (Book of Heaven and Hell, Borges and Bioy Casares), xxiv, 129, 323, 521
El libro de los seres imaginarios (The Book of Imaginary Beings, Borges and Guerrero), xxiv, 129, 246–47, 488, 495–96
El libro de sueños (The Book of Dreams, Borges), 129
Los Libros journal, 379, 383
Lida, Raimundo, 380–81
Lihn, Enrique, 255–56
"Límites" ("Limits," Borges), 256–57, 292–93, 434
"La lírica argentina contemporánea" ("Contemporary Argentine Poetry," Borges), 155, 156, 185
Literal journal, 379, 383
"La literatura alemana en la época de Bach" ("German Literature in the Age of Bach," Borges), 9–10
La literatura nazi en América (Nazi Literature in the Americas, Bolaño), 396
Literaturas germánicas medievales (Medieval Germanic Literatures, Borges and Vázquez), xxv, 85, 307–8
Littmann, Enno, 526–27
"Llamarada" ("Flare," Borges), 257–58, 265–66n.12
Locke, John, 457–58, 555
London, Jack, 44–45, 75, 76–80
Losada, Gonzalo, 6–7
"La lotería en Babilonia" ("The Lottery in Babylon," Borges)
    Aramaic, 443
    authoritarian style of decision-making in, 555
    biblical tradition, 118
    Borges's edits to, xvii
    conspiracy and surveillance in, 118–19
    Deleuze, 486
    Eastern bloc translations of, 427
    Judaism, 118–19
    Kafka, 118–19
    manuscript of, 119–20
    mathematics, 592
    populism, 118–19
    publication (1941) of, 116–17
    randomness of life, 359

Louis, Annick, 524
Louverture, Toussaint, 390–91
Lucentini, Franco, 407
Luchting, Wolfgang, 407–8
Lucretius, 280–81
Ludmer, Josefina, 375, 379, 401, 510
Lugones, Leopoldo
    Antología de la literatura fantástica, 242–43
    avant-garde reaction to, 374
    El hacedor, 126–27
    fascism, 382
    on "Germanophiles," 554
    Martín Fierro, 373
    suicide of, 116
Lukács, György, 429–30
Luke, Gospel of, 569–70, 598
Luna, Ricardo, 327
Luna de enfrente (Moon Across the Way, Borges)
    "A la calle Serrano" (Borges), 167
    Buenos Aires depicted in, 61–62
    criollismo, 61–62, 157–58, 168, 169–70
    design of, 62
    Flaubert quotations in, 24
    on metric recurrence in Borges's poetry, 166
    poems as basis of, 61–62
    prologue to reissued edition of, 85
    publication (1925) of, xxii, 55t, 57–58, 61–62
Luria, Isaac, 202–3
Lussich, Antonio, 186–87
Lyon, Ted, 334–35, 337, 338
Lyotard, Jean-François, 483, 495–96

Macbeth (Shakespeare), 567–68, 579–80
Machado, Manuel, 154
Macherey, Pierre, 381, 483
"Magias parciales del Quijote" ("Partial Enchantments of the Quixote," Borges), 323–24, 491–92
magical realism, 239, 247
Magnarelli, Sharon, 505–7, 514–15
Mahfouz, Naguib, 445–46, 451
Major, René, 483
Ma journal, 423–24
Mallarmé, Stéphane, 135, 135n.1, 143, 212, 485–86, 493–94
Mallea, Eduardo, 41, 76, 300n.3, 376n.6

Malvinas War (1982), 383, 414–15
"Mañana" ("Tomorrow," Borges), 424
"El Manifesto" (Borges, Alomar, and Sureda), 153–54
Mann, Heinrich, 41–42
Mann, Horace, 5
Mann, Mary Peabody, 5
Manual de zoología fantástica (The Book of Imaginary Beings, Borges and Guerrero), xxiv, 129, 246–47, 488
"Manuel Peyrou" (Borges), 292
Maples Arce, Manuel, 159–60, 375, 540
Marechal, Leopoldo, 39–40
Mariani, Roberto, 41–42
Marin, Louis, 483, 492
Martí, José, 390
Martínez, Guillermo, 435–36
Martínez Estrada, Ezequiel, 44–45, 244, 283–84, 379–80, 381, 541–42, 600, 607
Martin Fierro (Hernández), 185–86, 373, 390, 542
Martín Fierro journal
 avant-garde, 38–39, 374, 375
 Borges's literature reviews in, 36
 Borges's relationship with other leaders of, 39–40
 cessation of publication (1927) of, xxii
 Editorial Proa, 53, 54, 57
 editorial vision at, 38, 40
 Florida group, 38–39
 founding (1924) of, xxii
 Girondo, 38–39, 374–75
 humor in, 181–82
 "Manifiesto de Martín Fierro" (1924), 39
 Méndez, xxii, 38–39, 528
 ultraísta movement, 39
Marx, Karl, 278–79, 432–33, 497–98, 555n.2
Mašek, Jiří, 424
Maštarije (Serbo-Croatian translation of *Ficciones*), 432
Mastronardi, Carlos, 98
Matthew, Gospel of, 141, 146–47, 598, 603, 609n.5
Maurois, André, 381
Mauthner, Fritz, 17–18, 24, 460, 462
McGuirk, Bernard, 506–7, 510
McLuhan, Marshall, xvi

McVey, Alex, 506–7
Megáfono magazine, 375–76
Los mejores cuentos policiales (The Best Detective Tales, edited by Borges and Bioy Casares), xxiii, 76–77, 244, 250n.26
La memoria de Shakespeare (Shakespeare's Memory, book, Borges), xxvi, 302, 312–15
"La memoria de Shakespeare" ("Shakespeare's Memory," story, Borges), 313–14
Mendes de Souza, Marcelo, 394
Méndez, Evar
 Editorial Proa, 53–54, 57–59, 63, 70
 Martín Fierro journal, xxii, 38–39, 528
Mercader, Marta, 514
"La metáfora" ("The Metaphor," Borges), 155, 156, 179–81
"Metamorphosis" (Kafka), 101–2, 276
Mexico, 394–95, 434
Meyrink, Gustav, 41–42
Michaux, Henri, 75, 80–85, 82f, 83f, 86, 91
Mignolo, Walter, 473, 477
Miguel Cané Municipal Library
 Borges's financial support from work at, 7–8, 16–17, 40–41, 106–7, 114–16
 Borges's influence on book acquisitions at, 119
 Borges's joining the staff (1938) at, xxii, 115–16
 Borges's literary output during tenure at, 114–15, 116–21, 127
 Borges's public image as a writer, 114, 115, 130
 Borges's reading at, 120–21
 Borges's work tasks at, 106, 114, 116, 117–18, 119
 bureaucracy at, 118
 end of Borges's tenure (1946) at, xxii, 4, 97, 106–7, 121–24, 408
 location of, 115
 work environment at, 116, 117–18
"El milagro secreto" ("The Secret Miracle," Borges)
 banality of details in, 570–71
 Borges's interest in theatre, 333, 336
 Eastern bloc translations of, 428
 enigmas of time in, 458–59
 Hladik's wandering in, 193–94
 Judaism in, 418

"El milagro secreto" ("The Secret Miracle,"
    Borges) (*cont.*)
  Nazi violence in, 553
  publication (1943) of, 116
  The Qur'an, 442
  reading depicted in, 19
  time's stoppage in, 26–27
Miller, Henry, 408
Milleret, Jean de, 483
Mills-Court, Karen, 262–64
Milton, John, 342
"The Minions of Midas" (London), 76–80
Mir'ala'I, Ahmad, 446–47
Mitre, Bartolomé, 377–78, 600–1
Un modelo para la muerte (*A Model for Death*,
    Bioy Casares and Borges)
  characters in, 323–24
  detective story genre, 219, 221
  Suárez Lynch listed as author of, 325–26
  publication (1946) of, xxiii
  Seis problemas, 326
Moholy-Nagy, László, 423–24
Molas, Lorenzo, 41–42
Molinari, Ricardo E., 55*t*, 59*t*, 70n.4
Møller-Olsen, Astrid, 444
Molloy, Sylvia, 42–43, 379, 512
La moneda de hierro (*The Iron Coin*, Borges),
    xxvi, 291–92
Monory, Jacques, 495–96
Montaldo, Graciela, 194n.6, 383
Moraña, Mabel, 472–73, 474, 479
Moreno Heredia, Eugenio, 429–30, 434
Morgenstern, Christian, 528
Les mots et les choses (Foucault), xvi, 409,
    472, 511
La muerte y la brújula (*Death and the
    Compass*, book, Borges)
  Eastern Bloc translations of, 432–33
  publication (1951) of, xxiii
"La muerte y la brújula" ("Death and the
    Compass," story, Borges)
  bird's cry in, 568, 569–70
  crime solving in, 587
  Deleuze, 486
  detective genre subverted in, 226–28
  encrypted information in, 227
  end of, 227

first version (1942) of, 233n.19
labyrinths, 488
manuscript of, 119–20
mathematics, 592
The Pentateuch, 442
rabbi's death in, 514–15
reading depicted in, 19
"Las muertes eslabonadas" (London,
    translated by Borges), 76–77, 78–80, 79*f*
"El muerto" ("The Dead Man," Borges), 231n.6,
    426, 505–6, 508, 510–11
Mugica, René, xxiv, 546–48, 549n.9
Muller, Marta, 95–96
Municipal Prize (Argentina), 376
"La muralla y los libros" ("The Wall and the
    Books," Borges), 179–80, 211, 230, 277–79
Muschietti, Delfina, 255, 256, 259

Nabokov, Vladimir, 411
La Nación newspaper, 41, 47–48
"La nadería de la personalidad" ("The
    Nothingness of Personality," Borges), 9–
    10, 178–79, 185, 190, 417–18, 462
Nagyvilág magazine, 427–30
National Library of Argentina
  Borges's directorship of, xiv, 45, 98, 115,
    124–25, 381
  Borges's donations of annotated books to,
    15, 129
  Borges's dreams about, 127
  Borges's literary output during his tenure at,
    45–46, 115, 124–27
  Borges's public image as a writer, 114,
    115, 130
  end of Borges's tenure (1973) at, 128–29
  La Biblioteca magazine, 46–47, 126–27
  Mariano Moreno reading room at, 45
  salaries for employees at, 45–46
National Prize (Argentina), 197, 376–77, 381
Neruda, Pablo, 37–38, 391–92, 434
New Realism, 521–22
Nine, Lucas, xvi
Nixon, Richard, 389–90
Noether, Emma, 585
Nogués, Germinal, 337–38, 339
Nolan, Christopher, xvi
Nolasco Juárez, Guillermo, 86–87, 90

INDEX   635

Nosotros magazine, 40, 154–55, 374, 376, 377–78
"Nota sobre (hacia) Bernard Shaw" ("A Note on (toward) Bernard Shaw," Borges), 271
"Nota sobre Chesterton" (Borges), 44–45
"Nota sobre el Ulises en español" (Borges), 44–45
"Nota sobre Walt Whitman" ("Note on Walt Whitman," Borges), xv*t*, 24–25, 26, 44–45, 355, 447
Novalis, 41–42, 202
"Nuestra América" (Martí), 390
"Nuestras imposibilidades" ("Our Impossibilities," Borges), 376n.5, 541–42
"Nuestro pobre individualismo" ("Our Poor Individualism," Borges), 542, 554, 563
Nueva antología personal (*A New Personal Anthology*, Borges), xxv
"Nueva refutación del tiempo" ("A New Refutation of Time," Borges)
 Can Xue, 444–45
 contrast between naming and living in, 465
 humor in, 462–63
 identity of indiscernibles principles, 467–68
 imagined dialogues between philosophers in, 457–58
 ironic title of, 461–62
 limits of reason, 460–61
 on linguistic barriers, 465
 "Nota preliminar" in, 461
 publication (1947) of, xxiii
 "Sentirse en muerte," 465
 on time as substance, 459–60
"Las 'nuevas generaciones' literarias" (Borges), 378
Nueve ensayos dantescos (*Nine Dantesque Essays*, Borges), xxvi
Nueve poemas (*Nine Poems*, Borges), xxiv, 125–26
Nuevos cuentos de Bustos Domecq (*New Tales of Bustos Domecq*, Borges and Bioy Casares), xxvi, 219, 221, 323–24, 328–29

Oakeshott, Michael, 561
Obra poética, 1923–1966 (*Poetic Works, 1923-1966*, Borges), xxv

"La obra de Flaubert" ("The Work of Flaubert," Borges), 20–21
Obras completas (Borges)
 editorial decisions regarding, xvii, 127, 129, 416–17
 initial publication (1953) of, xxiv
 single-volume edition (1974) of, xvii–xviii, xxv
Obras completas en colaboración (Borges, Bioy Casares, and others), xxvi
Ocampo, Silvina
 advertising work for fermented milk (illustrations), 319
 Antología de la literatura fantástica, xxiii, 76–77, 236–37, 241, 242–43
 Antología poética argentina, xxiii
 Cuaderno San Martín, 65
 Cuentos breves y extraordinarios, 245–46
 Destiempo magazine, 44
 Los Anales de Buenos Aires magazine, 44–45, 244
 surrealism, 322
Ocampo, Victoria
 Bolaño character based on, 396
 on Borges's appointment to directorship of National Library, 124–25
 on Borges's departure from Miguel Cané Municipal Library, 122
 Borges's initial meeting of, xxii
 Editorial Proa, 54, 58, 70–71n.8
 Sur magazine, 43
 translation of foreign literature, 80–81
"Oda compuesta en 1960" ("Ode composed in 1960," Borges), 557–58
"Oda escrita en 1966" ("Ode Written in 1966," Borges), 558
O. Henry, 44–45, 77–78
Olea Franco, Rafael, 61–62, 161–62, 361–62
Oleríny, Vladimír, 428
Oliver, María Rosa, 16–17, 18–19, 29n.5
Omar Khayyam, 5, 278–79, 282, 447
O menino e o vento (*The Boy and the Wind*, Christensen), 548
Onetti, Juan Carlos, 434–35
Oppenheimer, Andrés, 343–45
"Una oración" ("A Prayer," Borges), 290–91
The Order of Things (Foucault), 409, 488–91, 494

INDEX

Los orilleros (*The Hoodlums*, film script
  written by Borges and Bioy Casares),
  xxiv, 219, 327, 331n.14, 543–44
Orlando (Woolf), 80, 507, 569
El oro de los tigres (*The Gold of the Tigers*,
  Borges), xxv, 45–46, 85, 414
Ortega y Gasset, José, 6–7, 376, 541–42
Ortelli, Roberto, 159
Ostroumov, Nikolai Petrovich, 526, 527
Othello (Shakespeare), 295–96
"La otra muerte" ("The Other Death," Borges),
  121, 360–62
Otras inquisiciones (*Other Inquisitions*,
  Borges)
  on Borges's "essential skepticism," 484
  as canonical Borges text, xvt
  editorial decisions regarding, 191–92
  epilogue of, 364
  French translation of, xxiv, 406
  on Kafka and Hawthorne, 276
  lectures that served as basis for, 110
  Paul's Letter to the Corinthians, 269–70
  publication (1952) of, xxiv
  Shih Huang Ti, 277–79, 283–84
"Otra vez la metáfora" ("On Metaphor Once
  Again," Borges), 180–81
El otro, el mismo (*The Other, The Same*,
  Borges)
  "A un poeta menor de 1899," 289–90
  "Baltasar Gracián," 263
  duplicity in, 463
  editorial decisions regarding, 257
  feminist responses to, 515
  "Insomnio," 258, 259
  "Límites," 292–93
  "Poema conjetural," 125–26
  publication (1964) of, xxiv
"El Otro" ("The Other," Borges), 9–10,
  307–8
"El otro duelo" (Borges), 303, 383
Ouspensky, Piotr, 320
Owen, Gilberto, 59t, 60fc

Pacheco, José Emilio, 394
Păcurariu, Francisc, 428
"Página para recordar al coronel Suárez,
  vencedor en Junín" ("A Page to

Remember Colonel Suárez, Victor at
  Junín," Borges), 256–57
Páginas escogidas collection, 431–32
Para las seis cuerdas (*For the Six Strings*,
  Borges), xxv, 261
"Parábola del palacio" ("Parable of the palace,"
  Borges), 556
"La paradoja de Apollinaire" (Borges), 44–45
El paraíso de los creyentes (*The Paradise of
  Believers*, film script written by Borges
  and Bioy Casares), xxiv, 219, 327, 543–44
Parodi, Cristina, xviii, 221, 226–27, 320–
  21, 323–24
Parpagnoli, Mario, 41–42
Partido Revolucionario Institucional
  (Mexico), 394–95
Pascal, Blaise, 26, 142, 193, 280, 486–87
Pastormerlo, Sergio, 189
Pater, Walter, 230
Paul of Tarsus, 269–70, 274–76, 283
Pauls, Alan, 188–89, 204
Pavić, Milorad, 433
Pavlović, Miodrag, 432–33
Paz, Octavio, 394–95
Peiper, Tadeusz, 423–24
The Pentateuch, 442
"Penumbra y pompa" ("Twilight and Pomp,"
  Borges and Bioy Casares), 328–29
Pereda, Estela, 514
Pereda Valdés, Ildefonso, xxii, 37–38, 169–70
Performance (film by Roeg and
  Cammell), 412–13
Perón, Eva, 46–47, 126, 345–46, 554, 562, 601,
  610n.13
Perón, Isabel, 414–15
Perón, Juan
  Borges's literary works criticizing regime of,
    102–3, 126
  Borges's political opposition to the regime
    of, 102, 122–23, 343–44, 345–46, 405, 414–
    15, 541–42, 554, 562
  Borges's public speaking during the reign
    of, 101–6, 122–23
  Borges surveilled during the regime of, 104
  death of Eva Perón, 46–47
  election (1946) of, 97, 408, 554
  fall (1955) of, xxiv, 98, 124, 381, 408

free speech restrictions under, 408
mass support for, 542
re-election (1951) of, 473–74
return to power (1973) of, 128–29
Rosas, 279–80
San Martín, 103
on traitors, 601
Unión Democrática's opposition to, 101–2, 122
writers' organizations and opposition to, 108, 380
"La perpetua carrera de Aquiles y la tortuga" ("The Perpetual Race of Achilles and the Tortoise," Borges), 192, 458–59
Perú, 393
"Las pesadillas y Franz Kafka" ("Nightmares and Franz Kafka"), 191
Pessoa, Fernando, xix
Peter (apostle of Jesus), 569–78, 611n.26
Petit de Murat, Ulises, xxii, 7–8, 40–41, 44–45, 76–77, 115, 538–39
Peyrou, Manuel
  Antología de la literatura fantástica, 242–43
  Borges's poem in honor of, 292
  Borges's reviews of works by, 217
  Cuentos breves y extraordinarios, 245–46
  Destiempo magazine, 44
  La Biblioteca magazine, 46
  Los Anales de Buenos Aires magazine, 44–45, 244
  psychotherapy with Kohan-Miller, 97
Pezzoni, Enrique, 25
"Die Pfeilketten" ("The Chain of Arrows," Koch-Grünberg), 529–32, 533
The Phaedrus (Plato), 135n.3, 270–71
"Pierre Menard, autor del Quijote" ("Pierre Menard, Author of the Quixote," Borges)
  amnesia in, 206
  as canonical Borges text, xiv–xv, xvt
  copying of *Don Quixote* in, 28, 406–7, 409
  on *Don Quixote* as palimpsest, 177
  engagement with imaginary books in, 198–202, 209–10, 486
  as fantastic literature, 236
  humor in, 264–65
  intellectual dead ends confronted in, 411–12
  Leibnitz, 467–68

meaning and manner of reading in, 280–81
  as obituary, 199, 205
  as paradigm of Borges's theory of literature, 409
  publication (1939) of, 116, 376
  reading defined in, 23–24
  as satire, 419
  transformation of *Don Quixote* in, 205, 206
  translation, 73
Piglia, Ricardo
  on Borges and erudition, 21, 204
  on Borges's fiction and uncertainty of personal memory, 118
  on Borges's intellectual and military lineages, 5–6, 602–3
  on Borges's literary production at National Library, 127
  on Borges's position in Argentine literature, 37–38, 382–83
  on "Emma Zuna," 225
  on "Insomnio," 259
Piñera, Virgilio, 431–32
Piñero, Sergio hijo, 55t
Pinochet, Augusto, xxvi, 394–95, 414–15
Pishbin, Shaahin, 447
Pissavini, Ernesto, 43
Pizarnik, Alejandra, 256
Plato
  Borges on the dialogic methods of, 270–71
  mimesis, 492
  oral exchange promoted over writing by, 135–36, 271, 285
  on perception, 270–71
  simulacra, 493–94
"Plato's Pharmacy" (Derrida), 487, 493
Poe, Edgar Allan, 121, 217–18, 220–21, 228–29, 230, 231n.5, 234n.25, 392–93, 569–70
"Poema conjetural" ("Conjectural Poem," Borges), 9–10, 102–3, 125–26, 256–57, 559, 563
"Poema del cuarto elemento" ("Poem of the Fourth Element," Borges), 256–57
"Poema de los dones" ("Poem of the Gifts," Borges), xiv, 126, 130, 262
Poemas, 1922–1943 (Borges), xxiii, 254
Poemas, 1923–1953 (Borges), 256–57
Poemas, 1923–1958 (Borges), 256–57

"La poesía" ("On Poetry," Borges), 271–72
Poirier, Richard, 411–12, 415
Poland, 423–24, 425–26, 432–33, 435–36
political theory
  anarchism, 559–60, 561–62
  authoritarianism, 552–53, 562
  Borges's criticism of Argentine
    democracy, 561–62
  Borges's dislike of partisan politics, 552
  patriotism *versus* nationalism in, 557–59
  populism, 562
Poniatowska, Elena, 363, 367n.19, 394
Popkin, Richard, 463
postcolonial studies
  Borges's cosmopolitanism, 473–74
  Borges's influence in, 471, 473–74
  Cold War, 474–75
  diversification at metropolitan
    universities, 476–77
  "El escritor argentino y la tradición," 474–
    75, 478–79
  gauchesque poetry, 473–74
  Latin America, 477–78
  Middle East, 476–77
  question of Borges's Argentine
    identity, 472–73
postmodernism, 411–12, 418–19, 471–72,
  477, 494–95
"La postulación de la realidad" ("The
  Postulation of Reality," Borges), 182, 189–
  90, 327–28, 463–64
pragmatism, 484–85, 497–98
Premat, Julio, 146, 185, 212, 262–63
Premiani, Bruno, 41–42
La Prensa newspaper, 375
Prieto, Adolfo, xxiv, 45, 379–80, 475
"El primer Wells" (Borges), 44–45
Prisma magazine, xxi, 7, 34–37, 154–55, 182–
  83, 374–75
Proa magazine
  beginning of publication (1922) of, 7, 36
  Borges's literature reviews in, xxi, 7, 36–37
  cessation of publication (1926) of, xxii
  editorial vision at, 36–37, 39, 374, 375
  format of, 36
  proposed revival of publication (1924)
    of, 39–40

Sur magazine, 37–38
  See also Editorial Proa
"Un problema" (Borges), 46
Prólogos con un prólogo de prólogos (*Prologue
  with a Prologue of Prologues,* Borges), xxv
"Prose poems for I. J." (Borges), 256–57
Proust, Marcel, 22–23, 337–38
"El proveedor de iniquidades Monk Eastman"
  ("Monk Eastman, Purveyor of Iniquities,"
  Borges), 356
public speaking by Borges
  alcohol, 99
  in Argentina's smaller cities, 99–100, 107–8
  at Colegio Libre de Estudios Superiores,
    xxiii, 15, 98–99, 100–1, 104–7, 108, 110
  at Collège de France, 414–15
  in Colombia, xxiv
  on Flaubert in Buenos Aires (1952), 22–
    23, 24–28
  on gauchesque poetry in Montevideo
    (1945), xxiii
  at Harvard University (1967-1968), xxv, 412
  income from, 16–17, 97, 106–8
  at Jewish institutions, 107–8
  on Kafka in Paris (1984), xxvi
  others' reading of Borges's written remarks,
    95–96, 110n.2
  Peronist regime in Argentina, 101–6, 122–23
  research and preparation for, 98–99, 109–10
  speaking style of Borges, 97–98, 105–6, 109
  on tango in Buenos Aires (1965), xxv
  in Uruguay, 95–96, 99–101, 104, 105, 108
"El pudor de la historia" ("The Modesty of
  History," Borges), 136, 143–44, 274
Puig, Manuel, 323–24, 347n.4
Punto de Vista journal, 379, 383

Quackenbush, L. Howard, 333, 336
queer criticism of Borges, 504, 505–6, 510–12
Qué es el budismo (*What is Buddhism,* Borges
  and Jurado), xxvi, 110
"Queja de todo criollo" ("Lament of Every
  Criollo," Borges), 185–86
Quevedo, Francisco de, 59–61, 168, 182, 202,
  273, 274–75, 282
Quichotte (Rushdie), 449–50, 451
Quijano, Alonso, 563

El Quijote de Avellaneda (1614), 365n.3
Quiroga, Horacio, 341–42, 392–93
The Qur'an, 135, 138, 140–41, 442, 568–69

"Rabón," 170, 174n.10
Rama, Ángel, 392–93, 474–75, 479
Readers Theater, 336–38, 346
reading by Borges
    archival records regarding, 15–16
    Borges's fictional depictions of reading, 19
    Buenos Aires bookstores and public
        libraries as sites of, 18–19
    father's library, 18–19
    French literature, 20–23
    literary genealogies of authors' "precursors"
        posited in, 22–23
    memory, 13, 16–18
    notebooks as record regarding, 17–18
    notetaking, 17–18, 20
    passing of time, 23–24
    referential nature of Borges's writing, 14
    re-reading, 23–28
    reviews by Borges as record regarding,
        16, 18–19
    on streetcars, 18–19
    travel compared to, 13
Rechain, Arístides, 41–42
Reger, Liselotte, 407–8
"Remordimiento por cualquier muerte"
    ("Remorse for Any Death," Borges), 424
"Réplica" (Borges), 153–54
Resnais, Alain, 412–13
Revista Mexicana de Literatura Borges issue
    (1964), 394
Revista Multicolor de los Sábados magazine
    Borges as co-director of, xxii, 7–8, 40–41,
        115, 538–39
    Borges's fiction in, 42–43
    Borges's literature reviews in, 41
    crime stories in, 77–80, 79f
    as *Crítica* newspaper's cultural supplement,
        40–43, 76
    editorial vision at, 41–42
    fantastic literature in, 76–77
    first issue (1933) of, 41–42
    Koch-Grünberg, 533
    Petit de Murat, 40–41

translation of foreign literature in, 76–80,
    91
    Xul Solar, 520, 523–33
Revolución Libertadora (Argentina, 1955), 124,
    380, 381, 602
"El rey de la selva" ("King of the Jungle,"
    Borges), xxi
Reyes, Alfonso, 37–38, 44, 58, 63, 70–71n.8,
    248n.7, 394–95
"Los reyes" ("The Kings," Cortázar), 244–45
Ricardou, Jean, 381
The Rime of the Ancient Mariner
    (Coleridge), 65
Ríos Patrón, José Luis, 380–81
Risso Platero, Ema, 99, 430–31
Rivera, José Eustasio, 393
Rivette, Jacques, 412–13
Robbe-Grillet, Alain, 406, 483
Rocca, Pablo, 95–96
Rodman, Selden, 341–42
Rodríguez-Luis, Julio, 239
Rodríguez Monegal, Emir
    Borges biography (1978) by, 415–16
    on Borges's global reputation, 392–93
    on Borges's public lectures, 95–96
    El Libro de Arena, 307
    on the "Parricide Generation," 379
Roeg, Nicolas, 412–13
Rojas, Pedro, 41–42
Rojas, Ricardo, 104–5, 194n.6, 273–74, 283–
    84, 373–74
Rojas Paz, Pablo, 36–37
Romania, 427, 428, 430–31, 432–33,
    435–36
Romero Brest, Jorge, 476, 539
Rosa, Nicolás, 379
"La rosa de Paracelso" ("The Rose of
    Paracelsus," Borges), 312
La rosa profunda (*The Deep Rose*, Borges), xxv,
    287–88, 296–97
Rosas, Juan Manuel de, 103, 160–61, 279–80,
    282, 305, 554
Rosato, Laura, 15, 45
Rose, H. R., 135–36, 136n.4, 146–47
Rossi, Attilio, 522
Royce, Josiah, 284–85, 491–92
Rozenmacher, Germán, 434–35

640   INDEX

"Las ruinas circulares" ("The Circular Ruins," Borges), 116, 198, 200, 379n.12, 427, 432–33, 442–43, 446–47, 449–50, 592

Rulfo, Juan, 394, 427–28, 474–75

Rushdie, Salman, 449–51, 452n.4, 473–74

"Rusia" (Borges), 153, 423–24, 561

Russell, Bertrand, 120–21, 202, 283, 284–85, 468, 588

Russian Revolution (1917), 4, 6–7, 153, 307–8, 427, 561

Sábato, Ernesto, 87, 377–78, 381

Sabsay-Herrera, Fabiana, 44

Said, Edward, 27, 441–42, 476–77

Saítta, Sylvia, 80–81

Sale, George, 138, 140–41, 146–47

Sánchez García de Paz, Isabel, 606

Sandburg, Carl, 41–42

San Martín, José de, 103, 305–6, 413–14. *See also Cuaderno San Martín (San Martín Notebook, Borges)*

San Montes lejos (Xul Solar), 519, 520

Santiago, Hugo, xxv, 327, 544, 545

Santos Chocano, José, 183–84

Sanz, Elviro, 153–54

Sarli, Isabel, 548, 549n.10

Sarlo, Beatriz
  on Borges and Kafka, 118–19
  on Borges and literature in translation, 74, 92n.3
  on Borges and postcolonial studies, 474, 478–79
  on Borges and sexuality, 512–13
  on Borges's fiction and "the West's skew toward the irrational," 118
  on Borges's nostalgia for Buenos Aires, 161–62
  on Buenos Aires literary landscape during 1930s, 76
  on the colonial condition and creativity, 392
  on *Contorno* and Borges, 383
  on "Emma Zunz," 226
  on *Evaristo Carriego*, 187–88
  on *Fervor de Buenos Aires*, 161–62
  on *Historia universal de la infamia*, 42–43
  on *Sur* magazine, 40–41

Sarmiento, Domingo Faustino, 5, 389–90, 391, 601

Sartre, Jean-Paul, 379–80, 406, 475

Sazbón, José, 381–82

Scholem, Gerschom, 135, 137–38, 140–41, 146–47

Schopenhauer, Arthur
  on "all those who ever said I," 178–79
  Borges's alignment with philosophy of, 461, 462, 465
  Borges's reading of, 24, 121
  on life and dreams, 207, 210
  Los Anales de Buenos Aires magazine, 44–45
  on reading *versus* talking with others, 144–45, 146–47

Schroeder, Barbet, 400

Schwob, Marcel, 41–42, 77–78

Sciascia, Leonardo, 407

Scorsese, Martin, 356

Scott, James E., 426–27, 480

Scotus Erigena, Johannes, 269–70, 271–72

Sebreli, Juan José, 379, 475

Secolul 20 magazine, 430–31

"La secta del Fénix" ("The Sect of the Phoenix," Borges), 279–80, 358–59, 510–11

Seis poemas escandinavos (Six Scandinavian Poems, Borges), xxv

Seis problemas para don Isidro Parodi (Six Problems for Mr. Isidro Parodi, Borges and Bioy Casares), xxiii, 68t, 69fc, 219–21, 320–21, 323–24, 378

Seneca, 277–78

"Séneca en las orillas" ("Seneca at the Outskirts," Borges), 186–87

"Sentirse en muerte" ("Feeling in Death," Borges), 187, 459, 465–67

"La señora mayor" ("The Old Lady," Borges), 305–6, 413–14

Séptimo Círculo collection, 218, 231n.2, 319, 323

Sérouya, Henri, 135, 137, 137n.7, 140, 146–47

Sessa, Aldo, 522

sexuality. *See* gender and sexuality

Shahnameh (Persian language epic), 447

Shakespeare, William
  All's Well That Ends Well, 295–96
  Julius Caesar, 608

Macbeth, 567–68, 579–80
Othello, 295–96
The Tempest, 392
Shaw, George Bernard, 24, 41–42, 120, 135, 146, 269–71, 411
Shelley, Mary, 321
Shimon bar Yochai, 357–58, 365n.6
Shklar, Judith, 553
Shock, Susy, 400
Siete noches (*Seven Nights,* Borges), xxvi, 110, 442–43
"Si la querés, usala" ("If You Want Her, Use Her," Pereda), 514
Silva, José Asunción, 393
"El signo" ("The Sign," Borges), 221, 325
Silesius, Angelus, 189
Silva Valdés, Fernán, 37–38, 59–61, 375
Silverman, Kaja, 513
"El simulacro" ("The Swindler," Borges), 46–47, 126, 562
Smith, Norman Kemp, 462–63
Smith, Paul Julian, 511
"Sobre el doblaje" ("On Dubbing," Borges), 489–90
"Sobre el 'Vathek' de William Beckford" ("On William Beckford's 'Vathek,'" Borges), 3–4
"Sobre la técnica de los cuentos fantásticos" ("On the Technique of Fantastic Tales," Bioy Casares), 322
"Sobre Oscar Wilde" (Borges), 44–45
"El soborno" ("The Bribe," Borges), 556
Sociedad Argentina de Escritores (SADE), xxiii, 103, 108
Socrates, 135–36, 141, 270–71
Solanas, Fernando, 545
Šoljan, Antun, 427
Sollers, Philippe, 493–94
Solomon (Old Testament king), 358
"Song of Myself" (Whitman), 85, 86, 87–88, 90
Sontag, Susan, xiii
Sorazábal, Juan, 41–42, 78, 79f
Sorrentino, Fernando, 334, 435–36
Sosnowski, Sául, 515
Soto, Luis Emilio, 37–38, 169–70, 376n.6
Soviet Union, 424–25, 428, 430–37
Spain, Borges's reception in, 408, 414–15

Spencer, Herbert, 105, 178–79, 559, 560, 564n.5
Spitzer, Leo, 181–82
Spivak, Gayatri Chakravorty, 441–42, 476–77
Stalin, Joseph, 426
Stamford Bridge, battle (1066) of, 351–52
Stanchina, Lorenzo, 41–42
"Starting from Paumanok" (Whitman), 86–87, 90
Steimberg, Alicia, 514
Steiner, George, xiii, 410–11, 415
Stevens, Wallace, 582
Stevenson, Robert Louis, 24, 74, 76, 222, 411, 538–39
Stoics, 276–78
Storni, Alfonsina, 156, 255
Sturluson, Snorri, 136, 272–73, 351–52, 358, 601
Suárez, Manuel Isidoro, 5–6, 160–61, 305–6, 600–1
Suárez Haedo de Acevedo, Leonor, xxi, 7–8, 305
Suárez Laprida, Isidoro, xxi, 7–8, 17–18, 305–6
Suchasnist, 426
Sun, Haiqing, 443–44
"La supersticiosa ética del lector" ("The Superstitious Ethics of the Reader," Borges), 136, 189
Sureda, Elvira and Jacobo, 7
"El Sur" ("The South," Borges), 5–6, 390, 427–28
Sur literary journal
   Borges's fiction in, 40–41, 116, 375–76
   Borges's reviews in, xxii, 16, 40–41, 276–77
   Borges's work on editorial board at, 40–41
   "Desagravio a Borges," 122, 376, 376n.6, 377–78
   editorial vision at, 43
   film criticism in, 538
   founding of, 376
   Proa magazine, 37–38
   special issue on Borges (1942) of, xxiii, 121
   translation of foreign literature in, 73–74, 80
Swanson, Phillip, 504
Swedenborg, Emanuel, 245–46, 324–25, 521, 522, 556–57
Swift, Jonathan, 27–28, 41–42, 183, 295–96, 432–33, 552
Sykes, Percy, 449–50
Szász, Béla, 426

642 INDEX

Taller de Arte Mural, 521–22
El tamaño de mi esperanza (*The Extent of My Hope,* Borges)
   compadrito, 165
   criollismo, 62–63, 157–58, 168, 184–85
   design of, 63
   essay format of, 62–63
   omission from *Obras completas* of, xvii
   publication (1926) of, xxii, 52, 55*t*, 56*f*b, 59–61, 62–63
Tel Quel journal, 409–10, 415–16
"Tema del traidor y del héroe" ("Theme of the Traitor and the Hero," Borges), 13–14, 116, 412–13, 541–42, 556, 587, 598–99
The Tempest (Shakespeare), 392
"Los teólogos" (Borges), 44–45, 325
"El testigo" ("The Witness," Borges), 221, 324–25
Teteryan, I. A., 434–35
Textos cautivos (Borges), xxvi, 8, 383
Textos recobrados (Borges), xviii, 8
Thibaudet, Albert, 21–23
"The Thing I Am" (Borges), 294–96
The Thousand and One Nights, 241, 442–44, 446, 448, 451, 526–27
Thurston, William, 585
Tiempo, César, 41–42, 170
"El tiempo y J.W. Dunne" (Borges), 207, 459
"Tigres azules" ("Blue Tigers," Borges), 312
"El tintorero enmascarado Hakim de Merv" ("The Masked Dyer, Hakim of Merv," Borges), 442–43, 448–49, 526–27
Tlaloc (Xul Solar), 519–20, 525
"Tlön, Uqbar, Orbis Tertius" (Borges)
   Antología de la literatura fantástica, 241, 242–43
   apocryphal texts, 354–55, 359–60
   Bioy Casares as character in, 320
   as canonical Borges text, xiv–xv, xv*t*
   Carthage, 25–26
   Eastern Bloc translations of, 432–33
   ending of, 145
   engagement with imaginary books in, 198
   as fantastic literature, 236, 246–47
   on idealism and reality, 181
   mirrors in, 396, 448–49
   Nazism, 389

   publication (1940) of, 116, 376
   reading in, 13–14
   recapitulation of Borges's previous work in, 193
   Russell, 283
   simultaneity, 569
   skepticism, 460
   unrestrained liberty, 37
   word choices in, 261
Todorov, Tzvetan, 239, 240, 249n.13, 609n.7
Torre Nilsson, Leopoldo, xxiv, 543–44, 546, 549n.8
Tournier, Michel, 493–94
Townley, Michael, 395, 396
Traba, Marta, 393
"Los traductores de Las 1001 Noches" ("The Translators of the 1001 Nights," Borges), 73, 191, 241–42, 526–27
"La trama" ("The Plot," Borges), 46, 556
translation
   appropriation of literature, 74, 92n.3
   commissioned translation, 80–85, 91
   definitions of, 75
   faithfulness to source texts, 602
   Faulkner, 74, 80, 86
   French translations of Borges, 406
   income for Borges from, xiv
   Kafka, 74
   "La busca de Averroes," 73
   "Las dos maneras de traducir," 73
   "Las versiones homéricas," 73
   literary pantheism, 73–74
   London (Jack), 76–80, 79*f*
   magazine work by Borges, 76–80
   metaphors, 73
   Michaux, 75, 80–85, 82*f*, 83*f*, 86, 91
   onomastics, 77
   "Pierre Menard, autor del Quijote," 73
   publishing discourse, 74–75, 78, 81, 86–87
   retranslation, 85–90
   Revista Multicolor de los Sábados magazine, 76–80, 91
   "scene of translation," 74, 77
   strategies of, 75, 77
   Sur magazine, 73–74
   Whitman, 75, 85–90, 89*f*
   Woolf, 74, 80, 91, 507, 569
   Xul Solar, 526–33

travels by Borges
   Brazil, xxv, 394
   Chile, xxv
   Colombia, xxiv
   Ecuador, xxvi
   Egypt, xxvi
   Europe, xxiv
   France, xxi
   Iceland, xxv
   Israel, xxv
   Italy, xxi, 7
   Japan, xxvi
   Mexico, xxvi
   Morocco, xxvi
   Peru, xxv
   Portugal, xxvi
   Spain, xxi, 7–8
   Switzerland, xxi, 6–8
   United Kingdom, xxiv
   United States, xxiv, 8, 381–82, 410, 412, 413
   Uruguay, xxii, 8
   West Germany, xxiv
"Tres versiones de Judas" ("Three Versions of Judas," Borges), 24, 116, 432–33, 597
"Trinchera" (Borges), 153, 561
"El truco" ("Truco," Borges), 183, 186–87, 466–67
Trueba, Fernando, 398, 400
"Two English Poems" (Borges), 256–57, 266n.18

Ubelaker Andrade, Max, 504
Ugarte, Manual, 105, 373–74
"Ulrica" ("Ulrikke," Borges), 309–10, 393, 505–6
Última Hora magazine, 34
"El último libro de Joyce" (Borges), 120–21
ultraísta movement
   Borges's break with, 601
   Borges's poetry, 153, 154
   González Lanuza, 37
   Inquisiciones, 59–61
   Martín Fierro journal, 39
   modernism, 153–54, 157
   Prisma magazine, 34–36
   Proa magazine, 36
   Spanish Baroque, 180–81

"Ultraísmo" manifesto (Borges), 34
Underworld (von Sternberg), 541–42
Unión Democrática (Argentine political party), 101–2, 122, 123
United Kingdom, Borges's reception in, 412–13
United States, Borges's reception in, 405, 410–12, 413, 418–19
University of Buenos Aires, Borges as professor at, xiv, 45, 127
Updike, John, 410–12, 415
Uruguay
   "Avelino Arredondo," 559
   Borges's reception in, 393
   Peronist regime's relations with, 104
   public speaking by Borges in, 95–96, 99–101, 104, 105, 108
   travel by Borges in, xxii, 8
"Utopía de un hombre que está cansado" ("A Weary Man's Utopia," Borges), 127, 128, 559–61, 563

Vaccaro, Alejandro, 34
Vajay, Szabolcs, 426
Valenzuela, Luisa, 514–15
Valéry, Paul, 87, 179–80, 184, 192–93, 202
Vallejo, César, 256, 341–42, 393
Vallejo, Fernando, 397–400
Varela, Alfredo, 434–36
Varela, Blanca, 256
Vargas, Chavela, 393
Vargas Llosa, Mario, 342–43, 343n.6, 344–45, 375
Vargas Vila, José María, 183–84
Vázquez, María Esther, 104, 106, 306, 312–13
Vea y Lea magazine, 47–48
Veinticinco Agosto 1983 y otros cuentos (*August 25, 1983 and Other Stories*, Borges), xxvi, 305–6
"Veinticinco de Agosto, 1983" (Borges), xxvi, 305–6, 312–13
Velázquez, Diego, 489
Venclova, Tomas, 434
Verdevoye, Paul, xxiii, 379n.12, 381, 406
Veríssimo, Luís Fernando, 400
"Las versiones homéricas" ("The Homeric Versions," Borges), 24–25, 73, 314

644 INDEX

"Versos con ademán de recuerdo" ("Verses That Gesture at Memory," Borges), 167–68

Vial, Sara, 395

Viața Românească, 427

Videla, Jorge Rafael, 395

Vignale, Pedro Juan, 170

"Una vindicación de la Cábala" ("A Defense of the Kabbalah," Borges), 192

"Una vindicación del falso Basílides" ("The Defense of Basilides de False," Borges), 192

Villarino, María de, 55*t*

Villaurrutia, Xavier, 37–38

Viñas, David, 379, 380

"Vindicación de Bouvard et Pécuchet" ("Vindication of Bouvard y Pécuchet," Borges), 24–25

La Virgen de los sicarios (Vallejo), 397–98, 399–400

Virgil, Borges's citations of, 287–88, 292, 294

VLTRA magazine, 34, 153–54, 155

Vogel, Daisi, 335–36

Volek, Emil, 471–72, 477

"La vuelta" ("The Return," Borges), 160–61, 167

Waisman, Sergio, 73–74

War on Drugs, 397–98, 400, 604

Wassner, Dalia, 512–13

Weil, Gustav, 241–42

Wells, H. G., 41–42, 44–45, 77, 80–81, 120–21, 182, 279–80, 411

West Side Story, 538

Whale, James, 320–21

Whistler, James McNeill, 189

Whitman, Walt
"all-embracing 'I,'" 178–79
Borges influenced by, 153
Futurism, 181–82
Neruda, 391–92
pantheism, 86
political theory, 561
self-figuration, 309
translation by Borges of, 75, 85–90, 89*f*
See also "Nota sobre Walt Whitman" ("Note on Walt Whitman," Borges)

Wilcock, Juan Rodolfo, 243–44, 327–28

Wilde, Oscar
art for art's sake, 388–89
on biography, 3–4
Borges's apocryphal quotes of, 353–54
Borges's championing of, 41–42
Borges's reading of, 74, 121
on Meredith and Browning, 351
on music, 353–54

Wilhelm, Richard, 241–42, 245–46

Wilkins, John, 191–92, 281–82

Williamson, Edwin, 301, 305, 417, 435–36, 504

Willoughby-Meade, Gerald, 245–46

Woodall, James, 128

Woolf, Virginia
Borges's translations of, 74, 80, 91, 507, 569
on connection between fiction and life, 419
Sur publishing house editions of, 80–81

Wordsworth, William, 191

Woscoboinik, Julio, 97

Xul Solar (Oscar Agustín Alejandro Schulz Solari)
Borges on seafarer image, 523
Borges's collaboration on books with, 531
Borges's prologue for Samos Gallery exhibition (1949) of, 520–21
Borges's purchasing of paintings from, 519–20
Editorial Proa, 54, 58, 523–24
El idioma de los argentinos, 523
El tamaño de mi esperanza, 63, 523
English and German language skills of, 524
library of, 8, 524–26, 528–29, 530
Los Anales de Buenos Aires magazine, 44–45, 521–22
Martín Fierro journal, 523–24
New Realism movement, 521–22
Revista Multicolor de los Sábados magazine, 520, 523–33
translations by, 526–33

Yates, Donald, xxiv, 410, 412–13, 574–75, 577

Yrigoyen, Hipólito, xxii, 377, 561

Yugoslavia, 432–33, 474

Yunque, Álvaro, 37–38, 41–42, 377

"El Zahir" (Borges), xv*t*, 44–45, 244–45,
366n.7, 417–18, 432–33, 447, 592–93
Zea, Leopoldo, 392
Zemborain de Torres, Esther, xxv, 106–7, 124
Zeno, 275, 458–59, 463, 464, 583–84, 588, 592

Zhuangzi, 444, 451
Zlatkova, Anna, 433
Zohar (Moses de León), 357–58
Zoroastrianism, 442–43, 449–50
Zorrilla, José, 242–43, 245–46